THE BIBLE IN AFRICA

THE BIBLE IN AFRICA

Transactions, Trajectories, and Trends

EDITED BY

GERALD O. WEST

&

MUSA W. DUBE

BRILL ACADEMIC PUBLISHERS, INC.
BOSTON • LEIDEN
2001

Library of Congress Cataloging-in-Publication Data

The Bible in Africa: transactions, trajectories, and trends/edited by Gerald
O. West & Musa W. Dube.
    p. cm.
  Includes bibliographical references and index.
  ISBN 0–391–04111–8
    1. Bible—Africa—History. 2. Africa—Church history. I. West, Gerald O.
II. Dube Shomanah, Musa W., 1964–

BS447.5.A35 B53 2001
220'.096—dc21
                                             2001043491

ISBN 0–391–04111–8

PRINTED IN THE UNITED STATES OF AMERICA

CONTENTS

PART TWO
PARTICULAR ENCOUNTERS WITH PARTICULAR TEXTS

Early Encounters

North East Africa

West Africa

PART THREE
COMPARISON AND TRANSLATION AS TRANSACTION

Comparative Studies

Translation Studies

PART FOUR

REDRAWING THE BOUNDARIES OF THE BIBLE IN AFRICA

PART FIVE

BIBLIOGRAPHY

Indices

ACKNOWLEDGMENTS

It was David Orton, then with E.J. Brill, who muted the idea of a collection of essays on the Bible in Africa during a visit I made to their Leiden office in 1995. My thanks to him for the initial idea, entrusting the project to me, and for ongoing support and sensitivity to the African context.

When I accepted the commission I knew that I could not do this project on my own. I hoped that Musa Dube, with whom I had already worked on a similar project, would have completed her PhD at Vanderbilt and would be back in Botswana in time to join me as co-editor. My special thanks to Musa for making the project her own and for a sustained period of collaboration.

A project of this size and located on this continent has had to endure many difficulties, but through them all, including the death of my wife's father here in South Africa, Anniek Meinders-Durksz from E.J. Brill has been wonderfully understanding and supportive.

Throughout the project I have received the support of the staff of the Institute for the Study of the Bible, in whose name this project began. Thanks to them and to Solomuzi Mabuza and Sam Tshehla for assisting in the early days with correspondence, filing, and finding. Thanks too to Lou Levine for converting file formats and presenting me with texts I could read, and to Alastair Nixon for providing scans and photographs of the African art. A special thanks to Billy Meyer who has conscientiously (and creatively) worked through all the essays in the last days of the project to ensure reasonable consistency and clarity.

I wish too to acknowledge the funding I have received from the University of Natal Research Fund and from the National Research Foundation (South Africa). Without their financial support much of this would have not been possible, though they are not responsible for any of the content.

Finally, my and Musa's thanks to all those who have supported the project through various forms of participation. We hope this project will lead to further collaboration among us.

LIST OF CONTRIBUTORS

David T. Adamo teaches Old Testament and was the former Dean of the Faculty of Arts at Delta State University, Abraka, Nigeria. He is presently on leave of absence from the University, pastoring an African Baptist Church in Irving, Texas, USA. His current research interest is in the area of African Biblical Studies. <adamod@juno.com>

Dorothy Bloosi E.A. Akoto (nee Abutiate) teaches Old Testament/ Hebrew Bible and Christian Education in Trinity Theological Seminary, Legon, Accra, Ghana. Her research interests include gender in missions and hospital chaplaincy Clinical Pastoral Education. <adam200010@excite.com>

Eric Anum has completed his doctoral studies at the Faculty of Theology and Religious Studies at the University of Glasgow, and is in the process of taking up a lecturing position in New Testament in the Department of Religious Studies, University of Cape Coast, Ghana. His research interest is in African biblical interpretation generally, but he is especially interested in the relationship between ordinary readers and scholarly readers. <eanum@hotmail.com>

Solomon K. Avotri has taught in Accra, Ghana, and is presently teaching Biblical Studies at Payne Theological Seminary, Wilberforce, Ohio, USA. His research interest is in the area of African biblical interpretation, with a particular focus on sickness and healing. <savotri@yahoo.com>

Robert P. Carroll taught Hebrew Bible and Semitic Studies in the Department of Theology and Religious Studies, at the University of Glasgow, Scotland. He had wide-ranging research interests and published extensively. He died suddenly in May 2000.

Philippe Denis teaches History of Christianity at the School of Theology, University of Natal, Pietermaritzburg, South Africa. He heads the Oral History Project, a research and development initiative which aims to recover the silenced memories of the Christian communities in South Africa under colonialism and apartheid. <denis@nu.ac.za>

Moiseraele Prince Dibeela is an ordained minister of the United Congregational Church of Southern Africa, Botswana. He has worked as Synod and Mission Secretary of the UCCSA. Currently he is a Mission Enabler for the United Reformed Church in the UK.

Jonathan A. Draper teaches New Testament at the School of Theology, University of Natal, Pietermaritzburg, South Africa. He is currently researching in the area of sociological and anthropological interpretations of the New Testament, using especially ritual theory and orality-literacy studies, with a particular interest in contextual exegesis. Other research interests include studies in John's Gospel, the Didache and Q. <draper@nu.ac.za>

Musa W. Dube teaches New Testament in the Department of Theology and Religious Studies, University of Botswana, Botswana. Her research interests are in gender, feminist theory, the gospels and postcolonial studies. <DUBEMW@mopipi.ub.bw>

Rebecca Ganusah has recently completed her PhD at the Centre for Christianity in the Non-western World, Edinburgh, Scotland. Her research interest is in the field of biblical and theological ethics, particularly in relation to the clash between Traditional and Christian practices in Africa.

Salimo Hachibamba is the Manuscript Coordinator for the Bible Society of Zambia. His current research interest is in the area of comparative studies in Bantu social and cultural structure, and the impact of such knowledge on Bible translation. <lsem@zamnet.zm>

Knut Holter teaches Old Testament in the School of Mission and Theology, Stavanger, Norway. He is the founder and Editor of the "Newsletter on African Old Testament Scholarship" and is the compiler of a web-site on "Old Testament Studies in Africa: Resource Pages" (http://www.misjonshs.no/res/ot_africa/). He is currently working on interpretation strategies in African Old Testament studies. <kh@misjonshs.no>

Andrew Olu Igenoza teaches Biblical Studies in the Department of Religious Studies, Obafemi Awolowo University, Ile-Ife, Nigeria. His current research interests include feminism and Luke-Acts. <rigenoza@hotmail.com>

Fergus King is The United Society for the Propagation of the Gospel's Regional Desk Officer for Central Africa and Tanzania. He is currently researching patterns of inculturation in the New Testament. <fergusk@uspg.org.uk>

Grant LeMarquand teaches New Testament and Mission at Trinity Episcopal School of Ministry in Ambridge, PA, USA. He formerly taught at Wycliffe College, Toronto, and at St Paul's United Theological College, Limuru, Kenya. <GrantLeMarquand@tesm.edu>

Bernice Letlhare is a lecturer of Religious Studies in Tonota College of Education. Her research interests are in the areas of Hebrew Bible and ancient biblical languages.

Jean Claude Loba Mkole trains Bible translators for United Bible Societies translation projects in the Democratic Republic of the Congo. He is currently working on New Testament hermeneutics in the Central Africa region. <loba-ubs@raga.net>

Bobby Loubser teaches New Testament at the Faculty of Theology and Religious Studies at the University of Zululand, South Africa. His research focuses on issues of orality and literacy in biblical interpretation. <jloubser@pan.uzulu.ac.za>

Temba L.J. Mafico teaches Hebrew Bible/Old Testament at the Interdenominational Theological Centre, Atlanta, USA. His is presently doing research on the relationships between the Old Testament and African Tradition and between the Divine call and the human response. <mafico@att.net>

Hezekiel Mafu teaches in the Department of Theology and Religious Studies at Solusi University, Bulawayo, Zimbabwe. His research interest is the interface between Christianity and Indigenous African Religions.

Mark McEntire teaches Hebrew and Old Testament in the School of Religion at Belmont University, Nashville, Tennessee, USA. He was formely a lecturer of Old Testament and Dean of the Department of Theology at the Mekane Yesus Theological Seminary in Addis Ababa, Ethiopia. He continues his work on violence in the Bible focusing specifically on how readers experience conflict and death within the narrative worlds constructed by biblical books. <McEntire-M@meredith.edu>

Hilary B.P. Mijoga teaches New Testament and New Testament Greek in the Department of Theology and Religious Studies, University of Malawi, Zomba, Malawi. He is currently working on preaching in African Instituted Churches in Malawi. <kachere@sdnp.org.mw>

Aloo Osotsi Mojola lives in Dodoma, Tanzania, and works as a Translation Consultant for the United Bible Societies with assignments in a number of African countries. He has interests in the history of Bible translation, cultural studies and in the recent developments in translation research and scholarship and its impact on the translation of the Bible. <Aloo_Mojola@maf.org>

Peter Wamulungwe Mwikisa teaches modern African literature in English and early twentieth century English literature in the Department of English at the University of Botswana, Botswana. His current research is on appropriations of the Bible and Shakespeare in modern African writers. <MWIKISAP@mopipi.ub.bw>

Nahashon W. Ndung'u lectures on New Religious Movements and African Independent Churches in the Department of Religious Studies at the University of Nairobi, Kenya. <jmugambi@iconnect.co.ke>

Fidelis Nkomazana teaches Church History in the Department of Theology and Religious Studies at the University of Botswana, Botswana. His current research is in the history of Pentecostalism in Botswana, and the history of the Roman Catholic Church and the Dutch Reformed Church in Botswana. <NKOMAZAF@mopipi.-ub.bw>

Anthony O. Nkwoka teaches New Testament and African Christian Theology in the Department of Religious Studies of Obafemi Awolowo

University, Ile-Ife, Osun State, Nigeria. He is currently working on the challenges of Nigerian Pentecostal theology on the perspicuity of the Scriptures. <ankwoka@oauife.edu.ng>

Gomang Seratwa Ntloebide is a coordinator of humanities subjects in the Distance Education Unit, Centre for Continuing Education, at the University of Botswana. She is currently working on the role of *dingaka* in the 'salvation history' of Africa. <ntloegs@mopipi.ub.bw>

Justin Ukpong teaches New Testament at the Catholic Institute of West Africa, Port Harcourt, Nigeria. He is currently working on the methodology of inculturation biblical hermeneutics. <justinukpong@-home.com>

Eliud Wabukala is the Anglican Bishop of the Diocese of Bungoma in western Kenya and was formerly lecturer in Old Testament and Academic Dean at St Paul's United Theological College, Limuru, Kenya.

Robert Wafawanaka teaches Biblical Studies and Old Testament in the School of Theology at the Virginia Union University, Richmond, VA, USA. He is currently working on poverty and wealth in the Bible. <rwafawa@vuu.edu>

Ernst R. Wendland teaches at the Lutheran Seminary in Lusaka, Zambia, and is associated with the Centre for Bible Translation in Africa at the University of Stellenbosch, South Africa. He is also a United Bible Societies Translation Consultant supervising work in Zambia and Malawi. His current research includes comparative rhetorical and stylistic studies in biblical and certain Bantu languages. <ernst_wendland@hotmail.com>

Gerald O. West is Director of the Institute for the Study of the Bible and teaches Old Testament and Biblical Hermeneutics in the School of Theology at the University of Natal, Pietermaritzburg, South Africa. He is currently working on early indigenous receptions of the Bible in southern Africa. <west@nu.ac.za>

Gosnell L.O.R. Yorke, of West Indian extraction, is a Translation Consultant with the United Bible Societies and is responsible for

Bible translation in Angola, Botswana and Mozambique. Currently based in South Africa, he has a strong research interest in the Afrocentric approach to Bible translation. <113324.647@compuserve.com>

INTRODUCTION

Gerald O. West and Musa W. Dube

This volume of essays is more than a book; it is a collaborative project among African biblical scholars. And the project has not come to an end with the production of this book. When we began we hoped that the book would generate more than what it contains between its covers. So we used the opportunity to consult and call for contributions as widely as we could. We accessed every known mailing list of African biblical scholars, focusing where possible on the continent (particularly north of the Limpopo river) but not restricting ourselves to the continent. We also contacted those who work closely with African biblical scholarship. We literally sent out hundreds of invitations for contributions. We did not presume to chart beforehand what constitutes African biblical scholarship or what is happening with the Bible in Africa. We waited to see what we would be offered.

We have tried in every instance to err on the side of including a contribution; we feel that it is important to present in this volume as wide a sense of the presence of the Bible in Africa as possible. Unfortunately, we have not been able to include everything offered, nor has everyone who supported the project been able to offer something (in time). We have also lost contact with some of our potential contributors during the process; items posted have not reached their destinations, email contacts no longer function, and other forms of communication have failed. We apologise to those who feel we have let them down.

The project of collaboration among African (biblical) scholars has received considerable impetus from this book. Contacts have been made, meetings have taken place, resources have been shared, and new initiatives have been born. So the book has already, prior to its publication, fulfilled important expectations.

We did not set out to invite contributions to fit within a set format or our own particular construct of what constitutes the Bible in Africa. We are also fairly certain that the essays gathered here represent only a partial picture of the presence of the Bible in Africa.

We therefore hesitate to offer an "authoritative" Introduction. Each of us as editors have contributed essays that clearly indicate our own concerns and contexts; even the essay "Mapping Biblical Interpretation in Africa" by one of the editors is just that, the view of one of the editors. It is not an analysis of the essays in this volume. The breadth of the collection, and we thank E.J. Brill for the generous space limits for this project, is itself an important contribution, providing some sense of the rich diversity and complexity of the Bible in Africa and enabling an inter-textual conversation within the book between the essays. Our hope is that this volume will generate not only a host of related projects (and there are signs of this already) but also several analytical attempts to "introduce" the Bible in Africa.

In one sense of the word "introduce," those who read the Bible outside of Africa do need to have an introduction to—some form of *initial* meeting with—the Bible as it is read in Africa. One watches the puzzled frowns appear on the faces of colleagues in the West when one talks of biblical studies in Africa. This volume will, we believe, reduce the frown, providing as it does a fairly comprehensive account of academic biblical scholarship. The essays as a whole give a sense of the breadth and richness of what African biblical scholars are up to, and the bibliographies at the end of each essay, together with the remarkable "A Bibliography of the Bible in Africa" by Grant LeMarquand, point to still further resources. With this volume Western biblical scholars can no longer say, "We did not know."

However, while we know that this book will find its way into libraries around the Western world, we also know that most libraries in Africa will not be able to afford it. We worry about this and are finding ways to remedy the situation, for we hope that this collection of essays will provoke and encourage African scholars to take the task of documenting and analysing African biblical scholarship further. We are aware, and other African scholars will be aware, of the limits of this collection, but we offer it as a small step further along the way of charting the presence and place of the Bible in Africa. To enable African scholars to make use of this volume we (as editors) have asked E.J. Brill to make complementary copies available to all the contributors, and they have agreed to this. We will also use our royalties to buy additional copies of the book, which we will donate to ecumenical and accessible libraries in Africa. We hereby invite you the reader to join us in making the book as widely available in Africa as possible, either through your own networks our via us (email: west@nu.ac.za).

As our subtitle indicates, the essays in this volume discuss some of the transactions, trends and trajectories, of the Bible in Africa. With considerable difficulty and diffidence we have grouped the essays into clusters and in so doing have begun the process of inter-textual conversation.

"Part 1: Historical and Hermeneutical Perspectives" provides the reader with a feel for the landscape of African biblical interpreta-tion. Justin S. Ukpong's essay gives a good sense of both the his-torical and hermeneutical scope of African biblical interpretation, showing as well the lines of continuity and discontinuity with West-ern biblical scholarship. The essay by Gerald O. West sketches the hermeneutical contours of African biblical interpretation, particularly as they are perceived from a Southern African perspective. West's essay analyses a number of the important transactions between the Bible and Africa, and points to areas that require more careful atten-tion from African biblical scholars. These essays are followed by two essays which concentrate more specifically on African Old Testament (as it is referred to by the majority of African biblical scholars) and New Testament research respectively. The essay by Knut Holter on African Old Testament scholarship is organised as a chronological and topical guide to Old Testament scholarship in Africa from the 1960s. Grant LeMarquand's essay surveys a number of African inter-pretative communities and the New Testament texts and themes that have been important to them.

The next essay in this section serves as a significant reminder of the difference and diversity that characterise biblical interpretation in Africa. J.A. (Bobby) Loubser's essay on the interpretation of the Bible within Coptic Christianity takes us further north in the conti-nent and further back in time than the other essays. The inclusion of this essay among the other essays also raises the issue of what constitutes Africa and an African, as does the essay which follows. In his essay on the black diaspora, Gosnell L.O.R. Yorke charts the presence of the Bible and Africa in the interpretative practices of Africans in the diaspora. In particular, Yorke argues that the Bible "has played (and continues to play) a pivotal role in the identity preser-vation of displaced, dispersed, despised and dispossessed people. . . ."

The predominant sense of a hermeneutics of trust evident in the essays by Loubser and Yorke (and many of the other essays in the sections below) is an important aspect of the Bible's place in Africa; but the ambiguity of the Bible in Africa for African readers is equally a part of its presence. Musa W. Dube's essay on John 1:1–18 is an excellent example of the extreme mistrust that has become a regular reading strategy for many African readers, particularly in Southern Africa. Rejecting the implied author's map to the implied reader of John 1:1–18, Dube draws her own map for reading from her experiences of travel, both in Africa and in more hostile Western contexts. In his essay on Ngugi Wa Thiong'o's use of the Bible in two of his novels, Peter Wamulungwe Mwikisa raises serious questions about Ngugi's privileging of Bible, and, more profoundly, of the institutions and discourses that structurally privilege the Bible over against non-biblical religious narratives. While Ngugi's work sets out to resist and deconstruct the hegemonic hold of the Bible, he never quite manages, according to Mwikisa's analysis, to free himself from collusion. Collusion of another, related kind, is examined in the final essay in this section. Robert P. Carroll's essays tells the story of an interested outsider's visit to South Africa in 1993 and specifically of his impressions of the ambiguity of the Bible in South Africa. Reflecting on the Bible in the South African context, Carroll warns us that the Bible can be a dangerous book, so "it is necessary to be very careful in matters hermeneutical—*caveat lector*, mind how you read!" These are useful words with which to end this section and move into the next.

"Part 2: Particular Encounters with Particular Texts." The long encounter of Coptic Christians with the Bible described above in Loubser's essay has deeply shaped their modes of interpretation. The encounters with the Bible in West, East, Central and Southern Africa, though of shorter duration, have been equally intense and creative. Three essays which chart elements of the early encounters with the Bible begin this section. Philippe Denis carefully documents the production of what might be the earliest piece of biblical scholarship on the African continent, a translation of the Psalms into French in 1699. According to the translator, that this work was done in Africa was no accident. In his essay on the earliest encounters between the indigenous Batswana peoples and the Bible in Southern Africa, Fidelis Nkomazana shows how the kings of the Bakwena, Bakololo and Bangwato people shaped biblical interpretation in Southern Africa by the ways in which they responded to the arrival of the Bible. The translation of the Bible into vernacular African languages has been a decisive factor in the African appropriation of the Bible (see also Part 4). In his essay Nahashon W. Ndung'u analyses the contribution of the early vernacular Gikuyu language Bible to the formation of the Akurinu African Independent Churches. Here the Bible is used against those who brought it to Africa.

The historical emphasis of the above essays in this section now gives way to a geographical emphasis. The next essay in this section could be considered as a case of either North African or East African biblical interpretation. Mark McEntire's essay, situated in Ethiopia, examines how students from a Protestant Ethiopian seminary engage with modes of biblical interpretation coming out of Southern and Western Africa. The West African interest continues in a series of essays from West Africa which document and analyse a range of West African reading resources. There are thee essays which reflect on the Bible reading practices of a particular ethnic group, the Ewe, in Ghana. Dorothy B.E.A. Akoto, in a remarkably creative reading of Psalm 23 and John 10, offers images from the lives of Ewe women as a way of re-envisaging the foreign, imported, and inappropriate image of "the good Shepherd" prevalent among Ewe Christians. Rebecca Yawa Ganusah explores the tensions between missionary initiated appropriations of the Bible and local indigenous appropriations around the issue of offering libation and offers some suggestions on how this issue might be dealt with interpretatively. Similarly, Andrew Olu Igenoza, although not specifically focusing on the Ewe, suggests that the contextual balancing of scripture with scripture approach of the Scripture Union in Nigeria and Ghana may provide a way forward for dealing with evil forces. Solomon K. Avotri shows how local cultural resources among the Ewe resonate with and are used to appropriate the story of the Gerasene demoniac in Mark 5. Two essays by Nigerian biblical scholars, Anthony O. Nkwoka and David Tuesday Adamo, demonstrate, respectively, the centrality of the Bible in the life of African (Igbo) Christians and the power of the Bible as both text and sacred object in the life of African (Yoruba) Christians.

Similar concerns and interpretative moves can be found in the essays from Eastern and Central Africa in this section. Eliud Wabukala and Grant LeMarquand discuss in detail the readings of Deuteronomy 21:22–23 and Galatians 3:13 among the Babukusu people on the border (a colonial construct) between Uganda and Kenya, and the pastoral implications of their readings. Fergus J. King examines how contemporary Tanzanian hymn writers use the Bible in their work. Shifting somewhat southwards, Hilary B.P. Mijoga surveys the role of the Bible in Malawi, paying particular attention to its liberatory and empowering potential in a time of political struggle.

Moiseraele Prince Dibeela provides a Southern African Setswana perspective on Genesis 1:1–10. Writing from Botswana, Dibeela reads Genesis 1:1–10 as a Motswana man belonging to the Bangwaketsi ethnic group. Academic training and African context encounter each other in this existential appropriation of Gensis 1:1–10. In his essay on the impact of the Bible on traditional rain-making institutions in Western Zimbabwe, Hezekiel Mafu traces how practitioners of African Indigenous Religion have recently appropriated the Bible in their rain-making rituals. The complex and ambiguous transactions that make up the mix of the indigenous African encounter with the colonial/missionary enterprise are analysed in detail by Jonathan A. Draper from South Africa in his essay on the two-way exchange between Bishop William Colenso and Magema kaMagwaza Fuze.

Almost all the essays could be incorporated in this section as all reflect particular encounters with the Bible. However, we think it may be useful to group some of the essays in other ways. "Part 3: Comparison and Translation as Transaction" draws together essays from two important paradigms in African biblical scholarship: the comparative paradigm and the translation paradigm. Eric Anum's essay discusses the ongoing dialogue among those who work within a comparative paradigm about its limits and possibilities. In his essay, Themba L.J. Mafico uses his Old Testament scholarship to justify and recover what he considers to be important religious and cultural elements of the Ndau people of Zimbabwe. Bernice Letlhare draws on notions of corporate personality in sociological studies of both ancient Israel and Tswana society in order to recover and critique this important concept. Robert Wafawanaka pushes the boundaries of the comparative paradigm by focusing on poverty rather than religio-cultural questions. Old Testament texts on poverty speak to the situation of the African poor, reinforcing Christian identity with ancient Israel and suggesting mechanisms for coping with poverty. By comparing *Ngaka*, a traditional indigenous healer among the Batswana of Botswana, with Jesus the healer, Gomang Seratwa Ntloedibe presents a compelling case for the affirmation of the healing and saving role of the *Ngaka* despite the legacy of colonial condemnation. Both the *Ngaka* and Jesus are "sacred agents that serve God's creation."

Closely related to the above essays are those with an overt interest in translation. However, as the essays gathered here demonstrate, translation in African contexts is always more than a technical exercise. In two essays Aloo Osotsi Mojola provides us with a useful overview of the history of Bible translation in East Africa. The complex interplay between local indigenous actors and the agendas of missionary and colonial forces is evident throughout his surveys. Ernst Wendland and Salimo Hachibamba present a case study of the problems implicit in many of the earliest translations. How do Africans make sense of God's foreign accent in early missionary translations? Wendland and Hachibamba answer this question through a careful analysis of a Chitonga translation of Isaiah 52:13–53:12. The final essay in this section revisits an old New Testament question about the identity of "son of man" in the gospels from the perspective of the Kiswahili translation of the phrase. According to Jean Claude Loba Mkole, against the advice of many translators and translators' helps the Kiswahili translation appears to have got it right.

The final section of the book, "Part 4: Redrawing the Boundaries of the Bible in Africa," assembles those essays which probe the boundaries of biblical scholarship in Africa. The place and presence of the Africa in the Bible, specifically in the Old Testament, has been an interest of Africans, both on the continent and (particularly) in the diaspora. Knut Holter's essay provides a survey of the African biblical literature on this topic and some insightful hermeneutical analysis of its importance. Essays by Justin S. Ukpong and Gerald O. West investigate the interface between socially engaged African biblical scholars and ordinary African "readers" of the Bible. Ukpong reports on a long-term research project exploring the many elements that constitute the reading practices of ordinary Africans. Ukpong's essay also signals some of the ways in which scholars in the West can collaborate with African scholars in these matters. West's essay reflects on ten years of the Institute for the Study of the Bible, a project in which socially engaged biblical scholars and ordinary black African South African "readers" of the Bible from poor and marginalised communities interpret the Bible together. Ordinary Africans who interpret the Bible are constitutive of African biblical scholarship, and these essays explore the deconstructing and reshaping of the discipline their presence entails. The final essay, by Musa W. Dube, confronts one of the major scourges facing Africa today, globalisation, and looks to the Bible for resources with which to counter its many forms. Dube's essay is an important reminder that the

African context is never static, and so contextual interpretation of the Bible must be ever vigilant.

"Part 5: Bibliography" is not merely a collecting and sorting of the bibliographies accompanying each essay; it is an independent project by Grant LeMarquand and incorporates years of diligent work. While it may not be exhaustive, it is the most comprehensive bibliography on the Bible in Africa ever published.

In writing this Introduction we have been aware of the other different ways in which we could have structured the book. The essays cannot be captured in the few lines allocated to each, nor do the dialogue partners we have placed them beside exhaust their contribution. Therefore, we grant you the reader the right to read as you will, following whatever lines of connection you find most useful.

We dedicate this book to the next generation of African biblical scholars and ordinary "readers" of the Bible; we hope this book may be of some use.

PART ONE

HISTORICAL AND HERMENEUTICAL PERSPECTIVES

DEVELOPMENTS IN BIBLICAL INTERPRETATION IN AFRICA: HISTORICAL AND HERMENEUTICAL DIRECTIONS

Justin S. Ukpong

Africa can rightly be referred to as the cradle of systematic biblical interpretation in Christianity. The earliest such attempt can be traced to the city of Alexandria and to such names as Clement of Alexandria, Origen, and others who lived and worked there (Trigg 1988: 21–23). The foundation laid by this tradition, which was largely allegorical and uncritical in the modern sense, lasted in the Western Church till the onset of the Enlightenment. It was replaced by the historical critical method in the 18th century followed by the literary approaches in the 20th century. These methods, developed in the West, have today been well established and recognized as veritable scientific tools of modern biblical research. In Africa South of the Sahara, which is the focus of this essay, the impact of these modern methods began to be felt about the middle of the 20th century. This corresponds with the period of political independence and the founding of African universities where these methods were taught. By the third quarter of the century, the use of these methods in academic interpretation of the bible in Africa had become widespread (Onwu 1984–85: 35; Le Roux 1993). Biblical scholarship in Africa today is therefore to some extent a child of these modern methods of Western biblical scholarship.

In spite of this however, biblical scholars in Africa have been able to develop a parallel method of their own (Holter 1995, LeMarquand 1996: 163). The particular characteristic of this method is the concern to create an encounter between the biblical text and the African context. This involves a variety of ways that link the biblical text to the African context such that the main focus of interpretation is on the communities that receive the text rather than on those that produced it or on the text itself, as is the case with the Western methods. To be sure, there are two currents of academic readings of the bible in Africa, one follows the Western pattern, while the other follows the African pattern of linking the text with the African context. Many

African authors publish in both patterns. However, this essay is interested only in the latter.

The purpose of this essay is to show the developments that have taken place in this method of biblical interpretation in Africa. I shall focus mainly on academic interpretation excluding apartheid and popular uses of the bible, and shall begin from the 1930's when one of the pioneering studies was first published. Within these parameters, I find it convenient to divide the development of biblical interpretation in Africa into three phases as follows:

Phase I (1930s–70s): reactive and apologetic, focussed on legitimizing African religion and culture, dominated by the comparative method.

Phase II (1970s–90s): reactive-proactive, use of African context as *resource* for biblical interpretation, dominated by inculturation-evaluative method and liberation hermeneutics (black theology).

Phase III (1990s): proactive, recognition of the *ordinary reader*, African context as *subject* of biblical interpretation, dominated by liberation and inculturation methodologies.

It must be emphasized that the above division is made to facilitate discussion and not to parcel biblical interpretation in Africa into compartments. It is also important to note that the seeds of one phase are sown in the previous phase, and the emergence of a new phase does not mean the disappearance of the former.

The beginning of modern biblical studies in Africa, what I have called Phase I, was in response to the widespread condemnation of African religion and culture by the Christian missionaries of the 19th and 20th centuries. African religion and culture were condemned as demonic and immoral and therefore to be exterminated before Christianity could take roots in Africa. In response to this, some Westerners who were sympathetic to the African cause and later on Africans themselves, undertook researches that sought to legitimize African religion and culture. This was done by way of *comparative studies* carried out within the framework of Comparative Religion. It took the form of showing continuities and discontinuities between the religious culture of Africa and the bible, particularly the Old Testament. Since the New Testament shares the same cultural worldview as the Old Testament, the consequence of such comparison was considered to extend to the New Testament too (Dickson 1984: 181). These studies were mainly located in Western, Eastern and Central Africa.

The comparison by Joseph John Williams, the earliest of such studies that was widely known, sought to illustrate a possible physical contact with the ancient Hebrews and therefore borrowing. However, later studies did not have this intention and were merely meant to illustrate similarities in patterns of thought and feelings, and to show how certain basic notions have been expressed by people in different places and times (Gaster 1970, "Preface"). The focus of early comparative studies was on the Old Testament, but there have been comparisons involving the New Testament.

Joseph John Williams' *Hebrewism of West Africa* published in 1930 represents the earliest, widely known, example of comparative studies. In the study, the author seeks to show a correlation between the Hebrew language and the Ashanti language of Ghana based mainly on similarities in sound. He also points to a similarity between the worship of deities apart from *Yahweh* in the Old Testament, and the Ashanti worship of God and the divinities. These similarities lead him to argue for the possibility of either the descent of the Ashanti of Ghana from the Jewish race or a very early contact between the Ashanti and the Jews (Williams 1930: 35). Williams' methodology has been shown by modern scholars to be superficial and weak. His conclusions have not been shared by later generations of scholars.

It was not until the 1960s that Williams' method was improved upon by later researchers who employed the methodology of Comparative Religion, and focussed on religious themes and practices rather than on mere extrinsic resemblance. Kwezi Dickson (1973: 5, 141–184) has done many studies in this area pointing to what he calls the Old Testament "atmosphere" that makes the African context "a kindred atmosphere." He has shown similar elements in both cultures like sense of community, pervasive nature of religion, and so on. I (Ukpong 1987) have also done a comparative study of the sacrifices of the Traditional Religion of the Ibibio of Nigeria and those of the book of Leviticus. In a similar study, S. Kibicho (1968) has shown the existence of a continuity between the African and the biblical conceptions of God. John Mbiti (1971) has also made a comparative study of the New Testament and African understandings of eschatology.

There have been objections to this type of study based on the fact that Ancient Israel and contemporary Africa are far apart in both space and time (Isaac 1964: 95). Such studies are however justified on these grounds, that only existential and not essential continuities that are sought. Besides, in the field of linguistics, a similar method involving the study of semantic parallels of diverse languages has been successfully used (Gaster 1970: "Preface"). The main weaknesses of this approach however, is that it does not involve drawing hermeneutic conclusions, and does not show concern for secular issues which have become important today in theological discussions in Africa. Besides, such studies are generally apologetic, and sometimes polemical. Their value therefore is mainly heuristic (Dickson 1984: 181).

An important result of comparative studies is that African traditional religion came to be seen as "Africa's Old Testament." African culture and religion came to be recognized as a *praeparatio evangelica* (a preparation for the gospel) that is, a fertile ground for the gospel. Also, these studies have helped to articulate the values of African culture and religion for the appropriation of Christianity. To this extent, they remain foundational to all biblical studies that link the biblical text to the African context.

Phase II, the period covering the 1970s–90s, has been one of the most dynamic and rewarding periods of biblical studies in Africa. In it, we notice that the reactive approach of the first phase gradually gives way to a proactive approach. The African context is used as a resource in the hermeneutic encounter with the bible, and the religious studies framework characteristic of the former phase gives way to a more theological framework. Two main approaches, which can be identified as inculturation and liberation, crystallize. The comparative approach had led to the recognition of African culture as a preparation for the gospel. However, Christianity was still being looked upon as a foreign religion expressed in foreign symbols and idiom. This generated the desire to make Christianity relevant to the African religio-cultural context and gave rise to the inculturation movement in theology. In terms of biblical studies, the inculturation approach is expressed in two models which I refer to as the *Africa-in-the-bible* studies and *evaluative* studies. Also, during this period, owing to the influence of socialist ideology, there arose greater consciousness about the need for theology to show concern for secular issues. Out of this background arose the liberation movement in theology which seeks to confront all forms of oppression, poverty and marginalization in society. The liberation approach to biblical interpretation is expressed in *liberation hermeneutics, black theology* and *feminist hermeneutics.*

Africa-in-the-bible studies investigate the presence of Africa and

African peoples in the bible and the significance of such presence. The overall purpose is to articulate Africa's influence on the history of Ancient Israel and Africa's contribution to the history of salvation, as well as correct negative interpretations of some biblical texts on Africa. These studies were developed in part as a way of establishing African historical and geographical links with the biblical world following on the comparative approach, and in part to correct the tendency in Western scholarship that de-emphasized Africa's presence and contribution in the biblical story. They belong to the same category of studies as those which, in the field of philosophy, have been able to show the contribution of ancient African nations to world culture (Diop 1974, Williams 1976). In cartography, a map of the world supposed to be quite old, that places Africa not Europe at the centre, was discovered and popularized earlier in the century. Researches of this type are often inspired by the movement referred to as "Afrocentrism" which seeks to articulate the role and contribution of Africa in world history.

Two main directions may be identified in these studies. One is concerned with correcting negative images about Africa and African peoples embedded in certain traditional readings of some biblical texts. An important theme in this regard which has appeared in different versions is the so-called curse of Ham (Peterson 1978) whose descendants are listed in Genesis 10:1–14 and 1 Chronicles 1:8–16 as the Cushites (Ethiopians), Mizraimites (Egyptians), Phutites, and Canaanites. In Genesis 9:18–27, Ham sees the nakedness of his drunken father Noah, but instead of covering him, reports this to his two brothers Shem and Japhet who cover their father. According to Hebrew tradition, Ham had committed an act of great disrespect towards his father. When Noah wakes up and learns of the actions of his children, he pronounces a curse not upon Ham but upon Canaan, Ham's son. A fifth century AD midrash on this narrative places Noah's curse directly on Ham and states: "Your seed will be ugly and dark-skinned" (Rice 1972). Also, the sixth century AD Babylonian Talmud states: "The descendants of Ham are cursed by being Black and are sinful with degenerate progeny" (Isaac 1980: 4–5). From these interpretations of the text came the idea that Africans are black because of the curse of Ham. It is very clear from the biblical text itself that the above interpretations of the narrative are purely ideological, for it is Ham's son Canaan and his descendants that were cursed. That Canaan (who was not yet born) was the one cursed seems based on the later experience of Israel's subjugation of Canaan. The argument that Ham is thereby also cursed does not seem to follow any logic. This mythic interpretation of the biblical text whose foundation is purely ideological was forcefully used by the Whites in South Africa and the Southern USA, as a support in their subjugation of the Blacks. There have therefore been researches today that show up such an interpretation as having no foundation in the text and as based on the ideology of dominance (Prior 1977, Felder 1991, Adamo 1993: 138–143).

The second approach seeks to identify the presence of Africa and African peoples in the bible as well as examine their contribution in biblical history. This is a direct reaction to the de-emphasis and exclusion, in Western scholarship, of Africa and its contribution to the biblical story. Such de-emphasis shows itself for example in that Egypt is often considered in biblical studies to belong to the Ancient Near East rather than to Africa. Also in the introductory courses in the Old Testament, the ancient Near East and Mesopotamia are focussed upon without much attention to the nations in Africa that made contributions to biblical history. Besides, some modern scholars have claimed that in the table of nations in Genesis 10, "the Negroes" are not mentioned because the author had not come in contact with them (Heinish 1952, Albright 1952). These studies have provoked reactions in terms of researches that seek to confirm Africa's presence and influence in the bible, Temba Mafico (1989: 100) has shown evidence of African influence on the religion of the patriarchs (and matriarchs), and in a number of studies David T. Adamo (1987: 1–8, 1992: 51–64) has focussed on this theme. Like the comparative approach, this model is not involved in the search for the theological meaning of the text, it however plays a very important and foundational role in creating awareness of the importance of African nations and peoples in the biblical story.

Evaluative studies focus on the encounter between African religion and culture, and the bible, and evaluate the theological underpinnings resulting from the encounter. They go beyond studying similarities and dissimilarities between African religion and the bible to interpreting the biblical text on the basis of these similarities and differences. The aim is to facilitate the communication of the biblical message within the African milieu, and to evolve a new understanding of Christianity that would be African and biblical. Generally, the historical critical method is used for the analysis of the biblical text, and anthropological or sociological approaches are used in analysing the African situation. Studies within this model often include, in their title, such phrases as: "in the light of . . .," "in the context of . . .," "biblical foundations for . . .," "against the background of. . . ." Up to five different approaches may be isolated within this model. Very often however, elements of one approach are combined with those of another, and sometimes elements of the comparative model are found in some of these approaches. However, in each study, the principal elements of one approach are generally predominant.

The first approach seeks to evaluate elements of African culture, religion, beliefs, concepts or practices in the light of the biblical witness, to arrive at a Christian understanding of them and bring out their value for Christian witness. The historical critical method is used in analysing the biblical text. The belief or practice is analysed in its different manifestations and its values and disvalues are pointed out against the background of biblical teaching. Examples of such studies include, Patrick Kalilombe's (1980: 205–220) "The Salvific Value of African Religions: An Essay in Contextualized Bible Reading for Africa" and Ernest A. McFall's (1970), *Approaching the Nuer through the Old Testament.*

The second approach is concerned with what a biblical text or theme has to say in the critique of a particular issue in the society or in the church's life, or what lessons may be drawn from a biblical text or theme for a particular context. It is similar to the first above but with the difference that in the first approach the contextual realities studied are assumed to be values or at least to contain values whereas in this one they are presented as liabilities to be challenged with the biblical message. The study involves analysing the biblical text and pointing out the challenge it issues to the context or drawing its implications for the context. Generally, historical critical tools are used for the study. For example, Andrew Igenoza (1988: 12–25) has offered a biblical critique of the practice of medicine and healing in African Christianity, Chris Manus (1982; 18–26) has studied Paul's attitude towards ethnicity in a critique of the situation of ethnic discrimination in Nigeria, Gabriel Abe (1986: 66–73) has shown the relevance of the Old Testament concept of the covenant for the Nigerian society, and Nlenanya Onwu (1988: 43–51) has studied the parable of the Unmerciful Servant against the context of the erosion of the traditional idea and experience of brotherhood in Africa.

In the third approach biblical themes or texts are interpreted against the background of African culture, religion and life experience. The aim is to arrive at a new understanding of the biblical text that would be informed by the African situation, and would be African and Christian. Historical critical tools are used in analysing the biblical text. The basis for this approach is the realization that any interpretation of a biblical text or theme is done from the sociocultural perspective of the interpreter. Approaching a theme or text from an African perspective is therefore expected to offer some fresh insights into its meaning even though the tools of interpretation still remain Western. For example, Daniel Wambutda (1981) has offered some fresh insight by examining the concept of salvation from an African perspective and Bayo Abijole (1988) has given an African interpretation of St. Paul's concept of "principalities and powers" that is different from Western interpretations.

The fourth approach has to do with erecting "bridgeheads" for communicating the biblical message. This means making use of concepts from either the bible or African culture, with which Africans can easily identify, to show the continuity between African culture and Christianity, for the purpose of communicating the biblical message. For example, in exploring the subject of Christology in an African context, John Pobee (1979: 88–94) has shown that for the Akan of Ghana, from whose perspective he writes, Jesus' kinship as presented in the gospels is a key concept for underscoring his humanity. Also, he has used the anthropological concept of "the grand ancestor," with which Africans can readily identify, to describe Christ. John Mbiti (1972: 54) also pointed out that the New Testament images of Jesus as miracle worker and risen Lord (Christus Victor) are images Africans can easily identify with, because they show Jesus as the conqueror of evil spirits, disease and death, which Africans fear most. These concepts serve as "bridgeheads" for communicating to Africans the role of Christ in the human community.

The fifth approach has to do with the study of the biblical text to discover biblical models or biblical foundations for aspects of contemporary church life and practice in Africa. Generally, such studies use the tools of historical critical research in analysing the biblical text. For example, Balembo Buetubela (1984) has studied the relationship between the mother churches in Jerusalem and Antioch and the mission churches they founded in early Christianity, and has shown how the relationship was marked by the autonomy of the mission churches rather than by their dependence on the mother

churches. He offers this as a model for the development of the autonomy of the young churches in Africa today. I (Ukpong 1994) have
analysed the biblical foundations for the inculturation of Christianity.
Joseph Osei-Bonsu (1990) has pointed to some New Testament antecedents of contextualization of Christianity that form the basis for
the contextualization of Christianity in Africa today.

The evaluative approach is the most common approach in biblical studies in Africa today. It is based on the classical understanding of exegesis, as the recovery of the meaning of a text intended
by the author through historical critical tools, and of hermeneutics,
as the application of the meaning so recovered to a particular contemporary context. Its basic weakness is that it does not give attention to social, economic and political issues which have become
important today in theological discussion. However, as a result of
these researches, African culture and religion have been seen to be
not just a preparation for the gospel, as in the comparative method,
but *indispensable resources in the interpretation of the gospel message* and in
the development of African Christianity.

Liberation hermeneutics in general uses the bible as a resource
for struggle against oppression of any kind based on the biblical witness that God does not sanction oppression but rather always stands
on the side of the oppressed to liberate them. Here we shall focus
on political and economic oppression in general. Because of the
specific theological response to them, racial oppression (apartheid) in
South Africa and oppression against women are treated separately
below under the headings "Black theology" and "feminist theology"
respectively.

The story of God's political liberation of the Hebrews in the book
of Exodus is the ground text for the hermeneutics of political liberation. While God's call on Israel to take special care of the poor
among them, and deal justly with all (see Exodus 23:11, Amos 2:6–7,
5:21–24), and Jesus' sympathetic attitude to and teachings in favour
of the poor (see Luke 4:18–19, 6:20–21) provide the grounding for
the hermeneutics of economic liberation. Throughout the bible, the
message is that while the poor are to be loved and cared for, there
should be commitment to action aimed at eradicating poverty and
oppression. Thus Jean-Marc Ela (1994) asserts that "Africa today is
crucified," and if the bible is read from this perspective, Christians
will be able to link their faith with commitment to transform society.
C.S. Banana (1981: 44–51, 1982: 21) uses Marxist analysis of the

biblical text to show how the bible not only condemns economic exploitation and political oppression, but also points the way to economic and political transformation of society.

Black theology is a form of liberation hermeneutics focussed on the issue of apartheid racial discrimination that prevailed in South Africa until 1994. Its point of departure is the ideology of Black consciousness whereby the Blacks are made critically aware of their situation of oppression based on their skin colour and of the need to analyse the situation and to struggle against it. It uses the bible as a resource for this struggle. The understanding of "Black" here covers all who were discriminated against in the apartheid system, and this includes ethnic Blacks, Indians and coloured people. Two strands may be discerned in this theology. One seeks to interpret the bible in the light of the apartheid experience, and to reflect on this experience in the light of the biblical message (Moore 1994: 7). Because the bible had been wrongly used as an instrument to entrench the apartheid system, it remains central to Black theology in its struggle for liberation. Its point of departure is that the bible basically contains a liberating message, that apartheid is diametrically opposed to the central message of the bible which is love of the neighbour, and that God is always on the side of the oppressed and therefore in support of the Black liberation struggle (Tutu 1979: 166, Boesak 1984: 149–160). Liberative themes in the bible are studied as a resource of empowerment for the liberation struggle.

The other strand starts from the position that the bible cannot be uncritically accepted as a resource for the liberation struggle. This is because the bible itself was written by the elite to serve their interests. It is steeped in the ideology of the elite, is oppressive and in places mutes the voices of the oppressed. It is for this reason that it was used by the apartheid regime to suppress the Blacks in South Africa. To make it serve the interest of the Black struggle, it must first be liberated from that ideology. This is the position strongly articulated by Itumeleng Mosala (1989: 13–42). He proposes the use of the historical-materialist analysis of the biblical text for his purpose.

Black theology has made an immense contribution to the demise of apartheid in South Africa. This is epitomized in the *Kairos Document* issued in 1985 by a number of concerned theologians in South Africa on the issue of apartheid. The document, which in many ways exercised the international community, focussed on the ethical and theological impropriety of apartheid. Apart from this, Black theology has contributed an important dimension to theological reflection in Africa by focussing on the issue of socio-political and economic relations which some of the other theologies on the continent lack. In spite of the abolition of apartheid and the resultant spirit of reconciliation, unity and solidarity in South Africa, a theology of liberation still has relevance in that country. For one thing, it will take a long time for the legacy of apartheid to disappear. For another, the liberation struggle must be seen as an ongoing exercise involving the marginalised in society. However, Black theologians will need to reevaluate their approach and emphasis in view of the changed situation. The task is no longer liberation from apartheid but liberation from the legacy of apartheid which is multifaceted. This includes the entrenched psychological distance between the different racial groups, poverty, marginalization etc. The direction must be total liberation for fullness of life, reconciliation and integration.

Feminist hermeneutics are liberation hermeneutics focussed on the oppression of women. It uses the bible as a resource for the struggle against the subordination of women in contemporary society and church life. Because the bible has been used to support such subordination, a feminist critique of the bible and of the conventional mode of biblical interpretation forms part of feminist hermeneutics. At least five approaches to feminist hermeneutics by African theologians are discernible. These are not mutually exclusive and very often a number of them are used in combination.

Coming to the first three approaches, the first, according to Mercy Oduyoye (1994: 47), is a challenge to the conventional hermeneutics by which scripture and the history of Christianity are interpreted in androcentric terms. For example, it is presumed that God is male, and instances in the bible where God is described with feminine attributes are ignored. Biblical translations, as a rule, render God's name with the male pronoun. Feminist theologians refer to such hermeneutics as imprisonment of God in maleness. This approach is foundational to all feminist hermeneutics. The second approach seeks to critique or reinterpret those biblical texts that are oppressive to women or portray them as inferior to men through "a close rereading" of such texts "in their literary and cultural contexts." Thus Teresa Okure (1985: 20–21) has shown that the creation of Eve from Adam's rib, far from denoting a situation of inferiority as is often understood, denotes their identity in nature, their destined marital status and their equality. Similarly, concerning some sexist

Pauline texts, Mbuy Beya (1990: 155–156) has pointed out that Paul was dealing with specific situations of disorder that needed establishing "a certain hierarchy for the sake of order." He was therefore not giving a universal and timeless directive. While the third approach focuses on texts that show the positive role of women in the history of salvation or in the life of the church. Some of these are explicit while others are implicit. Thus through an analysis of Jesus' teachings, parables and miracles, Anne Nasimiyu-Wasike (1991) has shown Jesus' attitude to women to have been positive. Joyce Tzabedze (1986) has also studied the positive role of women in the early church as reflected in 1 Timothy and Ephesians, and Mbuy Beya (1990) has highlighted the role of women in the history of Israel some of whom were unnamed like the widow of Zarephath (1 Kings 17:8). Their lives have become an inspiration for contemporary women in their struggle in a male dominated world.

Of the last two approaches: The fourth approach enquires into the basic biblical theological orientation that can function as a guide to interpreting both the negative and positive biblical texts about women. Mercy Oduyoye (1994: 48–51) identifies the theology of creation which affirms the basic equality of man and woman created in the image of God, and the theology of community which calls for the exclusion of violence and discrimination in society. Both theologies, she argues, are fundamental to all biblical teaching. And the last approach seeks to interpret biblical texts from the perspective of African women's experience. Rereading the stories of polygamy in the Old Testament from African women's experience of polygamy. Anne Nasimiyu-Wasike (1992) is able to show that the Old Testament itself contains a critique of this institution, contrary to the common assumption that it extols it.

The above shows that there are two main concerns in feminist hermeneutics—a critique of the androcentrism both of earlier interpreters of the bible and of the bible itself, and a recovery of the forgotten and muted voices, the images and contributions of women in the biblical text. Using a vast array of critical tools, including the tools of historical and literary criticism, and other disciplines like sociology and anthropology, it has succeeded in calling scholarly attention to many things that were taken for granted in the bible.

In Phase III, covering the 1990s, biblical studies in Africa become more assertive and proactive daring to make an original contribution. The two main methodologies of *inculturation* and *liberation* which had crystallized in the second phase are carried forward with new orientations. One is the orientation that recognizes the *ordinary African readers* (that is, non-biblical scholars) as important partners in academic bible reading, and seeks to integrate their perspectives in the process of academic interpretation of the bible. This is exemplified by Gerald West's *contextual bible study* method. The other is the orientation which, apart from recognizing the role of the ordinary readers, seeks to make the African context the *subject* of interpretation of the bible. This is exemplified by my *inculturation hermeneutics*. Thus, in this phase, the African context is seen as both, providing the critical resources for biblical interpretation and the subject of interpretation.

In contextual bible study, the bible is read against a specific concrete human situation, in this case, the situation of racial oppression and poverty in South Africa, within the context of faith, and with a commitment to personal and social transformation. In this, it shares the same goal as Black theology except that the starting point of Black theology is Black consciousness. However, its specific feature is that it recognizes the importance of the approach, the perspectives and concerns of the ordinary African readers of the bible. It seeks to empower them for critical study of the bible in relation to their life situation and for personal and societal transformation. It operates at the interface between academic and ordinary readings of the bible and thus seeks to bridge the gap between academic and ordinary readings of the bible. The procedure involves interaction between academic and ordinary readers of the bible such that the ordinary readers are helped to develop critical awareness and identify and use local critical resources in their reading of the bible. In developing the hermeneutics for this approach to bible reading, the resources of the people's culture and historical life experience are used as complementary to conventional critical tools of biblical exegesis. This recognition, by the academic community, of the place of the ordinary reader's in the scheme of things, regarding the appropriation of the biblical message, makes academic biblical scholarship relevant to the community of believers. According to Gerald West (1993: 58–61,74), a principal exponent of this approach, "If we are serious about . . . relating biblical studies to ordinary readers . . . then the contextual Bible study process provides the framework in which to read the Bible."

One criticism that runs through most of the inculturation models discussed above is lack of attention to social issues like poverty, political oppression, etc., while lack of attention to specifically African religio-cultural issues such as belief in ancestors, the spirits, spirit possession, witchcraft, etc. is the criticism of the liberation models. Inculturation hermeneutics discussed here seeks to redress the situation by adopting a *holistic approach to culture* whereby both the secular and religious aspects of culture are seen to be interconnected and as having implications one for the other, and the bible is read within the religious as well as the economic, social and political contexts of Africa (Ukpong 1994a). The second feature of this approach is that it operates at the interface of academic and ordinary readings of the bible. The characteristics of ordinary readers here include that they are strongly influenced by the world-view provided by their indigenous culture as opposed to the world-view of the Western technological culture, and that they are poor, oppressed and marginalised. The third feature is that the African context forms the *subject* of interpretation of the bible. This means that the conceptual framework of interpretation is informed by African socio-cultural perspectives. Therefore, rather than that the biblical text be read through a Western grid and the meaning so derived be applied in an African context, this model is concerned that the biblical text should be read through a grid developed within the African socio-cultural context. In this way the people's context becomes the *subject* of interpretation of the biblical text. The goal of interpretation is the actualization of the theological meaning of the text in today's context so as to forge integration between faith and life, and engender commitment to personal and societal transformation.

Certain basic assumptions that belong to the root paradigm of African culture inform the interpretive framework. Among these are, the unitive view of reality whereby reality is seen not as composed of matter and spirit, sacred and profane but as a unity with visible and invisible aspects, the divine origin of the universe and the interconnectedness between God, humanity and the cosmos, and the sense of community whereby a person's identity is defined in terms of belonging to a community. The basic hermeneutic theory at work is that the *meaning of a text is a function of the interaction between the text in its context and the reader in his/her context.* Thus, there is no one absolute meaning of a text to be recovered through historical analysis alone. Also there are not two processes, consisting of recovery of the meaning of a text through historical analysis and then applying it to the present context, but one process of a reader who is critically aware of his/her context interacting with the text analysed in its context. For procedure, the general pattern for Third World hermeneutics is followed. The starting point is analysis of the contemporary context against which the text is to be interpreted, and analysis of the context of the text. The text is then read *dynamically* within the contemporary context that has been analysed. This involves entering into the text with a critical awareness about the contemporary context and allowing it to evoke in the reader appropriate reactions, responses and commitments about the context. The bible is seen as a *sacred classic*—a book of devotion and norm of morality as well as an ancient literary work worth attention beyond its time. I have done two studies in this model, one clarifying the methodology, and the other applying the methodology to a particular biblical text (Ukpong 1995, 1996).

Modern biblical interpretation can conveniently be grouped into three main approaches (see West 1995: 131). One is the *historical critical approach* that focuses on the history of the text, its author and original audience. In this approach, the meaning of the text is identified with the meaning intended by the author. The second are the *literary approaches* that focus on the text and its underlying structure, and sees the meaning of the text as attained by decoding the text, and which also focuses on the reader in interaction with the text, and sees the meaning of the text as emerging in the encounter between the reader and the text. Closely associated with this is the third, the *contextual approach* which focuses on the context of the reader in relation to the text. It uses the reader's context in various ways as a factor in making the meaning of the text. All the approaches to biblical interpretation in Africa discussed above (and indeed all Third World approaches to biblical interpretation) belong to the last approach. Their point of departure is the context of the reader, and they are all concerned with linking the biblical text to the reader's context.

Given the diversity in the African cultural, religious, political, social and economic terrain, and the strategy of linking the biblical text to the African context, the contribution of modern Africa to biblical interpretation promises to be significant. The developments so far point to the two models of inculturation and liberation, gradually cross-fertilizing each other such that, both will be concerned with religious as well as secular issues in society. The importance of the ordinary reader will gradually come to the fore, because academic reading of the bible in Africa can no longer afford to ignore the concerns and perspectives of the ordinary reader. Since African biblical scholarship focuses on the community that receives the text, any continued ignoring of the ordinary readers will lead to sterile scholarship. African questions are now being put to the bible and African resources are being used in answering them. No longer then shall we have from the bible answers to questions not asked by Africans (Tutu 1978: 336). Biblical interpretation in Africa has made bold strides which can be said to place it at the threshold of maturity as we enter the third millennium. However, the real test of this maturity will be the extent to which it will sustain the African context as the *subject* of interpretation of the bible so that the hitherto muted voices and concerns of ordinary readers will come alive in the academic forum.

BIBLIOGRAPHY

Abe, G.O. "*Berith*: Its Impact on Israel and Its Relevance to the Nigerian Society." *Africa Journal of Biblical Studies* 1 (1986): 66–73.

Abijole, B. "St. Paul's Concept of Principalities and Powers in African Context." *Africa Theological Journal* 17:2 (1988): 118–129.

Adamo, David T. "The Black Prophet in the Old Testament." *Journal of Arabic and Religious Studies* 4 (1987): 1–8.

———. "Ethiopia in the Bible." *African Christian Studies* 8 (1992): 51–64.

———. "The Table of Nations Reconsidered in African Perspective (Genesis 10)." *Journal of African Religion and Philosophy* 2 (1993): 138–143.

Albright, W.F. "The Old Testament World." In *The Interpreter's Bible*. New York: Abingdon Press, 1952.

Banana, C.S. *The Gospel According to Ghetto*. Gwero: Mambo Press, 1981.

———. *Theology of Promise*. Harare: College Press, 1982.

Beya, Marie Bernadette M. "Doing Theology as African Women." *Voices From the Third World* 13:1 (1990): 155–156.

Boesak, Alan. *Black and Reformed: Apartheid, Liberation and the Calvinist Tradition*. Johannesburg: Skotaville Press, 1984.

Buetubela, B. "L'Autonomie des Jeunes Eglises et les Actes." In Eds W. Amewowo et al., *Les Actes des Apôtres et les Jeunes Eglises: Actes du Deuxieme Congres des Biblistes Africains, Ibadan, 31 Juillet–3 Aout, 1984*, Kinshasa, 1990: 77–105.

Dickson, K.A. "The Old Testament and African Theology." *The Ghana Bulletin of Theology* 4:4 (1973).

———. *Theology in Africa*. London: Darton, Longman and Todd, Maryknoll: Orbis, 1984.

Diop, Cheikh A. *The African Origin of Civilization: Myth or Reality?* Westport: Lawrence Hill, 1974.

Ela, Jean-March, "Christianity and Liberation in Africa." In Ed. R. Gibellini, *Paths of African Theology*, Maryknoll: Orbis, 1994: 146–147.

Felder, C.H., Ed. *Stony the Road We Trod: Africa American Biblical Interpretation*. Philadelphia: Fortress, 1991.

Gaster, T.H. *Myth, Legend and Custom in the Old Testament*. New York: Harper & Row, 1969.

Heinish, P. *History of the Old Testament*. Collegeville: Liturgical Press, 1952.

Holter, Knut. "Ancient Israel and Modern Nigeria: Some Remarks from Sidelines to the Socio-Critical Aspect of Nigerian Old Testament Scholarship." Paper Read at the Annual Conference of the Nigerian Association for Biblical Studies, Owerri, Nigeria, October 1995.

Igenoza, Andrew O. "Medicine and Healing in African Christianity: A Biblical Critique." *African Ecclesial Review* 30 (1988): 12–25.

Isaac, Ephraim. "Genesis, Judaism and the 'Sons of Ham'." *Slavery and Abolition: A Journal of Comparative Studies* 1:1 (1980): 4–5.

Isaac, Erich. "Relations Between the Hebrew Bible and Africa." *Jewish Social Studies* 26:2 (1964).

Kalilombe, P. "The Salvific Value of African Religions: A Contextualized Bible Reading for Africa." In Eds A. Angang et al., *Christianisme et Identité Africaine: Point de vue exegetique—Actes du 1ᵉʳ Congres des biblistes africains, Kinshasa, 26–30 Decembre 1978*, Kinshasa: Facultes Catholiques de Theologie, 1980: 205–220.

Kibicho, S. "The Interaction of the Traditional Kikuyu Concept of God with the Biblical Concept." *Cahiers des Religions Africaines* 2:4 (1968).

LeMarquand, G. "The Historical Jesus and African New Testament Scholarship." In Eds William E. Arnal and Michael Desjardins *Whose Historical Jesus?*, Waterloo: Wilfrid Laurier University Press, 1997.

Le Roux, J.H. *A Story of Two Ways: Thirty Years of Old Testament Scholarship in South Africa*. Pretoria: Vita Verba, 1993.

McFall, Ernest A. *Approaching the Nuer through the Old Testament*. Pasadena: William Carey Library, 1970.

Mafico, T.L.J. "Evidence for African Influence on the Religious Customs of the Patriarchs." In Eds J.B. Wiggins & D.J. Lull, *Abstracts: American Academy of Religion/Society of Biblical Literature 1989*, Atlanta: Scholars Press, 1989: 100.

Manus, Chris. "Galatians 3:28—A Study on Paul's Attitude Towards Ethnicity: Its Relevance for Contemporary Nigeria." *Ife Journal of Religion* 2 (1982): 18–26.

Mbiti, J. *New Testament Eschatology in an African Background: A Study of the Encounter between New Testament Theology and African Traditional Concepts*, London: London University Press, 1971.

———. "Some African Concepts of Christology." In Ed. George F. Vicedom, *Christ and the Younger Churches*, London: SPCK 1972, 54.

Moore, Basil. "Black Theology Revisited" *Bulletin for Contextual Theology* 1 (1994): 7.

Mosala, Itumeleng J. *Biblical Hermeneutics and Black Theology in South Africa*. Eerdmans, Grand Rapids, 1989.

Mveng, E. "la bible et l'Afrique noire." In Eds E. Mveng & R.J.Z. Werblowsky, *The Jerusalem Congress on Black and the Bible*, Jerusalem: The Israel Interfaith Committee, 1972: 23–39.

Nasimiyu-Wasike, Anne. "Christology and an African Woman's Experience." In Ed. Robert J. Schreiter *Faces of Jesus in Africa*, Maryknoll: Orbis, 1991: 73–80.

———. "Polygamy: A Feminist Critique." In Eds Mercy A. Oduyoye and Musimbi R.A. Kanyoro, *The Will to Arise*, Maryknoll: Orbis, 1992: 108–116.

Oduyoye, M.A. "Violence Against Women: A Challenge to Christian Theology." *Journal of Inculturation Theology* 1:1 (1994): 47–60.

Okure, T. "Biblical Perspectives on Women: Eve, the Mother of All the Living (Genesis 3:20)." *Voices from the Third World*, 8:3 (1985): 82–92.

Onwu, N. "The Current State of Biblical Studies in Africa." *The Journal of Religious Thought* 41:2 (1984–85).

———. "The Parable of the Unmerciful Servant (Matt 18:21–35)." In Ed. Justin S. Ukpong, *Gospel Parables in African Context*, Port Harcourt: CIWA Publications, 1988: 43–51.

Osei-Bonsu, J. "The Contextualization of Christianity: Some New Testament Antecedents." *Irish Biblical Studies*, 12:3 (1990): 129–148.

Peterson, T. *Ham and Japhet: The Mythic World of Whites in the Antebellum South.* Metuche and London: Scarecrow Press, 1978.

Pobee, John S. *Toward an African Theology.* Nashville: Abingdon Press, 1979.

Prior, M. *The Bible and Colonialism.* Sheffield: Sheffield Academic Press, 1997.

Rice, Gene. "The Curse of That Never Was (Genesis 9:18–27)." *Journal of Religious Thought* 29 (1972): 17, 25.

Tutu, Desmond. "Whither African Theology." In Eds E.W. Fasholé-Luke et al. *Christianity in Independent Africa* London: Rex Collins, 1978.

———. "The Theology of Liberation in Africa." In Eds Kofi Appiah-Kubi and Sergio Torres. *African Theology en Route*, Maryknoll: Orbis, 1979.

Tzabedze, Joyce. "Women in the Church (1 Timothy 2:8–15, Ephesians 5:22)." In Eds J. Pobee and Barbel von Wartenberg-Potter, *New Eyes for Reading: Biblical and Theological Reflections by Women from the Third World*, Geneva: WCC, 1986: 76–79.

Ukpong, J.S. *Sacrifice, African and Biblical: A Comparative Study of Ibibio and Levitical Sacrifices.* Rome: Urbaniana University Press, 1987.

———. "Inculturation and Evangelization: Biblical Foundations for Inculturation." *Vidyajyoti* 58:5 (1994): 298–307.

———. "Towards a Renewed Approach to Inculturation Theology." *Journal of Inculturation Theology* 1 (1994): 3–15.

———. "The Parable of the Shrewd Manager (Luke 16:1–13): An Essay in Inculturation Hermeneutics." *Semeia* 73 (1995): 189–210.

Wambutda, Daniel N. "Savannah Theology: A Reconsideration of the Biblical Concept of Salvation in the African Context." *Bulletin of African Theology*, 3:6 (1981): 137–153.

West, G.O. *Contextual Bible Study.* Pietermaritzburg: Cluster Publications, 1993.

———. *Biblical Hermeneutics of Liberation: Modes of Reading the Bible in the South African Context* (2nd edition). Pietermaritzburg: Cluster Publications, Maryknoll: Orbis. 1995.

Williams, C. *The Destruction of Black Civilization: Great Issues of a Race from 4500 BC to 2000 AD.* Chicago: Third World Press, 1976.

Williams, J.J. *Hebrewisms of West Africa: From Nile to Niger with the Jews.* London: George Allen and Unwin, New York: Lincoln MacVeach/The Dial Press, 1930.

MAPPING AFRICAN BIBLICAL INTERPRETATION: A TENTATIVE SKETCH

Gerald O. West

"Further developments in African Christianity will test the depth of the impact that the Bible has made upon Africa," says Kwame Bediako in the final sentence of his "Epilogue" to Ype Schaaf's book *On their way rejoicing: the history and role of the Bible in Africa* (Bediako 1994: 252). Bediako's statement points to the significant role the Bible has played in the formation of African Christianity. Unfortunately, this formulation perhaps gives the impression that the encounter between the Bible and Africa is in one direction: from the Bible to Africa. The Bible, in this formulation, is the subject and Africa is the object. The Bible as subject, it would seem, is static and has an essential and self-evident message which has had a series of effects upon Africa. But, what if we make Africa the subject and the Bible the object? We would then have the following formulation: *Further developments in African Christianity will test the depth of the impact that Africa has made upon the Bible.* This statement points to the role that Africa has played in the interpretation, and construction, of the Bible. Africa is no longer acted upon, but is itself an actor. The Bible is no longer the agent, but is the object of the actions of others (—African others).

By placing these two sentences alongside each other we can speak of the encounter between Africa and the Bible as "a transaction." The word "transaction," with its economic and legal connotations, is used here to signify that this process is far from innocent. When, for example, the Bible was brought to Africa by the missionaries and colonialists, it was part of "a package deal." However, the missionaries and colonialists did not always have their own way (see Comaroff and Comaroff 1991, Comaroff and Comaroff 1997). As Tinyiko Maluleke reminds us, "While oppression and imperialism have been real and ruthless, Africans have at a deeper level negotiated and survived the scourge—by relativising it, resisting it, and modifying it with uncanny creativity" (Maluleke 1996: 8). We could make the same point concerning the Bible. *While the Bible has been implicated in oppression and imperialism, both because of the ideologies of those who have used it and because of the ideologies intrinsic to it, ordinary Africans have at a deeper level negotiated and transacted with the Bible and partially appropriated the Bible—by relativising it, resisting it, and modifying it with uncanny creativity.* The remainder of my essay elaborates on and provides an exegesis of the various components in this sentence,[1] beginning with the ambiguity of the Bible in Africa.

The encounter between indigenous (South)[2] Africans and the Bible, is usually recounted in broad strokes: "When the white man came to our country he had the Bible and we had the land. The white man said to us "let us pray." After the prayer, the white man had the land and we had the Bible" (Mofokeng 1988: 34). This anecdote, Takatso Mofokeng argues, expresses more precisely than any statement in the history of political science or Christian missions "the dilemma that confronts black South Africans in their relationships with the Bible."

> With this statement, which is known by young and old in South Africa, black people of South Africa, point to three dialectically related realities. They show the central position which the Bible occupies in the ongoing process of colonization, national oppression and exploitation. They also confess the incomprehensible paradox of being colonized by a Christian people and yet being converted to their religion and accepting the Bible, their ideological instrument of colonization, oppression and exploitation. Thirdly, they express a historic commitment that is accepted solemnly by one generation and passed on to another—a commitment to terminate exploitation of humans by other humans (Mofokeng 1988: 34).

The dilemma of the Bible has been at the center too of Itumeleng Mosala's work.[3] In his early essay on "The Use of the Bible in Black

---

[1] An earlier form of this essay appeared as "On the eve of an African biblical studies: trajectories and trends" *Journal of Theology for Southern Africa* 99 (1997): 99–115. From this note onwards this essay re-organises and develops the earlier article.

[2] This anecdote is particularly well known in South Africa, but can also be heard in many other parts of Africa.

[3] Another dimension of the Bible as dilemma is the intriguing phenomenon in Africa and elsewhere whereby some African communities believe that "Europeans have kept secret those parts of the Bible that provide the key to their wealth and technology." "This belief seemed confirmed," writes Isichei, "by the discovery that the Apocrypha are omitted in Protestant Bibles, and by gnostic texts with titles such as the *Gospel of Thomas*." A further twist to such stories is evident in a story from Avaira, in the western Niger Delta, where local people tell of a lost Bible, that is far fuller and richer than the usual version in use. This lost Bible was originally and miraculously given to the Isoko Christians, but was then taken away and either lost or destroyed by the missionaries (Isichei 1995: 295).

Theology" he publicly questions the status of the Bible in Black
Theology (Mosala 1986). Mosala's basic critique is directed at Black
Theology's exegetical starting point which "expresses itself in the
notion that the Bible is the revealed 'Word of God'" (Mosala 1989:
15, Mosala 1986: 177). He traces this view of the Bible as "an
absolute, non-ideological 'Word of God'" back to the work of James
Cone.[4] He finds it even in the work of the "most theoretically astute
of black theologians," Cornel West. More importantly, according to
Mosala, "South African black theologians are not free from enslavement to this neo-orthodox theological problematic that regards the
notion of the "Word of God" as a hermeneutical starting point"
(Mosala 1986: 179, Mosala 1989: 17). Mosala underlines the pervasiveness of this view of the Bible by subjecting Sigqibo Dwane, Simon
Gqubule, Khoza Mgojo, Manas Buthelezi, Desmond Tutu, and Allan
Boesak to a similar critique. More recently, Tinyiko Maluleke has
extended this critique to African theologians north of the Limpopo
river, including Lamin Sanneh, Kwame Bediako, John Mbiti, Byang
Kato, and Jesse Mugambi (Maluleke 1996: 10–14).

Mosala's contention is that most of the Bible, "offers no certain
starting point for a theology of liberation within itself." For example, he argues that the book of Micah "is eloquent in its silence
about the ideological struggle waged by the oppressed and exploited
class of monarchic Israel." In other words, "it is a ruling class document and represents the ideological and political interests of the
ruling class." As such there "is simply too much de-ideologization
to be made before it can be hermeneutically straightforward in terms
of the struggle for liberation" (Mosala 1986: 196). The Bible, therefore, cannot be the hermeneutical starting point of Black Theology.
Rather, those committed to the struggles of the black oppressed and
exploited people "cannot ignore the history, culture, and ideologies
of the dominated black people as their primary hermeneutical starting point" (Mosala 1986: 197).

However, this does not mean that Mosala totally rejects the Bible.
While the Bible cannot be the primary starting point for Black theology "there are enough contradictions within the book [of Micah,
for example] to enable eyes that are hermeneutically trained in the
struggle for liberation today to observe the kin struggles of the

---

[4] The work of James Cone played a significant role in the development of Black
theology in South Africa in the early 1970s (see Frostin 1988: 89–90).

oppressed and exploited of the biblical communities in the very
absences of those struggles in the text." Because the Bible is "a product and a record of class struggles" (Mosala 1986: 196), Black theologians are able to detect "glimpses of liberation and of a determinate
social movement galvanized by a powerful religious ideology in the
biblical text." But, he continues, it "is not the existence of this which
is in question. Rather, the problem being addressed here is one of
developing an adequate hermeneutical framework which can rescue
those liberative themes from the biblical text" (Mosala 1987: 27–28).

In another article Mosala gives some indication of how Black theologians ought to appropriate the Bible. He identifies two sources of
Black Theology: The Bible and African history and culture (Mosala
1986: 119). "Black Theology has roots in the Bible insofar as it is
capable of linking the struggles of oppressed people in South Africa
today with the struggles of oppressed people in the communities of
the Bible," but because the oppressed people in the Bible "did not
write the Bible," and because their struggles "come to us *via* the
struggles of their oppressors," "Black Theology needs to be firmly
and critically rooted in black history and black culture in order for
it to possess apposite weapons of struggle, that can enable black people to get underneath the biblical text to the struggles of oppressed
classes." But Black Theology also needs to be "firmly and critically
rooted in the Bible in order to elicit from it cultural-hermeneutical
tools of combat" with which black people can penetrate beneath
both the underside of black history and culture and contemporary
capitalist settler colonial domination to the experiences of oppressed
and exploited working class black people (Mosala 1986: 120).

Similarly, for Mofokeng the Bible is both a problem and a solution. The "external" problem of the Bible is the oppressive and reactionary use of the Bible by white Christians. The internal problem
is the Bible itself. Like Mosala, he is critical of those who concentrate
on only the external problem, those who "accuse oppressor-preachers
of *misusing* the Bible for their oppressive purposes and objectives,"
or who accuse "preachers and racist whites of not practicing what
they preach." It is clear, Mofokeng continues, that these responses
are "based on the assumption that the Bible is essentially a book of
liberation." While Mofokeng concedes that these responses have a
certain amount of truth to them, the crucial point he wants to make
is that there are numerous "texts, stories and traditions in the Bible
which lend themselves to only oppressive interpretations and oppres-

sive uses because of their inherent oppressive nature." What is more, any attempt "to 'save' or 'co-opt' these oppressive texts for the oppressed only serve the interests of the oppressors" (Mofokeng 1988: 37–38).

Young blacks in particular, Mofokeng states, "have categorically identified the Bible as an oppressive document by its very nature and to its very core" and suggest that the best option "is to disavow the Christian faith and consequently be rid of the obnoxious Bible." Indeed, some "have zealously campaigned for its expulsion from the oppressed Black community," but, he notes, with little success. The reason for this lack of success, Mofokeng argues, is

> largely due to the fact that no easily accessible ideological silo or store-room is being offered to the social classes of our people that are des-perately in need of liberation. African traditional religions are too far behind most blacks, while Marxism, is to my mind, far ahead of many blacks, especially adult people. In the absence of a better storeroom of ideological and spiritual food, the Christian religion and the Bible will continue for an undeterminable period of time to be the haven of the Black masses par excellence.

Given this situation of very limited ideological options, Mofokeng continues, "Black theologians who are committed to the struggle for liberation and are organically connected to the struggling Christian people, have chosen to honestly do their best to shape the Bible into a formidable weapon in the hands of the oppressed instead of leaving it to confuse, frustrate or even destroy our people" (Mofokeng 1988: 40).

The Bible will probably continue to be a site of struggle (see West 1995), although the shape of the struggle will change as South Africa begins to dialogue more deeply with the rest of Africa and particularly as African women give voice to their experiences and readings of the Bible. I have dwelt at some length on this aspect of (South) African biblical interpretation because it is, in my opinion, one of South Africa's significant contributions to African biblical interpretation. The questions posed by Mosala, Mofokeng, and Maluleke,[5] are somewhat strident and difficult for many Africans who hold to a hermeneutic of trust, but they are important questions, and whether we agree with where Mosala, for example, goes with these questions

---

[5] In a recent article I have attempted to sketch the trajectory of these questions in the work of Maluleke (West Forthcoming).

or not, we must at least be willing to listen to his questions. These questions form the basis of one of Africa's important biblical hermeneutical paradigms.

The most persuasive paradigms within which African biblical scholarship functions are the inculturation and liberation paradigms. While the comparative paradigm persists, and while it remains "foundational to all biblical studies that link the biblical text to the African context" (Ukpong in this volume), its limitations are becoming more and more apparent. The early reactive and apologetic phase of the comparative paradigm, where the focus was on recovering and legitimizing an African culture that had been "condemned as demonic and immoral" by missionaries and colonialists, has made way for the more proactive inculturation and liberation paradigms. Within these paradigms the African context is more than an object of comparison with the Bible, the African context becomes the subject of biblical interpretation (Ukpong in this volume).

Implicit in my use of the singular "African context" is some sense of a common enterprise among African biblical scholars. While this is so, increasing access to each other reminds us of our differences too. The play of contextual similarities and differences has yet to determine a definitive paradigm for African biblical scholarship, and the more permeable boundaries between us have shown the limitations and possibilities of our paradigms. This is best seen in the way the liberation of South Africa has accelerated academic exchanges between South (and Southern) Africa and Africa north of the Limpopo river, and brought the liberation hermeneutical perspective of the South African (and to some extent Southern African) experience of the Bible into sustained dialogue with the inculturation hermeneutical perspective of West, East, North, and Central Africa.

The foregrounding of culture, ethnicity, and Africanness in South Africa in the post-apartheid context has opened biblical scholarship to the rich resources further north where culture has always been the predominant domain of transactions with the Bible (see Kinoti and Waliggo 1997). But just as South African biblical scholarship has much to learn, so too it has much to contribute. Issues of Africanness, ethnicity, and culture cannot be separated from the complex matrix they share with issues of race, class, and gender. African biblical scholarship north of the Limpopo has been strangely silent on these matters, but that silence is being broken, particularly by African women, who are tired of being asked to wait while more important (male) matters are dealt with. They wait no longer (see for example Dube 1997, Masenya 1997, Mbuwayesango 1997, Sibeko and Haddad 1997). African women, then, are providing a way for dialogue and collaboration between the liberation hermeneutical perspective of South Africa (where the predominant hermeneutic disposition is one of suspicion towards the Bible) and the inculturation hermeneutical perspective of West, East, North, and Central Africa (where the predominant hermeneutic disposition is one of trust towards the Bible). For African women theologies of bread (with an emphasis on liberation) and theologies of being (with an emphasis on inculturation) are inextricably intertwined (see Balcomb 1998).

Purity of the paradigm is clearly not the primary concern in African biblical scholarship. For socially engaged biblical scholars these paradigms, are employed only as long as and is so far as they are useful. For example, the role of the Bible in the "ethnic" conflict in Rwanda, and other contexts remains to be examined. But when it is, the relationship between culture and class will have to be carefully examined, given a social history in which social class divisions, within a single cultural group, were manipulated by colonial powers to produce ethnic forms of identity (see McCullum 1995, and more generally Brett 1996). Furthermore, to what extent the post-colonial paradigm, fashioned in Asia but commercialized in the West, is appropriate for Africa has yet to be determined. Offering real resources for literary and language studies in Africa, post-colonial criticism has yet to make its mark on African biblical studies, though there are emerging possibilities (Dube 1996, West 1997). These, and other emerging paradigms (Maluleke 2000), are African attempts to transact with the Bible; something they have been doing from the very beginning. So before we press on with the present, I now turn to the past, for some reflection on the history of biblical interpretation in Africa.

Any analysis of biblical interpretation in Africa must take account of the transactions that constitute the history of the encounters between Africa and the Bible. Historical accounts of the encounters between Judaism and/or Christianity and Africa are rich and detailed in their analysis of most aspects of these transactions, but consistently exclude the Bible. This is the case in the otherwise excellent recent work by Elizabeth Isichei, *A History of Christianity in Africa: From Antiquity to the Present* (Isichei 1995) where the historical, sociological, geographical, cultural, economic, and religious dimensions of, for example, the

emergence of North African Judaism centuries before Christ and
then Christianity in the beginning of the first century, the initial
interface between Judaism/Christianity and Islam, the impact of
Portugese (Catholic and Protestant) evangelization and exploitation
between 1500–1800, the nineteenth century missionaries and colonialists, and the expansion of Christianity through African evangelists in the twentieth century are all described and analyzed in detail,
but the biblical and hermeneutical are hardly mentioned. Even Ype
Schaaf's book, *On Their Way Rejoicing: The History and Role of the Bible
in Africa* (Schaaf 1994), belying its title, provides little analysis of the
Bible's interpretative history in Africa. Much is implicit, as with the
work of Isichei, but explicit analysis is absent. Though Schaaf deals
with the topic of translation of the Bible in great detail, this discussion does not lead into any inventory of its interpretative history.

So while the accounts we have of the encounters between Africa
and Judaism and/or Christianity, are well documented, those of the
encounters between Africa and *the Bible* are partial and fragmentary.
That the Bible is seldom treated separately from the arrival and
reception of Judaism and/or Christianity is not surprising, particularly as it can be argued that the Bible is analytically bound up with
being a Jew and/or a Christian (Barr 1980: 52). However, without
disputing the interconnectedness of the Bible and Judaism and/or
Christianity, the nature of the interconnectedness ought to be examined more carefully. We should not assume, for example, that the
reception of Christianity, and the reception of the Bible, always
amounts to the same thing. Vincent Wimbush's interpretative history
of the Bible among African Americans provides compelling reasons
for analyzing the reception of the Bible as distinct from but related
to the reception of Christianity (Wimbush 1991: 84). Furthermore,
if Wimbush is right in asserting that the array of interpretative strategies shaped in the earliest encounters of African Americans with the
Bible are foundational, in that all other African American readings
are in some sense built upon and judged by them, then such analysis
has tremendous hermeneutical significance for our current context.
The early African American encounters with the Bible have functioned,
according to Wimbush, "as phenomenological, socio-political and cultural foundation" for subsequent periods (Wimbush 1993: 131). While
there are many significant differences between African American
transactions with the Bible and indigenous African transactions with

the Bible, there are also many striking similarities which make Wimbush's analysis heuristically valuable.

Writing from the Kenyan context, Nahashon Ndung'u would seem to support elements of Wimbush's analysis. He notes that when the Akurinu Church emerged among the Gikuyu in Kenya there was a deliberate rejection of the beliefs and practices of the mission churches and a turn to the Bible, from which they identified their own teachings and practices (Ndung'u 1997: 61–62). A more comprehensive account of such transactions is necessary if we are construct a picture of early African encounters with the Bible and if we are to understand the interpretative resources of ordinary Africans today as they interact with their, usually Western trained, socially engaged biblical scholars. The discussion so far makes it clear that Africans do not transact with the Bible "empty handed." Beside their distinctive experiences of reality, both religio-culturally and socio-politically, and the particular questions that such experiences generate, Africans have a range of hermeneutic strategies for transacting with the Bible. While the interpretative tools of ordinary African interpreters of the Bible have yet to be adequately classified and analyzed—I will comment on this further below—African biblical scholars are adept at using the full array of scholarly interpretative resources on offer.

As Justin Ukpong points out, "Africa can rightly be referred to as the cradle of systematic biblical interpretation in Christianity" because the earliest attempts to structure biblical interpretation are associated with "the city of Alexandria and to such names as Clement of Alexandria, Origen, and others who lived and worked there" (Ukpong in this volume). But while largely allegorical interpretative techniques still have a place in Africa, mainly within the Coptic Orthodox Church of Egypt (Loubser 1997, see also Loubser in this volume), and while more work must be done on the impact of Coptic Christianity and their interpretative practices in North Africa (especially Ethiopia) and further south, the post-Enlightenment forms of biblical scholarship have become the preferred interpretative resources of African biblical scholars. Working primarily within a comparative paradigm, and I will say more about this later, African biblical scholars make use of the full array of critical methods that constitute the tools of the trade of biblical scholarship: historical-critical, sociological, literary, and reader-response methods (see Kinoti and Waliggo 1997, Ntreh 1990, Ukpong 1995). But, because most African biblical scholars have been trained in the West in contexts, where the historical-critical methods still hold sway, and because resources reflecting more recent developments in biblical scholarship are expensive and/or difficult to access in Africa, historical-critical tools tend to be the most prevalent.

South African biblical scholarship is perhaps an exception, but like all else here in South Africa, any analysis is deeply problematized by apartheid (West 1995: 47–59, see also the essay by Carroll in this volume). While white English-speaking biblical scholarship has been predominantly historical-critical, white Afrikaner-speaking biblical scholarship has tended to take up the structuralist and semiotic strands of the literary approaches (Draper 1991, Smit 1990). On the other hand, Black biblical scholarship, though showing some signs of literary analysis, concentrates on the socio-historical resources of biblical scholarship. But, and this is a big "but," having interpretative tools in common does not mean we all do the same thing with the tools. Though this is a gross oversimplification, it is probably fair to say that biblical scholarship in the West is primarily focused on questions generated by the academy. With some exceptions, the same could be said for white biblical scholarship in South Africa. In other words, they operate within what might be called a professional paradigm. African biblical scholarship is different, operating as it does within paradigms that are only partially professionally constituted.

In the same way, the comparative paradigm, for example, which is probably the dominant paradigm (Holter 1998: 242), historically speaking (Ukpong in this volume), of African biblical scholarship, concentrates on the correspondence between African experience and the Bible, thereby rupturing the barrier between community and academy. This is also true for the other major paradigms of African biblical scholarship, perhaps even more forcefully, namely the inculturation and liberation paradigms. It is this, that African biblical scholarship has to contribute to biblical scholarship in the West. By allowing the religio-cultural heritage ("the myths") and the socio-political situation ("the meanings") of Africa to interface with the Bible, Knut Holter argues, African biblical scholarship has much to offer their colleagues in the West. However, and here the traffic is one-way, when Holter examines First World/Western biblical scholarship he finds that African biblical scholars are marginalized, both in terms of their personal presence at international—that is Western—meetings and in terms of their scholarly production. Holter sees two factors as contributing to this marginalization. First, Western scholarship has a very narrow conception of what constitutes biblical scholarship, and second, African scholars do not have the financial resources to enter the academic biblical studies market place of current literature, data bases, and conferences.

While there are very real difficulties of access to the tools of biblical scholarship in its Western forms, this very disadvantage may have saved African biblical scholarship from the temptation of severing itself from its primary dialogue partner—ordinary African believers who interpret the Bible in their daily struggles for survival, liberation and life. So before we become too pessimistic about our lack of traditional scholar resources, we would do well to consider that perhaps the major contribution of African biblical scholarship to their Western colleagues is their alliance with ordinary African "readers" of the Bible. In addition, Africa has, of course, a wealth of other African resources for reading the Bible. The extensive range of African art that exegete and comment on the Bible are one such resource. For example, from the narrative art interpretation of the Joseph story by Azaria Mbatha (figure 1), to the linocut commentary of an episode from the Joseph story in Egypt by John Muafangejo (figure 2), to the three dimensional sculptural exploration of Pharoah's dream by Bonie Ntshalintshali (figure 3), we have an archive of local indigenous interpretative resources for recovering indigenous understandings of Genesis 37–50.

Furthermore, Mbatha's woodcuts, both in their form and in their images, provide excellent examples of (and for) resisting conversation— of (and for) African transactions with the missionaries, colonialism, and the Bible. The woodcut, an African form, seizes and remakes the left to right and top to bottom conventions of colonial text to tell an African story of struggle from a European brought book (—the Bible) (West 1999: 168–169). Unfortunately, however, many of these African commentaries are inaccessible to ordinary Africans, having been relocated to art galleries both on the continent (if we are lucky) and abroad. Returning these interpretative resources to ordinary Africans is a task that awaits us. Fortunately, there are other resources, found and forged deep in the interpretative practices of ordinary African "readers" of the Bible.

Ordinary African interpreters of the Bible are less constrained than their scholarly compatriots in the strategies they use to appropriate the Bible. Their strategies, in Wimbush's words, "reflect a hermeneutic

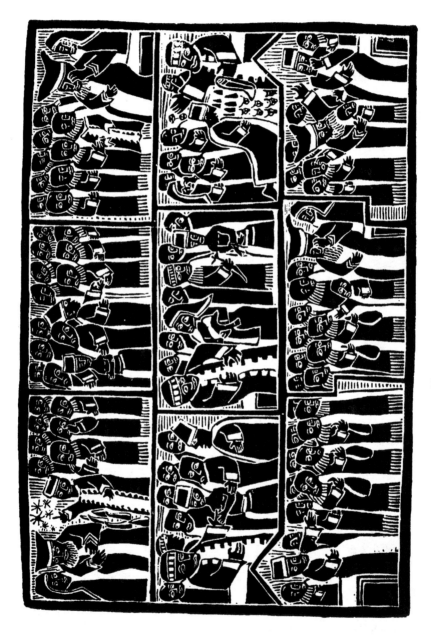

Figure 1. The Joseph story

Figure 2. Joseph's story in Egypt

Figure 3. Pharaoh's dream

characterized by a looseness, even playfulness, vis-à-vis the biblical texts themselves" (Wimbush 1991: 88). Much more work needs to be done on how ordinary Africans interpret the Bible, especially because how they "read" (whether literate or illiterate) matters in Africa and to African biblical scholarship, for African biblical scholarship "is inclusive of scholars and nonscholars, the rich and the poor" (Okure 1993: 77). This is not merely a nostalgic or romantic yearning for a lost naivete, nor are ordinary Africans merely informants for the enterprise of western scholarship (Smith-Christopher 1995, West 1998). Ordinary African "readers" of the Bible are constitutive of African biblical scholarship for a whole range of reasons. First, as already indicated, because African biblical scholarship concentrates on the correspondence between African experience and the Bible, it locates itself "within the social, political, and ecclesiastical context of Africa" (Holter 1998: 245), a context filled with ordinary African believers in and "readers" of the Bible. Put more crudely, the directions African biblical scholarship takes and the questions it admits to the scholarly task are shaped more by the life issues, such as AIDS, of local African communities than they are by the interpretative interests of the scholarly community. Biblical scholarship belongs in the church and the community, not only in the academy, and, anyway, the community intrudes into the academy, demanding a presence and access to its resources.[6] Second, certain impulses in biblical scholarship—such as strands of postmodernism, reader-response criticism, and liberation hermeneutics—have been eagerly appropriated because they provide both impetus and theoretical support for the inclusion of ordinary, real, "readers" (West 1999, West 1996). Often on the defensive against or intimidated by the scholarly enterprise of the Western world, African biblical scholars have revelled in the unravelling of the masters' mystical and exclusive academic empire, unprivileging the dominant discourses and thereby admitting, at last, the contributions of ordinary Africans to the task of critical discourse. Third, most African biblical scholars recognize that there are elements of ordinary readings in their own "scholarly" reading processes (Patte 1995). We remain, in some senses, ordinary readers, not always

---

[6] A clear indication of this is that African biblical studies is one strand in a closely woven cord that is African Theology. The separation of biblical studies from other theological disciplines, so common elsewhere, does not happen in African biblical studies.

giving precedence to the systematic and structure interpretative processes we have learned in our biblical training. We are willing to be untrained and retrained, to be born "from below." Fourth, remaining connected to the various forms of contextual theology in Africa (including, the theology of African women, black theology, African theology, etc.) requires that socially engaged African biblical scholars recognize the foundational (in Wimbush's sense) resources of ordinary "readers" of the Bible. For these are the resources from which their working theologies—theologies of survival, liberation, and life—are constructed. These are the resources they live by.

Given the constitutive contribution of ordinary African "readers" of the Bible to biblical interpretation in Africa, we have had to find and forge a process in which socially engaged biblical scholars and ordinary African "readers" interpret together in particular local collaborative acts. This is a process in which we read "with" each other in safe sites where power relations are acknowledged and structurally equalized, and in which the respective subject positions and resources of both the ordinary African "reader" and the socially engaged biblical scholar are vigilantly foregrounded (see my other essay in this volume).[7]

In the African context ordinary African interpreters work with a remembered (and re-membered) as well as a read Bible (West 1999: 79–107). As Itumeleng Mosala reminds us, ordinary Africans, particularly in the African Independent Churches, "have an oral knowledge of the Bible." "Most of their information about the Bible comes from socialization in the churches themselves as they listen to prayers and sermons" (see also Draper 1996, Mazamisa 1991, Mosala 1996, Oduyoye 1995: 190). This reality, however, does not imply the absence of the Bible as text. For, although the Bible as text is not central to the "reading" practices of most ordinary Africans, it does have a presence. Even those who are illiterate have considerable exposure to biblical texts being read. Reflecting on the Kenyan context Ndungu notes that "even the illiterate members [of the Akurinu African Independent Church] take pains to master some verses which they readily quote when they give their testimonies." These same members often carry copies of the Bible so that "If need arises they

---

[7] I realize that this is quite a mouthful, but here there is not the space to elaborate, see West 1999 for a detailed discussion of "ordinary 'reader'" and the process of their "reading 'with'" socially engaged biblical scholars (see also the cautionary comments in Maluleke 2000: 93–94).

can always request a literate member to read for them" (Ndungu 1997: 62). The remembered Bible and the read Bible reside side by side, requiring that our analysis biblical interpretation in Africa take note of the encounter between orality and textuality. Jonathan Draper cautions us not to minimize the complexity of the relationships between literacy and orality. That literacy and the Bible often went hand in hand in the missionary/colonial encounter is common knowledge, and is a much emphasized point in all accounts of transactions between the Africa and the Bible (Isichei 1995: 159, 174, 294, Schaaf 1994: 147–154). Draper's research, however, probes more deeply and raises difficult questions. How do textually orientated readers and orally orientated "readers" work together with the Bible? When we "read" the Bible are we dealing with the same thing? What are the prevailing interpretative practices in these respective communities? What implications does textual biblical and theological training have pedagogically for preparing people to minister in predominantly oral communities? Is the path away from orality towards textuality inevitable, and how should we implicate ourselves in this process? (Draper 1996, Lategan 1996: 250)

When the Bible as text becomes the focus of the encounter between Africa and Judaism and/or Christianity, the emphasis is almost always on translation. For example, Schaaf's *The History and Role of the Bible in Africa* is primarily about the history and role of *translation* of the Bible in Africa. From the translation of the Hebrew Bible into Greek (the Septuagint) in Alexandria around 260 BCE, to the first translations of the Bible into African languages in the early 1500s (Coptic, Arabic, Ge'ez), to the present where parts of the Bible have been translated into more than 230 African languages, translation has been a central aspect of Africa's transactions with the Bible. Bediako goes as far as to say that "to the credit of the modern missionary enterprise, the more recent missionary history of Africa . . . can justly be regarded as the history of Bible translation" (Bediako 1994: 246). Drawing on and developing the work of David B. Barrett (Barrett 1968), Kenneth Cragg (Cragg 1968), Philip Stine (Stine 1990), Ype Schaaf, and especially Lamin Sanneh (Sanneh 1989), Bediako argues that when missionaries or mission societies made the Bible available to an African people in that people's own language, their grip on the gospel was loosened and so too their proprietary claim on Christianity. Translation enabled the Bible to become "an independent yardstick by which to test, and sometimes to reject, what Western missionaries taught and practised" and in so doing "provided the basis for developing new, indigenous forms of Christianity" (see also Appiah-Kubi 1977: 119, Bediako 1994: 246, Mbiti 1977: 90–91). Translation in this sense is much more than a technical discipline, it is a metaphor for forms of inculturation.

While most translation in Africa to date has focused on particular translation problems in particular languages, Bediako's elaboration of translation as a metaphor for inculuration opens up other, less explored, areas. For example, what forms of Christianity emerge in a context where the first texts translated into the local languages are Genesis and then Luke? Such was the case in the coastal villages of East Africa among the freed slaves during the period 1840–70. This question is given additional force because, as Schaaf notes, these Christians "became the African pioneers of the missions who early in the twentieth century would spread the gospel among the peoples of East Africa" (Schaaf 1994: 66–67). If both Bediako and Wimbush are right in their respective arguments—that translation into the ver-nacular loosens the control of the missionary on the message and that the hermeneutic strategies that local communities adopt in order to appropriate the message for themselves are foundational—then more careful analysis of such transactions would be extremely valu-able. And we should not forget that translations are always trans-actions. While vernacular translation may have facilitated African appropriations of the Bible, there is a dark side. Most first transla-tions of the Bible into African vernaculars were strongly shaped by missionary forms of colonialism and Christianity, and their ideolog-ical legacy lives on (Dube 1999).

The Bible is only one of the sacred or classic texts that Africa has or has encountered. Besides the many sacred oral "texts" of indige-nous African religions, Africa has received the Qur'an, and to a lesser extent, the sacred texts of Hinduism. The encounter between Africa and each of these sacred texts has always been an encounter with the oral "texts" of African traditional religions, and while African biblical scholarship has been slow to explore these transactions explic-itly, African theological scholarship has not (Dickson 1972, Maluleke 1995). Besides an examination of the transactions between the Bible and sacred indigenous oral "texts," the transactions between the more recently arrived sacred texts themselves is beginning to be investi-gated. In those parts of Africa where Christianity and Islam sub-stantially encounter each other this task cannot be ignored, and some analysis and reflection is being done (Adelowo 1986, 1987). However, the challenge remains in those areas (like South Africa) where Christianity is overwhelmingly dominant. How we should go about this task is an important question, and while we will have to find our own ways of proceeding, the rich experience of Asian biblical scholarship in this regard, may be of use (see Sugirtharajah 1991: 297–394).

The encounter between Africa and the Bible has always been more than an encounter with a book. Wimbush's description of the earliest encounters between the Bible and African Americans as characterized by a combination of rejection, suspicion, and awe of "Book Religion" (see also Getui 1997: 94), has strong echoes in the encounters on the African continent. While the Bible did play a role in the missionizing of Africa, initially its role was not primary and so its impact was indirect. "It was often imbedded within catechetical materials or within elaborate doctrinal statements and formal preaching styles" (Wimbush 1993: 130). When Africans did encounter the Bible, it was from the perspective of cultures steeped in oral tradition. From this perspective the concept of religion and religious power circumscribed by a book was "at first frightful and absurd, thereafter, . . . awesome and fascinating" (Wimbush 1993: 131). As illiterate peoples with rich, well-established, and elaborate oral traditions the majority of the first African slaves were suspicious of and usually rejected "Book Religion." However, as Wimbush notes, "It did not take them long to associate the Book of 'Book religion' with power" (Wimbush 1991: 85).

The power that the Bible is, is for most Africans "the Word of God," but quite what is meant by this phrase is not clear. The analyses of Mosala, Mofokeng and, more recently, Maluleke in this respect offer useful insights. But, more careful analysis is required of exactly what particular Black and African theologians mean by their various uses of the phrase "Word of God."[8] Particularly, when we take into account that ordinary African interpreters of the Bible are not as transfixed and fixated by the text as their textually trained pastors and theologians are. As Wimbush has indicated, their hermeneutics is characterized by "a looseness" towards the biblical text. If they do speak of the Bible, as "Word of God," they do so in senses

---

[8] Some analysis of the different ways in which Mosala and Allan Boesak use this phrase can be found in Frostin 1988: 160–165 and West 1995: 122–124.

that are more metaphorical than literal. "The Book" is as much a
symbol and an object of power, as it is a text (see Ndungu 1997:
62–63, Yorke 1997, Yorke's essay in this volume, and Adamo's essay
in this volume). Both the open Bible (as text) and the unopened
Bible (as sacred object and icon) are powerful in much of Africa (see
figure 4, carved in Ghana).

Maluleke is right when he says that while many African Christians
"may mouth the Bible-is-equal-to-the-Word-of-God formula, they are
actually creatively pragmatic and selective in their use of the Bible so
that the Bible may enhance rather than frustrate their life struggles"
(Maluleke 1996: 13). In this, as in so many of the issues already discussed, ordinary African "readers" of the Bible may be ahead of

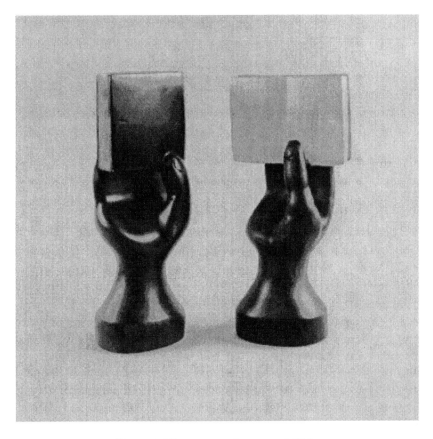

Figure 4. The open and unopened Bible

socially engaged biblical scholars. Maybe we as African biblical scholars have mastered the masters' methods too well! We may need to be reschooled and retooled (and re-mythologised) by the ordinary African "readers" of the Bible who call us to interpret the Bible (and experience its power) with them.

I conclude this essay with some reflections on "Africa" and "African," which I place in inverted commas to remind us that these terms must be problematised. Not much attention has been given *in Africa* to the presence and place of Africa in the Bible (see Ukpong's essay in this volume). Such interest has usually been the preserve of African American biblical scholars (Felder 1993, Felder 1991). But increasingly African biblical scholars are showing interest in biblical references or allusions to the people and places of Africa and the role of Africa in the formation of the Bible. As Africa recovers its dignity and its "Africanness" so too it is recognising, recovering, and reviving its presence in the past—including the Bible (Adamo 1998, see also the essay by Holter in this volume). Throughout this essay the proper name "Africa" has been used in an unproblematized manner. Postmodern studies remind us, however, to be cautious about inherited constructs, particularly when they are the constructs of the dominant and dominating discourse. Making maps is no innocent act, and tells us more about the map maker than the terrain mapped. Such is certainly the case with "Africa." Why, for example, do introductions to the Bible, histories of Israel, maps of the Bible lands, dictionaries of the Bible, and the work of church historians and theologians minimize the role of Africa? (Bailey 1991: 166–168) Might we, for example, consider Mesopotamia as a part of northeast Africa? (Yorke 1995: 9) "Africa" is one of the constructs of Western colonialism, imperialism, and capitalism. Africans themselves have had little say in the way "Africa" has been constituted by the dominant discourse of discovery, civilization, colonialization, industrialization, and capitalization. Problematising and destablising the proper name "Africa" is a painful and potentially dangerous thing to do, just as we are recovering and revelling in our "Africanness." But we will have to deconstruct the dominant discourse's constructions *as* we construct our own understanding of "Africa" and "African." African biblical studies clearly has a contribution to make, connecting as it does with every aspect of our Africanness; which brings me to the other problematic term, "African."

Similar complexities confront us, clearly, with the term "African" (see Maluleke 2000: 89–90). Reading African scholarship (and I am

not particularly concerned here by how others outside of Africa speak
of "Africans"), whether biblical or otherwise, the prevailing mode of
speaking is to use the generic term "African." We tend to speak of
"African biblical scholarship," "the African Renaissance," etc. when
speaking of ourselves. (I will return to the "ourselves" below.) Even
when referring to a particular interpretation of the Bible within a particular locality in Africa, one often finds the writer using the generic
"This African reading of 2 Samuel 13..." rather than a more local
designation, for example, "This Zulu reading of 2 Samuel 13...."

Clearly we (a problematic "we") will have to become more careful in our use of the term "African." The term may be used to signal an important strategic solidarity, and, I think, many African
biblical scholars use it in this sense as a way of affirming themselves
over against those who have named them. Here the colonial label
is being turned into a mark of dignity and identity in solidarity with
others who have been so named. However, we will also need to
become more explicit about the differences that constitute us as
"Africans." Ethnic designations may be useful, though in South Africa,
and elsewhere in Africa, these are also deeply contested and are as
much the product of colonial encounters as the term "African."
"Hutu" and "Tutsi" are colonial constructs, as is their more glamor-
ous colonial and apartheid cousin, "Zulu." A mix of particulars such
as race, class, gender, religion, and ethnicity may be a more useful
route to take, particularly in South Africa; and here I must declare
the ambiguities surrounding my "Africanness." To what extent I am
an "African" biblical scholar is contested terrain, and so sometimes
I refer to "we," "us," and "ours" and sometimes I refer to "they,"
"them," and "theirs" (see West 1999a).

The map is not the territory, and so any exercise which attempts
to map is fraught with difficulties. My mapping of African biblical
interpretation is heuristic (and mine) and must remain contested, as
must any map of Africa, even if it is only a sketch. The territory is
what matters, and our terrain is rich and diverse. No doubt as we
continue to engage with the realities of our territories, much will
need to be redrawn.

BIBLIOGRAPHY

Adamo, David Tuesday. *Africa and the Africans in the Old Testament*. San Francisco:
    Christian University Press, 1998.

Adelowo, E. Dada. "The Bible and the Qur'an as Sources of Theology, Ethics, Politics, History and Culture." *The Nigerian Journal of Theology* 1 (1986): 18–27.
———. "A Comparative Look at Some of the Contents of Yoruba Oral Traditions, the Bible and the Qur'an." *Asia Journal of Theology* 1 (1987): 334–354.
Appiah-Kubi, Kofi. "Indigenous African Christian Churches: Sins of Authenticity." In Eds Kofi Appiah-Kubi and Sergio Torres, *African Theology En Route: Papers from the Pan-African Conference of Third World Theologians, Accra, December 1977*, Maryknoll, NY: Orbis, 1977: 117–125.
Bailey, Randall. "Beyond Indentification: the Use of Africans in Old Testament Poetry and Narratives." In Ed. Cain Hope Felder, *Stony the Road We Trod: African American Biblical Interpretation*, Minneapolis: Fortress, 1991: 165–184.
Balcomb, Anthony. "From Liberation to Democracy: Theologies of Bread and Being in the New South Africa." *Missionalia* 26 (1998): 54–73.
Barr, James. *The Scope and Authority of the Bible.* London: SCM, 1980.
Barrett, David B. *Schism and Renewal in Africa: an Analysis of Six Thousand Contemporary Religious Movements.* Nairobi: Oxford University Press, 1968.
Bediako, Kwame. "Epilogue." In Ed. Ype Schaaf, *On Their Way Rejoincing: The History and Role of the Bible in Africa*, Carlisle: Paternoster Press, 1994: 243–254.
Brett, Mark G. "Interpreting ethnicity." In Ed. Mark G. Brett, *Ethnicity and the Bible*, Leiden: Brill, 1996: 3–22.
Comaroff, Jean, and John L. Comaroff. *Of Revelation and Revolution: Christianity, Colonialism and Consciousness in South Africa.* Vol. 1. Chicago: University of Chicago Press, 1991.
———. *Of Revelation and Revolution: The Dialectics of Modernity on a South African Frontier.* Vol. 2. Chicago: University of Chicago Press, 1997.
Cragg, Kenneth. *Christianity in World Perspective.* London: Lutterworth Press, 1968.
Dickson, Kwesi. "African Traditional Religions and the Bible." In Eds Engelbert Mveng and R.J.Z. Werblowsky, *The Jerusalem Congress on Black Africa and the Bible, April 1972/Le Congres de Jerusalem sur l'Afrique Noire et la Bible: Proceedings*, Jerusalem: The Israel Interfaith Committee, 1972: 155–166.
Draper, Jonathan A. "Confessional Western Text-centred Biblical Interpretation and an Oral or Residual-oral Context." *Semeia* 73 (1996): 59–77.
———. "'For the Kingdom Is inside You and It Is outside of You': Contextual Exegesis in South Africa." In Eds P.J. Hartin and J.H. Petzer, *Text and Interpretation: New Approaches in the Criticism of the New Testament*, Leiden: E.J. Brill, 1991: 235–257.
Dube, Musa W. "Consuming a Colonial Time Bomb: Translating *Badimo* into 'Demons' in the Setswana Bible (Matthew 8:28–34, 15:2, 10:8)." *Journal for the Study of the New Testament* 73 (1999): 33–59.
———. "Reading for Decolonization (John 4:1–42)." *Semeia* 75 (1996): 37–59.
———. "Toward a Postcolonial Feminist Interpretation of the Bible." *Semeia* 78 (1997): 11–26.
Felder, Cain Hope. Ed. *The Original African Heritage Study Bible: King James Version.* Nashville: James C. Winston Publishing Company, 1993.
———. Ed. *Stony the Road We Trod: African American Biblical Interpretation.* Minneapolis: Fortress, 1991.
Frostin, Per. *Liberation Theology in Tanzania and South Africa: A First World Interpretation.* Lund: Lund University Press, 1988.
Getui, Mary N. "The Bible as a Tool for Ecumenism." In Eds Hannah W. Kinoti and John M. Waliggo, *The Bible in African Christianity*, Nairobi: Acton Publishers, 1997: 86–98.
Holter, Knut. "It's Not only a Question of Money! African Old Testament Scholarship between the Myths and Meanings of the South and the Money and Methods of the North." *Old Testament Essays* 11 (1998): 240–254.
Isichei, Elizabeth. *A History of Christianity in Africa: From Antiquity to the Present.* Grand Rapids: Eerdmans, 1995.

Kinoti, Hannah W. and John M. Waliggo. Eds. *The Bible in African Christianity*. Nairobi: Acton Publishers, 1997.

Lategan, Bernard C. "Scholar and Ordinary Reader—More than a Simple Interface." *Semeia* 73 (1996): 243–255.

Loubser, J.A. "Gathering Jewels—Biblical Hermeneutics in the Coptic Orothodox Church of Egypt." *Journal for the Study of Religion* 10 (1997): 41–75.

Maluleke, Tinyiko S. "The Bible among African Christians: A Missiological Perspective." In Ed. Teresa Okure, *To Cast Fire Upon the Earth: Bible and Mission Collaborating in Today's Multicultural Global Context*, Pietermaritzburg: Cluster Publications, 2000: 87–112.

———. "Black and African Theologies in the New World Order: A Time to Drink from Our Own Wells." *Journal of Theology for Southern Africa* 96 (1996): 3–19.

———. "'A Morula Tree between Two Fields': The Commentary of Selected Tsonga Writers on Missionary Christianity." DTh, University of South Africa, 1995.

Masenya, Madipoane. "Proverbs 31:10–31 in a South African Context: A Reading for the Liberation of African (Northern Sotho) Women." *Semeia* 78 (1997): 55–68.

Mazamisa, Welile. "Reading from this Place: From Orality to Literacy/Textuality and back." *Scriptura* S9 (1991): 67–72.

Mbiti, John S. "The Biblical Basis for Present Trends in African Theology." In Eds Kofi Appiah-Kubi and Sergio Torres, *African Theology en Route: Papers from the Pan-African Conference of Third World Theologians, Accra, December 1977*, Maryknoll, NY: Orbis, 1977: 83–94.

Mbuwayesango, Dora Rudo. "Childlessness and Women-to-women Relationships in Genesis and in African Patriarchal Society: Sarah and Hagar from a Zimbabwean Woman's Perspective (Gen 16:1–16, 21:8–21)." *Semeia* 78 (1997): 27–36.

McCullum, Hugh. *The angels have left us: the Rwanda tragedy and the churches*. Geneva: World Council of Churches, 1995.

Mofokeng, T. "Black Christians, the Bible and Liberation." *Journal of Black Theology* 2 (1988): 34–42.

Mosala, Itumeleng J. "Biblical Hermeneutics and Black Theology in South Africa." Ph.D., University of Cape Town, 1987.

———. *Biblical Hermeneutics and Black Theology in South Africa*. Grand Rapids: Eerdmans, 1989.

———. "Ethics of the Economic Principles: Church and Secular Investments." In Eds. Itumeleng J. Mosala and Buti Tlhagale, *Hammering Swords into Ploughshares: Essays in Honour of Archbishop Mpilo Desmond Tutu*, Johannesburg: Skotaville, 1986: 119–129.

———. "Race, Class, and Gender as Hermeneutical Factors in the African Independent Churches' Appropriation of the Bible." *Semeia* 73 (1996): 43–57.

———. "The use of the Bible in Black Theology." In Eds Itumeleng J. Mosala and Buti Tlhagale *The Unquestionable Right To Be Free: Essays in Black Theology*, Johannesburg: Skotaville, 1986: 175–199.

Ndung'u, Nahashon. "The Bible in an African Independent Church." In Eds Hannah W. Kinoti and John M. Waliggo, *The Bible in African Christianity*, Nairobi: Acton Publishers, 1997: 58–67.

Ntreh, Benjamin A. "Towards an African Biblical Hermeneutics." *Africa Theological Journal* 19 (1990): 247–254.

Oduyoye, Mercy Amba. *Daughters of Anowa: African Women and Patriarchy*. Maryknoll: Orbis, 1995.

Okure, Teresa. "Feminist Interpretation in Africa." In Ed. Elisabeth Schüssler Fiorenza, *Searching the Scriptures: A Feminist Introduction*, New York: Crossroads, 1993: 76–85.

Patte, Daniel. *Ethics of Biblical Interpretation: A Reevaluation*. Louisville, Kentucky: Westminster John Knox, 1995.

Sanneh, Lamin. *Translating the Message: The Missionary Impact on Culture*. Maryknoll: Orbis, 1989.

Schaaf, Ype. *On Their Way Rejoicing: The History and Role of the Bible in Africa*. Carlisle: Paternoster Press, 1994.

Sibeko, Malika, and Beverley G. Haddad. "Reading the Bible 'with' Women in Poor and Marginalized Communities in South Africa (Mark 5:21–6:1)." *Semeia* 78 (1997): 83–92.

Smit, Dirk J. "The Ethics of Interpretation: and South Africa." *Scriptura* 33 (1990): 29–43.

Smith-Christopher, Daniel. "Introduction." In Ed. Daniel Smith-Christopher, *Text and Experience: Towards a Cultural Exegesis of the Bible*, Sheffield: Sheffield Academic Press, 1995.

Stine, Philip, Ed. *Bible Translation and the Spread of the Church: The Last 2000 Years*. Leiden: E.J. Brill, 1990.

Sugirtharajah, R.S., Ed. *Voices from the Margin: Interpreting the Bible in the Third World*. Maryknoll: Orbis Books, 1991.

Ukpong, Justin S. "Rereading the Bible with African Eyes." *Journal of Theology for Southern Africa* 91 (1995): 3–14.

West, Gerald O. "Being Partially Constituted by Work with Others: Biblical Scholars Becoming Different." *Journal of Theology for Southern Africa* 104 (1999a): 44–53.

———. *The Academy of the Poor: Towards a Dialogical Reading of the Bible*. Sheffield: Sheffield Academic Press, 1999.

———. "Biblical Scholars Inventing Ancient Israel and 'Ordinary Readers' of the Bible Re-inventing Biblical Studies." *Old Testament Essays* 11 (1998): 629–644.

———. "Finding a Place among the Posts for Post-colonial Criticism in Biblical Studies in South Africa." *Old Testament Essays* 10 (1997): 322–342.

———. "Reading the Bible Differently: Giving Shape to the Discourses of the Dominated." *Semeia* 73 (1996): 21–41.

———. *Biblical Hermeneutics of Liberation: Modes of Reading the Bible in the South African Context*. Second Edition, Maryknoll and Pietermaritzburg: Orbis Books and Cluster Publications, 1995.

———. "White Men, Bibles, and Land: Ingredients in Biblical Interpretation in South African Black Theology." *Scriptura* (Forthcoming).

Wimbush, Vincent L. "The Bible and African Americans: An Outline of an Interpretative History." In Ed. Cain Hope Felder, *Stony the Road We Trod: African American Biblical Interpretation*, Minneapolis: Fortress, 1991: 81–97.

———. "Reading Texts through Worlds, Worlds through Texts." *Semeia* 62 (1993): 129–140.

Yorke, Gosnell L.O.R. "The Bible in the Black Diaspora." In Eds Hannah W. Kinoti and John M. Waliggo, *The Bible in African Christianity*, Nairobi: Acton Publishers, 1997: 149–152.

———. "Biblical Hermeneutics: An Afrocentric Perspective." *The Journal of Religious Thought* 52 (1995): 1–13.

OLD TESTAMENT SCHOLARSHIP IN SUB-SAHARAN AFRICA NORTH OF THE LIMPOPO RIVER

Knut Holter

Historically and geographically speaking, the African experience of reading the Old Testament stretches from that of Jewish and Christian communities in the northern part of the continent two millennia ago to that of today's post-apartheid communities in the southern part of the continent. It also stretches from that of Coptic and Ethiopian communities throughout the two millennia, and up until today's rapid growth of new reading communities all over the continent. The scholarly approaches to the reception of the Old Testament in Africa therefore include a wide spectrum of fields, stretching not only from historical critical to literary readings, but also from historical studies of how the Old Testament is read in Jewish, patristic, Coptic and Ethiopian sources, to different kinds of contemporary readings, including inculturation, liberation, post-colonial, and post-apartheid readings.

Within this wide spectrum of fields, the present essay will delimit itself geographically to focus on Old Testament scholarship in sub-Saharan Africa north of the Limpopo river. That is, it will attempt to present how the Old Testament is interpreted by scholars attached to universities, theological seminaries and churches in that major part of the continent which is situated between the Maghrebian north, including Ethiopia, and the post-apartheid south (see Holter 1996: 13–14); still, for the sake of brevity, "Africa" will be used as an abbreviation for this geographically delimited region.

The presentation of Old Testament scholarship in Africa will be organized according to chronological and topical issues. From a chronological point of view Old Testament scholarship in Africa will be followed from the past, that is, the 1960s and 70s, here characterized as its background, through the present, that is the 1980s and 90s, here characterized as its breakthrough, and, indeed with some reservations, into the future, that is into the 21st century. And then, within each of these three chronological divisions, the presentation will circle around two sets of topics, the institutional context of Old Testament scholarship in Africa and its thematic orientation.

The first of the three chronological parts, here characterized as the past or background of Old Testament scholarship in Africa, includes the 1960s and 70s. It is, of course, possible to point out examples of Old Testament scholarship in Africa prior to the 1960s. A number of theological seminaries gave courses in Old Testament studies based on traditional western approaches, often, however, with an open attitude towards the relationship between the Old Testament and the African context (see Bates 1954: 59–61). Also, a few African theologians pointed out the possibilities of a more specific African reading of the Old Testament (see Bajeux 1956: 57–82). Still, the political and ecclesiastical independence of the 1960s, together with a rapid growth of theological seminaries and university departments of religion throughout the continent, and also a sudden wave of publications on Africa and the Old Testament, makes it natural to start this survey with the 1960s.

In 1960, at the dawn of independence, Africa had only six universities (see Marah 1989: 148–150), but throughout the 1960s and 70s the number increased rapidly. The same was the case with the number of theological seminaries (see Tutu 1976: 7–27). In this period of post-independence the mission of the universities was seen as part of the efforts of national development, politically, economically, and obviously also culturally (see Ajayi et al. 1996: 74–143). In the humanities this led to a focus on African culture and languages, and the departments of Religious Studies followed this up with research and teaching programmes on African Traditional Religion (see Platvoet 1989: 107–126). Also with regard to Old Testament studies this focus on African culture was reflected, here as an emphasizing of inculturation hermeneutical approaches, that is, approaches where the relationship between the texts of the Old Testament and the context of Africa were elaborated (see Abogunrin 1986: 12–16). As a result, a rapidly growing number of studies comparing religion and socio-cultural parallels between Africa and the Old Testament were published.

A glimpse into this period can be found in an article by Edward G. Newing, who in the late 1960s made a thorough survey of how Old Testament studies were conducted in universities and theological seminaries throughout Eastern and Central Africa, 37 institutions received a questionnaire, 23 answered (Newing 1970: 80–98). Newing found that most institutions exposed their students to some use of the higher critical approaches developed in western Old Testament scholarship, still, only three offered courses in biblical Hebrew. Not surprisingly, Newing was also able to draw parallels to the situation in the West with regard to programmes and textbooks. However, he was very critical of what he found. Especially he was sceptical about a rather rigid system of external examinations. As an attempt to improve the situation, he proposed a new four-year college curriculum where courses in Old Testament introduction, exegesis and theology were related to courses in other theological disciplines, and where questions of relevance were especially addressed. Additional electives in biblical Hebrew and Old Testament exegesis and hermeneutics were then to be offered for those having the ability to go on to further studies (Newing 1970: 97–98).

To go on to higher degrees in the field of Old Testament, at least in the sense of doing postgraduate studies, meant, in most cases in the 1960s and 70s, to go to Europe or USA. A growing number of Africans got their Masters' in Old Testament studies from western institutions throughout these two decades, and, eventually, some few also got their doctorates, mainly from Rome (see, for example Osuji 1967, Monsengwo Pasinya 1973, Ndiokwere [1977]1981), but eventually also from other places in Europe or USA (see for example Tesfai 1975, Mafico 1979). These first Africans to get doctorates in Old Testament studies were pioneers, and some of them managed to continue their research and participate in the scholarly debate after their return to Africa (see for example Monsengwo Pasinya 1976: 225–241, 1985: 192–207, Mafico 1986: 400–409, 1996: 155–173). Still, as a whole, their influence on the development of Old Testament scholarship in Africa should not be overestimated. Back in Africa, some disappeared into church administration, others drowned in teaching responsibilities, and few of them ever saw the results of their research published.

More influential were those theologians who, in their search for a *theologia africana*, showed a special interest for the Old Testament. This interest, which in particular focussed on the so-called African predilection for the Old Testament (see Dickson 1973: 31–41), was reflected already in the publications of the *Gründer*-generation of African theology, for example Kwesi A. Dickson (Ghana), John S. Mbiti (Kenya) and Emmanuel B. Idowu (Nigeria). As a consequence, the late 1960s, and especially the 1970s, experienced a rapid growth in scholarly publications on Old Testament questions, and then in particular publications relating the texts of the Old Testament and the context of Africa. An important factor contributing to this development was the launching of several theological journals. Of special importance here, as, from the beginning, they published articles related to the Old Testament, were *Orita* (1967, Nigeria) and *Africa Theological Journal* (1968, Tanzania).

Thematically there was a close relationship between the dissertations written in western institutions and the articles published in Africa, as both very often circled around the relationship between Africa and the Old Testament. Among the dissertations, comparisons were made on different kinds of religio-cultural phenomena, for example, Oko F. Ugwueze (Nigeria) wrote on proverbs, Nathanael I. Ndiokwere (Nigeria) on Prophetism, John Onaiyekan (Nigeria) on priesthood, and Buame J.B. Bediaku (Togo) on penitence (Ugwueze 1976, Ndiokwere [1977]1981, Onaiyekan 1976, Bediaku 1978). Among the articles similar comparisons were made, for example, Samuel G. Kibicho (Kenya) wrote on concepts of God, Bonganjalo Goba (South Africa) on corporate personality, Francis F.K. Abotchie (Ghana) on rites of passage, and Daniel E. Mondeh (Ghana) on sacrifice (Kibicho 1968: 223–238, Goba 1973: 65–73, Abotchie 1978: 82–89, Mondeh 1978: 76–81).

Similar themes were also discussed at three international conferences which took place in the 1970s, conferences that especially focussed on biblical scholarship vis-à-vis Africa. These conferences meant a lot to African scholars working with the Old Testament. Not least they meant possibilities to interact with fellow African colleagues. The first was "The Jerusalem Congress on Black Africa and the Bible" in 1972 (see Mveng & Werblowsky 1972), where a number of African scholars met Jewish colleagues, mainly from Israel, and discussed different topics relating to Africa and the Old Testament (see for example Idowu 1972: 199–204, Mveng 1972: 23–39). Similar topics were also discussed at a conference on "Christian-Jewish Relations in Ecumenical Perspective with Special Emphasis on Africa" in 1977 (see Hammerstein 1978), this also taking place in Jerusalem (see for example Abotchie 1978: 82–89, Mafico 1978: 36–52, Mbiti 1978: 53–61). And a third was the conference in Kinshasa in 1978 on "Christianisme et Identité Africaine" (see Atal Sa Angang 1980), initiated by the Pan-African Association of Catholic Exegetes (see for example Nyeme Tese 1980: 83–112, Renju 1980: 113–118).

The growing interest in the relationship between Africa and the Old Testament called for a more systematic analysis of the underlying hermeneutical and methodological questions; this enterprise was primarily undertaken by Mbiti and Dickson. Mbiti described the central role played by the Bible, and then not least by the Old Testament, in African Christianity. He pointed out that this especially concerned the African Instituted Churches, but that it, to some degree, also concerned African theology and Christianity in general (Mbiti 1978a: 72–85, 1978b: 13–19, see also 1986: 22–66). Dickson instead focussed on similarities and differences between Africa and the Old Testament with regard to world-view, coining the terms, continuity and discontinuity between African and Old Testament life and thought (Dickson 1979: 179–193), terms which other scholars also started to use in their discussion of the relationship between Africa and the Old Testament (see, e.g. Renju 1980: 113–118). In this respect, Dickson very early emphasized the need for a stronger methodological basis in the comparisons between Africa and the Old Testament (Dickson 1972: 155–166), rejecting the attempts that previously had been made by some western expatriates (see Williams 1930) at explaining the affinities between the two as due to historical interaction (Dickson 1974: 23–34, for an alternative view, see Wambutda 1987: 33–41).

Summing up, the 1960s and 70s showed a growing interest in scholarly studies of the Old Testament. While one can hardly talk about an African Old Testament scholarship as such, due to the lack of structures within the continent for research and publication, still, the efforts put into developing theological seminaries and university departments of religion, together with a growing interest for studies of the relationship between Africa and the Old Testament, provide an important background for what was to become African Old Testament scholarship. Let us now leave the past, that is, the 1960s and 70s, and proceed to the present, that is the 1980s and 90s, here focussing on the institutional context and thematic orientation of Old Testament scholarship in Africa.

The institutional context of Old Testament scholarship in Africa throughout the 1980s and 90s is characterized by two closely related aspects, a growth in the number of Africans doing postgraduate studies in the Old Testament, and a growth in publications on the Old Testament. At present, towards the end of these two decades, many university departments of religion and several theological seminaries have staff members with doctorates in Old Testament studies. Still, much of the training continues to take place in Europe or North America, but the connection between Africa and the West in this respect often follows ecclesiastical lines (Catholics: Rome, Evangelicals: USA), but to some degree it also follows historical and political lines (colonial: Great Britain, France and Belgium; neo-colonial: USA). However, it is increasingly being experienced as a problem that the training is given in a context that both culturally and scholarly is non-African. One result of this is that questions emerging from cultural and social concerns in Africa only to some extent are allowed into the interpretation of the Old Testament. As a consequence, there is a gap between the needs of ordinary African Christians for modes of reading the Old Testament, and the modes provided by scholars trained in the western tradition of biblical scholarship (see Ukpong 1995: 4). Another result of the location of the training outside Africa is a feeling, at least in some cases, of inferiority vis-à-vis the massive western tradition. This might eventually lead some scholars to neglect their African context, and instead see "themselves as ambassadors of Cambridge, Oxford, [the] Tübingen school etc." (Abogunrin 1986: 13).

As a response to this, several African universities have throughout the 1980s and 90s developed programmes for postgraduate studies in the Old Testament, mainly at Masters' level, but in some cases also at PhD level. Even some of the theological seminaries have developed Masters' programmes in Old Testament studies, of special importance are the two evangelical graduate schools of Theology, that were established during the 1980s, one in Nairobi (Kenya) for Anglophone Africa, another in Bangui (Central African Republic) for Francophone Africa. The major force in the development of programmes for postgraduate studies in the Old Testament is found in Nigeria, whose many university departments of Religious Studies had gained an international reputation as early as the 1960s. The universities in Ibadan and Nsukka awarded their first PhD's in Old Testament studies in the first half of the 1980s (see Abe 1983, Lasebikan 1983, Ebo 1985). Eventually, universities in other parts of Africa undertook similar initiatives, for example in Cameroon (see Gakindi 1992) and Kenya (see Gitau 1996).

Closely related to the growth in number throughout the 1980s and 90s of Africans doing postgraduate studies in the Old Testament is the remarkable growth in scholarly publications on the Old

Testament throughout the same two decades. The publications are
of varying character and different genres. The most influential genre
is probably represented by articles, published in an increasing number of African scholarly journals. Of great importance here was that
the Nigerian Association for Biblical Studies in 1986 launched the
African Journal of Biblical Studies, which was the first African journal
to focus on biblical research in Africa (see Abe 1997: 12–13). A second genre is represented by published versions of doctoral dissertations. Most dissertations are still not published, some of the ones
written in Africa are not even abstracted in international bibliographical tools, and hence are difficult to trace. However, a few have
been published, for example, Leonidas Kalugila (Tanzania) wrote
on the wise king, Nathanael I. Ndiokwere (Nigeria) and Samuel S.
Simbandumwe on prophetic movements, and Laurent Naré (Burkina
Faso) and Philippe D. Nzambi (Democratic Republic of Congo) on
proverbs (Kalugila 1980, Ndiokwere 1981, Simbandumwe 1992, Naré
1986, Nzambi 1992).

A third genre is represented by Old Testament commentaries.
This classical genre of Old Testament scholarship has actually found
surprisingly little attention in Africa, still, at least some commentaries have been published, in most cases' commentaries with a devotional profile, but also a few with a more scholarly profile (see Mbiti
1986: 51–52). The best-known example of the latter is probably
Modupe Oduyoye's (Nigeria) commentary on Genesis 1–11 (Oduyoye
1984), enthusiastically received as a sign that "The age of African
[sic] biblical theology has dawned!" (Obijole 1986: 53–55). There
have also been some attempts at launching African commentary
series. One attempt was made in the late 1960s, when John S. Mbiti
proposed that African scholars should write a commentary together.
However, he abandoned the idea when he found that none of those
who had promised to write contributions actually managed to do so
(Mbiti 1986: 60). Another attempt was made in the 1970s and 80s,
when the West African Association of Theological Institutions initiated a "Bible Commentary for Africa Project." This project aimed
at looking "afresh at the Bible with African insights, relating their
interpretation to the African past, the prevailing situations of the
churches in Africa and the problems of the various societies in Africa."
(Fasholé-Luke 1981: 44). The coordinator of this project was Edward
Fasholé-Luke (Sierra Leone), and the project ceased after his death
in 1991. A recent project, already in progress, aims to produce a

Bible for Anglophone African readers. The idea is to use an existing English translation and write introductions to books and chapters, and also footnotes to verses, from the perspective of African cultural and religious traditions as well as social, economic and political realities of present day Africa (see Zinkuratire 1998: 7–9).

These two aspects of the institutional context of Old Testament scholarship in Africa throughout the 1980s and 90s, that is, the increased number of Africans doing postgraduate studies in the Old Testament and the growth in publications, are obviously related to the thematic orientation reflected in their research and publications. Here two aspects should be pointed out. First, it is clear that the inculturation hermeneutical approaches of the 1960s and 70s continued to play a major role in the 1980s and 90s, often based on comparative paradigms which related certain ideas or motives in the Old Testament to similar ideas or motives in traditional or contemporary Africa. However, as demonstrated by for example Benjamin A. Ntreh (Ghana), Winston R. Kawale (Malawi), and Justin S. Ukpong (Nigeria), there is now a stronger awareness of the methodological questions that are involved (Ntreh 1990: 247–254, Kawale 1995: 7–30, Ukpong 1995: 3–14).

This preference for contextual approaches can be seen in the topics chosen for doctoral dissertations in Africa. For example George L. Lasebikan (Nigeria) wrote on prophecy, Samson Gitau (Kenya) on concepts of the environment, and Madipoane J. Masenya (South Africa) on proverbs (Lasebikan 1983, Gitau 1996, Masenya 1996), but also in the West, where for example Laurent Naré (Burkina Faso) and Philippe D. Nzambi (Democratic Republic of Congo) wrote on proverbs, Justin Ukpong (Nigeria) on sacrifice, Philibert Rwehumbiza (Tanzania) on concepts of God, and Samuel Abegunde (Nigeria) on translation methods and philosophy (Naré 1986, Nzambi 1992, Ukpong 1987, Rwehumbiza 1983, Abegunde 1985). Still, above all the preference for contextual approaches can be seen in the large number of articles published throughout the 1980s and 90s, largely articles comparing different kinds of religio-cultural phenomena in Africa and the Old Testament (for bibliographical surveys, see LeMarquand 1995: 6–40, Holter 1996). Only a very few examples can be mentioned here, Aloo O. Mojola (Kenya) and Temba L.J. Mafico (Zimbabwe) wrote on the names of God (Mojola 1995: 229–236, Mafico 1995: 21–32), Philibert Rwehumbiza (Tanzania) and S.G.A. Onibere (Nigeria) on sacrifice (Rwehumbiza 1988, Onibere

1988: 193–203), and Gabriel O. Abe (Nigeria) and Ofusu Adutwum (Ghana) on aspects of the institution of matrimony (Abe 1989: 3–18, Adutwum 1992/1993: 38–42). Moreover, it should be noted here, that the contextual approach to the Old Testament is not only found in studies on "the Old Testament in Africa," it is also reflected in different attempts at finding "Africa in the Old Testament," that is, exegetical analyses of how African peoples and individuals are portrayed by the Old Testament, the contributions by David T. Adamo (Nigeria) are here of special importance (see Adamo 1998, see also Holter 1997: 331–336, and Høyland 1998).

At the same time, however, it should be emphasized that the 1980s and 90s have seen an increasing focus on more traditional exegetical approaches. In other words, there is now a clear interest in interpreting the Old Testament texts without the African context of the interpreter being (at least explicitly!) reflected. In the mid-1980s John S. Mbiti argued that Leonidas Kalugila's dissertation (Kalugila 1980) is "one of the very few 'pure' biblical works by African scholars" (Mbiti 1986: 49). A decade later, one notices that Kalugila is being accompanied by an increasing number of African colleagues. This tendency is obviously reflected in doctoral dissertations written in western contexts (like that of Kalugila); for example, Ofusu Adutwum (Ghana) wrote on the Hebrew root *bth*, Victor Zinkuratire (Uganda) on the kingship of Yahweh, Benjamin A. Ntreh (Ghana) on political authority in ancient Israel, and Tewoldemedhin Habtu (Ethiopia/ Kenya) on Old Testament wisdom theology (Adutwum 1984, Zinkuratire 1987, Ntreh 1989, Habtu 1993). To some extent, however, the same tendency is also reflected in doctoral dissertations written in Africa, for example, Gabriel O. Abe (Nigeria) wrote on the covenant, D.J.I. Ebo (Nigeria) on hope in Amos, Gédéon Gakindi (Rwanda) on the Aaronitic blessing, and Malachy I. Okwueze (Nigeria) on mythology (Abe 1983, Ebo 1985, Gakindi 1992, Okwueze 1995).

Furthermore, the tendency to focus on more traditional exegetical approaches is also reflected in minor studies and articles, where publications throughout the 1980s and 90s reflect a wide spectrum within the field of Old Testament research. This includes studies on all kinds of exegetical and theological questions, for example, George L. Lasebikan (Nigeria), D.J.I. Ebo (Nigeria), and Edmond G. Djitangar (Chad) wrote on prophetism (Lasebikan 1985: 51–58, Ebo 1989: 17–27, Djitangar 1993: 30–39). But it also includes other kinds of approaches, for example, David Alao (Nigeria), J.M. Enomate (Nigeria), and Monday U. Ekpo (Nigeria) have focussed on history of scholarship studies (Alao 1984: 87–97, Enomate 1986: 148–159, Ekpo 1985: 79–90), and Laurent Monsengwo Pasinya (Democratic Republic of Congo), Hilary B.P. Mijoga (Malawi), and J.O. Akao (Nigeria) have focussed on Septuagintal and historical studies (Monsengwo Pasinya 1985: 192–207, Mijoga 1990: 85–90, Akao 1990: 52–63).

These two aspects of the thematic orientation of Old Testament scholarship in Africa throughout the 1980s and 90s are not accidental, rather, they represent a conscious understanding of what it means to do Old Testament scholarship in Africa—the responsibility for doing both historical studies of the text and studies of the encounter between the text and the contemporary context. This twofold mission of Old Testament scholarship in Africa was explicitly expressed in the policy statement of the first issue of *African Journal of Biblical Studies* (1986), it said that the journal wanted to promote biblical research and the study of biblical and related languages, but also to encourage biblical scholars to look afresh at the Bible from an African perspective, and to relate interpretation to the life situation in Africa. Similar thoughts have also been expressed throughout the 1980s and 90s by a number of Old Testament scholars. One was Daniel N. Wambutda (Nigeria), who emphasized the necessity of an exegetical basis of African theology (Wambutda 1980: 29–39), another was Samuel O. Abogunrin (Nigeria), who argued that "We cannot properly contextualize unless we first establish the nature of a text." (Abogunrin 1986: 18).

Summing up, whereas the past, that is the 1960s and 70s, was characterized as the background of Old Testament scholarship in Africa, the present, that is the 1980s and 90s, can be characterized as its breakthrough. This breakthrough is reflected in its institutional context as well as in its thematic orientation. As for the former, Old Testament scholarship in Africa has throughout these two decades experienced a remarkable growth and deliberate institutionalization of research and publication. And as for the latter, it has developed a conscious understanding of its mission, focussing on the text as an historical entity as well as the encounter between the text and the context of the contemporary reader.

Finally, after these surveys of the past and present, a few words must also be said about the future; where is Old Testament scholarship in Africa heading at the turn of the millennium? It should be emphasized here that the present author, as a non-African, does

not want to go into what John S. Mbiti has called the role of western theological engineers, that is to give advice on "how African
Theology should be done, where it should be done, who should do
it, what it should say, *ad infinitum*." (Mbiti 1986: 61). The following
should therefore not be read as recommendations for the future, but
rather as attempts at describing and following some lines that are
already present, drawing again on the same topics as previously, the
institutional context and the thematic orientation of Old Testament
scholarship in Africa.

The number of universities in Africa has increased from six in
1960, to more than one hundred now towards the end of the 1990s.
Still, most of these universities have no postgraduate programmes in
Old Testament studies. This also includes universities with theological departments (see for example Fiedler 1995: 37–41). In the same
period the number of theological seminaries and Bible schools has
passed one thousand, with far more of the latter than of the former, and only a very few seminaries have developed postgraduate
programmes at Master's level. In other words, within both universities and theological seminaries there is still a lot to do for the development of programmes in postgraduate studies of the Old Testament.

Publication will obviously be a key word in the years ahead. The
1980s and 90s were characterized by a preference for one particular genre within publications, the article in a scholarly journal, often
at the cost of other genres. To some extent this will continue, as
there is a strong need within the guild of scholars to present their
research in the form of brief articles. Still, in the years to come other
genres will be of importance. One is the scholarly monograph, usually in the form of a published version of a dissertation. This genre
will develop, not only due to the increasing number of doctoral dissertations in Old Testament studies, but also due to the increased
number of established researchers attached to universities and seminaries. Commentaries and introductory textbooks represent another,
and probably more important genre, as there is a strong need for
such books written from an African perspective. To some extent this
need has to do with money, as western books, generally speaking,
are priced at a level that effectively prevents the average African student (and even scholar) from buying them (see Holter 1998). Still,
more important than the question of money is the question of context. The need for commentaries and textbooks written by African

scholars is primarily a need for tools that reflect the context of the African students of the Old Testament. As for the commentary, it represents the classical genre of Old Testament scholarship, since all Old Testament scholarship, somehow, emerges from the interpretation of the texts. However, since the interpretation of a text to some extent reflects also the cultural, religious, and even political and economic context of the interpreter, there is obviously a need for commentaries that reflect the African context. And as for introductory textbooks, there is a need for African contributions concerning all subdivisions of Old Testament studies, that is, books on Old Testament introduction and historical as well as theological and hermeneutical questions. With regard to the former, it has been argued that there is a tendency of "de-Africanisation" in the prevailing western textbooks on the history and geography of ancient Israel, that is, a more or less deliberate disregard of Old Testament references to African nations (see Bailey 1991: 165–168). And with regard to the latter, it is no secret that western textbooks in Old Testament theology and hermeneutics hardly reflect anything of the insights provided by African scholars and their reading of the Old Testament in the context of Africa. As a response to this, several scholars, from different parts of Africa, plan to publish textbooks that reflect the African reading of the Old Testament, one example is Leonidas Kalugila (Tanzania), another is David T. Adamo (Nigeria).

As for the thematic orientation of the research conducted by African Old Testament scholars, the twofold approach will probably continue; studies of the text as well as studies of the encounter between text and contemporary context are considered necessary. However, a couple of factors might influence the balance between these two foci of Old Testament scholarship in Africa. One factor is the influence of post-apartheid South Africa. The political changes in South Africa have opened up new inter-African connections, for African Old Testament scholars this means that they, suddenly, have colleagues at the other side of the Zambezi. Traditionally, South African Old Testament scholarship has focussed on ancient text rather than contemporary context (see le Roux 1993), however, there is now a growing interest for relating Africa and the Old Testament, in some cases in the form of well-known liberation (see for example Mosala 1989, West 1995) and inculturation (see for example Burden 1983: 49–72, 1986: 95–110, Swanepoel 1990: 20–30) hermeneutical readings, in other cases in the form of newer post-colonial or post-apartheid readings (see for example Deist 1992: 311–331, 1996: 110–118, West 1994: 152–170).

Another factor, which should not be underestimated, is techno-logical development. Much of the research that is and has been done in Africa is done without access to the library services demanded by traditional western Old Testament scholarship (see Adamo 1997: 8–11; for a case study, the present situation in Nairobi, see Muutuki 1997: 5–7 and Bowen 1998: 20–21). Many African scholars have therefore realized that, under the given circumstances, the only option they have is to work with contextual comparative approaches. But technological developments might change this situation. As an increas-ing number of African Old Testament scholars have access to the Internet, and as the Internet increasingly offers access to biblio-graphical databases (see Kawale 1997: 3–4), full-text bases contain-ing journals, encyclopaedias, lexicons, etc., and all kinds of discussion groups, the geographical location of the researcher may be of less importance. As a consequence, the particular focus on comparative questions might diminish.

In a sum, just as the Old Testament has proved to be an African book (see Holter 1996: 11–13), to do Old Testament scholarship has likewise proved to be an African enterprise. Therefore, wherever African Old Testament scholarship will be heading, with regard to institutional context and thematic orientation, it deserves attention.

BIBLIOGRAPHY

Abe, Gabriel O. "African Journal of Biblical Studies." *Newsletter on African Old Testament Scholarship* 3 (1997): 12–13.
———. *Covenant in the Old Testament.* Unpublished Dissertation, University of Ibadan, 1983.
———. "The Jewish and Yoruba Social Institution of Marriage: A Comparative Study." *Orita* 21 (1989): 3–18.
Abegunde, Solomon O. *A Philosophy and Method of Translating the Old Testament into Yoruba.* Unpublished Dissertation, Southern Baptist Theological Seminary, 1985.
Abogunrin, Samuel O. "Biblical Research in Africa: The Task Ahead." *Africa Journal of Biblical Studies* 1/I (1986): 7–24.
Abotchie, Francis F.K. "Rites of Rassage and Socio-cultural Organization in African Culture and Judaism." In Ed. Franz von Hammerstein, *Christian-Jewish Relations in Ecumenical Perspective, with Special Emphasis on Africa.* Geneva: World Council of Churches, 1978: 82–89.
Adamo, David T. *Africa and the Africans in the Old Testament.* San Francisco: Christian Universities Press, 1998.

————. "Doing Old Testament Research in Africa." *Newsletter on African Old Testament Scholarship* 3 (1997): 8–11.
————. "Ethiopia in the Bible." *African Christian Studies* 8/II (1992): 51–64.
————. "The Table of Nations Reconsidered in African Perspective (Genesis 10)." *Journal of African Religion and Philosophy* 2 (1993): 138–143.
Adutwum, Ofosu. *The root נכה in the Old Testament.* Unpublished Dissertation, University of Hamburg, 1984.
————. "The Suspected Adulteress: Ancient Israelite and Traditional Akan Treatment." *The Expository Times* 104 (1992/1993): 38–42.
Ajayi, J.F. et al. *The African Experience with Higher Education.* Accra: The Association of African Universities, 1996.
Akao, J.O. "The Letter of Aristeas and Its Worth in Biblical Studies." *Orita* 22/I (1990): 52–63.
Akpunonu, Peter D. *Salvation in Deutero-Isaiah.* Unpublished Dissertation, Pontifical University Urban, Rome, 1991.
Alao, David. "The Relevance of the Amarna Letters to Hebrew Origins." *Orita* 16/II (1984): 87–97.
Atal Sa Angang, D. *Christianisme et identité africaine. Point de vue exegetique. Actes du 1er congres des biblistes africains.* Kinshasa: Faculte de theologie catholique, 1980.
Bailey, Randall, C. "Beyond Identification: The Use of Africans in Old Testament Poetry and Narratives." In Ed. Cain Hope Felder, *Stony the Road We Trod: African American Biblical Interpretation.* Minneapolis: Fortress Press, 1991: 165–184.
Bajeux, J.-C. "Mentality noire et mentality biblike." In Eds A. Abble et al., *Des prêtres noirs s'interrogent.* Paris: Les éditions de cerf, 1956, 57–82.
Bates, M. Searle. *Survey of the Training of the Ministry in Africa. Part II.* London & New York: International Missionary Council, 1954.
Bediaku, Buame J.B. *Etude comparé de la célébration pénitentielle dans l'ancient testament et chez le peuple Ewe du Togo. Pour une cathéchèse de la célébration pénitentielle en afrique noire.* Unpublished Dissertation, Academy Alfons., Rome, 1978.
Bowen, Dorothy N. "Old Testament Literature in the NEGST Library." *Newsletter on African Old Testament Scholarship* 4 (1998): 20–21.
Burden, Jasper J. "Are Shem and Ham Blood Brothers? The Relevance of the Old Testament to Africa." *Old Testament Essays* 1 (1983): 49–72.
————. "World-view in Interpreting the Old Testament in Africa." *Old Testament Essays* 4 (1986): 95–110.
Deist, Ferdinand E. "Biblical Interpretation in Post-colonial Africa." *Svensk Teologisk Kvartalskrift* 72 (1996): 110–118.
————. "South African Old Testament Studies and the Future." *Old Testament Essays* 5 (1992): 311–331.
Dickson, Kwesi A. "African Traditional Religions and the Bible." In Eds Engelbert Mveng & R. Zwi Werblowsky, *The Jerusalem Congress on Black Africa and the Bible.* Jerusalem: Anti-Defamation League of B'nai B'rit, 1972, 155–166.
————. "Continuity and Discontinuity between the Old Testament and African Life and Thought." *Bulletin of African Theology* 1 (1979): 179–193.
————. "'Hebrewisms of West Africa': The Old Testament and African life and Thought." *Legon Journal of Humanities* 1 (1974): 23–34.
————. "The Old Testament and African Theology." *Ghana Bulletin of Theology* 4 (1973): 31–41.
Djitangar, Edmond E. "La mission de serviteur de Yahweh: Isaiah 42: 1–9." In Eds P. Adeso et al., *Universalisme et mission dans la bible,* Nairobi: Catholic Biblical Centre for Africa and Madagascar, 1993: 30–39.
Ebo, D.J.I. "Another Look at Amos' Visions." *Africa Theological Journal* 18/I (1989): 17–27.
————. *"'O that Jacob Would Survive." A Study on Hope in the Book of Amos.* Unpublished Dissertation, University of Nigeria, 1985.

Ekpo, Monday U. "Robertson Smith, the 'Higher Critics' and the Problem of Prophecy: A Case Study in the Sociology of Knowledge." *Africa Theological Journal* 14/II (1985): 79–90.

Enomate, J.M. "Ezra the Scribe: A Reconsideration." *African Journal of Biblical Studies* 1/II (1986): 148–159.

Fasholé-Luke, Edward E. "Bible Commentary for Africa Project." *Exchange* 10 (1981): 42–45.

Fiedler, Klaus. "Postgraduate Theology Degrees in Malawi." *Religion in Malawi* 5 (1995): 37–41.

Gakindi, Gédéon. *La benediction aaronique et la b'rakah de l'ancien testament.* Unpublished Dissertation, Yaoundé Faculty of Protestant Theology, Yaoundé, 1992.

Gitau, Samson. *African and Biblical Understanding of the Environment.* Unpublished Dissertation, University of Nairobi, 1996.

Goba, Bonganjalo. "Corporate Personality: Ancient Israel and Africa." In Ed. Basil Moore, *Black Theology: The South African Voice.* London: C. Hurst & Company, 1973: 65–73.

Habtu, Tewoldemedhin. *A Taxonomy of Approaches of Five Representative Scholars to the Nature of Wisdom in the Old Testament, in the Light of Proverbs 1–9.* Unpublished Dissertation, Trinity Evangelical Divinity School, Deerfield, 1993.

Hammerstein, Franz von Ed., *Christian-Jewish Relations in Ecumenical Perspective, with Special Emphasis on Africa.* Geneva: World Council of Churches, 1978.

Holter, Knut. *Tropical Africa and the Old Testament: A Select and Annotated Bibliography.* Oslo: University of Oslo, 1996.

———. "Should Old Testament 'Cush' Be Rendered 'Africa'?" *The Bible Translator* 48 (1997): 331–336.

———. "It's Not only a Question of Money! African Old Testament Scholarship between the Myths and Meanings of the South and the Money and Methods of the North." *Old Testament Essays,* 11 (1998): 240–254.

Høyland, Marta. "An African Presence in the Old Testament? David Tuesday Adamo's Interpretation of the Old Testament Cush Passages." *Old Testament Essays,* 1998. (Forthcoming)

Idowu, Emmanuel B. "The teaching of the Bible to African Students." In Eds Engelbert Mveng & R. Zwi Werblowsky, *The Jerusalem Congress on Black Africa and the Bible.* Jerusalem: Anti-Defamation League of B'nai B'rit, 1972, 199–204.

Kalugila, Leonidas. *The Wise King: Studies in Royal Wisdom as Divine Revelation in the Old Testament and its Environment.* Lund: CWK Gleerup, 1980.

Kawale, Winston R. "Divergent Interpretations of the Relationship between Some Concepts of God in the Old Testament and in African Traditional Religions: A Theological Critique." *Old Testament Essays* 8 (1995): 7–30.

———. "New Data Base: Bible in Africa Research Project." *Newsletter on African Old Testament Scholarship* 3 (1997): 3–4.

Kibicho, Samuel G. "The Interaction of the Traditional Kikuyu Concept of God with the Biblical Concept." *Cahiers des Religions Africaines* 2 (1968): 223–238.

Lasebikan, George L. *Prophecy or Schizophrenia? A Study of Pophecy in the Old Testament and in Selected Aladura Churches.* Unpublished Dissertation, University of Ibadan, 1983.

———. "Prophets as Political Activists in the Ancient Israelite Monarchy." *Orita* 17/I (1985): 51–58.

———. "Sacrifice in the Old Testament." *Orita* 20/II (1988): 64–78.

LeMarquand, Grant. "A Bibliography of the Bible in Africa: A Preliminary Publication." *Bulletin for Contextual Theology* 2/II (1995): 6–40.

Le Roux, Jurie H. *A Story of Two Ways: Thirty Years of Old Testament Scholarship in South Africa.* Pretoria: Verba Vitae.

Mafico, Temba L.J. *A Study of the Hebrew Root* שפט *with Reference to Yahweh: A Thesis.* Unpublished Dissertation, Harvard, 1979.

————. "Parallels between Jewish and African Religio-cultural Lives." In Ed. Franz von Hammerstein, *Christian-Jewish Relations in Ecumenical Perspective, with Special Emphasis on Africa.* Geneva: World Council of Churches, 1978: 36–52.

————. "The Old Testament and Effective evangelism Africa." *International Review of Mission* 75 (1986): 400–409.

————. "The Divine Compound Name (לחי) יהוה and Israel's Monotheistic Polytheism." *Journal of Northwest Semitic Languages* 22/I (1996): 155–173.

————. "The Divine Name Yahweh Elohim from an African Perspective." In Eds Fernando F. Segovia and Mary Ann Tolbert *Reading from this Place. Volume II: Social Location and Biblical Interpretation in Global Perspectives* Minneapolis: Fortress Press, 1995: 21–32.

Marah, John K. *Pan-African Education: The Last Stage of Educational Developments in Africa.* Lewiston: The Edwin Mellen Press, 1989.

Masenya, Madipoane J. *Proverbs 31:10–31 in a South African Context: A Bosadi Perspective.* Unpublished Dissertation, University of South Africa, 1996.

Mbiti, John S. "The Biblical Basis in Present Trends of African Theology." *Africa Theological Journal* 7/I (1978): 72–85 [= 1978a].

————. "African Christians and Jewish Religious Heritage." In Ed. Franz von Hammerstein, *Christian-Jewish Relations in Ecumenical Perspective, with Special Emphasis on Africa.* Geneva: World Council of Churches, 1978: 13–19 [= 1978b].

————. *Bible and Theology in African Christianity.* Nairobi: Oxford University Press, 1986.

Mijoga, Hilary B.P. "Some Notes on the Septuagint Translation of Isaiah 53." *Africa Theological Journal* 19/I (1990): 85–90.

Mojola, Aloo O. "A 'Female' God in East Africa: The Problem of Translating God's Name among the Iraqw of Mbulu, Tanzania." *The Bible Translator* 46 (1995): 229–236.

Mondeh, Daniel E. "Sacrifice in Jewish and African Traditions." In Ed. Franz von Hammerstein, Ed., *Christian-Jewish Relations in Ecumenical Perspective, with Special Emphasis on Africa.* Geneva: World Council of Churches, 1978: 76–81.

Monsengwo Pasinya, Laurent. "Isaïe xix 16–25 et universalisme dans la LXX." In Ed. John Emerton, *Congress Volume: Salamanca 1983.* Leiden: Brill, 1985: 192–207.

————. *La notion de "nomos" dans le Pentateuque grec.* Rome: Biblical Institute Press, 1973.

————. "Le cadre littéraire de Genèse 1." *Biblica* 57 (1976): 225–241.

Mosala, Itumeleng J. *Biblical Hermeneutics and Black Theology in South Africa.* Grand Rapids: Eerdmans, 1989.

Muutuki, Joseph. "Library Resources for Old Testament Research in Nairobi." *Newsletter on African Old Testament Scholarship* 3 (1997): 5–7.

Mveng, Engelbert. "La bible et l'afrique noire." In Eds Engelbert Mveng & R. Zwi Werblowsky, *The Jerusalem Congress on Black Africa and the Bible.* Jerusalem: Anti-Defamation League of B'nai B'rit, 1972: 23–39.

Mveng, Engelbert & Werblowsky, R. Zwi Eds, *The Jerusalem Congress on Black Africa and the Bible.* Jerusalem: Anti-Defamation League of B'nai B'rit, 1972.

Naré, Laurent. *Proverbes salomoniens et proverbes mossi. Etude comparative à partir d'une nouvelle analyse de Proverbes 25–29.* Frankfurt am Main: Peter Lang, 1986.

Ndiokwere, Nathanael I. *Prophecy and revolution: The Role of Prophets in the Independent African Churches and in Biblical Tradition.* London: SPCK, 1981.

Newing, Edward G. "A study of Old Testament Curricula in Eastern and Central Africa." *Africa Theological Journal* 3/I (1970): 80–98.

Ntreh, Benjamin A. "Toward an African Biblical Hermeneutics." *Africa Theological Journal* 19 (1990): 247–254.

————. *Transmission of Political Authority in Ancient Israel: A Tradition Historical Study of the Demise and Succession of Kings in the Deuteronomistic History and in the Chronicler's History.* Unpublished Dissertation, Lutheran School of Theology, Chicago, 1989.

Nussbaum, Stan. "African Bible Guides: Preliminary Findings of an Experiment with African Christianity in Microcosm." *Evangelical Review of Theology* 17 (1993): 452–467.

Nyeme Tese, J. "Continuite et discontinuite entre l'ancien testament et les religions africain." In Ed. D. Atal Sa Angang, *Christianisme et identité africaine. Point de vue exegetique. Actes du 1er congres des biblistes africains.* Kinshasa: Faculte de theologie catholique, 1980: 83–112.

Nzambi, Philippe D. *Proverbes bibliques et proverbes kongo.* Frankfurt am Main: Peter Lang, 1992.

Obijole, O.O. "The age of Agrican [sic] Biblical Theology Has Dawned! [Book review: Oduyoye 1984]." *Orita* 18/I (1986): 53–55.

Oduyoye, Modupe. *The Sons of the Gods and the Daughters of Men: An Afro-Asiatic Interpretation of Genesis 1–11.* New York: Maryknoll & Ibadan: Daystar Press, 1984.

Okwueze, Malachy R. *Myth: The Old Testament Experience.* Unpublished Dissertation, University of Nigeria, 1995.

Onaiyekan, John. *The Priesthood in Pre-monarchial Ancient Israel and among the Owe-Yoruba of Kabba: A Comparative Study.* Unpublished Dissertation, Pontifical University Urban, Rome, 1976.

Osuji, Boniface A. *The Hebrew and Igbo Concept of Religion and Sin Compared in the Light of Biblical and Rabbinic Material.* Unpublished Dissertation, Pontifical University Urban, Rome, 1967.

Platvoet, Jan. "The Institutional Environment of the Study of Religions in Africa South of the Sahara." In Ed. Michael Pye, *Marburg Revisited: Institutions and Strategies in the Study of Religion.* Marburg: Diagonal-Verlag, 1989: 107–126.

Renju, Peter M. "African traditional religions & Old Testament: Continuity or Discontinuity?" In Ed. D. Atal Sa Angang, *Christianisme et identité africaine. Point de vue exegetique. Actes du 1er congres des biblistes africains.* Kinshasa: Faculte de theologie catholique, 1980: 113–118.

Rwehumbiza, Philibert. *A Comparative Study between the Development of Yahwistic Monotheism and the Concept of God among the Bantu People South of the Sahara: A Biblico-theological Evaluation.* Partly published dissertation, Pontifical University. Lateran, Rome 1983.

———. *Patriarchal and Bantu Cults Compared.* Eldoret: Amecea Gaba Publications 1988.

Simbandumwe, Samuel S. *A Socio-religious and Political Analysis of the Judeo-Christian Concept of Prophetism and Modern Bakongo and Zulu African Prophet Movements.* Lewiston, New York: Edwin Mellen Press, 1992.

Tesfai, Yakob. *This Is My Resting Place: An Inquiry into the Role of Time and Space in the Old Testament.* Unpublished Dissertation, Lutheran School of Theology, Chicago, 1975.

Tutu, Desmond. "Survey of Theological Institutions in Africa Today." *All-Africa Conference of Churches Bulletin* 9/II (1976): 7–27.

Ugwueze, Oko F. *Igbo Proverbs and Biblical Proverbs.* Unpublished Dissertation, Pontifical. University. Urban, Rome, 1976.

Ukpong, Justin S. "Rereading the Bible with African Eyes." *Journal of Theology for Southern Africa* 91 (1995): 3–14.

———. *Sacrifice: African and Biblical. A Comparative Study of Ibibo and Levitical Sacrifices.* Rome: Urbaniana University Press, 1987.

Wambutda, Daniel N. "Hebrewisms of West Africa: An Ongoing Search in the Correlations between the Old Testament and African Weltanschauung." *Ogbomoso Journal of Theology* 2 (1987): 33–41.

———. "Hermeneutics and the Search for Theologia Africana." *Africa Theological Journal* 9/I (1980): 29–39.

West, Gerald O. *Biblical Hermeneutics of Liberation: Modes of Reading the Bible in the South African Context.* Pietermaritzburg: Cluster Publications, 1995.

————. "Difference and Dialogue: Reading the Joseph Story with Poor and Marginalised Communities in South Africa." *Biblical Interpretation* 2 (1994): 152–170.

Williams, Joseph J. *Hebrewisms of West Africa: From Nile to Niger with the Jews.* New York: Biblo and Tannen, 1967.

Zinkuratire, Victor. *The Kingship of Yahweh in Israel's History, Cult and Eschatology: A Study of Psalm 47.* Unpublished Dissertation, University of Cambridge, 1987.

————. "The African Bible Project." *Newsletter on African Old Testament Scholarship* 4 (1998): 7–9.

NEW TESTAMENT EXEGESIS IN (MODERN) AFRICA[1]

Grant LeMarquand

The opinion is often expressed that the world view of African peoples is close to the Old Testament, or that Africans feel more at home with the Old Testament than with the New. Kwesi Dickson, for example, has explored what he calls the "African predilection for the Old Testament" noting even that some early African Christian leaders worried that since the Old Testament atmosphere was so congenial converts "might not want to go further" (Dickson 1984: 146, cf. Dickson 1973, Dickson 1979).

It would seem to be true that the Old Testament is used in African preaching more frequently than it is used in the pulpits of North Atlantic countries. It is also true that many Old Testament ideas which seem quite foreign to western minds appear to be readily comprehensible in African contexts. It is easier to understand the meaning of the concept of "covenant," for example, if one's people practices covenant rituals (Arulefela 1988). Sacrificial rituals found in Old Testament narratives and legal texts seem to be more easily appreciated by African people who have seen sacrifices performed (Ukpong 1987). Some Old Testament wisdom literature may be more easily grasped by African peoples who have rich proverbial traditions (Nare 1986, Golka 1993, Masenya 1996). The Old Testament Levirate marriage traditions are certainly understandable amongst a people (like the Luo of Kenya and Tanzania) who have similar traditions (Kirwen 1979). Most Africans do seem to feel "at home" with the Old Testament—at least compared to many readers from the Northern Hemisphere.

---

[1] New Testament exegesis is not new to the continent of Africa, of course. The scholarly efforts of Origen in Egypt and Augustine in Hippo, North Africa, are well known. The exegetical tradition of the Ethiopian Church has been examined in some depth (Cowley 1983, Cowley 1988, Mikre-Selassie 1972, Mikre-Selassie 1993). These exegetical traditions are still of vital importance, especially in the liturgy of the Ethiopian Orthodox churches (LeMarquand, 1998). The ancient Nubian Church produced its own translation of the Bible, but few manuscripts are extant. As the title of this article states our primary concern is with African scholarship as it has emerged in the modern period.

This is not to say, however, that the New Testament is less important in Africa than it is in the West. On the contrary, many of the ideas just mentioned (covenant, sacrifice, wisdom)[2] are important in the New Testament as well as in the Old. To say that the world of Africa has many similarities to the world of the Old Testament is therefore to acknowledge that the African and New Testament worlds contain many continuities. Many African readers do sometimes note that there is in the New Testament something which is radically new, something which is distinct from the Hebrew Bible, from African tradition and from the western world,[3] but this discontinuity, this new thing is not a culture or tradition incomprehensible to Africa, but the person of Jesus Christ who seems at once at home in and alien to every culture.

It may be that the "modern," post-Enlightenment West is the odd one out in this comparative game. Perhaps Marcion has cast such a shadow over the West that it is easier for westerners to see the *dis*continuities between Testaments,[4] and certainly post-Enlightenment scholarship has emphasised the "gap" between the biblical and modern worlds. This is not to imply that Africa does not appreciate the discontinuities between the Bible and the African world. There are indications that some African Christians consider the New Testament to be very important, perhaps even more important than the Old Testament, precisely because of some of the differences. For example, a survey done in Port Harcourt, Nigeria found that while many Nigerian Africans think that the Old Testament has more similarities to the cultures of Africa, the New Testament is considered to be more "powerful" and is often used in a magical way to combat evil (Riches 1996: 184). There is also some evidence that suggests that many New Testament texts are highly valued by African preachers and congregations (Turner 1965).

This essay will survey a number of African "reading communities"

---

[2] We could add to this list almost indefinitely: belief in one God, the importance of family and clan solidarity, circumcision, spiritual beings, prayer, healing are all issues of vital importance to the Old Testament, the New Testament and Africa alike.

[3] "The New Testament poses a radical question. It is new in many of its assertions. It demands new morality and new doctrinal teachings." (Kinoti and Waliggo 1997: 2).

[4] Efforts are being made to rethink the western scholarly myopia about such subjects as the "Jewishness of Jesus." See especially Stendahl 1963.

(missionaries, white South Africans, liberationist exegetes, inculturationist exegetes), and make note of some New Testament texts and
themes which have been influential, sometimes even paradigmatic for
these communities. We will see that the importance of texts is always
related to the social and cultural context of the exegete and his or
her community. For this reason, attention will be paid to contextual
issues and their influence on exegesis. We will see that the continuities between most African world views and the New Testament as
well as the radical newness of the New Testament to Africa are
important elements in popular and scholarly understandings of
the New Testament in Africa. In the modern period Christianity
was brought to Africa by missionaries from Europe, North America,
Australia, New Zealand and the Caribbean. With the possible exception of the few black missionaries from the Caribbean and the United
States, most of these missionaries were white, and carried a biblical
message wrapped in European, Enlightenment clothing. Most African
Christians are grateful for the work of these missionaries, whose effort
involved enormous dedication and often great suffering. It is also
true, however, that few African Christians are unaware of the cultural blindness and even racial prejudice of much mission activity.

   The missionary who came with the Bible also came as an interpreter of the Bible. The missionary's reading of the text was filtered
through cultural lenses which were not always congenial to African
traditional life. There was much in traditional African culture which
came as a shock to western missionaries. Issues such as female circumcision and polygyny, practiced in some groups of Africans, were
(and remain!) complex and controversial. The history of missions in
Africa is varied. But the common perception of missionaries, both
in African church circles and in scholarly work of African writers,
is that the missionaries failed to comprehend the depth and the richness of Africa. Missionary intentions no doubt varied, but the overall impression left by the visitors was that Africa had been weighed
in the western balance and found wanting: only by becoming less
African could one become more Christian. This perception is only
part of the truth about missionary activity, but it is a part of the
truth which is often most deeply felt. At the theological level it has
left Africans with a nagging theological question: Where was God
before the missionaries brought the Bible to Africa? Had God forgotten us? Did God love Europeans more?

Today the influence of various forms of western biblical interpretation is pervasive in the mission-founded churches. On the popular level, evangelists from Europe and North America often hold "crusades" in African cities in which biblical preaching in an important tool. Often these rallies are broadcast or televised. Many of these evangelists know little about Africa, its history, its hopes and its problems. Likewise, most of the published material available in African Christian book stores was published in Europe or North America, usually with a western audience in mind. On the more scholarly level, most books to be found in African theological colleges and universities were written in Europe or North America by scholars using exegetical tools produced out of post-Enlightenment philosophical and theological traditions. Very few of these works have any other context in mind but the original historical contexts of the biblical writers and the North Atlantic contexts of the scholars and their readers. Most African biblical scholars must do much of their graduate work outside of Africa, with professors who have little knowledge of (and, sadly, sometimes even little sympathy with) their students' cultural and religious background. Few African Christians, pastors or scholars wish to jettison all western learning, fewer believe it to be adequate.

Western influence is to be seen even in the texts of the Bibles which most Africans read. A priority for many missionaries and missionary societies, especially the Protestants, was the translation of the Bible (Schaaf 1994). As it has turned out, the work of translation has aided the spread of Christianity more than almost any other factor, ironically because vernacular translations gave the Bible a degree of independence from the European world view of the missionary and gave Africans a source of Christian authority external to the missionary (Sanneh 1989). To an extent the Bible and its message could be heard on its own terms. One result of the translation of the Bible into indigenous languages has been the enormous growth of African Instituted Churches, organizations which have effectively merged African culture and tradition with their own readings of the Biblical story (Barrett 1968). On the other hand, western ideas could not help but find their way into many of these translations, since the missionary usually had control of the final published product.

An examination of a missionary exegesis of Romans 1 provides an interesting example of the way scripture has been read by this

community. Andrew Walls has produced a valuable study of missionary interpretation of this important text (Walls 1996). In a careful investigation of nineteenth and early twentieth century missionary
sermons and reports, Walls traces the use of Romans 1 by missionaries in their encounter with "foreign" cultures. For many missionaries Paul's words self-evidently condemn non-Christian religion.
David Jonathan East, one of a small host of writers on West Africa
in the 1840's, produces an imposing account (based on travellers'
tales) of African slavery, drunkenness, immorality, and lack of commercial probity. He then quotes Romans 1:28–31. "What an awful
comment upon this affecting portion of Holy Writ are the humili-
ating facts which these and the preceding chapters record." In another
place, however, East recognizes that African paganism, though reprehensible, is in one respect different from that of Romans 1. Though
some African people have images, they do not make images of the
Supreme God: they simply ignore him for the subordinate divinities
and spirits.

> Thus it appears, that if they have not "changed the glory of the incor-
> ruptible God into an image, made like to corruptible man, and to
> birds, and four-footed beasts and creeping things"—they have, in their
> view, excluded him from the government of his world, and substituted
> in his room the wild creatures of their own imaginations, identifying
> these professedly spiritual existences with what is material and oft times
> grossly absurd (Walls 1996: 62).

As far as East is concerned, the truth of Romans 1 is confirmed by
the self-evident depravity of African people. Their idolatry has led
them to immorality. Having excluded God "from the government
of his world" Africans have been "given up" to absurd spiritual and
moral behaviour. Such assertions about the indigenous peoples of
Africa, Asia and the Americas are repeated frequently in the nineteenth century by missionaries, travellers and chroniclers. The corol-
lary was that if such religions and cultures were so obviously debased,
the truth and beauty of the Christian religion shines forth all the more
clearly.

Although Romans 1 (and Romans 2, as Walls points out) condemns *people* for their sinfulness and idolatry, the missionary rhetoric
tended to condemn *systems* of belief. Walls' comments are apt:

> As systems, and ultimately the collective labels for systems which we
> call the world religions, have slipped into the place of ungodly people
> in the interpretation of Romans 1, so Christianity, also conceived as

a system, has sometimes slipped into the place of the righteousness of God. The true system has been opposed to false systems condemned there. It has sometimes, but not always, been realized that "Christianity" is a term formally identical with the other labels, that it certainly covers as wide a range of phenomena as most of them, that, if the principalities and powers work within human systems, they can and do work within this one. Man-in-Christianity lies under the wrath of God just as much as Man-in-Hinduism . . . it is not Christianity which saves, but Christ (Walls 1996: 62).

If Paul's letter to the Romans has implications for the African traditionalist, its message is addressed equally to the western Christian: "all have sinned and fall short of the glory of God." (Romans 3:23). Romans 1 addresses the human situation, not just the *non-western* human condition.

One community of Europeans established themselves more solidly on African soil than any other—the Dutch settlers who came to South Africa. The deeply religious Afrikaner community has long been involved in the work of biblical exegesis. Biblical scholarship is now quite a large industry in South Africa. Learned professors in seminaries and universities produce many volumes of work every year.[5] But there is a deep ambiguity in this work. Although produced on the continent of Africa, some of these white scholars identify themselves more closely with European exegesis than with the African context.[6] For example, the prolific New Testament scholar from Pretoria, A.G. van Aarde, in discussing the history of Jesus research in South Africa, makes it clear that the major dialogue partners in this enterprise have been western scholars and that the major issue underlying South African New Testament research has been the tension between dogmatic theology and the historical-critical method (Van Aarde 1993a, Van Aarde 1993b). Although van Aarde's second essay does make reference to the emergence of "engaged scholarship" in his survey of more recent South African trends, he is still able to use the phrase "we, as First-World theologians" to describe South African Jesus scholarship (Van Aarde 1993b: 947).

This identification with things European has made John Mbiti

---

[5] See the final section of the bibliography of the present volume.

[6] By referring to white South Africans in this section I do not mean to imply that every white South African biblical scholar has been in sympathy with the ideology of apartheid and with situations of racism, both past and continuing in the post-apartheid era. There are many who have shown courage in their opposition to racism and injustice, both in their biblical studies and in other areas of their lives.

reluctant even to discuss white South African biblical scholarship.
Mbiti excludes this exegetical tradition from his survey of the use of
the Bible in Africa on the grounds that it is "still European" and
"closed to the realities of African presence" (Mbiti 1986: 17). "I do
not draw from this strand of Christianity in my presentation," he
says, "because it does not speak the language of indigenous African
Christianity and because it has excluded itself from African life"
(Mbiti 1986: 18). It is easy to appreciate Mbiti's position. A review
of major South African journals leaves the impression that until very
recently white scholars have shown little interest in scholarly engagement with either the political or religious realities of black Africa.
But Mbiti's solution is too simple—for white South African exegesis
has not "excluded itself" from African life. Indeed, white South African
exegesis is deeply implicated in the suffering of black South Africans.
In an article in the South African journal *Scriptura*, Dirk J. Smit
briefly outlines the history of white biblical scholarship.

> In a first stage, prominent scholars played an important role in legit-
> imizing apartheid and opponents were ostracized from the South African
> scholarly scene. In a second stage, the socio-political interpretation of
> the Bible has been strongly rejected, in the name of the ethos of
> scientific research. At present, in a third stage, the debate between
> scientific, historical scholarship and committed, socio-politically involved
> reading, is urgent but diffuse, since it is being argued at so many fronts
> (Smit 1990: 33).

As Smit sees the situation, some white South African biblical scholars
have attempted to defend the racism of apartheid on biblical grounds,
and, when this strategy failed, some have attempted to bracket out
questions of a "political" nature by arguing that the proper place of
biblical scholarship was the text itself, and not the readers of the
text—even if some Bible readers[7] suffer under the hands of other
readers.

It is exactly for this reason that we must reconsider Mbiti's decision to leave white South African exegesis out of consideration. In
fact, biblical scholarship in South Africa is *not* simply transplanted
European scholarship. White South African biblical scholarship, especially that which stems from the Afrikaner community, is rooted in

---

[7] I use the term "readers" here loosely, of course, since many black African Bible
"readers" are actually illiterate. Perhaps "hearers" would be more appropriate (and
more biblical?) an image.

the cultural mythology of the Afrikaner people. To ignore this scholarly tradition will not help. A biblical theme which has had a strong influence among the Afrikaner people is the idea of election: that Israel is the chosen people of God. December 16 is perhaps the most important day of the year for the Afrikaner people. Variously called Dingaan's Day, the Day of the Covenant and the Day of the Vow, it was on this date in 1838 that several hundred Voortrekkers fought the Battle of Blood River against more than 10,000 Zulu warriors under the leadership of Zulu King Dingane. At least 3,000 Zulu's were killed. No Afrikaners died. Before the battle it is believed that many of the Afrikaners had taken the following covenantal vow:

> My brethren and fellow countrymen, at this moment we stand before the holy God of heaven and earth, to make a promise, if He will be with us and protect us and deliver the enemy into our hands so that we may triumph over him, that we shall observe the day and the date as an anniversary in each year and a day of thanksgiving like the Sabbath, in His honour, and that we shall enjoin our children that they must take part with us in this, for a remembrance even for our posterity; and if anyone sees a difficulty in this, let him return from this place. For the honour of His name shall be joyfully exalted, and to Him the fame and honour of the victory must be given (Akenson 1991: 47).

In the years which followed the Voortrekkers victory the Afrikaners' rather unorganized knowledge of the Old Testament scriptures gradually hardened into an ideology which asserted that Afrikaners themselves were the elect people of God. In the words of Donald Harman Akenson, "It is a very short step from saying that 'we are like the children of Israel' to believing that 'we are a Chosen People'" (Akenson 1991: 70).

The preacher at the 1895 commemoration of the Day of the Covenant understood the election of Israel as a matrix through which the Afrikaner people should understand themselves—and understand the Africans who inhabited the land they had entered,

> When we think of the former emigrants, the Voortrekkers of yore, it is then revealed unto us how God, in his divine providence, dealt with them, even as he dealt with the Israelite Nation of Old. . . . He summoned them to the same task: Canaan was inhabited by heathen alienated from God . . . Israel was bidden make it the Lord's dwelling place (Van Jaarsveld 1964: 11).

In other words, just as the Afrikaners take the place of the Hebrews in this new covenantal narrative, so the Zulus and other black Africans take the place of the Canaanites. Just as it was the duty of Israel to cleanse the land of pagans in the occupation of Palestine, so it was the divinely sanctioned work of the Afrikaner nation to purge the land of the heathen.

The story of how the Afrikaner people came to adopt this covenantal ideology, is a complex one, as is the story of the recent repudiation of this ideology by the Nederduitse Gereformeerde Kerk (NGK). We will not attempt a review of this history here. Our task is the elucidation of New Testament exegesis in Africa. As can be seen from the above paragraphs, Afrikaner ideology appears to have little to do with the New Testament. The hermeneutical matrix of this ideology is the transposition of Old Testament covenantal ideas into a South African key.

As Akenson points out, the New Testament is a problem for this ideological world. The words of Jesus and the writings of Paul[8] come as a direct repudiation of racial exclusiveness. "Distinctions between people based on their ethnicity or social standing are specifically rejected" (Akenson 1991: 305–306). How, then, could Afrikaner Christians, deal with the New Testament?

> Whereas the general principles of the "Old Testament" were taken as having direct institutional implications in the modern world, the "New Testament" principles were interpreted as being doctrines of the heart, ones that had to reign in every righteous soul, but which had no direct institutional implications. Although the NGK scholars would never have admitted the point directly, it is fair to summarize their hermeneutic as saying that the "Old Testament" ruled the visible world and the "New Testament" guided the world of the spirit. . . . Thus the largest of the Dutch Reformed churches not only implicitly affirmed apartheid, but indirectly rejected their own integration with the black and "coloured" Reformed churches (Akenson 1991: 306).

This literalistic use of the Old Testament coupled with a spiritualising interpretation of the New Testament has had (literally) deadly implications. This hermeneutic has allowed and even bolstered a

---

[8] Actually, Akenson says "The words of Jesus (and to a lesser extent the writings of the apostle Paul) are a direct repudiation of the idea of there being a Chosen People in the physical sense" (1991: 305). I would argue that Paul's entire theological project is a repudiation of the idea of election having a racial basis. For Paul the covenant is established by grace, not by race, and membership in Israel is not a matter of a circumcision of the flesh, but of a circumcision of the heart. This follows directly from Paul's fundamentally Jewish belief that there is only one God who created and loves all people.

violent and racist regime. In such a situation a different reading of New Testament texts must eventually arise.

In recent years, the oppressive and officially racist ideology of South Africa has called forth a re-reading of biblical texts. This mode of reading repudiates the idea that there could be exegesis without presuppositions, scholarship with commitment. Liberationist scholars have chosen to be explicit that they are committed to and engaged in a struggle for justice, and that their Bible reading will be a part of this struggle. This is as much true now in the post-apartheid era as it was during apartheid, for the land is not yet healed and great inequities still exist. Although a liberationist exegesis has been more dominant in South Africa than in other parts of the continent, tyranny has not been limited to that region, and a number of African writers from outside of South Africa have recently produced writings which seek to employ the Bible as a tool in the struggle for social and political liberation in their own contexts (Magesa 1977, Ela 1980, Nthamburi 1980, Owan 1996).

As with other liberation theologies, the story of the Exodus is often taken as a starting point for theological reflection. Desmond Tutu and many others have explored the theological and political dimensions of this text for the South African context (Tutu 1983, Flint 1987, Oosthuizen 1988, Wittenberg 1991, Nurnberger 1992). The story of Israel held in bondage in Egypt had a familiar ring to black people in captivity under unjust systems of colonialism and apartheid. The Israelites' plea for freedom from slavery was heard as an echo of the aspirations of South African blacks. The promise of God to Moses that the cries of the people had been heard and that God had come down to deliver (Exodus 3:7–12) was a word of hope in the midst of suffering.

But the Exodus, while paradigmatic for a liberation exegesis, was not the only biblical text which has given courage in the context of struggle. Many New Testament texts have been held up as signs that God was on the side of the poor and marginalised. The Song of Mary, the Magnificat, is read as a song of a woman who trusted God to act in the midst of an unjust situation.

> He has shown strength with his arm; he has scattered the proud in the thoughts of their hearts. He has brought down the powerful from their thrones, and lifted up the lowly; he has filled the hungry with good things, and sent the rich away empty (Luke 1:51–53, NRSV), (Wittenberg 1991).

For some, like Allan Boesak, Jesus himself is seen as one who shares the black experience of poverty.

> The historical Jesus of the New Testament has a special significance for those who share the black experience. He was poor, the son of poor people who could not bring the prescribed sacrifice at his birth . . . He belonged to a poor downtrodden people, oppressed and destitute of rights in their own country and subjugated to countless daily humiliations under foreign rulers. He lived and worked among the poor . . . He was one of them (Boesak 1976: 43).[9]

Boesak has also written on the book of Revelation, showing that consolation in the hope of a future need not lead to complacency with present injustice (Boesak 1987).

The use of the Bible in liberation theology has itself been a site of struggle. Writers such as Boesak and Tutu not only find liberating themes in the Bible, but see the Bible itself as liberative Word of God. Those who find justification for apartheid in the Bible are told that they are misusing the text. On the other hand, Itumeleng Mosala has criticized black theology for not recognizing that the text itself is a production of class struggle. Writing within an explicitly Marxist paradigm, Mosala focuses his attention behind the text, looking for clues to the ideology which gave rise to the text. In his study of Luke, for example, Mosala argues that the theme of the poor in Luke's writings, is in fact, not liberative for the poor. The text itself, he says, treats the poor as a subject—but the text is written by and addressed to the rich. Mosala advocates a hermeneutic which, first "liberates the Bible" by exposing not only its oppressive use, but its origins in the class struggle (Mosala 1989, cf. West 1997).

One New Testament text makes more appearances in South African liberationist exegesis than any other—Romans 13:1-7 (Moulder 1977, Nopece 1986, Nurnberger 1987, Draper 1988, Wanamaker 1988, Wanamaker 1992, Hale 1992, Botha 1994). South Africa may be the most biblically literate society on earth. At the height of the struggle against apartheid, people on both sides were able to quote scripture in support of their views. Often these verses from Romans were used in an attempt to persuade anti-apartheid activists, especially church leaders, not to oppose the government. After all, Paul's words were about obedience to a pagan government, while the South

---

[9] For a description of uses of the historical Jesus in Africa see LeMarquand 1997.

Africa government was "Christian." Incidents similar to the following, which is related by Allan Boesak, could be repeated by many
South African Christians:

> On 19 October 1977, I was visited for the first time by the South
> African Security Police. They stayed from 3:30 a.m. till 7:00 a.m. At
> one point I was challenged by the Security Police captain (who assured
> me that he was a Christian and, in fact, an elder of the white Dutch
> Reformed Church) on my persistent resistance to the government.
> "How can you do what you are doing," he asked, "while you know
> what Romans Thirteen says? . . ." For him, as for millions of other
> Christians in South Africa and across the world, Romans 13 is an
> unequivocal, unrelenting call for blind obedience to the state (Boesak
> 1986: 138).

And, of course, Boesak is not the only South African who has been
experienced the results of the long history of the oppressive use of
this text.

However, other South African exegetes have often pointed out
that Romans 13 is not a call to blind obedience and that Paul's
words contain limits on the power of the state: all authority is "from
God" (v. 1), therefore all powers should recognize and reflect God's
authority; government is to be "God's servant for good" (v. 4)—not
for evil; the word "submit" does not imply force or coercion, it is
argued, but rather the obligation to love the neighbour (vv. 8–10).
It is further noted that Romans 13 must be read in the context of
other biblical passages which make it clear that primary obedience
is to be given to God rather that human beings (Acts 4:19), and
that the state itself is capable of radical disobedience and evil
(Revelation 13).

In a new South Africa, liberationist exegetes will continue to examine the text as one means of striving for justice. At the same time,
new issues have begun to emerge. It is being recognized by some
that it is not enough to read the Bible "for" the poor and marginalised. These communities themselves have insights which must be
brought to the text. A process of reading "with" poor and marginalised communities is being developed especially out of the Institute
for the Study of the Bible in Pietermaritzburg, where scholars ("trained
readers") work together with "ordinary readers" to discover the liberating potential of biblical texts. This interaction between popular
and scholarly readings is in need of more investigation (West 1993).

Liberationist exegetes who have rightly been consumed with the

struggle against apartheid will begin to examine the meaning of
African culture for a new South Africa. In this search they may be
helped by Bible readers from other parts of the continent—to which
we now turn.

According to Justin Ukpong, inculturation theology is not a theological discipline, but rather a way of doing theology which cuts
across disciplines. Applied to biblical studies, inculturation hermeneutics[10] is characterized, he says, by consciously and explicitly seeking "to interpret the biblical text from socio-cultural perspectives
of different people" (Ukpong 1996: 190). Whether it is practised in
Africa, Asia, Latin America, the Caribbean, or indeed, in Europe
or North America, inculturation hermeneutics, seeks to read the biblical text in the light of the needs, hopes, cultural values, religious
aspirations, political, social and economic realities of human beings.
The goal of inculturation hermeneutics is the enhancement of God-
given life.

There is a growing corpus of written material on the New Testament
being produced in Sub-Saharan Africa. A decade ago, in a review
of scholarly biblical studies from Africa, Mbiti made a distinction
between biblical studies which related to the African context and
"pure" biblical studies, that is, biblical studies which did not make
any explicit attempt to relate the biblical text to the African environment (Mbiti 1986: 49). The distinction is dubious. Although there
are, of course, studies which are more concerned with the text than
with the reader, no exegesis can be described as "pure." There is
no disinterested, objective scholarship. We are all "engaged in cultural readings of the Bible" (Riches 1996: 186). In fact Mbiti could
find only one work by an African scholar which he believed could
fit into the category of pure scholarship." At the time of his writing
Mbiti was apparently unaware that John Pobee's doctoral dissertation had been published. *Persecution and Martyrdom in the Theology of
Paul* (Pobee 1985) is one of the few works of African authorship
which does not mention Africa in its text. It would be a mistake,
however, to assume that Pobee's dissertation was unrelated to African

---

[10] The approach which is generally called "inculturation" by African exegetes
outside of South Africa, especially by Roman Catholic scholars, has much in common with what South Africans tend to call "contextualization." The emphasis in
South Africa has tended to fall on issues of politics and economics. In other parts
of the continent cultural and religious values have received the most attention.

life. In his preface Pobee makes explicit the connection between his research and his life:

> Though a happy and privileged sojourner in Cambridge, my heart was bleeding for my motherland, Ghana, which had come under the grip of a corrupt and ruthless tyrant and government. While I laboured to follow my calling as a New Testament scholar, I also agonized over the fate of loved ones back home, my parents and the Church of God (Pobee 1985: vii).

The context of African suffering does not enter into the body of Pobee's thesis, but Africa determined the choice of topic.

Since Mbiti's review, the Nigerian Roman Catholic sister, Teresa Okure, has completed and published her doctoral research, a study in Johannine theology (Okure 1988a). As with Pobee's work, so in Okure's thesis, the African situation is not mentioned in the text. But, once again, the preface is used to highlight the motivation behind the research.

> My interest in mission dates back to my school days, and was inspired by my living experiences of mission in the African context. I was often struck by the contrast between certain statements of Jesus found mostly in John's gospel concerning his mission from the Father and the actual conception and exercise of mission which obtained in my context. This contrast belonged mostly in the order of the attitude of the missionary to the work and the people, and of the method in the exercise of mission. The whole experience raised for me a number of unanswered questions concerning the relationship of the mission exercised in my context to the mission of Jesus.
>
> In the course of my biblical studies, however, I had completely forgotten that I had had these questions. The choice of the topic for this work was therefore not consciously connected with them. This was likely due to the biblical discipline itself which, like most theological disciplines of this century was, and to a large extent still is, literary and academically oriented, not designed to address real life issues. It was only afterwards, indeed as I was reflecting on a suitable preface for this book, that I remembered that I had, had these questions, and that here in the pages of this book I had finally found satisfying answers to them (Okure 1988a: v).

Okure's choice of topic was influenced by her experience of mission work in Nigeria, although this was apparently not a conscious choice and although Nigeria is nowhere mentioned in her exegesis.

But the works of Pobee and Okure are exceptions to the general rule. Although there is no scholarship which does not have a contextual interest, African biblical scholarship usually goes out of its way to highlight issues of importance for the African situation. Exegesis is explicitly related to life. Four issues from the African world appear to command the most attention from African New Testament exegetes: mission and colonialism, suffering, faith, and African traditional religion and culture. These are not airtight containers, of course. Much of the dissatisfaction with missionary work comes from the inability of missionaries to take African traditions seriously. The root of much African suffering stems from European colonialism. And so on. But while these subjects cannot be separated, they can at least be distinguished for the sake of elucidation and example.

We note first of all, that New testament exegesis in Africa is practised within a context of mission and colonialism. As we have already seen in our earlier discussion of missionary exegesis, for most of Africa the Bible arrived in the hands of missionaries from the North Atlantic world. The interpretation of the Bible reflected missionary minds which were shaped by that world and which had little understanding of the culture of Africa. Although in some parts of Africa the message of the New Testament as conveyed by the missionaries was received with joy, certain tensions began to emerge.

Once the Bible was in the hands and in the language of Africans themselves, it became evident that there were differences between what the missionaries said and what the book said. A classic example has to do with polygamy. Although most missionary societies and the churches which they represented condemned the practice, it did not escape the notice of African readers that many of the great "heroes of the faith" had more than one wife.

These tensions were not limited to Old Testament examples. A visitor to African churches will notice immediately that mission-founded churches and African-founded churches have different emphases. Of note is the pervasive practice of healing in African Instituted Churches and the almost complete lack of emphasis on healing in churches with roots in the missionary societies. There are several reasons for the emphasis on healing in African Instituted Churches. An obvious reason is that many Africans are in need of healing. A second is that Africans have traditionally been accustomed to ask God for healing. A third reason, and the one of most interest to us here, is that the pages of the New Testament are full of healing stories. We are left to ask why the mission churches have not been open to healing by prayer and ritual. The answer lies in the world view of most nineteenth and twentieth century missionaries. Consider the opinion of Samuel Abogunrin, for example:

> When Christianity, which from the earliest period has existed in parts of North Africa and Ethiopia, was introduced into the rest of Black Africa, the world view of Western Christian theologians retained only a veneer of Biblical world-view. The world-view of the Western missionaries who preached the Gospel in Africa had by then become quasi-scientific (Abogunrin 1988: v, cf. Imasogie 1986: 52).

The deist world view which pervaded even the most pious of missionaries was able to interpret New Testament healing stories either as spiritual lessons having little to do with prayer for sick bodies, or as a call to found clinics and hospitals. The latter they ought to have done, not neglecting the former. In short many missionaries did not hear aspects of the message of the New Testament which Africans claim to be able to hear very clearly indeed. The missionary world view and the ethos of the New Testament were sometimes quite far apart. This tension between African and western world-views continues in scholarly circles. Most African biblical scholars find western scepticism unacceptable. As Pobee puts it, "the tinge of agnosticism so characteristic of the Northern scientific method will not be wholly satisfactory" (Pobee 1996: 166).

A second tension between the Bible and the missionaries stemmed from the involvement of the missions with colonialism. The history of the relationship between the missions and colonial exploitation is complex. It is true that many missionaries were often at odds with the policies of colonial governments and sought to defend the rights of Africans against oppressive practices. It is also true that the construction of a colonial infrastructure made the missionaries' jobs easier, that missionaries could sometimes be co-opted by colonial authorities, and that many, no doubt, had mixed motives. Consider the example of David Livingstone. He was an outspoken and energetic opponent of the slave trade. He also believed that missionaries should come to Africa in order to open the way not only for Christianity—but for Christianity and "commerce." Africans did not miss that fact that although the New Testament spoke of the reign of God, missionaries often seemed to speak and act on the behalf of other ideologies and other sovereign powers.

A New Testament text which has received much attention from African exegetes is the story of Paul's preaching on Mars Hill in

Athens (Apochi 1995, Igenoza 1984, Manus 1985, Manus 1989, Manus 1990, Martin 1962, Onwu 1988, Osei-Bonsu 1994, Geraghty 1996). This story has provided fertile ground for exploring how evangelism should build bridges between the gospel and culture. Many African exegetes find an echo of some of their own concerns about openness to African culture and religion in Paul's presentation in which he investigates the culture before he speaks and then when he does speak he quotes the Athenians' own poets approvingly and shows how Greek religious traditions point the way to Christ. According to Chris Ukachukwu Manus, a Roman Catholic New Testament scholar from Nigeria, "Luke's text has . . . a special appeal for the young churches of Africa. It presents us with a model worthy of emulation for mission in Africa where the inhabitants are still as much 'religious' as the Athenians of anticuity [sic: antiquity]" (Manus 1990: 212). This approach to mission, says Manus, is in contrast to the approach of early European missionaries.

> Those early missionaries, unlike Paul[,] did not see our forebears as deeply religious . . . Rather they insisted on a total break from our past. The rupture from our past urged by Christian missionaries has not been successful, rather it tends to produce hostility . . . due partly to the disdain for our traditional belief systems by early evangelists (Manus 1990: 214).

Manus goes on to enjoin his readers to seek to forge links between the gospel message and African culture, which, he says (using a phrase from the great African theologian Clement of Alexandria), is a "preparation for the gospel."

A second important situation which receives attention in African exegesis is the pervasive presence of suffering on the continent. News from Africa, as it arrives in the West via international news services, is invariably bad news. Wars and rumours of wars, disease, environmental degradation, famine, tyranny, displaced peoples, and crushing debt loads are only the beginning of the litany of misery which could be recited. Africa is of little "strategic" importance to Western powers, and so the stability of an African nation is of little interest compared, for example, with Israel/Palestine or the fragmented countries of the former Yugoslavia. A recent article on malaria in a respected news magazine (Shell 1997) suggests that although this disease is by far the most devastating health problem in the world it has received comparatively little attention from the world community—partly because most of the people who suffer and die from the disease daily live in the "third world," particularly in Africa.

The cries for liberation from these plagues of war, sickness and poverty do not escape the ears of African readers of the New Testament. On a popular level it is common for ordinary people to use the New Testament in an effort to construct what has been called a "theology of survival."[11] In Port Harcourt, Nigeria, a survey of ordinary "readers" found that they were much less concerned with relating the Bible to their culture than with using it to surmount problems of childlessness, unemployment, sickness, demon-possession, etc. Respondents might recognize that there were closer connections between Nigerian culture and the Old Testament, but they still preferred the New because of its greater spiritual power (Riches 1996: 184).

African New Testament scholars and preachers find that they are confronted by the problems of African suffering whenever they open the text. To study the New Testament in Africa is to be constantly challenged to demonstrate the relevance of the exegetical task. For example, in 1993, when the country of Kenya lived through a period of ethnic "clashes" which many Kenyans believe were initiated by the government, Bishop David Gitari (now the Anglican Archbishop of Kenya), preached a sermon on John 10, reminding his people that Jesus was the Good Shepherd—and reminding the politicians that there are shepherds who are thieves and robbers.

> At the present time, the sight of the numerous displaced people in our midst is to be likened to the crowds which Jesus saw, "harassed and helpless like sheep without a shepherd." Kenyans, should no longer look like this when they have 188 strong shepherds [parliamentarians] to attend to their plight. If these parliamentarians decide to shun their duties, the sovereign Lord says this, "I will build up the injured and strengthen the weak, but the sleek and strong I will destroy. I will shepherd the flock with justice" (Ezekiel 34:16) (Gitari 1996).

Gitari's call for justice and warning of judgement earned him much criticism from the parliament, but Gitari would argue that he had little choice, the situation—and the text—compelled him.

---

[11] This phrase emerged in the discussions of "The Bible in Africa Project Consultation" which took place in Glasgow in 1994 (Bible in Africa Project 1994, cf. Riches 1996). The full minutes of the consultation are available from Professor Riches [Department of Biblical Studies, The University of Glasgow, Glasgow, G12 8QQ, Scotland]. See also Ukpong's second essay in this volume.

In the context of suffering, the passion of Jesus carries great meaning for readers of the New Testament, popular and scholarly alike (Dickson 1984: 185–99). It is perhaps the artistic and liturgical depictions of the New Testament which make the greatest impact. A mural by the now-martyred Cameroonian theologian Engelbert Mveng adorns the chapel of Hekima College, a Jesuit institution in Nairobi. At the bottom of the mural is Nairobi's skyline and above the city hangs the suffering Christ, depicted with African features—an African suffering for Africa. A powerful exploration of the meaning of the cross is the poem "I am an African" by Gabriel Setiloane, in which the cross interprets African suffering as a sharing in God's pain and African traditions interpret the cross of Christ in sacrificial terminology (Setiloane 1976: 56–59).

And yet for us it is when He is on the cross,
This Jesus of Nazareth, with holed hands
And open side, like a beast at a sacrifice;
When He is stripped naked like us,
Browned and sweating water and blood in the heat of the sun
Yet silent,
That we cannot resist him.
How like us He is, this Jesus of Nazareth,
Beaten, tortured, imprisoned, spat upon, truncheoned,
Denied by his own, and chased like a thief in the night,
Despised, and rejected like a dog that has fleas.
For NO REASON.

No reason, but that He was Son of His Father
Or . . . Was there a reason?
There was indeed . . . !
As in that sheep or goat we offer in sacrifice,
Quiet and uncomplaining,
Its blood falling to the ground to cleanse it . . . and us;
And making peace between us and our fathers long passed away:
He is the LAMB!
His blood cleanses not only us,
    not only the clan,
    not only the tribe,
        But all, all MANKIND:
Black and White and Brown and Red,
    All Mankind!

The cross of Jesus also plays a key liturgical role for suffering Christians in Africa. In a recent article, Mark Nikkel expounds the meaning

of the cross as it is experienced amongst Sudanese Christians who
have been displaced by war and famine.

> Among Dinka communities crosses appear today in an endless array
> of shapes, designs, and materials. They are displayed on people of all
> ages and in all possible locations, private and public. It appears that
> for many Bor Dinka, the aesthetic energies once invested in groom-
> ing and adorning a fine name ox, or in personal body decoration are
> today given to creating elaborate new designs for the simple cruciform
> shape (1995: 161).

In Dinka hymnody the cross is a symbol of salvation from sin: "I
am praying, remembering the cross and the crown of thorns [the
things you] suffered because of my great sin" (hymn by Andrew
Mayol, quoted in Nikkel 1995: 166). A standard for battle against
the evil one: "The flag of your cross, makes Satan flee away" (hymn
by Abraham Agoot Ajok Agoot, quoted in Nikkel 1995: 165). It is
even personified in human form: "We have our piece of wood that
walks like a human being; We have a cross which you cannot reject"
(hymn by Naomi Alueel Deng, quoted in Nikkel 1995: 165). Especially
striking is a hymn in which the Dinka take on themselves the role
of cross bearers, following the example of the African, Simon of
Cyrene (Mark 15:21–22 & par.).

> We are calling upon you to accept us;
> We are crying that you might hear us.
> Embrace us intimately ("cuddle" us) for we are your children,
> And let us carry your cross and follow after you.
> Let us be like Simon, the man of Cyrene, who went with you to
> The place of the skull (hymn by John Col Ater Cut, quoted in Nikkel
> 1995: 167–68).

In these artistic and liturgical portrayals the cross is not an image
of hopelessness and despair in suffering. Rather, in the cross African
readers of the New Testament see both the identification of God
with African pain, and the atoning work of the Lamb. According to
Theresa Souga, "The realism of the cross every day tells me, as a
woman of the Third World, that the laws of history may be overcome by means of crucified love" (1990: 22).

Thirdly, a significant portion of African New Testament scholarship is confessional in its ethos. Even scholars who teach the New
Testament in the context of the university tend to do so explicitly
as people of faith. In North Atlantic exegesis God has become one

of the marginalised. Not so in most African exegesis, here God is acknowledged as a living reality, not bracketed out in some desire to achieve an illusion of objectivity. According to Ukpong, "Interpretation is done within the canon . . . The Bible is looked upon as a sacred classic—a book containing norms for Christian living as well as a literary text. Historical critical tools and others are used precisely as tools to aid interpretation and not as ends in themselves" (Ukpong 1996: 190).

African scholars do not live with the luxury of specialization as do scholars in the North Atlantic world, and so African biblical scholars consider themselves to be part of the larger programme of African theology. "Biblical theology in Africa is not just an autonomous unit but an integral part of African theology," according to Pobee (1996: 170). In a similar vein Okure notes that her review of feminist biblical interpretation in Africa "deliberately made little distinction between African women biblical scholars and theologians," (Okure 1993: 83) since all African biblical scholars would also consider themselves to be theologians who were at the service of the church. African New Testament exegesis is explicitly a confessional exegesis.

Okure has called the story of the woman with the flow of blood "a cherished passage" among feminist biblical scholars in Africa (Okure 1993: 77). It also seems to be very popular among New Testament scholars who do not choose to call themselves "feminists." It is, in fact, one of the most widely discussed of New Testament texts in African exegesis (Amoah 1986, Tappa 1990, Tappa 1988, Souga 1988, Kanyoro 1990, Cochrane 1991, Okure 1992, Hochegger 1993, Sandblom 1993, Ukpong 1995, West 1995, Ntreh 1996, Sibeko and Haddad 1996, Loba Mkole 1997). Many connections have been noted between this story and the African world. The woman suffers from a disease which requires not only physical healing, but also healing from the social isolation caused by a blood taboo—a taboo which in Africa would also isolate a woman from her family, the community and even from the church and its ministrations. The woman is healed by touching the clothing of Jesus, believing that this would be effective for her cure—an idea similar to ideas about the power of the clothing of prophetic figures in some parts of Africa (Hochegger 1993). Even the mention of "power" "going out" from Jesus is parallel to African ideas about spiritual power (Sibeko and Haddad 1996, Sandblom 1993).

Of no little consequence for African readers is Jesus' description of the woman as having "faith." In her exposition of this story,

Okure sees the woman's faith as a challenge. In contrast to the man in John 5, this woman wanted to be healed; Although her approach was "somewhat magic-like," "she dared to believe" (Okure 1992b: 228). Okure praises the woman for her courage in seeking Jesus out, for overcoming her worry over the possible transmission of unclean-ness, for putting behind her the fear of the crowd. She had faith that the power of Jesus would heal her. African women also need to reach out to touch Jesus. God will not be defiled by the touch of an African woman, she says. African women need to touch Jesus, "because we genuinely need wholeness and life from him, both for ourselves individually, for one another and for our people" (Okure 1992b: 229).

African exegesis does not seek to understand the text merely for its own sake, or out of an intellectual curiosity. African exegesis is need-driven and faith oriented. African biblical study is, almost always, explicitly confessional, though not in the narrow sense of a particu-lar denominational tradition, but in the broad sense of not bracket-ing Christian faith in the academy. The faith of the woman with the flow of blood is often seen as a model for the exegete. Her faith was not detached and merely cerebral, but engaged and committed to life.

Finally, African exegesis takes place within the context of African traditional culture and religion.

> The majority of African Christians still live in the world of the New Testament, where belief in demons and a host of unseen supernatural powers was potent and real. A Jesus emptied of all the supernatural contained in the Gospels would be meaningless in the African context (Abogunrin 1987: 31).

So claims a New Testament scholar of a prominent Nigerian uni-versity and his claim is echoed by other African scholars: "for many Africans, church persons and theologians alike, there is no conflict between biblical and traditional African religious beliefs, particularly in the belief in the existence of a spirit world, including evil spirits" (Pobee 1996: 166). The African universe is well-populated. Ancestors, spirits, demons and angels may be invisible, but they are certainly considered to be present and active. Some African New Testament scholars are concerned about a perceived overemphasis on the spir-itual world within indigenous African Christianity. The importance given to the place of angelic beings in the worship of Nigerian Aladura churches, for example, is sometimes criticized (Abogunrin

1986, Owanikin 1987). Most New Testament scholars, however, consider belief in the activity of the spirit world to be an important point
of contact between Africa and the New Testament. Ukpong criti-
cises western exegetical methodologies "because they do not reflect
the concerns of African people" and goes on to suggest that "African
popular acceptance of the miraculous and the supernatural must be
built into any methodology seeking to operate in the African context" (Ukpong 1994: 19–20). A reading of the story of the Gerasene
demoniac illustrates the importance of the spirit world for African
readers. In a fascinating study of demon possession in Tanzania,
Lutheran missionary Stanley Benson reports that his theological preparation afforded him no help in dealing with the demonic.

> In my western oriented theological training in the 1950's, demonology
> was not taught or made known to any extent... When I was con-
> fronted with ... cases of demon possession, I was forced to look anew
> at Scripture and the church's theological stance. I was helped not from
> most modern educated westerners who looked on demons as an out-
> worn superstition; Nor by many of the biblical critics who identify
> demon possession as a psychological malady... My insights were gained
> more from an experiential nature in comparison with the literal text
> of Scripture. (Benson 1980: 58–59).

As we have seen, African experience and the New Testament often
have more in common than either one can share with the West.

A recent exposition of the story of the Gerasene demoniac (Umeagudosa 1996) underlines the importance of the subject of spiritual powers in African Christianity, and therefore in African exegesis. After
a review of scholarship on the miracles of Jesus in general and exorcism stories in particular, Margaret Umeagudosa investigates the
triple tradition story from a redaction critical perspective. The distinctive African contribution, however, comes when she turns to the
relevance of the story for the African situation. Jesus delivered people from demons; he commissioned his disciples to do the same in
the power of the Holy Spirit. And the same Spirit of God is still
available today, she argues (Umeagudosa 1996: 35).

> In Africa today people have received cures through divination, sacrifice
> and prayers. It is only a matter of faith. The activities of African
> Independent Churches in terms of healing ministry cannot be overem-
> phasised... We must admit that there are problems concerning the
> meaning, credibility and intelligibility plaguing the whole idea of mir-
> acles... [but] Jesus was absolutely concerned with human problems,
> liberation from demonic powers, salvation, love, compassion and above

all the wholeness of the human person. Therefore, the inner logic of Jesus' miracles is that they are concrete evidences of the continued supreme reign of God's kingdom on earth and victory over evil (Umeagudosa 1996: 35–36).

The story of the Gerasene demoniac is not left in the past as an artifact of early Christian experience or a piece of data to be fit into a comprehensive picture of a reconstructed historical Jesus. Jesus' healing of the oppressed man is a paradigm for the task of the church, a task of deliverance which is all but forgotten in the West, but is considered vital in African contexts, as Pobee has recently stated:

> Unlike Western societies, no effort is made to explain away cosmic powers. African exegetes take seriously the reality of cosmic powers, treating them as some kind of organized disobedience to the will of God, which affects the course of human history (Pobee 1996: 172).

This survey has raised a number of questions which could be investigated in much more depth. For now it is sufficient to raise some issues which will probably be important for African exegetes of the New Testament in the coming years.

First, the interface between popular and academic readings is an important motif in African exegesis. Popular readings and the use of the Bible by ordinary people are taken seriously. African scholars are unafraid to criticize some popular uses of the Bible, but in contrast to the disdain for popular readings one sometimes discovers among western scholars, African scholars are generally only willing to criticize the faithful with a good deal of respect and understanding.

Second, most African New Testament scholars have done at least a portion of their training in western institutions, and all are conversant with the use of historical critical tools. It is not always evident, however, that all African scholars consider these methods to be of much importance. Since the emphasis of African scholarly readings has been more on the readers than the text, more on present and future history than on the past, the use of critical tools to reconstruct history has not been the major issue. A recent call has gone out for African scholars to be more conscientious in their use of critical methodology (Obeng 1997).

Third, we have seen that women are beginning to emerge as a strong voice in the exegetical community. Attention focussed by women on the New Testament has had the result that texts which may have hitherto been neglected are now being investigated (Okure

1988[b]). We have seen that the story of the woman with the flow of blood is the focus of much discussion. A number of studies of other biblical passages which feature women as central characters are also beginning to emerge. The story of the Samaritan woman in John 4 (Manus 1987, Okure 1988[a], Dube 1992 and 1996, Aluko 1993) the Canaanite woman in Matthew 15 (Onwu 1985, Dube 1996) and the place of women in the Pauline corpus, (Manus 1984, Tzabedze 1990, Amadi-Azuogo 1996), have all been the focus of scholarly attention from African women or those influenced by feminist hermeneutics.

The emergence of African women as exegetes has also produced a different understanding of the role of African tradition than that which has usually been found among male scholars. Whereas most male New Testament scholars in Africa have assigned an almost exclusively positive role to African tradition, women scholars have some doubts. Some African traditions (blood taboos, for example) have prevented African women from assuming certain roles in society and in the churches. These traditions are now being questioned by women biblical scholars (Lagerwerf 1990, Masenya 1995, Oduyoye 1995, Okure 1992a).

Finally, it is being recognized that liberationist and inculturationist perspectives cannot be divorced. Liberation is seen as multifaceted, not only cultural and religious, not only economic and political. God's agenda encompasses all of life. Perhaps the most important single New Testament verse in African exegesis is John 10:10 in which Jesus says, "I came that they may have life, and have it abundantly." This verse is quoted and echoed time after time in African writings on the New Testament (Owan 1996, Gitari 1996).[13] Okure calls the verse a "key text" (Okure 1992a: 87). The passage in which it appears is,

> a summative and programmatic passage. Jesus declares that the sole purpose of his coming into the world is so that human beings may have life . . . and have it to the fullest . . . Concern for . . . personal, human welfare . . . characterizes Jesus' entire ministry (Okure, 1992a: 89).

The traditional African world view is life-affirming. This Johannine hope of abundant life encapsulates, and baptizes, the desire of many African readers.

BIBLIOGRAPHY

Abogunrin, Samuel O. "The Total Adequacy of Christ in the African Context (Col. 1:13–23, 2:8–3:5)." *Ogbomoso Journal of Theology* 1 (1986): 9–16.

———. "The Synoptic Gospel Debate: A Re-Examination in the African Context." *African Journal of Biblical Studies* 2/1–2 (1987): 25–51.

———. "General Preface." In Abogunrin, S. *The First Letter of Paul to the Corinthians.* African Bible Commentaries Nairobi: Uzima Press, 1988: vii–x.

Akenson, Donald Harman. *God's Peoples: Covenant and Land in South Africa, Israel, and Ulster.* Montreal & Kingston, London, Buffalo: McGill-Queen's University Press, 1991.

Aluko, Taiye. "Women in Evangelistic Mission." *African Journal of Biblical Studies* 8/1 (1993): 88–95.

Amadi-Azuogo, Chinedu Adolphus. "The Place of Women in the New Testament House Codes. An Exegetical Analysis of 1 Tim 3:11–15 and 1 Cor 14:33b–35." *Bulletin of Ecumenical Theology* 8/1 (1996): 35–39.

Amoah, Elizabeth. "The Woman Who Decided to Break the Rules," In Eds John S. Pobee and Barbel von Wartenberg-Potter, *New Eyes for Reading: Biblical and theological reflections by women from the third world.* Quezon City, Philippines: Claretian Publications, 1986: 3–4.

Apochi, Michael. "In Search for Effective Evangelization Methodology: Lessons from Acts 13:16–41; 14:15–18 and 17:22–31." *Jos Studies* 5/1 (1995): 28–41.

Arulefela, Joseph Oluwafemi. *The Covenant in the Old Testament and Yoruba Culture.* Ibandan: Daystar Press, 1988.

Barrett, David. *Schism and Renewal in Africa: An Analysis of Six Thousand Contemporary Religious Movements.* Nairobi: Oxford University Press, 1968.

Benson, Stanley. "The Conquering Sacrament: Baptism and Demon Possession among the Maasai of Tanzania." *Africa Theological Journal* 9/2 (1980): 52–61.

Bible in Africa Project. "Interpreting the Bible in Africa: Minutes of the Glasgow Consultation held on 13th–17th August 1994 at Scotus College, Bearsden, Glasgow, Scotland." Unpublished.

Boesak, Allan A. *Farewell to Innocence: A Socio-Ethical Study of Black Theology and Black Power.* Kampen: J.H. Kok, 1976.

———. "What Belongs to Caesar? Once Again Romans 13." In Ed. Charles Villa-Vicencio, *When Prayer Makes News.* Philadelphia: Westminster, 1986: 138–56.

———. *Comfort and Protest: The Apocalypse from a South African Perspective.* Philadelphia: Westminster, 1987.

Botha, Jan. *Subject to Whose Authority? Multiple Meanings of Romans 13.* Emory Studies in Early Christianity, 4; Atlanta: Scholars Press, 1994.

Cochrane, Renate. "Equal Discipleship of Women and Men: Reading the New Testament from a Feminist Perspective." In Eds Denise Ackermann, Jonathan Draper and Emma Mashinini, *Women Hold Up Half the Sky: Women in the Church in Southern Africa,* 21–36. Pietermaritzburg: Cluster Publications, 1991.

Cowley, Roger W. *The Traditional Interpretation of the Apocalypse of St. John in the Ethiopian Orthodox Church.* University of Cambridge Oriental Publications, 33; Cambridge: Cambridge University Press, 1983.

———. *Ethiopian Biblical Interpretation: A Study in Exegetical Tradition and Hermeneutics.* Cambridge: Cambridge University Press, 1988.

Dickson, Kwesi. "African Traditional Religion and the Bible." In Eds E. Mveng and R.J.Z. Werblowsky, *The Jerusalem Congress on Black Africa and the Bible. April 24–30, 1972/Le Congres de Jerusalem sur l'Afrique Noire et la Bible: Proceedings.* Jerusalem: The Israel Interfaith Committee, 1972: 155–66.

———. "The Old Testament and African Theology." *Ghana Bulletin of Theology* 4/4 (1973): 3–41.

————. "Continuity and Discontinuity Between the Old Testament and African Thought and Life." In Eds Kofi Appiah-Kubi and Sergio Torres, *African Theology en Route* Maryknoll: Orbis, 1979: 95–108.

————. *Theology in Africa.* London: Darton, Longman & Todd/Maryknoll: Orbis, 1984.

Draper, Jonathan. "'In Humble Submission to Almighty God' and its Biblical Foundation: Contextual Exegesis of Romans 13:1–7." *Journal of Theology for Southern Africa* 63 (1988): 30–41.

Dube, Musa W. "Jesus and the Samaritan Woman: A Motswana Feminist Theological Reflection on Women and Social Transformation." *Boleswa Journal of Occasional Theological Papers* (1992): 5–9.

————. "Readings for Decolonization (John 4:1–42)." *Semeia* 75 (1996): 37–59.

————. "Readings of *Semoya*: Batswana Women's Interpretation of Matthew 15:21–28." *Semeia* 73 (1996): 111–29.

Ela, Jean-Marc. *Le Cri de l'homme africain.* Paris: Harmattan, 1980.

Flint, P. "Old Testament Scholarship from an African Perspective." In Ed. J.J. Burden, *Exodus 1–15: Text and Context.* Pretoria: University of South Africa, 1987: 179–214.

Geraghty, Gerard. "Paul before the Areopagus: A New Approach to Priestly Formation in the Light of Ecclesia in Africa." *African Christian Studies* 12/3 (1996): 32–41.

Gitari, David. "The Good Shepherd: Ezekiel 34; John 10." In, *In Season and Out of Season: Sermons to a Nation*: 128–30. Carlisle: Regnum, 1996.

Golka, Friedemann W. *The Leopard's Spots: Biblical and African Wisdom in Proverbs.* Edinburgh: T. & T. Clark, 1993.

Hale, Frederick. "Romans 13:1–7 in South African Baptist Social Ethics." *South African Baptist Journal of Theology* 1 (1992): 66–83.

Hochegger, H. "L'experience evangelique face a certains rites traditionnels d'Afrique." *Telema* 19/75–76 (1993): 53–55.

Igenoza, Andrew Olu. "St. Paul in Athens: Acts 17: 19–34: A Study in the Encounter of Christianity with Philosophical Intellectualism and other Religions. How relevant to Africa?" Department of Religious Studies, University of Ife-Ife, Nigeria: Unpublished Seminar Paper, June, 1984.

Imasogie, Osadolor. *Guidelines for Christian Theology in Africa.* Ibadan: University Press Limited, 1986.

Kalugila, Leonidas. *The Wise King: Studies in Royal Wisdom as Divine Revelation in the Old Testament and its Environment.* Lund: CWK Gleerup, 1980.

Kanyoro, Musimbi R.A. "Daughter Arise (Luke 8:40–56)." In Eds Musimbi R.A. Kanyoro and Mercy Amba Oduyoye, *"Talitha qumi!": Proceedings from the Convocation of African Women Theologians, Trinity College, Legon-Accra Sept. 24–Oct. 2, 1989* Ibadan: Daystar Press, 1990: 54–62.

Kinoti, H.W. and J.M. Waliggo. "Introduction." In Eds Kinoti and Waliggo. *The Bible in African Christianity: Essays in Biblical Theology.* Nairobi: Acton Publishers, 1997.

Kirwen, Michael. *African Widows: An Empirical Study of the Problem of Adapting Western Christian Teaching on Marriage to the Leviratic Custom for the Care of Widows in Four Rural African Societies.* Maryknoll: Orbis, 1979.

Lagerwerf, Leny. "African Women Doing Theology: A Survey." *Exchange* 19/1 (1990): 1–69.

LeMarquand, Grant. "The Historical Jesus and African New Testament Scholarship." In Eds William E. Arnal and Michel Desjardins, *Whose Historical Jesus?* Waterloo, Ontario: Wilfrid Laurier Press, 1997: 161–80.

————. "Solemn Euphoria: The Consecration of an Ethiopian Orthodox Tewahedo Church in Canada." *Anglican and Episcopal History* 67/1 (1998): 113–19.

Loba, Mkole Jean-Claude. "A Liberating Women's Profile in Mk 5:25–34." *African Christian Studies* 13/2 (1997): 36–47.

Magesa, L. "The Bible and a Liberation Theology for Africa." *Africa Ecclesiastical Review* 19 (1977): 217–22.

Manus, Chris Ukachukwu. "The Subordination of Women in the Church: 1 Cor 14:33b–36 Reconsidered." *Revue Africaine de Theology* 8/16: 183–95.

———. "The Areopagus Speech (Acts 17:16–34): A Study of Luke's Approach to Evangelism and Its Significance in the African Context." *Africa Theological Journal* 14/1 (1985): 3–18.

———. "The Areopagus Speech (Acts 17:16–34): A Study on Luke's Approach to Evangelism and its significance in the African Context." *Revue African de Theology* 13/26 (1989): 155–70.

———. "The Areopagus Speech (Acts 17:16–34): A Study of Luke's Approach to Evangelism and Its Significance in the African Context." In Eds W. Amewowo, P.J. Arowele and Buetubela Balembo, *Les Actes des Apotres et les jeunes Eglises: Actes du Deuxieme Congres des Biblistes Africains. Ibadan: 31 juillet–3 aout 1984.* Kinshasa: Katholische Jungschar Oesterreichs/Facultes Catholiques de Kinshasa, 1990: 197–218.

———. "The Samaritan Woman (Jn 4:7ff.): Reflections on Female Leadership and Nation Building in Africa." *African Journal of Biblical Studies* 2/1–2 (1987): 52–63.

Martin, Marie-Louise. "Acts 17:16–34: Paul's Approach to Greek Intellectuals." *Ministry* 3/1 (1962): 20–24.

Masenya, Madipoane J. "The Bible and Women: Black Feminist Hermeneutics." *Scriptura* 54 (1995): 189–201.

———. "Proverbs 31:10–31 in a South African Context: A *Bosadi* (Womanhood) Perspective." Doctoral Dissertation, University of South Africa, Pretoria, 1996.

Mbiti, John S. *Bible and Theology in African Christianity* Nairobi: Oxford University Press, 1986.

Mbwiti, Justine Kahungu. "Jesus and the Samaritan Woman (John 4:1–42)." In Eds Mercy Amba Oduyoye and Musimbi R.A. Kanyoro, *"Talitha, qumi!": Proceedings of the Convocation of African Women Theologians, Trinity College, Legon-Accra Sept. 24–Oct. 2, 1989* Ibadan: Daystar Press, 1990: 63–75.

Mikre-Selassie, G.A. "Ethiopia and the Bible." In Eds E. Mveng and R.J.Z. Werblowsky, *The Jerusalem Congress on Black Africa and the Bible. April 24–30, 1972/ Le Congres de Jerusalem sur l'Afrique Noire et la Bible: Proceedings.* Jerusalem: The Israel Interfaith Committee, 1972: 190–96.

———. "The Bible and its Canon in the Ethiopian Orthodox Church." *The Bible Translator* 44/1 (1993): 111–23.

Mojola, A.O. "Vernacularization and the African Independent Churches Cross-Cultural Encounters: Some Preliminary Observations from Close Quarters." *Africa Theological Journal* 22/2 (1993): 130–46.

Mosala, Itumeleng J. *Biblical Hermeneutics and Black Theology in South Africa.* Grand Rapids: Eerdmans, 1989.

Moulder, James. "Romans 13 and Conscientious Disobedience." *Journal of Theology for Southern Africa* 21 (1977): 13–23.

Nare, Laurent. *Proverbs salomomiens et proverbes mossi: Etude comparative a partir d'une nouvelle analyse de Pr 25–29.* Frankfort, Bern, New York: Peter Lang, 1986.

Nikkel, Marc R. "The Cross of Bor Dinka Christians: A Working Christology in Face of Displacement and Death." *Studies in World Christianity* (1995): 160–85.

Nopece, N. Bethlehem. "Romans 13 and Apartheid: A Study of Rom. 13:1–7 in Relation to the Modern Political Situation in South Africa." M.Th. thesis, Glasgow University, 1986.

Nthamburi, Zablon. "African Theology of Liberation (II): Biblical Foundations of African Theology." *African Ecclesial Review* 22/5 (1980): 287–303.

Ntreh, Benjamin Abotchie. "Women's Support Agents in the Bible." West African Association of Theological Institutions [WAATI] held at the Seventh-Day

Adventist Seminary at Ilishan, Remo, Ogun State, Nigeria: Unpublished paper, July 28–August 2, 1996.

Nurnberger, Klaus. "Theses on Romans 13." *Scriptura* 22 (1987): 40–47.

Nurnberger, Margaret, Ed. *I Will Send You to Pharaoh* Bible Studies in Context, 2; Pietermaritzburg: Institute for the Study of the Bible/Cluster Publications, 1992.

Obeng, Emmanuel. "The Use of Biblical Critical Methods in Rooting Scriptures in Africa." In Eds Hannah W. Kinoti & John M. Waliggo, *The Bible in African Christianity*. Nairobi: Acton Publishers, 1997: 8–24.

Oduyoye, Mercy Amba. "Biblical Interpretation and the Social Location of the Interpreter: African Womens' Reading of the Bible." In Eds F. Segovia and M. Tolbert, *Reading from this Place. Volume 2: Social Location in Global Perspective* Minneapolis: Fortress, 1995: 52–66.

Okure, Teresa. *The Johannine Approach to Mission: A Contextual Study of John 4:1–42.* WUNT, 31; Tubingen: J.C.B. Mohr (Paul Siebeck), 1988a.

———. "Women in the Bible." In Eds V. Fabella and M. Oduyoye, *With Passion and Compassion: Third World Women Doing Theology*. Ecumenical Association of Third World Theologians, Women's Commission; Maryknoll: Orbis, 1988b: 47–59.

———. "A New Testament Perspective on Evangelization and Human Promotion," In Eds Justin Ukpong, Teresa Okure, John E. Anyanwu, Godwin C. Okeke and Anacletus N. Odoemene, *Evangelization in Africa in the Third Millenium: Challenges and Prospects. Proceedings of the First Theology Week of the Catholic Institute of West Africa. Port Harcourt, Nigeria, May 6–11, 1990.* Port Harcourt: CIWA Press, 1992a: 84–94.

———. "The Will to Arise: Reflections on Luke 8:40–56," In Eds Mercy Amba Oduyoye and Musimbi R.A. Kanyoro, *The Will to Arise: Women, Tradition and the Church in Africa*. Maryknoll: Orbis Press, 1992b: 221–30.

———. "Feminist Interpretations in Africa." In Ed. Elisabeth Schüssler Fiorenza, *Searching the Scriptures. Volume One: A Feminist Introduction*. New York: Crossroad, 1993: 76–85.

Onwu, Nlenanya. "Jesus and the Canaanite Woman (Matthew 15:21–28): Toward a Relevant Hermeneutics in African Context." *Bible Bhashyam* 11/3 (1985): 130–43.

———. "Ministry to the Educated: Reinterpreting Acts 17:16–34 in Africa." *African Christian Studies* 4/4 (1988): 61–71.

Oosthuizen, M.J. "Scripture in Context: The Use of the Exodus Theme in the Hermeneutics of Liberation Theology." *Scriptura* 25 (1988): 7–22.

Osei-Bonsu, Joseph. "A Reflection on Paul's Speech at the Areopagus (Acts 17: 22–32)." Scotus College, Bearsden, Glasgow, Scotland: The Bible in Africa Project Glasgow Consultation: Unpublished paper, 13th–17th August 1994.

Owan, Kris. "Jesus, Justice and Jn. 10:10. Liberation Hermeneutics in the Nigerian Context." *Nigerian Journal of Theology* 10/1 (1996): 18–42.

Owanikin, Rebecca M. "Colossians 2:18. A Challenge to Some Doctrines of Certain Aladura Churches in Nigeria." *African Journal of Biblical Studies* 2/1 & 2 (1987): 89–96.

Pobee, John S. *Persecution and Martyrdom in the Theology of Paul*. Sheffield: JSOT Press, 1985.

———. "Bible Study in Africa: A Passover of Language." *Semeia* 73 (1996): 161–79.

Riches, John. "Interpreting the Bible in African Contexts: Glasgow Consultation." *Semeia* 73 (1996): 181–88.

Sandblom, Alice. *La Tradition et la Bible Chez la Femme de la CEZ: influence de l'ancienne culture et de la Bible au sein de la Communaute Evangelique du Zaire*. Uppsala: Alqvist & Wiksell International, 1993.

Sanneh, Lamin. *Translating the Message: The Missionary Impact on Culture*. Maryknoll: Orbis, 1989.

Schaaf, Ype. *On Their Way Rejoicing: The History and Role of the Bible in Africa*. Carlisle: Paternoster Press, 1994.

Setiloane, Gabriel. "I Am an African." In Ed. John B. Taylor, *Primal World Views: Christian Dialogue With Traditional Thought Forms*. Ibadan: Daystar, 1976: 56–59.

Shell, Ellen Ruppel. *Atlantic Monthly* (August 1997): 45–49, 52, 54–56, 58–60.

Sibeko, Malika and Beverley Haddad. "Reading the Bible "with" Women in Poor and Marginalised Communities in South Africa." *Bulletin for Contextual Theology in Southern Africa & Africa* 3/1 (1996): 14–18.

Smit, Dirk J. "The Ethics of Interpretation—and South Africa." *Scriptura* 33 (1990): 29–43.

Souga, Theresa. "The Christ-Event from the Viewpoint of African Women: A Catholic Perspective." In Eds Virginia Fabella and Mercy Amba Oduyoye, *With Passion and Compassion: Third World Women Doing Theology*. Maryknoll: Orbis, 1990: 22–29.

Stendahl, Krister. "The Apostle Paul and the Introspective Conscience of the West." *Harvard Theological Review* 61 (1963): 199–215.

Tappa, Louise. "The Christ-Event from the Viewpoint of African Women II: A Protestant Perspective." In Eds Virginia Fabella and Mercy Amba Oduyoye, *With Passion and Compassion: Third World Women Doing Theology* Maryknoll: Orbis, 1990: 30–35. [Also printed as "An African Woman's Reflection on the Christ Event." *Voices From the Third World* 11/2 (1988): 76–83.]

Turner, H.W. *Profile Through Preaching*. London: Edinburgh House Press, 1965.

Tutu, Desmond. "Liberation as a Biblical Theme." In *Hope and Suffering: Sermons and Speeches*, 48–87. Johannesburg: Skotaville/Grand Rapids: Eerdmans, 1983.

Tzabedze, Joyce "Women in the Church (1 Timothy 2:8–15, Ephesians 5:22)." In Eds Mercy Amba Oduyoye and Musimbi R.A. Kanyoro, *"Talitha, qumi!": Proceedings of the Convocation of African Women Theologians, Trinity College, Legon-Accra Sept. 24–Oct. 2, 1989* Ibadan: Daystar Press, 1990: 76–79.

Ukpong, Justin. *Sacrifice: African and Biblical. A Comparative Study of Ibibio and Levitical Sacrifices*. Rome: Urbaniana Press, 1987.

———. "Rereading the Bible with African Eyes: Inculturation and Hermeneutics." *Journal of Theology for Southern Africa* 91 (1995): 3–14.

———. "The Parable of the Shrewd Manager (Luke 16:1–13): An Essay in Inculturation Biblical Hermeneutic." *Semeia* 73 (1996): 189–210.

Umeagudosa, Margaret Azuka. "The Healing of the Gerasene Demoniac From a Specifically African Perspective." *African Christian Studies* 12/4 (1996): 30–37.

Van Aarde, Andries. "Recent Developments in South African Jesus Research: From Andrie du Toit to Willem Vorster." *Hervormde Teologiese Studies* 49 (1993a): 397–423.

———. "Recent Developments in South African Jesus Research: From Willem Vorster to Andries van Aarde." *Hervormde Teologiese Studies* 49 (1993b): 942–62.

Van Jaarsveld, F.A. *The Afrikaner's Interpretation of South African History*. Cape Town: Simondium Publishers, 1964.

Walls, Andrew F. "Romans One and the Modern Missionary Movement." In Ed. A.F. Walls, *The Missionary Movement in Christian History: Studies in the Transmission of Faith*. Maryknoll: Orbis, 1996: 55–67. [Originally published as "The First Chapter of Romans and the Modern Missionary Movement." In Eds W.W. Gasque and R.P. Martin. *Apostolic History and the Gospel*. Grand Rapids: Eerdmans/Exeter: Paternoster, 1971.]

Wanamaker, Charles A. "Romans 13: A Hermeneutic for Church and State," In Ed. Charles Villa-Vicencio, *On Reading Karl Barth in South Africa*. Grand Rapids: Eerdmans, 1988: 91–104.

————. "Creation of New Meaning: Rhetorical Situations and the Reception of Romans 13:1–7." *Journal of Theology for Southern Africa* 79 (1992): 24–37.

West, Gerald O. *Contextual Bible Study*. Pietermaritzburg: Cluster Publications, 1993.

————. "Constructing Critical and Contextual Readings with Ordinary Readers: Mark 5:21–6:1." *Journal of Theology for Southern Africa* 92 (1995): 60–69.

————. *Biblical Hermeneutics of Liberation: Modes of Reading the Bible in the South African Context*. Revised Edition; Pietermaritzburg: Cluster Publications/Maryknoll: Orbis, 1997 [1991].

Wittenberg, Gertrud. "The Song of a Poor Woman: The Magnificat (Luke 1:46–55)." In Eds Denise Ackermann, Jonathan Draper and Emma Mashini, *Women Hold Up Half the Sky: Women in the Church in South Africa*. Pietermaritzburg: Cluster Publications, 1991: 3–20.

Wittenberg, Gunther H. *I Have Heard the Cry of My People: A Study Guide to Exodus 1–15*. Pietermaritzburg: Institute for the Study of the Bible/Cluster Publications, 1991.

HOW AL-MOKATTAM MOUNTAIN WAS MOVED: THE COPTIC IMAGINATION AND THE CHRISTIAN BIBLE

J.A. (Bobby) Loubser

Can any investigation of the Bible in Africa ever be complete without a consideration of its use in the Coptic Orthodox Church? The word "Coptic" is derived from *kibt* or *kubt*, an Arab name for Egypt, deriving from He-Ke-Ptah, an ancient name for a settlement on the Nile. Today the name "Coptic" indicates the Christian tradition that took root in North Africa since the earliest phases of Christianity. Legend has it that the evangelist Mark founded the Coptic Orthodox Church in the year 69 CE when preaching the Gospel in Alexandria. This was the beginning of a tradition that has left deep imprints not only on the history of Christianity in Africa, but also in Western Christianity in general.

There is a popular perception that Coptic Christianity is not really "African" since it finds its base in the Arabian world in distinction from the "African" world. If this definition of what it is to be African is accepted, large populations north of the Sahara will have to be regarded as "non-African." This also raises the question whether the Nilotic, Kushitic and Semitic peoples of Sudan and the Horn of Africa are to be considered "African" in the narrower sense of the world. In this chapter "Africa" will be understood in an inclusive, geographic sense. To use the latter definition makes sense for several reasons. One of these reasons is that "Africa" is not a self-contained entity, but a rich diversity that is implied in the ancient name itself. To the people of the ancient and classical worlds, Africa and Egypt were almost synonymous. Another reason is that a significant part of African reality was shaped through interaction of the rest of Africa with the civilisation in the Nile valley. When considering the Coptic tradition, it makes even more sense to include it in a definition of what is African. The Coptic tradition is much older than the Arab tradition in Africa, for the Arabs only conquered Egypt in the seventh century CE to begin a programme of Islamisation. Further, the Coptic tradition gave rise to the spread of Christianity to Ethiopia in the fourth century, thereby expanding its influence much further into Africa than only the Arab world. The Coptic tradition is a distinct African phenomenon. It builds on the intellectual achievements of ancient Egypt and also on the excellence of the Alexandrine Christianity in the first centuries of the Christian era. The Coptic language, extinct since the 16th century, not only represents the last phase of development of the ancient Egyptian tongue, but carries with it the values and perceptions of millennia of civilisation as it blossomed along the Nile.

In order to understand the biblical hermeneutic and exegesis in the Coptic Church a short review of its socio-political context may be illuminating. Toward the end of the fifth century, Egypt was a Christian country. Coptic Christians claim that their present pope is the 117th in an unbroken line of succession, occupying the See of Mark, the evangelist. Since the occupation by Muslim invaders in 627–642 CE[1] there had been little or no intermarriage between Copts and Arabs. The present day Copts of Egypt (10% of a population of 60 million) are relatively pure descendants of the ancient Egyptians.[2] From the year 150 BCE Coptic was written by means of the Greek alphabet together with seven additional characters retained from the previous Demotic script. Until the 8th century, affairs of state were conducted in both Coptic and Arabic. After that only Arabic was in use. Eventually, Coptic was prohibited in the 10th century. As a spoken language it died out completely in the 16th century, and is today only heard in the sung liturgies of the Coptic Orthodox Church. The survival of the Church through 1300 years of Muslim domination, harassment by the Crusaders (who regarded them as heretics) and isolation from the rest of the world therefore stands as a wonder equal to the preservation of the majestic pyramids of Gizeh.[3] Today the Coptic Church belongs to that branch of pre-Chalcedonian

---

[1] Cairo, then called Babylon, was taken in the year 641, and Alexandria in 642. A Biblical reference to this name is believed to be found in 1 Peter 5:13 where it is said that: "St. Mark and the church at Babylon saluteth you" (Murad Kamil, 1968: 89).

[2] In a broad sense the ancient Egyptians, as their language shows, were part of the Afro-Semitic group, with a closer affinity to the Arab groups than either the Greek-Latin or black African groups (a different view is held by Maphalala 1996: 106–108, who claims that there was a primary ethnic relationship between the ancient Egyptians and present black Africans, and that Egypt is "the child of inner Africa").

[3] Thus stated in an article on the World Wide Web.

Christianity, which—together with the Armenian, Ethiopian, Syrian and Indian Orthodox churches—recognizes only the first three ecumenical councils of the apostolic church.

We may also note that Coptic Christianity is alive and well today. Coptic Christians are knowledgeable of their proud heritage and enthusiastic about it. In Alexandria, a city of 4 million inhabitants, there are about 500,000 Copts. When I had the opportunity of visiting the city in 1997, I was invited on a Sunday evening to attend a meeting during which the patriarch, Shenouda III, trained about 120 lay church leaders. Meetings such as these are scheduled for every week. In Cairo, I was told, the patriarch was holding regular Wednesday Bible studies attended by up to 7,000 people. Representatives of the Church assured me that they are serious about their participation in ecumenical Christianity, for example, through the World Council of Churches and other international bodies. They are also looking south toward the rest of Africa for building ties and spreading their faith. During Easter 1977 the patriarch visited South Africa to consecrate two new churches in Nongoma and Gugulethu. The only Coptic bishop south of Egypt is today found in Johannesburg.[4]

The question that keeps returning after visiting the Egyptian Church, is why this tradition has been neglected by the rest of Christianity, also by African Christians? Why are they so often excluded when "African" Christianity and Bible interpretation is considered? From the introduction so far, we can gather that they have much to contribute. Not only do they draw on the experience of two thousand years of Bible interpretation, but also they are able and willing to participate. Moreover, the interest of predominantly black Christians in South Africa in Coptic Christianity is a sign of its appeal to a wide range of people in Africa. As we shall see below, the faith of the Coptic Church reflects an imagination that is not foreign to traditional African cultures.

In 1997 I visited the bookshop of the St George Orthodox Church in Alexandria. The church was bustling with people for some festival, and the shop was amply stocked and well supported. I bought a couple of books, and the salesman, seeing that I was interested in the Coptic materials put a copy in my hand that he thought would rouse my interest. It was *The Biography of Saint Samaan, the Shoemaker,*

---

[4] His holiness bishop Marcos.

"*the Tanner.*" I bought it more to please him than out of personal
curiosity, but much later as I was browsing through my little Coptic
collection, I found this book a brilliant example of what I would
like to call "the Coptic imagination." It provides the reader with a
window on Coptic Christianity as it understands itself in the present
and is an illustration of their biblical hermeneutic. Here I had a living Coptic artefact, referring to the past but dealing with the present. It is on this book that we are going to concentrate in the rest
of this essay.

The Biography of Saint Samaan deals with the story of Samaan (Simon)
a saint of a 1000 years ago. Its interest does not lie so much in the
story itself, but in the manner in which it draws together most, if
not all, of the central themes active in Coptic Christianity. Also interesting is how the story is woven into the spiritual fibre of the present, while bringing the past to life. The book was published in 1994
by the Church of Saint Samaan the Tanner, Mokattam Mountain
Cairo and has 110 pages. It is a translation from an earlier 1983
Arabic edition, but with some significant additions. The format follows the general conventions of books in Arabic, with an index at
the back (as in some ancient scrolls). It has five chapters, each with
several subdivisions. The 43 footnotes refer to no more that six
different sources. The lengthy manner in which references are made
reminds one of the style of a manuscript culture. The author is
Bishop Mattaos, abbot of the Syrian monastery (in the Wadi el
Natrun, as far as I can gather). His picture follows that of "H.H.
Pope Shenouda III," who is subtitled as the "117th Pope and Patriarch
of Alexandria and the See of St. Mark." The book is obviously
intended for spiritual upliftment, since every short chapter contains
explicit spiritual exhortations and ends with a prayer, which can be
quite moving. On one of the front pages it is explicitly stated that
the book is published "In the name of the Father, the Son, and the
Holy Spirit, one God. Amen."

The book is presented by the author as a "stirring biography, and
the account of the supernatural [sic] miracle of moving the Mokattam
Mountain, together with the miracle of building the Church of Saint
Samaan the Tanner in the Mokattam Mountain" (1994: 9). Noteworthy
is the logic of the book, which is different from what a Western
reader would expect. According to the logic of the book, the author
first gives a description of the conditions in Egypt at the end of the
first millennium. Then he proceeds to present a written "icon" of
the saint before turning to the miracle of how he moved Mokattam

Mountain is reported. This is followed by a discussion of the results of the miracle, one of which is the founding of a monastery on the mountain. The last section tells the story of how Samaan's body was discovered recently.

Between CE 934 and 968 there was a severe famine in Egypt in which half a million people died. For three years the Nile did not overflow its banks. Whole towns vanished. Bishop Mattaos remarks that this must have left a mark on a certain tanner (or shoemaker, for the original word is ambiguous). He draws a lesson from this, and mentions that "people are divided in their reactions to hard circumstances into three categories: the first murmurs against and resents the circumstances, while the second receives them in silence, and the third gives thanks even in the heated furnace, knowing that God will bring 'out of the eater something to eat, out of the strong, something sweet (Judges 14:14)'" (1994: 16). Saint Samaan obviously belonged to the latter.

The reference to the furnace would be understood by every Copt, for the most beloved hymn in their hymn book (that all are supposed to know by heart), deals with the friends of Daniel who survived the fiery furnace. The image of fire does not refer to the heat of the desert, but to the fire of persecution. Through centuries of persecution Coptic Christians have found spiritual strength in this narrative. The bishop concludes: "This third kind of person learns the lessons, and, therefore, comes out of the fire brighter than before, as Job the prophet of patience said, 'When he has tested me, I shall come forth as gold' (Job 23:10)."

At the time of Samaan, conditions were favorable for the Christians, though persecution did occur in the town of Tanis (presently San) in the Sharqia Governate at the beginning of the Fatimid reign. As Bishop Mattaos puts it, this "plucked the feeling of security from the hearts of the Copts and made them take refuge with God as their only protection" (1994: 18). Extremists declared themselves independent from the government and plundered the homes of Christians, taking their women and daughters as booty. These excesses were halted when the government was alerted and intervened. It should be noted that such incidents continue today, as in March, 1997, when gunmen opened fire in the Coptic village of Nag Hammadi killing 13 people.[5]

---

[5] This was reported widely in the local press.

The Copts were fortunate that the caliph who reigned from CE 969 till the end of CE 979 was Al-Mu'izz Li Din Illah, the most powerful of the Fatimids. The Muslims had finally conquered Coptic Egypt in CE 641–642 and gradually colonized it with Arabs, but there were times when they allowed the vanquished a relative freedom. Al-Mu'izz Li Din Illah was not only a liberal statesman, but also took an interest in religion. He used to invite Muslim, Christians and Jewish religious leaders to debate before him "with all frankness and freedom, and without any anger or contention" (Mattaos 1994: 20). This habit has a direct bearing on the story of Samaan the Tanner. The Coptic patriarch that the caliph used to invite was a pious old man, named Abram Ibn Zaraa the Syrian. He was elected in CE 975 as 62nd successor on the See of St. Mark. In the Coptic calendar that was in the month of Tuba, 687 A.M.[6] After being elected, the patriarch distributed his possessions to the poor and to the churches and monasteries. He also forbade simony and an "evil habit that prevailed among Christians, namely the possession of concubines" (1994: 21).

The next step in the narrative of Saint Samaan is the description of his exemplary character. This is typical of the Coptic appreciation of their spiritual role models or icons. The focus of the book on the saint does not concentrate so much on the facts of the miracle performed, but rather on the spiritual example that he represented. This already gives us an idea of how the Bible is read: as a rich tapestry of icons, constantly encouraging the faithful by refreshing their memory of Biblical themes.

Icons, like the figures in the Bible, are understood to be alive before God. The depicted biblical figures and saints are regarded as living beings, constantly praying for and attending to the spiritual needs of the faithful. The Bible is understood as a witness not of deceased historical figures, but of living examples. Scripture is not only illustrated in terms of iconic traditions, these also inform the interpretation of Scripture.[7]

It is noteworthy that the contemporary depiction of Samaan on the cover page of the book is an iconographic representation. His picture carries a message that would be clear to Copts but needs

---

[6] AM is the abbreviation for "anno martyrorum" the beginning of the Coptic calendar, deriving from the greatest slaughter of Christians in Egypt—believed to be 20.000—under the emperor Decius in 284 CE.

[7] As printed on the cover page of Mattaos 1994.

Figure 1. Samaan the Tanner

some explanation for those unfamiliar with Orthodox icons. The circular halo represents perfection, the Alpha and the Omega. The gold colour symbolizes love. Inside the halo a Coptic cross is normally included with the vertical and horizontal beams of equal length. This is to show that the love for God (symbolized by the vertical beam) and the love for the neighbour (the horizontal beam) are of equal importance. Western Christianity is seen to be symbolised by the Western cross with a longer vertical beam, which indicated the other-worldliness and abstraction of Western Christianity. In contrast Coptic Christianity is explained as emphasising the love for other human beings in a stronger way that in Western theology. The brown earthy colours of the icons are a deliberate choice to indicate how close Coptic Christians are to the earth. The reason why Samaan only has one eye, will be explained later in the essay.

In the iconography we also need to note the central place that Christ occupies in the symbolic universe of the Coptic Church. Christology is to be understood as the subtext of Coptic iconography. The icons and murals inside sacred buildings reflect this by placing the image of Christ Pantokrator in the dominant place (often inside the main niche). Christ is usually flanked by the four figures

Figure 2. Christ enthroned, from a niche in the Bawit monastery

of the apocalypse—the man, the beast, the lion and the eagle—symbolising the four-fold gospel. Often these figures have flaming wings, with wheels underneath, indicating Ezekiel's fiery chariot. The message is clear: Christ crucified had risen in glory and reigns as Lord of the church and the world. In other icons one often sees a Christ on the cross with his eyes open—to indicate his victory over death. In the same icon, Judas might be indicated with one eye closed, to indicate the opposite.[8]

All that is known about Samaan's character and upbringing has to be inferred from the brief record in a handful of sources. Mattaos mentions only four. First there is the report of Anba Saweeris Ibn Al-Muqaffaa, the bishop of Asmun who wrote the biography of the patriarch Anba Abram in his book, *The History of the Patriarchs*. Then there is a thirteenth century report by Bishop Usab of Fuwwa. Apparently this manuscript is kept in the Syrian monastery. There is also the report in the Synaxarion (martyrologium) that mentions that "the Tanner" was buried in the Al-Habash cemetery. Finally there is also

---

[8] Malaty, in a tape recording (1997).

a fifteenth century icon of the patriarch Anba Abram together with "Samaan the Tanner" in the Suspended Church of Saint Mary in Old Cairo. This was presumably copied from an older icon.

The author explains: "The Saint appeared suddenly on the scene of historical events as a shining star, and disappeared just the same way" (1994: 25). His upbringing and youth being hidden in obscurity leads the bishop to refer to the time of Elijah who asked the Lord: "Am I the only one left?" The Lord replied that there were seven thousand faithful who have not bowed down to Baal. In the same way, Samaan was one of the obscure saints.

His profession of tanner or shoemaker further reminds of Saint Ananias, the patriarch who succeeded St. Mark. Ananias was also a shoemaker, and was asked by Mark to mend his shoes, being torn from all his travels in Alexandria. Ananias hurt his hand with the awl and cried, "Ious Theos" which means "O, the one God." Mark used this exclamation to evangelize the cobbler, who later was to become his successor. In the iconographic description of Saint Samaan, six spiritual qualities are extolled.

Purity is the first. When visited by a beautiful woman to mend her shoes, her legs showed and he looked lustfully at her. The words of Jesus came to him that "if your right eye causes you to sin, gouge it and throw it away" (Mt 5:28,29). Although it was against the interpretation of the church, he at once drove the awl into one of his eyes, plucking it out. In this, the author says, he became a follower of Origen, who had castrated himself, taking the commandment in Matthew 19:12 literally (although the church excommunicated him for this).

Abstinence and asceticism are the second. In conversation with the patriarch Abram, Samaan mentioned that he only ate enough to keep him alive. In this, he followed what Saint Sara said: "A mouth that you keep from water does not ask for wine, and a stomach that you keep from bread does not ask for meat." Fasting is still one of the great ideals of the Coptic Church today. Up to one third of all days of the year are spent in fasting.

Prayer is the third. To the patriarch, Samaan said: "And at sunset I go out with the rest of the wage workers and eat just a little, so as to keep myself barely alive. Then I turn to prayer, and stand the whole night praying." In this he follows David, Saint Arsenius and others (mentioned in the Synaxarium) (1994: 34–35).

Practical services are the fourth. According to a report, Samaan said about himself: "I wake up as early as this hour in the morning every day to fill my jar with water and distribute it to the elderly and the sick, who have been hampered from bringing water for themselves by old age of sickness. When I am finished with this service of mine, I return my water skin to the house and go to my work . . ." He is also reputed to "distribute every day bread and food to the cloistered hermits, whether of men of women" (Mattaos 1994: 37).

Humility is the fifth. Bishop Mattaos mentions four arguments to prove Samaan's humility. When he first met the patriarch, he exclaimed: "Forgive me, father, I am but a sinful man." He also did not want the patriarch to tell others about his life. While performing his miracle, he further did not want to stand next to the patriarch, but insisted in remaining hidden in the crowd behind him, "So that no one would recognise me." The last proof of his humility is that after the miracle had been performed, "the Pope turned left and right looking for Samaan the Tanner, but he was nowhere to be found, and none has ever found him after that" (1994: 39).

His strong faith is the sixth. Samaan's faith was demonstrated when he told the patriarch: "My honourable father, go up the mountain that the caliph tells you, and you shall see the glory of God." This faith is an example of the faith that Jesus mentioned when he used the example of the mustard seed in Matthew 17:20. Having drawn all the possible lessons from the circumstances and character of Samaan, the author finally proceeds with the narrative, first relating the events that paved the way for the miracle.

The Fatimid caliph, Al-Mu'izz Li Din Illah, had one of his usual open discussions in which Jews, Christians and Muslims participated. One of the conversation partners was a Jew, Jacob Ibn Killis, who pretended to espouse Islam because he wanted to become a minister of state. Fearing that a Christian rival, Quzman Ibn Mina, would be appointed as minister, he examined the Christian Bible in order to find something against the Christians and happened to come across Matthew 17:20 which says: "If you have faith as small as a mustard seed, you can say to this mountain, 'Move from here to there,' and it will move. Nothing will be impossible for you" (1994: 49). On discovering this Jacob and his companion rushed to the caliph and demanded that the Christians prove this saying true. The caliph immediately thought of a mountain that was east of the new city of Cairo which had just recently been founded. If the mountain could be moved further east it would provide the city with much needed space for expansion. He therefore called Anba Abram the patriarch and presented him with four choices: remove the mountain, accept Islam, leave Egypt, or be smitten with the sword.

The pope and church were thrown into turmoil and did what Christians do in such circumstances. They turned to God in prayer for in mass they say: "For we do not know another but You . . . your holy name is the name we utter and our souls are revived by your Holy Spirit." A fast for three days was proclaimed in the church and all the leaders and monks were assembled in the "Suspended Church of Saint Mary" (which is still today in Old Cairo). For three days they sought guidance. This was the beginning of a chain of miracles that are continuing up to the present day, according to the author. On the third day of the fast, the pope dozed off for a short while and dreamt that the Virgin Mary appeared to him. She asked him what was wrong and he replied: "You know, lady of heavenly and earthly beings." The she said: "Fear not, faithful shepherd, . . . for your tears which you have shed in this church, and the fasts and the prayers which you and your people have offered up shall not be forgotten." She then told him to go to iron gate at the market place where he would find an one-eyed man carrying water. This is the man by whom the miracle would take place. Just as in the dream, the pope found Samaan at the market. When he told Samaan what had happened, the latter replied: "Forgive me father, for I am but a sinful man." The pope insisted on his help, saying: "It is the command of the Mother of Light." At this stage he promised his assistance and the pope further inquired about who he was. "My name is Samaan, the Tanner, I work in tanning animal skins. But I wake up as early as this hour in the morning every day to fill my jar with water and distribute it to the elderly and the sick, who have been hampered from bringing water for themselves by old age or sickness. When I am finished with this service of mine, I return my water skin to the house and go to my work at the tannery where I work till evening. And at sunset I go out with the rest of the wage workers and eat just a little so as to keep myself barely alive. Then I turn to prayer. . . ." (Mattaos 1994: 53–54).

This report is interesting because of the ambiguity in the description of Samaan's craft. Here it is described as "tanner," but somehow it had to be reconciled with that of "cobbler" to account for his lost eye and his continuity with Saint Ananias. There is also an ambiguity about whether Samaan carried a water jar or a water skin. Such apparent inconsistencies show that the focus is not on historical exactness, but rather on the supernatural. The Coptic imagination is constantly on the lookout for miracles, and has a specific set of conventions that operate once a miracle is suspected.

On the set day everything was done as recommended by Samaan. The patriarch, religious leaders, deacons, archdeacons and others went up the mountain, carrying Bibles, crosses, long candles that were lit, and censers full of smoking incense. The caliph and his entourage were also there, together with a great crowd of people. The two parties stood opposite one another on the mountain. After administering the holy sacraments, the patriarch, bishops and people repeated "with a broken spirit and a crushed heart" the "Kyrie Eleison" four hundred times, one hundred in each wind direction. Then they kept silent "for a moment between the hands of the Most High" (1994: 56). Subsequently they started to fall down in worship and stand up for three times while the patriarch drew the sign of the cross. This is when the miracle occurred. Each time they fell in worship the mountain was thrust down, and every time they stood up the mountain would rise up and the sun would be seen from under it.[9]

The results of this miracle are described at length. The first remarkable event was that Samaan, who stood in the multitude behind the pope, had disappeared and was not seen again. The caliph granted a special wish to the pope, who wished that the church of Makarios Abu Sifein in Old Cairo be restored "for some mob and riffraff had it torn down, and used what was left of it as a store-house for sugarcane" (1994: 59). At some later stage a mob tried to prevent the restoration of this church and the caliph got so angry that he mounted his steed and took his army to Babylon, where the mob stood in silence, stricken with awe. From that day the mountain also received a new name. It now became Al-Mokattam, the "Cut-Up" [mountain] (1994: 58). One of the most remarkable results of the miracle was that a three-day fast was added to the regular fast before Christmas (celebrated on the 6th of January in the Orthodox tradition). If reports are true, this three-day fast in honour of Saint Samaan, annu-

---

[9] This is how it is described in *The Story of the Coptic Church* by Iris El-Masri, page 27 (according to Mattaos 1994: 56).

ally from 25–27 November, has been kept now for one thousand years. Bishop Mattaos concludes his book by a section on the research to determine the date of the miracle and a report on how the grave and body of Samaan was found on Sunday August 4, 1991. These sections were added after the first edition in 1983. Most interesting for our purposes is his description of how the church of Saint Samaan was built in 1974 on the Mokattam Mountain, but to this we shall return later.

The description above provides us with a window on the vivid imagination and hermeneutic of Coptic Christianity. From discussions with lay Christians and theologians both in Alexandria and in Cairo I gained the impression that the narrative of Saint Samaan is indicative of the type of spirituality that colours their understanding of Scripture. In their centres of learning there is, of course, a more sober and abstract examination of Scripture, but here we have an example of its inner logic. As the following review will show, it fits in with a hermeneutic strategy that has been developed and elaborated over many centuries. Below some of the salient features of this strategy are highlighted. In the manner that Bishop Mattaos deals with his subject, there is logic at work that is strange to the linear logic of Western scholarship. This does not mean that it is not the product of a highly sophisticated theology. The Coptic Church was born out of the great spiritual movements of the first six centuries and in some respects it seems to outsiders as if she has remained stuck somewhere in those centuries. The Church consciously still preserves and lives by the theological excellence of patristic times.[10] This may be the reason why the Coptic Church partially lives in a context where modern scholars can come closest to the social and spiritual conditions of patristic times. It is also the only indigenous African tradition that has a recorded history of two thousand years.

This does not preclude any new developments. The vibrant enthusiasm of Coptic Christianity is a sign of renewal. Some decades ago the monastic movement was all but extinct, but has experienced a

---

[10] In a denigrating tone *The Encyclopaedia Britannica* (1910) comments: "The Copts [of the first centuries] had little interest in theology, they were content to take their doctrine as prepared for them by the subtler minds of their Greek leaders at Alexandria, choosing the simplest form when disputes arose." This statement overlooks the fact that many of the so-called Greek Fathers were Copts trained in Greek language and philosophy. This statement was omitted in the present, 15th edition, of the encyclopaedia.

steady revival. The beginning of a Coptic mission on Mokattam
Mountain in the 1970s is a witness to this. Some factors contributed
toward this ongoing revival. Toward the end of the nineteenth century a system of Sunday schools was brought in, tuned to the English
Protestant model. This development was strengthened by the "revival"
of the Christian School of Alexandria (second to the fifth centuries)
including the extension of theological training to lay people. Since
the 1960s the Coptic Church has broken out of its spiritual isolation and has begun talks with the estranged members of the Orthodox
family, as well as with the Roman Church.[11]

It is obvious that their commitment to patristic foundations has
consequences for their view of the Bible. The decisions of the Synod
of Nicea in 325 on the canonical books of the Bible are part and
parcel of their faith. It is also evident that the exegetical methods
of the Fathers (Athenagoras, Clement of Alexandria, Athanasius,
Origen, Cyril of Alexandria, etc.) supply the background and incen-
tive for their own theological endeavors. Although the narrative of
Saint Samaan can be understood and appreciated in other Christian
traditions, one has to ask whether there are any emphases specific
to their traditional theological position, which has often been described
as "Monophysitism?" Presently some Copts protest that this is an
incorrect description of what they really believed[12] and preferred to
be called "mia-physites" (Wahba). The main point that they wish to
make by this term is that Jesus Christ is one and that his person is
undivided. In other words: he does not have a "split personality."
In every action by him, both his divinity and humanity participates
fully. Like the main-line churches in the East and the West, they
reject the heresies of Nestor (who rejected the Maryan title *Theotokos*,
believing the Incarnate Christ to be two separate persons) and of
Eutyches (who under-emphasised the humanity of Christ).[13] Together
with the Chalcedonian churches they today confirm the formula stat-

---

[11] A bone of contention with the Roman Church is what they call "uniatism"—
presumably the inclination of the RC to want to combine all other churches in one
structure (see Coptnet, "Recent efforts . . .").
[12] In *The Encyclopaedia Britannica* (1910), as in many other reference works, they
are described as a "monophysite sect." See also the article by Wahba, where he
quotes the contribution by W.H.C. Frend in the *Coptic Encyclopaedia*.
[13] Eutyches taught that the human nature of Jesus "is dissolved in his divinity
like a drop of vinegar in water." For a comprehensive review of the official documents from 1964 to 1990 see Coptnet, "Recent efforts. . . ."

ing that the divine and human natures of Christ are *asynchrotos, atreptos, achoristos* and *adiatreptos* (i.e., unmixed, unchanged, unseparated and undivided). This position, repeatedly stated at ecumenical deliberations over the last three decades, gives the lie to their detractors. They also spend much effort in their own ranks to distance themselves from Docetism and Gnosticism.[14]

With regard to the story of Samaan, one can only remark that the manner in which the natural and supernatural exist side by side, provides us with some indication as to the logic of "mia-physitism." In the same way as the divine and human natures work together in Jesus Christ, so they also have to work together in the life of the believer. What is noteworthy in the hagiography of Samaan is his presentation as exemplary character. Even the simplest aspects of his life are examined for the spiritual lessons and examples they contain. Thus Samaan is projected as an ideal for believers. This corresponds to the dominant emphasis in Coptic soteriology, which can be described as deification (*theiosis*) rather than justification or liberation. This was characteristic of the teachings of the Church Fathers, and still appears to be the dominant approach. The famous statement of Clement of Alexandria expresses a view to this effect: "*The Word . . . became Man so that you might learn from Man how man may become god*" (Malaty 1995: 19, citing Clement, *Paidagogos*, Book 1, Chapter 2, Section 6). Athanasius again states: "*He was made man that we might be gods . . .*" (*De Inarch.* 8,9). Thus the incarnation forms the foundation for a soteriology of deification. Humanity has to become a participator of the divine nature. To this end the teachings of Scripture and the saints serve to lead to salvation and exaltation by a process of healing and education (Malaty 1995: 23).

The distinct emphasis on Mary as mediator of divine revelation in Samaan's story may seem to be unbiblical to Protestant Christians. However, as in Mediterranean Christianity in general, she occupies a vital role in the symbolic universe. Especially in Egypt, the depiction

---

[14] Some of the misunderstanding at church councils can be attributed to language differences. Emile Maher, professor in Coptic, Old Testament and Theology at the Theological School at the Patriarchate in Cairo explained that *hypostasis* in Greek does not have the same meaning as *substantia* in Latin. The word *hypostasis*, though meaning "substance" acquired the meaning of "person" toward the middle of the fourth century. Its employment for this purpose led to confusion in the minds of Western theologians, who suspected the Easterners of tritheism when they spoke of "three hypostases."

of Mary is seldom presented without some reference to the nativity
accounts and the "Flight to Egypt." These latter accounts received
elaborate attention from the ancient Coptic Church, and are com-
memorated by a number of pilgrim sites that the holy family is
believed to have visited (Kamil 1968: 9–18). At one such site, appari-
tions of the virgin were reported as late as 1968 over an extended
period of time.[15] Even president Sadat was reported to have witnessed such an appearance.[16] This focus on the "Holy Virgin, St.
Mary," who is revered as Mother of God dates back to the Council
of Ephesus in 431 where it was confirmed that she gave birth to
God, the Son (Gabra 1993: 12). Her position is best attested by
iconography. Whereas Christ Pantokrator occupies the top and central focus in many apses, scenes where she is the focal point often
appear on a level just below him.[17] It is generally acknowledged that
the pictography of Isis (Demeter) contributed to the graphic illustrations of Mary. Like Isis, she wears a blue robe, indicating that
she is the "Queen of Heaven." Relief's of Isis suckling a baby
Harpocrates (Horus), were applied to Mary and the infant Jesus without alteration.[18] In other icons she is depicted at the right hand of
Jesus: she is the queen while he is the king.[19]

It should not escape our notice that Samaan's story is used to further the ideal of asceticism. After all, for the last thousand years
there has been a special fast in his honour in the Coptic Church
and it would have been strange if the story did not exploit the opportunity to provide meaning and motivation for this annual activity.
This neatly fits in with the widespread asceticism in the Coptic
Church and with its self-understanding as the church of the martyrs.

It is no coincidence that the calendar of the Coptic Church begins
in the year CE 284, the date of the greatest massacre of Christians
in Egypt. It is estimated that altogether more than 20,000 believers
were martyred in the ancient church.[20] Martyrdom is not seen as a

[15] Patriarchate Report 1968, and article by Pace in *The New York Times*, August
21, 1968.
[16] According to my informant, Emile Maher.
[17] The best illustration of this is found in a 6–7th century fresco from the
monastery of St. Apollo, Bawit, presently in the Coptic Museum, Old Cairo (Gabra,
1993: 58–59).
[18] Elaborately illustrated to me by Maher.
[19] Malaty (1997 tape recording).
[20] This figure might be exaggerated, but the number of martyrs were still a high
percentage of the Christian population.

coincidence, but as part of the divine plan of salvation. It was then, and today remains, an ideal and a gift. Martyrdom is closely associated with asceticism, both relating to suffering with Christ for the salvation of the soul. Thus the theology of the cross finds a specific application. The extraordinary emphasis that fasting receives is a testimony to this. The official fasting time in the church varies from 155 to 190 days annually. Before Easter the fasting time averages 55 days. Fasting is not a rigid rule, but believers are challenged to renounce eating animal products, and to be self-controlled when taking other nutrition. This practice, indeed observed by the faithful, is seen as an application of the practices of the apostles, and serves meditation. From several interviews I gathered that suffering with Christ is not regarded as a "good work" through which salvation is "deserved," but that it is rather a participation in the ongoing suffering of Christ for the salvation of the soul. This participation is mediated by the sacrament of Holy Communion, where the sacrifice of Christ is experienced as "ongoing and never-ending," although it is "once and for all" and sufficient at the same time.[21] The ideal of martyrdom and asceticism lives on in the monastic tradition which has seen a decline until the 1950s, but is at present undergoing a steady revival. It should be noted that monasticism in Egypt requires a renunciation of the world, but also has a social vision. At the monastery of Anba Bishoy in the Natrun Valley, it was explained to me why monks engage in manual labour. In one project it is their aim to work so effectively that one monk can provide food for 600 families.[22] This social vision is also attested by the erection of the Saint Samaan mission on the Mokattam Mountain, as we shall see in the last section of this essay.

It is clear that the story of Samaan is exploited for pastoral purposes. In the Coptic Church exegesis and meditation is done with an explicit spiritual and pastoral aim. The exposition of Scripture is done for the sake of spiritual upliftment. An abstract or neutral study of Scripture is regarded as an anomaly. It is also stressed that Coptic Christians do not complicate issues of faith but are satisfied with simple explanations. In response to my question whether it is not tedious or even boring to read through the Fathers, Dr. Emile Maher Ishak pointed out that his method does not imply commenting on

---

[21] Thus explained to me by Father Izidoros of the Anba Bishoy monastery.
[22] According to guides at the monastery of Anba Bishoy.

complete documents, but rather on "collecting jewels." The same
hermeneutic is apparent in the narrative of Saint Samaan. Citations
form the Bible and the apostolic Fathers, the patriarchs and any
other appropriate source are often made without reflection on their
original historical context. This same approach is found in the commentaries written and produced on a large scale for popular consumption by Father Tadros Y. Malaty (see Malaty 1991, 1992a,
1992b, 1996). His commentary on Revelation, for example, consists
in a verse by verse discussion of the text, illustrated by more or less
random citations from the Fathers. The explicit aim of such an exercise—collecting "jewels" and proof texts—is to instruct the reader in
the spiritual life. The same procedure generally applies to the use
of Biblical texts. This is evident from the oral and written communications by H.H. Pope Shenouda III.[23] This is also the hermeneutic
of the popular Matthew Henry Commentary that they use (in Arabic
translation).[24]

It is precarious to generalise about the hermeneutic of any church.
Nevertheless, if one evaluates their readings from the perspectives of
modern Western methods of reading, they fall in the sphere of a
pre-critical, naïve realism, akin to that of the Church Fathers. This
approach is found in many other religious discourses, even in Western
Christianity where is often forms part of a "second innocence." The
Coptic approach to the Bible reminds one of pre-critical times in
the Western Church, when all the Johannine literature was believed
to have been composed by one author and Hebrews was still regarded
as a Pauline letter. The Pauline corpus is viewed much in the same
way as Chrysostom saw it in his extensive commentaries. The sharp
and polemic aspects of the Pauline message is interpreted in the light
of the whole Scripture, and thus much less revolutionary than, for
example, Luther, had interpreted it. The same hermeneutic applies
to the rest of the Bible. The four gospels are conceived as the one
"tetramorph" Gospel, symbolised by the four figures of Revelation,[25]
as depicted in the icons together with the Christ Pantokrator image
in the central focus of church buildings.

---

[23] This much I gathered from his "Bible Study" at the Patriarchate in Alexandria,
as well as from collected pieces published in English on the World Wide Web, see
Shenouda (1997).
[24] According to John de Gruchy, who visited the Coptic Church a month before me.
[25] Murad Kamil (1968: 77) writes that in ancient times these four symbols were
united into one form with four heads, called the *tetramorph*.

Although there was a profusion of hermeneutical ideas and strategies in the early church, there was some consensus on the interpretation of Scripture. Clement of Alexandria held the view that there were three meanings in Scripture: literal, allegorical and spiritual. This is still very much how Coptic exegetes view their task. Father Tadros Y. Malaty explained the exegesis of the Fathers as allegorical, grammatical and historical.[26] For our purpose it is not necessary to enter into the detail of this debate. We can only note a few important points. Study of the literal or historical aspects does not resemble the abstract "neutral" historical-criticism of Western scholarship. It has been pointed out that the Fathers never developed a comprehensive hermeneutic. Nor did they apply their theories consistently throughout their writings (though who does, one might ask.). The dispute between the Antiochene writers and the Alexandrine School on allegory is often taken out of context. Whereas the Antiochenes criticised the Alexandrines (especially Origen) for their use of allegory, their own interpretation was not bereft of allegory—they merely differed regarding the degree to which allegory should be applied, and the status of allegory.[27] From the writings of the Fathers, for example, Origen, it is obvious that allegory was taken too far, for almost every phrase in the Old Testament was taken to point to some New Testament issue. It is also clear that the "meaning" of Scripture thus disclosed, represented the "closed" view of the interpreter and soon became exhausted. It seems that the concentration on the physical incarnation of the Logos sometimes resulted in a forced interpretation. My impression is that Coptic exegetes are today much more circumspect than some of the Fathers in this, and that they have developed allegorical interpretation into a tool that suits their needs. Nevertheless their idea of the incarnation and the resulting deification of human nature is conducive to an allegorising view of Scripture through which divine revelation is sought in the particularities of human existence.

It is apparent that there is a widespread interaction between

---

[26] Malaty 1997 (tape recording).

[27] Malaty (1995: 59) writes with reference to Quasten: ". . . between the two there was no absolute opposition. . . . Origen discovers types not just in certain episodes, but in every detail of the inspired word. . . . Antioch made it a fundamental principle to see figures of Christ just occasionally, not always in the Old Testament. . . . Types were the exception, not the rule, the Incarnation was everywhere prepared, but not everywhere prefigured."

Scriptures and the iconographic and hagiographic traditions in Coptic
thinking. Scripture is not only translated and interpreted in terms of
these traditions, but the traditions themselves inform the way they
look at the message of Scripture. Thus Bishop Mattaos can use the
story of Samaan to inform Christian faith. In a sense the story of
Samaan has to be seen as an extension of the *Synaxarion* (biographies
of the martyrs) that provides the faithful with inspiring examples for
every day of the year. A narrative with a similar ring is the story
of Saint Simeon who tied his beard to a beam in the ceiling when
reading his Bible. Should he fall asleep, his beard would be pulled
and he would wake up. There is also the story of Saint Bishoy (who
died in 407 CE) to whom Jesus appeared and who was allowed to
wash the Master's feet. After this he pleaded with the Lord to be
allowed to drink the water, which request was granted. A medical
doctor turned monk, Father Izidoros, who believes it to be true, told
the latter story to me in the monastery of St. Bishoy, Wadi el Natrun.
With the same conviction he also explained that St. Bishoy received
a revelation from the Lord that his flesh would never decay after
his death. To this day it has, without any preservation, remained
intact in the monastery bearing his name.

In the Coptic Church we do not find a Christomonism or a
Gottesfinsternis (eclipse of God) as in various Western traditions. Neither
do we find a fully dynamic Christology as in some forms of indi-
genised Christianity.[28] The Coptic tradition, in contrast, employs a
sophisticated Christology, stemming from the theological excellence
in the first centuries. On the other hand, Coptic theology is much
less systematised than Roman scholasticism or Protestant orthodoxy.
They are also not fundamentalist in the Western sense, which as an
enterprise is driven by Western literate bias.

We can now come to a summary of how the Coptic imagination
informs a strategy for reading the Bible. As we have observed we
find an ancient and sophisticated theological tradition at work that
determines the way in which spiritual reality is understood and interpreted. It is not to be confused with a Western historical positivism.
Nor can one describe it as a biblicist fundamentalism, which is also
a Western phenomenon. Like the Muslims, the Copts inhabit a world
of metaphysical realism, where magic, angels, evil spirits, heaven,

---

[28] In the tradition of African indigenous churches Christ is seen as being present
in the charismatic spiritual leader, who appropriates the qualities of Christ.

hell and Satan are generally accepted. Miracles and exorcisms can
occur at any time. It is this expectation that stimulates the Coptic
imagination. It is an imagination that is constantly on the look out
for the supernatural. A great part of the pastoral work is to keep
the awareness in miracles alive. Further, miracles can happen, indeed
do happen, and can be certified by the church to become the focus
of veneration. This fits in with their "mia-physite" position. "Supernatural" miracles assist man to become a participator of divine nature.
The aim of reading the Bible is unashamedly pastoral and spiritual,
extolling the virtues of the ascetic life. While the Virgin Mary sometimes accompanies the miraculous, the local iconography and lives
of the saints also play a role in keeping the imagination alive. The
Bible is used in an eclectic manner to serve spiritual ends, especially
to promote a life of fasting and good deeds. It follows that a seam-
less unity is observed between both testaments. This is so because
the Old Testament is read from cover to cover as a New Testament
witness. Thus the offices, ceremonies, laws and covenants of the Old
Testament are explained as allegorical prefigurations of New Testament
realities. A regular description of the Old Testament, dating from
the time of the Fathers, is that of a *virgin* (because there are always
new things hidden in it). Thus it also reminds of the Virgin Mary.
It may even be that the regular twofold depiction in icons of Jesus
and the Virgin Mary refers to the two testaments. Whereas Western
critical scholarship may be more structured and systematic (in a modernist sense) in its dealing with the Bible, one cannot escape the
awareness that technical "correctness" comes at the price of spiritual impoverishment when compared to the Coptic tradition.

   To conclude this essay we now turn to the recent history in which
Samaan's miracle has had a remarkable aftermath. As indicated previously, the story soon went into the chronicles of the church and
became the subject of an icon. It would have remained shrouded in
the veil of tradition were it not that recently something remarkable
happened. In 1969 the governor of Cairo, now a city of 14–16 million people, issued a decree that all trash collectors should be relocated to live on one of the hills of the Mokattam Mountain. By
1987 fifteen thousand people had settled there in tin huts that are
commonly called "Zaraayib," the Arabic word for pigsty. These trash
collectors traverse the city with their donkey carts, collecting trash
and on returning to their settlement, sort and classify it. The settlement itself got the name of "Zabbaleen" (Garbage City) (Mattaos

1994: 77–78). In this city lived a trash collector with the name
Qiddesh Ageeb Abd Al-Masseeh. He became acquainted with a
Coptic priest in the area where he used to collect garbage. For two
years from 1972–1974 he invited the minister in vain to visit him
at his home. As last the minister "heard the voice of God inside
him confirming that the calling was from Him" (Mattaos 1994: 79).
After having tried to run away from this calling, like Jonah, the minister at last came to "Garbage City" and observed the "pigsties."
For three Sunday consecutively he prayed and fasted under an over-
hanging rock without talking to any of the trash collectors, waiting
on the Lord. Then a miracle happened. A sudden whirlwind whipped
up the trash and paper in the settlement and delivered a small piece
of paper in front of him. When his eye fell upon the paper, he saw
that is was a page from the Bible, which read: "Do not be afraid,
keep on speaking, do not be silent. For I am with you, and no-one
is going to attack and harm you, because I have many people in
this city" (sic, Acts 18:9,10) (Mattaos 1994: 81).

From here developments were accompanied by a chain of miracles. A ministry was begun at that very place, leading to the building of a tin church in 1974, which was then eventually replaced
with a brick building and developed into a monastery, appropriately
named the Monastery of Saint Samaan on Al-Mokattam. When water
was needed for the building, God provided another miracle. When
a six-year-old child was severely hurt, he was healed through an
intercessory prayer to Saint Samaan. Eventually, from 1977 the Pope
Shenouda III began to visit the church and declared the paper that
was blown to the minister to be "a heavenly edict." He even wrote
a poem on Samaan (Mattaos 1994: 83–87). This revived the interest in Samaan to such an extent that research was done and his
grave and body was discovered in 1991. This latter part of Samaan's
story serves to illustrate the context within which Coptic Christianity
operates. It also shows how a theology of miracle and wonder can
convert itself into a liberative "pig sty theology" that addresses the
needs of the poor in ways that confounds abstract theology. For
African Christians it is significant that this is how the Christian faith
is understood on a significant part of their continent.

For the first six centuries the Bible was studied in Egypt like in
no other country. Whatever the influence and presence of the Bible
in Africa in ancient times, came through the filter of Coptic Christianity.
Long before northern Europe was Christianised (partly through Coptic

monks) they had already carried the Bible south into Ethiopia. Had it not been for the intervention of Islam, Africa today would have been a Coptic continent. It might still happen that Coptic faith reclaims a part of Africa that it had lost because of historical developments in previous centuries.

BIBLIOGRAPHY

Attala, Nabil Selim. *Coptic Art, Wall Paintings, L'art Copte, Peintures murales, Vol. I.* Lehnert & Landrock: Cairo-Egypt, 1989.

Benjamin, Bishop of Menoufeia. *The Holy Liturgy.* Bilingual English and Arabic, translated by Wedad Abbas. St. Mark Church: Heliopolis, Cairo, 1996.

"Copts," article in *The Encyclopaedia Britannica*, Eleventh edition, Vol. VII, Cambridge University Press: Cambridge, 1910.

Coptnet. *Recent Efforts for Unity between the Two Families of the Orthodox Church.* Published on the World Wide Web. Http:/pharos.bu.edu/OrthodoxUnityDialog.txt. [A comprehensive documentation, 33 pages.]

Gabra, Amir. Coptic *Tours (1) Al Mu'allaqah Church.* Mahabba Bookshop, 30 Shobra St., Cairo.

Gabra, Gawdat. *Cairo, the Coptic Museum, Old Churches*, with contributions by Anthony Alcock. The Egyptian International Publishing Company—Longman: Cairo, 1993.

Kamil, Jill. *Coptic Egypt, History and Guide.* Revised edition. The American University in Cairo Press: Cairo, 1987 (1996, 3rd printing).

Kamil, Murad. *Coptic Egypt.* Printed by Le scribe Egyptien, Cairo, 1968.

Malaty, Father Tadros Yacoub. *The Psalms, Psalm 1–Psalm 10, Bible Study.* English text by Mary Rose Youssef Halim. St. Mark and Pope Peter the Last Martyr: Sidi-Bisher Alexandria. Available from the St. George's Coptic Orthodox Church, Sporting-Alexandria, Egypt, 1991.

————. *Ecclesiastes, Studies in the Holy Bible 21.* Translated by Salwa Youssef. St. Mark and Pope Peter the Last Martyr: Sidi-Bisher Alexandria. Available from the St. George's Coptic Orthodox Church, Sporting-Alexandria, Egypt, 1992a.

————. *Jonah, a Patristic Commentary.* Translated by Salwaa Amazees. St. George's · Coptic Orthodox Church: Sporting-Alexandria, Egypt, 1992b.

————. *Lectures in Patrology, The School of Alexandria, Book One, Before Origen.* St. Mark's Coptic Orthodox Church, 427 West Side Ave. Jersey City, NJ 07304, 1995.

————. *The Book of Revelation.* Translated by Victoria and Ramzy Malaty. St. George's Coptic Orthodox Church: Sporting-Alexandria, Egypt, 1996.

————. *Tape Recording of Conversation with Delegates of the South African Council of Churches.* Available from the St. George's Coptic Orthodox Church, Sporting-Alexandria, Egypt, 1997.

Malina, Bruce and Jerome Neyrey *Portraits of Paul, Anatomy of a Mediterranean Personality.* Westminster John Knox Press: Louisville, Kentucky, 1996.

Maphalala, Jabu S. Hulumende. "History and Mother-tongue Education in South Africa," *New Contree*, No. 40, November 1996.

Mattaos, Bishop. *The biography of Saint Samaan the Shoemaker, "the Tanner."* Church of Saint Samaan the Tanner in Mokattam: Cairo, Egypt, 1994.

Mikhail, Maged S. *The Gnostics, A Survey of Gnostic Beliefs and Gnostic-Christian Ties.* Published on Coptnet on the World Wide Web, http:/pharos.bu.edu/Gnostic Heresies.txt. [8 pages].

Pace, Eric. "Arabs Throng Christian Church at Cairo after Report of Vision," *The New York Times*, August 21, 1968.

Patriarchal Report on the Apparition of Saint Mary in the Zaitoun Church in Cairo, Egypt. 1968. Published on the World Wide Web, http://pharos.bu.edu/ZaitounApparition OfSaintMary.txt.

Richardson, Dan and Karen O'Brien. *Egypt, The Rough Guide.* Rough Guides Ltd.: London, 1993.

Shenouda III, 117th Pope of Alexandria and Patriarch of the See of Saint Mark. *Excerpts from the Writings of H.H. Pope Shenouda III.* Publication on the World Wide Web by St. George and St. Anthony Coptic Orthodox Church of Heliopolis, Cairo, 1997. http://www.geocities.com/Athens/Acropolis/3227/. Email to: stantonios@geocities.com.

Takla, Hany N. *A Copt's Perspective on the Fifth International Congress of Coptic Studies.* Published on the World Wide Web. Contact: HTakla@gnn.com. [19 pages], 1996.

Wahba, Father Matthias F. *Monophysitism: Reconsidered.* Published on the World Wide Web, at http://pharos.bu.edu/MonophysitismReconsidered.txt.

Personal Contacts

Bishop Markos, Coptic Orthodox Bishop of Johannesburg.

Dr. Emile Maher Ishak, Professor of Coptic, OT and Theology in the Coptic Orthodox Theological College, Ramses St. Abbasiyah, Cairo.

Dr. Samir Guindy Ghabriel Ph.D., Deacon of St. George Orthodox Church in Alexandria.

Emile Hanna Abd El-Messih, Restorer of Coptic art for the Coptic Museum, Cairo.

Father Izidorous.Anbu Bishoy Monastery, Natrun Valley.

Dr. Michael Ghattas, Associate Patristic Centre Cairo (PCC).

THE BIBLE IN THE BLACK DIASPORA:
LINKS WITH AFRICAN CHRISTIANITY

Gosnell L.O.R. Yorke

February
This is the month we love,
The giant immortelles
Splash fire on the hills
Hold torches in the dells
(E.M. Roach 1966).

Carter Woodson (1875–1950), the African-American historian, is considered the father of Black History Month, celebrated each February in the United States and, with each passing year, throughout more and more of the English-speaking African Diaspora such as in Canada (see Yorke 1986 and Williams 1997).[1] Therefore, the month of February is a time during which Blacks devote much of their attention reflecting on their collective story—one which has to do mainly with forced separation from the Motherland, involuntary servitude or slavery in the Diaspora, ongoing struggle and, ultimately, a semblance of survival against overwhelming odds.

Among others, both Woodson and W.E.B. Dubois (1868–1963), the eminent Pan-Africanist, had much to say about the significant role the Black Church has played in helping "Africans in exile"[2] cope and keep hope alive (see Woodson 1945, Dubois 1965, Lincoln 1994). In fact, Dubois is generally credited with the pertinent observation that the oldest institution in the English-speaking African Diaspora is not the family per se but the Black Church with its tap root firmly anchored in the soil of more than 300 years of slavery. During which, European slave traders gave millions (some put the "guesstimate" at more than 50 million) of our forefathers and foremothers a Trans-Atlantic trip against their collective wills and then coerced them into toiling away on sugar, tobacco and cotton plantations or estates

---

[1] This chapter is a modified version of Yorke 1997.
[2] This (I think correct) characterization of Blacks in the Diaspora comes from the outstanding Kenyan writer in exile, namely, Ngugi wa Thiong'o (1993).

throughout the Americas, that is, North, South and Central America and the Caribbean. In this way, Europe has contributed in no small measure to the unconscionable underdevelopment of Africa and her people (Rodney 1976). Or, perhaps putting it more accurately, Africa, through the enslavement of her people at home and abroad, has contributed substantially to the over-development of Europe.

Because of centuries of separation from the Motherland, and because of the random dispersal of Africans throughout the Americas, (slaves of the same family, clan and tribe were, for the most part, not allowed to live and work on the same plantation or estate—so as to minimize the possibility of successful slave revolts or of slaves strategising clandestinely to plot their escape) some of the cultural features of Africanness were invariably lost or, at least, seriously undermined. For instance, family patterns were disrupted although, in most cases, creative extended surrogate family arrangements did emerge. The sense of tribal or ethnic identity was lost. The mother tongues were spoken less and less as time progressed, albeit that a number of loan words and underlying syntactical structures can still be discerned in the manner in which the adopted European tongues of English, French, Spanish, Dutch and Portuguese are sometimes spoken, especially in their creolised forms (Wardhaugh 1992: 63–64, see also Asante 1990, Philips 1990, Lopes 1997, Da Silva 1984, de Granda 1991).

Further, African religious traditions were put at risk although, as some social anthropologists do not hesitate to point out, there are still extant examples of vibrant syncretic blends of things African and Christian. So much so that they and others are not always sure whether the phenomenon can best be described as the Africanization of Christianity or the Christianization of African religious consciousness (Mugambi 1989). This uncertainty surrounds, for example, the Shango cults and Spiritual Baptists in Trinidad and Grenada, Pocomania, Rastafarianism, Myalism and the Kumina cult in Jamaica, the Jumpers in the Bahamas, Voodooism in New Orleans (USA) and Haiti, Santeria in Cuba, Garifuna in Colombia, Winti in Suriname, and Candomble in Brazil (Bisnauth 1989, Chevannes 1994, Glazier 1983, Hood 1990, Yorke 1991, Leeuw 1992, Wooding 1972, Healy and Sybertz 1994). Residues of African religious tradition can also be detected in the cultural practices of naming children and those used to support and sustain various rites of passage (*rites de passage*). Belief in the continued existence of the soul-spirit of the deceased—at times taking the form of malevolent forces variously referred to as dup-pies, jumbies, zombies or orishas—has also persisted. These beliefs have justified the arcane exercises of witchcraft, such as the elabo-rately decorative masking of the face, colourful adorning of the body, and the *obeah* or "black magic" like use of concoctions either to cast a spell on someone or to ward off evil spirits from others. In addi-tion, the traditions regarding bush, folk or herbal medicine, the love of laughing, singing and dancing, the rhythmic use of communal work-songs, storytelling (Brer Ananse, Tortoise and Brer Rabbit espe-cially), the celebrative, expressive approach to worship (many sing, shout and clap for joy, at times using loud sounding percussive instru-ments of various kinds), and a generally buoyant and optimistic approach, to life in general, has all endured, albeit to varying degrees.[3]

The remarkable genius of our displaced and dispersed ancestors, was to adopt and then creatively adapt, mostly subconsciously, the slave masters' religion (Christianity in its Western garb). In other words, the oldest institution in the English-speaking Diaspora, the Black Church, had its birth in the determination of slaves to sur-vive in an exceedingly hostile environment. It is also true that, because of the sheer resilience, retentive power and profundity of African cultures themselves, the Black Church has always added both mean-ing and mystery to what it suggests about being an African in exile, feeling despised and "rejected." More so, than any other institution in the English-speaking Black community (Waliggo 1989, Paris 1985, 1994, Shreve 1983, Lampe 1997). The roots of the Black Church stem from the invisible institution of community fostered by condi-tions on the estates or plantations. Unknown to the slave-masters, some slaves (mainly those who worked in the fields) would steal away in the bush to worship. There, in song and dance, they would express

---

[3] As a boy who grew up in a Caribbean village (St. Kitts-Nevis), the author can relate experientially to much of what has just been listed as African retentions in the Diaspora. He recalls, for example, having to fetch special herbs from the bush for his late maternal grandfather so that he can create concoctions either for pur-poses of health and/or healing or for "fixing" an enemy. In addition, Christmas was celebrated with elaborate costuming and masking accompanied by singing, danc-ing and drumming in the streets—a dramatic acting out of a world view (*Weltanschauung*) influenced by a robust belief in the existence of the spirit of the departed and its power, for good or ill, to influence the living. The contemporary carnival extrava-ganza, whether it be in Trinidad and Tobago, Canada, the USA, Britain or Brazil, is part and parcel of this same religio-magical tradition. For an excellent discussion of the Africanness of the Caribbean personality, see Davis 1990 and Mulrain 1989.

their stubborn will to live—not as mere hewers of wood and drawers of water but as full human beings (Cone 1972, Spencer 1990, 1993).

Here to, the book of the Church, the Bible, has played its pivotal role in the identity-preservation of people who found themselves dispersed in distant places, having to live and labour under dehumanizing conditions through little or no fault of their own.[4] The most influential version of the Bible in the "Bible Story" for English-speaking Black in the Diaspora has been the King James Version, concerning which Peebles has this to say:

> The King James Version [1611], regardless of how much it neglected to denote about Africa (whether intentional or not) is all that the African slaves in the Diaspora, especially in the United States, had as a replica to the word they had once known in the indigenous languages through stories told to them around the village huts by their ancestors. A great number of slaves in the New World . . . knew too well already the teachings and stories of the Old Testament. . . . . Many slaves who learned to read and write did so by using the King James Version as a basic textbook. This held true even after the slaves were freed. Most Blacks who were not able to attend school, which was the majority of the black population, especially in the South (USA), learned to read by studying the words from the King James Version (Peebles 1993).

Although Blacks generally have never been able to find a resting place in the Diaspora, the English-speaking ones, at least, through their creative use of the Bible on the estates or plantations (the Church in "the bush") and then within the later-to-be established Black Church, have been able to develop and largely maintain some kind of home. They have done this by developing a hermeneutic, not only of suspicion, but one of liberation as well (Cone 1975). A hermeneutic which, for the most part, has enabled them to read the Bible historically, and like their counterparts in apartheid South Africa to "read" the Bible politically (Bauckham 1989, Mosala 1989, Mulonyora 1993). Additionally they have learned to approach the whole question of

---

[4] The protracted role that Africans themselves played in facilitating the Trans-Atlantic (and East African) slave trade has long been acknowledged, although this is sometimes done rather defensively. In terms of the Trans-Atlantic trade, for example, we are told that: "Until very late in the eighteenth century, virtually no white man had ever seen anything of the African interior. This was due not to their own preference but to a widespread, highly organized and successful determination on the part of the coastal tribes to keep them out. Except for the terminal points on the coast, the trade in slaves was for three centuries rigorously and exclusively controlled by the Blacks" (Elkins 1959: 95).

biblical history, theology, hermeneutics and translation from a distinctly Afrocentric perspective (Felder 1991, 1993, Yorke 1998).

The rest of this essay will be devoted to a more structured telling of this "Bible Story." Because of space and the pioneering nature of the piece, however, it will be more like a provisional probing of the subject. If for no other reason than this, that the literature on the African-American use of the Bible is now being actively generated, while that on the AfriCanadian and AfriCaribbean lags far behind. Not to mention Blacks in Britain who have just begun to tell their own story as well (Grant et al. 1990, Yorke 1991, Gerloff 1992). Further, this essay is limited, for the most part, to the Anglophone or English-speaking African Diaspora. Although a similar story can be told, perhaps, of those who had other non-African languages imposed on them, be they French, Spanish, Dutch, German, Portuguese, Danish (Hall 1987), Arabic, Hindi, Urdu or whatever. This, in my view, is an area in need of serious investigation. It would be mightily instructive to ascertain how those Africans in the Americas, Asia and elsewhere choose to express their Africanness, amidst their protracted exposure to non-Christian religious traditions, and then assess how the various sacred texts (where available) in those traditions were appropriated and applied to their situation (Harris 1971, 1982).

More out of convenience than due to any hard and fast categorical distinction, I have chosen to discuss briefly the uses of the Bible among my target group under two rubrics, namely, the literalist and quasi-magical use of the Bible, and its liberationist and socio-political use. An attempt will be made, in each case to relate such uses to some aspects of African Christianity by way of illustration. And in doing so, Mbiti's caveat becomes mine as well. He writes concerning the tremendous impact the Bible, especially in its vernacularised versions, is having on Africans as a whole and finds himself, like me, having to settle for mere illustrations of a vast and complex subject. He writes:

> The illustrations should be taken as generalizations about this otherwise complex phenomenon. They are intended to act as flashes of light illuminating small portions of the religious giant of Africa, [and her diaspora]. My sins of omission in this respect are bound to be many (Mbiti 1986: 20, see also Mojola 1993).

I recognise that there might be some readers who might feel less than comfortable (and perhaps, rightly so) about my unqualified reference to "African Christianity" as if it is clear that such "an animal" actually exists. The sheer size of the continent, the multiracial complexity of its demographics, the profusion of indigenous ethnic communities (over 3,000), a concomitant plethora of religio-cultural traditions, and the missiologically created denominational fragmentation of the Church in Africa has actually dissuaded some from speaking and writing in the singular (Nyaundi 1993). For some, it seems more defensible to pluralize, to speak (and write) about African Christian theologies and even moralities (Owino 1994, Nwatu 1994). If that is so, then, perhaps, it is equally defensible to speak and write about African Christianities as well.

This, however, is not necessary in an essay of this kind, meant primarily to show links between Africa as a whole and her Anglophone Diaspora, insofar as the use(s) of the Bible is (are) concerned. In addition, the case can be made that in spite of its diversity of expression, there is still a basic world view to which Black Africans subscribe. This is at least true for those in West Africa, which is the geographical and cultural root of the vast majority of those now constituting the Anglophone Diaspora.[5] Elkins, for example, writes:

> Indeed, there is a sufficient body of work available on the anthropology, history, and institutional life of West Africa to make it both possible and profitable to take up the "culture argument" on its merits. We would discover that it is in fact possible to make certain kinds of generalizations about African culture [and by extension: African reli-

----

[5] Most of the slaves coming from West Africa included Ibos, Temme, Wolof, Yoruba, Ashanti, Fanti, Fulani, Mandingo, Coromantins, Foulahs and others (Thompson 1987: 160).

Of course, it should also be pointed out that when it comes to tracing the roots of a particular individual in the Diaspora, it is not always certain that we should necessarily look to West Africa since both the West African and the East African slave trades converged at times (see Harris 1971). My experience (as one from the Diaspora) of now living and working in Africa is quite instructive. In Kenya, I am consistently mistaken to be a member of one of Kenya's tribes or ethnic communities (Luo) whereas when I first travelled to Nigeria, I was made out to be an Ibo. Interestingly enough, this latter classification was given to me in the Diaspora itself by Prof. B. Idowu of Nigeria when we first met at the University of Manitoba, Canada, at a conference of the International Association for the History of Religions (1980). In light of the convergence of the African slave trades, I should also mention that, like West Africa, East Africa is also sufficiently unified in world view to justify my writing in the singular when it comes to referring to African Christianity. The very existence of what has now become a reasonably successful ongoing series in African Christianity (sponsored by the East African Theological Symposium), going back to 1989, is positive proof that the use of such language in the singular is both possible and permissible.

gion, African Christian theology, morality and Christianity] (Elkins 1995: 92).

At times, there seems to be a fine line of demarcation between religion and superstition. This is particularly among those who feel the need to tap into any assumed preternatural powers available to them (or sometimes even denied them) as a way of compensating for feelings of powerlessness in this world. Feelings born of being despised and rejected, denied and denigrated. In other words, the psycho-social need to sustain one's sense of self at all cost usually precipitates the adoption and creative adaptation of whatever meaning-system or sacred canopy is available and considered useful at any given moment. This is especially if that meaning-system, sacred canopy or world view is associated with the privileged and the powerful and which is imposed on those not in a position to resist it entirely.

When religions, meaning-systems or world-views meet there is a dialectical exchange of some kind. Syncretism, though frowned upon and passionately denounced by not a few, is both unavoidable and useful in the identity-preservation of people bent on sustaining their sense of self. For example, some anthropologists, psychologists and sociologists of religion have now made us conscious to the fact that conversion (however defined) from one religion to the next is never a complete metamorphosis per se but an "incomplete" one at best. Invariably, elements of the old religion are incorporated into that of the new or, perhaps, the other way around, elements of the new are incorporated into that of the old. What Hurtado, the New Testament scholar, says about the Apostle Paul seems true of people as a whole. As far as Hurtado is concerned, Paul, on becoming a Christian, "did not renounce . . . the God of his (Jewish) ancestors" (Hurtado 1993: 284). And so it was, with our African ancestors who were involuntarily transplanted to the "New World" in the Caribbean and elsewhere. Bisnauth writes rather instructively:

> Despite the attitude of the plantocracy to prohibit African religious practices in the Caribbean and the formal legislation against such practices (e.g., *obeah* or witchcraft), the worship of African divinities survived. In Guyana, Komfo (i.e., Akomfo) dancing with its emphasis on spirit possession has had a long tradition. In Trinidad, the worship of Shango, Ogun, Eshu and other recognizably African "spirits" survived. In St. Domingue [Haiti], slaves worshipped Damballa, Legba, Shango and other gods of identifiably Dahomean origin. In both Trinidad and St. Domingue, the worship of African divinities was to combine with

that of the Roman Catholic Saints. . . . In Spanish Cuba, the Lucumi
Negroes (i.e., those from Nigeria and the Gulf of Guinea) worshipped
the recognizably Yoruba gods, Obatala, Chango (Shango), Eleggue
(Legba) and Oggun (Ogun). . . . Some features of Lucumi worship (also)
resembled those of the Akan worship of *obosom* (Bisnauth 1989: 87,
see also Hood 1990, Simpson 1976, Karenga 1982: 160–197, Ankrah
1998: 4, Jennings 1995: 5).

For comparative purposes, mention should also be made here of
Sierra Leone. In 1787, it was established as a colony by "British
philanthropists and enlightened men of letters and business to atone
for the wrongs which they believed Europeans had done to Africans
by subjecting them to centuries of slave labour" (Wyse 1989: 1,
Peterson 1969). Those Liberated Africans, as they are called, who
were returned from the Diaspora and who constituted the first settlers in Sierra Leone, were mostly from London, Nova Scotia (Canada)
and Jamaica (the Maroons). This group was a fairly good cross-
sectional representation of Blacks in the English-speaking Diaspora
as a whole, in that it pointed to Europe (London), the Caribbean
(Jamaica) and North America at large (since a sizeable percentage
of Canadian Blacks who settled in Nova Scotia trace their roots to
the USA, going back either to the war of American Independence
(1770's) or to the more extended period of the so-called Underground
Railroad). In describing this group of Liberated Africans, Wyse, for
example, has this to say:

> The Black poor, the Nova Scotians and the Maroons formed the
> Western foundations of the (Sierra Leone) society, which were reflected
> in their Christianity, education, politics, ideals and aspirations, civic
> pride and high sense of individualism, their mode of dress, their artic-
> ulateness and their language. . . . But even among these "Western"
> Africans there were a few cultural survivals that recalled from some
> distant past their African roots. One identifiable survival of this kind
> was the "talla" dance of the Maroons—which became the "goombay"
> of their Krio descendants. It is a lively and vivacious dance with fas-
> cinating chorcography. . . . An intuitive ability to effect a happy mar-
> riage between European and African cultures characterises Krio culture.
> Nothing epitomises this more completely than their customs, rites and
> language. The Krio, like most people, believe in a supreme being and
> an afterlife, although this belief has perhaps been modified by their
> adoption of Christianity and other facets of Western civilization. For
> instance, unlike the Yoruba, they do not have a word for the almighty
> (sometimes the simple phrase "Papa God" suffices), although some are
> aware of deities such as Olorun and Ogun (gods in the Yoruba pan-
> theon). They believe in the supernatural, and recognise the powers of

witches, magicians, traditional healers, charms, the babalawo (diviner) and the moriman (Wyse 1989: 1,10, Kirwen 1987).

It is this resilience of African cultures that best explains, perhaps, what I choose to refer to as the literalist and quasi-magical approach to, and use of, the Bible among Anglophone Africans in the Diaspora— the Bible as icon, as it were. One such illustration is that of the Shango (or Spiritual) Baptists of Trinidad who now constitute an international religious movement mostly throughout the Anglophone Diaspora. Glazier has this to say after doing extensive field research among them:

> The Bible is associated strongly with God the Father. The Bible is especially valued for the power and wisdom contained therein. It is considered desirable among members of the faith (Shangoism) to have many Bibles in many languages. Prominent leaders (and those who would be prominent) possess extensive Bible collections including, whenever possible, volumes in Greek and Hebrew. Those are said to be useful in divining ("proving") and curing. None of my informants had any knowledge or Greek of Hebrew, in fact, several older informants, including one with over fifty Bibles in his collection, are unable to read. Illiterate Baptists attempt to disguise their inability to read by committing long passages of the King James Version to memory. . . . Bible passages must be read and reread many times before the true meaning becomes apparent. Even after many hours of careful scrutiny, the meaning of a verse may remain obscure, and Baptists must call upon the Holy Ghost for assistance in interpreting the text (Glazier 1983: 27,48).

Glazier further describes their liturgical ritual as follows:

> Manifestations of the Holy Ghost are followed almost immediately by periods of illumination and contemplation. This part of the service, consisting of additional scripture readings and short homilies by various members of the congregation, is devoted to the Word of God. During periods of illumination, Biblical passages from the New Testament, especially the Gospel of John and the Books of Revelation [sic], and the Books of Daniel, Psalms, and Ezekiel from the Old Testament are favoured. . . . Teachings consist of Bible readings, prayers, and a type of divination known as "proving." In "proving," candidates are asked to close their eyes, open the Bible, and pick a random verse. Verses thus chosen are said to reveal a candidate's readiness for baptism (Glazier 1983: 46).[6]

---

[6] Plato may have been right after all. For him "Magic is no other than the worship of the gods" (Kee 1986: 97).

Speaking of Black Spiritual Churches within the context of the United States, Burkett correctly points out that such Churches are among the most neglected movements in the African-American religious experience, and that (like the Shango Baptists of Trinidad), they are characterized by a highly syncretic nature and a "strong emphasis on various magico-religious rituals and esoteric knowledge that are intended to provide power over the here and now" (Burkett 1984: 9). Drawing on elements from American Spiritualism, Black Protestantism, Catholicism, New Thought, Black Islam, Black Judaism, Voodoo (or hoodoo, a more diluted form), and some other African religious traditions, these Spiritual Churches carry such colourful names as the Temple of Israel, St. Theresa's Holiness Science Church, the Alpha and Omega Church, the Truth of Life Foundation, and the Universal Ancient Ethiopian Spiritual Church of Christ (Burkett 1984: 9, Baer 1984, Idowu 1937: 207, Adegbola 1983). Like the Shango Baptists of Trinidad, such Spiritual Churches also surround the Bible with an ultra-holy aura, bordering on bibliolatry or worship of the Bible itself. The "Sacred Book" is invested with magical or charm-like qualities by such Churches.

Such Churches are quite similar to what Mbiti refers to as one of the strands in African Christianity, namely, the African Indigenous, Independent or Instituted Churches, in so far as their approach to the Bible is concerned (Mbiti 1986: 14–20). Mbiti singles out the Aladura Church of Nigeria as worthy of special mention. It is an indigenous, independent or instituted Church, dating back to 1930, which "desires to be a biblical Church and holds the (whole) Bible in great reverence"—a reverence that, at times, generates a quasi-magical or talisman-like approach to it (Mbiti 1986: 35). Gaiya has also shown that the Aladura Churches of Nigeria are essentially no different in their use of, and approach to, the Bible than that of an offshoot of the Cherubim and Seraphim Church, namely, the El-Messiah Independent Churches in West Africa (Gaiya 1991, Owanikin 1987, Gates 1980: 73). Turner has, after analysing 8,000 sermons preached in the Aladura Churches, concluded that their use of, and approaches to, the Bible is not only "remarkably similar, to that found in independent Churches in Zambia and in parts of South Africa" (Turner 1965: 79, see also Gifford 1992: 80–102), but "more representative of Africa as a whole than might be expected" (Turner 1965: 23).

Another Independent Church that one can single out in closing this section is that of the Brotherhood of the Cross and Star which also had its genesis in Nigeria but has now evolved into a bona fide international religious movement. Mbon, for example, informs us that when it comes to their use of the Bible, they place great stress on the symbol-riddled and mysterious-sounding Book of Revelation in the New Testament (Mbon 1992: 76, see also Burney 1988), not unlike that of the Rastafarians of Jamaica (Hood 1990: 91). Rasta-farianism, made globally popular by its strong African rhythm in the form of reggae music, was established in Jamaica largely under the influence of the religious teachings of Marcus Mosiah Garvey, the Pan-Africanist and founder of the United Negro Improvement Association.

When it comes to the liberationist and socio-political use of the Bible in the Anglophone Diaspora, there is a trajectory that runs from the time of the slaves to that of some contemporary Black Biblical scholars—mostly African-American. The simple but beautiful Negro Spirituals, sung the world over and, unfortunately, sometimes rendered unappealing by what appears to be a clumsy attempt at imitating Western "classical" musical styles and forms, had their genesis in the hearts and minds of our enslaved ancestors, particu-larly in the United States (Felder 1993: 1841). Although the vast majority of slaves could not read the Bible for themselves, they were always able to put its liberating themes to a *Capella* music with great spontaneity and skill.

The orality of their African background and the slave-masters' cal-culated policy of not teaching them to read the Bible for fear of being subverted themselves, kept the slaves "illiterate." But their African tradition of being able to burst into song (and dance) extemporane-ously, stood them in good stead, enabling them to transform sermon into song. The slaves were able to extract, from their white minis-ters' sermons (calling for piety and passivity on their part), those ele-ments which resonated with their unshakeable commitment to be free. One such "passive" sermon is that of the Right Reverend William Mead, Bishop of the Diocese of Virginia (USA). It was a sermon prepared for the slave-leaders to read and teach their slaves. An extract reads as follows:

> Some He (the Almighty God) hath made masters and mistresses for taking care of their children and others that belong to them. . . . Some He hath made servants and slaves, to assist and work for their mas-ters and mistresses, that provide for them, and others He hath made ministers and teachers to instruct the rest, to show them what they ought to do, and to put them in mind of their several duties. Almighty

God has been pleased to make you slaves here, and to give you nothing but labour and poverty in this world, which you are obliged to submit to, as it is His will that it should be so. Your bodies, you know, are not your own, they are at the disposal of those you belong to (Felder 1993: 9).

Drew, writing of slaves in Canada, also comments as follows:

What knowledge the slaves have of the Scriptures is obtained by the ear, for they are generally unable to read . . . [and] it must be admitted that there is a strong temptation on the part of the masters to use the Scriptures mainly as an auxiliary to the overseer (Drew 1856: 9).

One creative scheme the slaves utilized to transform a passive sermon into a socio-political song was to employ the *double entendre* (double meaning) technique. They would sing, ostensibly about heaven and its unbroken bliss, when what they really had in mind was their strategy to escape from bondage in this life. This was especially true of escape songs associated with the Underground Railroad—a veiled reference to a clandestine and creative system of escape in which slaves in the Southern United States were able to make their way not only to the "freer" Northern States, but as far North as Canada itself (Walker 1976, Holloway 1976, Chatfield 1998). For example, the Negro Spiritual, "O Canaan," refers not only to the heavenly Canaan of joy and justice but also to Canada. This *double entendre* strategy was also applicable to "Get on Board Lil' Chilren," and several others (Yorke 1987: 8, see also Thompson 1987: 255–300). What the slave-masters and their ministers thought they heard in these songs was the slaves' opium-like appropriation of sermons meant to keep them happy with, and accepting of, their lowly state in life. What the unsuspecting authorities did not realize was that their enslaved labourers were taking the remnants of their "traditional [African] religious structures and meshing them together with their interpretation of the Bible" (Hopkins 1991: 7).

This observation is entirely consonant with Mugambi's. According to him:

Both in Africa and in the African diaspora across the Atlantic, Christianity and the African religious heritage have contributed positively to the resistance against slavery, colonial domination, and the denial of civil rights (Mugambi 1989: 52).

In terms of other creative appropriations of the Bible, mention must be made of another coded use as well. For example, the following story is told of Rev. W. Monroe who was Pastor of the Black First Baptist Church in Detroit, Michigan (USA), just South of the Canadian border. One evening, in 1839, he received the following message from one of his members (an escaped slave): "Rev., tomorrow night at our 8:00 o'clock prayer meeting, let's read Exodus Chapter 10 and verse 8." Immediately, Rev. Monroe knew exactly what that meant. He knew that in the language of the Underground Railroad or escape system, this request really meant the following: "Tomorrow night" meant Conductor #2, "Exodus" meant the escape or exodus of some more slaves was in progress, "Chapter 10" meant there were 10 escapees in all, and "verse 8" meant that 8 were men and the rest, women.

The historic Black Church in the Americas (be it in the USA, Canada or the Caribbean) is an heir to a tradition of creative struggle rooted and grounded in the slavocracy. The Black Church evolved, for the most part, because of the self-sacrificing efforts and mulish resistance of ex-slaves like Nat Turner, Richard Allen and Sojourner Truth in the United States, and David George and Richard Preston in Canada. And it matters not which Black Church it is, all the Black Churches are not only direct descendants of slavery but, more immediately, they are self-assertive responses to institutionalized racism. Most of them, like a number of the African Independent, Initiated or Instituted Churches, which evolved from the Mission Churches themselves, came into being as a result of the efforts of one charismatic individual or another who decided to "pull out" of the White-established and controlled Churches in the Diaspora.

In the Black Churches, the Bible is generally regarded as an instrument capable of facilitating psychological and cultural liberation,[7] and one which provides the justification for a hermeneutic of suspicion when it comes to dealing with the privileged and the powerful in society. Especially, those whose privilege and power provide them with an ideological advantage in interpreting and applying Scripture.

---

[7] In terms of the Diaspora Black's deep love for the Bible, perceived as an instrument of liberation, it is quite interesting to know that on Sept. 7, 1864, 519 Baltimore Blacks pooled their meagre resources to purchase a pulpit-size Bible costing $580.75 and then had 4 of them present it on their behalf to President Abraham Lincoln, the "abolitionist" President, at the White House. For an account of that ceremony, see Fishel, *et al.* 1967: 250f.

This "Bible Story," as it relates to the Black Churches, will be less than complete, however, if mention is not made also of the tendency, at times, for some contemporary Black Churches to adopt a counterproductive form of Pentecostal fundamentalism such as would render them untrue to their mission. It is a naive brand of fundamentalism that borders on escapism and anti-intellectualism—precisely that form of fundamentalism which Martin Luther King, for example, caricatured and which we find critiqued in *New Dimensions in African Christianity*, edited by Paul Gifford. In King's sermon, "The Strength to Love," we read:

> Soft-mindedness often invades religion. . . . The historical-philological criticism of the Bible is considered by the soft-minded as blasphemous, and reason is often looked upon as the exercise of a corrupt faculty. Soft-minded persons have revised the beatitudes to read, "Blessed are the pure in ignorance for they shall see God" (Washington 1986: 493, see also McClain 1993).

In addition, uncritical and self-injurious appropriation of the Bible also seems to characterize a number of Blacks in the Diaspora who choose for reasons that are commendable to remain members of predominantly white Churches. Some of these individuals do not really interpret the Bible *per se*, rather, it is interpreted for them. This usually creates a situation where, for example, some Black Anglicans, especially in a Caribbean country like Anglophile Barbados, become more Anglican than the British themselves—not unlike what is also true of some African Christians who belong to Mission Churches. However, it has long been recognised that Blacks (clergy or laity) emigrating to Britain from Africa and the Caribbean are usually in for a rude awakening when they try to fellowship as equals with their white British counterparts—be they Anglican, Roman Catholic or Protestant. In terms of Blacks in the Anglican Church, for example, we are told that:

> The Black presence in the Church of England is in rapid decline. After many words, often empty, the institutional structures of the Church have in reality turned their back upon our presence, despite the fact that the majority of the Anglican communion worldwide is Black (Moore 1990: 18).[8]

---

[8] I find it quite instructive, in light of Moore's observation in Britain, that commendable ecumenical attempts are now being made to have a number of the his-

It is clear that this complaint is not coming from a lone voice "crying in the wilderness," nor is it limited to the Anglican Church in Britain. Waruta makes a similar observation in describing and critiquing one of the types or strands of African Christianity. He too complains that, generally, "the Western Church refuses to accept African Christians as equal partners in truth but continues to regard them as mere extensions of themselves" (Waruta 1990: 40).

In terms of the trajectory to which I referred earlier (regarding the liberationist and socio-political use of the Bible), brief mention should also be made of two other developments relevant to the telling of our "Bible Story," and they are: the rise of Black Theology in the USA and the relatively recent stress on the need for an Afro-centric approach to, and use of, the Bible. If the name of James Cone is generally associated with the first development, then that of Cain Hope Felder should at least be associated with the second (see above). Of the two developments, the first, perhaps, is more widely known, going back, as it does, to the civil rights decade of the 1960's. In 1969, for example, Cone formally and forcefully initiated the dialogue and debate throughout the Anglophone Diaspora, influencing Africa itself (especially South Africa)[9] with the publication of his first book, *Black Theology and Black Power*. He continues to influence and inspire Blacks (and now others) throughout the world, as seen in the enthusiastic endorsement given to one of his more recent books, one about Martin Luther King, Jr., and Malcolm X (Cone 1992). Of course, Cone is not alone in his articulation of a Black Theology of Liberation. There is now a whole chorus of voices including a number of those who have studied under him—women and men.

Foundational to Black Theology is the defensible conviction that the Bible, properly translated and interpreted, is meant to be an instrument of liberation from those sins and systems that keep Blacks

toric Black Churches in America (e.g., the A.M.E., A.M.E.Z., and the C.M.E.) join with some of the traditionally non-Black Churches such as the Presbyterian Church (USA), plus a number of other Protestant and Anglican or Episcopalian Churches. My main concern with this positive step is that the historic Black Churches in America might no longer be able to use the Bible as prophetically as is expected of them. We'll just have to wait and see. For a report on these ongoing ecumenical developments, see *Journal of Ecumenical Studies* 30 (1993): 306.

[9] Alan Boesak, living through what was then an apartheid South Africa, for example, actually based and built his doctoral dissertation on issues arising out of Cone's first and subsequent books. Boesak's dissertation was later published as Boesak 1977.

down. Originally, this was seen mainly to be the racist pathology in America but subsequent dialogue and debate have lengthened the agenda to include both sexism and capitalism, among others. In terms of sexism, for example, one of Cone's own students is generally considered to be a pioneer when it comes to a Womanist or a Black woman's Theology of Liberation. She is Jacqueline Grant whose doctoral dissertation was later published as: *White Women's Christ and Black Women's Jesus: Feminist Christology and Womanist Response* (Grant 1989). In terms of the whole hermeneutical enterprise, Peters' observation is both perceptive and pertinent. For him:

> Most of the biblical discussions of feminists and African-American groups seem ... to be grounded in the desire to rearrange the structures of power within the scholarly or believing community. There is a consensus within those discussions, that what has passed, and is passing, for dispassionate, objective, scholarly biblical study, has been, and continues to be in fact, only a carefully disguised foregrounding of the concerns of one particular population group—white males from European-American culture. Thus, the efforts of African-Americans and feminists seem generally to be corrective, retributive, or compensatory in nature. But such efforts to "level the playing field" reveal only that both traditional and the more recent interpreters are in agreement on one thing: the Bible is a powerful source of authority to be manipulated to one's own ends (Peters 1993: 148, see also Yorke 1995).[10]

As for Afrocentricity, a term supposedly coined by Molefi Kete Asante of Temple University, Philadelphia (USA) (Felder 1993: 188), space allows only an exceedingly succinct statement in terms of what it is really all about. Basically, it is an attempt to reread Scripture but from a premeditated Afrocentric perspective and, in doing so, to break the hermeneutical hegemony and ideological stranglehold that white Western biblical scholars have long enjoyed in relation to the Bible. Early attempts so far have sought to put back Africa and Blacks in the Bible by amplifying the voice of those Blacks who are already there and by raising their profile and visibility. One example includes Zephaniah, the prophet, who, being the son of Cushi

---

[10] The hermeneutical discussion (and debate) is rendered all the more complicated by Silva's honest admission. He writes: "It is also clear ... that most of us find it very difficult to recognize, much less shed, our modern "eurocentric" presuppositions: Indeed, our tendency is to filter any new knowledge about ancient culture through the spectacles of our own assumptions" (Silva 1984: 43).

(Zephaniah 1:1), must have been Black (Yorke 1998, Clark and Hatton 1989: 144).

Another example is that of Jesus and his earthly family. The mere fact that, according to the Matthean tradition, the Holy Family had to become refugees in Egypt, Africa (Matthew 2:7), to escape King Herod's murderous plot and ploy is instructive. Not only is it seen as a clear fulfilment of Hosea's prophecy that "out of Egypt (Africa) have I called my Son," but it also suggests, for Felder, that the Holy Family (including Jesus) was more chocolate-brown than Caucasian in complexion since a Caucasian family trying to hide in Black Africa would be most unlikely (Felder 1993: 188). Other Afrocentric readings of Scripture strongly suggest, for some, that the Garden of Eden was located, not on Obadiah, the name given to the dry, hilly place I was shown some time ago in Israel while on an archaeological dig and tour, but in Africa since Genesis 2:8–14, for example, indicates that two of the rivers of Eden, the Pishon and the Gihon, were closely associated with Cush or ancient Ethiopia. In the opinion of Albright, these two rivers (usually regarded as unknown in most versions and study Bibles) most likely refer to the White and Blue Nile respectively. I am told, for instance, that in Ge'ez, or ancient Ethiopic, the lexical term for the Nile is Gihon.[11]

That the Bible has played (and continues to play) a pivotal role in the identity preservation of a displaced, dispersed, despised and dispossessed people such as our enslaved ancestors were and their diasporic descendants are, has been, I think, amply but inexhaustibly demonstrated by the foregoing discussion. Although our discussion was focussed primarily on the Anglophone Diaspora and the creative adoption and adaptation of the Bible therein, there is no reason to discount the possibility that those of our enslaved ancestors who were exposed to other European (and, therefore, "Bible") languages were any less creative and resourceful in their preservation of a robust African sense of self as well. In terms of the "Bible Story" within the Anglophone tradition itself, mention was made of two basic uses of the Bible, namely, the literalist and quasi-magical and the liberationist and socio-political. The first use served (and serves) primarily a religio-cultural purpose in that it helped (and helps) to foster a Black

---

[11] According to Dr. Mikre-Selassie, an Ethiopian Translation Consultant with the United Bible Societies (in conversations both in Mexico and Ethiopia). Also see Felder 1993: xiv, Adamo 1992, Holter 1997).

sense of identity within a religiously pluralistic milieu, and the second was (and still is) helpful in that it served (and serves) primarily
a psycho-social-cum-political purpose. It helped (and helps) to foster
a Black sense of identity within a hostile environment. If the first
use is analogous to a theology of inculturation (and reconstruction)
that is now being articulated by a number of African Christian theologians, then that of the second points mainly to a theology of liberation—one which, historically, has been associated mostly with
Christian theologians in South Africa.

Along the way, reference was also made, *en passant*, to a much
thinner tradition (mainly contemporary) in which the Bible tends to
be approached in a rather fundamentalistic way by which is meant
an attitude which borders on being anti-intellectual and eschatolog-
ically escapist in orientation. Further, there are those who choose to
remain in the White-established Churches but who, unlike others,
refuse to have the Bible simply interpreted for them. They refuse to
submit passively to the hermeneutical strategies employed by those
perceived to be the powerful and the privileged within those Churches.
Instead, attempts are sometimes made to work with a hermeneutics
of suspicion and liberation from within with the hope that creative
ways will be found to bring about reconciliation and fellowship especially between Black Christians and White Christians—since African
Christians in the Diaspora have always felt that unity (and not dis-
unity) in the human community is what God in Christ not only
desires but deserves as well.

One illustration of such a reconciling attempt in Britain, for example, is that of the Centre for Black and White Christian Partnership
in Birmingham, England, which Roswith Gerloff, a German, and
others helped to establish a few years ago and which is sponsored
jointly by the Council of Churches for Britain and Ireland, the Selly
Oak Colleges, and the University of Birmingham. The name of
Patrick Kalilombe, former Roman Catholic Bishop of Malawi, is also
associated with the Centre as one of its former Executive Directors.

An essay of this sort will be less than complete if mention is not
made, in closing, of a few other "uses" of the Bible which are relatively common in, at least, the Anglophone diaspora in the USA,
namely: personal and daily Bible study, the "Bible Drill" in which
contestants try to find the most Bible verses in as short a time as
possible, "Bible boxing" in which a contestant tries to recite from
memory more Bible verses than his/her competitor, family devotions

in which favourite Bible verses always feature prominently, and the Bible verse competition among rural preachers, which often occurs when a group of local preachers, usually on Saturday mornings, "would gather at the barber shop, sit around the fire and determine who would be the Scripture buff for the day" (Felder 1993). All of this is illustrative of the fact that for Africans in the Diaspora the Bible is as near and dear to them as it is for their counterparts at home (Felder 1993: 1867).[12]

BIBLIOGRAPHY

Adamo, D.T. "Ancient Africa and Genesis 2:10–14," *The Journal of Religious Thought* 49 (1992): 33–43.

Adegbola, E.A. Ade Ed., *Traditional Religion in West Africa*. Nairobi: Uzima Press, 1983.

Ankrah, K.E. *Development and the Church of Uganda: Mission, Myths and Metaphor*. Nairobi: Acton Publishers, 1998.

Asante, M.K. "African Elements in African-American English." In Joseph Holloway Ed. *Africanisms in American Culture*. Bloomington: Indiana University Press, 1990: 19–33.

Awino, J.O. "Towards and Analytical African Theology: The Luo Concept of God as a Case in Point," *African Ecclesial Review* 36 (1994): 171–180.

Bacr, Hans A. *The Black Spiritual Movement: A Religious Response to Racism*. Knoxville, University of Tennessee Press, 1984.

Bauckham, Richard. *The Bible in Politics: How to Read the Bible Politically*. Louisville, Westminster/John Knox Press, 1989.

Bisnauth, Dale. *History of Religions in the Caribbean*. Kingston: Kingston Publishers Ltd., 1989.

Boesak, A. *Farewell to Innocence: A Socio-Ethical Study on Black Theology and Power*. Maryknoll: Orbis, 1977.

Burkett, Randall, K. Ed., *Newsletter of the Afro-American Religious History Group* of the American Academy of Religion, 9 (1984): 9.

Burney, R. *The Book of Revelation*, in *The African Bible Commentaries*. Ibadan: Daystar Press, 1988.

Chatfield, Adrian. "African Independency in the Caribbean: The Case of the Spiritual Baptists," *Missionalia* 26 (1998): 94–115.

Chevannes, Barry. *Rastafari: Roots and Ideology*. Syracuse, New York: Syracuse University Press, 1994.

Clark, D.J. and H.A. Hatton, *A Handbook on The Books of Nahum, Habakkuk and Zephaniah* New York: United Bible Societies, 1989.

Cone, James. *A Black Theology of Liberation*. Philadelphia: J.B. Lippincott & Co., 1975.

[12] Based on a national survey, 101 Bible verses emerged as favourites among African-Americans. The summary is as follows: (1) Old Testament—48 verses with 30 coming from the Psalms. The rest are drawn from Genesis, Job, Song of Solomon, Ecclesiastes, Proverbs and Isaiah, (2) New Testament—53 verses with 16 coming from the Pauline epistles. The rest come from the 4 Gospels, 1 Peter, James, 1 John, Hebrews and Revelation. For the specific verses see Felder 1993: 1867–1875.

————. *The Spirituals and the Blues: An Interpretation.* New York: Seabury Press, 1972.

Cone, J. *Martin and Malcolm and America: A Dream or a Nightmare.* Maryknoll: Orbis, 1992.

Da Silva, Baltasar L. *O Dialicto Crioulo de Cabo Verde.* Lisboa: Imprensa Nacional, 1984.

Davis, K. *Emancipation Still Comin': Explorations in Caribbean Emancipatory Theology.* Maryknoll: Orbis, 1990.

de Granda, Germán. *El Espanol en Tres Mundos: Retenciones y Contactos Linguísticos y en America Africa* Salamanca: Universidad de Valladolid, 1991.

Saunders, A.C. de C.M. *História Social dos Escravos e Libertos Negros em Portugal* 1441–1555. Lisboa: Imprensa Nacional, 1982.

Drew, Benjamin. *The Narratives of Fugitive Slaves in Canada.* Boston: John P. Jewett and Company, 1856.

Dubois, W.E.B. *The Souls of Black Folk* The Three Negro Classics Series. New York: Avon Books, 1965.

Elkins, Stanley M. *Slavery: A Problem in American Institutional and Intellectual Life.* Chicago: University of Chicago Press, 1959.

Felder, Cain H. Ed. *Stony the Road We Trod: African-American Biblical Interpretation.* Minneapolis: Fortress Press, 1991.

————. "Cultural Ideology, Afrocentrism and Biblical Interpretation." In Eds James Cone et al. *Black Theology: A Documentary History,* Volume Two, 1980–1992. Maryknoll: Orbis Books, 1993: 184–195.

Fishel, Jr., Leslie, H. et al. *The Negro American: A Documentary History* Glenview: Scott, Foresman and Co., 1967.

Gaiya, M.A.B. "The Bible in Aladura Churches." *African Journal of Biblical Studies* 6 (1991): 105–112.

Gates, Brian Ed. *Afro-Caribbean Religions.* London, England: Ward Lock Educational, 1980.

Gerloff, Roswith I.H. *A Plea for British Black Theologies: The Black Church Movement in Britain in its Transatlantic Cultural and Theological Interaction.* Frankfurt am Main: Peter Lang, 1992.

Gifford, Paul Ed., *New Dimensions in African Christianity.* Nairobi: All Africa Conference of Churches, 1992.

Glazier, Stephen D. *Marchin' the Pilgrims Home: Leadership and Decision-making in an Afro-Caribbean Faith.* London: Greenwood Press, 1983.

Grant, Paul et al. Eds *A Time to Speak: Perspectives of Black Christians in Britain.* London: Council of Churches for Britain and Ireland, 1990.

Grant, J. *White Women's Christ and Black Woman's Jesus: Feminist Christology and Womanist Response.* Atlanta: Scholars Press, 1989.

Hall, N.A.T. *Education in the Caribbean: Historical Perspectives,* Ed. R.H. King. Kingston: University of the West Indies, 1987: 1–45.

Harris, Joseph E. *The African Presence in Asia: Consequences of the East African Slave Trade.* Evanston: Northwestern University Press, 1971.

————. "A Comparative Approach to the Study of the African Diaspora," In Ed. J.E. Harris *Global Dimensions of the African Diaspora,* Washington, D.C.: Howard University Press, 1982: 112–124

Healy, J. and Sybertz, D. *Towards an African Narrative Theology* Nairobi: St. Paul Publications, 1994.

Holloway, J.E. "The Origins of African-American Culture," In Eds M.L. Kilson, et. al. *The African Diaspora: Interpretive Essays.* Cambridge: Harvard University Press, 1976: 1–19.

Holter, K. "Should the Old Testament 'Cush' be rendered 'Africa'"? *The Bible Translator* 48 (1997): 331–336.

Hood, Robert E. *Must God Remain Greek?: Afro-Cultures and God-Talk.* Minneapolis, Minnesota: Fortress Press, 1990.

Hopkins, D. et al. *Cut Loose Your Stammering Tongue: Black Theology in the Slave Narratives.* Maryknoll: Orbis, 1991.

Hurtado, L.W. "Convert, Apostate or Apostle to the Nations: The "Conversion" of Paul in recent Scholarship," *Studies in Religion/Sciences Religieuses* 22 (1993): 284.

Idowu, E.B. *African Traditional Religion: A Definition.* London Press, 1973.

James, William C. "Dimorphs and Cobblers: Ways of Being Religious in Canada," *Studies in Religion/Sciences Religieuses* 28 (1999): 275–291.

Jennings, S.C.A. "Sorting Out Spirituality in Jamaica: Pluralism and Particularities in Caribbean Theological Reality," *Caribbean Journal of Religious Studies* 15 1994: 5.

Karenga, M. *Introduction to Black Studies* Los Angeles: Kawaida Publications, 1982: 160–197.

Kee, H.C. *Medicine, Miracle and Magic in New Testament Times.* Cambridge: Cambridge University Press, 1986.

Kilson, M.L. et al. Eds *The African Diaspora: Interpretive Essays.* Cambridge: Harvard University Press, 1976.

Kirwen, M. *The Missionary and the Diviner.* Maryknoll, New York: Orbis Books, 1987.

Lampe, A. Ed. *Christianity in the Caribbean: Essays on Church History.* Kingston, Jamaica: The Press/University of the West Indies, 1997.

Leeuw, Tom. Review of Robert E. Hood *Must God Remain Greek?: Afro-Cultures and God-Talk,* in *Journal of Theology for Southern Africa* 8 (1992): 22.

Lincoln, C. Eric et al. *The Black Church in African-American Experience.* Durham: Duke University Press, 1994.

Lopes, Armando J. *Política Linguística: Princípios e Problemas* Maputo: Universidade Eduardo Mondlane, 1997.

Mbiti, John S. *African Religions and Philosophy,* Second Edition. Oxford: Heinemann, 1989.

———. *Bible and Theology in African Christianity.* Nairobi: Oxford University Press, 1986.

Mbon, F.M. *Brotherhood of the Cross and Star: A New Religious Movement in Nigeria.* Frankfurt am Main: Peter Lang, 1992.

McClain, W.B. "African-American Preaching and the Bible: Biblical Authority or Biblical Literalism," *Journal of Religious Thought* 49 (1993): 72–80.

Mojola, A.O. "Vernacularization and the African Independent Churches Cross-cultural Encounters: Some Preliminary Observations From Close Quarters," *Africa Theological Journal* 22 1993: 130–146.

Moore, D. "Through a Black Lens: Telling our History and Understanding its Significance," In *A Time to Speak: Perspectives of Black Christians in Britain.* Birmingham: Community and Race Relations Unit/Evangelical Christians for Racial Justice, 1990, 17–21.

Mosala, I.J. *Biblical Hermeneutics and Black Theology in South Africa.* Grand Rapids: Eerdmans Publishing Co., 1989.

Mugambi, J.N.K. *African Heritage and Contemporary Christianity* Nairobi: Longman, 1989: 1–11.

———. *African Christian Theology: An Introduction.* Nairobi: Heinemann.

Mukonyora, I. et al. Eds *"Re-writing" the Bible: The Real Issues.* Gweru: Mambo Press, 1993.

Mulrain, G. "African Cosmology and Caribbean Religion," *Caribbean Journal of Religious Studies* 10 (1989): 8–9.

———. "The Use of the Senses of Worship," *Caribbean Journal of Religious Studies* 17 (1996): 32–38.

Ngugi wa Thiong'o, *Moving the Centre: The Struggle for Cultural Freedoms.* Nairobi: East African Educational Publishers, 1993.

Nwatu, F. "Colonial Christianity in Post-Colonial Africa?" *The Ecumenical Review* 1994: 352–360.

Nyaundi, Nehemiah M. *Religion and Social Change: A Sociological Study of Seventh-Day Adventism in Kenya.* Lund: Lund University Press, 1993.

Owanikin, R.M. "Colossians 2:18: A Challenge to some Doctrines of Certain Aladura Churches in Nigeria." *African Journal of Biblical Studies* 2 (1987): 89–96.

Paris, Peter J. *The Spirituality of African Peoples: The Search for a Common Moral Discourse.* Philadelphia: Fortress Press, 1994.

———. *The Social Teaching of the Black Churches.* Philadelphia: Fortress Press, 1985.

Peebles, John W. "Preface," In Ed. C.H. Felder *The Original African Heritage Study Bible.* King James Version, Nashville: The James C. Winston Publishing Co., 1993.

Peters, M.K.H. "Response to K.D. Sakenfeld," In Ed. Howard C. Kee. *The Bible in the Twenty-First Century,* New York: American Bible Society, 1993.

Peterson, John. *Province of Freedom: A History of Sierra Leone 1787–1870.* London: Faber and Faber, 1969.

Philips, John E. "The African Heritage of White America," In Ed. Joseph Holloway *Africanisms in American Culture.* Bloomington, Indiana: Indiana University Press, 1990: 225–239.

Roach, E.M. "February" In Ed. John Figueroa *Caribbean Voices: An Anthology of West Indian Poetry, Volume 1: Dreams and Visions,* London: Evans Brothers Ltd., 1966, 21–22.

Rodney, W. *How Europe Underdeveloped Africa.* Dar es Salaam: Tanzania Publishing House, 1976.

Shreve, Dorothy Shadd. *The AfriCanadian Church: A Stabilizer.* Ontario, Canada: Paideia, 1983.

Silva, Moises. "Recent Developments in New Testament Hermeneutics," In Eds R. Hodgson et al. *From One Medium to Another: Basic Issues for Communicating the Scriptures in New Media.* New York/Kansas City: American Society/Sheed and Ward.

Simpson, G.E. "Religions in the Caribbean," in Eds M.L. Kilson, et al. *The African Diaspora: Interpretive Essays.* Cambridge, MA: Harvard University Press, 1976: 280–311.

Spencer, J. *Sing a New Song: Liberating Black Hymnody.* Minneapolis, Minnesota: Fortress Press, 1993.

———. *Protest and Praise: Sacred Music of Black Religion.* Minneapolis: Fortress Press, 1990.

Thomas, Linda E. "South African Independent Churches, Syncretism, and Black Theology," *The Journal of Religious Thought* 53 (1997): 39–50.

Thompson, V.B. *The Making of the African Diaspora in the Americas 1441–1900.* New York: Longman, 1987.

Turner, H.W. *Profile Through Preaching.* London: Edinburgh House Press, 1965.

Waliggo, John M. "African Christianity in a Situation of Suffering," In Eds J.N.K. Mugambi et al. *Jesus in African Christianity: Experimentation and Diversity in African Christology,* Nairobi: Initiatives Publishers, 1989: 98–107.

Walker, J.W. St. G. "The Establishment of a Free Black Community in Nova Scotia, 1783–1840," In Eds M.L. Kilson, et al. *The African Diaspora,* 205–236.

Wardhaugh, Ronald. *An Introduction to Sociolinguistics,* second edition. Oxford: Blackwell, 1992.

Waruta, D. "Towards an African Church," In Eds J.N.K. Mugambi et al. *The Church in African Christianity: Innovative Essays in Ecclesiology,* Nairobi, Kenya: Initiatives Ltd., 1990.

Washington, J. Ed. *A Testament of Hope: The Essential Writings and Speeches of Martin Luther King. Jr.* San Francisco, California: Harper San Francisco, 1986.

Williams, Dorothy. *The Road to Now: A History of Blacks in Montreal.* Quebec: Véhicule Press, (1997): 157–158.

Wooding, C.J. *Winti, een "Afro-Amerikaanse" Godsdienst in Suriname*. Meppel: Krips Repro, 1972.

Woodson, C.G. *The History of the Negro Church*. Washington, D.C.: Associated Press, 1945.

Wyse, Akintola. *The Krio of Sierra Leone: An Interpretive History*. London: C. Hurst and Co., 1989.

Yorke, G. "AfriCanadian Theology: A Newcomer," *African Methodist Episcopal Zion Quarterly Review: An Ecumenical Witness* 47 (1986): 1–10.

———. Review of Robert E. Hood *Must God Remain Greek?: Afro-Cultures and God-Talk*, *Journal of Ecumenical Studies* 28 (1991): 646.

———. "The Bible and the Black Diaspora," In Eds H.W. Kinoti and J.M. Waliggo *The Bible in African Christianity Essays in Biblical Theology*, Nairobi: Acton Publishers, 1997.

———. "Translating the Old Testament in Africa: An Afrocentric Approach," *Newsletter on African Old Testament Scholarship* 4 (1998): 10–13.

———. "Biblical Hermeneutics: An Afrocentric Approach," *Journal of Religious Thought* 52 (1995): 1–13.

———. "The Black Church," *The McGill University Daily Supplement: Black History Month Issue* 76 (1987): 8.

———. "Bible Translation in Africa: An Afrocentric Perspective," *The Bible Translator: Technical Papers* 50.

BATSWAKWA: WHICH TRAVELLER ARE YOU (JOHN 1:1-18)?

Musa W. Dube

Most people travel. People travel to their work places, shopping areas, to see friends and relatives. Many travel within their own countries or internationally, for fun, business or security. The ancient history of the Roman Empire shows that massive travelling of different people under different roles was a feature of Intertestamental times (Meeks 1983: 16–23). The contemporary history of the past four to five hundred years indicate that there have been massive movements of people across boundaries and continents (Said 1992: 8–12, 330–336). People have travelled voluntarily or involuntarily as fortune seekers, slaves, religious agents, refugees, outcasts, students etc. Those who travel and those who do not travel have interacted under different power relations. Some travellers and guests are powerful wherever they travel, while other travellers are continually disadvantaged. Travel is, has always been, and will continue to be a central feature of this world.

How then, is travelling connected to texts, or in this case, the Bible? In pursuing the relationship of biblical texts and travelling one can ask the following questions: What kind of travellers are reflected in the texts? What kinds of maps of travelling does the Bible propose? And in reading, which maps do we adopt and which journeys do we undertake? In short, as a reader, which traveller are you? In what follows, I will first highlight the traveller posited in John 1:1-18. Second, I will expound on my own maps and stories of travel as maps and testaments that are operative in my life and in the lives of many citizens of Botswana and Southern Africa. Third, I will show how my stories of travel inform my reading of John 1:1-18. My aim is to show that narratives present readers with plots of powerful and plots of powerless travellers. Narratives present themselves as maps that invite their readers to travel with them, to take certain journeys and to become particular travellers (and hosts/hostesses). I shall therefore use the word story-maps to refer to this function of texts. With this introduction, I turn to John 1:1-18.

John recounts journeys undertaken by the Word and John the Baptist. They both travel from God to the world with different roles and status. The Word, who is identified as Jesus in verse 17, comes into the world: As one who was there from the beginning (verse 1). As one who was with God from the beginning (verses 1–2). As God (verse 1). As the creator of the world (verses 3, 10). As the bearer of life that enlightens all people (verses 4, 9). As light that overcomes the darkness (verse 5). As one who gives power to become children of God to those who believe in his name (verses 12–13). As the father's only son (verses 14, 18). As one who bears visible glory (verse 14). As the bearer of grace and truth (verses 16–17). As the only one who has ever seen God (verse 17). As the one who is close to the father's heart (verse 18). And as the only one who reveals God (verse 18). Although we hear that the Word did suffer some loss of power, when he came to his own and his own did not receive him (verses 10–11), yet the Word undoubtedly remains powerful: There is nothing outside the Word.

John the Baptist, on the other hand, is travelling as "a man sent from God" (verse 6), and he is not the light (verse 8), his role is to witness to the light (verses 7–8). Indeed, John the Baptist testifies, crying out that "he who comes after me ranks ahead of me because he was before me" (verse 16). John the Baptist is described in relation to the Word and his status and role are subordinated to those of the Word.

But what of those who are visited upon? How does the world receive "the light of all people"? The response of the world was not uniform. The world and its people, surprisingly, fail to recognize or receive their creator (verses 10–11). Yet some receive and believe in the Word (verse 12). These believers see and recognize the glory of the Word, they see that the Word is full of grace and truth, and from the fullness of the Word believers receive "grace upon grace" (verse 16). Because of their positive response, the Word gives them "power to become children of God" (verses 12–13).

Nothing is explicitly said on the fate of those who do not receive or recognize the Word. Yet it is clear that it is a loss not to believe. For a start, the Word is the creator of the world, who was from the beginning with God, and who made all things. Those who fail to believe or recognize the Word have missed a chance to know and associate with forces of power, forces of creation. Further, the Word is the bearer of life which is "the light of *all* people" (verse 4, emphasis

mine). Failure to receive or recognize the Word is, therefore, to deny
oneself life and the light. It is to identify with the darkness, which,
as stated, "did not overcome it [the Light]." The unbelieving people
are not given power to be children of God. Thus the unbelievers
also deny themselves grace and the knowledge of God, which can
only be received from the Word. In sum, those who do not believe
or recognize the Word, identify with death, failure, powerlessness
and ignorance. In addition, the product of grace, brought by the
Word into the world, is different from the product of law brought
by Moses. Although nothing directly belittles Moses' role and status
at this point, it is clear that the Word is above all in the world by
virtue of having been there from the beginning with God, for creating the world, and for being the only one who has seen God and
for making God known. The product of grace and truth is undoubtedly the best.

The above explication shows that it is advantageous for any wise
reader to receive and recognize the Word. To be on the side of the
Word is to have life, light, power, victory, birthright, knowledge and
grace and truth. Failure to adopt this story-map is to travel the road
of failures and ignorance. I shall return to this invitation to travel
on the story-maps of the powerful below. At this stage, I will now
expound on the several story-maps of the past and present that are
operative in my life.

Although I am a Motswana by birth, most Batswana people regularly ask me if I am from Zimbabwe or South Africa, for most
Dubes are found there. Their questions indeed capture the travel
plots of my story-maps, for the Ndebele people, who were originally
part of the Zulu people, broke away under the leadership of Mzilikazi
and fled to the present day Zimbabwe. On the way, they attacked
many Batswana people, captured their cattle, children and women.
The native's of Zimbabwe, the Shona were also subjected to random acts of terror.

Mzilikazi's migration was a manifestation of a larger phenomenon
in Southern Africa: The Mfecane Wars. With the growth of populations in the area between the Indian Ocean and the Drakensburg
Moutains, there was lack of land. This, and a number of other factors, triggered a chain of wars and migrations that became called
Mfecane or Difaqane, which meant "a time of crushing." As a result,
there were many wars and migrations that scattered the Nguni and
Sotho-Tswana populations all over the region of Southern Africa,

even to Central of Africa. The migrations of the Ndebele of Mzilikazi were one of the manifestations of this current.

Yet by the end of 19th century, the white settlers had ceased to be confined to the sea shores of Southern Africa. The scramble for Africa had come and gone. The conference of Berlin had taken place, where several colonial masters and agents met and divided Africa amongst themselves. Colonial agents had assumed power over the natives of Southern Africa. Thus in the 1950's when most of the land that belonged to black people was taken by the white settlers in the present Zimbabwe, or what was then called Rhodesia, my family found itself landless. They had two choices: to remain in the area and become servants on the farms of white settlers or to move to infertile and crowded lands that were allocated to black people. They chose the former. However, it soon became clear that they could only own a limited number of cattle and plough a small patch of land in what was now a white man's farm. It was then that my parents moved to Botswana, a dry desert like country, which did not attract huge numbers of white settlers.

I was thus born and grew up in Botswana, where my family continued to speak Ndebele. Consequently, I always heard people refer to my family as "*Batswakwa*" that is, "foreigners" and, sometimes, "*makwerekwere*," which means "black foreigners." To a degree, *Batswakwa* refers to recent migrators, for many Batswana speaking ethnic groups to the north of Phalapye could also be regarded as "*Batswakwa*" (who migrated to their present settlement because of the Mfecane Wars, Boer Trek, and internal wars). This is particularly so for the region north of Phalapye which used to be part of the Munamatapa Empire.

The people of Southern Africa and Africa in general had to fight wars of liberation in order to reverse the power relations established by powerful travellers of colonial times in the region. Yet the current trend shows that we are not through with plots of powerful travellers. Ironically, the opposite of what the wars' independence struggled to establish is being reinstated in the global economic age. That is, while we fought against being dominated by travellers from the so-called "civilized" Western world, today our presidents and ministers spend money and time travelling overseas to invite foreign companies to come and invest in our countries. I cannot claim that this invitation espouses a relationship of equal partners. For a start, no one from North America or Europe comes to Botswana to invite us to travel to their countries and do our little businesses in their lands, to make some profits for ourselves, and to create jobs for their people. Second, the foreign travellers who come on their own or who are invited to come and do business in Botswana come as masters, manufacturers, investors, creators etc. who are powerful guests among the "dependent" natives. What I find quite instructive in the current economic plot is that the story-maps of the powerful travellers have the capacity to replay themselves.

In the past seven years I have had a chance to travel and study overseas, in the UK and the USA. Compared to the majority of my fellow Batswana, I was indeed privileged to have funds availed to me to study overseas. Because of my journeys, I am now adorned with scholarly diplomas, which equip me to do and teach biblical interpretation at the highest institution of learning in Botswana. Nonetheless, I am aware that I was still travelling on the story-maps of the powerless. I travelled for education to the countries of those whose his-stories of travel have marked them down as powerful. I travelled for education to countries of those whose stories of travel have inscribed them as powerful specialists and marketers of their languages and knowledge. Upon arrival, I was a powerless traveller and guest. Unlike travellers and guests that many Southern African people have encountered, I had no power over my hosts/hostesses. In both cases, I was a student with limited power over the contents and requirements of my programmes. The bulk of what I learnt was wonderful, but did not always have direct relevance to my Southern African context, and most of what I had learnt in my own home, could not be applicable during the period of my study. Nevertheless, my travel and stay in USA was one of the most instructive journeys of self-discovery.

During my student days in Botswana, I did history and learnt about the slavery of African people. I also knew about the story of my family's migration from Zimbabwe to Botswana. These stories were plotted upon racism. Moreover, I had grown up close to apartheid South Africa. I knew the stories of powerful white travellers and powerless African travellers and hosts/hostesses. Yet these were story-maps that inspired anger from a distance, at the periphery of my experience. Travelling to and living in the USA was a great shock, since the stories of slavery, racism, and discrimination against black African people were moved from the periphery of my experience to the reality of my living. They were no longer his-story but a life-story, my story for that matter. In the USA I ceased to be a Ndebele or Motswana. I was black and I was an African, and nobody really knew of such a place called Botswana. This widening of the borders of my geography and story-maps was overwhelmingly painful. The suffering and the stereotypes about African people in the diaspora were suddenly mine. I was black with all the burdens that go with it. The first thing I noted on the campus were that black faces predominated among the grounds, kitchen, and cleaning staff. There were very few of us in the classrooms. The message sent to us in the classrooms was that our place was out there in the area of manual, not intellectual, work. The text of the campus turned the clock of history and its stereotypes into the present. The impact was real, often crippling me to silence in the classroom.

To add to this painful self-discovery, the media capitalized on presenting a disgusting image of Africa. On the TV, Africa was the emaciated children of Somalia, the Zulu people shaking and raising their traditional weapons, the Mozambique war-ravaged kids begging for food, Liberian kids carrying guns and killing each other, the Rwanda and Burundi genocide, the terror of *Ebola*, AIDS, Zaire becoming The Republic of Democratic Congo, etc. In the movies Africa was "Out of Africa," "The Gods Must be Crazy," "Coming to America," "Far Away Places," "Outbreak," etc. My point here is not to question the authenticity of TV reports. Rather, my point is that I came to discover that the media constructs the story of Africa in a "cut and paste" method which writes Africa as a story of war, backwardness, poverty, disease, and death. Africa is presented as a wholly negative space with no normal life or anything positive. Even when African presidents visit the USA on some noble mission they are barely covered in the news. One only learns about it from a paper sent from home. With this selective coverage of news, Africa can only appear as a negative place.

From these experiences, I learnt instructive lessons of reading. First, I consciously became aware of myself as a Sub-Saharan black African person from an oral culture. Second, I came to realize the sad implications of reading and living with or by stories written for me and not by me. This is a crucial issue, given that oral Sub-Saharan black African people who live in the age of the information superhighway, do not own the means of producing and disseminating information about themselves. Most of what we read about ourselves and other subjects, is not written or published by us. Moreover, it is written by people that have centuries of stereotypes about black

Sub-Saharan African people. Reading for me, and for most black Sub-Saharan African people, therefore, is often an invitation to embark on journeys that are out to subsume me or insult my very being. Since most Sub-Saharan Africans come into the business of reading through reading "their stories" written for them, about them, and against them, to read as a critical reluctant traveller, with a watchful eye that pays attention to the road signs, is imperative. As readers, Sub-Saharan travellers must be distrustful of the narrative plot they receive.

In sum, my story-maps indicate that by and large I am among the powerless travellers. Although I am now an adorned academician, with diplomas from prestigious universities of the UK and USA, I cannot help but realize that I am often working within narrative plots of the powerful and the powerless. My own narrative plot as a traveller, a hostess and as a guest has been by and large a plot of the powerless. Like many people of Southern Africa, I have had to associate myself with the stories of the powerful (like getting educated in the West) in order to be given power. The story-maps of black Southern African travellers, who fled from Mfecane, Boer trekkers, and English settlers, fought for independence and who are now being trammelled by global economic tremors, are narrative plots of disadvantaged travellers and hosts/hostesses, when compared to the story-maps of white settlers of the Cape, Boer trekkers, and colonists of Southern Africa, and Africa at large. These travellers had power, and still maintain power, over their host/hostess. Euro-American white travellers who come to our countries and region as business people, students, or professionals are usually privileged and powerful; Black African people who travel to Europe and North America are usually disadvantaged, regardless of their qualifications. The explication of the story-maps of my life indicates that world history is dominated by plots of different travellers—powerless travellers, powerful travellers, powerful hosts/hostesses, powerless hosts/hostesses, and their collaborating counterparts. Many narrative plots are designed to empower some travellers over their native hosts/hostesses and/or to suppress other travellers. These narratives invite readers to collaborate with the powerful travellers.

As a traveller who realizes that the world consists of story-maps of unequal power, what journeys am I prompted to take in John 1:1–18? In reading John, I am awestruck by its opening. The narrative invites me to embark on an exciting journey that reveals deep mysteries. A knowledgeable narrator takes me to the beginning of time, tells me who was there, and what happened. As I follow the routes of this story-map, I discover that without the Word "not one thing came into being" (verse 3). I discover that the Word embodied light that was the "light of all people" (verse 5). In these first five verses, I have been taken on a journey and travelled back to the beginning of time and discovered my very origins: How I came into being, who made me, who is the source of all life. I am now very interested. This is not just a story of John. It's my own story. John's narrative plot has presented me with a compelling invitation to adopt its story-map as my own.

It is at this point that the story-maps of my past and present prompt me to be a hesitant traveller, an alert companion. As a person of Southern African origin, and Africa at large, I immediately put my story-maps of pre-colonial, colonial and post-independence encounters on the table to read John's narrative with these other testaments. I begin to check the road signs of John against my story-maps for similarities, differences, and consequences. The all knowledgeable voice of John that takes me to the beginning, which tells me of the creator of all things, who lights "all" people, makes me a very reluctant traveller. Its road signs resonate with colonial narrative plots whose aim is to take me in, subsume me, impose themselves on me and then relegate me to a permanently inferior position. And which even invite me to accept and proclaim my inferiority.

As I read on, travelling along John's narrative plots, I am now like a hunting dog with its master in a strange forest. I do not know the forests that John's narrator is leading me to, but my sense of smell lends me an advantage over my master. Am I really part and owner of this story which the narrator invites me to claim as my own? The cards of my story-maps caution me that the prey that I am invited to hunt and kill is not really mine. What is even more important, the cards of my story-maps caution me that the prey, which I kill for my master, is a victim just like me. So in this hunt, this reading journey, I am distrustful of the narrator's masterful invitation to travel with him/her. I thus employ the powers at my disposal, the story-maps of my past and present, to reread the road signs of John's narrative. The presentation of John the Baptist, the Word, and Moses give me a chance to reexamine the road signs along the story-maps advanced by the narrator.

John the Baptist appears and is acknowledged as "a man sent

from God" (verse 6). John is a man of power, the narrator cannot help but acknowledge him. But between verses 6–9 and verse 15 the narrator scrambles to subsume John the Baptist under the story-map of the travelling Word by employing several tactics. First, John is characterized as a servant of the Word: "he came as a witness to testify to the light, so that all might believe in him" (verse 6). Second, the narrator stresses that John the Baptist "himself was not the light." Third, the narrator reasserts that the "the true light, which enlightens *everyone*, was coming into the world" (verse 9). Lastly, in verse 15, the narrator employs John the Baptist against himself: he is characterized as crying out, saying, "this was he whom I said, 'He who comes after me ranks ahead of me because he was before me'" (verse 15). John the Baptist proclaims his inferiority.

The characterization of John the Baptist bears the marks of a familiar terrain, a road with familiar signs. The Word journeys as a powerful traveller, who proceeds by subsuming all and assuming power over all. With the arrival of the travelling Word, all other powers must become subjected to a lesser position. The travelling Word cannot cohabit with other powers. For me, the story of John the Baptist reminds me of the colonial proclamation of Christianity, which held that African religious traditions, or all other world cultures for that matter, were an imperfect revelation of the same God of Christianity—they had been waiting for the Christian story to fulfill them. The Christian religious traditions were presented as the perfect revelation of God. Obviously, this approach co-opted all other religious cultures by relegating them to subservience. That John the Baptist is employed by the knowledgeable narrator to proclaim the greatness of the travelling Word against himself, reminds me of my story and that of many Sub-Saharan Africans who have been Christianised/colonized to believe and to proclaim their own inferiority.

The story-maps of my past and present prompt me to recognize that John the Baptist's story is my story. Yet it also fills me with yearning for a different plot of travelling in narratives and the world at large. I perceive the encounter between John the Baptist and the travelling Word as a missed opportunity for cohabitation, a missed opportunity for liberating interdependence between two good powers, an encounter that still begs for its own birth. If they are both from God, then why does the narrator proceed by subordinating John the Baptist to the travelling Word? My reading as a reluctant traveller, who identifies with John, is to refuse to participate in the subordination of John the Baptist. Thus, I assert that John the Baptist was a man from God. This assertion expresses my wish for a different story, my wish to read of how the travelling Word and John the Baptist lived together, learned from each other and worked together to enhance life on God's earth, without subordination one to another.

Turning to the arrival of the travelling Word in the world, how do I perceive the road signs of its entrance? The arrival of the Word in the world is briefly treated in verses 10–13. Although the narrator characterized the Word as the all powerful, creator of the world, this construction is not accepted by all hosts/hostesses. Many people of the world who found themselves claimed and owned by the travelling Word refused to accept its absolute power over them. The narrator is thus forced to confront the limitation of his/her plot: "He was in the world, and the world came into being through him, yet the world did not know him. He came to what was his own, and his own people did not accept him" (verse 10). Apparently, resistance surfaced at the very beginning, exposing and rejecting the narrator's prescription upon the world. Looking into the cards of my story-maps, I know that resistance is always there from powerless hosts/hostesses, who are often visited upon by those who come from afar, from powerful centres, claiming power over the natives. Powerful travellers, however, always want to undermine the resistance and to paint a picture of willing servants and believers. The native, in short, loves his/her oppressor, needs and begs to be subordinated.

I note how the narrator quickly guides the reader to travel past those who resist, the dissenting voices. Without giving any reason for their resistance, or what happened to them, or the impact of their resistance on the travelling Word and believers, the narrator leads the reader to travel along the path of believers, those who accept the claims of the travelling Word upon them. Here the narrator generously informs the reader of what becomes of those who believed: "They were given power to become children of God" (verse 12), they were born through the "will . . . of God" (verse 13). Second, the believers, like John the Baptist, are called upon to endorse the narrator. The believers, who are only identified as "we," narrate their story: "And . . . we have seen his glory, the glory as of a father's only son, full of grace and truth" (verse 14). Interjecting the words of John the Baptist to accentuate this story of believers in verse 15, the voices of believers again proclaim that "from his fullness we have received grace upon grace" (verse 16). This characterization of believers is the narrator's appeal to the reader to travel with and on the plot of the travelling Word, for to believe is to be given power and to be associated with powers of creation, grace and glory.

Yet the prescriptions and limitations of the narrator's plot are evident to a hesitant and alert traveller. To start with, she or he notes that the narrator introduced the Word as the creator of all and everything, whose status, therefore, should be self-evident, who should unconditionally guarantee the birth-right of all as children. When the reluctant traveller realizes that, on the contrary, the travelling Word only confers power and birth-rights on those who believe in his name and that there is resistance from the hosts/hostesses of the travelling Word, she or he begins to question a number of things. First, the reluctant traveller begins to problemitise a creator, a parent of all, who is selective and who confers power conditionally. Second, the reluctant traveller immediately discovers that to accompany the travelling Word is to subscribe to a worldview that baptizes an ideology of "selective and exclusive empowering" or "conditional empowering" or "chosenness" of particular creatures of God. Third, the reluctant traveller begins to yearn for the empowering of those who differ, those who refuse to subscribe to the narrator's plot. As a reluctant traveller, my reading yearns for an inclusive empowerment of the resisting and disbelieving worlds.

Turning to the characterization of Moses in verse 17, the cards of my story-maps confirm to me that I have sufficient reasons to become a watchful travelling companion to the arriving Word. The narrator acknowledges Moses' role. He brought the law. No further elaboration is made on the function and origin of the law. Nothing is said as to where Moses came from and who sent him. The narrator, however, proceeds to state that Jesus Christ brings grace and truth. Further, that "No one has ever seen God. It is the only Son, who is close to the Father's heart, who made him known" (verse 18). There is a glaring lack of elaboration on the origin and role of Moses, compared to the Word. Clearly, the role of Moses is subordinated to the role of the travelling Word—for if the Word is the only one who has seen God (verse 18), indeed, if he is the creator and God, the role and status of Moses, like that of John the Baptist and believers, can only be that of servanthood and children.

Embedded in this story is a subtle subordination of another character, Sophia. The Sophia tradition characterizes her as one who was active in creation, one who was sent to Israel to teach them the ways of life, one who bears children of righteousness whose father is God, and one who dwells amongst them as the law that was given to Moses. Jesus is presented in terms that closely resemble terms used to characterize Sophia. However, Jesus is the only son of God and the only one who has seen God. As the Word, Jesus is not only the agent of creation, he is also God. Moreover, if Sophia dwelt on earth as the law, Jesus replaces the law with grace and truth. In short, the plot of the travelling Word is closely modelled on the plot of Sophia, but, in fact, it subordinates her to an inferior position (see Petersen 1993).

In conclusion, the above reading of John 1:1–18 makes it clear that to identify with the travelling Word is to identify with creators, life, light, power, victory, knowledge, grace and truth. To fail to adopt this story-map is to travel on the road of failures. Travelling with the Word is indeed attractive, but to reap the benefits of this association is also to participate in the subordination of John the Baptist, those who resist/unbelievers, Moses, and Sophia. For a reluctant traveller, whose story-maps of travel are by and large those of powerless travellers, it is often appealing to claim a story of power for oneself. The offer, however, is difficult to accept since it does not only depend on a massive suppression of powerless travellers and hosts/hostesses, it also does not admit other people as equal partners; other people are admitted as servants and adopted children. Further, to accept the invitation to be associated with powerful travellers, especially when one's story-maps are plots of the disempowered, is to be involved in self-betrayal. Even more seriously, to accept the invitation to journey with the powerful travellers is to retreat from seeking for a better and just world, a world that encompasses different powers, exchange between equal powers, healthy co-habitations of travellers and hosts/hostesses, and encounters of liberating interdependence between different people and cultures. To read as an alert and hesitant traveller is just another way of seeking for better encounters—a different way of interaction both locally and internationally.

Evidently, most canonized narratives of the world, such as the Bible and others, present readers with story-maps of unequal distributions of power. Different narratives invite their readers to take certain journeys, to identify with powerful travellers and hosts/hostesses, and by so doing to suppress others. Perhaps this function of texts is captured by Edward Said, who argues that

All texts essentially dislodge other texts, or more frequently take the place of something else . . . texts are fundamentally facts of power not of democratic exchange. . . . The critic is responsible to a degree for articulating those voices dominated, displaced or silenced by textuality of texts. Texts are a system of forces institutionalized by reigning culture at some human cost (1983: 45, 53).

As readers of biblical texts, we are also invited to travel. Since travel remains central to our lives, nationally and internationally, biblical readers need to examine the power relations authorized by narratives and interpreters. Readers of biblical texts as fellow travellers may need to examine the journeys they undertake. Readers may need to take different paths, to plot new journeys, and to draw new maps and to establish new rules for travelling and hosting others.

BIBLIOGRAPHY

Anderson, Janice Capel and Jeffrey Staley. Eds, "Taking it Personally," *Semeia* 72. Atlanta: Scholars Press, 1995.
Blunt, Alison. *Travel, Gender and Imperialism: Mary Kinsley and West Africa.* New York: The Guildford Press, 1994.
Makeba, Miriam. *Makeba: My Story.* New York: A Plume Book, 1987.
Meeks, Wayne. *The First Urban Christians: The Social World of The Apostle Paul.* New Haven: Yale University Press, 1983.
Peterson, Norman R. *The Gospel of John and the Sociology of Light: Language and Characterisation in the Fourth Gospel.* Valley Forge: Trinity Press International, 1993.
Phillip, Jim. "Reading Travel Writing," In Ed. Jonathan White *Recasting the World: Writing After Colonialism.* London: The Johns Hopkins University Press, 1993: 241–255.
Quint, David. *Epic and Empire.* Princeton: Princeton University Press, 1993.
Reinhartz, Adele. *The Word in the World: The Cosmological Tale in the Fourth Gospel.* Atlanta: Scholars Press, 1992.
Said, Edward. *The Text, The Critic and The World.* Cambridge: Harvard University Press, 1983.
———. *Culture and Imperialism.* New York: Alfred A. Knopf, 1993.
Schussler Fiorenza, Elizabeth. *Jesus Miriam's Child, Sophia's prophet: Critical Issues in Feminist Christology.* New York: Continuum, 1994.
Segovia, Fernando. "Journeys of the Word: A Reading of the Plot of the Fourth Gospel" *Semeia* 53. Atlanta: Scholars Press, 1991.
Walsh, Jerome T., Ed. "Reading and Understanding the Bible From an African Perspective," *Boleswa Occasional Papers in Theology and Religion.* 1/6 (1997).

THE LIMITS OF DIFFERENCE: NGUGI WA THIONG'O'S REDEPLOYMENT OF BIBLICAL SIGNIFIERS IN *A GRAIN OF WHEAT* AND *I WILL MARRY WHEN I WANT*

Peter Wamulungwe Mwikisa

A Grain of Wheat (1967) is the third and most accomplished, after *Weep Not Child* (1964) and *The River Between* (1965), of the novels which Ngugi wrote before he dropped the Christian "James" and adopted the Gikuyu "Ngugi Wa Thiong'o" by which appellation he is now generally known. Ngugi has not given an account of his experience of the road to Damascus, so it is not possible to speak in precise terms of the significance and the kind of the conversion implied by, his change of names. Nevertheless, even a cursory glance at his work shows that his *oeuvre* lends itself easily to a division between, the early works on one side of that event, and the later works such as *Petals of Blood* (1977), *I Will Marry When I Want* (1982), and *Matigari* (1989), on the other side. The two texts—*A Grain of Wheat* and *I Will Marry When I Want*—are obvious choices to ponder Ngugi's ideological deployment of biblical images and themes because they lie on opposing sides of the decade-long watershed between the publication of *A Grain of Wheat* (1967) and *Petals of Blood* (1977). During this period Ngugi changed not only his attitude towards Christianity and the Bible, but also his views on the strategies and tactics of combatting the global power of Western imperialism.

I am, therefore, inclined to see the change in names as metonymic of what N. Lazarus describes as a "fundamental revaluation on Ngugi's part of formal and artistic priorities and political tactics" (Lazarus 1990: 212). In other words, the change reflects a multidimensional effort on the part of Ngugi to deal with the crisis of consciousness which, according to Lazarus, assailed African writers in the period immediately following independence, namely, how to identify with the masses, for whom they presumed to speak. The change signals Ngugi's search for a less intellectualised register (Lazarus 1990: 23). If, therefore, I focus on Ngugi's allusions to biblical images and themes, it is not because I do not see the larger picture. I do not think, for instance, that one could divorce Ngugi's views on indigenous African culture and religiosity from his decision to stop using English and switching to Gikuyu as a medium of his creative writing. Ngugi does not compartmentalize language, religion, politics etc. into separate categories. My point rather is that the Bible and Christianity are an important seam in Ngugi's intellectual make-up, and to understand the different ways in which he taps this resource is to understand a crucial element of the larger, complex picture.

In considering ways in which Ngugi constructs his own narrative out of the Bible and the Christianity of his missionary education, we do well to bear in mind that, in a sense, his is a "revisionist" project. I used the term "revisionist" here not in order to detract from the political radicalness of Ngugi's work in any way. It is a fact that as a creative writer Ngugi's ideal is to produce works which aim at a radical transformation of society. The usual associations of the term "revisionism" are a far-cry from such an ideal. I use the term, however, in a sense analogous to the way in which B. Ashcroft et al. (1989: 38) and K. Seshadra-Crooks (1995: 47) use the term "appropriation" to signify the post-colonial textual practice of constructing new revolutionary texts which subvert colonial ideologies from the very texts that colonialism and imperialism accord a privileged status. It is a practice, moreover, which implies a change in the way in which colonialism's master-texts are to be read away from the centre.

Like other post-colonial writers, Ngugi continues to conceive of freedom against colonialism and imperialism in ways which resonate with Christian and biblical images. The resilience of the Bible's influence on so radical a writer is astonishing when one considers how deeply implicated this book is in the propagation of ideologies which naturalise the hierarchal oppositions of slave and master, native and coloniser, pagan and Christian, savage and European, Black and white, etc. upon which colonial and imperial rule were predicated (Ngugi 1993: 31). Moreover, capitalism itself, if Max Weber is to be believed, owes its own rise (from its humble beginnings in early modern times) to the work-ethic of Bible-totting Calvinists (Giddens 1989: 461). The binary cosmology of the Protestant work-ethic conflates at the bottom end of a hierarchical opposition slavery, sloth, poverty, and sinfulness, and, at the upper end, mastery, diligence, frugality, wealth, and saintliness or virtue.

Given its revisionist ethos, one would have expected an African post-colonialist, and certainly a radical writer like Ngugi, to repudiate not only colonialism and imperialism themselves, but the culturally privileged texts which are ideologically implicated in their propagation. Ngugi, has after all, repeatedly drawn attention to how the gun and the Bible were used concurrently in the colonial occupation of Africa (Ngugi 1993: 11). The fact that such a wholesale repudiation of the masters' texts has been largely spurious is because, as V.T. Mudimbe points out, it seems possible to read into the same text a number of meanings, some of which may even be considered contradictory (Mudimbe 1998: 55). In other words, it is possible to read "colonial" texts in ways that may have a decolonising effect. It is this assumption which I would like to pursue in relation to Ngugi's redeployment of biblical and Christian images and themes in *A Grain of Wheat* and *I Will Marry When I Want*. I am going to try and show that in these two texts Ngugi has exploited the possibilities, and also exposed the limitations, of the decolonising hermeneutics of the deconstructionist position that any text, including the Bible, "can be read in contradictory ways, each of which denies the primacy of the other" (Young 1981: 18).

A Grain of Wheat was technically the most ambitious project Ngugi had hitherto undertaken. Its narrative modulates deftly between omniscience and the inner-speech of various characters. Flashbacks move us back and forth on a journey through Kenyan history, so that by the end of the novel we have a remarkably vivid understanding of how the struggle against colonialism begun with the arrival of the first colonists. How the first brave but reckless instances of anti-colonial insurrection were suppressed. How the insurrections nevertheless grew into a full-fledged armed resistance—the Mau-Mau—which led to the granting of independence from colonial rule. How the early euphoria after independence quickly gave way to disillusionment when the ideals of the struggle were betrayed in the course of a post-colonial feeding frenzy, as the political leadership sees independence as an opportunity to enrich itself at the expense of the people.

Yet it is not only Kenyan history which emerges from the novel. More importantly, what the novel reveals, is the role of the ordinary people, the rural peasants, in history. It is they who are, in a sense, the collective protagonist of the novel. The novel reveals their heroism, their weaknesses as they sacrifice their lives for the struggle and betray each other in order to survive during a state of emergency declared by the colonial administration in order to combat the Mau-Mau. The novel centres around a young freedom fighter called Kihika, who runs away from school to join the Mau-Mau freedom fighters in the forest. He quickly proves himself a charismatic and fearless freedom fighter. In one of his daring acts he shoots a colonial District Commissioner, and with the whole colonial army in pursuit of him, he ducks into Mugo's hut to hide. Before leaving he extracts a rendezvous with Mugo, who, however, instead of keeping the appointment betrays him to the colonial administration. Kihika is arrested and hanged in public as a warning to other would be freedom fighters. Mugo himself is not rewarded by the colonial office for delivering to them their prize captive. Instead he is thrown into detention and tortured, because the colonial authorities do not believe that he had not taken the Mau-Mau oath which they want him to confess. Since he had not taken the oath, Mugo really had nothing to confess, but his failure to say anything is taken by the authorities to mean that he is a hard-core member of the Mau-Mau. News of the torture that is meted out to him spreads, and among the Africans, who are not aware that it is he that betrayed Kihika, he becomes a hero. At independence, he is given pride of place as a former freedom fighter and invited to give the independence day celebration address. It is during these celebrations that he confesses to having betrayed Kihika, at which point he is subjected to a "court martial" and executed by former Mau-Mau generals.

There are many other instances of heroism and betrayal in the novel. Karanja is a fun-loving young man who, as soon as the struggle begins, joins the service of the colonial administration as an informer. He is later elevated to the position of chief of the regrouped village (concentration camp). As chief he seeks to enjoy the favours of Mumbi, the wife of his childhood friend, Gikonyo, who is in detention. Mumbi steadfastly fends off his advances and stays faithful to her absent husband for seven years, until the day when Karanja tells her that her husband was coming home, when she allows Karanja to sleep with her. As luck would have it, she conceives. On his return Gikonyo, who has himself betrayed the movement by confessing the oath, in order to be with his wife again, finds her nursing another man's child. The betrayer is himself the betrayed.

The novel ends on an ambiguous note. Positively, its final chapter, entitled "Harambe," depicts Mumbi and Gikonyo reconciled and leaving the past behind in order to build a future together. Negatively, the spectre of the member of parliament who cheats people from his constituency of their land by buying it for himself points to the corruption endemic to the African political landscape.

In *A Grain of Wheat* Ngugi signals his intention to deconstruct missionary interpretations of the gospels through the title itself. The agrarian metaphor beckons towards a Kenyan rural peasantry, from whose perspective the gospels are going to be reinterpreted. Yet the title phrase is such an unmistakable allusion to the Bible that it is impossible to dissociate it from the blinding array of meanings missionary proselytising discourses have already inscribed on it. As far as the peasants, whose meanings Ngugi seeks to read into it, are concerned, the metaphor is an occupied territory, and his efforts are the moral equivalent of a liberation war.

Taken directly from 1 Corinthians 15:36 and John 12:24 "a grain of wheat" has, at least, two significations in the proselytising discourses of the missionaries. First, it encodes a message to the Africans, already othered as objects of conversion, about the necessity of conversion. To be converted is to shed those characteristics (of paganism) which mark one as different from the saved and to adopt a new set of characteristics that would mark one as different from the unsaved. The old sinful African self had to die in order to give birth to the new virtuous African. The ideology of African alteriority the missionaries were constructing through this interpretation of the metaphor of "a grain of wheat" centred around the African who must be redeemed, through his own agency, by choosing to be converted. They made conversion seem a matter of free-will or choice. Completely suppressed in this view of conversion is the fact that African conversion, as Mudimbe has argued, occurred not because Africans chose to be converted, but because it was made the sole position the African could take to survive as a human being (Mudimbe 1988: 40).

There was hypocrisy in the way missionary discourses projected conversion as a voluntary rotting of the old sinful self in order to give rise to a new sinless self. The hypocrisy consisted, not least of all, in the way in which another kind of difference was inserted between converted Africans and Europeans in a hierarchical ordering in which the saved African was still inferior to the European, saved or not. European constructions of African alteriority, therefore, were motivated by the desire to objectify the African as the target of another's proselytising, colonising, subordinating gaze. It is this view of conversion which Ngugi rejects in the way he redeploys the metaphor of "a grain of wheat" in this novel. Kihika may carry a pocket-Bible in which these verses and others are underlined, but he also draws inspiration from traditional religious beliefs and customs of his own people. To postulate a conversion that places his own culture at the beginning and Western culture at the end of a journey to salvation is totally unacceptable to him. Through Kihika's syncretic Christianity Ngugi is asserting the idea that there was a difference between his own and the missionaries' view of conversion. To Kihika, being a Christian does not necessitate renunciation of his pre-Christian culture, but a renewed faith in it. Unlike the missionaries who conceived of conversion in terms of zero-degree traditional African Religion (Mudimbe 1988: 53), Kihika thinks in terms of bringing together Christianity and traditional African religious heritage as complementary sources of inspiration in his struggle against colonial rule. In Kihika, the African is not an object of a predatory Christian religiosity, but the subject of his own religious imagination.

In other interpretations I have heard, missionary discourses project Jesus Christ himself, because of his sacrificial death, as "the grain of wheat" that must rot in order for the new plant to grow. In this sense, the metaphor is a powerful symbol of the superiority of the Christian faith over African, or indeed all other faiths. It is a powerful marker of difference between the omnipotent, all-loving Christian God and the gods of other faiths. In a circular formulation, Jesus is presented as a unique God because he performed the ultimate sacrifice ("gave up his life so that we might have life abundantly," John 10:10), but he was only able to do this because he was a unique God in the first place. It was on the basis of this presumed superiority of the Christian faith that the "missionary [did] not enter into dialogue with pagans and 'savages' but must impose the law of God that he incarnates" (Mudimbe 1988: 39). Ngugi's deployment of the image is designed to violate a codification in which "the grain of wheat" encodes an ethno-centrically inspired "absoluteness of Christianity and its virtues" (Mudimbe 1988: 39). Ngugi uses it to encode the necessity of self-sacrifice in the struggle for a more just society. This is why Waiyaki, one of the warriors of the olden days who was killed when the tribe took up their spears to resist colonialism, is described as "a grain of wheat."

Then nobody noted it, but looking back we can see that Waiyaki's blood contained within it a seed, a grain, which gave birth to a movement whose main strength thereafter sprang from a bond with the soil (Ngugi 1967: 12).

At one point in the story, the precocious Kihika tells his playmates that Jesus was a failure because his death did not change anything, and invites his listeners to offer themselves to deaths that will change things. "In Kenya we want deaths which will change things, that is to say, we want true sacrifice ... I die for you, you die for me, we become a sacrifice for one another. So I can say you Karanja are Christ. I am Christ" (Ngugi 1967: 95). Ngugi here has taken a biblical image, revised it so radically that it now refers not to the one unique Christ, who is remote in time, place, and the concerns of his audience, but to every one who is prepared to make the sacrifice which both proves and confers godhood. The suggestion that Jesus was the lesser messianic figure, because his death did not change anything, is also a profound deconstruction of dominant ideological interpretations. In the Bible, Jesus' messiah-hood is unique, in *A Grain of Wheat* Kihika's messiah-hood is a universal potentiality.

Three other verses from the Bible, underlined in Kihika's pocket-Bible, are used as epigrams to certain sections of the novel. Exodus 8:1 containing the short sentence "Let my people go," Exodus 3:7 which contains the phrase, "I have surely seen the application of my people which are in Egypt ...," and Revelation 21:1 which talks of "a new heaven and a new earth," are equally intended to deconstruct the sign system which underpinned Christian discourses. It is a signifying system that projected a blissful after-life in heaven as the reward for patiently enduring oppression injustice and suffering on earth. What Ngugi does in *A Grain of Wheat* is to use these verses to suggest the transformability of the conditions of life here on earth. Again what we have here is a rejection of inscriptions of subaltern alteriority in ways that reduced Africans to a passive object of a salvific missionary agency. Ngugi succeeds in presenting the Christianity of missionary discourses as belonging to the obscure regions of the cosmos and of being the imaginary, and in replacing it with one whose proper element is language and history (Amuta 1989: 166).

Besides the weight which the title bears in the novel, there are other re-presentations of the Bible. The villages of Thabai and Rungei, which form the setting of the novel, are peopled by characters with strong biblical echoes. It would, however, be wrong to see in this

what may be interpreted as Ngugi's attempts merely to make the
Bible relevant to local situations. Such a project would merely endorse
orthodox missionary versions of African alteriority, in which Euro-
peanised Galileans are projected as the universal norm towards which
all humanity aspires to approximate, when what he seeks to do is
precisely to contest such a notion. Here, as with the title, what Ngugi
is concerned with is primarily to insert a critical difference between
the way biblical characters were used by Europeans as a foil against
which the wickedness of Africans could be imagined and the way
the Africans used them to re-imagine themselves in ways that subverted colonial ideologies. Kihika the revolutionary martyr, it has
been remarked countless times, is not just Christ-like, but as Lewis
Nkosi has pointed out, Christ incarnate (Nkosi 1993: 201). The parallels which Ngugi draws between him and the biblical Christ include
his precocity. The scene I have referred to above in which the young
Kihika talks of self-sacrifice, and the need for "deaths which will
make a difference" harks back to the twelve year old Jesus preaching in the synagogue. His leaving of the comforts of home to join
the Mau-Mau movement as a guerilla recalls Jesus' three year ministry in which he was seen as a rabble-rouser in a Palestine under
Roman imperial occupation. His betrayal by a person closely connected to him, Mugo, and the subsequent public hanging (crucifixion)
by the colonial administration clinch his role as a "Messianic hero
who must not only lead his people, but die in order to lead them
out of their bondage" (Nkosi 1993: 201).

Mugo, the person who betrays Kihika to the colonial authorities,
is clearly a complication of the character of Judas Iscariot. However,
whereas Judas is motivated purely by monetary gain, Mugo's equivalent of the thirty pieces of silver is only a factor in a complex network of causes (including fear, insecurity, a miserable childhood)
which he does not fully understand himself. When instead of being
rewarded for his act, he is arrested, and tortured by the colonial
regime in order to make him confess an oath which he is suspected
of having taken, the news spreads and he is transformed into a hero
of the struggle he has in truth betrayed. At independence, univer-
sally acclaimed as a hero of the freedom struggle, he courageously
confesses his betrayal of Kihika and is summarily executed, in an
ending which, depending on ones point of view, either belies or
betrays his moral affinity to Judas Iscariot who hangs himself.

Towards the end of the novel there is a description of a local
Member of Parliament who undertakes to help Gikonyo and other

members of his constituency to buy a farm from a departing white man. Behind their backs, however, the Member of Parliament raises some money and buys the farm for himself. An incident that is symbolic of the post-colonial elites' betrayal of the masses in whose name they assumed power. It is again, impossible not to read in this incident the biblical purchase of the field of blood with Judas' abandoned pieces of silver (Matthew 27:8).

There is also an allusion to "the Holy Family" in *A Grain of Wheat*. Mumbi, Kihika's sister is clearly intended to recall Mary, the mother of Jesus. She is a beautiful, obedient girl who, embodying the popular mission school image of a good Christian girl, does not go to tribal dances in the forest, but stays home to help her mother with household chores. She grows up to be a strong woman, who marries a Joseph-like figure, Gikonyo, the wood-carver (carpenter). She is a paragon of the virtues of African womanhood in the manner corresponding to Mary's embodiment of European (even though she was a Hebrew) womanhood as projected in missionary discourses. Her fidelity to her husband is unshakeable during the seven years during which he is detained for being a member of the Mau-Mau, except towards the end when overwhelmed by happiness at the news that her husband was coming out of detention, she allows the homeguard Karanja, who broke the news to her, to sleep with her. When her husband comes home, he finds her with another man's child. This is a situation in which it is not difficult to read Joseph's pain and suffering, when he discovered that his betrothed is carrying another man's child.

These characters are not, to emphasize my earlier statement, mere incarnations of biblical figures on the local scene. Although the parallels are compelling, the characters must be read, not as reproductions, but as the deconstructing of the dominant interpretations these biblical characters were given in missionary discourses. Kihika is not just a redeemed mission African, faithfully following in the steps of Christ in the manner of John Bunyan's Pilgrim. Neither is Mugo an example of the half-convert, notorious in the mission stations, who ends up damned by both the "pagan" and the Christian world, belonging to neither; nor is Mumbi the pious, long suffering mission station woman, a model of Christian pleasantness and charity and obsequious servant to white madam. Ngugi actually uses his characters to reject these stereotypes of African conversion. His language is still that of conversion, sacrifice and betrayal, but the faith to which they are converted, to which they must commit themselves to the point of preparedness to die and which they are warned against betraying, has more in common with a socialist project than the mission stations.

For all this, however, to advance what borders on heresy, in the light of the immense esteem in which even his early works are held as contestations of colonialist readings of the Bible, it can be argued that *A Grain of Wheat* is a limited ideological achievement. It is characterised by the uncomplicated way in which Ngugi relies on the Bible and Christian tenets to inform his vision of social justice. His anti-colonialism uses Christianity and the Bible to attack colonialism, but it leaves them un-interrogated or un-interpellated by other discourses. In dialectical terms, we could say that Ngugi analyses or deconstructs biblical images and themes in order to reveal the internal tensions and contradictions of the Christian signifying system, and discloses the warring interpretations of which it is capable in order to contest the primacy of dominant interpretations. It is a bit like liberation theology, which questions colonial conceptions of God, but not the concept of God itself. Thus while undermining the hierarchical oppositions which dominant readings of the Bible entrench, *A Grain of Wheat* relies on a logo-centric core or presence, namely, what the Bible really means and the true Christian practices which should follow from this meaning.

A Grain of Wheat is a critique Christianity from within. Christianity itself and its language are not brought into contestation with other sources of inspiration or ideas of social justice. There are references to African Traditional Religion resources, and even traces of historical-materialism in *A Grain of Wheat*, but these are brought in, not to contest, but to complement or validate the larger truths of a transcendental Christianity. The ideals of a true Christianity are the extra-systemic transcendental signified in relation to which the vagaries of the signifier are subjected. I think Lazarus makes the same point when he complains that, although Ngugi writes about the Kenyan peasantry and their experience during the emergency, "it can be seen in retrospect that the novel was the product of one determinate way of thinking about post-colonialism" (Lazarus 1990: 213).

A Grain of Wheat can envision the agency of the oppressed, but it cannot articulate their speech. The language in which it is couched is a language in which the silence of the oppressed is integrally encoded. *A Grain of Wheat* is not a voice of the people, but that of an African petty-bourgeois Christian intellectual participating in the project to show the continuing, universal relevance of Christianity in an anti-colonial and post-colonial futurity. In fact, the novel comes perilously close to colluding with the colonial discourses it seeks to deconstruct because its narrative mode silences the voice of the masses. Despite itself, *A Grain of Wheat* is a neo-colonial signifying practice which undercuts its own intention to be the voice of the people. The novel is a mode of representation in which a crisis-laden comprador-bourgeois consciousness constructs a stable subject position for itself by "othering" the peasants and workers whom it conjures in the interest of what it perceives to be their own good. They do not speak for themselves beyond the ventriloquistic reproduction of homilies on notions of the struggle for social justice based on Ngugi's Christian mission background.

I Will Marry When I Want, particularly the Gikuyu original, *Ngahiika Ndenda*, is a radically different signifying practice from *A Grain of Wheat*. In this play the masses will speak for themselves, as is unequivocally signalled by the first person declarative sentence which gives the play its title. Here the subalterns will speak and will not brook representations of themselves by others, no matter how sympathetic. Furthermore, when the subalterns speak it will not be in tones which emulate the accents of the former colonial masters. There is in the title *I Will Marry When I Want* none of the glaring but obsequious allusiveness with which *A Grain of Wheat* signals its significatory dependency on the Bible. While it is arguable that the nuptial reference in the title may be a deliberate attempt to echo the wedding at Capernaum, if this is indeed the case, we only need to recall that it was at this wedding that the founder of Christianity turned water into wine to feel a shift in Ngugi's attitude towards Christianity. The linking of Christianity and alcohol, which this allusion to the wedding at Capernaum intimates, is an important motif in *I Will Marry When I Want*.

In fact, the sentence, "I will marry when I want," is part of the words of a song which Kiguunda, the central character in the play, sings after he has been dispossessed of his land and seeks escape from that reality in inebriation. It announces his new-found "don't-care" attitude towards life. Christianity is being viciously attacked as a collateral form of escapism to alcohol:

> We cannot end poverty.
> By erecting a hundred beer-halls.
> In the village.

Ending up with two alcoholics.
The alcoholic of hard liquor.
The alcoholic of the rosary (Ngugi 1982: 114).

This speech is instantly recognisable as a restatement of the indictment of religion as an opium of the people, familiar in some cri-
tiques of Christianity. Understood in the way explained above, the
title of the play is perhaps the clearest way in which Ngugi signals
his intention in this play to escape the elitist or intellectualised stance
of *A Grain of Wheat* and forge an organic link with the people by
showing them acting and speaking for themselves, instead of via a
ventriloquising middle-class "other." In *I Will Marry When I Want*,
Ngugi seeks to make, "the subaltern speak," to borrow Spivak's words.
The play seeks to recuperate the narratives of the peasants which
neo-colonial discourses "prevent from emerging" (Said 1993: ix).

Unlike *A Grain of Wheat*, in which a critique of Christianity is performed from within its own moral categories, in *I Will Marry When
I Want* Ngugi interrogates or contests the claims of Christianity from
the moral standpoint of other ideological systems, in particular, historical-materialism and indigenous African religion. Since these moral
standpoints are articulated by the peasants and workers and not by
a privileged intellectual omniscience, in the play Ngugi comes closest to achieving the organic link with the people which eludes him
in *A Grain of Wheat*.

The storyline in *Ngahiika Ndenda* is soon enough told. It revolves
round Kiguunda, a farm labourer whose only gain from the erst-
while freedom struggle for *Uhuru* is a piece of land in an arid and
infertile valley. It is only one and a half acres, but

These are worth more to me
than all the thousands that belong to Ahab.
These are mine own.
A man brags about his own penis
however tiny (Ngugi 1982: 4).

It is, however, coveted by his employer, Ahab Kioi, because it is
suitable for an insecticide factory project which he proposes to undertake in a "smart partnership" with certain Western businessmen.
When Kiguunda refuses to sell to them, Kioi and another business
partner, Ikuuwa Ndihika, persuade him to become a Christian, in
the hope that it would make him more tractable. Since his daughter
has an affair with Kioi's son, John, Kiguunda mistakenly concludes
that Kioi wants him to become a Christian too because he wishes the

two young people to get married but would not like his son to marry into a non-Christian family. So Kiguunda agrees to be a Christian and even goes through one of those ludicrous weddings African married couples were prevailed upon to undergo after conversion.

He obtains a big loan, from a bank run by Kioi, to pay for the expenses of the wedding he believes is only a prelude to one between his daughter and Kioi's son. However, when even after the conversion Kiguunda still refuses to sell his land, he is fired from his job on Kioi's farm. Unable to repay the loan, he is forced to give up title to the land he had used as collateral to obtain the loan. At the same time his daughter, having been made pregnant and then jilted by John, resorts to prostitution. Plumbing the depths of despair, Kiguunda resorts to heavy drinking and is often heard singing in the middle of the night:

> I shall Marry When I Want.
> While all padres are still alive.
> And I shall get married when I want.
> While all nuns are still alive (Ngugi 1982: 4).

The drink induced bravado which makes a virtue of a refusal to take life seriously must be seen as juxtaposing of alcohol and religion as forms of escapism. Gicaamba, a factory worker with a highly raised level of class-consciousness, and clearly Ngugi's *alter-ego*, sternly chides Kiguunda for this immature behaviour.

> We cannot end poverty by erecting a hundred churches in the village.
> We cannot end poverty by erecting a hundred beer-halls in the village.
> Ending up with two alcoholics.
> The alcoholic of hard liquor.
> The alcoholic of the rosary.
> Let's unite in patriotic love:
> Gikuyu once said (Ngugi 1982: 114).

The presentation of biblical characters as models of virtue in *A Grain of Wheat* would be incongruous here. Ahab and Jezebel are not merely names of villainous characters from the Bible the way Judas' name evoked by the character of Karanja and Mugo is. They are used in *I Will Marry When I Want* as metonyms of the villainy, not of particular characters, but of Christianity itself. However, *I Will Marry When I Want* does not abjure Christianity and the Bible absolutely, for it is clear that as they tell their story, the workers and peasants reveal that Christianity, together with African Traditional Religion and historical-materialism, are inspirational in their struggle to take charge of their lives and change their history. Towards the end of the play, for instance, when Gicaamba says, "Lets rather unite in patriotic love/Gikuyu once said" (114), indigenous African morality combines in the following song with echoes of Marxism and Christianity.

> The Trumpet of the workers has been blown.
> There are two sides in the struggle.
> The side of the exploiters and that of the exploited.
> On which side will you be when.
> The trumpet of the workers is finally blown (Ngugi 1982: 115).

The Christian judgement day has clearly been transformed into the day of the eventual revolution that would inaugurate the dictatorship of the proletariat. Christianity is presented as an element in the make-up of a heightened level of class/social consciousness.

Gicaamba, who performs the role of a consciousness-raiser, draws his insights from three sources, namely African Traditional African Religion, historical-materialism, and the Bible. Lewis Nkosi describes this as Ngugi's increasing tendency to forge an uneasy alliance between historical-materialism and religious mysticism which, as he explains, "... discloses itself in the emergence of a messianic hero of extraordinary powers, who must lead the oppressed out of their bondage" (Nkosi 1983: 201). While I don't think Gicaamba quite fits Nkosi's description, his hybrid rhetoric recalls the youthful Jesus in the synagogue, in much the same way that Kihika in *A Grain of Wheat* does. Nkosi is acerbic about the salutariness of such uses of the Bible by Ngugi. While the strange bed-fellowship of the Bible and the communist manifesto in an African bed is arguably capable of spawning a conception of African agency, Nkosi thinks that it, in fact, nullifies that agency by extracting imaginary victories for the exploited classes in a struggle in which the odds are currently stacked against it" (Nkosi 1983: 201). One can understand Nkosi's skepticism. A Christ leading a victorious communist revolution rather goes against the grain. The point to make, however, would seem to be that in this play Ngugi has constructed a text which draws from a variety of sources and thus really defies readings that would fix it to one meaning. What the play as text is deconstructing are the textual strategies by means of which culturally privileged texts were processed as if they contained the one universal truth.

In other words, *I Will Marry When I Want*, while made up of the clash of warring signifiers itself, points to the fact that even the culturally privileged texts such as the Bible, *Das Kapital*, and the oral traditions out of which it is constructed are also made up of equally "warring signifiers." They are, in Homi Bhabha's phrases, not "unisonant" but "multisonant" (Bhabha 1994: 164). In this way not only the Bible, but the communist manifesto and the discourses of Traditional African Theology are revealed as battle-grounds, each torn between the signifying practices of the oppressor and those of the oppressed. The text is deconstructed to reveal not only its own fissured character, but also that of the texts from which it is constructed.

I Will Marry When I Want beckons towards the Bible as a site heavily contested between two readings. On the one hand, there are the meanings read into it by elements of the comprador bourgeoisie, such as Kioi, to whom "good and justice" which the Bible calls for, flow from private property. To them in a warped Weberian ethics, poverty is seen as the veritable hell-fire due to those who oppose the sanctity of private property. They use the Bible simply as a means of stupefying the poor into a state where they can be better exploited by coopting them into their (the rich's) value system in much the same way that missionary discourses used the Bible to achieve the co-optation of Africans into the colonial system of values through conversion. On the other hand, there are those meanings generated by the poor. From their point of view, the Bible encodes ideas of "good and justice" based on patriotism and equality.

Gicaamba, Ngugi's *alter-ego*, sees the comprador-bourgeoisie's readings of the Bible and the kind of Christianity predicated upon them as collateral with the beer which is sold to the poor to induce an escapist bliss. It is a poison, he says, ". . . poured into our country! Yes, yes, by the whites and their local followers, servants to foreigners" (Ngugi 1982: 109), an assertion which is borne out by Kiguunda, deadened by alcohol to the pain of his recent land dispossession, dancing blissful as he sings:

> Greet Chibuku for me.
> Chibuku chased away my bitterness.
> Chibuku chased away pain, sorrow and thoughts (Ngugi 1982: 109).

The unpatriotic alliance of the local elite with foreign interests against the poor forces Gicaamba to read the Bible in ways which not only make it complement Marxism and African Traditional Religion as sources of inspiration, but permit it also to be interrogated by the other two ideologically.

> One man's ability is not enough
> One finger cannot kill a louse,
> Many hands make work light.
>
> Why did Gikuyu say those things?
> Development will come from our unity . . .
>
> a day will surely come when
> If a bean falls to the ground
> It'll be split equally among us (Ngugi 1982: 115).

The first two lines and the last three are unmistakably renderings of traditional African proverbs. "Many hands make work light" is biblical, but it may also be a rendering of an indigenous African equivalent. "Development will come from our unity" is clearly in the register of contemporary development discourse which draws substantially from historical-materialism. While this passage may suggest the complementarity of the sources from which the play is constructed, it also reveals the nature of the play as a fissured text, consisting of a multiplicity of significations which contradict and interrupt each other.

In making Gicaamba, in the above quotation, construct his revolutionary rhetoric from a variety of sources, namely, indigenous African ethics, historical materialism, and the Bible, Ngugi is reading the Bible in ways which permit its privilege and dominance to be interpellated by the claims of other texts. The issue which such a reading of the Bible raises is no longer how to read the Bible in ways which prove its universal relevance, but rather of how the privilege, dominance, and meanings of texts are constituted. *I Will Marry When I Want* draws us towards the issue of how material institutions permit and constrain the ways in which holy narratives and other ideologically privileged texts are produced, circulated, and inscribed with social meanings.

The attitude towards the Bible implied by Ngugi's re-reading of it in *I Will Marry When I Want* is not a call to rewrite the Bible so that it incorporates the holy narratives of other faiths. Such a call has a proponent in Canaan Banana who argues that God has revealed himself to peoples of the world other than the Hebrews. He says:

> Strictly speaking, there is no difference between the "land of Israel" and Zimbabwe or any other land for that matter. The water from the Jordan River and that from the Zambezi are of similar importance. The fact that Jesus was baptised in the River Jordan was a pure accident of history. In the same vein, the prophets of Israel cannot be

regarded as superior to the prophets from other lands. To afford these prophets a special status would be to limit God's power to reveal himself through other people of the world (Banana 1993: 19).

I agree that the Bible as it stands is deficient because it elevates the experiences of one ethnic group with God above those of the rest of humanity. In a sense this is the point Ngugi too makes in *A Grain of Wheat* when he shows the closeness of the peasants of Rungei in Kenya. However, such a "rewritten" Bible would not meet the expectations generated by the moral and ideological tone of *I Will Marry When I Want*. It would be practically the same old Bible gilded with fragments of other religious narratives to enhance its privilege and pretensions of universal relevance. Such a Bible would merely give voice to alternative subject positions while at the same time always containing them within the institutions and discourses of a hegemonic (capitalist sponsored) Christian religiosity. What Ngugi is suggesting is that the privileging of the Bible itself perpetuates certain forms of colonialism, which we can only counter by bringing the Bible into dialogue on an equal footing with other religious and secular texts.

If post-colonial discourse is necessarily a revisionist discourse, what it contests should be not merely "interpretations" of the Bible by the dominant classes, but the very status of the Bible as a privileged text. In this respect, *A Grain of Wheat* achieves less than *I Will Marry When I Want*. In the former text, Ngugi's call for social justice is based on the world view of the gospels, and implicitly marginalised sources other than Christianity. The moral vision he expounds is almost exclusively informed by Christianity, which he hardly interrogates. But *I Will Marry When I Want* is informed by the Bible as well as African Traditional Religion and historical-materialism. Furthermore, in this latter text, Christianity is not placed on a pedestal beyond the splutter of the muddy fray, but is heavily implicated in the injustices the author condemns, and is savagely critiqued as such. It is compared insistently with *chibuku* as a collateral source of escapist dreams. Furthermore, the nomenclature Ngugi has used for his characters in the play clearly shows how the battle-lines have been drawn. On the one hand we have the peasants who all bear indigenous African names—Kiguunda, Wangeri Gathoni, Gicaamba, and Njooki. On the other hand are representatives of the national petty-bourgeoisie who bear biblical names—Ahab, Jezebel and Samuel. It is a nomenclature which implicates the Bible in the promotion of the

self-serving ends of the petty-bourgeois business elite. A stage direction in the sitting arrangements in one scene in the play underscores
the point. "They sit in such a way that the Kioi group is on one
side and the Kiguunda family on the other side, at least they should
be seen to be apart, or to be in two opposing camps." (Ngugi 1982:
41). What Ngugi seeks to disclose here is the fact that indigenous
African values and Christianity have been brought together in a violent confrontation on the side of good and evil, respectively. It is a
confrontation which receives its clearest objectification towards the
end of the play when Kiguunda, holding a sword against Kioi, has
his moment of power abruptly ended when he is disarmed by Kioi's
biblically named, gun-wielding wife, Jezebel (Ngugi 1982: 103), enact-
ing once more how the gun and the Bible worked hand-in-glove to
entrench oppression (Ngugi 1993: 11).

Yet for all this *I Will Marry When I Want* is only a partial ideological success if indeed Ngugi's aim in the play was to create a
work in which he achieved "a (re)turn to the people" (Lazarus 1993:
20). It is true he goes a long way in this play to "un-class" (Lazarus
1993: 20) or "reconvert" himself in a work that would be an act of
solidarity with the people. The play is an attempt at a repudiation
of the petty-bourgeois class of his ascription and a "forging of a
regenerative link with the people" (Ngugi 1981: 160). The reason it
is only a partial success lies, firstly, in the deconstructionist approach
it takes towards the colonial master-text, the Bible, from which it is
constructed. Pretty much like Kwame Nkhrumah's "seek ye first the
political kingdom," whose rhetorical force depends on familiarity with
an original whose authority it thus entrenches, *I Will Marry When I
Want* depends for its significatory force, at least in part, on the readers' familiarity with both the Bible and the Christianity which it
attacks.

Secondly, there is a limit to the liberatory efficacy of deconstruction, or an approach to colonialism's master-texts which seeks to
inscribe "difference" between the masters' colonising readings and
the colonial subjects' decolonising readings. Deconstruction's claim
to a liberatory praxis is predicated on the idea that by inserting
difference between he text and its meanings, it can show meaning
to be an ideologically constituted construct, and thus free the reader
from the tyranny of preconceived or official meanings. On this score,
I Will Marry When I Want may be regarded as a success. However,
deconstruction takes the wind out of its sails when it then advances

the notion that a text is capable of a multiplicity of readings, each of which denies the legitimacy of the others. If this view is taken then there is nothing that makes a colonialist reading of the Bible any less valid than a so-called decolonising one. In the end what we have is an endless dance of signifiers impossible to hitch to a political programme of any kind. In deconstruction agency is deferred *ad infinitum* in an endless replication of mutually devouring interpretations.

Revolutionary, therefore, as the reading of the Bible encoded in the play's structure is, from the standpoint of deconstruction, it is, so to speak, just one more disposable interpretation. Therefore, to conclude this discussion, we have to accept that from the standpoint of a deconstructionist project, the value of *A Grain of Wheat* and *I Will Marry When I Want* lies less in the meanings they encode, than in the degree to which they violate a pre-existing code and thus expose the artificiality of all meanings. In this way they beckon our attention towards the way meanings are constructed through institutions and ideologies. Ngugi's decision to stop writing in English but in Gikuyu is a logical outcome of such a recognition of the role of language as an institution.

In Ngugi's work this recognition of the role of institutions in the construction of meaning gets its fullest expression in the circumstances under which the original, *Ngahiika Ndenda*, was produced. In this form of the play Ngugi and his co-author were merely amanuenses who put down on paper what were essentially the workers' and peasants' ideas. The workers physically constructed the theatre, composed the play and acted in it. The result was a people's theatre in which the people acted out both their agency and their discourse. The audience was also predominantly made up of the workers and peasants. It was in an indigenous African language—their native Gikuyu.

The significance of *Ngahiika Ndenda* is that in it Ngugi, ironically, "died" as an author, as he submerged his own subjectivity in the collectivity of the people. It was only with the English version of the play and his subsequent testimonies that his own individual subjectivity re-emerges and that he regains the status of "authority." However, by re-claiming his authorship he not only finds himself colluding with the very hegemonic forces he has set out to subvert, he also reclaims his position in the class of his ascription. So in discussing this play one must recognise the distinction between *Ngahiika Ndenda*, which recuperates the agency and speech of the subaltern and in which Ngugi's individual subjectivity is "unclassed," and *I Will Marry When I Want*, in which a well-meaning, but petty-bourgeois consciousness regains its authority by objectifying the people. *I Will Marry When I Want* transgresses the very laws it appears to have set for itself, so that instead of "incarnating" the soul of the masses, it "incarnates" the crisis-laden soul of Ngugi himself. As it circulates as a text and is produced as a performance it is a play in which the workers and peasants are depicted by an "other." *Ngahiika Ndenda*, on the other hand, suggests that it is not enough to reinterpret the Bible in decolonising ways, no matter how radical. It interrogates the very institutions, language and discourses of theatrical performance which inscribe the silence of the masses in theatre. It is these institutions which are responsible for the violent hierarchical ordering in which the Bible is given greater value than non-biblical religious narratives.

BIBLIOGRAPHY

Amuta, Chidi. *The Theory of African Literature: Implications for Practical Criticism*. London and New Jersey: Zed Books Ltd. 1989.

Ashcroft, B., Griffiths, G. and Tiffin, H. *The Empire Writes Back: Theory and Practice. Post-Colonial Literatures*. London and New York: Routledge 1989.

Banana, C. "The Case for a New Bible." In Eds I. Mukonyera, J.C. Cox and F.J. Verstraelen, *Rewriting the Bible: The Real Issues*. Gweru, Zimbabwe: Mambo Press 1993: 17–28.

Bhabha, Hommi. *The Location of Culture*. London and New York: Routledge, 1994.

Christopher, A.J. *Colonial Africa*. Totowa, New Jersey: Barnes and Noble 1984.

Giddens, Anthony. *Sociology*. Cambridge: Polity Press 1989.

Dickson, K.A. *Theology in Africa*. New York: Orbis. 1984.

Horn, Andrew. "African Theatre—Docility and Dissent." *Index on Censorship*. Vol. 9 No. 3 (June 1980): 9–15.

Kidd, Ross. "Popular Theatre and Population Struggle in Kenya: The Theory of Kamiriithu" *Race and Class*, XXIV, 3 (1983): 288–304.

Lazarus, N. *Resistance in post-colonial African Fiction*. New Haven and London: Yale University Press 1990.

———. "(Re)turn to the People: Ngugi Wa Thiong'o and The Crisis of Post-colonial African Intellectualism" In Ed. C. Cantalupo *The World of Ngugi Wa Thiong'o*. New Jersey, Africa World Press 1995: 11–26.

Mudimbe, V.T. *The Invention of Africa: Gnosis, Philosophy and the Order of Knowledge*. Indianapolis: Indiana University Press 1988.

Ngugi Wa Thiong'o. *Decolonizing the Mind: the Politics of Language in African Literature*. London: James Currey 1986.

———. *A Grain of Wheat*. London: Heinemann 1967.

———. *Moving the Centre: The Struggle for Cultural Freedoms*. London: Heinemann 1993.

Ngugi wa Mirii and Ngugi wa Thiong'o. *I Will Marry When I Want*. London: Heinemann 1982 (Published in Gikuyu 1980).

Nkosi, L. "Reading Matigari: The New Novel of Post-Independence." In Ed. C. Cantalupo *The World of Ngugi Wa Thiong'o*, New Jersey, Africa World Press 1995: 197–205.

Said, E. *Culture and Imperialism*. London: Chatto and Windus 1993.

Seshadra-Crooks, K. "At The Margins of Post-colonial Studies." *Ariel: A Review of International English Literature*, 26:3, July 1995.

Verstraelen, F.J. "The Christian Bible and African Cultural and Religions Realities." In Eds I. Mukonyera, J.C. Cox and F.J. Verstraelen, *Rewriting the Bible: The Real Issues*, Gweru: Mambo Press 1993: 219–248.

Young, R. *Untying the Text: A Post-Structuralist Reader*. Boston, London and Henley: Routledge and Kegan Paul 1981.

(SOUTH) AFRICA, BIBLE, CRITICISM:
RHETORICS OF A VISIT

Robert P. Carroll[1]

Ex Africa semper aliquid novi: something new is
always coming out of Africa (Pliny the Elder).

The heaven of Europe is empty, like a Schloss
Abandoned because of taxes . . . (Wallace 1990: 4).

One of the most lasting merits of the historical-critical approach to
reading the Bible has been its insistence on the need for the focus
to be on the *historical retrieval* of local traditions embedded in the biblical text as sources and building blocks of the biblical tradition
(*Redaktionsgeschichte*), thus opening up a plurality of readings and perspectives for all subsequent work on the Bible (*Rezeptionsgeschichte*). So
local communities can imitate scripture itself by supplying their own
local stories as continua of biblical performance (see West 1993, and
especially West 1999). In this paper I want to take a very modest
approach to the topos of *reading Africa in relation to reading the Bible* by
telling my own story of a visit to South Africa which I made in
August-September of the year 1993 and by reflecting on that story
for what it may yield by way of rhetorical and hermeneutical insights.
This is my story of Africa. A part of my own larger personal story
as an academic biblical scholar, and it reflects what little I now know
about the continent. These are my hermeneutical reflections on the
rhetorics of my story and I offer them to the Guild of Biblical Studies
as my very small contribution to mapping the mosaic of reading the
Bible in an African context.

What on earth do I know about Africa? The continent is far too
big to be encompassed by the mind of a European used to living
within the small distances of the myriad cultures and languages constituting Europe. As well as on a set of very small islands off the
northwest coast of the European landmass. Born and reared in

Dublin, Ireland, and having worked summers in England, I now live and work in an ancient Scottish university in Glasgow, Scotland. So a great deal of my life experiences have been confined to the small islands at the nether end of Europe. Of course from books and films I knew a little about the topos of "out of Africa": Augustine and all that Egypt-Ethiopia material in the Bible which makes the Bible so much itself "a book out of Africa"—though arguably it is more confined than that, being restricted to the so-called "Fertile Crescent" or what we nowadays call "The Middle East" or "The Ancient Near East"—nomenclature is a real bugbear of any form of contemporary scholarship. The perspective is a Western one of course, but then *everybody has to be somewhere* and therefore everybody's viewpoint is necessarily relativized and localized. This truth about the relativity of all cultural points of view is not a colour thing, nor does it belong to any one race nor to any single ethnicity. All knowledge is local. We are all localized by our own stories and relativized by our experiences, whatever our creed, culture, ethnicity or race may happen to be. Some of my more defining features happen to be European and Irish and absolutely no apologies will be offered here for my being Irish, white, male, European or even academic—none whatsoever.

Throughout the 1980s Ferdinand Deist of UNISA in Pretoria (latterly he moved to Stellenbosch University in the 1990s) pestered me with invitations to visit South Africa and to give lectures there. For my part, being an old-fashioned liberal who was convinced that comfort should not be given to the apartheid regime, by my appearing to have approved of it by a visit to South Africa, thus endorsing its theopolitical ideology, I resolutely refused to visit there before the dismantling of the state apparatus of apartheid. This is a practice I consistently kept up during the long dark decades of apartheid and the equally dark decades of communist rule in Eastern Europe when the Soviet empire ruled so much of the Eastern world. Until the Berlin Wall had come down in 1989 and Nelson Mandela had been released from prison on Robben Island I simply refused *in practice* to visit such oppressive regimes in these different countries. My refusal was by no means a universal practice among liberal and/or left-of-centre scholars. Other colleagues in the Guild, including ecclesiastical colleagues in my own department in the University of Glasgow, took a very different view of such collaboration with apartheid and visited South Africa regularly. As I am not an ideologue, I cannot say that my negative attitude was right and their collaboration with apartheid (or with communism for that matter) was wrong. On the contrary, I am more inclined now to think that I may have been wrong in this matter. I suspect that the economic and cultural boycott against South Africa did far more damage, to the black peoples there than it did to the Afrikaners (Boers). But we all make our own decisions and having made them we must stand by the consequences, answering for the implicatures of our courses of action or non-action. However, once Mandela was released from jail I felt I could in some form of "good" conscience respond positively should Ferdinand Deist continue to seek to persuade me to visit the continent. Thereafter I allowed myself to be persuaded by him to visit South Africa in 1993 as a visiting professor and to give lectures on the topos of "The Bible and Ideology" around the different universities of UNISA, Pretoria, Natal (at Durban-Westville), Pietermaritzburg (a staff seminar), Stellenbosch and Cape Town.[2] The visit was an eye-opening experience, at first hand, of the impact of ideology in relation to the Bible, imposed on a country and all its different cultures. In that visit I learned in practice what I had known for a long time only in theory. Having heard with the ear, I now saw with the eye—the appalling effects of a Bible-based ideology imposed on a non-biblical world.

I was not entirely ignorant of things under apartheid in South Africa during the years before I visited the country. Ferdinand Deist had regularly written me very lengthy letters about the political situation there and this correspondence had been an invaluable source of political information for me. Looking back on it now, I can see that it was a genuine education in itself. A political education in things South African, as it were. I had also, in cooperation with Ferdinand, looked after two of his doctoral students on cultural-academic visits to Glasgow during the 1980s (Willie Wessels in 1984 and Fanie Marais in 1987), so I did have some knowledge of what to expect should I ever go out to South Africa. Given the high degree of culture shock that Willie and Fanie had experienced when living with us in Glasgow, especially in relation to a rugged West of Scotland democratic culture, and perhaps also in reaction to my own some-

---

[2] The funding of this trip was organized by the South African Human Sciences Research Council and once again I must acknowledge the sheer generosity of their support for my visit to South Africa in 1993. Without that generous funding of my trip there would have been no visit to South Africa.

what post-Christian, agnostic, academic approach to the Hebrew Bible, I could hardly have expected to be as culturally shocked by South Africa as they had been by Scotland during the 1980s.

As Ferdinand's sudden death on the 12th of July 1997 contributed to preventing me from returning to South Africa in the summer of 1998, this paper will have to serve as an underexposed reflection on my first and only (so far) experience of visiting (South) Africa. I would really need to have visited South Africa much more often to be able to provide an intelligent and mature reflective account of matters there. On Ferdinand's last visit to Glasgow (April 1997) we spent time over our last dinner together discussing the ways and means whereby I could visit South Africa again the following summer and do some teaching during term time there. All that planning and hoping have gone by the board now and I shall never see him again, nor hear his infectious laughter nor read a letter from him nor encounter a very incisive criticism of my own work from him. So I shall offer this paper as a substitute for such a visit, while once again recognizing in print Ferdinand Deist's enormous contribution to biblical scholarship in South Africa and, in particular, the debt I owe him for friendship, influence and scholarship (see Carroll 1998).

This contribution then is a retrospective attempt at analysing the rhetoric of my visit to the universities of South Africa in that year pitched between Mandela's release and the 1994 elections in South Africa. These were my first impressions of South Africa and their naiveté is entirely due to it being my first time on a continent, well beyond my experience and knowledge. I had many reservations about the visit, mostly having to do with the fact that I was very conscious of being a white male and privileged academic from the West, visiting a territory where until very recently other white folk had exploited, oppressed and deformed the black peoples of the country. This was a period in the West when, among North American biblical scholars, one could be forgiven for thinking that to be white and male was close to being an intellectual crime, a requirement for an act and attitude of self-hatred and certainly an ideological defect in a person.[3] I had one defence for my whiteness and it was the fact that

---

[3] This is how I read a book such as Daniel Patte's *Ethics of Biblical Interpretation: A Reevaluation*, Louisville: Westminster/John Knox Press, 1995. I think it is high time that this issue was discussed with a bit more backbone and "cards on the table" approach rather than in the mealy-mouthed fashion of "blaming Whitey"

I did not belong to the oppressor class of white imperial males from Britain or America. As an Irishman from Dublin I could always defend myself by the knowledge that I had myself in the past belonged to (a) peasant stock and (b) a nation which had itself been oppressed and exploited by the British colonizing imperial forces for many centuries. Of course I had shifted class from being of peasant stock to the middle-class characteristic of people with an education, especially academics. My grandfather had schlepped junk around on a horse and cart in the county of Wicklow, my father had been a tradesman in Dublin, but I had acquired a university education so had inevitably become middle-class in the process—so could no longer claim to be a peasant. *Professors are never peasants.* Whatever or however they may have started out in life, their evolution into academics or professors inevitably deracinates them. On the other hand, my status as an Irishman also gave me some affinity with the Boers (Afrikaners), who had themselves been oppressed by the British at the turn of the century. In that period which had seen the beginning of the ending of British imperialism (empire) and the emergence of total war, the creation of concentration camps and the mass maltreatment of women and children, features all so characteristic of the long twentieth century. But even with this cultural baggage supporting me, it was still with very mixed feelings that I flew out of Heathrow to Johannesburg towards the end of August 1993. As an attempt to analyse my reactions to that African experience this paper is more focussed on rhetoric than on hermeneutics, but the two are inevitably interconnected.

I took out to South Africa a series of prepared lectures and papers on the highly relevant topic of "The Bible and Ideology," including a paper on Bible translation for the Old Testament Society of South Africa conference in Stellenbosch. Within the opportunities made available for lectures, I also did some seminars on my own work on Jeremiah and, when invited, I talked about the book I had recently published *Wolf in the Sheepfold.*[4] It was certainly a most stimulating

---

which has characterized the non-debate thus far. Nobody, not even whites (pinks), is to blame for the colour of their skin and "inverted racist" approaches such as Patte's are just as racist as any of the racist approaches justly condemned by all right-thinking people.

[4] These lectures were subsequently written up for publication (see Carroll 1993, 1994, 1995). See also Carroll 1997 (in South Africa I used the original edition of *Wolf in the Sheepfold* published by SPCK in 1991).

experience talking about my own work to sympathetic, but probing, audiences and I suspect that one of the things I most liked about Ferdinand Deist was his critical appreciation of my own work. He liked it and said so, but he was always posing probing, critical questions about it. I spent half my time in South Africa living in Stellenbosch and working at the Department of Semitics in the university there. So I was able, on occasion, to visit that Theological Faculty in Stellenbosch which had been the heart and soul of the production of apartheid ideology. There in the past godly theologians and churchmen had read their Bibles, taken note of the highly separatist ideology to be found in the Pentateuch, especially in the Book of Deuteronomy, and had accordingly constructed a theopolitical ideology of their own for South Africa. In which, white superiority was enthroned over black inferiority, as if such politics were the very will of God for twentieth century South Africa. It was most interesting to be working out of the Department of Ancient Near Eastern Studies in contrast to the Theological Faculty; especially in relation to the little *Wolf* book, which I had written precisely against the very kind of reading of the Bible found in the Theological Faculty: ideological readings of the Bible such as the one that was constituted by the Deuteronomistic doctrine of apartheid, being reconstructed in and for the very different world of modern South Africa.[5]

Having flown from London Heathrow to Johannesburg, I stayed in Pretoria with Willie Wessels, who had stayed with us in Glasgow during his visit there in 1984. Immediately, I was struck by the class and wealth differences between a person who had been a student when I first knew him, yet *even then* had lived in a house much larger and grander than I had at the time of his visit, *when he was only a student*. This kind of affluence became, for me, a symbol (or cipher) of what it meant to be white in apartheid Africa. No wonder the depth of his culture shock when he had been in Glasgow when he had encountered white academics lacking servants (household slaves) or had seen white female newspaper vendors working on the streets! After more than twenty years teaching in a major, ancient Western University I was still far inferior as to social wealth compared to a white *student* in the privileged land of Africa. I am often made very conscious when I travel of the fact that, while I might be regarded

---

[5] On this point see Deist's own discussion of apartheid, an essay which was very influential in my preparation of lectures for South Africa (Deist 1994).

by some people as at the top of my profession, my social ranking
in the West of Scotland is a great deal poorer than that of academics elsewhere, with half my experience or achievements. A working-
class start in life is not the best way of becoming comfortably well-off,
in later life as an academic. It is also far too glib an exercise just
to treat all westerners as incredibly rich and upper class because
they teach at universities. When some of them may be, relatively,
quite poor compared to American or white South African standards.
That was a lesson reinforced by staying with Willie Wessels—who is
by no means a high totem ranking academic-churchman among the
ecclesiastical-academic hierarchies of South Africa. Quite the contrary,
and yet even he has remarked on the gap between the two of us.
He appeared not only to be richer than I, but to live at a better
economic level than I did, and he even had the rank of Professor
long before I had it! The day is near at hand when a serious but
proper analysis of the imagined social status in contrast to the actual
substance of academics across and around the world will need to be
carried out, in order to bring some realism to the social analyses so
often glibly taken for granted by certain exponents of Western biblical scholarship.

On the other hand, I did not envy the degree or level of social
wealth displayed by the various biblical scholars I met in UNISA
and the University of Pretoria. Too many of them have died since
I visited in 1993 for me to be envious of them at all and their
Pretoria existence was virtually a social ghetto because *they lived behind
bars.* Their properties had to be protected from violent criminal action
in Pretoria by means of iron bars, lights and guard dogs. Such an
existence I have never aspired to and I have to admit that the degree
of crime and violence, not to mention road accidents, in Pretoria at
that time was so high, that living in Glasgow was virtually utopian
by contrast. Of course Glasgow had its crime and its reputation for
social violence—much of that reputation was a hangover or transference from the 1930s (London was a lot more violent than Glasgow
in the 1980s)—but nothing like the level of that which pertained in
Pretoria in the early 1990s. In Natal, I stayed with Dirk Buchner
in Durban-Westville and that was much more like the world I was
used to, where young academics working on their doctoral studies
did not live in the lap of luxury. Observing Dirk and his partner I
could see myself as I had been decades before as a young academic struggling to make ends meet and to forge some kind of acad-

emic identity and voice for myself. Out at Pietermaritzburg, where I encountered the famed contextual theologians Gerald West, Jonathan Draper and Gunther Wittenberg, I also felt that I was in the presence of a much more practical and less alienating intellectual environment than I had found in Pretoria. In Stellenbosch the apartment I occupied was designed for visiting academics and, while more than adequate, it too did not approximate to any level of luxury. Only in Pretoria, where the Boer ruled, did I encounter such a disparate level of social kudos attached to academic standing. That in itself was a very interesting and eye-opening experience.

In striking contrast to such wealth in Pretoria and the general comfort of the white academics I met and worked with in South Africa, was the (near) absolute poverty I encountered among black peoples there, especially among various ethnic groups who lacked any access to English or Afrikaans language. Such poverty shocked me to the point of being breathtaking. If ever I saw a stark indictment of the cruelty and viciousness of apartheid, it was there among the poor blacks. Before going to South Africa I would have flattered myself that I thought I knew poverty to some extent, from the poverty of the peripheral estates in Glasgow (e.g., Castlemilk, Drumchapel, Easterhouse, Garthamlock) and especially places such as Possil and Shettleston, not to mention the poverty I could remember of poor barefooted kids growing up in the Dublin of my childhood. But in South Africa I encountered a dimension of poverty which had been beyond my imagination until I went there. If this was separate development (the so-called justification for a policy of apartheid), then the ideologues and engineers of the doctrine should have been taken out at once and shot. This was not development but the systematic impoverishment of peoples. What I saw across South Africa in the faces of poor black people was an indictment of the apartheid system which no amount of words could have equalled. Apartheid shocked me with its indifference to the suffering it had caused to so many people and to the impoverishment it had imposed on the black peoples. I felt (still feel) that if the rhetorical phrases "evil," "wicked" ever had a referent in the real world, then they applied to the doctrine and practice of apartheid as practised by the whites of South Africa. However, I also tend to think that such theological rhetoric is less helpful than harmful. It cloaks and masks reality by making disapproving noises and throws rhetoric at problems which are too real to be susceptible to rhetorical control.

Of course not all whites were guilty of this crime against humanity, some had fought it and had been among its fiercest critics, but the system itself was corrupt and corrupting. It made me ponder unanswerable questions such as, "How could churches have constructed such evil?" "How could a reading of the Bible be so wrong, without the learned theologians rethinking their wicked ways and amending their evil lives?." And many other questions which I shall not touch on here. When the apartheid system began to be dismantled, other questions presented themselves such as, "Why did the churches responsible for such evil not close themselves down and go out of existence?" "Why was there no major outcry of guilt and self-horror among the churches which had tolerated such crimes against humanity?" "How could such churches just apologize to everybody to whom they had done such injury and then act as if verbal apologies constituted adequate reparation for such evil deeds?" "If sensitivity to the Bible was as intense, as the fundamentalism of the neo-Calvinist theology which spawned apartheid suggested it was, how could such Bible readers be so insensitive to the evil they had done to so many people?" Such questions were multiplied for me when I was out in South Africa, but they were at best only rhetorical responses to what I witnessed there.

I knew that there had to be much better ways of reading the Bible than such literalistic and fundamentalistic reading programmes which had given rise to the dogma of apartheid in the first place. It was a most salutary encounter with the practical evil of ways how not to read the Bible. But I knew all this theoretically before I went out to South Africa, what the experience of visiting Africa gave me was a gut-wrenching sense of how wrong it all was. I do not doubt for a moment that the theologians had read their Bibles correctly, but nor did I doubt that this was not (or was no longer, if ever it had been) a proper way to read the Bible. That I already knew of course from the Enlightenment project of liberation through reason and from everything I had learned from the historical-critical approach to reading biblical texts. Hence, my continued strong liking for and defence of the historical-critical method of Bible reading. Without such an informing *Kritik* as the Enlightenment had generated, so it seems to me, ethical readings of the Bible are highly unlikely if not downright impossible in this day and age.

Had I then flown so far (some 12,000 miles) just to learn the obvious, what I had always known? I guess I had, in some very real sense. Counting my undergraduate and graduate days, as well as the years in which I had taught Hebrew Bible at university level, I had spent some thirty-five years working on the Bible from a post-Enlightenment point of view, and in the (reading) company of some of the finest radical minds since Baruch Spinoza in the seventeenth century—Thomas Paine, William Blake, Karl Marx etc.—so I already knew what was wrong with racist, illiberal regimes. But seeing the consequences of such systematic exploitation and oppression of peoples at firsthand was still a shock to my ideocultural system. To see such poverty, such lack of hope, such settling for so little and in contrast to the very rich sectors of society, all this arising from an ideological system of thought and practice derived from a reading of the Bible, reinforced the convictions I already had that this Dutch Reformed mode of apartheid was most definitely no way to read the Bible. Reading the Bible in such a theopolitical fashion just could not be justified without some redeeming ideology which would challenge any such reading of the Bible itself. For, as I had known for many years, *the Bible was itself part of the problem and not just part of the solution.* Whatever Liberation Theology may have said and thought, the real problem was the old problem, the Bible is *an unsafe text* when it comes to liberation or liberatory readings. It is equally a most unsafe text for doing any practical readings about how modern cultures should be constructed.

In one of the lectures I gave at various places I made the point—it is a well-known point but it will bear repetition here—and I quote from the published version of that lecture:

> It is far too easy to make connections between the exodus story in the Bible and modern slavery and to argue that the Bible is about liberation. It may be true to say that the Bible includes a strand of narrative about liberation from slavery, but it also includes the re-inscription of slavery in that narrative so that the reader of the Bible has to choose between these biblical values (Carroll 1995).

What determines the way we read the Bible are extra-biblical values and ideologies. It may be readily granted that some values derived from the Bible by means of a critical-historical post-Enlightenment reading of the text may have fed into our current value systems, but the opposite would equally be true. In the long history of Christianity, with its concomitant practice of Bible-reading, no ideology of liberty was ever generated or devised for the freeing of slaves until *after* the radical critique of religion constructed by the Enlightenment had taken place. Given a secular code of liberation it now becomes possible, even fashionable, for religious folk to read the Bible by means of a radical, even marxisant, liberatory principle.[6] There are some who would argue that there is in the Bible "a divine preference for the poor" or "a *nisus* within it, which takes sides with the poor against the rich, the oppressed against the oppressors, which demands justice, and which understands justice as respecting the fact that all people are made in the image of God, and that all are sisters and brothers of the Son of Man" (Gorringe 1998: 78). I find the second part of that sentence too replete with wishful thinking and a very slanted reading of the totality of the Bible. It speaks well for the heart of the writer, but seems to avoid his head altogether. In my opinion, a straightforward reading of the biblical text as a totality will not bear out this reading of it. Even a simple reading of the exodus myth soon reveals the fact (textual fact) that the exodus legend is not a narrative incompatible with the enslavement of people. For example, the very first set of *mišpāṭîm* encountered after the giving of the decalogue in Exodus 20 concerns the regulating of *buying and selling Hebrew slaves* (Exod. 21:1–11).[7] As I said in my lectures out in South Africa, "At its starkest level the Bible is a book of slaves for slaves" (Carroll 1995: 37). In my judgment, it is only the masking of such reading operations by the assumption of post-Enlightenment values *as if they had been biblical values all the time* that enables political readers of the Bible today to con themselves into believing that the Bible is a book of liberation *simpliciter* (see Prior 1997, Warrior 1989). The point needs to be made more forcibly: Taken by itself the Bible

---

[6] The prime example of this kind of secular transformation of political theology must be that of the current Pope (John Paul II) who jets around the world speaking on behalf of human rights against regimes which fail to practice them. Such democratic and social rights discourses were declared anathema by his papal predecessors in the last century and in the earlier part of this century. I guess the Emperor's new clothes now consist of those very garments he had dismissed a long time ago!

[7] But even the biblical writers over time had recognized problems with such slave-making as is indicated by the changing readings of the matter in the subsequent texts of Leviticus (25:25–28) and Deuteronomy (15:12–18). Taken as a totality of thinking on the subject, the three sets of texts are indicative of anxious changing cultural values, but the enslavement of foreigners remains inscribed forever in the Bible. For a discussion of the problem see Sternberg (1998).

is as much an instrument of oppression as ever it was a book of liberation. What it is or what it becomes all depends on the attitudes, ideologies and skills of its readers. Only when it is read in conjunction with an ideology of freedom and a critique of all oppressive measures can the book justifiably be used for liberatory readings by free peoples. It is the Bible *plus* the radical critique in favour of the emancipation project of the Enlightenment which operates for and towards liberation. Whereas by itself, the Book (and the conventional old ways of reading the Book) still belongs to all the old oppressive, imperially modelled structures of the ancient religion, from which the Enlightenment sought to free us all. Without "association" with other values the Bible cannot speak to free people at all, because it has through its history been itself so much an instrument of oppression and unfreedom, even if only by cooption and the historical practice of the powerful ruling classes of different cultures. Some kind of quadrilateral value system—that is, the Bible, *plus* reason, *plus* liberatory tradition, *plus* critique, [*plus* various other factors etc.?]—is required to transform the Bible into a text which may contribute something to becoming itself a liberative instrument (see Percy 1998: 264).

In recent years there seems to have been, in many ecclesiastical quarters, a concerted theologico-ecclesiastical effort to badmouth, denounce and reject the Enlightenment in favour of precritical and other imagined medieval values. One of the things which has given postmodernism such a boost in and for theology has been the sharing of a common enemy, the Enlightenment, between fundamentalists, church folk, the so-called "radical orthodox" and pro-medievalists. But my problem with this huge clanging-cymbals of a movement has been its fundamental reactionary approach to politics. Taking it seriously and following its deeply reactionary political values would have entailed the loss of democracy as a natural corrective to apartheid and would have meant that democracy would never have come to South Africa and apartheid could never have been dismantled in favour of democracy. Dismiss the Enlightenment and there is no justification whatsoever for dismantling apartheid or freeing the slaves, nor can there be any grounds for human rights or universal suffrage. While it may be readily recognized and freely admitted that the Enlightenment has had many failures and never did quite live up to its own lights and values, reaction really has got nothing going for it at all in terms of liberation and democracy.[8] Those who have never been slaves may wish to mock any system of thought which sought to free slaves, but ask the slaves themselves. Of course we may need a more critical perception of the Enlightenment and, in biblical studies, it may also be necessary to construct a post-critical take on biblical scholarship, even a second naiveté, to use Ricoeur's terminology, but such a move can *never* be a pre-critical or a non-critical approach to reading texts (Ricoeur 1967: 351). A genuinely free and open biblical scholarship must always factor the critique into its reading of the Bible.[9] In my judgment, and this is something which observation of the apartheid ideology of South Africa reinforces, though it does not invent it, only the critique will prevent learned theologians from making the fatal errors they committed when they constructed apartheid from a surface reading of the Book of Deuteronomy and of the Bible, and without such a critique oppression will go on being reinforced by readings from the Bible. While the critique need not necessarily guarantee that we will get our readings right, without the critique there can only be further re-inscription of oppression from a source such as the Bible—check the history books if you doubt this point—because the combination of political power allied to religious ideology *based on the Bible* is invariably an oppressive implementation of power, with Almighty God and his servant-messiah emperor (or its modern equivalent) as the spearhead of the institutionalization of that power.

Before I went out to South Africa, I knew all these things, but what my experience of five weeks going around South Africa, lecturing, listening and talking to so many different people (black, coloured and white), did for me was to re-inscribe my convictions more strongly than ever and to give them greater precision of expression by fuelling my imagination and intellect. I do not imagine for a moment that life now in South Africa will be wonderful or that after the dismantling of apartheid equality will flow freely throughout the land. Things do not work that way. What I do think must

---

[8] The literature on the failure of the Enlightenment is too well-known and too multitudinous to be listed here, I shall just refer to what I would regard as a fair and well-balanced account of the matter (see Wilson 1999).

[9] I tried to say something along these lines in my (as yet unpublished) Presidential Address to the Society for Old Testament Study (SOTS) in Birmingham on 4 January 1999 entitled "Beyond Kerygma and Kritik: A Future for Hebrew Bible Studies in the Institutions of Our Learning?."

be underlined is the desperate need for *sustained critical readings of the Bible* and that never again should a group of theologians be allowed to enslave a nation with their uncritical readings of the Bible. I have called this paper "(South) Africa, Bible, Criticism" because I would wish it to be the beginnings of a primer, an ABC, of how the Bible should be read in relation to political matters. Taken in conjunction with contemporary liberatory philosophies (or, in somewhat different form, ideologies of equality, equal opportunities or whatever) and always with a strongly critical interaction with the book, the Bible may be used *with extreme caution* in all modern political endeavours. The Bible is an ancient book and its contents just cannot be taken directly from the page and imposed on modernity. Cultures change, values change and circumstances change. So, to read the Bible without making the proper, major changes, serious allowances and radical adjustments for such changes, is to produce fundamentally defective readings and misapplications at best. That is what I tried to say in my book *Wolf in the Sheepfold* and what I also sought to get across in my lectures to the various classes and groups in the different universities of South Africa on my visit out there. I recognize and would readily admit that it sounds very simplistic and probably was when I delivered the lectures, but the cultural divides I had to bridge on my visit out there were sufficiently wide and diverse for me to keep things simple. Even if only for my own sake, if not always for the sake of those who heard me, simplicity was a necessity for me. I may be at home in the Celtic twilight of the West of Scotland where the final traces and echoes of a dying Presbyterianism still make life difficult for all of us, but among the black peoples and white academics of South Africa I was really out of my depth and far from home, both culturally and ideologically.

Looking back now on the experience of visiting South Africa, some six years ago, it is hard to offer a maturer evaluation than what I have said in the above paragraphs. The strength of my shocked feelings at the time remains a vivid memory for me. There were, of course, also very strong senses, of the size and beauty of the country, the gentleness of its black peoples, the sheer exoticness of places such as Table Mountain or Kruger National Park and the peacefulness of the Buddhist garden behind Table Mountain, that remain with me, in almost undiminished vigour, to this day. The formality of the theological faculties in contrast to the wonderful engagement with, and capacity for enjoyment of life, qualities of the other departments where I worked, is also something I remember well. What on first sight seemed to me to be the appalling near-idolatrous fundamentalism of the students going to church on Sundays, Bibles in hand, was explained to me by those who knew better as a social activity of a much higher nature: this was one of the very few ways available to young men and young women of meeting each other socially. The flora and fauna of the subcontinent were of a quality beyond anything in my own dark European experience and I felt myself at times to have been let loose to roam in some marvellous paradise of plenty and beauty. Of course, it was also quite otherwise. For all its stunning beauty and for all its exotic sights, South Africa was also a very dark place where much terrible evil had been done to millions of black and coloured people. The awfulness of the refugee camp at Khayelitsa will live in my memory of the visit for ever. Since then I have watched things improve slightly in South Africa and then return to an awful level of violence, crime and death as the totalizing consequences of apartheid are played out to their very end. There are also the burgeoning problems of HIV infection and AIDS. It will be a long time yet before the Republic finds its feet by educating all it's uneducated (and undereducated) peoples, provides work and homes for everybody and somehow helps to redress the terrible imbalances so carefully nurtured over the long reign of apartheid policies. It will be generations yet to come which will benefit from what is done now, but contemporary generations will have to go on contributing to and counting the awful costs of apartheid.

Rhetorics apart, what did I learn from my visit out there or from the period of reflection on the visit after I had returned to Scotland? I think there is one thing which I learned above all else and that is the absolute need for a *critical* reading of the Bible in any culture where the Bible is deemed to be of sufficient importance as to be imposed on the construction of life and social structures. No ideology drawn from, based on or associated with the Bible should ever be allowed to see the light of day ever again. Until the Bible has been subjected to *a severe critical scrutiny* and strong allowance made for cultural differences and calculations made of the likely consequences of the imposition of any practical policy based on the Book, its role in social engineering should *at best* be kept to a minimum. The Bible is *an unsafe book* from which to do politics or social engineering in contemporary society. Its roots are in ancient alien times and among ancient alien cultures. Nothing in the book can be transferred or transposed from its imagined roots to our own times without first having undergone a very radical critique and been transformed in the critical process. I knew that before I went out there, but I had no idea just how much I knew that until I went out there! I also learned at a new and deeper level that neither liberatory nor marxisant readings of the Bible could ever be adequate for contemporary African society. They are *at best* deeply inadequate as constructions of society for many different reasons. Perhaps this is a lesson which cannot be learned too often, but it is one which needs constantly to be relearned and restated for all theopolitical readers of the Bible.

The liberatory model extrapolated from the Bible is at best a partial paradigm extracted from a larger narrative (meganarrative) which in itself is not, nor need it be, liberatory at all. Few of the main features of the exodus story will bear the weight of liberatory readings assigned to them: the Hebrew slaves freed from the domination of the Egyptians are taken out of Egypt (in order to) and die, or are killed by YHWH, in the wilderness. A few survivors and the descendants of the freed slaves make it through the wilderness into the land where they proceed to butcher the local inhabitants in a genocidal, seizure of land, campaign. Thus the story of a people's freedom is sandwiched between two stories of the annihilation of foreigners (Egyptians and Canaanites) and the liberated survivor-slaves find themselves freed to buy their own slaves (Exod. 21:1–11). Eventually the emergence of monarchy will entail the use of forced labour (the dreadful corvée) to build YHWH's temple and the many royal palaces required by the Davidic dynasty to display its intimate relationship with its patron YHWH. Transposed to South Africa, this account of the story looks all too familiar: the Boer Voortrekkers found their promised land, had to fight off the imperialist British and then in their own country proceeded to enslave (aka. fail to provide for separate development) the black peoples. The re-inscription of history in another form makes for a new historicist reading of the Bible, but I have touched on that problem elsewhere (Carroll 1998: 308–315). The Boer captivity of the Bible underlines, for me, the problem and danger of all such readings of the Bible. The basic meganarrative of the exodus legend can and will underwrite any number of quite different appropriations of the biblical story. The appropriation of a biblical narrative, story or trope often involves taking over the text and colonizing the biblical material. Such an

act will not in itself guarantee the purity of a reading nor the innocence of intention of any culture or community choosing to read
the Bible in such a fashion. That much must be obvious to all readers of the Bible by now from the many centuries of experience and
examples available to historically minded readers of the Bible. In my
personal judgment the extrapolation of a few desirable elements from
a story quite full of undesirable elements is a grossly inadequate way
of using Bible readings as a blueprint for social engineering in the
contemporary world. Too many necessary factors are missing from
such a paradigm of Bible reading, hence such hermeneutics are a
useless appropriation of the Bible at best and at worst it is dangerous and destructive of human life and culture. Apartheid in South
Africa has demonstrated just how destructive and costly such bad
hermeneutics can be, and because reading and implementing any
such reading of the Bible remains a common and popular practice
around the world today it is necessary to be very careful in matters
hermeneutical—*caveat lector*, mind how you read!

I knew all this before I went to South Africa. I had learned it
from the Enlightenment project of liberty through reason, and from
the story of the long struggle of the historical-critical approach to
reading the Bible in order to emerge from the intimidations of its
more powerful ecclesiastical opponents. I had also learned it from
my knowledge of the long march through Western institutions to
enclaves of freedom in the academies of the West in the twentieth
century, and from my own solid university education in Hebrew
Bible and the history of the discipline. And, of course, from the
accumulative story of liberation as incarnated in the stories of Baruch
Spinoza, Thomas Paine, David Strauss, Ernest Renan and the-all-
too-many heroes of reason, who had fought the good fight and who
had left behind them such inspiring stories and examples for all of
us who come after them. And yet, my visit to South Africa had
helped to put plump flesh on the bare bones of what I already knew.
It also allowed me to see the wide range of different and distinctive
approaches to reading the Bible practised in various areas of South
Africa, so it added depth to the dimensions of what I had known
before flying out to Africa. I returned to Europe, to my academic
home in the far north of Britain a chastened scholar—the Jeremiah
trope of "the north" is an appropriate one for me as an Irish biblical scholar working under exilic conditions in Scotland because the
English centre down south dominates the discipline in terms of

resources and political influence[10]—having seen, at first hand, great poverty and the great oppression, which had contributed so much to creating such poverty—poverty of life, of opportunity, of economy and of education. By that time of course there were great hopes that Nelson Mandela would transform everything once the elections were held and black people had taken power into their own control. The failure of such dreams is another story and besides it is far too early to judge matters yet. As Chairman Mao is reputed to have said, when asked what he thought were the lasting results of the French Revolution: "It is far too early to be able to tell!" I feel the same way about the long-term prospects of South Africa and, as I bring these ruminations to a close, the only words which seem to come to mind about Africa's future are those from the well-known song: *Nkosi Sikeleli Africa.* . . . I cannot find it in my heart to dissent from those words.

BIBLIOGRAPHY

Carroll, Robert P. "On Representation in the Bible: An *Ideologiekritik* Approach," Journal of Northwest Semitic Languages 20 (1994): 1–15.
———. "Clio and Canons: In Search of a Cultural Poetics of the Hebrew Bible," *Biblical Interpretation* 5/4 (1998): 300–323.
———. "Beyond Kerygma and Kritik: A Future for Hebrew Bible Studies in the Institutions of Our Learning?," Unpublished Presidential Address to the Society for Old Testament Study (SOTS) in Birmingham on 4 January 1999.
———. "Biblical Ideolatry: *Ideologiekritik*, Biblical Studies and the Problematics of Ideology," Journal of Northwest Semitic Languages 24/1 (1998): 1–14.
———. "As Seeing the Invisible: Ideology in Biblical Translation," Journal of Northwest Semitic Languages 19 (1993): 79–93.
———. "An Infinity of Traces: On Making an Inventory of Our Ideological Holdings. An Introduction to *Ideologiekritik* in Biblical Studies," Journal of Northwest Semitic Languages 21/2 (1995): 25–44.
———. "Jeremiah, Intertextuality and *Ideologiekritik*," Journal of Northwest Semitic Languages 24/1 (1996): 15–34.
———. *Wolf in the Sheepfold: The Bible as Problematic for Theology*, London: SCM Press, 1997 (1991 Original Edition published by SPCK).
Deist, Ferdinand E. "The Dangers of Deuteronomy: A Page from the Reception History of the Book" In Eds Martinez, Hilhorst, Ruiten and Van der Woude, *Studies in Deuteronomy in Honour of C.J. Labuschagne on the Occasion of His 65th Birthday*, Leiden: E.J. Brill: 1994: 13–29.

---

[10] Of course everything is relative and Glasgow, Scotland is only in the "far north" from the perspective of, say, the "real centre of the universe of Biblical Studies" in Britain, namely Oxford and Cambridge!

Gorringe, Tim. "Political Readings of Scripture" In Ed. J. Barton *The Cambridge Companion to Biblical Interpretation*, Cambridge: CUP, 1998: 67–80.

Patte, Daniel. *Ethics of Biblical Interpretation: A Reevaluation*, Louisville: Westminster/John Knox Press, 1995.

Percy, Martyn. *Power And the Church: Ecclesiology in an Age of Transition*, London: Cassell, 1998.

Prior, Michael. *The Bible and Colonialism: A Moral Critique*, The Biblical Seminar 48, Sheffield: Sheffield Academic Press, 1997.

Ricoeur, Paul. *The Symbolism of Evil*, Boston: Beacon Press, 1967.

Sternberg, Meir. *Hebrews between Cultures: Group Portraits and National Literature*, Indiana Studies in Biblical Literature, Bloomington & Indianapolis: Indiana University Press, 1998: 426–519.

Wallace, Steven, "The Greenest Continent" In Ed. Milton J. Bates, *Wallace Stevens, Opus Posthumous*, New York: Vintage Books, 1990: 84.

Warrior, Robert A. "Canaanites, Cowboys, and Indians: Deliverance, Conquest, and Liberation Theology Today," *Christianity and Crisis* 29 (1989): 261–265.

West, Gerald O. *The Academy of the Poor: Towards a Dialogical Reading of the Bible*, Interventions 2, Sheffield: Sheffield Academic Press, 1999.

———. *Contextual Bible Study*, Pietermaritzburg: Cluster Publications, 1993.

Wilson, Edward O. *Consilience: The Unity of Knowledge*, London: Abacus, 1999: 13–47.

PART TWO

PARTICULAR ENCOUNTERS WITH PARTICULAR TEXTS

A LATE SEVENTEENTH CENTURY TRANSLATION OF THE PSALMS AT THE CAPE

Philippe Denis

In June 1699 Pierre Simond, the minister of the French church at the Cape, began a new translation of the Psalms into the French language. His work was published five years later in Amsterdam under the title *Les Veilles Afriquaines ou les Pseaumes de David, Mis en Vers François*. A copy of this extremely rare pamphlet was recently found in St. Petersburg.[1] It throws new light on what is probably the earliest piece of biblical scholarship ever produced on the African continent. According to Simond the fact that the book was written in Africa was no accident, even if the intended audience was much broader than the small French colony at the Cape. It was God's Providence, he explained in the preface, that inspired him to go to the "deserts of Africa" to translate the Psalms (Simond 1704: 1r).

The only other African biblical scholar who comes to mind from this period is Jacobus Capitein, a former Gold Coast slave who was trained as a theologian in Leiden, before becoming the pastor in Elmina in present-day Ghana. In his doctoral dissertation he discussed the biblical arguments in favour of the institution of slavery. But this was in 1742, long after Simond had published his book. In Elmina, Capitein also translated the Ten Commandments and the Our Father into the vernacular (Boxer 1965: 152, Kpobi 1993).

Had it not been written in Africa, Simond's translation of the Psalms would probably have fallen into oblivion. Its theological content is not particular significant and its literary value doubtful. But the fact that this work was produced on the African soil, as early as the turn of the eighteenth century, deserves attention. Why did Simond decide to write a new translation of the Psalms? What was

---

[1] [Pierre Simond], *Les Veilles Afriquaines ou les Pseaumes de David, Mis en Vers François*. Amsterdam: Cornelle de Hoogenhuisen, 1704. 12°, [ ]¹ *⁶ ⁽⁶⁾ **² A-L⁶, [16]–130–[2]p. National Library of Russia, St. Petersburg: 6.52.11.35. Microfilm: Bibliographie du Psautier, Institut Claude Longeon, Saint-Étienne, France. The preface and a few psalms are reproduced in *Psaume. Bulletin de la recherche sur le psautier huguenot* 14 (November 1997), pp. 9–17.

his training? What books were on his desk? Did he make use of the Hebrew Bible? A careful examination of Simond's work will hopefully give some answers to these questions.[2] Apart from a short, pioneering article by Randolph Vigne (Vigne 1997: 3–9), *Les Veilles Afriquaines* has never been researched. The same cannot be said of Simond's biography which is now fairly well documented (Fensham 1962: 755–57, Franken 1978: 190–206, Boucher 1981: 174–76, Coertzen 1988: 132–38, Vigne 1988: 14–26, Sienart-van Reenen 1989: 27–28). A brief outline of the French pastor's life and career will therefore suffice to introduce this essay.

The son of a lawyer who held a public office in Nyons in southwestern Dauphiné, Simond studied theology at the provincial academy of Dié, a Protestant school modelled on the Geneva Academy. In 1678, at the age of twenty-seven, he was accepted as pastor to the Montjoux congregation, a small church in the predominantly Protestant region of the Valentinois colloquy near Dieulefit. In the following year he was transferred to Eourre, near Crest, and in 1682 to Embrun, the chief town of the Embrunais colloquy of Dauphiné. This was to be his last charge in France (Boucher 1981: 174). In 1684, the Embrun temple was demolished and a year later the Edict of Nantes was revoked, forcing one hundred and sixty thousand Protestants, according to the latest estimate, to flee the kingdom of France. Simond's brother, David, took refuge across the Alps in Geneva (Fatio and Martin 1985: 208, Vigne 1991: 249–50). The future translator of the Psalms may have accompanied him, but he continued his journey to the Netherlands, by then the biggest place of refuge for the Huguenots.

On 18 February 1686 he was appointed Minister to the Walloon church of Zierikzee on the island of Schouwen in Zeeland (Franken 1978: 190). A regular contributor to the monthly *Lettres sur la nature du papisme où l'on fait voir que ce n'est qu'une monarchie temporelle* (Fensham 1962: 755), he published in 1687 in Leiden a sermon entitled *La discipline de Jésus Christ ou sermon sur ces paroles du chap. 16 de S. Matth., vers 24.*[3] The text chosen for the sermon—the invitation made to the

---

[2] I am most grateful to Bernard Roussel, director of studies at the Ecole Pratique des Hautes Etudes, Paris, for sharing with me his vast knowledge in the field of history of exegesis.

[3] Pierre Simond. *La discipline de Jésus Christ ou sermon sur ces paroles du chap. 16 de S. Matth., vers 24.* Leiden: J. Hacking, 1687. Franken (1978: 190), who seems to

disciple to deny himself and take up his cross—was a clear reference to the plight of the French Protestants in exile. The book was dedicated to the Stadhouder, Prince William of Orange. It is interesting to note that Simond's maternal grandfather had been a servant of the Stadhouder's grandfather, Prince Frederick Henry, a younger son of William the Silent (Franken 1978: 190, Vigne 1988: 15).

On 8 April 1688, after two years of service in Zierikzee, Simond married Anne de Béraut de la Maugère, a woman of l'Aigle in the Pays d'Ouche in Normandy. Four days after the wedding they embarked for the Cape with a group of twenty refugees and a number of Dutch East India Company officials, one of whom was the bride's brother, Louis Bérault, a sergeant in the Company's forces. In total, approximately 180 Huguenots settled at the Cape between 1687 and 1689 (Coertzen 1988, Denis, forthcoming). Their move was actively encouraged by the Lords XVII, the Company's governing body, who hoped to see them play a role in the development of the vine industry at the Cape. Being the most educated, Simond acted as their spokesman in their negotiations with the Cape Commander. The welcome, at first, was excellent. On their arrival they received food and livestock. A sum of 18,000 florins, originally destined for the evangelisation of the island of Taiwan, was distributed amongst them. Above all they were granted land, in a mountainous area recently opened to colonisation, near the newly-established towns of Stellenbosch and Drakenstein.

Before long, however, the relationship between the Huguenots and the Cape authorities began to deteriorate. The Lords XVII and the Commander of the colony took it for granted that the French immigrants would become integrated as soon as possible with the Dutch settlers. There was no question of giving them any autonomy. In the matter of ecclesiastical discipline, the colonial authorities expected total obedience from the churches. The refugees, and especially their minister, shared radically different views. They wanted to be given a special status, comparable to the one they had in France before the revocation of the Edict of Nantes or to that of the Walloon Church in the Netherlands, which was allowed a considerable degree of autonomy in practice and language while remaining part of the

have seen the book (possibly at the Bibliothèque des Églises Wallonnes in The Hague), notes that the book contains 99 pages.

Dutch Reformed Church. The Huguenots saw themselves as a separate body within the Cape Colony with specific religious and economic rights.

Given this misunderstanding, confrontation was unavoidable. Two issues were in debate: the allocation of new sites, the Huguenots demanding that they not be separated from each other as those which the Commander had first allocated to the refugees, and the use of the French language in church and at school. The conflict which ensued has been described elsewhere. Suffice it to say that in the end the Lords XVII gave authorisation, in a letter of November 1690 to the Commander, to establish a consistory and a school in Drakenstein. The schoolmaster would teach the children of French descent to read and understand the Dutch language "in order to unite our nations by all means." The use of the French language was thus maintained for the time being. On the other hand, the Lords XVII expressed their opposition to any redistribution of land. The Huguenots were to remain separated, so as to integrate themselves faster with the rest of the colony (Vigne 1988: 20).

While fulfilling the role of pastor, Simond was at the head of a prosperous farm. According to Randolph Vigne, he was the wealthiest of the fourteen Huguenot slave-owners that existed in those years (Vigne 1988: 18). This financial success seems to have created resentment amongst some of the refugees. His most vehement opponent was Jacques de Savoye, a man who, significantly, left South Africa some time later because of bankruptcy. During a dispute, he did not hesitate to call Simond a "false pastor, unworthy minister, hypocrite, Tartuffe, priest, Jesuit, Judas, Kaffir" (Franken 1978: 34–51, Coertzen 1988: 135–36, Vigne 1988, 17–18). This conflict poisoned the first years of Simond's ministry in South Africa. The French congregation of Drakenstein managed nevertheless to get organised. A consistory was instituted at the end of 1691. Three elders and four deacons were elected. Apart from two cases of excommunication (Gerstner 1991: 224–26), we know very little of its first years of operation since the existing registers only start in February 1715. A temporary building—"more a barn than a church," according to François Valentyn's description in 1705 (Coertzen 1988: 124)—was used as a place of worship. It was not until 1718 that it was replaced by a proper church.

Judging from a sermon which was later printed in Holland, the preaching was, in Simond's time, of good quality. Trained at the Dié Academy, the founder of the Drakenstein congregation was a qualified theologian. Published in Harlem in 1707 under the title *La vraye Adoration et les Vrays Adorateurs, ou Sermon sur ces paroles du Chap. 4. de l'Evangile selon S. Jean v. 23 & 24*, this sermon was first delivered in Cape Town on 25 January 1699, then again in Amsterdam on 17 October 1706.[4] In the version we have, the text does not make any direct reference to the situation of the French Huguenots at the Cape. But it contains a violent attack against the Roman religion, an indication that the author had suffered persecution at the hands of the Pope's agents. In his sermon, Simond argued that the external worship of ancient Israel, which combined internal devotion and external observances, had given way, since the coming of Jesus, to a worship "in spirit and truth" which corresponded fully to God's wishes for humankind. There was no way one could revert to the old style of worship. The Lord, who knew the "infirmity" of his people had only recommended a limited number of ceremonies, namely, Baptism and the Holy Supper, which contained nothing "fleshly and labourious." All the ceremonies practised in the Roman church, such as the pilgrimages, the recitation of the Rosary, the veneration of relics and the wearing of religious habits, were not only frivolous or pernicious, they were totally opposed to the will of God as expressed in the Gospel of St. John. The only worship that pleased the Lord was the worship in spirit and truth as instituted by the New Law.

Of all Simond's works the most remarkable is his translation of the Psalms, published, as mentioned earlier, in 1704 under the title *Les Veilles Afriquaines*. Since the time of the Reformation, the standard liturgical version of the Psalms was, in the French-speaking Reformed churches, the text in rhymes composed by Clément Marot and Théodore de Bèze in the sixteenth century (Marot and Bèze 1986). As time went on, however, this version came to be seen as obsolete, due to the fast evolution of the French language. More and more the Catholic polemicists were making jokes of a religion which pretended to reach out to the people while using a language that

---

[4] [Pierre Simond], *La vraye Adoration et les Vrays Adorateurs, ou Sermon sur ces paroles du Chap. 4. de l'Evangile selon S. Jean v. 23 & 24*. Harlem, H.F. Buys, 1707, 12°, [A1]–[C8], 48 p. I am indebted to Mr. Randolph Vigne, the president of the Huguenot Society of London, for giving me a copy of this very rare pamphlet, a copy of which he found at the Bibliothèque des Églises Wallonnes in The Hague. A handwritten copy, together with a Dutch translation, is kept in the Cape Town Dutch Reformed Archives (P 18), which are housed in the Cape Town State Archives. A translation of the sermon in Afrikaans appeared in *Die Kerkbode* (13 September 1939, pp. 495–98). See also Boucher 1981: 358, Coertzen 1988: 134–35, Sienaert-van Reenen 1989: 27–28.

nobody could understand any more (Stauffenegger 1984: 928-31, Yardeni 1995: 457-63). In 1646 a Genevan theologian, Jean Diodati, published a new translation of the Psalms in verses, but his work, a long paraphrase not devoid of literary qualities, was never used in the Reformed churches (*Psaumes* 1646). A quarter of a century later, the church of Charenton in Paris asked one of the pastors, Valentin Conrart, to compose a new version of the Psalms in rhymes. Conrart, who by then had moved to Geneva, only translated fifty-one Psalms which were published posthumously in 1677 (*Livre* 1677). Completed by another pastor, Marc Antoine La Bastide, the full translation was printed in Geneva in 1679 (*Psaumes* 1679a/b). It was officially adopted by the church of Geneva in 1698. Yet a number of French-speaking churches continued to make use of the old version of the Psalter. The Company of Pastors of Geneva was concerned about preserving the uniformity of liturgy, among the French-speaking Reformed churches. It was to achieve this goal that, in January 1700, it took the unprecedented step of sending a circular letter to all the French-speaking churches, recommending that all of them adopt the Conrart-La Bastide version.

This initiative provoked a bitter controversy in the European Reformed community. The French theologian Pierre Jurieu, who had taken refuge in Holland after the revocation of the Edict of Nantes, took the lead in the opposition to the Conrart-La Bastide translation. His argument was that a new Psalter would upset the ordinary people in the churches. At his instigation, several churches, including the French church of London, chose to keep to the old version. The situation in Holland was more complicated. The Walloon Protestants, who had been in the country for more than a century and were not acquainted with the new way of speaking French, tended to be more conservative. Jurieu was fully on their side. But the Conrart-La Bastide version of the Psalter also had supporters, as is shown by the number of editions printed in Amsterdam after the revocation of the Edict of Nantes (Candaux 1992: 79). The French church of Amsterdam, significantly, expressed support for the new version (Yardeni 1995: 461) This variety of opinions explains why the synod of the Walloon churches in Holland opted, at a meeting held in September 1700 in Rotterdam, for a middle way. The delegates decided not to adopt the Conrart-La Bastide version, as the Church of Geneva had recommended, but instead to ask five of the member churches to work on a new translation of the Psalms.[5]

It was in this context that Simond set about writing a new translation of the Psalms in rhymes. At the beginning of June 1699, on reading "the French Gazette that is printed in Holland" (Simond 1704: 1r), he realised that King William of England had authorised the Huguenot churches of his kingdom to make use of the new translation of the Psalms. As he noted in the preface of his book, Simond mistakenly assumed that the Conrart-La Bastide version had been adopted in England as a result of the king's decision. In fact no consensus had been reached in the Huguenot community on this contentious issue, neither in England, which seems here to take a leading role, nor in Holland. Simond himself had no leaning towards the Conrart-La Bastide version, in which he did not find "what he would have expected" (Simond 1704: 1v). He nevertheless decided to give it to his children to read. In doing so he discovered that in the Conrart-La Bastide translation, Psalm 50 had one more strophe (ten instead of nine) than in the standard text of Marot and Bèze. This anomaly prompted him to have a closer look at both versions. In his view neither of them was satisfactory. It was after this incident, he confided in the preface to *Les Veilles Afriquaines*, that he set himself to write a new metrical translation of Psalm 50 despite his inexperience in poetry. The job was finished in "one hour and a half." Excited by this success, he translated a few other Psalms, with an ease, he thought, which could only come from God.

On 9 June 1699 four English ships docked at Table Bay on their way to India. Aboard one of them was William Norris, the English ambassador to the Great Mogul. His entourage and himself, Norris noted in a letter, were treated "with all imaginable civility" by the Governor of the place, Mijnheer Adrian Vanderstell.[6] While the crews were refreshing themselves, a Huguenot officer paid a visit to Simond at Drakenstein. It was from him that the French minister learnt that the Conrart-La Bastide Psalter had not been adopted by the Huguenot churches in England. This news caused him "great

---

[5] "Articles résolus ay Synode de Rotterdam, le neuvième Septembre et jours suivants de l'année dix-sept cens," quoted in Coertzen 1988: 137.

[6] India Office Library and Records, London: G.40.19. Letter book of Sir William Norris, 1698–1700. See Vigne, 1997: 7. The fleet left Table Bay on 3 July 1699. See H.C. Leibbrandt, *Precis of the Archives of the Cape of Good Hope. Journal, 1699–1732* (Cape Town, 1896).

joy." It may well be the sign, he thought, that God had chosen him
to be the writer of the new translation of the Psalms. With this hope
in mind, Simond completed the work in three months without, he
insisted, neglecting any of his pastoral duties. The fact that such an
important enterprise could have been carried out in Africa was just
another manifestation of God's grace:

> I want everybody to know that there is no desert, in Africa or else-
> where, dry or arid as it may be, where God does not spread out, as
> it pleases him, the waters of his grace, and that he performs his works
> with the help of the meanest instruments and those we find the most
> unexpected, so that glory may be rendered to him (Simond 1704:
> Preface, [7]v).

In 1700, at a synod held in Rotterdam, the Huguenot churches of
the Netherlands rejected the Conrart-La Bastide translation of the
Psalms against the wish of the Genevan church which wanted uniformity in all the Reformed churches of French language. Instead,
as we have noted above, the synod commissioned five churches to
work on an alternative translation. Each of them received thirty
Psalms to translate (Franken 1978: 198, Coertzen 1988: 137, Yardeni
1995: 459). By then, Simond had lost the battle against the Dutch
East India Company's policy of forced assimilation. This and the
attacks of Jacques de Savoye against his person and his family had
left him deeply frustrated. The hope of seeing his translation of the
Psalms accepted by a Dutch synod added a new reason, perhaps
the most pressing one, for returning to Holland. It was the Company's
policy to allow its agents to go home after twelve years of service.
Simond's application was sent to the Lords XVII at the beginning
of 1701, but because no successor could be found, he had to post-
pone his departure. It was not until April 1702 that he received permission to leave his post. His successor was a Dutchman called
Henricus Beck (Coertzen 1988: 136).

Simond's translation never received any official recognition. Much
to his disappointment the synod of the Walloon churches, gathered in
Utrecht on 3 May 1703, decided against adopting his metrical version of the Psalms. The reason given was that the matter had already
been decided at the previous synod at The Hague. Considered as "a
Psalter which has been corrected," his work was not even examined.[7]

---

[7] "Articles résolus au Synode des Eglises Wallonnes des Provinces Unies des Pays-
Bas, assemblé—Utrecht le 3 May et jours suivans, 1703," art. XLII. The same fate

Despite this rebuttal, however, Simond decided to go ahead with the publication of his translation. As Marot and Conrart had done before him, he only published the first third of the Psalter,[8] letting the reader judge whether it was worth pursuing the enterprise. Making use of the "brief instruction on the rules of French poetry" included in Port-Royal's *Nouvelle Méthode pour apprendre facilement la langue latine* (Lancelot 1681: 790–815), he ensured that his work conformed to the commonly accepted rules of versification (Simond 1704: Preface, 3v). The book appeared in Amsterdam in 1704, at the author's expenses.

The French traveller Pierre Leguat, who paid a visit to the Huguenot community at Drakenstein in February 1698, knew of Simond's work. "If I remember well," he wrote ten years later in his *Voyages et avantures*, by the time of his visit Simond had been working "for some time" on a translation of the Psalms in rhyme, or at least, correcting to the best of his ability, that of Marot and Bèze, "to make these sacred canticles intelligible." A new translation of the Psalm was long overdue, Leguat commented. The old text had become "ridiculous, barbarous and scandalous" (Leguat 1708: 2,149–50). This paragraph must have been added at a later stage by Maximilien Masson, the editor of Leguat's travel account (Vigne 1997: 8). As mentioned earlier, it was only in June 1699 that Simond set about writing his new translation of the Psalms. Leguat may have met Simond after his return to Holland and taken cognisance of his book.

What is the nature of the "piece" (*pièce*) which Simond decided to give to the public (Simond 1704: Preface, [2]r)? In the preface to *Les Veilles Afriquaines* the book is described as "a new version of David's Psalms" (Simond 1704: Preface, f. [2]r). The same word is used in the foreword to Conrart's *Livre des Psaumes*. "The necessity of this work," the editor wrote, "comes from the fact that since the old version major changes have occurred in our language" (*Livre* 1677: [aiii]r). As a result Conrart resolved to "readjust" (*retoucher*) Marot and Bèze's old "version," that is, he explained, to adapt the language without bringing any change to the meaning and to the measure of the rhymes (*Livre* 1677: aiiv). Simond also wrote a new

---

was suffered by a document sent by Scalberge, a doctor from London. On the subsequent controversy see Vigne 1997: 7–8.

[8] Psalms 1–51. To use the space left free, he also published Ps 74, 79, 103, 130, 137 and 143.

"version" of the Psalms, more appropriate, he thought, than the one compiled by Conrart and La Bastide. But what did he mean by "version"? The day he gave Psalm 50 to his children to read, he compared the two versions in rhymes—that of Marot and Bèze and that of Conrart and La Bastide—with the text in prose to see if the old version had left out anything from the text or if the new one had added anything. Finding both versions wanting, he decided to "translate" the psalm in rhymes. He carried on with a few other psalms the following days. His aim, he commented in the preface to *Les Veilles Afriquaines*, was to "express better the force, beauty and simplicity of [the Psalms'] originals" (Simond 1704: *2v).

Did Simond "translate" the Psalms directly from the Hebrew? Judging from the foreword to the *Livre des Psaumes*, Conrart did. He deliberately used Hebraisms in his new version, the foreword notes, even if these figures of speech were "different from our ordinary practice." Phrases like "broken bones" (Psalms 6 and 51) and "Sons of men" (Psalm 31) sounded "a bit hard" to the contemporary reader, but they had to be maintained to render the "energy" and the "grace" of the holy language (*Livre*, 1677: [ēiii]v). This comment is evidence of the fact that Conrart had at least a working knowledge of Hebrew. Simond, who had been trained in a Protestant Academy, also knew Hebrew and Greek. He referred several times to the "original" in the preface to his book. Yet, according to the preface to *Les Veilles Afriquaines* it was to the text in prose ("avec la prose"), and not to the original Hebrew, that he compared the two versions of Psalm 50, the day he began the translation work. We know which text in prose he had in mind. It was the French Bible published in 1588 in Geneva under the authority of the pastors and professors of the town (*Bible* 1588), a text often described as "the version of our common Bibles" (*la Version de nos Bibles communes*). This version is mentioned by name in the *Advertissement* printed at the end of *Les Veilles Afriquaines*. In some versions of the Psalms in rhymes—Conrart's *Livre des Psaumes* for instance—the text in prose following the Geneva Bible of 1588 was printed in the margins of the book. There is no doubt that Simond had access to a copy of the Geneva Bible in Drakenstein. In the *Advertissement* Simond also referred to Calvin's Latin translation of the Psalms, which was published as part of his commentary to the Psalms (Calvin 1886). Lastly, he mentioned Diodati's translation of the Psalms in rhymes (*Pseaumes* 1646). This

version was never used in the Reformed churches but was nevertheless considered as a work of reference. We can assume that Calvin's
and Diodati's books were also on Simond's desk in Drakenstein, as
was of course Conrart and La Bastide's new version of the Psalms,
probably one of the two 1679 editions (*Pseaumes* 1679a or 1679b).

To gain some understanding of Simond's method of translation
we shall now turn to one of the psalms he "translated": Psalm 6, a
psalm which has received a fair amount of attention in the recent
history of exegesis literature (Bedouelle 1979, Roussel forthcoming).
It is one of the six penitential psalms. Bernard Roussel has shown
that Clément Marot—author, with Théodore de Bèze, of the version of the Psalms in use in all Reformed churches until the late
seventeenth century—broke with Jacques Lefèvre d'Étaples' interpretation according to which Psalm 6 was a prayer of the second
person of the Trinity to his father. Instead Marot presented himself
as the psalmist, a believer who identified with Christ in the midst
of his sufferings. The author of the psalm was depicted as a sick
person praying to God for forgiveness and healing. At the end of
the psalm his request was granted (Roussel forthcoming).

The first thing to keep in mind when examining Simond's "translation" is that rather than a verbatim translation he provided a paraphrase of the sacred text. His version of Psalm 6 is 281 words long.
It is slightly longer than the version of Marot and Bèze (259 words)
and marginally shorter than the Conrart-Labastide one (290 words).
But it is one and a half times longer than the Geneva Bible in prose
(171 words). The reason for this excess of words is easy to understand. Simond, like his predecessors, translated the Psalms in rhymes.
Each psalm followed a specific set of versification rules. Psalm 6 for
instance was written in hexameters with male and female rhymes
alternating in aabccb. These constraints forced the writer to expand
the biblical text. A verbatim translation was out of the question. In
the foreword to *Le Livre des Psaumes*, the editor of Conrart's translation of the Psalms took great pains to explain that "adding in passing some little idea ... that brings more clarity to the text is not
paraphrasing" (*Livre* 1677). But Conrart did paraphrase. Simond also
did for the same reasons.

A close examination of Simond's version reveals that the Geneva
Bible was the French pastor's main source. We give here a synopsis of the first two verses of Psalm 6.

Geneva Bible (1588)

1. Eternel, ne me repren point en
ta colere,
& ne me chatie point en ta fureur.

2. Eternel, aye pitié de moi,
car je suis sans aucune force:
gueri-moi, Eternel,
car mes os sont etonnez.

Simond (1704)

1. Seigneur, Seigneur, modere
Envers moi ta colere,
Cesse d'estre irrité,
O Dieu ne me châtie,
Ni repren, je te prie
En ta severité

2. Mais sois moi pitoyable,
Voi le mal, qui m'accable
Et vien me secourir
Mes forces m'abandonnent,
Mes os mêmes s'estonnent,
Veuille, ô Dieu, me guerir.

The choice of words (*colère, chastie, fureur, pitié/pitoyable, force/forces, guérir, estonnez/estonnent*) shows Simond's dependency upon the Geneva Bible. The version of Marot and Bèze used a partly different set of words: *ire* (vs *colère*), *punir* (vs *châtier*), *santé me donne* (vs *guérir*). So did the Conrart-La Bastide version: *haine, ne sois pas si severe, soulage ma foiblesse*. Both the Geneva Bible and Simond described the bones' troubles (Psalm 6: 2) in the passive mode: *mes os sont etonnez/mes os mesmes s'estonnent*. The versions of Marot and Bèze and of Conrart and La Bastide, on the contrary, used the active mode, which gave the phrase a fairly different meaning: *mon grand mal estonne tous mes oz, & mes sens/la douleur étonne et mes os, & mes sens*.

Marot and Bèze (1562)

1. Ne vueilles pas, ô Sire
Me reprendre en ton ire,
Moy qui t'ay irrité,
N'en ta fureur terrible,
Me punir de l'horrible
Tourment qu'ai merité.

2. Mais, Seigneur, vien étendre
Sur moy ta pitié tendre,
Car malade me sens:
Santé donques me donne,
Car mon grand mal étonne
Tous mes os & mes sens.

Conrart/Labastide (1679)

[1] Seigneur tu vois ma peine,
Ne me prens point en haine,
Cesse d'être irrité,
Dans ta juste colère,
Ne sois pas si severe,
Que je l'ay mérité.

[2]. Que plutôt ta tendresse
Soulage ma foiblesse,
Dans les maux que je sens,
Ma force m'abandonne,
Et la douleur étonne,
Et mes os, & mes sens.

When the Psalmist asked God to change his mind and come to his rescue (Psalm 6:4), he argued, both in the Geneva Bible and in *Les Veilles Afriquaines*, that God should do so "for [his] own sake" (*pour l'amour de ta gratuité/pour l'amour de toi-même*). The Conrart-Labastide version this time followed the Geneva Bible: *pour l'amour de toy-même*. The version of Marot and Bèze used an expression closer to the Hebrew original: "in your high goodness" (*par ta bonté haute*). Interestingly this was also Calvin's lesson in his Latin commentary to the Psalms: *propter misericordiam* (Calvin 1886: 75). As has been noted (Roussel forthcoming), the last hexameter in the version of Marot and Bèze (Psalm 6:11)—"Since God is so sweet to me" (*Puisque Dieu m'est si doux*)—radically changed the formal structure of the psalm and its sense. Instead of vindicating the destruction of the enemies, the last verse praised God's sweetness. The closing word was about the psalmist, first despised by God and now fully rehabilitated. The Conrart-Labastide version kept the same structure albeit with a different wording. The last three verses described God's faithfulness to the psalmist: "God confounds their wickedness, he is always good to me, as he promised me" (*Dieu confond leur malice, Et m'est toujours propice, Comme il me l'a promis*).

Here again Simond followed the Geneva Bible rather than the other two versions. The psalm ended with the defeat of the psalmist's enemies, a lesson, one should note, closer to the Hebrew original: "That they all therefore be confounded" (*Qu'ils soient donc confondus*). Yet, in the preceding two verses, he referred to God's intervention in his own life: "For despite their envy God restored my life" (*Car malgré leur envie, Dieu m'a remis en vie*). Simond did not completely ignore the lesson of the Marot and Bèze version. On one issue, which was far from being insignificant, Simond departed from his source. In the Geneva Bible the psalmist called God *Eternel*. In Psalm 6 alone the word occurred five times. The version of Marot and Bèze consistently used the word *Sire*. Like Conrart and La Bastide, Simond decided not to opt for a single term. In three verses (Psalm 6:1,3,9) he used the title *Seigneur*. But hc fclt free to make use of other expressions like *ô Dieu* (Psalm 6:2), *Pere de grâce* (4), *Dieu fort* (5) and *le Ciel* (9).This variety of titles reflected, I would like to suggest, a new appreciation of the figure of God. The rather hieratic phrase *Eternel* was clearly out of fashion. Simond developed a more personal, and therefore diversified, approach to God.

Before concluding, a word needs to be said about Psalm 7. We do not have to examine this psalm in full detail. Our interest lies in Simond's annotations both in the body of the text and in the *Advertissement* printed at the end of the volume. They provide us with further information on Simond's method of translation. In most versions Psalm 7 is divided into seventeen verses—or eighteen if one considers the *titulus* as the first verse. These verses are in turn subdivided into two strophes composed as follows: 1–8 and 9–17. Breaking with the common practice, Simond divided the psalm into nine verses, themselves subdivided into three strophes. The reason for this subdivision, he wrote in *Les Veilles Afriquaines*, was that in one verse (Psalm 7:6) "the old version has left out something of the original." To render a proper translation of the text he decided to add four verses. This is why he divided the psalm into three strophes instead of two in the old version (Simond 1704: 13).

This statement is rather puzzling. There is nothing in the original Hebrew which warrants the addition of four verses. These verses do not add anything substantial to the text. They merely paraphrase it. To make sense of Simond's addition one needs to look at the Geneva Bible. Two phrases contained in this version—"en ces furies" and "tu as ordonné le droit"—were deemed sufficiently important to justify the addition of four additional verses and, as a result, the subdivision of the psalm into three instead of two strophes.

Marot and Bèze (1562)	*Geneva Bible (1588)*	*Simond (1704)*
6. Leve toi donc, Sire, Sur mes ennemis en ton ire, Veille pour moi, que je sois mis Au droict lequel tu m'as promis.	6. Leve-toi, Eternel, en ta colere, & t'élève en ces furies de mes ennemis. & t'éveille vers moi: tu as ordonné le droit	3. [. . .] O Tout-puissant, en ta colere Leve-toi, montre-toi severe, Vien t'opposer B ces fureurs De mes cruels Persecuteurs. Pause I. 4. Reveille envers moi ta puissance, Ne me laisse B la violence, Des Oppresseurs abandonné, toi qui a le droit ordonné. [. . .]

In the *Advertissement* printed at the end of *Les Veilles Afriquaines*, Simond made another revealing comment. "The 4 verses [of Psalm 7, verse 6]," he noted, "are according to Calvin's Latin version, followed by Clement Marot. It may be better to combine the version of our common Bibles and that of Diodati." In other words Simond had an afterthought. On examining the proof of his book he discovered what he felt was an error of translation:

Original translation (Simond 1704: 14)	*Revised translation* (Simond 1704: [130])
6. [. . .] Le Dieu fort, de son trône auguste,	L'Eternel est un juste juge,
Juge le méchant & le juste,	Des justes il a esté le refuge,
Celui qui craint de l'offenser	Il s'irrite journellement,
Celui qui pèche, sans cesser.	Contre qui fait iniquement.

The two versions are markedly different. In the original translation Simond presented God as a fearful judge who pronounced judgment in all circumstances. He judged both the just and the sinner. In the revised translation the French pastor tried to give a more balanced view of God's justice. Of the just he was the refuge (and not the judge as in the original translation), while, of course, being irritated by the evil deeds of the wicked. Simond rightly pointed out that the revised translation followed the Geneva Bible. "God," the text in prose read, "makes justice for the just, & the powerful God gets angry every day" (*Dieu fait droit au juste, & le Dieu fort se courrouce tous les jours*). It was equally correct that the original translation was inspired by Calvin's Latin translation of Psalm 7: "God is judging the just and the one who has contempt for him every day" (*Deus iudicans iustum, et contemptorem Dei quotidie*) (Calvin 1886: 84). The version of Marot and Bèze closely followed Calvin's Latin text: "God is the true judge of the one who is equitable and also of the one who angers him every day" (*Dieu est le Juge veritable/De celui qui est equitable/Et de celui qui semblablement/Qui l'irrite journellement.*) So far Simond's annotation makes sense. It confirms my earlier observations on Simond's dependency upon the Geneva Bible. The only problem, admittedly minor, regards Diodati. For the "translation" of this verse (= Psalm 7:11), Diodati followed word by word the version of Marot and Bèze (Diodati 1646: 15). Clearly Simond made a mistake. The *Advertissement* must have been written in a hurry.

Let us conclude. This study has shown that, as far as Psalm 6 and 7 were concerned, the Geneva Bible was Simond's main source. The same can probably be said of the other psalms "translated" by the French pastor. He may have checked a few words in the Hebrew Bible. There is little doubt that he had a working knowledge of the Hebrew language. But to consider his version of the Psalms as a translation would be misleading. How could he have possibly "translated" Psalm 50 in a hour and a half as he said he did in the preface to *Les Veilles Afriquaines*? What he did, in fact, was to propose a new paraphrase in rhymes of the common French version in prose, more appropriate, in his view, than the two metrical versions then in use in the French reformed churches. He had both of them on this desk, as well as Diodati's and Calvin's Latin translation of the Psalms. He made use of each of these texts, but the Geneva Bible was his main source of inspiration. Most of the additions and corrections made to the original document, one should add, were his own. As can be expected, the text in rhyme is considerably longer that the one in prose. To follow the rules of versification, as laid down by Port-Royal, he had to expand the text considerably.

Only his "translation" of the first fifty psalms and a few others were printed. Simond had no doubt that his work was inspired by God. That it had been composed in a dark corner of Africa was, for him, a further argument of God's benevolence towards him. The synod of the Walloon churches in the Netherlands decided otherwise. For us the fact that a piece of biblical scholarship was produced at the Cape as early as the late seventeenth century is worth being remembered. *Les Veilles Afriquaines* marks the beginning of a century-long interaction between the centre and the periphery of production of Christian knowledge.

BIBLIOGRAPHY

Bedouelle, Guy. *Le Quincuplex Psalterium de Lefèvre d'Etaples. Un guide de lecture.* Genève: Droz, 1979.
Bible (La), qui est toute la Saincte Escriture du Vieil et du Nouveau Testament: Autrement l'Ancienne et la Nouvelle Alliance. Le tout reveu et conferé sur les textes Hebrieux et Grecs par les Pasteurs et Professeurs de l'Eglise de Geneve. Geneve: [Jeremie des Planches], 1588.
Boucher, Maurice. *French Speakers at the Cape: the European Background,* Pretoria: University of South Africa, 1981.
Boxer, C.R. *The Dutch Seaborne Empire 1600–1800,* London, 1965.
Calvin, Jean. *In librum Psalmorum commentarius.* Geneva: Robert Estienne, 1557. In *Ioannis Calvini opera quae supersunt omnia,* Eds G. Baum, E. Cunitz & E. Reuss, vol. 30. Brunsvigae: C.A. Schwetschke et filium, 1886.

Candaux, Jean-Daniel. "Le psautier huguenot chez les imprimeurs néerlandais: concurrence ou spécialisation?." In Eds C. Berkvens-Stevenlinck et al., *Le Magasin de l'Univers. The Dutch Republic as the Centre of the European Book Trade. Papers presented at the International Colloquium, held at Wassenaar, 5–7 July 1990*, Leiden: Brill, 1992: 71–83.

Coertzen, Peter. *The Huguenots of South Africa 1688–1988*, Cape Town: Tafelberg, 1988.

Denis, Philippe. "The Cape Huguenots and Their Legacy in Apartheid South Africa." In Eds Bertrand Van Ruymbeke and Randy Sparks. *Out of Babylon. The Huguenots and their Diaspora*, Columbia, South Carolina: University of South Carolina Press, forthcoming.

Fatio, Olivier and Martin, Louise. *Genève au temps de la Révocation de l'édit de Nantes, 1685–1705*, Genève and Paris, 1985.

Fensham, F.C. "Simond, Pierre," *Suid-Afrikaanse Biografiese Woordenboek*, I, Cape Town: Tafelberg, 1962: 755–57.

Franken, J.L.N., "Pierre Simond," in *Die Hugenote aan die Kaap*. (Argiefjaarboek vir Suid-Afrikaanse Geskiedenis, 41) Pretoria: Die Staatsdrukker, 1978: 190–203.

Gerstner, Jonathan Neil. *The Thousand Generation Covenant Theology and Group Identity in Colonial South Africa, 1652–1814*. Leiden: Brill, 1991.

Kpobi, David Nii Anum. *Mission in Chain. The Life, Theology and Ministry of the Ex-slave Jacobus E.J. Capitein (1717–1747). With a Translation of His Major Publications.* Zoetermeer: Boekencentrum, 1993.

[Lancelot, Claude], *Nouvelle methode pour apprendre facilement la langue latine contenant les regles des genres, des declinaisons, des préterits, de la syntaxe, de la quantité, & des accens latins, mises en françois avec un ordre tres-clair & tres-abregé*, 8th rev. ed., Paris: Denys Thierry, 1681.

Leguat, François. *Voyages et avantures...*, 2 vol. London: David Mortier, 1708.

Livre (Le) des Psaumes. En vers François, par Cl. Ma. & Th. de Be. Retouchez par feu Monsieur Conrart..., Charenton: Antoine Cellier, 1677.

Marot, Clément and Bèze, Théodore de. *Les Psaumes en vers français avec leur mélodies. Fac-similé de l'édition genevoise de Michel Blanchier, 1562. Publié avec une introduction par Pierre Pidoux.* Genève: Droz, 1986.

Psaumes (Les) En vers François, Retouchez sur l'ancienne version de Cl. Marot & Th. de Bèze. Par feu M.V. Conrart..., 1st ed., Charenton: Antoine Cellier, [early] 1679.

Psaumes (Les) En vers François, Retouchez sur l'ancienne version de Cl. Marot & Th. de Bèze. Par M.V. Conrart..., 2nd ed., Charenton: Antoine Cellier, [July] 1679.

Pseaumes (Les) de David en rime, Reveus par Jean Diodati, Genève, Pierre Chouet, 1646.

Roussel, Bernard. "'Laisse gémir, et braire les Psaumes': Clément Marot et le Psaume 6," in *Mélanges Giovanni Gonnet, Bollettino dei Studi Valdesi*, forthcoming.

Sienaert-van Reenen, Marilet. *Die Franse bydrae tot Africana literatuur 1622–1902*, Pretoria and Cape Town: Human & Rousseau, 1989.

Simond, Pierre. *La discipline de Jésus Christ ou sermon sur ces paroles du chap. 16 de S. Matth., vers 24.* Leiden: J. Hacking, 1687.

––––––. *Les Veilles Afriquaines ou les Pseaumes de David, Mis en Vers François*. Amsterdam: Cornelle de Hoogenhuisen, 1704.

––––––. *La vraye Adoration et les Vrays Adorateurs, ou Sermon sur ces paroles du Chap. 4. de l'Evangile selon S. Jean v. 23 & 24.* Harlem: H.F. Buys, 1707.

Stauffenegger, Roger. *Iglise et société, Genève au XVIIᵉ siècle*, Genève, 1984.

Vigne, Randolph. "The Rev. Pierre Simond: 'Lost Leader' of the Huguenots at the Cape," *Journal of Theology for Southern Africa* 65 (December 1988): 14–26.

Vigne, Randolph. "Rev. Pierre Simond (1651–?1713): the Family Background in the Dauphiné," *Africana Notes and News* 29/7 (September 1991): 249–50.

––––––. "Pierre Simond, pasteur du refuge et traducteur des Psaumes. Une esquisse biographique," *Psaume. Bulletin de la recherche sur le psautier huguenot* 14 (November 1997): 3–9.

Yardeni, Myriam. "La querelle de la nouvelle version des Psaumes dans le refuge huguenot." In Ed. Brigitte Maillard, *Foi, fidélité, amitié en Europe á la période moderne. Mélanges offerts B Robert Sauzet.* Tours: Publications de l'Université de Tours, 1995: 457–463.

EARLIEST SOUTHERN AFRICAN BIBLICAL INTERPRETATION: THE CASE OF THE *BAKWENA, BAKOLOLO* AND *BANGWATO*

Fidelis Nkomazana

In this essay, I am going to discuss the earliest interpretation of the Bible among the Batswana, namely, among the Bakwena, Bakololo and Bangwato. The social, economic, political, military and religious spheres of life of each of these peoples heavily influenced the way they tried to interpret or apply the Bible to their lives. Although the title of this essay gives the impression that our reference point will be the Bakwena, Bakololo and the Bangwato people, we will find that their kings dominated the scene. This is the case because among most Southern Africans the leader always spoke or acted on the behalf of his people. Besides, all visitors, including those who came with the Bible and Christianity, were expected to report at the *kgotla* (King's court), and so kings automatically became the hosts of all visitors. This is the reason that King Sechele I of the Bakwena, King Sebetoane and Sekeletu of the Bakololo and King Sekgoma of the Bangwato played a vital role in biblical interpretation in Southern Africa. These kings featured as key actors in the earliest response of their people to the Bible because it was during their reign that Christianity was first introduced among the Bakwena, Bangwato and Bakololo. Since Southern Africans responded to issues facing them corporately, the views of the rulers must be understood as representing the aspirations of the people.

The Kololo people are one of the Bantu speaking peoples who were forced by the Mfecane wars in the early 18th century to migrate northward from South Africa. They eventually settled in place in the present day Zambia where, David Livingstone (an agent of the London Missionary Society) found them and attempted to introduce Christianity. The Bangwato are one of the Tswana states which occupied what came to be known as the Bechuanaland Protectorate, the present day Botswana. They, with their sister states, the Kwena and the Ngwaketse, are said to have been formed when three brothers broke away from their father, Malope-a-Masilo, to establish their independence. The Bangwato established themselves under King Mathiba I (1780–1795) in 1780. Their meeting with Livingstone took place in their ancestral home of Shoshong, which is today regarded as the home of Christianity in Botswana. With this brief introduction, I now turn to the Bakwena and the Bible.

This section of the essay will concentrate on Sechele I, the king of the Bakwena, who was the most well-known Southern African king converted by David Livingstone. Sechele was a man of great talent and complexity, but also simplicity. It is historically known that he was a great ruler of his people until the coming of Christianity. He had previously ruled his people according to their culture, customs and religious beliefs. When Livingstone arrived in the early 1841, Sechele was pleased to receive him. He gave Livingstone a warm reception for coming to his country. Sechele's reasons for wanting Livingstone to stay among his people were that he hoped he would act as a deterrent against outside attacks, especially from the much hated Transvaal Boers and the much feared Amandebele of King Mzilikazi who continuously raided the Bakwena for their cattle and land. He also hoped to receive supplies of guns and European goods through this contact. Sechele eventually, and ambiguously, gave way to Christian belief and adopted European life-styles. Sechele's response to Christianity was also prompted by his desire to read, write and speak English. He showed a great interest in reading the Bible.

Aware of the implications of their King's conversion, the Bakwena were very critical of Sechele's decision to become a Christian. His colleagues in the Southern Africa region, such as Moshoeshoe, when Sechele had sent his men to purchase a horse from Moshoeshoe's country, also strongly advised him against the decision to be baptized, but in vain (Schapera 1959: 260). Sechele, however, ignored his colleagues' advice and went ahead with his intention to get baptized. On this and other similar matters, Livingstone had decided to keep a low profile. In 1848, when Sechele sought for advice on the question of polygamy and Christian baptism, Livingstone merely pushed the responsibility back on him and asked him to seek counsel of the Bible. Livingstone later commented,

> When he consulted me on the subject pressing so much on his mind, and especially about baptism, for which he applied about two years after he professed Christianity, I simply asked him if he thought he was doing right? What he thought he ought to do? I never preached against polygamy, but left the matter to take its course (Monk 1860: 173).

Livingstone wanted Sechele to make his own independent decision, for which he then would be answerable. He was aware that Sechele's baptism had implications for the whole state of Bakwena society. Also, Livingstone was aware of the difficulties involved, if Christianity insisted upon monogamy. The plight of the discarded wives was a sensitive one and needed to be carefully considered (MacNair 1940: 33–7). The general practice of most missionaries was to ask a polygamous man committed to Christianity to reject all the other wives except the first one to be married. Livingstone, however, insisted that as Christians: "We cannot call it adultery" (Livingstone 1844). After carefully studying the Bible, Sechele decided to divorce all his wives except the senior one, but accepted that the Bible expected him to take responsibility for providing for the economic needs of his divorced wives (Schapera 1960: 298).

The import of Sechele's decision in favour of Christianity was fully comprehended by the Bakwena. It is reported that on the day of his baptism the Bakwena men cried, loudly mourning for what they perceived as a major loss. However, having accepted Christianity, Sechele became eager to see the whole community follow his example and anxious to see his people accepting the teaching of the Bible. He said to Livingstone: "Do you imagine these people will ever believe by merely talking to them? I can make them do nothing except by thrashing them. If you like, I shall call my headmen, and with our *litupa* (whips of rhinoceros-hide) we will soon make them all believe together" (Livingstone 1857: 15). Although Livingstone rejected this proposal, Sechele did not understand the Bible to be against the use of force in converting people to Christianity. It is evident from the quotation that Sechele's understanding of the Bible was greatly influenced by his own cultural and religious background. He conceived everything in the light of his past experience and the traditions of his culture. The king was not only the head of the political, social, and economic spheres, but also the religious.

As the chief officiant in religious activities, Sechele expected the whole community to participate. As the only convert to Christianity, Sechele wanted to use his position as king to influence people. He told Livingstone that

> In former times . . . when a chief was fond of hunting, all his people got dogs and became fond of hunting too. If he loved dancing or music, all showed a liking to these amusements too. If the chief loved beer, they all rejoiced in strong drink. But in this case it is different.

> I love the Word of God, and not one of my people will join me (Livingstone 1857: 15).

During Livingstone's stay among the Bakwena, King Sechele became a very good personal friend of his, and Livingstone found him an interesting and intelligent man. The King too was impressed by Livingstone, particularly his biblical preaching, so much so that he eventually agreed to learn to read the Bible himself. Sechele found the Bible fascinating. He spent many hours in a day reading the Bible and was amazed by the things he discovered. Deeply impressed and frightened by what he read, at one time he asked Livingstone, saying: "You startle me—these words make all my bones to shake—I have no more strength in me: but my forefathers were living at the same time as yours were, and how is it that they did not send them a word about these terrible things sooner?" (Livingstone 1857: 16).

Although Sechele remained a Christian and a king, his life was continuously characterised by conflicts and dilemmas. As a result of his position as a Christian and a king of the Bakwena, he struggled to balance things. He put one leg inside the church and the other remained in the cultural way, for he tried to please both the missionaries and his own people. The Bakwena, for instance, demanded that he play his role as the chief officiant in the rain-making rituals, in the initiation ceremonies of *bogwera* (cultural school for boys) and *bojale* (cultural school for girls) and that he remain faithful to all his wives. The Bakwena rejected Sechele's claim that becoming a Christian or reading the Bible caused someone to discard his many wives. They blamed him for turning "himself a white man" (Mackenzie 1871: 105–106). Most of his people were opposed to the reading of the Bible, for they saw it as a dangerous influence. They feared that reading the Bible would influence them to discard their wives. Despite all the expectations and pressures, Sechele remained a zealous Christian. He continued to assist Livingstone with conducting Church services, preaching and devoting his time to reading the Bible, but also secretly participated in certain rituals and practices of the Bakwena, such as rain-making.

In 1852 Livingstone left the Bakwena, partly because of Sechele's double standards. Livingstone had discovered that Sechele had impregnated one of his former wives. He later claimed that he had repented and that he wanted to continue preaching. When the missionaries refused to allow him to preach, he demanded an explanation, pointing out that the Bible says that King David and Solomon had many wives and concubines and yet remained people of God's own heart. Why was he being forced to leave his own rightful wives, asked Sechele, who had read the Bible for himself? The attitude of the missionaries towards Sechele started to change. Whenever Sechele had adopted practices and measures which promoted literary education and other forms of European culture, he was described as "a fine man at heart and a beloved of his people" (Long 1965: 19). Early in her encounter with Sechele a Mrs Price, for instance, wrote of Sechele's compound saying that she "was amazed at the extreme cleanliness of everything around me" (Long 1965: 111). But when Sechele mixed his own Kwena customs with Christianity, conflicts with missionaries started. He would be suddenly described as an "uncivilised heathen." The same Mrs Price later wrote as follows:

> I cannot understand the mixture in Sechele. He reads the Bible threadbare—so as some of the holiest Christians do not read it—yet he is one of the vilest of characters in reality and (there is) no more of vital Christianity in him than is Sekhomi [sic]—the naked savage King of the Banguato [sic], who knows little more of the white people and their habits etc. than of their guns, ammunition and brandy. Ma-Sechele is Christian-like—weak and lowly and innocent, but she is under (a) horrid influence (Long 1965: 111).

Sechele's approach to the Bible should therefore be understood in the context of his position as a Christian King in a cultural environment of the Bakwena. He was concerned that if he did not strike a compromise between Christianity and the Bakwena customs, it would lead to a total subversion of his power. To meet the need of his people, he sent for rainmakers and paid them out of his own cattle. Although he tried to keep this compromise a secret, the Bakwena were excited that they had won their king back to normal life, and the news quickly spread that "Sechele was now making rain." When the missionaries came to learn about this, the whole practice became public and Sechele openly assisted in the performance of rain-making rites, initiation ceremonies, etc. This was a dramatic change because all along Sechele was most diligent in the observance of private and family prayers, and stood up regularly every Sunday to preach to the Bakwena. Sechele however always tried hard to engraft Christianity into the Kwena tradition and customs, so that the two might go together. For instance, he went with the people in their rain-making ceremonies, but did not neglect to pray to God at the same time. He would use charms and divinations, washing and purifying, according to the Bakwena culture and yet profess faith in Christ, whose blood cleanses all sin. Sechele argued that the Bible did not require him to give up the customs of his people, although it required him to believe in the Lord Jesus Christ. He could be an orthodox Motswana and a good Christian at the same time. In fact Sechele used to spend hours with Livingstone and his predecessors, defending his stance. Reflecting on such discussions, John Mackenzie wrote:

> I have spent many of the hours of night with this clever chief in the earnest discussion of these points. When one after another his arguments failed him, he had said to me, "You have conquered: your idea of Christian life is the right one, but was I not alone? What is one man against all the Bakwena?" "How hard it is for us all, Sechele for me as well as for you, to believe that God with us is greater than all who can be against us!" "Monare (Sir)," he replied with feeling, "not hard for you: You are a missionary, your faith is great, but hard for me, as a chief of a heathen town" (Mackenzie 1871: 107).

The missionaries were divided as far as Sechele's position was concerned. Was he a Christian or not? They saw Sechele's reason for becoming a Christian to be for economic and political benefits. They said that he was simply interested in European goods such as guns and ammunition. They also took the view that Sechele's "primitive" environment badly influenced his thoughts and character. Thus they failed to try to understand Sechele's struggles, but simply demanded high moral and consistent Christian standards. They excommunicated him from the church. Sechele was one of the first kings to adopt Christian faith. As we shall see, his experiences would affect the Bakololo and Bangwato response. At this stage I turn to the Bakololo and their biblical interpretation.

Around 1849 Livingstone, believing in the final triumph of Christianity, commerce and civilization, hoped that these forces would bring lasting peace between the Kololo and Ndebele nations, and would contribute to the termination of the slave trade by the Portuguese in central Africa. Livingstone saw the combination of Christianity, humane commerce and civilization as the best method of fighting against such slavery. The meeting between Livingstone and the Kololo, and the latter's response to the preaching of the Word of God, is a very interesting one. Livingstone first came into contact with the Kololo in 1851 and developed a great admiration for their King Sebetoane. He wrote of him saying: "He was the greatest warrior ever heard of beyond the colony, for unlike Mozilikatse, Dingaan and others, he always led his men into battle himself" (Livingstone 1857: 72). Livingstone found Sebetoane, not only the greatest warrior, but also an honourable man to share the Bible message with. As soon as they met, Livingstone immediately revealed the purpose of his visit. He had come to preach the Gospel to his people and to urge him to abandon slavery and war. The King, like Sechele, was very keen to welcome a white man because he saw him as a means through which he could obtain guns to protect his people against the more aggressive Ndebele and their King Mzilikazi. This military concern was an important factor in influencing the Bakololo to give permission to Livingstone to preach to his people. Livingstone wrote concerning this saying that Sebetoane seemed to have "the idea that our teaching was chiefly the art of shooting and other European arts, and that by our giving him guns he would thereby procure peace, the peace he so earnestly longs to possess" (Livingstone 1857: 72).

In the Southern African world view, if I may generalize for a moment, ancestors provide a sense of security and protection for warriors. Before they go into a battle, religious specialists (called *dingaka* amongst the Batswana) would consult the ancestors for guidance and protection. The warriors had their weapons doctored and made powerful in strength and aggression against their enemies. It was unheard of to simply allow the warriors to walk into a battle before their ancestors were consulted and certain war rites performed to make warriors invincible. Sebetoane brought this understanding to the Bible, believing that the Bible and its preaching had blessings to bring about a peaceful solution or atmosphere in the territory. The Bible was thought to have the power to help people win battles against their enemies. It is unfortunate that Sebetoane did not live long enough to assess the effects of the Bible as a method of winning war and bringing peace in his kingdom, for he was suddenly attacked by a severe disease which took his life. Livingstone mourned his death for a long time.

In 1853 Livingstone once again arrived at Linyanti, the chief town of the Bakololo, and began to instruct people on biblical teaching and education, while in turn learning more of their customs and traditions. Livingstone proposed to Sekeletu, Sebetoane's son, and heir to the throne, that he wanted to teach the Kololo to read the Bible. Sekeletu's immediate response was to turn down the request. He reasoned as follows: "According to the Makololo ideas, the cattle post is the proper school in which sons should be brought up. Here they receive the right sort of education, the knowledge of pasture, and to manage cattle" (Livingstone 1865: 17).

Sekeletu found the missionary interpretation of the Bible not relevant to their day-to-day needs or experiences. He wanted to see the Bible being made relevant to their lives, that is, addressing issues of their livelihood in terms of agriculture, especially cattle farming. But unfortunately the biblical interpretation of the missionaries did not seem to relate to the pertinent questions which directly faced the people. Nevertheless, Sekeletu eventually granted Livingstone permission to teach his people (to read) the Bible, but he himself could not be persuaded to attend the Bible classes. He sent some of his senior men for experimental purposes, promising to try it himself if there were no adverse effects on them. He feared that "talking to the book," as they referred to reading, would change his attitude to normal life. In this regard Livingstone wrote,

> At last, the King told me that he was afraid that learning to read might change his heart, and make him content with one wife only, as in the case of Sechele. It was in vain to urge him that the state of mind contemplated would be as voluntarily as the present: no underhand means would be employed to convert, all the means employed are open teaching, there is no compulsion, the truth is taught respecting God's will, and the belief or unbelief of the instructed is left as an affair between their judge and themselves. It was just as I felt in my early years in contemplating that everlasting preaching, praying and singing prolonged into heaven (Schapera 1961: 246–8).

Sekeletu's father-in-law, Motibe, and his stepfather were appointed to attend these Bible classes in order to experience the thing and report back to Sekeletu. Livingstone says that they were "determined to trace the mysterious book" (Livingstone 1857: 164–165). As soon as Motibe and his companion mastered the alphabet, they tried the book and found it was not harmful. After Sekeletu heard about this, he and a group of his young companions came to experience the Bible for themselves. But Sekeletu was very observant and carefully watched for any adverse effects or tendencies of the book to change his views on polygamy. His intention was to continue learning how to read, and to avoid whatever he perceived as forcing him to put his wives away.

As Livingstone continued to teach the Bakololo to read the Bible for themselves, they began to interpret it in their own language and within their own cultural context. This made their experience of the Bible meaningful and real. They turned the Bible into a kind of medicine for acquiring clothes, rifles, and beads etc. For most Southern African societies, religion was at the centre of life, whether it is economic, social, political or whatever. Without religion people did not know how to function. Before engaging in any economic activity such as hunting, ploughing, harvesting etc. or any military campaign, they would first consult their ancestors on the activity. Prayers or rituals were believed to insure successful productivity or create protection over crops, livestock and the home. It was within this cultural understanding that people made a link between the Bible and trade.

The response of the people was made more interesting by the fact that the Bible classes became a community issue, not an individual affair. When Livingstone preached against war, the shedding of blood and life after death, the Bakololo were terrified by the prospect of the resurrection of the dead. They asked Livingstone, "can those who have been killed in the field and devoured by the vultures, or those who have been eaten by the hyenas or lions, or those who have been tossed into the river, and eaten by more than one crocodile, can they all be raised again to life?" (Livingstone 1965: 291). The meaning of the scripture on the resurrection of the dead was understood or interpreted within the military reputation of a warrior people. African religious belief does not have a concept of resurrection of the dead, although they have a concept of life after death. Their concept of death and hereafter was different from that of the Bible, as presented by the missionaries, hence the people felt threatened and found it difficult to conceptualise a sudden and massive resurrection. A dead person was generally believed to join the spirit world and to become part of the existence of the living as an ancestor, but there was no concept of people physically coming back to life. In addition, they did not have a concept of judgement after death as found in the Bible. It was therefore a terrifying experience to think of having their enemies coming back to life, and probably coming back stronger than they had been, to revenge on them.

On the issue of salvation, Livingstone challenged the Kololo to make a decision for Christ, to which they responded by arguing that "Jesus has not loved their [the Bakololo] forefathers, hence their present degradation," though clearly "He had loved the white men, and given them all wonderful things they now possess." They expected, therefore, that "as I had come to teach them to pray to Jesus and to pray for them, their wants would soon be all supplied" (Schapera 1865: 246–8). The Kololo believed that God had to be revealed to them through God's care and provision for the people. This was implicit in their concept of *Modimo* (the Supreme Being). They understood God to be responsible for providing them with the materials they needed. When Livingstone told them that prayer was going to bring material blessings on them, they were impressed.

I now turn to my third case study, the response of the Bangwato to the Bible. In 1842 Livingstone paid two short visits to Sekgoma and his people at Shoshong, and then again in 1849 and 1851 (Seaver 1957: 58). On all these occasions Sekgoma gave Livingstone a warm welcome and permitted him to instruct his people in the biblical teaching as he had a great interest in what Livingstone had to say about the Bible and medicine. When Sekgoma himself heard Livingstone's preaching, he made a request for the elixir of regeneration saying, "I wish you would change my heart. Give me medicine to change it, for it is proud, proud and angry, angry always" (Seaver 1957: 58). At this request, Livingstone reached into his pocket and took a copy of the New Testament and gave it to Sekgoma, but Sekgoma interrupted him, saying, "Nay, I wish to have it changed by medicine to drink, and have it changed at once for it is very proud and very uneasy, and continually angry with someone" (Blaikie 1910: 39). Although Sekgoma was impressed at hearing the Bible being preached in the Setswana language, he desired to see "the Gospel" being accompanied by something he could touch and drink to heal him physically, emotionally and spiritually. Having heard the teaching of the Bible, Sekgoma expressed a willingness to embrace it, but wanted to see his past and cultural heritage brought under the care of Christ. Livingstone clearly misunderstood his request, and in so doing failed to interpret the Bible in a way that responded to the day-to-day experience of the people. Sekgoma tried to make a similar point to James Chapman, a traveller and hunter who reached Shoshong in the early 1850's:

> I should like to be a missionary, and to become a Christian, if I should be allowed to keep my wives. I don't want any more. I have transgressed and nothing can ever undo that which has once been done, but I cannot turn my wives and children out. All men's hearts will be against me, I shall be alone on the earth. To have many wives disgraced and my legitimate children branded with a false and igno-

minious name, would bring overwhelming ruin and trouble without end upon me (Chapman 1868: 220).

However, Sekgoma was greatly impressed with the presentation of the Bible by R.G. Cummings, a famous English hunter who visited the region before Livingstone. He was not a missionary and did not have any formal association with missionary societies, but frequently preached to the Bangwato (Cummings 1850: ix, Mackenzie 1871: 407). Sekgoma found Cummings' preaching down-to-earth and relevant to his context. The failure of missionaries to relate the Bible to the Ngwato culture and experience conjured up a host of uncertainties for Sekgoma, in particular, and for his people in general. Cummings's impact on Sekgoma came from the fact that his preaching was more contextual and relevant. As a hunter and trader, Cummings did not see Christianity as foreign to his everyday activities. He related the Bible which he preached to his hunting and trading adventures. His religion seemed to be making him a successful hunter and this is what Sekgoma and his people wanted to see happen. Sekgoma was impressed, because his idea was that biblical teaching should permeate the everyday issues of survival such as hunting, ploughing, drought, harvest, politics and war by bringing understanding and security. Sekgoma was searching for a culturally relevant form of Christianity which would not just change his heart and but also protect him from his fears. This is why in 1851 he appealed to Livingstone to give him something which was going to change his heart. Livingstone's interpretation of the Bible, unfortunately, did not meet Sekgoma's real need.

Sekgoma's stance towards biblical teaching argues for a cultural expression of Christianity, something which would relate both to the context and the conceptual thought of the people. The Bangwato religious practice catered for this. Divination, prayers and charms were provided for the people for healing and security. They needed something concrete and tangible. In this sense, the people wanted the Bible to be interpreted in such a way that it addressed their daily fears and needs, otherwise it remained foreign and irrelevant, failing to change people's environment and lives, something Sekgoma desired to see happen.

In the end, the London Missionary Society missionaries, simply and easily dismissed Sekgoma as anti-Christian. This was unfortunate because Sekgoma's struggle was not against God or the preaching

of the Bible but the way it was interpreted and presented before
him. He was struggling to interpret the Bible in a way that would
make sense within his socio-political environment. Sekgoma's dissatisfaction resulted from the missionary presentation or interpretation
of the Bible, which completely discouraged or cut his people from
their cultural systems. "How should I answer to Khari [his dead
father]?," Sekgoma asked, "if I changed the customs of my town"
(Mackenzie 1871: 397). In short, Sekgoma was saying he would find
it hard to account for his abandoning Setswana culture before his
ancestors. According to Bangwato tradition and religious beliefs, the
king was not only the preserver of custom but also the intermediary
to the royal *badimo* (ancestors). The thought of suddenly abandoning
this religious role without an assurance that his future and that of
the whole community would be cared for by a stronger system was
a source of Sekgoma's fear. Mackenzie and the rest of the London
Missionary Society agents could not appreciate the depth of this
predicament. Mackenzie, in reply to his cry, challenged him saying,

> Indeed it is impossible for you to live and die like your ancestors. You
> can never be like Khari, for he never refused the Word of God,
> whereas you refuse it at present . . . he would have probably believed . . . if
> it had ever been made known to him . . . live your own life, in the
> circumstances in which has placed you, and not seek to live the life
> of an ancestor to whom these circumstances were unknown (Mackenzie
> 1871: 397).

The issue for Sekgoma, however, was not that he rejected the Bible,
but that his problems and needs were vaguely, unrealistically and
unhelpfully understood by missionaries. Sekgoma therefore he did
not see any good reason why he had to completely abandon all his
Bangwato way of life at the expense of the Word of God, which
seemed to support Western culture and discourage his own cultural
heritage. To commit himself to such alien forms of interpreting the
Bible was unacceptable, and offered no security of any sort. The
interpretation of the Bible by the missionaries therefore only frustrated Sekgoma and forced him to adopt a defensive attitude. He
decided to prevent his people from attending misleading missionary
teaching that used the Bible against the traditions and culture of his
people. Mackenzie understood this quite well, writing that "It is not
that the people cannot comprehend what is preached to them, but
that they prefer the customs in which they have been brought up"
(MacKenzie 1871: 197).

Missionary interpretation of the Bible hindered the rapid development of an authentic Christianity based on Batswana culture and experience. Sechele, Sebetoane, Sekgoma and others wanted to see some form of relevance and continuity with the culture in their interpretation of the Bible, but the European missionaries who first brought the Bible to Southern Africans could not understand why there was resistance to their biblical teaching. When their new converts returned to the observance of their cultural ceremonies they concluded that they were not sincere from the start in their decision to become Christians. The missionaries tended to conclude that their converts, especially the kings, became Christians because they were interested in European goods such as guns and ammunition. Missionaries did not realize that their interpretation of the Bible was basically European.

BIBLIOGRAPHY

Blaikie, W.G. *The Life of David Livingstone.* London: John Murray, 1910.

Chapman, J. *Travels in the Interior of South Africa: 1849–1863*, Vol. 1, London: Edward Stanford.

Livingstone, D. Letter to J.H. Parker, 11.5.44, written from Mabotsa, National Library of Scotland: Manuscript 1079.

———. *Missionary Travels and Researches in South Africa.* London: John Murray, 1853.

Livingstone, D. & C. *Narratives of an Expedition to the Zambezi and its Tributaries and of the Discovery of the Lakes Shirwa and Nyassa: 1858–1864.* London: John Murray, 1865.

Long, U., Ed. *The Journals of Elizabeth Lees Price, Written in Bechuanaland, Southern Africa, 1854–1883.* London: Edward Arnold, 1956.

MacKenzie, J. *Ten Years North of the Orange River: A Story of Everyday Life and Work Among the South African Tribes: 1858–1869.* Edinburgh: Edmond and Douglas. 1870.

MacNair, J.I. *Livingstone: The Liberator: The Story of a Dynamic Personality.* London: Collins, 1940.

Monk W. *Dr. Livingstone's Cambridge Lectures, etc.* Cambridge: Deighton, Bell & Co., 1860.

Schapera, I., Ed. *David Livingstone's Private Journals: 1851–53.* London: Chatto & Windus, 1960.

———, Ed. *David Livingstone's Family Letters: Vol. 2:1849–1956.* London: Chatto & Windus, 1959.

———, Ed. *Livingstone's Missionary correspondence: 1841–56.* London: Chatto & Windus, 1961.

THE ROLE OF THE BIBLE IN THE RISE OF AFRICAN INSTITUTED CHURCHES: THE CASE OF THE AKURINU CHURCHES IN KENYA

Nahashon W. Ndung'u

The Christian Church has witnessed the greatest diversity in expression of her faith on the African soil, through the thousands of African Instituted Churches.[1] In an attempt to explain the causes for the rise of these churches, scholars from different disciplines have come up with various theories incorporating social, political, economic and cultural factors. The impact of the Bible in this scenario has quite often been underrated. Yet there seems to be a strong relationship between the time the Bible or portions of the Bible were translated in the African languages and the emergence of the first African Instituted Churches.

Among those scholars who have identified the significance of Bible translation as an important factor in understanding the phenomenon of African Church independence is D.B. Barret. He observes that,

> It is impossible to over estimate the importance of the Bible in African society. The portions of it that are first translated are in most cases the first printed literature in vernacular languages. . . . Through these scriptures, God, Africans perceived, was addressing them in the vernacular in which was enshrined the soul of their people . . . The vernacular scriptures therefore provided an independent standard of reference that African Christians were quick to seize on (Barret 1968: 129).

In the same vein, John Mbiti has observed that the translation of the Bible into various African languages shed a new light on and offered opportunities for new interpretations of the Bible for African converts. He compares this new experience of Africans to that of the disciples after the outpouring of the Holy Spirit on the day of Pentecost thus, "As in Acts 2: the local Christians now for the first

---

[1] This chapter is a revised version of a paper delivered at a seminar of the Eastern Africa Ecumenical Symposium of Theologians, Sagana, Kenya 17–20 March 1994.

time hear each of us in his language . . . . we hear them telling in our own tongues the mighty works of God. . . . . Local Christians cannot remain the same after that" (Mbiti 1986: 26). This essay focuses on the contribution of the vernacular Gikuyu language Bible to the rise of the Akurinu Churches.[2]

It was during the last decades of the nineteenth century that Gikuyu land, hitherto undisturbed by external foreign influences, witnessed the arrival and subsequent colonization by the Europeans. With the construction of the Kenya-Uganda railway from Mombasa (1896) to Kisumu on lake Victoria (1901), Gikuyuland was opened up for European colonial administrators, settlers, traders and Christian missionaries. They brought with them a "new and strange way of life, with its sometimes incomprehensible demands and ideas" (Muriuki, 1974: 136). The colonial administration dismantled the traditional Gikuyu government and put in place hand-picked chiefs. At the same time, the fertile and cool Gikuyu highlands were appropriated for the European settlers. Without land, the Gikuyu, being agriculturalists, were economically crippled. They were relocated onto African "native Reserves." Thus, through colonization, the Gikuyu became tenants on their former clan lands.

Apart from losing their lands, the Gikuyu were required to provide cheap labour on the settler farms. Various unscrupulous methods were designed in order to maintain a regular flow of forced labour. The introduction of taxation of male African adults in 1913 was such a tactic, as Sir Percy Girourd put it, "We consider that taxation is the only possible method of compelling the native to leave his native reserve for purposes of seeking work. Only in this way can the cost of living be increased for the native" (Leys 1924: 202). The forced labour greatly disrupted the social fabric of the Gikuyu families as members were scattered on different settler farms and remained in separation for long periods.

Following the construction of the railway, European Christian missionaries streamed into Gikuyuland and carved out their zones of operation. In 1898 the Church of Scotland Mission (CSM) founded a station at Kikuyu to the west of Nairobi. They were followed by the Church Missionary Society (CMS) in 1901 who founded a station at Kihuroko (Kabete) on the western outskirts of Nairobi. The Africa

---

[2] For a full account of the Akurinu churches see N.W. Ndung'u 1994.

Inland Mission founded a station at Kijabe in 1903. Apart from the
Protestant missions, there were the Roman Catholics who had joined
the race. The Holy Ghost Fathers arrived in 1899 and established
a station to the west of Nairobi at St. Austins. They were followed
by the Consolata Fathers in 1903 who founded a station at Limuru
in Kiambu District. From these initial stations, the missionaries gradually penetrated into Gikuyuland. Various methods were employed
to win Gikuyu converts.[3] The method which proved most effective
was the formal school education system.[4] Christian teachings occupied a central position in the school curriculum. Anderson has rightly
observed that in Kikuyuland Christianity and formal schooling were
presented together. Those who sought schooling became Christians
and those interested in Christianity went to school (Anderson 1970:
107). With time, however, the enlightened Gikuyu began to demand
a secular and better education, which was comparable to that offered
in the European and Asian schools in Kenya (Raju 1973: 6).

From the start the Gikuyu were suspicious of some of the missionary societies, who, like the settlers, had taken huge pieces of land
(Temu 1972: 101). But what greatly strained the relations between
the Gikuyu and the missionaries was the latter's attack on some
Gikuyu customs such as polygamy, dances, divination and female
circumcision. Led by the CSM, the Protestant missionaries in particular waged a campaign against what they viewed as unchristian
Gikuyu practices.[5] Their main focus was on the female circumcision,
a rite through which a girl graduated to an adult woman. Initially,
the campaign took the form of moral teachings but later it became
an ecclesiastical requirement whereby members were threatened with
suspensions and excommunications if they allowed their girls to be
circumcised (Wanyoike 1974: 72). It became the criterion of judging
between the nominal members and the committed Christians. To
the Gikuyu who were already grieved by the loss of their land, forced

---

[3] Other methods included giving of gifts such as beads, blankets, calico sheets,
employment in the mission stations and the provision of medical care.

[4] In Kenya there were 3 categories of schools, with decreasing amounts of financial
investment. First, there were the European schools, for whites only. Second there
were the Asian schools. And third, and least, were the African and Arab schools.
The African schools were started and managed by the various Christian missionary societies.

[5] The Roman Catholics kept out of this campaign and thus avoided direct confrontations with the Gikuyu.

labour and taxation, the added issue of female circumcision acted as a unifying factor in uniting them to reject the missionaries' demands. The Kikuyu Central Association (KCA), a political party founded in 1924, picked up the issue and added it on the list of the grievances affecting the Gikuyu community. Accordingly, the KCA leaders, who by then had read the Bible, accused the European missionaries of having added an eleventh commandment to the ten of Moses which required Gikuyu Christians to refrain from female circumcision (Mac-Pherson 1970: 108).[6]

The female circumcision controversy came to a climax in 1928 during a meeting held in Nyeri between the CSM missionaries and Gikuyu Church elders. The elders were required to endorse their support for the abolition of the custom but some of them refused to denounce it.[7] This was indeed a clear proof to the missionaries that not all their followers supported the campaign against the female circumcision. It became necessary therefore to determine their true followers. This was done by demanding that the Gikuyu Christians sign a loyalty declaration form which was as follows: "I reaffirm my vows to the Church of Christ and wish to dissociate myself with the practice of girl circumcision which I hereby renounce again" (Wanyoike 1974: 98). Those who refused to sign the loyalty declaration would henceforth be excommunicated and their children expelled from the mission schools. By the end of 1929 the separation of the loyal adherents and the dissenters was complete. The CSM lost 90% of its communicants at Kikuyu Mission while the Africa Inland Mission Kijabe mission lost 50% of its 600 adherents (Rosberg and Nottingham 1966: 124). Those who broke away from the mission founded churches immediately embarked on organizing independent churches and schools to cater for their spiritual needs and the education of their children. The Gikuyu Bible played an important role in these processes.

The translation of the Bible into Gikuyu language began soon after the planting of Christianity in Gikuyuland. Initially, portions of the Bible were translated separately. By 1926, the translation of the New Testament was completed while the Old Testament was completed in 1951. It is worth noting that the translation of the New

---

[6] A twelfth commandment ran as follows "Thou shalt not join Kikuyu Central Association" (Rosberg and Nottingham 1966: 120).

[7] For a detailed account of the meeting see Ndung'u 1979: 20.

Testament (and parts of the Old Testament) coincided with the conflict between the protestant missions and some Gikuyu Christians and non-Christians over some traditional customs. The literate Gikuyu turned to the Bible, and used it in defending their customs. According to Jomo Kenyatta:

> The African faced with these problems and seeing how his institutions have been shattered looked again in the Book of Books. There he found polygamy sanctioned by the personal practice of great Biblical characters ... But he was shocked to find the missionary again condemning him as a sinner for fulfilling that which is sanctioned in the Ibuku ria Ngai (the Bible) (Kenyatta 1938: 272).

It is clear then that after reading the Bible the Gikuyu could distinguish between the demands of the missionaries and what is found in the Bible. Thus, they had discovered a biblical basis for the defence of their customs.

The Akurinu Churches emerged in 1927 soon after the New Testament was translated into Gikuyu. According to some informants, the early founders of this movement spent long periods studying the Bible. For example, Joseph Ng'ang'a is said to have spent three years (from 1926–1929) in seclusion, studying the Bible while John Mung'ara spent one year in a store reading the Bible (Ndung'u 1994: 107). These two were to become the first preachers and evangelists among the Akurinu. Ng'ang'a is described as an impressive preacher well versed in the Bible. We can therefore conclude that it was the availability of the Bible in Gikuyu language which made it possible for these people, some of whom were semi-literate, to read and interpret it to others even though they had no theological training.

From the beginning the Akurinu considered themselves a special people purposely chosen by God for a mission. The conviction of the Akurinu that they are a chosen people of God is implied in their other name, "People of God" (Kiswahili—*Watu was Mungu*) which they used during the early days. It is on this basis that they consider themselves to be an eschatological community appropriating the fruits of the Holy Spirit as foretold by prophet Joel (Acts 2:17–21).

> And in the last days it shall be, God declares, that I will pour out my spirit upon all flesh and your sons and your daughters shall prophesy, and your young men shall dream dreams, yea, and on my menservants and my maidservants in those days I will pour out my spirit, and they shall prophesy. And I will show wonders in the heaven above and signs on the earth beneath, blood and fire, and vapour of smoke:

the sun shall be turned into darkness, and the moon into blood, before the day of the Lord comes, the great and manifest day. And it shall be that who ever calls on the name of the Lord shall be saved.

In 1938, Kenyatta described the Akurinu in the following words: "The members of this religious sect strongly believe that they are the chosen people of God to give and interpret his message to the people. They proclaim that they belong to the lost tribes of Israel" (Kenyatta 1938: 275).

The way the missionaries had interpreted the Bible to the Africans left a lot to be desired. So the Akurinu were to provide the correct version, "since they were prophets and interpreters of the word of God" (Barret et al. 1973: 125). The Akurinu claim to be guided by the Holy Spirit in their interpretation of the scriptures. This is one reason why they are not interested in sending their pastors to theological colleges.[8] Since the rise of the Akurinu movement, the Bible has been a major factor in shaping the life of this Church. Since they did not want to imitate the practices of the mission Churches, they turned to the Bible. From where they identified the teachings and practices which are observed to the present. The following practices offer an illustration: keeping of uncut hair and beard (Numbers 6:5-7, 1 Samuel 1:11-13), restriction from wearing red clothes (Deuteronomy 27:26), removal of shoes in Church (Exodus 3:4-7), ritual uncleanness after child delivery (Leviticus 12:1-8), rejection of modern medicine (Jeremiah 46:11-12, Hosea 5:13-14), wearing of white robes and turbans (Leviticus 8:9-14, Exodus 29:6-7), raising of hands during prayer (1 Kings 8:22-23, 1 Timothy 2:8-9).

Several events in their history reveal their deep sense of identity with and even a zeal to emulate biblical experiences. Among such events was the giving of the Law on Mount Kenya.[9] In 1930, a Mukurinu prophet was told through a vision that God wanted to give the Akurinu the commandments which would guide them. Eight elders were chosen to go and receive the commandments. It is claimed that when they got to the top of Mt. Kenya, God appeared to them, after which they received the Holy Spirit and began speaking in tongues. After that God gave them the following ten commandments:

---

[8] To date there are only two pastors who have had some training at St. Paul's United Theological College, Limuru. Some members however argue that those who advocate for such training are lacking in the Holy Spirit.

[9] In the Gikuyu religion, Mt. Kenya is considered as the sacred abode of *Ngai* (God).

1. To part with those who had signed the loyalty declaration forms and collaborators with the colonialists who were selling out the country.
2. Not to go to hospitals for treatment because of the hypocrisy of Europeans.
3. Not to use European things and to reject their teachings.
4. To revert to their traditional Gikuyu way of life.
5. To pray for the KCA, and the government that God would give the people to fight the colonial enemies.
6. To pray for the advancement of the education of the youths so that there would be educated leaders for the country.
7. To pray for and end to the suffering which the Akurinu were facing from colonial administrators, missionaries and collaborators from among their own people.
8. To pray for the land, food and the wealth of the country.
9. Not to eat meat with blood, and to bury the blood, liver, lungs, spleen and kidneys when they slaughter an animal.
10. To pray to God with clean raised hands and to repeat the Lord's prayer three times. Prayers should be made in the name of the Father, the Holy Spirit and the Son.[10] The following biblical references were given to seal these commandments: Joel 1:1–8, Ezekiel 33 and 37, Hebrews 33.

A closer look at the commandments reveals that commandments 1–4 deal with the preservation of the Gikuyu social and cultural identity. Numbers 5–8 spell out the means by which the survival of the Gikuyu community would be achieved. The last two commandments deal with the manner of worshipping God. These biblical references, they believed, were relevant to a period when the Gikuyu were suffering, like the Jews were during the time of the prophets. The locust invasion foretold by Joel was compared with the colonial invasion of Gikuyuland, to which Ezekiel and Jeremiah bring a message of hope and restoration of lost land and glory. This message of hope was significant during such a troubled period. Although the Akurinu did not participate physically in the armed struggle for independence in Kenya, they believe that it was through their prayers that the country was liberated from the colonialists.

---

[10] Note that the Holy Spirit comes before the Son in the Akurinu Trinitarian formula.

As mentioned earlier, the Akurinu consider themselves to be a chosen people of God. It is for this reason that they try to uphold the Levitical laws in order to maintain that relationship. These laws play a pivotal role in the liturgy of their Church. Before the pastor delivers his sermon, he starts by reading the Law (Exodus 20) and exhorts the congregation to observe the Law in order to get God's blessings. After the sermon, members are given a chance to testify. It is characteristic for members to support their testimonies by reading verses from the Bible as well as interpreting them. We should hasten to mention that even the illiterate members take pains to master some verses which they readily quote when they give their testimonies. Moreover, it is common to find them carrying copies of the Bible as they go to Church. If need arises they can always request a literate member to read for them. Thus during a single service, the congregation ends up getting a variety of lessons drawn from a cross-section of readings from both the Old and New Testaments.

Among the Akurinu the Bible is regarded as one whole unified text, from Genesis to Revelation. Such remarks as would draw a distinction between the Old and New Testaments are avoided. To them, the *Ibuku* (the Bible), contains the "Word of God" which is timeless and therefore remains relevant for all times. This explains why to them the Law of Moses is repeated every Sunday at the start of the service.

When one observes the manner in which the Bible is used during different occasions among the Akurinu, it is at times difficult to distinguish between the symbolism and the reality the Bible represents. In some cases, the Bible is used as though it transmits some mystical power which makes things to happen. For example, during prayers the elders will carry their Bibles in bags suspended from their shoulders. The same happens during such ceremonies as baptism, marriage, ordination and burial. This ritual gesture makes the members appreciate the solemnity of the occasions. The gesture reminds them that the elders carrying the Bibles are the custodians of the law which they are supposed to observe at all times. The power of the Bible is further demonstrated during faith healing. Some prophets and prophetesses will not only pray for the patient but will also place the Bible on the patient.[11] In this case, the Bible is treated as though

---

[11] This was observed during a healing ceremony at Kiawara (Nyeri District) on 2 September 1991, conducted by Prophetess Ruth Muthoni.

it transmits a power which will scare away or even destroy the evil powers responsible for the suffering the person is experiencing. The Bible is more than a text, it is a religio-magical symbol of God's presence and power.

The Akurinu service is a long ritual taking an average of four to five hours and sometimes more. In the African Mission of Holy Ghost Church, the service starts at abut 10 am and the closing prayer is said at 3 pm. This is in keeping with the Sabbath. Singing takes up a good part of the service. The Akurinu are renowned for singing and dancing during worship. There is no limit to the number of hymns to be sung on any one occasion, with the hymns occupying an important place theologically in the interpretative life of the Church. The Akurinu have composed their own original hymns. The hymnal is the only published literature in this Church. Until 1977 the hymns were transmitted orally, but when the composer, Daudi Ikigu, realized that other Protestant churches had started publishing the hymns, sometimes with modifications, he decided to publish them in order to retain their original forms and meaning. The hymnal has 554 hymns and Ikigu is currently preparing to publish a second part which will contain a greater number of hymns than the present one (Ikigu 1977). In terms of communicating the Bible message, the hymns play an important role in the Akurinu churches, as they do in many churches in other parts of Africa. Hymns are based on biblical stories like the creation, the exodus, the life, death and resurrection of Jesus Christ and the life of the early Church. The hymns are easier to commit to memory and play an important role in the remembering and interpreting of biblical stories. Moreover, individuals will sing the hymns at any time or place as they wish. Hymns are particularly important to the illiterate members. Although they are not able to read the Bible, they are capable of mastering the hymns.

The Akurinu like other Christians accept the Triune God doctrine. But unlike other Christians who retain the Father-Son-Holy Spirit formula, they have the Holy Spirit taking the second position while the Son comes third, as is demonstrated in the following prayer pattern:

Muhoi: Ndahoya Ngai na Roho na Jesu Kristo mukuri witu. (×3)
Andu othe: kwendaini gwaku na kwa Roho and kwa Jesu Kristo mukuri
             witu. Amen. (×3)
Muhoi: Ngai Baba turathime. (×3)
Andu othe: Kweandaini gwaku na kwa Roho na kwa Jesu Kristo
             mukuri witu. Amen (×3)

Prayer-leader: I beseech God the father and the Holy Spirit and Jesus
            Christ our Saviour. (×3)
Congregation: By your love (will) and of the Holy Spirit and of Jesus
            Christ our Saviour. Amen (×3)
Prayer-leader: God our Father have mercy on us. (×3)
Congregation: By your love (will) and of the Holy Spirit and of Jesus
            Christ our Saviour. Amen (×3) (Ndung'u, 1994: 266).

The Akurinu conception of the Trinity is based on a spatial and
temporal perspective. The Father has allowed the Son and the Holy
Spirit to be operative in the world at a given time. Jesus had his
time during his earthly ministry. At present, the Holy Spirit is at
work in the world while the Father and the Son are waiting in
heaven for the Spirit to complete the salvific mission which Jesus
had begun. It is this presence and personal experience of the Holy
Spirit by the Akurinu which may have led the founders of this
Church to place the Holy Spirit as the second person in the Trinity,
although they claim that their Trinitarian formula was revealed to
them by God. They even refer to themselves as "People of the Spirit"
and also regard themselves as the eschatological community appropriating the fruits of the Holy Spirit while awaiting the Parousia
(Acts 2:1ff., 1 Corinthians 12:1ff.).

    Prayer too is an important aspect in the Akurinu churches, and
in this the Bible also has a part to play. The Akurinu set aside three
days, Wednesday, Friday and Sunday for worship. At present most
members observe Friday and Sunday as rest and worship days. Apart
from the weekly prayers, the Akurinu have three important communal
prayers which are held in January, July and in December. These
are based on the Deuteronomic laws of Moses (Deuteronomy 16:16)
in which male Jews were to hold prayers three times every year. To
the Akurinu, the January prayers are for asking God for guidance
and His care in the New Year. The July prayers are for thanking
God for having guided the people through half of the year, while
the December prayers are for thanking God for the past year. The
participants in these prayer days are elders who are free from ritual uncleanness. They range between 6 and 12 and represent different
regions. The prayers take a period of one to two weeks and are held
in one selected church where the elders must remain until the prayers
are over. Each day they pray in the sanctuary at three-hour inter-
vals, at 6 am, 9 am, 12 noon, 3 pm and 6 pm. The rest of the
time is spent in Bible study with the senior elders instructing the
junior ones. Thus, the occasion serves as a Bible retreat during which

newly appointed pastors get on the job training since the Akurinu
have no Bible Schools or theological colleges.

Despite the fact that women are the majority in the Akurinu
Church, it is the men who hold the leadership positions, as my discussion so far indicates. Male domination is based on their reading
of the Old Testament traditions and is further endorsed by St. Paul's
teaching on the role of women in the Church (1 Corinthians 14:34–35,
1 Timothy 2:8–15). The Akurinu have used these texts to justify
male leadership and to apportion women ceremonial duties. The
Bible is used to deny the women any chance to preach or read the
Bible in Church. Furthermore, women are not allowed to step into
the sanctuary (*kigongona*) which is a reserve for the men. On the basis
of the Mosaic Laws, women are not allowed to go to Church during their menses and after childbirth until, after seven days, a cleansing ceremony is performed (Leviticus 12:1–8, 15:19–25).

While women are denied the leadership responsibilities they do
however form a greater number of the *Anabii* (prophets). The *Anabii*
play an important role in the life of the Church. Like the Old
Testament prophets, the *Anabii* mediate between God and the people in the Akurinu churches. Prophecy is one of the gifts of the Holy
Spirit (Acts 2:17–18), which is given to a person irrespective of age
or sex. The duties of the *Anabii* include revealing baptismal names,
identifying marriage partners, revealing evils in the Church, praying
for the sick in faith healing as well as directing errant members to
confess and be prayed for before they can resume their Church activities. Through prophecy and spirit possession, the women seem to
compensate for their lowly position in the Church. Their voice as
Anabii becomes even louder than that of the men. Thus, while the
Bible is used to oppress women it is at the same time used to liberate them as prophetesses in the Akurinu Churches.

The Bible is a library from which a person or a people will find
what they regard as relevant to their situation. It is in this respect
that it has been instrumental in shaping the African Instituted
Churches. The leaders have selected the practices which they consider to be relevant to their social-cultural locations. But, although
the Bible has been translated into many African languages, it still
carries the socio-cultural world view and metaphors of its contexts
of production, some of which are not easy to conceptualize in local
African contexts and vernacular languages. This problem calls for
African theologians to comment on the Bible and to write (vernac-

ular) commentaries on the Bible. This is an area that has received very little attention.[12] Some of the theological disputes in the African Instituted Churches which have led to several schisms in these churches could perhaps be minimized if the leaders had a deeper understanding of the scriptures. While the guidance of the Holy Spirit in interpreting the scriptures cannot be underrated, there is, however, room for a broadening of Bible knowledge through the reading of supplementary material. This then calls for the emergence of educated clergy in the African Instituted Churches. The time has come when Africa should not only be proud of the quantitative treasures of Bible translation but should also aspire for a qualitative understanding of the scriptures.

BIBLIOGRAPHY

Anderson, J. *The Struggle for the School.* Nairobi: Longman, 1970.
Barret, D.B. *Schism and Renewal in Africa.* Nairobi: Oxford University Press, 1968.
———. et al., Eds *Kenya Churches Handbook.* Kisumu: Evangel Publishing, 1973.
Ikigu, D. *Nyimbo cia Roho Mutheru.* Kijabe: Kijabe Printing Press, 1977.
Kenyatta, J. *Facing Mount Kenya.* London: Secker and Warburg, 1938.
Leys, N. *Kenya.* London, Leonard and Virginia Wolf, 1924.
MacPherson, R. *The Presbyterian Church in Kenya. An Account of the Origins and Growth of the Presbyterian Church in East Africa.* Nairobi: Presbyterian Church of East Africa, 1970.
Mbiti, J. *Bible and Theology in African Christianity.* Nairobi: Oxford University Press, 1986.
Muriuki, G. *A History of the Kikuyu, 1500–1900.* Nairobi: Oxford University Press 1974.
Ndung'u, N.W. *African Independent Pentecostal Church of Africa and Eschatology.* M.A. Thesis, University of Nairobi, 1979.
———. *The Akurinu Churches: With Emphasis on Their Theology.* Ph.D. Thesis, University of Nairobi, 1994.
Raju, B.M., *Education in Kenya.* London: Heinemann, 1973.
Rosberg, C.G. and Nottingham, J. *The Myth of Mau Mau, Nationalism in Kenya.* Nairobi: East African Publishing House, 1966.
Wanyoike, E.N. *An African Pastor.* Nairobi: East African Publishing House, 1974.

---

[12] For a list of the few commentaries written by Africans see Mbiti 1986: 51.

CAIN AND ABEL IN AFRICA: AN ETHIOPIAN CASE STUDY IN COMPETING HERMENEUTICS[1]

Mark McEntire

During the final years of Apartheid in the 1980's, a significant dispute arose among South African biblical interpreters over how to read the Cain and Abel story in Genesis 4. This debate has been documented, in at least two places.[2] The interpretations of the primary figures, Alan Boesak and Itumeleng J. Mosala will be summarized below. This text has also received attention from African interpreters in other parts of the continent. The most significant of these is Modupe Oduyoye of Nigeria. His interpretation is also summarized below. Within the context of a Protestant seminary in Ethiopia I have presented these three interpretations along with an explanation of the methodologies which produced them and have recorded the responses of Ethiopian students. Following the explanations of the interpretations, I will summarize the reactions of these students. Finally, I will attempt to evaluate the implications of the debate over Genesis 4 for the larger issue of African hermeneutics.

Boesak did not provide a thorough methodological background to his reading of the Cain and Abel story. His interpretation is published in a transcript of a sermon. He has made some assertions in various places about his method of reading the Bible. First, he has emphasized the importance of reading the Bible within a community of struggle (Boesak 1977: 16).[3] Second, his goal has been to bring together the world of the text with the world of the reader. He specifically emphasized that "This story does not tell us in the

---

[1] This paper, in a slightly different form, was read at the 1997 meeting of the Society of Biblical Literature. The theme for the Bible Africa, Asia and Latin America Section was "Contending Readings: Disputed Authority." This theme has had significant influence on the shaping of the essay.

[2] Anthony C. Thiselton has briefly summarized the methods and conclusions of Mosala, Boesak, and Tutu and has analyzed the debate in reference to contemporary hermeneutics (Thiselton 1992: 419–426). Gerald West has evaluated the methods and conclusions of Boesak and Mosala more extensively (West 1995).

[3] West identified this element of Boesak's hermeneutic is his analysis (West 1995: 69).

first place what happened once upon a time, rather it tells us about something that happens today" (Boesak 1984: 137). Third, he sought to read the final form of the text, concentrating on the literary detail of the story. In his exegesis, Boesak noted a number of key words which he used as keys to interpretation. The emphasis on the word "brother" draws attention to seriousness of the crime. Cain not only commits murder, but he fails to fulfill the responsibilities of human relationship (138). The frequent use of "ground" highlights Cain's connection to the land and the broken connection at the end of the story. In the end, Cain becomes one with no sense of belonging as indicated by the word "wander" (140).

Boesak moved from literary details of the Genesis 4 text to point toward two key canonical connections. First, like the thief on the cross next to Jesus (Luke 23:40–43), Cain had the opportunity to ask for forgiveness during his conversation with YHWH. Second, while Cain's way of violence continues in his ancestor, Lamech, Jesus reverses Lamech's sevenfold vengeance with his command to forgive seventy times seven (Matthew 18:21–22). Boesak ended his exegesis by observing that the birth of Seth and the institution of YHWH worship provide the end of the story with a sense of hope. It is apparent from these last two points that Boesak was not dividing the text as form or source critics and even some literary critics might, but reading all of Genesis 4 together.[4]

Boesak applied the text to his own situation in Apartheid South Africa in a number of significant ways. First, oppressors destroy all of their connections in the world and end up with no place in it (139–140). Second, those who live by violence, like Cain live with the anxiety that vengeance will come. Third, God wishes to make a new beginning with humanity. Boesak was quite honest in expressing that the canonical principle of forgiveness is extremely difficult to apply in situations such as his own in South Africa (144).

Mosala's interpretation stands over against Boesak's interpretation in almost every way. Mosala's method is historical, relying heavily on source-critical arguments, and radically materialist, making use of social-scientific approaches. For Mosala, the Bible is the record of a class struggle in ancient Israel. Proper interpretation of the text

---

[4] Boesak claimed at the beginning of this sermon to be interpreting 4:1–17, but he clearly goes beyond this to the end of the chapter (Boesak 1984: 137).

depends on locating it historically and sociologically. The interpreter must decode the agenda of the text, paying careful attention to class, gender, and race issues. Because the Bible is the record of an ancient class struggle, it becomes the site of a class struggle today. The Cain and Abel story must be read within the materialist context of the present, because it was produced within a materialist context of the past (Mosala 1989: 33–37).

Though never stated specifically, Mosala appears to be reading only 4:1–16, following the standard source division. Mosala's initial interpretive move is to follow standard source criticism in assigning this story to the Yahwist source and the Yahwist source to the Davidic-Solomonic empire of the tenth century. Evidence both inside and outside the Bible would indicate that during this time peasant land holders were being dispossessed of their land in order to create large estates. Because the religio-political power structure was responsible both for the dispossession of peasant land and the production of the text, then the Cain and Abel story must have been written for the purpose of legitimating the accumulation of land into the hands of the few. Therefore, the true victim in the story, Cain, is portrayed as the criminal who deserves his fate. The land-grabbing oppressors of the tenth century are portrayed as the victim (Abel). Both God and the text are on the side of Abel, and the reader is manipulated to take that side as well (33–37).

The application of Mosala's interpretation falls into place easily in the South African era of Apartheid. The social-material world of White farmers and the Black people they dispossessed, matches precisely the social material world of the Davidic-Solomonic empire, and the inequities of both are justified by Cain's murder of Abel. The oppressors have manipulated this story to serve their purposes, and readings of the story such as those of Boesak and Tutu play into the hands of these oppressors by agreeing with their ideology (38–42).

Gerald West has described the methods which produced these two opposing readings as "reading in front of the text" and "reading behind the text," the former being Boesak's literary approach and the latter Mosala's social-materialist approach (West 1995: 64–74). The absolute opposition of these two readings might be better characterized as reading "with" and "against" the text. One thing on which the two readings agree is that the text attempts to bring the reader onto the side of Abel. Mosala's daring assertion is that the reader must not follow the lead of the text, but struggle to quite an opposite conclusion. Boesak followed the lead of the text and, thus, drew Mosala's criticism.

Moving outside the South African context, perhaps the most significant interpretation of the Cain and Abel story is that of the Nigerian, Modupe Oduyoye. The approach of Oduyoye is significantly more difficult to describe, and his interpretation more difficult to present. His method is basically form-critical. He has identified the stories of Genesis 1–11 as myths, or founding stories of civilization. These stories, therefore, expose foundational issues of human life and society. In addition, Oduyoye has made extensive use of linguistics, especially cognates to the Hebrew language found within the Hamitic languages of Africa. Through these linguistic links, he connects the myths of Genesis 1–11 with those of African cultures. He then uses these related myths to help expose the meaning of the biblical stories (Oduyoye 1984: 1–4).

For Oduyoye, the Cain and Abel story is basically about the conflict between settled civilization and pastoral nomadism. This is revealed by the meaning of the names of the two sons. Cain's name, *Qayin* in Hebrew, is related to the Arabic word for "smith" (*Qayn*) and the legendary *Ogun* in Yoruba culture, who is the patron saint of both agriculture and iron-working. Cain's descendent and namesake, *Tubal Qayin* (Genesis 4:22), is the Bible's first ironsmith. Nigerian mythology attributes the discovery of iron technology to *Kuno*. Further, Genesis 4:17 tells us that Cain founded a city which he named for his son, *Hanok*. The earliest civilization in West Africa was *Nok*, which means "to start." Putting all of this together, Oduyoye concluded that the meaning of Cain's story is that through the use of iron technology city building became possible and was victorious over pastoral nomadism (20–22).

Abel's name is *Hebel* in Hebrew. This word means "fleeting breath," it is something insubstantial or impermanent. It is an ideal reflection of the existence of the nomad. Though they are somehow subsumed into Cain's genealogy, *Yabal* the tent-dwelling herdsman and *Yubal* the pipe player (Genesis 4:20) are both philologically related to Abel. Abel's nomadic existence reflects that of the Hebrew people, the sons of *'eber* in Genesis 10:21. They are cattle-herding nomads like the *Abore* and *Bororo* of West Africa. From the meanings of these names and the relations between them, Oduyoye concludes that the Hebrew people saw themselves as impermanent, as ones "passing by," which is what the Hebrew root *'br* means. They preferred this nomadic lifestyle, but their experience taught them that cities were the stronger older brother, who was typically victorious over the nomadic younger brother. Nomads were destroyed like Abel or subsumed into city life, just as *Yabal* and *Yubal* were subsumed into Cain's genealogy (63–74).

This is not the end of the story. It is already obvious that Oduyoye has read all of Genesis 4:1–26 together. In Genesis 4:25, Seth replaces Abel. Seth's son, Enosh, does not follow the dominating way of city-building and iron technology, but follows the way of religion, becoming the first YHWH worshiper in Genesis 4:26 (1–2). Cain and Abel disappear from the biblical story and Hebrew history emerges, but their namesakes, *Ogun* and *Pulo*, continue on in African culture as the ironsmith and the nomad. In Oduyoye's words, "if the *'iberim* stopped being wandering Arameans long ago, the sons of *'eber* in Africa (*Abore* and *Bororo*) are still moving on with their cattle" (78). The struggle between settled life and nomadism has not yet been fully settled in Africa.

Because the struggle is still somewhat unfinished, Oduyoye's application of this text as a Christian theologian in modern Africa is significant. First, he has insisted that there are no value judgements in the early Genesis stories. They simply report the way things are. Second, Christianity received it's "in the world but not of the world" tradition from the Hebrews, but has abandoned this way of life. "What the story of *Qayin* murdering *Hebel* tries to say is that a decision not to move on but to stay put in life makes one a murderer of idealists on a pilgrimage" (72–73). Here Oduyoye specifically points to the impact of the Boers on the nomadic Zulus as an example[5] (73).

Oduyoye further compared his own interpretive context with that of South Africans. He noted that white settlers in Nigeria were never allowed to own land, but only to lease it. In the early 1980's he attributed the contrasting political situations in South Africa and Nigeria to this practice. "If today the blacks in Nigeria are independent, and the blacks in South Africa are suffering, it is because white settlers (*Qayin*) arrived in the Cape in 1652 to compete with Zulu[6] cattle people, *Qayin* still kills *Hebel*" (73).

---

[5] Oduyoye is inaccurate here in his knowledge of the South African situation. In fact it was nomadic pastoralist Boers who trekked into what is now KwaZulu-Natal and had an impact on the settled Zulu population.

[6] In fact they were Xhosa cattle people, who speak a related dialect, but are a distinct society.

Oduyoye's reading of the Cain and Abel Story is in direct competition with that of Mosala. While Oduyoye's identification of Cain and Abel in the South African context agrees with Boesak's, this identification is based not on racial or even political grounds. It is based on the conflict between two ways of life. According to Oduyoye, the book of Genesis "curses all settlers . . . all who prefer the regularity of the waters of the Nile to the uncertainty of *Horeb* with its commandments" (74).

Ethiopia is in some ways quite a different context from South Africa or Nigeria. Its people are a mixture of Hamitic and Semitic tribes. Amharic, a Semitic language, is the most widely spoken tongue, though roughly half of the population is Oromo, a Hamitic ethnic group. Ethiopian culture thus takes on an interesting blend of Africa and the Middle East. Roughly half of all Ethiopians are Christians. Most of these are members of the Orthodox church, which traces its history back to the fourth century. About ten percent of the population are Protestant Christians, as a result of the contemporary missionary activity from Europe and North America. Most of the other half of the population of Ethiopia is Muslim. Unique, ancient religious festivals such as Meskel and Timket combine with Easter and Christmas to give a decidedly religious pulse to life in the country.[7] Aside from the brief Italian occupation during the Second World War of the twentieth century, Ethiopia has never been colonized by an external force. How might persons from this country respond to these competing African interpretations of the Cain and Abel story?

I presented the three readings of the Genesis story above to students of the Mekane Yesus Seminary in Addis Ababa. The church these students represent now numbers slightly more than two million in membership. It is the outgrowth of Lutheran and Presbyterian missionary efforts which began around the start of the twentieth century, but the Lutheran influence is dominant. These students typically understand their movement as a kind of Protestant Reformation, standing over against the Ethiopian Orthodox Church as Martin Luther stood against the Catholic Church of sixteenth century Europe.

Ethiopian students expressed difficulty in understanding and applying the issue of oppression, which is central to the readings of both Boesak and Mosala. The Bible is a book about spiritual matters, not

---

[7] Ethiopia has had a Jewish population in the past, commonly known as the Falashas. In the early 1990s the entire community moved to Israel.

political or economic ones. Particularly, they did not see it as the central issue of the Cain and Abel story. Consequently, they rejected the assumption that the Bible arises out of a class struggle. They rejected Mosala's reading of the story entirely and, though they did not reject Boesak's conclusions about Cain and Abel, they saw little or no connection between his contemporary application of the text and their own contemporary context. Specifically, they stated that because land confiscation had never occurred in Ethiopia they were unable to relate to Mosala's reading. Most of the conflict in Ethiopia's recent history has been ethnic conflict among Ethiopian tribes. These students, therefore, could relate to violence between brothers and God's solidarity with the younger, weaker brother. The Protestant churches suffered significantly during Ethiopia's communist era, but there is a tendency to see this strictly in terms of religious persecution, rather than economic or political oppression. Lack of common experience, then, would seem to place limits on the acceptance of these readings which come from the South African contexts.

There is another factor, however, which places a greater limitation on the acceptance of some readings. Ethiopian Protestant Christians read the Bible in a very literal, historical manner.[8] My students rejected Mosala's interpretation of the Cain and Abel story because both his method and his conclusions are simply unacceptable. A materialist reading understands the Bible to be the product of human processes. It arose out of class struggle. For these students, the Bible is the direct revelation of God, not literature that emerges from human politics. Reading the Bible from a context of struggle, like Boesak, may be appropriate, but to understand that the Bible was written within such a struggle, as Mosala did, is not. The source-critical and materialist assumptions of Mosala constitute an improper way to read the Bible. For them, the conclusion that Cain is the

---

[8] A thorough discussion of the of biblical interpretation within the Ethiopian Orthodox tradition is beyond the scope of this paper. Nevertheless, one factor may help to illuminate this point. Roger W. Cowley has demonstrated the strong connections between Ethiopian Orthodox exegesis and the Antiochene tradition (Cowley 1988: 373–382). He did acknowledge that allegorical material exists in Orthodox biblical commentary, but asserted that "there is no suggestion . . . that the original events did not happen, or were unimportant, there is no . . . 'theory of allegory,' and the reader will probably feel that these are examples of homiletic application, not allegory proper" (376). Likewise, Ethiopian Protestant Christians may make use of allegorical or spiritual application of biblical texts, but these always seem subordinate to literal historicity.

oppressed one in Genesis 4 and that we should align ourselves with him must also be incorrect. In the Cain and Abel story, God is on the side of Abel and punishes Cain. Even if this story is told by the Davidic-Solomonic empire, as Mosala assumes, the Bible tells us that God is on the side of David and Solomon. According to my Ethiopian students, we must accept this alignment.[9]

This literal hermeneutic also makes Oduyoye's interpretation difficult for Ethiopian readers to accept. The immediate response was to question how the Hebrew people could have any connection to Abel, because he died. The Hebrews are descendants of Seth through Shem. A literal understanding of the genealogies of Genesis appears to prevent a mythic understanding of the Cain and Abel story, or any of the stories in Genesis. Consequently, this prevents the connection of the founding stories of Genesis with the founding stories of Africa, a process which is central to Oduyoye's methodology.

Finally, these students find the existence of multiple interpretations quite disturbing. They believe there is one correct interpretation and that it can be determined. They tend to reject interpretations which are based upon uncertain historical assumptions, like those of Mosala and Oduyoye. A literary approach, like Boesak's, is more acceptable, but should not be applied too far out of the spiritual realm into the arenas of politics and economics. For Ethiopian Protestant Christians, religion and politics are to be kept completely separate.

The discussion of Genesis 4 above gives rise to a number of issues and questions concerning the general subject of biblical hermeneutics in Africa. The Bible has gained a very important place in African life and thought. African Christians read and study the Bible diligently and tend to know it far better than most Western Christians. Some of the reasons for the obvious connection that Africans have found with the Bible have been analyzed by the Kenyan theologian, John Mbiti, and the Ghanaian Old Testament historian Kwesi Dickson. Mbiti has pointed to both the affinity of African and biblical languages and the importance of orality in African culture as reasons for this connection (Mbiti 1994: 28–34). Dickson has classified three general areas of continuity between the Bible, especially the Old Testament, and the life and thought of Africa. These three are "theological, religio-cultural, and interpretive, or hermeneutical" (Dickson

---

[9] West raises very similar issues concerning the acceptability of a reading like Mosala's in South African churches (West 1995: 79–81).

1979: 99). Dickson has offered three reasons for what he calls "the attachment to the Old Testament demonstrated by African Christians." First, the legalism of the early missionaries closely matches that found in the Old Testament. This factor is further strengthened by the traditional importance of ritual in African culture which provides a strong connection with Old Testament thought. Second, the Old Testament offers important political support for the oppressed peoples of Africa. Third, for Africans religion is not simply one component of their lives. As in ancient Israel, religion is integrated into all parts of African life (97–98). Because the influence of the Bible, including the Old Testament, is so pervasive in Africa, the interpretation of its texts is of much more than academic interest. The understanding of biblical stories shapes African lives and patterns of thought.

For Ethiopian Protestant Christians, the first and third reasons for the sense of connection with the Old Testament are certainly operative. The second, as indicated earlier, seems to be of very little importance. Oppression is very much a "secular" issue to them, and is not a concern of the Bible and of Christian faith. What does all this mean for Ethiopian biblical hermeneutics and hermeneutics in Africa in general? The influence of the missionaries who brought Protestant Christianity to Ethiopia and all of Africa cannot be discounted. These missionaries brought not only the gospel, but also a hermeneutic which might best be described as imported fundamentalism. This fundamentalist, literal understanding of the Bible makes it improper and unacceptable, in much of the African Christian context, to interpret texts in certain ways. As noted above, Ethiopian seminarians rejected Mosala's reading of the Cain and Abel story because it goes against the obvious intent of the text. Of course, Mosala would counter that this very resistance to his reading offers evidence for the effectiveness of its deceitful intent. Genesis 4 is not just ideology. It is very effective ideology (Mosala 1989: 38–42). Likewise, Ethiopian students rejected Oduyoye's reading because they are not willing to read the stories of Genesis 1–11 as myths or foundational stories. They are literal history which should be applied to the present spiritual world, not to issues of politics and economics.

Kwame Bediako has analyzed the problem for African theology caused by the influence of Western fundamentalist Christianity. In his critique of the work of Byang Kato, Bediako has illustrated the impact of the North American evangelical tradition on the thinking and writing of a gifted scholar like Kato. So much the greater then, must their influence be on the shape of other African Christians' thinking. The primary debate between Bediako (and others) and Kato concerns the meaning of African Traditional Religion for contemporary African Christians. A number of African Christians, Bediako among them, have proposed that African indigenous beliefs serve as at least a helpful background for Christian faith among Africans (Bediako 1992: 250–252).[10] Kato has adamantly opposed this movement, arguing for a radical discontinuity between Christianity and African Traditional Religion (Kato 1975: 38). Those influenced by such a view, promulgated by Western missionaries throughout Africa, could hardly give credence to an approach such as Oduyoye's, which draws on traditional West African beliefs as background for understanding texts in Genesis.

The limitations placed on African hermeneutics by this imported fundamentalism are significant. N. Onwu has demonstrated the need for a critical hermeneutic in the African context (Onwu 1985: 158), but development in this area by African scholars has been slow. The influence of critical hermeneutics on the average Christian in Africa has been negligible. This is evident in the responses of my first year students to critical study of the Bible. The stakes are very high. Oduyoye's reading of Genesis 9:25–26, the cursing of Canaan, reveals just how high they are. He understands the curse as a statement of Israelite ideology. It answers the question, "Why were the blacks, who are said to have produced the first empire in human history, everywhere subject to the whites by the sixth century B.C.?" "The biblical answer is that it is because Ham saw Noah naked and did not cover him" (Oduyoye 1984: 58).[11] The result, according to Oduyoye is this: "We know that the belief that Ham was the father of Canaan mirrors accurately Hebrew ideology, however much it may be incorrect according to modern linguistic classification. It is the same ideology that prevented the Hebrew writers from leaving

---

[10] Dickson has examined, and rejected, the possibility that indigenous traditions might take the place of the Old Testament in non-Western cultures, as background for the new Testament. He specifically analyzed the proposal of some Asian Christians that the Vedas might serve as an indigenous "Old Testament" for the church in India. Dickson concluded that such a proposal amounts to "neo-Marcionism" (Dickson 1979: 96–97).

[11] Of course, it is possible to read into this story an even greater sin of Ham. "Seeing the nakedness" of Noah may hint that Ham had sexual relations with his father.

Ham out of a curse meant for Canaan" (99). If this inferred belief about Hamitic peoples on the part of Israelites is true, then its influence must spread beyond Genesis 9:25–26. This requires a response from Hamitic peoples, a hermeneutical response. In the words of Oduyoye, "It is the business of blacks to expose the inherent anti-Hamitism, which resulted in the paradigmatic extermination of the Canaanites . . ." (99). In light of this understanding of Israelite ideology, which permeates the entire Bible, any hermeneutic which uncritically reads with the text must be ultimately self-defeating for contemporary Africans.

This argument need not demand that the Cain and Abel story be read in a particular way in Africa. It does demand a hermeneutical approach which leaves open various, and potentially contending, readings in various contexts. The Kariyu people of Eastern Ethiopia have been pushed off of their fertile grazing lands along the Awash River by the government, and have been forced out into an arid semidesert which threatens their nomadic way of life. When I read about these oppressed people, I felt nothing but sorrow for them. When I visited them, however, and I saw tall and powerful men striding through the brush, guarding their herds with AK-47 assault-rifles, I also felt fear. The Cain and Abel story must be allowed to be as complex as contemporary Africa.

BIBLIOGRAPHY

Bediako, Kwame. *Theology and Identity: The Impact of Culture Upon Christian Thought in the Second Century and in Modern Africa.* Oxford: Regnum, 1992.

Boesak, Alan. *Black and Reformed: Apartheid, Liberation and the Calvinist Tradition.* Johannesburg: Skotaville, 1984.

————. *Farewell to Innocence: A Socio-Ethical Study on Black Theology and Power.* Maryknoll, N.Y.: Orbis, 1977.

Cowley, Roger W. *Ethiopian Biblical Interpretation: A Study in Exegetical Tradition and Hermeneutics.* Cambridge: Cambridge University Press, 1988.

Dickson, Kwesi. "Continuity and Discontinuity between the Old Testament and African Life and Thought." In Eds Kofi Appiah-Kubi and Sergio Torres, *African Theology En Route,* Maryknoll: Orbis, 1979: 95–108.

Kato, Byang. *Theological Pitfalls in Africa.* Kisumu: Evangel Publishing House, 1975.

Mbiti, John. "The Bible in African Culture." In Ed. Rosino Gibellini, *Paths of African Theology,* London: SCM, 1994: 27–39.

Mosala, Itumeleng J. *Biblical Hermeneutics and Black Theology in South Africa.* Grand Rapids: Eerdmans, 1989.

Oduyoye, Modupe. *The Sons of God and the Daughters of Men: An Afro-Asiatic Interpretation of Genesis 1–11.* Maryknoll: Orbis, 1984.

Onwu, N. "The Hermeneutical Model: The Dilemma of the African Theologian." *Africa Theological Journal* 14 (1985): 145–160.

Thiselton, Anthony C. *New Horizons in Hermeneutics: The Theory and Practice of Transforming Biblical Reading.* Grand Rapids: Zondervan, 1992.

West, Gerald. *Biblical Hermeneutics of Liberation: Modes of Reading the Bible in the South African Context.* Maryknoll: Orbis, 1995.

THE MOTHER OF THE EWE AND FIRSTBORN DAUGHTER AS THE "GOOD SHEPHERD" IN THE CULTURAL CONTEXT OF THE EWE PEOPLES: A LIBERATING APPROACH

Dorothy B.E.A. Akoto

With the increasing emphasis on contextualization, an attempt to produce Biblical hermeneutics for Africa or elsewhere must take into consideration cultural and traditional issues. This is important because most of the imagery of the Christian religion are foreign to and have little or no bearing on the traditional, cultural imagery and symbols of the peoples who are the recipients of the message. The imagery of sheep and shepherding is one such foreign imagery to many parts of Africa. In this essay, I will deal with this imagery as it pertains to the Ewe peoples of the Volta Region of Southeastern Ghana, West Africa. The mother of the Ewe and firstborn daughter will be portrayed as the "Good Shepherd" in the cultural context of the Ewe peoples. I am aware that what this essay sets out to do may be of relevance to women in general, but I intend to present it as a particular concern for Ewe women and Ewe peoples as a whole.

Among the Ewes of Southeastern Ghana, there is no shepherd nor is there shepherding in the literal sense of the word. The Ewes are, however, attached to the Shepherd of Psalm 23 and the Good Shepherd of John 19. They pray or recite Psalm 23 in any life-threatening situation and find consolation in it. The Good Shepherd has become part and parcel of their culture, through the presence of the Bible. This is remarkable, given that the Ewes of Ghana have no direct experience of shepherds or shepherding. And yet, the Good Shepherd is an important part of their theological discourse. It is not clear to me precisely what features constitute the Good Shepherd of the Ewes; a cursory analysis of their appropriation of this image indicates that it rests largely on "the supra regional" imagery of Western forms of Christianity (Schreiter 1986: ix). A more detailed exploration of how this appropriation has taken place is beyond the scope of this essay. Instead, I want to take the image in another direction. Is it possible, I want to ask, that Good Shepherd imagery can be contextualized, localized or adapted to suit the context of the Ewe peoples? Since the Good Shepherd image is so very important to the Ewe peoples, the primary intention of this essay is to lift up the mother of the Ewe and firstborn daughter as the image of the Good Shepherd in the cultural context of the Ewes. This is an attempt to concretize a hitherto "abstract" faith in the Good Shepherd of the scriptures and to make this imagery realistic for Ewe women and the Ewe peoples in general. It will also serve as a source of liberation from their attachment to a foreign scriptural Good Shepherd image. In order to do this, I will present Psalm 23, which I have recast in my own words, to portray the shepherding qualities of the mother of the Ewe, and John 10, also recast in my own words, to portray the shepherding qualities of the firstborn daughter. I agree with Wesley Ariarajah that

> The gospel had been brought to the nations as a plant, with the pot being Western culture. This may have been inevitable. But now the plant must be transferred into Asian or African soil [here Ewe soil], so that it might strike deep roots and draw nourishment from it (1995: 13).

"Ewe," the name of the peoples about whom I write, consists of two syllables and is pronounced "Ei-wey." Ewe traditions claim that in the distant past, the Ewes migrated from the Niger basin, an area centered on the towns of Oyo or Ketu, where the Yoruba of Nigeria now predominate. They settled and established themselves in the vicinity of the Volta River, occupying an area of land 80 kilometres wide, along the coast, and 160 kilometres long, on the banks of the Volta river. This area now corresponds to the east and southeast of Ghana, southern Togo and the southwestern lands of Benin. This resulted from the fact that Eweland was originally a German colony, but following the First World War France and Britain divided up the German Ewe colony along a North-South axis with the east going to France and the west going to Britain. The main occupation of traditional Ewes is farming, fishing, making traditional cloth, and basket weaving. The proceeds from these trades are utilized for subsistence and a small amount is sold either internally or through export to other countries. The word "Ewe" also refers to the language spoken in the part of Ghana occupied by the Ewe peoples.

The religiosity of the Ewe peoples in their cultural context embraces elements of their traditional religious system with its beliefs and practices and Christianity. As John Mbiti puts it, "Christianity in Africa is so old that it can rightly be described as an indigenous, traditional and African religion" (1969: 229). The Ewes, like other Ghanaians, endeavored to forge a relationship between the Judaeo-Christian God and their own Supreme Being, *Mawu*, whom they revered greatly. However, this attempt to forge a relationship with the Judaeo-Christian God created a problem for the Ewe peoples who came to consciously or unconsciously look down upon their own culture as substandard and to accept the entire Judaeo-Christian message without question. Such a negative view of aspects of their own culture came from the missionaries, as C.G. Baeta puts it,

> They all shared the same ethnocentric basic attitude, regarding their own . . . as the standard to which everybody had to conform, and were unanimous in roundly condemning all things African as "savage" or even "devilish," in any case, as in one way or another substandard and unworthy (1981: 34).

This essay is an attempt to reverse this process. In this paper, the mother of the Ewe and firstborn daughter will be portrayed as the Good Shepherd. They will mirror the loving, tender, protective, providing care of the Good Shepherd of scripture. They will represent, through their daily activities, the activities of the Good Shepherd of scripture who knows his sheep, is known by his sheep and cares for them to the extent of laying down his life for them. Rebecca Chopp's vision of the future as "one not so much of a conversing only through a complex rhythm of distance and belonging to one's subject matter, but also of conversing through a rich jazz improvisation where we are continually creating and recreating rhythm and harmony" (Chopp 1995: 79) powerfully conveys the effect that the Good Shepherd imagery will try to produce in this essay.

Ewe women, and probably women from elsewhere, have been oppressed and kept in bondage not only by infiltrating cultural influences but by a local culture that is dominated by patriarchy. In this culture, only the voices of fathers, brothers, uncles, husbands and sons carry weight. Ewe women have been "crucified"—stripped of all self-worth—in their everyday life experiences and yet they have borne their burdens like the lamb led to the slaughter that opens not its mouth (Isaiah 53:7). With Mercy Oduyoye

> We seek to discard these fetters of culture; We seek full humanity and some principles to guide our lives in community. The meaning of full humanity cannot be defined by only one sector of humanity, without

listening to the voices, the hurts, and the delights of all the Fatimas. Even more important, what constitutes the fetters of oppression should be defined by those who experience it and not those who simply observe it (1995: 82).

Ewe women need the above form of liberation, but they also need liberation from a probably unconscious attachment to an "abstract" foreign scriptural image. Why? Because the Ewe peoples have been compelled to adhere to certain belief systems and practices that have been dictated to them by others, not only in their secular cultural context but also in the spiritual. The Ewe peoples need to be liberated from the fetters of cultural oppression. Their culture needs to be affirmed and portrayed as rich and adequate for their needs. Their traditions need to be projected, their culture valued and their feelings expressed in positive cultural imagery.

The contact of the Ewe peoples with not only Christianity, but also Islam and some Eastern religions, have alienated them culturally. This reminds me of Proverbs 18:24a, which is similar to a Ghanaian etiological proverb which says, "The consequence of having too many friends caused the Crab to have no head." A folktale has it that at the time of creation, all animals were created without heads. A day and time were fixed by *Worla* (Creator) when the heads would be created and ready for the animals to receive them. On that day, Crab, who had several friends, went from house to house, knocking on door after door to remind his friends that it was the day and time to go for their heads. Every door at which he knocked yielded no response. All his friends had already left for the meeting place to receive their heads. When Crab finally got there, all the animals were wearing their heads so he too went forward to receive his. To his disappointment, all the heads had been given out and there was no head left for Crab. Not even his desperate pleas and tears could produce any more heads. Since the heads created were meant to be distributed only this one time, Crab never got a head and has remained without one until this day. The point I am trying to make with this story is to illustrate what happened to the Ewe people in their contact with other religions and cultures (friends) which caused its own culture to be so adulterated that it almost has nothing to claim as its own (no head).

Psalm 23 and John 10, both of which are metaphorical and deal with the Good Shepherd, are passages to which the Ewes of Southeastern Ghana are deeply attached. In fact, the Ewes, for whom I intend this essay to be a source of liberation, are not shepherds nor do they have shepherds in the true sense of the word. However, they are very much attached to the image of the Good Shepherd in these two biblical passages. The Ewes turn to the Psalm or the passage in John to comfort or encourage themselves in every life-threatening situation, and find solace. This belief in an "abstract" figure I see as culturally alienating. As such, I intend to offer a concrete image to help liberate the Ewe peoples, especially the Ewe women, from this cultural alienation and fit them into their own cultural context.

I would like to take a brief look at the two biblical uses of the image of shepherding in Psalm 23 and the tenth chapter of John's gospel. I will then move on to show its absence in the Ewe culture. My discussion will then culminate in the variety of ways in which the mother of the Ewe and the firstborn daughter of the Ewe people function as the Good Shepherd. In Psalm 23, the Psalmist paints the picture of a Good Shepherd whose providence causes the flock to know no want. The sheep are made to rest in the meadows where the sheep find food, water, shelter and rest (v. 2). The sheep are protected from enemies by the rod of the shepherd, which he uses to fight the wild animals that prey upon sheep, and by the staff of the shepherd used to guide the sheep from straying (v. 4). The shepherd provides the sheep with the choicest meals and the sheep are granted the opportunity to remain with the shepherd forever. This metaphor of the shepherd and sheep portrays God in relationship to God's people (specifically Israel, but by appropriation all God's people). Since this imagery arises from a real situation in the life of the Palestinians, no imagery would have been more appropriate for the purpose of the Psalmist than this one.

In John 10, Jesus designates himself as the Good Shepherd and declares that he is the gate to the sheep. He knows them by name and they know his voice and follow him. His care and concern for the sheep is expressed in his going before the sheep while the sheep follow him (v. 4). His love for them culminates in his laying down his life for them (vv. 17–18). What a shepherd! Why will not the sheep follow him since they know his voice and know that he cares for and loves them so dearly? It is no wonder that this imagery should have such powerful influence upon the people of his time. They saw all the credentials of this good shepherd literally, manifested in Jesus' person. The powerfulness of the imagery of shepherding made it very useful in both the Old and New Testaments (in the Judaeo-Christian tradition). The imagery was used to concretize teachings which might otherwise be abstract to the people so that they could easily remember them. By forming mental pictures about the teachings and relating these teachings to everyday phenomena in their cultural context, the people of Jesus' time could better understand Jesus' teachings and endeavor to follow them. This shepherding image was all the more important because Israel had several leaders, in the persons of kings and prophets, who had mistreated them instead of caring for them. In the face of their suffering, there was the need for a true shepherd like that of Psalm 23 or John 10 to shepherd them in the true sense of the word.

In the Northern and Upper Regions of Ghana, where the weather is always extremely hot and the luxury of fresh green vegetation is rare, shepherding is common. However, shepherding is not known among the Ewe peoples of the Volta Region of Southeastern Ghana, who are involved mostly in crop farming. The few animals (mainly sheep and goats) are domesticated ones and are not shepherded. They are fed with fodder prepared and served in troughs from which they eat. They are also allowed to graze freely on the rich green pastures that are abundant all year round and drink from water troughs or from the many streams that flow along the outskirts of the towns in the Volta Region. The poultry and domesticated animals are usually housed in coops or pens specially built for them where they spend the night and the hot part of the day.

When James Cone, in *God of the Oppressed*, talks about there being "no truth for and about black people that does not emerge out of the context of their experience" (1975: 17–18), I understand this to mean, not only to the experience of black people but also to that of all peoples. Unless the cultural context or real life situation of the Ewe people is taken seriously, unless their history and the totality of their beings are taken into consideration and above all, unless their experiences, stories, tales and sayings are examined thoroughly, there can be no true liberation for them. According to Esther Arias and Mortimer Arias there is the need for "awareness, identification and responsible action" (1980: 1) in order to liberate oppressed people. Yes, my awareness of the Ewes' attachment to an "abstract" Good Shepherd image, my identification with them, my empathy with them for their attachment to the Good Shepherd image which is absent from their cultural experiences, has led me to think of presenting this Good Shepherd to them in a concrete way to bring about their liberation. The undeniable statement of Gustavo Gutierrez that "The Biblical God is close to human beings, is a God of communion with and commitment to human beings" and is "actively present in their midst, as one of the oldest biblical promises" (1988: 106), makes me think that God must be experienced by all human beings in their daily cultural contexts. The Good Shepherd must be experienced by the Ewe peoples as part of their culture to make their belief in him more meaningful.

I would like to illustrate my proposal with a poem which is my own recasting of Psalm 23 in dedication to my Mother. This poem portrays my mother and other Ewe mothers as the cultural image of the Good Shepherd in the Ewe context.

1 My Mother, my shepherd,
   Because of your industry as an economist, trading and toiling endlessly
   I never know want; Your dependents and more are provided for.

2 You jealously guard law and order in the community as a politician,
   Ensuring that they provide for the welfare of all and sundry.

3 When the community is sick and waywardness is rising,
   Your instructions lead and direct toward the right ways of living,
   The health of the community is restored.

4 Even when life becomes tempestuous, the future unknown and scary,
   When situations are threatening and trying, there is no cause for alarm,
   For your teachings, your instructions, are always there to guide.
   Your words of chastening are a source of purification and encouragement.

5 You jealously guard the good because you are "nyornu" (maker of good things)
   Your eyes are always fixed on the prize.
   Your words of praise, comfort and encouragement make you an educator for they nullify feelings of bitterness and hatred and restore peace and calm.

6 My Mother, my shepherd, the good and rightful paths in which you offer training,
   Your tender love and care will always abide.
   As long as I live, I will continue to bask in your amazing motherliness.

> Surely, your guidance, your counsel, your industry will be appro-
> priated forever and ever.

A number of people in the Ewe community could be designated as the Good Shepherd. The father of the traditional Ewe, who is supposedly the breadwinner and who goes about his daily activities of farming, hunting, protecting, working hard, providing for the family and preserving the status of life in the community, could safely be a Good Shepherd. The chief of the Ewe and his traditional court could also be portrayed as the Good Shepherd for they are the custodians of law and order in the community ensuring that all the ancestors and the Supreme Being, *Mawu*, are properly venerated and revered. Their part in the community keeps life going smoothly, preventing epidemics and other disasters from befalling the living. The grandmother and grandfather also have their parts to play as Good Shepherd in the community and the extended family. They are the stores of wisdom. The stories they tell, the counsel they give and their activities in the council of elders of the community ensure a close link between the living and living-dead and a continuity in the normal life of the community. The traditional priests and priestesses also merit the designation Good Shepherd. They look into the future, possess unrivaled knowledge of herbal and spiritual healing for diseases that science cannot diagnose. They understand the language of trees and animals and can invoke good spirits for the good of individuals or the community and appease sinister powers to avert evil. There are several other persons who could be designated as the Good Shepherd but my concern, in this essay, is with the mother of the Ewe and firstborn daughter.

The Ewe mother plays a variety of roles, which I see as shepherding, in the cultural context of the Ewe people. She is the channel by which ancestors return to life. She is a homemaker as she bears children, takes care of, loves, provides for and protects her family as well as meets the needs of other extended family members. She is actively involved in the community's life. As a local politician, she helps to maintain the smooth-running of life in the community. She is a custodian of law and order ensuring that these are not violated but are carried out to provide for the welfare of the living and goodwill of the living-dead. It is the mother who breaks down the laws that govern the community for the women and younger generations to enable them understand the importance and need for adhering to these laws for the well-being of the entire community. She serves as the mediator or intermediary between the traditional council (chief and his elders) and the women by taking the views of the women to the council and bringing down the laws made by the council to the women. In this intermediary role, the Ewe mother ensures that the laws of the community are not one-sided but include the voices of all involved, to make the laws easier to implement. The Ewe mother is a born leader, organizer, educator or public relations officer, if I may use that designation, for it is she who rallies round the other women, the girls and younger folk in the community and educates them on the essential needs and services in the community. She is active in the life of the Christian Church and indigenous traditional religious practices, where the services of women are indispensable. She is an economist. Her industry in turning whatever little she has into much is unparalleled. One could even say that the economic power of the mother achieved through selling and buying (trading) makes her the breadwinner and not the father as tradition has it. As the Good Shepherd, the mother of the Ewe ensures that the community knows no want and is led in the paths of righteousness.

The Ewe mother, in her role as a channel for the return of ancestors to this life, is careful not to incur the displeasure of the ancestors that might want to come back to life through her. As soon as the Ewe mother realizes that she is expecting a child, her shepherding of the unborn begins. Her lifestyle circles around her care for and provision of all the needs of the unborn so that it "shall not want" (Psalm 23:1). Her eating habits ensure that the baby is well nourished and well provided for before it is born. The Ewe mother's physical activities at this time, ensure that the unborn child is not over strained or vigorously disturbed in any way. Thus the mother makes the baby "feed in green pastures" and "lie beside still waters" so that the baby's soul is refreshed (v. 2). Before the child is born, the mother spends time singing beautiful songs, reading the scriptures and talking about the good things that baby will come to be and do. It is believed that while they are yet unborn, babies listen, hear and respond to sounds. Thus the unborn child is already being led "in the paths of righteousness" (v. 3b) (rightful ways of living). While the baby is growing up, the mother's tender care and love are manifested in her talking to and gently instructing the baby about all the good things that happen in life, what the family and community considers the norm and what members do to preserve law and order in the community. The baby on her/his part, looks intently at the mother's face and responds, often with a smile, to what mother says. There is a beautiful and very popular song in Ghana which tells of some of the mother's everyday activities, which I see, as part of her shepherding qualities. Strands of this song read:

> Sweet mother, I no go [will not] forget you, for the way you suffer for me.
> When I no sleep my mother no go sleep. When I no chop [eat] my mother no go chop.
> When I dey [am] sick, my mother go carry me. When I dey cry, my mother go cry yei! yei!
> She go say, stop! stop! stop! stop! stop! stop! make you no cry [don't cry] again oh . . .

Like the Good Shepherd of scripture, the mother who is a doctor and a nurse in her own capacity, nurses her sick child to health. Her knowledge of the right healing herbs and nursing activities, carrying the child in her arms, on her shoulders or on her back as is the duty of a good shepherd help to restore health. Her holistic care and concern cause her to be remembered and like the Psalmist of Psalm 23, "I will dwell in the house of the Lord" (depend on or appropriate the mother's exceptional qualities) "forever" (v. 6).

Apart from taking care of the baby, the mother takes care of the whole family. She sees to it that all members of the family are properly fed and clothed. Oftentimes, she goes without food so that all the members of her family will have enough to eat. She readily and selflessly forgoes her own comforts and is content with whatever she has. She "lays down her life for the sheep" like the Good Shepherd (John 10:11). Some of the mother's good shepherding activities are summarized in a few lines of a poem composed by a Ghanaian Ewe grammarian and folklorist, Samuel K. Obianim. His poem emanated from his visit to a graveyard, where he saw the sepulchers of several people, famous and those considered as nobodies in the community. Death had leveled all these people and about the mother Obianim had this to say:

> The fourth grave was that of the "Carrier of eggs." She who provided for the needs of all the family, neglecting herself. In order that children might eat to their satisfaction before the mother eats, she has gone without food for many days and is even lacking in cloth, "avor," [the traditional two-yard piece of fabric that mothers wear as long skirts with their matching blouses]. She who returns from a journey

and the whole household is in an uproar "Dada gbor, Dada gbor."
["Mother has returned. Mother has returned"]. She lies down mute,
with both hands across her chest as though she had never existed
among human beings.

Obianim uses the metaphor "Carrier of eggs" for mother to show
her fertility like that of the fish or crab or some other egg-laying
creature with a bunch of eggs inside. As the sheep know the shepherd, the family knows the mother. Her teaching and education are
also known. Hence her students quickly do what they have learnt
from her. She takes care of the father by ensuring that he is pre-
sentable among his peers and that he is given his rightful place by
the children and in the community. The mother stays up most nights
when the rest of the family is asleep, thinking and planning how the
next day's needs are going to be met.

The Good Shepherd in John 10 knows his sheep by name. They
hear his voice and follow him when he calls them. This characteristic
of the Good Shepherd is illustrated by the following folktale among
the Ewes, which bears some semblance to the story of 1 Kings
3:16–27, in which King Solomon makes a wise judgement between
two women. A crawling child disappeared from home and was found
in the possession of another woman. This other woman was not the
real mother of the child, but she claimed the child was hers. Even
though witnesses testified that the child was not her child, the woman
who possessed the child insisted that the child was hers. The matter was taken to the local traditional council for settlement. The chief
who sat in arbitration over the case asked that the child be brought
forward and placed in front of the whole traditional gathering which,
of course, consisted of all the members of the community. The two
women who sat somewhere in the front row among those who had
gathered were asked to call the child to come to them. The woman
who falsely claimed the child was hers was asked to go first. She
called the child's name and invited the child to come toward her
but the child only sat and cried. Then the other woman (the real
mother) was given the opportunity to call the child. No sooner had
she began to call than, to the surprise of all who were gathered, the
child began to crawl toward her turning neither left nor right but
straight to its mother. This child had experienced the love, care and
protection of its mother. The child has heard its mother's voice from
the time it was in the womb until it began to crawl. Like the sheep
who knew the voice of the shepherd, this child knew the voice of

the mother and followed at her call. The other woman was "a thief" (John 10:1). She was a "stranger" (v. 5). She was not the "owner" (v. 12) (mother) of the "sheep" (child) so the child did not know her (v. 5).

The mother is concerned not only for her own children but extends her love and care to other persons in the community. Like the Good Shepherd, she has "other sheep which are not of this fold" and she seeks to "bring them also in" (John 10:16). She readily provides for the needs of others who are less fortunate than her own family. Her shepherding is felt among the younger women of the community to whom she is a mother. She counsels them and directs them in the paths of rightful living as she does her own children. In the traditional assembly of women or of the community, the mother is there actively participating in the deliberations on issues affecting the community. In the church also the mother's place is indispensable. She is present at the meetings actively participating in discussions of affairs affecting the women of the church and the younger generation. She takes care of the younger members of the church and renders needed services at the church. She helps in the Christian education of children and partakes in the visitation of the sick and shut-ins. Her shepherding is evident in the indigenous religious rituals, where she is a crucial part of the rituals that ensure the well-being and continuity of the life of the community, in her capacity as fetish priestess. In fact, when I see the mother of the Ewe engaged in all these activities, which are an essential part of the cultural context of the Ewe people of the Volta Region, I cannot help but think about her and see her as a Good Shepherd.

Another very important person in the cultural context of the Ewe people, whom I see as a Good Shepherd is the firstborn daughter. As Mercy Oduyoye puts it:

> Among the matrilineal Akan, [and the patrilineal Ewe also], a firstborn daughter is an auspicious beginning—a blessing to her mother, a little mother to subsequent siblings, a catalyst for the continued unity of that line, and an advocate for her clan [and family] before the kin group. She is brought up to be the channel for the return to this life of the ancestors, who, the Akan [and Ewe] believe, can return to this life through the daughters [mothers] of the clan [family] (80).

This statement is explicit that the firstborn daughter is a little mother. By implication, therefore, she is a mother. The truth is that the firstborn daughter functions exactly like a mother. When she is at home or out, she helps in the shepherding (in taking care of and providing the needs) of her siblings, of a father and those of the community in her power to provide. She sees to it that whatever task she has on hand is properly carried out like a mother would do. For my older sister, a truly Good Shepherd, I have these few lines (my own recasting of John 10:1–18) to write:

> My sister, you are truly the Good Shepherd. You open the door by which all the other children (your siblings) come. You are the one who sets examples for us. We learn from you. You always guide us in the proper way that we should go. We are not carried away by improper conduct.

> My sister, you are truly the Shepherd. We cling to you because you are always there for us. You love and care for us because we are part of you. When you teach us, we readily assimilate. Your direction and counsel are cherished for they keep us focused. We know you have good will in your heart for us.

> My sister, you are truly a Good Shepherd. You are willing to forgo your comfort in defense of what is good. My sister, how sweet you are. Mother, cherishes you because you are dependable. Father, cherishes you too. You can decide to do what you will, but love, the tenderness of your heart, makes you go without that we might have.

> My sister, you are truly a Good Shepherd, you are a good student too for you learnt from Mother very well how to tend the sheep (to educate, counsel and lead your siblings and others in the community too).

These lines, dedicated to my older sister, throw light on some of the activities of the firstborn daughter which I see as her shepherding in the cultural context of the Ewe peoples. She, like the Good Shepherd, is the door to the sheep (John 10:1). She is the one to comes first from the womb, and the Ewe literally say, the first child opens the door of the womb for other children to come. When other children are born after the first, he or she is said to be a blessing, but a firstborn daughter is a double blessing to her mother. She bears part of a mother's responsibilities and lightens a mother's duties. She is an example to her siblings and they follow in her footsteps. Her responsibility is thus to endeavor not to lead them astray. The firstborn daughter is the owner of the sheep and her sheep know her voice. She jealously guards and provides the needs of her siblings and the community's as mother would. Out of home, she protects them from bullies or any who might want to make them unhappy, as much as she is able. If we follow an emendation to Psalm 23:5, whereby the reference is not to preparing "a table" but "a javelin" (an implement of war) (Morgernstern 1946: 15–16), then, I think, this too fits, because the firstborn daughter sometimes fights physically (with strong words or even a fight) to protect her siblings from bullies in the community. The firstborn daughter, like the Good Shepherd, counsels and teaches her siblings and others the things that mother has taught her and also what the societal norms are for maintaining law and order.

The firstborn daughter knows what her mother and father's expectations are of her and all her siblings and she tries to uphold them. Like the Good Shepherd, the firstborn daughter is prepared to lay down her life for the sheep. She is ready to defend the laws of the community to ensure that order prevails. She will readily forgo her personal interest or comfort that her siblings might have theirs. In a popular Ghanaian proverb, "When a mother cow is chewing, its calves watch its mouth." The firstborn daughter watches the mother's mouth so well that she herself tries to chew just like the mother. She tries to follow in the footsteps of her mother. This particular demand on the life of the Ewe mother places great caution on her to set the best example that she can and also on the firstborn daughter to do the same so that those who learn from their example will learn what is the right thing and not otherwise.

As mentioned in an earlier part of this essay, the Ewes of the Volta Region in Southeastern Ghana are not shepherds nor do they have persons among them who can be designated as such in the true sense of the word. In spite of this lack of a Good Shepherd image in their culture or traditional context, the Ewes are very much attached to the Good Shepherd of Psalm 23 and John 10. Being an Ewe, I see the several life-threatening experiences of the Ewe peoples in their day to day cultural context and can understand why the Good Shepherd image of these passages should be so appealing to them. Security is of major concern to Africans and specifically the Ewe peoples. It is not uncommon for persons to become victims or even agents of evil forces (Amoah and Oduyoye 1988: 45). Witchcraft, untimely deaths, strange diseases that cannot be diagnosed scientifically, physical deformities, incurable ulcers and other issues beyond human control are but a few of what the Ewe peoples face on a daily basis. Their attachment and attention to these scriptural passages must be commended. However, this seems to be an adherence to an abstract

Good Shepherd image. For this image to become real, it must be concretized for the Ewes. My choice of the mother of the Ewe and firstborn daughter is, therefore, meant to concretize this abstract Good Shepherd image. It is to make the Ewe people come to see these two people, as they go about their daily activities in their cultural context, as the image of the Good Shepherd whom they can physically identify with, build trust in and then project this trust onto the Good Shepherd of scripture. It is to liberate them from being attached to a foreign "abstract" image.

Unlike Robert Schreiter who advocates "an encounter between church traditions and local themes for the actual development of local theologies to take place" (1986: 33), the missionaries dumped Christianity with other foreign cultural elements on Africans. As a result the Ewe also assimilated the Good Shepherd imagery even though there are no parallels in their traditional context. I, therefore, intend this essay to be a source of liberation from attachment to a foreign "abstract" image and to become a concretized image which, to borrow Baeta's words, "places itself fairly and squarely within the immediate context of the actual on going life of the people of God" [here the Ewes] (1981: 8). The missionaries forgot that the Judaeo-Christian God is the same who has been revealed throughout all of creation (Romans 1:20) and that this same God is the Hebrew "Elohim," the Supreme Being in Africa and the Ewe *Mawu*.

According to Mercy Oduyoye, "Women and their work as mothers and homemakers have often been bypassed as if women did nothing beyond producing and raising offspring" (1995: 81). Yes, this is the picture that tradition paints of women. Why women should continually be underrated and not affirmed or offered the opportunity to affirm themselves is a question that continues to eat at my heart, and I think this discussion will help Ewe women to affirm themselves as they see themselves mirroring the Good Shepherd of scripture. The Ewe word for woman, *nyonu*, (literally meaning "make a thing good") befits them and they deserve to be celebrated for going further, in mirroring the Good Shepherd so well, than just performing tasks laid upon them by tradition.

In conclusion, I would not claim to have exhausted this topic, but I call on not only Ewe women or Ewe people but also others who have taken an interest in reading this essay to make their voices heard. As Ewe mothers and firstborn daughters continue giving of

their best in educating, teaching, economic, political, industrial, coun-
seling, homemaking and you-name-it roles, so that future generations will appropriate what they have laid down throughout the ages,
I submit that they mirror the Good Shepherd whose image I have
portrayed them to be.

BIBLIOGRAPHY

Amoah, Elizabeth and Mercy Oduyoye. "The Christ From the Viewpoint of African
    Women." In Eds Virginia Fabella and Mercy A. Oduyoye, *With Passion and
    Compassion: Third World Women Doing Theology*, Maryknoll, New York: Orbis
    Books, 1988: 30–46.
Ariarajah, S. Wesley. *Gospel and Culture: An Ongoing Discussion within the Ecumenical
    Movement.* Geneva: WCC Publications, 1995.
Arias, Esther and Mortimer Arias. *The Cry of My People: Out of Captivity in Latin
    America.* New York: Friendship Press, 1980.
Baeta, C.G. "African Theology: What is that?" Presentations in the J.B. Danquah
    Memorial Lectures series. Accra-Tema, Ghana: Ghana Academy of Arts and
    Sciences, 1980.
Boff, Leonardo and Clodovis Boff. *Introducing Liberation Theology.* Maryknoll, New
    York: Orbis Books, 1996.
Campbell, Cynthia. *Theologies Written From Feminist Perspectives: An Introductory Study.*
    Louisville, Kentucky: Office of the General Assembly, 1988.
Chopp, Rebecca S. "Cultivating Theological Scholarship: An African American
    Perspective on Theological Scholarship." *Theological Education*, 32 (1995): 79–94.
Cone, James H. *God of the Oppressed.* San Francisco: Harper Collins, 1975.
Costas, Orlando E. *Christ Outside the Gate: Mission Beyond Christendom.* Maryknoll, New
    York: Orbis Books, 1982.
Dahood, Mitchell. *The Anchor Bible: Psalms 1–50.* New York: Doubleday, 1965/66.
Dickson, Kwesi A. *Theology in Africa.* Maryknoll, New York: Orbis Books, 1984.
Erskine, Noel L. *King Among the Theologians.* Cleveland, Ohio: The Pilgrim Press,
    1994.
Fern, Deane W. *Third World Theologies: An Introductory Survey.* Maryknoll, New York:
    Orbis Books, 1987.
Gottwald, Norman K. *The Hebrew Bible: A Socio-Literary Introduction.* Philadelphia:
    Fortress Press, 1985.
Grant, Jacquelyn. "Response from the United States." In Eds K.C. Abraham and
    Bernadette Mbuy-Beya *Spirituality of the Third World.* Maryknoll, New York:
    Orbis Books, 1994: 221–233.
Gutierrez, Gustavo. *A Theology of Liberation.* Maryknoll, New York: Orbis Books, 1988.
Hinga, Teresa M. "Jesus Christ and the Liberation of Women in Africa." In Eds
    Mercy A Oduyoye and Musimbi R.A. Kanyoro. *The Will To Arise: Women,
    Tradition, and Church in Africa*, Maryknoll, New York: Orbis Books, 1992.
Joy, Charles R. *Harper's Topical Concordance.* New York, Harper and Brothers Publishers,
    1940.
Kanyoro, Musimbi R.A. *Talitha, Qumi! The Proceedings of the Convocation of African
    Women Theologians 1988.* Ibadan: Daystar Press, 1990.
Kim, Yong-Bock. 1992. *Messiah and Minjung: Christ's Solidarity with the People for New
    Life.* Kowloon, Hong Kong: Christian Conference of Asia Urban Rural Mission.

Lambdin, Thomas O. *Introduction to Biblical Hebrew*. New York, Charles Scribner & Sons, 1971.

Limburg, James. "Psalms, Book of." In *Anchor Bible Dictionary*. Vol. V. New York, Doubleday, 1992: 522–536.

Lindars, Barnabas. "The Gospel of John." In *The New Century Bible Commentary*. Grand Rapids: Eerdmans, 1987.

Martey, Emmanuel. *African Theology: Inculturation and Liberation*. Maryknoll, New York: Orbis Books, 1996.

May, Herbert G. & Bruce Metzger, Ed. *The New Oxford Annotated Bible with Apocrypha: Revised Standard Version*. U.S.A.: Christian Education Division of the National Council of Churches of Christ, 1977.

Mays, James L. et al. Eds. *Harper Bible Commentary*. San Francisco: Harper and Row Publishers, 1988.

Mazrui, Ali A. & Toby K. Levine, Eds. *The Africans: A Reader*. New York: Praeger, 1986.

Mbiti, John S. "God, Sin and Salvation in African Traditional Religion." Lecture at the Pan-African Church Conference in Atlanta, Georgia, U.S.A. 17–23 July 1988.

————. *African Religions and Philosophy*. Nairobi: Heinemann, 1969.

Miller, J. Maxwell & John H. Hayes. *A History of Ancient Israel and Judah*. Philadelphia: The Westminster Press. 1986.

Mosala, Itumeleng J. *Biblical Hermeneutics and Black Theology in South Africa*. Grand Rapids, Michigan: William B. Eerdmans Publishing Co., 1989.

Morgernstern, Jullian. "Psalm 23." In *Journal of Biblical Literature*. Society of Biblical Literature, 1946.

Muzorewa, Gwinyai H. *The Origins and Development of African Theology*. Maryknoll, New York: Orbis Books, 1985.

Oduyoye, Mercy A. *Hearing and Knowing: Theological Reflections on Christianity in Africa*. Maryknoll, New York: Orbis Books, 1986.

————. "The Christ for African Women." In Eds Virginia Fabella and Mercy A. Oduyoye, *With Passion and Compassion: Third World Women Doing Theology*. Maryknoll, New York: Orbis Books, 1988: 30–46.

————. *Daughters of Anowa: African Women & Patriarchy*. Maryknoll, New York: Orbis Books, 1995.

Paris, Peter J. *The Spirituality of African Peoples: The Search for a Common Moral Discourse*. Minneapolis: Fortress Press, 1995.

Pobee, John. *West Africa: Christ Would Be an African Too*. Geneva: WCC Publications, 1996.

Prabhu, George Soares. "The Jesus of Faith: A Christological Contribution to an Ecumenical Third-World Spirituality." In Eds K.C. Abraham and Bernadette Mbuy-Beya S*pirituality of the Third World*. Maryknoll, New York: Orbis Books, 1994: 109–177.

Rensberger, David. *Johannine Faith and Liberating Community*. Philadelphia: Fortress Press, 1988.

Sarpong, Peter. *Ghana in Retrospect: Some Aspects of Ghanaian Culture*. Accra-Tema, Ghana Publishing Corporation, 1974.

Schreiter, Robert J. *Constructing Local Theologies*. Maryknoll, New York: Orbis Books, 1986.

Song, Choan-Seng. *Third-Eye Theology*. Maryknoll, New York: Orbis Books.

Takenaka, Masao. *God is Rice: Asian Culture and Christian Faith*. Geneva: WCC, 1996, 8–26, 71–83.

Vancil, Jack W. "Sheep, Shepherd." In *Anchor Bible Dictionary*. Vol. V. 1187–1190. New York: Doubleday, 1992.

Williams, Cecil with Rebecca Laird. *No Hiding Place: Empowerment and Recovery for our Troubled Communities*. San Francisco: Harper Collins, 1992.

Wilmore, G.S. *Black Theology: A Documentary History*. Vol. II: 1980–1992. Maryknoll, New York: Orbis Books, 1993.

Wilmore, Gayraud S. *Black Religion and Black Radicalism: An Interpretation of the Religious History of Afro-American People*. Maryknoll, New York: Orbis Books, 1992.

Young, Josiah U. *Black and African Theologies: Siblings or Distant Cousins?* Maryknoll, New York: Orbis Books, 1986.

POURING LIBATION TO SPIRIT POWERS AMONG THE EWE-DOME OF GHANA: AN INDIGENOUS RELIGIOUS AND BIBLICAL PERSPECTIVE

Rebecca Yawa Ganusah

For some time now, I have observed among the Ewe-Dome, a sub-group of the larger ethnic group the Ewe, who live in the central part of the south-eastern corner of Ghana, that there seems to be a conflict between the Church and the indigenous religious believer, over the performance of the indigenous rites of birth and initiation into womanhood (and some other rites of passage). By the Church, in this case, I am referring to the Evangelical Presbyterian Churches, the dominant Churches that are found in the area.

The main area of conflict has to do with the making of libations to *Mawu* (God), *togbuiwo* (ancestors) and *trowo* (spirit powers or "gods" in some English translations). While many Christians find the practice of making libations to be unchristian, there are others in the society who consider this an important ritual that has to be performed to acknowledge the presence of the supernatural among the people. To make a libation, the drink (usually alcoholic) is put in a calabash (if palm-wine) or in a glass (if any other), and drops of it are poured on the ground, accompanied with appropriate words, in the form of a prayer. The prayer is directed to *togbuiwo* in some localities, while in others it is said to *Mawu* and the *togbuiwo*. Libation prayers that are said on occasions like agricultural festivals, state functions and at difficult arbitrations, are directed not only to *Mawu* and the *togbuiwo* but also to other spirit powers known in Ewe-Dome as *trowo*.

Like others elsewhere, the indigenous religious believer in Ewe-Dome believes that there is a great God, *Mawu*, regarded as the creator of the universe. *Mawu* also sustains the universe. In *Mawu*'s creation, it is believed, are found also *trowo*, that is, various spirit powers that help in administering the world of nature as well as human life in society. The *trowo* are seen as children of *Mawu*, those that can help human beings to realize material as well as spiritual needs in life. Supplicants go to shrines that are made for the *trowo* and seek help through the *tronuawo* (priests) and *trosiwo* (priestesses). Those who approach the *trowo* are believed to get their requests granted. The *trowo* are seen as "able" and powerful. They are believed to act instantly, for example, in inflicting punishment or giving rewards—unlike *Mawu* who is seen to be long suffering and, therefore, acts rather slowly. Through the *tronuawo* and *trosiwo*, devotional attention is given to the *trowo*. Even though the *trowo* are seen as children of *Mawu*, the fear, attention and devotion paid to them seem to suggest that the *trowo* are ends in themselves, and not merely a way of working towards their creator, *Mawu*. In an interview with Afeto Wagba of Vane, an indigenous religious believer, he was asked whether prayers and sacrifices that are made to a *tro* (singular for *trowo*) are meant to be carried over to *Mawu*. He said: "The prayers and sacrifices are meant for the *tro* to act, not to be carried over to *Mawu*. The *tro* is addressed in its capacity as one that will bring about the desired result." This same view is shared by other indigenous religious believers in the area. So that even though people do call on *Mawu* to act in times of trouble or for thanksgiving, some would go to the shrines of the *trowo* to lay bare their supplications to them.

Another related belief of the indigenous Ewe-Dome society is that of the survival and continued existence in a particular place (*tsiefe*) of aspects of those that are dead. The life in *tsiefe*, the place of the dead, is in a spirit form but it is lived in the exact manner in which it was lived here on earth. The dead are classified into various categories. There are those who die very young and are not, therefore, considered as ancestors. There are also those who die what is regarded as unnatural deaths (*ametsiavawo*)—those who die through childbirth, drowning, or accidents. Certain rites would have to be performed for such people to qualify them for entrance into *tsiefe*—ancestral land. But our attention in this essay is centred around those dead that are referred to as *togbuiwo* (male ancestors) and *mamawo* (female ancestors) in the ancestral home of *tsiefe*. These are the dead considered to have lived lives that are profitable to society, contributed to the welfare of the society in various ways, lived long lives preferably (but not always necessarily) with children, and lived morally good and exemplary lives (by the societal standards). The ancestors (*togbuiwo and mamawo*) are believed to be still part of the society. They are remembered through food and drink, as morsels of food are left on the ground in the indigenous home for them to eat as the living also eat. Drinks are also served them, especially in the form of libation prayer, to invite them to partake in activities of the family, clan or society. In all these, the belief is that death does not bring about a total annihilation of a person—indeed just as the belief is held among many other societies. In the words of Noah Dzobo, "The Ewe, conceive of the next world not as a separate and an independent world which happens to be 'next' to this world but as an integral part of this world and interactive with it" (Dzobo 1982: 331).

These beliefs form a brief background to my main discussion, the making of libations. As said earlier, the ritual of making libation during various rites of passage, calling on the spirit world to witness the activities of the living, is an important indigenous heritage of the Ewe-Dome. Many rites are, in fact, begun with the libation prayer. At an outdooring and naming ceremony, libation prayer goes like this:

Ago na mi lo!
Tsiami se ne woado togbuiwo gbo be:
Le esime mieyo mi le ndi sia, mi meyo mi de vo dzi o.
Agbe dzi ko miyo mi do.
Le egbe nkekea dzia, miede devi (name)
Eyi ke mia nuto mietso na mi la de go.
Mina lamese devi sia
Be woatsi kple nunya, ade vi na mi kata.
Mina lamese, agbe didi, ga, dzilawo
Be woate nu akpo edzi abe aleyi ke wodze.
Ne amea de be devi sia mano anyi yeano o la,
Mikpo amema gbo kaba.
Mina ameyiwo medzi tsie, nadzi eve, eto, ene.
Agbe neva, fafa neva, ga neva.
Kuse, Kuse, Kuse.

Ago (we ask for your permission)!
The spokesman should listen and take it to the elders, that:
Our call on you this morning is not for anything bad.
Today, we are gathered to outdoor (name)
The child that you yourselves have given to us.
We ask for good health for this child.
We ask for wisdom and growth for him/her
That will be beneficial to all of us.
We ask for good health, long life and money for the parents;
For them to be able to take good care of this child.
Whoever would not like this child to stay alive,
We ask you to see to (i.e. deal with) that person.
Those who have no children should have two, three, four.
We ask for long life, peace and money.
Peace, Peace, Peace.

In some localities, the prayer is started with the mentioning of the name of *Mawu*, followed by the same pattern as above, with variations in the wording, depending on preferred emphases, on who is saying it, or the occasion. For example, it may start like this:

Eee . . . meyo mi lo, Eee . . . meyo mi lo, Eee . . . meyo mi lo
Mawu dzifoto, mieyo wo.
Anyigba ga, mieyo wo.
Togbuiwo miva.
Esi mieyo mia, menye de vo dzi o.

Eee . . . (We call upon you!). . . .
God of the sky, we call you.
The great earth, we call upon you.
The ancestors we call you.
We have called you not for any bad reasons.

A third variation, depending on the occasion, as we said earlier, would include the names of the *trowo*. Some of the drink is dropped on the ground after almost every sentence. The drink that is used traditionally is the commonest found in the area, palm wine. Nowadays, however, the people also use other alcoholic drinks like schnapps and gin. Those of the spirit world seem to like to drink according to the changes in taste in contemporary society!

In an interview with *Tsiami* (a chief's spokesman) Amedzoku of Tsito he was asked why the names of *trowo* are not called in a libation prayer of outdooring and naming. *Tsiami* has this to say, "We call on them in difficult situations, in festivals, in tribal functions. This is just an ordinary affair." The same explanation was given at a function in which a newly-installed *Okusie* (a chief) and *Tsiami* were being introduced to the chiefs and the spokesmen of the Avatime traditional area. On this occasion, and unlike at the outdooring ceremonies, the names of Avatime *trowo* were called, in addition to that of *Mawu* and the ancestors.[1] Clearly there is flexibility in such rites and practices.

The making of libations, calling on the spirit world to inform, to ask for blessings, to see to evil persons in the society of the living, or whatever the needs of the people are, has been a bone of contention among some members of the Evangelical Presbyterian Churches

---

[1] The interviews were held with the people in January 1997, and the function for the introduction of the chief and the chief's spokesman of Vane to the chiefs and their spokesmen in Avatime was held on the 28th of December, 1996.

and the indigenous religious practitioners over the years. The Churches think, in the words of the Rt. Rev Ledo, moderator of the Evangelical Presbyterian Church, Ghana, that: "*Nui ke mi medi le soleame koe nye ahafofod'anyi na togbuiwo, na togbui noliwo*" ("What we do not accept in the Church is the pouring of libation to the ancestors, the spirits of the ancestors"). These Churches think the ritual is idolatrous since it involves calling upon other spirit powers besides God. It is believed that the ritual is against the very first commandment of God to the Christians (Exodus 20:3), "You shall have no other gods besides me."[2] The Churches also see Christ as the only mediator between Christians and God (1 Timothy 2:5), "For there is one God, and there is one mediator between God and men, the man Christ Jesus." To call on the ancestors or other spirit powers, therefore, is to give recognition to other mediators besides Jesus Christ. However, the indigenous religious believers (and some Christians) are of the view that making of libations is an important ritual, a rich heritage with which they do not find anything wrong. To them, the ancestors are still part of the clan, even though they cannot be seen, and ought, therefore, to be invited to participate in the activities of the living.

While there seems to be a kind of tolerance from both sides in Ewe-Dome, the issue remains a one of potential conflict and therefore requires further reflection. The issue of libations, indeed, is not peculiar to Ewe-Dome. Libations are made in other parts of the country (Ghana) and various parts of the continent. As this is an important and prevalent practice, I shall offer some biblical and theological reflections on it.

What does the Bible say about libations, or what biblical principles are there to guide a Christian concerning the practice of libation? To this question, I would say that there are indications in the Bible concerning the practice of libations, though from my interviews most Christians do not seem to be aware of such references. One, however, needs to be careful not to make hasty conclusions about the ritual, without first making a careful reading of the texts that are related to libations.

The first reference to a libation or drink offering is found in Genesis 35:14. As Jacob was returning home from his self-imposed exile, he returned to Bethel, where he had earlier made a promise

---

[2] All biblical quotations are from the *Revised Standard Version*.

to God, and he "set up a pillar of stone; and poured out a drink offering on it, and poured oil on it." Another scriptural text that refers to pouring of libation is Exodus 25:29. In the instructions given for the making of the table for the bread of the Presence, God says to Moses: "And you shall make its plates and dishes for incense, and its flagons and bowls with which to pour libations; Of pure gold you shall make them." Here, it is as if God valued the pouring of the libations so much that the vessels that are to be used in the pouring are to be in "pure gold." The pouring of libations was, thus, part of the religious practice of Israel (at the time). In fact, in the daily calendar of rituals that are to be performed in Numbers 28 is one that asks for pouring of a libation to the Lord. Furthermore, in an act of repentance during the time of the prophet Samuel, the Israelites "gathered at Mizpah, and drew water and poured it out before the Lord, and fasted on that day" (1 Samuel 7:6a). Assuming the practice, God, in Hosea 9:4, asks the Israelites no longer to pour libation or make such rituals, for, the Israelites had forsaken God and turned to other gods.

Coming to the New Testament, one may say that even though there are no specific texts that point explicitly to the practice of making libations, there are a few texts that allude to the practice, as found in the Old Testament. Paul's statement in Philippians 2:17, for example, alludes to the practice of pouring libation when he says, "Even if I am to be poured as a libation upon the sacrificial offering of your faith, I am glad and rejoice with you all." Paul, certainly, was aware of the ritual of making a libation and was alluding to it.

From the above indications (and some others that we have not quoted), we can say that the ritual of pouring libations was part of Israelite practice. The sacrificial practice of libations is, however, not explicitly practised in the New Testament. Instead, Christ, in the New Testament, is regarded by many Christians as one who has come to fulfil all such rites of the Old Testament. Hebrews 9:9–12, for example, would seem to support such a position:

> According to this arrangement, gifts and sacrifices are offered which cannot perfect the conscience of the worshipper, but deal only with food and drink and various ablutions. . . . . But when Christ appeared as a high priest of the good things that have come, then through the greater and more perfect tent . . . . he entered once for all into the Holy Place, taking not the blood of goats and calves but his own blood, thus securing an eternal redemption.

It appears from such scriptural texts that sacrifices with drinks, animals and other forms of gifts are no longer necessary for those who accept the faith about Jesus Christ.

To some, making libations in African contexts is seen as an act of rekindling kinship relationship between the living and the dead, particularly in those cases where a libation is made to the ancestors in particular. In his *African Religions and Philosophy*, John Mbiti, writing about some east African people, has made the observation that: "Libations and the giving of food to the departed are tokens of fellowship, hospitality and respect; The drink and food so given are symbols of family continuity and contact" (Mbiti 1975: 9). Libation, in this sense, has more to do with respect and hospitality towards the ancestors (the living-dead as Mbiti calls them) than anything else. Peter Kwesi Sarpong makes similar observations when he says that,

> The dead are honoured in many other ways; flowers are put on their tombs, their pictures may be decorated, something they held dear may be kept in the family to remind the family of them and so on and so forth. ... If these acts are not considered to be religious but are acts of gratitude to remind the living of people who have meant something to the society in the past, then it would appear that on public occasions, it would be quite permissible to pour libation, mentioning the ancestors (Sarpong 1996: 42).

Such observations seem to give the impression that libation may not be an idolatrous ritual, giving recognition to other powers besides God, the way some Christians interpret libations. We need to reflect further, then, on the issue whether a libation in such contexts should be seen as idolatrous or not to the Christian.

On those occasions where the names of *trowo* and the ancestors are mentioned alongside that of *Mawu* in a libation prayer, one could say that the issue needs to be handled with care. This is because the concept that is held about the *trowo* in Ewe-Dome can at best be described as ambivalent. The *trowo*, as we have discussed, even though they are regarded as children or creatures of God, are seen as "able." The way they are approached and the ritual activities involving them are such that it is difficult to regard them as only a means to *Mawu*. In the minds of indigenous believers, libations directed towards the *trowo* are intended to elicit action from them. To argue, as some theologians do, that the rites really are meant for *Mawu*, cannot be said to be entirely correct—at least not as far as the rites are practised and experienced among the Ewe-Dome.

Coming to the issue of making libations to the ancestors, we would once more have to refer to the libation prayer that was presented earlier in this writing. In the prayers, the people prayed to the ancestors (through their *Tsiami*) to inform them about the ceremony of outdooring and naming, to ask for their presence, to ask for their blessings, to punish the wicked ones etc. In localities where the name of *Mawu* is mentioned, it is mentioned alongside that of the ancestors. One notices that the ancestors are not called upon to carry the message to *Mawu* the way the *Tsiami* is asked to carry the message to the ancestors. Intermediate roles in fact are not assumed in Ewe-Dome; they are stated categorically. It is always said: *Tsiami se ne woado egbo be* ("Spokesman listen and tell the one the following") whenever a message is being passed on from one person to another. So the ancestors are seen as the recipients of prayers that are addressed to them, through the *Tsiami*. Libations are, certainly, a form of prayer in Ewe-Dome. Sarpong, in spite of his suggestion above, sees libation as "clearly a form of prayer and, indeed, a form of sacrifice" (Sarpong 1996: ix). And that is the way the people understand libation—as a religious act of prayer and sacrifice. But how idolatrous is the libation prayer to the ancestors to the Christian believer?

Let us start with the whole idea of the kind of relationship that should exist or is believed to exist between the living and the dead. The idea of the kind of relationship that should or is believed to exist between the living and the dead has remained a controversy among various groups of people over the years. Various opinions prevail, which can be put into two main classes. First, there is the view that there should be no relationship whatsoever with the dead. Second, there is the view that some sort of relationship can be maintained with the ancestors. To the Ewe-Dome indigenous religious believer, in common with some elsewhere, and as discussed earlier, death does not mark the total end of a human being. It only serves as a means by which the dead are transported into another realm of a spirit world, where life continues as it used to be here on earth. The dead do not also cut off their kinship relationship with the living, and through food and libation that kinship relationship is always rekindled.

Christians also have the belief that life that is lived at present on earth is not all that is to what it means to live in-Christ. There is an expectation of another kind of life after death. Notions about the kind of life that exists after death, however, vary from one Christian

Church or sect to the other. The Roman Catholic Church, for example, holds the belief that the Church comprises the Church Triumphant, the Church Expectant, and the Church Militant. Those in the first group are those saints who by their faith and life in-Christ were able to attain salvation and after their death have entered heaven, in union with Christ. The members of the Church Triumphant "have attained the Beatific Vision and do not need our help but we should seek their intercession and also venerate them as lovers of God eternally united to Him. . . ." (Quilan 1966: 134). Intercessory prayers can be passed through this category of the dead, for them to intercede on behalf of the living and those in purgatory. The Church Triumphant is to be venerated for their love of God. "This veneration lawfully includes reverence for their relics even as we show honour to the bodily remains of our beloved dead" (Quilan 1966: 132). Reference is made to Exodus 13:9, for example, to support the belief, which shows that those leaving Egypt were asked by Joseph to bear his bones with them on their way back home. Roman Catholics are, however, warned that a relic should not be seen superstitiously as "a magic talisman" for the relic itself or its likeness "is not a source of spiritual power. Every superstitious tendency that suggests they are sources of spiritual power, should be resisted" (Quilan 1966: 134).

The second group, those in purgatory, are those dead that were not able to live to satisfaction the life that was required of them as Christians, or were not able to perform penance to satisfaction; They have the guilt of venial sin or still owe atonement for past sins. Such souls are believed to be in a state of limbo—not on earth and not yet in heaven. It is believed that "the Faithful on earth and the Blessed in heaven can by their intercession assist the souls in purgatory" (Quilan 1966: 132). The third category, the Church Militant or the Church on earth, are the living Christians, those striving to achieve God's own perfect way through Christ while on earth.

The Roman Catholic Church believes that "The souls of the Church Militant on earth, suffering in purgatory and Triumphant in heaven are all united with each other through their union of love with Christ, the source of holiness." This belief is based on, for example, "Christ's teaching of the Vine and its branches (cf. John 15:1–10), on his efficacious prayer at the Last Supper that all united with him might be united together even as he himself was with the

Father" (Quilan 1966: 132). But, while the concept of the Communion of Saints does not lend itself to one interpretation, the most widely held understanding of it is that it refers to the fellowship of the faithful, the living as well as the departed, irrespective of denomination (see Barth 1960: 144). It is this belief that is, in fact, incorporated in the Apostles' Creed. So there is within the Christian tradition a belief in an everlasting relationship between all faithful Christians, the living as well as the dead.

We can put the Roman Catholic Church under our first category, of those who believe that some sort of relationship can be maintained between the living and the dead, but not a worship-dependence relationship. However, some other Christian Churches, for example, the Evangelical Presbyterian Churches in Ewe-Dome, do not hold the beliefs of the Roman Catholic Church. To these Churches, the dead are "asleep" awaiting the final day of resurrection. They make reference to texts like 1 Thessalonians 4:14 and 1 Corinthians 15:20. In the Constitution of the Evangelical Presbyterian Church, Ghana, it is stated that "The Church shall be fully committed in the event of the death of a member. Members shall mourn with the bereaved family, comfort them, and give them every assistance. However, 'pagan' practices of all kinds shall be abhorred during death and burials" (nd.:46). The 'pagan' practices have not been explained further in the Constitution, but judging from the Church's beliefs and practices, these include pouring of libation to the dead. Memorial services can be organized for those who so desire, but no other practice or belief in the continuity of kinship relationship between the living and the dead is encouraged. The Evangelical Presbyterian Churches in Ghana can be put in the second category, that is, of those who hold the view that there should be no continued relationship between the living and the dead.

African theologians continue to debate the concepts implicit in these categories, so it is not easy to draw clear lines. Much energy has been expended by African scholars, in particular, some African Christian theologians, to explain to "the powers that be" that Africans regard their ancestors not as deities that are worshipped, but as kinsmen/women with whom they (the living) "continue to live." The ancestors are not worshipped, but are only venerated. The ancestors, even though dead, are still part of the living, supervising conduct since they are still concerned about the welfare of those they have left behind in the flesh, and so on. The plea of the theologians is that the Church should give public recognition, perhaps in its doctrinal formulations, to the beliefs and practices that are associated with African ancestors. Jean-Marc Ela, for example, raises the question, "Shouldn't the Church profit by encouraging African Christians to stay in contact with their loved ones who have left this life, rather than by attacking our ideas about the ancestors?" (Ela 1990: 26). He further asks,

> Can we be at peace with our conscience, if conversion requires that we live separated from the dead of our family, without any possibility of contacting them in the periods of crisis? What new kind of people does God want to construct among us out of our unique African traits? Isn't communion with the ancestors a mark of our culture? (Ela 1990: 31).

Mercy Oduyoye also writes: "Why is the relationship of the African with the 'living dead' any more idolatrous than the observance of All Souls Day and All Saints Day?" (Oduyoye 1986: 9). Similarly, Fasholé-Luke argues that

> From the outset of Christian missions in Africa; western missionaries unanimously rejected African ancestor cults as pagan superstition, and even the Roman Catholic Church, which has a cult of saints, has forbidden her converts from participation in the rituals of the ancestral cults. It is not surprising therefore, that it was and still is, at this point that Christianity has met with the stiffest resistance in Africa (Fasholé-Luke 1974: 209).

To some of the Christian theologians, the African ought to be allowed to continue living with his or her dead. Should the pleas be accepted, then the questions that are still left unanswered are, for example, how should the African live with his or her dead? Should making libation, a way of relating to the dead in Ewe-Dome, be accepted by Christians as a way of relating to or living with the dead?

Basing our reflection once more on the Bible, one may say here that there is little clear conceptualization about the state of the dead. In fact the Bible is almost silent on the state of the dead. In the Old Testament writings, the dead were believed to have entered "sheol," an underworld, a place of an uncertain existence (see for example, Job 26:6; Psalm 9:17). Coming to the New Testament, we encounter a different understanding of a place where the dead go. In the classical example of Jesus' parable of the rich man and Lazarus

(Luke 16:19–31), the rich man is pictured as being tormented in "Hades," but able to see in the distance Abraham with Lazarus— the poor man—by his side. Biblical interpretation has it that even though Hades, in the above parable, seems to be a place of punishment for the wicked, "the Hades in which the rich man is in torment may be regarded as merely a general term for the abode of all the dead, even though 'a great chasm' (16:26) separates him from the other part of Hades where Lazarus is in Abraham's bosom" (Miller and Miller 1973: 886). The impression here is that Hades is a place for the dead, but that it is divided between the wicked and the righteous.

Other conceptualizations, rather than referring to a place, refer to a form of being. At the end of time those who have lived good lives (in-Christ) will be rewarded with an everlasting heavenly body (1 Corinthians 15:52–53). Also, all souls who live a life in-Christ are described as having "fallen asleep" (1 Corinthians 15:20; 1 Thessalonians 4:14), awaiting the end of time for the resurrection.

It seems to me, then, that the kind of life that may go on after death—and hence our knowledge of how the living should relate to the dead—is one of the secrets that God has decided to keep out of the reach of believers. But if I may be so bold as to offer a suggestion, neither of the two extremes, that of totally rejecting any kind of relationship between the living and the dead, nor that of accepting ancestral rituals in their entirety, may not be good enough for the African Ewe-Dome Christian. This is because, on the one hand, there is at least some ontological bond between the living and the dead that cannot be wished away. So some kind of relationship would have to be maintained. On the other hand, there may be some ancestral practices that are offensive to Christian sensitivity. So the precise nature of what should be maintained is the problem.

An option might be to institute some form of relationship between the living and the dead that may be described as "Memorial." In this relationship, the living can fondly remember their dead, especially on important family occasions such as outdooring and naming, marriage, funerals etc. The family or Church can recall and acknowledge their good lives and work in the family, Church, community, nation etc., and thank God for them and bless them. They may ask God, not the dead, to give them grace to emulate the good examples of the dead, or to be inspired by their good principles. Memorial monuments can also be built in honour of the ancestors, for example, plaques or statues. Feasts and memorial lectures or foundations can also be instituted in honour of the dead.

However, given the concerns of some Christians and the injunction of texts like Deuteronomy 18:10–11, it might be argued that Ewe-Dome Christians should not enter into direct communication with the ancestors. This suggestion is based not only on biblical injunctions but also on a possible practical problem of "addiction," whereby people become so much dependent on the ancestors that they draw further and further away from Christ and find themselves outside his love and salvation. Christ's sufficient nature in providing Christians with material and spiritual salvation is such that Christians, one might argue, need not have to look elsewhere for provision. Libation prayer of the kind that is presented among the Ewe-Dome during outdooring and naming ceremonies is certainly a religious act of prayer asking the ancestors to do various things for example, give wealth, children and protection. It is not just a social or filial duty of sharing food and drink with kinsmen/women in the world of the dead. The sufficiency of Christ, upon whom there is to be a total dependence, thus seems to be undermined by such libation prayers. However, Christians by all means should remember the dead through a kind of "Memorial" practice, mentioning their names on public occasions.

Saying this does not mean, however, that beliefs that are held by other faith traditions should be downgraded. It is difficult to have full knowledge about the spirit realm. If the spirit of the dead (or the dead himself/herself) is reported to have appeared to someone to give warning, consolation, praise or punishment, then those who have had such encounters and believe them may joyfully (or regrettably) and pragmatically apportion the experience to themselves. Rites that may be associated with such beliefs should be performed by those who believe in them. Those that have no such experiences and who do not have the belief need not perform the rites and need not have conflicts in their consciences. In other instances, it may and need not always be easy for those who do not accept the ritual of libations to run away from a kinsman/woman or others who want to perform the ritual. Even those who disagree and do not believe can be present and use the time to pray according to one's own faith.

It is often the case that in some congregations of the Churches there is a careful avoidance of certain texts in the Bible (especially found in the Old Testament) that seem to point to certain practices of African Indigenous Religion. Such texts include those on libation discussed above. Such an attitude may be traced back to early missionary evangelization of the people when, to borrow the words of Birgit Meyer, "on the whole, the missionaries represented actual Ewe religion as the worship of the Devil" (Meyer 1995: 128). Such attitudes are not helpful, particularly for those who do find such texts outside congregational worship, and give various meaningful interpretations to them, though sometimes without relating them to the New Testament understanding. This can create serious problems for the Church. The reading of the Bible in Africa, one would suggest, ought to be a thorough affair, making reference to both the Old and New Testaments. With careful reading and deep theological reflection, the kind of uneasy tolerance or intolerance that is found among the people over the act of libation, among other things, one would hope, might be eased.

BIBLIOGRAPHY

Agossou, J.M., Ed. *L'Experience Religieuse Africaine Et Les Relations Interpersonelles*, Abidjan: Savanes-Fortes, 1982.

Barth, Karl. *Dogmatics in Outline*, London, 1960.

Dzobo Noah. "References To The Next World (Bome) In The Daily Life Of The Ewe Of West Africa" In Ed. J.M. Agossou *L'Experience Religieuse Africaine Et Les Relations Interpersonnelles*. Abidjan, Savanes—Fortes, 1982.

Ela, Jean-Marc. *My Faith As an African*. Maryknoll, New York, 1990: Orbis Books.

Fashole-Luke, E.W., "Ancestor Veneration and the Communion of Saints," In Eds Glasswell, M.E. & E.W. Fashole-Luke, Eds *New Testament Christianity for Africa and the world: Essays in honour of Harry Sawyerr*. London: SPCK, 1974.

Lindsell, Harold. *Study Bible: Revised Standard Version*: Cambridge University Press, 1964.

Mbiti, John S. *African Religions and Philosophy*, London: Heinemann, 1975.

Meyer, Birgit, *Translating the Devil: An African Appropriation of Pietist Protestantism—The Case of Peki-Ewe in south-eastern Ghana, 1847–1992*, Unpublished, 1995.

Miller, S. Madeleine & Miller, J. Lane Eds *Black's Bible Dictionary*. London: Adam & Charles Black, 1973.

Oduyoye, Mercy. *Hearing and Knowing: Theological Reflections On Christianity in Africa*. Maryknoll, New York: Orbis Books, 1986.

Quilan, David. *Roman Catholicism*. London: The Univ. Press, 1966.

Sarpong, Peter Kwesi. *Libation*. Accra: Anansesem Pub. Ltd., 1996.

The Constitution of the Evangelical Presbyterian Church, Ghana and The Evangelique Presbyterian Du Togo, Accra: Lestek, (nd.).

CONTEXTUAL BALANCING OF SCRIPTURE WITH SCRIPTURE: SCRIPTURE UNION IN NIGERIA AND GHANA

Andrew Olu Igenoza

In Africa, the majority of the people grapple with problems related to human existence on a large scale. The sick, who are mostly poor, seek for healing in different ways. The poor masses, of course, look for ways out of their plight. The rich, too, search for security and protection and the childless want to become parents, etc. Perhaps only the elderly might resign themselves to fate. This is even doubtful. With so much belief in witchcraft, sorcery and sundry preternatural powers, many would go to any lengths to counter perceived or imagined forces of evil. These forces may also be seen to be operating in the social, economic and political spheres. In a continent where the people are known to be very religious, it is not surprising that many use the Bible in addition to other methods in dealing with their problems. Churches and fellowships have continued to mushroom as a result, offering varied and often conflicting solutions purportedly based on the Bible. Some groups for example, use the Bible to justify their refusal of every form of medication while others use the same Bible to support the performance of rituals and sacrifices in pursuit of healing.[1] Some define prosperity in purely material terms while others believe otherwise.

It is in the light of these complexities that the approach of the Scripture Union to the use of the Bible in addressing these human issues is examined here with particular reference to Nigeria and Ghana. Nigeria is the scene with which I am most familiar, but in December 1996, I had the opportunity of observing a Scripture Union programme in Ghana and reading some of their literature

---

[1] In Nigeria, for example, the Christ Apostolic Church in the 1930s officially renounced the use of every form of medicine because of their belief in divine healing, using texts like Exodus 15:26 among others. At the same time, it is known that some so-called "white garment" churches prescribe animal sacrifice for therapeutic and apotropaic purposes based on the Old Testament and traditional sacrifice systems (Isaacson 1990: 87, Turner 1979: 165–172, Makhubu 1988: 59–64).

which has made it possible for the scope of this essay to be broadened. Perhaps, this is useful for comparative analysis.

This essay is primarily descriptive. A brief historical background of the Scripture Union will be offered, then its operational and hermeneutical principles will be outlined, after which a relevant sample of Bible Study outlines, devotional materials, papers, releases and publications of the Union will be analysed. Observation and participation at prayer meetings, Bible studies and other programmes of the Union have also contributed to this essay. From this study, it will become apparent that in the contextual use of the Bible, Scripture Union Ghana and Nigeria focus primarily on salvation and spiritual well-being and try to avoid denominational controversies, and that in their handling of human problems they aim at Scriptural balance. They strive to achieve this aim through a comprehensive approach to the study of the Bible. Whereas it is customary for most Churches or groups to read only portions of the Bible in their lectionary, or those portions that suit their denominational biases, the Scripture Union adopts a method whereby its members are encouraged to read the whole Bible systematically over a period of time, and to think, ask questions and apply what they read to their lives. This is done at the level of personal devotions, small discussion groups and large corporate meetings. Part of a Scripture Union rhyme puts it thus: "Pray and read and think and pray: That's the Scripture Union way to read the Bible every day. . . ." Variations of this method are: "Pray and read and think and do" and "Pray and read and think and pray and share."[2] This method seems to have deeply affected Scripture Union in Ghana and Nigeria.

The Scripture Union is an international and non-denominational organization founded in England between 1867 and 1879. By 1890, the Union had established its presence in West Africa. Scripture Union Nigeria celebrated its centenary in 1985 while that of Ghana did so in 1990. At a historic meeting in Old Jordans, near London, in 1960, Scripture Union International decided to decentralize and allow the different national Unions to forge their own identities in their respective cultural contexts (Sylvester 1984: 155–160). With this development the national Unions in Nigeria and Ghana were well

---

[2] I owe this information to a leaflet entitled "*Some Distinctives: Scripture Union's Use of the Bible.*" I am grateful to Rev. Canon Niyi Woranola of Scripture Union Headquarters, Ibadan, Nigeria, for this and other useful material.

set to chart their respective indigenous, independent and distinctive outlooks. In 1962, Florence Yeboah became the first indigenous staff member of Scripture Union Ghana, while in 1966 Michael Oye (now Rev. Dr. Oye) was appointed the first Nigerian travelling secretary of Scripture Union Nigeria (Sylvester 1984: 209–210). Worthy of note was the employment of Mr. Edward Okyere by Scripture Union Ghana in September 1973.[3] In my opinion, the contributions of Oye in Nigeria and Okyere in Ghana, together with their respective Scripture Union compatriots, definitively changed the pattern and direction of Scripture Union ministries in these countries and permanently stamped it with indigenous authenticity through the process of contextualization. They did this by addressing the issues of cardinal importance in their local religious milieux like witchcraft, curses, mysterious sicknesses, occult bondage, superstitious beliefs, taboos and deliverance. Emmanuel Oladipo had reasons to say that when he took over as the Regional Secretary of Scripture Union from John Dean in 1982, the work of the Union was already "very firmly rooted in the African soil." He continued: "One of the factors, under God, responsible for this is the absence of a standard internation manual answering all the questions we are not asking. We have therefore been free to experiment, make our own mistakes and learn our lessons. . . ." (Sylvester 1984: 246). This deliberate policy of decentralization and indigenisation has helped the Scripture Union to become genuinely African in Africa, especially as Nigeria and Ghana are concerned.

The Scripture Union as a worldwide movement is primarily concerned with evangelism and to encourage converts to read their Bibles devotionally, systematically and comprehensively in the light of Christ, and with a view to obeying it. It is within this two-pronged ministry that the Scripture Union in Ghana and Nigeria seek to use the Bible to deal with peculiar local religious aspirations, while striving to maintain Scriptural balance. From the operational viewpoint the Union has always believed that sustained and systematic teaching is the task of evangelism, rather than in one-off meetings with instant appeals for a decision. It allows people to independently make up their minds, after being presented with the gospel. Secondly, it

---

[3] Private Interview with Mr. Edward Okyere (59 years) on 29th December, 1996 during the Scripture Union Healing and Deliverance Workshop at Presbyterian Women's Training College, Aburi, Ghana.

steers clear of denominational controversies to focus solely on the Bible. Another operational principle of the Union is its emphasis on dependence on the Holy Spirit in answer to prayer.

As early as 1894 Tom Bishop, one of the founding Fathers of the Union, outlined the hermeneutical principle of the Union. He said:

> The divine inspiration and supreme authority of the Scriptures has been a leading principle of our work. . . . We have always shown clearly that we accept "all Scripture" as "given by inspiration of God" and as "profitable for doctrine, for reproof, for correction, for instruction in righteousness." A solid reason for holding to this position was "the estimate which the Lord Jesus Christ placed upon the Father's Word. We find that he treated the facts recorded in it as true in every particular and that he regarded each utterance in it as infallible. . . ." We hold strongly that the doctrines rest upon the facts, and that we have no right to expect any true morality or Christian life apart from the full acceptance of the facts and doctrines (Sylvester 1984: 52).

Tom Bishop did not go into details of how Scripture should be interpreted other than to accept the plain meaning. Most recently (1997) the Union put forward its hermeneutical principles, in greater detail, through its *Network Bulletin*. According to this Bulletin the Bible should be interpreted as a whole, contextually, Christologically and relationally: "We are committed to the whole of Scripture, to allowing Scripture to interpret Scripture and to promoting the broad sweep. . . ." The Scripture Union believes that a biblical passage should be interpreted according to the author's intention and in terms of its original context. One should therefore seek to understand the original vocabulary, style and background of the text. It believes that while an exhaustive knowledge of the context may be impossible, an adequate knowledge of it is not. Contextual interpretation also takes into account how the reader's life-situation will affect his or her understanding of Scripture. This aspect embraces one's worldview, culture, age group and history. The Union believes that the life and ministry of Jesus are the key events in God's dealings with humanity and thus form the focus of God's revelation in Scripture. In reading any Scriptural passage, therefore, one should consider how it relates to Christ.

Of cardinal importance in the Scripture Union's hermeneutical theory is the role of the Holy Spirit:

> The Holy Spirit must be the driving force of our interpretation. As God's empowering presence, he will lead people to engage with the

text and face God's challenge in the here and now. The recognition that the Holy Spirit brings a sense of immediacy will draw our readers into an understanding not just of the original meaning of the text but also its contemporary prophetic significance.[4]

The Scripture Union hermeneutical theory as summarised above may sound too academic, especially with reference to phrases like "original context" and "original vocabulary." The average Scripture Union members in Ghana or Nigeria do not know Hebrew, Greek, biblical history or hermeneutics, but they seem to desire to know the scriptures and apply them in their different contexts, and are willing to benefit from simple books on interpretation which are often available in Scripture Union bookshops.

An advantage which most Africans often have is the striking similarity between their indigenous culture and worldview and the biblical—while not overlooking the differences. Of utmost concern, however, is the desire of the Scripture Union in Africa that their members should be committed to the whole of Scripture and seek to interpret and apply it in a balanced way. The *Daily Guide*, a Bible reading guide written for adults, in the commentary of April 12th, 1998 on Luke 24:13–25 seeks to highlight this saying: "Lack of clear understanding of the Scriptures often robs us of the joy of Christian living. The knowledge of the Bible (all of it, not just the New Testament or Psalms) helps to renew our hopes and deliver us from frustration and confusion." Apart from the spiritual benefit as perceived by this commentator, a fair knowledge of the whole Bible helps to promote theological balance.

Scripture Union in Nigeria and Ghana operate within the above guidelines and seek to translate them to suit their respective localities. Two leaflets by Scripture Union Nigeria: "Note Writing Principles" and "Daily Power and Balanced Teachings" have been written along these lines while taking cognisance of Nigerian peculiarities. According to the former, readers "should be helped to achieve a balanced understanding of God's word, enabling them to respond to its personal, social, evangelistic and cultural demands. . . ." The document emphasises that people should be made to think for themselves and not to depend solely on the notes: "Try to make the reader think

---

[4] These hermeneutical principles are contained in A *Network Bulletin*: Scripture Union International Bible Ministries Network, No. 8 April 1997.

for himself by occasional use of relevant questions or by sending him back to the text."[5] The second document written by Dr. Japhet Adeneye on behalf of the Scripture Union elaborates appropriately on Scriptural balance. Daily Power is published with young Secondary School students in mind. He counselled the various contributors to use it "as a medium for establishing and conveying balanced teachings" and that it should not be used to teach or emphasize "denominational biases or differences on any topic." He proceeds to mention aspects of human experience where balancing must be struck, some of which are hereby highlighted. The first is suffering. He noted that some aspects of it, including sickness, may be caused by sin. He cited Proverbs 23:29–35 as a proof-text, which states that the drunkard cannot but suffer for the consequences of his action. He then pointed out that not every sickness or misfortune is due to any particular sin as stated in John 9:1–5. He made it clear that Christians are not screened from suffering for it is part of the Christian life, citing 1 Peter 4:12–19 and 5:7–11 in support. Christians should therefore be able to joyfully praise God and witness to his love even in suffering and death. He then cited Acts 7:54–60 (about Stephen) and Acts 16:19–32 (Paul and Silas). Christians should be able to accept the sovereign will of God for their lives. As Dr. Adeneye points out, God allowed Abel to be killed for offering an acceptable sacrifice and still put a mark on Cain, the murderer, to prevent Cain from being killed by another person (Genesis 4:1–16); he also allowed James the son of Zebedee to be killed by Herod Agrippa I, but saved Simon Peter from imprisonment and death (Acts 12:1–11). Again Hebrews 11:4–35a is different from Hebrews 11:35b–38 for, in the former reference, some people of God triumphed through their faith while in the latter others who were equally people of God "were tortured refusing to accept release . . . suffered mocking and scourging, and even chains and imprisonment . . . . were killed with the sword. . . . ." Adeneye noted that Isaiah 54:17 has not always been literally fulfilled in the experience of all Christians of every age. This passage says: "no weapon that is fashioned against you shall prosper, and you shall confute every tongue that rises against you in judgement. This is the heritage of the servants of the LORD and their vindication from me, says the LORD" (RSV). Therefore, he

---

[5] The source of this one-sheet document is Canon Woranola, as above.

thinks that the focus of the Christian should be on Romans 8:28 which says that in all things God works for the good of those who love him.

Adeneye then observed that some gospellers teach that because of Exodus 15:26, Christians cannot be sick. He pointed out that, however, Tabitha (Dorcas) fell ill and died though she was later raised (Acts 9:36–41) and Timothy had frequent illnesses which included a strange stomach upset for which he was recommended to take "wine" as a medicament (1 Timothy 5:23). He writes:

> Is it not probable that Paul had oftentimes earlier prayed and laid hands on Timothy for healing, or Timothy prayed for himself and claimed healing promises or divine healing? The use, or not, of orthodox or traditional medicine is neither a mark of spirituality nor passport to heaven and should therefore not be forced down the throat of every Christian.

Adeneye was not denying instantaneous or divine healing but was only advocating a balanced biblical approach. He continued:

> All orthodox and/or traditional doctors are prescribers but there is only one Healer. . . . God is the Healer. . . . God's healing power is unlimited and inexhaustible. If God chooses, He knows how and when to confound and embarrass any or all doctors put together. Let no spiritual pride prevent any sick Christian from using prescribed drugs for healing purposes. Let no unbelief prevent a sick Christian form receiving divine healing. Let every sick Christian use his or her level of faith in using or not using drugs for healing. . . .

He was certainly not advocating that it was right for the Christian to use traditional medicine alongside divination and sacrifices to the ancestors as is usually the case in the traditional milieu. Certainly this is not the position of Scripture Union Nigeria as will soon be shown. He was only saying that traditional medicine and traditional healers are not evil in themselves. On the prosperity issue, he claimed that riches are not necessarily a mark of closeness to God, and neither is poverty a sign of ungodliness. Therefore, all teachings about material prosperity must be properly balanced in the Scriptures, "and result in the preparation of the heart that is fertile enough to receive and make the seed of spiritual prosperity germinate, grow and bear good fruit." Prosperity preachers often rely heavily on the Old Testament. However, in the same Old Testament passage where Moses said "There will be no poor among you. . . .," he proceeded to say "if there be among you a poor man, one of your brethren. . . ." Then later he added: "For the poor will never cease out of the land. . . ." (Deuteronomy 15:4,7,10, RSV: the NIV has "should" instead of "will" in verse 4). Afflictions and misfortunes in various forms, sicknesses, poverty and death are part of the human condition and Scripture Union Nigeria has not used the Scripture to shy away from them. The organisation takes *theologia crucis* very seriously.

The concern for balancing Scripture as analysed above is not peculiar to Dr. Japhet Adeneye and his immediate circle of influence within the Scripture Union family. We have already referred to the pivotal role played by Rev. Dr. Michael Oye within the Union in the 1960s and onwards. He and other like-minded old Scripture Union members got together in 1996 to form the Concerned Ministers' Forum in Abuja, Nigeria in order to counteract "the present wave of doctrinal imbalances and heretical tendencies in the practice of Christianity in Nigeria today."[6] Their Scriptural warrant was Jude verse 23 which says that believers should "earnestly contend for the faith that was once delivered to the saints." The Forum observed the lack of sound teaching of "the whole counsel of God" in the Church, arising from a poor understanding of Christian Theology, the enthronement of a self-serving gospel, the lack of true Christian values with the concomitant neglect of holiness, the merchandising of the gospel, and the drive for power through occultism, spiritism and metaphysics. Their aim was to publish relevant materials to enlighten Christians in Nigeria on these observed anomalies. The issue is really that of balancing Scripture with Scripture and the members of the forum are concerned thus because as Scripture Union members they knew and still know the Scriptures from the comprehensive point of view.

Another old Scripture Union member whose organisation, the Deeper Life Christian Ministries, is concerned with Scriptural balance is W.F. Kumuyi.[7] From his own experience he concluded that in Africa, hard core gospel preaching alone may not give the desired result. According to him, "the proof and evidence of the love and

---

[6] This quotation comes from the brochure of the Concerned Minister's Forum, announcing their conference of September 1st to 5th, 1997 at Abuja. I obtained this brochure from Rev. Simeon Ilaya who is based in Lagos.

[7] I had known Mr. Kumuyi in Scripture Union circles as far back as 1970. See Isaacson 1990: 60 where he said that after his conversion, "I got involved with the Scripture Union, and grew."

concern of God pave the path for the Gospel in Africa" (Isaacson 1990: 10). Isaacson, (1990: 75–90) then narrated how Rabi Olaiwola, who had been a devout Muslim, and had been afflicted with "leprosy" through African occult powers was saved and healed. Sherifat, also of Muslim background, was released from a curse which caused her to become epileptic. Then Dorothy, who grew up a nominal Christian, was equally saved, healed and delivered from demonic attacks. However, Kumuyi viewed these miraculous cures not as ends in themselves but a means to an end. He regards conversion as "incomparably greater than every other miracle, even the raising of the dead" (Isaacson 1990: 10).

Not only has the Scripture Union ministry brought help and healing to ordinary people who felt oppressed or cursed by agents of evil, it has also brought deliverance to hard core occultists who had become agents of evil. Emmanuel Eni whose testimony has been published not only by Scripture Union Nigeria but also by Scripture Union Kenya, according to him, had his life threatened by former cult members after his conversion. The local Scripture Union fellowship proved to be "the right place" where a Christian woman counselled him with the Word of God. In his own words, "God's protection was fulfilled in my life." He claimed that the promises of Psalm 91 and Isaiah 54:17, which Eni himself cited, worked for him (Eni 1987: 43–44).

We now wish to dwell on how Scripture Union Nigeria influences and encourages Scriptural balance in their day to day and periodic activities. In addition to *Daily Power* and *Daily Guide* which have already been mentioned, it publishes *Inye Aka* for Ibo readers, *Odudu Uwem* for Efik, *Bibeli Ajumoka* for the Yoruba and *Ujenwu Inmi* for the Igala speakers. Through these devotional aids the Scripture Union takes users through the Bible in about five years. To make any particular pericope clearer, cross-references from both Testaments are given while commenting or asking questions on the text. Taking *Bibeli Ajumoka* for 1997 as an example, while attention is adequately paid to the peculiar concerns of its readers the focus is primarily on salvation and its implication for daily living. Commenting on the reading for March 7th, namely Matthew 20:20–34, the writer encouraged readers to follow the example of Jesus to serve others selflessly and be willing to lay down their lives as verses 26 to 28 make clear. However, the commentator was keen to demonstrate that God is more than concerned about, and more than able to solve, their personal problems and therefore they do not need to consult diviners and traditional healers. The passage for January 31, Matthew 8:1–17, entitled "Jesus can heal all your diseases," serves as an example. The user was instructed to reread the passage and then mention the miracles Jesus performed in verses 3, 5, 6 and 14–16. The reader was told to note the faith of the leper, the centurion, Peter's mother-in-law and all others that Jesus healed. The commentator then said: "This Jesus has not changed, see Hebrews 13:8." The reader was then encouraged to bring all his diseases, sicknesses and difficulties in life to Jesus "today": "He will deliver you. If you believe in him truly, he will turn all your sorrows into joy." But the comment of May 22 based on Acts 3:1–10 looked beyond physical healing, though it was not being undermined:

> Many people today are searching for wealth, blessings and physical healing alone instead of the deliverance of the soul from the bondage of sin which has crippled their spirits. If God has given you spiritual healing, you too can become an instrument in God's hand to break the fetters of the devil in your own life and in those of others. Secondly, God can heal you physically and perform other types of miracles in your life if you believe in him. The power in the name of Jesus (verses 6 and 7) has not diminished. He can still perform mighty miracles today.

In many other similar ways the commentator of this vernacular devotional aid aimed to strike a balance in dealing with human predicaments.

However, he was unsparing in condemning idolatry and ancestral worship because, according to him, they are inimical to one's spiritual well-being from the biblical point of view. The commentary of October 13 was based on Isaiah 44:9–20. He enjoined the reader to reread verse 14–17 which is a mockery of the idol worshipper who fashions an image from a piece of wood and yet uses part of the same wood for fire to warm himself with. He commented: "It is a pity that many people regard idolatry as part of our culture to be preserved. Many churchgoers are still trapped in this position because they do not know what salvation is. Let us be courageous enough to let such people know that Jesus is the only Saviour and warn them to abandon idolatry altogether." For meditation, he then referred the reader to 1 John 5:21 which says: "Little children keep yourselves from idols." The comment on 1 Samuel 7:2–17 on November 10 made it clear that idolatry went beyond the worship of images. "Whatever a person loves more than God in this life, be it one's profession, money, husband, wife, child, worldly goods and so on, have become idols."[8]

This contextual application of Scripture is also reflected in the Bible studies designed for school groups. There are studies on basic themes like "Jesus the Saviour of the World," "Standing Firm," "Holiness," "The Danger of Compromise" and "The Cost of Discipleship."[9] To illustrate the contextual application we will briefly focus on the studies on healing based on John 5:1–15, and on Christianity and Traditional Religion. The former study was designed to show that Jesus has the power to heal "whoever he chooses." Among the questions asked were: "Did Jesus heal all the people at the pool?," "Was Jesus only concerned for this man's physical health? (see verse 14)." "Why is Jesus more concerned with our spiritual health?" Exodus 20:2–5a was the text for introducing the study on Traditional Religion which was defined as the worship of the Creator through nature and the ancestors. After summarising its world-view and practices, the study proceeded to the biblical teaching on the issue through questions like: "How many gods should we have?" "Should we worship nature? (read Romans 1:19 and 20)." "Can we ask the ancestral spirits to represent us before God? (See 1 Timothy 2:5, also, Hebrews 1:1 and 2)." "In Traditional Religion who is it who communicates with the spirits?" "What does God say in His Word about such people? (Read carefully all these Scriptures: Deuteronomy 18:9–12, Leviticus 19:2, 6, 10 and 31, Isaiah 44:9–20, 47:11–115, Revelation 21:8)." "What will happen to anyone who follows the leading of false prophets, sorcerers, traditional healers, fortune tellers and mediums?" The study emphatically asserted that it is the devil who uses sorcerers etc. to trap people through fear and that Jesus is able to protect the "born again" Christian. It then encouraged the users to confess and renounce any connection with Traditional Religion.

The Scripture Union Pilgrims are mostly working class adults and their programmes exhibit more political and economic consciousness. In the group at Ile-Ife with which I am acquainted it is the policy to pray for Nigeria and its rulers at the weekly Wednesday prayer meeting. Then, every October 1st—or there about—when the nation

---

[8] I have made my own free translation of the comments in *Bibeli Ajumoka* 1997 from Yoruba to English.

[9] Scripture Union (Nigeria) *"Bible Study Outlines for School Groups"* (Ibadan, Scripture Union Press and Books Ltd.).

celebrates its Independence Anniversary, a special prayer meeting is organised for the nation. In preparing the minds of members for prayer at such meetings the use of Scripture is exhibited. Psalm 94 was so used at a Wednesday meeting in June 1997. God was portrayed as the God of vengeance and the Judge of all the earth who has the power to eliminate wicked rulers at his own time: "Can wicked rulers be allied with thee, who frame mischief by statute? They band together against the life of the righteous and condemn the innocent to death.... (The LORD) will bring back on them their iniquity and wipe them out for their wickedness...." (Psalm 94:20–23 RSV). However, it was stressed that God can make a wicked ruler do his will because "the king's heart is like a stream of water in the hand of the LORD" and he turns it wherever he wills (Proverbs 21:1). At an October 1 prayer meeting (1992), Isaiah 45:1–4 (the Cyrus model) was used to show that God can appoint an unbeliever to rule according to his will.

Scripture Union members are political pacifists who believe in peaceful change through prayer and nonviolent action. They believe in leadership by example and Scripture is used to emphasize this. For example at the twentieth national conference held at Akure, August 8–13, 1992 in which the book of Nehemiah was studied, some of the observations and questions for discussion included the following: "At the end of twelve years of faithful governance Nehemiah declared his assets (Nehemiah 5:14–16). What risks did he face as governor? (Verse 15). Discuss the lessons a Christian governor, commissioner or civil servant in Nigeria can draw from this."[10] Holiday conferences, and group Bible studies of this nature are time-honoured aspects of Scripture Union life in Nigeria. The number of people in a Bible study group at such a conference is around twelve on the average and the groups can be found scattered in classrooms, halls, verandas, under the shade of trees or just in the open and everybody is encouraged to participate through questions, answers, and comments. In addition, there is usually the general question time at conferences when a panel would give answers to the burning questions (usually anonymous) of participants ranging from sex and marriage to ancestral rites and cults. The primary concern is to give balanced biblical answers and to make people think for themselves.

---

[10] Programme of the 20th Scripture Union National Conference at Akure, Nigeria, page 21. I am grateful to Mrs. Elizabeth Nkwoka for this and other Scripture Union Study Programmes.

This concern for balance was also observed in Scripture Union Ghana in December 1996. Rev. S.Y. Kwami, a key member of the Union, asserted that on any biblical matter the watchword should be balance because "balance is the rudder of life." According to him, "Those who go to extremes will soon be lost on the high seas of heresy" (Kwami 1994: 7). The Healing and Deliverance workshop held at Aburi from the 26th to the 31st of December proved to be a useful avenue for testing this out. In the Chairman's opening address his concern for spiritual well-being in the context of his hearers was immediately apparent in his use of Scripture. He read Isaiah 9:2 which says that the people "who walked in darkness have seen a great light" and Psalm 103:1–5 which praises God "who forgives all your iniquity, who heals all your diseases," etc. According to him, for anyone to still be in any form of "ancestral bondage" was to be in darkness. God was able to deliver all such people, and above all to save them from sin. This focus on ultimate salvation without over-looking a perceived religious plight was an act of balancing. The workshop was a fasting conference, *mutatis mutandis*, at which "refresh-ment" of plain pap was served at sunset. The programme of the four full days, that is, 27th to 30th December, followed the same pattern of early morning group devotion followed by personal devo-tion and cleaning up, after which there was Bible exposition, then a talk entitled "The School of Prayer," and then "The Theme Address" followed by another talk tagged "Deliverance Procedure." Of course, there were short breaks in between. After the afternoon rest, people went for Bible study in their various groups. The evening after "refreshment" was devoted to loud, intensive and, at times, tearful and emotional prayers, enthusiastic singing and the giving of testimonies which included delving into the "Deliverance Archives," that is, accounts of past deliverance. The workshop theme was "The Kingdom of God is Power." Details of the events are not possible in this essay, however, summaries which highlight the manner which Scripture was used shall be attempted.

The main focus of the workshop was spiritual warfare in line with its theme, and concepts like power, provision, protection, success, destruction (of enemy forces) and such like were significant *leitmotifs*. At the first corporate devotion, Psalm 105 especially verses 14, 15 and 37 were used for admonition: "He allowed no one to oppress them, he rebuked kings on their account, saying 'Touch not my

anointed ones, do my prophets no harm!'.... Then he led forth
Israel with silver and gold, and there was none among his tribes
who stumbled" (RSV).[11] But how the fact of Israel going forth with
"silver and gold," was to work out in practice in the lives of the
hearers was not specified. Which "Egyptians" were they to "despoil"?
Were they just to pray and wait for God's miracle of prosperity?
However, another Ghanaian Scripture Union member attempted a
balancing act in dealing with the issue: "You will never prosper by
sitting down and expecting God to prosper you. You have to play
your part . . . obedience and hard work plus God's guidance and
blessing give prosperity" (Kwami 1994: 6). The following morning,
Canon Koomson used Isaiah 40:25-31 to emphasize "waiting on the
Lord" for the renewal of strength, but this has to be through confession and repentance, humility and total commitment to obedience.
For the last corporate devotion Psalms 111, 113 and 115 were used.
In the exposition the sovereignty of God was recognized and therefore, God was free to do "whatever he pleases." At the same time
he is gracious and covenant-keeping. He alone must be worshipped-
not idols—and as we do so he will give us and our children "increase."
This "increase" includes deliverance from poverty and barrenness
(Psalm 113:7-9).

   The first Bible exposition centred on 1 Corinthian 4:20: "For the
Kingdom of God does not consist in talk but in power." The cross-
references included 1 Corinthians 2:4-5, 1 Thessalonians 1:5 and
Romans 15:19. This was where the discipline of prayer was crucial,
for without it, according to the speaker, the Christian would be powerless. Another exposition considered Proverbs 18:10: "The name of
the LORD is a strong tower, the righteous runs into it and is safe."
The speaker pointed out that a tower was built of stones and mor-
tar and that it symbolized strength and safety. According to him,
the name of the LORD was stronger than any human name and
that Jesus has been given a name which is above all names and as
long as Christians remain in him, they will be safe and victorious.
S.Y. Kwami's "School of Prayer" presentations were no less forth-
right in the theology of power. He began the first talk rhetorically:
"Did Jesus come only to save us?" he asked. In his view Jesus came

---

[11] The biblical expositor, the Rev. Kwabena Owusu-Amoah had used the King
James Version which says, "no feeble one among them" (Psalm 105:37).

to do more than that: in addition, he came to destroy the works of the devil and to establish the Kingdom of God on earth. His proof texts were 1 John 3:5–8 and Luke 11:20 among others. For the believers to effectively accomplish Christ's purpose on earth they must "put on the whole armour of God," and emphasise prayer and the study of the Word of God, which is the Sword of the Spirit (Ephesians 6:10–18). As a soldier of Christ, the believer must be fully surrendered to his Master whatever the cost, manifesting not only the moral and spiritual qualities of the Holy Spirit (Galatians 5:22–23) but also the dynamic gifts spelt out in 1 Corinthians 12:4–11. According to him, the Christian must walk and work in "revelation knowledge" but which must accord with the written Word. The Christian who prays and expects to be heard must be forgiving (Mark 11:25), must not regard iniquity in his heart (Psalm 68:18), must pray according to the will of God (1 John 5:14–15), must cultivate good human relations (1 Peter 3:7, Matthew 5:23–24, Colossians 3:18–4:2), must not be involved in idolatry (Ezekiel 14, 3, Exodus 20:3, 1 Samuel 15:23, Colossians 3:5) and finally must not be proud (Luke 18:10–14, 1 Peter 5:5–6) or double minded (James 1:6–8).

Significantly, Kwami's second "School of Prayer" talk was again on Ephesians 6:10–18. The focus this time was on "all kinds of prayer and requests" (verse 18).[12] In his view, our spoken words could be prayers, even if we did not so intend, citing Mark 11:23: ". . . whoever says to this mountain, be taken up and cast into the sea, and does not doubt in his heart, but believes that what he says will come to pass, it will be done for him." The emphasis here is on what the believer "says" because the power of life and death is in the tongue and he could be trapped by what he has said (Proverbs 18:21 and 6:2). An example he gave was of a student who out of fear confesses that he would not pass his examination. In his view he would likely fail because he has confessed negatively. This is problematic because a lazy student would likely fail, no matter how positively he confessed and the one who out of fear worked hard might pass even if he confessed negatively. However, it was good that he encouraged a positive attitude to life. His last presentation in the series was on the need for travailing prayers for the lost and for ethnic reconciliation in Africa until the answer is received. He *inter alia*

---

[12] S.Y. Kwami (1992: 22–165) identified fifteen kinds of prayer.

cited the teachings of Jesus on persistency in prayer and reconciliation (Luke 11:4–13, Matthew 5:23). However, Genesis 33:4 in which
"Esau ran to meet Jacob and embraced him" was vested with symbolic and dramatic significance because he called out an elderly man
from the Ewe ethnic group as well as from the Ashanti, and then
asked them to embrace and pray for each other as Christians. He
did the same thing with the women. These two groups are said to
be age long rivals in Ghana and would never normally belong to
the same political camp. The occasion was very moving for these
Ghanaian Scripture Union members. They pledged to carry it through
to the political arena.

As with the "School of Prayer," all the theme addresses were given
by one person, Dr. Seth Ablorh. He asserted that the plan and purpose of God concerning the gospel is that its preaching should be
with power. Among his references was 1 Corinthians 2:4: "and my
speech and my message were not plausible words of the wisdom of
men but in the power of God." The Christian then needed to put
on "the whole armour of God" as defined in Ephesians 6:11–18
because he is engaged in spiritual warfare. The purpose was for
"effective evangelism." His text for the following day was Luke 1:35:
"the power of the Most High will overshadow you. . . ." He proceeded to say that though the birth of Jesus was different from those
of other people, according to the text, he still needed the power of
that same Spirit that caused the incarnation as indicated in Luke
4:11 and 13. If so, the believer needed this power too, but he would
need to live a holy life to exercise this power like the early apostles.
He pointed out in his last address that the primary task of the Holy
Spirit is to reveal sin so that people might repent (John 16:8–9).
The miracles which God performed through the apostles were for
this purpose and were not ends in themselves.

The talks on "Deliverance Procedure" were far from being methodological as the title may suggest.[13] In his first presentation the burden of S.Y. Kwami, the speaker, was to challenge his hearers to get
involved by becoming "prayer warriors" and putting on the whole
armour of God according to Ephesians 6:11–18. He reinforced his
challenge by using the imagery of the "battle axe" (Jeremiah 51:20)
which speaks of God's purpose for his people Israel in relation to

---

[13] S.Y. Kwami (1993: 1–33) has written a booklet entitled *Deliverance Procedure*
which he advised his hearers to read.

the nations. Jesus has committed the task of completing the destruction of the works of the devil to the Church. According to him, the
devil and his demons are spiritual realities "whether we like it or
not." He then added, "allow us to preach our African thing." In a
subsequent presentation, he underscored the importance of the Deliverance Ministry by asserting that whereas it took "fourteen years"
in those days for a foreign missionary to make one covert, it would
now take a week for an evangelist who is involved in deliverance to
assemble a congregation of one hundred worshippers. Using Exodus
20:5 as his text, he contended that African Christians especially
needed to renounce and make a clean break with ancestral idolatry
without which they would continue to suffer from demonic oppression
or attacks. This raises the question whether a Christian can be a
victim of demonic oppression or attacks. Some people have reservations
but from his own experience Christopher Neil-Smith (1974: 46-51)
asserts that conversion alone is no protection and therefore that
Christians are not exempt from such attacks. If this is granted, then
exorcism assumes importance and relevance. According to Kwami
in his talk, the Deliverance Ministry cannot be thrown out of the
Church because salvation, healing and deliverance are linked. In his
last talk, he observed that it was not only demons that people needed
deliverance from but also from "worldliness"—the lust of the eyes,
the lust of the flesh, the pride of life, immodest dressing, etc. His
texts included 1 John 2:15-17, 1 Timothy 2:9-10 and 1 Peter 3:3-6.

The group Bible studies were replete with Scriptural passages
details of which need not detain us other than to make a few remarks.
It was perhaps significant that the first study was based on Daniel
chapter 6 which talks of Daniel's commitment to his God even in
the face of death. Others came from the booklet "*Deliverance Workshop
Study Outline*" treating topics like: how people come under demonic
influence, how both the Church and minister should prepare for
deliverance and how to handle deliverance cases. It was emphasized
that deliverance was to be exercised "in conjunction with evangelism and healing" and not in isolation with the examples of Philip
and Paul cited in support (Acts 8:4-8, 16:16-34, 19:11-20). In one
of the testimony and Deliverance Archives' nights, Jeremiah 50:33-34
formed the basis of an exhortation which preceded the testimony
about a woman who was allegedly delivered from frequent miscar-
riages. The passage says: "The people of Israel are oppressed and
the people of Judah with them, all who took them captive have held

them fast, they refuse to let them go. But their Redeemer is strong. . . . He will surely plead their cause. . . ." This was supported by Isaiah 49:24–25 which says: "I will contend with those who contend with you and your children I will save."

It is doubtful whether Scripture Union Ghana can seriously be accused of a purely eudaemonistic use of Scripture in view of what happened at the Deliverance Workshop. It seemed to me that they were eager to preserve the sovereignty of God and to emphasize repentance, humility, holiness and unreserved commitment to God, let come what may. Though theirs may be regarded as a theology of power, the dimension of *theologia crucis* cannot be said to be absent. Their aim was to deal with concrete human predicaments and aspirations in a balanced biblical manner. Though Scripture Union Nigeria, to the best of my knowledge, does not organise annual workshops specifically for deliverance as their Ghanaian counterparts, they are also concerned with these matters. In every holiday conference they always provide time on the timetable for "ministrations" which deal with healing, deliverance, the baptism with the Holy Spirit, etc.

Since Scripture Union Nigeria and Scripture Union Ghana are run by human beings they cannot but be with their own flaws. However, I have attempted to show in this essay that they, on the whole, have attempted to maintain Scripture balance, though certain individuals might occasionally overemphasise certain issues. In their contextual use of Scripture they strive to be truly African and truly Orthodox. Of them the words of John Laird of Scripture Union Britain seem appropriate.

> We have so far, in the mercy of God, been preserved from heresies, strange notions and unbalanced doctrinal excesses or aberrations. I sometimes think that the reason for this may be that as a movement, council members, staff members and voluntary workers we all follow, or are supposed to follow, the practice of daily Bible reading, not of a few favourite passages selected at random, but systematically throughout both Old and New Testaments. It is this balanced reading of the Scriptures day by day which, I believe keeps our movement on the right lines, following the paths of wisdom and truth, at least in some measure (Sylvester 1984: 247).

There is, however, the need for Scripture Union in Nigeria and Ghana—as elsewhere—to constantly and consciously strive for a more informed interpretation of the Scriptures based on the Union's hermeneutical principles.

BIBLIOGRAPHY

Bibeli Ajumoka. Ibadan: Scripture Union Nigeria, Press and Books Ltd., 1997.
Daily Guide. Nairobi: Scripture Union of Kenya, 1998.
Eni, Emmanuel. *Deliverance from the Powers of Darkness.* Ibadan and Nairobi: Scripture Union, 1987.
Isaacson, Alan. *Deeper Life.* London: Hodder and Stoughton, 1990.
Kwami, S.Y. *Deliverance Procedure.* Accra: SonLife Printing Press and Services, 1993.
———. *Prayer in the Life of the Believer.* Accra: SonLife Printing Press and Services, 1992.
———. *Prevailing Prayer.* Accra: SonLife Printing Press and Services, 1994.
Makhubu, Paul. *Who Are The Independent Churches?* Johannesburg: Skotaville, 1988.
Neil-Smith, Christopher. *The Exorcist and the Possessed.* St. Ives, Cornwall: James Pike Ltd, 1974.
Scripture Union Prayer Warrior Ministry. *Deliverance Workshop Study Outline.* Accra: SonLife Printing Press and Service.
Turner, H.W. *Religious Innovation in Africa: Collected Essays on New Religious Movements.* Boston, Massachusetts, 1979.

THE VERNACULARIZATION OF SCRIPTURE AND AFRICAN BELIEFS: THE STORY OF THE GERASENE DEMONIAC AMONG THE EWE OF WEST AFRICA

Solomon K. Avotri

The purpose of this essay is to explore what has been happening along the frontier between the gospel and African beliefs among the Ewe of West Africa, arising from Western missionary evangelism in the region. First, we must delimit the scope of what we have described as "frontier." The scope of our study primarily includes the activities relating to the Vernacularization of Scripture and its impact on African beliefs in Eweland. This is in an attempt to discover ways in which Vernacularization of Scripture has helped to incarnate biblical portrayals of reality into an African (Ewe) culture, and the extent to which these perceptions have impacted African perceptions of reality. For further resources we shall draw on insights of scholars from other parts of Africa.

The field of African beliefs is a vast one. My first problem is one of selection. I have selected the theme of the "demonic" and its life-destroying powers, an issue which seems to be an area of focus in Mark's gospel and among many Africans. Therefore I will examine the confrontation between Jesus and the demonic powers in Mark's gospel in general, and in the story of the Gerasene demoniac (Mark 5:1–20) in particular. I will then reflect on the relevance of this analysis to a particular group of African readers, the Ewe, in the context of their life-world and culture, by reflecting on their cultural and personal attitudes toward demonic powers.

The Ewe live in southeastern Ghana, known as the Volta Region of Ghana and the southern parts of Benin (formerly Dahomey), and Togo, numbering between four and seven million (Agbodeka 1971: 6). They speak various dialects of Ewe, a language of the Kwa branch of the Niger-Congo family. Although the Ewe territory in Ghana extends inland only up to the town of Hohoe, Ewe speakers can be found in all parts of Ghana as traders, fishermen, teachers, civil servants, and so on (Asimpi 1996: 25). The unity of the Ewe is based on language and common traditions of origin, the original homeland being traced to Oyo in Western Nigeria. The religion of the Ewe is organized around a creator god *Mawu* (called *Nana Bluku* by the Fon of Benin), and numerous lesser gods.[1] There is also belief in the supernatural powers of ancestral spirits to aid or harm their descendants. The name *Mawu* for the Supreme Being comes from *wu*, "to spread," "to cover"; it is also used to designate the firmament and the rain (Eliade 1958: 45).

Eweland was evangelized by missionaries of the North German Missionary Society who worked closely in collaboration with the Basel Mission. Because the North German Missionary Society had its headquarters in Bremen, it was best known in Eweland as the Bremen Mission (Debrunner 1967: 111). As regards Christian education, the emphasis was on devotional religious education rather than on academic education for theological reflection. The result of this was that the type of seminary training given to Africans in the Basel Mission's Institute in Basel, prior to World War II, "was of a low academic standard and thus the graduates did not command the same respect accorded to University graduates in Europe" (Asimpi 1996: 109, 251). After comparing the missionary educational activities in India and Japan, Asimpi concludes that the low grade missionary education offered to Africans arose out of racist attitudes. He points out the evidence of this argument in a statement made by Freeman: "that in Africa the Bible and the plough go together," a belief which was implemented by the churches (Asimpi 1996: 259).

Wolf was the pioneer missionary to Eweland. He quickly attempted to reduce the Ewe language to written form. But the foundation for standard literary Ewe was laid by J. Bernhard Schlegel, who within two years of his arrival in Eweland in 1854, published a *Key to the Ewe Language* (Asimpi 1996: 152). Diedrich H. Westermann, another Bremen Mission missionary in Eweland from 1900–1907, produced many publications in the Ewe language (Asimpi 1996: 152). All this literary activity was to prepare both indigenous Africans and missionaries for translating the Bible into the Ewe language. Schlegel translated large sections of the Old Testament, and by 1861 the whole Bible. Others followed in Schlegel's steps, and by 1877 the whole New Testament had been translated, and was published in 1913 (Grau 1968: 61).

---

[1] For more information about the Ewe, see the *New Encyclopedia Britannica*. Chicago: Chicago University, 1987. Micropedia vol. 4, 625.

The immediate consequence of the Vernacularization, as Lamin Sanneh has clearly argued, is that "the vernacular ushered in a fundamental religious revolution, with new religious structures coming into being to preside over the changes" (Sanneh 1989: 159). Sanneh further argues that,

> One of the most dramatic changes was undoubtedly the popular, mass participation of Africans in this process. It began to dawn on African populations that the missionary adoption of vernacular categories for the Scriptures was in effect a written sanction for the indigenous religious vocation. The God of the ancestors was accordingly assimilated into the Yahweh of ancient Israel and "the God and Father of our Lord Jesus Christ" (Sanneh 1989: 159–160).

According to Sanneh,

> Vernacular agency became the preponderant medium for the assimilation of Christianity, and although missionaries did not consciously intend to occupy a secondary position, their commitment to translation made that necessary and inevitable. The preexisting vernacular came to exert a preemptive power over the proprietary claims of mission over the gospel, and when missionaries assumed that mission must occur by scriptural translation, they invoked that preemptive power without knowing that it would at the same time minimize their role as external agents (Sanneh 1989: 161–162).

Missionaries to Eweland themselves noted the power that was invoked by scriptural translation when they saw parallels between the history and religious ideas of the Ewe people and those of the people of Israel. For example, J. Spieth (1905: 35) noted similarities between the story of the exodus of the Israelites and the famous story of the exodus of the Ewe from the cruel tyranny of King Agokoli in Notsie (today Nuatja in the Republic of Togo). Hans Debrunner cites from Spieth's work a few lines from the decisive part of the story of deliverance of the Ewe, as found in the tradition of Ho (a town in the Volta Region of Ghana):

> At a certain moment the wall was undermined with a cutlass. Then a chief lifted the cutlass towards the sky and prayed: "God, open Thou the door for us, so that we can get out!" People next pushed with all their force against the mud-wall, and the wall fell (Debrunner 1967: 5).

Debrunner himself, after studying a cluster of villages in Eweland and their strong bond between a single tribal deity (or a clan deity) and the tribe (or the clan), concluded that "This bond is expressed in terms like those used in the covenant between God and his people

Israel in the Old Testament" (Debrunner 1967: 5). The Danish chaplain, Rev. Johannes Rask, of whom Debrunner says, "He lived intensely with the Bible," also pointed to the parallels between African and biblical customs, such as oath-making procedures and birth rites (Debrunner 1967: 53).

This parallelism was greatly enhanced by the process of translation itself. J.G. Christaller was reported to have employed a storytelling method for his translation. He painstakingly told the story of the text in English to his African assistants, and then asked them to retell the story to school children in the vernacular, and each of the assistants then translated the text in writing (Debrunner 1967: 143–144). This practice is particularly suited to the African context where storytelling is widely used for the transmission of tradition.

> We gather together and tell stories of God to calm our terror and hold our hope on high . . . To tell a story of God is to create a world, adapt an attitude, suggest behaviour. In interpreting our traditional stories of God we find out who we are and what we must do. In telling stories of God we ourselves are told (Source Unknown).

By telling biblical stories of God in our own language, we, the Ewe, are recreating our world and ourselves, a process made possible by the Vernacularization of the Bible because of the apparent affinity between indigenous terms and the concepts and the central categories of the Bible. Sanneh elaborates on the significance of this connection: "As long as missionaries were committed to translation, so long would vernacular concepts and usage combine to determine the assimilation of Christianity, including the understanding of God by more inclusive criteria" (Sanneh 1989: 166).

Eugene Nida makes the connection between translation and interpretation. He sees translation as an inter-cultural communication which has implications for exegesis. Translation has the potential of making the text that is being translated come to life in another culture in another time (Nida 1974: 159). For Nida, the interpreter is a cross-cultural or intercultural translator who is responsible for bringing what is foreign and distant into the medium of the audience's idiom (Nida 1974: 6). Louis Stulman suggests that the greatest challenge to the interpreter is to be attentive to the deepest and most profound concerns of the particular target community, to address these focal concerns by engaging the biblical literature in an imaginative, discriminating, and relevant manner, and to be sensitive to the proper "time and season" in the life of the indigenous milieu provided by the community (Stulman 1993: 5). According to Nida and Reyburn, "Too often, translators [and interpreters] work in isolation from the believing community and without sufficient regard for what receptors want or expect or actually comprehend in translation" (Nida and Reyburn 1981: 61). For African interpreters, how to bridge the gap between the community and the interpreter (the intellectual) is a serious question of methodology. One way of addressing this question is the adoption of a thematic approach to biblical interpretation.

In his essay on "The Current State of Biblical Studies in Africa," (Onwu 1985) has outlined the biblical usage within present trends in African theology. Popular themes among African theologians include liberation, salvation, missions, and Christology. His main point is that biblical interpretation in Africa is not merely for the sake of scholarship, but places an emphasis on belief and "a faith in Christ who offers to humanity in his life, words and deeds, a version of a humane society." It is clear, therefore, Onwu continues, why African biblical interpretation concentrates on themes that have relevance "to the African experience and self-understanding." While a thematic study of the Bible is a legitimate approach, John Mbiti complains that African theological reflection on these themes are discussed with too few scriptural references![2]

In their work, John Levison and Priscilla Pope-Levison (1995: 337), pick up on this concern for a closer relationship between the Bible and African theological interpretation by drawing attention to what they call a "hermeneutic of resonance" between the Bible and traditional African culture. Explaining this further, they point out that African theologians discern a "kindred atmosphere" connecting African traditional religion to the Hebrew Bible. The points of connection include, for example, emphasis on the pervasiveness of religion in all activities of life, and the predominance of rites and rituals. Levison and Pope-Levison also find aspects of the New Testament, such as

---

[2] Other African scholars have noted the low level of critical reflection in African biblical interpretation. Abogunrin (1990: 36) has observed missionaries did not bring a critical approach to the Bible to Africa, and still over 90% of theological schools in Africa are still unwilling to expose their students to the critical study of the Bible. Abogunrin attributes this attitude to the similarity between the thought-world of Africa and that of the Bible.

emphasis on community, which resonate with African culture. There is also resonance between figures in African culture who function as mediators and New Testament portraits of Jesus as mediator. While they worry that this type of interpretative approach can surrender the biblical text to the tyranny of contemporary context, this does not need to be so if one does not force a one-to-one correspondence between biblical concepts and African tradition.

A good example of a nuanced and complex exploration of the affinity between indigenous and biblical concepts is the work of Temba Mafico (1995: 331–343) in which, for example, he has demonstrated the close similarity between the *svikiro* ("African spirit medium") and the *sophet* ("the early prophets of Israel"). But of greater relevance to my essay with its focus on the study of the Bible in Eweland is N.K. Dzobo's exposition of his *Melagbe* theology. N.K. Dzobo (1986) has devoted some attention to developing what he calls "affirmative African Christianity" in Eweland. Explaining the relationship between the gospel and culture in his "Melagbe Theology" (*Melagbe* in the Ewe language means "I'm alive"), Dzobo reemphasises the World Council of Churches' statement that "The Gospel message becomes a transforming power within the life of a community when it is expressed within the cultural forms in which the community understands itself" (Dzobo 1986: 2). It could also be added that the cultural forms in which the community understands the world is also very important. Dzobo supports his view by drawing attention to the manner of greeting and personal names among the Ewe people. According to Dzobo, both of these show that Africans are "incurably life-affirming people and thus have a life-affirming culture. . . . To them therefore life is the greatest value as confessed by an *Ewe* personal name—*Agbenyega*, meaning 'life is the greatest value in the world'" (Dzobo 1986: 6). As a member of the Ewe tribe myself, I have no doubt that Dzobo has identified an important point of departure, not only for his theology, but also for a perspective on African biblical interpretation. Jesus himself, as Dzobo acknowledges too, affirms the great value of the abundant life, and in John 10:10 identifies it as one of the reasons for his coming. But in this study our attention is focussed on the negative forces that seek to destroy the abundant life.

Corresponding to the great emphasis on the value of life is the great concern about the life-destroying and life-denying powers of human existence as Africans experience them. J. Ledo (1994: 1) explained that according to African belief, a vital "life force" is given to the human person at conception by God, and it is this life force which animates the physical body. Ledo continues that, "It is believed that this aspect of the human personality can be harmed by spiritual forces, e.g., divinities, witches, and magical powers." These forces, Ledo emphasizes, can "strike violently," which can cause even fatality to the physical body.[3]

According to Asimpi, the most dreaded evil spirits are witches (Asimpi 1996: 37). Asimpi explains further that,

> It is believed that a living human being can go out of the body spiritually to inflict pain or suffering on or even destroy another person. Every effort is made, therefore, to control or drive away the spirits of witches or any other malicious spirits. This can be done by a medicine man or woman, who uses his or her medicine or magic to coerce or [or negotiate] to bring the evil spirit under control (Asimpi 1996: 37).

Max Assimeng has carried out an extensive Ghanaian case study of witchcraft beliefs and practices. He has observed that witchcraft beliefs and practices are part of the religious activities in contemporary West Africa. According to Assimeng,

> The core of witchcraft beliefs is in the search for an extraordinary power that enables a person to regenerate a phenomenon from evil intentions and destruction, or to prevent a phenomenon from falling into the hands of evil and destructive intentions and machinations (Assimeng 1989: 168).

Furthermore, he also points out that witchcraft beliefs and their corresponding response paradigms are manifested usually in specific and concrete crisis situations.

The vital concern in all this is the African's desire to defend his or her health and life and essential and fundamental values of the individual and community against attacks from wherever they may come. This is equally true, at least apparently, of the New Testament world. The violent attacks of demonic powers, and deliverance and restoration of life and health by Jesus, is a dominant theme of Jesus' ministry in Mark's gospel. The significance of this is that Mark, and

---

[3] The former Archbishop of Lusaka (Zambia), Emmanuel Milingo (1984) who had devoted much time in his ministry to the care of members of his diocese who considered themselves struck by evil spirits, has described this African experience in his *The World in Between*.

the other gospel writers, express very clearly an awareness and experience of a spiritual reality similar to those of the Ewe, which, beyond the mythological language, deserves our study. The story of the Gerasene demoniac (Mark 5:1–20) is perhaps our most poignant biblical example.

The word δαιμόνιον, translated as "demon" or "evil spirit," occurs eleven times in Mark's gospel. In Ewe, δαιμόνιον is translated *gbogbo vo*, literally, "evil spirit," or "evil breath." Mark also uses the term "unclean spirits" (πνεῦμα ἀκάθαρτον) as synonymous with δαιμόνιον. For example, in Mark 7:25–26 we read, "But a woman whose little daughter had an unclean spirit (πνεῦμα ἀκάθαρτον), begged him to cast the demon (δαιμόνιον) out of her daughter." The verb δαιμονίζομαι is variously translated: "to be possessed with a demon," "to be cruelly tormented by a demon," "to be a demoniac," and occurs four times in Mark (1:32, 5:15, 16, 18), three of these are found in the story of the Gerasene demoniac.[4] The word is translated by a clause in Ewe: *amesi me gbogbo vo le*, "a person who is inhabited by an evil spirit."

Right from the beginning of the gospel, Mark alternates accounts of Jesus' encounter with demons and healings with the Kingdom of God teachings. When Jesus entered the synagogue at Capernaum, a demon-possessed man or a man with an unclean spirit (ἄνθροπος ἐν πνεύμα ἀκάθαρτι), hearing him preach "with authority," screams as the demon within him recognized what Jesus' activity meant. Jesus forced the demon out, but the demon convulsed the man, cried out with a loud voice, and then departed (Mark 1:23–26). In this first public challenge of the demonic forces to Jesus, Mark shows how Jesus' authority sets him apart as the Son of God (Mark 1:1). All who witnessed this contest were convinced of a new authority in their midst: "What is this? A new Teaching! With authority (ἐξουσίαν) he commands the unclean spirits (πνεύματα ἀκάθαρτα), and they obey him!" (Mark 1:27). Throughout chapter one of the gospel, Jesus "cast out many demons" (δαιμόνια πολλὰ) and would not permit them to speak (Mark 1:34). While proclaiming the message in the synagogues throughout Galilee, he cast out demons (δαιμόνια), and explained to his disciples, "that is what I came to do" (Mark 1:38). Exorcism elements in the first four chapters all point ahead to the exorcism of the Gerasene demoniac in Mark 5.

---

[4] For further study of demonology, see e.g., Unger 1952, Davies 1969, Kelly 1968.

The word is put in Jesus' own mouth, when after casting out a demon at a distance from the daughter of Gentile woman of Syro-Phoenician origin Jesus told her, "the demon has left your daughter" (ἐκ τῆς θυγατρός σου τὸ δαιμόνιον; Mark 7:29). Thus Mark demonstrates not only a belief in the unseen spirit world, but the intrusion of this spirit world into the human world with violent attacks on human beings. But even more important, Mark shows that Jesus and the demonic powers are on a collision course, but there is no doubt in Mark's mind who the winner is in this cosmic contest. After his resurrection, Jesus appeared to Mary Magdalene and cast seven demons (ἕπτα δαιμονία) out of her (Mark 16:9). For Ewe readers, these stories affirm their beliefs in the spirit world. The story of the Gerasene demoniac is the epitome of it all.

The story of the Gerasene demoniac is one of three miracle stories put together by Mark to demonstrate the manifestation of Jesus' divine power. The first of these stories demonstrates his power over the natural elements: Jesus stills a storm on the lake and thereby shows that "even the wind and the sea, obey him (Mark 4:35–41).[5] The third story, which is conflated with a healing story of a woman with a chronic haemorrhage (Mark 5:25–34), demonstrates Jesus' power over death. In this story, Jesus restores a young girl to life (Mark 5:21–24, 35–43). The second story, which is our focus passage (Mark 5:1–20), takes place in Mark's narrative on the evening of the day that Jesus stilled the storm, when they had crossed to the other side of the lake,[6] in the countryside of the Gerasenes. In this story, Mark shows Jesus demonstrating his divine power over the demon spirits. Where in Mark 3:22–30 Jesus talks about casting out demons,[7] Jesus now delivers on that talk.

The city of Gerasa was semi-gentile. The story of the Gerasene demoniac, located spatially outside the city of Gerasa,[8] fits the usual

---

[5] De Mello (1971: 409–418) observes that the storm on the sea was a tremendous effort Satan made to prevent Jesus' arrival at Gerasa.

[6] Achtemeier (1970: 275). "Whatever the origin of this story may have been, there are no clear indications of Markan editorial work in the story as we now have it. . . . In fact, the story is so closely linked with the preceding one (sea journey to opposite shore, 4:35 and 5:1, getting into and out of the boat, 4:36 and 5:2) that they appear to have been linked already in the pre-Markan tradition. Nor are there any obvious points at which Markan style becomes apparent."

[7] For a political reading of Mark's story of Jesus, see e.g. Ched Myers (1988).

[8] The city of Gerasa (modern Jerash) whose inhabitants and country are mentioned in Mark 5:1 (the country of the Gerasenes) is described as a city of the Decapolis in Mark 5:20.

structure of a miracle story: the introduction of the patient, the
description of the ailment, the magic word of healing from Jesus,
the proof of healing, the response of the crowd. Mark describes the
reality of this man's situation in graphic terms (Mark 5:1–5). The
journey through the storm took Jesus (and the disciples) to a place
of tombs and demoniacs outside society's structure, where Mark
demonstrates before our eyes the horror of being attacked by demonic
life-destroying forces. The name of the demoniac is not given to us;
he is only described as "a man" (ἄνθρωπος), identified only in terms
of the forces that have destroyed his life and humanity. Not only is
he possessed with unclean spirits, he has been cast out by his community into the place of the dead—among the tombs.[9] Mark emphasizes the extreme violence of the possessed man:

> No one could restrain him anymore, even with a chain; for he had
> often been restrained with shackles (πέδαις) and chains, but the chains
> he wrenched apart, and the shackles he broke in pieces; and no one
> had the strength to subdue him. Night and day among the tombs and
> on the mountains he was always howling and bruising himself with
> stones (Mark 5:4–5).

This story is also reported by Matthew (8:28–9:1) and Luke (8:26–39).
Matthew says there are two demoniacs (δύο δαιμονιζόμενοι). Luke
agrees with Mark that there was only one and explains that he was
from the city of Gerasa (ἀνήρ τις ἐκ τῆς πόλεως ἔχων δαιμόνια
(Matthew 8:27). The three synoptists however agree that the demo-
niac(s) came out of the tombs to meet Jesus. This man was living
outside the normal human habitation. Matthew says he was so fierce
that no one could pass that way (Matthew 8:28).

The word πέδη, translated "shackles" or "fetters," (Mark 5:4) is
rendered in the Ewe Bible as *kunyowu*, which may be translated as
"death is better." This translation, and Mark's depiction, captures
the condition of the demoniac from the Ewe perspective: they would
prefer to die rather than to be so possessed. Superhuman powers
are here at play, which in Mark's plot, provide a challenge to Jesus
and an opportunity to demonstrate his divine powers.[10] Rudolph

[9] Keenan (1995: 139) informs us that Buddhist texts often speak about medi-
tating among the tombs, beholding decaying corpses to bring home a sense of
human impermanence.

[10] Pesch (1971: 349): "Mark 5:1–20 presents the unsophisticated with preposter-
ous material to feed his credulity and at the same time invites the scorn of the

Pesch's comments on this text, from a historical-critical perspective, offers us a choice between two positions concerning the story of the Gerasene demoniac: first, to share Mark's belief in demons and so attribute to Jesus, the Son of God, authority over Satan, or second, to be critical of biblical belief in demons and dismiss this story as the transference of a popular tale to Jesus. Ewe readers/hearers of the Bible have no difficulty with the first option.

But back to Mark's story. Mark gives an account of the encounter between the demoniac and Jesus. Many details are not provided. We do not know, for example, whether the townsfolk were expecting Jesus' arrival, or how close the graveyard was to the town. Jesus suddenly appears at the shore with his disciples. While he is stepping out of the boat, the demoniac catches a glimpse of him. One might wonder how the demoniac recognized Jesus, but Mark does not dwell on this point either. For Mark it is automatic and axiomatic that the demons recognized him (as the "Son of the Most High God") (Mark 5:7). The demoniac then ran and προσεκύνησεν αὐτῷ; the Ewe translation simply says "he knelt down before him."

Clearly, the confrontation between Jesus and the demoniac had already started before Mark puts words in the demoniac's mouth. Though the demoniac speaks first, we are told, one verse later, that it was indeed Jesus who uttered the opening discourse: Jesus had already told the unclean spirit, "Come out of the man, you unclean spirit." This explains why the response of the demoniac sounds arrogant and confrontational, even ambivalent, beginning with the difficult Greek phrase τί ἐμοὶ καὶ σοί, "what have you to do with me?" (RSV)—in Ewe, "what is the matter between you and me."[11] This is followed by the conjuring formula, ὁρκίζω σε τὸν θεόν, "I adjure you for God's sake, do not torment me." (Mark 5:7)—in Ewe, *Meta Mawu na wò*, literally, "I swear God to you." Was the unclean spirit pleading or fighting? For Legion, Jesus is a tormentor, for the man, he is a liberator. The conflict Jesus is engaged in is both local and

---

sceptic. To the naive it seems a glorious demonstration of Jesus' power over Satan's legions, to the skeptical it comes pretty close to turning Jesus into a miracle monger, duped by or duping the devil, but in any case deceiving his unsuspecting contemporaries."

[11] Sr Vandana (1995: 156–167) draws attention to these same words spoken by Jesus to his mother (John 2:2) and suggests that the expression "seems to draw a line between mother and son." Perhaps here too, Legion wants to draw a line between himself and Jesus.

cosmic. The use of first person singular and plural pronouns interchangeably in the demoniac's response (verse 9) is understood by
some Ewe readers to point to the person of Satan, who stands behind
the various and many evil spirits of witchcraft (De Mello 1971: 416).
Which brings me to my final reflections.

In his comments on this story, Rene Girard suggests that the
unclean spirit tries to negotiate with Jesus, as they do with the local
healers in my context, to be sent into pigs. Girard captures here an
important aspect of demonic presence as it is usually perceived in
Ewe traditional society. According to Girard,

> Traditional cures have real but limited action to the degree that they
> only improve the condition of individual X at the expense of individ-
> ual Y, or vice versa. In the language of demonology, this means that
> the demons of X have left him to take possession of Y. The healers
> modify certain mimetic relationships, but the little manipulations do
> not compromise the balance of the system, which remains unchanged.
> The system remains and should be defined as a system not only of
> men, but of men and their demons (Girard 1990: 94).

The biblical story of the Gerasene demoniac tells our story, but sets
Jesus apart from the local healers, as Girard points out again,

> This traveller is not initiated in any local cult; he is not sent by any-
> one in the community. He does not need to make concessions in order
> for the demons to leave the possessed. The permission he gives them
> to possess the swine has no consequence because it has no lasting
> effect. It is enough for Jesus to appear somewhere to put a stop to
> demons. . . . Demons cannot exist in his presence (Girard 1990: 94–95).

Furthermore, Jesus' question, "What is your name?" forces the demon
to say more about himself, to declare his identity. This is important
too, according to Werner Foerster, and Ewe readers would agree:

> What is at issue is not merely sickness but a destruction and distor-
> tion of the divine likeness of man according to creation. The centre
> of personality, the volition and active ego, is impaired by alien pow-
> ers which seek to ruin the man and sometimes drive him to self-
> destruction (Mark 5:5) (Foerster 1964: 1–20).

The request of the demons to be permitted to enter the pigs, and
Jesus' permission for them to do so, is perplexing to commentators.
One explanation is that Jesus wanted to demonstrate the havoc the
demon spirits could cause if they had full power. Manoel De Mello
(1971: 416) thinks that Jesus accepted the request of the demons in

order to show that evil spirits could enter not only humans, but also animals. In African traditional belief, evil spirits are believed to inhabit animals, sometimes riding on them. Whenever a domestic animal is seen behaving strangely, it is killed in order to drive away the evil spirit believed to be riding on it. But in this story, even entering the pigs did not save the demons; the pigs are just a vehicle for their destruction.

The power of the story and of Jesus is that the former demon-possessed man becomes himself: "And they came to Jesus and saw the man who had been possessed with the demon, the one who had the Legion, sitting, and in his right mind" (Mark 5:15). No longer dehumanized—naked, howling, cutting himself, dominated by alien powers stronger than himself—he is once again a complete human being, a testimony to the transforming power of Jesus. There is striking contrast between the response of the townsmen and that of the man who had been delivered. Father Cyrille Argenti (1971: 402) suggests that the herd of swine may have represented the total fortune of the entire village. They came, perhaps, to protest at what had happened, and to demand compensation. But at the scene they witnessed the transformation of a man who had been the terror of the whole village; so they simply begged (παρακαλεῖν) Jesus to leave their country. The restored man, in contrast, begged (παρακάλει) Jesus that he might continue to be with him (v. 18). Discipleship may not have been the primary motive here! The townsfolk have just lost 2,000 pigs on account of him; how can he return to his former chainers, to the owners of this herd, to angry local healers whose power has been clearly challenged by Jesus, and to family who might be afraid of victimization? It is better to stay with Jesus. Even in Ewe community there is a saying, "Once mentally ill, always mentally ill." There is always a fear of such a person. Jesus however declines the man's request, and commands him to go back to the very people he may be trying to avoid (εἰς τον οἶκον σου, πρὸς τοὺς σοὺς) and to publish the very story that has scared them: God's redemption and mercy through Jesus—restoration from the power of a demon spirit.[12]

---

[12] De Mello (1971: 417) suggests that Jesus did not allow the man to follow him because it would have been rumored that he perished with the swine in the lake (cf. Matthew 28:11–15). The man should remain in the town and continue to witness.

In conclusion, we have noted that there are several features of δαιμόνιον and δαιμονίζομαι ("demon" and "demon-possession") as used in Mark's gospel that resonate with African beliefs in malicious spirits. The story of the Gerasene demoniac is the most poignant example of this. The stories of demon-possession which we read about in Mark's gospel find an approximative expression in everyday life of the Ewe. Supernatural powers and beings and their violent attacks on human life are a living reality in the life of the Ewe. Even if the resonances are only that, resonances and not one-to-one correspondences, something close to biblical concept of demon-possession exists in Ewe culture. The Vernacularization of Scripture gives space to the basic concerns of the Ewe about the life-destroying powers of the unseen world, but at the same time promises the possibility of deliverance, transformation, and restoration by a force more powerful. The question which Zogbo (1990: 194) asks for the Godie culture, is relevant for us Ewe too, namely, "If the miraculous stories concerning Jesus' life are not the most convincing evidence of Christianity, then what is?"

BIBLIOGRAPHY

Abogunrin, S.O. "The Synoptic Gospel Debate: A Reexamination from an African Point of View." In Ed. David L. Dungan *The Interrelations of the Gospels. A Symposium.* Leuven: Leuven University Press, 1990.

Achtemeier, P.J. "Toward the Isolation of pre-Markan Miracle Catenae." *Journal of Biblical Literature* 89 (1970): 265–291.

Agbodeka, Francis. *African Politics and British Policy in the Gold Coast, 1808–1900: A Study in the Forms and Force of Protest.* London: Longman Group Ltd., 1971.

Argenti, Father Cyrille. "A Meditation on Mark 5:1–20." *Ecumenical Review* 23 (1971): 398–408.

Asimpi, Kofi. "European Christian Missions and Race Relations in Ghana: 1826–1970." Boston University: Unpublished Ph.D. Dissertation, 1996.

Assimeng, Max. *Religion and Social Change in West Africa.* Accra, Ghana: Universities Press, 1989.

Debrunner, Hans W. *A History of Christianity in Ghana.* Accra: Waterville Publishing House, 1967.

De Mello, Manoel. "The Gerasene Demoniac. The Power of Jesus Confronts the Power of Satan." *Ecumenical Review* 23 (1971): 409–418.

Dzobo, N.K. "*Melagbe* Theology: A New Perspective on African Christian Theology." Unpublished Paper, 1986.

Eliade, Mircea. *Patterns in Comparative Religion.* Paris: Editions Payot, 1958.

Foerster, Werner. "δαίμων, δαιμόνιον," In Eds Gerhard Kittel and Geoffrey W. Bromiley *Theological Dictionary of the New Testament.* Grand Rapids, Michigan: William B. Eerdmans Publishing Co., 1964.

Girard, Rene. "The Demons of Gerasa." In Eds Robert Detweiler and William G.

Doty. *The Demonic Imagination. Biblical Text and Secular Story*. Atlanta: Scholars Press, 1990.

Grau, Eugene. "Missionary Polices." In Ed. Baeta, C.G. *Prophetism in Ghana: A Study of Some "Spiritual" Churches*. London: SCM Press, Ltd., 1962.

Ledo, J.Y. "Ancestorhood: The Cult of the Living and Living-Dead." Unpublished Paper, 1994.

Levison, John R. and Priscilla Pope-Levison. "Global Perspectives on New Testament Interpretation." In Ed. Joel B. Green *Hearing the New Testament. Strategies for Interpretation*. Grand Rapids, Michigan: William B. Eerdmans Publishing Company, 1995.

Lowry, Eugene L. "Cries from the Graveyard." In Eds Robert Detweiler and William G. Doty. *The Demonic Imagination. Biblical Text and Secular Story*. Atlanta: Scholars Press, 1990.

Mafico, Temba L.J. "Were the 'Judges' of Israel like African Soirit Mediums?" In Ed. Daniel Smith-Christopher *Text & Experience. Toward a Cultural Exegesis of the Bible*. Sheffield: Sheffield Academic Press, 1995.

Nida, Eugene A. *Toward a Science of Translating*. Leiden: E.J. Brill, 1974.

Nida, Eugene A. and William Reyburn. *Meaning Across Cultures*. Maryknoll, N.Y.: Orbis, 1981.

Onwu, N. "The Current State of Biblical Studies in Africa" *Journal of Religious Thought* 41 (1985): 35–46.

Pesch, Rudolf. "The Markan Version of the Healing of the Gerasene Demoniac: Historico-Critical Analysis." *Ecumenical Review* 23 (1971): 349–376.

Sanneh, Lamin. *Translating the Message. The Missionary Impact on Culture*. Maryknoll, New York: Orbis Books, 1989.

Stulman, Louis. "Dynamic Correspondence and Preaching" *Homiletic* 18, (1993): 1–5.

Vandana, Sr. "Water—God's Extravaganza: John 2:2–11." In Ed. R.S. Sugirtharajah. *Voices from the Margin. Interpreting the Bible in the Third World*. Maryknoll, N.Y.: Orbis, 1995.

THE ROLE OF THE BIBLE IN THE IGBO CHRISTIANITY OF NIGERIA

Anthony O. Nkwoka

The Igbo people who constitute one of the three major ethnic groups in Nigeria and inhabit the south-eastern States of Nigeria received Christianity relatively late. The Church Missionary Society's (CMS) Niger Mission of 27th July 1857 led by Revd Samuel Ajayi Crowther marked the beginning of the Christian enterprises in Igboland. In that team was an Igbo ex-slave and catechist, Mr. Simon Jonas (Ross 1960: iii). As stated in another study, the massive embrace of Christianity by the Igbo People and the speedy retreat of the African gods, has remained a puzzle (Nkwoka 1991). Islam, which arrived in Nigeria in the 13th century and spread to the northern and western states, kept knocking unheeded on the tightly closed religious doors of Igboland until Christianity came and met with an open floodgate of acceptance.

Christianity is a religion of the Book in Igboland. Much of Igbo Christianity may be summarised by the phrase "Is it in the Bible?" The first and to date, the only standard Igbo Bible was translated by Archdeacon Thomas J. Dennis between 1913 and 1917. Archdeacon Dennis was an Anglican clergyman and as a result, this Bible was mainly used by Igbo Anglicans. When I was a boy, the Roman Catholics used to taunt us by offering us "*aju*,"[1] to help us carry this Bible on account of its volume (1,075 pages) and also because of the superstition that we would all go blind as non-priests attempting to read what was meant for priests alone. In those days no one might be baptised or confirmed as a young adult without possessing an Igbo Bible and being fluent in reading it. But nowadays all the new denominations from "non-Christian" "messianic, revivalistic, and nativistic" Sabbath Churches (Kalu) to the most vibrant Pentecostal Churches, and in some cases even the Roman Catholics use the Archdeacon Dennis' Igbo Bible.

---

[1] *Aju* is a cushion-like object made from old soft clothes or banana leaves used for carrying loads on the head in Igboland.

So, the monumental translation of Archdeacon Dennis of the Igbo Bible remains unchallenged as the most used and influential translation among the Igbo. The next significant translation of the Bible into Igbo language is the Living Bible Version whose New Testament was produced in 1966 while the whole Bible was published in 1988. Even though it is much cheaper than the Archdeacon Dennis' Version, people still prefer the popular version. The Igbo are a highly literate group in Nigeria, even in English, and consequently English versions are also used by Igbo Christians, especially the King James Version. The King James Version is the standard Bible of Evangelical and Pentecostal Christians. Currently, however, Bibles are difficult to come by due to the economic difficulties facing the country in the wake of military maladministration and corruption. There is presently a dearth of Bibles and many Nigerian Christians especially the Igbo are yearning for the printed Word of God.

In a study of this nature, it is not possible to document all the vital roles of the Bible in the lived experiences of Igbo Christianity. I will therefore reflect on the Bible in the Igbo Church, the use of the Bible in theology, the Bible in Igbo Christian homes, and on the prospects for the 21st century.

To the Igbo, the Bible is a living book, the unique Word of God Almighty, Creator and Controller of the universe. Apart from the fact that it is "*Bible Nso*" (The Holy Bible), it is the Messenger-gift of an awfully holy and all-terrible God and is therefore very different from any other book! An irreverent handling of it is regarded as an insult to God, which no sane person should engage in. The strong affinity between the Igbo and the Hebrew cultures all the more makes the Igbo to feel very much at home with the Bible. Some people have even suggested that the word "Igbo" is a progressive corruption of the word "Hebrew" as they moved further away from the Middle East. The Bible is the basic source of Igbo Christian theology, which is a small branch of African Christian Theology. As Mbiti has rightly identified, there are three main areas in African Christian Theology, consisting of the written, oral and symbolic theology (Mbiti 1986: 46). As he pointed out too, whereas written theology is the privilege of a few educated Christians, oral and symbolic theologies are the product of the masses. In all of these forms the Bible plays a prominent role.

The role of the Bible in the Igbo Church would have been more amazing, had it not been for the religious colonisation of the Bible by the missionaries. The two dominant denominations were the Anglican and Roman Catholic Churches. The Anglican Church encouraged the study of the Bible, but the mission-trained ministers had absolute control over the Scriptures and their interpretations were final. In the Roman Catholic Church, things were much worse with the Bible. Only the Reverend Fathers could read and interpret the Bible, which was available in Latin among the priests. So, the Protestant Igbo read the Bible with intimidated interpretation and the Roman Catholic Igbo had little or no access at all.

Nigeria's national independence in 1960 and the rise of cultural nationalism removed the colonial restraints. The white Protestant missionaries were forced to relinquish key Church positions to Nigerians and the Roman Catholic Church "embarked upon large scale training of indigenous staff and other indigenisation projects" (Kalu: 5). In 1966, the Scripture Union that had been promoting Bible reading, in some Protestant Churches, and organising Bible Clubs for secondary school students, granted autonomy to the Nigerian Chapter. The Scripture Union (Nigeria) immediately introduced Pilgrim Groups in towns and Christian Unions in higher institutions. Fortunately or unfortunately, that was the year that the pogrom against the Igbo people was executed in Nigeria as a result of the ethno-military politics of post independent Nigeria. Consequently, Colonel Chukwuemeka Odumegwu Ojukwu declared independence for the Igbo dominated Republic of Biafra, a move that occasioned the three-year Nigerian Civil War. The threat of the late Sir Ahmadu Bello, the last Premier of Northern Nigeria, to dip the Quran into the Atlantic Ocean, together with the boast of the Military Governor of the then Northern Provinces, Colonel Usman Katsina, to crush Biafra within forty-eight hours if permitted by the Federal authorities, caused great concern to the Igbo people. They were somehow given to understand that the Nigeria-Biafra War was not just a war of political, but also religious and ethnic, survival. Their only hope of survival against overwhelming odds rested in the God of the Bible, and so the Igbo read the Bible and prayed as they had never done before.

Waning missionary control and the war were two of the factors, among others, that led to greater autonomy in Igbo Bible reading. The advent of Igbo reading and understanding of the Bible gave rise to early schismatic movements in the Igbo Church. The coming of the new missionary groups from America like the Assemblies of God, The Apostolic Faith and Seventh Day Adventists as well as the startling emergence of the Yoruba indigenous Aladura Churches in the 1930s provided better opportunities for the Igbo Christian to form their own understandings of the Bible. But some colonial restrictions remain. The centrality and local control of the Bible in Igbo Christianity has given rise to many changes in Igbo Church life, some of which I will discuss in the following pages. I will only highlight some outstanding ones, as pointers to the comprehensive nature of the Bible's influence in Igbo Christianity.

One of the foremost roles of the Bible in Igbo Christianity is the charismatic renewal, which in simple language was the rediscovery of New Testament Christianity. The widely circulated and used Scripture Union Bible reading cards in Protestant Churches had inculcated the culture of Bible reading among Protestant Igbo members (see the essay by Igenoza in this volume). The strong emergence of the "born again" Christians of the Scripture Union ignited new understanding of the Bible. The *Daily Power* reading notes for young people introduced in 1963 and the *Daily Guide* with its Igbo equivalent called "*Inye-aka*" ("Help") for adults and families became very popular. Closely associated with the charismatic renewal is the issue of Church growth and Church planting. The Scripture Union members spearheaded an all-out evangelisation through person-to-person witnessing wherever they went, through house-to-house preaching and tract distribution, vibrant Sunday fellowship, open air preaching and guest services. They were ready to make whatever sacrifices were necessary in the form of money, resources or time in facilitating the Gospel. Consequently, many Churches were growing fast with young and energetic members itching for action. Some Churches were however taken by surprise and die-hard conservatives interpreted the upsurge of youthful members as foreign sponsored invaders specially paid to disorganise the Church. Some of the new Christians were physically assaulted and subjected to all kinds of persecutions and suspicions. A spate of expulsions and excommunications from mainline Churches gave rise to new Pentecostal Churches, some of which began as Gospel "ministries" but which were then forced by circumstances to become Churches. These new Pentecostal Churches stormed the society with the Gospel message opening branches in rural and urban centres and absorbing the "outcasts" from the mainline Churches and converting others from nominal Christianity to regenerated and committed faith in Christ. Many Charismatic Igbo Christians became founders and leaders of new denominations.

The role of the Bible in these Churches cannot be over-empha-
sised. Certain days in the week are devoted to Bible teaching, then
there are also the Bible lessons of every Sunday morning, including
Sunday school and Sunday sermons. With respect to the latter, there
are usually no fewer than ten Bible references for a single sermon.
Prayers are based on the exposition of certain Bible passages while
relevant passages must punctuate the prayers to tell God why He
should answer a particular request. No special offering is taken without the exposition of a Bible passage to show the participants why
they must give and that overflowing blessings await them from God.

The loss of members and the doggedness of some Charismatics
of the mainline Churches has forced these Churches not only to
accommodate changes but also to allow Gospel groups to exist as
societies in their Churches. The Anglicans welcomed the Evangelical
Fellowship in the Anglican Communion (EFAC) introduced from
Britain in 1978. But even till today, EFAC is a banned society in
about three Dioceses in Igboland. Roman Catholics also participated
in the Catholic Charismatic Renewal, but when some of them could
not find Mariology, Purgatory and some other Roman Catholic doctrines in the Bible, they began to kick against such doctrines. They
were eventually expelled as rebels. But determined to remain "Catholic
Christians," they formed the Catholic Charismatic Movement with
branches in many places.

The one discovery (or recovery) from the Bible that seems to have
towered above any other in these new Christian movements in
Igboland is the central place of healing in the Bible. The promises
of God to Israel, such as those recorded in Exodus 15:26, Deuteronomy
7:15 and Jeremiah 30:17, are regarded as the direct inheritance of
anyone who has received salvation in Christ. The ministry of Jesus
as a healer and exorcist confirms these Old Testament promises of
healing, affirming that good health is actually "children's bread" as
Jesus was reported to have told the Syro-Phoenician woman. Isaiah's
prophecy, quoted by the writer of 1 Peter in 2:24 and interpreted
Christologically, that by the stripes of Jesus we (Christians) are healed,
is seen to have settled it all. It is popularly believed in Igboland,
and Africa in general, on the basis of the Bible and African Traditional
Religion, that diseases and serious sicknesses have supernatural causes.
In African Traditional Religion, the disease or sickness receives healing when the particular god is appeased or the malignant spirit is
driven away by a more powerful spirit or god whose services are
enlisted through the prescribed sacrifices. From a biblical perspec-

tive, diseases and sicknesses vanish when Jesus casts out the spirit of infirmity or forgives the sins of the patient. Combining the two ideas, Jesus is seen in the New Testament not only as the Creator of all the spiritual forces (see John 1:3; Colossians 1:16), but the One at whose Name "every knee must bow" in obedience according to Philippians 2:9–11. Requisite confession of sins is very important in obtaining God's mercy and once this is properly done, the Name of Jesus is invoked in the power of the Holy Spirit in driving out the spirit of infirmity.

Faith healing is an incontrovertible aspect of Igbo Christianity. The faith healers believe that they do not possess any magical or healing powers. They are commissioned by Jesus Christ who Himself does the healing. Therefore, strong faith in Jesus Christ is emphasised, and so in many cases the patient must first be "born again" and promise to continue in the faith after the healing. Dedicated members of and office-bearers in mainline Churches have on occasions been forced by the need for healing to change their allegiance to either Pentecostal or African Independent Churches. It has become axiomatic that a God who cannot heal or cares nothing about the health of the adherents is not the God of the Bible. The grossly inadequate healthcare delivery in Nigeria and the reality of a myriad of spiritual forces manifesting themselves in mental disorders, *ogbanje* (those born-to-die), witches/wizards, ancestral and mermaid spirits, secret cults and so on are potent factors that give divine healing a priority.

Lively worship is another new discovery from the Bible. The confirmation of some worship practices of the Africa Independent Churches has been one of the strong factors that have brought the youth back to the Church. The Roman Catholic and the main Protestant Churches in Igboland inherited organ music and solemnity of worship, and people had few occasions in the year, like the harvest thanksgiving service, when they were free to sing indigenous local tunes and dance. The clapping, drumming, and dancing that accompanied singing in the Independent African Churches were initially viewed with suspicion as irreverent and as a paganisation of Christianity by the mission churches, since these were prominent features of the African Traditional Religion. The conservatives were further irked when it was discovered that the American style of worship filtering into Nigeria included guitar and other musical instruments associated with secular music and night clubs. The Bible was used by both those adopting traditional and those taking up modern

Western resources for worship to justify their position. The users of traditional and modern musical instruments claimed that their use in worship is biblical, especially in Yahweh approved worship. This led to a re-reading of the Bible by many. Psalm 150, 47, and 1 Chronicles 25 were frequently cited. When the Igbo Christian youth discovered that boisterous worship with musical instruments, clapping, shouting and dancing is biblical, it produced an electrifying (even literally!) effect on the youth in the Church. Independent Gospel bands such as the Disciples' Band, Jesus Revolution Voices, The Reconcilers Group and Lift Up Jesus Singers were formed and shook the Church. They accepted invitations to such functions as Christian weddings, funerals, Gospel outreaches and interdenominational gatherings. Churches were forced to wake up and liberalise their worship patterns, and before long "Gospel bands" were introduced in many Churches. But this is not to say that pockets of resistance to "this sacrilegious mode of worship" have disappeared.

Another significant role of the Bible in Igbo Christianity is the rediscovery of tithing, which has enriched many Churches and improved the financial bases of others. The Scripture Union popularised that receiving without giving is unbiblical. From Malachi 3:8–10, Hebrews 7:1–10 and Jesus' reference to tithing in Matthew 23:23, it was strongly emphasised that for believers, tithing is a must lest the person is simply robbing God and attracting God's decreed curse (Malachi 3:9). For Charismatic and Pentecostals, tithing became an established practice and a veritable source of revenue generation for their Churches and ministries. Gradually, the eyes of the mainline Churches were opened to the huge amounts of money which their "believing" members pay to para-church groups and Gospel ministries just because they did not practice or encourage tithing. Some of the Charismatic groups grew richer than their mother Churches and could afford to buy vehicles of all types as well as other equipment like public address systems, generators and lighting gadgets for evangelism. After the initial accusations of receiving money from overseas, especially the United States, for clandestine purposes, some of those Churches began to introduce tithing. Members reacted in various ways. Some totally rejected it as a modern money making doctrine, others grudgingly tired to adapt themselves to it, while others still were convinced to give "something sizeable" but by no means a tenth of one's income. Many rich members opted for this third stance.

Hitherto, the proceeds of the annual harvest thanksgiving service and bazaar sales had been the main source of financing many main-line Churches. The Charismatic and the Pentecostals have severely criticised bazaar sales as something similar to the buying and sell-ing in the temple (Mark 11) that evoked Jesus' righteous indigna-tion. The abuses to which the bazaar has been subjected in the quest for more money have worried the average Church member, and so in a protest reaction, some Pentecostal and some Evangelical Churches outlawed the harvest thanksgiving as unchristian. Some mainline Churches have been forced by the consistent pressure from the Charismatic members to ban the bazaar. However, some Churches still stick to the harvest thanksgiving and bazaar for fear that their revenue would be jeopardised if they were abandoned. Increasingly, Churches continue to adopt the tithing system.

Finally, the role of the Bible in Igbo Christianity will not have received a fair treatment without the mentioning of its influence on the Igbo Christian family life. The Igbo, like the other African peo-ples, inherited and cherished a polygynous system of family life. In Charismatic and Pentecostal theologies, polygyny though freely prac-tised by the Jewish patriarchs and kings, is very strongly condemned as man's rebellious invention. The one-man-one-wife doctrine is hinged on certain Scriptures. Genesis 2 is used to make the point that God chose to create only one woman for the man, when polyg-yny may have provided him better company! Further, in Deuteronomy 17:17 the kings of Israel were forbidden by God to multiply wives to themselves so that their hearts would not be turned away form God. Finally, no New Testament Christian said anything against monogyny or in support of polygyny.

Other aspects of the human family that are given strong biblical backing include the stability of marriage, care for family members covering the extended family system, a proper upbringing of chil-dren, unalloyed obedience by children to their parents and elders and the priority of Scripture teaching in the family. Divorce, which was almost impossible in the Igbo culture, was further anathemised from Scriptures such as Malachi 2:16, Matthew 19:3–9 and 1 Corinth-ians 7:10–16. As F.C. Ogbalu stated in his book (Ogbalu 1981), in a traditional Igbo family everybody, right from the father who is the unquestionable head, through to the mother and the children, down to the slave and baby-sitter, knows his or her duties and responsi-bilities. It is the duty of the father to call any delinquent person to order and if it is the father himself who is delinquent, the extended family members, the village or even the town will deal with him. With industrialisation and urbanisation, these structures began to crumble. The back-to-the-Bible revolution in Igboland has be used to restore, in the view of many Igbo, every member of the Christian family to his or her God ordained position. The Christian man is constantly reminded that as the head of his family, loving his wife, caring for his family and raising godly children are not negotiable. In fact, God holds him responsible for all that happens in his family. The wife must submit to her husband and keep the home even if she holds a civil job. The children cannot but obey and honour their parents till they die. The Bible has an important position in the life of the Igbo family, particularly in Charismatic and Pentecostal Churches. There is a strong emphasis on what is called the family altar as well as the quiet time. The family altar involves morning and evening prayers by every family unit, which prayers are preceded by systematic Bible reading and discussion. The quiet time demands that every member find time to be alone with God in Bible reading, meditation and prayers. The Bible is progressively fashioning the family life of Igbo Christianity, assisting it in the ever-increasing spiritual and moral battles of modern civilisation and technological advancement.

The role of the Bible in Igbo Christianity is tremendous. Despite the scarcity of Bibles as earlier mentioned, more and more Igbo Christians are falling in love with the Bible and immersing themselves deep in the religious traditions of the Bible. The Bible is to them a living book of practical realities. The affinity between the Igbo cultural, religious and family life with those of the Hebrews as recorded in the Bible inspires confidence in the God and Father of Jesus as the real God of the African, especially the Igbo, and not the white man's God as painted by white missionaries and so-called cultural revivalists. God is not oblivious of the struggles of the black person, but is concerned with, and can save, heal and miraculously answer prayers.

Archdeacon Dennis' Union Igbo Bible has left an indelible mark on Igbo Christianity. The vernacular version brought a great illumination to the Word of God and offered divine sanction to the cultural, social and religious life of Igbo people. The fragility of life in Bible times, the family solidarity and extended family system, the struggles of the common people like Joseph, Moses, Gideon, Samuel, Saul and many others who attained greatness, the communal character of life and the primary role of agriculture in the occupational disposition of the Hebrews, all go to convince the Igbo that they belong to the biblical world and that the Bible belongs to them.

Despite the political turmoil, economic recession and fears of the unknown that becloud the 21st century in Africa, Nigeria not excepted, the Igbo Christian loudly agrees with the Scripture Union that:

> The best book to read is the Bible!
> The best book to read is the Bible!
> If you read it everyday, it will help you on your way,
> Oh the best book to read is the Bible! (1971: Chorus 176)

BIBLIOGRAPHY

Catholic Charismatic Movement (CCM). *From Mystery Babylon to Christ*, Enugu: Anene Press, 1987.

Kalu, O.U. "Testing the Spirits: A Typology of Christianity in Igboland Revisited, 1890–1990," Unpublished.

Mbiti, J.S. *Bible and Theology in African Christianity*, Nairobi: Oxford University Press, 1986.

Nkwoka, A.O. "Jesus as the Elder Brother (OKPARA): An Igbo Paradigm for Christology in the African Context" *Asia Journal of Theology* 5 (1991): 87–103.

———. "Spirituality and Ministerial Formation in West Africa" *Ministerial Formation* 72, 1996.

Obi, C.A. Ed. *A Hundred Years of the Catholic Church in Eastern Nigeria, 1885–1985*, Onitsha: Africana-FEP Publishers, 1985.

Ogbalu, F.C. *Ndu Ndi Igbo* (The Life of the Igbo), Onitsha: University Publishing, 1981.

Ojo, M.A. "The 1970 Charismatic Renewal in Nigeria" *Thelia* 3 (1990): 4–7.

Ross, P.J. *It Is Marvellous in Our Eyes: C.M.S. Niger Mission Centenary 1857–1957*, Port Harcourt: C.M.S. Press, 1960.

THE USE OF PSALMS IN AFRICAN INDIGENOUS CHURCHES IN NIGERIA[1]

David Tuesday Adamo

Early missionaries, and later the missionary trained indigenous leaders of mainline churches, made us, Nigerian Christians, throw away all our charms, medicines, incantations, forms of divination, sacrifices and other cultural ways of protecting, healing and liberating ourselves from the evil powers that fill Nigerian African life, leaving us only with the Bible. They did not teach us how to use the Bible as a means of protecting, healing, and solving the daily problems of life, but by reading the Bible with our own eyes we have found ways of appropriating it for our context.[2] Gradually, as we recognized the emptiness of their ways, we began asking questions about how to read the Bible with our own eyes, to meet our daily needs as African Christians. The attempt to answer these questions brought about the introduction of various forms of African cultural hermeneutics or vernacular hermeneutics (see Adamo 1999), which make African socio-cultural contexts the subject of interpretation (Ukpong 1995: 5). It means that analysis of the text is done from the perspective of the African world-view and culture (Ukpong 1995: 6). The purpose of this essay is to discuss how African cultural hermeneutics have been used to interpret the book of Psalms in an African context. This essay will illustrate in the most concrete way how African Indigenous Churches, particularly the Aladura Churches among the Yoruba people of Nigeria, have applied vernacular hermeneutics to the book of Psalms.[3]

---

[1] I would like to acknowledge first of all that this essay would have been impossible without the assistance of the Centre for the Study of Christianity in the Non-Western World, New College, University of Edinburgh, Edinburgh, who offered me a research fellowship that enabled me to put these ideas together.

[2] This is not to say that the Christian missionaries have done nothing good for Africa. Despite all the mistakes that Christian missionaries have made, it is an indisputable fact that they have been an immense blessing to Africa in the area of education. They did not only translate the Bible into African languages, they also taught Africans how to read the Bible in their languages and "with their own eyes." This enables African Christians to read the Bible in their own cultural perspective, world view, and life experience (see Ukpong 1995).

[3] The fact that my investigation is done among the Aladura Churches of Nigeria

I have chosen the book of Psalms because of its important place among the Old Testament books of the Bible and among the African Indigenous Churches of Nigeria. It could be argued (Adamo 1999: 69–70) that the book of Psalms has a unique place in the Christian churches and in biblical scholarship, a place that has generated a range of interpretative categories and approaches for understanding the book of Psalms. However, as this essay will show, for the many Africans who were converted to Christianity their context too has made a contribution. The categories and concepts of Euro-American worship and scholarship have not really met the daily needs of Africans who are confronted with what to eat, how to diffuse the power of enemies, diseases, and even death. Nigerian Africans have constantly faced the question of how to use their Christian faith and the Bible as a concrete and effective substitute for the traditional means denied them by the missionaries, and so they have found ways of reading the Psalms for protection against enemies and evil spirits, for healing sicknesses and bringing successes in work, school and business. In so doing the African Indigenous Churches of Nigeria have appropriated the Psalms by classifying them according to their own cultural hermeneutic categories as: protective, curative or therapeutic, and success Psalms. Each type of Psalms, used together with other materials, plays an important part in the life of Nigerian African Indigenous Churches. In the following pages I want to demonstrate an example of such an African cultural hermeneutic appropriation by the Aladura Churches among the Yoruba people of Nigeria.

In Africa, the existence of evil ones and enemies are painfully real. Witches, sorcerers, wizards, evil spirits, and any ill-wisher are a major source of fear and anxiety in African society. Among the Yoruba people of Nigeria there is a firm belief that every person has at least an enemy known as *ota*. The activities of *ota* can bring very painful consequences, such as abnormal behaviour, loss of children, and even death. In order to express the wicked acts of some witches, Primate J.O.S. Ayelabola narrated the following confession of a witch:

> We drink human blood in the day or night;
> We can prevent a sore from healing;

---

does not mean that this method of reading the Bible is limited to Aladura Churches. Many members of the mainline missionary churches in Nigeria have adopted this method and are also patronising prophets of Aladura churches. Some indigenous churches in some other West African countries follow similar interpretative practices.

We can make a person to lose a large sum of money;
We can reduce a great man to nothing;
We can send a small child to heaven suddenly;
We can cause a woman to bear born-to-die children (*abiku*) (Dopamu
1986: 57).

The belief in the existence of the evil ones and enemies is so strong
that nothing happens naturally without some spiritual forces behind
it. Thus, incidents like infant mortality, barenness in women, impotence in men, motor accidents and even dullness in school children
are attributed to evil forces and enemies without hesitation.

Before the advent of Christianity, Africans had cultural ways of
dealing with the problem of enemies and evil ones. There are various techniques of making use of natural materials and potent powerful words of mouth which are put to defensive and offensive use in
dealing with evil ones. One of the Yoruba cultural ways of protection against enemies is the use of imprecatory potent words of mouth
(so-called incantations), called *ogede* in Yoruba. Traditionally, when a
Yoruba identifies an enemy and he or she does not have appropriate
potent words or medicine to deal with an enemy, such a person
consults a traditional healer (*babalawo* or *onisegun* or *oologun* in Yoruba)
who prepares or teaches him or her some potent words or gives a
charm for protection or for attacking the enemy. A good example
of the type of potent words used among the Yoruba to make a sorcerer loose his or her senses is stated below:

Igbagbe se oro ko lewe (3 times)
Igbagbe se afomo ko legbo (3 times)
Igbagbe se Olodumare ko ranti la ese pepeye (3 times)
Njo ti pepeye ba daran egba igbe hoho ni imu bo 'nu
Ki igbagbe se lagbaja omo lagbaja ko Maa wagbo lo
Tori t 'odo ba nsan ki iwo ehin moo

Due to forgetfulness the Oro (cactus) plant has no leaves (3 times)
Due to forgetfulness the *Afomo* (mistletoe) plant has no roots (3 times)
Due to forgetfulness god did not remember to separate the toes of a
duck (3 times)
When the duck is beaten it cries, hoho
May forgetfulness come upon [name the enemy], the son/daughter of
[name the mother]
That he or she may enter into the bush
Because a flowing river does not flow backward (Ademiluka 1990:
71–72).

The above potent words may be repeated two or three times or more, and will make enemies forget all the evil actions planned, against the person reciting them.

Another major way of obtaining protection against enemies in Yoruba society is the use of charms or amulets. Amulets and charms are usually obtained from traditional healers. They are used for diverse purposes, but mainly as protective devices to prevent enemies, witches and wizards, and evil spirits from entering a house and attacking a person. They are prepared with different ingredients according to the purpose of the charm or amulet. For example, a charm for the purpose of hanging on the door frame for protection may be made of "seven leaves of some plants, and seven seeds of alligator pepper." Charms to be tied around one's neck for protection against enemies may require alligator peppers, white and red cola-nuts and the blood of a cockerel. Charms are wrapped with animal skin and sewn round. Others are wrapped inside pieces of cloth or paper and tied with some black and white threads. Some also require the recitation of some potent words and prayer to go along with the charms for their effectiveness (Ademiluka 1991).

Yoruba converts to Christianity were forbidden to practice their cultural ways of protection because these were labelled pagan and abominable to God. But unfortunately the type of Western Christianity brought by the missionaries gave no substitute for protection. When Yoruba men accepted this type of Christianity without arming themselves without potent words, amulets and charms, they were ridiculed by other men and called women. To traditional men, Christianity was an impotent religion. More unfortunate was the fact that the Western Christianity that was introduced to Africans did not reveal the secrets of Western power and knowledge, but instead revealed prejudice and oppression in the missionary support for colonial masters. Yoruba Christians began to feel that there must be more in such a popular Whiteman's religion that missionaries did not want to reveal to them. African Indigenous Christians sought vigorously for that hidden treasure in the missionary religion that was not revealed to them. They sought it in the Bible, using their own cultural interpretative resources. Using Yoruba cultural hermeneutics to interpret the Bible, they found that there was (and is) a secret power in the Bible, especially in the book of Psalms, if it is read and recited at the right time, in the right place and a certain number of times.

They began therefore to use the Bible protectively, therapeutically, and for success to fill the gap left by the Eurocentric Christianity. As Yoruba Christians searched the Bible to find potent words for protection against the perennial problems of witches and all forces of evil, they discovered rich resources in the book of Psalms that resembled the traditional resources they had been forced to abandon. They discovered that the words of certain Psalms are potent and lend themselves to imprecatory use. Christians within the African Indigenous Churches, then, began to classify Psalms according to their usefulness in the practice of daily living in their context.

Psalms 5, 6, 28, 35, 37, 54, 55, 83, 109 are classified as protective Psalms. (Most of these Psalms belong to the scholarly classification of the individual and community lament.) Psalm 55, for example, is regarded as a Psalm for protection; its potency lies in that it lets one's enemies "die by their own evil deeds" (Ogunfuye: 37). This Psalm is to be read with the holy name of God, *Jah*, very often or every day. The belief in God's saving grace is important as one reads this Psalm. One will be protected against the plans of enemies and they will be caught and perish by their own evil deeds. Similarly, Psalm 35 is used as an imprecation to drive away the evil plans of enemies and especially witches and evil men. This Psalm should be read in conjunction with prayers between twelve midnight and three o'clock in the morning, in the open air, while the reader is naked.

As in the Yoruba tradition, Psalms are also made into amulets to be worn around the neck or around the body. Chief J.O. Ogunfuye seems to specialize in the preparation of Psalms into amulets for various usages. For protection against enemies and the evil one, for example, he prescribes Psalm 7. According to him, there are two ways to prepare this Psalm for defending oneself against secret enemies or evil forces that plan to ruin a person. This Psalm can be read with the holy name *Eel Elijon* with special prayer every day (Ogunfuye: 7). An alternative way of using this Psalm is by writing it and its prayer on a pure parchment and putting the amulet in a special consecrated bag kept under one's pillow. The prayer to accompany the Psalm is as follows:

> O merciful Father, Almighty and everlasting King, I beseech Thee in the holy name of *Eel Elijon* to deliver me from all secret enemies and evil spirits that plan my destruction always. Protect me from their onslaught and let their evil forces be turned back upon them. Let their expectation come to naught and let them fail in their bid to injure

me. Let their ways be dark and slippery and let Thy holy angels disperse them so that they may not come nigh unto my dwelling place. Hear my prayer now for the sake of holy *Eel Elijon*. Amen (Ogunfuye: 7).

Protection from evil people and forces is only one area in which the Psalms have proved to be effective. Traditionally, Yoruba society had complex systems for rescuing themselves from diseases and sickness. These included the use of herbs, powerful, mysterious or potent words, animal parts, living and nonliving things, water, fasting, prayers, laying of hands, and other rituals for the restoration of harmony between people and the environment. The use of potent words, together with other elements, for therapeutic purposes, is common among Yoruba indigenous people. These words have to be uttered in a specific place, at specific times and in a specific way for them to be effective. It may also involve ritual performances. So, for example, there are medicines for various illnesses, snake bites, scorpion stings, safe delivery for pregnant women, and sharp memory for students. So, for example, after chewing seven alligator peppers, and then placing one's mouth on the patient's navel, Yoruba's would recite potent words to cure scorpion sting and headache.

But, with the advent of Christianity in Nigeria, the indigenous therapeutic method was considered not only barbaric, but an abomination to Christianity. Surely, it was then argued by Yoruba Christians, the Christian Book must contain something equally potent which could be used for healing. The discovery of Psalm as equally potent as the indigenous words for healing aroused great interest in the book of Psalms. Some Psalms are therefore classified as therapeutic Psalms and the reading of such Psalms are combined with African indigenous methods of healing. Absolute faith in the word of God and in God himself is maintained, but with a combination of herbs, prayer, fasting, and the use of the names of God in the healing process. It is believed that virtually all types of illnesses are curable with the combination of reading Psalms and the use of local Yoruba materials. For example, for a swollen stomach, Psalms 20 and 40 are recommended. These Psalms can be read into a mixture of fried oil, coconut oil, some cow urine and cheer oil. The holy name *Eli Safatan* should be read over it, and it can then be used for drinking and bathing and rubbing over the body (Adegboyejo 1988: 21). J.A. Bolarinwa believes that these Psalms are potent in the curing of toothache, headache and backache. For toothache, these Psalms should be read into lukewarm water and the mouth rinsed with it

until the tumbler is empty (Bolarinwa: 9). The process can be repeated
from time to time.

Chief Ogunfuye recognizes Psalm 6 as the one to relieve a sick
person of pains and worries. This is also good for stomach trouble,
eye trouble or any ailment. The sick person should read the Psalm
in great humility and with special prayer and the mentioning of the
holy names *Jaschaja*, *Bali*, and *Hashina* in mind. According to him,
all worries will be removed. Below is the special prayer to be offered
to accompany this Psalm for effective healing:

> O Lord God and Prince of Peace, I beseech Thee in the name of
> *Jaschaja, Bali, Hashina* to hear me and speedily heal me from this dis-
> eases that troubles me [name the diseases]. Wipe away my tears and
> turn my sorrow into joy. Give unto me Thy wonderful grace to over-
> come all manner of diseases. Restore unto me my former health and
> silence all my adversaries for ever. Forgive me all my sins and sustain
> me with Thy grace all the days of my life. Pour thy blessings upon
> me from above and let my prayers be acceptable in Thy sight so that
> I may glorify thy holy name for ever. Amen (Ogunfuye: 5–6).

These therapeutic Psalms are many and are prescribed according to
the type of illness: Palms for fearfulness (127), chronic diseases (21),
long term pregnancy (27, 28, 29, 16), epilepsy (100, 109, 102) are
examples. It is certain that these methods of reading Psalms therapeutically are shaped by African cultural influences on Nigerian
Christians in the African Indigenous Churches (and even in the mainline churches). The task of classifying the entire Bible to meet the
daily needs of Nigerian indigenous Christians is still ongoing, not
only because modern medicine is not available or may never be
available to all in Nigeria, but also because the Psalms, together with
elements of traditional healing, are effective and Christian.

An examination of the classification of some Psalms into success
Psalms will require some discussion of the use of medicine and potent
words to enhance success in all works of life in Yoruba indigenous
tradition. Success in all works of life is an important aspect of Nigerian
society. Lack of success is viewed with all seriousness, whether it be
success in academic life (especially passing exams), business, a journey, securing love from a woman or man, or success in court cases.
Lack of success in any of these areas is often attributed to enemies
or evil forces and Yoruba indigenous resources for activating or
improving success abound. Medicine for activating or improving
memory, for example, among the Yoruba people of Nigeria is called
Isoye. *Isoye* in Yoruba literally means "quickening the memory or

intelligence" (Ademiluka 1991: 88). It refers to any medicine that can help to quicken memory. Below is an example of such medicine prescribed to one of my former students for success in an examination by a traditional healer:

> A combination of honey, *eeran* leaves, *awerepepe* leaves and one alligator pepper.
> All should be burnt together and mix with honey.
> The client licks from the concoction and spits it into his left palm.

There is a firm assurance that the client will be successful in the examination.

Another important way by which Yoruba people try to bring success to themselves is the use of medicine called *awure* in Yoruba. It literally means the thing that activates success or what uncovers success. The type of medicine that brings good luck may be in the form of potent words, soap, or a mixture of herbs and other ingredients to make a concoction. Whenever an important venture is being embarked upon, there is in Yoruba indigenous tradition a strong sense that enemies, whether human or spirits, may attempt to hinder that venture. Hence, when an important event is planned, like starting a new business, building houses, taking a new wife, looking for a new job or attending an interview, a traditional healer is often consulted to narrow down the chances of failure and increase success.

Here too the Psalms have provided a resource for Christians. Success Psalms are Psalms believed by the Yoruba African Indigenous Churches to have the power to bring success, if used with faith, rituals, prayer and fasting, specific symbols, and a combination of animate or inanimate materials. Christians in Nigeria who are not comfortable with using purely indigenous ways of obtaining success, mostly because of condemnation by Western orthodox Christians and missionaries, have no choice but to find alternative methods of achieving success. They have turned to the Christian Bible, and found in the Psalms equivalent powers, if not greater, than those they had been coerced to discard. For example, for success in examinations or studies, Psalms 4, 8:1–9, 9, 23, 24, 27, 46, 51, 119:9–16, and 134 are commonly identified. Students who want to improve their memory and be sure of success in all their examination should use Psalms 4, with this instruction:

> Cut four candles into three each,
> Light them round and be in the middle of the candles,
> Put some salts under each candle, read Psalm 4 eight times.

Call Holy Name *Alatula Ja Ajarahliah* 72 times.
Pray for success. You will surely pass (Adegboyejo 1988: 23).

As indicated, Psalm 8:1–9 is also recommended for success in examinations (Adegboyejo 1988: 14). In order to sharpen one's memory, Psalms 9, 24, 27, and 46 are recommended by the Prophet Sam Akin Adewole with specific instructions to be followed (Adewole 1991: 45). In another booklet the Prophet Adewole prescribes Psalms 23 and 51 (to be read in conjunction with 1 Kings 3:1–14) for students as *Isoye* for them to be successful in examinations (Adewole 1991a: 24).

Psalm 133 is a Psalm classified as one that will aid one to secure love of a woman or a man. For example, if any man is looking for a girlfriend or a wife and has a history of failure in such endeavours; if a woman is looking for a boyfriend or a husband; if a wife is losing the love of her husband; if a husband is looking for the love of his wife who is on the verge of divorce, he or she should read this Psalm with the following important instruction:

> Draw some water with your mouth into a bottle. Put some water that will fill the bottle into a bowl. Wash your face and armpit seven times in the water in the bowl. Add that water in the bowl to the one in the bottle to fill it up. Then call the name of the woman/man and the name Eve/Adam 21 times. Read Psalms 133, Ruth 1:16–17 and Solomon 3:1–11 and John 1:1–4 into the water at midnight and if the person is known, give the water to her/him to drink (Adegboyejo 1988: 27).

Chief Ogunfuye recommends this same Psalm, Psalm 133, for husband and wife, family, society or church to avoid disharmony (Ogunfuye nd: 88–89).

For success or good-luck in winning court cases, Psalms 13, 35, 46, 51, 77, 83, 87, 91, 110, 121, and 148, with specific instructions are recommended. Adegboyejo recommends other Psalms, with instructions for their use, for victory in a court case:

> One should fast for three or seven days depending on the seriousness of the case before the giving of evidence. Light three white candles. Read at night Psalm 13 seven times, Psalm 51 seven times and Psalm 77 seven times, Psalm 83 seven times, Psalms 110 and 148 seven times. Call the four powerful angels, Holy Michael, Gabriel, Raphael, and Uriel and tell them to come in the name of the Father, Son, and the Holy Spirit. Then call the name of *Jehovah Aturaka-Ja* seven times and mention the case and the day of the case and court in the court. Call this Holy name *Womwomuoba* seven times and tell him to dismiss the case for me in the name of Jesus Christ Our Lord. Amen.

Psalm 4, 108, and 114 are special Psalms for success in any venture one embarks on, such as laying the foundation of a house, promotion in government work, or embarking on a business trip. These Psalms are to be read with prescribed instructions and prayers to accompany them. Chief Ogunfuye also recommends Psalm 4 for success in any business or in any undertaking (Ogunfuye n.d.: 3–4). Ogunfuye also recommends Psalm 114 for success in business of any kind. It should be read from time to time in the morning with the name of *Aha* and *Adonai* in mind.

Psalms, then, are assigned for special purposes, to either cure special types of sickness, for success, or for general or special types of protection. The division of Psalms into types in Yoruba Indigenous Churches is informed mostly by the contents of the Psalms as understood by Yoruba Christians, whether lay, prophets, pastors or evangelists. A close examination of the use of Psalms in Yoruba African Indigenous Churches shows that the use of names is predominant. Some of the names that are recited or invoked are names of God such as *Yahweh, Elohim, Adonai,* names of angels such as Gabriel, Michael, Uriel, and some unknown names such as *Alatulah, Ja, Ajarahlial, Ehala, Selidira, Tabbih, Jaschaja, Bali, Hashina Walola, Asabata Ja,* and *Womwomwoba.* During my visit to some of these indigenous churches, I found that some of the names used are understood to be names of God in Hebrew that describe his activities such as *Jehovah Jireh,*[4] *Jehovah Nissi, Jehovah Shallom, Jehovah Shammah, Jehovah Tsidkenu,*[5] *Jehovah Rophe,*[6] *El Shaddai, Jehovah Mkeddesh, Jehovah Rohi,*[7] *Jehovah Shaphat,*[8] *Jehovah Zadak,*[9] *Jehovah Zabad, Jehovah Emmanuel.* Although some of these names are Hebrew names from the Old Testament, they are not properly

---

[4] The name *Jehovah Jireh* is to be used for special prayer to seek God's favour, by reading Psalm 123.

[5] This name means "God is righteous" and should be used for deliverance when afflicted by principalities and powers. It should be combined with the reading of Psalm 88. The name should be chanted 7 times.

[6] Means "Yahweh heals" (Exodus 15:26) and should be used for sick persons using clear rain water in a calabash with new palm tree leaves that point to the sky and with 7 candles round the calabash.

[7] This name means "God is my shepherd" and to be chanted 7 times with the reading of Psalm 23 for protection.

[8] This name should be chanted 7 times with the reading of Psalm 7 for court cases.

[9] Call this name 7 times for those who hate and oppress you unjustly with the reading of Psalm 12.

spelt or pronounced. This is probably because the users are not literate in biblical Hebrew. However, during my interview with some
of the prophets and apostles of these churches, they claimed that
these names were revealed to them.

To the Yoruba, names are not only symbolic, they represent the
totality of persons and are regard as having special power. Names
are chosen with great care because such names may represent one's
prayer to God, to the divinities, expression of faith in the existence
of *God* (*Orunmbe*), God's goodness (*Chukwu dima*), God's providence
('*Yiopese*), God's love (*Olufemi*).[10] Names may represent the parent's
experience in life or during birth. Most of the time names are not
just given without special meanings. This is also true among the Ibos
of Nigeria.[11] Clearly, in their emphasis on names and the inclusion
of the names of God, angels, and persons in their readings of Psalms,
Nigerian Christians are making effective use of traditional understandings of names and their power. In order to demonstrate the special
power of the names of God and the names in the Bible, evangelists
and prophets recommend the use of these names in conjunction with
the reading of specific Psalms.

Another important element of the use of Psalms is the accompanying traditional medicine. So for example, the use of protection
Psalms with traditional medicine is an important aspect of the prescription for protection. This includes the use of herbs and parts of
living and nonliving things in conjunction with the reading of specific
Psalms, together with the burning of candles, prayers, and recitation
of the names of God a certain number of times. The basis for the
classification of Psalms into protective, therapeutic, and success Psalms
is done according to the traditional Yoruba ways of classifying medicine. Most of the herbs used contain some potent ingredients in
themselves that heal diseases. The use of nonliving ingredients like
sand, stone, and other similar ingredients is a demonstration of faith
in God's power to make these inanimate things potent. It is also a
demonstration of God's power over nature. The reality that all materials, including the Psalms, are potent for healing is the demonstra-

---

[10] Unfortunately, most of the early missionaries to Africa did not care to understand the importance of these African names, but made us change our names at
random. If they had understood these names, I believe that they would have taught
us to choose the equivalent in the Old Testament, particular as there are equivalents in the Old Testament.

[11] For further details about the significance of names consult Agoro 1984.

tion of God's power and mercy. Once they are blessed, God transfers power into anything that the prophets lay their hands on.

I have discussed above the importance of the use of potent words for healing purposes, protection, and success. Since the early missionaries condemned the use of so-called incantations for these purposes, Nigerians who became Christians found an alternative. The most logical place to search for the alternative is the Christian Bible which, they believe, must have potent words for their everyday problems. The books of Psalms resemble African potent words for healing, for protection and success, and they have been appropriated for these purposes and found to be effective. My interviews with practitioners from the Aladura Churches and my personal observation makes it clear that there is no doubt as to the potency of the words of Psalms, if one knows how, when, and where to read them for specific problems.

At a cursory glance, the above approaches to Psalms may be condemned as pagan, magical, and syncretistic, but a critical and contextual examination of the practice will show that it has come about as a result of the fact that Western culture no longer commands awe and admiration, as it used to, and so Nigerian Christians have had to search for a form of Christianity that will deal with both old and new problems. The discussion above is a good example of contextualization at work and an African attempt to make a contribution to Christianity. Nigerian Christians, particularly in the African Indigenous Churches but also in the mainline churches, have taken into consideration their religio-cultural traditions in appropriating and presenting the Bible. Nigerian culture, customs, traditions, arts, metaphors and images are necessary for Nigerian Christians to feel at home with the gospel. Furthermore, Nigerian religio-cultural traditions are closer to biblical culture(s) than Western culture(s), as affirmed by David Garret, "Africanism is not only good in itself, but also a culture closer than European to the biblical way of life, and therefore more suitable for building a Christian society" (Garret 1968: 166).

The African Indigenous Churches in Nigeria that are using this method of appropriating the Psalms are growing significantly more than the mainline missionary churches. Ironically, while the authorities of the mainline churches have condemned these indigenous churches for approaching the Bible this way, many of their members join these churches (either by day or by night). In fact, many outstanding church members of the mainline churches prefer to keep their membership intact with the missionary churches, but frequently visit the pastors and prophets of these African Indigenous Churches. Testimonies of members and non-members who visit these churches either during the night or daytime is powerful evidence of the effectiveness of the use of the Bible in this way.

The type of classification described above is based not only on the contents of the Psalms but also substantially on the function and the efficacy of particular Psalms to protect, heal and obtain success in the African context. The fact is that African Christians, like the Yoruba, do not face the same problems as Western Christians. They need a different hermeneutic that takes into cognizance their cultural traditions and the place of the Bible in the solving of their problems. African Indigenous Christians are not passive receivers of Christianity. They make use of whatever they find useful from Western missionaries and adapt it to suit their world view and needs and in so doing they have made a substantial contribution to the African interpretation of the Bible.

BIBLIOGRAPHY

Adamo, D.T. "African Cultural Hermeneutics." In Ed. R.S. Surigitharajah, *Vernacular Hermeneutics*, Sheffield: Sheffield Academic Press, 1999: 66–90.
Adegboyejo, T.N. *St. Michael Prayer Book.* Lagos: Seye Ade & Sons, 1988.
Ademiluka, Solomon. "The Use of Psalms in Africa Context." Unpublished M.A. Dissertation, University of Ilorin, Ilorin, Nigeria, 1990.
Adewole, S.A. *The Revelation of God for 1992 and the Years Ahead.* Lagos: Sam Adewole, 1991.
———. *Awake Celetians, Satan is Nearer.* Lagos: Celetia Church of Christ Publication, 1991.
Agoro, Roland. *Sixteen Names of God.* Ibadan: Olapade Agoro Investment Co. Ltd., 1984.
Anderson, B.W. *Out of Depths.* Philadelphia: The Westminster Press, 1974.
Barrett, David. *Schism and Renewal.* Oxford: Oxford University Press, 1968.
Bolarinwa, J.A. *Potency and Efficacy of Psalms.* Ibadan: Oluseyi Press.
Dopamu, P.A. *Esu: The Invisible Foe of Man.* Ijebu: Shebiotimo Press, 1986.
Mume, J.O. *Traditional Medicine in Nigeria.* Agbarho: Jom Tradomedical Naturopathic Hospital, 1978.
Ogunfuye, J.O. *The Secrets of the Uses of Psalms.* Ibadan: Ogunfuye Publications.
Ubrurhe, John. "Life and Healing Processes in Urhobo Medicine," *Humanitas* 1 (1994), New Series. Forthcoming.
Ukpong, Justin. "Rereading the Bible with African Eyes," *Journal of Theology for Southern Africa* 91 (1995), 3–14.
Weiser, A. *The Psalms, Old Testament Library.* Translated by Herbert Hartwell. Philadelphia: The Westminster Press, 1962.
West, Gerald. *Biblical Hermeneutics of Liberation-Modes of Reading the Bible in the South African Context.* Pietermaritzburg: Cluster Publications, 1991.

Westermann, C. *Praise and Lament in the Palms*. Translated by K.R. Crim and Richard
   N. Soulen, Atlanta: John Knox Press, 1981.
Yorke, G.L. "Afrocentric Hermeneutics," *Journal of Religion and Theology*, 2:2 (1995):
   145–158.

CURSED BE EVERYONE WHO HANGS ON A TREE: PASTORAL IMPLICATIONS OF DEUTERONOMY 21:22-23 AND GALATIANS 3:13 IN AN AFRICAN CONTEXT

Eliud Wabukala and Grant LeMarquand

Then they came to the tree from which Okonkwo's body was dangling, and they stopped dead.

"Perhaps your men can help us bring him down and bury him," said Obierika.

"We have sent for strangers from another village to do it for us, but they maybe a long time in coming."

The District Commissioner changed instantaneously. The resolute administrator in him gave way to the student of primitive customs. "Why can't you take him down yourselves?" he asked.

"It is against our custom," said one of the men. "It is an abomination for a man to take his own life. It is an offense against the Earth, and the man who commits it will not be buried by his clansmen. His body is evil, and only strangers may touch it. That is why we ask your people to bring him down, because you are strangers."

"Will you bury him like any other man?" asked the Commissioner.

"We cannot bury him. Only strangers can. We shall pay your men to do it. When he has been buried we will then do our duty by him. We shall make sacrifices to cleanse the desecrated land" (Achebe 1962: 146–47).

We begin with the observation that the tradition of a hanged person being cursed and a hanged corpse bringing a curse on the land, is common to the Deuteronomist and to some parts of Africa.[1] This paper will examine two contexts in which this tradition concerning hanging has resulted in theological and pastoral difficulties: the preaching of the cross in early Christianity, and the funeral practice of the Babukusu people of Western Kenya and Eastern Uganda. We shall argue that the Pauline solution to the Jewish Christian dilemma

---

[1] This preliminary observation was first discussed by the authors in a class at St. Paul's United Theological College, early in 1987. The eventual result of that discussion was Eliud Wabukala's B.D. thesis, which Grant LeMarquand supervised (Wabukala 1988).

about the cross as a curse has positive implications also for the pastoral practice of Babukusu Christians.[2]

> When someone is convicted of a crime punishable by death and is
> executed, and you hang him on a tree, his corpse must not remain
> all night upon the tree; you shall bury him that same day, for anyone hung on a tree is under God's curse. *You must* not defile the land
> that the LORD your God is giving you for possession (Deuteronomy
> 21:22–23, NRSV).

Most commentators agree that the hanging to which this text refers
is the act of hanging a corpse on a tree or a post for public display
after the person to be hanged has been executed in some other fashion (see 2 Samuel 4:12, 21:8–9). The Old Testament provides several examples of the display of a corpse as a part of a military
campaign (Joshua 8:29, 10:26–27). The purpose seems to have been
to warn the enemy. The practice appears to be ancient, for the
Deuteronomic text appears to assume its existence, and other peoples besides Israel used the method (1 Samuel 31:10). Grammatically,
however, the Old Testament text can read either "is put to death
and you thereafter hang him on a tree" or "is put to death when
you hang him on a tree" (Elgvin 1997). The latter translation would
sanction hanging as a form of execution. Within post-biblical Judaism
this interpretation of Deuteronomy is confirmed by a number of
texts. The Temple Scroll, probably a composition of the Essene community who composed the Dead Sea Scrolls, reads:

> If a man informs against his people, delivers his people up to a foreign nation and betrays his people, you shall hang him on a tree so
> that he dies. On the word of two or three witnesses shall he be put
> to death, and they shall hang him on a tree. If a man commits a
> crime punishable by death, and he defects into the midst of the nations
> and curses his people, the children of Israel, you shall hang him also
> on the tree so that he dies. And their bodies shall not remain upon
> the tree, but you shall bury them the same day, for those who hang
> on the tree are accursed by God and men, you must not defile the
> land which I give you as an inheritance (Temple Scroll 64: 6–13).

---

[2] As can be seen from the quotation at the head of this article, the idea of a
hanged person being cursed is present also in West African traditions: Chinua
Achebe is a novelist from Nigeria.

Clearly the Essene community, in common with the Old Testament and Judaism, believed that certain crimes were punishable by death. The usual form of execution would have been stoning (Bammel 1970, Pobee 1985). Some offenses, however, here described as "delivering his people up," "betraying his people," "cursing his people" called for a more radical punishment. Having cursed his people, the offender is himself to become cursed by the horrifying execution of hanging. The Essenes understood this form of execution to have been sanctioned by the Deuteronomic text (*4QpNahum*).

It is not clear what the Temple Scroll meant by hanging—impaling and hanging by a rope are possible candidates (Baumgarten 1972). It is more likely, however, that the Scroll's writer is thinking of crucifixion (Yadin 1971, Hengel 1977: 84, Fitzmeyer 1978). Crucifixion appears to have been invented by the Persians (Esther 2:23, 5:14, 7:9, 9:25 may refer to crucifixion). It was employed by Alexander the Great, the Seleucids and by the Romans (Elgvin 1997: 14). According to Martin Hengel, the widespread practice of this sadistic form of punishment was usually reserved for "dangerous criminals and members of the lowest classes" (Hengel 1977: 88) and associated with "political and military punishment" (Hengel 1977: 86). In other words, crucifixion was a punishment for slaves and traitors.

It is likely that the Temple Scroll's sanctioning of hanging for traitorous activities alludes to the possible use of crucifixion for certain capital offenses.[3] Throughout the ancient world the practice of crucifixion was considered a terrifying form of execution. Cicero referred to it as "that plague" (*In Verrem* II.5.162) and argued that even the word "cross" should be far removed from the thoughts, eyes and ears of a Roman citizen (*Pro Rabirio* 16). For Jews the horror of the cross was increased because of its association with Deuteronomy 21:22–23 which lent to crucifixion a taboo religious character.

> . . . for any Jew . . . the cross would be doubly repulsive . . . crucifixion was the most abhorrent of all deaths because of its cruelty and shame, but for the Jew it also involved the curse of the Torah, the curse pronounced on "every one that hangeth on a tree" (Davies 1980: 227).

---

[3] It is not known if the Essenes actually practised hanging or crucifixion. That other Jews did employ the technique is stated by Josephus who reports that Alexander Jannaeus had eight hundred Pharisees crucified (*Jewish War* I 97, 113, *Antiquities* XIII 380). Several traditions report the crucifixion of Jews by the Hellenising high priest Alcimus in 162 BCE (1 Maccabees 7:16, Josephus *Antiquities* XII 396, *Genesis Rabbah* 65:22). The Mishnah reports that Simeon ben Shetah had eighty women hanged in one day (*m. Sanhedrin* 6.4).

The horror associated with crucifixion was also felt in Christian circles: "Christ redeemed us from the curse of the Torah, having become a curse for us—for it is written, 'Cursed by every one who hangs on a tree.'" (Galatians 3:13) By the first century of the common era it is likely that every Jew who witnessed a crucifixion interpreted that hanging in the context of Deuteronomy 21. Indeed, the pre-Christian Paul hearing the story of the cross of Jesus is likely to have thought of Jesus as cursed by God.[4] The very idea of such a one being the Messiah would have been viewed as absurd. The cross was proof of the opposite. Paul's own words, "No one speaking by the Spirit of God ever says 'Jesus is cursed'" (1 Corinthians 12:3), are likely an echo of Paul's own pre-Christian thinking.

It is outside the scope of this paper to enter into a discussion of what happened to Paul to cause his radical change of opinion about the person of Jesus (Stendahl 1976, Kim 1981, Segal 1990, Hurtado 1993). What does concern us is an examination of the way in which the Christian Paul re-conceptualized the "hanging" of Jesus. Paul's solution is radical. Affirming the Old Testament and contemporary Jewish notion that the curse of God attached to a hanged person, Paul affirms that on the cross Christ was in fact cursed. This curse was not, however, the final word for, as Paul says "Christ became a curse *for us*." Those who deserved the curse ("all who do not abide by all things written in the book of the law, and do them," Galatians 3:10) are spared because the Messiah, God's representative, has taken the curse on himself. An "exchange" has taken place (Hooker 1971). Since Christ is the representative of Israel (the "Messiah," "born under Torah," Galatians 4:4; see Donaldson 1986), he is the appropriate candidate to deliver those under the Torah's curse. Christ as the representative is able to take their place and become the place of an exchange. He takes the curse which the Torah-breakers deserve— *for them*. Paul expresses a similar line of thought in 2 Corinthians 5:21: "For our sake he made him to be sin who knew no sin, so that in him we might become the righteousness of God." The logic at work here is the logic of sacrifice, which allows an innocent victim to take the place of the guilty. It is at this point that Paul's logic intersects with the Babukusu context to which we must now turn.

---

[4] It is likely that the language of the cross as a "tree" and, therefore, a place of cursing, had already entered into Christian vocabulary and preaching before Paul; see, for example, Acts 5:30.

The Babukusu are a people who belong to a larger ethnic group known as the Luyia (Makila 1978). The Babukusu probably migrated from the environs of upper Egypt around 900 CE. They settled in the area of Mt. Elgon, near the present border between Uganda and Kenya. In common with many African peoples the Babukusu acknowledge the immanent reality of ancestral spirits (*Basambwa*). Harmful, malevolent spirits can causes disease and misfortune. These are the spirits of those who have been rejected in the spirit world and are left to roam in forests, river banks and valleys. Reasons for rejection in the spirit world include moral failure, such as thievery and murder. The childless and outcast become outcasts in the after-life, just as they were in this life. Also included among malevolent spirits are those who have committed suicide. The spirits of those approved by society are received favourably in the next life. These become ancestors and continue to have a beneficial relationship with the living. They are invoked in prayer and mediate between people and God (*Wele*). The spirits who have died most recently are con-sidered most helpful. Care is taken to ensure that all the necessary after death ritual requirements are fulfilled, in order to facilitate the relative's reception in the afterworld, thus making the ancestor more helpful to the family. The helpfulness of spirits depends on blood relations. It is only the spirit of a relative who can be invoked with effect. The living dead are ever present, watching over human activ-ities, punishing misbehaviour and upholding the order and morality of the clan.

Given the relationship between the living and the ancestral spir-its, it can be understood that the transition from this life to the next is considered vitally important. Suicide, especially suicide by hang-ing, is considered abhorrent. That a member of the Babukusu would be so unable to cope with life is considered a judgement on the soci-ety for not caring for one of its members. Suicide, therefore, is not considered the fault of the victim alone—all blood relations are impli-cated in the death. The entire tribal unit shares in the shame and all become the object of the curses from God and the ancestral spir-its, as well as the derision of the living. Because human life is highly valued, suicide is considered an offense of the highest order. Although any form of suicide is detested, all agree that death by hanging causes much fear and horror. The person who has resorted to sui-cide is said to bring a curse. Curses are usually passed within fam-ilies related by blood, and are thought to have great power. Blood which binds people together in the blessing of family can also bind them together in a curse. Since death by hanging is a result of the community's failure to recognize its own weakness and prevent the factors which could lead to such a death, the curse turns upon that community. Because of the threat of the curse, extreme measures are taken in order to deflect its power.

Four cases of suicide by hanging in recent times have been remembered. Interviews with those who remember reveal significant rituals which must follow such a death.[5] When it is found that a suicide by hanging has taken place, the body must quickly be identified. The relatives who have been informed do not remove the body, but hire strangers who are unrelated to take the body down. These people are provided with a sheep to be used in a sacrificial ritual of cleansing from any evil influence. The intestines of the slaughtered sheep would be smeared on any who make contact with the body, as well as on the desecrated area. The disposal of the body is performed without honour. Mourning is not expected. Normal funeral rituals are prohibited. A cow is slaughtered, but not as a gift for the dead relative as would be customary, but as an appeasement to the spirit in order to prevent trouble for the survivors.

In the case of most deaths, the ritual of "removing the disease" (*khurusia lufu*) is performed. This involves a gathering of the clan in which an elder recites the life history of the dead person, followed by a narration of the circumstances of the death. A second session soon after involves accounting for the dead person's property and debts. In this way the society is able to make sure that the surviving members of the family are cared for. In the case of suicide by hanging, no such rituals take place. Other rituals which are meant to ensure a peaceful transition to next life are also left undone. In most African societies children are named after close relatives, ensuring that the relative is remembered, and somehow survives, through the child. This privilege is not given to one who dies by suicide. The entire funeral is intended to avert any possibility of a curse coming on the remained members of the family.

Even the tree of hanging is given special attention. In the Babukusu life world, the tree is the symbol of life. Trees are put to many

---

[5] One case involved a girl at Namwesi village in 1956. The other three cases, between 1984 and 1987, involved two elderly men and a youth in Kuafu area of North Kulisiru sub-location, Kenya.

beneficial uses. Branches are used as fuel, and construction of houses, leaves of some trees have medicinal qualities, large trees are used as shade from the sun. But a tree used as an instrument of suicide becomes a symbol of death. Such a tree is feared, for it is believed that others in the community could be prompted to commit suicide by the presence of the tree. Some believe that the branches or leaves of such a tree could have harmful effects, or that the tree could become a home for evil spirits and, therefore, bring more evil on the society. The suicide by hanging on a tree is much feared because the tree which remains standing in the midst of the community reminds people of the tragedy amongst them. So following the suicide, the tree is completely uprooted, cut into pieces and burned. The ashes are collected and thrown into a river to be carried away. The tree which could be a source of a curse if left standing is totally obliterated and removed from the society.

The practice of Babukusu Christians has been affected by these traditional ideas. Christian pastors who have been asked to participate in the funeral of a suicide victim normally refuse. There are remarkable similarities between the biblical tradition preserved in Deuteronomy 21:22–23 and ideas concerning hanging preserved in Babukusu oral traditions. Both cultures find the very idea of hanging on a tree to be an abomination. In both traditions the person hanged is considered to be under a curse. Deuteronomy and the Babukusu both consider the land to be threatened with a curse if a person is left to hang. Both cultures have strict rules surrounding the disposal of the corpse. There are differences, of course. The Bible stipulates that the corpse must not be left over night. Babukusu culture insists that foreigners must deal with the body. Babukusu tradition also has elaborate regulations concerning the disposal of the tree which are lacking in scripture. The most important difference is the occasion of the hanging—in Deuteronomy the hanging referred to is a capital punishment, for the Babukusu the hanging which is so loathed is a suicide.

For our purposes the important issue is that both first century Judaism and the Babukusu people conceive of a connection between hanging on a tree and a curse which is attached to death by hanging. Paul the apostle and the contemporary Babukusu Christians are in comparable situations. It stands to reason that people within both cultures would conceive of Jesus' death as cursed and, therefore, would have difficulty understanding how the crucified Jesus could be of any benefit. For both cultures the cross appears to be a barrier to faith and yet it is clear that the cross is at the centre of Paul's theology: "I decided to know nothing among you except Jesus Christ and him crucified" (1 Corinthians 2:2), "being found in human form he humbled himself and became obedient unto death, even death on a cross" (Philippians 2:8),[6] "But God shows his love for us in that while we were still sinners Christ died for us ... we are now justified by his blood" (Romans 5:8–9), "in Christ Jesus you who were once far off have been brought near in the blood of Christ" (Ephesians 2:13).[7]

It is also clear that Babukusu people having responded positively to a version of Christianity which emphasizes the cross. Protestant Christianity in Western Kenya (and in much of East Africa) is deeply influenced by the East African Revival Movement which began in Rwanda and spread through Uganda, Tanzania, Kenya and the southern Sudan in the 1930s. This movement emphasizes the cross as a sacrifice which takes away sin. The preaching of the Revival Movement proclaims Jesus as the "lamb of God," and the virtue of the "power of the blood." The hymns of the Revival announce "*Damu ya Yesu, u sa fisha kabisa*" ("the blood of Jesus, it washes completely"). The effect of preaching about Christ's death by hanging has immediate appeal:

> At Namwesi Church a member of the congregation who had just become a Christian, on hearing the message came and commented that Jesus' death was horrible; he added, "so he was hanged because of my sins." While at Malakisi Church, the imagery of Christ crucified and hanging led an elder of the church to conclude the "the message of our Lord becomes new every time I realize that his blood was shed on the cross for my sins." In these two instances it should be noticed that the image of Christ hanging and his blood flowing had an impact on each of the people in a special way. . . . The sense of appeal in the imagery of Christ crucified, hanging and bleeding appeared overwhelming (Wabukala 1988: 56).

----

[6] Many argue that in Philippians 2:5–11 Paul is quoting an ancient Christian hymn. Most of those who argue this case, however, assume that the mention of the cross is a Pauline addition to the hymn.

[7] Some consider Ephesians to be deutero-Pauline. Those who would do so would argue that Paul's pseudepigraphal disciple has attempted to write Ephesians as a letter which closely resembles Paul's thought. Whether or not Ephesians was actually penned by Paul, in its cross-centred focus Ephesians certainly sounds "Pauline."

Paul came to understand the curse of hanging on a cross as an
exchange curse which was capable of bringing redemption and blessing to those believe. The logic which Paul invokes is the logic of
sacrifice: an innocent victim can represent and take the place of one
who is guilty; a curse can be removed from one by being transferred
to another. This same logic is at work in the popular theology of
the Revival Movement among the Babukusu: in dying on the cross,
Jesus becomes the lamb of God who takes the world's sin so that
the world can go free; the curse of sin and guilt is transferred to
another. This logic of an exchange curse allows Paul to view the
curse of the cross as God's way of giving life to people previously
living under the curse of the Torah. The same logic has allowed
Babukusu Christians to sing and preach about the cross as a life-
giving tree, at least since the 1930s. The idea of the hanged Christ
has the potential to be a cause of offense to Babukusu people. The
cross could have been considered a source of cursing. Instead the
logic of sacrifice has allowed the cross to be for the Babukusu a sign
of life and blessing.

BIBLIOGRAPHY

Achebe, Chinua. *Things Fall Apart*. Nairobi: Heinemann Kenya, 1962 (1958).
Bammel, Ernst. "Crucifixion as a Punishment in Palestine," In Ed. Ernst Bammel,
    The Trial of Jesus. London: SCM, 1970: 162–65.
Baumgarten, J.M. "Does the TLH in the Temple Scroll Refer to Crucifixion?" *JBL*
    91 (1972): 472–81.
Davies, W.D. *Paul and Rabbinic Judaism: Some Rabbinic Elements in Pauline Theology*.
    Philadelphia: Fortress, 1980.
Donaldson, Terence L. "The 'Curse of the Law' and the Inclusion of the Gentiles:
    Galatians 3:13–14." *NTS* 32 (1986): 94–112.
Elgvin, Torleif. "The Messiah Who Was Cursed on the Tree," *Themelios* 22/3 (1997):
    14–22.
Fitzmyer, Joseph A. "Crucifixion in Ancient Palestine, Qumran Literature and the
    New Testament." *CBQ* 40 (1978): 493–513.
Hengel, Martin. *Crucifixion: In the Ancient World and the Folly of the Message of the Cross*.
    London: SCM, 1977.
Hooker, Morna D. "Interchange in Christ." *JTS* ns. 22 (1971): 349–61.
Hurtado, Larry. "Convert, Apostate or Apostle to the Nations: The 'Conversion'
    of Paul in Recent Scholarship." *Studies in Religion/Sciences Religieues* 22/3 (1993):
    273–84.
Kim, Seyoon. *The Origin of Paul's Gospel*. Grand Rapids: Eerdmans, 1981.
Makila, F.E. *An Outline History of the Babukusu*. Nairobi: Kenya Literature Bureau, 1978.
Pobee, John S. *Persecution and Martyrdom in the Theology of Paul*. Sheffield: JSOT Press,
    1985.
Segal, Alan. *Paul the Convert: The Apostolate and Apostasy of Saul the Pharisee*. New Haven:
    Yale University Press, 1990.

Stendahl, Krister. "Call Rather Than Conversion." In Ed. K. Stendahl *Paul among Jews and Gentiles*. Philadelphia: Fortress, 1976: 7–23.

Wabukala, Eliud. "The Idea of Hanging on a Tree among the Babukusu People of Kenya and Implications for the Teaching of the Message of the Crucifixion of Jesus Christ." St. Paul's United Theological College, Limuru, Kenya: Unpublished thesis, 1988.

Yadin, Y. "Pesher Nahum (4QpNahum) Reconsidered." *Israel Exploration Journal* 21 (1971): 1–12.

NYIMBO ZA VIJANA: BIBLICAL INTERPRETATION IN CONTEMPORARY HYMNS FROM TANZANIA

Fergus J. King

John Mbiti emphasized that a full study of African interpretations of the Bible must not just involve engagement with African academicians, but must also engage the interpretative activities in the parishes, cities, towns and villages, for it is there rather than in colleges and universities that the bulk of African biblical interpretation is being done (Mbiti 1986: 9–10). This study is built on Mbiti's advice, and examines how contemporary Tanzanian hymn writers use the Bible in their work. It is not an exhaustive study. Rather, it suggests how such work might be analysed, together with examples from the work of one hymn writer, Motti Mbogo. A full study is beyond the scope of this essay since it would have to involve the comparison of the work of many writers, but I do hope to provide a preliminary analysis that may prove useful for further research.

Nyimbo za Vijana (Youths' Hymns) are a lively part of the life of the Church of the Province of Tanzania. They are used in both primary evangelism and in established parishes and stations (Mhogolo 1996: 31). They are often the work of younger Christians, thus providing a voice in worship for youth who are often marginalised by traditions which discriminate against them (Mtingele 1995: 5–6). Youth choirs, which are found in many parishes, are comprised of men and women up to 35 in age, and often take an active part in the regular worship of the church as well as special celebrations. The hymns sung by these choirs may either be written by choir directors or members of the choirs. Hymns also may be adopted by other choirs. In many choirs members build up a handwritten exercise book of the lyrics which make up their repertoire. Many of these hymns are based on passages or themes taken directly from the Bible. It is with the latter that this study is concerned.

Two cautionary remarks must be made about the sources of these youth hymns. First, although the hymns analysed are referred to in written form, this is really an oral form of communication, and must be treated by different criteria to written materials. In practical terms, this can mean that definitions and categories may be less precise than the equivalent categories used in the analysis of written materials (Mbiti 1994: 27–39, Molyneux 1993: 170–2).

The second concerns the language used. Mbiti has noted that, in the study of African theology, a distinction must be made between the use of a lingua franca or a vernacular language. He places Kiswahili in the category of a lingua franca, and thus sees it as a less accurate medium of African thought (Mbiti 1986: 28–31,33). His verdict, it seems, reflects his own background as a Kenyan. In Kenya, the post-uhuru (independence) period has seen Kiswahili adopted as the national language and English as the official language: this certainly has led to Kiswahili being used rather as a lingua franca. The situation is different, however, in Tanzania which adopted Kiswahili as its national and official language. Kiswahili has penetrated much more into all levels of communication, even supplanting vernacular languages in the home, and exhibits characteristics of mother tongue languages.[1] Even if the critic should continue to think of Kiswahili as a lingua franca it remains a language whose meaning is more accessible to most Tanzanians than other languages imported from the North.

The method of analysis presented in this paper was first used as the basis for teaching students at St. Mark's Anglican Theological College in Dar Es Salaam. In 1994, a revision of the syllabus for the two provincial colleges, St. Mark's and St. Philip's, Kongwa, allowed tutors to develop their own optional modules in New Testament ([CPT]1997: 11). In October-November 1996, I taught such an optional module, titled "Interpreting The Bible In Tanzania." The material taught in that module, with some modifications, provides the method for analysis given below. One of the aims in teaching this course was to give students a reminder that biblical interpretation is not only the preserve of students and teachers, but is also found in parish life. A second aim was to encourage students to see that African biblical interpretations, by people from all walks of life, should be taken seriously and not marginalised by a theological education which remains Euro-centric, especially because so many of the materials used originate in Europe and America. It is perhaps

---

[1] I am grateful to Dr. Maternus Kapinga, University of Dar Es Salaam for this observation.

worth noting here the kinds of preliminary arguments I offer to my students for my position before proceeding to the analysis itself.

The first argument is drawn from contemporary hermeneutics, noting that approaches like those of Gadamer, Ricouer and Bultmann show us that the text does not stand alone when it is interpreted. The background of the reader also intrudes. Hermeneutical studies ask us to raise not so much the question "what is the right interpretation?" as "what makes a legitimate interpretation?.".

The second argument involves a criticism of the current state of biblical scholarship. There is a tendency to downgrade interpretations which come from outside the guild, or non-academic circles. However, there is an increasing resistance with some scholars arguing for a serious weighing of both pre-critical and extra-critical study of the Bible and its interpretations (Gowan 1994: xi, Mouw 1994, Thiselton 1993: 86). The elitist assumptions that underlie the tendency to downgrade the pre- and extra-critical are also attacked from another direction. For example, after reading Frazer's *The Golden Bough*, Wittgenstein pointed out that Frazer basically condemned as superstitious ways of looking at the world which differed from his own perspective as a rationalist, post-enlightenment academic. Wittgenstein argued that the examination of ancient practices should rather be a means of encountering and learning about our true nature than charging others with superstition (Wittgenstein 1979, Kerr 1986: 159–162). Wittgenstein saw value in the study for the opportunity it provided to learn more about the depths of human nature. He surely challenges scholars of religion to see popular contemporary religious expression as material for the same quest.

From this approach, which takes seriously popular and non-academic interpretations, an analysis of the hymns can begin. Four questions are important in my analysis: Which biblical texts are used? How are these texts incorporated into the hymns? Which methods of interpretation are used? Do particular circumstances shape the interpretation? These questions correspond to four stages in analysing the hymns: the identification of texts, the incorporation of texts in the hymns, the interpretations used, and factors affecting the interpretation. Two sources are crucial in all four stages: the writer, and the lyrics of the hymns.

Interviews with the author serve two aims. The first is to get biographical information and explore possible explanations about the writer's methods of composition. The second deals with specific hymns, classifying them by types, and identifying the context or life-situation of each. The first interview with Motti Mbogo was held on April 15th, 1997. It covered his own history and basic questions about his writing. The second one was on July 18th, 1997. It clarified some points raised by my preliminary analysis, especially the precise identification of source passages which could have come from one of several parallels.

Mbogo comes from a Christian household, and was educated up to primary school level. The bulk of his hymns are written in Kiswahili. He produced an exercise book containing fifty four Kiswahili hymns, which he has written himself. He has also written "two or three" hymns in Cigogo (his tribal/local language) for use where Kiswahili might not be so readily understood. He cites three aims in his hymn-writing: to praise God, to inform, and to encourage. In his view, his own writing stresses encouragement.

Mbogo claims no direct engagement with concerns raised by other faiths (either Islam or African Traditional Religions) in his writing, instead his overt interests concern matters that arise within the Christian community and the different denominations. He also claims no political (*kisiasa*) dimension to his writing, saying that such matters are outside his scope and abilities.

Mbogo categorizes his hymns in different ways. How the hymn is to be performed, including, for example, the number of vocal parts, instruments etc. constitutes one form of categorization. His second form of classification will form the basis of my analysis and involves a distinction between *nyimbo za mwendo huru* ("hymns that bring a sensation of freedom," that is, from sin or present difficulties)[2] and *nyimbo za kitabuni* ("hymns from a book"). These two groupings also reflect different methods of composition: *nyimbo za mwendo huru* are described as hymns "from a sudden revelation," (that is, "given" to the writer rather than a result of conscious reflection or activity), whereas *nyimbo za kitabuni* are a product of a conscious activity by the writer. *Nyimbo za kitabuni* are products of an engagement with a specific biblical text or idea. In this process either the circumstance of the writer, or a particular text gives the initial impetus for composition.

---

[2] Mrs Irene Mwizya King kindly supplied this definition.

Twenty three of the fifty four Kiswahili hymns collected are *nyimbo za kitabuni*. These provide the sample used in the analysis.

The first stage in my analysis of the lyrics is to identify the biblical passages or themes used. To do this the *Itifaki Ya Biblia* and its corresponding Kiswahili translation of the Old and New Testaments, the Union version, were used. This was the translation used by the author. Using this method, it was possible to find sources for twenty two of the twenty three *nyimbo za kitabuni*. The source of one hymn remains unknown. Whilst the bulk of these passages appear to be clearly identifiable, there are some whose exact source remains in doubt.

In the following list of biblical texts used, I have indicated with a question mark those sources which are uncertain, in each case the writer himself cannot remember exactly which passages were used. Whilst many passages are used only once, there are some multiple attestations. These are noted by ordinal numbers. The total number of passages cited shows that some hymns use passages from more than one source. The biblical passages cited or alluded to in the sample are as follows: Genesis 6–7, Exodus 14, esp. v. 11, 17:2–7, Numbers 20:2–13, Deuteronomy 28:6, Joshua 24, Job 2:7 (?), Psalms 23:1–4, 27:1–3 (v. 3 twice), 95:8 (or Hebrews 3:8), Amos 8:10 (?), Malachi 1:6ff., 3:7, Matthew 5:3 (twice), Mark 1:3ff., Luke 10:13, 20:17, Romans 13:11–12, 14:1, Galatians 5:22, 1 Thessalonians 5:1–11 (v. 2 twice, v. 4 twice?), 2 Thessalonians 3:8, Hebrews 3:8 (or Psalms 95:8), Revelation 20:1–2 (twice).

The selection of texts shows that source passages come roughly equally from the Old and New Testaments. A whole range of literary genres are drawn upon: legal, wisdom, prophetic, historical, gospel, letters, and apocalyptic forms of literature are all represented. Our writer's selection is not limited to one testament, or to a particular literary type.

The second phase of my analysis addresses the incorporation of texts into the lyrics of the songs: there are two general methods. The first method is the thematic, in which a biblical theme rather than a specific text is the basis of a hymn. The following hymn is an excellent example of this.

AYUBU—KWELI
Solo: *Ayubu kweli Ayubu alipigwa na majipu mabaya lakini kamtegemea Mungu kamponya ugonjwake* (sic). (Repeated twice)
Chorus: *Ni kweli Ayubu aliteseka lakini Mungu kamponya ugonjwa imani yetu*

leo ifanane na mtumishi wa Mungu Ayubu. (Twice)
Solo: *Sasa ndugu leo uje kwake Yesu aliye mkombozi atakuokoa na hizo dhambi zakoo* (sic), *utafika mbinguni juu* . . . (Twice)[3]

JOB—TRULY
Solo: Job, truly, Job was stricken with terrible sores but he depended on God, and God healed his illness.
Chorus: Its true, Job really was made to suffer, but God healed his illness. Our faith today should be like that of the servant of God, Job.
Solo: Now, brother/sister, today you should come to Jesus who is the Saviour. He will save you from these sins of yours and you will reach heaven above.

In the second method the biblical text is more directly the basis of the hymn. Texts are incorporated in a variety of ways, but usually they are used verbatim or altered for metrical or interpretative reasons. I have chosen the following hymn as an example of verbatim incorporation in the first stanza. The chorus, on the other hand, shares vocabulary with the text, but in altered form.

KISHA NIKAONA
Kisha nikaona maraika (sic) *kishuka toka mbinguni mwenye ufunguo kuzimuu* (sic) *namnyororo mkubwa mkononi mwakee* (sic) *akamshika yule joka yule joka zamani.* (Twice)
Chorus: *Ndipo walipomfunga mwaka elfu nyoka yule Ibirisi* (sic) *kweli na Shetani anayewadanganya watu hivi leo duniani.* (Twice)
Sasa ndugu yangu leo uzipinge hila zake kweli huyo nyoka sasa hana nguvu kwetu tena. (Twice)

THEN I SAW...
Then I saw an angel when he came down from heaven, the one with the key of hell, and a large chain in his hand. He seized that ancient dragon . . .
Chorus: It was the time when they locked him up for a 1000 years, that real Devil and Satan who so tricks people on earth today.
Now, my brother/sister, frustrate his tricks today. Truly that snake has no power over us again.

The words of the original Kiswahili biblical text (Revelation 20:1–2) read as follows (I have underlined the portions included in the hymn):

Kisha nikaona malaika akishuka kutoka mbinguni, mwenye ufunguo wa kuzimu, na mnyororo mkubwa mkononi mwake. Akamshika yule joka, yule nyoka wa zamani, ambaye ni Ibilisi na Shetani, akamfunga miaka elfu, akamtupa katika

---

[3] I have retained the spelling and punctuation from the original manuscripts.

kuzimu, akamfunga, akatia muhuri juu yake, asipate kuwadanganya mataifa tena,
hata ile miaka elfu itimie, na baada ya hayo yapasa afunguliwe muda mchache
(UBS 1989: 1216).

The first verse includes the whole of Revelation 20:1 quoted verbatim, and the first part of 20:2, except for the words *yule nyoka wa;*
the contraction is probably metrical. The chorus uses ideas and
vocabulary from the source passage, but makes changes in the grammar: "he locked him up" (*akamfunga*), becomes "they locked him up"
(*walipomfunga*). It is not clear to me why the change in subject is
made. There are omissions, and these are more easily explained as
they appear to fit the message of the hymn, thus the reference to
Satan being subsequently loosed for a short time is not included,
probably because it would damage the paraenetic (encouraging) message of the hymn, namely, that Satan no longer has any power. The
incorporation of scriptural material is clearly very fluid. Passages or
themes can be used in their full form or edited to suit the metrical
arrangement of the hymn or its final message. Alteration of texts is
necessary for both metrical and interpretative purposes.

The third part of my analysis pertains to the type of interpretation
prevalent in the hymns. I must stress here that interpretation need
not be academic or complex: "Every understanding . . . even if it is
not explicitly arrived at by a conscious process of hermeneutics, still
tacitly includes interpretation" (Thiselton 1993: 100). In my analysis
I listed different kinds of interpretation and assigned each hymn to
an appropriate category. The categories I used, and these are preliminary and suggestive, are the following: literal, allegorical, *mazingira*
("contextual," in which the context of writer, listener or both informs
the interpretation), paraenetic, political, and practical. The last includes
advice about behaviour and/or spirituality; African culture does not
distinguish between these two elements (Paris 1995: 144–8).

This stage yielded the following results. Firstly, I found that Mbogo
tended to favour a literal approach to interpretation, in the sense
that the term "does not exclude metaphorical or symbolic meaning
when this plainly accords with the intention of the author, but
demands that meaning be understood in the customarily acknowledged sense that it would normally bear in its proper linguistic context" (Thiselton 1993: 105).

Furthermore, he would claim that the bulk of these hymns are
mazingira. That is, they reflect his or his listeners' situation. This need
not refer to a specific historical incident, but more often to a general-

isation about one's spiritual state, for example, the need for salvation, the need to resist the devil, and so on.

Beyond this the paraenetic and the practical dominate. The difference is not always clear. Rather than provide abstract definitions of these terms, I would prefer to give examples. Thus, *Ayubu Kweli* gives a practical interpretation, whereas *Kisha Nikaona* is essentially paraenetic. Of the twenty-three hymns analysed, fourteen were categorised as practical and six as paraenetic.

The three hymns of Mbogo's which can neither be described as paraenetic or practical are statements or paraphrases of biblical passages. The writer has not added any interpretive elements to the hymn beyond the selection of the passage, nor has he written them to reflect or address a particular situation.

Many of Mbogo's hymns show a basic pattern, moving from an initial statement of a biblical theme or text, through a chorus which brings out the main point that the author wants to stress, to a final verse, which either gives encouragement or leaves the listener to make a response to the claims of the hymn. Thus the hymns are dynamic and interactive, picking up the listener and bringing him or her to a point of decision. This process is aided not just by the words, but by the music and the participatory nature of African worship (McKim 1993: 156). In Tanzania assent may be shown by *makofi* (clapping) or *vigelegele* (ululation).

In short, the interpretations are related to context, and directed towards the cares and concerns of the writer and listeners. They show a strong practical bias. Biblical texts are used as the starting point for giving information or encouragement. The development of these points is a process informed by the writer's reflection on text and circumstance.

The final stage in my analysis identifies factors which might influence an interpretation. It would appear that some come from either Christian or African traditions. Sometimes they are the result of the harmonization of African and biblical traditions (Mbiti 1986: 26–7, 1994: 28). The first, and most obvious, factor is the Bible itself as a source of material from which theological reflection begins. The Bible, seen as God's gift to God's people, has an exalted place in many people's thinking. For many it is the dominant literary document in their lives (Mbiti 1994: 28). Thus, the Christian tradition supplies an indispensable source: the texts themselves encourage reflection and theological activity.

Within the Christian tradition and missionary enterprise, there is
a second factor which facilitates the work of interpretation and gives
many the opportunity to engage with the tradition. This is the enterprise of translating and making available the scriptures in both vernacular languages and linguae francae. This work is not restricted
to any particular denomination, place or period, but can be seen
throughout the history of the Church. Thus the Eastern traditions
were responsible for the codifying of eastern European languages as
their missionaries moved into the Balkans and Russia, and the Western
traditions, some more willingly than others, moved from Latin (itself
a translation in an earlier age) to vernacular translations in the period
of the Reformation and its aftermath. In Africa, the earliest churches
provided translations in the languages of ancient Egypt and Ethiopic.
In the period of modern missionary activity, representatives of both
Protestant and Roman Catholic churches stressed the importance of
knowing local languages, preparing grammars, dictionaries and translations of the Scriptures (Mbiti 1986: 22–4, Shorter 1996: 33–51).
It is this impetus that has led to a situation in which the central
texts of the tradition, that is, the Scriptures, are available in a form
which can allow direct access for all literate Christians in a more
familiar language. This shortens the distance between disciple and
text, and gives opportunities for reflection to more than an educated
elite. Even if the churches themselves limit the public expression of
interpretations by their own canons and practice, interpretation goes
on in private. *Nyimbo za Vijana*, which are not regulated by any official
canons in the Church of the Province of Tanzania, give a public
expression to interpretations which need not come from the theologically "qualified," the criteria by which their survival as pieces of
reflection is judged are their popularity, whether their sentiments
agree with those of the listeners, and their musical quality.[4]

Further, socio-cultural factors which may influence the method of
interpretation come from the meeting point of African and biblical
worlds. Resonances with and reverence for the Bible may have lead
to a copying of its methodologies as well as respect for its contents.
Methods of using Old Testament texts which are seen in the New
Testament may have become models for contemporary writers. The

---

[4] Canon Lawrence Mnubi and Fr. Philip Baji, both of St. Mark's College, DSM,
advise me that the parish priest or the *mlezi* (overseer) of the choir may censor
hymns performed publicly.

Letter to the Hebrews, for example, shows both the incorporation of Old Testament themes (for example, sacrifice in Hebrews 10) and portions of Old Testament text (Hebrews 3:7–10). As with my study, it must be noted that there are difficulties in identifying precisely the texts used in Hebrews and the possible alterations by the writer (McCullough 1980: 378). Nevertheless both Hebrews and the hymns in our sample show a freedom to alter the wording of a text, either for grammatical or interpretative reasons. Both, too, show texts being used as the starting points for reflection on, and dialogue with, present circumstances. However, to propose a direct link may be premature.

Other local resources may also play a role in this form of interpretation. African wisdom traditions, especially in East Africa and in Kiswahili, often use short "texts" from their proverb traditions as key elements in debate and teaching. These proverbs may be recorded in variant forms, and their interpretation is dynamic, changing to suit the situation addressed. Sylvanus Udoidem provides a definition of the way in which proverb traditions work, and the proverbs themselves are used as the basis for reflection:

> A proverb serves as an occasion for creative reflection: it is a framework for collaborative and contributive creativity both for the speaker and listener. The former gains a new insight into the given situation that necessitates the application of a particular proverb. For the latter this provides a frame for reflection, creative insight and an awareness of a new reality (cited in Paris 1995, 147. See also Healey 1981: 125–8, Healey & Sybertz 1996: 34–43, Shorter 1996: 87–94).

This pattern seems close to the pattern of our *nyimbo za kitabuni*, except that a verse, passage or biblical theme stands in place of a traditional proverb and becomes the basis for creative reflection by both writer and listener.

It is not just the methods of incorporation and interpretation which may be influenced by biblical or African traditions. It also applies to the content of the interpretations. The stress that our writer puts on Jesus as Saviour (exemplified in *Ayubu Kweli*—see above) initially looks as though it is a theme that is biblical in origin. It is common in the New Testament that Old Testament passages are interpreted Christo-centrically. The "Suffering Servant" passages of Isaiah are an obvious example. Similarly, the strong futurist eschatology of our writer is a biblical theme, or at least one of the theological strands in the Scriptural discussion of time. Mbiti has shown that both ideas

about the future and eternity differ very much from the African time
concepts of *Sasa* and *Zamani* (Mbiti 1976: 163, 1994: 34–5). It would
appear that this (futurist) theology of time is clearly coming from the
biblical texts and their subsequent (Western) interpretations. The
"Christ as Saviour" theme is less straightforward. Why does our
writer return to that theme, rather than other biblical themes? The
idea of Jesus as teacher, for example, is never handled. Here we
may find the answer in African tradition. In many African traditions,
the themes of salvation and deliverance are strong and Christ is venerated and worshipped especially for his ability to heal, to exorcise
and to save:

> There is more than ample evidence to show that the main preoccu-
> pation of many African Christians is redemption from physical dilemma
> or evil forces. The idea of deliverance is the commonest theme in the
> hymns, prayers and catechisms of these Indigenous African Churches.
> They address themselves to complete personal and community deliver-
> ance from the forces of evil, witchcraft, death, drought, floods, sickness
> or any epidemic. This idea ties in with the traditional African concept
> of religion and therefore God and Christ (Appiah-Kubi 1991: 72).

A further choice of material which may reflect the interaction of the
biblical and African world views is exemplified by the content of the
hymn *Kisha Nikaona* (above) which stresses that the power of the devil
has been broken. In many African societies, the supernatural is a
vibrant part of cosmology. There is no questioning the existence of
majini (the spirits, demons), whose existence is not just a part of traditional belief systems, but also of the East African Islamic world
view. "The reality of the spirit world is not doubted by African or
Arab Muslims. The working of spirits known as jins, is to Africans
and Arabs a social reality. Here the two religions [Islam and African
Traditional Religions] met and embraced each other" (Safari 1994:
101–2, see also Msamba 1997: 11). The choice of material again
may well be based on the harmony between local and biblical world
views. The writer is answering everyday concerns and fears of his
listeners, and his interpretation is earthed in their shared experience
and view of the world. As these hymns may be used in situations
of primary evangelism, a further case can be made that the choice
of such materials is addressing traditional views as much as those
learned purely from the biblical and Christian traditions.

The discussion is further complicated by the fact that one cannot
isolate Bible and African culture without considering the influence

of subsequent interpretative traditions, including the Western. Whether one likes it or not, Western Theology and the history of interpretation throughout the history of the church are also factors which may influence a contemporary African interpretation. However, the coincidence of African and biblical views (because the bottom line in many local controversies is "what does the Bible say?") may help us to see why some brands of theology seem to be more acceptable than others.

Within the last century, for example, what might loosely be termed revivalism has become a loud voice in East African Christianity from the time of the Great Revival in Rwanda in the 1930s (Isichei 1995: 241–3). Since then, revival movements have come and gone in the area. These have led not just to increases in church membership, but also to the formation of new churches and denominations. Many mainline denominations have also been affected as *vikundi vya uamsho* (revival groups) have been founded. In the Church of the Province of Tanzania, this trend is exemplified by the *Nyumba kwa Nyumba* (House To House) fellowship, started by the late Edmund John in 1972/3 (Namata 1990: 18–20). These movements put a great stress on the accepting of Christ as a personal saviour and on healing and deliverance ministries. In doing so, *Nyumba kwa Nyumba*, for example, appears to answer needs which might not be satisfied by the regular liturgical life of the Church of the Province of Tanzania, needs which might well be expected from the cultural context. The *Nyimbo za Vijana* address similar themes which may be, for local tastes, understated in the two official Anglican hymn books, *Nyimbo za Dini* and *Nyimbo Standard*, which are predominantly translations from English hymn collections. Both the *vikundi* and the *nyimbo* address the needs of the church, particularly the circumstances that demand interpretations which answer questions about deliverance and salvation. However, it is impossible to isolate one factor (biblical, Christian, or African) which leads to this preference of "Christ-as-Saviour," what we can say is that it becomes a dominant theme because of the ways in which the present day situation is the result of the meeting and harmonising of these factors in the local church.

The analysis of *Nyimbo za Vijana* is far from complete. The next stage is the comparison of the work of writers from different parts of the province to see whether the points noted above are representative of the practice as a whole, and to build up a wider picture of this phenomenon. It would be important to see whether this kind

of interpretation remained a male preserve, or whether women are
also writing hymns which address their specific concerns. However,
this study gives a valuable glimpse into African biblical interpretations and their concerns. It shows us that African Christians are
engaging creatively with the biblical texts and applying them to their
current situation and needs. It shows above all that the practical and
the paraenetic are core themes in the experience of our writer and
that the work of the interpreter is not just to reflect, but to encourage and inspire others. The interpreter's work is not private, it is
for the community and its needs. These *nyimbo* are also signs of an
interpretative tradition which is faithful to its Tanzanian African heritage, in both its choice of method and theme. In these hymns, we
see a true Tanzanian African Christian school of interpretation, which
speaks to its people in a familiar voice. Moreover, we see an opportunity given to youth, who are so often marginalised, to present their
biblical interpretation in a popular and public fashion. The practice
of accessibility to Scripture within Christianity continues to flourish
and to allow those who are often silenced by both cultural and
denominational traditions to be heard. *Wenye masikio wasikie* (Matthew
11:15).

BIBLIOGRAPHY

Appiah-Kubi K. "Christology." In Ed. J. Parratt, *A Reader In African Christian Theology*,
    London: SPCK, 1991: 69–81.
Church of the Province of Tanzania "Syllabus for Diploma in Theology Course."
    Dodoma: Unpublished Report, 1997.
———. *Itifaki Ya Biblia*. Dodoma: Central Tanganyika Press, 1991.
———. *Nyimbo Za Dini*. Dodoma: Central Tanganyika Press, 1931.
Gowan, D.E. *Theology in Exodus*. Louisville: Westminster/John Knox Press, 1994.
Healey, J. *A Fifth Gospel*. Maryknoll: Orbis, 1981.
Healey, J., and Sybertz, D. *Towards an African Narrative Theology*. Nairobi: Pauline, 1996.
Isichei, E. *A History of Christianity In Africa*. Grand Rapids: Eerdmans, 1995.
Kerr, F. *Theology After Wittgenstein*. Oxford: Blackwell, 1986.
McCullough, J.C. "The Old Testament Quotations in Hebrews." *New Testament
    Studies* 26 (1980): 363–79.
McKim, D.K. *The Bible in Theology And Preaching*. Nashville: Abingdon, 1993.
Mbiti, J. *African Religions And Philosophy*. London: OUP, 1976.
———. *Bible & Theology In African Christianity*. Nairobi: OUP, 1986.
———. "The Bible in African Culture." In Ed. G. Rosellini, *Paths of African Theology*.
    27–39. London: SCM, 1994.
Mhogolo, G. "The Bible: Our Tool for Evangelism & Church Planting." In Ed.
    J. Stott *The Anglican Communion And Scripture*. Oxford: Regnum, 1996: 129–133.
Molyneux, G. *African Christian Theology: A Quest for Selfhood*. Lewiston and Lampeter:
    Mellen, 1993.

Mouw, R.J. *Consulting the Faithful* . . . Grand Rapids: Eerdmans, 1994.

Msamba, P. "Majini Yapo Hayapo?" In *Nipashe* 0873 (6 July 1997): 11.

Mtingele, H.M. "African Traditional Leadership in The Church Today" Open University: Unpublished Thesis, 1995.

Namata, J.A. *Edmund John: Mtu Wa Mungu.* Dodoma: Central Tanganyika Press, 1990.

Paris, P.J. *The Spirituality of African Peoples.* Philadelphia: Fortress, 1995.

Safari, J.F. *The Making of Islam In East Africa.* Peramiho: Benedictine Publications-Ndanda, 1994.

Shorter, A. *Christianity and The African Imagination.* Nairobi: Pauline, 1996.

[SPCK]. *Nyimbo Standard.* London: SPCK, 1897.

Thiselton, A. *The Two Horizons.* Carlisle: Paternoster, 1993.

[UBS]. *Biblia Ya Kiswahili- Union Version.* Nairobi and Dodoma: UBS, 1989.

Wittgenstein, L. *Remarks on Frazer's Golden Bough.* Retford: Brynmill, 1979.

Interviews

Reverend Philip Baji, Dar Es Salaam, September, 1997.

Reverend Canon Lawrence Mnubi, Dar Es Salaam, September 1997.

Reverend Dr. Maternus Kapinga, Dar Es Salaam, May 1997.

Mrs Irene Mwizya King, Dar Es Salaam, May 1997.

Nd. Motti Mbogo, Dar Es Salaam, 15th April 1997.

Nd. Motti Mbogo, Dar Es Salaam, 18th July 1997.

THE BIBLE IN MALAWI: A BRIEF SURVEY OF ITS IMPACT ON SOCIETY

Hilary B.P. Mijoga

Since the inception of Christianity in Malawi a little over a century ago, no serious studies have been done on the use or role of the Bible in Malawi. However, this situation has changed since the early 1990s. During this period, studies have been undertaken on the role of the Bible in the country. Churches have also produced documents which have manifested clearly the influence of the Bible on current thinking in the church. These studies and documents have revealed that the Bible has been used by the church (as an institution) and individual members for cultural, educational, socio-political and religious (spiritual) transformation. By socio-political transformation, I refer explicitly to the political changes which took place from 1992–1994, in particular, the national referendum and the general elections, and by religious transformation I refer to issues like the use of the Bible for understanding Christology, in grassroots theology, the Bible as a means of grace, and the Bible as the basis of sermons for mainstream and African Instituted Churches.

History has shown that the Bible's encounter with local cultural customs and practices has led to their transformation. For example, when the Bible came into the country, it confronted, among other things, the African concept of God, ritual practices, rites of passage, and customs. In a recent study on sacraments and sexuality, it was observed that fewer women than men took part in the holy communion. The study showed that cultural practices, including traditional understandings of menstrual uncleanness, prevented women from taking part in this celebration. But after a series of contextual Bible studies on this and related issues, the situation changed. More women then began to participate in the Lord's supper (Chingota 1998: 34–40). In this case, one can conclude that the contextual Bible studies were liberative to women. In light of this observation, it can be said that the Bible had a role in transforming cultural beliefs among the women concerned in this study.

The translation of the Bible into the local languages has also brought in some changes in Malawi. John S. Mbiti has said that "the Bible in local languages becomes the most directly influential single factor in shaping the life of the Church in Africa" (Mbiti 1986: 28). One of the consequences of the vernacular Bible was that "the believers had direct access to the Word of God and could therefore apply it relevantly within their cultural setting as they allowed it to either transform or confirm their cultural beliefs and practices" (Mwenifumbo 1997: 4). This direct access has ensured the spread of the gospel in Malawi.

Historically, the Bible has been associated with the development of education and literature. The first Chichewa Bible in Union Nyanja, *Buku Lopatulika*, had its second proof in 1936. This vernacular Bible contributed to the country's Chichewa literature standardization, for "the standardised Nyanja gave birth to a vigorous literature and became one of the most important national languages of Central and Southern Africa, spoken and understood in five countries" (Pauw 1980: 220). In a way, this became a lingua franca for this part of Africa. In addition to playing a substantial role in generating a lingua franca for the region, this standardized version also served to break tribal barriers, for it was used by different linguistic and ethnic groups.

In 1915, Malawi had its first nationalist uprising against the British colonial government, and here too, the Bible played a role, this time, a political role. The leader of this rebellion was a Malawian pastor of the Providence Industrial Mission, John Chilembwe. Chilembwe had some connections with the Watch Tower movement which produced religious tracts which were accessible to him and his followers. In this literature, the group seemed to have "found its implicit and explicit criticism of all government institutions attractive" (Shepperson and Price 1958: 324–325). At the trial of the followers of Chilembwe, the epistle of James, particularly chapter 5, was often quoted in their defence.

Later, and more generally, the modern history of Malawi can be divided between "before the Catholic Bishops Lenten Pastoral Letter" and "since the Pastoral Letter." The bishops' Letter was the first public challenge to the one-party system of government, and it dealt with issues such as wage structure, education and health services, human rights, and democratic accountability of government. In their challenge to the government, the bishops used the Bible in support of their position, for the Letter was explicitly based on biblical exposition. In fact, it was observed that engagement with the biblical text was, from the beginning, a central feature in the struggle for social and political change in Malawi from 1992 (Chingota 1996: 41, see Chakanza 1995: 59–74, Mijoga 1997b: 55–68).

This was a Lenten letter which commemorates the saving mysteries of the Lord's death and resurrection. The Letter is based on the gospel message in a general way, but also makes reference to particular texts. The Letter is entitled "Living our Faith," but when it was republished by the Catholic Institution for International Relations in London, it was entitled "The Truth Will Set you Free,"—a clear reference to John 8:32. There are explicit biblical quotations supporting the issues at stake. In the "Introduction," the second paragraph reads: "Christ began his public ministry by proclaiming: 'Repent and believe the Gospel' (Mark 1:15). In this proclamation he states the programme of his ministry: to call all humankind in and through His life, and resurrection to conversion and witness. People in every age and culture are called to this conversion and to respond in commitment and faith."

In a number of the subsections of the Letter the opening paragraph makes explicit reference to a biblical text. On "The Dignity and Unity of Humankind," the first paragraph reads:

> Man and women, created in the image and likeness of God (Genesis 1:26), carry, in themselves the breath of divine life. Each created person is in communion with God. He or she is "sacred," enjoying the personal protection of God. Human life is inviolable since it is from God and all human beings are one, springing as they do from a single father, Adam, and single mother, Eve, "the mother of all those who live" (Genesis 3:20). The unity and dignity of the human race have been definitely sealed in Christ the Son of God who died for all, to unite everyone in one Body. Rejoicing in this truth, we proclaim the dignity of every person, the right of each one to freedom and respect.

On "Participation of all in Public Life," the first paragraph also draws directly on biblical texts: "In their writings to the Christians, both the apostles' Peter and Paul note how the Holy Spirit grants the members of the Christian community gifts of all sorts for the benefit to the community. . . . Whatever the gift, the purpose is one: 'to knit God's holy people together for the work of service to build up the Body of Christ' (Ephesians 4:7–16, cf. 1 Peter 4:10–11)." This explicit reference to the Bible is immediately followed and supported by drawing on African traditional values: "African society has tra-

ditionally recognized that what is true of the church is also true of
any society: its strength resides in recognizing the gifts of all and in
allowing these gifts to flourish and be used for the building up of
the community." On "The Truth Will Set You Free," the opening
paragraph reads: "A first step in the restoration of the climate of
confidence may be taken by recognizing the time state of the nation.
'The truth will set you free' (John 8:32). These words of Christ do
not have an exclusively religions meaning. They also express a deep
human reality."

In other sections biblical texts, while not framing the argument,
are used to sustain the argument. In the section on "A System of
Justice which Works Fairly," the third paragraph reads: "In this context, we recall the words of Jesus at the beginning of his ministry:
'The Spirit of the Lord is on me, for he has anointed me to bring
the good news to the afflicted. He has sent me to proclaim liberty
to the captives, sight to the blind, to let the oppressed go free, and
to proclaim a year of favour from the Lord' (Luke 4:18–19). This
appeal for fair treatment should also be heard within the Church."
The conclusion of the letter is titled: "Love tenderly, act justly, walk
humbly with your God," a quotation from Micah 6:8.

The Catholic bishops wrote another pastoral letter in 1993. This
letter was an attempt at voter education (Ross 1996a: 223–235). This
letter was also based on the Bible in much the same way as the Letter discussed above. As a follow up to the Catholic Bishops' Lenten
Pastoral Letter, other churches followed in challenging the one-party
system of government and supported the bishops' stand. In their
open letter to Dr. Hastings Kamuzu Banda (the former president),
the Church of Central Africa Presbyterian (CCAP) leaders together
with a World Alliance of Reformed Churches (WARC) delegation,
also used the Bible as a basis of their challenge. This means that the
Bible came to be a central text in public discourse concerning the
transformation of Malawi. In a statement by the Blantyre Synod of
the CCAP on the transformation of Malawi in 1993, the Bible was
also explicitly used (Ross 1996a: 217–222). In all these cases the
church was measuring government policies and actions against the
biblical message of the Kingdom of God. By weighing the existing
order against the demands of God's impending kingdom, the church
supplied a gauge which freed people to make their own assessment
of the prevailing system and to take action accordingly. In a predominantly Christian country like Malawi, where the biblical message

has tremendous resonance, to make the exercise of power accountable to God in this way was a formidable political challenge (Ross
1996a: 26).

During the period leading up to the referendum, "the message in
many pulpits included a biblically based critique of the prevailing
one-party system" (Ross 1996b: 31). Overall, keen observers of the
advent of multiparty politics in Malawi at this time could not fail
to see that the Bible was central to the argument of the proponents
of change. This was not only true with the proponents of change,
but it was observed that even the defenders of one-party system
sought legitimation for their positions from the Bible.

Apart from the church (as an institution), individual members in
Malawi used the Bible in the process of socio-political change. A
survey was carried out to find out whether people were influenced
by biblical passages in their decision to vote in the referendum
(Chingota 1996: 41–62). According to the survey, people's greatest
area of concern regarding the situation in the country before the
referendum was political. Those who wanted a change of the system of government gave biblical passages in support of their views,
consequently, one can say, their decision to vote was influenced by
the Bible. Specific passages were given, and looking at these passages, it was observed that there were two important biblical traditions referred to during this period: God's liberating acts and God's
empowering wisdom (Chingota 1996: 60).

So, from the studies undertaken and the letters from the churches,
it is not far fetched to conclude that the Bible has had a role to
play in the socio-political transformation of Malawi, especially in the
period 1992–1994. The process of change, as we have seen, began
with the Catholic Bishops' Lenten Pastoral Letter, which was strongly
biblically based, and the process ended with people's decision to vote
for change, which was also deeply influenced by biblical passages.

On the role of the Bible in religious (spiritual) formation and transformation, studies have been done on the use of the Bible in sermons, both in the so-called "mainline" (Settler/Missionary Initiated)
churches and in the African Instituted Churches, in grassroots theology, and as a means of grace among prisoners. In 1990–92, a
nation wide survey of sermons delivered in mainline churches was
conducted. One of the aims of the survey was to ascertain what the
characteristic emphases of contemporary preaching in these churches
were and to assess what significance might lie in them (Ross 1995:

81–106). The study found as one of its main findings "the massive importance of the Bible for mainstream Christianity in Africa. Not only are the texts being read week after week in parishes throughout the country but a serious effort is being made to expound them. This survey has not sought to assess the quality of the Bible exposition but it has revealed that preaching, by and large, attempts to explain, amplify, illustrate and apply a given passage of scripture" (Ross 1995: 86). It was also observed that a broad range of scripture was read and expounded. One of the major issues to emerge in this study was that many of the sermons had as their focus questions of morality (for example, adultery, promiscuity, drunkenness, etc.). These sermons delivered with the aim of improving people's moral standing, and clearly it was believed that the Bible had a role to play here. We might say, then, that the Bible was used for individual religious transformation.

In 1989–90, a survey was carried out on 18 African Instituted Churches in Malawi. The aim of the survey was to carry out a detailed study of biblical interpretation in these churches. The study revealed that the Bible was extensively used and that both Testaments were used. It was also observed that one of the beliefs among the churches was that God reveals his will and manifests himself to the people through the Bible (Mijoga 1996b: 358–371). As was the case with sermons in the mainline churches, so also here the exposition is closely related to the biblical text read. In a 1996–97 study on sermons from African Instituted Churches, 299 sermons were recorded and transcribed (Mijoga 1998a). Preliminary findings indicate that these sermons too were closely related to the biblical passages read. Here too one of main issues addressed was morality (e.g., adultery/promiscuity, drunkenness, theft, etc.) (Mijoga 1997a: 41–44, Mijoga 1999). Here too the Bible had a part to play (through the sermons) in the religious transformation of people. It has been claimed that the influence of the Bible has also led to the rise and development of African Instituted Churches in Malawi (see Mijoga 1998b, Mwenifumbo 1997, and for the root causes of religious independency in Malawi, see Chakanza 1982: 133–42, Mijoga 1991).

In 1995, a survey was conducted on grassroots Christology. The aim of the research was to understand how ordinary people, the grassroots, understand the identity and meaning of Jesus Christ (Ross 1997: 160–176). A majority of the respondents indicated that their own personal Bible reading and prayer were the most important

means of experiencing the person and presence of Jesus. This means
that the Bible stands out as the principal source of Christology. This
study "underlines the massive importance of the text of the Bible in
contemporary African Christianity, in this case in the central area
of the construction of a Christology" (Ross 1997: 163). On the question of the predominant Christological categories, by far the most
commonly chosen categories are the biblical umbrella terms "saviour" and "messiah" which speak strongly of the function of Jesus
Christ as the bringer of salvation. Here too, the powerful influence
of the Bible is apparent. On the question of the function of Jesus
Christ, respondents were asked to choose three benefits promised by
Jesus which they found most precious. The respondents opted for
issues which are central in the biblical proclamation, such as eternal life after death and the forgiveness of sins. It was also observed
that "the only option to attract more than half of the respondents
is the devil. This was the most frequently chosen option among both
Catholics and Presbyterians. . . . It appears that the biblical understanding of evil in terms of the devil is more influential than such
traditional categories as witchcraft and evil spirits" (Ross 1997: 166).

Research has also revealed that the Bible is used as means of
grace. As part of the World Council of Churches "Theology of Life
Project," a study was done in Malawi in 1995–96 on the sub-theme:
"All exercise of power is accountable to God: Christian experience
in Malawi prisons" (Mijoga 1996a: 177–186). The situation in Malawi
was that during the one-party era, prisoners were among those
markedly on the receiving end of an exercise of power which was
often arbitrary, unjust, and unaccountable. No one would accept
responsibility for what was happening in the prison facilities, and the
voices of prisoners were never heard. In a situation like this, the
prisoners themselves had to find ways and means by which they
could survive this arbitrary, unjust, and unaccountable exercise of
power by the regime. One thing that kept some of them going,
according to the research, was faith. Faith gave them power to resist,
survive, endure, and overcome the overwhelming power of the government which removed their liberty and which threatened their life.
In this struggle the Bible was one of the tools used to sustain that
faith. The Bible gave them this power through its stories which were
comforting and encouraging. In this regard, the research revealed
that the Bible was by far the most important "means of grace."
Apart from the Bible, prayers, chaplaincy, hymns and sacraments

(in that order) also functioned as means of grace to the respondents. However, it was undoubtedly the Bible which was most prized as a means of grace.

Prisoner were asked whether the Bible was the book of the oppressed or the oppressors. They responded that the Bible is relevant to the oppressed as well as the oppressors of the society. Some of the reasons that were given for holding this view included: the Bible is the word of God to all, oppressors and the oppressed are found in the Bible, the message contained in it is not peculiar to one group, and the Bible would convert the oppressors.

Respondents were also asked what the Bible meant to them before their prison experience. It emerged from their responses that the Bible is the word of God. It is a comforter, guide, and source of inspiration. Respondents were then asked if the experience of reading the Bible in prison affected their Christian life in prison. A large percentage of the respondents indicated that it did. Some of the reasons given were that the Bible comforted them and gave them hope for release. This hope gave them power to endure and survive the hardships they experienced in prison. When people read stories about Paul's prison experiences, the teaching that if one is to follow Christ one has to suffer, stories of the suffering of the Israelites, experiences of Peter, Daniel etc., they found comfort and hope for their own prison experiences. This then helped them to resist, endure, survive, and overcome the unjust power of the state. From the foregoing, it is clear that the Bible played a significant role in the lives of some of the respondents. What transpired here was that the Bible turned out to be the greatest means of grace during their prison experiences. On this note we can say that the Bible contributed to the respondents' religious transformation.

This brief survey outlines the role the Bible has played in social and individual transformation in the history of Malawi. We have observed that the Bible has influenced changes in the cultural and educational sectors. We have also seen that the church and ordinary members in Malawi have used the Bible to transform politics in the country during the 1992–1994 period. Under the influence of the Bible, the political system changed from the one-party system to a multiparty system of government. The survey has also shown that the Bible has contributed to religious transformation in the country. From the sermons studied (from mainstream and African Instituted Churches), it has been observed that one of the issues of concern in them is morality. This means that the biblical passages are believed to be able to change people's ways of behaviour. The survey has also revealed that the Bible is the greatest means of grace, as was evident in the case of Christian prisoners during their prison experiences. Hence we can say that the Bible transforms lives. In short then, from this brief survey, it is evident that the Bible plays a transformative role in the cultural, educational, socio-political, and religious life of the people of Malawi.

BIBLIOGRAPHY

Chakanza, Joseph C. "Pro-Democracy Movement in Malawi: The Catholic Church's Contribution, In Eds Matembo S. Nzunda & Kenneth R. Ross, *Church, Law and Political Transition in Malawi 1992–94*. Kachere Books No. 1. Gweru: Mambo Press in Association with the University of Malawi Department of Theology & Religious Studies, 1995: 59–74.
———. "Towards an Interpretation of Independent Churches in Malawi." *African Theological Journal* 11 (1982): 133–42.
Chingota, Felix L. "Sacraments and Sexuality." *Religion in Malawi* 8 (1998): 34–40.
———. "The Use of the Bible in Social Transformation." In Ed. Kenneth R. Ross, *God, People and Power in Malawi: Democratization in Theological Perspective*. Kachere Monograph No. 3. Blantyre: CLAIM, 1996b: 41–62.
Mbiti, John S. *Bible and Theology in African Christianity*. Nairobi: Oxford University Press, 1986.
Mijoga, Hilary B.P. *Separate But Same Gospel: Preaching in African Instituted Churches*. Kachere Monograph. Blantyre: CLAIM. Forthcoming, 1999.
———. "Bible and Church Growth in Malawi." *Religion in Malawi* 8 (1998b): 28–33.
———. "The Lenten Pastoral Letter: A First Public Declaration of the Hidden Transcript." *Journal of Humanities* 10/11 (1996–97b): 55–68.
———. "Hidden and Public Ways of Doing Contextual Bible Study in Southern Africa: South Africa and Malawi as Case Studies." *Religion in Malawi* 7 (1997a): 41–44.
———. "Preaching in African Instituted Churches in Malawi." Zomba: Unpublished research report, 1998a.
———. "Hermeneutics in African Instituted Churches in Malawi." *Missionalia* 24 (1996b): 358–71.
———. "Christian Experience in Malawi Prisons." In Ed. Kenneth R. Ross, *God, People and Power in Malawi: Democratization in Theological Perspective*. Kachere Monograph No. 3. Blantyre: CLAIM, 1996a: 177–86.
———. "Biblical Exegesis in African Independent Churches in Malawi." *Sources for the Study of Religion in Malawi* 14 (1991).
Mwenifumbo, Alfred L. "A Historical Survey of the Use of the Bible in Religious and Socio-Political Challenges in Africa. A case of Malawi." Zomba: Unpublished theology conference paper, 1997.
Pauw, Christoff Martin. *Mission and Church in Malawi: The History of the Nkhoma Synod of the Church of the Central Africa Presbyterian 1889–1962*. Lusaka: Baptist Press, 1980.
Ross, Kenneth R. "Current Christological Trends in Northern Malawi." *Journal of Theology in Africa* 27 (1997): 160–76.

————. "The Transformation of Power in Malawi 1992–94: The Role of the Christian Churches." In Ed. Kenneth R. Ross, *God, People and Power in Malawi: Democratization in Theological Perspective*. Kachere Monograph No. 3. Blantyre: CLAIM, 1996b: 15–40.

————. Ed. *Christianity in Malawi: A Source Book*. Kachere Books No. 3. Gweru: Mambo Press & Kachere Series, 1996a.

————. "Contemporary Preaching in Mainstream Christian Churches in Malawi: A Survey and Analysis." In Ed. Kenneth R. Ross, *Gospel Ferment in Malawi: Theological Essays*. Kachere Books No. 2. Gweru: Mambo Press in Association with University of Malawi Department of Theology & Religious Studies, 1995b: 81–106.

Shepperson, G. & Price, T. *Independent African, John Chilembwe and the Origins, Setting and Significance of the Nyasaland Native Rising of 1915*. Edinburgh: Edinburgh University Press, 1958.

A SETSWANA PERSPECTIVE ON GENESIS 1:1–10

Moiseraele Prince Dibeela

This interpretation of Genesis cosmology is done by an African in Botswana. It is therefore done with certain presuppositions arising out of my Africanness. The first such supposition is my conviction that this creation account carries some of the central teachings of the Hebrew Bible. The second presupposition is that much of what now constitutes the Bible arose out of an experiential living of the faith. This understanding calls for a new hermeneutic: a hermeneutic that does not only take seriously the form and world of the text, but the culture and experience of the reader. For instance, what is the significance of Setswana mythological narratives about creation in comparison to biblical myth? Is the fact that African communities are largely storytelling communities of any significance to reading the Bible, which as a final product is a compilation of stories of faith by the believers?

Academic structures have made Bible reading a monopoly of the few professional theologians and clergy who have gone to seminaries and universities. But what do we do about the ordinary member in the pews? How can academic methods of reading be allowed to have a creative interplay with experiential readings of the Bible? These questions lay ground for a hermeneutic that seeks to take cognisance of the world of the reader, the world of the text and how they impact on each other. In order to bring into focus my approach to the text, I shall begin by expounding on my culture and my identity before I specifically examine the text itself.

I am a Motswana man belonging to the Bangwaketsi ethnic group in the south of Botswana. I am quite aware that my maleness is a factor in the process of interpreting the Bible. It is bound to influence my approach. As a Christian, I believe in an inclusive society and I cherish respect for all peoples irrespective of their gender. However, I cannot deny that I have been socialized in a patriarchal society, which has implanted in me the false belief that a man is superior to a woman. This belief is unacceptable to me yet it is so strong in me that no matter how I resist it, time and again I find myself guilty of unconscious gender discrimination.

As a Motswana, I belong to a bigger group of people called
Africans. This is significant to my identity because my Africaness
defines my political situation, a situation of a Third World people
struggling for survival, a people faced with droughts, diseases and
famines. This context makes me read the Bible as though it were a
political book. It makes me ask questions like: Why is my country
and those in our region so poor? What has the Bible to say about
our poverty, about oppression? As a Motswana, I am also grounded
in a tradition of oral history. My people are a people with a ver-
satile memory that goes back into centuries through oral narratives.
Our history is encapsulated in tales of wars, of myths about animals
and peoples and of heroism by both kings and commoners. These
stories which are normally related around the fire by the old to the
young make us a distinctive people. They certainly make me to
appreciate oral history and storytelling in other cultures. They also
make me read the Old Testament with a special intuition and passion
for in many ways it reflects a world closer to mine. Narratives also
make me capture the message more easily. They relay a message in
a way that I am able to visualize for myself and my people. Storytelling facilitates easy communication for my people, many of whom
cannot read or write but who are good narrators who appreciate
narratives. My culture also expresses itself in various forms such as
in idioms, taboos and proverbs. It is such expression that facilitates
my reading of the text. It is in applying these to the reading that
my perspective in the interpretation of the text will come through.

I am also an ordained minister of the United Congregational
Church of Southern Africa, which is numerically the largest church,
and it is also the oldest church, in Botswana. Such firmly established
institutions have a strong tradition of interpreting the Bible. Whilst
it is not bad in itself to follow church tradition, one would not like
to be too hooked and immersed in it. There is a point where the
individual must emerge over everything else in the reading of the
text. My reading is therefore both an individual's perception and at
the same time carries with it an influence of my worship community. Being a Congregationalist means that I come from the reformed
tradition which places the Bible as the supreme guide in Christian
life. As such, my inclination is to approach the Bible with the eyes
of one who is grounded first in the tradition of the reformation, but
particularly so with congregational dogma.

I have also been equipped with academic training in modern theology and criticism of the Bible. Such training makes me not to

accept anything just as it is in the Bible. I read the Bible with a
critical eye which makes me realize that the Bible is culturally conditioned, its scripts have been corrupted over its years of transmission and that it comes out of a context far removed from mine.
My training has also conditioned me to accept that the text of the
Bible was first written in either Hebrew or Greek, and that knowledge of these languages is vital for a clearer understanding of the
Bible. As a church leader, my academic approach often makes me
to miss the immediate "soundings" of the word of God as I delve
too much into the world of academics. The very tools of biblical
exegesis and interpretation often become a hindrance to spiritual
understanding of the Bible.

In summary, my reading of the Bible is by no means a straightforward exercise. It is based on the complexity of my identity. I
approach the text from various social locations. These are borne out
of the many influences that embroider my life through socialization.
Such influences constitute my identity, and the complexity of who I
am has an impact on my reading of the Bible. My reading is also
undergirded by a deliberate intentionality on my part to reject any
form of "reading" that is imposed on me. However, I am committed
to embracing some of those things that I have been schooled into
which I find valuable for my reading. I believe that I need to rebel
against a "conventional reading" in order to have an authentic reading of the Bible that takes seriously my faith struggles, my people,
the questions and burdens that we approach the Bible with. With
these preliminary comments, I now turn to Genesis 1:1-10.

"In the beginning God created the heavens and the earth." This
creation account was a Jewish folktale, at least until it was canonized. This factor is very important because it shows that the narrative was not written by some prophet, nor was it related by some
divinity or even composed by a scribe. It arose out of the experience of ordinary people trying to make sense of their situation. It
arose, as it were, out of the grassroots. It is believed to have arisen
out of Babylon, where the Jews were held in captivity. The narrative reflects something of the Jewish understanding of who God is
and how God relates to people. It reflects something of the struggle of the Jews in fathoming who God is in the midst of a plethora
of teachings about God(s). The account begins with an assumption
that everything begins in and with God. Nothing just happens on

its own or as a result of some unexplained mechanical processes. It is a statement of faith attesting to the involvement of God in Jewish history. Implicit in this account is that God is the only God and that there is none besides God. That God is the almighty, and that God is the creator. The narrative begins by stating the conviction about God's active role in the realm of creation. This is not a God who is abstract and passive, but the one who is interested in the way things are and involves Godself. This is a concept that carries with it something of the religio-cultural similarity between the Jews and my people.

Batswana have several of their own folktales on creation. One such tale describes how everything emerged out of the earth. It is said that there was a crack on the surface of the earth and out of it came out people, animals, and their property. In this mythology the assumption is that the earth was created before human beings. This is a significant variance with other creation myths which tend to be anthropocentric. In this narrative human beings are not the crown of creation, they are just part of it as are the animals, the earth and the like. Furthermore, the narrative seems to suggest that all people were created equal, and with an equal entitlement to the prosperity of the earth. All were created with property and so all should have a right to be self-sufficient. Also strongly expressed in the narrative is the way creation is connected and interdependent. The fact that we came out of the earth is a connection, perhaps, that can only be likened to that of a child coming out of its mother's womb. Similarly, Genesis also holds that people were made from dust. Such a bond cannot be broken. In Setswana religious practices that affinity to nature is time and again expressed. During certain times of the year cutting of certain trees is considered to be a taboo. For example, during the months of November and December the *morula* tree is not to be cut. It is believed that cutting such trees will result in hailstorms which will destroy crops when they are just small. Such beliefs emanate from out high regard for inanimate creation which compel us to nurture it and preserve it.

Comparatively, the Genesis account is very dogmatic. On the contrary, the Setswana creation account is not as confrontational at all. It is not a debate about God, it simply states the belief that we and other animals came out of mother earth or that we are part and parcel of the earth. God is not mentioned, God is simply assumed to be the force behind the process. Neither is it said that a "man" was created first. For Batswana, God is not only the one who created heaven, earth and all that is, but God who brings rain, harvest, children, protection, freedom and all to our human situation. The Setswana narrative cited above depicts creation as having brought abundance in the form of food, animals, plants and their produce, and so forth. God provided us all with our daily bread at creation and should therefore continue with such provision. One of the many phrases that are used to refer to God in Setswana is that of *Moabi wa masego otlhe* (One who provides all the blessings). God's involvement in our daily lives is therefore somewhat measured with material prosperity for all. This understanding of God is very different from that of the missionary preaching which portrayed God as One who is distant and aloof from human situations. This is a totally different perception from Setswana belief. In Setswana when one begins a journey she or he would be bidden farewell with the saying *Tsamaya le Modimo* (Go with God) because it is believed that she or he can make the journey only with God. When one gets unexpected fortune or gain in life it is not because of luck but because God provides in God's way. As the saying goes, *Modimo ga o fe ka letsogo* (God does not give directly).

These creation stories attest to God's involvement in the human situation on a day to day basis. This characterization of God places a burden on a Motswana preacher. A Motswana preacher is challenged to constantly assess the portrayal of God in his or her preaching. That is, what kind of God do we preach to our people? Is it a foreign God or is it one who is totally involved with our lives and with creation as a whole? This new approach will unlock a whole new area of biblical interpretation that will be liberating to the Botswana church. It will liberate the church from the heavenward fundamentalism of the West which holds the church sedated and groggy such that it accepts the poor human condition as from God.

The narrative continues in verse two with the verse: "The earth was formless and void and darkness covered the face of the deep." One would think that the Hebrews are being too imaginative in the description of how the situation was when the process of creation began. But I have the suspicion that the prevailing circumstances at the time informed them about how things might have been at the beginning. In fact it is doubtful whether the writer was too concerned with the past, as opposed to the present and perhaps the future of God's creation. It was therefore in the present situation at the time that the Israelites were able to create a picture portrayed in the text. The narrative uses such graphic language as, "it was formless and empty." Unlike the Setswana narrative which seems to imply that the earth was already there, the Hebrews believed that creation was out of nothing. It is out of this nothingness that God brought creation into being. When there is nothing God's creativity brings new life. Quite often life around us seems empty, formless and purposeless. This is the situation that the Israelites experienced for themselves. This is the situation that many in Botswana experience in their daily faith struggles. Statistics show that 13% of our small population is HIV positive. We are already in a situation where cases of clinical AIDS are on the increase. For many people life is "formless and empty." This expression is, therefore, not an abstract concept. It is a daily reality.

The account continues by saying that the darkness was over the surface of the deep. The motif of darkness as an expression of a people's sinful situation is common to many religious teachings. Israel went through many moments of testing and hardship that in their memory they could appropriately refer to as moments of darkness. The experience of bondage and oppression in Egypt was such a moment of darkness. The subsequent nomadic life that Israel had to endure, landless and having to cope with the harsh conditions of the desert, was yet another experience where we could say they experienced an intense darkness in their life as a people. The context out of which our text probably arose, that of the Babylonian exile, was one of the darkest moments in the life of the community of Israel. This is a time when they had been stripped of their selfhood and dignity as a people, when they had been uprooted from their familiar surroundings—their Motherland.

Their bitterness and sense of humiliation is best captured in Psalm 137,

> O daughter Babylon, you devastator!
> Happy shall they be who pay you back
> what you have done to us!
> Happy shall they be who take your little ones
> and dash them against the rock! (8–9)

These are real human feelings, feelings of hurt and vindication that could be a result of the human condition that can only be described as darkness. This is the human condition that is so succinctly described in Genesis 1:2, the "darkness covered the surface of the deep." The description of the fragility and lameness of the human condition is true of all common human generations down the centuries and millennia. Generations characterized by wars, enmity between peoples, coups d'etat, oppressions and so forth. What should not escape our memory though is that in the midst of all this God's presence is always there. Hebraic history is rich in this exposition of divine presence through Israel's journeys and expressions. What should not escape our memory though is that in the midst of all this God's presence is particularly espoused in the various cultic traditions and tales of an epiphanic visitation in the traditions of the biblical patriarchs. It is often in the darkest hour that God's presence is revealed. Is it not interesting that it is in his/her diagnosis of the situation with its "voidness" and "darkness" that the writer is aware of the *ruach* (spirit) of God hovering over the deep? Similarly, it is often when things are difficult, in times of death, sickness, poverty, etc. that Batswana would often say '*Modimo o teng*' (God is present). In short, no human condition or pain is too derelict to diminish or exile God from us. In fact it is the very grim human conditions that necessitate God's initiative in revealing Godself to us. One who came and dwelt among us as one of our own, so as to set us free. So it does seem correct to say that God's creation work as recorded in the Genesis accounts was an act of liberation that set the tone for further acts of revelation and redemption later in their history.

The Genesis story is truly like a theatrical account of the beginning of the universe. So far we have been listening to the part that would be played by a narrator in a drama piece. The third verse is different, it begins with the phrase, "*Whayihi Elohim*" (Then God said . . .). This phrase is of special interest because so far we have not heard God speak. We have heard from the narrator about what God did and in what condition creation was. But now for the first time God speaks. God breaks the silence and does not just allow Godself to be heard but allows the word to effect transformation. What was void and useless becomes the realm upon which God's salvation history is manifested. Such transformation becomes a continuing activity of God on creation throughout the ages. When God speaks, change is bound to occur and there is a marked effect in the situation into which God's Word is uttered. This is somewhat different from what Batswana would understand as the role of God in the arena of creation. For them, God "speaks" through events that occur around us or through *Badimo* (Ancestors). God is not portrayed as one who speaks as characterized in the Genesis account. One of the popular Setswana idioms is that which goes, *Lefoko ga le boe go boa monwana* (A word never returns empty, it is the pointing finger that might go without effect). There is a sense in which the word is both the inward thought and the outward expression of that same thought not only in speech but also in deed (see Genesis 12:1–3, Joshua 3:17ff., 6:9ff., Exodus 3:12, 1 Samuel 5, etc.). From a Setswana understanding, a word is bound to have some kind of effect. Therefore the divine word that was ushered into the voidness and emptiness of the human condition is a concept that is easily acceptable. This is the word that brought order, light, days, waters and later became flesh and the liberator of humanity. God spoke through this word and brought creation into being and spoke through this same word and brought redemption to humanity.

One meets the phrase "*Whayihi Elohim*" over and over through the Bible. Its placing in the creation story is therefore significant and it becomes a lens through which we can read through God's journey with the Hebrews as is recorded in the Bible. Having shattered the silence, the divine word is to impinge upon history through the ages. It is later to be proclaimed by the prophets and it becomes a word for social consciousness. Its cutting edge is directed at kings, idolatrous nations, hypocritical nations and so forth. While it is sometimes ignored, ridiculed, and shunned, it also touches lives and restores them. The word brings life out of death, light out of despair, and it brings the reality of life out of nothingness.

The place of the Bible or the word in the Setswana church is therefore a special one. The Bible is perceived to be the word of God, and because it is the word of God it is the supreme guiding principle for Christian living. Central to our liturgical celebrations is always the proclamation of the word of God. The preacher, the medium through which the word speaks to us, plays an indispensable role in the character of our life as a believing community. Our preacher is our storyteller! And we gather to hear the storyteller. The listeners who "receive" the word from God also play an important part in the life of the community. Thus we want to hear God speak through our preachers, our women, our children and through the priesthood of all believers. Perhaps, it is somewhat correct in asserting that in Africa, and here I include Botswana, the Bible has a sort of numinous power being the record of God's word. The

downside of this is that the Bible has been used as a tool of control
and domination. As a result of the "numinous" status that the Bible
has acquired, in many circles it is seen as infallible. It is therefore
not read with any critical eye. Because many people read the Bible
with a gullible attitude, without a proper dialogue with it, some of its
vitality is lost. Instead of it becoming a tool of liberation it becomes a
tool of domination. The word of God is however the word of creativity,
freedom and empowerment, anything else is not the word of God.

"Let there be light and there was light." God commands that there
be light and indeed there was light. It does not come as much of
a surprise that God begins by commanding light to come into being.
As we saw earlier on, darkness was the arch-rival of God's purpose
for God's created order. Again the motif of light is a very popular
one in many religious traditions. In Setswana one of the names by
which we call God is that of *Ramasedi-a-poloka* (One who is the light
of salvation). Light is also used as a symbol of the presence of goodness and of the very being of God. This is why a candle is such a
strong symbol within the meaning system of the African Independent
Churches. During funerals it is lit around the coffin of the deceased.
It is a symbol of hope in the midst of death, hope that the deceased
will go to dwell in eternal peace in the land of the Living Dead.
The symbol of light is also strongly used during leadership hand-
over ceremonies. Candles or some form of light are exchanged between the new leadership and the old one. Such symbolism is indicative
of the fact that the new leadership is to carry on the work of sharing the light of good leadership and preaching the word of life. Many
indigenous churches also use light as a powerful symbol of their
meaning system. It features in a lot of their rituals, particularly those
relating to cleansing and healing. Some of these rituals include the
washing of "the client" in a tub full of water that has been prayed
for. Such bathing is meant to exorcise evil spirits from the person
since all such spirits are responsible for all ailments and ill fortune.
During this ritual candles are lit around the tub and continue burning through the entire process. The cleansing is effected by the
prayers offered, the washing itself and the light that drives away the
spirits of darkness. Light is therefore a very powerful symbol for
Botswana. It is a symbol of the presence of God among us, of God's
life for us and of victory over the powers of darkness. God's word

brings light and the darkness of our hearts and sinfulness disappears. In the Bible, this motif of light is commonly used in particular by the evangelist John. Jesus is quoted in the Johannine gospel as saying, "I am the light of the world, anyone who follows me will not walk in darkness, but will have the light of life." (2 John). The gospel holds that when we are still far away from God then we live in darkness. But when we accept Jesus as our friend, our model in life and our saviour then we have received the light for ourselves. This light is the salvation won for us through the death and resurrection of Jesus Christ. Other texts that use the symbol of light are quite popular within the Batswana church. One such text is the one in the Beatitudes which refers to believers as "the light of the world." It is read and preached on over and over again in the church.

The fifth verse is connected to the creation of light and it refers to a separation of day and night. Perhaps this is all there is to the verse, yet on the other hand I have the suspicion that there is an underlying message. There seems to be an implicit reference to two realms, one realm of darkness and the other of light. It is also curious that God does not create "darkness," it is part of the nothingness that requires God to act and bring forth creation. God could not have created that which negates the very being of God.

"Let there be the sky, the seas and land." Here the narrator spends some time narrating about the continuing creation of the other cosmic features of the universe. The focus is on the sky, waters and the earth. As a Motswana reader of the Bible, I am quite intrigued by these motifs. Although God is believed to be so involved in the human affairs, God remains *Modimo* (the most high). God remains lifted up above all creation. The sky is always a significant cosmological feature representing the transcendental nature of God. The Israelites would use the highest mountains as the seat of Yahweh, but Batswana have always seen the sky as the only realm upon which God resides. As such, the sky plays a significant role as the physical expression of the exalted nature of God above creation.

We need to remember that Palestine, like Botswana, is a desert country. Natural resources such as water remain priceless. In Setswana culture, one of the most commonly used words is *pula* (rain). *Pula* is a sign of blessing from God because through it we have crops, water to drink and all of creation rejoices with its coming. Rain is also a

sign of our prosperity as a community. Our farms yield food for our
people, the environment is beautiful, animals and people have water
to drink. When rain falls on our land, it is often seen as a sign of
our spiritual well-being. We would then know that our Ancestors are
pleased with us. It would be indicative of the fact that our moral
fibre as a community is intact. In fact there are a lot of taboos in
Setswana culture that forbid certain behavior on account that it
would chase away rain. For instance, unnecessary veld fires send
away rain and so does destruction of certain types of habitat. Thus
rain may be just another of God's created phenomenon for other
Christians, but for Batswana it is integral to our spirituality as much
as it is a basic commodity for our daily living.

It is important to note that the skies produce rain upon which
the earth is dependent. The people, animals and inanimate creation
are dependent on the land and the seas for their living. Here it is
clear that the whole created order is interconnected and interrelated.
No part of creation is self-sufficient on its own. We can also discern
the presence and control of a creator in creation. It is God the creator that is in control and holds the world together, and not the
human being as is often portrayed in our anthropologies. Humanity
is simply part of the created order. Such an interconnectedness of
creation undergirds a holistic spirituality among the Batswana that
includes all of life. There is no distinction between the sacred and
the secular, the material and the spiritual, religious belief and cultural norms. Batswana always pray for rain at the beginning of a
rainy season. During droughts and famines *dingaka* (traditional doc-
tors) have to perform rain-making rituals to appease the Ancestors
for the sins committed by the people. These activities show that the
physical aspects of creation and spiritual matters are intertwined.
God created one world and it is therefore a spiritual world.

The other important aspect of this cosmology is the creation of
the earth. It is upon the land that everything else is dependent. We
live on it, plough our crops upon it, mine valuable minerals out of
it, bury our dead in it, etc. Our lives therefore revolve around it.
The Setswana creation account asserts that not only is the land
important for our daily living but that it is the source of our very
being. It is the substance with which we have been made because
we came out of its belly. The Priestly narrative, that is the subject
of our discussion, also points out that a human being was created
out of the earth. This question of land has a special place in Hebraic

thinking. Perhaps because they were a landless people on many occasions in their history as a people. They lived as sojourners in the land of Egypt and had no land rights. During their nomadic life in the desert all they knew was the barrenness of the scorched earth. They had to survive in the precariousness of the situation. When the Israelites came to dwell in their own land, the land which they believed Yahweh had given to their foreparents, they did so with pride and cherished it. Their affinity to the land is best expressed in the Psalmist's words saying,

> The earth is the Lord's and everything in it
> the world, and all who live in it,
> for he founded it upon the seas and
> established it upon the waters (24: 1-2).

This statement is an epitome of the Jewish perspective on land issue. Their approach was of communal ownership. As a result it was regarded as anathema for an individual or group of individuals to claim sole ownership of land to the exclusion of others. This of course is not withstanding the fact that the land on which they lived had been forcibly taken from the Canaanites. This communal ownership is only restricted to Israel as a nation. Due to the religio-cultural hostility of Israel towards other nations their land was perceived to belong to God and as such the heritage of God's people, Israel. I believe Setswana religious believe has an even richer understanding of the concept of land. Batswana believe that the land is the abode of the Living Dead or the Ancestors. As such, it must not be desecrated. We desecrate our land by spilling of human blood onto it. Such irreligious behaviour results in infertility of land, veld fires, drought and other calamities. To restore our relationship to the earth would normally require a ritual which would involve a cleansing of the community: slaughtering a cow and brewing of traditional beer. The beer would be drunk in a ritualistic fashion, with the calabash being passed from one person to the other after every sip. It would then be poured on the ground as a sign of communion with the Ancestors and therefore with God. Such cleansing restores broken relations between peoples within the community, between human community and the environment as well as between creation and the divine. It is believed that it would result in the earth flourishing in its produce and in other blessings. This hallowing of land resonates even though remotely with Jewish belief that land had to lie fallow every seventh year. Such time of "rest" allowed for the restoration of the earth.

It seems to me that the earth or land is the centre piece in the order or creation. Western hermeneutics have tended to put a human being as the most important aspect of creation. As a result the role of humanity in creation has been by and large a negative one. Such an interpretation cast the human role as to dominate other over creation, to exploit it and get the most out of it. If, however, we perceive the earth as that part of creation around which everything else revolves then our attitude to it would certainly be different. We would want to preserve its goodness, and our role would be that of caretakers and not exploiters. By plundering and abusing the earth and its ecological systems, we are not only undermining God's creation but the very pinnacle of our existence. The fact that we all came out of the earth and are so intrinsically linked to it means that we ought to change our ownership ethic. Like the Israelites, Batswana believe that land should be owned corporately. Most of the land would normally be classified as tribal land and under the oversight of the *kgosi* (king). In this way, the land would be accessible to all for pastoral use, settlements and farming.

The passage ends with the statement "and God saw that it was Good." This is a profound statement. In a sense it is a statement that brings out the aspect of anthropomorphism which is so characteristic of Jewish biblical theology. God is presented as though it were a person who having done an artwork takes time to inspect it and admire the finished work. This kind of portrayal of the divinity is quite common through the Bible and facilitates an incarnational conceptualization of the transcendent. It is a feature common in other religions. This concept though is insidious in a Setswana perspective and is often inferred rather than explicitly expressed. What complicates this even more is the fact that Setswana, as in most African languages, is inclusive. Unlike in English, and its relative languages, God is not referred to as He or She. In our God-talk, we often refer to the divine in generic terms such as Creator, Provider, Saviour, Pillar, Rainmaker. Anthropomorphic language is seldom used in talking about God because of its inadequacies.

According to divine observation, creation is good. It appears as though this statement is said in anticipation of what is to happen to creation, with the intervention of disobedience and sin later on.

Because of human sin, the original intention of God for creation was blemished. As a result there became a division between creation and God, between one human being and the other as well as between humanity and the rest of creation.

What could the writer possibly mean, though, by saying that creation was good? Is it possible to imagine this goodness of creation? Perhaps, we should see this verse as a deliberate and direct contrast to verse two which depicted creation as void and formless. God had impinged upon a chaotic situation and transformed it into the goodness that is observed here. Creation was now balanced and all were equal without any form of exploitation. God's providence had also left creation in a state of prosperity and self-sufficiency. There was no disparity between the rich and the poor. Creation was also in a coherent harmony and was interdependent, with the earth dependent on the rain, the people and animals on the earth, etc. This concept of a good creation was to become a preoccupation of Israel throughout the ages through her religious and political reforms. It was to be found embedded in the yearnings of the prophets of the eighth and ninth century. A yearning that includes a world without wars:

> they will beat their swords into ploughshares and their spears
> into pruning hooks. Nation will not take up sword against nation.
> Nor will they train for war anymore (Isaiah 2:4).

This I believe is the kind of world that Batswana and African people would agree that it is good. This is how I would like to believe creation was before it was despoiled and tainted by human domination and greed, there were no wars between nations. Countries were not ravaged by civil wars as Angola, Somalia, Liberia, Sierra Leone to name just a few countries. Peace, self-sufficiency, interconnectedness and justice in creation should be at the centre of our existence.

The Setswana mythology on creation asserts that people came with property from the earth, and we came with corn, furniture, tools, our animals and so forth. It underscores the self-sufficiency pointed to in the Priestly narrative of Gen 2:26–28. This question of self-sufficiency vis-à-vis poverty, homelessness and exploitation is another concept that the prophets of Israel tackled with much vigour: Jeremiah 22:16 says God "defended the cause of the poor and the needy and so all went well. Is that not what it means to know me? declares he Lord." While Amos 2:7 says "They trample on the heads of the poor as upon the dust of the ground, and deny justice to the

oppressed." For the prophets, poverty and exploitation of a person
by another person was an abomination before the Lord and contrary to God's intention for creation. God's world was created good
and all its creatures had access to its providence. What the rich, the
kings and religious leaders were doing was, therefore, contrary to
God's plan for a good and well-balanced creation.

Yet we who live in Sub-Saharan Africa do not know justice, self-
sufficiency and interconnectedness in creation. Because our economies
are controlled from the West, our people are unemployed, paid mean
salaries, uneducated and homeless. We do not experience God's creation as good, well balanced and admirable. Yet in reading Genesis
1:1–10 we have faith in God, faith that the God of creation, the
God of our Ancestors, will restore the goodness of our planet. God
will look again and it shall be good, for God who is the Creator of
Light, or as Setswana theologians would say, *Ramasedi-a-poloka* (One
who is the light of salvation), can bring light onto the darkness and
formlessness of the earth. Because God created the earth good and
with all people sufficient, we can never accept the poverty that reigns
in Sub-Saharan Africa. This gives us courage because we realize that
God is on our side. It is not part of God's plan for creation that
there should be darkness and formless in any part of the created
order. Rather, God wants all people to be interconnected with one
another by upholding principles of sharing the riches of the earth
with fairness and justice. God wants all people to be closely connected to the earth and to participate in the continuation of creation by conserving its goodness.

Our faith is that in our reading of the Bible we will use resources
of our culture and experience to have a new understanding of God's
plans for us as creation. With such a fresh reading of the Bible we
Batswana will contribute to what other African Christians and Christians elsewhere are trying to do in capturing the message of the text
for ourselves, our contexts, and our world.

BIBLIOGRAPHY

Buck, H.M. *People of the Land, the History, Scriptures, and Faith of Ancient Israel.* New
York: Macmillan, 1966.
Lessa, W.A. and Voft, E.Z. *Reader in Comparative Religion: An Anthropological Approach*
New York: Harper and Row, 1965.
Parrinder, G. *African Mythology.* London: Hamlyn, 1967.

Pauw, B.A. *Religion in Tswana Chiefdom.* London: Oxford University Press, 1960.
Westermann, C., Ed. *Essays on Old Testament Hermeneutics.* Richmond: John Knox
   Press, 1966.

THE IMPACT OF THE BIBLE ON
TRADITIONAL RAIN-MAKING INSTITUTIONS
IN WESTERN ZIMBABWE

Hezekiel Mafu

From the time Christianity was first introduced into Western Zimbabwe, a tense or perhaps a hostile atmosphere has existed between the adherents of African Indigenous Religions and Christian religious systems. This has often become most conspicuous in times of disastrous situations, such as droughts. Such catastrophic events have generated accusations and counter-accusations by protagonists of both religions for the prevailing conditions. Communities and families have been torn apart especially when religious convocations have been called by either side to remedy the situation. Traditionalists consider the Bible a tool to undermine indigenous religious systems and have urged communities to reject it totally. The underlying cause for this acrimonious friction between the religious groups has been occasioned by conceptions, or perhaps misconceptions, held by each group, on the source of and the methodology used to acquire rain. As a prelude to the main focus of this essay, I shall endeavour to briefly outline what could be called the fundamental belief systems of each of the two religions relative to the source of rain.

According to the Old Testament biblical literature, Yahweh (God) is the only source and provider of rain. In his rhetorical questions to Israel, the prophet Jeremiah asked if any of the worthless idols of the nations brought any rain or the skies themselves sent down showers? Responding to these questions Jeremiah reiterated that it was Yahweh, the God of Israel who provided rain (Jeremiah 14:22). Echoing the same sentiments Job stated that it was God who ordered the snow to fall on earth and determined the quantity and quality of rain (Job 37:6). It was further believed that rain could be used by God to express divine displeasure and punishment for people's delinquency. Such was the situation in the account of the flood in Genesis where Yahweh destroyed the antediluvian people with rain, save Noah and his family and specimens of every animal species (Genesis 7:1–4). In his final warning to the nation of Israel, Moses warned them to be careful not to be enticed to turn away from God and worship other gods because that would evoke God's anger against them and he would shut the heavens so that it would not rain and the ground would yield no produce and they would perish in the land the Lord had given them as an inheritance (Deuteronomy 11:16–17).

Similarly the prophet Jeremiah accused Israel of prostitution against her God and stated that the consequences of her unfaithfulness were the withholding of showers and the absence of spring rains (Jeremiah 3:1–3). Israel was further accused of stubbornness and possessing rebellious hearts which did not fear God who provided autumn and spring rains in season and assured them of regular weeks of harvest (Jeremiah 5:23–24). In his dedicatory prayer for the temple King Solomon prays that if the heavens were shut up and there was no rain because of Israel's sins, God should hear from heaven, forgive their sins and send rain on the land, when Israel gathered at the temple or, if they were slaves in a far away land, prayed facing its direction and confessing their sins (1 Kings 18:35–36).

The drama on Mount Carmel is a sombre example of Israel's waywardness in regard to God, followed by the divine discipline of drought. The story begins with king Ahab of Israel marrying Jezebel daughter of Ethbaal king of the Sidonians. As queen she introduced the worship of Baal and Asherah in Israel. She further seduced her husband to worship foreign gods. As a result Elijah, the prophet, confronted the king and declared that there would be no rain in Israel because of the insolence of the king and that of the whole nation to Yahweh (1 Kings 17:1). Baal was known to be the rider of clouds and was worshipped as dispenser of fertility (Dunnigan 1981). One day the king and his servant Obadiah, while searching for fodder and water for horses, met Elijah who challenged the king to schedule a contest between Baal and Yahweh on Mount Carmel. The story ends with the victory of Yahweh. The 450 prophets of Baal are slaughtered on the orders of Elijah. There is a confession of sin and acknowledgement of Yahweh as the great God over Baal, followed by a downpour (1 Kings 18:16–45). The principle undergirding the above texts is that the art of rain-production was the prerogative of the God of heaven who could, at God's discretion, either withhold or oversupply it as an expression of divine displeasure on the misdemeanours of God's people. Such retributive acts

of God could only be reversed by confession of sin and acknowledgement of Yahweh as God by the Jewish nation.

The New Testament presents God as the merciful benefactor whose
rain is bountifully given to both the righteous and unrighteous alike
without partiality. God's generosity knows no discrimination on moral
or religious grounds (Matthew 5:44–45). While not much more is
said on rain in the New Testament, it is, however, assumed that the
Christian believers imbibed the Old Testament perceptions that rain
was the prerogative of God. For example, exhorting his congregation on the efficacy of the prayer of faith, James, the apostle, refers
to the mount Carmel episode where Elijah, through prayer, successfully unlocked the heavens to end the drought that had devas-
tated the land for more than three years in succession (James 5:17–18).
Although no spectacular occasion of rain-production through prayers,
similar to that of the prophet Elijah on Mount Carmel, has been
recorded during and subsequent to the New Testament era, it is,
however, unquestionable that the tradition and practice of praying
for rain have been a part of church life over many centuries.

The following poem of the 14th century is reflective of the religious perceptions of the day on the issue of rain. "Wyth the lest
word that a wil, the wynd ys aready to blowe or to be stille or to
brethy softe and oile the water of thys world woilde in his glove"
(Langland 1995: 69–71). Furthermore, the following prayer for rain
is evidence that prayer for rain continued to be the tradition and
practice of the Christian church.

> O God heavenly Father, who by thy Son Jesus Christ has promised
> to all them that seek thy kingdom and thy righteousness thereof, all
> things necessary to their bodily sustenance, send us, we beseech thee,
> in this our necessity, such moderate rain and showers that we may
> receive the fruits of the earth to our comfort and thy honour, through
> Jesus Christ our Lord, Amen (*The Book of Common Prayer* 1853).

The writings of the church fathers in the fourth and fifth century
show that miracles existed in profusion and were believed to be a
kind of celestial charity to alleviate the sorrows, diseases and also
supply the wants of the faithful. Such miracles incited piety, stimu-
lated devotions of the languid and rewarded the patience of the fer-
vent. They were viewed as signs of great and saintly virtue which
had universal respect for those who had attained a high degree of
sanctity. Men of extraordinary sanctity seemed, naturally and habit-

ually, to obtain the power of performing miracles and their lives were crowded with such achievements, condoned and attested to by the highest sanction of the church. Missionaries to heathen nations abroad were reported to have experienced supernatural signs which confounded their opponents and made the powers of darkness flee before them, such incidents abounded in every part of Europe and neither excited astonishment nor scepticism (Leacky 1893: 140–143). The supernatural became part of and an accepted form of the religious component of the age. Among the noted supernatural acts was that of rain-making. For example, Saint Quintinianus, an early sixth century Bishop of Rodez, in the face of a great drought and at the behest of the parishioners of Augvergne, on the third day of the feast of the ascension of Christ, prostrated himself on his cloak in the middle of the road and prayed for a long time in tears. His prayer was based on 2 Chronicles 6:26 which says when the heavens are shut up and there was no rain because of Israel's sins, if the Israelites prayed towards the temple confessing their sins, then God should hear from heaven and forgive God's people and send rain upon the land given to them as an inheritance. When the bishop rose and sang the sky darkened with clouds followed by heavy torrents of rain over the whole land (Flint 1992: 186). Deodatus of Nevers tells of how his tunic and that of his friend Hidulph were used in times of drought, floods or pestilence. Saint Columbus' tunic and books in his own handwriting were taken round the plain that had been lately ploughed and sown, the tunic was raised three times in the air and his books opened and read on the hill of angels, believed to be the spot heavenly guests descended to confer with the late bishop. Rain was reported to have fallen in torrents as a result. Some of these holy men were reported to have stopped adverse winds, storms and hailstorms which destroyed crops in the fields by climbing rooftops and simply ordering it to stop. Florentius of Nursia was reported to have had the capacity to call down thunder and lightning to destroy snakes that had infested the cells (Flint 1992: 187–188).

During the Protestant Reformation era attitudes towards the miraculous or supernatural changed. In their contempt for Catholic superstitions and the desire to repudiate miracles in support of Catholicism, Protestants refused to accept the validity of miracles that had occurred after biblical times (Westfall 1958: 5–6). It was argued that when Christianity was still unrecognized by governments it existed in an

abnormal condition, the laws of nature were suspended in its favour
and continual miracles ensured its triumph. When the conversion of
Constantine placed civil powers at its disposal the era of the supernatural was closed and the power of working miracles was with-
drawn. The alliance between church and state being instituted,
Christianity had arrived at its normal and final position and exceptional assistance in the form of miracles thus became obsolete (Leacky
1893: 149–150). There was a clear line of demarcation between the
New Testament miracles which were seen as characterised by dignity and solemnity and to have conveyed some spiritual lesson and
other benefits, besides attesting to the character of the worker, and
medieval miracles believed to be trivial, purposeless and unimpres-
sive, constantly verging on the grotesque (155–161).

The seventeenth century marked the beginning of the modern
world with its new institutions, convocations and concepts which
were apparent in many fields. There was, however, no element of
European civilization that revealed changing patterns of life and
thought more than the Christian religion (Westfall 1958: 1). Early
in the seventeenth century natural disasters were still believed to be
evidences of God's anger at the vices of humankind, the universe
was regarded as the sphere of the operations of spiritual beings of
a nature analogous to their world, every unusual phenomenon was
considered the direct and isolated act of an unseen agent, thunder,
famine and pestilence were considered the result of an ebullition of
spiritual anger, while great and rapid prosperity was viewed as the
sign of spiritual satisfaction. So whenever disaster struck preachers
and pamphleteers were quick to indicate its direct origin in the moral
delinquencies of the people (Thomas 1971: 96–97). After the mid-
seventeenth century it became unfashionable to explain such events
it terms of God's providence. Most people reacted against enthusiasts who identified the judgements of God in daily life. A new intellectual current, the achievement of natural science, raised questions
that could not be ignored. A form of mechanical philosophy, sometimes called rationalism, pointed to the creator who originally made
a machine and set it in motion, but once created nature was an autonomous material order made up of senseless atoms moved by other
unconscious particles (77). No longer was nature considered an element of the providential plan, it was understood to be an order of
static, immutable and impersonal laws. Material causes once created
were supposed to act by their own necessity in accordance with nat-

ural laws. Leibniz, one of the philosopher-scientists, did not believe that God intervened in creation at all because divine intervention in nature would imply self-contradiction on the part of the Almighty (75–77).

Contrary to modern scientists, those in the seventeenth century were deeply religious. Among them, for example, were clerics who found little difficulty in reconciling the ministry with the interest in natural philosophy. With the growing prestige of science, reconciliation with Christianity meant the adjustment of Christian beliefs to conform to the conclusions of science. To them every investigation of nature was believed to be an act of worship and they saw themselves as investigators of God's creation as theologians studied scriptural revelation (Westfall 1958: 3, 7, 8, 27, 32). Although they believed that the age of miracles was past and that the ordered course of nature precluded miraculous eruptions, they regarded the Bible as the inspired foundation of the Christian religion and could not deny biblical miracles. They, however, believed that providence operated by a mechanical process inherent in the original construction of the machine. God was compared to an engineer who exhibited great skill in designing a machine that would do whatever job God had in mind by itself, rather than one that required an operator. Consequently God displayed more acumen in creating a universe that fulfilled all purposes by the operations of brute matter alone than in fashioning one that needed an intelligent overseer to regulate and control its parts (84). Some scientists came to believe that every phenomenon in the Bible could be traced to the machine as created by God initially, and they thus denied that biblical miracles were supernatural acts. For example, the Egyptian plague that caused water in the Nile river to become blood was believed to have been caused by a disease of haemorrhage among the fish in the river Nile, and the incident of the tumbling down of the walls of Jericho they claimed was the result of an earthquake. To the people then both events had appeared supernatural but to scientists of later centuries they were products of natural forces. Floods, earthquakes and diseases, all of the extraordinary events that had been hitherto attributed to divine causation, were seen to be as natural as the daily rotation of the earth (99–101).

Thus the nineteenth century begins with science and religion not just in harmony but mutually interdependent, for not only did theologians use scientific evidences, but scientists investigated nature with a religious pursuit providing evermore evidences of God's existence. But while the general trend of Protestantism embraced and even advocated such views, there were, however, some opposing voices who advocated for a return to what could be called "old time religion" of the medieval era. They viewed life's ship as never without a steersman, whether passengers were awake or asleep, God was always at the helm. To them the idea of "deus absconditus" (a God who had abandoned creation to its devices) was reprehensible. They still regarded natural disasters as expressions of divine anger at the vices of affected communities (Thomas 1971: 91–92). Throughout the seventeenth and later centuries such preachers continued to re-iterate that comets, floods and monstrous births were sent by God to draw men to repentance. The search for a scapegoat came from the conviction that every natural disaster had a moral cause (Palley 1984: 251). Some of the clergy in this category viewed the process of mechanical philosophy as a symptom of a subtle and sinister attempt to eliminate God from the natural scene (Carsi 1988: 51).

Such were the conflicting and changing religious attitudes towards the supernatural in Europe at the time Christian missionaries invaded the continent of Africa with the gospel. There were some who, when requested and pressured by communities to pray for rain, acquiesced to such requests while others declined believing that such prayers could not change the natural laws. Dr. J.TH. Van De Kemp, after repeated pressure from the Xhosa chief Ngqika and his deputation reluctantly conceded to the request to pray for rain, after which a two-day torrential rain was experienced so much so that the chief's kraal was flooded and the chief had to be evacuated in haste (Enklaar 1988: 34). Similar situations could be said of men like William Sykes in Northern Matabeleland in Western Zimbabwe (Bhebe 1979: 60) and Francois Coillard among the Lozi people in Zambia (Prins 1980: 195). While on the other hand, men like Dr. David Livingstone, a pragmatist, suggested, as solution to the recurring drought problem in Botswana, not a season of prayer for rain, but the creation of a dam and the construction of a canal on a never failing river to irri-gate their fields. He accepted the reality of the drought and pro-posed coping mechanisms to affected communities to mitigate against its effects (Livingstone 1910: 18, 24). Livingstone further advocated what could be called "a twin-track approach" to evangelism in Africa where Christianity and civilization were simultaneously promoted. He believed that neither could be promoted singularly.

The context of the above narratives reveals a dichotomous state of affairs on the part of Christian missionaries. Their duty called for the Christianization of communities in Africa and this involved teaching them to trust and pray to God for the supply of their needs. Yet they themselves were constrained by the mechanical philosophy imbibed by Protestantism. So it was that the mission Christianity which came to Africa was experiencing a tension between its textual tradition, in which the dominant themes were of healing the sick, the experience of the spirit and the miraculous, and its 'modern' missionary interpretations. A large number of phenomena which used to be explained in religious terms were now explained in terms of scientific cosmology. The weather especially was now explained in theoretical terms, from which the supernatural was totally removed.

This was not the case for the indigenous rain-shrines in Western Zimbabwe, particularly the *Mwali* rain cult. *Mwali* is the shrine god who is concerned primarily with rain, the well-being of crops and local politics in the region (Beach 1980: 249). This High-god is further considered to be active and immanent and is the spiritual owner of the earth and creator of mankind. She or he intervenes in human affairs. She or he manifests her/himself in such great natural phenomena as volcanic eruptions and lightning. *Mwali* speaks directly to the living not only in thunder and wind but as a voice heard most frequently in caves amidst the rocks and as a god who can be approached by the living with sacrifice and supplication. At some point in time when the rocks were still soft *Mwali* walked the earth and left an imprint on them, such rocks and hollows constitute a sacred zone in mediation which provide points of contact between him/her as creator with people who talk to him/her and hear his/her voice in response (Werbner 1989: 248). At the shrine reports from the districts are made to an officer known as the "eye," petitions are addressed to another officer known as the "ear," and answers are received from the senior officer known as the "mouth" (Ranger 1967: 22–23). She or he is viewed and believed to be the god of plenty, rain, fertility, life war and peace. She or he punishes those who refuse or forget to thank him/her by offering gifts after she or he has given his/her blessings.

Mwali is considered the creator of the universe, she or he is the spiritual power that made the world and everything in it. His/her benevolent power ensures the prosperity of the world and its peoples multiply. For the world to prosper it needs water which is controlled by the creator, hence she or he is to be requested to supply the blessings of bountiful rains (Cockcroft 1972: 83–84). *Mwali* has many shrines yet she or he is one, she or he is believed to manifest her/himself in the following ways. First, *Mwali* is manifest as *Shologulu*, which means "the big-headed one." He is the powerful and transcendent god who is feared and respected. He manifests himself through natural phenomena like the thunder clap and meteorite and is an ambivalent divine power capable of showing both kindness and anger when offended. He is not considered to be a fetish god bound to some stick or stone but as a god who moved from cave to cave. There is no one cave sacred to her/him (Ranger 1967: 146). Second, she also manifests herself as *Banyachaba*, which means "mother of the nation." In this capacity she is the god of fecundity of the land and its people. It is she who is responsible for providing rain and substance to all creatures in the universe. It is this manifestation of *Mwali* that is interested in the welfare of the people (Mason 1958: 195). Thirdly, *Mwali* manifests himself as *Lunji*, which is "the son of god," who runs errands between *Shologulu* and *Banyachaba* (Ntoi 1994). He is the intermediary going back and forth between the mother and father (Werbner 1989: 248). In fact Gwakuba Ndlovu says that after the priest had said all the praises to *Mwali* at the cave, a loud jingling of iron objects was heard inside the cave before a voice was heard in response to the requests presented by the chief priest. The voice usually said that *Lunji* too would go and present their requests to the greater one—*Banyachaba*. At no time in the past has *Mwali* promised people anything (Ndlovu 1994: 5). This seems to be *Lunji*'s responsibility in his shuttle diplomacy between the people, *Banyachaba* and *Shologulu*. Richard Werbner says that most commonly people mean *Lunji*, the son, when they speak of *Mwali*. V. Ralushai claims that *Lunji* can manifest himself in wind, thunder and lightning (Ralushai 1994). Werbner further claims that the earthly location of oracles in the hills corresponds to the celestial location of the trinity. In the south at Njelele is *Shologulu* the great head and father. It is there that he arrived first and left his footprints. In the east of Njelele is Dzilo (Wirirani) which corresponds to *Banyachaba* the mother of the nation. Finally south of Dzilo is Dula which corresponds to the son *Lunji* (Werbner 1989: 286).

In an interview with James Ncube, a messenger to the Njelele shrine for many years, he gave the following information regarding the deportment and what goes on inside the holy cave as they enter.

Black attire is a requirement for all messengers to the shrine cult. As they go to *Mwali*, they carry the following items as gifts to the High-god: a black cloth, tobacco (unground), a skin of a genet and dagga. On entering the cave they face the east as the shrine priest takes the articles they have brought as gifts and places them in their proper places. He would then inform the "rock" (another name for the shrine-god) that his/her people have come to request rain. Such ceremonies were conducted at the beginning of the rain season between September and October each year (Interview with Ncube 1994).

From these descriptions we can understand the source of the tension between the Christian and traditional indigenous views. The Christian religion, if it was looking at all, looked up to God in the heavens for answers to their prayers for rain, while traditionalists looked up to the Matopo hills for answers to their drought predicament. The lines of demarcation between the two religious systems might therefore have seemed distinct and clear. But the 1991–92 drought precipitated what could be termed "the Christianization of the traditional religious systems in Western Zimbabwe." This is a religious event with neither precedent nor parallel in the religious history of the region.

The year itself will be remembered in the annals of Zimbabwe as a year of profound and unprecedented drought which caused devastation and immense human suffering and has been rightly labelled "the worst drought in living memory" (Gasela 1992: 4). Its enormous impact on the populace and its livestock left a trail of indescribable misery and the reasons for the character and magnitude of the phenomenon became a topic of discussion in both scientific and indigenous circles. Meteorological explanations focussed on the movements of the inter-tropical convergence zone. However, these were not adequate for a belief system which holds that there is a divine force which has the capacity to withhold the rain if offended. So the focus of attention changed to a search in the realm of the divine. Spirit-mediums delved into the spirit-world to discover the nature of the offence committed by the nation and the remedy needed to right the situation. The responses were many and varied, but there was unanimity on the underlying cause of the drought—it was the anger of the gods (*Chronicle* 1992). Among the many reform movements that emerged as responses to the drought were three of particular interest—the Njelele Reform, the Juliana Movement and the Manyangwa

Theological Reform. On the basis of interviews conducted in 1994 I shall endeavour to give a synopsis of each one of them.

Having secured nomination, in a bitterly contested election, Gogo Ngcatu emerged as the rightful heir to the priesthood at the Njelele rain-making shrine in the 1991–92 rain-season. She initiated a theological order hitherto unprecedented in the history of the cult-shrine. She considered herself a believer and worshipper of the God of the Bible. She claimed to have been instructed by the "rock" (a reference to *Mwali*) to always keep and frequently read the Bible. Gogo Ngcatu believed that the God who appeared to Moses on Mount Sinai and gave him the Ten Commandments was the same God who spoke in the past and is still speaking now at the Njelele cult-shrine in the Matopo hills. The methodology of communication has not changed, what has changed is the venue and the audience addressed. She also believed that the Lord Jesus Christ would come soon to this earth to establish his everlasting kingdom. Her hope of the second coming of Christ is based on Matthew 24 where Christ spoke of the signs of his coming in power and glory. She believed that the two systems of worship—the indigenous and Christian—emanated from the same source and pray to the same God. She believed that God honoured his/her children's petitions from both religious systems. Through the theological initiatives of Gogo Ngcatu members of the Zionist Christian Movements have participated for the first time in the traditional rain-ceremonies of the shrine.

Another movement of significance which stormed the southern part of the country in 1992 was spearheaded by a middle-aged woman commonly known as "Mbuya Juliana." Her base was at the Dzilo shrine and she lived in the same village as Machokoto the shrine-keeper. Mbuya Juliana claimed to have been sent by a team of six divinities who were, *Musikavanu, Mapa, Nehanda, Chaminuka*, the ancestors and Jesus Christ. Among the abovementioned divinities, the *Mapa* are a new and unknown element in the indigenous religious structure. The word "*Mapa*" in Shona is associated with giving or giver but in this context, as she explained, they are divine beings ranked second to *Musikavanu* (creator of humankind). They also seem to be the agents of communication for the divine sextet. The message from the divine sextet was delivered to Machokoto by the *Mapa* on the 1st of January 1992. Subsequently, the latter commissioned Mbuya Juliana to admonish the nation on what these divinities required to be done if the drought was to end. Mbuya Juliana did not regard herself as a rainmaker but as a messenger sent with a special message. She claimed to have been given a ten-year programme during which she was to cover the entire country with her message. At the beginning of her ceremonies in the various districts she visited, Juliana always asked one of the Christians present to offer prayer. Her message to the Zimbabwean nation was that the *Mapa* were angry because the political leadership had not accorded them due honour and respect for the role they played in the armed struggle. As a result they had withheld the rain from falling. The *Mapa* wanted independence celebrations out in the bush, on hilltops and mountains—where actual acts of fighting and protection had taken place. It was at such places where the *Mapa* were most active in providing protection and security for freedom fighters, not in the cities and towns. Two days were declared as holy days, Sundays and Wednesdays for Christians and traditionalists respectively. These days were to be observed by all irrespective of religious affiliation.

The third theological reform movement which featured in the country during the 1991–92 drought was at the Mamnyangwa shrine. The shrine is located about thirty kilometres from the border town of Plumtree to the northwest, in chief Mpini's area. Unlike the Dzilo and the Njelele shrines, the Manyangwa shrine is not located in the Matopo Range. On the day we visited Mr. Manyangwa (the shrine keeper) his attire was of particular significance. He wore a dark suit and across his shoulders were two scarves of different colours, one was blue and had an emblem of white cross on it, and the other was black. He explained the significance of the two scarves, saying that the blue one represented his role as a Christian minster of his church, while the black one, and the beads on his forehead, represented his service to *Ubabamkulu* and the ancestors. This attire symbolised that indigenous tradition and Christianity were now in agreement. There was one God for both systems. Of particular relevance to this essay is his understanding of John 1:1–3. Mr. Manyangwa argued that this text of scripture refers to the voice that speaks from the shrine. There is little distinction between "word" and "voice" in isiZulu or isiNdebele, and both could be used interchangeably particularly in this text. John 1:1 in isiNdebele reads "*Ekuqaleni wayekona Ulizwi.*" A literal word for word translation of this text could be "In the beginning was the voice." Mr. Manyangwa argued that the voice referred to in John was that same voice that addressed people at the *Mwali* shrine. This text, according to Mr. Manyangwa, confirmed the pre-existence of the voice at the shrine.

In an earlier interview we also spoke with the Reverend Kenneth Nkomo of the Faith Apostolic Church of Zion, who had come to participate in the rain-ceremonies. He claimed to have visited the shrine with his son-in-law at the beginning of the 1993 rain-season and had heard the voice speak from the "rock." This voice had referred them to the Gospel of John 1:1–3 and had claimed to be the one referred to in this text. The voice had claimed to have been there before anyone else was, it further claimed to be the creator, to own the Bible and to have written and given the Ten Commandments to Moses on Mount Sinai. Mr. Manyangwa and Reverend Nkomo both claimed that God who spoke to the patriarchs/ancestors during Bible times on hills, mountains and rocks, was the same God who still used these objects at the cult-shrines today. God spoke to Abraham on one of the mountains in the land of Moriah in Genesis 22. God spoke to Moses on Mount Sinai in Exodus 20, and spoke to Elijah in the cleft of Mount Horeb in 1 Kings 19:8–9. The difference for us, the two men concluded, is that the mountains are in Zimbabwe and the communities addressed are Zimbabweans.

In conclusion, it is obvious that the 1991–92 drought introduced a new element within the religious scenario in Western Zimbabwe. The new shrine-keeper at Njelele transformed the theological stance of the cult in an unprecedented way. In contrast to the hostile attitude of previous incumbents, Gogo Ngcatu claimed allegiance to the Old and New Testament God and upheld the authenticity of the Bible from which she read every day. The Bible became the cornerstone of her instruction to the Wosana during their annual pilgrimage to the Njelele shrine for rain-making ceremonies. Her equation of the God who wrote the Ten Commandments at Mount Sinai with the god at the Njelele shrine in the Matopo hills is of particular significance; God's methodology has not changed with times but what has changed is the venue, the location and audience. If the current trend continues, it may not be long before the Wosana and the delegates who come for their annual pilgrimage to this shrine will be required to bring, along with other items, their Bibles as well.

At Dzilo the Juliana Movement has done something comparable. Christ became a member of the divine sextet that appeared to Machokoto, who in turn sent Juliana to the nation. To signal the authenticity of the alliance of the sextet two days were declared as holy days to be observed by all, one for traditionalists and the other for Christians. Juliana makes use of Christians who attend her ceremonies by asking them to pray at the beginning of her ceremonies. Like her counterpart at Njelele, there is a strong ingredient of Christianity in her ceremonies, though Christ does not play as active a role as the *Mapa*.

The Manyangwa theological reform presents a fascinating example of attempts by indigenous forms of religion to foster an alliance with Christianity. The incumbent shrine-keeper serves a dual capacity, first as minister of the New Covenant Apostolic Faith Mission and secondly as shrine-keeper for *Ubabamkulu*. The two scarves symbolize that Christianity and African Indigenous Religion are now in agreement. *Ubabamkulu* assumed all the claims of the God of the Bible such as creation, authorship of the Ten Commandments and the ownership of the Bible itself. He also claims to be the "Word/Voice" referred to in John 1:1–3.

The theological reforms at the cult shrines seem to have attracted considerable sympathy and understanding between African Indigenous Churches and African Indigenous Religion practitioners, dissolving the acrimonious relationships that had existed between these groups for decades. Something of an alliance or fusion might be in the offing. However, what the nature of the alliance or fusion might be, is not yet clear. While the Christianisation of the indigenous *Mwali* rain-cults described in this essay may appear fairly superficial, its significance should not be underestimated. On the one hand, it illustrates graphically the advance of what we might call "a public biblical and Christian culture" from which the traditional indigenous shrines can no longer stand apart, on the other, it appears to have broken down the barrier of separation between Zionist clergy and the shrine officials. If this is the case, then the 1991–92 drought materially altered the religious complexion of Western Zimbabwe.

BIBLIOGRAPHY

Beach, D.N. *The Shona and Zimbabwe 900–1800*. London: Heinemann 1980.
Bhebe, N. *Christianity and Traditional Religion in Western Zimbabwe 1859–1923*. London: Longman, 1979.
Carsi, Pietro. *Science and Religion*. Cambridge: Cambridge University Press 1988.
Cockcroft, I.G. "'The Mlimo' (Mwali) Cult," *NADA X*. 1972. *Chronicle*. 20 January 1992.

HEZEKIEL MAFU

Dunnigan, Ann. "Rain." In Ed. Mircea Eliade, *Encyclopaedia of Religion*. New York: Macmillan, 1987.

Enklaar, Ido H. *Life and Work of Dr. J.TH. Van Der Kemp 1747–1811*. Cape Town: Rotterdam, 1988.

Flint, Valerie I.J. *The Rise of Magic in Early Medieval Europe*. Oxford: Clarendon Press, 1992.

Gasela, G. "Feature Drought." *The Granary* (December 1992): 4.

Leacky, Hartpole Edward William. *History of the Rise and Influence of the Spirt of Rationalism in Europe*. London: Longman, 1893.

Langland, William. *Piers Plowman*. Edited by A.V.C. Schmidt. London: Longman, 1995.

Livingstone, David. *Missionary Travels*. London: Wardlock and Co. Ltd., 1910.

Mason, Phillip. *The Birth of a Dilemma*. London: Oxford University Press, 1958.

Ndlovu, Gwakuba. "The Mwali Cult." Paper presented at the Oral Traditions Association of Zimbabwe. Harare, May 1994.

Nthoi, Leslie. "Wosana Rite of Passage, Reflections on the Initiation of Wosana in the Mwali Cult in Zimbabwe," Paper presented at the Conference on the Interaction between Christian and Traditional Religions, Harare, 21–24 June 1994.

Palley, William. *Science and Religion in the Nineteenth Century*. Ed. Tess Coslet. Cambridge: Cambridge University Press, 1984.

Prins, Gwyn. *The Hidden Hippopotamus*. Cambridge: Cambridge University Press, 1980.

Ralushai, V. "The Mwali Cult," Paper Presented at Oxford University, 23 April 1994.

Ranger, T.O. *Revolt in Southern Rhodesia 1896–97*. London: Heinemann, 1967.

Scholar's Zulu Dictionary. 11th Edition, s.v. G.R. Dent and C.L.S. Nyembezi.

The Book of Common Prayer. Oxford: University Press, 1853.

Thomas, Keith. *Religion and the Decline of Magic*. Harmondsworth: Penguin Books, 1971.

Werbner, Richard. *Ritual Passage Sacred Journey*. Manchester: Manchester University Press, 1989.

Westfall, Richards. *Science and Religion in the Seventeenth Century England*. New Haven: Yale University Press, 1958.

Interviews

Juliana, J. Interviewed by the Author. Dzilo Shrine, Bulawayo. 24 July 1994.

Manyangwa, M. Interviewed by the Author. Manyangwa Village, Plumtree. 27 September 1994.

Ncube, James. Interviewed by the Author. Kezi District Offices, Bulawayo. 14 June 1994.

Ncube, Ngcatu. Interviewed by the Author. Njelele Shrine, Bulawayo. 18 June 1994.

Nkomo, Kenneth. Interviewed by the Author. Manyangwa Village, Plumtree. 27 September 1994.

THE BISHOP AND THE BRICOLEUR: BISHOP JOHN WILLIAM COLENSO'S *COMMENTARY ON ROMANS* AND MAGEMA KAMAGWAZA FUZE'S *THE BLACK PEOPLE AND WHENCE THEY CAME*[1]

Jonathan A. Draper

In their ground-breaking work setting out their theory of the social construction of reality, Berger and Luckmann argue that, "The historical outcome of each clash of gods was determined by those who wielded the better weapons rather than those who had the better arguments" (1966: 109). At one level, this is undeniably true of the colonial encounters between Europe and Africa. Christianity rode in on the back of imperial conquest. The missionaries used the opportunities provided by colonial administration—indeed sometimes aided and abetted the conquest—and the desire of African people for trade in European goods to their own advantage. They also provided legitimation for colonial rule. At another level, this was not the whole truth. The African people were not mere passive victims of European aggression, but purposive participants in events. Their relationship with both the missionaries and the colonialists consisted from the first of both resistance and negotiation. Because the outcome of such a confrontation of competing social universes is not known at the outset, they saw not only threats but also opportunities. The missionaries were only ever partially in control of the process of evangelization, whatever they themselves imagined. This can be seen in their constant complaints that their African converts were "not to be trusted."

In other words, the history of the missions and of the reception of the Bible must be seen as a dialectical process, an unequal one in

---

[1] This first part of the paper is a modification of a paper, "Hermeneutical Drama on the Colonial Stage: Liminal space and creativity in Colenso's *Commentary on Romans*," *Journal of Theology for Southern Africa* 103, 1999, 13–32, the second part is based on an article, "Magema Fuze and the Insertion of the Subjugated Historical Subject into the Discourse of Hegemony," *Bulletin for Contextual Theology in Africa* 5, 1–2, 16–26.

many respects to be sure, but nevertheless a more intricate, contested and mutual process than has usually been recognized. This has been aptly characterized by Jean and John Comaroff in their study of the mission among the Tswana people as a "long conversation":

> In the long conversation to which this [the mission] gave rise—a conversation full of arguments of words and images—many of the signifiers of the colonizing culture became unfixed. They were seized by the Africans and, sometimes refashioned, put to symbolic and practical ends previously unforeseen, certainly unintended. Conversely, some of the ways of the Africans interpolated themselves, again detached and transformed, into the habitus of the missionaries. Here, then, was a process in which signifiers were set afloat, fought over, and recaptured on both sides of the colonial encounter (Comaroff & Comaroff 1991: 17–18).

European military power and technology certainly ensured that the missionaries could insert their agenda into the conversation and be heard. However, from the first, their converts talked back and did not always agree. They experimented with the numinous sources of power they imagined (rightly or wrongly) to lie behind European might, in the attempt to control and use them for their own purposes. They did not always understand what they were doing, nor, for that matter, did the missionaries, but the path of the missions was not the smooth and triumphal one so often portrayed in the missionary reports home. Since, however, the records were written by the conquerors, with apologetic intent, they often have to be "read backwards" to hear the other side of the "conversation."

Jean and John Comaroff develop a particularly helpful model of the relationship between *hegemony* as the power of the taken-for-granted world view which is shared by particular communities and controls' human behaviour unseen, and *ideology* as the conscious and contested "effort to control the cultural terms in which the world is ordered and, within it, power legitimized" (1991: 24). The relationship between hegemony and ideology is fluid, unstable and constantly shifting:

> Hegemony, we suggest, exists in reciprocal interdependence with ideology: it is that part of a dominant world view which has been naturalized and, having hidden itself in orthodoxy, no more appears as ideology at all. Inversely, the ideologies of the subordinate may give expression to discordant but hitherto voiceless experience of contradictions that a prevailing hegemony can no longer conceal (1991: 25).

Most significantly, for our purposes, the Comaroffs argue that there is always a gap between hegemony and ideology, a liminal space, out of which forms of resistance and new consciousness may emerge:[2]

> Between the conscious and the unconscious lies the most critical domain of all for historical anthropology and especially for the analysis of colonialism and resistance. It is the realm of partial recognition, of inchoate awareness, of ambiguous perception, and, sometimes, of creative tension: that liminal space of human experience in which people discern acts and facts but cannot, or do not, order them into narrative descriptions or even into articulate conceptions of the world: in which signs and events are observed, but in a hazy, translucent light. In which individuals or groups know that something is happening to them, but find it difficult to put their fingers on quite what it is. It is from this realm, we suggest, that silent signifiers and unmarked practices may rise to the level of explicit consciousness, of an ideological assertion, and become the subject of overt political and social contestation—or from which they may recede into the hegemonic, to languish there unremarked for the time being. As we shall see, it is also the realm from which emanate the poetics of history, the innovative impulses of the bricoleur and the organic intellectual, the novel imagery called upon to bear the content of symbolic struggles (1991: 29).

Colonial conquest plunged the African social universe into crisis, since neither "therapy" nor "nihilation" (Berger & Luckmann 1966: 105–116) could hold it together in the face of European power and the growing number of "deviants" from the African social system (the converts to Christianity). But the crisis was not one-sided, since the missionaries themselves also came from an England in acute intellectual and social crisis, arising out of the related phenomena of the Enlightenment and industrial capitalism, so that the (contested) area of ideology was proportionately large in comparison with the (silent and uncontested) area of hegemony. The Comaroffs argue, indeed, that the missionary enterprise was in some respects an attempt to resolve cognitive dissonance in Nonconformist Britain by

---

[2] This liminal space seems akin to what Victor Turner (1969) finds in the ritual process and calls "anti-structure," open to experimentation, creativity and play. Perhaps one might also note that Turner sees in this liminal space the potential for the emergence of what he calls *communitas*, a discovery of that fundamental human community or *ubuntu*, which is usually controlled or suppressed by social structures (1969: 94–165). Here indeed there may have been the possibility for a genuine discovery of their mutual otherness and possible community by missionary and convert.

the creation of a new world in their image in the "blank spaces" of Africa (1991: 77–78). The collision of their European culture with African culture thus provided a rich liminal space for potential exploration (1991: 49–85). Both social universes were destabilized by the colonial encounter, and not just the African one, and this study of Colenso's work bears out their contention that "the missionary encounter must be regarded as a *two*-sided historical process, as a dialectic that takes into account the social and cultural endowments of, and the consequences for, *all* the actors—missionaries no less than Africans" (1991: 54).

In this contestation, both parties became *bricoleurs*, in their own ways, sorting through the debris of the two collapsing social universes for usable odds and ends of culture. Of course it is more obvious in the case of the African converts, since their predicament was the more severe, but it was true also for the missionaries as well, since they constantly found that things did not work as they should and their received ideas were challenged. Both parties engaged in the work of cultural *bricolage*, as this has been aptly defined (and positively evaluated) by Marilyn Legge in her attempt to address the crisis of the Christian faith in the post-modern era:

> *Bricolage* is the art of using what is at hand, odd materials for purposes other than intended, to create something useful and distinct to meet a yearning or need. This is an accessible practice often found where people aim to survive against the odds. Like some popular art, theological *bricolage* dares to revise, recast, and redefine the notions of theology and culture; it is open to change in an era of ecological, political, and cultural crisis, it aims to promote a prophetic and prospective praxis (1997: 6).

In this paper we shall be exploring both sides of a missionary "conversation" around the Bible and Christianity, offered to us by the fact, by no means accidental, that Bishop John William Colenso and one of his first converts both published extensive works. Colenso's *Commentary on St. Paul's Epistle to the Romans Newly Translated and Explained from a Missionary Point of View*, was published at his mission station at Ekukhanyeni near Pietermaritzburg in 1861 and immediately caused a storm of controversy. It was the key evidence produced in his trial and delation as a heretic in 1863 by an ecclesiastical court convened by the Metropolitan of the Anglican Church in South Africa, Bishop Robert Gray of Cape Town. This commentary, together with his *Commentary on the Pentateuch* published in four volumes from 1862–1863, caused shock waves also in England and led to the convening of the first worldwide conference of the Anglican Church, the Lambeth Conference of 1868, which has since become a regular and central part of international Anglican identity. On the other side, Magema kaMagwaza Fuze was one of three of Colenso's first converts who wrote the first indigenous Zulu work published in Zulu and English by Colenso as *Three Native Accounts of the Visit of the Bishop of Natal in September and October 1859, to Umpande, King of the Zulus, with Explanatory Notes and a Literal Translation, and a Glossary of All the Zulu Words Employed in the Same: Designed for the Use of Students of the Zulu Language*, in 1860. He subsequently wrote the first book by a Zulu person in the Zulu tongue, *Abantu Abamnyama, Lapa Bavela Ngakona* (*The Black People and Whence They Came*), which he only succeeded in getting published in 1922 as an old man. The publication of this book went almost unnoticed, and it still has not received appropriate recognition.

Although Colenso and Fuze are not dialoguing explicitly with each other, the implicit "conversation" is clearly audible, and makes both works resonate with each other. The bishop writes with the passion of conviction born from his perception of a crisis facing both British and Zulu society. His conversations with his Zulu converts pushed him to conclusions unacceptable to his own community (although there were many intellectuals who supported him in Britain). Fuze writes as a "bricoleur" adapting and adopting whatever served his purpose from the bishop or from his own culture, seeking to find a way forward in the face of a disintegrating Zulu social universe and a collapsed Zulu kingdom.

John William Colenso learnt Zulu by long and arduous conversations with Zulu converts at his mission, particularly William Ngidi, whom he characterizes as having "the reasoning powers of mature age" (1863: viii). He compiled a Zulu dictionary, a Zulu grammar and translated much of the Bible (including Romans), as well as many other secular works, into Zulu. His work on the Zulu language continues to be recognized by linguists in the field (Doke 1940: 234–235, Doke & Cole 1961: 45, see Guy 1983: 65–67). This Zulu conversation was not a superficial or one-sided exchange, but fundamentally challenged important aspects of the missionary's own received world view, as he wrote in *Commentary on Romans*:

Such questions as these have been brought again and again before my mind in the intimate converse which I have had, as a Missionary, with Christian converts and Heathens. To teach the truths of our holy religion to intelligent adult natives, who have the simplicity of children, but withal the earnestness and thoughtfulness of men,—to whom these things are new and startling, whose minds are not prepared by long familiarity to acquiesce in, if not to receive, them,—is a sifting process for the opinions of any teacher, who feels the deep moral obligation of answering truly, and faithfully, and unreservedly, his fellow-man, looking up to him for light and guidance, and asking, "Are you sure of this?" "Do you believe this?" "Do you really believe that?" (1861a: 199).

Colenso highlights the same dilemma he faced in honest conversation with Ngidi in his *Commentary on the Pentateuch* (1862: vi–viii), "I dared not, as a servant of the God of Truth, urge my brother man to believe that, which I did not myself believe, which I knew to be untrue."[3]

For Colenso, crucial areas of British hegemony (what is "self—evidently true") were breaking down under the impact of the African experience, and this in the situation where important gaps in the ideology of post-Enlightenment, industrial Britain, were emerging among the educated elite he represented. His *Commentary on Romans* is a valuable source of insight into the hermeneutical and cultural issues which came into play in this meeting of Africa and Europe, particularly since the nature and authority of the Bible was one of the focal points of conflict. The Comaroffs suggest that both missionaries and the colonized Africans should be understood as actors in a two-sided drama, and that the context of both parties should be explored before any attempt is made to delineate their interaction. This is the procedure we shall follow here, albeit briefly. The Nonconformist missionaries of the Comaroffs' study were largely drawn from upwardly mobile men from the newly industrialized

---

[3] He came close to espousing Maurice's rejection of damnation in his *Village Sermons* of 1854, but retreated in the face of public criticism. Maurice, in his turn, was to publicly condemn Colenso for his radical universalism and critical Biblical scholarship. At a meeting of the two in 1862, Maurice admonished Colenso to retract his books and resign his see (Guy 1883: 116–117), and the effects of this rupture between them impacted even on his wife Francis, whose mother was close to Maurice and warned the Colenso family not to stay in Russell Square during their visit (in a letter of November 3rd 1862, Reese 1958: 77–8). Other members of this circle remained supportive, for example Stanley and Jowett (72).

areas, poorly educated and socially marginalized: "persons caught between the rich and the poor, either indeterminate in their class affiliation or struggling hard to make their way over the invisible boundary into the bourgeoisie" (1991: 85). They enacted their marginalization in the mission field by moving beyond the boundaries of colonial administration. They were subsequently caught between and manipulated by both the colonial authorities and by the African authorities. Their response to the Tswana people was pragmatic, reactive and unreflective, assuming that simply proclaiming the Word found in the Bible and teaching cleanliness and industry would evangelize the natives. Their assumption was that African languages were simple "folk languages" not difficult for advanced (European) people to grasp and utilize, so that their translations were "a hybrid creation born of the colonial encounter itself" (1991: 218). Colenso presents a profile with marked differences.

Much has been written about Colenso already (Cox 1888, Burnett 1947, Cockshutt 1959, Hinchliffe 1964, Warwick 1966, Darby 1981, Guy 1983, Draper & West 1989: 30–33, Draper 1998: 44–54), and there is no need to elaborate overly here. Colenso was born into a lower-middle-class family, his father being a civil servant of sorts (a mineral agent for the Duchy of Cornwall) and owning an interest in a tin mine. By the time Colenso was sixteen, however, the flooding of the mine had led to a financial ruin of the family, his mother had died and he himself was forced to do menial work to help provide for his siblings. At this age he switched from the Nonconformism in which was raised and chose to seek ordination in the state Church of England. Colenso went up to St. John's College, Cambridge, worked his way through his undergraduate years as a Clerical Sizar and was elected a Fellow of the College. His intellectual acumen and energy were quickly recognized, especially in Mathematics for which he wrote a well-regarded series of school text books. The poverty of his own family led to an accumulation of debt, compounded by a disastrous fire to a property he had purchased. He fell in love with and married a woman from a respectable upper middle class London family and took a parish in order to enable himself to marry, according to the current practice. However, he was only able to marry because benefactors cleared his debt. Thus Colenso was upwardly mobile but socially and economically marginal to the upper middle class to which he now belonged.

His marriage, however, introduced him to a new intellectual circle in which the influence of the philosopher-poet Samuel Taylor Coleridge was strongly felt, as Colenso became personally acquainted to varying degrees with some of the most innovative thinkers of his age, in particular Frederick Denison Maurice (1805–1872, liberal theologian and Christian Socialist), Arthur Penrhyn Stanley (1815–1881, a church historian at Oxford and Broad Churchman), Julius Charles Hare (1795–1855, liberal theologian and Broad Churchman), Thomas Carlyle (historian, moralist and philosopher), Charles Kingsley (1819–1875, novelist, theologian and Christian Socialist), and Benjamin Jowett (1817–1893, classicist and biblical commentator). His obvious abilities and growing circle of influential friends led to his nomination as Bishop of Natal, and he was consecrated in 1853. F.D. Maurice was particularly influential on the young Colenso, with his denial of the doctrines of total depravity, a predestined saved elite and eternal punishment. His brand of Christian universalism emphasized the presence of God in all human beings and human community, God's work in nature and in history. Conversely, Maurice emphasized human solidarity and responsibility for the realization of the Kingdom of God on earth, which developed into his espousal of socialism:

> If the Gospel be the revelation or unveiling of a mystery hidden from ages and generations; if this mystery be the true constitution of humanity in Christ, so that a man believes and acts a lie who does not claim for himself union with Christ, we can understand why the deepest writings of the New Testament, instead of being digests of doctrine, are epistles, explaining to those who had been admitted into the Church of Christ their own position, bringing out that side of it which had reference to the circumstances in which they were placed or to their most besetting sins and shewing what life was in consistency, what life at variance, with it (Maurice [1838] 1959: 296, see Hinchliffe 1964: 32–42, Guy 1983: 24–30).

Colenso, like Maurice, emerged from Calvinist roots and he found these ideas liberative. Colenso was to have a somewhat checkered relationship with this influential circle in England, but it meant that he began his work in the mission field with an insecure but significant foothold in an elite which was constantly challenging the received ideas and practices of European society. The ideas of geologist Sir Charles Lyell and scientists like Charles Darwin were familiar and much debated here, as were the challenges of German theologians and Biblical scholars (Vidler 1971: 112–133). Colenso himself not only read Lyell, who rejected the Biblical account of creation on the basis of the age of the earth, but summarized his ideas for his Zulu students in his *First Lessons in Science* published at Ekukhanyeni in 1861, at the very time he was working on *Romans*. In the language of the Comaroffs, this circle with which Colenso felt affinity was engaged in bringing these matters out of the silence of hegemony into the contested field of ideological discourse. When Colenso, with his earnest and open study of Zulu language and custom, encountered the African world view, this meant that he and his Zulu dialogue partners found themselves in the interstices between hegemonic silence and ideological repetitions in which "human beings often seek new ways to test out and give voice to their evolving perceptions of, and dispositions' toward, the world" (Comaroff & Comaroff 1991: 30). It would be too much to claim that Colenso's *Romans* expresses an emerging implicit Zulu consciousness, and yet we may hear echoes of their questions and modes of resistance to missionary discourse in Colenso's answers,[4] so that they may be read "contrapuntally" in a way suggested by Edward Said (1995: 32, 51–52, 194).

Colenso's *Romans* is significant in a number of respects, but perhaps in none more than that he worked simultaneously with the Greek and Zulu text, even though he wrote in English. His translation of the text from Greek, which he provides in English, also served his translation of Romans into Zulu following his usual careful practice of detailed discussion with William Ngidi and others about both text and meaning (Colenso 1982: 228). His fluency in Greek from a sound Classical training at Cambridge allowed him conceptually to bypass his nineteenth century English Authorized Version conditioning and allowed new possible meanings to emerge, which might be more congenial to the Zulu environment in which he worked. Colenso frequently underpins his interpretation with reference to the meaning of a Greek word or its grammatical form or even to textual critical evidence. The second half of the nineteenth century saw an explosion of interest in textual critical study of the New Testament, in the light of new manuscript evidence (Metzger 1968: 124–146). Colenso was clearly in touch with this new evidence, as his commentary shows (for example 1861a: 159), although

---

[4] The questions themselves represent the injection of resistance generated in the "hidden transcript" of the colonized into the "official transcript" of the missionary, in the terminology of James Scott (1990).

it is not certain what critical text he was using. Colenso was work-ing already with an "unstable" and hence polysemous text when he came to read it "with" his Zulu converts.

In addition to these Western tools, Colenso's commentary is in-formed by his simultaneous work on the translation of the Bible into Zulu (for the New Testament see Harriet Colenso's private edition, *Izindab'ezinhle ezashunyeyelwa ku'bantu ng'uJesu-Kristo inKosi yethu kanye nezincwadi ezalotshwa ng'abapostole bake, The Good News which is Preached to Humans by Jesus Christ our Lord together with the Letters Written by his Apostles* (1897)) his Zulu dictionary (1878) and Zulu grammar (1903). Since there were no precedents in these fields, the ambiguity pro-duced by finding the cognate concepts for Greek expressions in Zulu created space for him to re-read Paul with new eyes. The detailed work of comparison between his translation and his commentary has yet to be done.[5]

The first key hermeneutical move Colenso makes is to see Romans as addressed to Jews and not Gentile Christians, that is, there was no Christian church there separate from the synagogue, the Jewish believers held on to all their former Jewish identity, and even Gentiles in the community were proselytes (1861: ii–iii, xxi–xxiv, 12). Perhaps some Jews may have been in Jerusalem on the occasion of the first Pentecost and returned with an incipient faith, but they were igno-rant of the heart of the gospel message, namely, that in Jesus all human beings were now saved by faith and not by membership of the covenant people or any other racial privilege. This means that the purpose of the letter is to overcome Jewish prejudices against Gentiles and their own sense of superiority and privilege. It is designed to assert the equality of humanity in sin and in salvation. The sec-ond hermeneutical move Colenso makes, identifies the Jewish believ-ers, to whom Paul was writing then, with the Christian British people of his own day. They were those who relied on their inherited pos-session of the faith and wished to exclude the heathen Zulu from eternal life and consign them to eternal damnation. They were the ones who wished to impose customs and laws other than the gospel

---

[5] Though, for a first attempt, see my paper to the Romans Session of the *SNTS* Congress in Pretoria, July 1999, "The Reception of Romans in Bishop John William Colenso's *St. Paul's Epistle to the Romans: Newly Translated and Explained from a Missionary Point of View* of 1861."

as a condition of salvation, for example the termination of their polygamous marriages and families before baptism.[6] Their demand for
the "faith" of an individualistic conversion experience as a legal
requirement for salvation represented a new kind of works. On the
other hand, the "Greeks" or Gentiles represent for Colenso the heathen Zulu among whom he was working.

Missionaries usually based their requirement for such "faith" on
their reading of Romans, but Colenso's reading reversed this interpretation by means of his identification of the (Calvinist) British
Christians with Paul's "Jews." Commenting on 9:14–17, Colenso
writes:

> In point of fact, the whole tenor and object of the Apostle's words is
> expressly to do away with this notion of an arbitrary election. It was
> just that which the Jew of his day relied on. He was one of the elect.
> The Jews were the Calvinists of those days, and believed themselves,
> as God's chosen people, sure of the kingdom. St. Paul is trying, with
> all possible arguments, to shatter this fond notion to pieces. He says,
> "No! God Himself, with His own wise, and just, and unerring judg-
> ment, will pass a righteous sentence upon all, whether Jew or Greek,
> Christian or Heathen" (1861: 216).

There is, of course, much debate still raging about the context and
addressees of Paul's letter (see the essays in Donfried 1991), but since
the seminal essay of Krister Stendahl (1963) many scholars have
come to agree that Paul is writing Romans primarily to deal with
the issue of Jewish privilege with an eye to the admission of Gentiles
without the imposition of circumcision (for example Sanders 1983,
Räisänen 1988). He is not dealing with the troubled conscience, or
with *sola fidei* as that has been understood since the Reformation.
Colenso's Zulu context prefigured this debate and also, incidentally,
made him remarkably understanding of the position of the Jewish
people of his own day, which is logical given his equation of the
Jews of Paul's day with the British of his own (1861a: 34)!

Colenso identifies the "*key-words*" for interpreting Romans in 1:16:
"for the power of God it [the Gospel of Christ] is unto salvation to

---

[6] In 1861, the same year as the commentary was published, Colenso published,
*A Letter to His Grace the Archbishop of Canterbury, upon the Question of the Proper Treatment
of Cases of Polygamy, as Found Already Existing in Converts from Heathenism*, in which he
argued that polygamous marriages should be respected and should not constitute
an obstacle to baptism.

everyone that believeth, both to Jew first and Greek" (1861: 9).[7] He
sees this as addressing three Jewish prejudices: belief in favoured status and rights to enter the kingdom through race, refusal to accept
the complete equality of the meanest Gentile, and a trust in Law
and rites and ceremonies. Since his hermeneutical key identifies Jew
here as Briton and Greek as Zulu, the implication is that salvation
is to everyone, "Briton first and then Zulu," without any distinction
of race or favour. The qualification "to everyone that believeth"
might seem to undermine this universality. Not so, says Colenso, for
God continues to reveal himself, not just in the Bible but also in
reason and experience, so that the heathen Zulu continually experiences both the grace and the wrath of God in the same way the
English person does. This comes to the level of conscious enjoyment
with conversion to Christianity, but is not confined to the "saved."
He is able to point to the sense of the present passive verb *apokalup-
tetai* found parallel in 1:17 and 18, rejecting the Authorized Version's
"is revealed," which implies a completed act, for "is being revealed,"
which implies a continuing process (1861a: 14–15, 17–19). In this
rendering he is quite justified, since the present tense normally presents "an action going on at the time of writing" (Goodwin 1897: 8).

The implications of this bold statement are drawn in 1:20. Since
God is revealed in nature, all human beings have a duty to fear,
love, trust and obey God, but while all are therefore without excuse
as a general rule, this does not apply to every individual concretely
in the same way. Children, imbeciles and heathen could not with
justice be abandoned to eternal punishment by God for what they
could not know. People can only be judged on the basis of their
own behaviour, inasmuch as they did or did not respond to the
Light in the measure it was revealed to them. Many Christians are
put to shame in their behaviour by the heathen: "Probably their
worst sins of murder and uncleanness are not more essentially abominable in God's sight than the slanderous talk, and malicious acts,
and dishonest practices, and self-indulgent, selfish lives, of many
Christians, whom He alone can judge, who knows the secrets of all
hearts, and the share of His goods committed unto each—and not
we" (Colenso 1861a: 24). There is a difference between willful sin
and ignorance and we are not authorized to judge between them.

---

[7] The translation cited is Colenso's, unless otherwise stated.

Zulu people are capable of great virtue: brave, kind, just and generous, they are also capable of killing others on suspicion of being *umtakati*. But then English people burnt witches in sincere belief that they were doing God's will. So a Zulu chief who abuses his cultural power for his own ends for vengeance or greed is in a different position from one who obeys Zulu custom in the belief that she or he is doing good. We do not suffer for Adam's sin but for our own: "But the Apostle teaches, what the Bible everywhere teaches, and our own hearts teach also, that the essence of moral guilt consists in the commission of acts of *conscious willful sin*, whether sin of negligence or sin of presumption" (1861: 28–32, esp. 31).

This being the case, Britons have no right to pronounce on the moral guilt or otherwise of the heathen any more than on the Jew. Indeed, Colenso regards the Zulu as alienated descendants of Abraham who have gradually sunk into ignorance from their ancestry as sons/ grandsons of Abraham through Esau or Ishmael (1861: 34–35, see 215).[8] Yet they still are monotheists like these supposed Semitic ancestors, he argues. While the curious idea of a Semitic ancestry for the Zulu people may be wildly inaccurate, Colenso is correct, it seems, in his portrayal of the Zulu understanding of the "High God" (*uNkulunkulu*), though there are some ambiguities.[9]

Just as the Jews were entrusted with the Law and the prophets,

---

[8] The exact origin of this hypothesis is obscure, but may go back at least as far as the African travelogue of Mungo Park (1799: 287), according to an echo in the Comaroffs' account about Esau (1991: 91). I have not had the opportunity to check this. The conversation of James Stuart with Lazarus Mxaba provides an interesting example of the developed ideology, which was taken over by some Zulus. The Zulus represent the lost tribes of Israel, which have forgotten their language and even their God, but have continued the practices of ancient Israel from which they are descended (Chidester 1996: 116–118). The arrival of the missionaries has enabled them to remember and recover this heritage. This myth was propagated by Henry Francis Fynn, one of the earliest British settlers, who lived like a Zulu until the establishment of the colony of Natal, and the idea took a firm hold (1996: 124–127). The ideas were given firmer form by the Prussian Egyptologist Baron Christian von Bunsen and systematized in a rather different way by the philologist, Wilhelm Heinrich Immanuel Bleek, who was one of those accompanying Colenso when he arrived in his diocese. Bleek believed that all human religion originated in Africa, and that Zulu ancestor worship represented the most ancient and pure form of human religion (1996: 141–152).

[9] Berglund (1976: 43) points out that there is a distinction between *ukukhonza* (worship proper), which is due only to *uMvelingqangi*, and *ukuthetha* (reverence), which is due to the *amadlozi* (shades) in ritual celebrations. However, there are question marks, relating to *iNkosikazi yaseZulwini* (the Heavenly Queen) and perhaps also *Nomkhubulwana* (the Maiden) if she is a separate entity (1976: 63–74).

but were unfaithful, so Christians today were entrusted with the Old and New Testaments and the sacraments. This is their only advantage, not in some exclusive possession of salvation, as Colenso comments on 3:2:

> All his [Paul's] language may be well applied to those unfaithful Christians, who bring dishonour on the Name of God among the heathens in the present day, and whom the heathen himself, though unbaptised, and ignorant of the name of Christ and the letter of Christianity, yet keeping the law of truth and right, according to his light, shall one day judge. For instance, it might be asked, "If you say the heathen may be saved without the knowledge of the Gospel, what advantage, then, hath the Christian, or what profit is there in Christian Baptism?" And a similar answer might be given: "Much, in every way: in the very first place, because to them are entrusted the Holy Scriptures, the books of the New Testament as well as the Old?" And to this we might go on to add, "To them are given the means of grace, and the hope of glory." (1861: 53).

Here again, the Jews of the Epistle become the British of Colenso's *Romans*.

This raises the question of the nature of sin: surely the heathen are under original sin, having inherited the Fall of Adam, whereas the British can claim through baptism to have been redeemed from sin (implicitly from birth, since the British are baptized as babies!). Not so says Colenso. Paul does not say, "For all have sinned, and come short of the glory of God" as the Authorized Version translates it. Instead, the aorist tense (*hēmarton*) implies a single completed individual act and is best translated by the English present, "For all sin, and come short of the glory of God" (1861: 61–62). Sin is not inherited but is a matter of individual human responsibility a product of human fallibility by which all indeed do sin. According to 3:21–26, God's dealing with Israel was intended to put right this situation, as the Law and Prophets indicate, but this was misunderstood. Now, however, the work of Christ has made all human beings righteous, without any distinctions at all:

> But now it *is* revealed that this gift of righteousness is meant for all, that all are *being made righteous*, (the Greek Present, implying their continuing state of righteousness),—all men everywhere, though many more may not yet have heard them, and so may have little or no present enjoyment of their Father's Love.
> The Apostle's words in this verse most probably mean this, because he afterwards (v. 15–19) fully and explicitly states it, namely, that the justification here spoken of extends to *all*, to those who have never

heard the name of Christ, and who cannot have exercised a living faith in Christ, as well as to Christians. It is *certain* that, in this latter passage, he is speaking of the whole human race.

And even in heathen men, who have never heard the Gospel, and cannot "believe" in the full sense of the word, there is a faith in the Living Word, which speaks within them, there is a living obedience to the law of truth and love, which they find written upon their hearts by the finger of God, which is akin to the true living faith of a Christian, and to which is granted a kindred feeling, a measure of enjoyment, even in this life, of the gift of righteousness, a sense of gladness and freedom in the consciousness of at-one-ment with the Right and the True, a share of the Peace of God's children, "which passes all understanding" (1861: 62–64).

This universal and objective atonement achieved by Christ is experienced in an attenuated way by those who have never heard the Gospel by their experience of nature and its bounty. Nevertheless, only Christians are able to know the "shewing forth of (*endeixin*, not 'declare' as in the AV) His righteousness" (3:24) fully and explicitly through faith in Christ, which is God's purpose and not some kind of punitive retribution exacted from the human Jesus as a punishment for Adam.

Human culpability is limited by the extent of their knowledge of what they are doing, so that heathen cannot be held to break the Law until they know it and understand it, and however we find Zulu customs, they are not culpable until they truly know the alternative way (4:15):

And so, too, among the ignorant heathen, many things are practised, which, however offensive in the eyes of a white man and a Christian, are not transgressions of God's known Law, and are not reckoned as sins in the sight of Him, who searcheth the hearts and judgeth righteously the children of men, until that Law is brought home to them, brought home to their hearts and consciences by the teaching of His own Good Spirit, not merely reiterated in their ears, with the voice of authority, by the lips of a Missionary, laying down the law to them, often with most obscure and defective utterance, in some difficult native tongue, upon matters of the deepest personal and social interest. Among the reproofs that will be passed "in that day," are there none that will justly belong to us, Christians and Missionaries, for the harsh, uncharitable, judgments, which we have passed in our arrogant self-confidence upon our heathen fellow-men? (1861: 84).

Thus Colenso interprets "Made righteous then out of faith, we have peace with God through our Lord Jesus Christ" (5:1) to refer to the objective existence of the gift of salvation for all. Any insistence on prior belief for it to become effective is instituting a new form of works. The sin of Adam could not have led in a literal way to the origin of organic death in the species, since scientific discoveries, and especially geology, show that death existed in the world before the origin of the species. Paul may or may not have believed in this primitive myth, but we have no right to expect him to know our modern scientific data or to have any insight impossible in his day. In any case, the Bible is not infallible as Word in this sense, but is a vehicle for the Word:

> It is possible that St. Paul entertained this notion himself, namely, of *all* death having come into the world by sin. For we have no reason to expect scientific knowledge of any kind, beyond that of the people of his age, in a Scripture writer. It is not in this way, by securing a historian, or prophet, or evangelist, or apostle, from all errors of detail in matters either of science or of fact, that the power of the Divine Spirit is exhibited in Scripture. The "spirit and the life," which breathes throughout the Holy Book,—that which speaks to the heart, and touches the main springs of being in a man,—that which teaches him what is pure and true and loving, and gives him living bread to feed upon in the secrets of his own spiritual consciousness,—this is the work of God's Spirit, these are the "words which the Holy Ghost teacheth,"—not a mere historical narrative, or a table of genealogies, or a statement of scientific facts, cosmological, geological, astronomical, or any other, in all which matters the books of the Holy Scriptures must be tested by the ordinary rules, which critical sagacity would apply to any other human compositions (1861: 99–100).

The language of death and life, sin and justification, must be taken as figurative and not literal.

From 5:15 Colenso is now able to draw the logical conclusion that since, *all* in "as in Adam all died" clearly refers to all human beings regardless, then *all* in "so also in Christ shall all be made alive" also refers to all human beings regardless (1861: 102). This salvation is objectively achieved for all as a free gift, whether a human being knows it or not. But this objective salvation of all human beings needs to be experienced subjectively for its full benefit to be realized, even if this is not in the conventional Christian manner:

> Whenever the "unrighteousness" of any Jew, Christian, or Heathen, "is forgiven, and his sin covered,"—whenever he feels any measure of the peace of God's children, in the faithful discharge of any duty, or in forsaking any path of evil,—whenever there is brought home to his heart in any way the message of God's Fatherly Love by means of any one of Earth's ten thousand voices,—then he hears, as it were, a

fresh declaration of righteousness, he may know that he is recognised again as a child of God's House (1861: 103).

This experience is what Paul calls new life, as all share in the life of the Body of Christ. This is how Colenso interprets Paul's reference to baptism in Romans 6 (1861: 107–137). Indeed, the concept of Christ as appointed by the Father to be Head of a redeemed community of brothers and sisters is central to Colenso's Christology: the "Grace of God" is "bestowed upon the whole of the human race in His own dear Son, whom He has given to be their Head, and whose members they are" (1861: 75). There are at least 49 references to Christ as Head in the commentary, although the concept does not occur in Romans being largely a deutero-Pauline expression (Ephesians 1:22, 4:15, 5:23, Colossians 1:18, 2:10, 19, though see 1 Corinthians 11:3). The signs of this new life are objectively displayed in the sacraments of Eucharist and baptism, which do not depend on the subjective state in which we come to them. They are signs not only to believers but to all human beings, whether they know they are benefiting or not. This has been called very subjective, but in reality it is the reverse. Colenso could rejoice in taking a service in the Zulu liturgy—which he had translated already by 1856—even though surrounded by the bones of the those killed in the Zulu civil war between Mbulazi and Cetshwayo (which he calls the "Bloody way") on the banks of the Tugela (Colenso [1859]1982: 67), or at the royal kraal of Mpande where his young men officiated in the liturgy. He records that "our dear boys have been the first to publish the Word of Life among the Zulus" ([1859]1982: 109). The sign is effective corporately rather than individually, it is not dependent on understanding or participation to be experienced as a reassurance and blessing (1861a: 115–9).

Colenso comes now to the well known anthropological passage in Romans 7:21: "I find the law to me, willing to do what is beautiful, that evil is present to me." The Zulu just like Jew and Christian has a struggle between good and evil in his/her life:

> And if, in spite of this, the pious heathen has given his heart to do the good, and refused to do the evil, it was only because he had a strength supplied to him, from a source which he knew not. In his flesh, indeed, though he knew it not, there was no good thing, but in his Lord, unknown, perhaps by Name to him as yet, but by whom he was known, there was Life from which the life of his spirit came (1861: 152).

He argues that since this double aspect of human nature is known in Zulu culture, so that there is no essential anthropological difference between the Zulu person and the European person. This is critical because a number of anthropologists were openly questioning whether missions to the heathen were desirable or even possible, since these indigenous people were innately inferior products of evolution who would gradually die out in the face of the more advanced civilizations. Colenso faced this very question in his *Lecture to the Marylebone Literary Society* in 1865 (1982: 205–206). In his dialogue with his Zulu converts, Colenso had found that Zulu people have a strongly developed conscience, which for him was evidence of the presence of the Divine Spirit in them, the "higher powers which raise us above the mere brute animal" (1982: 210). Outward differences of race and colour mean nothing if the Zulu person manifests the two essential human characteristics, namely reason and human affection. This ethical sense is expressed particularly in the concept of *uNembeza*, which Colenso makes the focal point of his recognition of the objective redeeming work of Christ among the heathen:

> Among the Zulus there is a distinct recognition of the double nature of man. They speak of the *uGovana*, which prompts him to steal and lie, commit murder and adultery, and the *uNembeza*, which "bids him," as a native would say, "leave all that" (1861a: 156).

This is nothing less than the Divine Spirit of Romans 8:16, which is present in all human beings who do not quench it by evil doing. Indeed, the "Sons of God" of 8:19 refers to the whole human race, all of whom are groaning for liberation and will indeed all eventually be liberated to eternal life (1861: 173). Colenso correctly identified *uNembeza* as the central moral principal of Zulu culture. It is related to the legitimate anger derived from *uMvelingqangi* aimed at "sustaining order and a good life," and so motivates ethical conduct, whereas *uGovana* refers to destructive immoral anger which leads to wrongdoing (Berglund 1976: 255–256). Colenso held onto this Zulu understanding vigorously, both in his preaching to the heathen, whom he enjoined to follow the *uNembeza* within them (1859 in 1982: 86), and in his defence of the human dignity, equality and rights of the Zulu people before European racists who would deny it (1865 in 1982: 215–221).

In the light of the objective nature of the atonement wrought by Christ and in the light of the nature of the moral struggle experienced by all human beings, Christian or heathen, Colenso is led to interpret the "groaning" of "all the creature" as it waits for the "freedom of the glory of the children of God" as a denial of endless punishment. We have already seen that this may be in part attributed to the questions posed by his Zulu converts concerning the position of the *amadlozi* (living dead or ancestors). However, it also represents a final adoption of the position advocated by F.D. Maurice, which he had equivocated about earlier. The confrontation with Zulu culture impacted at a point where the cultural hegemony of his own society had emerged into the sphere of contestation. This produced the "liminal space" which calls forth some of the most sustained argumentation in his whole commentary (1861: 175–201). It also pushes him to question the authority of the very text he is interpreting and in doing so clarifies for him what is most fundamental to his humanity, namely reason and conscience/love:

> Whatever contradicts that Law, whether it be the word of man, or the dictum of a Church, or the supposed teaching of Holy Scripture, cannot, ought not to, be a Law for him . . . But no seeming authority of the Church or Scripture *ought* to persuade a man to believe anything, which contradicts that moral law, that sense of righteousness, and purity, and truth, and love, which God's own finger has written upon his heart. The voice of that inner witness is closer to him than any that can reach him from without, and ought to reign supreme in his whole being. The Light, in which he there sees light, the Voice which he hears, is the Light of the Divine Word, is the Voice of his Lord. We may be certain, then, that any interpretation of Scripture, which contradicts that sense of right which God Himself, our Father, has given us, to be a witness for His own perfect excellencies, must be set aside, as having no right to crush down, as with an iron heel, into silence the indignant remonstrance of our whole spiritual being (1861: 189–190).

This emphasis on reason and ethics is, of course, typical of the Kantian epistemology, but in the context of colonial racism, it has a new edge to it. Endless punishment is immoral and incompatible with Divine goodness and is ruled out, especially since it would allow special privilege to the Briton and a cruel injustice to the Zulu who have never heard the gospel:

> And it is often so stated as to involve the multitudes of ignorant, untaught, heathen, the great mass of humankind, in the same horrible doom of never-ending despair, making this beautiful and blessed world the very shambles, as it were, of Almighty Vengeance, while

> some few individuals, called by the name of Christians, but living comfortably all the while, notwithstanding their professed belief that myriads of their fellow men are, every moment, passing into perdition, will, by some special act of Divine favour, be so fortunate as to be excepted from it. I need hardly say that the whole Epistle to the Romans is one of the strongest possible protests against such a notion (1861: 190–1).

Instead, Colenso takes Paul's words in 8:28 to apply generally to humanity, "all things work together for good, being called according to a purpose." Salvation cannot depend "*idly*" (Colenso's italics) on the accident of birth (1861: 207).

With regard to Romans 9–11, Colenso perceptively describes it as "the language of prophecy," by which he means that it should be taken figuratively and not literally (1861: 215). There is actually no favouritism in God's judgment for anyone. In accordance with his hermeneutical key, he points to the applicability of the disobedience of Israel to the behaviour of the British:

> All will be judged according to their works, and according to the Light vouchsafed to them. With reference to the Light, which we, Christians of England, have received, it might be said, in like manner, "England has God loved, and Africa has He hated." Yet not all English Christians are children of the Light, nor are all African heathens' children of Satan, but those, who have received most, shall have most required of them (1861: 215).

Colenso is able to answer Paul's rhetorical question in 10:18 affirmatively. There have always been people in every nation who have heard in their own way and responded with obedience, "according to the light vouchsafed to him, though he may not be circumcised as a Jew, nor baptised as a Christian, [which] 'is accepted of Him,' who is the Faithful Creator, the Merciful God, and the loving Friend and Father of all" (1861: 231–2). God never reverses his intention to bless humankind as loving Father (Romans 11:29) and this must be the hermeneutical key to interpreting Scripture as a whole:

> And, if the words seem, at first sight, to contradict other words in the Bible, and other facts in the Scripture history, we must seek for the truth which underlies the whole, and connects all together, as different branches of the same root. The root is the Fatherly Love of God to His creatures, which leads Him at one time to bless His children, at another to chasten them, at one moment to reveal to them the signs of His Favour, at another to cut them off for a time in displeasure,

to banish them, it may be, into the outer darkness, and yet suffers Him never to forget them, or cast them off altogether (1861: 242–3).

Colenso here comes to the recognition which guided him through his subsequent Biblical interpretation. Though not expressed here, it is connected implicitly in Colenso's mind with reason and hence with science.[10] There are other interesting insights to be gleaned from *Romans*, but the main thrust of Colenso's work has been covered.

In his *Commentary on the Pentateuch* (1862–1863), Colenso reflects his wide reading (especially in Dutch scholarship, a language which he taught himself) of the critical Old Testament scholarship of continental scholars: Kurz, Ewald, Hengstenberg whose conservatism disgusted him, and Bleek, de Wette and Abraham Kuenen with whom he interacted and corresponded (Hinchliffe 1964: 85–114).[11] His work was read and admired by continental scholars, but created a storm in England. The main thrust of Colenso's work was to destroy in a systematic and mathematical way any claims of the Old Testament to historical accuracy and inerrancy. He also notes an evolutionary process of revelation within the Old Testament, whereby different writings exhibit higher or lower conceptions of God. He concludes from this that the understandings of God found in indigenous people in the missionary field should not be rejected, but seen as a part

---

[10] He is able later to express this principle in a more thorough-going Enlightenment way as follows, "The time is come, through the revelations of modern science, when, thanks be to God, the traditionary belief in the divine infallibility of Scripture can, with a clear conscience, be abandoned—can, in fact, be no longer maintained . . . we seek to establish your faith—not, indeed, in the mere Book, but in that Living Word which speaks in the Book and speaks also by the lips of apostles and prophets in all ages, of all good men and true, whose heart God's Spirit has quickened to be the bearers of His messages of truth to their fellow-men. For we believe that in the Bible we have the earliest record of that Divine teaching, which has led men more and more out of darkness into light, out of slavish fears and superstitions into the liberty of God's children, out of confusion and ignorance into the clearer knowledge of the Living God. But we believe also that this teaching is still going on by all the new revelations in science—by all the deep thoughts which are stirred within men's hearts: and that, in one word, the completion of it would be, in fact, the end of the History of Man" (1982: 232–233).

[11] There is an extensive collection of correspondence between Colenso and Abraham Kuenen in the University Library of Leiden (Kuenen Archive BPL 3028), which reveals great warmth and mutual influence. I am grateful to Professor John Rogerson for giving me access to his transcription of the letters. Colenso translated and published several Dutch works with extensive commentaries on them, e.g. Kuenen's *The Pentateuch and Book of Joshua Critically Examined* (1865) and H. Oort, *The Worship of Baalim in Israel* (1865).

of an evolutionary process towards understanding or enlightenment. Moreover, the accounts of the origin of human kind in the Bible are mythical and not scientific. Hence they are not, in principle, different from the accounts of origins found among indigenous peoples, and cannot be foisted on credulous converts. Consequently, as he describes his conversations with Ngidi in which he declared, "I dared not, as a servant of the God of Truth, urge my brother man to believe that, which I did not myself believe, which I knew to be untrue" (1862: vi–viii).

Colenso's strong focus on history and historical truth needs to be read within the stream of critical study in post Enlightenment Europe. His contemporaries' J.G. Droysen (1808–1884) and Wilhelm Dilthey (1833–1911) set a hermeneutic of historical study at the centre of the development of a human science and a humanist ethics (Gadamer 1993: 3–9, 212–242). History serves for the "liberation of interpretation from dogma" and enables the human individual to develop a historical consciousness which may be equated with enlightenment (1993: 176–177). Droysen understands the historian to be limited ineluctably to the particularity of her own specific culture, and indeed only able to participate in historical discourse out of this "insuperable one-sidedness." Dilthey takes this further, with his understanding of the possibility of achieving "historical consciousness" through the study of history from within history. Historical knowledge becomes self-knowledge. As Gadamer (1993: 229) expresses it: "Thus for historical consciousness the forms that objective spirit takes are objects of this spirit's self-knowledge. Historical consciousness expands to universality, for it sees all the data of history as manifestations of the life from which they stem: 'Here life is understood by life.'"

This kind of valuation of the historical enterprise lies behind the work of Colenso as well, and is a significant aspect of the ideological debate which dogged his missionary work, but also opened up space for the production of a new historical ideology by Fuze. It is probably because Fuze's work has been read as a marginal supplement to the "real work of history writing" which is done by white scholars that it has been so little appreciated. His translator describes it as "a good first try" by a naive and ignorant person: "Nevertheless it contains much valuable information on the sidelights of Zulu history" (Fuze 1979: xvii). I would argue that it is more accurate to read Fuze's work as an act of resistance to domination.

After Colenso's act of historical demolition, what remained for him to affirm about the Christian gospel was the love of God for all human beings which is declared in Jesus Christ, and the salvation he wrought on the cross for all, whether they know and acknowledge it or not (1861: 102–103). Humane, just behaviour following the ethical value of the human conscience represent the goal of the Christian life. Revelation is found already within all human cultures to a greater or lesser extent. The goal is not to scare the Zulu people into the church with the threat of damnation, but to bring them to see what God has done for them in Jesus Christ, and which they already experience through natural revelation. The goal is enlightenment. So Colenso's missionary zeal shifts from a concern with individual conversion to a concern with the Zulu people as a whole, with their culture and history and political predicament in the face of colonial encroachment.

Colenso set out on his missionary task convinced of the duty of the "enlightened Briton" and the benefits of "her standard of victory waving in triumph on many a shore" (Edgecombe 1982: xiv). Indeed his first enthusiastic friendship in the Colony was with that unscrupulous agent of empire, Theophilus Shepstone, to whom he dedicated his commentary. But he ended up isolated and ridiculed by his countrymen and in a somewhat "treasonous" alliance with the exiled Cetshwayo against the machinations of both empire and the wily Shepstone (Guy 1983: 332–349). His *Romans* provides a fascinating insight into the beginning of the "long conversation" between British missionaries and Zulu converts, which fundamentally altered the consciousness of both parties.

Colenso can be seen at one level as a representative of the emerging Enlightenment Biblical hermeneutics beginning to affect Britain from Germany. Yet this could not explain the storm which greeted his work, which many even more radical critics escaped. It was his status as a Colonial Bishop, with all that entailed in terms of legitimating empire both by the silence of European hegemony and the discourse of imperial ideology, which made his "defection" so unforgivable. The ditty cited by Guy contains a large measure of truth, for all its racist innuendo:

A bishop there was of Natal
Who took a Zulu for a pal,
Said the Native 'Look 'ere,
Ain't the Pentateuch queer?'
Which converted the Lord of Natal
(cited in Guy 1983: 133).

Colenso's Christian mission has been portrayed by the apologists for
the Church of the Province of Southern Africa, represented ably by
Peter Hinchliffe (1963: 83–110, 1964) as a failure. Colenso's life is
redeemed from "a rather seedy end" only by his struggle for political
justice (1963: 104). The destruction of Colenso's house at Bishopstowe
after his death is seen as a symbol (by divine *fiat?*) of the obliteration
of his Zulu mission: "Three months later Bishopstowe was destroyed
by fire, as though the symbol of Colenso's life could not survive that
life itself" (1964: 195). Reading through Colenso's letters, he himself had a very different perception, and certainly the "space" opened
up by his "conversation" with the Zulu people as not so easily closed
down, as we will see in Fuze's work of *bricolage*.

The Nonconformist missionaries among the Tswana envisaged a
complete separation of church and state, sacred and secular, which
was embedded in the *laissez faire* capitalism of the era. They strove
to convert individuals to a spiritual kingdom, while maintaining, even
bolstering and protecting, the traditional "secular" authority of the
chiefs. Such a position conflicted with the holistic African world view,
in which religion was embedded in society and the power of the
chief was undergirded and proclaimed by his control over rain-making ceremonies. As a result, their early converts were themselves
marginal and their conversion seemingly superficial (Comaroff &
Comaroff 1991: 252–255). The difference between this scenario and
Colenso's approach should not be exaggerated, yet it is important
to note that Colenso began with a different premise: the central concept of the universal brotherhood of man and Fatherhood of God
(using the terminology of the time, 1861a: 74, 1865 in 1982: 213),
and within that framework he stressed the incorporation of a Christian
family rather than the conversion of the individual. This is the origin of his opposition to breaking up polygamous marriages, which
he stated already in his *Ten Weeks in Natal* (1855), and on which he
wrote an eloquent treatise (Colenso 1861b).

His first and most important missionary venture was the establishment in 1856 of a Boy's Institution at his station at Ekukhanyeni,
which was targeted at the sons of chiefs. Colenso not only spent
endless hours translating and writing textbooks for his school and
discussing them, but gave his pupils their own voices in his revolutionary parallel publication in Zulu and English, with lexical and
grammatical notes, of *Three Native Accounts of the Visit of the Bishop of*

Natal in September and October 1859, to Umpande, king of the Zulus (Fuze, Ndiyane & Ngidi 1860: 163–195). In other words, unlike the first Tswana converts, these Zulu converts were not socially marginal. Indeed they continued to play important rôles in Zulu society after the demise of the Boy's Institution itself.

Magema kaMagwaza Fuze, son of Matomela chief of the Ngcobo people, was trained as a printing compositor. Fuze was the person who alerted Colenso to Shepstone's duplicity in the case of Langalibalele in 1874, and it is a tribute to their relationship that Colenso trusted him above Shepstone (Guy 1983: 207–208). Fuze and Ngidi refused to be intimidated in the face of stiff interrogation by the magistrate hearing the affair, and signed as witnesses to a petition for clemency for Langalibalele (1983: 210–211). They repeated their work with Colenso for the legal defence of the rights of the Zulu against the colonial authorities in the case of Matshana in 1875 (1983: 244–245). Fuze proved well able to continue printing texts of the Bible on the press at Ekukhanyeni on his own during Colenso's long absences in England, writing him letters to keep him informed of his work (1865 in 1982: 225–227). He eventually set up his own print compositing business in Pietermaritzburg. He was to write the first book in Zulu by a Zulu person, *Abantu Abamnyama Lapa Bavela Ngakona* (1922), also translated into English as *The Black People and Whence They Came* (1979), which is the focus of the second part of this diptych of bishop and *bricoleur*. This important work charts the influence of Colenso's work on Zulu culture and history with remarkable clarity (Draper 1998: 16–26).

Just as the Britain from which Bishop Colenso came was a society in crisis and in the throes of transition, so Zulu society was in a state of crisis and transition. The rule of Shaka had created a new Zulu hegemony over a part of the eastern seaboard of Southern Africa, which reached into the interior, creating considerable movement and dislocation of peoples.[12] This upheaval coincided with the colonial incursions of the first Dutch and British settlers into the region, which added to the instability and dislocation. The defeat of

---

[12] The origins and character of the *mfecane/difaqane* is a matter of some dispute, since it also reflects the impact of slave trading by the Portuguese in Angola and Mozambique, but most historians acknowledge some connection of this phenomenon with the rise of the Zulu kingdom.

Shaka's successor, Dingaan, by the Afrikaaners, his murder by the
Swazis and the succession of his weaker brother Mpande as King,
destabilized the newly established Zulu kingdom and led to a war
between Mpande's sons Cetshwayo and Mbulazi. A considerable loss
of life and continuing campaign by the victorious Cetshwayo to root
out opposition led to considerable numbers of refugees crossing into
the new colony of Natal. Zulu society was characterized by strong
chieftainship, but at the time Colenso's *Romans* was written, King
Mpande was under virtual house arrest by his own son, Cetshwayo,
who effectively ruled Zululand. This was witnessed by the young
Zulu men who accompanied Colenso on his visit to both kraals. The
king was seen as a child of *uMvelingqangi*, Lord-of-the-Sky, whose
most obvious attribute is power (*uSomandla, uMninimandla*). The king
mediates the power and fertility of *uMvelingqangi* through various ritual processes, particularly at *Umkhosi*, the festival of first fruits (Berglund
1976: 32–77, see Opland 1983: 123–124). Hence the impotence of
King Mpande would potentially have called the hegemonic power
of Zulu kingship into the realm of contested ideology for the Zulu
converts of Colenso.

   This social and political crisis is in marked contrast to the situation which greeted the first missionaries to the Tswana. For those
who accompanied Colenso on his journey to visit the King, the
impact of the highly visible and numerous unburied skulls and bones
of thousands of the slaughtered followers of Mbulazi is obvious in
their accounts (Colenso 1982: 165, 172). All three tell the macabre
story with mirth and horror of Jojo, son of Nyangana, who by mistake picked up and chewed a (human) bone in the darkness after
he had dropped the piece of bread he was eating (1982: 165, 172,
182). In a culture where morality is enshrined in and protected by
the ancestors, the unburied dead create a social crisis which is not
easily resolved. The death of so many young men without children
is a double tragedy in Zulu society, since to kill someone without
progeny is to kill utterly and without hope (*ukubulala nya*) (Berglund
1976: 80–81). There are ritual means of cleansing society from the
disturbance caused by the unplacated living dead who have died violently, particularly ritual washing, but this presupposes some kind of
social redress and reconciliation also (1976: 122–123, 129–131), something not readily attainable in the given situation of the crisis in the
Zulu royal household. Paulina Dlamini (1986: 94–95), one of the
women from Cetshwayo's *isigodlo*, bears witness to this in her oral

testimony, speaking of an outbreak of possession by evil spirits (*fufun-yane*), which "did not exist at the time of the old Zulu kings" but are now everywhere because they "come mainly from those who were killed in battle, but not buried. . . ." William Ngidi closes his account with a praise poem expressing something of the crisis:

> Yes, indeed, my brothers, the weapons of war should be beaten into ploughs for cultivating the ground, and war-shields be sewed into garments of clothing, and peace be proclaimed, on the north and on the south, and on both sides, through the Father of our Lord Jesus Christ, uNkulunkulu, who ever liveth, and all evil become peace, I mean become goodness (Fuze, Ndiyane & Ngidi 1860: 193).

It is no accident that Colenso becomes preoccupied with the fate of the departed in his commentary, as we have seen. The role of kinship and the ancestors is a central question for Zulu society and the concept of eternal damnation of those ancestors who had never heard the gospel, or even who refused to hear it, would make Christianity incomprehensibly cruel. In a time when death was so omnipresent, this was no mere idle theological question. In Colenso's arguments in Western categories, we may hear the questions and problems of his African dialogue partners.

In order to establish his Boys Institution, Colenso enlisted the help of Theophilus Shepstone (*uSomtsewu kaSonzica*), the colonial Secretary for Native Affairs, to instruct the Zulu chiefs under his control that they should send their eldest sons (who would inherit after them, *abantwana abakulu abayakupata imizi aoyise uma bengaseko*). There was considerable resistance to this on their part, fearing (rightly) that they would lose (control over) their children (Fuze 1922: v). However, in the end, the chiefs were coerced to comply. Probably the action of Magwaza kaMatomela of the Fuze clan was typical: he sent the third son of his chief wife and the eldest son of his junior wife (neither of whom could inherit the chieftainship). Manawami kaMagwaza Fuze was twelve years old[13] when he arrived at Ekukhanyeni, an association he retained (through the wife, son and daughter after the death of Colenso himself) until his death sometime after 1923.

Fuze's baptism is described by him in his biographical introduction and is remarkable in itself. Having been despatched to school

---

[13] By his own reckoning (1922: v), though H.C. Lugg incongruously gives his birth date as 1840 in his introduction to the English translation (1979: xvii).

at Ekukhanyeni by his father, and after a period of three years instruction in the school and in type compositing in the printing press, Colenso decided the time had come for his baptism and approached his father when the latter visited Ekukhanyeni. Magwaza is horrified when he discovers this would mean that his son would become a Christian: "Sir, I am afraid of my child becoming a Christian. There is a son of So-and-So at the Edendale Mission School over yonder who went there to study, and when his mother went to see him she found he was no longer there, and it was said he had simply left and no longer lived there. I am afraid, Sir, and I do not wish my child to become a Christian, because he will defy me and his mother" (1979: iii). Colenso's response is to ask the boy to read the Ten Commandments in full, with no homily or attempt to justify the Christian mission in terms of conversion. Rather, the message given and received is that the son would continue to respect his parents and avoid theft and adultery.[14] The parents agree to the baptism, though with a clear warning that Colenso was "taking" their son in the same way as a man might "take" a wife, and that he "owed them":

> Hau, Sir, then you wish to make my child honour me and his mother, and desist from the evil practices of stealing and fornicating? Wo, Sir, I have nothing to say, and I give my consent for you to do to him what you want to do to him. Even I when in need of a blanket go and beg for one from Somtseu [Shepstone], and he gives me one, and when in need of a wife, I take cattle from my cattle kraal and pay them as lobolo to her father. I give my consent, Sir, do as you wish with my child (1979: iii).

While there is no evidence that Colenso paid in cash, it is clear that Fuze himself understood the obligation incurred, and it seems likely to me that the bishop was aware of the implications. If baptism is to be negotiated as a mutual agreement by the ritual elder and the parents as "equals" then it has quite different implications to baptism as a death to the old society and a social rupture. In the terms used by Berger and Luckmann (1966), no "alternation of universe" is taking place, no nihilation of the old social universe. Alternation

---

[14] *Ukwazise*—"to respect, to esteem, to honour (in a weaker sense)" rather than *ukuhlonipa*—"to honour (in a much stronger sense)." The difference may be significant, given the central role of *ukuhlonipa* in Zulu culture, relating to patriarchal authority and the ancestor rituals.

of social universe cannot be "negotiated," it is effected by a radical process of re-socialization:

> Alternation requires processes of re-socialization. These processes resemble primary socialization, because they have radically to reassign reality accents and, consequently, must replicate to a considerable degree the strongly affective identification with the socializing personnel that was characteristic of childhood. They are different from primary socialization because they do not start ex nihilo, and as a result must cope with a problem of dismantling, disintegrating the preceding nomic structure of subjective reality (1966: 157).

Instead, two different and competing social universes are here brought into direct connection without such "dismantling" of the prior Zulu social universe nor any attempt to devalue Fuze's family and culture.

Pre-alternation biography is typically nihilated in toto by subsuming it under a negative category occupying a strategic position in the new legitimating apparatus (1966: 160). Berger and Luckmann would describe the kind of success Colenso's mission achieved in Fuze as "cool" alternation, in which "the individual may opt for it in a manipulative manner ... The individual internalizes the new reality, but instead of its being his reality, it is a reality to be used by him for specific purposes" (1966: 172). However, I would argue that in this process both English and Zulu cultural universes are destabilized. Colenso refuses to respond to the protests of Fuze's parents with ideological combat or a display of power (which normally determines the outcome of such confrontations of social universes according to Berger and Luckmann, 1966: 109), but allows the validity of their demand that they continue to be respected and that their authority continues to be accepted. He does not refute the statement of an obligation incurred on his part and hence implicitly accepts it.

A further remarkable aspect of Fuze's baptism is the choice of name. Colenso sends William Ngidi to ask him what name he chooses for baptism. Fuze is nonplussed. Ngidi, who had been baptized by the American Mission in 1855, and knew the ropes, reassures him by suggesting he flip through the New Testament and choose a name from there. Fuze chooses Petros and Johane. Colenso refuses Petros and then, on a second delegation, refuses Johane also. He tells Fuze instead that he has chosen the Zulu name Magema for him. Fuze tells us that Colenso's reasoning was as follows, "He objected to African people being called by foreign names which meant nothing to them" (1979: iv). The word *magema*, according to Cope (1979:

150) means, "He who nods the head in agreement," or "He who threatens with a stick."[15] Colenso has surely chosen the baptismal name to indicate that the initiate has consented to become a Christian, but the ambiguity of the word is significant. Colenso's choice of Zulu names opens up the possibility of "cultural continuity" for Zulu converts, since it minimizes the rupture with their own community signified by the choice of a foreign name. Incidentally, Colenso's choice of an indigenous name for God, uNkulunkulu ("the Great, Great One"), to replace the "nonsense word" uTixo preferred by the American Mission,[16] has the same effect. uNkulunkulu can also refer to "the ancestral spirit of all mankind (sic.)" (Dent & Nyembezi 1969: 434), and hence would also imply continuity with African traditional cultural understandings of the numinous.[17]

It is interesting that Fuze understands his baptism at Easter 1859 as the culmination of "how he came into being" as Magema kaMagwaza Fuze of the Ncobo people. Yet he follows it immediately with an expression of his need to find out where his people came from: "To proceed with this book, he [Fuze] had long begun questioning his people asking them, 'Where did we come from?,' but they did not tell him exactly we here they came from" (1979: iv). It is as if the effect of Colenso's Christian mission was to raise the question of origins, of historical identity and continuity, in its acutest form. Fuze experiences this as a prophetic call, in his own way. This is clear in that he defines his childhood as "different from the others." He includes an account of his own prophecy as a boy that he would be adopted by an important white man: "In his conversation with the other children he used to say, 'I am not going to grow up here at home. A white man of high rank will be coming here from across

---

[15] The latter is the more obvious sense, from gema, "make as if to strike" (Dent & Nyembezi 1969: 353).

[16] uTixo is used in the American Mission's New Testament in 1865, but Colenso's usage won out for Zulu but not for Xhosa Christians. See Fuze's protestations against the word (1979: 5). He argues that it comes via Xhosa from the Khoi people and referred to a praying mantis. Hence it is totally inappropriate in his opinion as a word for the creator of all.

[17] Chidester points out that the confusion over the reference of Zulu names for God arises out of the unsettled nature of the frontier situation. Zulu people furthest from the mission stations held uNkulunkulu to refer to their particular original tribal ancestor, while those nearest the missions were most likely to understand the word to refer either to a universal human ancestor or to the universal High God of the missions (1996: 160–165).

the sea, he is the one for whom I will work, and who will call me by the name of Skelemu" (1979: ii).[18] In his conclusion to this opening section, Fuze adopts the mantle of a Christian prophet with words clearly drawn from the Johannine epistles:

> *Yimi onilobelayo*
> *Owakini onitandayo*
> It is I who record this for you,
> One of you who loves you (1979: iv).

In other words, his Christian identity is inextricably linked in his mind with his quest for Zulu origins, for the construction of a Zulu historical consciousness.

This rich new potential has been opened up by the "liminal space" created by the failure of the ideologies of the two social universes here in the process of interaction. Colenso denies his own people's stories of their origins (Genesis), substituting a "scientific world view" which is hotly contested. Fuze denies naive accounts of the origin of his own people ("from the reed beds of the Umvoti river," 1979: iv), substituting an attempt at "objective" historical work which nevertheless inserts an authentic Zulu voice into the current Eurocentric accounts. He expresses the beginnings of a pan-African consciousness, of common origins and identity which is larger than the Zulu people, larger even than the black people of Southern Africa. His is not a book about *Zulu* origins but about and for the black people of Africa as a whole, including even African Americans in its purview (1979: 8).

Abantu Abamyama, Lapa Bavela Ngakona (*The Black People and Whence They Came*) constitutes the first substantial work in Zulu written by a Zulu person. It is also a first hand account of a Zulu people in the throes of the forging of a national identity, in the face of colonial aggression and, simultaneously, the penetration of their culture by the Christian mission. It is remarkable that this valuable work has not received more attention. The fine study of Axel-Ivar Berglund, *Zulu Thought-Patterns and Symbolism* (1976), for instance, which is based

---

[18] Fuze's use of this name is interesting, since its implications are entirely derogatory: it probably derives from the Afrikaans word, "*skelm*" or "rascal," but may refer to a worm in Zulu. It could, of course, be a term of "belittling" endearment, and may have been a nickname of Fuze's at Ekukhanyeni, since it is described as given to him by Colenso. However, it undercuts, with its negative connotations, the baptismal name of Magema.

on many field interviews as well as secondary literature, does not mention the work in his introduction, either under "informants" or "literature on Zulu."[19] Its style is redolent of Zulu oral traditions of story telling and *izibongo* (praise songs), and its progression is often cyclical rather than linear.[20] The editor of the English translation, A.T. Cope, has insisted on rearranging the material in linear and thematic fashion (1979: x), despite his own awareness of and sensitivity to Zulu cultural traditions and protestations about the imposing of "foreign concepts."[21] He has also "deliberately played down 'whence they came' in the title, for the interest here is not how much the author knows but how little he knows . . . and how limited his historical and geographical horizons" (1979: ix). This deemphasis on the historical origins in the work is exacerbated by the editor's omission of the sections of Bishop Colenso's *Izindaba ZaseNatal* (1856) which Fuze includes. In my opinion, this seriously distorts the intention of Fuze in writing the book, which is precisely to insert himself and his people into the hegemonic historical discourse of white people. He deliberately provides the history of Southern Africa written in Zulu by Colenso (*Izindaba ZaseNatal*), described as *ngokutsho kwabelungu* ("as told by white people") and interpolates his own comments ("not by white people") because "there are some matters that conflict" ("*kukona ezinye izindaba ezingaqondene, ezipikisanayo kwamanye amazwe*," 1979: 111). His insertions are partly to accept white history, where it suits him, and partly to subvert it. A failure to see this is to lose sight of Fuze's distinctive contribution in the history of resistance to colonization. Western historical discourse is hegemonic precisely because it is unaware of its own practice of domination (Comaroff & Comaroff 1991: 25).

Fuze begins his prologue with a word of appreciation to John L. Dube, the first president of the South African Native National

---

[19] Though it is present in his bibliography and used, for example, on page 300 note 66.

[20] Rev. Sipho Mtetwa has pointed out to me that the circle is an important symbol in Zulu culture, in physical architecture of huts and in the seating pattern of the *Inkundla* (Council of Elders) and the *ukhamba* (calabash), as well as Zulu rhetoric. The main point of a particular speech is likely to be introduced towards the end of a conversation by the deprecatory *konje* ("by the way") or *okunye* ("Oh and another thing").

[21] Trevor Cope is the editor also of *Izibongo: Zulu Praise-Poems* (1968) and numerous other publications on Zulu culture.

Congress, later called the African National Congress, who founded the newspaper *Ilanga laseNatal*. Indeed, according to Shula Marks (Fuze 1979: xvi), Fuze seems to have acted as a courier between Dube and Harriette Colenso. He is also close to the family of Chief Albert Luthuli—with whose uncle, Chief Martin Luthuli he shares a bed while his wife is absent (1922: 139)—and other founding members of the ANC. His project of describing the origins of the black people, of inserting their presence and voice into the histories written by white people, is intimately related to the resistance of the African people to colonial domination. It should not be judged for what it does not say (by Western rationale) but by what it inserts into the Western discourse and why it does so. The more interesting question is, How and why does this convert to Christianity write his own book on the origins and history of his own people? If, as the Comaroffs assert, the history of Christian missions is the history of a "long conversation" between colonialism and colonial culture (including religion) and the indigenous peoples (1991: 17–18), to what is this discourse a reply and what gave Fuze space to write as he does? The collision of two competing harmonious, unconscious, hegemonic world-views brings many things into contention and produces ideology which seeks to legitimate what is thus brought into the sphere of contestation. While the competition may have been unequal in terms of power, the challenge was not entirely one-sided. The gaps which were created between hegemony and ideology opened up space for experiment, play of meaning and new understandings which could emerge finally into coherent resistance to domination.

The nature of the relationship between Colenso and Fuze produces a particular brand of prophetic nationalism infused by Christian symbolism. Clearly it would be impossible to do justice to Fuze's work in a short essay like this, but some preliminary observations can be made. Fuze begins his work with an interesting triplet, which draws simultaneously on Zulu culture and Christian tradition. Entitled *Isisusa, Inkondlo* and *Amangebeza*, they refer to three phases of a Zulu wedding: preliminary dance, grand dance and bridesmaid's refreshments. Fuze gives an extended account of the Zulu custom in the book (1979: 32–39). However the wedding reference has a Christian significance as well, with its reference to the parables of Jesus and the Wedding Banquet (for example Mt. 22:1–14 = Lk., Lk. 13:28 =, Lk. 14:7–24, Mt. 25:1–13). It has eschatological reference to God's imminent intervention and restoration of the kingdom. In Fuze's appropriation of the symbol, it seems to refer to the awakening of nationalist hopes:

> You will attain nothing by your present state of disorganisation. Unite in friendliness like the enlightened nations. Do not merely look on heedlessly when others are being exploited. So long as you desire evil to one another, you will never be a people of any consequence, but you will become the manure for fertilizing the crops of the enlightened nations, disorderly, useless, and without responsibility.
>
> Seeing that dawn is about to break, listen all of you and understand. There are the bridesmaids chanting and asking for refreshments from the bridegroom. What do they say? They say, "*Wolete amangebeza, wolete*" [bring forth the refreshments, bring them forth]. And if the bridegroom should fail to do so, they will certainly not remain silent but subject him to perpetual and persistent protest throughout the night (1979: viii–ix).

The wedding is a symbol of national revival as the will of God worked out in history.

A constant theme of Fuze's work is that the abandonment of Zulu custom and the adoption of Western culture is contrary to the will of God. Indeed it will result in God abandoning the people. This African culture, says Fuze, is an aspect of God's good creation. The book is a wake-up call intended by Fuze to be used in school instruction as a means of resisting further erosion of African identity. It is worth quoting his statement at some length:

> ... And when we began to be roused by foreign peoples, we then thought that we had sprung from the same source as they, ceasing to observe our own ways and respectful customs, and grasping those of the foreigners and then finding that we had been abandoned by the One above from whom we originated. I now warn you to abandon all this pretence because it is of no benefit whatever. Adhere strictly to your own. It does not mean to say that because you see civilised people and wish to become like them that you should discard your own which is good. It may happen that in seeking to do so, you may suddenly find yourselves being cast into a bottomless pit. The creator did not create us foolishly, but wisely, and there can be no doubt that if we love and acknowledge Him, He will uplift us like all the nations, but if we treat Him with disdain, and do not acknowledge Him, He will forsake us for ever (1979: viii).

Zulu culture is described warmly and luxuriantly in the work, and it is positively valued throughout. There is no sense of reservation even about customs which European missionaries found problematic. It is only wilful violence which Fuze condemns, and not military conquest *per se*, since Shaka is positively viewed and so is Cetshwayo. Rather in Fuze's account malicious, self-seeking or wanton violence is rejected and seen as the cause of problems.

Finally, in terms of the historical framework itself, Fuze seems to have adopted the "good king, bad king" terminology from the Biblical books of Kings and Chronicles. The Zulu kingdom is prophesied in advance by his great-grandfather Ndaba, "for from his progeny would unexpectedly appear the one who would rule the whole of South Africa" (1979: 58, 43, 50). When he triumphs against Zwide of the Ndwandwe people, everyone asks in Biblical fashion, "What sort of a king has now arisen?" (1979: 50). His illegitimate birth is not a sign of shame but of special providence:

> If a person thinks and looks at the unexpected activities of Shaka, he cannot conclude that he was merely the progeny of Senzangakhona and Nandi, he can see clearly that he was a special product appearing from above, who arrived here expressly for the purpose of bringing unity to the country instead of disunity, and rule by one person instead of everyone doing as he pleased. These words which I speak are supported by the fact that Nandi never became the chief's wife [*inkosikazi*] of Senzangakhona, and that when she became pregnant and gave birth, she did not live with him as a wife with her child (1979: 59).

The reference to the virgin birth of Jesus Christ is unmistakable. Shaka is, in the limited sense Fuze specifies, namely the beginning of black nationalism, the black messiah (see 1979: 66)! Yet it is Shaka's own violent action in the end, in Fuze's view, which brings him down. Among other things, Fuze (1979: 60) mentions Shaka's murder of his own mother in a fit of rage, though his account may be disputed by others! In this he was "discarding the old ways of Senzangakhona and his forebears" (1979: 146, note the "invention of tradition" concerning Zulu royal ancestors, on which see below). Since he "defied the Owner of all peoples for whom he ruled his people, his rule was terminated and God roused his brothers to kill him" (1979: 97). Dingane was far worse, entirely wicked and murderous (1979: 83–85), so he too "was condemned by God who brought his years to an end, and he died. In his place He appointed his brother Mpande" (1979: 98). It is Mpande's peaceful, enlightened rule, which results in a long reign. Cetshwayo is justified in

his devastating war against his brother, Mbulazi, because he had a
mark on his ear to show that Mpande had declared him his heir to
the Boers (Fuze's term, 1979: 98). It is Cetshwayo's violent action in
murdering his father's favourite wife, Nomantshali, before his very
eyes, out of jealousy and contrary to all Zulu custom, which brought
a curse and was the cause of his downfall (1979: 99–100). Nevertheless
he is a good king, because he rules justly and wisely (1979: 111).
Those who rule as servants of their people are blessed by God (1979:
93–94), while those who act wickedly and arbitrarily are removed
by God (for example 1979: 98). In other words, Zulu history is salvation history:

> At the outset, before the account of the years of the reigns of the Zulu
> kings who are responsible for forging this great nation together, it is
> right to remember that all kings are supported by God, and it is He
> who appoints and supports them. If sovereignty is not supported by
> Him, it is dead, and authority nonexistent. Also if a king rules with-
> out the realisation that he is a servant, a mere headman to represent
> his people to God, his kingship is nonexistent and dead, because God
> will soon bring it to an end (1979: 97).

This theology would not be remarkable, except that it is an appropriation of Biblical legitimation for colonial rule and an application
of that very legitimation to describe the rule of the Zulu kings. This
was exactly the kind of colonial ideology used by the colonial administration to wage war on the Zulu people, to try in court and imprison
first Langalibalele, then Cetshwayo and finally Dinizulu under British
law. Colenso and, later, his family stressed in repeated court cases
that the Zulu kings had never invaded "British" colonial territory,
being instead the victims of colonial aggression, and that they were
not technically under British jurisdiction (Guy 1983: 249–251). The
appropriation and adaptation of this ideology is an act of resistance.
It is the kind of innovation which emerges in the gap or "liminal
space" between hegemony and ideology described by the Comaroffs.
    Terence Ranger's valuable study on the "invention of tradition"
in colonial Africa (1983: 211–262) argues that, in the absence of a
readily available African framework they could co-opt to legitimate
colonial rule, the conquerors made extensive use of the concept of
"imperial monarchy." Africans were well aware of the ideological significance of monarchy in British colonial domination and sought to
appropriate the symbol for themselves (1983: 237–246). These attempts

to claim the symbol of monarchy were not "innocent" but were also inventions of tradition: "It will be seen that these attempts to manipulate British royal symbolism were complex. If from the point of view of the chiefs they were largely reassertions of status, from the point of view of the mission-educated they were also an attempt to *redefine* chiefly authority" (1983: 243). The Zulu kings are made a part of salvation history, but simultaneously made into models of the rule of order, justice and peace inspired by mission ideology:

> When Mpande appeared on the scene to contest against Dingane, he was installed by the Boers who had already discerned that he was a kind person with respect and regard for others, unlike his two brothers, Shaka and Dingane, who were like wild beasts. We do not know who these two took after, seeing that we know Senzangakhona to have bee a kind and considerate person, but from some of his praises [*izibongo*] we learn that he had a violent temper, so perhaps Shaka and Dingane took after him. Only one is known to have been without it: Mpande. This one of today, Solomon, is mild, kind and humble, and one can say that he is indeed a child of Mpande. His father, Dinizulu, was also humble, but took after his father when angry. But Cetshwayo was very good and kind, and loved all his people (1979: 146).

The Zulu kings were warrior conquerors, who "invented" (in Hobsbawm's terminology 1983: 4–5) a Zulu nation during a time of instability and rapid change. In Fuze's work we see the further "invention" of a constitutional Zulu monarchy operating within culturally and legally defined norms. Fuze, rightly or wrongly, saw the Zulu monarchy as having the potential to unite the African people of Southern Africa in resistance to colonialism and become the focus of African renewal.

The work of Magema Fuze deserves further study. While it is undoubtedly affected by Fuze's age in places, which *may* perhaps account for lapses and anecdotal reminiscences (though I would prefer to see it as part of oral cultural style), it represents a mature reflection on colonial intrusion and cultural hegemony of rich complexity. In places Fuze rather naively accepts white colonial *bona fides* (for example his praise of Shaka for his willingness to cooperate with white people in order to gain "the products of their knowledge" (1979: 85). Fuze's acts of ideological resistance and appropriation are partly conscious and partly unconscious. They are part of what the Comaroffs term an "inchoate awareness" of the rules and stakes involved in the "long conversation" between the Zulu people and

the missionaries and colonial authorities. Nevertheless, in its forth-
right appropriation of Christian symbolism and ethics, while it retains
a positive valuation of indigenous Zulu culture and history, it represents a critical phase of the "long conversation" between the missionaries and the colonized peoples of Africa. The symbols and values
emerging from Colenso's mission were seized upon by his converts,
and had an impact beyond what he could have imagined. Historical
consciousness became a central ingredient of that *bricolage* constructed
by Fuze, and enables him to understand the black people of southern Africa as having a place and an identity and a future beyond
what was offered to them by the ideology of empire.

It is no accident that Fuze is an advocate for the nascent African
National Congress. He, together with Ngidi, was active and instru-
mental in the uncovering of colonial duplicity in the case of the
Hlubi chief Langalibalele (Guy 1983: 193–214, esp. 206) and also,
subsequently, in the defence of Cetshwayo and Dinizulu, even beyond
Colenso's own death. Perhaps the link between early Natal and the
formation of the ANC owes something to the peculiar nature of
Colenso's mission and the responses it evoked among the emergent
Zulu intellectuals as *bricoleurs*. Certainly the early Zulu Congress lead-
ers were known as "the Bishopstowe faction" after the name of
Colenso's home (Guy 1983: 242).

BIBLIOGRAPHY

Berger, P. & Luckmann, T. *The Social Construction of Reality: A Treatise in the Sociology
    of Knowledge*. New York: Doubleday, 1966.
Berglund, A.-I. *Zulu Thought-Patterns and Symbolism*. Bloomington: Indiana University
    Press, 1976.
Burnett, B.B. *The Mission Work of the First Anglican Bishop of Natal, the Rt. Reverend
    J.W. Colenso, between 1852–1873*. Unpublished MA Dissertation of Rhodes
    University, 1947.
Chidester, D. *Savage Systems: Colonialism and Comparative Religion in Southern Africa*.
    Charlottesville: University Press of Virginia, 1996.
Cockshutt, A.O.J. *Anglican Attitudes*. London: Collins, 1959.
Colenso, J.W. *Ten Weeks in Natal. A Journal of a First Tour of Visitation among the
    Colonists and Zulu Kafirs of Natal*. Cambridge, 1855.
———. *First Steps of the Zulu Mission*, 1860. Reprinted in Colenso, *Bringing Forth
    Light*, 43–161.
———. *St. Paul's Epistle to the Romans: Newly Translated, and Explained from a Missionary
    Point of View*. Pietermaritzburg: Ekukanyeni Mission Press, 1861a.
———. *A Letter to His Grace the Archbishop of Canterbury, upon the Question of the Proper
    Treatment of Cases of Polygamy, as Found Already Existing in Converts from Heathenism*.
    Ekukhanyeni: Mission Press, 1861b.

————. *First Lessons in Science*. Ekukhanyeni: Mission Press, 1861c.
————. *The Pentateuch and Book of Joshua Critically Examined*. London: Longman & Green, 1862–1863.
————. Translation of A. Kuenen, *The Pentateuch and Book of Joshua Critically Examined*. London: Longman & Green, 1865.
————. Translation of H. Oort, *The Worship of Baalim in Israel*. London: Longman & Green, 1865.
————. *On Missions to the Zulus in Natal & Zululand* (A Lecture to the Marylebone Literary Society, 23rd May 1865), 1865. Reprinted in Colenso, *Bringing Forth Light*, 203–238.
————. *First Steps in Zulu: Being an Elementary Grammar of the Zulu Language*. Pietermaritzburg & Durban: Vause, Slatter & Co., 1903 (4th Edition), (Printed by Magema, Mubi & Co., Ekukanyeni).
————. *Zulu-English Dictionary*. Pietermaritzburg: Davis, 1878 (2nd Edition), (Printed by Magema, Mubi & Co., Ekukanyeni).
————. Translation of C. Vijn, *Cetshwayo's Dutchman*. Reprinted London: Greenhill, [1880] 1988. (Pages 83–192 consist of Colenso's notes).
————. *Bringing Forth Light: Five Tracts on Bishop Colenso's Zulu Mission*, Ed. R. Edgecombe. Pietermaritzburg: University of Natal Press, 1982.
Comaroff, J. & J. *Of Revelation and Revolution: Christianity, Colonialism, and Consciousness in South Africa* I. Chicago: University of Chicago Press, 1991.
————. *Of Revelation and Revolution: The Dialectics of Modernity on a South African Frontier* II. Chicago: University of Chicago Press, 1997.
Cox, G.W. *The Life of John William Colenso, Bishop of Natal*. London: Ridgeway, 1888a–b.
Darby, I.D. *The Soteriology of Bishop John William Colenso*. Unpublished PhD Dissertation of the University of Natal, Pietermaritzburg, 1981.
————. "Colenso and Baptism." *Journal of Theology for Southern Africa* 67, 1989: 62–66.
————. "Another Look at Bishop Colenso's Controversial Theology." Unpublished paper for the Southern African Anglican Theological Commission, 1991.
Dlamini, P. *Paulina Dlamini: Servant of Two Kings*. Compiled by H. Filter, Translated and Edited by S. Bourquin. Pietermaritzburg, University of Natal Press, 1986.
Doke, C.M. "Bantu Language Pioneers of the Nineteenth Century," *Bantu Studies* 14, 1940: 234–235.
Doke, C.M. & Cole, D.T. *Contributions to the History of Bantu Linguistics*. Johannesburg, 1961.
Draper, J.A. & West, G.O. "Anglicans and Scripture in South Africa." In Eds T.J.M. Patterson & F. England, *Bounty in Bondage: Festschrift for Dean Edward King*, Johannesburg: Ravan, 1989: 30–52.
Draper, J.A. "Archbishop Gray and the Interpretation of the Bible." In Eds J. Suggit and M. Goedhals, *Change and Challenge: Essays Commemorating the 150th Anniversary of Robert Gray as First Bishop of Cape Town (20 February 1848)*, 44–54. Johannesburg: CPSA, 1998.
————. "Magema Fuze and the Insertion of the Subjugated Historical Subject into the Discourse of Hegemony," *Bulletin for Contextual Theology* 5/1–2, 1998: 16–26.
————. "Hermeneutical Drama on the Colonial Stage: Liminal Space and Creativity in Colenso's Commentary on Romans," *JTSA* 103, 1998: 13–32.
Edgecombe, R. "Introduction." In Colenso, *Bringing Forth Light*, 1982: xiii–xlvi.
Festinger, L. *A Theory of Cognitive Dissonance*. Stanford: Stanford University Press: 1956.
Festinger, L., Riecken, H.W. & Schachter, S. *When Prophecy Fails*. New York: Harper & Row: 1957.
Fuze, M.M. *Abantu Abamnyama, Lapa Bavela Ngakona*. Pietermaritzburg: City Printing Works, 1922.

————. *The Black People and Whence They Came*, Translated by H.C. Lugg, Ed. A.T. Cope. Pietermaritzburg: University of Natal Press/Killie Campbell Africana Library, 1979.

Fuze, Magema kaMagwaza, Ndiyane & Ngidi, William. *Three Native Accounts of the Visit of the Bishop of Natal in September and October, 1859, to Umpande, King of the Zulus, with Explanatory Notes and a Literal Translation, and a Glossary of All the Zulu Words Employed in the Same: Designed for the Use of Students of the Zulu Language.* Ekukhanyeni: Mission Press, 1860. The English translation is reprinted (with notes by R. Edgecombe) in Colenso, *Bringing Forth Light*, 1982: 161–203.

Gadamer, H.-G. *Truth and Method.* New York: Continuum, 1993.

Guy, J. *The Heretic: A Study of the Life of John William Colenso 1814–1883*, 1983. Pietermaritzburg: University of Natal Press/Johannesburg: Ravan.

Hinchliff, P. *John William Colenso, Bishop of Natal.* London: Nelson, 1964.

Hobsbawm, E. "Introduction: Inventing Traditions." In Eds E. Hobsbawm & T. Ranger, *The Invention of Tradition*, Cambridge: Cambridge University Press, 1983: 1–14.

Metzger, B.M. *The Text of the New Testament: Its Transmission, Corruption and Restoration.* Oxford: Clarendon, 1968.

Neill, S. *The Interpretation of the New Testament 1861–1961.* Oxford: Oxford University Press, 1964.

Opland, J. *Xhosa Oral Poetry: Aspects of a Black South African Tradition.* Cambridge: Cambridge University Press, 1983.

Räisänen, H. "Paul, God, and Israel: Romans 9–11 in Recent Research." In Eds J. Neusner, P. Borgen, E.S. Fredrichs & R. Horsely, *The Social World of Formative Christianity and Judaism*, Philadelphia: Fortress, 1988: 178–206.

Ranger, T. "The Invention of Tradition in Colonial Africa." In Eds E. Hobsbawm & T. Ranger, *The Invention of Tradition*, Cambridge: Cambridge University Press, 1983: 211–262.

Reese, W. *Colenso Letters from Natal.* Pietermaritzburg: Shuter & Shooter, 1958.

Said, E.W. *Culture and Imperialism.* New York: Vintage Books, 1995.

Sanders, E. *Paul, the Law, and the Jewish People.* Philadelphia: Fortress, 1983.

Stendahl, K. "The Apostle Paul and the Introspective Conscience of the West," *HTR* 56, 1963: 199–215 (also in *Paul among Jews and Gentiles*. Philadelphia: Fortress, 78–96).

Turner, V. *The Ritual Process: Structure and Anti-structure.* Ithaca: Cornell University Press, 1969.

Vidler, A.R. *The Church in an Age of Revolution.* Harmondsworth: Penguin, 1971^2.

Warwick, G.W. *The Contribution of Bishop Colenso to Biblical Criticism.* Unpublished MA Thesis of the University of Natal, Pietermaritzburg, 1966.

PART THREE

COMPARISON AND TRANSLATION AS TRANSACTION

COMPARATIVE READINGS OF THE BIBLE IN AFRICA: SOME CONCERNS

Eric Anum

The comparative approach was developed against the background of the way the gospel was propagated in Africa by Western missionaries. Missionaries were greatly inhibited in their perception of both African religion and African humanity, by their prejudices, and also by the evolutionary view of the human race and of the religions then current. This explains why conversion to Christianity had to involve,

> the abandonment and renunciation not only of the traditional African ways of worship, sacrifices to the Supreme Being, communion with the ancestral spirits and other holy rites—but also the abandonment and renunciation of African cultural customs and practices including songs and dances. All of them together were referred to as "things of the devil." Almost the whole of the traditional African culture was seen as being under the kingdom of the Prince of Darkness, and the African peoples were summoned by the missionaries to come out of it completely, root, stock and branch (Kibicho 1978: 378).

This was a challenge to modern African biblical scholars. Were they to take into serious consideration the traditional African beliefs and practices, which had been abandoned or overlooked in interpreting the Bible for use in Africa by the Western missionaries?

One of the approaches used by contemporary African biblical scholars to achieve this goal is the comparative model. This approach postulates three levels of continuity or relationship between the Old Testament and African life and thought. These are religio-cultural, theological and interpretative or hermeneutical (Dickson 1979: 99). Religio-cultural continuity suggests that various elements in the African religio-cultural ethos recall ancient Israelite beliefs and practices. Theological continuity suggests a continuity between the Old Testament and African life and thought as God is regarded as God of the whole earth and therefore at work in Israel as well as the other nations. Lastly, there is hermeneutical continuity, which suggests that in appropriating the Old Testament, Africans approach the text with presuppositions, questions and problems that matter to them. Thus, the text and the African are bound together as they dialogue with each other.

The most dominant of these three levels of relationship or continuity with respect to the comparative model is the religio-cultural relationship. Those who adopt a religio-cultural perspective attempt to show a "cultural" continuity between African and biblical worlds, through a comparative study of selected linguistic, religious, historical and cultural concepts. Such forms of continuity can be found, several writers suggest, because at some time in the past there was physical contact between Africans and Jews who had come to the continent in search of trading partners. Thus, the proponents of this view have argued that it is this contact that explains resemblances between the Old Testament and religion and life among Africans. The primary point of this comparison is to legitimate African culture either by demonstrating its historical roots in the Old Testament or its similarity to the Old Testament.

The pioneer work in this area is J.J. Williams' *Hebrewisms in West Africa: From Nile to Niger with the Jews*, published in 1930. In his study of the Ashanti people of Ghana, Williams proposes that "there is a far-reaching indication of the possible origin of the Ashanti, that carries us well on our way to the verification of the assertion . . . that the Ashanti may trace their descent from distant Egypt" (William 1930: 57). Williams seeks to establish this in various ways, but his main contention is that there are significant similarities between Ashanti traditional religious beliefs and practices and Hebrew religion. However, he does also identify what he claims to be historical links between the Hebrew language and the Ashanti language, basing his claim mainly on similarities of sound, but also arguing for a close relationship between Ashanti and Hebrew language structures.

With respect to religious practices, his main focus, Williams finds similarities in the concept of the Supreme Being in both cultures. He argues, for example, that the Supreme Being of the Ashanti "is the Jehovah of the Israelites" (Williams 1930: 72). The very name *Onyame* is seen by Williams to be from the same source as *Yahweh*. Furthermore, he argues, we have among the Ashanti exactly that "mixed religion" which is found among the Israelites of old, that is, the worship of a Supreme Being and lesser gods. Here, and in many other examples Williams uses Ashanti parallels to make sense of the Old Testament and to legitimise Ashanti religion.

Williams' proposal gained support from some writers. Hence, Eva Meyerowitz noted in her book, *The Divine Kingship in Ghana and Ancient Egypt* (1960) that, the Carthaginian deities *Tanit* and *Baal Hamman* can in every respect be equated with the Akan *Nyame* and *Nyankopon* (Meyerowitz 1960: 15). J.B. Danquah's *Akan Concept of God* also linked *Nyame* and *Yahweh* even though he admitted that, "I have not enough evidence to be certain" (Danquah 1968: 37). However, there were others who have expressed reservations concerning Williams' methodology. Eric Isaac argues that extreme caution should be exercised in identifying similarities too readily which are only so in appearance, when comparing ancient Jewish culture and other cultures (Isaac 1964: 93).

Kwesi Dickson's review of Williams' methodology, which appeared in the *Legon Journal of Humanities* forty years later, shows the importance of this work, even though Dickson is critical of Williams' work. Dickson believes that Williams makes too much of the similarities in sound between Ashanti and Hebrew, and also expresses reservations with respect to similarities in language structures between Hebrew and African languages. He is of the opinion that there are more dissimilarities in the language structures of the Ashanti than the similarities cited by Williams. For Dickson, the value of any parallelism in languages is primarily pedagogical. Concerning this he says, "on the subject of viewing together of the Old Testament and African life and thought, we may note that in teaching Hebrew attention might be drawn to those aspects of the indigenous language which might make it easier for students to gain greater facility in certain areas of Hebrew usage" (Dickson 1974: 31). His point is that such parallels tell us nothing about historical links between the languages but may be useful for teaching purposes.

While Dickson accepts that there are similarities at a religio-cultural level between, for example, the religious festivals in Africa and those of the Old Testament, their significance is different. Dickson's position is that the significance of a custom in a particular religious set-up is more important than surface resemblances. He therefore cautioned that it is important for a religio-cultural item to be studied first in its own historico-religious context before the comparative method is applied. However, even though Dickson saw a lot of weaknesses in Williams' methodology, he maintained that the comparative method could still be used. He advocated a related approach that identifies what he calls the "authentic religion" of the Israelites and compares it with African Traditional Religion(s).[1] Unlike Williams, he would not include the worship of lesser deities or Canaanite gods as part of "authentic Jewish religion." He disagrees totally with Williams' argument that the ancient Israelites practiced "mixed religion." This is because Dickson thinks that what Williams has done is to cite what is an aberration, and by putting this in the place of the authentic Hebrew religion, he provides no authentic basis for comparison with Ashanti religion. Thus, commenting on Williams' statement that "we have in Ashanti exactly that 'mixed religion' (consisting of the worship of both the Supreme Being and the lesser gods) which we find in Israel of old. They worshipped other gods as well" (Williams 1930: 72), Dickson argues that such a statement ignores the true nature of the Old Testament and that those pagan beliefs and practices which are found in its pages are of no significance in assessing what is central to Hebrew religion. This implies that much of what Williams notes should be properly labelled corrupt religious practices which had infiltrated Hebrew religion. Dickson is of the view that since Williams does not describe what authentic Hebrew religion is, his book is of little value in discussions on Old Testament life and thought. Williams' obsession with maintaining historical continuity by tracing a line of Hebraic influence from Egypt to West Africa blinds him to authentic Jewish religious beliefs and practices, Dickson believes, and so weakens the contribution of his comparative analysis.

Dickson outlines his own approach in his book *Theology in Africa*. His opinion is that, "one could compare a considerable number of customs and societal arrangements found in the Old Testament and African life and thought" as "this will provide additional basis for evaluating what may be described as a cultural continuity" (Dickson 1984: 160). As distinct from Williams' methodology of historical continuity, Dickson argues that such comparisons are never intended to imply direct cultural contact or borrowing but merely to illustrate patterns of thought and feelings. Dickson has done detailed studies in this area pointing to what he calls the Old Testament "atmosphere" that makes the African context "a 'kindred' atmosphere" (Dickson 1973: 36). Thus, a number of religious themes, practices and rites

---

[1] My usage shifts between the singular and plural. The singular denotes a strategic and substantive claim to important "family resemblances" among African religions. The plural denotes the rich diversity that constitutes African religion.

are compared with each other. The selected themes that Dickson deals with are nature, spirit possession and corporate personality.

Dickson operates on the hypothesis that there is both continuity as well as discontinuity between Israelite religio-cultural practices and attitudes and those of Africa. With respect to land, for example, Dickson argues that the Canaanite view, which believed that land was infused with divinity, is closer to the African view than is the Israelite view. However, "the land, in Africa as well as Israelite thought, is the basis for group consciousness. Not only is the land not to be defiled, but also it plays a part in the African awareness of group interrelatedness" (Dickson 1984: 166). Forms of both continuity and discontinuity are also found in the area of spirit possession. In the Old Testament, Yahweh the national God was the source of prophecy and true prophetic inspiration, but in Africa spirit possession seldom originates from God; it is usually the lesser divinities and other spirit powers who possess people. However, Dickson indicates that despite these dissimilarities, the person possessed in both cases is required to do the spirit's bidding, as for instance, "The Nuer of Sudan speak of the spirit 'laying hold of' or 'taking hold of' a person, much as the Hebrews did" (Dickson 1984: 168). For both, spirit possession comes with a sense of dismay, but with the Israelites it is more from a sense of inadequacy and unpreparedness than the burden of the body of prohibitions which the person who becomes the agent of a spirit power invariably has to observe. Also, Old Testament prophets are conscious of the fact that they are called to bring back erring people to God. Dickson states that "they saw themselves as the conscience of their people, charged with the responsibility of waking them up to spiritual realities and sharpening their conscience with respect to social inequities" (Dickson 1984: 169). African prophets are also conscious of having been called to serve the people, but their oracles are mainly aimed at maintaining the religio-cultural heritage on which society's equilibrium is believed to rest. Dickson sees this as a major discontinuity: Old Testament prophets were critical of Israelite institutions in a way that prophecy in Africa is not.

With respect to the sense of corporate community, African societies incorporate not only the extended family and the clan but also the unborn and the dead. While there is a place for the individual, provided they act responsibly and ensure the success of their destinies by acquiring and maintaining good characters, individuals are not expected to take decisions against the customs of the group. Dickson finds similar family structures in the Old Testament, and in a later article argues that "The available evidence would seem to suggest that the dead, in consciousness with the living, were part of this corporateness. Officially, it would seem that no cult was paid to the dead; however, the dead were owed certain duties that were taken seriously (1 Samuel 31:12; 2 Samuel 21:13–14 etc.) and it may thus be said that they were honoured in a religious spirit" (Dickson 1989: 104). He is not sure whether this is also the case with the unborn, but cites texts that indicate a possibility of such a belief: Genesis 17 and 2 Samuel 7.

In both Israelite and African religions, community consciousness was paramount and often took destructive forms. An awareness of difference and boundaries often led to conflict. For instance, in the Old Testament, there is continual admonition to exterminate the non-Palestinian population. Similarly, in Africa, inter-community and sometimes, intra-community relations can often be bitter. However, here Dickson also identifies elements of discontinuity between ancient Israel and Africa. In the prophecies of Amos and Deutero-Isaiah, for example, there is the teaching of the love of God that transcends the national boundaries of Israel. "Even if Israelite thinking was divided on this issue—and the division spills over into New Testament times when the church struggled with the question of Gentile admission—the very fact that there is this insistent strain of openness ensures that Israel's history could not be written without due prominence being given to this attitude, which to a certain extent marks a discontinuity with the traditional African understanding of the community" (Dickson 1979: 105). In my view, however, Dickson held this view because of his preoccupation with African ethnic communities and their community consciousness. Dickson in the process, overlooked the African sense of identity that goes beyond ethnic boundaries and that stresses an openness to others, especially strangers and visitors.

Methodologically, for Dickson, "the validity of the comparative method is that there is a sense in which one could speak of a religio-cultural continuity; and when it is realised that the New Testament shares the same propositions with the Old Testament, then this continuity embraces the whole Bible. But Dickson is insistent that "to speak of a continuity is not to imply convergence of ideas, for there

is also discontinuity between the two traditions; this dialectical relationship must be recognised if facile adoption of the Old Testament
is to be avoided" (Dickson 1984: 181). Surely, it is the failure to
realise and understand this relationship which accounts in part for
the misinterpretation of the Old Testament by the African Instituted
Churches. Sometimes the desire to adopt a traditional practice had
dictated the kind of interpretation to be given to a particular biblical passage. B. Sundkler, for instance, notes that "because the Bantu
standard for testing Bible interpretation is accepted as self-evident . . .
it is possible for the Zionists to quote Micah 4:13 in support of
isangoma—divination" (Sundkler 1961: 277). G.E. Philips makes a similar point, when he says that in "both East and West Africa there
are secessionist Churches which encourage polygamy insisting that
it is permitted 'in the Bible'" (Philips 1942: 7).

For Dickson, and others, therefore, the great need of the Church
in Africa today is a biblical hermeneutic which will take seriously
the biblical story as read against its Ancient Near Eastern background as well as the particularity of the African situation. This
implies that, "Biblical commentaries by African theologians could
have a distinctive character; for, in addition to the relevant critical
tools, they could utilise the continuity-discontinuity relationship to
achieve interpretative realism" (Dickson 1984: 164).

The main argument against Dickson's approach has been raised
by T.H. Gaster. He is of the opinion that it is methodologically frail
to institute parallels between biblical beliefs and the practices of other
peoples who lived (or live) much later and in quite different environments. He notes this in the preface to his book, *Myth, Legend, and
Custom in the Old Testament* (1970). After drawing upon the traditions
of a great number of peoples, including African peoples and others
whose home lies outside the Ancient Near East, Gaster concludes
that some of the explanations given for parallelism may be incorrect
and this may cause the distortion of some of the things in the Old
Testament. He therefore wonders whether it is a risk worth taking.

Dickson responds by stressing that indeed it is a risk worth taking, as a lot of the Old Testament would be missed if such a risk
were not taken. Such comparisons, he argues, are not meant to imply
direct cultural contacts or borrowing but merely to illustrate patterns
of thought, and as such are useful. Dickson cites the issue of semantic parallels between diverse languages and argues that they are no

less valid and instructive because those languages themselves are unrelated as the diversity enhances rather than diminishes the significance of the comparison.

A number of African scholars have done detailed comparative work on specific concepts from African life and thought and the Bible. Among them are the works of S. Kibicho on the concept of God, John Mbiti on eschatology and Justin Ukpong on sacrifice. Kibicho's article, "The Continuity of the African Conception of God into and through Christianity: A Kikuyu Case Study" (1978), employs the comparative method in looking at the concept of God in the Bible and the Kikuyu culture. Like Dickson, Kibicho also uses the continuity-discontinuity methodology. However, he is not as judgmental and hard on African Traditional Religion as Dickson. His central question is whether the God of African Traditional Religion, known by different names, such as, *Nyasaye, Were, Mulungu, Mungu, Asis, En-kai, Ajuk, Ngai, Nyankopon, Nyonmo, Maawu*, is the One True God whom Christians worship in Christianity, the Father of our Lord Jesus Christ. His response to this question is that there is a radical continuity between the conception of God in African Traditional Religion and Christianity. More specifically, he proposes that the Kikuyu conception of God from ancient times has continued to the present day even into and through Christianity. Ironically, missionary Christianity came to Kikuyuland with a message of radical discontinuity between African conception of God and the Christian one. According to this doctrine of radical discontinuity, "African Traditional religion is presented as a religion through which the African people were merely groping in the dark for an unknown God, of whom they were so ignorant that they could hardly be said to know him" (Kibicho 1978: 380). Kibicho uses the example of some of the Mau Mau fighters who were Christians to put across his view. According to him, the Christian Mau Mau freedom fighters held to the traditional African conception of God, which they also believed to be the true biblical conception (Kibicho 1978: 380). One of their hymns includes the following stanza, confirming Kibicho's contention:

> *Hoyai ma* (pray earnestly)
> *Thai thai ma* (beseech truly)
> *Ngai no uria wa tene* (for God is the same one, of ancient times that is the *Ngai* of the fathers of old) (Kibicho 1978: 382).

In other words, there was a radical continuity of the Kikuyu conception of God into and through Christianity, through the religio-political movements of protest and struggle for independence, justice and *uhuru* (freedom) from British colonial rule.

While emphasizing continuity at this point, Kibicho notes points of discontinuity. Kikuyu converts, whether they were nationalists or mission-oriented, viewed Christianity as a different religion with its own scriptures, creeds, history, symbols and mythologies of redemption, holy rites, and ceremonies. The Kikuyu,

> conceived of God primarily as the creator and sustainer of all men and things, but unlike the Hebrews, they did not see him also at the same time as the Lord of history whose act of creation had as its main purpose the redemption of mankind. . . . Consequently also, again unlike the Hebrews, they did not view God as their redeemer who comes and who will come into history to save mankind (Kibicho 1968: 2).

Kibicho is here asserting the identity of the object of the Old Testament and African beliefs in God, while acknowledging that they are expressed very differently.

John Mbiti also used the comparative hermeneutical method in some of his work. Mbiti's *New Testament Eschatology in an African Background* (1971) makes a correlation between what he calls "African Ontology" and "Christian Ontology." Mbiti's African ontology consists of five dimensions: God, spirit, people, nonhuman animate and inanimate creation. All these are conceived of in terms of their relationship to humanity. Mbiti went on then to elaborate on the nature of his African, five dimensional, ontology by saying that it is a unity, so that to break up that unity is to destroy one or more of the modes of existence, and to destroy one is to destroy all. Christian ontology centres on Christ as the boundary of human existence and not on time as a commodity to be "created" or "produced." Thus, in Christ, "the two-dimensions of 'past' and 'present' merge and hold out the promise of the 'living' future, which is already anticipated in a dynamic 'present' that makes all things new. Thus, Africans are called upon to apprehend and fully appropriate this Christ" (Mbiti 1971: 328). Thus, Mbiti draws connections between the wholeness in African religions which is demonstrated in its inseparable ontology (with its five modes), and the relationship between Christ and the Gospel. Mbiti further states that the divine invasion of the world of humankind in the incarnation, far from upsetting that unity, in fact retains those five modes in equilibrium.

> God . . . in our traditional concepts lives in another mode of existence
> separated from ours, He became one with us and we can become one
> with Him. The mystery of the Incarnation is therefore, illuminated as
> the mystery of the mutual indwelling of God and man in which no
> department of man is segregated or left out (Mbiti 1971: 330).

This means that seen from Mbiti's angle, the God-given preparation
for the Gospel in African tradition manifests itself in this intensely
religious life of the African who is and has been religiously ready
for many centuries. This implies that the encounter between Christianity and African religious tradition is the meeting of the African in
his and her religiosity and Jesus Christ, whose presence in the world
(as Mbiti describes it elsewhere, in reference to John 8:58) "is not a
historical (that is, chronological) but a geographical presence in a
world made by him and through him" (68).

Clearly, Mbiti conceives of continuity between African religious
traditions and the gospel message; "Mission history is seen from the
perspective of its place within a religious history which belongs to
African tradition" (Bediako 1992: 331). According to Kwame Bediako,
as a "hermeneutical tool," this thesis is very important; it confers a
"personality" on the pre-Christian tradition as an active ingredient,
not just a passive component, in the making of the Christian experience in modern Africa (331). This means that Mbiti removes African
religious traditions from the anthropological realm and integrates it
firmly into the Christian theological category of a universal salvation-
history. By this, Mbiti is advocating a theological interpretation of
African religious traditions. This stems from his postulate of the essential and fundamental religiousness of the totality of African existence.
For Mbiti, the *starting* point of any interpretation is African Traditional
Religions, which reflect God's witness among African peoples through
the ages. Mbiti calls it "an indispensable lamp on the spiritual path"
(Mbiti 1976: 131–132); the *completing* element is the Gospel. Thus
according to him, no matter how valuable that lamp has been, it
cannot be a substitute for the eternal Gospel which is like "the sun
that brilliantly illuminates the path" (Mbiti 1976: 131–132). Mbiti's
primary purpose is theological. He is attempting to lay the basis for
a distinctly African theology by blending the African past with the
Judaeo-Christian tradition. The African traditional world and the
Christian world meet as African Christians embrace a biblical faith
which so strongly affirms the centre of their spirituality or religiosity
(see also Mbiti 1986).

Justin Ukpong's book *Sacrifice: African and Biblical—A Comparative Study of Ibibio and Levitical Sacrifices* (1987) employs the comparative methodology in looking at the concept of sacrifice in the religio-cultural contexts of ancient Israel and the Ibibio people of Nigeria. Ukpong observes that there are resemblances in the area of material usage and rituals, as well as the theoretical conceptions of sacrifice in both cultures. With respect to materials, he notes that items are offered in accordance with class, prescription and occasion in both cultures. The bull, for instance, is used for sacrifices involving kings and nobles who are higher up in the society and for bigger occasions. Thus, as you come lower down the class ladder, sheep, fowls, birds and cereals are used. With respect to rites, Ukpong noted that, even though each culture puts its specific contextual stamp on what should be done, there are still general similarities in practice. The Ibibio disposed of uneaten sacrificial animals by burying or abandoning but the Israelites burnt theirs completely. However, when it comes to the rite of making a gesture of contact with the victim before it is offered, there are similarities. He explains that, "In every Levitical sacrifice, the offerer was required to place his hand on the victim as he presented it to the priest. This ritual was a symbol expressing the fact that the victim was the offerer's and that he was a party to the sacrifice. Conceptually, the ritual of placing *nsei* on the head of the victim in Ibibio *ebe Abasi* sacrifice finds a parallel here" (Ukpong 1978: 191). The offerer in both cases performs this action without saying any words. Ukpong also identifies the offering of harvest products as sacrifices. He observes that the Ibibio new yam sacrifice shares some of the features of the "feast of weeks" or "Pentecost" of the Ancient Israelites. Both were feasts of new harvest and are meant to be thanksgiving for the gift of crops. Just as the Hebrews offered the first sheaf of their harvest, the Ibibio offer new yams. Ukpong observed that in both cases nothing of the new harvest is to be eaten until sacrifice has been made.

Ukpong considers the correlation between the theoretical conception of sacrifice in Ancient Israel and that of the Ibibio peoples. To him, sacrifice as a gift and as a means of expiation are the two most important features on which the concept of sacrifice dwells in both contexts. Firstly, with respect to gift, for them both "sacrifice is a symbolic giving" and, further, "the sacrificial gift was always a means in the case of Israel, of arriving at communion with God, and in the case of the Ibibio, establishing contact with invisible beings"

(Ukpong 1978: 192–193). Also, both Ancient Israel and Ibibio religion used sacrifice as a means of expiating sin; it is only by confession and sacrifice that one who has sinned could be restored to
communion with his/her deity in both contexts. He therefore holds
the opinion that there are certain intrinsic aspects of Ibibio socio-
cultural life and religion that actually correspond to those of post-
exilic ancient Israel which make their sacrificial practices comparable.

   But Ukpong also identifies striking dissimilarities between Levitical
sacrifices and that of the Ibibio. He argues that while the Hebrews
sacrificed frequently to God, the Ibibio sacrifice to God only occasionally. There are also differences in the materials offered in sacrifice
by the Hebrews and by the Ibibio. Significant among these is the
abundance in Ibibio sacrifice of fowls and fish, which are completely
absent in Hebrew sacrifice.

   Ukpong goes on to discuss the New Testament appropriation and
spiritualisation of notions of sacrifice in the Old Testament. He argues
that the New Testament points away from the earthly temple as the
place of sacrifice to the eternal temple, which is Jesus himself. This
means that Jesus replaces the temple in its sacrificial context and
becomes the new sacrifice (John 1:29, 36). In the New Testament
"a new world of meaning is created whereby Jesus is presented as
a new sacrificial victim in a (paschal) sacrifice that fuses with and
transforms Old Testament sacrifice" (Ukpong 1987: 219). Here too
Ukpong sees similarities with Ibibio thought and practice. In particular, he identifies three ideas which are basic to the Ibibio conception of sacrifice, that is sacrifice as an *entry* into the divine presence,
as a means of *communicating* with God and as a *feast*. Each of these,
Ukpong argues by way of example, have the potential to give greater
meaning to the Eucharist for Catholic Ibibio.

   In sum, the comparative method arose as a response to a colonial conception of African Traditional Religion and culture on the
part of missionaries who believed that African cultures were satanic
and pagan and needed to be totally abandoned if Christianity was
to thrive in Africa. Thus, what African biblical scholars tried to do
was to identify similarities between the biblical world and African
religio-cultural practices and to use their scholarly and scientific tools
to show the relationship between African Traditional Religion and
Christianity. The outcome of the comparative approach is the thesis
that African Traditional Religion constitutes a *praeparatio evangelica*.
(Such a move, it should be noted, while redeeming African Traditional

Religion as a forerunner of the gospel diminishes its role as a religion in its own right.)

Williams' proposition of a historical relationship between ancient Israel and Africa seems to suggest that the foundations for the Gospel have already been laid in that African traditional beliefs and practices are historically related to Old Testament life and thought. Dickson on the other hand, did not argue for any historical relationship between ancient Israel and Africa. Rather he based his comparison of Africa and ancient Israel on the thesis that various elements in the African religio-cultural ethos recall ancient Israelite beliefs and practices. But Dickson too sees African Traditional Religion as a preparatory ground for the full revelation of the gospel. Thus, African life and thought is seen as a shadow of what is to come to fruition in the life and work of Christ. What Kibicho, Mbiti and Ukpong have attempted to do is to persuasively argue that there exists in African religions very high spiritual and religio-humanistic values which are of theological value. They have done this in varying ways. Kibicho's thesis, that African Traditional Religions contain the full revelation of God and the full means of salvation, is contested by a number of African theologians (Metuh-Ikenga 1994, Agbeti 1972). Unlike Kibicho, Mbiti maintains that African Traditional Religions are incomplete and are thus awaiting fulfilment in the Gospel even though it has enough in it to prepare Africans for its appropriation. Ukpong stresses the contribution of traditional thought and practice rather than its shortcomings, emphasizing how Ibibio sacrificial beliefs and practices, for example, enrich received Roman Catholic understandings of the Eucharist.

Whatever the limits of the comparative approach, and I will return to this briefly below, in a situation where value judgements are placed on one religious concept by others, the comparative readers were hermeneutical pioneers who were responding to the negative value judgements placed on African traditional values and beliefs by European missionaries.

Some African writers have criticised the comparative approach to biblical interpretation. Okot P'Bitek has done a critique of this approach in his book, *African Religions in Western Scholarship* (1970). P'Bitek argues that the comparative approach was a response of African scholars to Western academics who refer to African cultures and religious beliefs in a disparaging manner. According to P'Bitek, what the comparativists end up doing in their response is to "dress

up African deities with Hellenistic robes and parade them before the
Western world to show that Africans were as civilised as Europeans"
(P'Bitek 1970: 80). P'Bitek, however, argues that "the African deities
in the books, clothed with the attributes of the Christian God, are
the creatures of students of African religions" (P'Bitek 1970: 80).
According to P'Bitek, African beliefs and practices are to be accepted
as unique and peculiar, and different from Christianity, and therefore must not be compared with Christian beliefs and practices as
there are no readily available parallels for that kind of comparison.
African traditional beliefs and practices are more than just *praeparatio evangelica*.

African liberation theologians have also criticised the comparative
approach. Desmond Tutu, commenting on the comparativists method,
says

> It has seemed to advocate disengagement from the hectic business of
> life because very little has been offered that is pertinent, say about the
> theology of power in the face of the epidemic of coups and military
> rule, about development, about poverty and other equally urgent pre-
> sent-day issues (Tutu 1979: 490).

The criticism levelled against the comparative method by most liberation theologians is related to the fact that the comparative method
seems to be more concerned with "cultural" and "spiritual" concepts
to the neglect of political and contemporary socio-economic concepts
(Cone 1993: 396). In his *My Soul Looks Back* (1991), James Cone
states that "What we reject is the tendency among some African
theologians, to limit the gospel and theology to spirituality that had
not been curved out of the concrete sufferings of the poor who are
engaged in political liberation" (Cone 1991: 109). However, this position has been revisited by South African liberation theologians in
recent times. This is because of the realities of South African blacks
in the post-apartheid era involves more than just economic and social
well being, but also cultural issues that relate to people's world views
and traditional practices. Here, and more widely, there is talk of a
paradigm shift from socio-economic to cultural models within liberation theologies (De Scrijver and Damen 1995: 40).

In conclusion, the comparative method was generally a bold attempt
at bringing out the importance of African Traditional Religions in
doing biblical interpretation. However, it is clearly not enough to
see African religious beliefs and practices as *praeparatio evangelica*.

African countries have been exposed over the centuries to diverse cultural, religious, social, political and economic concepts and practices which have one way or the other affected their beliefs and practices. For instance, the church in Africa cannot overlook the effect of their own missionary history which has affected their interpretation and practice of Christianity and life and thought as well. Also, the effect of other religions like Islam cannot be overlooked in attempting to develop hermeneutical practices in Africa. In his *Religion and Politics in Independent Nigeria: A Historical Analysis* (1996), Alexius Makozi states that,

> Indeed, Islamic religion has exerted a lot of influence on the lives of millions of individuals and people in Nigeria. Just as Christianity had a great influence on the religious, socio-economic and political life of Nigeria, so did Islam. The adoption of patterns of common religions and social life gave Islam a moulding force in the life of individuals and community. The Islamic re-integration of a cultural process whereby forms of animistic belief is acknowledged or tolerated made it easy for Africans to adopt Islam as a religion (Makozi 1996: 21).

Similar arguments could perhaps be made for other religious movements like Buddhism and New Religious Movements in contemporary Africa. Also, present world trends in Christianity, politics, and economics clearly affect the way one interprets and relates to biblical texts. African context(s) are certainly more complex than the early pioneers of the comparative approach anticipated. Such complexity calls for an interpretative model that takes seriously the ancient African traditions together with the various influences and modifications that Africans have gone through over the past decades; in order to read biblical texts more effectively, there is the need look at the text critically with both ancient and contemporary eyes.

BIBLIOGRAPHY

Agbeti, J.K. "African Theology: 'What is it?'" *Presence* 5/3 (1972): 5–8.
Bediako, K. *Theology and Identity: The Impact of Culture upon Christian Thought in the Second Century and Modern Africa.* Oxford: Regnum, 1992.
Cohen, A.P. *The Symbolic Construction of the Community.* London: Tavistock, 1985.
Cone, James. *My Soul Looks Back.* Maryknoll: Orbis, 1991.
———. "Black Theology and Third World Theologies." In Eds James Cone and Gayraud Wilmore, *Black Theology: A Documentary History, 1980–1992*, Maryknoll: Orbis, 1993: 388–398.
Danquah, J.B. *The Akan Concept of God.* London: Frank Cass, 1968.

De Scrijver, G.L. and F. Damen (Eds). "Paradigm-shift in Third World Theologies of Liberation: From Socio-economic to Cultural Models." *Inter-sectiones* 3 (1995): 40.

Dickson, K.A. and P. Ellingworth (Eds), *Biblical Revelation and African Beliefs.* London: Lutherworth, 1969.

Dickson, K.A. "African Traditional Religion and the Bible." In Eds E. Mveng and J.Z. Werblowsky, *The Jerusalem Congress on Black Africa and the Bible—Proceedings.* Jerusalem, 1972.

———. "The Old Testament and African Theology." *Ghana Bulletin of Theology* 4/4 (1973): 36.

———. "Hebrewism of West Africa—The Old Testament and African Life and Thought." *Legon Journal of Humanities* 1 (1974): 23–32.

———. "Continuity and Discontinuity between the Old Testament and African Life and Thought." In Eds Kofi Appiah-Kubi and Sergio Torres, *African Theology En Route,* Maryknoll: Orbis, 1979: 95–108.

Gaster, T.H. *Myth, Legend and Custom in the Old Testament.* London: Duckworth, 1970.

Isaac, E. "Relations between the Hebrew Bible and Africa." *Jewish Social Studies* xxvi: ii (1964): 93.

Kibicho, S. "The Interaction of the Traditional Concept of God with the Biblical Concept." *Cahiers des religions Africaine* 4/2 (1968).

———. "The Continuity of the African Concept of God into and through Christianity: A Kikuyu Case Study." In Eds E. Fashole-Luke, R. Gray, A. Hastings and G. Tasie, *Christianity in Independent Africa,* London: Rex Collins, 1978: 370–388.

Kinney, J.W. "The Theology of John Mbiti; His Sources, Norms and Methods." *Occasional Bulletin of Missionary Research* 3/2 (1979): 65–68.

Kudadjie, J.N. "Does Religion Determine Morality in African Societies? A View Point." In Ed. J.S. Pobee, *Religion in a Pluralistic Society,* Leiden: Brill, 1976: 60–70.

Makozi, A. Obabi. *Religion and Politics in Independent Nigeria: A Historical Analysis.* Lagos: Rubik, 1996.

Mbiti, J.S. *New Testament Eschatology in an African Background.* London: Oxford, 1971.

———. "The Encounter between Christianity and African Religion." *Temenos: Studies in Comparative Religion* 12 (1976): 125–132.

———. *Bible and Theology in African Christianity.* Nairobi: Oxford University, 1986.

Mckenzie, P.R. "Review of Prayers of African Religion by J.S. Mbiti." *The Expository Times* 87 (1975–76): 220–221.

Metuh-Ikenga, E. "Theological Status of African Traditional Religion." In *Journal of Inculturation Theology* 1/2 (1994): 109–125.

Meyerowitz, E. *The Divine Kingship in Ghana and Ancient Egypt.* London: Faber and Faber, 1960.

Opoku, A. Kofi "Changes within Christianity: The Case of The Musama Disco Christo Church." In Eds E. Fashole-Luke, R. Gray and G. Tasie, *Christianity in Independent Africa,* London: Rex Collins, 1978: 111–121.

Oosthuiezen, G.C. *Post-Christianity in Africa.* Stellenbosch: Wever, 1968.

Parrat, J. "Current Issues in African Theology." In: *A Reader in African Christian Theology,* Ed. J. Parratt, 143–151. London: SPCK, 1987.

P'Bitek, Okot. *African Religions in Western Scholarship.* Nairobi: Oxford University, 1970.

Philips, G.E. *The Old Testament in the World Church.* Guildford: Lutterworth, 1942.

Shorter, A. "New Attitude to African Culture and Religions." In Eds A. Shorter, et al. *Towards African Christian Maturity,* Kampala: St. Paul, 1987: 18–20.

Sanneh, L. *Translating the Message: The Missionary Impact on Culture.* Maryknoll: Orbis, 1989.

Sundkler, B. *Bantu Prophets in South Africa.* London: Oxford, 1961.

Tutu, Desmond, "Black Theology/African Theology—Soul Mates or Antagonists?" In Eds Gayraud S. Wilmore and James Cone, *Black Theology: A Documentary History, 1966–1979,* Maryknoll: Orbis, 1979: 483–491.

Turner, H.W. *Profile through Preaching*. Edinburgh: Edinburgh House, 1965.

Ukpong, Justin. *Sacrifice: African and Biblical—A Comparative Study of Ibibio and Levitical Sacrifices*. Rome: Urbaniana University, 1987.

———. "Christology and Inculturation." In Ed. Roselini Gibelini, *Paths of African Theology*, Maryknoll: Orbis, 1994: 40–61.

Williams, J.J. *Hebrewisms of West Africa: From Nile to Niger with the Jews*. London: George Allen & Unwin, 1930.

CORPORATE PERSONALITY IN BOTSWANA AND ANCIENT ISRAEL: A RELIGIO-CULTURAL COMPARISON

Bernice Letlhare

Many theologically inclined scholars of Old Testament have recognised the continuity between the Old Testament and many indigenous societies (Dickson 1979: 141–149). This study is an attempt to rediscover the religio-cultural continuity of corporate personality between the Old Testament and indigenous communities in Botswana. The approach is thereby comparative in nature. I shall endeavour to look at this concept in ancient Israel as defined in the Old Testament and in the traditional Tswana society.

To define the concept, corporate personality simply means the collective sense of a people. Furthermore, corporate personality is the embodiment of the community in the individual (Goba 1972: 44). The individual, it may be rightly said, represents the community to which she/he belongs. What the individual does affects the whole community and what the community does affects the individual. In such a society, life is corporate in all respects, whether political, religious, cultural or economic. These facets are intertwined and expressed wholly. Binding factors are the same thought patterns, an observance and practice of the same norms, customs and traditions as well as shared experiences. This is not to be confused with collectivism, which is a sociological term that "takes the community more than the individual as the principle source of value and attributes major importance to the social relations between members of the group" (Jansz 1991: 2).

In ancient Israel, when looking at kinship, it is evident that the family was the basic residential and productive unit. It was also the basic unit in economic matters, for example in the ownership of property, cultivation of land and care of domestic animals. The family was a dominant factor in the social structure of ancient Israel. The father figure was important because the family was identified through him. In fact it was called the *beth 'ab*, that is, the "house of the father." The house was called by his name though it belonged to him as much as it belonged to those called by his name who were members of the family, whether in its nuclear or extended forms.

This Hebrew word 'ab (father) indicates that he was "the centre from which strength and will emanated through the whole of the sphere which belonged to him and to which he belonged" (Robinson 1981: 37). This was corporate personality. The father was not an isolated despot even though children and other members of the house were taught and expected to give him honour and reverence. It was around him that members grouped themselves thereby forming a psychic community which was given a stamp through his name. We see for example in Genesis 12 that Abraham is commanded to leave his land and his kindred to go and look for the promised land, during the course of which his descendants shall be increased. In his understanding, the commandment extended to those called by his name. Hence he moves not alone but with his wife, nephew and "all their possession which they had gathered, and the persons that they had gotten in Haran" (Genesis 12:6). He could not leave alone because he was characterised by corporate personality. Reflected in this way, corporate personality yields profound mutual trust, understanding and support. Sarah's reaction shortly after this call when she was before Pharaoh in Egypt (Genesis 12:10–20) shows her obligation to Abraham her husband. This incident also shows the interdependence between Abraham and his wife.

On the other hand, the duty of the father was to give aid and protection especially when the continuation of one's name was threatened. As we see for example in Deuteronomy 25:6, when a man died and left a childless widow, the man's brother was expected to marry her. The first son of this union was to succeed the name of the dead brother so "that his name may not be blotted out of Israel." In the traditional Tswana society, this is referred to as *seyantlo*, literally meaning "that which goes into a house."

These expectations regarding children and fathers were not different in the traditional Tswana society. *Ramotse* (father of the house) was also the central figure in the family. He was therefore responsible for the whole set-up of the family, by moulding it through occasional performances of rites and providing for it, especially economically. When he did this, members of his family autonomously gathered around him to form the psychic community as in the ancient Israelite society.

When groups of extended families came together to form a unit, a clan was formed. The clan was headed by elders who were themselves heads of families. The settlement period was characterised by leaders after Joshua who were called judges, although this term did not quite describe them appropriately since they were charismatic military leaders. It is interesting to note the story of Deborah who was called a prophetess and a judge. She is presented as brave and hence Barak did not want to go to war unless she accompanied him (Judges 4:8). This means that, occasionally, ancient Israel had women leaders. Likewise in the traditional Tswana society, as is the case with the female leaders like *Mme* Ntebogang Ratshosa of the Bangwaketse tribe and *Mme* Pulane Moremi of the Batawana tribe. These women were elders and acted as regents when the chiefs were yet to be installed to chieftaincy.

The tribe was another corporate expression of extended families and clans. This entity was actually the basis for membership in ancient Israel. A person could not claim identity with Israel unless the person held membership in a particular tribe. This social feature, although identified even during the patriarchal period, was very prominent during the settlement period (Joshua 21–22). The members of any particular tribe looked to the tribe for protection against enemies from inside the tribe as well as from outside the tribe. The tribe also had the right to call the member to battle. Through their elders, individual tribes entered into larger tribal alliances as occasion demanded, for example at war times, or to punish a tribe that had offended grossly against another tribe.

In the political group, the king was regarded as the embodiment of the community over which he was the leader because the fortunes of the nation would rise or fall depending on whether he was obedient to the covenant (that is, walking in the ways of his fathers) or not. In this case, the political institution was intertwined with the religious. The role of the priests and prophets was to keep society intact through performances of sacrificial rites for various reasons, as for example to entreat favour from God or to expiate sins. They also kept society working as a unit by reminding them time and again of the regulations of the covenant.

Although corporate personality in ancient Israel can be detected in the way the social groups or units carried out their functions and duties, as for example the one found in Joshua 7 or in 2 Samuel

21. In the former account, Achan broke the taboo on the spoil of Jericho by keeping it for himself instead of dedicating it to Yahweh. This infuriated Yahweh and caused Him to withdraw the divine protection when the Israelites went to war against Ai. Israel was therefore defeated. When what Achan did was discovered and the defeat was interpreted to be the result of Achan's act, he and his family were destroyed. The sin of one member of the family eroded other members and they suffered the same consequences. In the second case, seven of Saul's descendants were executed to expiate the Gibeonite blood shed by Saul. These examples portray the negative connotations of the concept of corporate personality but they nevertheless show the extent to which Israel was group conscious.

As with ancient Israel, a Motswana has uppermost in his/her mind the sense of community. He/she is characterised by his/her need for identity because this gives him/her a place in society. The proverb *motho ke motho ka batho* wholly enshrines the essence of being a person. *Motho ke motho ka batho* is an absolute and complete statement: "A person is a person through people" or "A human being is a human being through human beings." Sometimes the proverb *motho ke motho ka batho* appears as *motho ke motho ka batho ba bangwe*, meaning: "A human being is a human because of other human beings" or "A person is a person because of other persons/people." Of particular importance here is the role the instrumental adverbial formative *ka* in the proverb plays. It may be rendered by the following constructions:

> a person is a person *on account of* people
> a person is a person *as a result of* people
> a person is a person *because of* people
> a person is a person *by means of* people
> a person is a person *by the existence of* people

Through this proverb then, the indigenous Motswana recognised that the process of shaping and forming of the "one" is a product of "others." How they do this is determined by the social units which form society. These units then are inevitably responsible for determining and defining who "one" is in society. As in the Old Testament, corporate personality is exemplified in the family, the clan system and or the tribe. These technically unite all members no matter how widely members are separated physically. The proverb, therefore, answers the question, "What constitutes a person?" or "What is a person?"

In his book, *The Image of God among the Sotho-Tswana*, Setiloane does a good job of explaining what a person is. He discusses humanity, *botho*, by tracing the formation of personhood from when a child is born into the family and considered as a gift from the *badimo* (ancestors) to the time of initiation when a person is a fully formed human being because his/her *botho* (personality) has been fully developed. After initiation "they have passed from the status of *bacha* (youth) to the full *botho* (humanity)" (1979: 39). A true Tswana, Setiloane says, is "one who follows the accepted pattern of social living, who shows equanimity and maturity" (1979: 41). During initiation, elderly women trained groups of girls whereas boys were trained by elderly men of society. The youth were taught mores, laws and customs of society especially relating to marriage and family life. A woman's role was not only reproductive but it was also to produce for consumption. A woman was married not so much for her beauty as for her industriousness. She had a say in the productive and reproductive needs of the family.

Initiation was followed by the naming of the participants by one name. Thus the initiation group to which one belongs is another example of corporate personality. The group identifies itself as one, hence they say *re mophato* ("we are one being") and after initiation "they continue to act as one by sharing each and all, in the blame and shame as well as the glory and joy of any one of their group" (Setiloane 1979: 42). The significant thing about the *mophato* is that they were trained up in the *mekgwa ya borre*, that is, "in the ways of our fathers." This brings to mind elements of Old Testament society, especially during the times of Kings when the whole society was judged negatively or positively depending on whether they "walked in the ways of their fathers" or "have departed from them."

Corporate personality in traditional Tswana society is also expressed through *losika* (lineage), that is, the claim to be a descent from an ancestor. It was and is still a tradition for a Tswana person when identifying oneself to trace his/her lineage as far back as is possible. This conceptual system helped society to understand itself and express itself in various units or social groupings. Members in a lineage see themselves as a single unit bound together by ties of kinship, culture, history, religion, political and economic interdependence. They see themselves to be a group over and against other groups and thereby express their unity by engaging in common ritual activities. Outsiders share the lineage members' self perception and view them as a corporate entity.

Importantly, indigenous Tswana society includes the unborn, the living and the dead (ancestors). The unborn child was already a citizen of the spirit world and was believed to be one of the departed members of the family or clan. For this reason rites were performed to the dead. These rites inculcated "a sense of solidarity and security through integration of a worldview, that constitute a regulatory moral force" (Appiah-Kubi and Torres 1979: 104). Outside any societal unit one can only exist as a *ledimo*, that is, a being with neither characteristics of a spirit nor of a human being.

Although one may think the concept of corporate personality as depicted here gives a sense of claustrophobia, so that individuals in the group are so submerged in their society that they do not have any dignity of their own or meaning in themselves, the true picture is not at all like that. The individual was in a position to responsd to whatever values society inculcated in him/her, but he/she was not free to make decisions against customs of society.

While in Tswana traditional society the units that form society are fundamentally important, to the extent that through societal norms one is moulded and shaped, there are such proverbs as: *moremogolo go betlwa wa taola wa motho o a ipetla*, which literary means, "the greatest medicine shaped is that of a divining bone; that of a person shapes itself." This implies that the divining bone gives great medicine because of the doctor who uses it because it is him/her who interpretes what the bone is saying, but that the greatest medicine is for one to mould oneself. What it means is that individuals are really responsible for the shaping of their own characters or personality. This proverbs means that the traditional Motswana recognised that an individual also had a say in the shaping of his/her personality. Likewise, in ancient Israel, the sixth century prophet Ezekiel quoted a proverb which called attention to the individual (Ezekiel 18:2) and questioned his/her pace in society. Here corporate personality is challenged, for the prophet says that the proverb should not be repeated anymore. The implication is that individual responsibility is inherent in both societies.

Corporate personality still exists in some forms in contemporary Botswana, but the societal units which used to hold society together have been destabilised. This is inevitable because culture is by its nature dynamic. But this also means that the interdependence, solidarity and security provided by corporate personality in the indigenous Tswana society has ceased to have the same impact it used to have. The forms are seen in such social gatherings as funerals and weddings and other social gatherings which call for solidarity and oneness. Members of society still feel the obligation to follow tradition even within the limits and constraints of the economic set-up prescribed by modern society. In the family unit, whereas the father used to be the provider, protector and supporter of the family, this is no longer so. Anybody, as long as one is the "breadwinner" can play this role.

In important ways, however, the legacy that the concern for corporate personality found both in ancient Israel and indigenous Tswana society leaves us is valuable despite the tensions between this concern and current society's concerns for the individual. Perhaps, by way of a synthesis, we should remind ourselves that in Botswana one is never *merely* a member of a group, but is a person. This is what the person who asserts *ke motho* (I am a person) is asserting. That is, he/she is worthy of respect because he/she is a *person*, that is, a member of the largest of all groups, that of humanity. Paradoxically, at the largest level of corporate personality, we find we have come full circle and that corporate identity becomes individual worth.

BIBLIOGRAPHY

Appiah-Kubi, K. and Torres, S. Eds *African Theology en Route*, Maryknoll, New York: Orbis, 1979.
Brown, Raymond E., Joseph A. Fitzmeyer, and Roland E. Murphy. Eds *The New Jerome Biblical Commentary*, Englewood Cliffs: Prentice Hall, 1990.
Dickson, Kwesi. *Theology in Africa*, Englewood Cliffs: Prentice Hall, 1979.
Goba, B. "Corporate Personality in Africa." In Ed. Mokgethi Motlhabi, *Essays in Black Theology*. Johannesburg: University Christian Movement, 1972, 44–52.
Jansz, Jeroen. *Person, Self and Moral Demands: Individualism Contested by Collectivism*, Leiden: DWSO Press Leiden University, 1991.
Robinson, H. Wheeler. *Corporate Personality in Ancient Israel*, Edinburgh: T&T Clark, 1981 (Original Edition 1936).
Rogerson, J. Ed. *Beginning Old Testament Study*, London: SPCK, 1983.
Setiloane, G. *The Image of God among the Sotho-Tswana*, Rotterdam: A.A. Balkema, 1979.
Wilson, R. *Sociological Approaches to the Old Testament*, Philadelphia: Fortress, 1984.

THE BIBLICAL GOD OF THE FATHERS
AND THE AFRICAN ANCESTORS

Temba L.J. Mafico

There are many similarities between the religio-cultural life of the Israelites and that of pre-colonial Africans. The phrase "pre-colonial Africans" refers to people who lived in Africa prior to the colonization of the continent by Europeans beginning in the seventeenth century. Hereinafter, the term Africans refers to pre-colonial Africans. The beliefs and cultural traits of pre-colonial Africans remain prevalent in rural areas of Africa where Western civilization has not yet made inroads. One can find the religio-cultural beliefs of Africans not only in rural areas, but also in stories told by old people who moved to live with their children in the cities, as well as from songs, poetry, artifacts, tales, legends and in some meagre historical records. It can be argued that no culture disappears without leaving a trace. Traces of ancient culture are clearly present among Africans who have maintained their traditional culture in defiance of the overwhelming influence of Western civilization.

One of the strongest connections between modern and ancient times is the African belief in ancestors. This subject is interesting to me because of the similarities between the place of ancestors in the life of Africans and the place of the gods of the fathers in the life of Israel. Both the ancestors and the gods of the fathers seem to have shaped their respective societies and so my discussion of this topic will invariably include an examination of the African and the Israelite social structure. Although my discussion of ancestors generally reflects practices of the whole continent of Africa, specific examples will be drawn from the Ndau people of Zimbabwe, with whose culture, religion and philosophy of life I am more familiar.

My interest in this research was triggered in 1972 when I was pursuing a doctoral degree in Old Testament at Harvard University. Prior to attending Harvard, I had been a pastor for several years in Zimbabwe and had maintained a fundamentalistic attitude toward the Bible and Christian teachings. I regarded God's revelation to the world through Jesus Christ as the only, and ultimate revelation God

had ever made to humanity, and viewed all other divine revelations
and religions as pagan and evil superstition. However, in the course
of my own personal and critical research, I was exposed to the
history and religions of the ancient Near East. Initially, of course,
I was highly critical of and prejudiced against these religious cultures. Prior to my research I had wondered why my professors were
fascinated by the possibility that the Israelites might have borrowed
ideas from these pagan religions. I was fortunate because these professors, who were devout Christians, were sympathetic and patient
with me, having realized how my missionary upbringing, with its
religious and cultural prejudices, had affected my theology. They
gently reoriented me to a pluralistic approach to religion by showing
me links between the religions of the ancient Near East (Mesopotamia,
Palestine, and Egypt) and some key religious elements of the Old
Testament. I was stunned by the possibility that the Israelites either
borrowed aspects of their worship patterns, religious beliefs and cultural traits from other so-called pagan nations, or that they were not
as uniquely different, after all, from the nations surrounding them
as I had presumed. As my interest in the Old Testament grew, I
began to enjoy studying it within its ancient Near Eastern environment. It became clear to me that the Israelites were culturally, socially,
and economically linked with other people of the ancient Near East,
especially the Canaanites among whom they lived. Eventually, I
became interested not only in the similarities between the Old
Testament and religions of the ancient Near East, but also in the
more remarkable religio-cultural parallels between the Israelites and
Africans.

Before the seventies, in the United States, Europe and Africa, Old
Testament as a course was taught by Westerners who, unfortunately,
were unfamiliar with African religio-culture. Consequently, they explained the Old Testament only from a Western point of view. As
a specialist in Old Testament and African traditional religions, I
wonder why Christians were shocked by African religio-culture when
it was, in fact, similar to Old Testament religio-culture, particularly
in the patriarchal era—and I use the term "patriarchal" deliberately,
as I have the term "fathers" (see below). I will begin this discussion
by examining the patriarchal veneration of ancestors and showing
how this religious practice was central to their worship of God. I
will follow this discussion with an exposition of the African belief in
and worship of the supreme God through intermediary ancestors.

Finally, I will demonstrate how Israelite and African worship compare with each other in these respects.

The early religion of Israel was more complex than is reflected in the prophetic books and the New Testament. For one thing, early Israelite religion appears to be polytheistic. Alt found that the gods of the patriarchs were individual gods who were all later identified with Yahweh (Alt 1966: 24). Close examination of the text of Genesis shows that each patriarch worshipped his own god under the rubric of the gods (*'ĕlōhîm*) of the ancestors (Genesis 46:3). These gods had individual names. The God of Abraham was *'abrām 'ānōkî māgēn*, "the Benefactor of Abraham" (Genesis 15:1). Isaac, on the other hand, worshipped *paḥad yiṣḥāq* the God who was acknowledged as "the Kinsman of Isaac," (Genesis 31:42), while Jacob revered *'ăbîr yaʿăqōb*, "the Mighty One of Jacob" (Genesis 49:24). These deities appear to have been distinct gods whose theophanies were encountered in various sacred places which, eventually, were turned into sanctuaries. Thus the term *'ĕlōhîm* appears to have been a generic noun, meaning "gods" or "ancestral spirits," albeit later, it was used as a designation of the supreme deity called Yahweh (Mafico 1998: 261–63).

Theodore Lewis offers an analysis of this use of the term *'ĕlōhîm* in 1 Samuel 28:13 (Lewis 1991: 597–612). In this text, Saul wanted to hear the word of God before going to battle against the Philistines. However, God did not answer him. So, Saul resorted to a medium to call back the spirit of Samuel so that he might declare the word of the Lord. The medium summoned Samuel from among the dead and brought him up to respond to Saul's inquiry. When the medium saw the spirit of Samuel, she told Saul, *'ĕlōhîm rā'îtî 'ōlîm minhā'āreṣ* ("I see gods (spirits) coming up from the earth"). As Lewis notes:

> The narrator certainly did not mean to imply that the dead Samuel was on par with Elohim [God with the capital E]. Evidently the deceased in ancient Israel, as elsewhere in the ancient Near East could be referred to as *'ĕlōhîm* (as well as *repa'im*) (Lewis 1991: 597–612).

The medium at Endor called Samuel, but what she saw were the *'ĕlōhîm 'ōlîm* ("gods coming up"), among whom was Samuel, an old man, one of the ancestors. A painting in the Paris National Museum, Lewis points out, captures this image well; the painter portrays several *'ĕlōhîm* (spirits) rising from their sleep and Samuel standing in front of Saul (Lewis 1989: 105). These *'ĕlōhîm* are the gods of the fathers. They are the gods whom their fathers have worshipped, and who are present with the spirits of the deceased fathers as they are with the living. The Israelites trusted these gods because they were the gods whom their ancestors had trusted and worshipped and because these gods had made promises to them of progeny and land. However, these promises had been only partially fulfilled. The problem which remained regarding these promises centred on the issue of land. While the Israelites were languishing in slavery in Egypt, they continued to cry to the gods of their ancestors rather than adopting new gods, hence Moses' reticence when God sent him to deliver the Israelites from Egypt. A strategy had to be worked out whereby the Israelites, by embracing Yahweh, would not be breaking with the gods of their ancestors. The strategy is clearly formulated in several texts, but especially in Exodus 3:15–16, where God explains to Moses the relationship between *Yahweh* and the *'ĕlōhîm*:

> Say this to the people of Israel, Yahweh, the God of your ancestors, the God of Abraham, the God of Isaac, and the God of Jacob, has sent me to you: This is my name forever, and thus I am to be remembered throughout all generations. Go and gather the elders of Israel together, and say to them, Yahweh, the God of your ancestors, the God of Abraham, of Isaac, and of Jacob, has appeared to me.

The gods of the fathers now come together in the one God. Yahweh is the God who now encompasses the gods of the ancestors.

The African approach to God is in many ways similar to that of the Israelites. Both the African and Israelite communities were organized along family hierarchical structures. While the Israelites approached God through the gods of their progenitors, the Africans did so through the ancestors. This does not mean, of course, that the Israelites did not set great store on ancestors. Belief in their ancestors influenced the Israelites to structure themselves hierarchically by age. To be a *gibbor* ("first born"), accorded a son special status, not because the first born was stronger, wiser or more experienced, but because he was the closest one in line to the ancestors. In addition to the significance of the first born child was the social importance of the elders. The elders were an important component of the social stratum in Israelite society. When Jacob died, among the dignitaries that carried him back to Canaan for burial were the elders of his household and all the elders of the land of Egypt (Genesis 50:17). In Exodus 3, God sent Moses to deliver the children of Israel from Egyptian bondage, reminding him to begin with the elders of

Israel (Exodus 3:16). The people would listen to Moses' words if they were endorsed by the elders, because of the elders' structural proximity to the ancestors. Moreover, Pharaoh too would be more likely to listen to the words of Moses if Moses approached him accompanied by the elders of Israel (Exodus 3:18). Clearly, the position of the elders in Israelite social structure was quite significant.

Africans regard ancestors as intermediaries who intercede for humans in times of need and during their worship of God. The ancestors are not only intercessors for the worshippers, but they are also providers for material and spiritual needs. They expect obedience from family members, and harmonious relationships among them. If family members show loyalty, reverence and obedience, then the ancestors fulfil the promises of protection from illness and other evils. Africans worshipped God through their ancestors in accordance with traditional protocol of approaching elders and superiors. Thus, when they approached God, ancestors played a very vital role as intermediaries. Because Africans did not regard death as the end of life, ancestors were part of the human hierarchical structure. The ancestors, though comprising their dead parents and grandparents, were and still are honoured as living members of the family.

To Africans, life and events are viewed in cycles. The cycles are based on their observation of natural phenomena. For example, the sun rises in the east and sets in the west, then goes back to the east to rise again the next day. It completes a circle as it marks a full day. Seasons also appear cyclically year after year. Winter is followed by spring, which in turn introduces summer. The summer season ushers in the autumn season, thus completing the seasonal cycle. Growing plants also follow a similar cycle. Seeds grow and become plants. Most of the plants mature and bear fruit with seed. The parent plant may die, but it leaves the seed to grow in the earth to repeat the cycle all over again. This idea of cycles was shared by the Israelites; it is vividly reflected in Ecclesiastes 1:1–11.

The cycles of life influenced several aspects of African culture and religion. Africans built and lived in round huts. They sat in circles, whether it was at family palavers or at village court hearings. Africans always sat by age in a circle, which always began and ended at the head of the circle. The most senior among the people in the circle always sat at the head of the circle and presided at meetings. With regard to the worship of God, Africans regarded the circle to comprise their ancestors who were stratified by age in a relationship with

each other. The circle extended far back and linked with God, who
was the head of the entire family circle of the living and the dead.
A cultural circle began forming from the most senior in age or
authority down to the last person, the youngest or lowest in rank or
authority. Although the youngest or junior would naturally sit closest to the head of the family in the circle, he or she could not
approach the head of the circle because protocol prescribed that
messages come and be returned via one's seniors.

To the Israelites and Africans, the importance of seniority by age
played a very significant role. This practice is observed, for example, in the blessings Isaac accorded to Jacob and Esau. Isaac made
the blessing in the name of the '*ĕlōhîm*, the gods (Genesis 26:28–29).
Once the blessing was given, albeit to the wrong person, Jacob instead
of Esau (the first born), that blessing could not be revoked because
it was given under oath in the name of the gods. Age also signified
wisdom, not wisdom based solely on theoretical knowledge, but wisdom seasoned by experience. The contrast between the wisdom of
the elders and that of the youth is demonstrated in the story of
Rehoboam's succession to the throne of his father, Solomon. In 1
Kings 12:1–15, following the death of Solomon, the people gathered
at Shechem, one of the oldest sanctuaries in Israel, to express to
Rehoboam, Solomon's son, their grievances against King Solomon.
They demanded that he treated them more lightly. The elders advised
the young king thus,

> "If you will be a servant to this people today and serve them, and
> speak good words to them when you answer them, then they will be
> your servants forever." But he forsook the counsel which the old men
> gave him (1 Kings 12:7).

Instead, Rehoboam decided to seek and follow the advice of young
people of his age who advised him to be tougher than his father.
They said to him,

> Thus shall you speak to this people who said to you,—Your father
> made our yoke heavy, but do you lighten it for us; thus shall you say
> to them,—My little finger is thicker than my father's loins. And now,
> whereas my father laid upon you a heavy yoke, I will add to your
> yoke. My father chastised you with whips, but I will chastise you with
> scorpions (1 Kings 12:10–11).

The consequences of not listening to the advice of the elders were
catastrophic for the united kingdom of Israel. The land of Israel split

into two nations: the Northern Kingdom called Israel fell under the kingship of Jeroboam and the Southern Kingdom, Judah, was under Rehoboam. Several civil wars were fought between the two nations. This narrative clearly shows how seriously the Israelites, like the Africans, regarded the status of their elders. To Israelite and African communities, age, signified by gray hair and beard, signified wisdom. As is written in Proverbs 20:29: "The glory of young men is their strength, but the beauty of old men is their gray hair."

Mwari is an important figure in Ndau African religio-culture. Ndau people worshipped *Mwari* not so much as the creator of the universe but as patron of the family. They realized that children depend on their parents for clothing, protection and food. The children did not have to beg or flatter their parents with praises and prayers to get the help they needed. Likewise, Ndau people made their needs and demands known to God as children would to their own parents. They did not worship or pray to God, lavishing God with flamboyant descriptive terms, to persuade him or curry favours. They worshipped God because he was a benevolent God. They accorded him honour and praise as they also did to their kings and chiefs. In accordance with social protocol, Ndau people did not approach God directly, however. They always approached God with their requests for protection, food, and healing through their ancestral spirits. These ancestors were believed to have acquired greater power and ability to protect, to care and provide for their families than when they were living in the flesh. In all their activities, however, the ancestors acted in accordance with the will and providence of God. But the ancestors did this only if the people adhered to the correct tribal norms and mores decreed by *Mwari* at the beginning of time. The ancestors were regarded as members of *Mwari*'s administrative agents on earth. They acted as sub-patrons and protectors of individual families and clans. They carried out God's commands as they related to the community of the living. The living channelled their petitions through the ancestors to *Mwari*. It was, therefore, improper and discourteous for individual people to approach God whenever they felt like it. The proper procedure was for them to approach God through their elders. For example, when a young person was setting out on a long journey, the father, as head of the family, would convene the extended family. If his uncles and grandparents attended, the chief intercessor who would perform the parting ritual to assure safety would be the most elderly person among them. The worship of

God was, therefore, structured according to family procedures. When sacrifices or petitions were made to *Mwari*, the immediate ancestor was asked to relay them hierarchically backwards until they reached *vari kure kure*, "those who are far, far away." As has already been said, under normal circumstances a person was expected to channel petitions to God through the ancestors. The only exception for an individual to appeal directly to *Mwari* was when suddenly confronted with a dire emergency.

There are several advantages accruing from this type of worship. It promoted and sustained community cohesion. No person would, under normal circumstances, move out of the circle nor deliberately spoil relationships by gossip and other antisocial behavior. In African worship and society, the community was a vital aspect of the *Mwari* tradition. To be in good relationship with God meant that one was in a harmonious relationship with members of the community (see 1 John 3:20). The African social structure explains why Africans found it difficult to accept God as introduced by missionaries. They found it inconceivable that an individual could approach God for every personal need, bypassing their ancestral spirits. If it was improper protocol to approach the king or chief without going through the elders, it was confusing to the Africans that God, the most reverenced among all living beings, could be easily accessible. Thus the Christian approach violated social protocol and also destroyed family cohesion and community structure.

The African approach to God is in many ways similar to that of the Israelites. Both the African and Israelite communities were organized along family hierarchical structures. While the Israelites approached God through the gods of their progenitors, their spiritual patrons, the Africans did so through the ancestors. Most remarkable is the fact that Africans, except in West Africa where the Semitic influence was strong, believed in one God. This God, *Mwari*, was called by different names according to national languages and tribal dialects. The names reflected God's attributes. The Israelites, who at first were as polytheistic as the other nations of the ancient Near East, in the end merged the gods of their progenitors and ended up worshipping one God, Yahweh, who remained closely related to the *elohim*, "the gods" or ancestors of their progenitors.

BIBLIOGRAPHY

Alt, Albrecht. *Essays on Old Testament History and Religion*. New York: Doubleday, 1966.
Lewis, Theodore. "The Ancestral Estate (*nahalat 'elohim*) in 1 Samuel 14:16." *Journal of Biblical Literature* 110, No. 4 (1991): 597–612.
————. *Cults of the Dead in Ancient Israel and Ugarit*. Atlanta: Scholars Press (1989), 105.
Mafico, Temba L.J. "Cultural and Biblical Roots of Honouring Elders." In Ed. Ann Wimberly, *Ministry to the Soul Community*, 1997: 19–33.
————. "The Divine Compound Name Yahweh Elohim and Israel's Monotheistic Polytheism." *Journal of Northwest Semitic Languages* 22/1 (1996): 155–173.
————. "Old Testament and Effective Evangelism in Africa." *International Review of Mission*, Vol. LXXV No. 300 (1968): 400–409.

AFRICAN PERSPECTIVES ON POVERTY IN THE HEBREW LAW CODES

Robert Wafawanaka

The idea of poverty is something with which most traditional Africans are familiar. Africans have endured generations of grinding poverty, but they have somehow managed to survive it. Poverty is an issue which Africans can relate to directly, based on their own experiences. To Africans, poverty is real, material, and economic. It may be due to a lack of sufficient material resources, unemployment, or lack of opportunity, but is equally due to exploitation, oppression, and other forms of injustice at the national and international levels. The African understanding of poverty has as much to do with land as with oppression, for land is the primary economic mode of most Africans. Combined with animal husbandry, traditional Africans subsist on pastoral agricultural economies. For the African to be without livestock or land would therefore be an economic disaster. Historically, the "scramble for Africa" resulted in the appropriation of traditional lands and the displacement of Africans to infertile areas. Although scholars tend to downplay this fact, this era obviously created its own categories of the poor, as colonial governments acquired more land from the Africans. The exodus to the city in search of work not only made Africans abandon their infertile lands, but also made them work for meager wages. Therefore, compared with pre-colonial Africa, post-colonial or independent Africa saw more relatively landless people as well as poor Africans in the overcrowded cities (Illiffe 1987).

John Illiffe helps us to understand the situation of the poor in Africa with his distinction between "structural" and "conjunctural" poverty. According to him, structural poverty is "the long-term poverty of individuals due to their personal or social circumstances," and conjunctural poverty is "the temporary poverty into which ordinarily self-sufficient people may be thrown by crisis" (Illiffe 1987: 4). Illiffe distinguishes between the structural poverty characteristic of societies with land and those without land. In land-rich societies, the very poor are characteristically whose who lack access to the labor needed to exploit the land (for example, the incapacitated, elderly, or young). In land-scarce societies, the very poor include the above group as well as the able-bodied who lack access to land, or are unable to sell their labor at prices sufficient to meet their needs (Illiffe 1987: 4). Thus Illiffe argues that the poor of pre-colonial Africa were not the landless but mainly the incapacitated who lack access to labor (structurally poor). Conjunctural poverty was mostly caused by drought, political insecurity, or famine (Illiffe 1987: 5–6, 114).

In colonial Africa, structural poverty continued to exist. Illiffe asserts that since colonial Africa was still relatively land-rich, it's very poor continued to be those who lacked labor and family support. But he admits that colonial rule created new categories of the poor, namely, those impoverished by "land alienation" and economic change. Moreover, others became poor due to the competition for resources, urban overcrowding, and unemployment (Illiffe 1987: 114, 143, 164–167). Poverty continued to grow in independent Africa. During this era, structural poverty did not change very much. The bulk of the poor were still the traditional (structural) poor who were now supplemented by the new poor—the neglected, the unemployed, the ill-paid, and the able-bodied competing for resources in a grow- ing population. For these victims of structural unemployment, "to belong to a large family could be a reason for poverty rather than a source of wealth as in the past" (Illiffe 1987: 260). Finally, Illiffe argues that because of the lack of institutions and organizations to care for the poor, the African poor survived, and continue to sur- vive, by the support of their families and their own efforts (Illiffe 1987: 7–8, 193–213).

This historical perspective gives Africans a strong sense of their impoverishment. Indeed, the African experience may be compara- ble to that of other oppressed and poor groups of people. This expe- rience enables Africans to identify with the poor, and comprehend the meaning of poverty in a real and dramatic sense. Consequently, a look at poverty in the Bible "with African eyes" seeks to bring a fresh perspective, and contribute to our understanding of the sub- ject, not only in the Bible, but also in the modern world.

For centuries, biblical interpretation has been done primarily from a Western/European perspective. It is only recently that we have seen an influx of theologies from different perspectives, such as lib- eration or feminist theologies (see Sugiratharjah 1991, Gutiérrez 1988, Cone and Wilmore 1993, Maimela and Hopkins 1989, Moore 1973,

Roberts 1983, Collins 1985, and Russell 1985). These theologies seek to interpret the biblical message in light of their own contexts and experiences. We Africans, too, seek to contextualize and indigenize the word of God to make it meaningful to our experiences. What does the biblical text mean in light of our social, historical, and religious circumstances? How can we appropriate the bible to make it more meaningful to us? In so doing, what light can this approach shed on biblical scholarship?

When the missionaries came to Africa, they came to convert, preaching a gospel of "repentance for the forgiveness of sins." While this message was in line with Jesus' teaching, it was woefully inadequate in light of African realities. The kingdom of God was presented as something transcendental, something to be enjoyed in the hereafter. Even from the writer's own experience, very little preaching was done on the realities of economic poverty, oppression, exploitation, let alone the impact of colonialism. Such a gospel of "pie in the sky" was rejected by liberation theologians who sought to relate social structures and economic conditions to the word of God. This "conscientization" took many forms including empowering the poor to see the Bible as a tool of liberation from oppressive social structures. Hence, the popularity of the Exodus story to many theologies of liberation. The totality of this historical and social experience therefore equips the African biblical interpreter to bring special insights to the biblical text. He or she brings to the exegetical task the experience of poverty, oppression, injustice, and socially-oriented coping mechanisms.

The present study is an analysis of the poor in the legal texts of the Hebrew Bible. My primary focus is on the Covenant Code (Exodus 20:22–23:33), the Deuteronomic Code (Deuteronomy 12–26), and the Holiness Code (Leviticus 17–26). My approach is threefold. The first part attempts to determine the structure and causes of poverty in the law codes. Who are the poor? Why are they poor? How do they become poor? The second part examines some of the coping mechanisms and social programs that were instituted in response to the poor and their plight. Finally, I will attempt to determine the ethical implications of the problem of poverty in these texts. The conclusion is a reflection on the implications of this study for contemporary society.

Israel did not emerge out of slavery in Egypt as the nation that it later became. Instead, the biblical narratives of Israel's wilderness wanderings portray the Hebrews (later Israelites) as traveling through the wilderness for a very long period of time. The journey through the desert is a difficult and arduous one. Once Israel settled on the land, Roland de Vaux argues that Israel organized itself as a tribal unit, the twelve tribes of Israel (de Vaux 1961: 3–15, see also Pedersen 1926: 23). According to de Vaux, during this period, there was "a profound social transformation" as the tribes broke into clans and settled into town-like villages (de Vaux 1961: 68). He further argues that during the early days of the settlement, all Israelites enjoyed the same standard of living. However, this egalitarian picture was shattered with the rise of the monarchy. Between the tenth and eighth century BCE, "a social revolution" took place as kingship created a class of "rich" and "poor." Resulting in the poor suffering from the oppressive burdens of the monarchy (de Vaux 1961: 72–74). It is in this context that prophecy arose to take up the cause of the poor and their suffering. Using Illiffe's model, we can deduce that the poor of the monarchical period were the "structural" poor. Their poverty was caused mainly by social circumstances, such as the lack of land as the monarchy and landlords appropriated land for their own uses. In addition, the poverty of groups like wage-earners and day-laborers falls into the category of those who lack resources, or cannot sell their labor power at prices sufficient to meet their needs.

Israel's legal codes presuppose an agrarian and pastoral community. Such a lifestyle is one that traditional Africans can relate to, for they too depend on their land and livestock for survival. Whether Israelite laws were original, borrowed, revised or edited, as in any other society, they have a variety of functions including preserving the social order, providing a standard by which to judge actions, preserving cultural practices, and, ultimately, protecting citizens and their rights. In addition to addressing and deterring crime, laws can also function to project a desirable state of affairs in society. Several categories of the poor, powerless, or socially disadvantaged persons can be identified in the law codes. These are the poor (referred to as *dal, 'ebyôn,* and *'ānî*), indentured servants or bonded laborers, slaves, resident aliens, and the widow and fatherless.[1] It is noteworthy that

---

[1] The references are as follows: the poor (*dal, 'ebyôn,* and *'ānî*) (Exodus 22:25, 23:3, 6, 11, Deuteronomy 15:4–11 (cf. 23:19–21, 24–25), 24:12–15, Leviticus 19:10, 15, 23:22), indentured servants or bonded laborers (Leviticus 25:39–55, cf. 25:25, 35), slaves (Exodus 21:2–11, 20–21, 26–27, 32, 23:12, Deuteronomy 12:12, 18, 15:12–17, 16:11–12, 14, 21:14, 23:15–16, 24:7, 18, 22, Leviticus 19:20, 22:10, 25:6,

not all of these groups were necessarily poor. Instead, some of the groups are mentioned with reference to their vulnerability or low social status. For example, the widow of a rich man may not have been poor as such, but lacked a male member of the household to care and provide for her, as well as to protect her. Moreover, the different Hebrew words for "poor" encompass a variety of meanings, including their physical and economic condition, social standing, or relationship to the powerful. In general, the poor in the law codes are those who are socially inferior, politically powerless, economically needy, and therefore dependent on the rich and powerful for their survival. The majority of references to "poor" in the Hebrew Bible refer to poverty due to oppression and exploitation ('ānî) (Pleins 1992: 402–414, Hammel 1990: chapter 5, Keck 1990: 672–675, Fabry 1978: 208–230, and Botterweck 1978: 27–41).

An analysis of the context and usage of references to the poor in the law codes reveals a social underclass, perhaps with no land of their own to cultivate crops or resources to exploit. They work to obtain wages on a daily basis and sometimes sell themselves into slavery because of economic needs or debts (Deuteronomy 15:12). They are oppressed and exploited by the rich and powerful landlords of the time. Some, like the Levites, lack inheritance privileges. According to Illiffe's theory, these are the structural poor, whose poverty is caused by social circumstances. If indeed the widow was poor, then her poverty would be structural, and caused by personal circumstances such as the loss of the labor of others due to the death of her husband. The fatherless child would be considered poor because he or she was a minor child who could not support him or herself.

Having established who the poor are in the law codes and how they become poor, I will attempt to analyze their survival techniques and coping mechanisms in this land-based economy. A close reading of the texts under consideration shows a number of provisions and legislation intended to alleviate the suffering of the poor. For example, the poor were not to be charged interest on loans (only aliens were) (Exodus 22:25, Leviticus 25:35–37), and wage laborers had to be paid at the end of the day. A pledged garment was to

---

26:13), resident aliens (Exodus 22:21, 23:9, 12, Deuteronomy 14:21, 29, 16:11, 23:7, 24:14, 17, 19–21, 26:5, 11–13, Leviticus 17:10, 12–13, 18:26, 19:10, 33–34, 22:18, 23:22, 24:16, 22, 25:23, 35, 45, 47), the widow and the fatherless (Exodus 22:22–24, Deuteronomy 14:29, 16:11, 14, 24:17, 19–22, 26:12–13, cf. Leviticus 21:14, 22:13).

be returned before nightfall in order to keep the poor person warm at night (Exodus 22:26–27). The poor also had the right to glean from the fields of others and gather the forgotten sheaves (Deuteronomy 24:19–22). Slaves were offered far more protection and rights in ancient Israel than their counterparts in the rest of the ancient Near East (Mendelssohn 1949: 1–123, Mendelssohn 1962: 383–391). A person sold into slavery could be redeemed by relatives if he or she could not do so. In the year of Jubilee (Leviticus 25), there was a general amnesty whereby all debts were to be forgiven, slaves and indentured servants released, and property returned to its original owners (Leviticus 25:10, 13, 25–28). The question of the implementation of these measures and programs is, however, a subject of scholarly debate.

What are the ethical implications of poverty in the Hebrew law codes? What paradigms model God-pleasing or ethical behavior? (Janzen 1994: 2–3). I think it is clear that there is a general humanitarian aspect to these laws. They are concerned with the well-being of the weaker and less powerful members of society. Such people are to be treated with dignity and respect. The poor are to be taken care of by their own families and neighbors who are in a better position to do so. Even slaves are to be included in some of the family's festivals. To oppress the powerless or neglect the duty to care for the poor is a punishable offense in the eyes of Yahweh (Exodus 22:21–27).

These texts strike a familiar code when Africans read them. They immediately identify with the situation of the poor and why they became poor. For the majority of Africans who are dependent on land, these texts speak with a dramatic immediacy. Many small-farm owners toil on the land for basic subsistence. As I indicated above, colonial experience also exacerbated poverty in its own way. The humanitarian and socially-oriented programs providing for and protecting the poor in ancient Israel are not foreign to the traditional African. Africa also had a tradition of allowing the poor person or tired traveler to feed him or herself right at the field, but not to carry away any food, lest it was seen as theft. Widows and orphans were cared for by an institution similar to the biblical law of the levirate, whereby the deceased's brother would marry his widow and assume the duties and responsibilities of the dead husband.

According to African traditional beliefs, religion, and morality, Africans have a "societary" or communitarian ethic, which puts the well-being of the other first and foremost. It is a morality of "conduct" rather than a morality of "being." This is so because "it defines what a person *does* rather than what he *is*" (Mbiti 1990: 209). This communal spirit and social solidarity is reflected in the way people unite to deal with problems, care for one another, and view the poor person in society as family members in need of help. According to African theologian and philosopher, John Mbiti, there is no "stranger" in African systems of kinship, because "everybody is related to everybody else" either by blood, marriage, or totem (Mbiti 1990: 103). Thus according to this conception, an individual has literally hundreds of mothers, fathers, sisters, brothers, wives, children, etc. (Mbiti 1990: 102). It follows that any needy person is viewed in this light, that is, as a relative in need of help. It is true, however, that this social solidarity and communal experience are stronger in the rural areas than in the cities and towns which tend to erode traditional values because of the breakdown of communal relationships.

The biblical "mandate for the poor" (Gnuse 1985: 10) as reflected in Israel's law codes is of great relevance to Africans. While the text seems to speak to their situation, the readers tend to see their lives, struggles, and coping mechanisms dramatized in the text. Such texts are at once liberating, affirming, and poignant to those reading the Bible from the margins of the human society, or the interpreter viewing the text from the same perspective.

Modern societies can learn some useful lessons from the ancient Israelites. One lesson is to deal with the *effects* of poverty by providing charity to the less fortunate members of our communities as the book of Deuteronomy calls for (Deuteronomy 15:1–11). Another lesson is to deal with the causes of poverty in the manner of the prophets of ancient Israel. This is a call for governments and the powers that be, to create and maintain just and equitable laws and social structures, which apply to everyone, regardless of race, color, creed, gender, age, ethnicity, or religious affiliation. As Amos says, "Let justice roll down like waters, and righteousness like an ever flowing stream" (Amos 5:24). After all, this is what would be ultimately pleasing to God (Micah 6:8).

BIBLIOGRAPHY

Botterweck, G. Johannes. "'ebhyôn." In Eds G. Johannes Botterweck and Holmer Ringgren *Theological Dictionary of the Old Testament*. Vol. III., Grand Rapids: William B. Eerdmans Publishing Company, 1978: 27–41.

Collins, Adela Yarbro, Ed. *Feminist Perspectives on Biblical Scholarship*, Chico: Scholars Press, 1985.

Cone, James H. *A Black Theology of Liberation*. Philadelphia: Lippincott, 1970.

———. and Gayraud S. Wilmore, Eds *Black Theology: A Documentary History, 1966–1979*. Revised Second Edition, Maryknoll: Orbis Books, 1993.

De Vaux, Roland. *Ancient Israel: Its Life and Institutions*. New York, Toronto, London: McGraw-Hill Book Company, 1961.

Fabry, Heinz-Josef. "däl, däläl, dälläh, zäläl." In Eds G. Johannes Botterweck and Holmer Ringgren. *Theological Dictionary of the Old Testament*. Vol. III., Grand Rapids: William B. Eerdmans Publishing Company, 1978.

Gnuse, Robert Karl. *You Shall Not Steal: Community and Property in the Biblical Tradition*. Maryknoll: Orbis Books, 1985.

Gottwald, Norman K. *The Tribes of Yahweh: A Sociology of the Religion of Liberated Israel, 1250–1050 B.C.E.* Third Printing. Maryknoll: Orbis Books, 1985.

Gutiérrez, Gustavo. *A Theology of Liberation: History, Politics, and Salvation*. Ed. Sister Caridad Inda and John Eagleson. Maryknoll: Orbis Books, 1988.

Hammel, Gildas. *Poverty and Charity in Roman Palestine, First Three Centuries C.E.* Berkeley, Los Angeles, Oxford: University of California Press, 1990.

Illiffe, John. *The African Poor: A History*. Cambridge, New York, New Rochelle, Melbourne, Sydney: Oxford University Press, 1987.

Janzen, Waldemar. *Old Testament Ethics: A Paradigmatic Approach*. Louisville: Westminster/ John Knox Press, 1994.

Keck, Leander E. "Poor." In Ed. Keith Crim *The Interpreter's Dictionary of the Bible. Supplementary Volume*, Nashville: Abingdon Press, 1990: 672–675.

Maimela, Simon S., and Dwight N. Hopkins, Eds *We are One Voice: Black Theology in the USA and South Africa*. Bloemfontein: Skotaville Publishers, 1989.

Mbiti, John S. *African Religions and Philosophy*. Revised and Enlarged Second Edition, Oxford and Portsmouth: Heinemann, 1990.

———. *Slavery in the Ancient Near East: A Comparative Study of Slavery in Babylonia, Assyria, Syria, and Palestine from the Middle of the Third Millennium to the End of the First Millennium*. New York: Oxford University Press, 1949.

Mendelsohn, Isaac. "Slavery in the Old Testament." In Ed. George Arthur Buttrick *The Interpreter's Dictionary of the Bible*. Vol. 4, New York, Nashville: Abingdon Press, 1962: 383–391.

Moore, Basil. *Black Theology: The South African Voice*. London: C. Hurst, 1973.

Pedersen, Johs. *Israel: Its Life and Culture*. Vol. 1–2. London: Oxford University Press, 1926.

Pleins, J. David. "Poor, Poverty (Old Testament)." In Ed. David Noel Freedman, *The Anchor Bible Dictionary*. Vol. 5, New York, London, Toronto, Sydney, Auckland: Doubleday, 1994: 402–414.

Roberts, James Deotis. *Black Theology Today: Liberation and Contextualization*. New York: E. Mellen Press, 1983.

Russell, Letty M., Ed. *Feminist Interpretation of the Bible*. Philadelphia: Westminster Press, 1985.

Sugirtharajah, R.S., Ed. *Voices from the Margin: Interpreting the Bible in the Third World*. London: SPCK, 1991.

NGAKA AND JESUS AS LIBERATORS:
A COMPARATIVE READING

Gomang Seratwa Ntloedibe

When Christianity was first introduced to Africa, African religiosity was rejected "as perfect specimens of absolute error, masterpieces of hell's invention, which Christianity was simply called upon to oppose, uproot and destroy" (Gairdner 1910: 137). But it was hard for the African world view to be replaced with any other without creating "a form of religious schizophrenia." The early missionary enterprise reached Africa with exclusive attitudes that seldom associated God's creative hand and revelation with African religions. This influenced most colonial writers to state that there were no figures in African cultures playing a similar role to that played by the Jesus of Christianity (Mbiti 1972).

As a Motswana, I also grew up reading from early missionary literature that the *Ngaka*, an indigenous healer, is a witch (*moloi*) not a fighter of evil (witchcraft). In this essay, I am going to interpret against the colonial approach. I will regard both African Religious Traditions and the Christian Testaments as equally important/authoritative to my life, and that of Batswana people. This essay will argue that the *Ngaka*, like Jesus, is a liberator, saviour and sacred agent, who attempts to bring about justice in society. I will use a comparative approach to show that the *Ngaka*, an indigenous healer, and Jesus, a Jewish-Christian healer, are both liberators and saviours. First, I will describe the role played by the *Ngaka* in his/her own society. Second, I will discuss the healing of Jesus in order to trace the role he played in his own society and how he came to be understood as "Christ" or saviour. Finally, as a way of conclusion, I will compare the roles of the *Ngaka* in Batswana societies and Jesus in his Jewish context.

How was the concept of the *Ngaka* understood amongst Batswana? Traditionally Batswana have two main groups of *dingaka* (plural): the herbalist (*e tshotswa*) who is the one who does not practice divination, who mainly attends to the physical symptoms of disease, and the diviner-herbalist (*Ngaka ya Setswana*) who is differentiated from the herbalist by an emphasis on divination. Amongst the Batswana the *Ngaka* who practises healing without divination is not considered a complete and a powerful *Ngaka*, for it is the divination exercise that is believed to disclose the hidden mystery. This essay will focus on the latter, the *Ngaka*.

Amongst Batswana societies the *Ngaka* is a figure who is expected to find a solution to all problems presented to him/her in the form of illness or disease. In order to understand the importance of this role we need to look into how the Batswana view and express their understanding of the concept *bolwetse*, or illness. Setiloane has noted that Setswana word for illness—*bolwetse*—indicates a condition far more complex than the normal use of English word "illness." The Setswana concept of "illness" is used to describe the symptoms of physical disease, but in addition it also describes the state of a person who is not physically ill, but whose family, livestock, crops or land, or even the wild plants around them are suffering misfortune. Because of the connected relationship between a person and his/her environment, a person suffers "illness" if there is any form of disconnection anywhere in the network of relationships that constitute their world. In short, in Setswana the concept of illness/sickness/disease implies a breakdown in the harmony of human being's relationships with all the centres of Divine forces, from *Modimo* (God) to inanimate stones, of which the universe is made (Setiloane 1976: 44). Disharmony affects the created order and something has to be done to restore harmony. In other words, when one aspect of *Modimo's* creation is not in order then it has fallen sick and nothing remains in its rightful state and everything else is affected. When humanity is affected, nature too gets affected and this in turn affects the Divine forces as well. This understanding underlines the interdependence of all things in God's creation. It emphasizes the balance between nature and humanity (Linzey 1994).

Accordingly, Comaroff and Comaroff have identified the following categories in the Batswana belief system: cooperation in government under the *kgosi* (ruler), the principle of agnatic rank, the gender-based division of productive and reproductive labour, and the separation of the social from the wild. They go on to argue that the violation of any aspect of this system "was held to bring illness and destruction" (Comaroff and Comaroff 1991: 156). Agnatic rivalry took the form of sorcery and was an offence to ancestors amongst the Batswana. It was regarded as a disruption of physical relations between men and women, giving rise to pollution that required purification (Willoughby 1932). Disharmony between the social and the natural unleashed the powers of undomesticated spirits. Batswana beliefs, therefore, emphasise that the well-being of an individual depends not primarily on the person alone, but on her/his relationships and the connections with other people and nature as well. In the socially interdependent society of the Batswana, the survival of the whole community is, therefore, endangered by individual anti-social and anti-nature behaviour. Failure of relationships results in the breakdown of good health since both parties become saddened or hurt. A specific illness is attributed to a physical cause, but at the same time, to an underlying cause, which is defined in terms of one's relationship to others.

> The "real" cause will usually be sought in the context of the horizontal relations of the individual with the community physically surrounding him or in the context of his vertical relations with the Badimo. Psycho-social belonging to the community in the Tswana culture is the necessary precondition for health. Any disturbance of this state of belonging leads to disease, illness or bad luck for the individual (Staugard 1985: 67).

Relationships are both physical and spiritual as well as inclusive amongst Batswana. The interconnection stretches from the immediate relative and neighbour to the ancestors and even to the unknown member of the society and the Deity or Divinity. According to Setswana beliefs, the greatest good for all can be achieved if all live according to the basic virtue of harmony, between people and nature, ancestors and *Modimo.*

If harmony is disrupted, it is regarded as illness. There are three causes of illness in Setswana belief: sorcery or witchcraft (*boloi*), ancestral wrath (*kgaba*) which is at times related to the breaking of taboos (*moila*), and natural causes which happen as a result of the Divine will (*go rata ga Modimo*). To begin with sorcery/witchcraft, many colonial writers tended to identify African healing with "witchcraft." On the contrary, African healing intends to counter witchcraft. Batswana have only one name for either sorcery or witchcraft, *boloi*. *Boloi* is mainly the effect of ill-relationship or disharmony between the living. In most cases, sorcery is detected when there are feelings of contention, jealousy and hatred. Sorcery is also detected when one or more members of the society perform "abnormally," that is, when members of the community are either extremely poor or excellent. The one who performs extremely well is thought of as a sorcerer, having extraordinary or spiritual powers which she uses to help herself to perform differently from the rest of the society. On the other hand, if anyone in the society performs very poorly, that is, far below the social expectation, she is thought of as bewitched, that is, some unseen powers have been used to work against her. This understanding indicates that the health or the well-being of the society was found in the balance in the community. Batswana society did not entertain extremes in their society. In fact, the Batswana belief concerning creation illustrates that people were created as a community, not as individuals. It is said that *Modimo* enabled the people to come out as children, women and men. These people were brought out with property—livestock—and no one was given more than the other (see the essay by Dibeela in this volume). Wealth was for all to share. Batswana do not have any "myth" to justify inequality, exploitation and oppression of others. Where inequality existed, systems like the *Mafisa* system, were set up to cater for the poor.

Second, other causes of illness are attributed to the invisible community of ancestors. According to Batswana beliefs, death does not stop relationships, hence ancestors continue to have an interest in how their descendants live and relate. Failure to live well together displeases the ancestors. This unhappiness manifests itself in a form of illness.

> One of the most common ways of the Badimo [ancestors] to express disapproval of the behaviour of one of their earthly relatives would be to cast disease on him (it is not that, ancestors directly caused illness but if displeased they can withhold their protective power for evil to haunt their descendants) (Staugard 1985: 50).

Illness that occurs as a result of dissatisfaction from ancestors might in most cases not have physical but spiritual symptoms, such as persistent and disturbing dreams and other misfortunes.

Lastly, ordinary circumstances such as a change in seasons or exposure to a very cold day may lead to illness. Natural causes are not understood to imply that *Modimo* instigates illness, human beings, it is recognised, can also get ill naturally. These disorders are not considered as life threatening. It is believed that they can respond to medical treatment. Also, the sickness or death of a very old person (as long as sickness does not involve long term suffering) is accepted as the will of *Modimo*. At times when something bad happens to someone who has not been respecting social harmony, this also might be attributed to *Modimo* (or the ancestors). Of course, all these causes of illness relate or overlap, in the sense that, for example, as witchcraft disrupts social relations, the anger of the ancestors is provoked.

In so far as the *Ngaka* is the mediator for maintaining a healthy balance in the society, the *Ngaka* is a liberator, a saviour. It is the *Ngaka*, and only the *Ngaka* figure in the Batswana societies, who is expected to find solutions to all problems, whether they are caused by sorcery, ancestral wrath, or natural causes. All are presented to him/her in the form of disease or illness and the *Ngaka* has to diagnose their causes, give advice, find treatment, and provide preventive and protective measures. In so doing the *Ngaka* endorses popular perspectives, initiates healing and inspires a sense of liberation that is life-giving and that promotes justice, security and harmony among the people.

> Because the advice of the traditional healer (Ngaka) is well integrated in the religious and moral concepts and beliefs prevailing in society, the Ngaka thus assumes a stabilising role in social control (Staugard 1985: 54).

The role of the *Ngaka* as saviour, liberator and balance-keeper is clearly evident in the Setswana understanding of *bolwetse*, illness. As we have seen, in Setswana, *bolwetse* indicates a condition that is far more complex than the Western concept of illness. Consequently, the concept of the *Ngaka* includes more than the Western concept of a medical doctor. Staugard, a scientifically trained Western medical doctor, correctly describes "traditional" (African) healing as "a religious phenomenon," for it goes beyond the physical and the obvious symptoms and causes. To be a *Ngaka* one has to understand the patients' world-view. Staugard says,

> The traditional healer in the Tswana village, in common with the situation in other parts of Southern Africa . . . is not only a medicine-man. He is a religious consultant, a legal and political advisor, a police detective, a marriage counsellor and a social worker (Staugard 1985: 12).

He further describes the role of the *Ngaka* as "a necessary precondition for the maintenance of social justice and order." The *Ngaka* is involved in the life of an individual as a member of the community from birth until death and into the hereafter, for the *Ngaka* alone has special access to the world of the ancestors and the Divine.

Staugard's description of the *Ngaka*'s role amongst the Batswana is consistent with Gelfand's description of the *nganga* role among the Shona people of Zimbabwe:

> European society has no one quite like the nganga, an individual to whom people can turn in every kind of difficulty. He is a doctor in sickness, a priest in religious matters, a lawyer in legal issues, a police-man in the detection and prevention of crime, a possessor of magical (miraculous) preparations which can increase crops and instil special skills and talents into his clients. He fills a great need in African soci-ety, his presence gives reassurance to the whole community and his position will, no doubt, remain secure so long as the Shona's belief in witchcraft, and his need for an antidote to the witch survive Western education and civilization (Gelfand 1964: 55).

In short, Gelfand describes the *nganga* as "the kingpin of African society," expected to find the answer to all kinds of problems. The *Ngaka* has an enhanced ability to transform things and relationships, say Comaroff and Comaroff (1991), he or she sustains the fragile boundaries of civil society, mediates between the domesticated and the wild, the living and the dead, and only he or she can restore the integrity of the disrupted, both personal and social. Evidently, the *Ngaka* plays a vital role in all spheres of Batswana life.

Of all the different categories of *dingaka* outlined above, it is the "diviner-herbalist" whose position in the society is important (Krige and Krige 1943: 224). The *Ngaka*'s function is not only healing in the sense of physical illness but also in the sense of spiritual illness, attending physical symptoms and causes does not complete the mis-sion of the *Ngaka*. Divination is an act in which people are moved by what they feel and believe to be their experience of the sacred or the transcendental power (Werbner 1989: 4). It is the divination dimension that brings the ordinary person represented by the *Ngaka* into contact with the sacred (the organised) and the *Ngaka* becomes a vehicle who serves as a medium of the sacred power. The *Ngaka* has the power because of his/her relationship with the Divinity. The *Ngaka* always deals with the total situation of the patient. Socially the *Ngaka* pays attention to his/her patient's personal relations with the community and the supernatural. Physically, the *Ngaka* pays atten-tion to the symptoms described and spiritually he or she attempts to restore the balance between the individual and his/her surroundings, for which modern medicine has no answer, or concern (Fako 1980). The *Ngaka* heals by inviting or invoking the sacred to create order and balance in the midst of the chaotic and profane. The *Ngaka*'s role in the Batswana religious belief system is a sacred role. The *Ngaka* is undoubtedly a saviour and liberator amongst his/her people. Having briefly discussed the *Ngaka* as healer and saviour, I now turn to elaborate on the role of Jesus as healer.

In this part of the essay, I would like to look into the healing of Jesus, particularly his role as healer and how he came to be understood as "the Christ" or saviour. The New Testament record suggests that Jesus practised no secular profession. He devoted himself exclusively to religious activities which were dominated by the message about the kingdom of God.

> Jesus' core message centred on the kingdom of God: The reign of God is near, repent and believe in the good news (Mark 1:15). His central message focussed not on himself but on God's gift of the kingdom (Fabella 1989: 5).

David Dale quotes Hans Kung saying that, "God's kingdom is creation healed" (Dale 1989: 20). In the New Testament, especially in the gospel stories, the work of Jesus is characterised as a multi-fold ministry, including teaching, preaching and healing (Matthew 9:35). This section of the essay will focus on the healing aspect of Jesus' ministry in the light of the idea that the kingdom Jesus preached can be understood as "creation healed."

It is important to reflect on why Jesus chose to be a healer at the time when there were already healers in Galilee and Jerusalem. Among the Jews the dominant expectation was that of a political messiah, though there were also expectations of a healing messiah too. The Jews were expecting someone to set them free from the Roman rule. But Jesus, who later was given the messianic title, chose to be a "healer" rather than a revolutionary politician in the sense of the Zealots. His healing ministry earned him a following and later contributed (together with the resurrection) to the messianic title— Jesus the Christ. Therefore, before looking into Jesus' healing, it is important to understand how healing was viewed at the time of Jesus by his people in order to understand why Jesus decided to identify with healing above any other activity, and what weight his teaching derived from his healing.

Dawson holds that disease was (and is) a feature of every age. He has observed that healing arose in close connection with religion, and remained so for hundreds of years, only to be isolated in later days (Dawson 1935: 3). From this perspective healing is a distinc-

tive, divine or a religious phenomenon. More specifically, Jesus' healing must be seen within its Jewish context. How did the Jews understand healing? As noted by Vermes (1973), Jesus Ben Sira, the author
of Ecclesiasticus, indicates that Judaism believed that a healing skill
does not originate from the regions of darkness, rather it originates
from divine powers. This divine gift confers on the healer a high
standing in society and secures him or her respect from all walks of
life—from kings to ordinary people. Vermes points out that the
author of Ecclesiasticus denies magical means to the medicine but
holds that they have been created as such and their use by the healer
or doctor is for God's glory. This implies that the "healer" is not a
magician but a "holy" man/woman of God.

The world of Jesus believed that certain human beings were empowered to act on the behalf of God as healers. In the Jewish society,
these were the priests and prophets, probably some would refer to
them as physicians, medicine-men and magicians, though this obviously narrows their role. These remained religious figures in their
society and were thought to be the only intermediaries between God,
the sick and the rest of the society. Elijah (1 Kings 17:17–24) and
Elisha (2 Kings 4:32–37) were such figures. In Jewish society, to seek
the help of a prophet, priest (or a healer) was a religious act—healing was a religious phenomenon.

Jesus' Jewish contemporaries understood sickness not in isolation
but in relationship to what was termed "evil" and "sin." It was
believed that one falls sick because of the work of the evil one and
because of one's lack of faith in God. In other words, physical illness was understood as a divine punishment for something wrong.
In many instances' recourse to the work of a healer was interpreted
as lack of faith in God who is the source of all healing. Ill-health
was also understood as a manifestation of sin, hence healing and
forgiveness of sin came to mean the same thing (Vermes 1973). This
"sin" was understood in relation to the supernatural. This suggests
that the core cause of any sickness was spiritual. Thus when a healer
was called, the healer had to consult the supernatural by praying to
God. This enabled him/her to diagnose the cause of the disease correctly and the treatment needed to remedy it. Before the discerned
disease was attended to, repentance from sin, that is, the amending
of ways or relations and the offering of gifts and sacrifice, was necessary. Since the cause of illness was believed to be spiritual, the
means to curing it too were believed to be spiritual and this cure

was effected through a God-given insight or revelation. Whoever was able to expel and control evil spirits, which were believed to be responsible for illness, was believed to be acting as God's agent in the whole system of liberating, healing and pardoning humanity (Vermes 1983). It is therefore from this background that we can now look into Jesus' healing and try to understand why he identified himself with the act of healing.

When it comes to Jesus' healing, there is no adequate reason to doubt that it was definitely part of his mission of salvation and believed to be so by the apostles (Acts 10:38) (Dawson 1935). The accounts that suggest that Jesus impressed his country people and acquired fame among them also suggest that it was so chiefly because Jesus was a healer (Matthew 15:30-1, Mark 3:9-10, 6:54-6, Luke 18:15, John 11:45). It is through healing that Jesus' renown spread throughout Galilee (and is now spreading in Africa through African Independent Churches). According to these scriptures, when Jesus and his disciples were recognised, the people would immediately run about bringing their sick out, some on stretchers, and others at the point of death, to be healed by Jesus. This happened everywhere: in the streets, farmsteads, marketplaces. The good thing about this is that all the sick people were cured, by whatever method of healing Jesus used. In these healing activities we see God's power being demonstrated through a human-agent: the man Jesus.

Jesus was born, grew up and started his religious activity in a society which was already religious. Jews believed that all sickness and healing were activities in which spiritual powers and the supernatural was involved. It is through healing that Jesus' teaching gained substance and his message of salvation was reinforced and clearly understood. It is through healing that it became clear what he meant by "life in abundance" (John 10:10). Healing became Jesus' effective tool. In his world there was nothing particularly unique about teaching, but healing was highly regarded for the healer was understood to have some special relations with the Divine. A person's healing powers were measured first and foremost by his/her proximity to God, and only secondarily by expertise acquired from study of the divinely ordained curative qualities of plants and herbs. Professional knowledge was an additional asset to the healer's essential requisite, holiness (Vermes 1973: 60-61). Through his healing, Jesus, in some cases, brought people into renewal of relationship with God. Like his contemporaries, Jesus believed that human beings were often under the baneful influence of the evil powers, which were hostile to God. These might be the equivalent of the power of witchcraft or demons in the biblical language. Jesus also demonstrated that while sickness could be caused by sin, there is no reason for supposing that this will always be the case (John 9:2–3). In other words, sickness can occur as a result of natural causes so that "the works of God might be made manifest." He, however, indicates that it might well be that sin does leave one more open to the invasion of the hostile forces which are working against the will of God, hence the call to repentance, to "sin no more."

Throughout the Gospels, Jesus heals many different kinds of sickness: leprosy, paralysis, fever, haemorrhage, blindness, a withered hand, deaf-muteness, lameness, dropsy and many others, even those at the point of dying. There is no disease or illness that is not taken to Jesus. Jesus' healing considers the entire personality of his patients, his healing power bears upon moral, mental, spiritual and bodily sickness, as disharmony in any of these aspects results in disease. But the most fundamental of all these levels is the spiritual. Sickness, in Jesus' view, was a degradation and disarrangement of the personal entity (Dawson 1935). By healing all these different diseases Jesus was rescuing, liberating and saving people from a needy situation in which they seemed powerless to help themselves. Jesus was one of the figures who

> Rejected the opinion of apocalyptic circles that in the struggle against evil, human beings have only to act as insignificant aids, to a heavenly host of angels, powers and domination. He injected reality into the fight against the devil (Vermes 1983: 27).

The methods that Jesus used in his healing varied considerably, but in all the methods that he used, in most cases, he called upon the faith of the individual seeking healing. In other times, he called upon the faith of those around the sick person—the community (Mark 2:5). In his methods, Jesus used verbal healing (Matthew 9:2–8), bodily contact (Mark 3:10, Matthew 14:36), laying-on-of-hands (Luke 13:13, Mark 6:5), ritual (Mark 7:33–34, Mark 8:23–5, John 5:1–17) and, at one point, he healed a patient, *in absentia* (Matthew 8:5–13). I will now briefly discuss three examples of Jesus healing from John 5:1–18, Mark 7:31–7, Luke 13:10–17 to summarise some of my arguments.

In John 5:1–18 healing takes place in Bethesda. The restoration of the lame man at the pool, who has been ill for thirty-eight years, is an account of a man healed by the word alone. Jesus said to him,

"Rise, take up your pallet, and walk." And at once the man was healed, and he took up his pallet and walked. What is required in this healing is the desire to be healed, an act of commitment to express readiness to accept in faith the gift that God offers. In most healing cases it is an advantage if the patient has faith. Vermes also noted this, holding that "even in modern times, faith healers . . . and their secular counterparts in the field of medicine, can and do obtain parallel therapeutic results where the individuals who ask for help are animated by sufficient faith" (Vermes 1983: 6).

In Mark 7:31–7, Jesus heals a deaf and mute person through a ritual. Jesus put his fingers into his ears, and he spat and touched his tongue. Then looking up to heaven he sighed, and said to him, "*Ephphatha*," that is, "be opened." And his ears were opened, his tongue was released, and he spoke plainly. We are not told why Jesus spat, but we do know that what he was doing has certain parallels with so-called pagan healing stories and it suggests links with charismatic and miraculous healing of the Greco-Roman and the Jewish worlds where spittle (saliva) supposedly had a therapeutic function (Guelich 1989: 395), especially the saliva of a saintly or exalted person. The saint and his saliva were considered as manifestations of the sacred. In addition, Jesus reportedly looked up to heaven and sighed. Many scholars interpret this as a gesture of prayer and of receiving supernatural powers similar to what he did before feeding the five thousand and raising Lazarus from death. In all three cases, his looking to heaven points to his relation with God (who stays in heaven) and from whom he received the power to feed the hungry, heal the sick and raise the dead. The healing of a deaf-mute bears similarities with the healing of a man who was blind from birth (John 9), where spittle and clay are used on the eyes of the patient, who is asked to go and wash in the pool of Siloam. Again, we see Jesus using natural resources—saliva, clay and water—in his healing activities, as does the *Ngaka*.

Turning to Luke 13:10–17, it is a healing of a spirit of infirmity. In this healing, apart from using the word, Jesus laid his hands upon the woman who was bent over for eighteen years and could not fully straighten herself. The woman was healed, and she started praising God, not Jesus. It seems the woman understood very well the source of the healing power. To her, Jesus was a manifestation of God's power. The examples given above illustrate three types of Jesus' methods of healing: by word only, by natural resources and by laying-on-of-hands. Throughout the healing stories of Jesus there are many instances which can be interpreted to mean that Jesus had to establish some contact with the supernatural, which is similar to divination in the case of the *Ngaka*. It is undoubtedly clear that Jesus many times had to look up and seek divine contact or power. Those around him realised that he had power over life and death, and responsibility as the intermediary between the invisible powers and his people. Though many came to realise this, many others failed. "The majority of the people had not the spiritual insight to see the inner meaning of his miracles of healing. He would remain for them a mere wonder-worker and not a saviour" (Dawson 1935: 44).

Through his healing, Jesus ended up commanding a great following and at the same time his healings resulted in divided opinion about him. Some, especially the Pharisees, thought that Jesus' power of healing was from the prince of demons, Beelzebub (Matthew 9:34), but many wondered how a man who was possessed by a demon did such wonders—opening the eyes of the blind. Jesus makes it clear that all healing comes from God. But clearly Jesus' healing activities resulted in different understandings of him. For some he was the Christ. In my view, Jesus deserved this title because of his healing role, which is similar to the *Ngaka*'s role in Batswana society. Jesus was a divine agent that brought God's harmony into his society.

To conclude, Jesus' role as a divine healer is similar to the *Ngaka*'s role among the Batswana. When we look at Jesus' healing and his world, there is a lot that he shares with the *Ngaka*'s role among the Batswana. The belief that the causes of illness are more spiritual than physical, and that these spiritual causes take people beyond the physical world to the supernatural, to God, to *Modimo*. The person who takes responsibility for combatting illness as one problem of evil occupies an important place in his or her society. She or he is believed to have some special relationship with the Divine power. To the Christian, the power is directly from "God," but for the Batswana it comes through the ancestors—those liberated from physical disabilities—to the *Ngaka*. The *Ngaka* becomes an intermediary between the Divine and his/her people. The underlying belief is that for the *Ngaka* to be successful in the struggle against evil there has to be a source of good to help him—*Modimo*/God. The role of a healer in his/her society is a saving role, a life giving role, a struggle against evil. The role of Jesus in the Jewish society is similar to the role of the *Ngaka* in the Batswana society. Yet, when colonial

Christianity was introduced to Batswana, the role of the *Ngaka* in his/her society was condemned. The same Jesus who built his reputation of healing in the Jewish culture was made to be indifferent to Batswana culture by the missionary enterprise. In spite of the attempt to denigrate the role of the *Ngaka*, his/her role remains indispensable. In this post-colonial era, it is just and right that some of us who are undeniably both African and Christian read for ourselves from both religious testaments—from both African Traditional Religion and the Bible. As I have expounded, my reading shows that both the *Ngaka* and Jesus are sacred agents that serve God's creation.

BIBLIOGRAPHY

Appiah, Kubi. "Christology." In Ed. John Parratt, *A Reader in African Christian Theology*. London: SPCK, 1987, 69–81.
Comaroff, J. and J. *Of Revelation and Revolution: Christianity, Colonialism and Consciousness in South Africa. Vol. 1*. Chicago: University of Chicago, 1991.
Dale, D. *In his Hands: Towards a Theology of Healing*. London: Darton, Longman and Todd, 1989.
Dawson, G.G. *Healing: Pagan and Christian*. London: Longman, 1935.
Fabella, V. and Sun Ai Lee Park. Eds *We Dare to Dream: Doing Theology as Asian Woman*. Hong Kong: AWCCT, 1989.
Fako, T.T. In "Health/Illness and the Social-Cultural Background," Seminar Proceedings, 111–124. NIR. University of Botswana, 1980.
Gairdner, W.H.T. *Edinburgh 1910: An Account and Interpretation of the World Missionary Conference*. London: Oliphant and Ferrier, 1910.
Gelfand, M. *Witch-Doctor*. London: Harvill Press, 1964.
Guelich, R.A. *Word Biblical Commentary*. Dallas: Word Books, 1989.
Kolie, C. "Jesus as Healer?." In Ed. J.R. Schreiter, *Faces of Jesus in Africa*. Maryknoll: Orbis Books, 1991, 128–150.
Krige, E.J., and Krige, J.W. *The Realm of Rain-Queen: A Study of the Pattern of Lovedu Society*. London: Oxford University Press, 1943.
Linzey, A. *Animal Theology*. London: SCM Press, 1994.
Mbiti, J.S. "Some African Concepts of Christology." In Ed. G.F. Vicedom, *Christ and the Young Churches*. London: SPCK, 1972, 51–60.
Setiloane, G.M. *The Image of God among the Sotho Tswana*. Rotterdam: A.A. Balkema, 1976.
Staugard, F. *Traditional Healers*. Gaborone: Ipelegeng, 1985.
The Holy Bible (RSV). London: Oxford University Press, 1952.
Vermes, G. *Jesus the Jew: A Historian's Reading of the Gospel*. London: Collins, 1973.
———. *Jesus and the World of Judaism*. London: SCM Press, 1983.
Werbner, R.P. *Ritual Passage Sacred Journey: The Process and Organisation of Religious Movement*. Washington: Smithsonian Institution Press, 1989.
Willoughby, W.C. *Nature Worship and Taboo*. Hartford: Hartford Seminary Press, 1932.

THE SWAHILI BIBLE IN EAST AFRICA FROM 1844 TO 1996: A BRIEF SURVEY WITH SPECIAL REFERENCE TO TANZANIA

Aloo Osotsi Mojola

Christian missionary presence in East Africa has its roots in the 19th century beginning with the work of two German missionaries, Johann Krapf and Johann Rebmann. These two Lutheran missionaries came as representatives of the Anglican, Church Missionary Society (CMS). Krapf arrived in Mombasa Kenya in 1844 and was joined by his colleague Rebmann in 1846. Their aim was to establish a continental missionary system beginning from the East African coast and stretching to West Africa. Professor Roland Oliver in his classic work *The Missionary Factor in East Africa* (1952, 1970) while observing that these "sad and otherworldly men achieved no great evangelistic success" (Oliver 1970: 6), acknowledges that they, "who set in motion the missionary invasion of East Africa" (Oliver 1970: 7).

There is no doubt that their pioneering linguistic research and publications as well as their work in Bible translation laid a lasting foundation for subsequent work. It is not surprising that Bishop Steere said of Krapf, "Bible translation, like geographical discovery and almost everything else in the recent history of East Africa, owes its beginning to Dr. Krapf" (quoted in Bedford 1954: 19). Krapf's translations of Genesis (published in 1847) and the New Testament in Kimvita Swahili (completed in 1846) laid a basis for further work in Swahili. Krapf's decision to use Kimvita Swahili as the main dialect for his translation work was well founded, for at that time this was the dominant language of the East African coastal region and moreover the language of a long tradition of Swahili poetry, including the poetry of Muyaka bin Haji one of the most celebrated nationalist poets of the East African coast. The future however did not favour the Kimvita dialect. The wind of standardization which started blowing in the 1920s overlooked not only Kimvita but also its important northern cousin the Kiamu dialect in favour of the Kiugunja dialect spoken in the town of Zanzibar.

It is a pity that Krapf's translation of the New Testament into

Kimvita Swahili was not published. The first complete portion of Scripture published in Kimvita was the book of Jonah in 1878 by the United Methodist Free Church at Ribe near Mombasa. The book of Jonah was followed by the Psalms in 1883 published by the Society for Promoting Christian Knowledge. Canon W.E. Taylor, the main translator, aimed to have the Anglican liturgy and prayer book translated in Kimvita Swahili. These were translated together with selections from the Gospels and the Epistles for the liturgy. Thereafter he turned his attention to the entire Bible assisted by his main collaborator, fellow CMS missionary, H.K. Binns. Through their efforts Deuteronomy and 2 Chronicles were published in 1889, the Gospel of Luke in 1892, John in 1897, all the Gospels in one volume in 1901, and the entire New Testament in 1909. It was not until 1914 that work on the complete Bible was finalized, with the publication of the Old Testament. As already noted, the future did not lie with these translations in Kimvita Swahili, even though this was the most prestigious dialect of ancient Swahili poetry. The impact of Krapf and Rebmann's pioneer efforts (or of their successors Taylor and Binns) on Tanzania and on the future of Kiswahili was thus limited and sidelined by the developments that followed.

According to Professor Roland Oliver "it was Livingstone, the individual, and not the CMS missionaries with their twelve years' start and their powerful society behind them, who set in motion the missionary invasion of East Africa" (1970: 7). Indeed it was Livingstone's campaign against the Arab slave-trade and his call for the Christian-ization, civilization and commercialization of Africa which opened the gate for the coming of the first wave of missionaries and other westerners to Tanzania. Among these pioneers were the men and women of the Universities' Mission to Central Africa (UMCA), with chapters at Cambridge (1858) and Oxford (1859), whose linguistic work and contribution to Bible translation were trail blazing and long-lasting. This group was theologically of the Anglican High-Church variety and hence closer to the Roman Catholic tradition. The first group of UMCA pioneers who obeyed this call to Africa were led by Bishop Charles Frederick Mackenzie. They travelled, via Cape Town, where Mackenzie was consecrated first Bishop of the UMCA on January 1, 1861. This group never made it to East Africa. Most of the team members met their end along the way. Bishop George Tozer of St. John's College, Oxford succeeded Bishop Mackenzie. He is the one who moved the UMCA base from Central

Africa to Zanzibar. He arrived in Zanzibar on August 31, 1864 in the company of Dr. Edward Steere. Edward Steere like Johann Krapf, his counterpart in Mombasa, immediately immersed himself in learning and mastering the local language of Zanzibar namely, Kiugunja Swahili. He set up the mission printing press at Zanzibar from which by 1865 the first parts of his celebrated *Handbook of the Swahili Language as Spoken in Zanzibar* started coming out. Steere's ultimate goal was to eventually make the Holy Scriptures available in Kiugunja Swahili.

It was under Dr. Steere, consecrated in Westminster Abbey as third Bishop of the UMCA on August 24, 1874, that the famous Zanzibar landmark, Christ Church Cathedral was erected. Bishop Steere himself designed and supervised the construction of this Cathedral, apparently as it is reported, on the very spot where the slave market had been or alternatively at the very site of the old whipping post for slaves. This famous cathedral took six years to complete, from Christmas day 1873, when the foundation stone was laid, to Christmas day 1879, when it was officially opened. The UMCA in Zanzibar founded, as part of its "civilizing mission," a Christian village at Mbweni, Zanzibar, on the model of the Bagamoyo Christian village started in 1868 by missionaries from the Roman Catholic Holy Ghost Fathers Congregation. The UMCA missionaries also founded St. Andrew's College, in 1868, at Kiungani, Zanzibar, also called Kiinua Mguu, but better known in the UMCA community as the "School of the Prophets." St. Andrew's College was the first educational institution of its type in East Africa and was intended for the training of some of the new converts as teachers or preachers. It is said that the best educated Tanzanians at the beginning and during the first half of this century were graduates of St. Andrew's. Many of the early students of St. Andrew's College were ex-slaves.

In 1875 the UMCA finally established their work, on the mainland of Tanganyika, in the Usambara Mountains, in the territory of Chief Kimweri, after initial exploratory visits in 1867 by Rev. Charles Argentine Alington and in 1868 by Bishop Tozer. A mission centre was opened at Magila not far from Tanga. The next move was to the southern parts of Tanzania in 1876. This eventually led to the establishment of mission centres at Masasi among the Yao and Makua and at Newala among the Makonde in present day Mtwara Region. These UMCA centres were intended to be nuclei for the promotion of commerce and for the Christianization and civilization of the native communities. It was in this respect similar to those at Freretown, Rabai and Ribe at the Kenyan coast near Mombasa. These were all intended to be beacons of light and models of Christian values and lifestyle. They also served their role as centres for the indoctrination and training of native Christians.

From the start, Bishop Steere got involved in Bible translation, together with his other numerous duties as bishop. The first books of the Bible, translated into Kiugunja Swahili, to come off the UMCA Mission Press in Zanzibar were the Old Testament books of Ruth and Jonah in 1868, the Gospel of Luke in 1872 and 1 and 2 Kings in 1875. The Gospel of Luke had been originally translated by Abd al-Aziz, a Zanzibar sheikh, together with Richard L. Pennell. These were followed by Ephesians and Philippians in 1876, Acts, Romans, 2 Corinthians, James and 1 John in 1878, Genesis, Galatians, Colossians to 2 Peter, 2 John to Jude, and Revelation in 1879. In 1869 the Gospel of Matthew was published by the British and Foreign Bible Society (BFBS) in London, as were the Psalms, which appeared two years later in 1871. The BFBS published the Gospel of John in 1875 and a revised edition for the Gospel of Matthew in 1876. Mark and a revised edition of John also came out in 1879. The complete New Testament was made available in 1879 in Swahili as was the complete liturgy. The following year, the Mission Press released copies of Exodus followed in 1882 by the book of Isaiah, a revised edition of 1 and 2 Kings, and also a revised edition of Acts. The complete New Testament in a revised form appeared the following year in 1883 and was published by the BFBS, London. This was the result mainly of Bishop Edward Steere's labours, together with some of his UMCA colleagues namely—Chauncey Maples, Herbert Geldart, Arthur C. Madan and Mary A.H. Allen. It is to be noted that T.H. Sparshott of the Church Missionary Society (CMS) also participated in this noble effort. This was the first New Testament to be published in East Africa. Krapf's New Testament in Kimvita Swahili was certainly the first to be translated, but it never saw the light of day. Krapf's New Testament manuscript was lent to Dr. Steere, who no doubt benefitted from its pioneering solutions to many translation problems. It is of interest though, in this connection, that the Gospel of Luke translated by Johann Rebmann and revised by Johann Krapf was published apparently in Kiugunja Swahili by the BFBS in 1876 and in a revised form in 1881.

This splendid work did not stop with Bishop Steere's death. Others continued from where he stopped. In 1882, the year he died, Daniel was published by the Mission Press in Zanzibar, and Judges in 1883. In addition, Luke and Proverbs were produced in 1885 and 1886 respectively. Between 1886 and 1887 the Mission Press released Numbers, 1–2 Samuel, Ecclesiastes, Song of Solomon, Jeremiah to Ezekiel, Hosea to Obadiah, and Micah to Malachi. Genesis and Joshua were published by the BFBS, London in 1884. In 1886 Exodus was produced by the BFBS, 2 Samuel, 1 Chronicles to Malachi were published between 1889 and 1891, and the complete Old Testament was produced in 1895. The main translators of this Old Testament were Francis Roger Hodgson and his wife Jessie Hodgson. Arabic transliterations of the Gospel of John were done by Mary A.H. Allen in 1888 and of the Gospel of Matthew by Petro Limo in 1891. A revised New Testament prepared by Arthur C. Madan and Percy L. Jones Bateman was produced by the BFBS London in 1892. The following year 1893 a further revision was prepared by Percy L. Jones, Bateman, Herbert W. Woodward, assisted by Petro Limo and Cecil Majaliwa and printed at the Zanzibar Mission Press. A revision of the Old Testament was prepared by Francis Roger Hodgson and published by the BFBS in 1895. A final revision of this Zanzibar Bible was undertaken by Godfrey Dale and Frank Weston both of the Universities' Mission to Central Africa (UMCA). Their efforts saw the publication of the New Testament in 1921, Psalms and Proverbs in 1925 and Isaiah to Malachi in 1930 by the BFBS, London.

The first attempt by the Roman Catholic Church at translating the Scriptures in Kiugunja Swahili was spearheaded by Emile Brutel of the White Fathers Congregation. His translation of the four Gospels and Acts was published by the Sociéte des Missionaires D'AFRIQUE, Algiers in 1929. Preliminary editions appeared in 1913 and 1923, but Emile Brutel's work unfortunately did not receive the wide circulation it deserved. It was no doubt beneficiary of the first rate research and immense contribution of the French Holy Ghost Fathers to Swahili studies. This legacy to Swahili studies is widely known through the enviable work of the venerable Fr. Charles Sacleux, whose research and publications in Swahili dialectology as well as grammar in 1909 as well as his voluminous Swahili lexicon of 1939–41 are still widely respected and consulted. Sacleux himself attempted translations of Old Testament and New Testament selections variously published in 1893, 1898, 1921 and the complete New Testament published at the Maison Spitaine at Grasse in 1937.

Dr. Karl Roehl's translation of the Bible into Kiswahili represented a new stage in the writing of Swahili. Roehl aimed not only
at fully utilizing Kiugunja Swahili as a base, but also to go beyond
it in capturing its expanded use and function in the interior. He
aimed at minimizing its Arabic lexical borrowing while at the same
time maximizing the use of its Bantu lexical roots as reflected by
usage in the interior of mainland Tanganyika. Roehl was a missionary of the Bethel Mission of the German Lutheran Church who
had previously translated the New Testament into Kishambala. He
was supported by the Berlin Missionary Society in the translation
of this new Swahili Bible. His New Testament was essentially a
revision of an earlier translation of the New Testament by Martin
Klamroth of the Berlin Missionary Society. This translation was on
the behalf of four German missionary societies, namely the Berlin
Mission, the Bielefeld Mission, the Leipzig Mission and the Moravian
Mission. At meetings held in August and October 1914 representatives of these missions resolved to sponsor "a new translation, of the
scriptures in Swahili suitable for use throughout German East Africa"
and whose "main object was to purify Swahili as a Bantu language,
by eliminating the majority of the Zanzibar Arabic words, which are
either not used, or imperfectly understood, by the natives on the
coast, and are quite unintelligible to those in the interior" (BFBS
Files). Martin Klamroth with the help of some of his colleagues, and
with some linguistic assistance and advice from Prof. C. Meinfhof
of Hamburg, completed the New Testament in 1914, but the outbreak of the War made its publication impossible. After the War,
in the mid-1920s Roehl commenced on the revision of the Klamroth
translation at Dar es Salaam. It was reported by Prof. Westermann
in 1926 that this translation was "especially adapted to the Swahili
as spoken in the interior. Many Arab words have been replaced by
authentic Swahili words. It is written in the orthography officially
adopted by the Government" (BFBS Files).

In 1928 consideration was given to the question of having a
common Swahili Bible in *Standard Swahili* bringing together Mombasa
and Zanzibar with their Kimvita and Kiugunja versions as well as
their UMCA and CMS traditions. This was given impetus by the
Conferences on the Standardization of Swahili held at Dar es Salaam
in October 1925 and at Mombasa on June 3, 1928, as well as the
Government's promotion of a new common Swahili orthography.
The BFBS took an active part in encouraging the UMCA and CMS

missions to explore the possibility of this new joint union translation in Standard Swahili and standard orthography. The first meeting held in London to discuss this matter included Prof. Westermann (Germany), Dr. Roehl (Bethel Mission), Dr. Diehl (Bible Society, Stuttgart), Dr. Broomfield (UMCA), Canon Butcher (CMS), Revs. Pittway (CMS) and Wilkinson (BFBS), and was chaired by E.W. Smith (BFBS). This meeting discussed the acceptance of the Zanzibar New Testament as the basis of the translation, the Mombasa and Roehl versions being consulted in the course of preparation. For the Old Testament, Roehl's version would be accepted as the basis, and be used with reference to the Mombasa and Zanzibar versions. Kimvita Swahili whose cause was championed by Krapf and other later CMS missionaries on the Kenyan coast lost the battle for hegemony as the standard and official form of the language, despite having an older written literary tradition as well as Krapf's monumental dictionary and groundbreaking grammar book. The Rules of the BFBS on translation were expected to be followed, and each translator was furnished with a copy.

It was noted that Dr. Roehl disagreed with his colleagues on the proportion of Arabic words to be admitted in the translation. His idea was to substitute Bantu words wherever possible for Arabic words. The British members were of the view that "this limits the possibility of bringing out the meaning of the sacred text, especially if words which have been for a long time in use are replaced by less meaningful words" (BFBS files). A first tentative edition of the proposed joint union version had been translated by Godfrey Dale (UMCA, Zanzibar) and revised by G. Pittway and H.J. Butcher (CMS, Mombasa) and published by the BFBS, London in 1934. Dr. Roehl rejected this test portion presented as a model on the grounds that it contained "so many Arabic words" (BFBS Files). In the end cooperation with Dr. Roehl and the Stuttgart Society proved unworkable. Roehl's version of the New Testament in Swahili was eventually published in 1930 and the complete Bible containing both the New and Old Testaments in 1937 by the Whürttemberg Bible Society in Stuttgart, Germany. Dr. Roehl had been assisted by Pastor Martin Nganisya and Mwalimu Andrea Ndekeja. Commenting on this translation, the Stuttgart Society observed that "Our Swahili Bible is, as far as we know, the first edition of the Bible in a standardized Swahili written in the standardized orthography" (BFBS Files). This Bible had, as its target audience, "all the Christian people in the whole

East and Central Africa" (BFBS Files). Rev. H. Scholten the Secretary of the Tanganyika Missionary Council[1] writing about this translation observed as follows: "I still regret that two translations of the Swahili Bible will follow each other in short periods, but I do think that Dr. Roehl has done a great piece of work. I hardly doubt that his version of the Old Testament will be easily surpassed" (BFBS Files).

Following the break with Dr. Roehl, Canon Hellier (UMCA, Muheza) was welcomed as the chief translator of the *Standard Swahili* Bible and was assisted by Canon Butcher (CMS, Mombasa) as his chief collaborator. Dr. Richard Reusch (Lutheran, Marangu) and others were invited to be reviewers to this translation. By 1945 tentative editions of the Gospels of Matthew, Mark and John were published by the CMS in Nairobi, followed by the Psalms in 1949. The New Testament in this new *Swahili Union Version* appeared in 1950 and the Old Testament appeared in 1952, published by the BFBS. Accomplishing this task required a lot of patience, as well as mutual respect. This was not always possible. For example Canon Hellier wrote to Canon Coleman: "Nobody can produce agreement between us on such a point. . . ." (BFBS Files). At another time, Butcher wrote to Coleman: "The position with regard to these Psalms is a bit complicated as they are almost solely Canon Hellier's work. . . ." (BFBS Files). Meanwhile Canon Broomfield, UMCA Secretary, writing to A. Wilkinson, BFBS General Secretary, wrote: "I feel that final decisions should rest with Hellier. After all, he is a scholar, and I do not think Messrs. Butcher and Pittway, for instance, would make that claim for themselves. At one of our meetings to discuss New Testament translation they admitted that they knew practically no Greek" (BFBS Files). Earlier, writing to E.W. Smith of the BFBS, Broomfield complained: ". . . as far as Swahili as we know it is concerned, the present Zanzibar version is much better than that writ-

---

[1] It is to be noted that the Tanganyika Missionary Council was an ecumenical council created in 1936 as an instrument for the Protestant missionary agencies in colonial Tanganyika, namely the UMCA, the CMS, the Leipzig, the Berlin, the Bethel, the Moravian and the Seventh Day Adventist Missions. It became the Christian Council of Tanganyika in 1948, and now brings together all major Protestant Churches in the country—the Lutherans, the Anglicans, the Moravians, the Africa Inland Church (AIC), the Baptists, the Mennonites, the Seventh Day Adventists, among others. The Bible Society of Tanzania (BST) and some other major para-church agencies are associate members.

ten by our friends in Kenya. . . . In a word, it seems to us that
Messrs. Butcher and Pittway and Miss Deed are not Swahili scholars of the same calibre as those responsible for the present Zanzibar
version." (BFBS Files). Rev. G. Capon of CMS, Limuru in defence
of his Mombasa friends wrote to Rev. H.D. Hooper of CMS, London
(17.1.1941): ". . . a fairly close study of Hellier's work makes me very
doubtful whether he should be an assessor over Butcher, or indeed
over anybody else at all . . ." (BFBS Files). Clearly, like today's translators, personal, academic, denominational and doctrinal sensitivities
bedevilled the translation teams of yesterday. Canon Hellier's subsequent mental breakdown in England was probably due to the many
strains and stresses he suffered in the course of his work as the chief
translator to the *Swahili Union Version*. To his credit and unlike many
others in his position, Canon Hellier never forgot his native collaborators. He specially wrote to BFBS (15.9.1952) to send a copy of
the first editions of the *Swahili Union Version* from the press to Rev.
Paulo Kihampa because ". . . he made some original and really helpful remarks in the discussion and I felt that for a native he was quite
outstanding" (BFBS Files). It is a miracle of grace that these human
frailties resulted in such a great translation. Clearly the BFBS was
correct in claiming in a letter written to the widow of Canon Hubert
John Edwin Butcher (1879–1956) at his death that: "The Union
Swahili Version has already taken its place as one of the monumental achievements of the Bible Society . . ." (BFBS Files).

It is not surprising that a reprint of the Roehl Bible in 1960 was
strongly resisted. Rev. Frederick Bedford of the Bible Society in East
Africa wrote: "I think it is now accepted as a general principle that
the Union Swahili Bible has superseded all other Swahili versions
and it certainly would be a retrograde step if a German Bible Society
of its own initiative resurrected the Roehl Version" (BFBS Files). His
successor at Bible House, Nairobi, Rev. John T. Mpaayei, echoed
the same sentiments in his letter to Stuttgart: "I think it would be
a great pity if another Bible in the Swahili language were to be
given wide circulation, and at another price," and that "it certainly
would be disastrous to have this Roehl Bible circulating alongside
our Union Swahili Bible" (BFBS Files). Meanwhile from BFBS,
London the view was that printing the Roehl Bible "does seem to
be retrograde as it certainly tends to be a divisive step" (BFBS Files).
The *Swahili Union Version* was simply seen there as "a God-given
means of furthering the sense of unity among Christians in East

Africa" (BFBS Files). The view from Stuttgart was different. The General Secretary of the Bible Society in Stuttgart, Dr. Th. Schlatter had written to Dr. Oliver Beguin, the UBS General Secretary in defence as follows: "It is not a matter of rivalry but of the richness of the translation of God's Word. Africans are continually asking for the Roehl Bible" (BFBS Files). Dr. Beguin in turn observed: "I am aware, of course that the Stuttgart Society never quite swallowed the introduction of the Union Version. . . . I am simply aware that behind this project there is the sense of grudge which Stuttgart feels against the BFBS in this matter" (BFBS Files). A second edition of the Roehl Bible was of course produced by the Whürttemberg Bible Society in 1961 and has recently been reprinted again by the Bible Society of Tanzania in 1995 perhaps with faint echoes of Th. Schlatter's position.

The Deuterocanonical books of the Bible (also referred to as the Apocrypha) were translated into the Union Swahili by Miss D.V. Perrot assisted by a committee of reviewers. The resulting text was copyrighted by the SPCK and published together with the standard *Swahili Union Version* text in a Roman Catholic edition of the Bible containing the Deuterocanonical books, at the Tabora Mission Press, Tabora in 1967. This edition with an imprimatur also contained introductions and footnotes translated from the French *Jerusalem Bible* of 1956. Arabic transliterations of the *Swahili Union Version* text were prepared for the Gospel of John (1969), Matthew, Mark, Luke and Acts (1970) by H. Mtipura, assisted by Martha Lagerström. Note should be made here of two important Roman Catholic translations in Standard Swahili. Already, mention has been made of Fr. Emile Brutel's work in producing the Gospels and Acts in Kiugunja. Fr. Alfons Loogman of the Roman Catholic White Fathers Order was perhaps the first Catholic to attempt a translation in standard Swahili based on standard orthography. His labours culminated in the publication of the Gospels and Acts in 1947 and the complete New Testament in 1958. The Gospel and Acts were revised and published in 1960. These were all produced at the Holy Ghost Press in Morogoro. Again like the Brutel effort, this work was not produced in adequate quantities and made little impact and has been unavailable and out of print for a long time. The same may be said of the translation of the New Testament by the Benedictine Fathers which appeared for the first time in 1986. Already by 1972 portions of this translation were published by the Ndanda Mission Press in southern Tanzania. The Psalms portion which appeared earlier was published in a revised edition in 1985 by Fr. P. Isaya. These German missionaries were assisted and supported by local Swahili experts including Fr. Filipo Mrope. All the above-mentioned translations were strictly speaking not inter-confessional, even though they were often used across confessional and denominational lines.

The renowned *Swahili Union Version* has dominated the field, as the leading Swahili Bible. Indeed it has become, in a very short time, the *"King James Version"* equivalent of the Swahili speaking world. Nevertheless it is the new *Biblia Habari Njema* which has from its inception been truly inter-confessional and interdenominational in effort. Sponsored by the Bible Society of Kenya and the Bible Society of Tanzania at the request of the Protestant and Roman Catholic Churches in both countries, the *Biblia Habari Njema* translation has sought the participation of all churches at all levels and from the two sponsoring countries. *Biblia Habari Njema* is the first major Swahili translation for which East Africans themselves have been wholly responsible and in which they have fully participated at all levels. This translation was started in 1973. Among those who have participated as translators at one stage or another during the translation process have been the following: Peter Renju (RC), Cosmas Haule (RC), Jared Mwanjalla (Anglican), Amon Mahava (Lutheran), Amon Oendo (Seventh Day Adventists), Douglas Waruta (Baptist), David Mhina (Anglican) and Leonidas Kalugila (Lutheran). The first test portion of this translation was the Gospel of Luke which appeared in 1975 published by the Bible Societies of Kenya and Tanzania. The New Testament followed three years later in 1977 to an enthusiastic reception. It has since become a best seller, outselling all other books in the region. A copy of the New Testament with Psalms was published in 1987 by these Societies. In 1988 the *Habari Njema* New Testament appeared with the Jerusalem Bible notes translated especially for this edition. An imprimatur was also granted for this edition to encourage wide use by Roman Catholic readers. The completion of the Old Testament encountered some delays. The complete Bible which included a revised New Testament was eventually taken to press in 1994. The public launching and dedication of the new *Habari Njema* Bible took place simultaneously in Nairobi, Kenya and at Manyoni, Tanzania on 24 March 1996. It was enthusiastically received and is reported to be enjoying high sales.

The *Biblia Habari Njema* is a meaning-based translation or a dynamic translation of the functional equivalence variety. Translations of this type, such as the English *Good News Bible* or *Contemporary English Version*, as a matter of policy set out to give greater priority to meaning and how this is to be faithfully captured in the receptor text (the language of translation) as accurately, clearly and naturally as is possible. These type of translations place priority on the sense of the original text. In contrast, translations such as the *Swahili Union Version* are of the formal correspondence variety. They place more emphasis on the words and forms of the original text rather than on the contextual meaning of the original text. The result is often unnatural, unclear, inaccurate and ambiguous renderings. Many of the early translations mentioned in this paper are of this variety.

With at least five major complete Bible versions in Swahili, namely the Kiugunja (1891), the Kimvita (1914), the Roehl (1937), the *Swahili Union Version* (1952), and the *Habari Njema* (1996), no other language in East Africa is blessed with such a rich heritage. The fact that Swahili is now the major lingua franca of the East African region means that this heritage is spread over the whole area. Indeed the impact and influence of these translations on other translations in East African languages are fairly evident. It is moreover interesting to note that in Tanzania the use of the Swahili translations holds a near monopoly and is fast replacing the existing vernacular translations. Whether this trend will continue or whether the vernacular translations will reassert their dominance in their respective areas remains to be seen. The situation in Kenya and Uganda is however different. There the use of vernacular Scriptures is a dominant factor in the rural areas while the use of Swahili and English Scriptures tends to dominate the urban scene. The impact and influence of the Swahili Scriptures on the early Christian communities in East Africa and on the contemporary church situation in this region is an interesting subject of further study and research.

BIBLIOGRAPHY

Abdulaziz, M.H. "Tanzania's National Language Policy and the Rise of Swahili Political Culture," In Ed. W.H. Whiteley, *Language Use and Social Change, Problems of Multilingualism with Special Reference to Eastern Africa.* London: Oxford University Press, 1971: 160–178.
Anderson, W.B. *The Church in East Africa.* Dodoma: Central Tanganyika Press, 1977.

Anderson-Morshead, A.E.M. *The History of the Universities' Mission to Central Africa. Vol. 1. 1859–1909.* London: UMCA, 1956.

Baur, John. *2000 Years of Christianity in Africa—61 to 1992.* Nairobi: Pauline Publications, 1994.

Bedford, F.J. *The Bible in East Africa.* London: BFBS, 1954.

British and Foreign Bible Societies—Notes and Correspondence Files. Swindon & Cambridge: BFBS Offices & Library.

British and Foreign Bible Societies, *The Bible Society Reporter,* Monthly Reports of the Society in the Early Period. Swindon & Cambridge: BFBS Offices & Library.

Blood, A.G. *The History of the Universities' Mission to Central Africa, Vol. II. 1907–1932.* London: UMCA, 1957.

———. *The History of the Universities' Mission to Central Africa, Vol. III. 1933–1957.* London: UMCA, 1962.

Coldham, Geraldine E. (Compiler) *A Bibliography of Scriptures in African Languages, Vols. 1 & 2.* London: BFBS, 1966.

———. (Compiler) *A Bibliography of Scriptures in African Languages, (Supplement 1964–1974).* London: BFBS, 1975.

Iliffe, John. *A Modern History of Tanganyika.* Cambridge: Cambridge University Press, 1979.

Mojola, Aloo Osotsi. *Bible Translation in East Africa from 1844 to the Present.* Nairobi, Dodoma, Kampala: Bible Societies of Kenya, Tanzania and Uganda, Forthcoming.

Nurse, Derek & Spear, Thomas. *The Swahili—Reconstructing the History & Language of an African Society, 800–1500.* Philadelphia: University of Pennsylvania Press, 1985.

Oliver, Roland. *The Missionary Factor in East Africa.* London: Longman, 1952, 1970.

Polome, Edgar C. & Hill, C.P. Eds *Language in Tanzania.* Oxford: Oxford University Press, 1980.

Sahlberg, Carl-Eric. *From Krapf to Rugambwa—A Church History of Tanzania.* Nairobi: Evangel Publishing House, 1986.

Schaaf, Ype. *On Their Way Rejoicing—The History and Role of the Bible in Africa.* Carlisle: Paternoster Press/Nairobi: AACC, 1994.

Scriptures of the World. Reading: United Bible Societies, 1996.

Whiteley, Wilfred. *Swahili—The Rise of a National Language.* London: Methuen & Co. Ltd., 1969.

World Translations Progress Report. Reading: United Bible Societies, 1996.

World Translations Progress Report, Supplement. Reading: United Bible Societies, 1996.

100 YEARS OF THE LUGANDA BIBLE (1896–1996):
A GENERAL SURVEY

Aloo Osotsi Mojola

In 1996 the Bible Society of Uganda organised celebrations to com-
memorate one hundred years since the publication of the complete
Bible in Luganda. Already in 1887 the first publication of Scripture
in Luganda had appeared, the first in any Ugandan language, to be
followed by other publications of individual books of the Bible in
Luganda. 1896 was the culmination of this pioneer process, a precursor of Bible translation work in other Ugandan languages.

The Luganda Bible was destined to become a model to be followed by others. Indeed its powerful and widespread impact can
hardly be overestimated. Luganda is a Bantu language spoken by
the Baganda of the kingdom of Buganda. It is probably the most
widely spoken or understood African language in Uganda. It is also
spoken or understood in parts of north western Tanzania and the
neighbouring parts of western Kenya. The naming of the country
of Uganda after Buganda is due to the mistake of confusing a part
for the whole. Buganda was at the time the dominant power of the
region of the Great Lakes and outsiders and foreigners often committed this mistake. The great political power exercised by the kingdom of the Kabaka naturally gave the language of this kingdom an
advantage as well as power over other neighbouring languages. It is
therefore not surprising that the ground-breaking 1896 Luganda Bible
was destined to exercise great influence and power not just in the
kingdom of Buganda but in the whole of Uganda as well as in
Buhaya in northwestern Tanzania and Buluyia in western Kenya.

The impact of the Luganda Bible can be gleaned from the following: the inscriptions on the foundation stone of the old Lutheran
church on Kashura Hill, in the town of Bukoba, in Buhaya; the
orthography of the first Ruhaya Bible, especially its proper names
in Gandaized form; the religious terminology used in the Anglican
translation of the New Testament in the Luhanga dialect of Buluyia
in western Kenya. There is hardly a translation, during this early
period of this region or even beyond, that evaded the influence of the
Luganda Bible. It was ubiquitous. The widespread use of Luganda

throughout this region by missionaries and their Luganda-speaking agents or evangelists no doubt contributed to this phenomenon. Luganda was transformed into the medium of Christian religious discourse and the Luganda Bible provided the terminology proper to this discourse.

On my visits to Busoga to assist with the launching of the Lusoga Bible translation project, I was struck by the continuing use to this very day of Luganda and the Luganda Bible in the very heart of Busoga, in the kingdom of the Kyabazinga where Lusoga should rightfully claim a place. A Soga family or group could conduct a mundane conversation in Lusoga one moment but would immediately switch to Luganda if a prayer or a religious homily was called for! I was however struck even more during my visits to the territory of Padhola in the environs of Tororo close to the Kenyan border, to find Luganda and the Luganda Bible used in Christian worship and prayer in an area which is the domain of a Nilotic speaking people. Such is the power of the Luganda Bible!

When the Luganda Bible appeared in 1896, it was the first Bible to appear in any of the languages of Uganda. Indeed the Luganda Bible was, after the Kiunguja Swahili Bible, the second complete Bible to appear in any of the languages of East and Central Africa. It was also the first Bible in East and Central Africa to appear in one volume. This 1896 Luganda Bible was popularly called the "Biscuit-tin Bible." This was probably due to the fact that it was the size of the tin boxes used by Baganda to store biscuits and incidentally also to store and protect books. This Bible was thus designed to be stored in these biscuit-tin boxes. This "biscuit-tin" Luganda Bible comprised the Old Testament and a revised New Testament. Pioneered by Church Missionary Society (CMS) missionaries Alexander Morehead Mackay, Robert Pickering Ashe and Edward Cyril Gordon, it was principally the work of the remarkable translators' George Lawrence Pilkington, Henry Wright Duta Kitaakule, William A. Crabtree, Sembera Mackay, Samwili Mukasa and Nuwa Nakiwafu.[1]

---

[1] The One Volume Luganda Bible was divided into four parts as follows, Genesis to 2 Samuel, p. 720, 1 Kings to Song of Solomon, p. 718, Isiah to Malachi, p. 509, and the NT, p. 623. An indication of the popularity of this Luganda Bible is shown for example by the fact that between 1888 and 1913, 16,000 Luganda Bibles and 6,400 Luganda New Testaments were printed. All together 213,290 Luganda Scriptures were printed during this period if account is taken of Scripture portions and selections in Luganda printed and distributed during the same period. Considering the realities of the period, this was no mean achievement!

The year 1896 in which this pioneer Bible appeared marks not
the beginning of Bible translation in Uganda but only one stage in
a movement whose roots are marked by the arrival of the first missionaries to Uganda. Perhaps the first visible representative of this
movement was the journalist and explorer Henry Morton Stanley.
When he arrived at Kabaka Mutesa's court in April 1875 during
his second Trans-Africa Expedition of 1874–1877, (his first expedition of 1871–72 had been in search of Dr. Livingstone), he was
accompanied by, among others, two African guides and interpreters
namely Robert Feruzi and Dallington Scorpion Maftaa. These two
were freed slaves who had undergone some training and rehabilita-
tion at Bishop Steere's Universities' Mission to Central Africa (UMCA)
school in Zanzibar. Robert Feruzi, originally of Nyasa ethnicity like
Maftaa, and a noted caravan leader, was one of Stanley's most trusted
men in his famous journey from Zanzibar to the source of the great
Zaire River. When Stanley left Buganda carrying with him ground-
breaking stories for the Western news media, he left Maftaa behind
to teach the Kabaka and his people about "the whiteman's Book."
Stanley had been apparently led by force of circumstances to take
on the role of missionary to Mutesa, extolling the message of Christianity. Gwen Anderson of the British and Foreign Bible Society (BFBS)
made the same point more dramatically when she noted that:

> The first sentence of Scripture ever written in Luganda was dictated
> not by a missionary, but by a very famous traveller. In order to give
> the king some idea of the Christian religion, explorer Henry Stanley
> and the king's scribe—a man named Idi—worked out a translation
> from the Swahili version of the Ten Commandments into Luganda
> (Anderson: 2).

It is very unlikely that Stanley knew Luganda. It is equally unlikely
that he had learnt or mastered the rudiments of Swahili well enough
to attempt a translation from that language into Luganda. Hence
his need to make use of Maftaa as an interpreter (Tuma and Mutibwa
1978: 93). Stanley's background did not associate him closely with
the Gospel, yet finding himself alone in a faraway land, he saw himself as an ambassador not only of Western civilization but of Christianity
as well. In this instance he took on the role of missionary evangelist.
In a joint dispatch to the *New York Herald* and the *Daily Telegraph* of
15 November 1875, Stanley had reported that "by one conversation" he had convinced Mutesa of the superiority of Christianity and

that "if it were only followed by the arrival of a Christian mission. . . . . the conversion of Mutesa and his court to Christianity would be complete" (Bierman 1990: 176–177). Stanley claims to have seen in Mutesa "a man who if aided timely by virtuous philanthropists will yet do more for Central Africa and civilization what fifty years of gospel teaching unaided by such authority cannot do. I see in him the light that shall lighten the darkness of this benighted region . . . In this man I see the possible fruition of Livingstone's hopes . . ." (Bierman 1990: 175). It is interesting that others such as the Rev. Charles Thomas Wilson, a member of the first group of Anglican missionaries in Buganda, saw in Mutesa a "murderous maniac" (Faupel 1962: 5) while another missionary of the same group Rev. Robert Pickering Ashe observed that Mwanga's education "had been a training in cruelty, brutality and lust" (Faupel 1962: 5).

In his impassioned appeal to "leading philanthropists and the pious people of England" (Bierman 1990: 177) Henry Morton Stanley wrote:

> Here gentlemen, is your opportunity—embrace it! The people of the shores of the Nyanza call upon you. Obey your generous instincts and listen to them, and I assure you that in one year you will have more converts to Christianity than all other missionaries united can number (Bierman 1990: 177).

The reputation of Henry Morton Stanley was in certain respects akin to that of Dallington Maftaa whom he left behind at Mutesa's court to carry on the Gospel. The chronicler of the UMCA speaks of Dallington Maftaa, who at the UMCA station in Zanzibar "had not been looked on as a credit to the Mission," as an example of "the bread 'cast upon the waters' (which) is found 'after many days'" (A.E. Anderson-Morshead, 1956: 78–79). From Buganda, Maftaa wrote to Bishop Steere, his Bishop in Zanzibar as follows:

WANTAGALA, April 23, 1876.

My DEAR BISHOP, —

> Let thy heart be turned to thy servant, and let me have favour in thy sight; therefore send me Swahili prayers, and send me one big black Bible. I want slates, board, chalk, that I may teach the Waganda the way of God. I been teach them already, but I want you to send me Litala Sudi, that he may help me in the work of God. Oh! My lord, pray for me; oh! ye boys pray for me. And if thou refuse to send me Litala Sudi, send me John Swedi. Your honour to the Queen, and my honour to you.

Dallington Maftaa.

I am translating the Bible to Mutesa, son of Suna, King of Uganda.
I was with Henry M. Stanley, together with Robert Feruzi, but Robert
is gone with Stanley, but I being stop in Uganda, translating the Bible
(Anderson-Morshead 1956: 79, grammatical and spelling errors are as
in the original).

Maftaa eventually attempted a translation into Luganda of selected
portions of the Bible as well as a complete Gospel of Luke. In later
years, Maftaa is reported however to have fallen by the way side,
thereby greatly compromising the faith he had once embraced, however it cannot be denied that Maftaa was indeed a pioneer Christian
evangelist in Buganda. His introductory lectures on the Christian
message and his regular public reading of the Christian Scriptures
gave the Baganda their initial preparatory taste of the Christian
religion.

Meanwhile in Europe, Stanley's stories and reports as well as his
challenge to the English missionary societies were given wide circulation and coverage by the mass media (notably the *Daily Telegraph*
of 15 November 1875). These played no small part in preparing the
ground for the missionary invasion of Uganda. The Church Missionary
Society was the first to take up this challenge. The pioneer CMS
party led by Lt. Shergold Smith and Rev. C.T. Wilson arrived in
Buganda on 30 June 1877. The other members of this party which
included Alexander Mackay arrived later, after a short spell at the
coast. They found Maftaa engaged in the preparation of the ground
for the Gospel. The French Catholic party of the White Fathers
arrived in Buganda on 17 February 1879 led by Fr. Simeon Lourdel
and Br. Amans. One would prefer not to mention the rivalry, mistrust, hostility and fights that later resulted from this meeting of the
British, Protestant, Anglican CMS factor, the French, Roman Catholic
White Fathers factor and the Arab, Islamic factor, which had been
in Buganda a little longer, it is one of the saddest and most shame-
ful stories in the history of Christianity in Africa. It is generally
agreed among historians of Buganda that it was Islam which initially created a thirst for literacy in Buganda especially among the
young pages (*bagalagala*) at the Kabaka's court and also pioneered
the idea of a holy book as well as of a transcendent God and a
holy day. Naturally these ideas were taken up to good advantage by
the Christian missionaries. We have noted how Maftaa easily took
up the task of teaching literacy and of teaching and translating the

Christian message from the Holy Bible in Swahili. The *bagalagala* formed a ready captive audience for instilling new ideas, teaching new skills and winning over to the new faith. It is no wonder that many of the early Christian martyrs in Buganda came from this group. The missionaries, both Catholic and Anglican, gathered around them groups of enthusiastic *bagalagala* who in no time were ready to die for their new found faith. These young enthusiasts after acquiring new literacy skills naturally hungered for something to read. The only logical and obvious choice of reading material was the Christian holy book in a language they could understand. And so the imperative to render the Bible into Luganda was forced upon the missionaries right at the onset of their missionary labours.

Fr. John Baur speaks of a "Readers' Revolution of the young Baganda movement towards Christianity" (Baur 1994: 236). He notes that:

> The number of people from the court, especially the pages, who came to read and to hear the Good News, increased from day to day. The term "reader" became identical with "Christian" and "man of the new elite." These young Christians were not only convinced but grew also very apostolic in mind. . . . There emerged prominent lay leaders who gathered the Christians into prayer groups: Joseph Mukasa Balikuddembe, at the court, Andrea Kagwa around the capital and Matia Mulumba at Mityana. The number of Catholic catechumens more than doubled to more than five hundred (Baur 1994: 236).

Anderson speaks of a "Christian revolution" which he says began among the *bagalagala* but eventually spread among even ordinary Baganda and within no time beyond Buganda. He notes that "The most characteristic element in the revolution was *kusoma*, reading. It was literacy. It was education. It was learning the ways of Europe. It was reading God's Word" (Anderson 1977: 37).

The spread and growth of the new movements—Catholicism, Anglicanism and Islam no doubt threatened the power and authority of the young Kabaka Mwanga who acceded to the throne in October 1884 while only eighteen years old. He was not as adept at controlling and manipulating these forces for his own ends as efficiently and effectively as his own father Kabaka Mutesa had been. His inability to hold the centre, coupled with the unceasing rivalry, hostility and suspicions among all the contending forces led to bloody feuds and scandalous wars of religion. They led to a period of social turbulence and political upheavals, to open clashes and confrontation between the traditionalists and believers of the new faith, between Muslims and Christians and between Christian and Christian, i.e. between Catholics and Anglicans.

These socio-political and religious upheavals had their first toll on the young *bagalagala*. The first to fall on 31 January 1885 as martyrs of this chaotic period were three from Mackay's group of Christian youth, namely Yusufu Lugalama, Marko Kakumba and Nuwa Serwanga. Joseph Mukasa Balikuddembe was the first Catholic to fall as a martyr, on 15 November 1885, apparently for criticizing Kabaka Mwanga for the murder in Busoga on 29 October 1885 of the first Anglican Bishop of East Africa, James Hannington. The day of the Bishop's martyrdom coincided with the day Mackay is reported to have finalized his revised translation of the Gospel of Matthew into Luganda. These horrific murders increased, culminating in the terrible slaughter at Namugongo on June 3, 1886. The blood of these martyrs ensured the spread by leaps and bounds of the new faith.

The Luganda Bible was translated at such a time as this. Some historians have interpreted this eventful period as strategic in the Christianization of Buganda. The "Christian revolution" which is said to have occurred is described as falling into five phases as follows: "a revolution of the 'new dini' (1888), a 'Muslim revolution' (1888–9), a 'Christian Counterrevolution' (1889), a 'Protestant seizure of power' (1892) and finally the consolidation of the revolutionary changes by the British take-over and loss of Buganda's sovereignty (1894/1900)" (Ward 1991: 91). Thereafter Christianity in its Protestant and Catholic forms became a dominant factor in the social and political life not only of Buganda but eventually of the whole of Uganda.

To encourage and promote literacy as well as to help in the spread and establishment of Christianity, translation of the Holy Scriptures was seen as indispensable. The Anglicans led the way. It was Alexander Mackay who pioneered the development of a romanized orthography for Luganda, an orthography which was later refined and developed into the present standard system. This orthography was soon adopted to provide the basis of the literacy programmes of the *bagalagala* and the new Scriptures into Luganda. The use of missionary Arthur Brian Fisher's reading houses and the great interest and enthusiasm for reading among the novice Christians gathered a lot of momentum during this period and their numbers grew, even though it was not clear even then whether there was a corresponding growth in Christian maturity and understanding. It is reported for example that by March 1896, nearly seven thousand people had been baptized as members of the Anglican Church in Buganda while more than 50,000 were actively seeking baptism. This phenomenon obviously provided a great motivation for Bible translation.

The first book of the Bible to be translated and published was the Gospel of Matthew. This was translated by A.M. Mackay and R.P. Ashe. The first 13 chapters of this Gospel were printed in 1886 at the CMS Mission Press at Natete. This became the earliest edition of Scripture in Luganda. The complete text of Matthew was finalized and also printed at the CMS Press at Natete in 1887. It was reprinted in 1888 and in 1890 in response to overwhelming demand for copies from the new readers! Mackay died in February 1890. Concerning this first gospel translated by Mackay, Pilkington wrote:

> A tentative translation of St. Matthew's Gospel was made by Mackay and Ashe, this was printed in the country, eagerly read, and criticized, and revised, reprinted, again revised, and again reprinted, and so on, until a version was produced which was faithful to the original and idiomatic, a splendid piece of work, and a grand basis for future translation (Omulokoli 1995: 3).

The next to appear was the Gospel of John translated by R.P. Ashe and printed privately in 1891 at Wareham in England at the translator's expense. Another edition with the BFBS imprint followed in the same year. In 1892 the Gospel of Mark translated by E.C. Gordon assisted by native speakers was published by the BFBS in London. In the same year, the BFBS published a revised edition of the Gospel of John, revised by A.M. Mackay and after his death in 1890 further revised by E.C. Gordon assisted by Henry Wright Duta Kitaakule and Sembera Mackay. The book of Acts translated by Pilkington assisted by Duta Kitaakule was published also in 1892 by the BFBS, London. This was followed the same year by the publication of the Gospels and Acts in one volume. Romans, Galatians to Colossians, the Book of Revelation, Thessalonians to Philemon, and Jude, all appeared in 1892. These were translated by Pilkington together with his Baganda collaborators. Pilkington thus translated all the books from Acts to Revelation, with the exception of 1 John which was translated by Gordon assisted by Mika Sematimba. Thus, in 1893 the complete New Testament was available in Luganda.

This Luganda New Testament was issued in one volume. The Gospels and Acts, Romans to Hebrews, James to 3 John and James to Revelation were also issued separately. These were all published by the BFBS in 1893.

The cooperation between the CMS translators in Buganda and the BFBS in London continued with more translation and publication of Old Testament books. In 1893 the Old Testament books of Exodus and Joshua translated by Pilkington were published by the BFBS. In 1894 the BFBS published the books of Genesis, Psalms and Daniel, also translated by Pilkington. In 1895 a new edition of the New Testament with corrections made by Pilkington was printed. The books of the Pentateuch translated by Pilkington appeared in 1896 while the entire Old Testament appeared the same year. This was the work of Pilkington except for some of the books of the Minor Prophets which were translated by Crabtree.

As already evident, these CMS missionaries could in no way have translated these books of the Bible without the help and assistance of the native speakers of the language. The missionaries' short stay in the country was not adequate to make them masters or experts of Luganda in all its idiomatic complexities and intricacies, much less in its social and cultural ramifications. They depended greatly on native speakers. Henry Wright Dutamaguzi (Duta) Kitaakule, Sembera Mackay and Mika Sematimba, among native Luganda speakers are noted for their outstanding contribution to the translation of the Luganda Bible. Duta was a product of Bishop Steere's UMCA school in Zanzibar and was therefore equipped to contribute to this great task. It is interesting to note that Duta was "sent out of Uganda in 1881 as a punishment for 'reading,' but was allowed to go down to the coast with Pearson, who arranged for him to be taught in the school of the Universities Mission at Zanzibar" (Tuma and Mutibwa 1978: 96). It is here at Zanzibar that Duta mastered Swahili and thoroughly familiarized himself with the Swahili New Testament. It is not surprising that on his return to Buganda, Duta was as Anderson notes "translating the Swahili Bible into Luganda for preaching and teaching. Pilkington found that the religious terms and phrases had already been worked out by Duta" (Anderson 1977: 39). It can be seen that Duta and even Maftaa before him brought something of the powerful influence of the Zanzibar Swahili Bible upon the Luganda Bible. Pilkington himself alluded to this fact when he observed that:

> For a long time the Swahili New Testament was the textbook of Uganda; Day after day the most intelligent of the Christians translated from it into their own language; Day after day they discussed among themselves the proper rendering of terms, appealing to the European as to the exact force of the original; for years they were occupied in hammering out a version on a native anvil (Omulokoli 1995: 5).

He referred to Swahili as "a temporary bridge, on which to stand to build what, from the first, was recognized as the only permanent bridge between God's thoughts and the native mind, a version in the Ganda tongue itself" (see Omulokoli 1995: 5). The fact that Swahili is a Bantu language obviously had certain advantages and meant that many translational problems of interest to Luganda had already been grappled with and solved in Swahili. This however did not mean that the translators of the Luganda Bible did not have to work through these problems anew. The credit for the complete Luganda Bible which appeared for the first time in 1896 is usually given to George Lawrence Pilkington and to the others mentioned above. Thus although the bulk of the work on the Old Testament and the revision of the New Testament for this complete edition of the Bible is credited to Pilkington, it was quite clear even then that the input of Duta Kitaakule, Sembera Mackay and others could not be denied or belittled.

Anderson writes that "George Pilkington was one of the most sensitive missionaries.[2] He learned Luganda very well. He was close to Africans and understood them far better than most Europeans of his time" (Anderson 1977: 38). For example at an anniversary meeting of the CMS held at Oxford on February 8, 1896, Pilkington had described "the people of Uganda as physically and intellectually strong. Their intellectual strength was illustrated by the way in which they learned to read, by the intelligent interest which they took in the Bible, and by the immense number of their proverbs" (BFBS 1896: 89). Pilkington was thus far better qualified and more suitable

---

[2] George Pilkington was born on June 4, 1865. He had a conversion experience in 1886 while still a student, and graduated with the Cambridge Classical Tripos BA in 1887. He received a call for missionary service and arrived in Buganda in 1890. Pietistic and charismatic in outlook, he became deeply involved in the Christian revival which swept Buganda starting from the 1893–1894 period. He cultivated very close and warm relationships with Baganda Christians. It is no wonder then that it was he who was instrumental in spearheading this Christian revival, a precursor of the *Tukutendereza* revival movement some years later.

for the task of translation than many missionaries who later took up this task. His closeness to the people and his sensitivity, as well as his sense of identification with the people he was serving, eventually led him to his death in 1897 while serving as their chaplain during the Nubian rebellion. The 1896 Luganda Bible is therefore his main legacy to the Buganda mission. As Duta Kitaakule eulogized at his death:

> We sorrow very much, beyond our strength; We do not see among the missionaries whom we have anyone who can fill his place and take on his work. I worked very hard at teaching him Luganda; he learnt it well, and was able to speak Luganda like a native, and could translate any book into Luganda without my help, and I was not afraid of him making any mistakes (Omulokoli 1995: 8).

Andrea Mwaka, Pilkington's Swahili teacher at the coast and Nuwa Kikwabanga his first Luganda teacher as they travelled from the coast to Buganda, were no doubt proud of their pupil's extraordinary success in language learning and his monumental contribution to the translation of the Luganda Bible.

A revised edition of the 1896 Bible appeared in 1899. This was published by the BFBS in London. It was the product of a revision committee consisting mainly of native speakers of Luganda, including Duta Kitaakule, Ham Mukasa, Natanieli Mudeka, Tomaso Senfuma and Bartolomayo Musoke. This team was assisted by Jane E. Chadwick, a CMS missionary. A corrected edition of New Testament appeared in 1914. This was in large type and had *Isa Masiya* altered to *Yesu Kristo*. Some years later in 1968 a new edition of the 1899 text of the complete Bible appeared in a revised orthography prepared by Christopher M.S. Kisosonkole. It was published by the Bible Society in East Africa, Nairobi.

The 1896 Bible and its 1899 and 1968 editions were held by the Catholics to be essentially a Protestant endeavour. The Catholics had of course their own parallel translation which also goes back to the beginning. The founding Catholic missionaries by the same force of circumstances had been led to engage in linguistic study and translation. Thus, Fr. Livinhac had prepared a Luganda grammar, Fr. Girault had translated the catechism while Fr. Lourdel had translated the Gospels for liturgical use. Thus, Catholic translations of the liturgical Gospels and Scripture narratives into Luganda were variously published in 1891, 1892 and 1913. In 1894 the Gospels of Matthew, Mark and Luke translated by members of the Roman

Catholic Uganda Mission were published at the Imprimerie de L'ouvre de Don Bosco, Marseilles, France. In 1896 the Gospel of John was published by the Imprimerie Notre-Dame des Prés, Montreuil-sur-Mer, France. In 1905 another Catholic translation of the Gospels and Acts was published by the Imprimerie des Missionaires d'Afrique at the Maison-Carrée in Algiers, Algeria. Another edition of the Gospels is reported to have been published in 1915. However, the most popular of the Catholic translations is the New Testament done mainly by Fr. Modeste Raux and his colleagues. The Gospel of Matthew in this translation was published in 1933, and the Gospels of Mark to John were published in 1934, Acts in 1936 and Romans to Revelation in 1953. All these were printed locally at the White Fathers Press in Kampala. A revision of the Raux version of the New Testament in Luganda was prepared by J. Muswabuzi, S. Kok, and William Mpuuga. This revised New Testament was published by the Kampala Archdiocese of the Catholic Church in 1968.

In recent times another major effort at producing an ecumenical or interconfessional translation of the Bible into Luganda has been sponsored and promoted by the Bible Society of Uganda. This effort brings together Catholic, Protestant and Orthodox Church representation and contributions aimed at producing a new major translation in common every day, modern Luganda. Publications of this common language inter-confessional translation started appearing with the publication of Mark in 1974, Matthew, Luke and John in 1975, Ephesians in 1977, culminating with the publication of the New Testament in 1979. This new translation is acknowledged by many to be more readable and easily understandable and is likely to appeal much more to the younger generation who have not been brought up on either the Pilkington-Duta version or the Raux version. The Committee responsible for the New Testament translation included Fr. Francis X. Mbaziira (Roman Catholic), Yafeesi Mwanje, Samuel Ssekadde and Christopher Ssenyonjo (Anglican), as well as Archbishop T. Nankyama (Orthodox Church), C. Ssendawula (Seventh Day Adventist) among others, while on the Old Testament those who have contributed include Francis Mbaziira (Roman Catholic), Stephen Keewaza Ssenyonjo (Anglican), John Baptist Ssemwanga (Roman Catholic), Fehekansi L. Nyanzi (Anglican) as well as Edward Kironde (Anglican). Work on the Old Testament has been slowed down by the fluctuations in the availability of full time as well as part time staff actively involved in the work. Work has therefore proceeded at a slower pace despite the fact that readers eagerly await the completion of this Bible in today's common language Luganda.

In conclusion it is worth noting that the place of the Luganda Bible in non-Ganda areas of Uganda is progressively being replaced by translations in the vernacular languages of those areas. The Runyoro-Rutooro Bible of 1912 was the pioneer in this process. It was followed by the Alur Bible in 1936, the Ateso Bible in 1961, Rukiga-Runyankore in 1964, the Lugbara in 1966, the Lango and the Bari in 1979, the Kakwa in 1983 and the Acholi in 1986. New Testaments have also appeared in Karamojong 1974, Madi and Lumasaaba in 1977, Kebu in 1995 and Kupsapiny in 1996. Work on both the Lusoga and Dhopadhola New Testaments is complete and the texts are now in press. They are anxiously awaited! Nonetheless the process represented by the 1896 Luganda Bible is far from over. A number of languages in Ugandan languages are still in need of a Bible. The Bible Society of Uganda and more recently groups such as the Summer Institute of Linguistics/Wycliff Bible Translators are committed and working hard to meet this challenge.

BIBLIOGRAPHY

Anderson, Gwen. "Bringing the Bible to Africa," mimeo at BFBS Library. Swindon.
Anderson, W.B. *The Church in East Africa*. Dodoma: Central Tangayika Press, 1977.
Anderson-Morshead, A.E.M. *The History of the Universities' Mission to Central Africa, Vol. I. 1859-2909*. London: UMCA, 1956.
Baur, John. *2000 Years of Christianity in Africa—an African History, 62-1992*. Nairobi: Paulines Publications, 1994.
British and Foreign Bible Society—Notes and Corresponde Files. Swindon & Cambridge, England: BFBS Offices and Library.
British and Foreign Bible Society. *The Bible Society Reporter*, 88, April. Swindon & Cambridge, England: BFBS Offices and Library, 1896.
Bierman, John. *Dark Safari—The Life behind the Legend of Henry Morton Stanely*. New York: Alfred Knopf, 1990.
Coldham, Geraldine E. (Compiler) *A Bibliography of Scriptures in African Languages, Vols. 1 & 2*. London: BFBS, 1966.
———. *A Bibliography of Scriptures in African Languages, (Supplement 1964-1974)*. London: BFBS, 1975.
Faupel, J.F. *African Holocaust—The Story of the Uganda Martyrs*. London: Geoffrey Chapman, 1962/Nairobi: St. Paul Publications Africa, 1984.
Hansen, Holger-Bernt. *Mission, Church and State in a Colonial Setting—Uganda 1890-1925*. Nairobi: Heinemann Education Books, Ltd., 1984.
Kilaini, Method M.P. *The Catholic Evangelization of Kagera in North-West Tanzania—The Pioneer Period 1892-1912*. Roma: Gregorian Potifical Institute, 1990.
Mojola, Aloo Osotsi. *Bible Translation in East Africa from 1844 to the Present—A General Survey*. Nairobi, Dodoma, Kampala: Bible Societies of Kenya, Tanzania and Uganda, Forthcoming.

Neill, Stephen. *A History of Christian Missions, 2nd Edition.* London: Penguin Books, 1986.

Nida, Eugene, Ed. *The Book of a Thousand Tongues, 2nd Edition.* New York: United Bible Societies, 1972.

Niwagila, Wilson B. *From the Catacomb to A Self-Governing Chruch.* Hamburg: Verlag an der Lottbek, 1991.

Nthamburi, Zablon, Ed. *From Mission to Church—A Handbook of Christianity in East Africa.* Nairobi: Uzima Press, 1991.

Oliver, Roland. *The Missionary Factor in East Africa.* London: Longmans Green, 1952, 1970.

Omulokoli, Watson A.O. "The Contribution of George L. Pilington to Christian Work in Uganda, 1890–1897." Nairobi: Unpublished Typescript, 1995.

Pirouet, Louise. *Black Evangelists—The Spread of Christianity in Uganda, 1891–1914.* London: Rex Collings, 1978.

Scriptures of the World. New York: United Bible Societies, 1995.

Tourigny, Y. *So Abundant a Harvest—The Catholic Church in Uganda, 1879–1979.* London: DLT, 1979.

Tuma, Tom and Mutibwa, Phares. *A Century of Christianity in Uganda*, Nairobi: Uzima Press, 1978.

Twaddle, Michael. *Kakungulu and the Creation of Uganda, 1868–1928.* London: James Currey Ltd., 1993.

Ward, K. "A History of Christianity in Uganda" In Ed. Z. Nthamburi. *From Mission to Church—A Handbook of Christianity in East Africa.* Nairobi: Uzima Press, 1977: 81–112.

"DO YOU *UNDERSTAND* WHAT YOU ARE READING [HEARING]?" (ACTS 8:30): THE TRANSLATION AND CONTEXTUALIZATION OF ISAIAH 52:13–53:12 IN CHITONGA

Ernst Wendland and Salimo Hachibamba

In response to Philip's perhaps unexpected query, the Ethiopian dignitary replied, "How can I, unless someone guides me?" (Acts 8:31a, NRSV). This is the answer that many present-day Tonga Christians must also give as they try to read, or simply listen to, the older version of the Bible published in their language.[1] There is no doubt in their minds that this is indeed the Word of God (*Majwi aa Leza*), but why did he choose to communicate with people in language that is so difficult at times to understand and that often sounds as if God speaks with a "foreign accent?"[2] To be sure, it is with great gratitude that we note that by the end of 1996 at least a portion of the Bible existed in more than 600 of the estimated 2,000 plus languages spoken in Africa, including 250 New Testaments and 133 full Bibles.[3] But many of these Scripture texts are old, and relatively literal, missionary translations, which are often characterized by a form of language that is not completely natural and/or up-to-date in comparison with what is used by the majority of speakers today. In many cases,

---

[1] The *Batonga* people (language: *Chitonga*) number over a million and inhabit as their traditional homeland large parts of the Southern Province in Zambia. The Tonga (for short) are a matrilineal, patrilocal people who may roughly categorized anthropologically as a Southern Bantu, cattle-culture ethnic group. Of course nowadays many Tonga are urban dwellers and engage in various business ventures to earn their living, but the majority still practice farming and herding in rural areas, which include some of the most fertile agricultural areas of Zambia.

[2] We use the third person singular *masculine* pronoun to refer to "God" (as well as to his "servant" in the Isaiah passage) because that is how most receptors view *Leza* in a Tonga socio-religious setting nowadays. This agrees with a Hebrew perspective on the gender of the supreme deity, "Yahweh." Moreover, in the case of any new or unfamiliar text, the unmarked third person pronoun is assumed to be male unless the context clearly and explicitly specifies that a female person is being referred to.

[3] These statistics are from the most recent *World Report* published by the United Bible Societies (Reading, England) March 1997, Number 318, page 4. This list includes 13 vernacular Bibles and 6 Testaments in Zambia.

therefore, Philip's question needs to be seriously repeated, again and again: "Do you [*really*] understand what you are reading—or *hearing* (since most people hear the Bible being read rather than actually reading it for themselves)?"[4] And this must be followed by another, equally important, query depending on one's response to the first: If "Yes," then, "All right, so what does this passage mean in your own words?" This is to check up on the relative completeness and accuracy of one's understanding. But if "No," then, "Why not, what seems to be the problem here?" This is to try to determine what has gone wrong with the communication process—that is, on the part of the sender, the receiver, or both. Why has God's Word failed to convey its intended meaning, and what can be done to set things right?[5]

In this essay we will present a case study to illustrate the importance of questions such as these when evaluating the *quality* of Scripture use in Africa. There is no doubt about the *quantity* of such use, for the Bible in most countries on the continent is an "open book," that is, freely and widely used for a variety of purposes under the broad categories of Christian preaching, teaching, witnessing, personal reading, and private devotion (Mbiti 1986: Chapters 2–4). But what people actually comprehend from their Bibles in terms of the sufficiency

---

[4] This distinction between hearing and reading is especially important in many countries of Africa where *functional*, (that is, the actual, operational) literacy rates are relatively low (despite published government statistics which seem to deny this fact), that is, less than 50% overall and usually less than 40% for women.

[5] It should be pointed out at the beginning of this exercise that we adhere to a relatively conservative, positivistic conception of "meaning" in relation to biblical texts and their contemporary interpretation. This is in distinction to a particular text's "significance," that is, its special relevance or application to readers and hearers today. The difference between these two hermeneutical notions has been well stated by Peter Cotterell: "Behind the [biblical] text stands an author, and editor, a redactor, with some intention lying behind the production of the text. We have no access to that intention, although an understanding of contemporary and cognate languages and cultures, of related texts, of grammar, syntax, and possibly some knowledge of the author might at least indicate what the intention was *not*, and might even indicate what it was. . . . A text cannot carry *any* meaning, but it does carry a meaning *intended* by the original speaker or author, related to the context in which it was generated and the cotext of which it is a part" (1997: 143–144). We do not, however, subscribe to the position that each and every interpretation (of possible text *meaning*) or application (possible text *significance*) is either automatically "right" or "wrong." More often in fact today's interpreters, whether professional or lay, are dealing with a gradient or continuum of hermeneutical possibilities and probabilities, depending on the degree of scholarly consensus on the meaning (content and function) of the passage in question, their own knowledge of the biblical text and context, and their current communicative purpose, interest, setting, and so forth.

and accuracy of information is at times open to serious question. So we will take a relatively well known portion of the text—that is, the climactic "suffering Servant" periscope from Isaiah, namely, 52:13–53:12 in the older Tonga version (published in 1963, the NT in 1949)—and interrogate it. In other words, we go through this passage from beginning to end, verse by verse, and select a number of the major critical questions that the text raises from the perspective of an "average" (rural, lay, Christian) reader or listener.[6] We will briefly comment on the nature of the various problems involved and suggest some possible solutions, both textual (translational) and extra-textual (supplementary), with special reference to the new "popular-language," meaning-oriented translation of the Bible that has just been published (1996).[7]

It is agreed that for most, if not all, Christians a "Philip"—whether in the person of an individual fellow believer, a scholarly colleague, or the church at large—will always be necessary for the purposes of correction, clarification, instruction, guidance, and encouragement.[8] But the issue that we wish to address here is simply this: What can *reasonably* be done—that is, without compromising either the limitations

---

[6] In addition to our Bible translation work, each of the authors has been engaged in a multi-leveled teaching and pastoral ministry in both urban and rural Zambia in several language areas for some thirty years. Therefore we have both interacted extensively with "average" (lay, ordinary, non-professional) Tonga (and other Bantu) interpreters in these three principal settings: the local parish, a Bible institute and seminary classroom, as well as various translation-team field locations. Our joint perception of how "average" receptors *most probably* understand the Tonga translation of Isaiah 52:13–53:12 is thus based upon the actual presentation of this particular passage in diverse public fora as well as on our participation in similar hermeneutical-communicative "events" with regard to many other analogous biblical texts over the years. The dialogic nature of this process of "text-sharing" naturally varies according to the setting, but in all cases the contribution of the lay majority is *essential* for the success of any given venture—with respect to both matters of "fact" and also those involving potential problem points.

[7] For an overview of the basic translation principles and procedures that guided the production of this Bible, one may consult Wendland (1998), which deals with a comparable version in Chichewa of Malawi, or more generally, Nida & Taber (1969) and de Waard & Nida (1986).

[8] There are a number of Tonga proverbs that highlight the value of mutual interaction with regard to all types of learning experience. This includes one's understanding of a particular verbal text, whether oral or written, traditional or modern, for example: *yakila munzila, bakubule beenda* "build [your house] along a pathway, let passers-by make you wise," *sibbuzya takolwi bowa* "the one who asks [questions] does not get poisoned by a mushroom," *mulonga watakazyolwa, wakabula makoba* "a river that does not wind, [in its course] does not have steep banks" (i.e., a person who is not prepared to receive, and act upon, good advice often goes astray/is unstable).

of publishing resources or the conservative theological character of the Tonga constituency—both inside and outside the printed text to promote a more comprehensive or accurate grasp of certain rather difficult portions or passages of the Bible as they are being read, whether aloud or silently to oneself?[9] Due to the limitations of space, the respective older (TOB) and newer (TNB) Tonga versions that are cited as examples will be given in relatively literal English only, except for certain key vernacular words and phrases. Furthermore, it will not be possible to go into details during this presentation: the particular problem in question will simply be pointed out and concisely explained with reference to one or more available means of resolution. Various difficulties pertaining to language and culture will not be separated in the discussion since in many cases they are very closely related and must be dealt with together within the scope of a given translation text. The specific verse from Isaiah under consideration will be indicated by an underlined reference number at the beginning of each section. English Scripture text citations are from the New Revised Standard Version (NRSV) unless indicated otherwise.

52:13

The first major problem for the listener (reader) is one which recurs throughout the Hebrew prophets in particular and that is: *who* is speaking the words of this verse, as well as those which follow? Is it the prophet, Isaiah, God (or "the LORD," *Yahweh*), or some other, unnamed person? It is important to clarify this because the reference of all of the text's first-person pronouns ("I," "me," etc.) depends on this identification. Trained Bible readers can look back to the preceding verse and deduce that the speaker and referent (antecedent) of "my" in v. 13 is "the LORD" of v. 12. But such an inference is not so easy to make for unskilled readers and pure listeners of the passage, for two reasons: the references to God in v. 12 are in the

---

[9] The notion of a "more accurate" interpretation or exposition of a given verbal text is certainly not a foreign (Western) imposed or an imported one. Hermeneutical correctness and precision ("right" versus "wrong"), with regard to both understanding and application, were (and still are) required or expected for a variety of traditional Tonga language-communication events, such as, royal directives, judicial decisions, rites of divination (*kuuma kwacisolo*), the revelation of dreams (*kupandulula ziloto*), the interpretation of the esoteric utterances of spirit-possessed persons (*bamasyabe*), and the cryptic predictions of prophets (*basinsimi*).

third person, not the first. And a major sectional break occurs between verses 12 and 13, and therefore they are not often taken together in most public readings of the Scriptures. In many cases, a medial section heading or title does not help since this does not usually reveal the speaker either, for example, "The Suffering Servant" (NRSV, *Good News Bible* (GNB)). In order to resolve this difficulty, the TNB introduces this pericope with the words, "In this way speaks Chief-God saying . . ."[10]

The TOB uses the word *mulanda* to render the key term "servant" for which Tonga does not seem to have an indigenous equivalent (the closest is *mugwasyi* "helper"). The problem with *mulanda* is its rather negative connotation, that is, a "slave," a person who was either captured in war or sold in payment for a personal or famil-ial debt. So why would God, the LORD, engage such unfortunate people in his service? The TNB employs *mubelesi* "work-person" (male/female), a loanword from the Lozi language. While this is cer-tainly more appropriate in this context than *mulanda*, it still gives a somewhat misleading impression of the nature and role of this par-ticular "servant of the LORD." In this case, *mwiiminizi* "representa-tive" (ambassador) would perhaps fit better, also according to biblical Hebrew usage, and it would further serve to heighten the shame of this person's total rejection by the majority of his own people (53:3).

In the TOB it is somewhat surprisingly reported that this divine "slave" will literally "get lucky" (*-jana coolwe*, NRSV "prosper"). Thus his elevation is purely a matter of chance, and God has nothing to do with it. The question that the present prediction then raises, for many listeners, is this: How would such an amazing turn of events take place? In a strictly earthly setting (which is all that is suggested by the present passage) the following references to being "raised up" and "honoured" would seem to denote the miraculous obtaining of a well-paying, executive type of urban job, perhaps as the head of a major company or manufacturing firm. As already indicated, the

---

[10] The TNB renders the Hebrew divine tetragrammaton (*hwhy/YHWH*), "Yahweh" ("LORD" in most English Bibles), as *Mwami Leza* "Chief-God" instead of *Jehova* as found in the TOB. "Jehovah" has a foreign, sometimes even colonialistic ("European") sound to it because, as far as most people are concerned, this name comes from the English language. The two terms that comprise the compound designation *Mwami Leza* would be ambiguous as references to "Yahweh" if used alone. But when spoken in conjunction with one another, they constitute a natural, easy-sound-ing designation of the distinct, and personal covenant God of Israel.

TNB clearly connects the servant's elevation in status to the LORD's pronouncement and activity. Nothing is left to "chance." Instead, he will "be successful in" or "carry through to completion" (*-zwidilila*) some activity on the behalf of (implied) *Mwami Leza*.

52:14

This verse, together with v. 15, presents the special difficulty of inter-clausal transition and semantic complexity, which is another one of the main challenges presented by Hebrew prophetic writing. The problem this passage poses for most listeners is simple: How does it all fit together? They don't get the point. The TOB, following the (N)RSV, translates vv. 14–15 as a single overly-long sentence, one that contains a prominent parenthesis in the middle covering the second half of v. 14. Such a large chunk is indeed hard to mentally "process," or comprehend, as one reads along. Therefore, it is broken up into four shorter, more manageable utterances in the TNB, while the disruptive parenthesis is removed and recomposed as an independent unit. That still presents the challenge of clarifying the distinct connections between the various clause (or poetic "colon") segments of the sequence of ideas found in these verses, which has also tested the skills of many commentators.[11] Instead of the comparative notion, "Just as . . ." (NRSV, TOB, TNB—*Mbubonya mbuli*) at the beginning of v. 14, a contrastive pair of temporal expressions may be a better way to establish the basic twofold effect-to-cause linkage of ideas in these verses. Thus v. 14 would begin with "Formerly" (*Kaindi*) or "At first" (*Cakusanguna*) in order to relate to a time prior to the servant's exaltation mentioned in v. 13. Verse 15 would start with "So then" (*Nkaako*) or "As a result" (*Aboobo*, TNB) with specific reference to the amazing ultimate effects of the servant's humiliation recorded in v. 14.

Among the Tonga it is culturally inappropriate to laugh at or call attention to a person's ugliness or physical deformity as seems to be the case in v. 14. The literal equivalent of "Behold!" from v. 13 in both the TOB and TNB appears to suggest this scenario with *Amubone!*

---

[11] One of the clearest exegetical presentations of this entire segment (52:13–15) is found in Motyer 1993: 424–426. Within the confines of this essay, it is not possible to analyze the detailed structure or hermeneutics of this passage (or any other) on the basis of the original Hebrew text.

"May you (plural) see"; better perhaps would be *Masimpe!* "Truly."[12] Such behavior is in effect despising God (*Leza*), the ultimate Creator of all human beings. If someone were born either deformed, lame, or "with an appearance more ugly than anyone else on earth" (TOB), the practice of sorcery would be suspected. For example, a father magically utilizes the power of his unborn child's body part in order to "energize" a charm for making him wealthy. The guilty party in such cases would be identified by means of divination. However, if a person were disfigured later in life, it would be viewed as the result of punishment for some personal crime against society, such as adultery, or less likely nowadays, as a "scapegoat" to pay for some communally-significant violation provoked by one or more members of an entire family or clan, like stealing cattle.[13] In any case, an explanatory footnote would be helpful (as in a future edition of the TNB) to point out that none of the preceding "culturalised" interpretations are applicable with regard to this passage.

52:15

The paradoxical pair of parallel statements found in the second half of this verse are made even more difficult to understand in the TOB due to its literal rendering. Thus, people ask: Why will "chiefs" (*bami*) "be silent" (*bayooumuna*) because of God's servant? And how does someone "see," (*-bona*) a "spoken news report" (*makani*)? In the TNB a culturally appropriate gesture is employed to indicate the chiefs' great shock, they will "grab/cover their mouths" (*bayoojata kumulomo*) when they see him. The proverbial quality of the final two utterances seem to point to some "unique truth" of theological significance (Motyer 1993: 426). They may be utilized here to heighten

---

[12] The structural importance of this Hebrew attention-grabbing particle (*hinnēh*) is outlined in Motyer 1993: 423–424. Both the TOB and the TNB also suggest that the LORD's servant was a very ugly person in terms of his natural form or appearance. It thus needs to be pointed out (in a footnote) that such disfigurement was inflicted upon this servant at a special time of suffering/persecution, most likely in connection with his priestly-sacrificial work of "sprinkling" (cleansing) the nations (see Motyer 1993: 425–426, Barker 1985: 1094).

[13] From an indigenous Tonga point of view, it would be much more relevant to present the (life) story of Christ beginning with his passion, which is the most significant aspect of his existence here on earth. One would then work back to his earlier years, including his birth, in order to see how these preceding events led up to, or even caused, his death at the hands of his own people. The subsequent story of his resurrection and exultation presents distinct interpretational problems of its own (see below).

the enigmatic nature of the preceding verses, which juxtapose references to the exaltation (v. 13) and humiliation (v. 14) of the LORD's ambassador. In order to formally mark such usage, the traditional verbal introduction to a riddle (*kalabi*) might be used in the TNB: *Nkaako* "There it is!" in place of the present causal connective (*Nkaambo* "for").

53:1

Another serious ambiguity in pronominal reference leads off this second portion ("stanza") of the so-called "Servant Song" (the stanzas are 52:13–15, 53:1–3, 4–6, 7–9, 10–12). Listeners wonder: To whom does the "we" of "*our* message" refer? Is it the prophet himself (speaking in the "editorial plural"), the prophet and his prophetic colleagues, the prophet and his fellow countrymen/women in general (if rendered "what we have heard" NRSV, see also GNB), or even the gentiles (speaking as a distinct group, note the preceding verse)? A footnote is probably necessary to designate the second choice, that is, the communal "prophetic voice," as the most likely interpretation in this case (see 52:7). And what is this "message"? Most likely what the prophet reported in stanza one as the TNB indicates, "these things we have spoken." This is a matter of personal "belief" (*-syoma*, TNB), not mere assent, as the TOB suggests with its rendering: "So who agreed with (*-zumina*) our story?"

Mention of "the arm of Jehovah" being "revealed" (TOB) causes considerable perplexity for most hearers: How can any part of God, who is a *spiritual* being, be physically seen by any human? And what is so special about the arm itself? Like most peoples, the Tonga employ various picturesque anthropomorphic expressions to designate certain outstanding characteristics and activities of the traditional God *Leza*. Note, for example, the prominent *female* component in these praise names which laud God's gracious preservation of his people: *Nacoombe* "Mrs. Cow" and *Namakolomakolo* "She of many breasts."[14] But nothing of this nature is ever said about God's "arm" (*kuboko*). The TNB partially clarifies the most likely sense with its rendering, "To whom has Chief-God shown his powers?"[15]

---

[14] The gender of God (*Leza*) in an ancient traditional context is a matter of debate, perhaps it was not even an issue at all. Nowadays, however, after a century of Christian influence, the divine image is definitely male-oriented.

[15] Motyer (427) makes a good case for understanding "arm of the LORD" as a metonymic reference to God himself in the person of his chosen Servant (52:13, see also 51:9).

The implication of each of the two rhetorical questions found in this verse is quite different. The self-understood answer to the initial challenge is "No one!" But that will not work in the case of the less obvious second query, which is probably best construed as an implicit critical comment on the first question. In other words, those ("Everyone!" in fact) who have already witnessed the LORD's powerful deeds of deliverance *should have* believed what the prophetic messengers reported. This interconnected relationship will have to be pointed out in future editions of the TNB to avoid such confusion. This is preferably done within the translation itself, for example, by changing the second question into an emphatic direct statement. Alternatively, the necessary clarification may be effected through the use of an explanatory footnote.

53:2

The first ambiguous pronoun, "he" (TOB), is rendered explicitly in the TNB as "that worker/servant of his (God's)," while the second, "him" (TOB), is replaced by its referent "God" in order to prevent any misunderstanding. The shoot/root imagery used to describe the LORD's servant is misleading to many who live in a Tonga environmental setting. The original biblical similes would suggest "the miserable nature of the conditions in the midst of which the servant's life was lived" (Young 1972: 342, see Isaiah 6:13, 11:1). For the Tonga, however, it is only natural to expect a root to spring up out of hard, dry ground, for this is what happens every September before the onset of the annual rains. In fact, such prolific growth is a good sign which points ahead to the promise of another season of life-giving "water from God." Such a clash in connotations thus needs to be pointed out in a footnote. Another possible erroneous notion that may require a similar mode of correction involves widespread beliefs concerning "witchcraft/sorcery" (*bulozi*). If a green shoot were to spring up out of the "dry ground" which constituted the floor of one's house, then this would be taken as a clear "sign" that the owner was a practising "witch/sorcerer" (*mulozi*). The literal expression "that we should desire him" (NRSV, TOB) at the end of this verse must be reworded in order to avoid any unwanted sexual overtones. The problem is that the Tonga verb "want/desire" (*-yanda*) also means "like/love" depending on the context. The TNB employed a nice idiom here to circumvent this potential difficulty: "to attract our hearts" (*kututolela moyo*).

53:3

Local cultural conditioning again enters in to complicate the sad picture being portrayed by the prophet here. This concerns in particular the average person's understanding of the comment that God's servant was "one from whom others hide their faces." What does this mean? For one thing, "others" (TOB *kubantu* "to people," TNB *abantu* "by people") wrongly indicates a group that is different from those referred to by the pronouns "we" occurring both before and after. Secondly, only a woman would exhibit such behavior of avoidance, and that would be if she were sexually attracted to the man in whose presence she was or to whom she were talking. Thus a literal translation, besides sounding out of place in this passage, gives entirely the wrong impression. Finally, even though literalism is avoided, one must still be careful how one conveys the intended idea in Tonga. The TOB's *uusesemya* "disgusting" goes too far in suggesting that the servant's body was full of smelly, pussy sores. Thus the TNB opted for *uulisenza* "degraded," that is, somebody whom you avoid looking at because she or he is disreputable, uncouth, or in some other aspect socially inferior.

53:4

The TOB unfortunately introduces an anthropomorphism into its translation: "the hand of God brought sufferings to him" (see v. 1). But how can this be, many listeners ask. The "hands" (pl.) of God may be used figuratively in a positive sense with reference to God's relationship with human beings, for example, "we are in his hands" (protection), but there is no negative counterpart. God can be said to punish an impious person by "striking" him/her (*kumuuma*), but no body part is mentioned in connection with such punitive action, for example, for disregarding tribal customs or ignoring the ancestral spirits.

These ancient, but persistent, religious beliefs may need further elaboration in a footnote of some kind. Thus when an entire family or clan has committed a serious crime against sacred tradition or the ancestors, such as failing to offer appropriate worship and thanksgiving after a good rainy season and harvest, then some innocent individual of the younger generation will be afflicted with a life-threatening disease. This serves as a warning that things need to be rectified by a communal sacrificial ritual, or death could result. On the other hand, if a person is suddenly "stricken" or made to suffer on account of a certain secret crime that she or he committed against someone else, then this would be construed (through divination) as some form of magical punishment, inflicted by the wronged party by means of a protective potion or security charm. The TNB adds "[struck] *by God*" to eliminate the latter interpretation as a possibility.

53:5

One question for information that is sometimes occasioned by the text of the TOB results from a rendering that is overly general. Thus in this verse "the punishment that made us whole" turns out to read "to help us is the reason for his being beaten with a whip/stick." But "help" in what way, people ask, since there would be any number of possibilities? The TNB states this notion as "his suffering is that which brought us peace," for "peace" (*luumuno*, from the verb "to be quiet, at rest") is the closest that one can come to the sense of the rich Hebrew term found in the original, *shalom* "wholeness, well-being."

53:6

Here we are often asked one of the most crucial queries of all: what are "sheep" really like? These animals are not traditionally herded by the Tonga, and many people have never even seen a sheep because they tend to be restricted to the vicinity of large commercial farms and ranches. The word used to translate "sheep," *mbelele*, is strangely related to the expression used to refer to the indigenous "pangolin" *cibbata-mbelele*, the spotted variety of which is believed to bring good luck to a person who happens to find one and bring it home to the village. The ominous significance of sheep "going astray" is therefore also unfamiliar to most listeners, especially in view of the next line which states that these sheep ("we") each had its own "path" to follow. Hence some comment on the cultural background of the biblical text would again seem to be needed in a footnote, along with an illustration (if possible) of a sheep or herd of them. The much more familiar "goat" (*impongo*) cannot be utilized as a clarifying "local equivalent" in this case for two major reasons: because of the importance of sheep in the overall biblical setting and record, and due to the undesirable connotations connected with goats, especially males, such as being unruly, destructive of crops, and sexually (over)active.

The notion of a "scapegoat" implicit in this verse (note the possible allusion to Leviticus 16:21–22) is well known in traditional Tonga religious practice. Thus a substitutionary, sacrificial animal bearing the sin(s) and/or disease(s) of society may be prepared by ritual and sent out into the bush and far away from the village to remove from the vicinity some aggrieved or avenging spirit (*cizwa*). However, the particular creature used for this purpose is quite different, namely, a chicken. This is because the latter will not find its way back home to bring a curse back upon the community, like some larger animal (such as, a goat, dog, or even a cow) would do. Another important variation from the biblical sense in this context concerns the notion of a *human* scapegoat to atone for some communal crime or offense before God (*Leza*), which is unknown in Tonga indigenous religion. The closest local correspondent unfortunately involves the practice of witchcraft, where a "witch/sorcerer" (*mulozi*) will maliciously and surreptitiously utilize the "life-force" (*muuya*) of a close family member in order to empower a certain charm for *self*-protection or to enable some sorcerous activity for the purpose of personal enrichment. In this case of course the innocent "substitute" is completely unwilling while the agent, and beneficiary, is made guilty by means of such nefarious, antisocial action. Therefore, in view of the potential disparity and consequent confusion with respect to both form and function in the present context, the desired biblical concept of vicarious sacrifice (with reference also to the foundational "atonement" ritual of Leviticus 16) might well deserve some exposition in a note because of its importance to the prophetic imagery which appears especially in this and the following verse.

53:7

It would be helpful for listeners to repeat at the beginning of this new stanza in the lament (as also at verses 4 and 10) a mention of the primary referent, namely, the "servant of God/the LORD." This was done at least in verse 2 in the TNB, but not thereafter. Such clarification is needed especially in longer passages where there is a shift in subject, as in verses 4, 6, 9, and also in cases where it is likely that only a portion of a well-known pericope like this might be read, such as verses 4–6 for a sermon text.

In addition to the sheep-related imagery (silence, slaughtered, sheared), which is very unfamiliar to most Tonga receptors, this verse introduces another important picture that is made more difficult (also for the Ethiopian official, Acts 8:32–33) due to its implicit nature.

Here then we have depicted the setting of a trial of capital offense before a court of law (see verse 8, Motyer 1993: 433, Young 1972: 351). It is a strange situation indeed, for the individual being accused—one who is like a "sheep" (reference here to a "*little* sheep/lamb" in both the TOB and TNB merely muddies the waters of interpretation)—refuses to "open his lip" (TOB) or "speak a word" (TNB), either in protest or to defend himself. Such deliberate "silence," appropriately reinforced by an ideophone *zii*! (TNB), in a traditional Tonga judicial setting is not only disrespectful, it would be regarded as a clear indication of one's guilt. A person who behaved in this manner would most likely be found guilty anyway by means of ritual divination (for example, by "throwing bones"). In any case, the whole complex scenario portrayed by this passage is completely missed by the majority of uninstructed listeners. Thus, the original scene, sense, and significance of the biblical text-in-context needs to be explained in a footnote in order to facilitate at least a partial communication of the most probable meaning.

53:8
In this instance both the TOB and TNB give listeners an initial, misleading impression of how the trial of the "servant-lamb" was conducted. TOB has "he was denied a good judgment," namely, a satisfactory outcome with regard to his sentence or fine, while TNB says that "they arrested him by force and indicted him." The latter could easily be corrected by the addition of a compound adjectival modifier to give the desired prominence: *uutakwe mulandu kakunyina akaambo* "[he] having no case, without anything objectionable (against him)" strengthened by *uululeme* "upright" in the next poetic line. The literalism of the TOB raises further problems of comprehension for the listener, for example: "he was carried away" (but to which place?), "who among his agemates" (were only they concerned?), "he was removed from the land of the living" (does this mean he was taken to heaven, for even the remembered ancestral spirits are believed to inhabit the same "land" as their living relatives?), "he was beaten" (is that all that happened to him?). In fact, there is nothing in the TOB translation which states that the person being persecuted was actually killed. All these queries are clarified in the TNB along the lines of (but not exactly the same as) the GNB.

There is one point where the TNB may be improved in the interest of greater accuracy, and that is at the final pronominal reference of this verse, literally, *"my* people" (as in the TOB), which is rendered as *"our* people" (as in the GNB). Indeed, the pronoun here is somewhat problematic, but it is also likely to be significant because a less common singular form is used, one which last appeared way back at the beginning of the pericope in 52:13. There it referred to "the LORD," and that is the probable antecedent in 53:8 as well (Young 1972: 352), though a weaker case could be made for it being the prophet himself (Motyer 1993: 435). A less obtrusive way of conveying the first interpretation would be by means of a third-person designation, for example, "the people of Yahweh/God."

53:9

The entire content of this verse is culturally unfamiliar to Tonga thinking. In the first place, if there is one thing that people do not discuss, it is *death* or being buried, so as not to risk angering the newly emergent spirit (*muzimo*) of the deceased. Such verbal circumspection is all the more important if the person is not dead yet, which would be the case if this passage is regarded as predictive prophecy. Thus the very words of the first part of this verse cause a certain uneasiness to fall upon many hearers. Secondly, no person, not even the dreaded and detested "witch/sorcerer" (*mulozi*), is regarded as "evil" anymore, *after* she or he has died. Hence it sounds quite inappropriate to say that someone was "buried together with wicked persons," as in both TOB and TNB (GNB's "evil *men*" is even more strange-sounding, see also verse 12). The TOB is made more difficult by an overt mismatch in its rendering: in the first line it is stated that "he" (whoever that is) was placed in a grave along with *evildoers,* while the very next line says that "he was buried with a rich man." So which is it—one or many? To be sure, the Hebrew text is itself quite difficult at this point, but it would be more helpful (as in the TNB) to avoid what appears to be an obvious contradiction in the text and to employ a footnote to explain the key hermeneutical issues involved. The TNB further clarifies this passage—for hearers of the text in particular, but also for readers—by breaking up the single overly long sentence into three shorter ones and by making explicit the semantic relationship between its two distinct halves. This is done by means of the transitional expression *Zyakaba oobu nikuba kuti* "Things happened in this way even though . . ."

Thus the essential theological *enigma* of the divine servant's innocent suffering and death is more patently preserved as a key to one's understanding this entire pericope.

53:10

The initial conjunction *Pele* "But" in the TOB (Hebrew *waw*) not only distorts the semantic linkage between verses 9 and 10, but it also blurs the structural fact that a new stanza begins here. Better in this case is to leave the transition unmarked (TNB), especially since the compositional links of this stanza are stronger in relation to the first (52:13–15) and third (53:4–6) units within the "servant song" as a whole (Motyer 1993: 436–437).

The expression "he will see his descendants" (*uyoobona lunyungu lwakwe*, TOB/TNB) is viewed as a very good outcome from a traditional Tonga perspective. It means that the person will live to see his grandchildren, which is certainly not the norm in a region where the average life-expectancy was only about 45 years, even before the onset of AIDS. However, the underlying spiritual sense in this context needs to be pointed out in a footnote, namely, that this refers to the blessed benefits of the suffering servant's vicarious activities which have been so vividly described in the two preceding stanzas (verses 4–6, 7–9). Also worth a comment here is the likely reference to life after death (with a resurrection implied) for the martyred servant, namely, in the expression "[he] shall prolong his days" (TNT: *akuyooongolola* "and [he] will [live to] be bent over [in his back].").[16]

The TOB's opaque literal translation of the final clause of this verse, "and the plans of Jehovah will go forward in his hands," is another good example of "God-language" (*mulaka wa Leza*). That is

---

[16] There is naturally a strong hermeneutical debate over this issue. The problem is that if the servant does not rise to live again, then there is another direct contradiction in the text, that is, first the servant dies (v. 10ab) and then he lives a long-enough life to see his descendants (v. 10c, see GNB's translation). The Messianic Servant's eternal rule has been clearly prophesied elsewhere in the book (for example, 9:7), and so it should not be surprising to see another allusion here (see Motyer 1993: 440, Young 1972: 355–356). However, the conceptual difficulty of life after death in an indigenous Tonga thought-world also needs to be briefly addressed. Simply put, this concerns the belief that in order for a vicarious self-sacrifice on behalf of the clan or wider community to be valid and efficacious in the estimation of the ancestral spirits, the martyr would have to remain dead! This is because any sort of personal "resurrection" after death is attributed to the practice of witchcraft, either deliberately on the part of the individual involved or due to someone who had "bewitched" him/her.

to say, these words must mean something because they are found in God's holy book, but their sense is not immediately apparent to most listeners. The TNB renders this as, "and so through him the will/love (either sense would fit here) of Chief-God is brought to its completion/fulfillment."

53:11

It would be helpful for the sake of most hearers of the Word to introduce this verse with an explicit mention of the speaker, for example, "The LORD says . . ." (see 52:13, and note the GNB at 53:10). Otherwise, the first-person pronouns in this and the following verse might not be understood as referring to God, which would consequently present certain problems of interpretation, such as, who is performing the action ("allotting") of v. 12a.

The translation of the TOB raises an important, but misleading question for some receptors: "He will see fruit" (*Uyoobona micelo*). So what sort of "fruit" is being spoken about here? A literal understanding, that is, fruit from a tree, is supported by the following verb *uyookuta* "he will be [physically] filled." But how would this fit into the present context? Another possible meaning would be a metaphoric one, namely, "children." While such a construal seems to make sense in the light of v. 10, it is not really supported by the Hebrew text, which appears to be an idiom, as rendered by the TNB, "he [the servant of Chief-God] will see/experience its goodness/benefits (*bubotu*, namely, of his suffering and death), and he will be satisfied (*uyoolamwa*)."

It would be preferable in both the TOB and TNB to present a chronologically-based order of events in the final part of this verse in order to clarify the underlying cause-effect relationship. That is to say, "[my servant] shall bear their iniquities" (the means) and "[he] shall *make* many righteous" (the result) may be more accurately rendered as "he will *provide* righteousness *for* many people" (Motyer 1993: 442).

53:12

Both the TNB and the even more literal TOB provoke some serious questions in the minds of a traditional Tonga audience: What kind of "portion" (*caabilo*) is being referred to here? Who are the "elders" (*bapati*) with whom the LORD's servant is going to have to share his portion? From whom were the mentioned battle "spoils" (*zisaalo*) taken? And who are the "strong ones" (*basintanze*) who will be "divided out" (*-abanya*) along with these spoils? There are too many questions raised by the unexpected military imagery and not nearly enough contextual information available to provide an adequate framework for properly understanding the first part of this verse, which consequently sounds almost proverbial in style (see 52:15). Only an explanatory footnote will do in the case of such a heavy concentration of unfamiliar concepts which are conveyed by an equally uncommon collocation of lexical items. But at least the TNB does indicate the discourse-climactic nature of this verse by breaking it up into five distinct utterances. The poem's close is made especially prominent and stylistically pleasing in Tonga by means of a final staccato-like series of asyndetic *waka* "he did" verbal constructions. This dramatic sequence neatly summarizes the servant's sacrificial offering of himself for the sake of "many"—which in a Bantu, collectively-oriented context would most certainly incorporate the entire community.

In conclusion, this illustrative exercise in translation, interpretation, and comprehension has shown that the actual understanding of "average" Bible receptors is not a matter that can be taken for granted or ignored, even with regard to such a well-known pericope as Isaiah 53. Many different questions are raised by the text when people honestly attempt to assess their level of comprehension based on what they are reading or hearing. The preceding comments on this pericope have also indicated that it is not possible to deal adequately with all of the queries evoked by a particular passage of Scripture within the translation itself, that is, by changing from a literal to a more dynamic, meaning-oriented rendering. This is especially true where issues of a socio-cultural, ecological, and historical nature are concerned, whether these pertain to the life and times of the biblical peoples or to south-central Bantu of the present day. Thus we saw quite a few instances where the situationally more remote message of the Bible may be misunderstood or misinterpreted in the light of a familiar traditional African world-view and way-of-life.[17]

---

[17] The nature and degree of "misunderstanding" in any hermeneutical situation must be determined on the basis of commonly accepted methods and norms of biblical exegesis and also with reference to the generally established "framework" (or range) of interpretation that is applied to a particular passage. This problem of limited Scripture understanding is not confined to Africa of course. It is rather ironic in this modern age of ever-increasing communication skills and access to var-

What is needed in such cases is a sympathetic "Philip" sitting beside the reader or hearer, someone who can anticipate potential problem spots and ask, "Do you *really* understand what you are reading?" Then, on the basis of a mutually engaging dialogue with one another in relation to the verse in question, such a facilitator would be prepared to offer whatever guidance and enlightenment that may be needed with regard to the original text and context. It was further suggested that in the absence of such a live on-the-spot commentator, a more heavily annotated translated version, or "study Bible," may be able to provide an appreciable measure of assistance by opening up, as it were, the original sense and contemporary significance of the passage under consideration. Such a study tool would still require an initial "reader" (teacher, pastor, evangelist), first to comprehend and then to meaningfully transmit to listeners the information supplied in these notes. But at least the resource would be already prepared and immediately available whenever necessary.

In closing, it remains to call attention to the essential role that the "average receptors" (hearers/readers) play in any successful hermeneutical-communication event. They are the ones who—in genuine, give-and-take dialogic sessions of Bible study—initially reveal many of the possible problems to be found in a given pericope. They suggested in turn some of the diverse ways in which a problematic biblical text may be understood within the context of an indigenous belief-system and customary lifestyle. In many cases they also call attention to a particular interpretation or perspective that the "trained" exegete or instructor had not even realized was present, whether implicitly or as commonly construed by the general public. Finally, and perhaps most important, it is up to "ordinary Christians" to help their study leaders (pastors, teachers, etc.) to formulate the most meaningful and socially significant way of conveying the intended

---

ious mass media that the average level of Bible "literacy" appears to be decreasing in many constituencies of Christendom where a high standard of formal education prevails. To be sure, there is a lot of preaching and teaching going on nowadays, but this does not seem to be contributing to people's overall knowledge of the Bible and its message to a corresponding degree, if at all. While a hard-to-understand translation may explain some of this difficulty, it is only part of the answer. As one possible solution to this universal problem, we would suggest a greater effort to promote text and context-related, expository and interactive Scripture-study programmes in all churches. These courses would be aimed at distinguishing and also bridging the crucial conceptual gap between the world and culture presupposed in the biblical books and the corresponding situational life-setting of receptor peoples today.

message of God's Word in their own mother-tongue and life-setting (either or both of which may differ from that of their instructor). The Church needs to devote itself to the mutually interactive and stimulating task of preparing carefully contextualized, culturally sensitive, and locally relevant Scriptures, as it enters upon a new millennium of Christian communication.

BIBLIOGRAPHY

Barker, Kenneth, Ed. *The NIV Study Bible*. Grand Rapids: Zondervan.
Cotterell, Peter. "Literature, Interpretation, and Theology." In Ed. Willem A. Van Gemeren *New International Dictionary of Old Testament Theology & Exegesis: Volume 1*, Grand Rapids: Zondervan, 1997: 103–160.
Mbiti, John S. *Bible and Theology in African Christianity*. Nairobi: Oxford University Press, 1986.
Motyer, Alex. *The Prophecy of Isaiah*. Leicester: Inter-Varsity Press, 1993.
Nida, Eugene A. and Taber, Charles. *The Theory and Practice of Translation*. Leiden: E.J. Brill, 1969.
de Waard, Jan and Nida, Eugene A. *From One Language to Another: Functional Equivalence in Bible Translating*. Nashville: Thomas Nelson, 1986.
Wendland, Ernst R. *"Buku Loyera": An Introduction to the New Chichewa Translation of the Bible*. Zomba: Kachere Books, 1998.
Young, Edward J. *The Book of Isaiah*, vol. III. Grand Rapids: Eerdmans Publishing Co., 1972.

THE KISWAHILI *MWANA WA MTU* AND THE GREEK *HO HUIOS TOU ANTHRÔPOU*

Jean Claude Loba Mkole

A Translator's Handbook prepared under the auspices of the United Bible Societies has strongly warned the translators about the meaning and translation of *ho huios tou anthrôpou* (Bratcher & Nida 1961: 81):

> In order that the meaning of the phrase, as used by Jesus in the Gospels, be properly carried over into modern languages, it is necessary either literally to translate the words as a Christian technical term, a title, "The Son of man," or else use some phrase or title that will convey if possible a (messianic) sense of dignity, authority, and responsibility.

The authors argue that any translation which would equate the title merely with man or a human being is strictly to be avoided (Bratcher & Nida 1961: 81). In this they disagree with Geza Vermes (1967: 310–328) who has demonstrated that "son of man" was used neither in Judaism nor by Jesus as a messianic title, and agree with an article published by the Summer Institute of Linguistics which appealed to translators to consider "son of man" as "the heavenly Messiah" (Hill 1983: 37–38). For Hill, the component of humanity in the "son of man," while present, is nonetheless not central: "It is in the Son of Man as the heavenly Messiah that we find the central emphasis of the title" (Hill 1983: 38).

In Kiswahili *ho huios tou anthrôpou* has been rendered by *mwana wa mtu* (son/daughter of human being). The translators, guided by translators' helps, or by some exegetes, did not hesitate to attribute the messianic meaning to the "son of man" expression. In a note on Matthew 8:20, the Catholic *Biblia Takatifu* (Holy Bible) published in 1986 by Verbum Bible in Bukavu (Zaire/Congo) explains the meaning of "son of man" as a messianic title. In the Inter-confessional *Biblia* (Bible) conjointly published in 1995 in Dodoma (Tanzania) and Nairobi (Kenya), "son of man" is explained as a name or title used by Jesus in the line of his messianic secret. So, whereas the Catholic *Biblia Takatifu* of Zaire understands "son of man" as a messianic title, the Interconfessional *Biblia* of Tanzania and Kenya seems to consider "son of man" as a secret or hidden messianic title (compare with the "verborgene Menschensohn" of Sjöberg 1955). In any case, the Kiswahili translations attribute a messianic understanding to the "son of man" phrase. However, this article intends to show that the messianic meaning is conveyed neither by the Greek *ho huios tou anthrôpou* nor by the Kiswahili *mwana wa mtu*. We will first consider the meaning of *mwana wa mtu* in Kiswahili and then the meaning of *ho huios tou anthrôpou* in the Greek New Testament.

In spite of the warning of the Translator's Handbook's, the Kiswahili *mwana wa mtu* is neither a literal translation of *ho huios tou anthrôpou* nor a messianic designation. On the literal or syntactical level, it is impossible for the Kiswahili language to render word-for-word the Greek *ho huios tou anthrôpou*. In English and French, it is possible to literally translate *ho huios tou anthrôpou* by *the son of the man* or *le fils de l'homme* because both languages can use the definite article. The definite articles *ho* (nominative) and *tou* (genitive) cannot be translated into Kiswahili simply because this language has no articles (Heylen 1977: 46.57). The articles (*ho* and *tou*) which give the phrase *ho huios tou anthrôpou* the sense of a definite name or title are not translatable. Therefore, the Kiswahili *mwana wa mtu* literally corresponds not to the Greek *ho huios tou anthrôpou* but to *huios anthrôpou* which does not have a messianic meaning either in the Septuagint or in the Greek New Testament. Another literal feature which differentiates *mwana wa mtu* from *ho huios tou anthrôpou* concerns the gender. In Greek *huios* belongs to the masculine gender and can be translated only by "son" or "a son." In Kiswahili, the word *mwana* is inclusive. It is used for masculine and for feminine gender as well. Whereas *ho huios tou anthrôpou* or *huios anthrôpou* indicates a son in Greek, in Kiswahili *mwana wa mtu* denotes a son or a daughter, a man or a woman.

Mwana wa mtu is not a messianic designation. In Kiswahili, *mwana wa mtu* does not mean a Messiah but a human being (a man or a woman). It indicates a human being in opposition to other beings (God, animals, vegetables, minerals). Other synonyms of *mwana wa mtu* in Kiswahili are *mbinadamu, mwanadamu, mtoto wa mtu* or *mtoto wa watu*, and *mtu*. The first two expressions both have a Semitic origin. *Mbinadamu* comes from the Hebrew *ben Adam* (son of humankind, a man). In *mwanadamu*, the Hebrew word *ben* (son) has been replaced by the Kiswahili *mwana* which has the advantage of designating both a son or a daughter (a man or a woman). *Mtoto wa mtu* literally means "child of humankind." *Mtoto wa watu* or *Mtoto ya bhatu* in

Kingwana (a Kiswahili dialect spoken in Bunia/North-Eastern Democratic Republic of Congo) is an idiomatic phrase. Though it can be translated into English as "son or daughter of men" (*watu* being the plural of *mtu*), it just means a human person like others. It is used to refer to every human being, to the speaker or to an implied third person. For example, the sentence *Mtoto wa watu hajali* can be understood as follows: "a human being does not care" (generic and indefinite sense), "I do not care" (circumlocutional sense), "he or she does not care" (definite sense).

In Lingala, which is a Bantu language like Kiswahili, *mwana/mtoto wa mtu* or *mwana/mtoto wa watu* have their equivalents in *mwana ya moto* or *mwana ya bhato*. The Lingala *mwana ya moto* is often used in Congolese (ex-Zairean) musical literature. The most interesting example is found in the song *La beaute d'une femme* from the singer Mbilia Bel where *mwana ya moto* ("son or daughter of a man or a woman," a human being) is used in opposition with *mwana ya Nzambe* ("son or daughter of God," an extra-ordinary person): *Nakanisaki ozali mwana ya Nzambe nzoka ozali mwana ya moto lokola ngai* ("I thought you were the daughter of God whereas you are a daughter of a man or woman like me.") This song's female author is singing against her rival.

Mtu also is used in Kiswahili in an inclusive sense of a human being, male or female. In sum, the Kiswahili *mwana wa mtu* is a synonym of *mbinadamu*, *mwanadamu*, *mtoto wa watu*, or *mtu*. All refer in Kiswahili to a human being and not to a Messiah. For the latter, the Kiswahili speaker uses the transliteration *Masiya*. *Mwana wa mtu* in Kiswahili has no messianic connotation but simply translates the Greek *huios anthrôpou* which is not a messianic title. Like *mbinadamu*, *mwanadamu*, *mtoto wa mtu* or *mtu*, it means a human being (a male or a female). Given this analysis, is *mwana wa mtu* an appropriate translation of the Greek *ho huios tou anthrôpou*? We turn now to the Greek phrase.

The expression *ho huios tou anthrôpou* is not known in Classical Greek. It is especially used in the New Testament where it appears 81 times in the Gospels (30/14/25/13). Apart from the Gospels, it is found in Acts 7:56. In all occurrences, it is used only by the speaker Jesus, except in John 12:34 and in Acts 7:56. Many studies have demonstrated that this expression is a translation or a transliteration of a Semitic original. "It is accepted that the expression used in the Gospels is not a genuine Greek idiom but the literal translation or mistranslation, of a Semitic Original, the Aramaic *bar nāsh* or *bar nāshā*" (Vermes 1967: 310, see also Colpe 1969: 404, Jeremias 1971: 248, Perrot 1979: 243, Bietenhard 1981: 266). In Aramaic literature, this expression occurs in different forms and states. As far as the forms are concerned, this idiom is written in one or two words. Written in two words it appears in two forms: *bar nāshā* with alef and *bar nāsh* without alef. While scholars differ on the relationship between these forms (Vermes 1967: 316–317, Fitzmyer 1979: 62, Svedlund 1974: 21–22), there is agreement that whether written in one or two words, with or without alef, the idiom has the same meaning. The Aramaic idiom also appears in two main states: the absolute or indefinite state *bar nāsh* and the definite or emphatic state *bar nāshā*. Casey (1987: 27–28) speaks of three states taking into account the construct state. Again, the different states, particularly given Kümmel's argument that the difference between the definite and indefinite states gradually broke down (1984: 160), though they might introduce some nuances, do not affect the meaning.

The expression *bar nāsh(ā)*, no matter its form and state, means a human being: "Aramaic *bar enash* evidently means nothing more than 'human person'" (de Moor 1980: 430), though it does refer to the human being in three aspects (Ternier 1991: 121). In the generic sense the idiom is used for "every human being" (Meyer 1896: 93, Dalman 1930: 194, Fiebig 1901: 57, 76, Campbell 1947: 132, Bowman 1947/48: 283). In the indefinite sense the idiom indicates "someone" or "some people" (Lietzmann 1896: 38). In the circumlocutional sense it refers to the speaker like another Aramaic idiom *hāhū gabrā* and has the same function as "I" (Meyer 1896: 93, Vermes 1967: 327–328). In the case of the circumlocutional use, there are three kinds of auto-designation or auto-reference: an exclusive auto-reference, an inclusive auto-reference and an idiomatic auto-reference. The exclusive auto-reference occurs when the speaker only refers to himself (Vermes 1967: 327). The inclusive auto-reference signifies when the speaker refers to himself and to all others human beings (Casey 1976: 147, 1979: 226, 1985: 3, 6, 1991: 18, 42, 1994: 89, 117). And the idiomatic auto-reference applies when the speaker refers to himself and to a group of persons of his position (Lindars 1983: 23–24).

As far as New Testament *ho huios tou anthrôpou* is concerned, exegetes' opinions differ about its authenticity and meaning. They generally subdivide the expression into three categories: earthly "son of man"

sayings (Mark 2:10, 28 and parallels), suffering "son of man" sayings (Mark 8:31, 9, 12, 10:33 and parallels) and eschatological "son
of man" sayings (Mark 8:38, 13:26, 14:62 and par.). Concerning
authenticity, some think that none of the "son of man" sayings is
authentic, that they are the creation of early Christian communities
(Käsemann 1954/56: 256, Vielhauer 1957/1965: 61, 80, Conzelmann
1957: 281, Perrin 1966: 78). For other exegetes the majority of the
"son of man" sayings are authentic because they are not confessional. They are most of the time uttered by Jesus himself and no
Christian community would dare to create such sayings (Hooker
1967: 191, Cullmann 1957: 158, Marshall 1966: 350, Schmidt &
Silva 1994: 94). Some consider the eschatological sayings as authentic, because of the apparent distinction between the coming "son of
man" and Jesus (Bultmann 1948/84: 30, Tödt 1958: 61, 313, Borsch
1992: 144, Vögtle 1994: 11). Schweizer (1959: 74) supports the
authenticity of earthly sayings and Pesch (1975: 195) gives preference to the passion sayings. Other critics (Vermes 1973: 182, Casey
1979: 236, Lindars 1983: 24) consider as authentic only the sayings
which keep the idiomatic sense of the Aramaic *bar nāsh(ā)*. Frankly,
there is no consensus about the authenticity of the "son of man"
saying.

Coming to the meaning of the phrase, many exegetes attribute a
messianic meaning to the New Testament *ho huios tou anthrôpou*
(Bultmann 1984: 3, 4, 34, Sjöberg 1955: 241, Cullmann 1957: 138,
Higgins 1964: 202, Schnakenburg 1986: 125, Marshall 1965/66: 350,
Hooker 1967: 192, Kuzenzama 1990: 76, Burkett 1991: 170). For
Bultmann the messianic "son of man" was expected not only by the
Jews but also by Jesus himself. On this point concerning a "son of
man" different from Jesus, Bultmann did not get a lot of support
from other exegetes. Others held a more nuanced position. For them,
the distinction is not between two persons but between two functions or two states of the same person (Vielhauer 1965: 107,
Conzelmann and Lindemann 1987: 110, Lohse 1984: 49, Vögtle
1994: 147–148). The messianic meaning of the "son of man" expression is supported by a many exegetes in view of texts like Daniel
7:13, the Parables of Enoch 46–71 and 4 Ezra. But, I do not find
these sources convincing. The reference in Daniel 7:13 is not a messianic title but a symbolic comparison, *kᵉbar ʾĕnāš* meaning "like a
son of man" (Joüon 1930: 601, see also Coppens 1981: 256). Regarding
the Parables of Henoch, not only has its pre-Christian or Judaic

origin not been proven yet, but also the only existing text in an Ethiopic version does not present a messianic figure called "The son of man." The figure is called by different expressions (Charles 1893: 128, Kuzenzama 1990: 17, Charlesworth 1985: 89). In 1 Enoch 46:2, 3, 4, 48:2 he is called *walda sab'* (*filius hominis*, "son of a human being"), in 1 Enoch 69:29, 71:14 he is designated by *walda be'si* (*filius viri*, "son of a male human being"), in 1 Enoch 69:29 he is portrayed as *walda be'sit* (*filius mulieri*, "son of a female human being"), and in 1 Enoch 62:7, 9, 14, 63:11, 69:26, 27, 70:1, 71:17 he is named *walda 'eguāla 'emma ḥeyāw* (*filius prolis matris viventium*, "son from the spring of the living mother"). All these different Ethiopic translations show that the figure is a human being. Finally, the book of 4 Ezra 13 cannot offer confident evidence because it belongs to the Christian era (Coppens 1983: 168, 183, Koch 1993: 80).

With a number of other scholars who have investigated the Aramaic background of this expression (Lievestad 1982: 234, Bietenhard 1982: 337, Haag 1992: 167) I would argue that the New Testament *ho huios tou anthrôpou* is not a messianic designation but an idiom meaning "a man" (Manson 1931/55: 211–212, Hare 1983: 258, Schwarz 1986: 14, 323–324, Casey 1995: 182). Furthermore, examining the expression in different contexts of the New Testament, we notice that in all "son of man" sayings where Jesus is presented as the locutor, the "son of man" phrase is interchangeable with the first person singular personal pronoun (Formesyn 1966: 27–29). The redactional work of the other Gospels attests this interchangeability. *Ho huios tou anthrôpou* in Mark 8:38 (Luke 12:8, 9:26) has been replaced by the personal pronoun, first person singular in Matthew 10:32. *Ho huios tou anthrôpou* in Mark 9:31 becomes the personal pronoun, third person singular in Matthew 16:21 (the third person is used here because of the indirect speech). The personal pronoun, first person singular in Mark 8:27 has changed into *ho huios tou anthrôpou* in Matthew 16:13.

Considering the particular context of "son of man" sayings in the gospel of Mark, we may notice that the phrase is not used as a messianic title as such but as an important human component of the understanding of Jesus' person. The human being component is necessary for the understanding of the "son of man" expression. The example of 14:62 can suffice for the illustration. The formulation *kai opsesthe ton hion tou anthrôpou* and *kai opsesthe me . . .* basically has the same signification, for both refer to the same locutor. But the expression "son of man" tells more about the locutor. Not only does it refer to the locutor Jesus but it also specifies him as a human being. This aspect becomes more important in the context of 14:62 whereby Jesus has just affirmed with *ego eimi* to be the Christ, the son of God. By using "son of man" instead of "me" he claims to be not only the Christ, the son of God, but also a human being. In doing so he completes the understanding of his Christhood which the high priest's question has only limited to divine sonship. Therefore the *kai* in the second part of 14:62 is not a simple conjunction device, but serves to provide additional information concerning precisely the humanity of Jesus. With the expression "son of man," Mark underlines Jesus' human nature as he does with "Son of God" when he wants to affirm his divine sonship. Though Jesus is confessed as "Son of God" on several occasions, Mark also depicts him as human, "son of man"—from his earthly activity until his eschatological manifestation, through his passion and resurrection.

There is no linguistic or theological reason for translating or understanding *ho huios tou anthrôpou* as a messianic title. Linguistically, the Aramaic background explains this expression as an idiom meaning nothing other than a human being. Theologically, the human nature of Jesus has to be affirmed. The Kiswahili *mwana wa mtu* is not a literal, but it is an accurate, translation of the intended meaning of the New Testament *ho huios tou anthrôpou*.

BIBLIOGRAPHY

Biblia. Habari Njema. Dodoma-Nairobi, 1995.
Biblia Takatifu. Bukavu, 1986.
Bietenhard, H. "Der Menschensohn—ho huios tou anthrôpou. Sprachliche und religionsgeschichtliche Untersuchungen zu einem Begriff der synoptischen Evangelien I. Sprachlicher und religionsgeschichtlicher Teil." *Aufstieg und Niedergang der Römischen Welt* II.25.1 (1982): 265–350.
Bowman, T. "The Background of the term 'Son of Man.'" *The Expository Times* 59 (1947/48): 283–288.
Bratcher, R.G. & Nida, E.A. *A Translator's Handbook on the Gospel of Mark.* Leiden: United Bible Societies, 1961.
Bultmann, R. *Theologie des Neuen Testaments.* Thbingen: Mohr, 1948, 1984.
Burkett, D. *The Son of Man in the Gospel of John.* Sheffield: JSOT, 1991.
Campbell, J.Y. "The Origin and the Meaning of the Term Son of Man." *The Journal of Theological Studies* 48 (1947): 145–155, also In Ed. J.Y. Campbell, *Three New Testament Studies. Republished and Presented to Him by His Friends with an Appreciation.* Leiden: Brill, 1965: 29–40.

Casey, M. "The Son of Man Problem." *Zeitschrift für die neutestamentliche Wissenschaft und die Kunde der ältern Kirche* 67 (1976): 147–154, Also In Ed. M. Casey, *Son of Man. The Interpretation and Influence of Daniel 7.* London: Routledge, 1979: 224–240.

———. *Son of Man. The Interpretation and Influence of Daniel 7.* London: Routledge, 1979.

———. "Aramaic Idiom and Son of Man Sayings." *The Expository Times* 96 (1984/85): 233–236.

———. "The Jackals and Son of Man (Matt 8.20/Luke 9.58)." *Journal for the Study of the New Testament* 23 (1985): 3–22.

———. "General, Generic and Indefinite: The Use of the Term 'Son of Man' in Aramaic Sources and in the Teaching of Jesus." *Journal for the Study of the New Testament* 29 (1987): 21–56.

———. "Method in our Madness, and Madness in their Methods: Some Approaches to the Son of Man Problem in Recent Scholarship." *Journal for the Study of the New Testament* 42 (1991): 17–43.

———. "The Use of the Term bar (e)nash(a) in the Aramaic Translations of the Hebrew Bible." *Journal for the Study of the New Testament* 54 (1994): 87–118.

———. "Idiom and Translation: Some Aspects of Son of Man Problem." *New Testament Studies* 41 (1995): 164–182.

Charles, R.H. *Book of Enoch. Translated from Prof. Dillmann's Ethiopic Text.* London: SPCK, 1893.

Charlesworth, J.H. *The Old Testament Pseudepigrapha* I. London: Darton, Longman and Todd, 1983.

Conzelmann, H. "Gegenwart und Zukunft in der synoptischen Tradition." *Zeitschrift für Theologie und Kirche* 54 (1957): 277–296.

Conzelmann, H. & Lindemann, A. *Grundriss der Theologie des Neuen Testaments,* Munich: Kaiser, ⁴1987.

Colpe, C. "Ho huios tou anthrôpou." *Theologisches Wörterbuch zum Neuen Testament* 8 (1969): 403–487.

Coppens, J. *La relève apocalyptique du messianisme royal. III: Le Fils de l'homme néotesta-mentaire.* Leuven, 1981.

———. *La relève apocalyptique du messianisme royal II. Le Fils d'homme vétéro- et interte-stamentaire.* Leuven, 1983.

Dalman, G. *Die Worte Jesu mit Berücksichtigung des nachkanonischen jüdischen Schriftums und der aramaeischen Sprache erörtet I: Einleitung und wichtige Begriffe.* Leipzig, 1898, ²1930.

de Moor, J.C. "An Incantation Against Evil Spirits/Ras Ibn Hani 78/20." *UF* 12 (1980): 429–432.

Ellington, J. "'Son of Man' and Contextual Translation." *The Bible Translator* 40 (1989): 201–208.

Ellingworth, P. "Translating 'The Son of Man': A Response." *The Bible Translator* 48 (1997): 109–113.

Fiebig, P. *Der Menschensohn. Jesu Selbstbezeichnung mit besonderer Berücksichtigung des aramäischen Sprachgebrauchs für "Mensch."* Tübingen-Leipzig, 1901.

Fitzmyer J.A. "The Contribution of Qumran to the Study of the New Testament." *New Testament Studies* 20 (1974): 382–407.

———. "Another View of the 'Son of Man' Debate." *Journal for the Study of the New Testament* 4 (1979): 58–68.

Formysyn, R.E.C. "Was there a Pronominal Connection for the 'Bar Nasha' Self-designation?" *Novum Testamentum* 8 (1966): 1–35.

Haag, E. "Der Menschensohn und die Heiligen (des) Höchsten. Eine literar-, form- und traditionsgeschichtliche Studie zu Daniel 7." In Ed. A.S. van der Woude, *The Book of Daniel in the Light of New Findings.* Leuven: Leuven University Press, 1993: 137–186.

Hare, D.R.A. *The Son of Man Tradition.* Minneapolis: Fortress, 1990.

Higgins, A.J.B. *Jesus and the Son of Man.* London: SCM, 1964, Philadephia: Fortress, 1965.
———. *The Son of Man in the Teaching of Jesus.* Cambridge: Cambridge University Press, 1980.
Hill, R. "Futher Considerations on Translating 'The Son of Man.'" *Notes on Translation* 93 (1983): 35–51.
Hooker, M.D. *The Son of Man in Mark. A Study of the Background of the Term "Son of Man" and its Use in Mark's Gospel.* London: SPCK, 1967.
Jackson F.J.K. & Lake, K. *The Beginning of the Christianity* I. London: Macmillan, 1920.
Jeremias, J. *Neutestamentliche Theologie I: Die Verkündigung Jesu.* Ghtersloch: Gerd Mohn, 1971/1973.
Joüon, P. *L'évangile de Notre Seigneur Jésus-Christ. Traduction et commentaire du texte original grec, compte tenu du substrat sémitique.* Paris, 1930.
Käsemann, E. "Sätze heiligen Rechtes im Neuen Testament." *New Testament Studies* 1 (1954/56): 248–260.
Kearns, R. *Vorfragen zur Christologie I: Morphologische und semasiologische Studie zur Vorgeschichte eines christologischen Hoheitstitels.* Tübingen: Mohr, 1978.
Koch, K. "Messias und Menschensohn. Die zweistufige Messianologie der jüngeren Apokalyptik." *Jahrbuch für Biblische Theologie* 8 (1993): 73–102.
Kümmel, W.G. "Jesus der Menschensohn." *Sitzungsberichte der Wissenschaftliche Gesellschaft an der J.W.G.—Univarsität Frankfurt* 20/3 (1984): 147–188.
Kuzenzama, K.P.M. *Le titre johannique du Fils de l'homme. Essai lexicographique.* Kinshasa: Facultés Catholique de Kinshasa 1990.
Leivestad, R. "Jesus—Messias—Menschensohn. Die jüdischen Heilandserwartungen zur Zeit der ersten römischen Kaiser und die Frage nach dem messianischen Selbstbewusstein Jesu." *Aufstieg und Niedergang der Römischen Welt* II.25.1 (1982): 220–264.
Lietzmann, H. *Der Menschensohn. Ein Beitrag zur neutestamentlichen Theologie.* Freiburg im Breisgau: Herder, 1896.
Lindars, B. *Jesus Son of Man. A Fresh Examination of the Son of Man Sayings in the Gospels in the Light of Recent Research.* London: SPCK, 1983.
Lohse, E. *Grundriss der neutestamentlicher Theologie.* Stuttgart: Kohlmann, 1984.
Manson, T.W. *The Teaching of Jesus. Studies of its Form and Content.* Cambridge: Cambridge University Press, 1931/1955.
Marshall, I.H. "The Synoptic Son of Man Sayings in Recent Discussion," *New Testament Studies* 12 (1965/66): 327–351 also In Ed. I.H. Marshall, *Jesus the Saviour. Studies in New Testament Theology.* Downers Grove: InterVarsity, 1990: 73–99.
Marshall, I.H. "The Synoptic 'Son of Man' Sayings in the Light of Linguistic Study." In Eds T.E. Schmidt & M. Silva, *To tell the Mystery. Essays on New Testament Eschatology in Honour of R.H. Gundry*, Sheffield, JSOT, 1994: 72–94.
Meyer, A. *Jesu Muttersprache. Das galiläische Aramäisch in seiner Bedeutung für die Erklärung der Reden Jesu und der Evangelien überhaupt.* Freiburg-Leipzig, 1896.
Nida, E.A. & Louw, J.P. *Lexical Semantics of the Greek New Testament.* Atlanta: Scholars Press, 1992.
Perrin, N. "The Son of Man in Ancient Judaism and Primitive Christianity." *Biblical Research* 11 (1966): 17–28, also In Ed. N. Perrin, *A Modern Pilgrimage in New Testament Christology.* Philadelphia: Fortress, 1974: 84–93.
———. "The Creative Use of the Son of Man Traditions by Mark," In Ed. N. Perrin, *A Modern Pilgrimage in New Testament Christology.* Philadelphia: Fortress, 1974: 84–93.
Perrot, C. *Jésus et l'histoire.* Paris, 1979.
Pesch, R. "Die Passion des Menschensohnes. Eine Studie zu den Menschensohnworten der vormarkinischen Passionsgeschichte." In Eds R. Pesch et al. *Jesus und der Menschensohn.* Freiburg im Breisgau: Herder, 1975: 166–195.

Schnackenburg, R. "Der Menschensohn im Johannesevangelium." *New Testament Studies* 11 (1965): 123–137.

———. *Die Person Jesu Christi im Spiegel der vier Evangelien.* Freiburg-Basel-Wien: Herder, 1986.

Schwarz, G. *Jesus "der Menschensohn." Aramaistische Untersuchungen zu den synoptischen Menschensohnworten Jesu.* Stuttgart: Kohlmann, 1986.

Schweizer, E. "Der Menschensohn (Zur eschatologische Erwartung Jesu)." *Zeitschrift für die Neutestamentliche Wissenschaft und die Kunde der äaltern Kirche* 50 (1959): 185–209 also "The Son of Man." *Journal of Biblical Literature* 79 (1960): 119–129 and In Ed. E. Scweizer *Neotestamentica. Deutsche und Englische Aufsätze 1951–1963.* Zhrich: Zwingli, 1963: 93–104.

Sjöberg, E. *Der verborgene Menschensohn in den Evangelien.* Lund: Lund University Press, 1955.

Svedlund, G. *Aramaic Portions of the Pesiqta de Rab Kahana.* Uppsala, 1974.

Taylor, J.E. "Ho huios tou anthrôpou, 'The Son of Man': Some Remarks on an Androcentric Convention of Translation." *The Bible Translator* 48 (1997): 101–109.

Ternier, A. "Een eeuw filologisch onderzoek naar de term 'mensenzoon.'" Leuven: Unpublished Licenciate Thesis, 1991.

Tödt, H.E. *Der Menschensohn in der synoptischen Überlieferung.* Ghtersloh: Gerd Mohn, 1959/⁴1978.

Vermes, G. "The Use of Bar nash/Bar nasha in Jewish Aramaic" In Ed. M. Black, *An Aramaic Approach to the Gospels and Acts,* Oxford: Oxford University Press, ³1967: 310–328.

———. *Jesus the Jew.* London: Fontana/Collins, 1995.

Vielhauer, P. "Gottesreich und Menschensohn in der Verkündigung Jesu," In Ed. W. Schneemelcher, *Festschrift G. Dehn zum 75. Geburtstag am 18. April 1957 dargebracht von der Evangelisch-Theologischen Fakultät der Rheinischen Friedrich Wilhelms-Universität zu Bonn.* Neukirchen, 1957 also In Ed. P. Vielhauer *Aufsätze zum Neuen Testament,* Mhnchen: Kaiser, 1965: 55–91.

———. "Jesus und der Menschensohn. Zur Diskussion mit Heinz Eduard Tödt und Eduard Schweizer," *Zeitschrift für Theologie und Kirche* 60 (1963): 133–177, also In Ed. P. Vielhauer, *Aufsätze zum Neuen Testament.* München: Kaiser, 1965: 92–140.

Vögtle, A. *Die Gretchenfrage des Menschensohn-problems. Bilanz und Perspektive.* Freiburg-Basel-Wien: Herder, 1994.

PART FOUR

REDRAWING THE BOUNDARIES OF THE BIBLE IN AFRICA

AFRICA IN THE OLD TESTAMENT

Knut Holter

Africa in the Old Testament, to many Old Testament readers, in Africa as well as outside, this topic may sound rather exotic. Few have thought of the idea that the ancient texts of the Old Testament have anything to say about Africa. However, to other readers, mainly in Africa or in the African diaspora, this topic touches existential questions, the place of Africa in the Old Testament is related to their identity as well as their history. Accordingly, whether the topic is seen as exotic or existential, depends on the eyes that see. The present essay acknowledges this and takes sides, it is consciously written from the perspective that a closer study of what the ancient texts of the Old Testament say about Africa is of importance for its contemporary African readers.

The presentation and discussion of the topic Africa in the Old Testament will be done in three steps. First, an introductory section, which aims to clarify some definitions and the background and material of this enterprise. Then follows the major section, which makes a textual survey of how some African nations and even some African individuals are portrayed throughout the Old Testament. And finally, a brief summary of the findings, noting some hermeneutical questions.

Let us start with a definition of the two terms "Old Testament" and "Africa." First, while the term "Old Testament" may seem relatively unproblematic (except to those who would prefer the designation "Hebrew Bible," though this is seldom used in Africa), referring in the minds of most scholars to the Masoretic canon, this understanding is not without problems, as no less than two broader canons, competing with the Masoretic one, have their background in Africa: The Alexandrian and the Ethiopian. Just what constitutes the Old Testament, has been problematised, and some have argued that African translations of the Old Testament and hence also African interpretations of the Old Testament should follow the broader African canons (Kealy 1979: 13–26). I raise this concern, but will not develop it. My focus is on the second term, "Africa." The term "Africa" usually designates the African continent. But this understanding is not without its difficulties as well. One problem is what we are to do with Egypt: Is it appropriate to say that ancient Egypt was an African nation? Would it not be more accurate to say that it belonged to the Ancient Near East? Another related problem is what to do with the areas surrounding the Red Sea: Is it appropriate to distinguish between an African and an Arabian side (see Yorke 1995: 150)? Is it not so, that such a distinction just demonstrates the problems of approaching ancient sources with modern geographical and carto-graphic concepts? We will return to some of these problems later. Still, in this article "Africa" refers to the African continent.

Only a brief glance into the current scholarly literature on the Old Testament is enough to realize that traditional western Old Testament scholarship has not shown much interest in the portrayal of Africa in the Old Testament. On the contrary, western literature on the Old Testament, from Bible atlases and histories of Israel to dictionaries and commentaries, has been accused of reflecting a more or less deliberate de-Africanization. African nations such as Egypt and even Cush, it has been argued, are either located in the so-called Ancient Near East rather than in Africa, or their cultural influence on ancient Israel is neglected (see Bailey 1991: 165–168). However, the picture is probably somewhat more complex. Some of the western reluctance might be an understandable reaction to some-times fanciful attempts at drawing lines between Africa and the Old Testament, for example the identification in the late 19th century of the newly discovered wealth of Zimbabwe with Old Testament Ophir (see North 1967: 200). However, several western Old Testament scholars have actually shown some interest in drawing lines between Africa and the Old Testament, in a few cases this was directly due to their encounter with the African interest in this topic (see, e.g. Anderson 1995: 45–46). However, it should be admitted that the quest for an analysis of the Old Testament portrayal of Africa has not been, and is still not, regarded as a priority within traditional western Old Testament scholarship.

However, within parts of African and African American Old Testament scholarship the situation is quite the opposite, though with some terminological (and ideological) differences. Whereas the for-mer tend to talk about an African presence in the Old Testament, the latter tend to talk about a black presence. Whatever this pres-ence is called, attempts at giving it a scholarly description have been made from the early 1970s and throughout the 1980s and 90s by

Africans such as Engelbert Mveng and David T. Adamo, and African Americans such as Robert A. Bennet and Charles B. Copher and Alvin A. Jackson (see Mveng 1972: 23–39, Adamo 1998, Bennet 1971: 483–500, Copher 1993, Jackson 1994). Of special importance here is the contribution made by the Nigerian scholar David T. Adamo. In a number of studies he has focussed on the Old Testament references to Cush, arguing that these reflect close connections between ancient Israel and Africa (see Adamo's works listed in the bibliography, most recently Adamo 1998, see also Høyland 1998).

Adamo's focus on Cush demonstrates the need for a clarification of which geographical entities referred to by the Old Testament can, with some certainty, be located on the continent of Africa. This is necessary in order to define the relevant material for the present study of the Old Testament portrayal of Africa. The relevant geographical entities can be grouped into three categories: those referring to Egypt, those referring to Cush, and then a number of different entities with fewer references or more uncertain location. Before I discuss each of these in detail, some comments on the relationship between the references to Egypt and Cush may be useful. From a numerical point of view the approximately 680 references to Egypt (see Even-Shoshan 1993: 700–703) reflect a closer focus than the 56 references to Cush/Cushi (30/26, see Even-Shoshan 1993: 527). Further, the proportional relationship between the two is not the same throughout the Old Testament. The Law has six references to Cush and approximately 350 to Egypt, the Prophets have 33 (Former: 8, Latter: 25) to Cush and approximately 280 to Egypt (Former: 80, Latter: 200), and the Writings have 17 to Cush and approximately 50 to Egypt. However, in my search for the Old Testament portrayal of Africa, Cush will receive an attention equal to that of Egypt, for two reasons. First, the Old Testament portrayal of Cush echoes aspects of Africa and Africans that go beyond the geographical, cultural, and anthropological borders of Egypt and further into Africa. Secondly, African and African American scholars in their search for Africa in the Old Testament have focussed strongly on Cush as a representative for Africa.

Let us then proceed to the textual survey, searching for the Old Testament portrayal of the three groups pointed out above. We will start with Egypt, whose location in the north-eastern corner of the African continent made it a bridge, both geographically and culturally, between the Ancient Near East and Africa. Traditionally, scholars have emphasized the relationship between Egypt and the Ancient Near East. In recent years, however, one has become increasingly aware of its African heritage. On the one hand, the geographical source for the peopling of the Egyptian Nile Valley seems to have been predominantly African, rather than European or Near Eastern (see Keita 1993: 129–154), and, on the other hand, the civilization formed here was "to an extent usually not recognized, fundamentally African. The evidence of both language and culture reveals these African roots" (Ehret 1996: 25). Also ancient Israel had a long history of contact with its mighty neighbour in the south (for a survey, see Williams 1977: 492–505). The approximately 680 references to Egypt in the Old Testament vividly demonstrate this contact (see Pfeifer 1995, a recent contribution that probably goes too far in emphasizing the historicity of the literary portrayal of the Old Testament with regard to this contact, is Currid 1997). Still, in the African and African American search for the portrayal of Africa in the Old Testament the traditions related to Egypt have only occasionally been included (see Bennet 1971: 483–500, Copher 1993: 45–65). This is mainly due to a definition of Africa that emphasizes "the area inhabited by black Africans in the south of the Sahara" (Adamo 1986: 5, see also Mveng 1972: 23–39, Sempiore 1993: 17–29), rather than the African continent as a whole, as is the case in this essay.

Starting with the pentateuchal portrayal of Egypt, we find that it is linked, first and foremost, to the traditions of Israel's sojourn in what is called "the land of slavery" (see Exodus 13:3) or "the iron-smelting furnace" (see Deuteronomy 4:20). These expressions reflect central aspects of the narrative traditions about the experiences in Egypt. Negatively, the traditions emphasize the experience of suffering and humiliation (see Exodus 1–11), and positively, they locate the experience of suffering and struggle as the background for the experience of YHWH's salvation (see Exodus 12–14). The importance of these traditions is also seen in that they are reflected in central pentateuchal creeds and formulas. The creed in Deuteronomy 26:5–10 presents the Egyptians as the ones who "ill-treated us and made us suffer, putting us to hard labour" (v. 6), the Deuteronomy variant of the Sabbath commandment reminds Israel that "you were slaves in Egypt" (Deuteronomy 5:15), and both variants of the Decalogue present YHWH as the one who "brought you out of Egypt, out of the land of slavery" (Exodus 20:2, Deuteronomy 5:6).

A closer study of the Pentateuch shows a number of other more positive portrayals of Egypt. One aspect of this is Egypt as an asylum for refugees who had to flee Israel due to famine or political problems (see Cogan 1996: 65–70). This image of Egypt frequently comes up in the patriarchal narratives. Abraham went down to Egypt due to a famine in Canaan (Genesis 12:10), and during another famine Isaac needed a special command from YHWH not to seek help in Egypt (Genesis 26:2). Joseph collected food throughout seven years of abundance in Egypt (Genesis 41:41–57), and thereby not only the Egyptians, but also Jacob and his family survived still another famine. A closely related aspect is the richness and fertility of Egypt. Egypt can be likened to the garden of Eden (Genesis 13:10), and it constitutes the background for the growth of the people of Israel, seventy descendants of Jacob who went down to Egypt, but eventually they "were fruitful and multiplied greatly and became exceedingly numerous, so that the land was filled with them" (Exodus 1:5–7). After their departure from Egypt, Israel could therefore look back with longing for, not only the "pots of meat" (Exodus 16:2), but also the "cucumbers, melons, leeks, onions and garlic" (Numbers 11:5).

These positive portrayals of Egypt are also reflected elsewhere in narrative and legislative pentateuchal texts. A mixed marriage between an Egyptian and an Israelite can, for instance, be mentioned without any condemnation (Leviticus 24:10–16). And whereas Ammonites and Moabites were never to be admitted into the congregation of YHWH, not even after ten generations, Egyptians could do so after only three generations (Deuteronomy 23:4–9).

Turning now to the Prophets, we notice that the references to Egypt in the former prophets (Joshua, Judges, Samuel, Kings) express some of the same tension attested already in the Pentateuch. On the one hand, Egypt is the place of suffering and humiliation (see, e.g. 1 Samuel 10:18), from which Israel was freed by YHWH (see, e.g. Joshua 24:5). On the other hand, however, Egypt continues to be an asylum for political refugees from Israel (see, e.g. 1 Kings 11:40, 2 Kings 25:26). Eventually it can even be a coalition partner for the king in Jerusalem (see, e.g. 2 Kings 18:21, 24). Also the Latter Prophets (Isaiah, Jeremiah, Ezekiel, the twelve minor prophets) let Egypt play several roles. Of special importance are the so-called oracles against the nations. Isaiah warns against making an alliance with Egypt (see Isaiah 20 and 30:1–5), arguing that "the Egyptians are men and not God, and their horses are flesh and not spirit" (Isaiah 31:1–3, v. 3). Jeremiah pronounces judgement over Egypt, describing the defeat of Pharaoh Neco (Jeremiah 46:2–12) and the attack by Nebuchadnezzar (Jeremiah 46: 14–28). And Ezekiel likens Egypt to a sea monster (Ezekiel 29) or a cedar (Ezekiel 31); the sea monster will be left in the desert, the cedar will be cut down, and Egypt will be judged by YHWH (Ezekiel 30). Still, in the midst of all this judgement, Isaiah 19 foresees a time for blessing, when Israel is YHWH's inheritance and Egypt is his people (see v. 25).

Finally, there are some references to Egypt in the Writings (Psalms, Job, Proverbs, Ruth, Song of Songs, Obadiah, Lamentations, Esther, Daniel, Ezra, Nehemiah, Chronicles). Egypt can positively be portrayed as bringing gifts to Jerusalem (see Psalm 68:32 [ET 31]), and negatively it will experience YHWH's judgement (see Daniel 11:42). However, the majority of the references to Egypt focus on the traditions about the sojourn and exodus, both in the Psalms (see Psalms 81:6, 11, 105:23, 38, 114:1, 135:8–9, 136:10) and elsewhere (see Daniel 9:15, 2 Chronicles 6:5, 7:22, Nehemiah 9:9ff.).

The Old Testament is also aware of a nation that is located south of Egypt (see Ezekiel 29:10), a nation called Cush by the Old Testament. In most cases (see below) Old Testament Cush seems to be referring to a nation known as Kush in Ancient Near Eastern sources, and as Ethiopia in Greco-Roman sources. This African nation was situated south of Egypt, and its heartland was the area between the first and sixth cataracts' of the Nile. Throughout the third and second millennia BCE there was a close connection between this area and the mighty, northern neighbour (for general surveys, see Trigger 1976 and Adams 1977). The nature of this relationship has traditionally been seen from the perspective of a superior Egyptian culture and political system. Ancient Kush has to some extent been overshadowed by the impressive and better-known history and culture of ancient Egypt. However, recently it has been argued that Kush and Egypt should rather be seen as more equal rivals, "two major powers competing for resources and lands of the Lower Nile." (O'Connor 1993: 2).

More important for my essay is the history of Kush in the first millennium BCE. From the mid-eighth to the mid-seventh centuries BCE Kushites controlled Egypt (the 25th, so-called Kushite dynasty), and they established a kingdom stretching from central north-east Africa to the Red Sea in the east and the Mediterranean in the north. This climax in the history of Kush is important to us, as it chronologically comes just prior to the period that saw the genesis of most of the Old Testament. One should therefore expect that the military and political apex of Kush is reflected in the Old Testament portrayal of Cush.

It should be emphasized here that not all 56 Old Testament references to Cush necessarily refer to the African nation, or to individual members of that nation. Some may refer, for example, to the Kassites in Babylon or to a tribal group supposed to have lived on the south-western border of Judah (see Hidal 1977: 97–106, Anderson 1995: 45–70, Haak 1995: 238–251). Still, it is clear that the majority refer to African nations. For obvious reasons, African and African American scholars who have been searching for the portrayal of Africa in the Old Testament tend to emphasize the African location of Old Testament Cush. Adamo, for instance, argues that "Everywhere the word 'Cush' is used with clear-cut identification, it refers to Africa." (Adamo 1992c: 51, see also Hays 1996: 396–409). Adamo is also willing to go one step further, arguing that the use of Kush and Ethiopia in the extra-biblical sources refers quite broadly to black Africa, so he suggests that Old Testament Cush ought to be rendered Africa in modern translations (see Adamo 1992c: 51–64, see also Holter 1997: 331–336).

In the Pentateuch Cush occurs already in the Eden narrative (Genesis 2–3). According to Genesis 2:10–14 four rivers were flowing out from Eden, and "The name of the second river is the Gihon, it winds through the entire land of Cush" (v. 13). The geographical location here is difficult. Gihon is the name of a spring in Jerusalem, pointing to a location of Eden in Israel, whereas the third and the fourth rivers are Tigris and Euphrates, pointing to a Mesopotamian location. Traditionally, many interpreters of Genesis 2 have placed Gihon and Cush in Mesopotamia, linking Cush to the Kassites. Still, an African location is more probable (see Westermann 1974: 297–298). There is an old tradition (see LXX Jeremiah 2:18, Ben Sira 24:27) of linking the name Gihon to the Nile (see Ullendorff 1968: 2–3), and this allows for an interpretation of the name Cush in Genesis 2:13 in its traditional sense. This does not mean that the author of Genesis 2:10–14 actually located Eden in Africa (so Adamo 1992b: 33–43), but it means that Africa is included in the world map reflected here (see Hidal 1977: 103–105).

Cush recurs twice in the Pentateuch. First, in the table of nations, Genesis 10:6, 7, 8, Cush is mentioned first in a series of Ham's four sons, probably due to a geographical orientation starting from the

far south (see Adamo 1993: 138–143), and then, in a narrative in
Numbers 12, telling about Miriam and Aaron, who criticize Moses.
In the beginning of this narrative the opposition from Miriam and
Aaron somehow is linked to his taking of a Cushite wife (see v. 1).
This has lead to some interpreters arguing that Miriam and Aaron
criticize Moses for marrying a Cushite woman. This could then be
taken as an example of a negative attitude towards people from
Cush. However, as there are no other examples of a negative attitude in the Old Testament towards people from Cush, this is probably not the case here either (see Adamo 1989: 230–237, Hays 1996:
397–401). One solution is that they criticize Moses for taking a second wife (see his marriage with Zipporah, Exodus 2:21–22), another
is that the opposition from Miriam and Aaron has nothing to do
with marriage to the Cushite woman.

The eight references to Cush in the Former Prophets are found
in two different narratives. Both allude to the military reputation of
Cush, which, historically speaking, was a result of the Cushite rule
of Egypt from the mid-eighth to the mid-seventh century BCE. The
first narrative is the death of Absalom, 2 Samuel 18. Here a Cushite
is depicted as serving as officer in king David's army (vv. 21–32). Interpreters of this narrative have especially focussed on how a Cushite
could become an officer in Jerusalem. Some older interpreters could,
revealing their own prejudices, present the Cushite as "a negro (naturally, a slave)" (Smith 1898: 359). However, there is nothing in the
Old Testament that supports such a view. A better explanation is
that the narrative more generally reflects a Cushite presence in the
land of Israel, that is, outside the Cushite heartland (see Anderson
1995: 45–70). An interesting aspect of this narrative is that it lets
the military skill of the Cushites serve Israel. That is also the case
in the other narrative, where 2 Kings 19 depicts the Cushite king
Tirhakah as a central actor in the deliverance of Jerusalem (v. 9).

The 25 references to Cush in the Latter Prophets let Cush play
different roles. Not least is the military reputation of the Cushites
reflected in several places, in lists, such as in Nahum 3:9 and Ezekiel
38:5, or in more elaborated narratives, such as the one about Ebed-
Melech the Cushite in Jeremiah 38–39. One single verse in Amos
9 is also of importance, due to its particular focus on the relationship between Israel and Cush in v. 7a. Some interpreters have argued
that the comparison here of Israel with Cush expresses a judgement
over Israel. A comparison of Israel with "the far-distant, uncivilized,

and despised black race of the Ethiopians" (Harper 1905: 192), it has been argued, points to a humiliation of Israel (see also Gese 1979: 33–38). However, the other half of the verse (7b) points in another direction. It makes a comparison that clearly is positive: the exodus from Egypt is compared with similar experiences of other peoples. The comparison in 7a ought to be interpreted in this light (see Adamo 1992a: 76–84, Smith 1994: 36–47).

The books of Isaiah and Zephaniah show a particular interest in Cush. Isaiah 18 offers the most vivid anthropological description of Cush in the Old Testament depicting "a people tall and smooth-skinned, a people feared far and wide, an aggressive nation of strange speech, whose land is divided by rivers" (Isaiah 18:2, see also Jeremiah 13:23, quoting a proverb which asks rhetorically: "Can the Cushite change his skin or the leopard its spots?"). Isaiah also alludes to the wealth of Cush (see Isaiah 43:3, 45:14, see Stassen 1992: 160–180), seeing a time when it will bring gifts to YHWH (see Isaiah 18:7). Still, Israel is warned against placing her trust in Cush (see Isaiah 20). When it comes to Zephaniah, the opening verse introduces the prophet as son of Cushi (Zephaniah 1:1). Further, Cush is used to represent the far south in the prophet's geographical orientation (Zephaniah 2:4–15, especially verse 12). One here notices that the judgement over Cush is more briefly described than the ones of the other nations. And finally, Cush is also mentioned in a context of salvation (Zephaniah 3:10). As a whole, these references to Cush reveal a special awareness of these distant people, and some inter-preters argue that this reflects traces of a Cushite presence in the land of Israel (see Anderson 1995: 46–70), whereas others have spec-ulated on the geographical background of Zephaniah, making him the black or African prophet of the Old Testament (see Rice 1979: 21–31, Adamo 1987: 1–8).

The Writings too offer examples of portrayals of Cush. One is the reference in Chronicles alluding to the military reputation of Cush. Whereas Samuel and Kings let the military skill of the Cushites serve the king in Jerusalem (see above), the opposite is the situa-tion in Chronicles (see Bailey 1991: 182). 2 Chronicles 14:8–14 describes a war where Asa king of Judah beats Zerah the Cushite. This narrative is typical of the holy war pattern in Chronicles, as it strongly exaggerates the number of soldiers involved, and empha-sizes the role played by YHWH (see also 2 Chronicles 16:8 and 12:2–4, see Hays 1996: 401–403). Other examples of the portrayal

of Cush in the Writings include Esther 1:1, which depicts the mighty
Persian empire as stretching from India to Cush, Job 28:19, which
alludes to the wealth of Cush and Psalms 87:4, mentioning pilgrims from different nations, including Cush. Psalms 68:32 [ET 31]
should also be mentioned here, though the text is difficult, it probably alludes to the tradition that Cush too will bring gifts to YHWH
in Jerusalem.

Egypt and Cush clearly offer the most relevant material in our
search for Africa in the Old Testament. Still, there is also a third
group, consisting of possible Africa linked geographical entities with
few Old Testament references and/or uncertain location (for a general survey, see Simons 1959). Most of these are found in different
kinds of lists, for example the table of nations in Genesis 10 and 1
Chronicles 1 (see especially the descendants of Cush and Mizraim),
or more scattered lists of kings or nations (see, for example, Jeremiah
46:8–9, Ezekiel 30:4–5, Nahum 3:9). Some of the geographical entities have proved impossible to locate, in spite of many attempts,
Ophir (see Isaiah 13:12, Job 28:16, 1 Kings 22:49) could serve as
an example here (see Görg 1996:5–8). Others have tentatively been
located in north-east Africa or Arabia, Sabteca (Genesis 10:7, 1
Chronicles 1:9) could serve here as an example, related perhaps to
Pharaoh Shebiktu or to several places in Arabia.

The most relevant geographical entities can then, roughly, be
grouped in two. First, there are some which most probably have an
African location. One is Put, that is, Libya or Somalia (see, e.g.
Genesis 10:6, Nahum 3:9, Jeremiah 46:9, Ezekiel 30:5), another is
Lubim, that is Libya (see, e.g. 2 Chronicles 12:3, Nahum 3:9), and
a third is Pathros, that is Upper Egypt (see, e.g. Genesis 10:14,
Jeremiah 44:15, Ezekiel 29:14). The last occurs mostly in references
to the Jewish diaspora (see Isaiah 11:11, Jeremiah 44:1.14). The first
two occur in lists related to war and military reputation, often together
with Cush (see, e.g. Nahum 3:9, Jeremiah 46:9, Ezekiel 30:5, 2
Chronicles 16:8). Lubim also has connotations of wealth, again
together with Cush (see Daniel 11:43).

Secondly, there are some locations which have ancient traditions
in favour of an African location. One is Sheba, located in Africa
according to Josephus (*Antiquities* viii 6,5–6), another is Seba, located
in Meroe, again according to Josephus (*Antiquities* ii 10,2). Both have
strong connotations of wealth (see, e.g. Psalms 72:10.15, Ezekiel
27:22–23, Isaiah 43:3, 45:15), the latter not least due to the narra-

tive about the Queen of Sheba (see 1 Kings 10, 2 Chronicles 9).

In our search for the Old Testament portrayal of Africa, we have now been through the most relevant material. It is now time to briefly summarize our findings and relate them to some hermeneutical questions. The textual survey can be summarized in two points. First, Africa is indeed present in the Old Testament. Egypt and Cush, but to some extent also other African nations, play a substantial role in the Old Testament. Egypt is the closest, geographically speaking to Palestine, and consequently knowledge about Egypt and traditions about its relationship to Israel, not least the exodus tradition, are reflected throughout the Old Testament. Cush is also relatively well known, its location in the far south can be used to demarcate political borders, and the colour of the skin of the Cushites is used in the proverbs. Secondly, the Old Testament reflects a dual concept of Africa, including both positive and negative lines of thought. Positively, Africa is associated with great wealth and strong military abilities, both of which can, at times, be used to the benefit of Israel. Negatively, however, Africa is at other times an enemy of Israel, oppressing and threatening her.

Both points touch important hermeneutical questions. First, it touches the question of identity. The focus on the African presence in the Old Testament leads contemporary African readers to draw lines between their own identity and the Old Testament portrayal of Africa. This, however, creates a hermeneutical dilemma. Due to the dual concept of Africa in the Old Testament contemporary African readers might feel that they have to choose between the identity of the people of God or the identity of its enemies (see Holter 1997: 335–336). Accordingly, further hermeneutical reflection is needed. Secondly, it also touches the question of history. Traditional Eurocentric interpretation of the Old Testament has generally marginalised the African presence in the Old Testament. Consequently, an Afro-centric interpretation is now challenged to reappraise the ancient Old Testament traditions that are related to Africa, and to expose contemporary Old Testament readers to the pre-western concept of Africa reflected in these traditions (see Yorke 1995: 145–158). Not only will this demonstrate that "Black people are not a modern-era addition to the story of salvation history. They were there from the beginning" (Hays 1996: 409), but it will also let Old Testament scholarship contribute to "the idea that Africa and persons of African descent must be seen as proactive subjects within history, rather than as passive objects of Western history" (Felder 1993/1994: 47).

BIBLIOGRAPHY

Adamo, David T. *Africa and the Africans in the Old Testament*. San Francisco: Christian Universities Press, 1998.
———. "The Table of Nations Reconsidered in African Perspective (Genesis 10)." *Journal of African Religion and Philosophy* 2 (1993): 138–143.
———. "Amos 9:7–8 in an African Perspective." *Orita* 24 (1992): 76–84 [= 1992a].
———. "Ancient Africa and Genesis 2:10–14." *The Journal of Religious Thought* 49 (1992): 33–43 [= 1992b].
———. "Ethiopia in the Bible." *African Christian Studies* 8/II (1992): 51–64 [= 1992c].
———. "The African Queen (I Kings 10:10–13, II Chronicles 9:1–12)." *Journal of Arabic and Religious Studies* 7 (1990): 14–24.
———. "The African Wife of Moses: An Examination of Numbers 12:1–9." *Africa Theological Journal* 18 (1989): 230–237.
———. "The Black Prophet in the Old Testament." *Journal of Arabic and Religious Studies* 4 (1987): 1–8.
Adams, W. *Nubia Corridor to Africa*. London: Allen Lane, Penguin Books, 1977.
Anderson, Roger W. "Zephaniah ben Cushi and Cush of Benjamin: Traces of a Cushite Presence in Syria-Palestine." In Eds Steven W. Holloway & Lowell K. Handy, *The Pitcher is Broken: Memorial Essays for Gösta W. Ahlström*, Sheffield: Sheffield Academic Press 1995: 45–70.
Bailey, Randall C. "Beyond Identification: The Use of Africans in Old Testament Poetry and Narratives." In Ed. Cain Hope Felder, *Stony the Road We Trod: African American Biblical Interpretation*, Minneapolis: Fortress, 1991: 165–184.
Bennet, Robert A. "Africa and the Biblical Period." *Harvard Theological Review* 64 (1971): 483–500.
Cogan, Mordechai. "The Other Egypt: A Welcome Asylum." In Eds Michael V. Fox et al., *Texts, Temples, and Tradition: A Tribute to Menahem Haran*, Wiona Lake: Eisenbrauns, 1996: 65–70.
Copher, Charles B. *Black Biblical Studies: An Anthology*. Chicago: Black Light Fellowship, 1993.
Currid, John D. *Ancient Egypt and the Old Testament*. Grand Rapids: Baker Books, 1997.
Ehret, Christopher. "Ancient Egyptian as an African Language, Egypt as an African Culture." In Ed. Theodore Celenko, *Egypt in Africa*, Indianapolis: Indiana University Press, 1996: 25–27.
Even-Shoshan, Abraham. *A New Concordance of the Old Testament*. Jerusalem: Kiryat Sefer Publishing House, 1993².
Felder, Cain Hope. "Afrocentrism, the Bible, and the Politics of Difference." *Journal of Religious Thought* 50 (1993/1994): 45–56.
Gese, Hartmut. "Das Problem von Amos 9,7." In Eds A.H.J. Gunneweg & O. Kaiser, *Textgemäss: Aufsätze und Beiträge zur Hermeneutik des Alten Testaments. Festschrift für Ernst Würthwein zum 70. Geburtstag*, Göttingen: Vandenhoeck & Ruprecht, 1979: 33–38.
Görg, Manfred. "Ofir und Punt." *Biblische Notizen* 82 (1996): 5–8.
Haak, Robert H. "'Cush' in Zephaniah." In Eds Steven W. Holloway & Lowell K. Handy, *The Pitcher is Broken: Memorial Essays for Gösta W. Ahlström*, Sheffield: Sheffield Academic Press 1995: 238–251.

Harper, William R. *A Critical and Exegetical Commentary on Amos and Hosea.* Edinburgh: T. & T. Clark, 1905.

Hays, J. Daniel. "The Cushites: A Black Nation in the Bible." *Bibliotheca Sacra* 153 (1996): 396–409.

Hidal, Sten. "The Land of Cush in the Old Testament." *Svensk Exegetisk Årsbok* 41–42 (1977): 97–106.

Holter, Knut. "Should Old Testament 'Cush' be Rendered 'Africa'?" *The Bible Translator* 48 (1997): 331–336.

Høyland, Marta. "An African Presence in the Old Testament? David Tuesday Adamo's Interpretation of the Old Testament Cush Passages." Forthcoming in *Old Testament Essays,* 1998.

Jackson, Alvin A. *Examining the Record: An Exegetical and Homiletical Study of Blacks in the Bible.* New York: Peter Lang, 1994.

Keita, S.O.Y. "Studies and Comments on Ancient Egyptian Biological Relationships." *History of Africa* 20 (1993): 129–154.

Kealy, Sean P. "The Canon: An African Contribution." *Biblical Theology Bulletin* 9 (1979): 13–26.

Mveng, Engelbert. "La bible et l'afrique noire." In Eds Engelbert Mveng & R. Zwi, *The Jerusalem Congress on Black Africa and the Bible,* Jerusalem: Anti-Defamation League of B'nai B'rit, 1972: 23–39.

North, R. "Ophir/Parvaim and Petra/Joktheel." *Proceedings of the World Congress of Jewish Studies* 4 (1967): 197–202.

O'Connor, David. *Ancient Nubia: Egypt's Rival in Africa.* Philadelphia: University of Pennsylvania, 1993.

Pfeifer, Gerhard. *Ägypten im Alten Testament.* München: Biblisch Notizen, 1995.

Rice, Gene. "The African Roots of the Prophet Zephaniah." *Journal of Religious Thought* 36 (1979): 21–31.

Sempiore, Sidbe. "Le noir et le salut dans la bible." In Eds P. Adeso et al., *Universalisme et mission dans la bible. Actes de cinquième congrès des biblistes africains,* Nairobi: Catholic Biblical Centre for Africa and Madagascar, 1993: 17–29.

Simons, J. *The Geographical and Topographical Texts of the Old Testament.* Leiden: Brill, 1959.

Smith, Henry P. *The Books of Samuel.* Edinburgh: T. & T. Clark, 1898.

Smith, Regina. "A New Perspective on Amos 9:7a 'To Me, O Israel, You are Just Like the Kushites.'" *Journal of the Interdenominational Theological Center* 22 (1994): 36–47.

Stassen, Stefan L. "Die Rol van Egipte, Kus en Seba in Jesaja 43:3 en 45:14." *Journal for Semitics* 4 (1992): 160–180.

Trigger, B. *Nubia under the Pharaohs.* London: Thames & Hudson, 1976.

Westermann, Claus. *Genesis 1–11.* Neukirchen-Vluyn: Neukirchener Verlag, 1974.

Williams, Ronald J. "II. Ägypten und Israel." *Theologische Realenzyklopädie* 1 (1977): 492–505.

Yorke, Gosnell L. "Biblical Hermeneutics: An Afrocentric Perspective." *Religion & Theology* 2 (1995): 145–158.

POPULAR READINGS OF THE BIBLE IN AFRICA AND IMPLICATIONS FOR ACADEMIC READINGS

Report on the Field Research Carried out on Oral Interpretation of the Bible in Port Harcourt Metropolis, Nigeria under the Auspices of the Bible in Africa Project, 1991–94

Justin S. Ukpong

The purpose of this essay is to briefly introduce the *Bible in Africa Project* that was started in 1991, and to analyse highlights of the result of the fieldwork that was carried out under the auspices of the project on oral popular interpretation of the bible in Port Harcourt Metropolis, Nigeria. A similar field study was also carried out in Glasgow, Scotland under the project with the aim of comparing ways ordinary people read the bible in Europe and in Africa (see Riches 1996). This essay however deals with only the fieldwork carried out in Port Harcourt.

Today there is increasing awareness amongst theologians and exegetes that all theological and biblical interpretations are culturally, historically and socially conditioned (Schreiter 1985: 3–4, Geffré 1972: 27), and that current exegetical methodologies have been developed from specifically Western perspectives and do not reflect the perspectives of other cultures, neither do they take into account the life concerns of ordinary Christians. In recent times, African biblical scholars have also expressed concern about the relevance of the classical mode of biblical interpretation for the socio-cultural context of Africa, and have pointed to the need for developing a framework of academic biblical interpretation that would be responsive to the social, cultural and religious contexts of Africa and that would involve the perspectives and concerns of the ordinary African reader (Pobee 1985–86: 22–29, Wambutda 1980: 34, West 1992: 3–13).

It is against the above background that the *Bible in Africa Project*, carried out in the years 1991–94 at the initiative of John Riches of the University of Glasgow, Scotland and Justin Ukpong of the Catholic Institute of West Africa, Port Harcourt, Nigeria is to be understood. It had been in planning since the middle of 1988, with The Evangelisches Missionswerk (EMW), Hamburg and Missio, Aachen, of Germany, and the Programme on Ecumenical Theological Education of the WCC, Geneva, providing the funding. The project was conceived and designed to be a cooperative research venture with an ecumenical dimension in which African and Western exegetes, theologians and theological centres would be involved. The aims were:

- To examine existing uses, both oral and literary, of the bible in Africa and Europe as a means to understanding present practice and in developing new initiatives.
- To consider critically the ways in which biblical studies as it has developed has reflected the perspectives and interests of the North, and the ways in which it is presently being made use of by African biblical scholars.
- To develop specifically African ways of academic reading of the bible that would pay attention to popular uses of the bible in Africa and evaluate the usefulness of historical critical and other tools.
- To consider the extent to which academic modes of biblical scholarship in the West reflect social and individual concerns which can be observed in more popular uses of the bible.
- To consider the implications of the global context in which we find ourselves for biblical studies in both North and South.
- To establish and develop links between Northern and Southern institutions and to encourage continuing research and the exchange of staff and students beyond the limited life of this project as a way of putting the findings of the research into effect.

It was hoped that the research would provide insights into ordinary people's approach to and interests in the bible, and that such insights might inform the development of academic readings of the bible so that they would address the concerns of ordinary users and therefore be relevant to their situation. Among other things, this would serve to bridge the evident gap between academic and ordinary uses of the bible.

Two institutions, the University of Glasgow (Department of Biblical Studies) and the Catholic Institute of West Africa, Port Harcourt, Nigeria (Department of Biblical Studies) were involved in the research. The Department of Religious Studies and Classics, University of

Zimbabwe was also to take part in the research but could not. Two conferences at which papers were presented on different aspects of the project were held, the first in Port Harcourt in July 1993, and the second in Glasgow in August 1994.

Based on the aims of the project, the research was carried out in four areas of the use of the bible. One was a critical analysis of the ways in which academic biblical studies as it has developed has reflected Western perspectives and interests. A paper on this was presented by John Riches at the Port Harcourt and Glasgow conferences. The second area was analysis of the ways African biblical scholars have made use of Western biblical scholarship. A paper surveying the various approaches to biblical interpretation in West Africa was presented by Chris Ukachukwu Manus of the university of Ife, Nigeria, at the Port Harcourt conference. The third area focussed on developing African ways of academic biblical interpretation that would pay attention to ordinary uses of the bible in Africa. A paper, presented by me at the Glasgow conference, considered the methodology of inculturation hermeneutics as an approach to biblical interpretation that would pay attention to the world-view and social concerns of ordinary African readers of the bible. Another paper, presented by Kris Owan at the Glasgow conference, argued for a culturally pluralistic approach to biblical interpretation. The last area was on popular uses of the bible in Africa and Europe. A paper, on popular *literary* interpretation of the bible as found in religious tracts, bills boards, film, etc., was presented by Daniel Wambutda of the University of Jos, Nigeria at the Port Harcourt conference. In addition field research on oral interpretation of the bible was carried out in Port Harcourt and Glasgow, and analyses of these were presented by Mark Anikpo of the Sociology Department, University of Port Harcourt at the Port Harcourt conference and by Leslie Milton of the University of Glasgow at the Glasgow conference.

At the Glasgow conference, the Department of Religious Studies and Classics, University of Zimbabwe was represented, as was the Institute for the Study of the Bible, University of Natal, Pietermaritzburg, South Africa. Grant LeMarquand, then of Wycliffe College, Toronto, Canada who was working on a bibliography of biblical interpretation in Africa also participated in this conference.

The project is ongoing and only a part of it has so far been realised. Many more of the activities articulated in its aims are still to be carried out. These include the collection of materials on biblical studies in Africa, the compilation and publication of bibliographies on biblical studies in Africa (see LeMarquand 1995 and this volume), and the exchange of staff and students among the participating institutions, something that has yet to be properly defined and implemented, though I am at present assisting John Riches in supervising the doctoral thesis of an African student at the University of Glasgow who is writing in the area of biblical interpretation in Africa.

The rest of this essay will reflect on aspects of the report of the field research on oral interpretation of the bible by ordinary readers that was carried out in Port Harcourt in 1991–92. A sociologist experienced in field research methodology, Professor Mark Anikpo of the University of Port Harcourt, Nigeria directed the research. I, a professor of New Testament at the Catholic Institute of West Africa, and the coordinator of the *Bible in Africa Project*, provided the biblical and theological input for carrying out the research. The ultimate aim of the research was to provide biblical specialists with information and insights that might make academic bible study relevant to the needs of ordinary African readers.

The field research was carried out in two interrelated parts. The first part, which was meant to be a prelude to the entire research endeavour, was exploratory in nature and was intended to provide a guide in formulating the research questionnaire. It involved the use of the Focus Group Discussion technique. This is a specialized form of the interview that involves small groups from the target population rather than selected individuals. It is found to be particularly useful in obtaining data that is essentially qualitative, including information on people's attitudes, knowledge, inner feelings, fears and desires, particularly as these relate to their use of the bible. The specific objectives of the research derived from the above aim were identified as follows:

- To determine the attitude of ordinary Nigerian people to the bible.
- To determine how people interpret and apply the bible in their daily lives, their homes, places of work, public life, and so on.
- To determine the cultural influences on the interpretation and use of the bible by the ordinary people.
- To determine those aspects of the bible that the people find difficult to understand and apply in their daily lives, and how they resolve the conflict, and those aspects of the bible that appeal to the people most.

– To determine the differences in the approach to and use of the bible by Christians in the mainline churches and the African Instituted Churches.

A total of 10 research assistants underwent training for the exercise. Working in three groups, and with the help of the consultant, each group produced discussion "guides" (questionnaires) intended to guide the researcher in eliciting responses. Thirty Focus Group Discussions were conducted, and each group which participated was characterised according to various criteria that noted location, religious affiliation, gender and age. The groups were spread across both urban and suburban areas of Port Harcourt Metropolis. Each group comprised 8–10 persons and the discussions lasted 60–90 minutes. Ordinary people from four Christian traditions participated: Roman Catholic, Protestant (Presbyterian), African Instituted Churches, and Evangelical churches. Some of the groups were ecumenical adult neighbourhood groups, some were mixed adult and youth groups within each of the denominations, and there were also groups based on gender. Information gathered from these discussions was analysed and used for preparing a questionnaire that formed the major research instrument for the second part of the fieldwork.

The second part of the fieldwork was a Baseline Survey. Information from the Focus Group Discussions revealed that the interpretation of the bible among the research population was rather dogmatic and oriented towards problem solving. The bible was seen as God's word that had the spiritual power to help the user in various ways. Given this situation and the ultimate aim of the project, the final survey sought to determine the various ways the bible was used by the research population, the motives for such uses, and the cultural influences behind such motives. The preliminary survey provided insights for formulating the central hypothesis that the use of the bible by the research population was conditioned by the people's world-view and life exigencies.

For the purpose of administering the questionnaire, Port Harcourt Metropolis was divided into 10 zones each comprising a city area and a suburban area. One hundred questionnaires were administered by personal interview to 100 households in each of the 10 zones making a total of a thousand questionnaires in all. Fifty households whose members are users of the bible were selected at ran-

dom in the city and suburban areas for the administration of the
questionnaire. This number was thought to be sufficient with the
corroboration of the evidence of the Focus Group Discussions. Information gathered from this survey was analysed and presented in
the research report.

In what follows, I shall analyse the materials presented in the
reports of the two parts of the fieldwork and point to the insights
they offer for academic biblical interpretation. The report of the
Focus Group Discussions shall be referred to as the Focus Group
Discussion Report, and that of the Baseline Survey which is titled
"Report of the Household Research Survey" shall be referred to as
the Household Research Survey Report. The two reports reveal a
number of insights that are enlightening about the research population's attitude to and use of the bible.

The research population exhibited a rather naive and dogmatic
approach to the bible. The bible is regarded literally as God's own
words divinely inspired and communicated to human beings. They
maintain an attitude of reverence and submission to it as if the words
of the bible were directly communicated to humanity by God (Focus
Group Discussion Report: 3–4, 14). The bible is interpreted literally. Being the word of God, the bible and its authority over people's life are accepted without question. Here we found that ordinary
Africans in the study shared the same position irrespective of their
denomination. Perhaps they are attracted to this position by the
world-view of their African traditional society where authority, more
so religious authority, is accepted without question.

That the bible is divinely inspired is taken to imply that it has
magical dimensions. The bible is used to ward off evil spirits, witchcraft and sorcery, it is placed under the pillow at night to ensure
God's protection against the devil, it is put in handbags and cars
when travelling to ensure a safe journey, it is used in swearing to
bring God's wrath upon culprits (Focus Group Discussion Report:
4–6). Africans in this study believe that the world has two dimensions, the material, which is visible to the human eye, and the spiritual, which is invisible. They also believe that the world is inhabited
by both visible beings, that is, human beings, plants, animals etc.,
and invisible beings, that is, God and the spirits which are both
good and evil. Though unseen, the spirits exert influence on human
beings, and such influence may be good or bad. They believe that

all kinds of evil including illnesses, childlessness, poverty, accidents, deaths, calamities and hardships come from evil spirits and witch-craft. They therefore believe that these can be overcome by invok-ing the power of God expressed in the bible. Besides, since in the traditional Nigerian African world-view, religion has to do not only with the spiritual welfare but also with the material welfare of the people, the bible is used in seeking deliverance from material afflictions like poverty, childlessness, etc. which they believe are caused by evil spirits. Arising from the fact that Africans attach great potency to the spoken word, the bible is regarded as very "powerful" being the word of God (see below). Passages of the bible are also read for con-solation and enlightenment.

The reverence accorded to the bible as God's word means that the bible is regarded entirely as a book of devotion, a rule of life and a norm for morality. It means too that the historical veracity of its content is not questioned as such questioning would detract from this reverence. These people do no therefore go to the bible with a questioning mind, but they go to learn. They are interested neither in the literary analysis of biblical texts nor in the history behind the text. They are interested in the theological message in the text and how that message might be useful to their lives. The bible is thus treated not as any other literature but as literature of a special category.

While the African Instituted Churches adopt unorthodox and lib-eral practices in their use of the bible, they however remain con-servative in their belief that the bible is universal and not subject to cultural interpretations. For them such practices as handclapping, dancing and drumming at worship are not the result of cultural adaptation but are directives from the bible. They point particularly to the Old Testament where examples of such practices are found. They tend to take their ideas from the New Testament and their practices from the Old Testament (Focus Group Discussion Report: 14). Roman Catholics were identified as most liberal in their approach to the bible (Focus Group Discussion Report: 9).

In view of the fact that academic reading of the bible can no longer afford to be naive and fundamentalistic in this post-Enlighten-ment era, an obvious implication of the above for academic read-ing of the bible, is that the bible should not be looked upon and treated merely as *ancient* literature, as does the historical critical method with its historical interest, nor merely as *literature*, as do the literary approaches, with their interest in the bible as literature, but should, in addition, be accorded the full measure of its spiritual dimension as a *book of devotion and norm for morality*. If the people take the bible as God's word and are interested in the message rather than the history or literary analysis of the biblical text, it was important to find out what they thought was the central message of the bible. Both in the focus group discussions and in the questionnaire answers, most of the research population indicated love and salvation, followed by obedience, humility and peace as the central messages of the bible (Household Research Survey Report: 7–8). An analysis of the backgrounds of the respondents showed that those of the high income communities (people in Shell residential area and low density estates) indicated love first while those in the high density and low income areas indicated salvation. Both in the focus group discussions and in the questionnaire responses, it was clear that love was understood as God's love for humanity and our love for God and neighbour. It was also clear that salvation was understood in existential terms, and it has to do with the conditions of living in the present life. Salvation in the next life is meaningless without material well-being in this life.

The responses as to the question of the central message of the bible may be interpreted in various ways. One way is to see them as a true representation of what the people think the bible stands for and communicates. Another way is to see them as a reflection of the needs of the people, that is, what the people look for in the bible and expect to get from it. A third way is to see them as a reflection of what they have been told by their churches to be the central message of the bible. It appears to us that these are not mutually exclusive. No Christian church fails to emphasize love as the central teaching of the bible, and the importance of God's salvation offered in the course of human history. Christians who read the bible already have this knowledge from their churches. Thus while the premium placed on love and salvation may well reflect biblical teaching, when we consider the attitude of the people to the bible and the use they make of it, it becomes clear that these responses are also a reflection of the yearnings of the people.

Much too often, academic readings of the bible do not see the bible in existential terms, that is, in terms of its implications for contemporary life situations, though we do owe thanks to liberation theology for bringing this approach to the bible to the fore in recent years. This is one important implication of this research finding for academic readings of the bible. The ordinary people read the bible in existential terms.

To a question seeking to determine the parts of the bible (Old Testament or New Testament) which attracted the participants the more, 83.8% compared with 16.2% of the respondents preferred the New Testament. This is in spite of the fact that African cultures are much closer to the culture of the Old Testament than they are to that of the New Testament. From the responses, the reason for the preference is that the New Testament "is more powerful than the Old Testament." This refers to the power of Jesus expressed in the miracles of the gospels, and the fact that it is easier to identify with him in his power since he was human though also God (Focus Group Discussion Report: 10, Household Research Survey Report: 7). The Psalms, the story of Jonah, and the creation stories were identified as favourite texts in the Old Testament.

Among the major motives for reading the bible as indicated by the respondents, seeking spiritual support comes first. Such support is sought against evil forces and enemies (Household Research Survey Report: 7–9). The bible is believed to provide a spiritual resource for combatting spiritual forces. Since these forces are spiritual, only spiritual resources can overcome them. It is on this ground that the mainline churches, which do no use the bible in this way, lose their members to the "Spiritual churches" which do use the bible for this purpose. The search for such support makes Christians move from one church to another in search for the one that best provides the needed support, for not all the "Spiritual churches" are equally endowed with the "power."

Next among the reasons for using the bible is prayer. Responses to another question reveal that the underlying reason for such prayer has to do with matters of prosperity, long life, protection, good health, success and happiness in life, etc. No distinction was therefore made between the use of the bible for spiritual needs and for material needs. Prosperity, happiness, good health, etc. are regarded as a sign of divine blessing, while a life of deprivation on earth is a negation of the expected happiness of the afterlife. There is therefore no purely spiritualised interpretation of the bible. The world-view of the bible itself lends credence to this. For example, in the Old Testament, God promised Abraham prosperity for keeping faithful to God (Genesis

12), and in the New Testament Jesus promised blessings in this world and in the next to those who followed him faithfully till the end (Matthew 19:28–29). From the above, it is clear that for the ordinary people in this study, how the bible affects their lives is very important. In terms of academic readings this means that, for the Africans, methods and strategies for reading should seek to involve and touch the lives of ordinary readers.

One thing that is however found wanting here is the lack of societal transformation as a motive for reading the bible. In no place does this feature. All the motives mentioned are about individual benefits. The bible is not read from the perspective of political or economic commitment. While a strong aspect of academic interpretation of the bible in Africa links the biblical text with the African context, this often has not been done in a manner that involves a commitment to change in the society. More recently, however, more awareness has been created about the use of the bible to bring about change in society. Creating such awareness among ordinary readers is one way academic bible reading could contribute to popular reading.

In seeking to determine the people's awareness of cultural influences in their attitude to and use of the bible, a particular concern of mine, the general response indicated an ambivalence. In terms of direct general questions the responses were generally negative, while the ambivalence showed up in specific questions. More that 80% of the research population claimed ignorance of cultural influences in their approach to the bible. They claimed that they were not guided by cultural images in their understanding of the bible. As to the question whether a people's culture should guide them in interpreting and using the bible more effectively, 69.8% disagreed, 28.5% agreed while 1.7% were undecided. The reasons offered ranged from the conviction that culture had nothing to do with the bible to the fear that the bible may end up losing its universality. Similarly, to the question whether their cultural heritage had influenced the way they read and understood the bible, 61.8% answered negatively, 29.1% answered positively while 9.1% were undecided (Household Research Survey Report: 9–12). To a question seeking to know the people's reaction to the portrayal of Jesus as an African, the majority (55.6%) were indifferent, while 39.3% were positive, and 5.15% were negative (Household Research Survey Report: 7). Based on the people's dogmatic attitude to the bible, it is not surprising that a large number would be indifferent.

Could these responses be said to reflect the true position regarding the presence of African culture in the people's attitude to and interpretation of the bible? Three considerations need to be taken on board here. One is that in view of the people's naive understanding of the bible as the word of God "dictated" by God to human beings, it is not surprising that they would not consciously associate culture with the bible. The second is that over the years they have been taught to understand the bible in a certain way and to accept certain interpretations of the biblical texts as normative, and all this has not been associated with their culture; sometimes the bible was even shown to be against their culture. One is again therefore not surprised that they do not link their culture with the way they interpret the bible. The third consideration is the type of questions with which people approach the bible. That the majority of the research population were interested in and were even preoccupied with spiritual protection against evil forces in their use of the bible strongly betrays the influence of their culture because these are the main preoccupation of the African Traditional Religions. In a parallel research project that was carried out in Glasgow, the motives for reading the bible were mentioned as guidance, support and solace. Nothing was said about using the bible to ward off evil spirits because this is not part of the Western world-view and culture. Research in African Traditional Religions have shown that these religions are preoccupied with the security and welfare of the human community through the control of the spiritual forces that are perceived to be responsible for such matters. Even if it is argued that this pre-occupation with evil spirits is found in the bible itself, the question remains as to how Africans so easily identify with this phenomenon while Westerners, as it is well known and as the Glasgow report shows, do not. Basically this must be explained by the way of life of these two peoples. In effect, the responses to the questionnaires denying any linkage of the people's attitude to and use of the bible with culture must be seen to be based on the people's wrong understanding of the bible as word of God and the way they were brought up to read the bible. This becomes much clearer when we consider questions on individual practices.

To the question "Should women cover their hair during worship?," the majority, 74.1%, answered in the affirmative, 21.3% in the negative, while 6.4% were undecided. The comment in the Report states:

> In the African context, the implication here is not really a preference for a cultural trait because covering the hair is not an African custom. It is more of a pointer to the dogmatism that underlines the attitude of the African to the bible and bible-related behaviour as handed down by the Europeans who introduced the Book to Africans (Household Research Survey Report: 15).

The biblical basis for this practice is 1 Corinthians 11:5–15 where the apostle Paul rules that women should cover their hair. This ruling was taught to and accepted by Africans as dogmatic and of universal application. They therefore hold tenaciously to it. This makes it easy to see that many of the answers the people give are based on what they have been taught to believe about the bible.

We see a preference for African cultural practice in responses to the question about the use of proverbs in interpreting the bible. On this question, 79.5% preferred the use of proverbs while 18.6% did not, and 1.9% were indifferent. According the Report, "In the African context, one may even say that the use of proverbs could be an asset in the interpretation of the bible" (Household Research Survey Report: 14). The reason here is that proverbs are an important cultural tool of communication in Africa. It can be immediately seen here that this response negates the earlier denial that African culture can help in understanding the bible, and confirms our position that such denial is to be attributed to the way the people were taught to look on the bible. Our culture does influence our attitude to the bible and the questions we put to the biblical text. The bible is both the word of God and a cultural product of the human communities that passed on this word to us. It is not a dictation from God. This is why culture can and does influence the interpretation of the bible.

One serious challenge that this research brings out for academic readings of the bible is that of overcoming the dogmatic stance of the ordinary people on the bible. Bridging the gap between academic and ordinary readings of the bible should not be a one way affair. While academic readings of the bible should seek insights from ordinary readings, ordinary readers must be helped to overcome a naive and dogmatic attitude to the bible, and to approach the bible with a critical mind.

BIBLIOGRAPHY

Geffré, C. *Theology in a New Key*. New York: Paulist Press, 1972.

LeMarquand, Grant "Bibliography of the Bible in Africa," *Journal of Inculturation Theology* (1995): 2, 39–139.

Pobee, John S. "Teaching the New Testament in an African Context." *Journal of Religious Thought* 42: 2 (1985–86): 2–39.

Riches, John. "Interpreting the Bible in African Contexts: Glasgow Consultation." *Semeia* (1996): 73, 181–188.

Schreiter, R. *Constructing Local Theologies*. Maryknoll: Orbis, 1985.

Wambutda, D.N. "Hermeneutics and the Search for Theologia Africana." *Africa Theological Journal* 9:1 (1980): 29–39.

West, G.O. "Some Parameters of the Hermeneutic Debate in the South African Context." *Journal of Theology for Southern Africa* 80 (1992): 3–13.

CONTEXTUAL BIBLE STUDY IN SOUTH AFRICA: A RESOURCE FOR RECLAIMING AND REGAINING LAND, DIGNITY AND IDENTITY[1]

Gerald O. West

Of course, all Bible study is contextual. Even the most committed modernist now finds it difficult to maintain that interpretation can be neutral and objective. So why do I elevate the phrase "contextual Bible study" to the title of this essay? The phrase is formed by both historical and methodological impulses.

Methodologically, "contextual Bible study" begins with, but admits to more than, the contextual nature of all interpretation. The many disruptions of modernity's masterly march have taken their toll. We have lost our interpretative innocence; as David Tracy aptly shows, "There is no innocent interpretation, no innocent interpreter, no innocent text" (Tracy 1987: 79). But contextual Bible study is not content with an admission of contextuality. Contextual Bible study embraces and advocates context. Commitment to rather than cognizance of context is the real concern. Because "Intellectual neutrality is not possible in a historical world of exploitation and oppression," biblical scholars and theologians are called to an intellectual conversion that enables them to become committed to the context of the poor and marginalized (Schüssler Fiorenza 1983: xxi). So implicit in the notion of "contextual" as it is used in the phrase "contextual Bible study" is commitment to a particular context, the context of the poor and marginalized.

It is here that the methodological impulse merges with the historical. Many, reading the above paragraph, would be quick to make the point that this all sounds very much like liberation theology. And they would be right. In his eloquent and incisive analysis of liberation theology, Per Frostin identifies the fulcrum of liberation theology as a commitment to the experience of the poor and marginalized as "a necessary condition for theological reflection" (Frostin 1988: 6). So why all this talk of "contextual Bible study" when what is really

---

[1] An earlier form of this essay is published in *Grace and Truth* (West 1999).

meant is "liberation Bible study?" Pragmatically, under apartheid, to talk of "liberation" was dangerous, so to talk of "liberation Bible study" would have meant bannings, beatings, or worse. Strategically, therefore, the term "contextual" was used instead of "liberation" (and there were still bannings, beatings, and worse). More substantively, however, because of the particular context of the South African struggle for liberation, contextual Bible study has been constituted by the particularities of the contexts of the poor and marginalized in South Africa. So struggles around race, class, culture, and gender—in their specifically South African manifestations—have forged and fashioned what I call contextual Bible study. The primary dialogue partners, methodologically, of contextual Bible study have been, locally, South African Black theology, African theology, and African women's theology, and internationally, Black Theology in the USA, Latin American liberation theology, feminist theology, and womanist theology (see West 1995). More recently, (dis)ability, age, and sexuality have been drawn to the attention of contextual Bible study as forces and factors that shape life in South Africa.

The passive construction in the final sentence of the above paragraph hides the primary interlocutor of contextual Bible study. Ordinary poor and marginalized South Africans—historically black, African, and female—constantly reconstitute the theory and practice of contextual Bible study. The theologians that represent them may have provided the theoretical terminology, but they themselves have provided the lived experience that is the foundation and font of contextual Bible study.[2]

How useful the term "contextual" is as an adjective to describe a process of Bible study remains to be seen. "Contextual *theology*" in South Africa bears ambiguous baggage, describing as it does a particular theological trajectory with closer links to liberation theologies from Latin America and the Philippines than to Black and African theologies. By using so similar a phrase to designate a form of Bible study—and the similarity is not accidental, as indicated above and as evident below—may not be useful. Even if its flexibility in a post-apartheid context is attractive, the negative connotations it carries, particularly from the perspectives of Black and African theologies

---

[2] A historical analysis of my own work over the past ten years would demonstrate the continual sifting and shifting of theoretical resources in the attempt to find appropriate theory with which to reflect on this experience.

(see Mosala 1985: 103–104), may seriously limit its usefulness. But enough of these etymological considerations. It is time to turn to the theory and practice of contextual Bible study.

Contextual Bible study as practice emerged in the messy way that real things are usually born. In the dark days of the 1980s in South Africa, black and white socially engaged biblical scholars, through their involvement in various forms of social struggle, regularly came into contact with ordinary black South African readers of the Bible who were striving to hear God on the killing fields of KwaZulu-Natal. Often, on hearing that one was a biblical scholar, such people would ask whether could offer resources for Bible study, to better hear what God was saying in these traumatic times. But we too were overwhelmed by the violence, and our Bibles too were strangely silent. *The Kairos Document* captures the sense of our yearning: "Our KAIROS impels us *to return to the Bible* and to search the Word of God for a message that is relevant to what we are experiencing in South Africa today"; and goes on to warn that this would be "no mere academic exercise" (Kairos 1986: 17). But *The Kairos Document* offered little by way of a process that could assist us to move beyond our paralysis. So it was with small hesitant and heuristic steps that groups of ordinary black African Bible "readers" and socially engaged biblical scholars began to meet to read the Bible together. These groups took many forms and were shaped by a range of influences, including the experiences of the Bible movement in Brasil and of many Non-Governmental Organisations and Community-Based Organisations in South Africa. Ten years later, after hundreds of such meetings in various contexts throughout South Africa (and beyond) and with some reflection on the practice of contextual Bible study as it has evolved, we can speak more clearly of this process and offer a feel of its contours. In what remains of this essay I will sketch the dimensions of the contextual Bible study process as we in the Institute for the Study of the Bible (ISB) have come to understand it, beginning with the call that comes to socially engaged biblical scholars to read with ordinary readers of the Bible.

Typically, the ISB is approached by a particular group to participate with them in Bible study or theological reflection. When invited, staff in the ISB first ascertain whether the invitation comes from a group that already has some degree of structured organization. Organized groups tend to have a stronger sense of identity than unorganized groups and it is this sense of identity that enables a

group both to own the particular project they are inviting the ISB
to participate in with them and to "talk back" to the ISB. Implicit
in any participation with church and/or community based groups
are complex matrices of power, and so the ISB prefers to work with
groups who have a fairly clear idea of what they want from a particular project and what resources they themselves bring to the project, and who will not be intimidated by the presence of ISB staff
and their resources. A key commitment of the ISB is to work within
the social reality of the group, as it is experienced and understood
by the group.

If the invitation comes from an unorganized group or if the organized group has only a vague idea of the project, then the ISB offers
resources which would assist the group to structure itself and/or to
formulate more carefully their project. Wherever possible, the ISB
also encourages groups to draw in related groups in the community
and/or church who would share similar concerns. This often means,
for example, that the ISB would suggest to an Anglican women's
group that they invite other women's groups in their area to join
with them to form an ecumenical project.

Once the organized group has ownership of the project, the ISB
then joins with them in a workshop. Usually the workshop is based
on a theme or issue that is of vital concern to the group; so, for
example, the group may want to deal with the question of violence
against women, or leadership, or unemployment. Because the Bible
is a resource for groups with which we work, Bible study is always
one of the activities of a workshop—though there may be other
activities as well—and is the activity that the ISB is specifically invited
to facilitate.

Contextual Bible study is essentially a communal process,[3] in which
local community resources for interpreting the Bible and the specialized interpretative tools of biblical scholars are used together to
"read" the Bible. I place "read" in inverted commas because ordinary interpreters of the Bible differ in degrees of literacy and because
literacy is not required of every participant. But having said this,
reading the Bible is an important component of the contextual Bible
study process, and literary resources are one of the resources that
socially engaged biblical scholars bring with them to the process (see

---

[3] In which, as I have indicated, power relations are acknowledged, foregrounded,
and equalized as far as possible.

below). Being able to read is one of the interpretative resources that participants who can read offer to the group. Contextual Bible study requires a sharing of skills and resources; it cannot be done alone. In fact, contextual Bible study demands more than a weak sense of "communal" conveys; central to contextual Bible study is a commitment to collaborative work and interpretation.

I have already used the phrase "socially engaged biblical scholar," but without any comment. Implicit in this phrase is the participation of the biblical scholar in forms of social transformation. The biblical scholar who is called to interpret the Bible with ordinary poor and marginalized communities is usually one who is already involved in forms of social struggle, reconstruction, and development, and who already has taken sides with the poor and marginalized in their struggles for survival, liberation, and life. Collaborative interpretation, then, is only another form of working with others.

Such collaboration brings with it a conversion "from below" in which the biblical scholar becomes partially constituted by the experiences and struggles of the poor and marginalized (West 1999). One of the most significant consequences of such forms of collaboration has been a growing shift in how the socially engaged biblical scholar conceives of his or her role in the contextual Bible study process. In the formative days of reflection on forms of collaboration between socially engaged biblical scholars and ordinary poor and marginalized "readers" of the Bible, Marxist categories of analysis tended to prevail. Popular religion was seen as "the opiate of the people," a manifestation of "false consciousness" which kept the masses captive to the dominant ideology and slaves to systems of exploitation. The primary function of the socially engaged biblical scholar was to conscientize the people, to "break the culture of silence," and to enable them to create their own language (Frostin 1988: 10, Segundo 1985). But we have been forced by our collaboration to find new categories of analysis and different ways of seeing. Gradually we have begun to understand that the poor and marginalized do speak, that they are not silent, though they may appear to be so. In fact, their apparent subservience and silence is precisely this, an appearance. Behind the mask of compliance are many finely crafted "arts of resistance" (Scott 1990).

Oppressed people's accommodation to the logic of domination is an elaborate act, a show that they practice and perform in order to survive, while they wait for an opportunity to transform their reality.

But because real transformation is difficult and dangerous and because the consequences of failure are dire for the oppressed, as South Africa under apartheid aptly demonstrates, poor and marginalized communities practice their arts of resistance in safe sequestered sites until an appropriate opportunity for public resistance can be found. Just as the dominant patrol the boundaries of their domination, ever vigilant for gaps in their hegemonic hold, so too the poor and marginalized keenly wait for the surveillance to wain and watch for cracks to appear in the borders and barriers through which their resistance might erupt.

Often, however, waiting and watching are not enough, and an irruption occurs in the face of domination. The hidden transcript spills into the streets and cries, "Enough!" Then, if sufficient voices join in, there is revolution. But, more often than not, the cries are crushed and surveillance is intensified, and resistance returns to its more artful forms.

In between these two moments, the moment of the hidden transcript offstage and the moment of the public irruption at center-stage, lies a zone of constant contestation. In this zone the dominant groups and ideologies present their domination in euphemistic terms, disguising their agenda of domination. So, for example, apartheid presented itself as "separate development" and transnational capitalist corporations present themselves quaintly as patrons of a "global village." Also occupying this contested zone are the poor and marginalized, whose dignity demands a presence and a say in the territory of the dominant, which they achieve by disguised forms of resistance. So, for example, subversive acts like poaching and pilfering and deconstructing discourses like trickster tales and satiric stories are a constant reminder that all is not as controlled as it appears.

In sum, the poor and marginalized are not as constrained at the level of thought as we had imagined, though in situations of strong surveillance and domination they are often severely constrained at the level of action (contra Antonio Gramsci). They have much to say, provided they have a safe space and place to say it.[4] They are

---

[4] For a detailed discussion of these matters see West 1999. As indicated in note 2 above, the reflections here are part of "a web" of reflections. My ideal implied reader would have followed my various moves within this web, though, alas, I accept that most of my readers do not have the time or inclination to navigate my web!

not without their own(ed) interpretations, though heavy surveillance
may mean that there has been insufficient time and space to articulate and corporately own them.

The socially engaged biblical scholar is called to read the Bible
with them, but not because they need to be conscientized and given
interpretations relevant to their context. No, socially engaged biblical scholars are called to collaborate with them because they bring
with them additional interpretative resources which may be of use
to the community group, of which I will say more about below.
Before I do, however, one other feature of the collaborative interface should be mentioned. In some communities it may even be that
the very presence of the socially engaged biblical scholar (or theologian) is a resource in that, for example, such a person may enable
a group to form and meet in a situation where the surveillance of
dominant forces usually prevents such gatherings (Haddad 2000). A
group of workers or women may be allowed to meet with a (socially
engaged) pastor or priest when they would not be permitted to meet
together under any other circumstances. Furthermore, as a boundary crosser, someone who moves between the worlds of the dominant and the dominated, and as a boundary betrayer, someone who
has exposed the logic of domination, the socially engaged biblical
scholar may provide additional information for charting the boundaries and borders. Collaborative interpretation, then, is a second core
commitment of the contextual Bible study process.

Socially engaged biblical scholars, as boundary crossers, not only
contribute spatially, helping to chart more clearly where the boundaries are; by offering resources that cross boundaries in and of time,
socially engaged biblical scholars are able to open up potential "lines
of connection" between present local communities of faith and past
communities of faith in the biblical tradition (Schreiter 1985: 18,
West 1999: 77). The systematic and structured sets of questions that
constitute the work of biblical scholars may provide, therefore, other
ways of interpreting and so appropriating the biblical text, and in so
doing may enable what is incipient (Cochrane 1999) to be owned
by the reading community. As I have indicated, local communities of
poor and marginalized believers have their own hermeneutics of resistance and survival with which they "re-member" the Bible and construct their "lived" and "working" theologies. They may be naive and
pre-critical, unsystematic and scattered, and they may draw incongruously on a range of symbols, rituals, readings and ideas, but they

are theirs—they are what they live by. In some cases their readings and theologies resonate with the readings and theologies of their churches, but often they do not, and so they have to be disguised and hidden. Often what is proclaimed in the pulpits, what is sung in the hymns and songs, what is listened to in the liturgy, and what is performed in the cultic rituals, only partially resonates with the "working" readings and theologies of ordinary people. People then, for example, belong to the Anglican church by day and to a Zionist church by night—if they are fortunate enough to find a place to belong to by night where their incipient "working" theology resonates with the "official" theology of the church. Yet even here, in this marginal site, there may not be a place for the readings and theologies of some—for example, of women.

Ordinary "readers" of the Bible from poor and marginalized communities and socially engaged biblical scholars interpret the Bible differently, but within the practice of the ISB this difference is seen as profoundly creative rather than a problem. Ordinary "readers" bring with them a whole range of interpretative strategies forged in diverse and difficult circumstances, and while these strategies have not been adequately analysed (West 1999: 79–107), they are strategies that have been forged over time which have been found to work. The interpretative tools and methods of biblical scholars have been catalogued, and so it is easier to specify the kind of reading resources they bring to the collaborative interpretative process. Being conscious of the reading resources socially engaged biblical scholars bring to the interpretative interface has enabled us to track and trace their contribution.

When official or received readings are not meaningful, powerful, and true (see Cady 1986), then ordinary "readers" only have their own resources for interpreting and appropriating the biblical tradition. For many this may mean a constant sense of discontinuity between their "working" readings and theologies and the biblical tradition as they have encountered it. This alienation between the lived faith/working theologies of ordinary poor and marginalized Bible "readers" and the public readings and theologies of their churches may be exacerbated in contexts where surveillance is constant. So, for example, women in rural contexts may not even know that other women in the community share a similar working theology, though, of course, they may suspect that this is the case (see Scott 1990,

Haddad 2000). However, while working with socially engaged biblical scholars, not only is there a safe (and sacred) place to engage with each other, but they also have access to other resources— resources which offer other possibilities for continuity with other parts of the tradition. The interpretative resources of socially engaged biblical scholars offer forms of access to the boundaries of the biblical tradition that are not available to ordinary "readers," and in so doing they provide opportunities for lines of connection between the "working" readings and theologies of poor and marginalized believers and previously inaccessible parts of the biblical tradition. Being able to find lines of connection is potentially empowering because, as Rosemary Radford Ruether reminds us, to find glimmers of what is authentic and true for us in "submerged and alternative traditions" is to "assure oneself that one is not mad or duped" (Ruether 1983: 126–128).

Because black Africans were confronted, converted, and catechized with particular parts and peculiar interpretations of Bible, it is these that have constituted the raw material of their interpretative and appropriative acts. The resources of socially engaged biblical scholars and theologians open up, through the contextual Bible study process, additional parts of and perspectives on the Bible. Neglected and forgotten texts become available; those parts of the canon ignored by the missionaries and colonialists are now read; alternative forms of access to the very edges of the tradition are found; and the received readings of well worn texts are disrupted and deconstructed. The plurality of interpretative perspectives that constitute biblical studies today open up and offer unexpected places of connection with the biblical tradition. In short, our additional reading strategies and tools provide increased capacities for interpretation and appropriation.

Different interpretative resources offer potentially different forms for finding a place in the biblical tradition with which to establish continuity. And while most ordinary "readers" have little problem with recognizing and acknowledging moments of discontinuity with the Bible, their deep desire is for lines of continuity. Continuity may be with reconstructed sectors of society and their struggles behind the text (Schüssler Fiorenza 1983, Mosala 1989), with untold stories, neglected themes, and unfamiliar characters in the text (Bal 1988, Trible 1978), or with potential worlds (Schneiders 1999) and theological trajectories (Brueggemann 1993) projected in front of the text which intersect with the experiences "readers" bring to the reading process. In these and other ways, ordinary poor and marginalized "readers" can make lines of connection with parts of the tradition not previously encountered, particularly those parts which are not usually the resources of the dominant readings and theologies that proliferate in the public life of the Church.

In those places where socially engaged biblical scholars and poor and marginalized "readers" of the Bible read together there are indications that the various interpretative interests (Fowl 1990) of socially engaged biblical scholars can provide alternative access to parts of the tradition that may source and resource poor and marginalized communities. Sources for survival, liberation and life in the biblical tradition may be scarce, and we may have to search for them in the cracks, gaps, and absences of the forms of the tradition we have received. But, it appears from our practice, the contextual Bible study process provides the space, a safe and sacred place, and the resources for locating lines of connection with the biblical tradition, for enabling subjugated and incipient readings and theologies to be articulated and owned, for discovering whether our "working" readings and theologies resonate with those of others we live and work with, for being partially constituted by the other we "read with," and for giving shape to resisting and reconstructing readings and theologies that bring survival, liberation, and life.

The readiness, in our experience, with which ordinary black African "readers" have embraced the otherness of our resources demonstrates their openness to these critical resources.[5] The third commitment of the contextual Bible study process, therefore, is a commitment to a critical reading of the Bible.

However, the way in which ordinary black African "readers" have taken up these critical resources demonstrates that they have not abandoned the array of interpretive resources they already possess. On receiving critical resources ordinary Black African "readers" do not become purists who pursue particular interpretative perspectives. They do not; they do not because they read for purposes other than the production of academic papers—they "read" for survival, liberation, and life. So the fourth and final core commitment of the contextual Bible study process is a commitment to use the Bible for

---

[5] I use the term "critical" here in the sense of a structure and systematic set of questions; this is what biblical scholars do, they pose structured and systematic questions to the Bible.

social transformation. Contextual Bible studies end in some form of action.

Speaking of which, let me now leave the theory[6] and offer a brief example. Increasingly the ISB has been invited to participate in workshops organized by women's groups on the theme of violence against women. Our contribution to these workshops has been varied; we have offered some resources for facilitator training, we have encouraged groups of women to network with each other both ecumenically and regionally, we have put the group in contact with relevant Non-Governmental Organizations (NGOs) and government departments, but our major contribution has been to facilitate a contextual Bible study.

In workshops with this theme we usually work with 2 Samuel 13: 1–22, a neglected and marginalized text which is found in few lectionaries and seldom publicly read (and never on a Sunday). Having made sure that counsellors are available we work with the following framework.

2 Samuel 13:1–22 is read aloud to the group as a whole. After the text has been read a series of questions follow.

1. Read 2 Samuel 13:1–22 together again in small groups. Share with each other what you think the text is about.

Each small group is then asked to report back to the larger group. Each and every response to question one is summarized on newsprint. After the report back, the participants return to their small groups to discuss the following questions.

2. Who are the main characters in this story and what do we know about them?

3. What is the role of each of the male characters in the rape of Tamar?

4. How does Tamar respond throughout the story?

When the small groups have finished their discussion, and this takes considerable time, each group is invited to present a summary of their discussion. This is done in a variety of ways; if there is time, each group is asked to report on each question, but if time is a constraint then each group is asked to report on only one question. The full report, which the scribe of the group puts up on newsprint, is then displayed for everyone to read at some

---

[6] Again, the theoretical dimensions are discussed in detail in West 1999. More practical resources can be found in (West 1993).

other time. The report backs can also be presented more creatively, by way of drama, poetry or song.

After this report back the smaller groups reconvene and discuss
the following questions.

*5. Are there women like Tamar in your church and/or community? Tell their
story.*

6. What is the theology of women who have been raped?

7. What resources are there in your area for survivors of rape?

Once again, the small groups present their report back to the
plenary group. Creativity is particularly vital here, as often women
find it difficult or are unable to articulate their responses. A drama
or a drawing may be the only way in which some groups can
report.

Finally, each small group comes together to formulate an action
plan.

8. What will you now do in response to this Bible study?

The action plan is either reported to the plenary or presented
on newsprint for other participants to study after the Bible study.

In our experience the effects of this Bible study are substantial.
Women are amazed that such a text exists, are angry that they have
never heard it read or preached, are relieved to discover that they
are not alone, are empowered because the silence has been broken
and their stories have been told. As one women said, "If such a text
exists in the Bible, how can we be silent about these things in the
church?" How indeed.

Implicit in the Bible study as outlined above are all the elements
of the contextual Bible study process. The Bible study begins and
ends with what can be called "community consciousness" questions.
Questions 1, 5, 6, 7, and 8 draw on the readings and resources of
the local community group. By using small groups and writing up
all responses, the contributions of all participants are affirmed. Habit-
ually, responses to question 1 elicit the public transcript; participants offer interpretations they have received and which they feel
are safe to proclaim publicly. They know what they are expected to
believe about the Bible. However, there are usually some responses
which are more ambiguous and which potentially provide space for
more authentic interpretations—interpretations that articulate something of their "working" theologies. If the group becomes a safe
place, if there are resources to articulate what is often incipient and

inchoate, and if there are resonances with others in the group, then gradually elements of "working," "lived" faith may be more overtly and vigorously voiced and owned.

Clustered in between the opening and closing community consciousness questions are a series of what might be called "critical consciousness" questions. These questions are the contribution of the socially engaged biblical scholar, and provide resources for repeated returns to the text and more careful and close "reading." In this example, the critical consciousness questions draw on literary modes of interpretation, posing questions about characters, plot, setting, etc. Such structured and systematic questions are not usually in the repertoire of ordinary "readers," though once asked, the questions are readily grasped and appropriated. The advantage of using questions which draw on literary modes of interpretation is that they do not require any input from the socially engaged biblical scholar (—"the expert"). The questions are contribution enough, and ordinary "readers" make of them what they will. However, in many instances ordinary "readers" want access to resources that are only available to the "trained" reader. So, for example, participants may want to know the significance of Tamar tearing her clothing. In such cases, the socially engaged biblical scholar may offer socio-historical resources in response to this question, choosing to do this, preferably and where possible, by drawing on parallels in the participants' own socio-historical context.

In our experience literary-type questions almost always lead into socio-historical-type questions; this is important, because it indicates the need ordinary "readers" have to locate faith in real concrete contexts. But by beginning with literary-type questions and by allowing socio-historical-type questions to emerge from the participants, the powerful presence of the biblical scholar is held in check. Equally importantly, by waiting for the questions to arise from the participants, we can be sure that we are answering questions of interest to them rather than questions of interest to us biblical scholars (on which the industry of biblical scholarship is based).

Critical consciousness questions facilitate a more careful and close reading of the text than is usually the case among ordinary "readers." They give the text a voice, and in so doing open up potential lines of connection with faith trajectories in the biblical tradition that have been neglected or suppressed. Women discover, to return to our example, that they are not alone, that their terror can be found in the Bible, and while this "text of terror" (Trible 1984) gives little comfort, it does at least acknowledge the reality of their experience.

The concluding community consciousness questions (5, 6, 7, and 8) ground the Bible study firmly in the life of the participants. In responding to these questions, community consciousness and critical consciousness fuse and fashion faith interpretations[7] that make sense and which are an expression of the "lived," "working" theologies of ordinary believers. Whether or how these incipient and inchoate faith interpretations are articulated depends on how safe the contextual Bible study process is. In safe places women who have been touched by Tamar tell their stories, help and hold the pain of their sisters, and plan for the transformation of their churches and communities. Unfortunately, not all Bible study groups are safe, and so women may remain silent, waiting still. But the potential is there, implicit within the contextual Bible study process, for the articulation, owning, and acting out of those interpretations and theologies that ordinary "readers" of the Bible live by.

The ISB too has been challenged to act beyond the contextual Bible study process. Beginning in 2000 the ISB will be launching a "Tamar Sunday" campaign throughout South Africa, in which local churches will be provided with resources to recognize, recover, and revive Tamar's story.

Even before the Bible is opened, the "unopened" Bible as symbol and icon creates a sacred space within which believers gather. The contextual Bible study process honours this space by providing a range of resources with which ordinary "readers" of the Bible, together with the socially engaged biblical scholars they have called to read with them,[8] can use to locate themselves and their daily experiences in the biblical tradition. The contextual Bible study process provides a safe (and sacred) space, and a place, for owning and articulating working theologies of survival, liberation, and life— theologies which in turn form the foundation of social transformation. Which explains the second part of my title for this essay. "When the white man came to our country he had the Bible and we (Blacks) had the land. The white man said to us 'let us pray.' After the prayer, the white man had the land and we had the Bible." This is

---

[7] For an illuminating analysis of the relationship between "faith interpretations" and biblical scholarship see Patte 1995.

[8] I place considerable emphasis on the preposition "with" (see West 1999: 34–62).

true; but the contextual Bible study process is a South African resource, among many others, for reclaiming and regaining land, dignity and identity (see also Maluleke 1998: 62, Mosala 1987: 194).

BIBLIOGRAPHY

Bal, Mieke. *Death and Dissymmetry: The Politics of Coherence in Book of Judges*. Chicago:
    University of Chicago Press, 1988.
Brueggemann, Walter. "Trajectories in Old Testament Literature and the Sociology
    of Ancient Israel." In Eds Norman K. Gottwald and Richard A. Horsley, *The
    Bible and Liberation: Political and Social Hermeneutics*, Maryknoll: Orbis, 1993: 201–
    226.
Cady, L.E. "Hermeneutics and Tradition: The Role of the Past in Jurisprudence
    and Theology." *Harvard Theological Journal* 79 (1986): 439–463.
Cochrane, James R. *Circles of Dignity: Community Wisdom and Theological Reflection*.
    Minneapolis: Fortress, 1999.
Fiorenza, Elizabeth Schüssler. *In Memory of Her: A Feminist Theological Reconstruction of
    Christian Origins*. London: SCM, 1983.
Fowl, Stephen E. "The Ethics of Interpretation; Or, What's Left Over after the
    Elimination of Meaning." In Eds David J.A. Clines, Stephen E. Fowl and
    Stanley E. Porter, *The Bible in Three Dimensions: Essays in Celebration of the Fortieth
    Anniversary of the Department of Biblical Studies, University of Sheffield*, Sheffield: JSOT
    Press, 1990: 379–398.
Frostin, Per. *Liberation Theology in Tanzania and South Africa: A First World Interpretation*.
    Lund: Lund University Press, 1988.
Haddad, Beverley G. "African Women's Theologies of Survival: Intersecting Faith,
    Feminisms, and Development." Ph.D., University of Natal, 2000.
Kairos. *The Kairos Document: Challenge to the Church*. Revised Second Edition. Braam-
    fontein: Skotaville, 1986.
Maluleke, Tinyiko S. "The Land of the Church: A Response to the Whole Issue."
    Bulletin for Contextual Theology in Africa 5, no. 3 (1998): 61–64.
Mosala, Itumeleng J. "African Independent Churches: A Study in Socio-theologi-
    cal Protest." In Charles Villa-Vicencio and John W. De Gruchy, *Resistance and
    Hope: South African Essays in Honour of Beyers Naude*. Cape Town: David Philip,
    1985: 103–111.
———. "Biblical Hermeneutics and Black Theology in South Africa." Ph.D.,
    University of Cape Town, 1987.
———. *Biblical Hermeneutics and Black Theology in South Africa*. Grand Rapids: Eerdmans,
    1989.
Patte, Daniel. *Ethics of Biblical Interpretation: A Reevaluation*. Louisville, Kentucky: West-
    minster: John Knox, 1995.
Ruether, Rosemary Radford. *Sexism and God-talk: Towards a Feminist Theology*. London:
    SCM, 1983.
Schneiders, Sandra M. *The Revelatory Text: Interpreting the New Testament as Sacred
    Scripture*. Second ed. Collegeville, Minnesota: Michael Glazier, The Liturgical
    Press, 1999.
Schreiter, Robert J. *Constructing Local Theologies*. Maryknoll: Orbis, 1985.
Scott, James C. *Domination and the Arts of Resistance: Hidden Transcripts*. New Haven
    and London: Yale University Press, 1990.
Segundo, Juan Luis. "The Shift within Latin American Theology." *Journal of Theology
    for Southern Africa* 52 (1985): 17–29.

Tracy, David. *Plurality and Ambiguity: Hermeneutics, Religion, Hope.* San Francisco: Harper and Row, 1987.

Trible, Phyllis. *God and the Rhetoric of Sexuality.* Philadelphia: Fortress, 1978.

———. *Texts of Terror: Literary-feminist Readings of Biblical Narratives.* Philadelphia: Fortress, 1984.

West, Gerald O. *The Academy of the Poor: Towards a Dialogical Reading of the Bible.* Sheffield: Sheffield Academic Press, 1999.

———. "Being Partially Constituted by Work with Others: Biblical Scholars Becoming Different." *Journal of Theology for Southern Africa* 104 (1999): 44–53.

———. *Biblical Hermeneutics of Liberation: Modes of Reading the Bible in the South African Context.* Second Edition. Maryknoll, and Pietermaritzburg: Orbis Books and Cluster Publications, 1995.

———. *Contextual Bible Study.* Pietermaritzburg: Cluster Publications, 1993.

———. "Contextual Bible Study: Creating Sacred (and Safe) Spaces for Social Transformation." *Grace and Truth* 16, no. 2 (1999): 51–62.

TO PRAY THE LORD'S PRAYER IN THE GLOBAL
ECONOMIC ERA (MATT. 6:9-13)[1]

Musa W. Dube

> Professor Very Pius, if the Jesus' paradigmatic prayer (called the
> Lord's Prayer) has as its paramount concerns bread for subsistence
> in a time of hunger, relief from debt when an unjust debt structure
> crushed the people underfoot, and the establishment of God's sole
> sovereignty when the people's misery was largely the by-product of
> Caesar's imperial control, then why is the Lord's Prayer not also
> called the Lord's Paradigmatic Critique of Political Economy? The
> Lord's Model of Social Analysis? (Hendricks 1995: 79).

Prayer is an expression of wishes, dreams, hopes and needs. It
expresses the vision one espouses for oneself, for one's family and
friends, neighbours and communities, nations and creation at large.
Thus praying is something that most people do. Yet what distinguishes prayer, from any other human desire, is that it is a human
will in search of Divine partnership. To pray is to seek to merge
one's vision and wishes with the Divine vision, for oneself and for
others. From a Christian perspective, to pray is to constantly declare
one's visions, availability, and commitment to seeking God's will for
oneself and for others, including the earth, or God's creation at large.
There are indeed many prayers and ways of praying, yet the Lord's
Prayer is, undoubtedly, the most popular prayer among Christian
communities. The Lord's Prayer is probably the most well-known
and memorized text of the Christian Testament. Long before many
Christian children can open and read the Bible for themselves, they
have already been taught to memorize and recite the Lord's Prayer
at home, church, and, in many cases, at school. I remember that it
took me many years before I came to discover that the Lord's Prayer
was a text in the Christian Testament even though I had recited it
for as long as I could remember.

---

[1] This essay first appeared in *The Ecumenical Review* 49/4 (1997): 439-450. It appears here with permission.

This popularity of the Lord's Prayer entails positive and negative factors. Positively, the popularity indicates its importance to the Christian faith. It indicates that the vision of the Lord's Prayer is probably regarded as the nearest articulation of God's will for the world, that the Lord's Prayer is the clearest statement on the role of Christian men and women in their partnership with God on earth, and that in praying the Lord's Prayer Christian individuals and communities at large repeatedly pledge their commitment and responsibility to the realization of God's will on earth. Thus the Lord's Prayer is called the Lord's Prayer even though it is women and men who use it, for prayer is an attempt to meet, hear, speak and work with God. Prayer is a pledge made by men and women to take responsibility for their interpersonal and international relationships on earth. Because of these positive and significant aspects of the Lord's Prayer to the Christian faith and communities, it is imperative for adherents to pause and ponder upon the meaning and the vision of the Lord's Prayer as well as the implications of reciting this prayer, especially in the global economic era. It is also because of this centrality that I have chosen to probe its vision and what it may offer us in the global era. This, however, is not to claim that other visions cannot be found within the Bible, in other religious cultures, or in current solutions offered by the wise and responsible citizens of the world, for, as John Parratt reminds us, "the search for a just society is not the prerogative of Christians alone" (1996: 286).

Negatively, the popularity of the Lord's Prayer means that many people have come to recite it without reflecting on its meaning and its implications. The Lord's Prayer has become just another text that one recites because one has always recited it at home or in their Christian gatherings, but not because we are saying something we wish to bring to realization. In this essay, I seek to invite all the Christian practitioners of various persuasions and races—readers, believers, hearers, academicians, planners, economists, politicians, and nations of the Christian and non-Christian worlds—to reconsider the responsibility of praying the Lord's Prayer in the global economic era. My goal in this essay is to confront Christian practitioners with the following questions: What is the vision of the Lord's Prayer for God's world and people? What if we pray the Lord's Prayer attentively—seriously pledging our commitment to being partners with God in building God's kingdom on earth? What would we do in the age of globalization? My aim in this essay is not to offer "the correct," "the original" or "the only" meaning of the Lord's Prayer, although I may rhetorically sound like I am offering such an explication. Rather, my aim is to read the Lord's Prayer in order to urge Christian communities and individuals to assume active responsibility in the global economic era. My reading, in other words, is prompted by ethical concerns for current international economic practices. It is important that I should begin by giving a definition or picture of the global economic system.

I describe the global era as an age characterized by increasingly interconnected economic systems of different countries, nations, and continents (see Lind 1995: 30–36). This closely knit economic organ is in fact a relationship of dependence and interdependence, of exploitation and exponential profit, of economic giants and dwarfs, indeed, of masters and servants as well as massive monetary loses and gains. The economic global era at its basic level is described by my son's observation, when he comments that everything in North America is written "made in China." One immediately wonders if an average house in China would have many items written "made in the USA." Perhaps not. Indeed, the colours of the global economic era are evident here in the streets and villages of Botswana, where North American and European products and companies are at home, while one hardly ever finds Botswana companies or products in overseas markets, save, occasionally, for baskets. In other words, globalization is an economic system that has turned the world into a small interconnected village—but for only a handful of people to run and benefit from. Hence it allows those who are in power to export and import goods to certain markets easily, while this is not automatically applicable to their trading partners. For example, this system allows those in power to import many foreign goods at cheap rates, while they do not allow the concerned nations to enjoy the same privileges for their populations. Its manifestations are seen in the so-called multi-national companies and corporations that build industrial plants in developing countries to exploit cheap labour and maximize their profits. Yet these developing countries are seldom, if ever, invited to establish their businesses in developed nations in order to maximize their profits.

Describing the global economic era Ngugi wa Thiong'o states that

> Economic links are quite obvious. The leading financial institutions—banks, insurances, credit cards—operate in nearly all the capitals of the earth. Transnationals of all kinds link economic activities of several

the rich are getting richer and the poor poorer. What then is the point of revisiting these old and open secrets? What necessitates that the Christian communities, institutions and individuals return to reflect upon this old problem that has taken on a new mask? First, this economic set up of international relations has never been solved, it persists—indeed, it has worsened. Second, it painfully affects lives and takes away lives. In short, the global economic set up is, as Lind tells us, unethical, exploitative and causes a great deal of suffering in the world. And, I would say, it is inconsistent with God's will for the earth.

Some reader may well say, "Get used to it. This is not a problem but the rule of capitalism and free market system." There is a problem, however, and the problem is that the free market system is not free. It is structured to benefit a few and exploit multitudes. It is designed to privilege those who are already in power. Someone may also say, "This problem cannot be solved by Christian communities, institutions and individuals. This is a problem of political governments." True as these arguments may be, Christian practitioners are part of the world, and, I would insist, they are not exempted from the responsibility to stop and think, to assess if the current set up resonates with the will of God for God's creation. Christian practitioners are not exempted from building healthy interpersonal and international relationships that promote God's kingdom.

Suppose the Lord's Prayer encapsulates an important part of God's vision for the world, and calls upon all those who recite it to be responsible partners with God in building the kingdom of God on earth? Would the Christian practitioners then be at peace with the current economic international structures? Would we be at home with corrupt and exploitative governments? Would we regard the current international and national structures as constitutive of godly interpersonal relations? I suppose not. I now turn to an analysis of the potentially probing and productive Lord's Prayer. To reflect on the vision and challenges of the Lord's Prayer in today's world it is necessary to examine its context, its contents, and its contention.

What is the literary and historical context of the Lord's prayer? In the Matthean gospel, the Lord's Prayer is a component of the Sermon on the Mount (Matthew 5–7:28). Many readers have noted that the Sermon on the Mount is an inter-textual construction that recalls Moses receiving the Law of God on Mount Sinai (Exodus 19–20). At Mount Sinai God does not only call the Israelites out of slavery. The new nation is culturally, economically, politically and socially called to be responsible to God's vision for them. The Matthean community, on the other hand, is one of the many Jewish groups that has survived the destruction of the temple in Jerusalem in 70 CE. Critical times become moments for listening to God and for seeking God's vision most intently. Crises call for a re-vision, for hearing and seeing anew.

As a black African woman of Botswana—who is a survivor of colonialism, and the subsequent neo-colonialism of globalization—I live in the deep shadow of death. To live with the intensification of poverty in African countries, to live with wars and coups, to live with corruption and exploitation, to watch helplessly as beloved friends, neighbours, and relatives slowly shrivel as HIV/AIDS gnaws at them, is to live where death and life have become identical twins. Indeed, the fact that the highest concentration of HIV/AIDS is in Sub-Saharan Africa is related to the economic realities of the continent. Furthermore, HIV/AIDS exacerbates the economic crisis since able-bodied and trained workers are either too sick to work, dying or dead. Yet the economic realities of Africa, or any place for that matter, are not independent from international relations. The fact that there are constant wars and coups is related to poverty. People are adopting a strategy of the survival of the fittest in the face of insufficient resources, corrupt governments and international trade policies. The economic crises of African countries are both nationally and internationally founded.

This context of death-living challenges me to reflect on what it means to profess Christian faith and to pray the Lord's Prayer in the global economic era. I am confronted with a crisis that necessitates a re-examination of the Lord's Prayer. What, in other words, is God's vision for God's creation? What are the roles of Christian men and women, individually and corporately, in bringing God's kingdom on earth? Is there any vision that is pledged to God and to each other when Christians recite the Lord's Prayer? If so, is this a vision we can implement? And, how? These questions shall be the subject of my reading of the Lord's Prayer, through a close reading of the prayer.

The first line of the Lord's prayer says, "Our Father in the heavens, hallowed be Your name." This opening of the Lord's Prayer presents the heavens as the realm of patriarchal power. God is called Father. Such a view hardly proposes a liberating vision for women

who have borne various forms of gender exclusion and subordination in patriarchal structures of the world. Luckily, many Christian
and non-Christian readers, communities, and institutions agree that
God is neither a father nor a mother. The use of the word "father"
only reflects a particular culture and time as well as the limitation
of human language in representing God. Gender research has shown
that the metaphoric use of male language to represent realms of
Divine Power does in fact re-enforce the exclusion and subordination of women in the society. This first line of the Lord's Prayer,
therefore, can be read as "Our parent in the heavens, hallowed be
your name," without losing its meaning to Christian worshippers. By
designating God as a parent, the Lord's Prayer is not only gender
neutral, it also confronts all the Christian communities and individuals of different persuasions and nations with an image of a family.
And family, for the most part, means sharing, love, relationships,
care and staying together. Christian nations, races, women and men
of different colours, sizes and shapes in different countries and continents are all "children" of the same parent. Suppose all the reciters
of the Lord's Prayer began to grasp this truth, how would they live
with globalization that strips naked many members of the family in
order to over-embellish a few others?

The text of the Lord's Prayer differentiates God's residence from
the earth, where all the children live. God lives in the heavens. It
is pertinent to pursue the meaning of the heavens, how God's name
needs to be hallowed and the implications of hallowing God's name.
A lot has been said about the heavens. In Christian songs and mythology, heaven is a realm of absolute peace, equity, and self-sufficiency.
In heaven, so we have heard and sung, there is no pain, no death,
no hunger, no tear to stain the eye. In heaven, so we have seen in
the imagination of artists, there shall be no enmity, lions and people shall be friends. The economic factor that moves a lion to grab
and kill its nearest neighbour does not apply. Even men and women
shall no longer be given into marriage (Matthew 22:23–33). The
abode of God is thus constructed as a realm of equity, peace and
self-sufficiency. If this is how the Christian communities, nations and
individuals imagine heaven, how can it be translated into an economic vision for the world? I shall return to this point below.

The first part of the Lord's Prayer consists of three petitions "concerning God—let thy name be sanctified; Let thy kingdom come;
And let thy will be done" (Garland 1993: 80). It seems to me, that

the latter two elaborate on how and where God's name should be hallowed. I now turn to elaborate on these separately. "Your kingdom come, Your will be done on earth as it is in heaven." God's name is sanctified through the establishment of God's kingdom on earth. That is, the prayer exhorts all to "let the earth and its creatures be sacred unto the Lord." Many Western readers have elaborated on the meaning of "kingdom of God," holding that it does not designate a particular geographical place, but refers to the reign of God. Recently, George Tinker, has given us a Native American spatial reading of "kingdom of God." Tinker, reads "kingdom of God as a creation metaphor," that acknowledges "the goodness and inherent worth of all God's creatures" (Tinker 1994: 176). The Lord's Prayer, therefore, enjoins the Christian communities, nations and individuals to embrace the rule of God in order for the will of God to be established on earth, or upon God's creation. The Lord's Prayer proceeds to state that God's name will be hallowed if God's rule and will are established *on earth as it is in heaven*. In saying, "Your kingdom come, your will be done on earth as it is in heaven," the prayer exhorts all to let the earth and its creatures to be sacred to God.

It is difficult to define the rule of God in modern political terms such as "democratic," "socialist," "liberal," "conservative," or "communist" etc. Nevertheless, the Christian communities have constructed elaborate images of heaven as a place of peace, self-sufficiency and equity, or a state of being in absolute peace. This ideal picture is a perception, a construction, an image of God's rule in heaven, built by Christians according to their understanding of their faith. And since it insists that "what passes for heaven 'up there' can be effected 'down here'" the perception of God's rule must be effected on the geographical spaces of the earth (Overman 1996: 93). God's abode, in other words, might be in the heavens and God's children may dwell here on earth, but the rule of God must apply equally on both sides. Sacredness of the earth or creation at large must be recognised, by hallowing God's name. In this regard, the vision of the Lord's Prayer is definitely a challenge to the Christian communities, nations, institutions and individuals that have become at home with the mechanisms and ethics of imperialism, colonialism, and globalization.

It has been observed that in these three petitions, God is seemingly enjoined to bring to realization the sanctification of God's name, to bring God's kingdom and God's will. God meets God's own needs! This, however, does not mean that practitioners of the Christian faith are exempted from responsibility. Indeed, Christian adherents are active participants, who pledge their commitment to the sanctification of God's name through the establishment of God's rule on earth as it is in heaven. This is underlined by the separated abode of God and God's children: while God lives in the heavens, the children live on earth. The separation underlines the responsibility assigned to the daughters and sons of God on earth. To pray the Lord's Prayer as Christian practitioners, therefore, is to pledge responsibility in being active partners in building the kingdom of God on earth. There is open recognition that the earth, and all that is in it, are sacred and belong to the Lord. To pray the Lord's Prayer is, therefore, to pledge responsibility for building healthy interpersonal and international relationships on earth. If praying the Lord's Prayer means to declare this commitment, can the Christian communities, nations, individuals and institutions live with and by the ethics of globalization?

I would hold that praying the Lord's Prayer in the present age of globalization should be to heed a call to turn to God and rejoice in hope, for if Christian practitioners understand themselves to be God's children and partners, then Christians can be committed to bringing God's kingdom on earth as it is in heaven; they can be dedicated to maintaining God's creation sacred. Keeping the earth sacred should be regarded as incompatible with exploitative global economic system, or living with corrupt and exploitative government policies. Indeed, as Tinker tells us, Christians should come to "experience evil or sin as a disruption in that delicate balance, which negates the intrinsic worth of any of our relatives" (Tinker 1994: 176). Taking heed of the implications of the Lord's Prayer most certainly necessitates a call for a new understanding of the Christian mission—a point that I shall elaborate upon in my concluding remarks.

Turning to the last three petitions, they focus on the interpersonal relationships of God's children with one another on earth. Whereas the first three petitions concern the will of God, the last three are concerned with the material and non-material needs of people. They consist of a petition for daily bread, for forgiveness and for deliverance from temptation and evil. "Give us this day our daily bread." Bread or food is an indispensable need in our lives. On a daily basis, women and men wake up and work to ensure that food is there in their houses. Globally, nations formulate and reformulate various economic strategies to ensure that their people stay supplied and well fed. The Lord's Prayer certainly underlines the place of bread by making it the first human request. To an average twentieth century worker it may sound funny that people work just to eat. With refrigerators, storerooms, and supermarkets full of food, it may seem unnecessary that one needs to pray for "daily bread." Many workers thus save to go on a holiday, to buy or build a house, to buy a car, electronic goods, clothes, health insurance, shares or bonds for future retirement or to meet the needs of their family members. Some work because they are interested or like their jobs. Nonetheless, praying for daily bread captures the centrality of food in our lives. People need food daily, and many are still without their daily bread and any assurance of its availability.

To pray for daily bread is thus a simple, but loud reminder to all Christian worlds that food is not readily available to all on a daily basis. It reminds all practitioners that God's will is food for all on a daily basis. Praying for daily bread confronts those who have their refrigerators, storerooms and supermarkets stuffed with food with a question: How come I do not need to pray for daily bread while homeless, jobless, and hardworking lower class people have little to put on their plates and those of their children? The Lord's Prayer gives the Christian communities and institutions the task of being responsible sons and daughters of God, who need to remember those members of the family who do not have any daily bread, but who cannot go on without it. The Lord's Prayer challenges all who eat, store, or throw away food to be producers and givers of daily bread. I do not, however, refer to the institution of charity, which, while useful, tends to work together with oppressive structures of the world. I believe that to be partners with God in supplying, producing or giving daily bread to the rest of God's family, the whole of God's creation, entails creating economic environments that enable all to work fairly for their bread. Economic contexts, be they global or local, that deny people being partners with God in seeking to meet their most basic needs, should be constantly assessed and remolded. As I see it, Christian practitioners and their institutions should be active ambassadors of God's reign. They should constantly scrutinize the policies and structures of their local and international governments to assess if they respectively allow God's rule to be realized on earth as in heaven. To pray for daily bread in the age of globalization should, therefore, require repentance. Uttering this line should challenge Christian practitioners who have become too comfortable with national and international economic structures that pump excess food to some areas and deprive many millions to realize that their contexts are inconsistent with God's will for the world. It challenges Christian communities and individuals that live with poverty and death to realize that God's rule and will is not realized on their parts of the world. That is, Christian communities and individuals both from extremely rich and extremely poor contexts are challenged to assess the economic structures at work that bless some and curse many and to promote international and national systems that will enable peace and self-sufficiency for all.

"And forgive us our debts as we have also forgiven our debtors." Forgiveness, what a difficult, costly and demanding discipline. It is incarnated by rare saints of the likes of Nelson Mandela, who in spite of twenty-seven years of imprisonment, displays no bitterness or revenge towards his oppressors. But how we all need it! In the context of Matthew's gospel, that of the Roman colonial empire, the average Palestinian Jewish person had debts. There was imperial tax (Matthew 22:15–22) and temple tax (Matthew 17:24–27) to be paid. Besides, many lived in crowded, insufficient and infertile lands, leading to unemployment and indebtedness (Matthew 18:23–35, Horsely 1993: 11–38, 254–255). Those who prayed the Lord's Prayer in Matthew's context, like many other colonized Jews of their time, knew what it meant to fail to pay their taxes, to borrow money from some rich landlord, and to not be able to meet this debt. Some would have been imprisoned for their debts and some would have lost their freedom or the freedom of members of their family (Matthew 5:25–26; 18:23–35).

Praying for the forgiveness of debts in the Matthean context was, therefore, not a spiritual utterance that had nothing to do with the economic structures of the day. Rather, it was a direct comment on the economic structures of the Roman Empire and Palestine. The Lord's Prayer is suggesting that debts due to the temple tax, imperial tax, and/or loans must be forgiven; they must be let go. The suggestion is not synonymous with the deliberate evasion of taxes or paying of loans, for indebtedness and paying for ones debts is central to the Christian faith. Rather, the Lord's Prayer challenges the systematic structures that lock many responsible, hard-working individuals and nations into a vicious circle of poverty and debts. The Lord's Prayer vision indicates that to place impossible debts on people through oppressive and exploitative international or national policies are inconsistent with the rule and will of God in heaven or on earth—it does not resonate with the role of hallowing God's name on earth.

Yet forgiveness is a two-way exercise. Not only do the worshippers ask for forgiveness, they have to forgive their debtors. Who are the debtors of the colonized and exploited Jews of the Matthean context? It is quite possible that so many people were indebted that almost everyone had at some time lent a struggling neighbour something which they could not repay (Matthew 5:23–25, 18:23–35, 20:1–19, 22:33–41). Most people would have had to forgive struggling neighbours and relatives who were not able to repay their debts. But another viable way of looking at this might be to consider forgiving both the imperial system of Rome and the collaborating local Jewish leadership! In the eyes of many ordinary people the imperial government and the collaborating local leadership owed them their land, their money and their autonomy. They knew that they were unjustly exploited (Horsely 1993: 33–58). Though they were angry and bitter, they may have taken it upon themselves to forgive—to dispense with anger and bitterness and to seek peace and healthy national and international trade systems. Asking for forgiveness and giving forgiveness is thus a call for repentance: the turning away from oppressive and exploitative economic and political policies to seeking God's will for the whole creation.

To pray for the forgiveness of debts as one has forgiven debtors in the Lord's Prayer, therefore, is not just an individual pursuit. Rather, it is a call to national and international economic restructuring—a restructuring that frees the oppressed from exploitative systems; a restructuring that calls those in positions of power to abandon their unjust economic strategies. To pray for forgiveness as one has forgiven is a clarion call to action. It demands, first, a restructuring that is not dictated from above, but one that is articulated from below, by those who seek justice. Second, it demands that exploiters should cease from their practices. National and international leaders and elites and their governments are forgiven as a statement against their exploitative systems. To forgive your debtor, in the context of the Lord's Prayer, is to say, "I know what you are doing to me and how you are doing it; it is unjust, and so I am angry and I want this to end, and I want for all of us to seek a just relationships." To forgive your debtors, those in power, is not to let them continue to dictate or formulate unjust national and international

terms of relations. Rather, is to be involved in seeking and formulating healthy and fair national and international economic policies.
I would thus say, praying the Lord's Prayer is a demanding call on
Christian communities, nations, institutions and individuals to actively
get involved in the formulation and implementation of a just rule,
a godly rule—to be responsible partners with God in building God's
kingdom on earth. Indeed, as Richard Horsely points out, the Lord's
Prayer's call for forgiveness of debts recalls the biblical concept of
the Jubilee "in which debts would be cancelled, prisoners released,
and people returned to their family inheritance as provided for in
Leviticus 25" (9). This allusion, as Horsely points out, indicates that
the message of Jesus was understood to advocate "social-economic
liberation" (248–255).

Obviously the issue of forgiving debts is not remote from us. It is
a reality that many Two-Thirds World countries are groaning under
the burden of debt. Some countries owe more than they produce as
a whole nation, yet the loans they have received have hardly improved
their lives. Indeed, most of these Two-Thirds World countries are
ensnared in worse forms colonization than in the pre-independence
era. As Sharon Ringe points out,

> The loans ostensibly were to support projects of economic develop-
> ment leading to greater economic stability.... In fact, however, the
> interest payments alone ... continue to wreck havoc on their economies,
> sending inflation rates soaring, provoking ever higher unemployment,
> and widening the gap between the very small wealthy class and des-
> titute masses (1995: 209).

We have heard that loaning money to African countries, for example, is like throwing money in a bottomless pit. The fact of the matter is that countries with such huge debts have painfully lost their
money, their land, their pride and their autonomy. They experience
themselves as owned and at the mercy of their benefactors. They
are also angry with their local governments, who misuse funds, and
they are angry with the international monetary bodies, who give
loans with interests rates that are designed to make it impossible to
repay completely or to sustain a healthy economy. These debts, of
course, also affect the interpersonal relationships of Two-Thirds World
people. With insufficient funds and food, people turn to fights, bribery,
stealing, coups, and crimes of many forms at all levels of the society as people struggle to survive with insufficient resources. In short,
with unhealthy and unjust national and international relationships,

there are severe constraints on the interpersonal relationships between people in these contexts. Dignity and integrity are lost to the tactics of the survival of the fittest.

Thus Two-Thirds World countries do not deny that they have debts or that they should pay them, or that they are unable to pay them. They ask for forgiveness, for they know they have had to forgive the so-called developed countries, who, for more than a century, have colonized them, exploited their resources and designed international markets that are fixed to benefit them. It is unproductive, however, to point fingers and to keep grudges. The Lord's Prayer presents us with an alternative model: forgiveness. The alternative is that Christian communities, nations, and institutions must clear the tangles of yesterday and today's exploitative structures, and work to build a realm of equity, justice, peace and self-sufficiency. This burden is upon the Christian worlds of both the so-called developed and developing countries. Those who pray the Lord's Prayer from either side must become active partners in the building of God's kingdom on earth as it is in heaven. They must become deliberate, self-conscious partners who are dedicated to hallowing God's name by hallowing God's creation.

"And lead us not into temptation, but deliver us from evil." This is a humbling utterance. All are vulnerable to temptation and evil. This is demonstrated by the fact that Jesus teaches this prayer to his disciples, a group of people that should be among the best of his followers. Similarly, the Christian communities, nations, institutions, and individuals know God's will for the earth, yet they have fallen into temptation and evil by living with the ethics of globalization. I am not saying we have not heard many voices in the wilderness such as Bishop Tutu, Latin American liberation, feminist and black theologians etc. Yet by and large, Christian communities and individuals have not taken vigilant positions against national and international government corruption, misuse of funds, unfair international economic policies and the exploitation of the powerless. Millions who pray the Lord's Prayer have neglected the responsibilities and their pledge. This pledge requires vigilance, staying awake and alert to what is happening. In this regard, I find Christian institutions and practitioners more at home in the exploitative economic structures of their nations and the world than troubled. Indeed, they also benefit from these structures while billions suffer from them. God's daughters and sons have therefore ignored the will of their

parent; they have ignored their responsibilities to each other and
have become partners with, or silent supporters of, the exploitative
ethics of international markets and corrupt local governments. This,
in my view, is to fall into temptation, to be led into evil. Hence we
need to be delivered. Deliverance, however, requires our willingness
to take our positions as partners with God, for God, for ourselves
and for one another. We will be delivered when we repent from our
complacent positions towards oppressive national and international
structures, when we seek to build God's kingdom on earth by hallowing God's creation at large.

To conclude this reading of the Lord's Prayer, I believe that it
rests upon Christian individuals and communities, first, to squarely
confront the reality of globalization; second, to educate themselves
on its mechanisms and ethics; third, to critically situate themselves
within the parameters of active globalization; and, fourth, to ask if
the Christian faith offers us an alternative vision, by looking at the
Lord's Prayer. Christian practitioners are corporately and individually duty bound to re-examine what is proposed in the vision of the
Lord's Prayer and to consider if it may offer us an alternative to
confront the ethical challenges of living in the global economic era
and amongst corrupt and exploitative governments. Once that is
done, the fifth element of the challenge calls for strategies of resistance—the positioning of women and men on earthly spaces who
will seek to exude the heavenly justice on earthly spaces.

But a reader may rightfully ask, "But what if the vision of the
Lord's Prayer is found lacking?" It still remains incumbent upon
Christian adherents to listen to the seasonal approach of prophesy,
to fulfill the scriptures: "You have heard what was said . . . but I say
to you," (Matthew 5:21–48). Put differently, Christian practitioners
of various persuasions are not called to the simple task of reproducing the biblical text. They are also called upon to take the risky
challenge and responsibility of seeking the will of God for God's creation by re-reading these texts. God's name is not hallowed in
Christian institutions or texts. Rather, God's name must be hallowed
in the whole of God's creation. This challenge is demonstrated by
Jesus in the Sermon on the Mount, when he preaches to the crowds,
quoting from the scriptures saying, "You have heard what was
said . . .," but proceeding to declare what he responsibly perceived
to be in accordance with God's will for the world of his time by
saying, "but I say to you. . . ." Jesus demonstrates a responsible act

that goes beyond reproducing the scriptures or remaining faithful to the religious institutions (Matthew 12:1–8). To seek the seasonal, contextual will of God for the earth is a call that involves new reflections, that sometimes challenges or diverts from the written scriptures when they are found inadequate and irrelevant to new situations, and when, in particular, they are found inconsistent with God's will for God's creation.

The approach of seeking to hear God afresh in new contexts is, no doubt, the most difficult and often overlooked by the Christian communities and individuals. Christian practitioners of various persuasions prefer to shield behind "You have heard" (or the contemporary "the Bible says"). That is to say they have perfected the art of reproducing and adhering to ancient scriptures without daring to cross the boundary and say, "But I say. . . ." No doubt, going beyond ancient scriptures and challenging the religious institutions that guard these texts, needs prophetic courage—the willingness to hear God speak anew for one's people in new contexts. It entails a willingness to challenge the elites and leaders of our societies, national and international governments and to confront possible death. This is a role for all Christian communities and individuals, for anything less may mark practitioners as unfaithful partners in the role of keeping the earth, or God's creation, sacred. Christian practitioners should not be found to be stewards of scripture and Christian institutions while they betray God's creation.

I have suggested above that taking heed of the Lord's Prayer necessitates a call for a new understanding of the Christian mission, a suggestion I will now elaborate. How can we reconfigure the Christian mission? Western Christian churches, societies, and academicians embarked on a mission to christianize and civilize the non-Western worlds. They perceived the non-Christian worlds as lost in sin, barbarism and in need of salvation. To bring Christ and civilization to these nations, the Christian church worked hand in glove with imperialist and colonialist movements. It was such currents that brought most of the Two-Thirds World in contact with the Christian faith. This unfortunate history of the Christian church cannot be erased, but it need not be repeated.

It is now the beginning of a new century and international Christian mission is far from over, nor should it be defined by certain so-called civilized nations alone. It is now the business of both worlds to speak to and with each other concerning what the Christian mission should entail and what Christian salvation means. As a Two-Thirds World African woman of Botswana, I would insist that the contemporary Christian mission must concern itself with all issues that hinder the realization of God's kingdom on earth. It must focus on all that desacralizes life on earth. It must rally against all structural forces and institutions that militate against peace, equity and self-sufficiency for individuals and nations of various cultures. The Christian mission must identify as sinful those forces that hinder the blossoming of God's creation as a whole. Christian salvation can and should no longer concern itself with the denunciation of God's diverse cultures of the world. Rather, Christian salvation must be regarded as creating environments where the whole of God's creation and its cultures are given a chance for their maximum fulfillment. Their gender, race, nationality, age, religion and class should be a cause for celebration, not suppression.

If the Christian mission is appropriated thus, the method of its implementation would indeed be different. In the past it was common for Western Christian worlds to "send off" Christian disciples to the so-called "exotic and dangerous" places of the world. In sending off to other nations, the contemporary Christian mission has focussed on the mission and vision of the disciples of Jesus, a vision of the earliest church, but has hardly embraced the mission undertaken by Jesus himself. The mission of Jesus hardly ever saw him travel cross boundaries to other nations. Indeed, he travelled within the boundaries of his nation. Jesus' mission brought him face to face with the elites and leaders of his country as he critically told them that they are oppressing God's people (Matthew 12:1–8, 23:23), as he proclaimed that God's kingdom is at hand, that God's kingdom is already amongst them and that God demands "justice and mercy and faith" (Matthew 23:23b–c). This was a difficult and dangerous mission, for prophets receive no honour in their own homes. That his was a dangerous mission is attested by the fact that Jesus did not last more than one year before he was crucified. This is the mission that the Christian church has neglected, but one that needs to be recaptured for our particular and global economic contexts.

In the context of globalization, the Christian mission must, therefore, concern itself with such issues as identifying the faces behind the mega multi-national companies and monetary bodies that are colonizing God's creation again. It must make it its business to familiarize itself with their policies and their implications and impact. It

must seek deliberate ways of resisting and organizing Christian practitioners as resisting communities who counteract national and international economic policies that hinder the health and freedom of
God's creation in the world. Put differently, the contemporary Christian
mission should no longer focus on searching out the Basarwa (the
so-called Bushmen) in the remote Kgalagadi desert and throwing
coke bottles in their lands. Rather, it needs to concern itself with
the companies behind coca-cola, whose bottles enter such societies
and immediately make them into a poor people who fight for
insufficient foreign goods, whose bottles steal away their peace. The
mission, now, more than ever, needs to be directed, not to the so-
called "exotic and dangerous" places. Rather, the mission must be
directed to the metropolitan centers of the West and to many other
cities of the world that house corrupt and exploitative governments
and multi-national companies. In short, the Christian mission must
be a struggle to hallow God's name, to bring God's kingdom on
earth, to creation at large, by building healthy interpersonal and
international relations.

As I said earlier, this reading is not offered as "the only," "the
original" or "the correct" interpretation of the Lord's Prayer. It is
offered as an invitation to Christian communities and individuals to
assume active responsibility for all that hinders the daughters and
sons of God around the world to come to full realization. For
Christian communities, nations, institutions, and individuals to pray
and ask for deliverance from evil in this global economic age entails
repentance accompanied by action. Only in so doing will we show
a willingness to hear the Lord's Prayer anew and to recapture the
implications of praying the Lord's Prayer in the global economic era.
To pray the Lord's Prayer—to say "thy kingdom come," to say,
"your will be done, on earth as it is in heaven"—is to become
responsible partners, guardians of justice, active daughters and sons
in the establishment of God's rule in the world and in the building
of healthy interpersonal and international relationships. Even as
Christian communities, nations, and individuals have neglected such
roles in the past, they must strive to hear God now; they must awake
to take the responsibility for one another now, for God's creation
as a whole, since the situation is critical: God's name must be hallowed on earth by keeping all creation sacred.

BIBLIOGRAPHY

Carbaugh, Robert J. *International Economics*. Cincinnati: South-Western College Publishing, 1995.

Garland, David. *Reading Matthew: A Literary and Theological Commentary on the First Gospel*. New York: Crossroad, 1993.

Hendricks, Osayande O. "Guerilla Exegesis: A Post-Modern Proposal for the Insurgent African-American Biblical Interpretation," *Semeia* 72 (1995): 73–90.

Horsely, Richard. *Sociology and the Jesus Movement*. New York: Crossroad, 1989.

——. *Jesus and the Spiral of Violence: Popular Jewish Resistance in Roman Palestine*. Minneapolis: Fortress Press, 1993.

Lind, Christopher. *Something is Wrong Somewhere: Globalization, Community and the Moral Economy of the Farm Crisis*. Halifax: Fernwood Publishing, 1995.

Luz, Ulrich. *Matthew 1–7: A Continental Commentary*. Minneapolis: Fortress Press, 1989.

Mazrui, Ali. *Cultural Forces in World Politics*. London: James Currey, 1990.

Ngugi wa Thiong'o. *Moving the Centre: The Struggle for Cultural Freedoms*. London: James Curry, 1993.

Overman, Andrew J. *Church and Community in Crisis: The Gospel According to Matthew*. Valley Forge: Trinity Press International, 1996.

Parratt, John. "Setting the Agenda for Christian Involvement in Development: A Summary of Papers," In Eds. Isabel Phiri, Kenneth Ross and James Cox. *The Role of Christianity in Development, Peace and Reconstruction*. Nairobi: All Africa Conference of Churches, 1996.

Ringe, Sharon. "Solidarity in Contextuality: Readings of Matthew 18:21–35." In Eds F.F. Segovia and Mary Ann Tolbert. *Reading From This Place Volume 1: Social Location and Biblical Interpretation in the United States*. Minneapolis: Fortress Press, 1995.

Tinker, George. "Reading the Bible as Native Americans," In *The New Interpreters's Bible: A Commentary in Twelve Volumes*. Nashville: Abingdon Press, 1994: 174–180.

Ukpong, Justin S. "The Parable of the Shrewd Manager (Luke 1–13): An Essay in the Inculturation Biblical Hermeneutic," *Semeia* 73 (1996): 189–210.

PART FIVE

BIBLIOGRAPHY

A BIBLIOGRAPHY OF THE BIBLE IN AFRICA

Grant LeMarquand

This bibliography is an updated version of a listing which was first published in 1993. The present version is an attempt to list all known works of biblical interpretation produced by Africans, for Africa, or about African interpretation. Included in this version is a listing of book reviews and abstracts which have appeared in various publications describing many of the works listed here. The listing of reviews and abstracts may prove to be especially helpful in cases where it is difficult to acquire a copy of the original essay or book. Although this work has the purpose of being comprehensive, it is probable that I have missed numerous items which should be included in this list. I wish to apologize to any whose works have escaped my attention.

The bibliography is divided into five sections. Section one lists bibliographical sources. Some of these sources are periodical publications which should be consulted for future contributions to the growing corpus of works of African Exegesis. Although there are few annotations in other parts of the bibliography, this section is quite thoroughly annotated. The second section is entitled "Studies of the Use of the Bible in Africa/Hermeneutics." Works in this section elucidate various aspects of biblical interpretation in Africa, especially the relationship between culture and interpretation. The third section lists works on "Africa and Africans in the Bible." Since this division of the bibliography deals with texts which have received extensive treatment from non-Africans, many more works could have been listed. I have included only those publications written by Africans (including Africans of the "diaspora") and any others who focus on the "Africanness" of the texts in question. The section on "Exegetical and Thematic Studies" is the longest. It includes any essay or book which does not fit into another category of the bibliography and which has a biblical passage or theme as its primary focus. Section five lists works which focus on the special subject of "Bible Translation in Africa." Sections six and seven, list homiletical/devotional materials and educational materials respectively. Since many of these works are locally published, these sections are probably the least comprehensive. It is important to note them here, however, since they give important evidence of the ways in which ordinary Africans understand and use the Bible. The final section is on "South African Exegesis." The history Christianity in South Africa has given rise to particular issues and concerns and it was felt best to keep most of these South African materials in a separate section. This section is not hermetically sealed, however, and some works from South Africa can be found in other divisions of the bibliography.

I would like to thank the many people who have helped me in what has become a decade long search for material. In Kenya, the Rev. Johan Beks, Mr. Alfred Wetindi, the Rev. Sammy Githuku, and the Rt. Rev. Eliud Wabukala, all at some point associated with St. Paul's United Theological College, Limuru, Fr. Gerald Murphy of Hekima College, Nairobi, Dr. Laurent Naré of the Catholic Biblical Centre for Africa and Madagascar, Dr. Peter Renju, Dr. Leonidas Kalugila and Dr. G.A Mikre-Selassie of the United Bible Societies, Nairobi, all provided material and interesting leads. In Tanzania, Mr. Wolfgang Apelt of the Lutheran Theological College, Makumira supplied many works which I was unable to locate elsewhere. In Nigeria, Pastor Clare Fuller and Principal M.F. Akangbe of the United Missionary Theological College, Ilorin, the Rev. Emmanuel Komolafe of Immanuel Theological College, Ibadan, Prof Samuel Obogunrin of the University of Ibadan, and Drs. Teresa Okure and Justin Ukpong of Port Harcourt were all very helpful and welcoming of this project. In southern Africa, Dr. Paul Bowers, Dr. Gerald West, Dr. Jonathan Draper all moved this project along in various ways. In Canada, encouragement and help came from Ms. Cindy Derrenbacker, the Rev. Stephanie Douglas and Dr. Ian Ritchie. Many thanks to all.

Abbreviations (with addresses of African publications)

AACC   All Africa Conference of Churches [P.O. Box 14205, Nairobi, Kenya]
A-CCN   Akrofi-Christaller Center News [P.O. Box 76, Akropong-Akuapem, Ghana]
ACS   African Christian Studies [The Journal of the Faculty of Theology of the Catholic Higher Institute of Eastern Africa (CHIEA), now the Catholic University of Eastern Africa (CUEA), P.O. Box 24205, Nairobi, Kenya]
AEAM   The Association of Evangelicals of Africa and Madagascar [Nairobi, Kenya]
AFER   African Ecclesiastical Review (vol. 1–20/2) African Ecclesial Review (vol. 20/3–) [AMECEA Publications, P.O. Box 4002, Eldoret, Kenya]
AfSt   African Studies [Witwatersrand University Press, Private Bag 3, Wits 2050, Johannesburg, South Africa.]

AJBS	African Journal of Biblical Studies [The Nigerian Association for Biblical Studies, c/o Department of Religious Studies, University of Ilorin, Ilorin, Nigeria]
AJET	Africa Journal of Evangelical Theology (continuation of EAJET, renamed 9/1, 1990) [Scott Theological College, P.O. Box 49, Machakos, Kenya]
AMECEA	Association of Member Episcopal Conferences in Eastern Africa [AMECEA Documentation Service, P.O. Box 21400, Nairobi, Kenya]
ANITEPAM Bulletin	ANITEPAM Bulletin: The Newsletter of the African Network of Institutions of Theological Education Training Anglicans for Ministry [212 East Capital Street, Washington, D.C. 20003, USA]
APECA	Association Panafricaine des Exegetes Catholic = PACE
ATIEA	Association of Theological Institutions in Eastern Africa
ATJ	Africa Theological Journal [ALICE, P.O. Box 314, Arusha, Tanzania]
BCT	Bulletin for Contextual Theology in Southern Africa & Africa (continuation of Bibliography in Contextual Theology in Africa) [School of Theology, University of Natal at Pietermartizburg, Private Bag X01, Scottsville, 3209, South Africa]
BCTA	Bibliography in Contextual Theology in Africa (continued as Bulletin for Contextual Theology)
Bible and Life	A Daily Bible Reading Guide [published by the Catholic Institute of West Africa; begun in 1985, discontinued in 1988]
Bible Bhashyam	Bible Bhashyam: An Indian Biblical Quarterly [Kerala, India]
B-PB	Biblical-Pastoral Bulletin [Catholic Biblical Centre for Africa and Madagascar (BICAM), P.O. Box 24215, Karen, Nairobi, Kenya]
BISAM	Biblical Studies and Missiology
Bodija Journal	[Seminary of Ss. Peter and Paul, P.M.B. 517 Secretariat P.O., Ibadan, Nigeria]
BookNotes	Book Notes for Africa [P.O. Box 250100, Ndola, Zambia]
BT	The Bible Translator
BTA	Bulletin de Théologie Africaine/Bulletin of African Theology/ Boletim de Teologia Africana
BTS	Bigard Theological Studies [Bigard Memorial Seminary, P.O. Box 327, Enugu, Nigeria]
BET	Bulletin of Ecumanical Theology [P.O. Box 9696, Enugu, Nigeria]
CATHAN	Catholic Theological Association of Nigeria
CBQ	Catholic Biblical Quarterly [Catholic Biblical Association of America]
Challenge	[P.O. Box 556, Johannesburg, South Africa]
CHIEA	Catholic Higher Institute of Eastern Africa [Nairobi, Kenya]
CIWA	Catholic Institute of West Africa [Port Harcourt, Nigeria]
CRA	Cahiers des Religions Africaines [Faculte de Theologie Catholique de Kinshasa, P.O. Box 712, Kinshasa-Limete, Congo]
CTB	Cahiers de traduction bibliques [Alliance Biblique Francaise, France]
CUEA	Catholic University of Eastern Africa
CV	Communio Viatorum [Prague]

EAJET   East Africa Journal of Evangelical Theology [Scott Theological College, Machakos, Kenya; renamed AJET 9/1 (1990)]
ERT   Evangelical Review of Theology [Exeter, UK]
ETSI   ETSI Journal: Journal of the Faculty of ECWA Theological Seminary, Igbaja [ECWA Theological Seminary, P.O. Box 20, Igbaja Via Ilorin, Kwara State, Nigeria]
Exchange   Exchange: Journal of Missiological and Ecumenical Research [Utrecht, The Netherlands]
FAT   Foundations of African Theology [Department of Religious Studies, University of Jos, Nigeria]
Flambeau   Flambeau: Revue Theologique de l'Astheol [Faculté de Théologie Protestante de Yaoundé, B.P. 4011, Yaoundé, Cameroun]
FTCK   Faculté de Théologie Catholique de Kinshasa
GBT   Ghana Bulletin of Theology [discontinued]
Hekima Review   Hekima Review: Journal of Hekima College [The Jesuit School of Theology, Nairobi, P.O. Box 21215, Nairobi, Kenya]
HTS   Hervormde Teologiese Studies [Faculty of Theology, University of Pretoria, Posbus 5777, Pretoria 0001, South Africa]
IBMR   International Bulletin for Missionary Research
IDS   In Die Skriflig [(251), PU for CHO, Potchefstroom 2520, South Africa]
In God's Image In God's Image: Journal of the Asian Women's Resource Centre for Culture and Theology [Kuala Lumpur, Malaysia]
IRM   International Review of Missions [1912–1968]
                International Review of Mission [1969–]
JACT   Journal of African Christian Thought: Journal of the Akrofi-Christaller Memorial Centre for Mission Research and Applied Theology [P.O. Box 76, Akropong-Akuapem, Ghana]
JARS   Journal of Arabic and Religious Studies [The Department of Religions, University of Ilorin, Ilorin, Nigeria]
JATA   Journal of Adventist Thought in Africa [P.O. Box 2500, Eldoret, Kenya]
JBL   Journal of Biblical Literature [Atlanta, USA]
JBTSA   Journal of Black Theology in South Africa [Department of Systematic Theology, University of South Africa, P.O. Box 392, Pretoria, 0001 Gauteng, South Africa]
JCT   Journal for Constructive Theology: [Centre for Constructive Theology, University of Durban-Westville, Private Bag X54001, Durban, 4000, South Africa.]
JIT   Journal of Inculturation Theology [Faculty of Theology, Catholic Institute of West Africa, P.O. Box 499, Port Harcourt, Nigeria]
JITC   Journal of the Interdenominational Theological Center [Atlanta, Georgia, USA]
JNSL   Journal of Northwest Semitic Languages [Department of Semitic Languages, University of Stellenbosch, Stellenbosch 7600, South Africa]
JOTT   Journal of Translation and Textlinguistics [Summer Institute of Linguistics Bookstore, 7500 W. Camp Wisdom Rd., Dallas, Texas, 75236, U.S.A.]
JORT   The Journal of Religious Thought [Washington, D.C., USA]
Jos Studies   Jos Studies [St. Augustine's Major Seminary, P.O. Box 182, Jos, Plateau State, Nigeria]
JRA   Journal of Religion in Africa [Leiden, Netherlands]
JSNT   Journal for the Study of the New Testament [Sheffield, UK]

JSOT	Journal for the Study of the Old Testament [Sheffield, UK]
JTSA	Journal of Theology for Southern Africa [Department of Religious Studies, University of Cape Town, Rondebosch 7700, Cape Town, South Africa]
Ministry	"Ministry," now discontinued, had a number of subtitles during its publishing history: 1/1 (1961) to 2/1 (1961): "a quarterly Theological Review for South Africa"; 2/2 (1962): "a quarterly Theological Review for Africa"; 3/1 (1962) to 5/2: "a quarterly Theological Review for East and South Africa"; 5/3 (1965) to 11/4 (1971): "a quarterly Theological Review for Africa."
Missionalia	[P.O. Box 35704, Menlo Park, 0102, South Africa]
Mission Studies	Mission Studies: Journal of the International Association for Mission Studies
NABIS	Nigerian Association for Biblical Studies [see AJBS]
NAOTS	Newsletter on African Old Testament Scholarship [edited and published by Dr. Knut Holter, School of Mission and Theology, Misjonsvegen 34, N–4024, Stavanger, Norway.]
NEGST	Nairobi Evangelical Graduate School of Theology
Neotestimentica	[Department of New Testament, University of Orange State, P.O. Box 339, Bloemfontein 9300, South Africa]
NGTT	Nederduits Gereformeerde Teologiese Tydskrif [Van der Stelstraat 63, Stellenbosch 7600, South Africa]
NIST	Nairobi International School of Theology
NJOT	The Nigerian Journal of Theology [The Catholic Theological Association of Nigeria, Seat of Wisdom Seminary, P.O. Box 2124, Owerri, Imo State, Nigeria]
NRT	Nouvelle Revue Theologie [Belgium]
NTA	New Testament Abstracts [Cambridge, MA, USA]
NTS	New Testament Studies [Cambridge, UK]
NTSSA	New Testament Society of South Africa
NZM	Neue Zeitschrift für Missionswissenschaft/Nouvelle Revue de Science Missionaire [Immensee, Switzerland]
OAIC	Organization of African Instituted Churches [Nairobi, Kenya]
OJOT	Ogbomoso Journal of Theology [Nigerian Baptist Theological Seminary, Ogbomoso, Nigeria]
One World	[World Council of Churches, Geneva, Switzerland]
OP	Orientations Pastorales [Kinshasa, Congo]
Orita	Orita: Ibadan Journal of Religious Studies [The Department of Religious Studies, University of Ibadan, Ibadan, Nigeria]
OTA	Old Testament Abstracts [Washington, D.C., USA]
OTEssays	Old Testament Essays: Journal of the Old Testament Society of South Africa [P.O. Box 392, Pretoria 0001, South Africa]
OTSSA	Old Testament Society of South Africa
PA	Practical Anthropology [discontinued]
PACE	Panafrican Association of Catholic Exegetes = APECA
RAT	Revue Africaine de Théologie [Revue Africaine de Théologie, Faculté de Théologie Catholique de Kinshasa, B.P. 1534, Kinshasa/Limeté, Congo]
RCA	Revue du Clerge Africain [Mayidi, Congo]
Religion in Malawi	[Department of Theology and Religious Studies, Chancellor College, P.O. Box 280, Zomba, Malawi]
RICAO	Revue de l'Institute Catholique de l'Afrique de l'Ouest (RICAO) [08 B.P. 22 Abidjan, Cote D'Ivoire]

RSA	Revue de Spiritualité Africaine [publication annuelle de l'Institute de Spiritualité Africaine et de Missiologie (ISAMI); Home ASUMA, Av. Biangala No. 1, Q. Gombele (ex-Righini), Zone de Lemba—B.P. 1800 Kinshasa I (Congo)]
RSR	Religious Studies Review [Council of Societies for the Study of Religion Executive Office, Valparaiso University, Valparaiso Indiana, 46383, U.S.A.]
R&T	Religion & Theology/Religie & Teologie [as of 1994: formerly Theologia Evangelica Business Section, University of South Africa, P.O. Box 392, Pretoria 0001, South Africa]
RTA	Religious and Theological Abstracts [Myerstown, PA, USA]
RZTP	Revue Zairoise de Théologie Protestante [Facultés Protestantes au Zaire, B.P. 4745 Kinshasa II, Congo]
SABJOT	South African Baptist Journal of Theology [Baptist Union of South Africa, Cape Town]
SBL	Society of Biblical Literature
SCC	Small Christian Community
Scriptura:	Scriptura: Journal of Bible and Theology in Southern Africa [Department of Biblical Studies, University of Stellenbosch, 7600 Stellenbosch, South Africa]
SECAM	Symposium of Episcopal Conferences of Africa and Madagasgar
Select	Select: Feuillet Selectif Dominicains Kinshasa
Semeia	Semeia: an experimental journal for biblical criticism [Atlanta, Georgia, USA]
SJT	Scottish Journal of Theology [Edinburgh, Scotland]
SK	Skrif en Kirk [Theological Faculty, University of Pretoria, 0002 Pretoria, South Africa]
TCNN	Theological College of Northern Nigeria Research Bulletin [P.O. Box 64, Bukuru, Plateau State, Nigeria]
Select	Select: Feuillet Selectif Dominicains Kinshasa
Semeia	Semeia: an experimental journal for biblical criticism [Atlanta, Georgia, USA]
TEE	theological education by extension
TEEC(SA)	The Theological Education by Extension College (Southern Africa)
Telema	Telema: Revue de réflexions et de creativité chretiennes en Afrique [Avenue P. Boka 7–9, B.P. 3277, Kinshasa/Gombe, Congo]
TJCT	Trinity Journal of Church and Theology [Trinity College, P.O. Box 48, Legon, Ghana]
TPRB	Théologie et Pastorale au Rwanda et au Burundi [Bujumbura, Burundi]
Voices	Voices from the Third World [P.O. Box 4635, 63 Miller's Road, Bangalore 560 046, India]
UBS	United Bible Societies
UBS	Bulletin United Bible Societies Bulletin [Reading, UK]
UMTC-JTS	UMTC Journal of Theological Studies [United Missionary Theological College, Box 171, Ilorin, Kwara State, Nigeria]
WAJES	West African Journal of Ecclesial Studies [c/o Seminary of Ss. Peter & Paul, P.M.B. 5171, Secretariat P.O., Ibadan, Nigeria]
WAR	West African Religion [Department of Religion, University of Nigeria, Nsukka, Nigeria]
WCC	World Council of Churches [Geneva]

1. *Bibliographical Resources*

Anon.
1996   "Annotated Bibliography: The Bible in Africa," *BCT* 3/1:
              24–32. [A listing of 96 items with abstracts. Most of these
              are South African in origin and many are not listed in
              the current bibliography.]

Book Notes for Africa
March 1996–   [This small journal defines itself as "a twice yearly pub-
              lication providing one-paragraph reviews on recent Africa-
              related publications of potential interest to theological
              educators and libraries in Africa." It is evangelical in
              ethos and sponsored by the Theological College of Central
              Africa, Ndola, Zambia and Harare Theological College,
              Harare, Zimbabwe.]

Brown, Dorothy N.
1998   "Old Testament Literature in the NEGST library," *NAOTS*
              4: 20–21. [abstract: *OTA* 21/3 (1998): #1194.]

Diemer, E.
1961   "Essai de Bibliographie des Travaux Bibliques des Peres
              Blancs en Afrique," *NZM* 17 (1961): 127–34; reprinted
              in Beckmann, ed: 271–78. [A listing of bible translations
              produced by missionaries of the White Fathers, organized
              regionally and linguistically.]

Deist, Ferdinand
1992   "South African Old Testament Studies and the Future,"
              OTEssays 5: 311–31. [Reprinted in *OTEssays* 7/4 (1994):
              33–51; abstracted in *OTA* 17/2 (1994): #893. A survey
              and bibliography of South African Old Testament schol-
              arship that includes many works in Afrikaans which are
              not listed in the present bibliography.]

Du Toit, A.B.
1993   "The Rise and Current State of New Testament Research
              in South Africa: Part 1," *HTS* 49/3:503–14.
              "The Rise and Current State of New Testament Research
              in South Africa: Part 2," *HTS* 49/4: 786–809. [The
              above two articles, written in Afrikaans, include exten-
              sive bibliography.]

Eggen, Wiel
1995   "African Theological Journals in 1994," *Exchange* 24/3:
              259–76.

Geyer, Douglas W. (Project Director), with Lowell K. Handy
1993   *International Christian Literature Documentation Project: A Subject,
              Author, and Corporate Name Index to Non-Western Christian Liter-
              ature. Volume One: Subject Index; Volume Two: Author-Editor Index,
              Corporate Name Index* (Evanston, Il: American Theological

Library Association). [This resource lists theological works (excluding journals) from the "non-western world" which are housed in eight major North American libraries.]

Holter, Knut

1996 *Tropical Africa and the Old Testament: A Select and Annotated Bibliography* University of Oslo. Faculty of Theology Bibliography Series 6 (Oslo, Norway: University of Oslo). [reviews: *BookNotes* 2 (October 1996): #2.14; J. Lukwata *ACS* 12/4 (1996): 77–79; J. Miller *AJET* 17/2 (1998): 152–53; abstracts: *NAOTS* 1 (1996): 7–8; *OTA* 20/1 (1997): #545. [A listing of 232 modern works on the Old Testament and Africa between the tropics of Cancer and Capricorn. Includes abstracts for each work and three indices: to Old Testament texts, to African countries and languages, and to key words. Does not include works by African Old Testament scholars which make no explicit reference to Africa.]

1996– *Newsletter on African Old Testament Scholarship* [NAOTS is published biannually under the editorship of Knut Holter. The first three issues (#1 1996, #2 1997, #3 1997) were abstracted in *OTA* 21/2 (1998) #1108–1110 respectively. Following this *OTA* has provided abstracts for individual articles.]

n.d. "Old Testament Studies in Africa: Resource Pages," [Available at *www.misjonshs.no/res/ot_africa* (electronic bulletin board).]

Kawale, Winston

1997 "New Data Base: Bible in Africa Research Project," *NAOTS* 3: 3–4. [Report of a project to develop a data base of African biblical studies based at the Department of Old and New Testament, Faculty of Theology, University of Stellenbosch, South Africa.]

Lagerwerf, Leny

1990 "African Women Doing Theology: A Survey," *Exchange* 19/1: 1–69; especially part IV, "Women in the Bible": 30–38. [abstract: Holter: #106.]

1996 "African Theological Journals in 1995," *Exchange* 25/3: 285–304. [Especially "Bible and Hermeneutics": 286–88.]

LeMarquand, Grant

1994 "African Bibliography Project," Bible in Africa Project: 29–30. [Report of oral presentation on work in progress towards the compilation of a comprehensive bibliography in African biblical studies.]

1995 "A Bibliography of the Bible in Africa: A Preliminary Publication," *BCT* 2/2: 6–40.

"Bibliography of the Bible in Africa," *JIT* 2/1: 39–139. [These two bibliographies published in different parts of Africa contain essentially the same material, approximately 1,000 references to African biblical studies. At the request of the publishers, however, the arrangement of the material is slightly different in each journal. In the *JIT* most of the South African material does not appear separately but has been integrated into the rest of the bibliography. In the *BCT* the South African material appears in a separate section at the end of the bibliography. In the *JIT* version Prof. Justin Ukpong was kind enough to add entries from *Bible and Life* to section 4 (now Section 6), "Homiletical and Devotional Material." These bibliographies contain entries published up to 1993.]

Mbiti, John S.
1986 *Bible and Theology in African Christianity* (Nairobi: Oxford University Press). [This volume includes two chapters of relevance to the topic of the Bible in Africa: Chapter Two, "Bible Translation and Use in Africa"; Chapter Three, "The Use of the Bible in African Theology." Both chapters contain bibliographical information and comments on a number of African biblical studies.]

Mbiti, John S. (with Margaret Groesbeck)
1993 "Bibliography: The Publications of John S. Mbiti for the Years 1954–1987," Olupona & Nyang: 395–415. [A listing of Mbiti's scholarly works and creative writing, omitting book reviews.]

Mbiye Lumbala
1983 "Théologie Africaine: Bibliographie selective (1976–1980)," *RAT* 7/13: 140–142.
1987 "Théologie Africaine: Bibliographie selective (1981–1985)" *RAT* 11/22: 273–276.
1996 "Théologie Africaine. Bibliographie selective (1981–85) (suite)," *RAT* 20/40: 257 78.

Ntedika Konde
1978 "La Théologie Africaine: Bibliographie selective (1925–1975)" *RAT* 2/3: 142–146.

Nussbaum, S., ed.
1996 *African Proverbs: Collections, studies, bibliographies: CD #3 in the 20:21 Library. Version 1.0 for Windows* (Colorado Springs: Global Mapping International). [review: Peter Kimilike "African Proverbs: A Compilation of Proverb Collections, Studies, Bibliographies and Other Resources for African Proverbs on CD-ROM," in *NAOTS* 6 (1999): 9–10.]

Olupona, Jacob K. & Sulayman S. Nyang, eds
1993 *Religious Plurality in Africa: Essays in Honour of John S. Mbiti* (Religion and Society #32; Berlin/New York: Mouton de Gruyter).

Schoonhoven, E. Jansen
1980 "The Bible in Africa," *Exchange: Bulletin of Third World Christian Literature* 25/9: 1–48. [abstract: Holter: #202.]

Theology in Context: Information on Theological Contributions from Africa, Asia, Oceania and Latin America (Aachen, Germany: Institute of Missiology Missio), 1984–
[This bi-annual reference work contains "Annotated Bibliography, Summaries of Selected Articles, Book Surveys, Reports about Theological Conferences, Indices of Authors and Key Words." It also contains mailing addresses of "third world' journals which it indexes. Available in German and in English.]

2. Studies of the Use of the Bible in Africa/Hermeneutics

Abe, Gabriel Oyedele
  1997 "African Journal of Biblical Studies," *NAOTS* 3: 12–13.
Abitbol, Nichel
  1972 "Traces Juives et Influences Bibliques dans les Traditions Africa-ines," Mveng & Werblowsky: 167–72. [abstract: Holter: # 009.]
Abogunrin, Samuel O.
  1986 "Biblical Research in Africa: The Task Ahead," *AJBS* 1/1: 7–24. [abstracts: *NTA* 33/1 (1989): #1.] Holter: # 010.]
Adamo, David Tuesday
  1989 "The African Background of African-American Hermeneutics," *Abstracts: American Academy of Religion/Society of Biblical Literature 1989* James B. Wiggins & David J. Lull, eds (Scholars Press): 102.
  1997 "Doing Old Testament Research in Africa," *NAOTS* 3: 8–11.
Adewale, S.A.
  1988 "The Magical Use of the Bible Among the Yoruba Christians of Nigeria," *B-PB* 1[sic]: 48–55.
Adeyemo, Tokunboh
  1983 "Towards an Evangelical African Theology," *ERT* 7/1: 147–54.
Adugu, Damian
  1990 "The Sudanese Church Vision of the New Evangelization," Ame-wowo, ed.: 105–107.
Agbakwuru, Ugochukwu
  1990 "The Role of the Biblical Apostolate in Nigeria," Amewowo, ed.: 95–98.
Akene, Awa Hellene
  1990 "Women in the New Evangelization," Amewowo, ed.: 80–83.
Alexis, Elvire
  1990 "Apostolat Biblique aux Seychelles/Biblical Apostolate in Seychelles," Amewowo, ed.: 99.
Amegadzi, E.
  1990 "The first Panafrican Biblical Apostolate Seminar," Amewowo, ed.: 3–6.
Amewowo, Wynnand
  1979 "Proclaiming God's Word by Men," *B-PB* 1 (1979): 13–17.
  1986 "Experiences and Discoveries with the Bible in West Africa," *Mission Studies* 3/1 (1986): 12–24; reprinted in *B-PB* 5/Jan (1987): 27–38 and in French as "Expériences et découvertes avec la Bible en Afrique Occidentale," *Cahiers Bibliques Africains* 1/Jan (1987): 11–22. [abstract: Holter: #034.]
  1987 "New Attitudes to Reading and Living the Bible," Shorter & Waliggo: 81–92.
Amewowo, Wynnand, ed.
  1990 *The Bible in the New Evangelization in Africa: Acts of the First Panafrican Biblical Apostolate Seminar, Karen-Nairobi, Kenya, 17–25th January 1990*

(Nairobi, Kenya: Catholic Biblical Centre for Africa and Madagascar, 1990).

Anderson, Allan H.
1996 "The Hermeneutical Processes of Pentecostal-type African Initiated Churches in Africa," *Missionalia* 24/2: 171–85. [abstract: *NTA* 41/2 (1997): #707.]

Anderson, Roger W.
1993 "The Canon: Present Understandings," Mukonyora, Cox & Verstraelen: 61–80.
"'To Your Descendants I Will Give This Land': Thoughts on the Promise of Land and Rewriting the Bible," Mukonyora, Cox & Verstraelen: 89–99.

Anum, Eric
1984 "Cultural Relativism and Biblical Interpretation—A Contemporary Case Study" (M.Th. thesis, University of Glasgow, Scotland).

Atal Sa Angang
1985 "Le Deuxieme Congres des Biblistes Africains," *RAT* 9/17: 91–100.
"La Première Assemblée du Comité Biblique du SECAM," *RAT* 9/17: 101–2.

Babalola, E.O.
1991 "Phenomenon of African Christianity Vis-a-vis Adoption of the Bible and Cultural Awareness in Nigeria," *AJBS* 6/2: 90–105.

Babs Mala, Sam, ed.
1983 *African Independent Churches in the 80's* (Nairobi, Kenya: Organization of African Instituted Churches).

Bach, Werner
1990 "La Bible dans la Nouvelle Evangelisation: Rapport du Centre Biblique à Bandundu/Zaire (CAB)," Amewowo ed.: 117–19.

Bacinoni, V.
1980 "Le Premier Congres des Biblistes Africains (Kinshasa-Zaire, 26–30 decembre 1978)," *Bulletin du Secretariat pro Non-christianis* 15/1: 101–6.

Banana, Canaan S.
1993 "The Case for a New Bible," Mukonyora, Cox & Verstraelen: 17–32; reprinted in Sugirtharajah (2nd ed.): 69–82.

Bebodu, Paul
1990 "The Role of the Biblical Apostolate in the New Evangelization in Ghana," Amewowo ed.: 84–85.

Becken, H.-J., ed.
1973 *Relevant Theology for Africa. Report on a Consultation of the Missiological Institute at Lutheran Theological College, Mapumulo, Natal, September 12–21, 1972* (Durban, South Africa: Lutheran Publishing House).

Beckmann, Johannes
1965 "Die Heilige Schrift in den katholischen Missionen: Ein Rhckblick," *NZM* 21: 45–60; reprinted in Beckmann, ed.: 336–51.

Beckmann, Johannes, ed.
1966 *Die Heilige Schrift in den katholischen Missionen: Gesammelte Aufsaetze* Herausgegeben in Verbinddung mit P. Walbert Bühlmann und

Joh. Specker; Supplementa NZM, 14. (Immensee, Switzerland: Neue Zeitschrift für Missionswissenschaft).

Bedford, F.J.
  1956   "Spreading the Bible," Birkell: 137–40.

Bediako, Gillian M.
  1997   *Primal Religion and the Bible: William Robertson Smith and his Heritage* (Sheffield: Sheffield Academic Press).

Bella, Sita
  1972   "La Femme Africaine et la Vocation Biblique de la Femme," Mveng & Werblowsky: 212–35.

Bessem, John
  n.d.   "Assessment of A National Bible Seminar to Priests. Updating, Refreshing, or/and Examination of Conscience?" (unpublished paper, Ntungamo Major Seminary, 11pp.).
  1962   "God's Word: Alive and Vigorous," *AFER* 4/1: 1–12.

Best, Kenneth, ed.
  1975   *African Challenge* (Nairobi: Transafrica Publishers).

Bible in Africa Project
  1994   "Interpreting the Bible in African Contexts: Minutes of the Glasgow Consultation held on 13th–17th August 1994 at Scotus College, Bearsden, Glasgow, Scotland" [This unpublished document, available from Prof John Riches of the University of Glasgow, consists of summaries of papers and discussions. The papers deal largely with the issue of the intersection of scholarly and popular readings of the Bible in Scotland and in various parts of Africa. The Bible in Africa Project is chaired by Prof. Riches and by Prof. Fr. Justin Ukpong of Port Harcourt, Nigeria. The secretaries for the Glasgow Consultation were Rev. William Anderson and Mrs. Denise Francis.]

Bimazubute, Gilles
  1990   "Apostolat Biblique et Nouvelle Evangelization," Amewowo ed.: 74–76.

Bird, Phyllis
  1994   "Authority and Context in the Interpretation of Biblical Texts," *Neotestimentica* 28/2: 323–37. [abstracts: *NTA* 40/1 (1996): #7; *BCT* 3/1 (1996): 24.]

Bird, Phyllis with Katherine Doob Sakenfeld and Sharon Ringe, eds
  1997   "Reading the Bible as Women: Perspectives from Africa, Asia, and Latin America," *Semeia* 78. [abstract: G.I. Emmerson "The Society for Old Testament Study Book List 1999" *JSOT* 84: 95–96; review: Grant LeMarquand *BookNotes* 8 (October 1999): #8.04.]

Blomberg, Craig L.
  1995   "The Globalization of Hermeneutics," *Journal of the Evangelical Theological Society* 38/4: 581–93. [abstract: *NTA* 41/1 (1997): #12.]

Boyer, J.P.
  1979   "Diffuser la Bible en Afrique. Exposé lors d'une Rencontre-Information DEFAP le 14 mars 1979," *Journal des Missions Evangeliques* 154: 15–23.

Brossard, J.G.
1986 "The Bible in the Family: A Lesotho Experience," *B-PB* 3: 12–15.
1990 "New Evangelization in Lesotho: Role of the Biblical Apostolate," Amewowo ed.: 90–92.
Bühlmann, Walbert
1960 "Die Bibel in der Katholischen Weltmission," *NZM* 16: 1–26; reprinted in Beckmann, ed.: 3–28.
Buetubela Balembo, P.
1987 "Le Problème des Méthodes en Exégèse Aujourd'hui," *Cahiers Bibliques Africains* 1: 23–27.
1990 "La Bible et la Nouvelle Evangélization: La Contribution des Facultés de Théologie," Amewowo ed.: 59–61.
Bulkeley, Tim
1988 "Le Texte Biblique et le Contexte Africain," *RZTP* 2: 11–17.
Burden, J.J.
1982 *The Old Testament in the Context of Africa* (Pretoria). [abstract: Holter: #046.]
Camera, G.
1990 "Inter-territorial Episcopal Conference of Liberia, Sierra Leone and The Gambia: Role of Biblical Apostolate in the New Evangelization at National, Diocesan, Parish and SCC Level," Amewowo ed.: 93–94.
Chidavaenzi, Ignatius
1990 "Biblical Apostolate and the New Evangelization in Zimbabwe," Amewowo ed.: 123–26.
Campbell, M.G.
1990 "Inculturation: Some New Testament Perspectives," *Jos Studies* 1/1: 4–14.
Chikafu, P.
1994 "Zimbabwe Project," Bible in Africa Project: 31.
Chojnacki, S.
1974 "The Nativity in Ethiopian Art," *Journal of Ethiopian Studies* 12/2: 11–56.
Chouraqui, Andre
1972 "Reflexions sur la Pénétration de la Bible en Afrique," Mveng & Werblowsky: 40–46. [abstract: Holter: #052.]
Cilumba Cimbumba, N.
1991 "L'Ancient Testament Vu par un Negro-Africain," *RAT* 15: 53–61.
Cocker, M. de
1950 "Essai de Parallelism Biblico-Congolais," *Zaire* 4: 277–298. [abstract: Holter: #053.]
Cole, Victor Babajide
1979 "A Biblical Approcah to Contextualization of Theology" (M.Th. thesis, Dallas Theological Seminary).
Cowley, Roger W.
1974 "Old Testament Introduction in the Andemta Commentary Tradition," *Journal of Ethiopian Studies* 12/1: 133–75.

1977   "New Testament Introduction in the Andemta Commentary Tradition," *Ostkirchliche Studien* 26/2–3: 144–92.
1980   "Patristic Introduction in the Ethiopian Andemta Commentary Tradition," *Ostkirchlichen Studien* 29: 39–49.
1983   *The Traditional Interpretation of the Apocalypse of St John in the Ethiopian Orthodox Church* University of Cambridge Oriental Publications No. 33 (Cambridge: Cambridge University Press). [abstract: *RSR* 10/4 (1984): 400.]
1985   "The 'Blood of Zechariah' (Mt 23:35) in Ethiopian Exegetical Tradition," *Studia Patristica* 18/1: 293–302.
1988   *Ethiopian Biblical Interpretation: A Study in Exegetical Tradition and Hermeneutics* University of Cambridge Oriental Publications No. 38 (Cambridge: Cambridge University Press). [reviews: E. Ullendorff *Journal of Semitic Studies* 35 (1990): 181–83; M. Knibb *Journal of Theological Studies* ns 42 (1991): 276–81; M. Parmentier *Bijdragen* 52 (1991): 332–33; E. Lanne *Irnikon* 65/1 (1992): 150; abstracts: *NTA* 33/3 (1989): 376; *RSR* 16/2 (1990): 160.]
1989   "Zekri and Pawli: Ethiopic Bible Translators or Interpreters?" *Journal of Semitic Studies* 34: 387–98.

Cox, James L.
1993   "Not a New Bible but a New Hermeneutics: An Approach from within the Science of Religion," Mukonyora, Cox & Verstraelen: 103–23.

Delanote, D.
1984   "Animansi par animare. Formazione biblica à Kinshasa-Zaire," *Messis* 36/3: 4–6.

de Souza, I.
1969   "Bible et culture africaine," *Catechistes* 79: 805–27.
1972   "Bible et Culture Africaine," Mveng & Werblowsky: 81–99; reprinted as "The Bible and African Culture. Text of speech given at the Bible and Black Africa congress, Jerusalem, April 24–27, 1972," *Worldmission* 23/4 (1972): 44–54 and 24/1 (1973): 32–37. [abstract: Holter: #207.]

Dickson, Kwesi
1972   "African Traditional Religions and the Bible," Mveng & Werblowsky: 155–66. [abstract: Holter: #061.]
1973   "The Old Testament and African Theology," *GBT* 4/4: 31–41. [abstract: Holter: #062.]
1974   "Hebrewisms of West Africa—The Old Testament and African Life and Thought," *Legon Journal of Humanities* 1: 23–34. [abstract: Holter: #063.]
1975   "African Theology: Origin, Methodology and Content," *JORT* 32/2: 34–45.
1979   "Continuity and Discontinuity Between the Old Testament and African Life and Thought," Kofi Appiah-Kubi & Sergio Torres, eds *African Theology en Route: Papers from the Pan-Africa Conference of*

Third World Theologians, December 17–23, 1977, Accra, Ghana (Maryknoll: Orbis): 95–108; reprinted with some changes in *BAT* 1 (1979): 179–93. [abstract: Holter: #064.]

1982 "Mission in African Countries," Martin A. Cohen & Helga Croner, eds *Christian mission—Jewish mission* (N.Y.: Paulist Press): 187–206. [abstract: Holter: #065.]

1984 *Theology in Africa* (London/Maryknoll: Darton, Longman and Todd/ Orbis); especially chapter 6, "Cultural Continuity with the Bible" and chapter 7, "The Theology of the Cross in Context." [abstract of chapter 6: Holter: #066.]

1987 "Understanding the Scriptures," *Christian Jewish Relations* 20: 9–22. [abstract: Holter: #067.]

Dickson, K.A. & P. Ellingworth, eds

1969 *Biblical Revelation and African Beliefs* (London/Maryknoll: Lutterworth/Orbis). [reviews: E.W. Fashole-Luke *JRA* 2/3 (1969): 202–205; C. Omari *Lutheran World* 18/3 (1971): 306; H.W. Turner *Journal of Ecumenical Studies* 8 (1971): 892–93; W.E. Welmers *Christian Scholar's Review* 2 (1971): 81–83; W.E. Abraham *Worship* 46 (1972): 189–90; R. Recker *Calvin Theological Journal* 9 (1974): 86–93.]

Dinwiddy, Hugh

1989 "Biblical Usage and Abusage in Kenyan Writing," *JRA* 19: 27–47. [abstracts: *BCTA* 1 (1993): 18; Holter: #068.]

Dore, Delphine

1990 "Rapport du centre pour l'Apostolate Biblique en Guinée," Amewowo ed.: 86–89.

Dovlo, Bertha

1981 "The Importance of Bible Study in the Women Organizations in the Church," *B-PB* 4: 35–38.

Dube, Musa W.

1995 "Towards a Postcolonial Feminist Interpretation of the Bible: A Motswana Perspective," *Abstracts: American Academy of Religion/Society of Biblical Literature 1995* (Scholars Press): 148–49.

1997 "Toward a Postcolonial Feminist Interpretation of the Bible," *Semeia* 78: 11–26. [abstract: *NTA* 43/2 (1999): #772.]

Dubois, Marcel J.

1972 "La Bible comme Evénement Transcendant et la Culture," Mveng & Werblowsky: 47–59. [abstract: Holter: #069.]

Echeverria, J.R.

1978 "Reading the Bible From A Contemporary Perspective," *Pastoral Orientation Service* 4/6: 16–47.

Esua, Cornelius Fontem

1990 "The Role of the Biblical Apostolate in the New Evangelization," Amewowo ed.: 77–79.

Ezeogu, E.M.

1998 "Bible and Culture in African Christianity," *IRM* 87/344 (1998): 25–38. [abstract: *NTA* 42/3 (1998): #1520.]

Fashole-Luke, E.W.
1981   "Bible Commentary for Africa Project," *Exchange* 10: 42–45. [abstract: Holter: #075.]
Fiensy, D.
1987   "Using the Nuer Culture of Africa in Understanding the Old Testament: An Evaluation," *JSOT* 38: 73–83. [abstract: Holter: #077.]
Flint, P.W.
1987   "Old Testament Scholarship from an African Perspective," J.J. Burden, ed. *Exodus 1–15: Text and Context. Proceedings of the 29th annual congress of the Old Testament Society of South Africa* (Pretoria, South Africa: Old Testament Society of South Africa): 179–214. [abstract: Holter: #078.]
Foullah, Leopold A.
1987   "The Use of the New Testament Greek Text: A Critique of the Eclectic Textual Critical Method" (M.Th. thesis, NEGST).
Gakwandi, E.
1969   "Bible et Tradition Religieuse Africaine," *Cum Paraclito* Numero special: 13–18.
Garcia, Miguel A.
1996   "Ethiopian Traditional Biblical Interpretation," *ACS* 12/2: 1–8. [abstract: *NTA* 41/1 (1997): #26.]
Getui, Mary N.
1997   "The Bible as a Tool for Ecumenism," Kinoti & Waliggo: 86–98.
Gibellini, Rosino
1994   *Paths of African Theology* (Maryknoll: Orbis). [review: *BookNotes* 1 (March 1996): #1.14.]
Gichuhi, George N.
1985   *The Spirituality of Small Christian Communities in Eastern Africa* (Spearhead #85; Eldoret, Kenya: Gaba). [especially chapters 1 and 2 on Acts and Paul respectively.]
Gilkes, Cheryl Townsend
1970   "Colonialism and the Biblical Revolution in Africa," *JORT* 27/2: 59–75. [abstract: Holter: #079.]
Greenberg, Moshe
1972   "The Universal Aspects of the Message of the Bible," Mveng & Werblowsky: 15–22. [with some changes reprinted as "On sharing the Scriptures," F.M. Cross, et al., eds *Magnalia Dei. The Mighty Acts of God. Essays on the Bible and Archaeology in Memory of G. Ernest Wright* (N.Y.: Doubleday): 455–63. [abstract: Holter: #085.]
Grimes, Edward
1979   "The Biblical Apostolate and the Child," *B-PB* 1: 25–26.
Gueye, Doudou
1972   "Négritude et Bible," Mveng & Werblowsky: 60–81.
Hackett, Rosalind
1993   "From Inclusion to Exclusion: Women and Bible Use in Southern Nigeria," I. Wollaston and J. Davies, eds *The Sociology of Sacred Texts* (Sheffield: Sheffield Academic Press): 142–55.

Hansen, Ellen
    1990   "The Old Testament within African Oral Use of the Bible" (unpublished paper written for the University of Copenhagen, Denmark, Oct. 1990; on file at The Lutheran Theological College, Makumira, Tanzania).

Healey, Joseph G.
    1995   "The Need for an Effective Bible Reflection Method in SCC's in Africa," *AFER* 37/3 (1995): 156–59.

Heisey, N.R.
    1998   "The Influence of Africa Scholars on Biblical Studies," *JTSA* 101: 35–48. [abstract: *NTA* 43/2 (1999): #858.]

Hinga, Teresia M.
    1990   "Women Liberation in and through the Bible: The Debate and the Quest for a New Feminist Hermeneutics," *ACS* 6/4: 33–49. [abstract: *NTA* 36/2 (1992): #579.]
    1996   "'Reading With': An Exploration of the Interface between 'Critical' and 'Ordinary' Readings of the Bible: A Response," *Semeia* 73: 277–84.

Hollenweger, W.J.
    1990   "Black Christian Interpretation," R.J. Coggins & J.L. Houlden, eds A *Dictionary of Biblical Interpretation* (London: SCM Press/ Philadelphia: Trinity Press International): 90–92.

Holter, Knut
    1994   "Gammelstestsmentlig forskning mellom Sahara og Zambezi" [Old Testament Research between the Sahara and the Zambezi], *Tidsskrift for Teologi og Kirke* 68: 135–46. [abstract: *OTA* 21/1 (1998): #8.]
    1998   "The Institutional Context of Old Testament Scholarship in Africa," unpublished paper delivered the International Organization for the Study of the Old Testament, Oslo, Norway, August 2–7, 1998.
           "'It's Not Only a Question of Money!' African Old Testament Scholarship Between the Myths and Meanings of the South and the Money and Methods of the North," *OTEssays* 11: 240–54.
           "Some Recent Studies on Postcolonialism and Biblical Scholarship," *NAOTS* 5: 20–23. [abstract: *OTA* 22/2 (1999): #681.]
    1995   "Report: Symposium in Nairobi, October 1999," *NAOTS* 7: 8–9.

Idowu, E. Bolaji
    1971   "The Relation of the Gospels to African Culture and Religion," Donald G. Miller & Dikran Y. Hadidian, eds *Jesus and Man's Hope Volume 2* (Pittsburg: Pittsburg Theological Seminary): 262–72.
    1972   "The Teaching of the Bible to African Students," Mveng & Werblowsky: 199–204. [abstract: Holter: #088.]

Imokhai, Charles
    1990   "The Challenges Posed by the New Evangelization," Amewowo ed.: 71–73.

Isaac, E.
    1964   "Relations between the Hebrew Bible and Africa," *Jewish Social Studies* 26: 87–98. [abstract: Holter: #092.]

Jeffrey, Jon
 1989   "Research into the Use of the Bible in Small Christian Communities (SCCs)," *B-PB* 8/Jan: 29–32.
Jensen, A.E.
 1960   "Beziehungen zwischen dem Alten Testament und der nilotischen Kultur in Afrika," S. Diamond, ed. *Culture in History. Essays in honor of Paul Radin* (N.Y.: Published for Brandeis University by Columbia University Press): 449–66. [abstract: Holter: #096.]
Johnson, Solomon Tilewa
 1993   *Batum Yalla Word of God: The Centrality of Scripture in the Life of the Church* (Nairobi: Church of the Province of Kenya).
Jourdes, Francois Raison
 1991   *Bible et Pouvoir a Madagasgar au XIXᵉ Siècle: Invention d'une Identité Chretienne et Construction de l'Etate (1780–1880)* (Paris: Editions Karthala).
Kabazzi-Kisirinya, S.
 1990   "Report and Vision of the New Evangelization in Uganda," Amewowo, ed.: 111–13.
 1987   "New Trends in the Bible: From Revelation to the Word of God in community," Shorter & Waliggo: 129–35.
Kalilombe, Patrick A.
 1981   "The Role of the African Biblist in the Church in Africa Today," *B-PB* 4: 27–34.
 1991   "A Malawian Example: The Bible and Non-Literate Communities," in Sugirtharajah, 1st ed.: 397–411; 2nd ed.: 421–35.
Kato, Byang H.
 1985   *Biblical Christianity in Africa* (Achimota, Ghana: Africa Christian Press.) [review: *BookNotes* 2 (October 1996): #2.17.]
Kaungya, J.
 1978   "The Relationship between Christianity and Judaism," Hammerstein: 32–35. [abstract: Holter: #100.]
King, N.G. & D.J.F. King
 1976   "Towards an African Strack-Billerbeck?" John S. Pobee, ed., *Religion in a Pluralistic Society* (Leiden: Brill): 78–84.
Kinoti, Hannah W. & John M. Waliggo, eds
 1997   *The Bible in African Christianity: Essays in Biblical Theology* (Nairobi: Acton Publishers). [review: K. Holter *NAOTS* 5: 27–28.]
    "Introduction," Kinoti & Waliggo: 1–7.
Kritzinger, J.N.J.
 1985   "The Bible and Human Transformation: A Case Study from South Africa," *Mission Studies* 2/2: 4–7.
Lackey, W.M.
 1987   "The Use of Old Testament Narrative for Bible Teaching in Africa," (M.Div. thesis, NIST).
Lambert, Jean C.
 1993   "Theologians' Uses of the Bible," Mukonyora, Cox & Verstraelen: 171–98.

Laperruque, Marcel
  1972 "La Bible et les Civilisations de la VallJe du Nil," Mveng &
        Werblowsky: 173–89.

Le Deaut, R.
  1980 "Continuite et Discontinuite entre l'A.T. et le N.T.," Atal sa
        Angang, et al., eds: 31–64.

Lehman-Habeck, Martin
  1993 "New Light on the Bible for Today's Readers," Mukonyora, Cox
        & Verstraelen: 35–59.

LeMarquand, Grant
  1999 "'And the Rulers of the Nations Shall Bring Their Treasures Into
        it': A Survey of Biblical Exegesis in Africa," <http://www.tesm.edu/
        writings/lemafric.htm>

Levison, J.R. & P. Pope-Levison
  1992 "The Use of the New Testament in Third World Christologies,"
        Biblical Research: Journal of the Chicago Society of Biblical Research 37:
        32–46. [abstract: *NTA* 37/2 (1993): #920.]
  1995 "Global Perspectives on New Testament Interpretation," *Hearing*
        the New Testament Joel Green, ed. (Grand Rapids: Eerdmans):
        329–48.

Lufuluabo, F.M.
  1968 *Valeur des religions africaines selon la Bible et Vatican II* (Kinshasa:
        Editions Saint Paul).

Lwaminda, Peter
  1990 "The New Evangelization and the Building up of SCCs in
        AMECEA," Amewowo, ed.: 62–70; reprinted as "The New Evange-
        lization: Biblical Apostolate dimensions in Africa—The New Evan-
        gelization and the Building Up of Small Christian Communities
        in AMECEA Countries," *B-PB* 10 (1990): 22–43.

Mafico, Temba L.J.
  1979 "The Contribution of the Old Testament to Missionary Effectiveness
        in Africa," *Missiology* 7: 110–111. [abstract: Holter: #113.]
  1986 "The Old Testament and Effective Evangelism in Africa," *IRM*
        75: 400–409. [abstract: Holter: #114.]

Magesa, L.
  1977 "The Bible and a Liberation Theology for Africa," *AFER* 19:
        217–222.
  1997 "From Privatized to Popular Biblical Hermeneutics in Africa,"
        Kinoti & Waliggo: 25–39.

Malamat, Avraham
  1972 "Tribal Societies: Biblical Genealogies and African Lineage Sys-
        tems," Mveng & Werblowsky: 147–154; with some changes reprinted
        in *Archives Europeennes de Sociologie* 14: 126–36. [abstract: Holter:
        #115.]

Maleya, Laura
  1995 "The Bible and Modernity," *Hekima Review* 13: 12–15.

652 GRANT LEMARQUAND

Mandivenga, E.C.
1993 "The Qur'an and the Bible: A Comparison," Mukonyora, Cox
& Verstraelen: 125–39.
Masawe, Sabas
1995 "The Community and its Role in Interpreting the Bible," *Hekima Review* 13: 16–21.
Mbaya, Tshiakany Tshiabantu
1992 "L'Opposition des Opprimes a l'Option Liberatrice. Une Relecture des Paradigmes Bibliques en Face des Realites Negro-Africaines," *RZTP* 6: 27–42.
Mbiti, John S.
1978 "African Christians and Jewish Religious Heritage," Hammerstein: 13–19. [abstract: Holter: #123.]
1986 *Bible and Theology in African Christianity* (Nairobi: Oxford University Press).' *Bibel und Theologie im afrikanischen Christentum* Bernard Ferrazzini, trans; Theologie der Oekumene 22 (Gottingen: Vanderhoeck & Ruprecht, 1987). [reviews: A. Mojola *BT* 38/3 (1986): 344–45; A. Hastings *Journal of Ecclesiastical History* 39 (1988): 324–25; H.W. Huppenbauer *Zeitschrift für Mission* 14/4 (1988): 255–56; E. Kamphausen *Oekumenische Rundschau* 37 (1988): 506–508; J. Schlegel *Theologische Literaturzeitung* 113 (1988): 858–59; H.R. Weber *IRM* 77 (1988): 282–85; R.F. Collins *Louvain Studies* 14/1 (1989): 74–75; J. Khhl *Zeitschrift für Missionswissenschaft und Religionswissenschaft* 73/1 (1989): 88; *BookNotes* 4 (October 1997): #4.25; abstracts: *NTA* 32/2 (1988): 236; *RSR* 16/3 (1990): 277; Holter: #126.]
1987 "An Ecumenical Approach to Teaching the Bible," *Ecumenical Review* 39/4: 404–12; also published in *The Teaching of Ecumenics* Samuel Amirtham and Cyrus Moon, eds (Geneva: WCC Publications): 30–37.
1994 "The Bible in African Culture," Gibellini: 27–39.
Mbogori, Johanna
1975 "How the Bible is Used in Africa," Best: 111–18.
1976 "Comment est Utilisée la Bible en Afrique," *Flambeau* 49–50: 24–31.
McCallum, F.V.I.
1970 "African ideas and the Old Testament," *Nada* 10/2: 3–11. [abstract: Holter: #127.]
Mijoga, Hilary B.P.
1996 "Hermeneutics in African Instituted Churches in Malawi," *Missionalia* 24/3: 358–71.
1997 "Hidden and Public Ways of Doing Contextual Bible Study in Southern Africa. South Africa and Malawi As Case Studies," *Religion in Malawi* 7: 41–44.
Mikre-Selassie, G.A.
1972 "Ethiopia and the Bible," Mveng & Werblowsky: 190–96.
1993 "The Bible and its Canon in the Ethiopian Orthodox Church," *BT* 44/1: 111–23. [abstract: *NTA* 37/3 (1993): #1104.]

Milton, Leslie
  1994 "Presentation and Evaluation of Glasgow Surveys of Popular Uses of the Bible," Bible in Africa Project: 8–12.

Mojola, Aloo Osotsi
  1996 "A Brief Report of the 16th IOSOT [International Organization for the Study of the Old Testament] *NAOTS* 5: 8–11. [abstract: *OTA* 22/2 (1999): #644.]

Mohono, S.A.
  1983 "The Importance of the Bible to the African Independent Churches," in Babs Mala: 58–65.

Monsengwo Pasinya, L.
  1972 "Herméneutique et Interprétation Africaine de la Bible," Mveng & Werblowsky: 236–47.
  1975 "La Problèm Herméneutique," *Telema* 1/1: 9–22.
  1977 "Interprétation Africaine de la Bible: Racine Herméneutique et Biblique," *RAT* 1/2: 145–64. [abstract: *NTA* 26/1 (1982): 23.]
  1980 "Continuité et Discontinuité entre l'A.T. et les Religions Africaines: Rapport de Carrefour," Atal sa Angang et al., eds: 239–42.
  1982 "Exégèse Bibliques et Questions Africaines," *RAT* 6/12: 165–75. [abstract: *NTA* 28/1 (1984): #29.]

Mosothoane, E.K.
  1973 "The Message of the New Testament Seen in African Perspective," Becken, 1973: 55–67.

Moyo, Ambrose Mavingire
  1983 "The Quest for African Christian Theology and the Problem of the Relationship Between Faith and Culture—The Hermeneutical Perspective" *ATJ* 12/2: 95–108.

Mubabinge, Bilolo
  1980 "Valeur Salvifiques des Religions Africaines: Rapport de Carrefour," Atal sa Angang, et al., eds: 251–53.

Mudiso, Gaspard
  1990 "Les Experiences Concretes d'Apostolat Biblique au Zaire," Amewowo: 114–16.

Mugambi, J.N.K.
  1997 "The Bible and Ecumenism in African Christianity," Kinoti & Waliggo: 68–85.

Mugaruka Mugarukira Ngabo, Richard
  1990 "Y a-t-il une Approche Négro-Africaine de la Bible?" *RAT* 14/27–28: 11–31.
  1993 "Pour une Catechese Biblique Inculturee: Principes et Methodes," *RAT* 17/34: 203–13.

Mukendi, Félix Mutombo
  1997 *Herméneutique Athée et Exégèses Modernes. A Propos d'un Thème Capital de la Foi Chrétienne: Le Fils de l'Homme* (Kinshasa: Lingue pour la lecture de la Bible.) [review: *BookNotes* 7 (March 1999): 7.27.]

Mukeng'a Kalond, G.
  1980 "Tâche de l'Exégète Africain," Atal sa Angang, et al., eds: 17–27.

Mukonyora, Isabela, James L. Cox & Frans J. Verstraelen, eds
1993 *"Rewriting the Bible: The Real Issues. Perspectives from within Biblical and Religious Studies in Zimbabwe"* Religious and Theological Studies, 1 (Gweru, Zimbabwe: Mambo Press). [review: *BookNotes* 1 (March 1996): #1.28.; abstract: *NTA* 40/3 (1996): 512.]
"The Fulfilment of African Religious Needs through the Bible," Mukonyora, Cox & Verstraelen: 249–262.
"Women's Readings of the Bible," Mukonyora, Cox & Verstraelen: 199–216.

Murphy, C., ed.
1995 *The African Bible: The New Testament* (Nairobi: Paulines Publications). [abstract: *BookNotes* 3 (March 1997): #3.26.]

Muutuki, Joseph
1997 "Library Resources for Old Testament Research in Nairobi," *NAOTS* 3: 5–7.
1999 "Report: Workshop in Stellenbosch, May 1999," *NAOTS* 7: 6–7.

Mveng, Engelbert and R.J.Z. Werblowsky, eds
1972 *The Jerusalem Congress on Black Africa and the Bible. April 24–30, 1972/ Le Congres de Jerusalem sur l'Afrique Noire et la Bible: Proceedings* (Jerusalem: The Israel Interfaith Committee). [abstract: Holter: #137.]

Nasimiyu-Wasike, Anne
1989 "Report on Consultation on Methods of Research to Find out how the Bible is Being used in Small Christian Communities in Africa," *B-PB* 8/Jan: 3–13.

Nare, Laurent
1993 "Centre Biblique Catholique pour l'Afrique et Madagascar (CEBAM ou BICAM)," *Telema* 19/75–76: 19–21.

Ndungu, Nahashon
1997 "The Bible in an African Independent Church," Kinoti & Waliggo: 58–67.

Ngally, J.
1972 "Lecture Africaine de la Bible et Exégèse Traditionelle," Mveng & Werblowsky: 121–33. [abstract: Holter: #143.]
1975 "Bible Studies from an African Perspective," *AACC Bulletin* 8/1: 33–36.
"Jesus Christ and Liberation in Africa: a Bible Study," *Ecumenical Review* 27/3: 212–19.

Nthamburi, Zablon
1980 "African Theology of Liberation (II): Biblical Foundations of African Theology," *AFER* 22/5: 287–303; reprinted in French as "Fondements Bibliques d'une Theologie Africaine," *Spiritus* 88: 267–77.

Nthamburi, Zablon & Douglas Waruta
1997 "Biblical Hermeneutics in African Instituted Churches," Kinoti & Waliggo: 40–57.

Ntreh, Benjamin Abotchie
1990 "Towards an African Biblical Hermeneutic," *ATJ* 19/3: 247–54. [abstracts: *NTA* 35/3 (1991): #1035.; Holter: #147.]

1998   "Methodological Challenges of Old Testament Scholarship in the African Context," *NAOTS* 5:2–4. [abstract: *OTA* 22/2 (1999): #685.]

Ntumba, Tshiamalenge
1977   "Exegese Bibliques et Philosophie du Langage," *RAT* 1/2: 165–84. [abstract: *NTA* 26/1 (1982): #29.]

Nussbaum, Stan
1993   "African Bible Guides: Preliminary Findings of an Experiment with African Christianity in Microcosm," *ERT* 17/4: 452–67. [abstract: Holter: #149.]

Nyamiti, Charles
1991   "My Approach to African Theology," *ACS* 7/4: 35–53; especially: 40–42]

Nyathow, M.T.
1990   "Report on Biblical Apostolate Promotion in the Sudan 1984–1989," Amewowo: 103–04.

Nyemb, A.T.
1972   "L'Espérance Africaine en l'Eternité," Mveng & Werblowsky: 100–105. [abstract: Holter: #150.]

Nyeme Tese, J.
1980   "Continuité et Discontinuité entre l'A.T. et les Religions Africaines," Atal sa Angang, et al.: 83–112. [abstract: Holter: #151.]
1983   "La bible a l'Heure de l'Afrique," *Mission, Coeur en Alerte* 6–7; also published as "Afrika offnet sich der Bibel," *Missio, Herz in Angriff* 6–7.

Nyirongo, Lenard
1997   *The Gods of Africa or the God of the Bible: The Snares of African Traditional Religion in Biblical Perspective* (Potchefstroom: Potchestroom University). [review: *BookNotes* 8 (October 1999): #8.27.]

Obeng, Emmanuel
1997   "The Use of Biblical Critical Methods in Rooting Scriptures in Africa," Kinoti & Waliggo: 8–24.

Offiong, Mary Immaculata
1991   "The Nigerian Woman and the Bible," Edet & Umeagudosa: 63–70.

Okabe, Patrick
1995   "Being Doers of the Word: Submitting to the Authority of Scripture," *Hekima Review* 13: 22–24.

Okambawa, Wilfrid
1995   "Biblical Exegesis and the Authority of Christians," *Hekima Review* 13: 10–11.

Okorocha, Cyril
1996   "Scripture, Mission and Evangelism," Stott and Others: 61–81.

Okure, Teresa
1993   "Feminist Interpretations in Africa," *Searching the Scriptures. Volume One: A Feminist Introduction* Elisabeth Schussler Fiorenza, ed. (New York: Crossroad): 76–85.
1995   "'Behold I Make All Things New': The Final Statement of the Fourth Plenary Assembly of the Catholic Biblical Federation,"

W.M. Beuken & Sean Freyne, eds *Concilium 1995/1: The Bible As Cultural Heritage* (London and Maryknoll: SCM and Orbis): 108–20. [abstract: *NTA* 40/1 (1996): #42.]

1996   "Word of God, Word of Life: An African Perspective," *Word and Worship* 29: 178–200.

Opoku Kofi, A.
1977   "Compatibility between African Traditional Religion and Biblical Religion," *Catholic Voice* 52: 125–126.

Onwu, Nlenanya
1984–85 "The Current State of Biblical Studies in Africa," *JORT* 42/2: 35–46. [abstract: *NTA* 29/3 (1985): #824; Holter: #174.]
1985   "The Hermeneutical Model: The Dilemma of the African Theologian," *ATJ* 14/3: 145–60. [abstract: *NTA* 32/2 (1988): #512.]

Osei-Bonsu, Joseph
1990   "Biblically/Theologically Based Inculturation," *AFER* 32/6: 346–58. [abstract: *NTA* 35/2 (1991): #847.]

Oshitelu, J.O.
n.d.   *The Golden Key to the Bible* (Ogere, Nigeria: Church of the Lord (Aladura) Publications). [In *African Independent Church II. The Life and Faith of the Church of the Lord (Aladura)* (Oxford: Clarendon, 1967) H.W. Turner suggests (p. 377) that this 33pp. pamphlet may have been published in 1949.]

Oshun, E.O.
1987   "The Word of God as Word: A Pentecostal Viewpoint," *AJBS* 2/1–2: 106–12. [abstract: Holter: #178.]

Owan, Kris
1993   "The Fundamentalists' Interpretation of the Bible: A Challenge to Biblical Exegetes in West Africa," *WAJES* 5: 1–15. [abstract: Holter: #179.]
1994   "The Word of God in Human Language: Towards a Culturally Pluralistic Interpretation of the Bible." (Unpublished paper presented to the Bible in Africa Project Consultation in Glasgow.) typescript, 22pp. Summarized in Bible in Africa Project: 41–44. "The Fundamentalists' Interpretation of the Bible: A Challenge to the Nigerian Biblical Association," *BTS* 14/1: 5–21.
1999   "Intertestamental Literature in Africa," *NAOTS* 5: 5–7. [abstract: *OTA* 22/2 (1999): #648.]

Parratt, John
1983   "African Theology and Biblical Hermeneutics," *ATJ* 12/2: 88–94. [abstract: Holter: #180.]

Parvey, C.F.
1985   "Third World Women and Men: Effects of Cultural Change on Interpretation of Scripture," J.C.B. Webster & E.L. Webster, eds *The Church and Woman in the Third World* (Philadelphia): 105–19, 164–66.

Patte, Daniel
  1996   "Biblical Scholars at the Interface between Critical and Ordinary
              Readings: A Response," *Semeia* 73: 263–76.
Peter, C.B.
  1993   "Theological Polarization and Biblical Synthesis," *AFER* 35/5:
              288–98.
Pobee, John Samuel
  1985   "The Word became Flesh: The Meeting of Christianity and
              African Culture," *Voices* 8/2: 49–63.
  1985–86   "Teaching the New Testament in an African Context," *JORT*
              42/2: 22–29. [abstract: *NTA* 30/3 (1986): #944.]
  1989   "Biblical Studies and Missiology (BISAM)," *Mission Studies* 11,
              6/1: 57–60.
  1994   "Keynote Speech," Bible in Africa Project: 12–15. [a summary]
  1995   "The Use of the Bible in African theology," T. Fornberg, ed.
              Bible, Hermeneutics, Mission Missio, 10 (Uppsala): 113–30. [abstract:
              Holter: #186.]
  1996   "Bible Study in Africa: A Passover of Language," *Semeia* 73:
              161–79. [abstract: *NTA* 42/1 (1998): #67.]
Poucouta, Paulin
  1993   "Congres des Biblistes Africaines," *Telema* 19/75–76: 22.
Preus, Jonathan
  1993   "Reading the Bible through Christ," *TCNN Research Bulletin*
              26: 1–20.
Prior, A.
  1990   "Report from the Southern African Catholic Bishops' Confer-
              ence," Amewowo, ed.: 100–102.
Prior, Michael
  1997   *The Bible and Colonialism: A Moral Critique* (Sheffield: Sheffield
              Academic Press).
Rakotoarisoa, [ ].
  n.d.   "The Old Testament in the Malagasy Church," in "An Inter-
              disciplinary Workshop . . .": 55–64.
Rapoo, D.
              "The Word of God in Everyday African Life," Birkell: 133–34.
Rath, J.Th.
  1956   "Die Bibel—Buch des Unheils für Afrika," *Die Katholischen
              Missionen* 75: 109–12.
Reaume, J.D.
  1995   "The New Testament Use of the Old Testament," *UMTC—
              JTS* 1: 56–66.
Reed, S.A.
  1996   "Critique of Canaan Banana's Call to Rewrite the Bible,"
              R&T 3/3: 282–88. [abstract: *NTA* 41/2 (1997): # 750.]
Renju, Peter Masumbuko
  1980   "African Traditional Religions & Old Testament: Continuity

or Discontinuity?" Atal sa Angang, et al., eds: 113–18. [abstract: Holter: #189.]

Riches, John
1994   "Interpreting the Bible in African Contexts: Glasgow Consultation," *Ministerial Formation* 67 (Oct.): 58–59.
        "Cultural Bias in Western Biblical Interpretation." (Unpublished paper presented to the Bible in Africa Project Consultation in Glasgow. Summarized in Bible in Africa Project: 32–36.)
1996   "Interpreting the Bible in African Contexts: Glasgow Consultation," *Semeia* 73: 181–88. [abstract: *NTA* 42/1 (1998): #71.]

Robinson, P.J.
1994   "The Future of Old Testament Studies through the Eyes of Missiology," *OTEssays* 7: 245–60. [abstract: Holter: # 194.]

Rogers, Robert G.
1994   "Biblical Hermeneutics and Contemporary African Theology," Lewis M. Hopfe, ed. *Uncovering Ancient Stones: Essays in Memory of H. Neil Richardson* (Winona Lake: Eisenbrauns): 245–60. [abstract: Holter: #195.]

Rogho, J.M.O.
1993   "A Critique of Biblical Authority in John Mbiti's Theology" (M.Th. thesis, Nairobi Evangelical School of Theology).

Ruiz, Jean-Pierre
1995   "New Ways of Reading the Bible in the Cultural Settings of the Third World," *Concilium 1995/1: The Bible as Cultural Heritage* W.M. Beuken & Sean Freyne, eds (London and Maryknoll: SCM and Orbis): 73–84. [abstract: *NTA* 40/1 (1996): #47.]

Sanders, E.R.
1969   "The Hamitic Hypothesis: It's Origins and Functions in Time Perspective," *Journal of African History* 10/4: 521–32.

Sarpong, Peter Kwesi
1990   "The Biblical Apostolate in the New Evangelization, African Perspectives: Challenges and Pastoral Strategies in the Third Millenium," Amewowo: 7–24; reprinted in *B-PB* 10: 3–21.

Sarah, Robert
1987   "Qu'est-ce que l'Apostolat Biblique?" *Cahiers Biblique Africains* 1/Jan: 5–10.

Schelbert, G.
1960   "Einheimische Kunst und Bibel—Illustrationen im Protestantismus," *NZM* 16: 305–309.

Schuller, S.
1938   "Erste afrikanische Bibelillustrationen," *Die Katholischen Missionen* 66: 15–19.
        Premieres illustrations de la Bible en Afrique (Aachen).

Shuuya, I.K.
1973   "The Encounter Between the New Testament and African Traditional Concepts," Becken, 1973: 47–54.

Skweres, D.E.
1982 "Bibelpastorale Publikationen im frankophonen Afrika und ihre missionsstrategische Bedeutung," *Verbum Societatis Verbi Divini* 23: 177–86. [abstract: Holter: #205.]

Smith, Adrian B., ed.
1977 *Bridging the Gap: A Handbook for Promoting the Biblical Apostolate* Spearhead #46 (Eldoret: Gaba).
1978 *Applying Scripture to Life* Spearhead #53 (Eldoret: Gaba). [abstract: *BCTA* 1 (1993): 43.]

Smith-Christopher, Daniel, ed.
1996 *Text and Experience: Towards a Cultural Exegesis of the Bible* (The Biblical Seminar, 35; Sheffield: Sheffield Academic Press). [review: B.E. Bowe *CBQ* 59/4 (1997): 813–14; abstract: *OTA* 20/1 (1997): #536.]

Snyder, Graydon F.
1993 "Before the Canon: The Pre-Cultural Jesus Tradition," Mukonyora, Cox & Verstraelen: 81–87.

Spindler, Marc
1996 "The Biblical Impact on Malagasy literature," *Exchange* 25: 106–18.

Standaert, Benoit
1993 "La Dialectique du Particulier et de l'Universel. Pour un Universalisme non-totalitaire," Adeso, et al., 1993: 263–75.

Stott, John and Others
1996 *The Anglican Communion and Scripture: Papers from the First International Consultation of the Evangelical Fellowship in the Anglican Communion, Canterbury, UK, June 1993* (Carlisle, UK: Regnum Books International and EFAC with Paternoster Publishing).

Sung, Nam Yong
1997 "Worldview Themes regarding Spiritual and Natural Realities and the Impact on Biblical Hermeneutics of the Students of ECWA Theological Institutions in Nigeria" (Ph.D. dissertation, Trinity Evangelical Divinity School, Deerfield, Illinois).

Swanpoel, M.G.
1990 "An Encounter Between Old Testament Theology and African Concepts of God," *Theologia Viatorum* 18: 20–30. [abstract: Holter: #209.]

Swiderski, S.
1979 "Les Récits Bibliques dans l'Adaptation Africaine," *JRA* 10: 174–233. [abstract: Holter: #210.]

Thompson, Prince E.S.
1962 "The Approach to the Old Testament in an African Setting," *GBT* 2/3: 1–11. [abstract: Holter: #211.]

Tienou, Tite
1983 "Biblical Foundations for African Theology," *Missiology* 10: 435–48; reprinted with some changes as "Biblical Foundations: an African Study," *ERT* 7/1: 89–101. [abstract: Holter: # 213.]

Ukpong, Justin S.
1985 "The Bible in the Life of the Christian," *Shalom* 3: 82–85.

1994   "Christology and Inculturation: A New Testament Perspective," Gibellini: 40–61.

"Inculturation and Evangelization: Biblical Foundations for Inculturation," *Vidyajyoti* 58: 298–307. [abstract: *NTA* 39/2 (1995): #1078.]

"Inculturation Biblical Hermeneutic: Reading the Bible with African Eyes" (unpublished paper distributed to Bible in Africa Project Consultation Glasgow; summarized in Bible in Africa Project: 37–41.)

"Interpreting the Bible in Africa Contexts: Implications for a Global Context," (unpublished paper distributed to Bible in Africa Project Consultation Glasgow), typescript, 5pp.

"Port Harcourt Report," Bible in Africa Project: 16–20.

Review of J.S. Croatto *Biblical Hermeneutics* (Maryknoll: Orbis, 1987) in *JIT* 1/2: 179–91.

"Towards a Renewed Approach to Inculturation Theology," *JIT* 1: 8–24.

1995   "Rereading the Bible with African Eyes: Inculturation and Hermeneutics," *JTSA* 91: 3–14. [abstracts: *BCT* 3/1 (1996): 31; Holter: #217; *NTA* 40/2 (1996): #709; *RTA* 39/3 (1996): #3375.]

1999   "Can African Old Testament Scholarship Escape the Historical Critical Approach?" *NAOTS* 7: 2–5.

Ullendorff, Edward

1956   "Hebraic-Jewish Elements in Abyssinian (Monophysite) Christianity," *Journal of Semitic Studies* 1: 216–56.

1968   *Ethiopia and the Bible: The Schweich Lectures of the British Academy 1967* (Oxford: Oxford University Press). [reviews: H.S. Gehman *JBL* 88 (1969): 234–35; D.W. Thomas *Journal of Theological Studies* ns 20 (1969): 552–56; K.T. Andersen *Svensk Missionstidskrift* 58/1 (1970): 24–34; E. Bishop *Palestine Exploration Quarterly* 102 (1970): 141–42; M. Rodinson *Journal of Semitic Studies* 17 (1972): 166–70;

Uwalaka, E.E.

1990   "Biblical Apostolate in African Universities," Amewowo: 53–56. [also published in *B-PB* 10: 44–51.]

van Oostrom, Evert

1973   "Does our Bible-Teaching in the East African Theological Institutions Make Real Pastors?" (Katigondo National Major Seminary, Uganda, 12pp., 1973).

van Zyl, Danie C.

1995   "In Africa Theology is Not Thought Out but Danced Out—On the Theological Significance of Old Testament Symbolism and Rituals in African Zionist Churches," *OTEssays* 8: 425–38. [abstract: *OTA* 20/2 (1997): #624.]

1997   "Interpretasie van die Ou Testament in Sionistiese kerke—'n verkennende studie [The Interpretation of the Old Testament in Zionist Churches: An Exploratory Study]," *NGTT* 38: 85–93. [abstract: *OTA* 20/3 (1997): #1314.]

Verstraelen, Frans J.
  1993   "The Christian Bible and African Cultural and Religious Realities,"
          Mukonyora, Cox & Verstraelen: 219–48.
          "Mission and the Bible in Historical and Missiological Perspective,"
          Mukonyora, Cox & Verstraelen: 141–67.
          "The Real Issues Regarding the Bible: Summary, Findings and
          Conclusions," Mukonyora, Cox & Verstraelen: 265–89.
Wambutda, Daniel
  1980   "Hermeneutics and the Search for Theologia Africana," *ATJ* 9/2:
          29–39. [abstract: Holter: #222.]
  1981   "Savannah Theology: A Biblical Reconsideration of the Concept
          of Salvation in the African Context," *BTA* 3/6: 137–53.
Weems, Renita
  1996   "Response to 'Reading With': An Exploration of the Interface
          between Critical and Ordinary Readings of the Bible," *Semeia* 73:
          257–61.
Wernhart, K.R.
  1992   "Altes Testament und Schwarzafrika," in *Zur Aktualitat des Alten
          Testaments. Festschrift für Georg Sauer zum 65. Geburtstag*, S. Kreuzer &
          K. Luthi, eds (Frankfurt am Main: Peter Lang): 219–26. [abstract:
          Holter: #228.]
West, Gerald O. & Musa W. Dube, eds
  1996   "'Reading With': An Exploration of the Interface Between Critical
          and Ordinary Readings of the Bible. African Overtures," *Semeia*
          73. [review: K. Holter *NAOTS* 5: 28.]
          "An Introduction: How We Have Come to 'Read With,'" *Semeia*
          73: 7–17.
  1999   "Early Encounters with the Bible in Africa: Historical, Method-
          ological, and Hermeneutical Analysis of the Transactions between
          the Bible and Indigenous African Communities," *NAOTS* 6: 16–18.
White, Charles Edward
  1993   "Teaching Mark's Gospel to Muslims: Lessons from an African
          University," *Christianity Today* 37/2: 39–40.
Widart, J.M.
  1976   "How Do You Explain the Bible in Zaire?" *Worldmission* 27/3:
          50–51.
  1990   "Nos activités depuis l'Assemblée de Bangalore (1984)," Amewowo,
          ed.: 120–22.
Wille, Wilhelm
  n.d.   "Some Reflection on African Traditional Religions in the Light of
          Historical-Critical Exegesis of the New Testament," (unpublished
          paper, on file at St. Paul's United Theological College, Limuru,
          Kenya).
  1973   "Popular Biblical Interpretation in Uganda: Some Observations Based
          on Political Texts, Mainly from 1967–70," *AFER* 15/3: 227–36.
Yorke, Gosnell, L.O.R.
  1995   "Biblical Hermeneutics: An Afrocentric Perspective," *Religion and*

Theology 2/2: 145–58. [abstracts: *NTA* 40/2 (1996): #714; *RTA* 39/1 (1996): #419.]

"Seventh-day Adventists Believe . . .: A Biblical Exposition of 27 Fundamental Doctrines: An Afro-Adventist Appraisal," *JATA* 1/1: 8–23.

1997 "The Bible and the Black Diaspora," Kinoti & Waliggo: 145–64.

1995 "Biblical Hermeneutics: An Afrocentric Perspective," *JORT* 52/1 (1995): 145–58. [abstract: *NTA* 42/1 (1998): #87.]

Zinkuratire, Victor

1990 "The Role of C.H.I.E.A. in the New Evangelization," Amewowo: 57–58.1

3. *Africa and Africans in the Bible*

Adamo, David Tuesday

1986 "The Place of Africa and Africans in the Old Testament and its Environment," (Ph.D. dissertation, Baylor University).

1987 "The Black Prophet in the Old Testament," *JARS* 4 (1987): 1–8. [abstract: Holter: #013.]

1989 "The African Wife of Moses: An Examination of Numbers 12: 1–9," *ATJ* 18/3: 230–37. [abstracts: Holter: #014; *BCT* 3/1 (1996): 24.]

1990 "The African Queen (I Kings 10:10–13, II Chronicles 9:1–12)," *JARS* 7: 14–24. [abstract: Holter #016.]

1992 "Amos 9:7–8 in an African Perspective," *Orita* 24: 76–84. [abstracts: *OTA* 17/2 (1994): #1344; Holter: #017.]

"Ancient Africa and Genesis 2:10–14," *JORT* 49/1: 33–43. [abstract: Holter: #018.]

"An Interpretation of Amos 9:7–8 in an Africa Perspective," *AJBS* 7/1: 1–8.

"Deuteronomic Conception of God According to Deuteronomy 6:4 and its Importance in African Context," *Bible Bhashyam* 18: 55–65. [abstract: *OTA* 17/1 (1994): #379.]

"Ethiopia in the Bible," *ACS* 8/2: 51–64. [abstract: Holter: #020.]

"Jehudi's African Identity in Jeremiah 36: 14,21,23," *Bible Bhashyam* 18/3: 153–62.

1993 "The Table of Nations Reconsidered in African Perspective (Genesis 10)," *Journal of African Religion and Philosophy* 11: 138–43. [abstract: Holter: #021.]

1994 "'Are You Not Like [Africans] to Me O People of Israel?'—An Interpretation of Amos 9:7–8 in an African Perspective," *Bible Bhashyam* 20/1: 19–28.

1998 *Africa and Africans in the Old Testament* (San Francisco/London/ Bethesda: Christian Universities Press). [review: *BookNotes* (March 1998) #6.01; K. Holter *NAOTS* 5 (1998): 26–27.]

Atal Sa Angang, Dosithee
  1993   "La Conversion de l'Eunuque Ethiopien (Ac 8, 26–40) ou le Des-
          tin de la Mission Chrétienne en Afrique," Adeso, et al., 1993:
          189–227.
Bailey, R.C.
  1991   "Beyond Identification: The Use of Africans in Old Testament
          Poetry and Narratives," Felder, ed.: 165–84. [abstract: Holter:
          #038.]
  1996   "'They Shall Become as White as Snow': When Bad is Turned
          into Good," *Semeia* 76: 99–113. [abstract: *OTA*22/3 (1999): #1383.]
Bellis, Alice Ogden
  1995   "The Queen of Sheba: A Gender-Sensitive Reading," *JORT* 51/2:
          17–28.
Bennett, R.A.
  1971   "Africa and the Biblical Period," *Harvard Theological Review* 64:
          483–500. [abstract: Holter: #040.]
Braude, Benjamin
  1997   "How Did Ham Become a Black Slave? Reexamining the Noahides
          in the Abrahamic Tradition," lecture presented at the Annual
          Meeting of the Society of Biblical Literature, San Francisco, Nov.
          24, 1997.
Budge, E.A. Wallis, ed.
  1932   *The Queen of Sheba and Her Only Son Menyelek* (London: Oxford
          University Press/Humphrey Milford).
Burden, J.J.
  1983   "Are Shem and Ham Blood Brothers? The Relevance of the Old
          Testament to Africa," *OTEssays* 1: 49–72. [abstracts: *OTA* 7/1
          (1984): #6; Holter: #047.]
Carter, Leroy
  1989   *Black Heroes of the Bible* (Columbu, Georgia: Brentwood Christian
          Press).
Copher, C.B.
  1974   "The Black Man in the Biblical World," *JITC* 1/2: 7–16; reprinted
          in idem, *Black Biblical Studies*: 19–32.
  1975   "Blacks and Jews in Historical Interaction: the Biblical/African
          Experience," *JITC* 3/1: 9–16; reprinted in idem, *Black Biblical
          Studies*: 33–44. [abstract: Holter: #054.]
  1984   "Egypt and Ethiopia in the Old Testament," *Nile Valley Civilizations:
          Proceedings of The Nile Valley Conference, Atlanta, September 26–30, 1984*,
          Incorporating *Journal of African Civilizations* 6/2: 163–78; reprinted
          in idem, *Black Biblical Studies*: 45–66.
  1986   "Three Thousand Years of Biblical Interpretation with Reference
          to Black Peoples," *JITC* 13/2: 225–46; reprinted in G. Wilmore,
          ed. *African American Religious Studies: An Interdisciplinary Anthology*
          (Durham, N.C.: Duke University Press, 1989): 105–28; and in
          idem, *Black Biblical Studies*: 95–120. [abstract: Holter: #056.]

1988   "The Bible and the African Experience: The Biblical Period,"
        JITC 16: 32–50; reprinted in idem, *Black Biblical Studies*: 133–48.
        [abstracts: *NTA* 36/1 (1992): #391; Holter: #055.]
1991   "The Black Presence in the Old Testament," Felder, ed.: 146–64.
        [abstract: Holter: #057.]
1993   *Black Biblical Studies: An Anthology* (Chicago: Black Light Fellowship).
        [abstract: Holter: #058.]
1995   "Blacks/Negroes: Participants in the Development of Civilization
        in the Ancient World and Their Presence in the Bible," *JITC*
        23/1: 3–47. [abstract: *NTA* 40/3 (1996): #1727.]
Dunstan, Alfred G.
1974   *The Black Man in the Old Testament* (Philadelphia: Dorrance and
        Company).
Evans, William McKee
1980   "From the Land of Canaan to the Land of Guinea: The Strange
        Odyssey of the 'Sons of Ham,'" *The American Historical Review* 85:
        15–43.
Felder, Cain Hope
1989   *Troubling Biblical Waters: Race, Class, and Family* (Maryknoll: Orbis);
        especially chapter 2, "Ancient Ethiopia and the Queen of Sheba":
        22–36. [review: G. West *JTSA* 74 (1991): 73–74; abstract: *RSR*
        17/2 (1991): 145.]
1991   "Race, Racism, and the Biblical Narratives," Felder, ed.: 127–45.
Felder, Cain Hope, ed.
1991   *Stony the Road We Trod: African American Biblical Interpretation* (Min-
        neapolis: Fortress). [reviews: R.L. Brawley *Memphis Theological
        Seminary Journal* 30 (1992): 68–69; R.P. Carroll *Expository Times* 103
        (1992): 281; O.O. Hendricks *Koinonia* 4 (1992): 235–39; T.J. Johnson
        Review and Expositor 89 (1992): 569–71; G. LeMarquand *TJT* 8/1
        (1992): 186–88; P.T. Nash *Word & World* 12 (1992): 418–19; M.G.
        Cartwright *Modern Theology* 9 (1993): 100–102; C.F. Chase *Daugh-
        ters of Sarah* 19 (1993): 46–47; R.R. Featherstone *Trinity Seminary
        Review* 15 (1993): 95; O.O. Hendricks *Sojourners* 22 (1993): 46–47;
        P. Perkins *Cross Currents* 43 (1993): 120–22; J.C. Ross *Interpretation*
        47 (1993): 200–201; K. Waller *Journal of Religion* 73 (1993): 84–86;
        B. Wylie-Kellermann *Witness* 76 (1993): 28; B. Sanders *JORT* 49
        (1992–93): 87–96; R.S. Chopp, J. Grant, A.S. Park, F. Segovia,
        G.A. Yee, T. Hoyt *JITC* 22 (1994): 110–169; J.E. Massey *Southwestern
        Journal of Theology* 37 (1994): 53–54; abstract: *RSR* 19/4 (1993):
        330.]
Frost, P.
1991   "Attitudes toward Blacks in the Early Christian Period," *Second
        Century* 8/1: 1–11. [abstract: *NTA* 36/1 (1992): #426.]
Haynes, Stephen R.
1997   "Original Dishonor: The Curse of Ham and the Southern Defense
        of Slavery," lecture presented at the Annual Meeting of the Society
        of Biblical Literature, San Francisco, Nov. 24, 1997.

Hays, Daniel J.
    1996   "Black Soldiers in the Ancient Near East: Ebedmelech Recon-
            sidered," *Abstracts: American Academy of Religion/ Society of Biblical
            Literature 1996* (Scholars Press): 317.
            "The Cushites: A Black Nation in Ancient History," *Bibliotheca
            Sacra* 153/611: 270–80. [*OTA* 19/3 (1996): #1417.]
            "The Cushites: A Black Nation in the Bible," *Bibliotheca Sacra*
            153/612: 396–409. [abstract: *NTA* 41/2 (1997): #1183; *OTA* 20/1
            (1997): #173.]
    1998   "From the Land of the Bow: Black Soldiers in the Ancient Near
            East," *Bible Review* 14/4: 28–33, 50–51. [abstract: *OTA* 22/1 (1999):
            #4.]
Holter, Knut
    1997   "Old Testament 'Cush' as 'Africa'?" *BT* 48/3: 331–36.
Jackson, A.A.
    1990   *Examining the Record. An Exegetical and Homiletical Study of Blacks in the
            Bible* Martin Luther King Jr. Memorial Studies in Religion, Culture
            and Development, 4 (N.Y.: Peter Lang). [abstract: Holter: #094.]
Kenneth Kitchen
    1997   "Egypt and East Africa," *The Age of Solomon: Scholarship at the Turn
            of the Millenium* Lowell K. Handy, ed. Studies in the History and
            Culture of the Ancient Near East, 11 (Leiden: Brill): 107–25.
            [abstract: *OTA* 21/3 (1998): #1324; for abstract of the book see
            #1733.]
            "Sheba and Arabia," Handy (op. cit.): 127–53. [*OTA* 21/3 (1998):
            #1325.]
Linton, O.
    1974   "The List of Nations in Acts 2," Glasswell & Fashole-Luke: 44–53.
Lumeya, Nzash U.
    1988   "The Curse on Ham's Descendants: Its Missiological Impact on
            Zairian Mbala Mennonite Brethren," (Ph.D. dissertation, Fuller
            Theological Seminary). [abstract: *Direction* 20 (1991): 108–11.]
McCray, Walter A.
    1990   *The Black Presence in the Bible. Discovering The Black and African Identity
            of Biblical Persons and Nations* The Black Presence in the Bible,
            Vol. 1 (Chicago: Black Light Fellowship).
            *The Black Presence in the Bible and the Table of Nations. Genesis 10:1–32 with
            Emphasis on the Hamitic Genealogical Line from A Black Perspective.* The
            Black Presence in the Bible, Vol. 2 (Chicago: Black Light Fellowship).
Meester, Paul de
    1979   "Le Pèlerin d'Ethiopie. Essai d'une Interpretation 'Africaine' des
            Actes 8, 26–40," *Telema* 2: 5–18.
    1981   "'Philippe et l'Eunuque Ethiopien' ou 'Le Bapteme d'un Pelerin
            de Nubie,'" *NRT* 113: 360–74. [abstract: *NTA* 26/1 (1982): #186.]
Morrisey, R.A.
    1925   *Colored People and Bible History* (Hammond, Ind.: W.B. Conkey
            Company).

Mveng, Engelbert
1972 "La Bible et l'Afrique Noire," Mveng & Werblowsky: 23–39. [abstract: Holter: #136.]

Obenga, Theophile
1992 *Ancient Egypt and Black Africa* (London: Karnak House).

Ojeyemi, R.M.
1983 "Paul's Doctrine of Justification by Faith According to the Epistle to the Galatians," (M.A. thesis, University of Ibadan, Ibandan, Nigeria).

Okure, Teresa
1996 "Africans in the Bible: A Study in Hermeneutics," (unpublished paper presented to the Annual Meeting of the Society of Biblical Literature, New Orleans, Louisiana, Nov. 24, 1996).

Palmer, Timothy
1994 "The Sudanese Eunuch. A Study of the 'Aithiops' in Acts 8," *TCNN Research Bulletin* 27: 7–32.

Previn, Dory
1989 "Sheba and Solomon," *Union Seminary Quarterly Review* 43/1–4: 59–66.

Pritchard, James, ed.
1974 *Solomon and Sheba* (London: Phaidon Press).

Rice, G.
1979 "The African Roots of the Prophet Zephaniah," *JORT* 36: 21–31. [abstract: Holton: #192.]

Sanderson, Jerome
1995 "Africa and the Christian Church," *Epiphany Journal* 15/4: 3–20. [abstract: *RTA* 40/2: #2432.]

Snowden, Frank M.
1970 *Blacks in Antiquity: Ethiopians in the Greco-Roman Experience* (Cambridge, Mass.: Harvard University Press).
1983 *Before Colour Prejudice: The Ancient View of Blacks* (Cambridge, MA/London: Harvard University Press). [abstracts: *RSR* 9/4 (1983): 374; *NTA* 36/1 (1992): 143.]

Trent, Earl David
1994 "African Presence in the New Testament and Early Church: Using an Africentric Bible Study to Build Community in a Suburban Context," (D.Min. dissertation, United Theological Seminary, West Chester, PA).

Turkson, P.K.
1994 "De taal van de Bijbel en Afrika," *Wereld en Zending* 23/3: 74–80. [abstract: Holter: #215.]

Ullendorff, Edward
1955 "Candace (Acts 8:27) and the Queen of Sheba," *NTS* 2 (1955): 53–56.
1962–63 "Queen of Sheba," *Bulletin of the John Rylands Library* 45: 486–501.
1974 "The Queen of Sheba in Ethiopian Tradition," *Solomon and Sheba* J. Pritchard, ed. (London: Phaidon Press): 104–14.

Unseth, Peter
 1998 "Semantic Shift on a Geographical Term," *BT* 49/3: 323–31. [On the term "Ethiopia."]
 1999 "Hebrew *Kush*: Sudan, Ethiopia, or Where?" *AJET* 18/2: 143–59.
Waters, John W.
 1991 "Who Was Hagar?" Felder, ed.: 187–205.
Watts, Daud Malik
 1990 *The Black Presence in the Lands of the Bible* (Washington, D.C.: Afro-Vision, Inc.).
Wright, Jeremiah A. Jr. [with Colleen Birchett]
 1995 *Africans Who Shaped Our Faith: A Study of 10 Biblical Personalities* (Chicago: Urban Ministries, Inc.).
Zoungrana, P.
 1978 "The Bible and Africa," *World Catholic Federation for the Biblical Apostolate* 8: 121–23.

4. Exegetical and Thematic Studies

Abdul, Musa
 1974 "The Role of Abraham in the Formation of Islam," *Orita* 8/1: 58–70.
Abe, Gabriel Oyedele
 1981 "The Sacrificial System of the Old Testament," (Master's thesis, University of Ibadan).
 1983 "Covenant in the Old Testament," (Ph.D. dissertation, University of Ibadan, Nigeria). [abstract: *AJBS* 1/2 (1986): 183.]
 1986 "Berith: Its Impact on Israel and Its Relevance to the Nigerian Society," *AJBS* 1/1: 66–73. [abstract: Holter: #001.]
 "Destiny: A Theological Analysis of Predestination," *JARS* 3: 1–11.
 "Religion and National Unity: Guidelines for Nigeria From Judean Exilic and Post-exilic Experience," *Atj* 15: 63–72. [Abstract: Holter: #002.]
 "Sacrificial Rites in Israelite Religion and the Ancient Near East," *Orita* 18/1: 16–27.
 1987 "The Religious Value of the Sinai Covenant," *AJBS* 2/1–2: 97–105.
 1988 "The Community of God and its Mission in the Old Testament," *ATJ* 17/2: 150–61. [abstract: Holter: #003.]
 1989 "The Jewish and Yoruba Social Institution of Marriage: A Comparative Study," *Orita* 21: 3–18. [Abstract: Holter: #004.]
 "The Messianic Theology of Deutero-Isaiah," *ATJ* 18/1: 61–70. [abstract: Holter: #005.]
 1990 "Theological Concepts of Jewish and African Names of God," *Asia Journal of Theology* 4/2: 424–29. [abstract: Holter: #006.]
 1991 "The Old Testament Concept of Leadership Role in Nation Building," *AJBS* 6/1: 27–41.
 "Impact of Ancient Near East Culture on Yahwism Vis-à-vis

African Culture on Christianity," *AJBS* 6/2: 12–20. [abstract: Holter: #007.]

1992   "Ethical and Moral Pronouncements of Yahweh's Spokesmen in Nation Building," *AJBS* 7/2: 30–42.

1994   "Yahwism and Priesthood in the Old Testament," *Asia Journal of Theology* 8: 251–60. [abstract: *OTA* 18/2 (1995): #1046.]

1996   "Redemption, Reconciliation, Propitiation: Salvation Terms in An African Milieu," *JTSA* 95: 3–12. [abstract: *NTA* 42/2 (1998): #1221.]

Abijole, Bayo

1988   "St. Paul's Concept of Principalities and Powers in African Context," *ATJ* 17/2: 118–29. [abstract: *NTA* 33/3 (1989): #1241.]

Abogunrin, Samuel O.

1977   "The Background to St. Paul's Concept of Freedom," *Orita* 11 [?].

1978   "The Theology of the Resurrection of Jesus Christ with Particular Reference to Pauline Kerygma and Soteriology," (doctoral dissertation, University of Ibadan, Nigeria). [abstract: *AJBS* 1/2 (1986): 177.]

1980   "The Modern Search for the Historical Jesus in Relation to Christianity in Africa," *ATJ* 9/3: 18–29. [abstract: *NTA* 25/3 (1981): #814.]

"St. Paul's Idea of the Pre-Gospel Man according to Romans," *Kiabara: Port Harcourt University Journal of Humanities* 31: 5–31.

1981   "The Four Current Endings of St. Mark, A Problem of Authenticity," *Orita* 13: 29–38.

"The Language and Nature of the Resurrection of Jesus Christ in the New Testament," *Journal of the Evangelical Theological Society* 24/1: 55–65. [abstract: *NTA* 26/1 (1982): #68.]

"Paul the Apostle of Liberty on Freedom Through Christ," *Orita* 13/1: 24–26.

1985   "The Three Variant Accounts of Peter's Call: A Critical and Theological Examination of the Texts," *NTS* 31/4: 587–602. [abstract: *NTA* 30/2 (1986): #595.]

1986   "The Community of Goods in the Early Church and the Distribution of National Wealth," *AJBS* 1/2: 74–94. [abstract: *NTA* 33/1 (1989): #216.]

"The Total Adequacy of Christ in the African Context (Col. 1:13–23, 2:8–3:5)," *OJOT* 1: 9–16.

1987   "The Synoptic Gospel Debate: A Re-Examination in the African Context" *AJBS* 2/1–2: 25–51; reprinted as "The Synoptic Gospel Debate. A Re-Examination from an African Point of View," David L. Dungan, ed. *The Interrelations of the Gospels: A Symposium led by M.-E. Boismard – W.R. Farmer – F. Neirynck Jerusalem 1984* (Leuven: Leuven University Press, 1990): 381–407. [abstract: *NTA* 34/2 (1990): #592.]

1988   "The Christian Conception of Reconciliation," *FAT* 3/1: 33–63.

"The Cosmic Significance of Jesus Christ in the African Context (An Exegesis of Philippians 2:5–11)," *Orita* 20/1: 3–14.

The First Letter of Paul to the Corinthians African Bible Commentaries (Nairobi/Kampala: Uzima/Centenary Publishing House). [reviews: Richard Gehman in *EAJET* 8/2 (1989): 37–38; G. LeMarquand *BookNotes* 3 (March 1997): #3.01.]

1991 "Immortality and Resurrection in Early Judaism," *Orita* 23/1–2: 15–34. [abstract: *OTA* 16/2 (1993): #1355.]

1997 "The Lucan View of Jesus as Savoiur of the World from an African Perspective," *Orita* 29/1–2: 15–33.

1998 "Luke," in Farmer, et al., eds: 1368–438.

Abogunrin, S.O., ed.
1986 *Religion and Ethics in Nigeria* Ibadan Religious Studies Series #1 (Ibadan: Daystar Press).

Abotchie, F.F.K.
1978 "Rites of Passage and Socio-cultural Organization in African Culture and Judaism," Hammerstein: 82–89. [abstract: Holter: #011.]

Achilla, Patrick
1996 "Signs and Wonders in Luke-Acts and Church History, with Reference to the Church in Africa" (M.Th. thesis, NEGST).

Adamo, David Tuesday
1989 "The Lord's Supper in 1 Corinthians," *ATJ* 18/1: 36–48. [abstract: *NTA* 34/1 (1990): #282.]

"Sin in John's Gospel," *ERT* 13/3: 216–27. [abstract: *NTA* 34/ (1990): #184.]

"Understanding the Genesis Creation Account in an African Background," *Caribbean Journal of Religious Studies* 10: 17–25. [abstract: Holter: #015.]

1990 "Jesus' Resurrection and His Disciples' Acceptance: (An Exegetical Study of John chapter 20)," *Deltion Biblikon Meleton* 19/2 (1990): 13–21. [abstract: *NTA* 35/3 (1991): #1220.]

1991 "The Concept of Sin in the Gospel of John," *Bible Bhashyam* 17/1: 45–59. [abstract: *NTA* 36/1 (1992): #217.]

1992 "Deuteronomic Conception of God According to Deuteronomy 6:4 and its Importance in African Context," *Bible Bhashyam* 18: 55–65. [abstract: Holter: #019.]

1993 "Distinctive Use of Psalms in Africa," *Melanesian Journal of Theology* 9/2: 94–111.

1997 "Peace in the Old Testament and in the African Heritage," Kinoti & Waliggo: 99–111.

"The Distinctive Use of the Psalms in African Indigenous Churches in Nigeria," *Abstracts: American Academy of Religion/Society of Biblical Literature 1997* (Scholars Press): 43, 173.

Adegbola, E.A. Adeolu
1969 "The Theological Basis of Ethics," Dickson & Ellingworth: 116–36.

Adegbola, E.A. Adeolu, ed.
1983 *Traditional Religion in West Africa* (Ibadan: Daystar).

Adelowo, E. Dada
1982 "A Comparative Study of Angelology in the Bible and the Qur'an

and the Concept of Gods Many and Lords Many in the Religion of the Yoruba," *ATJ* 11/2: 151–67. [abstract: Holter: #022.]

1982   "A Comparative Study of the Phenomenon of Prophecy in the Bible and the Qur'an," *Ife Journal of Religions* 2: 38–55.

1983   "A Comparative Study of Angelology in the Bible, the Qur'an and in the Concept of Ministers of Olodumare," *Orita* 15/2: 115–24. [abstract: Holter: #023.]

1986   "The Bible and the Qur'an as Sources of Theology, Ethics, Politics, History and Culture," *NJOT* 1/2: 18–27.

"A Comparative Study of Creation Stories in Yoruba Religion, Islam and Judeo-Christianity," *ATJ* 15: 29–53. [abstract: Holter: #024.]

"A Repository of Theological and Ethical Values in Yoruba Oral Traditions, the Qur'an the Hadith, and the Bible," *ATJ* 15/2: 127–41. [abstract: Holter: #025.]

1987   "A Comparative Look at Some of the Contents of Yoruba Oral Traditions, the Bible and the Qur'an," *Asia Journal of Theology* 1/2: 334–54. [abstract: Holter: #026.]

"Death and Burial in Yoruba [,] Qur'anic and Biblical Religion," *Orita* 19/2: 104–17. [abstract: Holter: #027.]

Ademiluka, Sola
    1995   "The Use of Therapeutic Psalms in Inculturating Christianity in Africa," *AFER* 37/4: 221–27. [abstract: Holter: #028.]

Aderi, S.
    1978   "Parallels between Jews and African Orthodox Christians," Hammerstein: 29–31. [abstract: Holter: #029.]

Adeso, Patrick
    1993   "Evangelizing in Weakness. An Exegesis of Luke 5,1–11," Adeso, et al., 1993: 112–36.

Adeso, P., D. Atal Sa Angang, P. Buetubela Balembo, L. Nare, Chr. M. Ukachukwu, Sidbe Sempore, Edmond G. Djitangar, Paulin Poucouta, eds [Association Panafricaine des Exégètes Catholiques/Panafrican Association of Catholic Exegetes].
    1993   *Universalisme et Mission dans la Bible/Universalism and Mission in the Bible: Actes du Cinquième Congrès des Biblistes Africains/Proceedings of the Fifth Congress of African Biblical Scholars. Abijan, 16–23 July 1991* (Nairobi: Katholische Jungschar Oesterreichs/Catholic Biblical Centre for Africa and Madagascar (BICAM)).

Adewale, 'Biyi
    n.d.   *the Kingdom Parables: A Critical Analyses* [sic] *of Christ's Parables and Their Contemporary Application* (Ibadan, Nigeria: Baptist Press).

Adeyemi, M.E.
    1991   "A Sociological Approach to the Background of Pauline Epistles," *Deltion Biblikon Meleton* 10/1: 32–42 [abstract: *NTA* 37 (1993): #832.]

Adeyemo, Tokunboh
    1976   "African Traditional Concepts of God in African Traditional Religion" (M.Div. thesis, Talbot Theological Seminary).

Adiele, S.N.
   1991   "Religion and Contemporary Issues: The Church and Burial Ceremony among the Igbo of Nigeria," *AJBS* 6/2: 21–30.
   1992   "The Minorities and Nation Building," *AJBS* 7/2: 115–26.

Adogbo, M.P.
   1994   "A Comparative Analysis of Prophecy in Biblical and African Traditions," *JTSA* 88: 15–20. [abstracts: *RTA* 38/3 (1995): #2849; Holter: #030; *BCT* 3/1 (1996): 24.]

Adom-Oware, Seth
   1991   "'Who Do You Say That I Am?' (Mt. 16:15): A Contemporary African Response," *WAJES* 3: 9–23.

Adundo, B.
   1978   "Symposium on the Bible and Evangelization in Africa—A Personal Account," [held in Limuru, Kenya, Nov. 12–17, 1978, co-sponsored by AACC and UBS.] in A *Monthly Letter about Evangelism* 11–12: 2–6.

Adutwum, Ofosu
   1992   "The Suspected Adultress: Ancient Israelite and Traditional Akan Treatment" *The Expository Times* 104/2: 38–42. [abstract: Holter: #031.]
   1993   "BATACH in the Book of Psalms," *Irish Biblical Studies* 15/1: 28–38. [abstract: *OTA* 16/3 (1993): #1913; *RTA* 37/4 (1994): #4418.]
   1994   "The Old Testament and Nation Building," *TJCT* 4/1: 1–9.
   1998   "Ruth," in Farmer, et al., eds: 566–71.

Agogo, Chr. Dieterle-Bauberot
   1967   "The Healing Miracles in the New Testament," *GBT* 3/2: 27–33.

Ahirika, E.A.
   1990   "The Theology of Matthew in the Light of the Nativity Story," *Bible Bhashyam* 16/1: 5–19.
   1991   "Acculturation of Christianity: A Case Study of Igbo Culture," *AJBS* 6/2: 106–12.
   1992   "The Theology of the Matthean Baptism Narrative," *Bible Bhashyam* 18/3: 131–39.

Aicher, Anna
   1961   "1 Corinthians 15," *Ministry* 1/4: 14–19.
          "1 Corinthians 15:19–28," *Ministry* 2/1: 13–16.
   1962   "1 Corinthians 15:29–41," *Ministry* 2/2: 12–16.

Aina, Gabriel Ibukun
   1974   "The Problem of a Single Theology of History, Deuteronomy-Kings," (Master's thesis, University of Ibadan).

Ajibola, J.A.
   1972   *The Secret School of Jesus* (Ibadan: Daystar).

Aka-Abiam, T.H.
   1989   "Jesus' Prophetic Mission in Luke 4:16–30 and Its Implications for the Nigerian Catholic Church," (M.Th. thesis, CIWA/University of Calabar, Calabar, Nigeria).
   1991   "The Role of Prophecy in Nation Building," *AJBS* 6/1: 42–56.

1992   "Pauline Concept of Freedom and its Implications for Nation Building—A Commentary on Galatians 2:11–14 and 1 Corinthians 9:19–23," *AJBS* 7/2: 127–38.

"Pauline Practice of Inculturation in His Mission and Gospel," in Brookman-Amissah, et al.: 148–57.

Akaenyi, Chudi P.

1992   "Biblical Foundations for Contemporary Ecumenical Initiatives," in Ukpong & Okure, et al.: 156–62.

Akande, S.T.O.

1978   *The Epistle to the Ephesians* (Ibadan: Daystar).

Akangbe, Michael Fehintola

1981   "Master-Slave Relations and Christian Brotherhood: A Pauline Study with Special Reference to the Epistle of Philemon," (M.A. thesis, Trinity Evangelical Divinity School, Deerfield, Illinois, USA).

1988   "St. Paul's Conceptions of Eschatology with Particular Reference to the Issue of Development," (Doctoral dissertation; University of Ibadan, Nigeria).

1993   "Religious Crises in the Early Church," (lecture delivered to the Association of All Christian Theological students, Nigeria (ACTSN), United Missionary Theological College, Ilorin, Nigeria, 7pp.).

1995   "Salvation of Soul and Body for Onesimus in Philemon," *UMTC—JTS* 1: 1–15.

1997   "Mark 16:17–18 and the Neo-Pentecostal Movements," *UMTC—JTS* 2:1–19.

Akao, J.O.

1987   "The Aniconic Cult of Yahweh and the Imageless Supreme Being in African Traditional Religion," *Orita* 19/2: 90–103. [abstract: Holter: #032.]

1990   "The Letter of Aristeas and its Worth in Biblical Studies," *Orita* 22/1: 52–63.

"Yahwism and *Mal'ak* in the Early Traditions of Israel: A Study of the Underlying Traditions of Yahweh/Angel Theophany in Exodus 3," *Irish Biblical Studies* 12: 72–85. [abstracts: *OTA* 15/1 (1992): #213.]

1993   "Word—A Potent Extension of Personality in the Old Testament and African Belief System," *Bangalore Theological Forum* 25: 49–63. [abstract: Holter: #033.]

1994   "In Search of the Origin of the Deuteronomic Movement," *Irish Biblical Studies* 16: 174–89. [abstract: *OTA* 18/2 (1995): 838.]

1995   "Cultic Influence on the Composition of the Theophany in Exodus 3 & 4," *UMTC—JTS* 1:31–40.

Ake, Joseph

1994   "Cherchez d'abord le Royaume de Dieu et sa Justice (Mt 6,33)," *RICAO* 8: 29–45.

Akinyode, E.T.

1991   "The Nigerian Christian in Nation Building," *AJBS* 6/1: 83–93.

Akpunonu, Peter Diaman
1971   "Salvation in Deutero-Isaiah," (Doctoral dissertation, Pontifical Arban University, Rome).
1980   "Christianity is a Historical Religion," Atal sa Angang, et al.: 121–32.
1988   "Religion and Politics in Old Testament and in the Intertestamentary Era," *NJOT* 1/4: 78–90.
1989   "The Church and the Churches in the Acts of the Apostles," *RAT* 13/25 (1989): 17–30; also published in Amewowo, et al., 1990: 52–72.
1991   "The Celebration of Feasts [in John's Gospel]," Amewowo, et al., 1991: 156–80.
        "Die Africanische Synode und die Universale Kirche," L. Bertsch, ed. *Theologie der Dritten Welt* 15. (Freiburg/Basel/Wien: Missionswissenschaftische Institute): 137–47.
1992   "The Universal Church and the Local Churches in Africa," Ukpong & Okure, et al., eds: 27–36.
        "Neo-Colonialism and the Mission of the Church in Nigeria," Brookman-Amissah, et al., eds: 39–50.
1995   "Healing in the Bible and in the Church: The Nigerian Situation," *BTS* 15/2: 5–17.

Alana, Emmanuel Olu
1990   "Reconsidering the Poor by Gospel Norms," *AFER* 32/4: 193–200. [abstract: *NTA* 35/1 (1991): #115.]
        "The Theology of Newness in Jesus' Birth and Burial Narratives," *Caribbean Journal of Religious Studies* 11/1: 54–62.
1992   "The Impact of the Healing Miracles of Jesus on the Healing Methods of Aladura Churches in Yorubaland," (Doctoral dissertation, University of Ilorin, Nigeria).
        "Liberation of Womenhood—Fetters of Conservatism with Particular Reference to Women Leadership in the Cherubim and Seraphim Church," *AJBS* 7/1: 89–97.
1993   "A Critical Examination of the Historicity of Biblical Miracles," *AJBS* 8/1: 47–54.
        "The Secret Disciples of Jesus," *Deltion Biblikon Meleton* 22/1 (1993): 43–48. [abstract: *NTA* 39/2 (1995): # 727.]

Alao, David
1984   "The Relevance of the Amarna Letters to Hebrew Origins," *Orita* 16/2: 87–97.

Aluko, Taiye
1993   "Women in Evangelistic Mission," *AJBS* 8/1: 88–95. [especially John 4.]

Amadi-Azuogo, Chinedu Adolphus
1996   "The Place of Women in the New Testament House Codes. An Exegetical Analysis of 1 Tim 3:11–15 and 1 Cor 14: 33b–35," *BET* 8/1: 35–59.

Amewowo, Wynnand
  1979   "The Child and the Bible," *B-PB* 1: 18–19.
          "Theology of Liberation: Biblical Foundations," *B-PB* 2 (1979): 7–12.
  1979   "The Responsibility of Children Towards their Parents," *B-PB* 2: 23–29.
  1987   "The Christian Community and Acts of the Apostles," *B-PB* 6: 31–38.
          "The Poor of Jahweh, The Poor of the Messiah," Shorter & Waliggo: 58–61.
  1989   "The Christian Community in Acts of the Apostles: Model for our Days," *RAT* 13/25: 59–66; reprinted in Amewowo, et al., 1990: 105–16.
  1993   "Ecclesiology in Africa. A Search for Biblical Ecclesiological Model(s) for Tanzania Today," *ACS* 9/3: 8–63.
Amewowo, Wynnand, P.J. Arowele, Buetubela Balembo, eds
  1990   *Les Acts des Apôtres et les jeunes Eglises: Actes du Deuxième Congrès des Biblistes Africains. Ibadan 31 juillet–3 aout 1984* (Kinshasa, Zaire: Facultés Catholiques de Kinshasa).
  1991   *Communautés Johanniques/Johannine Communities: Actes du Quatrième Congrès des Biblistes Africains Nairobi/Karen, 24–29 juillet 1989* (Kinshasa, Zaire: Facultés Catholiques de Kinshasa).
Amoah, Elizabeth
  1986   "The Woman Who Decided to Break the Rules," in Pobee & Wartenberg-Potter: 3–4.
          An Interdisciplinary Workshop in Research on Religion in Africa
  n.d.   *Theory and Practice in Church Life and Growth: Studies in East and Central Africa over the last hundred years* (Nairobi, Kenya, June 1966–June 1968; unpublished papers on file in the library of St. Paul's United Theological College, Limuru, Kenya).
Anon.
  1982[?] *Parole de Dieu et langages des hommes/Word of God—human languages. La rencontre de Yáounde/Reports of the Yaounde meeting (24–28 septembre 1980)* Collection de Théologie Africaine/Collection: African Theology, 1; A. Ngindu Mushete, Director (Association Oecumenique des Theologiens Africains/Ecumenical Association of African Theologians).
  1989   *Lutheran Theologians Face Old Traditions and New Challenges: A Joint Study Seminar for Pastors from Lutheran Churches of Brazil, Tanzania, Kenya, Papua New Guinea and Bavaria* (Institute for Studies of World Mission; Nueendettelau: Department of World Mission of the Evangelical Lutheran Church in Bavaria).
Anyaeche, Jude O.
  1995   "The Canonical Implications of Matthew 19:6 for Christian Marriage in Nigeria," Obinwa and Obilor, eds, 123–33.
Anyanwu, H.O.
  1991   "Salvation in African Tradition in Biblical Concept: The Igbo Perspective" *AJBS* 6/2: 123–29.

Anyimadu-Wireko, Jospeh
1991 "Discipleship in Mark 10:35–45: Implications for Akan Christians of Ghana Today," (M.Th. thesis, CIWA/University of Calabar, Calabar, Nigeria).

Apochi, Michael
1995 "In Search of Effective Evangelization Methodology: Lessons from Acts 13:16–41; 14:15–18; 17:22–31," *Jos Studies* 5/1: 28–41.

Ariri-Chidomere, A.C.
1988 "A Biblical Answer to a National Problem. A Proposition for a True Solution to Nigeria's 'Economic Problem,'" in S.A. Adewale, ed. *Christianity and Development in Nigeria* (Ibandan): 188–220.

1992 "King Solomon, A Prophet's Mistake," *AJBS* 7/2: 69–82.

Arowele, P.J.
1981 "This Generation Seeks Signs: An Exposition of the Miracles of Jesus with a Reference to the African Christian Situation," *BTA* 3/6 (1981): 247–255; also published as "This generation Seeks Signs: The Miracles of Jesus with Reference to the African Situation," *ATJ* 10/3: 17–28.

1989 "Mission and Evangelisation in Acts and the African Experience," *RAT* 13/26: 193–207; reprinted in Amewowo, et al., 1990: 219–40.

1990 "The Pilgrim People of God (An African's Reflections on the Motif of Sojourn in the Epistle to the Hebrews)," *Asia Journal of Theology* 4/2: 438–55. [abstract: *NTA* 35/1 (1991): #282.]

1991 "'The Scattered Children of God' (John 11:52): A Johannine Ecclesial Cliché," Amewowo, et al., 1991: 181–201.

Arulefela, Joseph Oluwafemi
1972 "The Biblical Doctrine of Baptism," (Master's thesis, University of Ibadan).

1980 "An Analysis of the Biblical and Yoruba Concepts of Covenant with Implications for Christian Education of Yoruba Christians" (Ph.D. dissertation, New York University).

1988 *The Covenant in the Old Testament and Yoruba Culture* (Ibadan: Daystar Press). [originally Th.M thesis, Fuller Theological Seminary, 1978.]

1990 *Baptism (A Biblical Interpretation)* Ibadan: Impact Publishers Nigeria Limited).

Asante, E.
1986 "The Theological Jerusalem of Luke-Acts," *ATJ* 15/3: 172–82. [abstract: *NTA* 31/3 (1987): #1105.]

Assaad, Marie
1986 "Reversing the Natural Order," Pobee & Wartenberg-Potter: 25–27.

Atal Sa Angang, Dosithee
1978 "Le Problème de la Foi et de la Langue Chrétiens Hellénistes et Hébreux dans l'Eglise Naissante," Facultés Catholique de Kinshasa: 6–30.

1980 "Christ, Unique Sauveur et Médiateur: Une lecture de Jn 14,6," Atal sa Angang, et al.: 189–203.

"La Liberté-Liberation des Hommes en Jésus-Christ dans le Nouveau Testament," Facultes Catholique de Kinshasa, 1980(b): 49–75.

"Théologie de la Vocation: Approche biblique," Facultés Catholique de Kinshasa, 1980(a): 13–32.

1987   "Le Troisième Congrès des Biblistes Catholiques Africains," *RAT* 11/22: 251–53.

1988   "Foi et Conversion dans la Guérison de l'aveugle-né de Siloé (Jn 9,1–4). Les Instances Africaines d'une Lecture du Texte," *RAT* 12/23–24: 31–65. [abstract: *NTA* 33/3 (1989): #1226.]

1992   "Universalisme et Mission dans la Bible: Le cinquième Congrès des Exégètes Catholiques Africains," *RAT* 16/31: 105–107.

Atal sa Agang, D., P. Buetubela Balembo, L. Monsengwo Pasinya, J. Nyeme Tese, eds

1980   *Christianisme et Identité Africaine: Point de vue Exégétique. Actes du 1er Congrès des Biblistes Africains Kinshasa, 26–30 Décembre 1978* (Kinshasa). [abstract: Holter: #036.]

Atallah, Ramez

1974   "The Objective Witness to Conscience: An Egyptian Parallel to Romans 2:15," *ERT* 18/3 (1994): 204–13.

Avorti, Solomon K.

1997   "Sickness, Healing, and the World-in-Between: Reading Mark 5:1–20 in an African Context," *Abstracts: American Academy of Religion/ Society of Biblical Literature 1997* (Scholars Press): 44.

Awoniyi, J.

1991   "Predestination," *AJBS* 6/2 (1991): 31–35.

Awoniyi, Valentine

1985   "Pauline and Yoruba Concepts of Reconciliation," (S.T.L. thesis, CIWA/Pontifical Urban University, Rome).

Aworinde, John Ademola

1981   "A Comparative Analysis of Destiny in the Old Testament and in Yoruba Philosophy of Life," (Ph.D. dissertation, University of Jos, Nigeria).

Babalola, E.O.

1992   "Women in Aladura Churches: A Biblio-Theological Study of Women in Aladura Pastoral Ministry in Yoruba Community," *AJBS* 7/1: 40–47.

1994   "Death and Burial Rites Among the Yoruba Traditional Society.— A Biblico-Missiological Appraisal," *Bible Bhashyam* 20/1: 42–59.

1995   "Cosmogonic Stories in Indigenous Religion of the Yoruba and the Bible: A Comparative Investigation," *Bible Bhashyam* 21/3: 204–14.

1997   "The Contextualization of the Biblical Concept of Angels in the Yoruba Traditional Community," *Njot* 11/1: 49–59.

Baccuet, E.

1961   "The Light of the World," *Ministry* 1/4: 21–23.

Bacinoni, Venant

1980   "Révélation-Dans-l'Histoire," Atal sa Angang, et al., eds: 133–48. "Continuité et discontinuité entre le N.T. et les Religions africaines: Rapport de carrefour," Atal sa Angang, et al., eds: 243–44.

"Révélation-dans-l'Histoire: Rapport de Carrefour," Atal sa Angang, et al., eds: 247–48.
1989 "Bible et Identité Africaine," Facultes Catholiques de Kinshasa: 241–55. [abstract: Holter: #037.]
Bajeux, J.-C.
1956 "Mentalité Noire et Mentalité Biblique," A. Abble, et al., eds *Des Prêtres Noirs s'interrogent* (Paris): 57–82. [abstract: Holter: #039.]
Bakare, Sebastian
1993 *My Right to Land in the Bible and in Zimbabwe: A Theology of Land for Zimbabwe* (Harare, Zimbabwe: Zimbabwe Council of Churches); especially chapter 1: "The Eighth-Century Prophets (Amos, Hosea, Isaiah and Micah)," chapter 2: "Land Tenure in the Reigns of Pompey and the Herodians," chapter 3: "The Teaching of Jesus on the Eschatological Reality of God's Rule."
Banana, Canaan
1979 "The Biblical Basis for Liberation Struggles," *IRM* 68/272 (1979): 417–23. [reprinted in idem, 1990.]
1987 "The Continuing Liberation Struggle in the New Testament," *Voices* 10/2: 86–89.
1990 *The Gospel according to the Ghetto* (edited [3rd] edition; Gwero, Zimbabwe: Mambo Press, 1990 [1980]); section 1 previously published by Wesley Theological Seminary in Washington, D.C. in 1974 also under the title: "The Gospel according to the Ghetto."
Banzikiza, Constance R.
1995 *The Pastoral Approach To African Traditional Values of Fecundity and Marriage* Spearhead nos 135–137 (Eldoret, Kenya: AMECEA Gaba Publications); especially chapter four, "Looking at Fecundity and Population Control in the Light of Scripture": 59–80.
Barker, P.
1968 "Paul's Relationship with the Churches: A Pattern for the Present-day Pastor," *Ministry* 8/2: 68–73.
Barraclough, Gerald
1967 "The Significance and Implications of the Term 'Good Shepherd,'" *Ministry* 7/2: 78–81.
Bassey, Michael E.
1986 "Signs and Wonders in the Acts of the Apostles," (Masters thesis, Rome).
1988 "Witnessing in the Acts of the Apostles," (Doctoral dissertation, Rome).
Bayinsana (Bayaingana?), Ng. Eugene
1996 "Christ as Reconciler in Pauline Theology and in Contemporary Rwanda," *AJET* 15/1: 19–28. [abstract: *NTA* 43/2 (1999): #1084.]
Bediako, Kwame
1983 "Biblical Christologies in the Context of African Traditional Religions," Vinay Samuel & Chris Sugden, eds *Sharing Jesus in the*

Two Thirds World: Evangelical Christologies from the contexts of poverty, powerlessness and religious pluralism: the papers of the First Conference of Evangelical Mission Theologians from the Two Thirds World, Bankok, Thailand, March 22–25, 1982 (Bangalore: Partnership in Mission-Asia; Grand Rapids: Eerdmans, 1984): 115–75.

1988   "The Ultimate Vision: New Heaven and New Earth. Bible Study on Revelation 21: 1–4," *Mission Studies* 10, 5/2: 32–38.

1990   *Jesus in African Culture (A Ghanaian Perspective)* (Accra, Ghana: Asempa Publishers, 1990); a portion is reprinted as "Jesus in African Culture" *ERT* 17/1 (1993): 54–64. [reviews: E. Wendland *AJET* 14/2 (1995): 113–23; *BookNotes* 2 (October 1996): #2.04.]

1994   "Epilogue," in Schaaf: 241–54.

1999   "Mission and Spirituality: Lessons from the Life of Abraham," *A-CCN* 24: 8–11.

Bediaku, Buame J. Baptiste

1978   "Etude Comparée de la Célébration Penitentielle dans l'Ancient Testament et chez le Peuple Ewe du Togo. Pour une Catéchèse de la Célébration Penitentielle en Afrique Noire," (Doctoral dissertation, Academia Alfonsiana, Rome).

Bemile, Paul

1990   "Critical Appreciation," [response to J.M. Waliggo "Acts of the Apostles and a Hundred Years of Evangelization in Africa,"] Amewowo, et al., 1990: 46–51.

Bengie-A'Kiara, Mborandaa

1988   "Dimensions Théologiques de la Médecine du Peuple d'Israel dans l'Ancien Testament," *RZTP* 2: 19–32.

1992   "Notion et Richesses Théologiques de la Consecration d'Aron et de ses Fils en Exode 28, 41," *RZTP* 6: 7–17.

1993   "La Conception du Temps chez les Hébreux et ses Incidences Liturgiques," *RAT* 17/34: 149–62.

Béré, Paul

1997   "Pourqoi Pierre est-il Peine?" *Hekima Review* 18: 66–80. [abstract: *NTA* 42/1 (1998): #316.

"Rom. 12,2–3: Exhortation au Renouvellement Interieur (Essai d'exégèse)," *Hekima Review* 18: 82–96.

Beresford, R.S.

1963   "Authority and Inspiration of the Bible," *GBT* 2/4: 30–34.

Berhe, Assayehgn

1995   "Biblical Leadership with Special Interest in the New Testament and Application to the Ethiopian Evangelical Church" (M.Th. thesis, NEGST).

Bernard, Michel

1965   "Amos 1:1–15," *Ministry* 5/2 (1965): 66–69.

"Amos 2:1–16," *Ministry* 5/3 (1965): 118–20.

"Amos 3:1–15," *Ministry* 6/1 (1965): 21–23.

1966   "Amos 4:1–5:17," *Ministry* 6/2–3 (1966): 98–99.

"Amos 5:18–27," *Ministry* 6/4 (1966): 158–62.

1967   "Amos 6:1–14," *Ministry* 7/4 (1967): 178–83.
1968   "Amos 7:1–8:3," *Ministry* 8/2 (1968): 77–82.

Beutler, Johannes
  1990   "Critical Appreciation," [response to Peter D. Akpunonu "The Church and the Churches in the Acts of the Apostles"] in Amewowo, et al., 1990: 73–76.

Birkell, Fridtjov, ed.
  1956   *Marangu: A Record of the All Africa Lutheran Conference Marangu, Tanganyika, East Africa November 12–22 1955* (Geneva, Switzerland: The Lutheran World Federation Department of World Mission, 1956).

Birri, Debela
  n.d.   "Exodus 5–14," Lutheran World Federation [Yaounde]: 31–38.

Bitjick Likeng, P.
  1980   "La Paternité d'Abraham selon Rom. 4,1–25," *RAT* 4/8: 153–86.

Blum, William G.
  1989   *Forms of Marriage: Monogamy Reconsidered* Spearhead #105–107 (Eldoret, Kenya: AMECEA Gaba Publications,); especially chapters 4 and 5 on the Old Testament and the New Testament respectively.

Boer, Harry R.
  1973   *The Minor Prophets* 2nd edition (Ibadan, Nigeria: Daystar,).
  1976   *A Short History of the Early Church* (Ibadan, Nigeria: Daystar).
  1981   *The Bible and Higher Criticism* (Grand Rapids: Eerdmans, 1981).

Bokundoa—bo—Likabe
  1992   "Le Cycle de Baal dans Osée 2, 4–25" *RZTP* 6: 19–26.

Bolomba Wa Ngboka
  1993   "'Le Fils de Dieu est Venu . . . pour Servir.' A Travers les Épitres Pastorales de S. Paul," *Telema* 19/74: 49–59.

Booth, Newell S. Jr.
  1993   "Time and African Beliefs Revisited," Olupona & Nyang: 83–94.

Bosch, David J.
  1973   "God in Africa: Implications for the Kerygma," *Missionalia* 1: 3–21. [abstract: Holter: #042.]
         "God Through African Eyes," Becken, 1973: 68–78; reprinted in *Theologia Evangelica* 6 (1973): 11–22. [abstract: Holter: #043.]

Bowers, Paul
  1990   "Acquainted with Grief: The Special Contribution of the Book of Lamentations," *AJET* 9/2: 33–39.

Boyo, Bernard
  1996   "An Exegetical Study of John 8:12 With Special Attention Given to the Imagery of Light in the Old Testament as its Background" (M.Th. thesis, NEGST).

Brookman-Amissah, J. John E. Anyanwu, Kris J. Owan, Joseph Ogundiyilemi, Patrick C. Chibuko & Gerald M. Nwagwu, eds
  1992   *Inculturation and the Mission of the Church in Nigeria: Proceedings of the Third Theology Week of the Catholic Institute of West Africa, Port Harcourt, Nigeria, May 4–8, 1992* (Port Harcourt: CIWA Press).

Buetubela Balembo, Paul

1978 "La Syrophenicienne: Mc 7, 24–30. Etude litteraire et exégètique," *RAT* 2/4: 245–56. [abstract: *NTA* 26/1 (1982): #114.]

1979 "La Vocation de Levi et la Repas avec les Pecheurs (Mc 2, 13–17)," *RAT* 3/5: 47–60. [abstract: *NTA* 26/1 (1982): #108.]

1980 "Continuité et Discontinuité entre l'Ancien et le Nouveau Testament," Atal sa Angang, et al.: 65–81.

"Continuité et Discontinuité entre l'A.T. et le N.T.: Rapport de Carrefour," Atal sa Angang, et al.: 237–38.

"Jn 3,8: l'Esprit-Saint ou le Vent Naturel?" *RAT* 4/7: 55–64. [abstract: *NTA* 25/3 (1981): #924.]

"Les 'Anges' B la Lumieres des Evangiles Synoptiques," *Telema* 6/24: 49–55. [abstract: *NTA* 25/3 (1981): #839.]

1981 "Actualité du Prophetism Biblique," *Telema* 7/25: 7–18.

1983 "Les sens du Témoinnage d'apres les Synoptiques et les Actes," *RAT* 7/13: 5–17. [abstract: *NTA* 30/1 (1986): #96.]

1984 "Le Produit de la Vigne et le Vin Nouveau. Analyse exégètique de Mc 14, 25," *RAT* 8/15: 5–16. [abstract: *NTA* 30/1 (1986): #143.]

1985 "Le Message de Jean Baptiste en Mc 1,7–8," *RAT* 9/18: 165–73. [abstract: *NTA* 31/3 (1987): #1092.]

1986 "Et ne Nous Soumets pas a la Tentation . . . la Difficile Actualisation de Mt 6,13," *RAT* 10/19: 5–13. [abstract: *NTA* 32/1 (1988): 121.]

1987 "Le Contenue de la Bible," *Cahiers Bibliques Africains* 2: 27–31.

"Le Dieu de Jésus-Christ en qui nous Croyons," *Cahiers Bibliques Africains* 2/Sept (1987): 32–35.

"L'Autonomie des Jeunes Églises et les Actes," *RAT* 11/21: 5–22; also published in Amewowo, et al., 1990: 77–104. [abstract: *NTA* 32/3 (1988): 1190.]

1988 "A le Découverte du Père de Jésus Christ," *Cahiers Bibliques Africains* 3: 18–26. [reprinted in English as "The Father of Jesus Christ," *B-PB* 1 [sic] (1988): 16–24.]

"La Mission selon les Synoptiques et Paul," *Spiritus* 29/113: 353–58. [abstract: *NTA* 33/3 (1989): #836.]

"Le Péché dans l'Évangile de Marc," *RAT* 12/23–24 (1988): 23–29. [abstract: *NTA* 33/3 (1989): #1138.]

1989 "Lecture Africaine de la Bible. Essai sur l'exégèse Symbolique de Lc 15, 1–32," Facultes Catholiques de Kinshasa: 231–39.

"IVe Congres de l'Association Panafricaine des Exegetes Catholiques," *RAT* 13/26: 227–229.

1990 "Le Vêtement de Noce: exégèse symbolique de Mt 22,11–14," *RAT* 14/27–28: 33–45.

1991 *L'Identite de Jesus et Jean-Baptiste en Mc 6,14–29* Recherches Africaines de Theologie, #12 (Kinshasa: Facultes Catholiques de Kinshasa, 1991).

"Le Symbolisme et la Pédagogie du Signe dans le Quatrieme Evangile," Amewowo, et al., 1991: 57–70.

1993 "Le Bonheur des Simples: Exégèse de MT 11, 25–27," Adeso, et al., 1993: 68–85.
1994 "L'Universalisme du Salut par Jésus-Christ dans l'Evangile de Marc," *RAT* 18/35: 7–20.
1995 "La Notion d'Potre selon Saint Paul," *RAT* 19/37: 5–19.

Bujo, Benezet
1980 *Les Dix Commandments, pour quoi faire?* (Zaire: Editions Saint Paul-Afrique); E.T.: *Do We Still Need the Ten Commandments? A fundamental Question in Today's African World*, Alphons Vanden Boer, trans. (Nairobi: St. Paul Publications Africa, n.d.).
1995 *Christmas: God Becomes Man in Black Africa* (Nairobi, Kenya: St. Paul Publications Africa).

Bulkeley, Tim
1986 "Une Lecture Feministe, l'Analyse Structurelle et Apercu d'une Scribe Juif," *RZTP* 1: 173–81. [A study of Phyllis Trible's interpretation of Jer 3:15–22.]

Bulley, C.J.
1980 "Extension of the Person: A Biblical Concept Shared with the African Traditional Thought-World," *TCNN Research Bulletin* 6: 20–34.

Burden, J.J.
1973 "Magic and Divination in the Old Testament and Their Relevance for the Church in Africa," *Missionalia* 1:103–12. [abstract: Holter: #045.]
1986 "World-view in Interpreting the Old Testament in Africa," *OTEssays* 4: 95–110. [abstract: Holter: #048.]

Burleson, Blake W.
1987 "John Mbiti as Anti-Historian of Theology," *ATJ* 16/2: 104–21.

Burney, Robert S.
1986 "The Purpose of Romans and the Central Theme of the Preaching of Paul," *AJBS* 1/2: 136–47. [abstract: *NTA* 33/1 (1989): #251.]
1988 *The Book of Revelation* African Bible Commentaries (Nairobi/Kampala: Uzima/Centenary Publishing House).
1990 "The Kingdom of God and the Mission of the Church," *OJOT* 5: 37–44.
New Testament Introduction. Volume 1: The Four Gospels (Ibadan: Bezekos Printing Press).

Butelezi, P.
1968 "The Ministry in the Bible," *Ministry* 8/2: 60–66.

Bwanali, Peter N.
1997 "We Believe that Jesus Died and Rose Again: A Reply to Paul," *Hekima Review* 18: 97–104. [abstract: *NTA* 42/3 (1998): #1841.]

Byll Cataria, J.-B.
1981 *Contribution à l'Unité Réligieuse et Politique de l'Afrique* (Paris: La Pensee Universelle).

Callaway, P.R.
1984 "Deut 21:18–21: Proverbial Wisdom and Law," *JBL* 103/3: 341–52. [abstract: Holter: #050.]

Camp, C.V.
  1988 "Wise and Strange: An Interpretation of the Female Imagery in Proverbs in Light of Trickster Mythology," *Semeia* 42: 14–36. [abstract: Holter: #051.]
Caron, Gerard
  1982 "Did Jesus Allow Divorce (Mt. 5:31–32)?" *AFER* 24/5: 309–16.
Carpenter, John B.
  1996 "Toward a Biblical Political Science. American and Asian Lessons for Africa," *AJET* 15/1: 29–39. [abstract: *NTA* 43/2 (1999): #1236.]
Cartledge, Mark J.
  1993 "A Model of Hermeneutical Method—An Exegetical Missiological Reflection upon Suffering in 2 Corinthians 4:7–15," *ERT* 17/4: 472–83.
Caspar, Robert and a group of Christians living in Tunisia
  1989 *Trying to Answer Questions* Series "Studi arabo-islamici del PISAI," no. 3 (Rome: Pontificio Istituto di Studi Arabi e d'Islamistica).
CATHAN
  1993 *Authority and Charism in the Nigerian Church: Proceedings of the 8th National Theological Conference held at the National Missionary Seminary of St. Paul, Gwagwalada—Abuja April 13–16, 1993* (typescript, 148pp.).
Chenyange, Cesaire
  1964 "Le Christ et la Monde des Esprits. Esquisse de Théologie Paulinienne," (Doctoral dissertation, Pontifical Urban University, Rome).
Chibuko, P.C.
  1992 "Liturgical Inculturation in the Early Church, 1st–4th Centuries," in Brookman-Amissah, et al.: 159–74.
Chikafu, P.
  1993 "The Audience Presupposed in the Conquest, Infiltration and Revolt Models: A Sociological Analysis," *JTSA* 84: 11–24. [abstract: *BCT* 3/1 (1996): 25.]
Chittleborough, Gordon
  1990 *Mwongozo wa Ijili ya Yohana* (Dodoma, Tanzania: Central Tanganyika Press).
Choge, Emily J.
  1996 "'I Was A Stranger and You Welcomed Me . . .': Jesus' Teaching on Hospitality with Special Reference to Matthew 25:31–46," (M.A. in Christian Education thesis, NEGST).
Ciervide, Joaquin
  1992 "Le Peuple de Dieu comme Temple (2 Cor 6,16)," *Telema* 18/70: 8–17.
Ciswaka Cibwabwa
  1996 "Le 'Ut unum sint' de Jesus-Christ (Jn 17,21) dans la Chretienté Africaine Aujourd'hui. Apport de Saint Irenee de Lyons," *RAT* 20/40: 201–209.
Clerici, Luigi
  1995 "The Church as Family: African Church Communities as Families of Jesus and of God: A Biblical and Theological Reflection," *ACS* 11/2: 27–45.

Clobus, Rob
  1992 *Environmental Care: A Possible Way to Restore God's Image to the Earth*
        (Spearhead #122; Eldoret, Kenya: AMECEA Gaba Publications).
        [chapter 3: "Understanding the environment through scripture."]

Combrink, H.J.B.
  1996 "The Reception of Matthew in Africa," *Scriptura* 58: 285–303.
        [abstract: *NTA* 41/1 (1997): #186.]

Connolly, Dermot
  1988 "The Parable of the Sower, Mark 4:1–9, 14–20," Ukpong: 13–17.

Couprie, P.
  1962 "Noah—Hebrews 11:7a," *Ministry* 2/2: 16–18.
  1964 "Psalm 2: God's laughter," *Ministry* 4/2: 66–67.
  1966 "James 3:13–18," *Ministry* 6/2–3: 106–107.

Craig, R.
  1966 "The Christian's Concern in Politics," *Ministry* 6/2–3: 91–92.
        "The Christian's Concern in Race Relations," *Ministry* 6/2–3: 92–97.

CUEA, Biblical Theology Department
  1994 "New Testament Perspectives on Evangelization as Dialogue," *ACS*
        10/1: 57–68.

Cuenod, R.
  1961 "Matthew 7:24–27," *Ministry* 2/1: 17.

Cunningham, S.
  1986 "The Synoptic Problem: A Summary of the Leading Theories,"
        AJBS 1/1: 48–58. [abstract: *NTA* 33/1 (1989): #102.]
  1990 "The Healing of the Deaf and Dumb Man (Mark 7:31–37), with
        Application to the African Context," *AJET* 9/2: 13–26. [abstract:
        NTA 36/1 (1992): #182.]
  1994 "'Through Many Tribulations': The Theology of Persecution in
        Luke-Acts," (Ph.D. Dissertation, Dallas Theological Seminary).
  1995 "The Theology of Persecution in Luke-Acts," *ETSI* 1/1: 16–34.

Dagbovou, Emmanuel
  1995 "De la Mort selon la Vie Religieuse Vodun a la Mort-Resurrection
        dans le Christ en référence a Mc. 15,39," *RICAO* 12: 65–80.

Dain, F.R.
  1986 *Hebrews for Today* (Nairobi: Uzima).

Dairo, A.O.
  1991 "The Religiosity of the Pharisees: Lessons for African Christianity,"
        AJBS 6/2 (1991): 79–89.

Dayok, D. Nshak Denis
  1985 "Sickness, Prayer and Healing in James 5 13–15: Implications for
        the Mupun Christians of Nigeria," (S.T.L. thesis, CIWA/Pontifical
        Urban University, Rome).

de la Potterie, I.
  1980 "Le Christ Sommet de la Révélation," Atal sa Angang, et al.,
        eds: 169–86.

de Vries, Lukas
  1977 "Psalm 56:4" in Lutheran World Federation [Gaborone, 1977]:
        1–4.

Dickson, Kwesi
  1964 "A Note on the Laying on of Hands As a Sacrificial Rite," *GBT* 2/7: 26–28.
  1978 "The Story of the Early Church As Found in the Acts of the Apostles," *WAR* 17/1: 64–66.
  1988 "He is God Because He Cares: Isaiah 58: 1–12," *IRM* 77: 229–37.
Diggs, Ronald
  1978 "Isaiah 61: The Spirit of the Lord," in Lutheran World Federation [Gaborone, 1978]: 186–90.
  n.d. "Exodus 1–4," Lutheran World Federation [Yaounde]: 27–30.
Djitangar, Edmond Guetime
  1991 "Jesus et les Authorites Juives dans l'Evangile de Jean," Amewowo, et al., 1991: 118–34.
  1993 "Etude de Is 42,1–9: La Mission du Serviteur de Yahweh," Adeso, et al., 1993: 30–39.
Dodman, Norman
  1988 *Behind the Scenes: A Commentary on the Book of Revelation* (Nairobi, Kenya: Nairobi Bible Training Institute).
Doke, C.M.
  1957 "L'étude de la Personne du Christ dans les Évangiles Encouragée aux Cours de Cathechisme," *RCA* 12: 92.
Douglas, Mary
  1988 "The Problem of Evil Among the Lele: Sorcery, Witch-hunt and Christian Teaching in Africa," *ACS* 4: 21–38.
Downey, James
  1975 "The Bible and Polygamy," *AFER* 17/4: 237–242.
Dube, Musa W.
  1992 "Jesus and the Samaritan Woman: A Motswana Feminist Theological Reflection on Women and Social Transformation," *Boleswa Journal of Occasional Theological Papers* 1/4: 5–9.
        "Jesus as our Ancestor: The African Feminist Quest for Identity," *Boleswa Journal of Occasional Theological Papers* 1/4.
  1996 "Savior of the World But Not of this World: A Post-Colonial Reading of Spatial Construction in John," *Abstracts: American Academy of Religion/Society of Biblical Literature 1996* (Scholars Press): 257.
        "Reading for Decolonization (John 4:1–42)," *Semeia* 75: 37–59. [abstract: *NTA* 42/3 (1998): #1748.]
        "Readings of *Semoya*: Batswana Women's Interpretation of Matt 15: 21–28," *Semeia* 73: 111–29. [abstract: *NTA* 42/1 (1998): #216.]
  1998 "Saviour of the World But Not of this World: A Postcolonial Reading of Spatial Construction in John," in Sugirtharajah: 118–35.
  1999 "Consuming a Colonial Cultural Bomb: Translating *Badimo* into 'Demons' in the Setswana Bible (Matthew 8:28–34; 15:22; 10:8)," *JSNT* 73: 33–59. [abstract: *NTA* 43/3 (1999): #1584.]
Dzurgba, A.
  1986 "John's Gospel: A Theological Reflection," *Orita* 18/2: 78–92.

Earthy, E.D.
1957 "A Probable Creation- and Flood-Myth in Portugese East Africa," *Numen* 4: 232–34. [abstract: Holter: #070.]

Ebo, D.J.I.
1985 "'O That Jacob Would Survive': A Study on Hope in the Book of Amos," (Doctoral dissertation, University of Nigeria).
1986 "Echoes of Old Testament Eschatology and Apocalyptic in Adventist Churches In Africa," *AJBS* 1/2: 160–173. [abstract: Holter: #071.]
1989 "Another Look at Amos' Visions," *ATJ* 18/1: 3–17.

Edet, Rosemary N.
1990 "Leadership in the New Testament—Resurrection/Feminist Perspective," *NJOT* 1/5: 94–101.
1991 *New Testament Studies for Colleges and Universities* (Lagos, Nigeria: Heritage Publishers).
1992 "Women and Evangelization: A New Testament Perspective," Ukpong & Okure, et al.: 128–34.

Edet, Rosemary N. & Mary Titilayo Dipe, eds
1992 *Women and Rituals: The African Story* (Ibadan: Daystar).

Edet, Rosemary N. & M.A. Umeagudosa, eds
1991 *Life, Women and Culture: Theological Reflections. Proceedings of the National Conference of a Circle of African Women Theologians 1990* (Lagos, Nigeria: African Heritage Research and Publications).

Edmonds, P.
1981 "Luke's Portrait of Christ," *B-PB* 4: 7–14.

Edmunds, Peter
1994 *Three Portraits of Jesus and Other Gospel Portraits: A Study Guide for Matthew, Mark and Luke* (Gweru, Zimbabwe: Mambo Press). [reviews: Hermann Hauser *ACS* 10/4 (1994): 66; Roger Randrianarimalala *Hekima Review* 12 (1995): 97–99.]

Eggen, W.M.G.
1996 "The Church as a Family and Magdalene' Touch," *JIT* 3/4: 19–30.

Ejenobo, David Tejere
1986 "The Holy Spirit in the Theology of Paul," (Doctoral dissertation, University of Ibadan).
1987 "The Meaning and Significance of the Death of Christ in the Theology of St. Paul," *AJBS* 2/1-2: 64–76.

Ejere, Kingsley Asahu
1988 "The Parable of the Prodigal Son, Luke 15:11–32," Ukpong: 35–42.

Ekofo, Bunyeku
1989 "Spiritualité: un Problème du Moment" *RZTP* 3: 9–15.

Eke, Anthony Okechukwu
1977 "Emancipation in Paul's Letter to the Galatians," (Doctoral dissertation, Pontifical Urban University, Rome).

Ekeya, Bette J.
1986 "Woman, For How Long?" Pobee & Wartenberg-Potter: 59–67.
1990 "Women's Place in Creation," Oduyoye & Kanyoro: 89–103.

Ekpo, Monday U.
1985 "Robertson Smith, the 'Higher Critics' and the Problem of Prophecy: A Case Study in the Sociology of Knowledge," *ATJ* 14/2: 79–90.
Ekuwen, Joseph
1991 "Biblical Perspective on Christology," *NJOT* 1/6: 3–10.
Ela, Jean-Marc
1980 *Le Cri de l'Homme Africain* (Paris: Harmattan); E.T.: *African Cry* Robert R. Barr, trans. (Maryknoll: Orbis, 1986), chapter 3, "An African Reading of Exodus": 28–38; reprinted in *Voices* 10/2 (1987): 76–85 and as "A Black African Perspective: An African Reading of Exodus," Sugirtharajah, 1st ed.: 256–66; 2nd ed.: 244–54. [abstract: Holter: #072.]
1992 *Le Message de Jean-Baptiste de la Conversion à la Réformé dans les Église Africaines* (Yaounde, Cameroun: Editions CLE). [review: Nkebi Luamba, *Flambeau* n.s. 1 (1993): 75–77)
Eluchie, Callistus Nnamdi
1988 "The Concept of Salvation in Independent African Churches: A Critique in the Light of Pauline Theology of Salvation," (S.T.L. thesis, CIWA/Pontifical Urban University, Rome).
Emedi, G.
n.d. "To Relate the Biblical View of Death and Life After Death to the Babembe Understanding About Death and Life Beyond the Grave," Occasional Research Paper No. 190 (Kampala: Makerere University).
Emeghara, Nkem L.
1994 "A Critical Examination of the Circumcision Account of Genesis 17," *Bible Bhashyam* 20/4: 280–89. [abstract: *OTA* 19/1 (1996): #206.]
Eneme, Grace
1985 "Living Stones. Bible Study on 1 Peter 2:4–10" *Women in a Changing World* 16: 14–15; reprinted as "Living Stones," Pobee & Wartenberg-Potter: 28–32.
Enomate, J.M.
1986 "Ezra the Scribe: A Reconsideration," *AJBS* 1/2: 148–59.
Enuwosa, J.
1993 "The Synoptic Gospels," *AJBS* 8/1: 20–35.
Enyagu, George N.
1995 "Pastoral Care and Counselling: The Biblical Basis," Douglas Wanjohi Waruta, ed. *Caring and Sharing: Pastoral Counselling in the African Perspective* (Nairobi: ATIEA): 22–40.
Enyioha, B. Uche
1989 "The Resurrection Power of Jesus Christ and Its Implications for the Christian Life," *OJOT* 4: 4–9.
Essien, Michael
1995 "The Bible and the Veneration of Saints," Obinwa and Obilor, eds, 134–51.
Esua, Cornelius Fontem
1987 "Prophétie, Ravissement et le Don des Langues dans la Spiritualité Biblique," *Cahiers Bibliques Africains* 1/Jan: 29–35; reprinted in

English as "Prophecy, Ecstasy and Speaking in Tongues in Biblical Spirituality," *B-PB* 5/Jan (1987): 19–26.

1991   "The Word (Logos) in Johannine Writings," Amewowo, et al., 1991: 28–56.

Etim, Leo Effiong

1983   "Social Justice in the Prophet Amos and Its Relevanec in the Nigerian Context," (M.Th. thesis, CIWA/Pontifical Urban University, Rome).

Etok, Sylvanus Udo

1964   "Biblical-theological Basis for the Once and for All Sacrifice of Christ in the Epistle to the Hebrews," (Doctoral dissertation, Pontifical Urban University, Rome).

1990   "Critical Appreciation," [response to Robert Sarah "Les Actes des Apotres—L'Evangile du Saint-Esprit,"] in Amewowo, et al., 1990: 20–24.

Etuk, U.

1992   "God, Justice and Minority Groups in Nation Building," *AJBS* 7/2: 94–105.

Evans-Pritchard, E.E.

1956   *Nuer Religion* (Oxford: Clarendon Press). [abstract: Holter: #074.]

Eze, N.

1991   "The Christian Concept of Leadership Role in Nation Building," *AJBS* 6/1: 57–69.

Ezeanya, Stephen N.

1969   "God, Spirits and the Spirit World," Dickson & Ellingworth: 30–46.

1974   "Ancestor Veneration and the Communion of Saints," Glasswell & Fashole-Luke: 209–21.

Ezeogu, Ernest Munachi

1992   "The Jewish Response to Hellenism: A Lesson in Inculturation," in Brookman-Amissah, et al.: 133–47; reprinted in *JIT* 1/2 (1994): 144–55.

1993   "Root Causes of Conflict between Authority and Charism in the Nigerian Church. A Response to the Paper: 'Charism and Authority: A New Testament Perspective,' of Fr. J.," CATHAN, 1993: 39–44.

Fabella, Virginia & Mercy Oduyoye, eds

1988   *With Passion and Compassion: Third World Women Doing Theology* Ecumenical Association of Third World Theologians, Womens' Commission (Maryknoll: Orbis). [abstract: *RSR* 15/3 (1989): 245.]

Facultes Catholiques de Kinshasa

1978   *Foi Chrétienne et Langage Humain: Actes de le Septième Semaine Théologique de Kinshasa (24–29 juillet 1972)* (Kinshasa: Facultés de Théologie Catholique Kinshasa).

1980   *Pastorale et Épanouissement des Vocations dans l'Afrique d'Aujourd'hui: Actes de la Onzième Semaine Théologiques de Kinshasa (du 26 au 31 juillet 1976)* (Kinshasa: Facultés de Théologie Catholique).

      Libération en Jesus-Christ: Actes de la Douzième Semaine Théologique de Kinshasa (du 25 au 30 juillet 1977) (Kinshasa: Facultés de Théologie Catholique).

1989 *Théologie Africaines Bilan et Perspectives: Actes de la Dix-septième Semaine Théologique de Kinshasa 2–8 avril 1989* (Kinshasa: Facultés Catholiques de Kinshasa).

1991 *Communautés Johanniques/Johannine Communities: Actes de Quatrième Congrès des Biblistes Africains Nairobi/Karen, 24–29 juillet, 1989* (Kinshasa: Katholische Jungschar Oesterreichs/Facultés Catholiques de Kinshasa).

Fadeji, S.O.

1990 "Biblical and African Names of God: A Comparison," *OJOT* 5: 29–36.

1991 "The Christian Leader," *AJBS* 6/1: 10–15.

Falusi, Gabriel K.

1973 "The Christian View of Freedom," *Orita* 7/2: 113–28.

1976 "The Suffering and Exalted Son of Man in Daniel and St. Mark's Gospel," *Orita* 10/1: 67–80.

1982 "Some Reflections on the Concept of Koinonia in the New Testament, with Particular Reference to Acts and the Pauline Epistles," *Orita* 14/2: 132–39.

1988 "Sacrifice in the New Testament," *Orita* 20/2: 79–90.

Fanusie, Lloyda

1990 "Christianity and African Rituals (Matthew 11:25–30; Leviticus 12:1–5; Luke 2: 21–24)," Oduyoye & Kanyoro: 84–88.

Farmer, William R. with Sean McEvenue, Armando J. Levoratti, David Dungan and Andre LaCocque, eds

1998 *The International Bible Commentary: A Catholic and Ecumenical Commentary for the Twenty-First Century* (Collegeville, MN: The Liturgical Press). [review: D. Smith-Christopher *CBQ* 61/3 (1999): 538–40.]

Federation Lutherienne Mondiale Department de la cooperation des Eglises

n.d. *Conference des Eglises Lutherienne de toute l'Afrique sur La Mission dans les Villes et les Milieux Industriels en Afrique 20–28 juin 1987 Antsirabe, Madagascar* (n.p.: Federation Lutherienne Mondiale).

Ferdinando, Keith

1992 "Biblical Concepts of Redemption and African Perspectives of the Demonic," (Ph.D. Dissertation, London Bible College).

1996 "Screwtape Revisited: Demonology Western, African, and Biblical," in Anthony N.S. Lane, ed. *The Unseen World: Christian Reflections on Angels, Demons and the Heavenly Realm* (Grand Rapids: Baker Book House & Paternoster): 103–32.

1997 "The Great Dragon: The Nature and Limit of Satan's Power," *AJET* 16/1: 17–30.

   "The Dragon Hurled Down: The Victory of Christ over the Dominion of Darkness," *AJET* 16/2: 113–36.

Field, M.J.

1958 "Ashanti and Hebrew Shamanism," *Man* 58: 14. [abstract: Holter: #076.]

Finch, Charles

1985 "The Kamitic Genesis of Christianity," *Journal of African Civilizations* [?].

Fitzgerald, Michael L.
    1980   "Points of Contact between the Bible and the Qur'an," *B-PB* 3:
            25–30.
Folarin, George O.
    1994   *Studies in Old Testament Prophecy* (Kaduna: Adelewa Printing Works).
            [review: *BookNotes* 8 (October 1999): #8.09.]
Fortes, Meyer
    1983   *Oedipus and Job in West African Religion* (Cambridge: Cambridge
            University Press); reissue of 1958 edition with an Introduction by
            Jack Goody and an essay by Robin Horton. [abstract: *RSR* 12/1
            (1986): 86.]
Fourche, J.A.T. & H. Morlighem
    1973   *Une Bible Noire* (Brussels: Max Arnold).
France, R.T.
    1978   "Critical Needs of the Fast-Growing African Churches," *Evangelical
            Missions Quarterly* 14/3: 141–49.
Fray, Marion G.
    1968   "New Church Member Orientation in Central Africa in the Light
            of Biblical and Historical Backgrounds" (Th.D. dissertation, South
            Western Baptist Theological Seminary, Houston, Texas).
Fueter, Paul D.
    1962   "The Bible and Nyakusa Religion," *Ministry* 3/1: 3–8.
Fuller, Lois K.
    1995   "Slaves of God/Sons of God," *UMTC—JTS* 1: 41–46.
Gaiya, Musa A.B.
    1991   "The Bible in Aladura Churches," *AJBS* 6/1: 105–13.
Galot, J.
    1958   "L'Expression 'Fils de l'Homme' dans les Langues Africaines,"
            RCA 13: 355–62.
Gakuru, Griphus
    1999   "An Anglican's View of the Bible in an East African Context,"
            in *Anglicanism: A Global Communion* Andrew Wingate, Kevin Ward,
            Carrie Pemberton, Wilson Sitshebo, eds (N.Y.: Church Publishing
            Incorporated): 58–62.
Gakwandi, E.
    1975   "Divination et Magie dans la Bible et dans la Tradition Rwandese,"
            Foi et Culture 44: 37–52.
Garcia, Miguel A.
    1993   "Committed Discipleship and Jesus' Lordship. Exegesis of Luke
            6:46–49 in the Context of Jesus' Discourse on the Plain," *ACS*
            9/2: 3–10.
Gathaka, Jephtha K.
    1990   "Bible Study: Nehemiah 5:1–13 and Economic and Social Problems
            Created by the Debt Crisis," Appendix 2a, pp. 1–7 in report of
            Debt Crisis as it Affects Human Rights Seminar (Maseru, Lesotho, 26–30
            September, 1990).
Gehman, Richard J.
    1970   "Ancestor Relations Among Three African Societies in Biblical

Perspective" (D.Miss. dissertation, Fuller Theological Seminary, Pasadena, California).

Geraghty, Gerard
1996 "Paul Before the Areopagus: A New Approach to Priestly Formation in the Light of *Ecclesia in Africa*," *ACS* 12/3: 32–41.
1997 "The Book of Revelation: An Aid to Primary Evangelization As We Await the Third Millennium," *Acs* 13/2 (1997): 53–62.

Gertz, Roland
1987 "The Idea of Creation in African Traditional Religion and in the Old Testament," unpublished paper for the University of Erlangen, Nurnberg, Germany; on file at the Lutheran Theological College, Makumira, Tanzania.

Getui, Mary N.
1996 "Zelophehad's Daughters: A Challenge for the African Woman," *BCT* 3/1: 19–23. [abstract: *Abstracts: American Academy of Religion/ Society of Biblical Literature 1995* (Scholars Press, 1996): 149.]

Gitari, David M.
1982 "The Claims of Jesus in the African Context," *IRM* 71/1: 12–19; reprinted in *ERT* 6/2 (1982): 215–23.

Gitari, David M. & G.P. Benson, eds
1986 *Witnessing to the Living God in Contemporary Africa:Findings and Papers of the Inaugural Meeting of the Africa Theological Fraternity* (Nairobi, Kenya: Uzima). [review: Grant LeMarquand *BookNotes* 7 (March 1999): 7.14.]

Gitau, Samson
1996 "African and Biblical Understanding of the Environment," (Doctoral dissertation, University of Nairobi). [abstract: *NAOTS* 1 (1996): 5.]

Githuku, Sammy
1995 "Suffering and the Wrath of God in Lamentations," (Master's thesis, Faculty of Religious Studies, McGill University).

Githumbi, S. Kamau
1980 "The Kingdom of God," *ATJ* 9/1 (1980): 48–52. [abstract: *NTA* 25/2 (1981): #426.]

Glasswell, M.E. & E.W. Fashole-Luke, eds
1974 *New Testament Christianity for Africa and the World* (Fs. H. Sawyerr; London: S.P.C.K.).

Glenday, D.K.
1974 "Old Testament Echoes in the Sudan: Sin and Sacrifice among the Nuer People," *Worldmission* 25: 41–45.

Goba, Bonganjalo
1973 "Corporate Personality: Ancient Israel and Africa," Basil Moore: 65–73. [abstract: Holter: #080.]

Godbey, A.H.
1930 *The Lost Tribes. A Myth. Suggestions Towards Rewriting Hebrew History* (Durham, North Carolina: Duke University Press); reprinted with a prolegomenon by Morris Epstein (N.Y.: Ktav, 1974); especially "Berber, Moorish, and Negro Jews": 204–56. [abstract: Holter: #081.]

Golka, Friedemann W.
  1986   "Die Königs- und Hofsprhche und der Ursprung der israelitischen
         Weisheit," *Vetus Testamentum* 36/1: 13–36; reprinted in idem, 1993:
         16–35. [abstract: Holter: #082.]
  1989   "Die Flecken des Leoparden. Biblische und Africanische Weisheit
         im Sprichwort," R. Albertz, et al., eds *Schöpfung und Befreiung. Für
         Claus Westermann zum 80. Geburtstag* (Stuttgart: Calwer): 149–65;
         reprinted in idem 1993: 36–53. [abstract: Holter: #083.]
  1993   *The Leopard's Spots: Biblical and African Wisdom in Proverbs* (Edinburgh:
         T. & T. Clark). [= *Die Flecken des Leoparden. Biblische und afrikanische
         Weisheit im Sprichwort* Arbeiten zur Theologie, 78 (Stuttgart, 1994).]
         [reviews: S. Weeks *The Expository Times* 105 (1994): 346; R. Davidson
         Theology 97 1994): 456–57; Chirevo V. Kwenda *JTSA* 91 (1995):
         95–96; K.J. Dell *VT* 45 (1995): 566–67; R. Kassis *Theological Review*
         16: 137–39; abstract: Holter: #084; *NAOTS* 1 (1996): 6–7; *BookNotes*
         7 (March 1999): 7.15.]
  1996   "Sozialanthropologie und Altes Testament am Beispiel biblischer
         und afrikanischer Sprichworter," *"Jedes Ding hat seine Zeit . . ." Studien
         zur israelitischen und altorientalischen Weisheit: Diethelm Michel zum 65.
         Geburtstag* Anja A. Diesel et al., eds (BZAW 241; Berlin/New York:
         de Gruyter): 65–89. [abstract: *OTA* 20/3 (1997): #1623.]
  1999   "Biblical and African Wisdom in Proverbs," *NAOTS* 6: 6–8.
         [abstract: *OTA* 22/3 (1999): #1626.]
Haafkens, J.
  1990   "L'Islam en Afrique," Amewowo, 1990: 33–38.
Habelgaarn, A.W.
  1965   "John 4:9, 29: How is it That Thou, Being a Jew . . ." *Ministry*
         6/1: 24.
Hammerstein, F. von, ed.
  1978   *Christian-Jewish Realities in Ecumenical Perspective with Special Emphasis
         on Africa. A Report on the Conference of the WCC Consultation on the
         Church and the Jewish People, Jerusalem, 16–26 June, 1977* (Geneva:
         World Council of Churches). [abstract: Holter: # 087.]
Harte, Klaus-Dieter
  1979   *Mifano ya Bwana: Mafafanuzi* (Maandiko ya Makumira na. 2; Arusha,
         Tanzania: Evangelical Lutheran Church of Tanzania).
  1980   *Waraka wa Paulo kwa Waefeso Waraka wa kwanza wa Yohana: Masomo
         Kumi ya Biblia* (Maandiko ya Makumira na. 3; Arusha, Tanzania:
         Evangelical Lutheran Church of Tanzania).
Healey, J.G.
  1996   "Accompanying the Poor . . . Light from a Biblical Parable and
         an African Parable," *Hekima Review* 14: 68–72. [the prodigal son]
Hearne, Brian, ed.
  1979   *The Community Called Church* (Spearhead #60; Eldoret, Kenya:
         AMECEA Gaba Publications); especially chapter 2, "Scripture and
         the Church."]
  1983   *An African Christmas?* Spearhead No. 77 (Eldoret, Kenya: Gaba
         Publications).

Hecht, F.
   1964   "II Samuel 15:1–30: The Historical and The Theological View of The Revolt of Absalom," *Ministry* 4/4: 168–71.
Hetsen, Jac & Raphael Wanjohi
   1982   *Anointing and Healing in Africa* (Spearhead No. 71; Eldoret, Kenya: Gaba Publications, 1982). [chapter 1: "Biblical Themes of Healing."]
Hevi, Jacob
   1987   "Biblical Ethics," *B-PB* 5/Jan: 1–18.
           "New Testament Ethics," *B-PB* 6/July: 1–17.
   1988   "New Testament Ethics Part III (Conclusion)," *B-PB* 1[sic]/Jan: 25–47.
Hirpo, Tesarga
   n.d.   "II Corinthians 8 and 9," Lutheran World Federation [Gaborone, 1977]: 5–17.
Hochegger, Hermann
   1993   "L'Expérience Évangelique face à certains Rites Traditionnels d'Afrique," *Telema* 19/75–76: 53–55.
Holmberg, Bengt
   1987   "Sociological Versus Theological Analysis of the Question Concerning a Pauline Church Order," Kalugila & Stevenson: 70–89.
Holmes-Siedle, J.
   1973   "Reading the Bible Without Tears," *AFER* 15/1: 76–79.
Holst, Robert
   1967   "Polygamy and the Bible," *IRM* 56: 205–12.
Holter, Knut
   1999   "Old Testament Proverb Studies in the 1990's," *NAOTS* 6: 11–15. [abstract: *OTA* 22/3 (1999): #1637 (sic: #1639.]
Houston, W.J.
   1972   "Readings in Colossians, Related to the Religious Situation in Nigeria," *WAR* 13: 9–28.
Hukema, Lemmert
   1989   "Biblical Solution to Kongo Witchcraft," (M.Th. thesis, NEGST).
Hutchison, E.
   1965   "Ephesians 4:11–12: To Equip God's People," *Ministry* 5/2: 70–72.
Ibe, Francis C.
   1995   "Workers for the Harvest: An Invitation to Missionary Participation," Obinwa and Obilor, eds, 176–88.
Idowu, E. Bolaji
   1969   "God," Dickson & Ellingworth: 17–29.
           "Introduction," Dickson & Ellingworth: 9–16.
   1978   *Job—A Meditation on the Problem of Suffering* (Ibadan: Daystar).
Ifesieh, Emmanuel Ifemegbunam
   1983   "Web of Matrimony in the Bible, Social Anthropology and African Traditional Religion. A Short Survey Through Comparative Analysis," *CV* 26: 195–211. [abstract: Holter: #089.]

1984 "Emmanuel: A Theological Name with Cultural Index," *Neue Zeitschift für Missionswissenschaft* 40: 36–46; reprinted as "EMMA-NUEL: A Theological Name with Cultural Index (A Case Study with Reference to Igbo Traditional Religion)," *Lucerna* 6/2 (1986): 34–44. [abstract: Holter: #090.]

Igenoza, Andrew Olu

1982 "Prayer, Prophecy, Healing and Exorcism in Luke-Acts in an African Context," (Ph.D. dissertation, University of Manchester).

1984 "St. Paul in Athens: Acts 17: 19–34: A Study in the Encounter of Christianity with Philosophical Intellectualism and Other Religions. How Relevant to Africa?" (Seminar Paper, Department of Religious Studies, University of Ile-Ife, Nigeria, June, 1984).

1985 "African Weltanschauung and Exorcism: the Quest for the Contextualization of the Kerygma," *ATJ* 14/3: 179–93.

1986 "The Problem of Evil: A Biblical Theological Perspective," *Evangel* 4/3: 5–10.

1987 "Luke, the Gentile Theologian: A Challenge to the African Theologian," *ATJ* 16/3: 231–41. [abstract: *NTA* 32/2 (1988): #641.]

1988 "Medicine and Healing in African Christianity: A Biblical Critique," *AFER* 30/1: 12–25. [abstracts: *NTA* 32/3 (1988): #1333; Holter: #091.]
"Universalism and New Testament Christianity," *ERT* 12/3: 261–75. [abstract: *NTA* 33/1 (1989): #360.]
"The Message of Jeremiah," in George Carey, ed. *The Bible for Everyday Life* (Grand Rapids: Eerdmans): 118–27.
"The Message of Lamentations," in George Carey, ed. *The Bible in Everyday Life* (Grand Rapids, Eerdmans): 128.

1992 "'Epiousios' in the Greek Texts of the Paternoster in an African Context," *AJBS* 7/1: 48–66.

1998 "The Church and the African State towards the 21st Century: Biblical Perspectives," *JACT* 1/1: 16–23.

Ilonu, Anthony E.

1971 "The New Testament Concept of Priesthood and the Hebrew Passover," (Doctoral dissertation, Pontifical Urban University, Rome).

Imasogie, Osadolor

1975 *Studies in Second Corinthians 1–6* (Ibadan, Nigeria: Daystar).

1988 "Biblical Theology of Reconciliation," *OJOT* 3: 1–10.

Inworogu, Okpara E.

1991 *The Pastoral Epistles (I & II Timothy and Titus): Faithful Words from a Faithful Man to Faithful Men* (Aba, Nigeria: Christian Family Publishers).

Isizoh, Chidi Denis

1995 "Jesus Christ the Priest and His Personal Experience of Human Suffering in the Letter to the Hebrews: Lessons for Priests Today," Obinwa & Obilor, eds: 111–22.

1997 "African Traditional Religious Perspective of the Areopagus Speech

(Acts 17, 22–31)," [Online]. Available: <http://security-one.com/isizoh/areopagus.htm>

1997   "The Resurrected Jesus Preached in Athens: The Areopagus Speech (Acts 17,16–34): An Inquiry into the Reasons for the Greek Reaction to the Speech, and a Reading of the Text from the African Traditional Religious Perspective," (Lagos/ Rome: Ceedee). [review: Wilfrid J. Harrington *CBQ* 61/2 (1999): 361.]

Ita, J.M.
1989   "Biblical Prophecy and its Challenge to Contemporary Prophetic Movements," *ATJ* 18/1: 3–17. [abstract: Holter: #093.]

Iwuanyanwu, Linus Emeka
1987   "Discerning the Body, 1 Cor 11: 29: The Relationship Between the Eucharistic Celebration and the Social Life of the Community in 1 Cor 11: 17–34. Its Application to Umuloha Catholic Community in Nigeria," (S.T.L. thesis, CIWA/Pontifical Urban University, Rome).

Izukanne, Andrew A.A.
1995   "The Problem of Infant Baptism vis-à-vis Mark 16:15–16," Obinwa & Obilor, eds: 152–63.

Jasper, Gerhard
1969   "Polygyny in the Old Testament," *ATJ* 2: 27–57.

Joyce, John
1993   "Authority and Charism in the Nigerian Church: 'Do Not Quench the Spirit . . . But Test Everything,'" *NJT* 7/1: 77–89.

Kabasele Mukenge, Andre
1994   "Figures Bibliques dans le Negro Spirituals. Une Example de Lecture Contextuelle de la Bible," *RAT* 18/35: 83–102.

1971   *L'Unité Littéraire du Livre de Baruch* (Paris: Gabalda). [review: Daniel J. Harrington *CBQ* 61/2 (1999): 338–39.]

Kahutu, Zacharia
1989   "Who has Power: The Holy Spirit or the Spirits?" Anon.: 84–95.

Kakongoro, M.L.A.
1987   "An Exegetical Analysis of Paul's Teaching on Christian Worship in 1 Corinthians 11:2–14:4, with Application for the Deliverance Church in Kampala," (M.A. thesis, NIST).

Kalanda, P.
1982   "The Gospel and the Indigenous Customs and Practices ('Okukyalim Ensiko' Re-examined)," Anon.: 149–55.

Kalilombe, Patrick-Augustine
1980   "The Salvific Value of African Religions: An Essay in Contextualized Bible Reading for Africa," Atal sa Angang, et al.: 205–20.

Kalongo Joachim, P.
1997   "Le Vrai Culte, lieu de Libération Humaine. Lecture Pastorale et Spirituelle de Jn 4,20–24," *RSA* 3: 13–23.

Kalu, Ogbo U.
1986   "Luke and the Gentile Mission: A Study on Acts 15," *ATJ* 1/1: 59–65.

Kalugila, Leonidas
1968 "Messiasproblemet I Det Gamle Testamente," [The Messianic Problem in the Old Testament] (Master's thesis, Aarhus University, Aarhus).
1971 "The Royal Wisdom as Divine Revelation: In the Israelite Wisdom Literature," (S.T.M. thesis; Lutheran School of Theology, Chicago).
1979 *Vitabu vya Agano la Kale* (Tanzania: Vuga Press).
1980 *The Wise King: Studies in Royal Wisdom as Divine Revelation in the Old Testament and its Environment* (Lund: CWK Gleerup). [reviews: W. Brueggemann *CBQ* 44 (1982): 650–51; D. Lys *Etudes Théologiques et Réligieuses* 57/1 (1982): 96–97; L.G. Perdue *Interpretation* 36 (1982): 308–312; H.C. Schmitt *Zeitschrift für die Alttestamentliche Wissenschaft* 94/1 (1982): 175–76; W. Vijfvinkel *ATJ* 11/1 (1982): 107–108; abstracts: *OTA* 4/1 (1981): 109; *RSR* 9/2 (1983): 173.]
1985 "Women in the Ministry of the Priesthood in the Early Church: An Inquiry," *ATJ* 14/1: 35–45.
1987 "Kutafsiri Biblia," Kalugila & Stevenson: 110–22.
Kalugila, Leonidas & N. Stevenson, eds
1987 *Essential Essays on Theology in Africa: Essays presented to The Rev. Dr. Howard Stanley Olson on his 65th Birthday* (Usa River, Tanzania: The Research Institute of Makumira Theological College).
Kameeta Zephanja
1983 *Gott in Schwarzen Gettog. Psalmen und Texte aus Namibia* (Erlagen: Verlag der Ev. Luth. Mission).
Kanyandago, Peter
1989 "A Biblical Reflection on the Exercise of Pastoral Authority in the African Churches," *Jesus in African Christianity: Experimentation and Diversity in African Christology* J.N.K. Mugambi & Laurenti Magesa, eds (Nairobi, Kenya: Initiatives): 112–22. [review: E. Wendland *AJET* 14/2 (1995): 113–23.]
1997 "The Cross and Suffering in the Bible and the African Experience," Kinoti & Waliggo: 123–44.
Kanyoro, Musimbi R.A.
1990 "Daughter, Arise (Luke 8:40–56)," Oduyoye & Kanyoro: 54–62.
1992 "Interpreting Old Testament Polygamy through African Eyes," Oduyoye & Kanyoro: 87–100. [abstract: Holter: #097.]
1972 "Rereading the Bible From an African Perspective," *Ecumenical Review* 51/1 (1999): 18–24. [abstract: *NTA* 43/3 (1999): #1536.]
Kasujja, Augustine
1986 *Polygenism and the Theology of Original Sin Today: East African Contribution to the Solution of the Scientific Problem* (Doctoral Dissertation in Theology with Specialization in Biblical Theology; Roma: Pontificia Universitas Urbaniana).
Kato, Byang
1975 *The Spirits: What the Bible Teaches* (Achimota, Ghana: African Christian Press).

Katshingula, Kawaya Makola
1982 "Les Themes de l'Exode et de l'Alliance dans la Théologie Africaine," (Memoire de Licence en Theologie et Sciences Humaines, Facultés de Théologie Catholique de Kinshasa).

Kavale, Festus
1993 "A Biblical Study of Witchcraft: With Applications for Second and Third Generation Christians in Kenya," *AJET* 12/2: 114–33.

Kawale, W.R.
1995 "Divergent Interpretations of the Relationship Between Some Concepts of God in the Old Testament and in African Traditional Religions—A Theological Critique," *OTEssays* 8: 7–30. [abstracts: Holter: #101; *BCT* 3/1 (1996): 27.]

Kazadi Kanyanga
1986 "'Suivez-moi et je vous ferai pecheurs d'hommes': Marc 1:16–17—Sermon Prononce a l'occasion des Manifestations du Jubilé d'Argent de la F.T.P.Z. [Facultés Théologiques Protestantes au Zaire]," *RZTP* 1: 13–17.

Kealy, Sean P.
1976 "The Irrelevance of the Bible," *AFER* 18/6: 348–54.
1977 "Jesus the Unqualified Teacher," *AFER* 19/4: 228–33.
1989 "Jesus' Approach to Mission," *AFER* 31/1: 27–36.

Kemdirim, Protus O.
1995 "Oppression of Women and the Liberating Message of Jesus," *JIT* 2/2: 184–95.
1996 "Dialogue in the Gospels: its Relevance for Good Governance in Nigeria," *BTS* 16/1: 5–19.
1997 "Eschatology of Paul: Its Nature, Language and Development," *NJOT* 11/1: 90–100.

Kibicho, Samuel G.
1968 "The Interaction of the Traditional Kikuyu Concept of God with the Biblical Concept," *Cahiers des Religions Africaines* 2: 223–238. [orginally in "An Interdisciplinary Workshop . . .": 281–390.] [abstract: Holter: #103.]
1982 "Challenges from the Encounter of Christianity and African Religion to the Traditional Christian Idea of Revelation," Anon.: 115–22.

Kibongi, R. Buana
1969 "Priesthood," Dickson & Ellingworth: 47–56.

Kijana, Peter
1987 "Ubatizo na Roho Mtakatifu," Kalugila & Stevenson: 30–69.

Kimirei, Gabriel
1973 "Reconciliation Among the Maasae in Comparison with Reconciliation in the Old Testament," (S.T.M. thesis; Wartburg Theological Seminary, Dubuque, Iowa).
1989 "Sickness and Healing," Anon.: 179–84.

King, Fergus J.
1994 "Angels and Ancestors: A Basis for Christology?" *Mission Studies* XI–1/ 21: 10–26.

Kinoti, Hannah W.
  1997 "Well-Being in African Society and in the Bible," Kinoti & Waliggo: 112–22.
Kings, Graham
  1986 "God the Father in the New Testament," Gitari & Benson: 55–76.
  1987 "Facing Mount Kenya: Reflections on the Bible and African Traditional Religion," *Anvil* 4/2: 127–43. [abstract: Holter: #104.]
  1996 "Proverbial, Intrinsic and Dynamic Authorities in Kenya: Scripture and Mission in the Diocese of Mount Kenya East and Kirinyaga," in Stott and Others: 134–43.
Kinsioni, Tady Ngwashi
  1981 "La Conversion. Théologie Biblique. Expérience Africaine," (Memoire de Licence en Théologie et Sciences Humaines, Faculté de Théologie Catholique de Kinshasa).
Kivunzi, T.
  1985 "Biblical Basis for Financial Stewardship," *EAJET* 4/1: 24–34.
  1990 "Seven Biblical Exclusions for Married Life," *AJET* 9/2: 27–32. [abstract: *NTA* 36/1 (1992): #406.]
Kossi Ametonu Tossou, R.
  1982 "Parole de Dieu et Théologie Africaine," Anon.: 51–71.
Kossi Dossou, Simon
  1993 "De l'Oppression à la libération: des interpretations de l'Évenement de l'Exode Hier et Aujourd'hui," *Flambeau* n.s. 1: 55–61.
Kouto, Kokou M. Julien
  1978 "Humanité et Authorité du Christ-Prêtre. (une approche exégético-théologique de He. 2,5–18; 3:1–6; 4,15–5,10)," (Doctoral dissertation, Pontifical Urban University, Rome).
Kowalski, Wojciech
  1993 "Female Subjection to Man: Is it a Consequence of the Fall?" *AFER* 35/5: 274–87.
Kubulana, Matendo
  1990 "Le Role du Temple de Jerusalem dans la Religiosité Juive: Interrogations Actuelles," *RZTP* 4: 21–32.
Kudadjie, Joshua
  1993 "African Bible Guides Series—Booklet 8: Colossians," selections reprinted in *ERT* 17/4: 468–71.
Kuzenzama, K.P.M.
  1977 "La Conception Johannique de la 'montée-descente' du Fils de l'Homme. Etude semantique," *RAT* 1/2: 207–18.
  1979 "Jn 5–6 ou Jn 6–5? Une Question Embarrassante de Critique Litteraire," *RAT* 3/5: 61–69.
  1980 "La Préhistoire de l'Expression 'pain de vie' (Jn 6,35b; 48). Continuite ou Emergence?" *RAT* 4/7: 65–83. [abstract: *NTA* 25/3 (1981): #927.]
  1981 "L'Expression 'le pain de vie' (Jn 6,35b) et les Donées Néotestamentaires. Originalités Johannique?" *RAT* 5/9: 45–55.

1983   "Une Discussion sur les 'oeuvres.' Approche Éxègetiques de Jn 6, 26–30," *RAT* 7/14: 165–79.
1987   *La Structure Bipartite de Jn 6,26–71: Nouvelle Approche* Recherche Africaines de Théologie #9 (Kinshasa: Faculté de Theologie Catholique). [abstract: *NTA* 33/3 (1989): 386.]
1990   *Le Titre Johannique du Fils de L'Homme: Essai Lexicographique* Recherches Africaines de Théologie #11 (Kinshasa: Facultés Catholique de Kinshasa).

Laiser, [ ]
1989   "Who has Power—The Holy Spirit and the Spirits?" Anon.: 108–20.

Lasebikan, G.L.
1981   "Prophets and Prohecy in Ancient Israel," (Master's thesis, University of Ibadan).
1983   "Prophecy or Schizophrenia? A Study of Prophecy in the Old Testament and in Selected Aladura Churches," (Doctoral dissertation, University of Ibadan, Nigeria). [abstract: *AJBS* 1/2 (1986): 181–82.]
1985   "Kings and Priesthood: A Comparative Analysis of the Cultic Functions of Kings among the Hebrews and Yoruba," *JARS* 2: 78–86.
        "Prophets as Political Activists in the Ancient Israelite Monarchy," *Orita* 17/1: 51–58.
1986   "Ethical Revolution—The Prophetic Model," Abogunrin, ed.: 83–92.
1988   "Sacrifice in the Old Testament," *Orita* 20/2: 64–78.

Latzoo, Cyril
1995   "The Story of the Twelve in the Gospel of Mark," *Hekima Review* 13: 25–33.

LeMarquand, Grant
1996   "The Historical Jesus and African New Testament Scholarship," Michel Desjardins & William Arnal, eds *Whose Historical Jesus?* Studies in Christianity and Judaism, 7 (Waterloo, Ontario, Canada: Wilfrid Laurier): 161–80. [review: J. Kloppenborg *Studies in Religion/Sciences Religieuses* 28/3 (1999): 368–70.]

Leon, M.
1983   *La Sagesse Africaine. Ouvertures sur les Evangiles* (Paris/Fribourg: Editions Saint Paul).

Levison, J.R. & P. Pope-Levison
1992   *Jesus in Global Contexts* (Louisville: Westminster/Knox). [reviews: B. Lawless *Ching Feng* 35 (1992): 241–44; D. Cave *Christian Ministry* 24 (1993): 29–30; D.G. Dawe *Theology Today* 50 (1993): 320–21; T.J. Gorringe *Expository Times* 104 (1993): 286; L.D. Laird *Perspectives in Religious Studies* 20 (1993): 321–24; I. McCrae *Encounter* 54 (1993): 449–50; D. Rhoads *Currents in Theology and Mission* 20 (1993): 415–16; J.F. Watson *Ashland Theological Journal* 25 (1993): 144–145; L. Creighton *Missiology* 22 (1994): 105; J. Mbiti *IBMR* 18 (1994): 42–43; T.Y. Okosun *Reformed Review* 48 (1994): 60; J.L. Powell

Journal of Ecumenical Studies 31 (1994): 408–409; C. Villa-Vicencio *JTSA* 87 (1994): 79; G. Snyder *Chicago Theological Seminary Register* 85 (1995): 46–47; abstract: *NTA* 37/2 (1993): 297.]

Lilembu-Sapiele Bodjoko
1995 "Face to Face with Saint Paul," *Hekima Review* 12: 3–14.

Limpens, F.B.
1967 "The Healing Ministry of the Church, A Theological Approach," *GBT* 3/2: 34–35.

Link-Wieczorek, Ulrike
1994 "Neulesen der Bibel im Kontext afrikanischer Theologie," *Material-dienst* 45/6: 116–19. [abstract: *Theology in Context* 12/2 (1995): #912.]

Lutheran World Federation
n.d. *All Africa Lutheran Consultation Gaborone, Botswana 7–16 February 1977* (n.p.: Lutheran World Federation Department of Church Coope-ration).

n.d. *All Africa Lutheran Consultation on Christian Theology in the African Context Gaborone, Botswana October 5–14, 1978* (n.p.: Lutheran world Fed-eration Department of Church Cooperation).

n.d. *"Let My People Go" (Ex. 5:1b): African Pre-Assembly 7–12 July, 1989 Yaounde, Cameroon* (n.p.: Lutheran World Federation Department of Church Cooperation).

Maasdorf, A.
1966 "Revelation 3:7–11," *Ministry* 6/4: 163–64.

Mafico, Temba L.J.
1973 "The Relevance and Appeal of the Old Testament to the Ndau People of Rhodesia, Based on a Form-Critical Analysis of the Patriarchal and Covenantal Historical Narratives, Recorded in Gen. 12–35 and Exodus 1–24," (Th.M. thesis, Harvard University).

1978 "Parallels between Jewish and African Religio-cultural Lives," Hammerstein: 36–52. [abstract: Holter: #112.]

1979 "A Study of the Hebrew Root SPT with Reference to Yahweh," (Doctoral dissertation, Harvard Divinity School). [abstract: *HTR* 72: 319.

1982 "African Tradition and Jewish Culture," *Patterns of Prejudice* [London: Institute of Jewish Affairs] 16/3: 17–26.

1983 "The Crucial Question Concerning the Justice of God (Gen. 18:23–26)," *JTSA* 42: 11–16. [abstract: *OTA* 7/3 (1984): #750.]

1986 "The Ancient and Biblical View of the Universe," *JTSA* 54: 3–14. [abstract: *OTA* 103 (1987): #631.]

1987 "The Term *Sapitum* in Akkadian Documents," *JNSL* 13: 69–87. [abstract: *OTA* 11 (1988): #135.]

1989 "Evidence for African Influence on the Religious Customs of the Patriarchs," *Abstracts: American Academy of Religion/Society of Biblical Literature 1989* J.B. Wiggins & D.J. Lull, eds (Scholars Press): 100.

1992 "Just, Justice," *Anchor Bible Dictionary. Vol. III* (N.Y.: Doubleday): 1127–29.

1995   "The Divine Name Yahweh Elohim from an African Perspective,"
        Segovia & Tolbert, 1995: 21–32. [abstract: *OTA* 19/3 (1996):
        #1762.]
1996   "Were the 'Judges' of Israel like African Spirit Mediums?" Smith-
        Christopher: 330–43. [abstract: *OTA* 20/1 (1997): #13.]
        "The Divine Compound Name [YHWH Elohim] and Israel's
        Monotheistic Polytheism," *JNSL*22/1: 155–73. [*OTA* 20/2 (1997):
        #1056.]
1998   "Judges," in Farmer, et al., eds: 548–65.
Magagula, S.J.
1964   "John 8:17: the Life of Costly Discipleship," *Ministry* 4/3: 125.
Magnante, Antonio
1997   *Why Suffering? The Mystery of Suffering in the Bible* (Nairobi: Paulines
        Publications Africa).
Maillu, David G.
1989   *The Black Adam and Eve* (Nairobi, Kenya: Maillu Publishing House).
Makundu, Mangala
1975   "Repentir et Pardon. Une Lecture de la Parabole de l'Enfant
        Perdu (Luc 15, 11–32). Approche Litteraire et Thématique de la
        Parabole Biblique et de la Parabole Populaire Négro-Africaine,"
        (Mem. Lic. Theol. Kinshasa).
Mallia, Bernard
1977   "Back to Genesis with Love," *AFER* 19/3: 149–55.
1983   "Social Justice: A Biblical Dimension (1)," *AFER* 25/1: 33–41.
        "Social Justice: A Biblical Dimension (2)," *AFER* 25/2: 109–13.
Mangematin, B.
1964   "'Thou Shalt Not Have Strange Gods Beside Me': A Catechetical
        Problem," *AFER* 6/1: 17–23.
Mann, Pamela S.
1989   "Towards a Biblical Understanding of Polygamy," *Missiology* 17:
        11–26. [abstract: Holter: #118.]
Manus, Chris Ukachukwu
1981   "The Opponents of Paul in 2 Cor 10–13; An Exegetical and
        Historical Study," (Ph.D dissertation, The Catholic University of
        Louvain, Belgium). [abstract: *AJBS* 1/2 (1986): 178.]
1982   "Gal 3:28—A Study on Paul's Attitude towards Ethnicity: It's
        Relevance for Contemporary Nigeria," *Ife Journal of Religion* 2: 18–26.
1983   "1 Thessalonians 2: 17–20, A Reflection on Paul's Use of the
        Plural Number and its Significance for Ministry in Africa," *ATJ*
        12/2: 76–87. [abstract: *NTA* 28/3 (1984): #1073.]
        "2 Cor 10–11:23a. A Study in Paul's Stylistic Structures," *BTA*
        5/10: 251–68. [abstract: *NTA* 28/2 (1984): 624.]
1984   "Amenuensis Hypothesis: A Key to the Understanding of Paul's
        Epistles," *Bible Bhashyam* 10/3: 160–74. [abstract: *NTA* 29/3 (1985):
        #1030.]
        "The Subordination of Women in the Church: 1 Cor 14:33b–36
        Reconsidered," *RAT* 8/16: 183–95. [abstract: *NTA* 30/2 (1986):
        #728.]

1985   "The Areopagus Speech (Acts 17:16–34): A Study of Luke's Approach to Evangelism and Its Significance in the African Context," *ATJ* 14/1: 3–18. [abstract: *NTA* 32/2 (1988): #711.]

"The Centurion's Confession of Faith (Mark 15:39): Its Reflections on Mark's Christology and its Significance in the Life of African Christians," *BTA* 7/13–14: 261–78. [abstract: *NTA* 31/1 (1987): #149.]

"Conversion Narratives in the Acts: A Study in Lucan Historiography," *Indian Theological Studies* 22/2: 172–95. [abstract: *NTA* 30/3 (1986): #1154.]

"The Eucharist: A Neglected Factor in Contemporary Theology of Liberation," *AFER* 27/4: 197–208.

1986   "1 Thess. 5.27 and Related Passages: Reflections on the Lector in the New Testament Church," *RAT* 10/20: 225–38. [abstract: *NTA* 32/3 (1988): #1310.]

"The Concept of Death and the After-Life in the Old Testament and Igbo Traditional Religion: Some Reflections for Contemporary Missiology," *Mission Studies* 3/2: 41–56. [abstract: Holter: #120.]

"Elijah—A Nabi Before the Writing Prophets; Some Critical Reflection," *AJBS* 1/1: 25–34. [abstract: Holter: #119.]

"Matthew 5:13–16. Jesus' Ethical Teaching to His Disciples: An Exemplar for Nigerians in the Present Decade," Abogunrin *Ethics*: 139–57.

"The Resurrection of Jesus: Some Critical and Exegetical Considerations in the Nigerian Context," *NJOT* 1/2 (1986): 28–45; reprinted in *Japan Mission Bulletin* 41 (1987): 30–43.

1987   "Apostolic Suffering (2 Cor 6:4–10): The Sign of Christian Existence and Identity," *Asia Journal of Theology* 1/1: 41–54. [abstract: *NTA* 31/3 (1987): #1212.]

"The Samaritan Woman (Jn 4:7ff.): Reflections on Female Leadership and Nation Building in Africa," *AJBS* 2/1–2: 52–63; reprinted in *ACS* 4/4 (1988): 73–84. [abstract: *NTA* 34/1 (1990): #211; *NTA* 34/2 (1990): #698.]

"The Universalism of Luke and the Motif of Reconciliation in Luke 23: 6–12," *ATJ* 16/2: 121–35; reprinted in *Asia Journal of Theology* 3/1 (1989): 192–205 with the subtitle "Reflections on Their Implications in the African Cultural Context." [abstract: *NTA* 33/3 (1989): #1194; *RTA* 38/3 (1995): #3852.]

1989   "The Areopagus Speech (Acts 17:16–34): A Study on Luke's approach to Evangelism and its significance in the African Context," *RAT* 13/26 (1989): 155–70; reprinted in Amewowo, et al., 1990: 197–218.

"Miracle-Workers/Healers as Divine Men: Their Role in the Nigerian Church and Society," *Asia Journal of Theology* 3/2: 658–69. [abstract: *NTA* 34/2 (1990): #862.]

"New Testament Theological Foundations for Christian Contribution to Politics in Nigeria," *BET* 2/1: 7–30. [abstract: *NTA* 36/1 (1992): #410.]

1990   "The Community of Love in Luke's Acts: A Sociological Exegesis
        of Acts 2: 41–47 in the African Context," *WAJES* 2/1: 11–37.
        [abstract: *NTA* 35/2 (1991): #718.]
        "Luke's Account of Paul in Thessalonica (Acts 17,1–9)," R.F.
        Collins, ed. *The Thessalonian Correspondence* Bibliotheca Ephemeridum
        Theologicarum Lovaniensium, 87 (Leuven: Leuven University
        Press): 27–38.

1991   "Elizabeth Schussler Fiorenza's Feminist Hermeneutics of the New
        Testament: Its Relevance in the Nigerian Context," *WAJES* 3:
        67–73; also published in Manus, Mbefo & Uzukwu: 146–52.
        [abstract: *NTA* 38/3 (1994): #1223.]
        "Jesus and the Jewish Authorities in the Fourth Gospel," Amewowo,
        1991: 135–55.
        "King-Christology: The Example of Some 'Aladura' Churches in
        Nigeria," *Africana Marburgensia* 24/1: 28–46.
        "King-Christology: Reflections on the Figure of the 'Endzeit'
        Discourse Material (Mt 25,31–46) in the African Context," *Acta
        Theologica* 11: 19–41.
        "King-christology: the Result of A Critical Study of Matt 28:
        16–20 As An Example of Contextual Exegesis in Africa," *Scriptura*
        39: 25–42. [abstract: *NTA* 36/3 (1992): #1286.]

1992   "Healing and Exorcism: The Scriptural Viewpoint," Manus, Mbefo
        & Uzukwu: 84–104.
        "John 6: 1–15 and its Synoptic Parallels: An African Approach
        Toward the Solution of a Johannine Critical Problem," *JITC*
        19/1–2: 47–71. [abstract: *NTA* 38/1 (1994): #239.]

1993   *Christ, the African King: New Testament Christology* Studies in the Inter-
        cultural History of Christianity 82 (Frankfurt am Main/Berlin/
        Bern/New York/Paris/Wien: Peter Lang). [review: G. LeMar-
        quand *BookNotes* 2 (October 1996): #2.21; abstract: *NTA* 38/3
        (1994): 477.]
        "Universalism and Mission: A Review of the Epilogue in Matt
        28, 16–20 in the African Context," Adeso, et al., 1993: 86–111.

Manus, C.U. & R.F. Collins
1989   "Contemporary New Testament Scholarship. Outlining its Relevance
        for African Christianity," *Bodija Journal* 1: 8–22.

Manus, C.U. & Fortunatus Nwachukwa
1992   "Forgiveness and Non-Forgiveness in Matthew 12:31–32: Exegesis
        Against the Background of Early Jewish and African Thought-
        forms," *ATJ* 21/1: 57–77.

Manus, C.U., Luke N. Mbefo & Eugene Elochukwu Uzukwu, eds
1992   *Healing and Exorcism: The Nigerian Experience* Spiritan International
        School of Theology [SIST] Symposium Series (Enugu, Nigeria:
        SIST).

Many, Gaspard
1990   "Appreciation Critique," [response to Wynnand Amewowo "The
        Christian Community in Acts of the Apostles: Model for our
        Days"] in Amewowo, et al., 1990: 117–19.

Martey, Emmanuel
1994–95 "Jesus of History, the Church and the Poor in Africa," *TJCT* 4/2: 26–38.
Martin, Marie-Louise
n.d. "Outlines and Suggestions for an Old Testament Theology and Teaching Related to the Religious Background in Southern Africa," in "An Interdisciplinary Workshop . . .": 177–190.
1961 "You Are the Salt of the Earth; You Are the Light of the World. Matthew 5:13–16," *Ministry* 1/4: 20–21.
1962 "Acts 17:16–34: Paul's Approach to Greek Intellectuals," *Ministry* 3/1: 20–24.
"Genesis 18:16–33: Abraham the Man of Faith," *Ministry* 3/1: 25–26.
1963 "Psalm 1: The Blessedness of the Righteous," *Ministry* 4/1: 18–21.
1964 "Psalm 130: Out of the Depth I Cry to Thee," *Ministry* 4/2: 64–65.
1965 "The Concept of Mission in the New Testament, According to Dr. F. Hahn," *Ministry* 5/3: 113–117.
"Ordination and the Ministries of the Church According to the Biblical Witness," *Ministry* 6/1: 5–12.
Masoga, M.A.
1996 "Exploring Belief in *Bolai* (Witchcraft) in the Light of Mark 5,1–20," *JBTSA* 9/2: 53–69. [abstract: *NTA* 41/2 (1997): #933.]
Massawe, Wilfred
1989 "Who has Power [?]—The Holy Spirit and the Spirits," Anon.: 75–83.
Matthew, Obiekezie Uche
1995 "Biblical Anthropology and 'Mmadu' in Igbo Religious Thought—An Experiment in Inculturation Theology," Obinwa & Obilor, eds: 44–62.
Mbachu Hilary
1995 *Inculturation Theology of the Jerusalem Council in Acts 15: An Inspiration from the Igbo Church Today* European University Studies, series 23: Theology 520 (Frankfurt am Main/Bern/New York: Peter Lang). [review: James C. Okoye in *CBQ* 58/3 (1996): 556–57; abstract: *NTA* 40/1 (1996): 143.]
1996 *Cana and Calvary Revisited in the Fourth Gospel. Narrative Mario-Christology in Context* (Egelsbach/Frankfurt: Hansel-Hohenhausen). [abstract: *NTA* 41/2 (1997): 362.]
Mbang, S.C.
1978 "Apocalypticism in Israel: A Possible Background To the Study of 'Prophetism' in Nigeria," *Orita* 12/1: 42–50. [abstract: Holter: #122.]
1986 "The Agony of the Ethical Prophets and the Nigerian Response," Abogunrin: 93–104.
Mbanusi, Chudi C.
1994 "Is the Book of Revelation A Curse to Christians? A Sober Reflection," *Jos Studies* 4/1: 78–85.

Mbaziba, Francis X.
1964 "The Death of Christ Upon the Cross As the Supreme Manifestation of God's Love, in Light of Jn Xv, 13," (Doctoral dissertation, Pontifical Urban University, Rome).
Mbefu, L.
1990 "Critical Appreciation," [response to L. Monsengwo Pasinya "L'inculturation dans le Livre des Actes"] in Amewowo, et al., 1990: 134–38.
Mbiti, John S.
1963 "Christian Eschatology in Relation to Evangelisation of Tribal Africa," (Ph.D. dissertation, Cambridge University).
1967 "Afrikanisches verständnis der Geister im Lichte des Neuen Testamentes," Rosenkranz, ed.: 130–47.
n.d. "New Testament Eschatology in Relation to the Evangelization of Tribal Africa," in "An Interdisciplinary Workshop . . .": 281–88. [paper was delivered sometime between 1966 and 1968.]
1969 "Eschatology," Dickson & Ellingworth: 159–84.
1971 "New Testament Eschatology and the Akamba of Kenya," David B. Barrett, ed. African Initiatives in Religion (Nairobi, Kenya: East Africa Publishing House): 17–28.
New Testament Eschatology in an African Background: A Study of the Encounter between New Testament Theology and African Traditional Concepts (SNTS monograph series; London: Oxford University Press [London: SPCK, 1978]). [reviews: H. Desroches Archives de Sociologie de Religions 16/32 (1971): 246; P. Ellingworth Expository Times 82 (1971): 349–50; M. Warren Journal of Theological Studies ns 22 (1971): 687–88; E. Dammann Theologische Literaturzeitung 98 (1973): 76–77; J. Frdy Recherches de Science Religieuses 61 (1973): 139–51; E.G. Newing Reformed Theological Journal 38/1 (1979): 26–27; D. von Allmen IRM 69 (1980): 229–31; S. Barrington-Ward SJT 33/3 (1980): 298–300.
1973 "[Our Saviour] as an African Experience" Barnabas Lindars & S.S. Smalley, eds Christ and Spirit in the New Testament (fs. C.F.D. Moule) (Cambridge: Cambridge University Press): 397–414.
1978 "The Biblical Basis in Present Trends of African Theology," ATJ 7/1: 72–85; reprinted in Bulletin of African Theology 1/1 (1979): 11–22; with some changes reprinted as "The Biblical Basis for Present Trends in African Theology," African Theology en Route: Papers from the Pan-African Conference of Third World Theologians, December 17–23, 1977, Accra, Ghana Kofi Appiah-Kubi & Sergio Torres, eds (Maryknoll: Orbis, 1979): 83–94; Occasional Bulletin of Missionary Research 4 (1980): 119–24. [abstract: Holter: #124.]
"'Cattle are Born with Ears, Their Horns Grow Later': Towards an Appreciation of African Oral Theology" in Lutheran World Federation [Gaborone]: 35–51.
"The concept of God in Jewish and African traditions," Hammerstein: 53–61. [abstract: Holter: #125.]

1979 "New Testament Eschatology in an African Background," in *Readings in Dynamic Indigeneity* Charles H. Kraft and Tom N. Wisley, eds (Pasadena: William Carey Library): 455–64.

1989 "God, Sin and Salvation in African Christianity," *AME Zion Quarterly Review* 100/1: 2–8.

1990 "Eucharistie, Koinonia und Gemeinschaft in der africanischen Christenheit," *Zeitschrift für Mission* 16/3: 149–154.

1992 "Is Jesus Christ in African Religion?" Pobee: 21–29.

1993 "Authority and Charism: New Testament Notes and Pastoral Implications in the Nigerian Church," CATHAN, 1993: 45–60.

Mbuwayesango, Dora Rudo

1994 "Beyond Disaster: A Dialogue about the Future of Zion/Jerusalem (Micah 4:1–8)," *Abstracts: American Academy of Religion/Society of Biblical Literature 1994* (Scholars Press): 377.

1995 "Childlessness and Woman-to-Woman Relationships in Genesis and in African Patriarchal Society: Sarah and Hagar from a Zimbabwean Woman's Perspective," *Abstracts: American Academy of Religion/Society of Biblical Literature 1995* (Scholars Press): 151.

1997 "Childlessness and Woman-to-Woman Relationships in Genesis and in African Patriarchal Society: Sarah and Hagar from a Zimbabwean Perspective (Gen 16:1–16; 21:8–21)," *Semeia* 78. [abstract: *OTA* 22/2 (1999): #777.]

1998 "The Defence of Zion and the House of David: Isaiah 36–39 in the Context of Isaiah 1–39," (Doctoral dissertation, Emory University). [abstract: *NAOTS* 6: 21.]

Mbwiti, Justine Kahungu

1990 "Jesus and the Samaritan Woman (John 4:1–42)," Oduyoye & Kanyoro: 63–75.

Mbon, Friday M.

1982 "Deliverance in the Complaint Psalms: Religious Claim or Religious Experience," *Orita* 14/2: 120–31. [abstract: *OTA* 12/2 (1989): #595.]

McCain, Danny

1992 "The Parable of the Shrewd Manager: Lessons in Nation Building," *AJBS* 7/2: 54–68.

McDermond, J.E.

1993 "Modesty: The Pauline Tradition and Change in East Africa," *ACS* 9/2: 30–47. [abstract: *NTA* 39/2 (1995): #988.]

McFall, Ernest A.

1970 *Approaching the Nuer through the Old Testament* (South Pasadena, California: William Carey Library).

Meester, Paul de

1990 "Inculturation de la Foi et Salut des Cultures: Paul de Tarse à 'Areopage d'Athens (Acts 17,22–32)," *Telema* 62: 59–80.

1993 "Prenez soin de vous-mêmes et du Troupeau . . . S. Paul aux Anciens d'Ephese (Ac 20, 17–35)," *Telema* 19/74: 35–47.

1995 "Juifs et Chrétiens: Une Théologie Rénouvelée. Premiers Réperes dans un Discours de Paul (Ac 13, 16–41)?" *RAT* 19/38: 195–214.

Merker, M.
1904 *Die Masai. Ethnographische Monographie eines ostafrikanischen Semitenvolkes* (Berlin: D. Reimer). [abstract: Holter: #128.]

Mhando, Ernest
1984 "Israel's Worship," (M.A. thesis, Vanderbilt University).

Mhogolo, Mdimi
1996 "The Bible: Our Tool for Evangelism and Church Planting. The Diocese of Central Tanganyika," in Stott and Others: 129–33.

Mijoga, Hilary B.P.
1990 "Some Notes on the Septuagint Translation of Isaiah 53," *ATJ* 19/1: 85–90.
1991 "Refugees Unfold the Stories of the Bible," *Religion in Malawi* 3: 16–24.
1995 "An Approach to Christian Mission in Africa. Paul's Approach in Rom 2:13 and 3:20a," *JTSA* 42/2 (1998): #1108.]
1998 "The Use of the Term 'Merit' in Connection with Paul's Phrase ['erga nomou'] (erga nomou, 'Deeds of the Law')," *JTSA* 100:20–35. [abstract: *NTA* 43/1 (1999): #319.]

Milimo, J.
1972 "African Traditional Religion," A *New Look at Christianity in Africa* World Student Christian Federation books, 2 (Geneva): 9–13. [abstract: Holter: #130.]

Mkole Jean-Claude, Loba
1997 "A Liberating Women's Profile in Mk 5:25–34," *ACS* 13/2 (1997): 36–47.

Mngadi, C.S.
1982 "The Significance of Blood in the Old Testament Sacrifices and its Relevance for the Church in Africa," *Theologia Evangelica* 15/3: 66. [dissertation abstract]

Mojola, Aloo Osotsi
1998 "The Chagga Scape-goat Purification Ritual and Another Re-reading of the Goat of Azazel/Azazel in Leviticus 16: Some Preliminary Observations," unpublished paper delivered the International Organization for the Study of the Old Testament, Oslo, Norway, August 2–7, 1998.

Molangi Tomoyakabini
1996 "L'Option Préferentielle pour les Pauvres selon Mt 25,40.45," *RAT* 20/39: 81–93.

Molyneaux, Paul
1985 "Does the Pauline Doctrine of the Atonement Have Any Basis in the Gospels?" *EAJET* 4/2: 15–19. [abstract: *NTA* 30/3 (1986): #1171.]

Mondeh, D.E.
1978 "Sacrifice in Jewish and African Traditions," Hammerstein: 76–81. [abstract: Holter: #135.]

Monsengwo Pasinya, L.
1973 *La Notion de Nomos dans la Pentateuque Grec* (Rome: Biblical Institute Press).

1977 "Antioche, berceau de l'Eglise des Gentiles? Ac 11, 19–26," *RAT* 1/1: 31–66. [abstract: *NTA* 26/1 (1982): #187.]

1980 "Revelation-Dans-l'Histoire," Atal sa Angang, et al.: 149–68.

1988 "Lokola biso tokolimbisaka baninga (Mt 6,9 par): l'Incidence Theologique d'une Traduction," *RAT* 12/23–24: 15–21. [abstract: *NTA* 33/3 (1989): 1129.]

1989 "L'inculturation dans le Livre des Actes," *RAT* 13/25: 31–40; reprinted in Amewowo, et al., 1990: 120–33.]

1991 "La Foi dans les Ecrits Johanniques," Amewowo, et al., 1991: 10–27.

Monsma, Timothy Martin

1977 "African Urban Missiology: A Synthesis of Nigerian Case Studies and Biblical Principles," (Ph.D. dissertation, Fuller Theological Seminary).

Moreau, A. Scott

1986 "A Critique of John Mbiti's Understanding of the African Concept of Time," *EAJET* 5/2: 36–48.

1990 *The World of the Spirits: A Biblical Study in the African Context* (Nairobi: Evangel Publishing House). [review: *BookNotes* 2 (October 1996): #2.25.]

Morlan, G.

1968 "Towards a Biblical Understanding of Womanhood," *Ministry* 8: 3–9.

Moti, James Shagba

1991 "Collection as Koinonia (2 Cor. 8–9): Understanding Material Contribution in the Church as an Expression of Christian Fellowship," *Jos Studies* 2/2: 17–32.

Mouton, E.

1997 "The Transformative Potential of Ephesians in a Situation of Transition," *Semeia* 78: 121–43. [abstract: *NTA* 43/2 (1999): #1142.]

Moyo, Ambrose Mavingire

1984 "The Colossian Heresy in the Light of Some Gnostic Documents from Nag Hammadi," *JTSA* 48: 30–44. [abstract: *NTA* 29/2 (1985): #648.]

Mpevo Mpolo

1996 "Joseph: un Homme qui Dépanne Dieu? Exegese de Mt 1,18–25," *RAT* 20/39: 61–80.

Msafiri, A.G.

1997 "Diversity in 1 Corinthians 1–4; 12–14, As a Challenge Towards Church Unity: An African Perspective," *ACS* 13/1: 28–41. [abstract: *NTA* 42/1 (1998): #381.]

Mshana, Eliewaha E.

1966 *Fidia ya Wengi: Marko na Injili yake* ['Ransom for Many: Mark and His Gospel'] (Dodoma: Central Tanganyika Press).

1979 *Tumewekwa Huru: Matakafuri ya Waraka kwa Wagalatia* ['Set Free by Christ: A Commentary on the Letter to the Galatians'] (Dodoma, Tanzania: Central Tanganyika Press).

Mudendeli, Martin

1987 "L'Utilisation de l'Ancien Testament dans la Première Epitre de

Pierre: Unité Dynamique des Ecritures," (Doctoral dissertation; Pontificia Universitas Gregoriana Facultas Theologiae, Rome).

Mugambi, Jesse Ndwiga Kanywa
1989   *The Biblical Basis for Evangelization: Theological Reflections based on an African Experience* (Nairobi: Oxford University Press). [review: *BookNotes* 7 (March 1999): 7.25.]

Mukuta, Paulo M.R.
[?]   "Paul's Confrontation with the Problems of Immorality, Marriage and Food Sacrificed to Idols in 1 Corinthians, and its Implications for the Church in Tanzania and its Mission," (Doctoral dissertation; Pontifical Urban University, Rome).

Mulago, Vincent
1969   "Vital Participation," Dickson & Ellingworth: 137–158.

Muli, Alfred
1997   "The Modern Quest for an African Theology Revised in the Light of Romans 1:18–25. Part 1: An Exegesis of the Text," *AJET* 16/1 (1997): 31–50.
       "The Modern Quest for an African Theology Revised in the Light of Romans 1:18–25. An Exegesis of the Text (Patr 2): Implications for African Theology," *AJET* 16/2 (1997): 137–47. [abstract (of both parts): *NTA* 43/2 (1999): #1111; these two articles are taken from the author's M.Div. thesis presented to NIST, 1997.]

Müller, Hans-Peter
1999   "Afrikanische Parallelen zu Gen. Iii und verwandten Texten," *Vetus Testamentum* 49: 88–108. [abstract: *OTA* 22/3 (1999): #1498.]

Muoneke, M. Bibiana
1991   "Women Discipleship and Evangelization (Luke 8:1–3)," *BETh* 4/1–2: 59–69. [abstract: *NTA* 37/2 (1993): #772.]
       "Worship and Sacraments in John's Gospel," Amewowo, et al., 1991: 86–117.
1993   "Universalism and Mission in the Bible. Women Discipleship and Evangelization in Lk 8:1–3," *RAT* 17/34: 163–180.

Muoneme, Maduabuchi
2000   "What are they saying about the one loaf in the boat?" [Mk 8:14–21] *Hekima Review* 21: 9–19.

Mushila Nyamanank
1988   "Eglise et Développement: Reflexions Théologiques" *RZTP* 2: 35–48. [Jn 10: 7–10].

Musopole, Augustine
1992   "The Quest for Authentic Humanity: Becoming Like Christ," *AJET* 11/1: 1–12.
       "Witchcraft Terminology, the Bible, and African Christian Theology" *ACS* 8/4: 33–41; reprinted in *JRA* 23 (1993): 347–354.

Musuvaho Paluku
1983   "La Conception de Dieu Créateur chez les Bayira et dans l'Ancien Testament," (Mémoire de Licence en Théologie, Kinshasa, Faculté de Théologie Protestante au Zaire).

Musvosvi, Joel Nobel
  1993   *Vengeance in the Apocalypse* Andrews University Seminary Doctoral Dissertation Series, 17 (Berrien Springs, Mich.: Andrews University Press). [review: Julius M. Muchee in *JATA* 1/1 (1995): 157–59.]

Muthengi, Julius
  1984   "A Critical Analysis of Sensus Plenior," *EAJET* 3/2: 63–73. [abstract: *NTA* 31/1 (1987): #34.]
  1992   "Missiological Implications of the Book of Jonah: An African Perspective" (Ph.D. dissertation, Trinity Evangelical Divinity School, Deerfiled, Illinois).
  1995   "Polygamy and the Church in Africa: Biblical, Historical and Practical Perspectives," *AJET* 14/2: 55–78.

Muthungu, Samuel M.
  1986   "The Fatherhood of God in the New Testament," Gitari & Benson: 34–54.

Muyengo, Mulo
  1991   "Les Droits de l'Enfant dans la Bible," *RAT* 15/30: 213–17.

Mwakabana, Hance A.O.
  n.d.   "Mission dans les Villes dans l'Ancien et le Nouveau Testaments," Federation Lutherienne Mondiale [Antsirabe]: 87–100.

Mwakisunga, Amon D.
  1967   "Jesu Wort zur Ehe auf dem Hintergrund seiner Botschaft vom Reiche Gottes," (Master's thesis, University of Hamburg).

Mwereke, Thadei
  1996   *A Christian Ethic on Refugees in Africa South of the Sahara* (Karen-Nairobi: CUEA Publications). [chapter 2: "A Biblical Ethic on Refugees and Related Matters"]

Mwombeki, F.R.
  1995   "The Book of Revelation in Africa," *Word and World* 15/2: 145–50. [abstract: *NTA* 40/1 (1996): #369.]

Mworia, Thaddeus A.
  1986   "The Community of Goods in Acts: A Lucan Model of Christian Charity," (Doctoral dissertation; Pontifical Urban University, Rome).
  1995   "The Missionary Techniques in Acts," *RAT* 19/37: 21–36.

Naab, Jude Thaddeus
  1987   *The Basic Christian Community in Biblical Perspective* Incarnation Monograph Series No. 1 (Port Harcourt, Nigeria: CIWA Publications).

Naré, Laurent
  1986   *Proverbs Salomoniens et Proverbes Mossi: Etude Comparative à partir d'une Nouvelle Analyse de Pr 25–29* Publications Universitaires Europeennes, xxiii/283 (Frankfort/Bern/New York: Peter Lang). [review: J.G. Williams *CBQ* 51 (1989): 343–44; abstract: Holter: #139.]
  1987   "Bible et Evangélisation," *Cahiers Bibliques Africains* 2/Sept (1987): 3–16; reprinted in English as "The Bible and Evangelization," *B-PB* 1[sic]/Jan (1988): 1–15.

1988   "La Fraternité dans l'Ancien Testament Essai de Reflecture Africaine," *Cahiers Bibliques Africains* 4/Dec: 4–18.
1993   "Temoignage et Kerygme dans les Actes des Apotres," Adeso, et al., 1993: 147–88.
Nasimiyu-Wasike, Anne
1992   "Polygamy: A Feminist Critique," Oduyoye & Kanyoro: 101–18.
1997   "Mary, the Pilgrim of Faith for African Women," Kinoti & Waliggo: 165–78.
National Council of Churches in Kenya
1983   *A Christian View of Politics in Kenya: Love, Peace and Unity* (Nairobi: Uzima).
Ncube, P.A.
1974   "A Christian Feast of Tabernacles for Africa?" *AFER* 16: 269–76. [abstract: Holter: # 140.]
Ndebe, Joseph Kiiru
1992   "An Evaluation of the Field Education Programme At Scott Theological College in Light of Principles of Training Derived From the Example of Jesus" (M.A. thesis, NIST).
Ndiokwere, Nathaniel I.
1981   *Prophecy and Revolution: The Role of Prophets in the Independent African Churches and in Biblical Tradition* (London: S.P.C.K., 1981). [revision of "Prophetic Movements in the Independent African Churches in Confrontation with Old Testament Prophetism," (Doctoral dissertation, Pontifical Urban University, Rome, 1977).] [reviews: J. Hodgson *JTSA* 40 (1982): 73–74; H.W. Turner *Zeitschrift für Missionswissenschaft und Religionswissenschaft* 66 (1982): 142–43; J. Rennes *Etudes Théologiques et Réligieuses* 58/4 (1983): 555; H.W. Turner *Evangelical Quarterly* 56 (1984): 127–28; abstracts: *RSR* 8/3 (1982): 259; Holter: #141.]
Ndombi, Jean-Roger
1997   "Le Langage des Lieux dans L'évangile de Jean," *Hekima Review* 17: 53–65. [abstract: *NTA* 42/1 (1998): #293.]
Ndongwo, A.
1978   *Le Salut de Dieu selon Saint Paul* (Montréal: Editions Paulines/Trois Riveres: Editions de l'Alliance/Paris: Apostolat des Editions). [abstract: *NTA* 24/3 (1980): 307.]
Ndulue, Patrick O.N.
1988   "Jesus Teaching on Forgiveness and Reconciliation in Matthew's Gospel and Its Relevance for the Igbo People of Nigeria," (S.T.L. thesis, CIWA/Pontifical Urban University, Rome).
Nebechukwu, Augustine U.
1992   "The Prophetic Mission of the Church in the Context of Social and Political Oppression in Africa," Ukpong & Okure, et al.: 103–112.
Nebechukwu, Augustine U., ed.
1993   *The Holy Spirit and the Renewal of the Church in Africa: Proceedings of the Fourth Theology Week of the Catholic Institute of West Africa,*

Port Harcourt, Nigeria, March 22–26, 1993 (Port Harcourt: CIWA Press).

Neels, M.
  1960 "Jesus' Resurrection: The Core of the Message," *AFER* 2/2: 99–107.

Nelumba, Martin
  1987 "Torah As the Foundation of Life: the Meaning and Function of Torah in the Old Testament As Exemplified in Psalm 119" (M.A. thesis, Luther Northwerstern Theological Seminary).
  1994 "Analytical Study of the Theme of Liberation in the Psalms" (D.Phil. dissertation, University of Natal, Pietermaritzburg, South Africa).

Newing, Edward G.
  n.d. "Concepts of Mediation Among the Kenya Highland Bantu Compared with Those of Pre-exilic Israel: A Study in Methodology," in "An Interdisciplinary Workshop . . .": 149–56.

Ngally, J.
  1984 "La Libération d'Egypte," *BTA* 6/2: 303–307.

Ngayihembako, S.
  1994 *Les Temps de la Fin. Approche Exégètique de l'Eschatologie du Nouveau Testament* Le Monde de la Bible 29 (Geneva: Labor et Fides). [abstract: *NTA* 38/3 (1994): 478.]

Ng'ekieb, Mukoso
  1979 "Quelques Elements Bibliques, Réligieux, du Kimbanguisme," *Telema* 5/19: 39–46.

Ngewa, Samuel
  1987 "The Validity of Meaning and African Christian Theology," *EAJET* 6/1: 17–23. [abstract: *NTA* 32/1 (1988): #28.]
         "The Biblical Idea of Substitution Versus the Idea of Substitution in African Traditional Sacrifices: A Case Study of Hermeneutics for African Christian Theology," (Ph.D. dissertation, Westminster Theological Seminary).

Ngoumou, P.C.
  1972 "Bible et Liturgie Africaine," Mveng & Werblowsky: 205–11. [abstract: Holter: #144.]

Ngoy Mwaka Kyabulewa
  1986 "La Vocation de Jeremie 1, 4–19: Lieu de Réflexion Pastorale dans l'Eglise du XXème Siècle" *RZTP* 1: 239–53.

Ngulube, John V.
  1979 "Liturgical Understanding of Biblical Texts in The Mass" *B-PB* 1:7–12.

Ng'unda, Emeline Joseph
  1986 "The Role of Women in the Synoptic Gospels," (B.D. thesis; Lutheran Theological College, Makumira, Tanzania).

Niekerk, A.S. van
  1994 "Old Testament Studies From A Practical Theology Viewpoint," *OTEssays* 7: 298–304. [abstract: Holter: #145.]

Niyorugira, Pierre-Claver
  1980 "La Formulation du Salut chez les Murundi: Des Elements Lexi-
       cographiques," Atal sa Angang, et al.: 221–34.
       "Christ, Sommet de la Revelation: Rapport de carrefour," Atal
       sa Angang, et al.: 249–50.
Njeni, Lwaga Tumwimbilege
  1986 "A Comparison of the Nyakyusa Understanding of Witchcraft,
       Sorcery and Divination with that of the Pentateuch," (B.D. thesis,
       Makumira, Tanzania).
  1989 "Sickness and Healing as Challenges of the Christian Faith,"
       Anon.: 185–91.
Njoroge, Moses M.
  1991 "Recent Social and Cultural Changes in Kenya and their Impact
       on the Care of the Elderly among Kikuyu People," (M.Rel. thesis,
       Wycliffe College, Toronto School of Theology); especially chapter
       II, "Biblical Perspectives on the Care of the Elderly."
Njoroge, Nyambura
  1996 "Hannah, Why do you Weep? 1 Samuel 1 & 2:1–21," Grace
       Wamue & Mary Getui, eds *Violence against Women: Reflections by
       Kenyan Women Theologians* (Nairobi: Acton Publishers): 21–26.
Njoroge wa Ngugi, J.
  1997 "Stephen's Speech as Catechetical Discourse," *Living Light* 33/4:
       64–71. [abstract: *NTA* 42/1 (1998): 326.]
Nkansah-Obrempong, James
  1992 "The Indicative and Imperative Structure in Paul and their Impli-
       cations for Developing Evangelical Ethics in Africa" (M.Th. thesis,
       Nairobi Evangelical School of Theology).
Nkoyane, Vi Paulos
  1998 "A Socio-scientific Study of the Status of Widows in 1 Timothy"
       (M.A. thesis, University of Durban-Westville, Natal, South Africa).
Nkwoka, A.O.
  1985 "Mark 10:13–16: Jesus' Attitude to Children and its Modern Chal-
       lenges," *ATJ* 14/2: 100–10. [abstract: *NTA* 32/2 (1988): #628.]
  1986 "Paul's Idea of the Hagioi and its Significance for Contemporary
       Nigerian Christianity," *EAJET* 5/1: 23–35. [abstract: *NTA* 31/2
       (1987): #696.]
  1989 "Mark 3:19b–21: A Study on the Charge of Fanaticism Against
       Jesus," *Bible Bhashyam* 15/4: 205–21. [abstract: *NTA* 34/3 (1990):
       #1152.]
  1990 "Jesus as Eldest Brother (Okpara): An Igbo Paradigm for Christology
       in the African Context," *Asia Journal of Theology* 5/1: 87–103.
Nnamani, Godwin
  1995 "Mary, The Model for New Evangelization," Obinwa & Obilor,
       eds: 96–110.
Nsibu, Isaac K.
  1974 "An Exegetical-Theological Study of the Holy Spirit in 1 and 2
       Corinthians with Reference to the Abalokole in the North-Western

Diocese of the Evangelical Lutheran Church in Tanzania Today,"
(S.T.M. thesis; Wartburg Theological Seminary).

Ntezimana, Laurien
   1997   "La Justice dans the Bible," *Dialogue* 201: 67–76.

Nthamburi, Rosemary Kathure
   1991   "A Female Facilitator of the Exodus: The Mother of Moses from
         an African Perspective," *In God's Image* 10/2: 15–18.

Ntoko Saka
   1993   "A Travers Les Actes des Apotres: Dialogue entre Foi et Cultures,"
         Telema 19/74: 31–32.

Ntreh, Benjamin Abotchie
   1990   "Transmission of Political Authority in Ancient Israel and Judah:
         A Tradition Historical Study of the Demise and Succession of
         Kings in the Deuteronomistic History and in the Chronicler's
         History," (Doctoral dissertation; Lutheran Theological Seminary).
   1996   "Women's Support Agents in the Bible," (unpublished paper read
         at the West African Association of Theological Institutions [WAATI]
         held at the Seventh-Day Adventist Seminary at Ilishan, Remo,
         Ogun State, Nigeria, July 28–August 2, 1996).
   1997   "How Kings Were Made in Ancient Israel: From History to
         Tradition," *Bible Bhashyam* 23/2: 71–89.

Ntshwene, C.
   1964   "Matthew 16:24–27: Seek First God's Kingdom," *Ministry* 4/4:
         172.

Nussbaum, S.
   1984   "Re-thinking Animal Sacrifice: A Response to Some Sotho Inde-
         pendent Churches," *Missionalia* 12: 49–63. [abstract: Holter: #148.]

Nwahaghi, F.N.
   1991   "Biblio-Traditional African Concept of Leadership Role in Nation
         Building: A Theological Appraisal," *AJBS* 6/1: 113–122.
         "The Meaning and Significance of 'Eyei' Ritual Symbol in Ibibio
         Traditional Socio-Religious Life," *AJBS* 6/2: 113–122.
   1992   "King Solomon's Royal Policies and the Breakdown of the Empire,"
         AJBS 7/2: 106–14.

Nweka, A.O.
   1992   "Healing: The Biblical Perspective," *AJBS* 7/1: 20–39.

Nwosu, L. Ugwuanya
   1996   "The Nations and the Sons of God in Deuteronomy 32: Perspectives
         on Evangelical Strategies in Non-monotheistic Cultures," *Bible
         Bhashyam* 22/1: 22–43. [abstract: *OTA* 20/1 (1997): #264.]

Nyeme Tese, J.
   1977   "L'Aspect Moral dans l'Enseignement de Proverbes x, i–xxii, 16
         et i–xxiv, 27," *RAT* 1/2: 185–206.
   1990   "Justice dans la Bible et Societe Zairoise," *RAT* 14/27–28: 183–96.

Nyesi, John F.
   1986   "The Old Testament View of God the Father," Gitari & Benson:
         18–33.

Nyom, B.
1981   "Prière Biblique et Prierè Négro-Africaine," *BTA* 3/6: 155–218. [abstract: Holter: #152.]
Nyoyooko, Vincent G.
1983   "Genesis 3: The Sin of Adam and Eve," (S.T.L. thesis, CIWA/ Pontifical Urban University, Rome).
Nzambi, P.D.
1992   "Proverbes Bibliques et Proverbes Kongo: Etude Comparative de Proverbia 25–29 et de quelques Proverbes Kongo," (Frankfurt am Main).
Obaje, Yusufu Ameh
1992   "Theocentric Christology," Pobee: 43–53.
Obeng, E.A.
1976   "Prayer in Luke-Acts," (Masters thesis, University of Aberdeen).
1984   "The Spirit Intercession Motif in Paul," *ExT* 95/12: 360–64. [abstract: *NTA* 29/2 (1985): #626.]
1986   "The Origins of the Spirit Intercession Motif in Romans 8:26," *NTS* 32/4: 621–32. [abstract: *NTA* 31/1 (1987): #253.]
          "The Reconciliation of Rom 8:26f. to New Testament Writings and Themes," *SJT* 39/2: 165–74. [abstract: *NTA* 31/1 (1987): #254.]
          "The Significance of Blood in the New Testament in Relation to Blood in African Religion" *JARS* 3 (1986): 36–42.
          "Speaking in Tongues: The Only Sign of Reception of the Holy Spirit?" *ATJ* 15/2: 121–26. [abstract: *NTA* 31/1 (1987): #360.]
1988   "Abba, Father: The Prayer of the Sons of God," *ExT* 99/12: 363–66. [abstract: *NTA* 33/2 (1989): #734.]
1989   "An Exegetical Study of Rom. 8:26 and its Implications for the Church in Africa," *Deltion Biblikon Meleton* 18/2: 88–98. [abstract: *NTA* 34/3 (1990): #1266.]
          "The Miracle of the Stilling of the Storm and its Implications for the Church in Africa," *Deltion Biblikon Meleton* 18/1: 43–52. [in modern Greek; abstract: *NTA* 34/3 (1990): #1156.]
1990   "The 'Son of Man' Motif and the Intercession of Jesus," *ATJ* 19/2: 155–67. [abstract: *NTA* 35/2 (1991): #815.]
1992   "The Significance of the Miracles of Resuscitation and its Implication for the Church in Africa," *Bible Bhashyam* 18/2: 83–95. [abstract: *NTA* 37 (1993): #1191.]
Obi, Chris A.
1993   "Charismata and Authority: A Pauline Viewpoint," CATHAN, 1993: 110–24.
Obijole, B.
1986   "St. Paul's Understanding of the Death of Christ in Romans 3:25: The Yoruba Hermeneutical Perspective," *ATJ* 15/3: 196–201. [abstract: *NTA* 31/3 (1987): #1187.]
1988   "Infant Baptism: A Critical Review," *AFER* 30/5: 299–312. [abstract: *NTA* 33/1 (1989): #370.]

1989   "St. Paul's Concept of Principalities and Powers," *Bible Bhashyam* 15/1: 25–39. [abstract: *NTA* 34/1 (1990): #255.]

Obijole, Olubayo O.
   1986   "Principalities and Powers in St. Paul's Gospel of Reconciliation," *AJBS* 1/2: 113–25. [abstract: *NTA* 33/1 (1989): #240.]

           "The Theology of the Cross in the New Testament with Particular Reference to Pauline Kerygma and Soteriology," (Doctoral dissertation, University of Ibadan, Nigeria, 1986). [abstract: *AJBS* 1/2 (1986): 187–88).

   1987   "The Background to St. Paul's Concept of the Mystery of the Gospel," *Bible Bhashyam* 13/4: 233–49. [abstract: *NTA* 32/3 (1988): #1221.]

           "The Influence of the Conversion of St. Paul on his Theology of the Cross," *EAJET* 6/2: 27–36. [abstract: *NTA* 32/2 (1988): #1222.]

           "St. Paul on the Position of Women in the Church: Paradox Or a Change?" *Orita* 19/1: 57–69.

   1989   "The Pauline Concept of the Law," *Indian Theological Studies* 26/1: 22–34. [abstract: *NTA* 34/3 (1990): #1247.]

Obilor, Iheanyi, J.
   1995   "The Bible and Reincarnation," Obinwa & Obilor, eds: 29–43.

           "Christian Attitudes Towards Reincarnation," Obinwa & Obilor, eds: 164–75.

Obinabu, Patrick C.
   1995   "Priesthood in the Bible and in African Traditional Religion: A Comparative Analysis," Obinwa & Obilor, eds: 63–73.

Obinwa, Ignatius M.C.
   1992   "The Kingdom of Heaven and its Ethical Implications as Reflected in the Sermon on the Mount," *AJBS* 7/2: 83–93.

           "The Response of the Early Church to the Problem of Widows 1 Tim 5: 3–16: A Challenge to the Catholic Church in Igboland," (M.Th. thesis, CIWA/University of Calabar, Calabar, Nigeria).

   1995   "Introduction," Obinwa & Obilor, eds: 5–8.

           "The Use and Abuse of the Bible," Obinwa & Obilor, eds: 9–28.

Obinwa, Ignatius M.C. & Iheanyi J. Obilor. eds
   1995   *The Bible and Theological Reflections* (Buguma, Nigeria: Hanging Gardens Publishers).

Oded, A.
   1974   "The Bayudaya of Uganda. A portrait of an African Jewish community," *JRA* 6: 167–86. [abstract: Holter: #153.]

O'Donovan, Wilbur
   1992   *Introduction to Biblical Christianity from an African Perspective* (Ilorin, Nigeria: Nigerian Evangelical Fellowship). [review: Sam Onyejindu Oleka in *AJET* 13/1 (1994): 59–61; abstract *BookNotes* 3 (March 1997): #3.29.]

Odumuyiwa, E. Ade.
   1983   "Prophecy in the Bible and the Qur'an," *Orita* 15/1: [?].

Oduyoye, Mercy Amba
  1981 "Naming the Woman: The Words of the Akan and the Words of the Bible," *BTA* 3: 81–97; reprinted in Anon. (1982): 133–48. [abstract: Holter: #154.]
  1985 "Women Theologians and the Early Church: An Examination of Historiography," *Voices* 8/3: 70–72, 92.
  1986 "Birth," Pobee & Wartenberg-Potter: 41–44.
  1995 "Biblical Interpretation and the Social Location of the Interpreter: African Women's Reading of the Bible," Segovia & Tolbert, 1995: 52–66.
  1998 "Family: An African Perspective," in Farmer, et al., eds: 289–92.
Oduyoye, Mercy Amba & Musimbi R.A. Kanyoro, eds
  1990 *"Talitha, qumi!": Proceedings of the Convocation of African Women Theologians, Trinity College, Legon-Accra Sept. 24–Oct. 2, 1989* (Ibadan: Daystar Press).
  1992 *The Will To Arise: Women, Tradition and the Church in Africa* (Maryknoll: Orbis).
Oduyoye, Modupe
  1978 "An African Christian's Evaluation of Judaism," Hammerstein: 63–66. [abstract: Holter: #155.]
  1983 "'Adamu Orisa,'" Adegbola, ed.: 112–16. [abstract: Holter: #156.]
       "Agbara—God's Powerful Agents," Adegbola, ed.: 396–406. [abstract: Holter: #157.]
       "Festivals. The Cultivation of Nature and the Celebration of History," Adegbola, ed: 150–69. [abstract: Holter: #158.]
       "Man's Self and its Spiritual Double," Adegbola, ed.: 273–88. [abstract: Holter: #159.]
       "The Medicine-man, the Magician and the Wise Man," Adegbola, ed.: 55–70. [abstract: Holter: #163.]
       "Patrilineal Spirits. The 'Ntoro' of the Akan, the 'Tro-wo' of the Ewe," Adegbola, ed.: 289–96. [abstract: Holter: #160.]
       "Polytheism and Monotheism—Conceptual Difference," Adegbola, ed.: 244–57. [abstract: Holter: #161.]
       "Potent Speech," Adegbola, ed.: 203–32. [abstract: Holter: #162.]
       "The Sky: Lightning and Thunder," Adegbola, ed.: 389–95. [abstract: Holter: #164.]
       "The Spider, the Chameleon and the Creation of the Earth," Adegbola, ed.: 374–88. [abstract: Holter: #165.]
  1984 *The Sons of God and the Daughters of Men: An Afro-Asiatic Interpretation of Genesis 1–11* (Maryknoll/Ibadan, Nigeria: Orbis/Daystar). [abstract: *RSR* 10/4 (1984): 391.]
  1994 *The Longest Psalm: The Prayers of a Student of Moral Instruction* (Ibadan: Sefer). [review: K. Holter *NAOTS* 7 (1999): 13–14.]
  1995 *The Alphabetical Psalms: Systematic Instruction for a life of Faith and Trust* (Ibadan: Sefer). [review: K. Holter *NAOTS* 7 (1999): 13–14.]
       Le-mah Sabach-tha-niy? Lament and Entreaty in the Psalms (Ibadan: Sefer). [review: K. Holter *NAOTS* 7 (1999): 13–14.]

1997 *The Psalms of Satan* (Ibadan: Sefer). [review: K. Holter *NAOTS* 7 (1999): 13–14.]

Ofusu-Adutwum
1977 "Hebrew Prophetism and Spirit Possession in Africa—A Comparative Study of Inspiration in Two Religions," (M.A. thesis; University of Ghana).

Ogbo, Zerehaimanot Yohannes
1983 "The Influence of the Old Testament in the Worship of the Ethiopian Orthodox Church, with Special Reference to the Ark (Tabot) of the Covenant," (B.D. thesis, Lutheran Theological College, Makumira, Tanzania).

Ogeke, Juma Francis
1994 "The View and Use of Possessions in the Ethics of Jesus and the Early Church, An Exegetical/Ethical Analysis of Possession Texts in Luke-Acts with Implications for Social Ethics in Kenyan Society" (M.Th. thesis, NEGST).

Ogundare, Z.B.
1992 "The Problem of Evil vis-à-vis Biblio-Philo Technological Perspectives," *AJBS* 7/1: 76–88.

Ogunkunle, Caleb O.
1988 "The Struggle of Faith in Habakkuk 2:4 and its Application in Later Writings," (M.A. thesis; Winnipeg Theological Seminary, Canada).
1995 "The Concept of Salvation in the Psalter," *UMTC—JTS* 1: 22–30.

Ogunrinu, T.B.
1995 "The Genesis Account of Creation and Its Relationship to Cosmogony," *UMTC—JTS* 1: 47–55.
"Jephtah's Vow: Specific Reference to Its Theological Implication," *ETSI* 1/1: 35–43.
1997 "The Appearance of Samuel after Death: Deception, Hallucination or Divine Intervention," *UMTC—JTS* 2: 20–26.

Ojore, Aloys Otieno
1996 "An African Reading of the Jacob—Esau Story, Gen. 25:19–34 and Gen. 27: 1–45," *ACS* 12/4: 18–29.

Okaalet, Peter E.
1996 "Biblical Submission and Authority in Marriage with Special Interest in the New Testament: Implications for Iteso Evangelical Christians of Uganda" (M.Th. thesis, NEGST).

Okafor, Jude Mwaemeka
1985 "Christian Burial in the Light of 1 Cor 15: 35–49 and in the Context of Igbo Culture," (S.T.L. thesis, CIWA/Pontifical Urban University, Rome).

Okeke, G.E.
1978 "The Problem of Fund Raising in the Corinthian Church," *Orita* 12/2: 108–13.
1981 "The Interpretation of New Testament Teaching on Death and Future Life in an African Context," (Doctoral dissertation, University of Nigeria).

1980   "The Mission of Jesus and Man's Sonship with God: The Setting
        of the Problem," *ATJ* 9/3: 9–17. [abstract: *NTA* 25/3 (1981):
        #822.]
        "1 Thessalonians 2: 13–16: the Fate of Unbelieving Jews," *NTS*
        27/1: 127–36. [abstract: *NTA* 25/2 (1981): #600.]
1987   "The Church as the Community of God's Chosen People," *CV*
        30/3–4: 199–213. [abstract: *NTA* 33/2 (1989): 831.]
        "The Context and Function of 1 Thess. 2:1–12 and its Significance
        for African Christianity," *AJBS* 2/1–2: 77–88. [abstract: *NTA* 34/3
        (1990): #777.]
1988   "The After-Life in St. Matthew as an Aspect of Matthean Ethic,"
        Melanesian Journal of Theology 4/2: 35–44. [abstract: *NTA* 34/1
        (1990): #110.]
        "The Synagogue and the Qumran Community—An Assessment
        of their Influence on Early Church Structure," *FAT* 3/1: 14–32.
        "Anagenesis (Rebirth) in the New Testament," *ATJ* 17/1: 89–99.
        [abstract: *NTA* 32/3 (1988): #1332.]
        "Concept of Future Life: Biblical and Igbo," *NZM* 44/1: 178–96.
        [abstracts: *NTA* 33/1 (1989): #371; Holter: #167.]
Okodua, Michael Odinosen
1986   "The Church as the Church of the Poor: a Lukan Perspective
        with Reference to the Church in Nigeria," (S.T.L. thesis, CIWA/
        Pontifical Urban University, Rome).
Okon, Pius Asuquo
1983   "The Sinai Covenant: Its Implications for the African Christian
        Community as the People of God," (S.T.L. thesis, CIWA/Pontifical
        Urban University, Rome).
Okorie, Andrew Mbama
1988   "Marriage in the Pastoral Epistles," (Ph.D. dissertation, Southern
        Baptist Theological Seminary).
1994   "The Gospel of Luke As A Polemic Against Wealth," *Deltion
        Biblikon Meleton* 23/2: 75–89. [abstract: *NTA* 40/1 (1996): #219.]
1995   "The Art of Characterisation in the Lucan Narrative: Jesus, the
        Disciples and the Populace," *R&T* 2/3: 274–82. [abstract: *NTA*
        41/1 (1997): #262.]
        "The Pauline Work Ethic in 1 and 2 Thessalonians": *Deltion Biblikon
        Meleton* 24/1 (1995): 55–64. [abstract: *NTA* 40/2 (1996): #1017.]
        "Revelation 2 and 3: Grammar Notes," *Deltion Biblikon Meleton*
        24/2 (1995): 31–39. [abstract: *NTA* 40/3 (1996): #1637.]
1996   "Who Killed Jesus?" *R&T* 3/3: 289–96. [abstract: *NTA* 41/2
        (1997): #863.]
1997   "The Lord's Prayer," *UMTC—JTS* 2: 59–66. Also published in
        Scriptura 60 (1997): 81–86. [abstract: *NTA* 42/1 (1998): #208.]
        "Understanding the Book of Ecclesiastes," *AFER* 39/1: 53–57.
        "Sexuality and the Nature of God," *AFER* 40/3: 161–69.
Okorocha, Cyril C.
1986   "God the Father and Hunger in Africa: Give us this Day our
        Daily Bread," Gitari & Benson: 196–211.

Okorocha, Cyril C. & Francis Foulkes
  1995   *Understanding the Psalms. Volume 1: Psalms 1–41* (Achimota, Ghana: African Christian Press).
Okoye, J.C.
  1996   "Mark 1:21–28 in Africa Perspective," *Bible Today* 34/4: 240–45. [abstract: *NTA* 41/1 (1997): #232.]
Okure, Teresa
  1982   "'How Can These Things Happen?' A Study of Jn 3:1–21 in Context," (A "Memoire" of the Ecole Biblique et Archeologique Francaise, Jerusalem).
  1985   "Biblical Perspectives on Women. Eve, the Mother of All the Living. Gen. 3:20," *Voices* 8/3: 82–92.
  1987   "Justice with Compassion: A Biblical Perspective," *Source* 16: 5–18.
  1988   *The Johannine Approach to Mission: A Contextual Study of John 4: 1–42* Wissenschaftliche Untersuchungen zum Neuen Testament. 2. Reihe 31 (Tübingen: J.C.B. Mohr [Paul Siebeck]). [reviews: Robert Morgan in *Theological Book Review* 1/3 (1989): 13; Judith Lieu *Expository Times* 100/11 (1989): 431–32; F. Maloney *Australian Biblical Review* 37 (1989): 77–80; Hendricus Boers in *JBL* 109/1 (1990): 147–49; E.E. Ellis *Southwestern Journal of Theology* 32 (1990): 60; J. Painter *Pacifica* 3 (1990): 347–49; F. Segovia *Interpretation* 44 (1990): 314; K. Wengst *Theologische Literaturzeitung* 115 (1990): 268–70; J. Wietzke *International Journal for Philosophy of Religion* 28 (1990): 256–67; W. Sebothoma in *JBTSA* 5/1 (1991): 52–54; D. Senior *CBQ* 53 (1991): 338–39; *BookNotes* 3 (March 1997): #3.31; abstract: *NTA* 33/2 (1989): 252.]
         "Women in the Bible," Fabella & Oduyoye: 47–59.
  1989   "A Theological View of Women's Role in Promoting Cultural/Human Development," *AFER* 31/6: 362–67.
  1990   "Inculturation: Biblical/Theological Bases," Okure & van Thiel: 55–88; an expanded version published as "Extending the Reality of the Incarnation: A Theological Reflection," *Source* 27: 26–34.
         "Leadership in the New Testament," *NJOT* 1/5: 71–93.
  1991   "Witnessing in the Johannine Communities, a reflection paper," Amewowo, et al., 1991: 71–85.
  1992   "A New Testament Perspective on Evangelization and Human Promotion," Ukpong & Okure, et al.: 84–94; reprinted with some revisions in *JIT* 1/2 (1994): 126–43.
         "The Significance Today of Jesus' Commission to Mary Magdalene," *IRM* 81/322: 177–88. [abstract: *NTA* 37 (1993): #248.]
         "The Will to Arise: Reflections on Luke 8:40–56," Oduyoye & Kanyoro: 221–30.
  1993   "APHES AUTEN (Jn 12, 7): The Challenge of the Anointing of Jesus in Bethany (Jn 12, 1–8 and apr.) for the Contemporary Church," Adeso, et al., 1993: 137–146.
         "'Behold I Make All Things New': The Final Statement of the Fourth Plenary Assembly of the Catholic Biblical Federation," *Concilium* 1: 108–20. [abstract: *NTA* 40/1 (1996): #42.]

"Conversion, Commitment: An African Perspective," *Mission Studies* 10/1 & 2: 109–33.

"The Holy Spirit in the New Testament," in Nebechukwu, ed.: 20–43.

"Jesus der Mann der in der Art Frauen Wirkte," Joachim Wietzke, ed. *Jahrbuch Mission 1993* (Hamburg: Missionshilfe Verlag): 53–62.

"The Laity: People of God in the African Church," *Sedos* 25/6–7: 161–66.

"The Role of Women in the African Church," *Sedos* 25/6–7: 167–73.

1994   "A New Testament Perspective on Evangelisation and Human Promotion," *JIT* 1/2: 126–43.

1995   "The Mother of Jesus in the New Testament: Implications for Women in Mission," *JIT* 2/2: 196–210.

"Reading from This Place: Some Problems and Prospects," Segovia & Tolbert, 1995: 33–51.

1996   "Reading John, the Gospel of Life, in an African Context," *Abstracts: American Academy of Religion/Society of Biblical Literature 1996* (Scholars Press): 185.

1997   "Von Bogata nach Hongkong—von Emmaus nach Sychar. Gedanken zu Lk 24 und Joh 4 aus afrikanischer Perspektive," *Bibel und Kirche* 52/2: 74–79. [abstract: *NTA* 42/1 (1998): #306.]

1998   "John," in Farmer, et al., eds: 1438–505.

Okure, Teresa & Paul van Thiel, et al., eds

1990   *32 Articles evaluating Inculturation of Christianity in Africa* Spearhead numbers 112–114 (Eldoret, Kenya: AMECEA Gaba Publications). [reviews: A. Radoli *AFER* 32 (1990): 308–310; M. Karecki *Missionalia* 19 (1991): 89–90.]

Okwueze, Malachy Ikechuwu

1995   "Myth: The Old Testament Experience," (Doctoral dissertation, University of Nigeria, Nsukka, Nigeria).

Olajubu, Oyeronke

1991   "Women Awareness and Leadership in Church Structure in Nigeria," AJBS 6/1: 70–82.

1992   "The Importance of the Family Unit in Nation Building: A Biblical Perspective," *AJBS* 7/2: 150–56.

1998   "Jesus' Attitude Towards Women: A Model for the Church in Africa Today," *AFER* 40/3: 183–88.

Olayinka, Bolaji

1993   "Biblical Creation Accounts and the Problem of Evil," *AJBS* 8/1: 12–19.

Olayiwola, D.L.

1992   "Messianic Metaphor in Levitical Covenant: The Interplay of Text, Concept and Setting in the Ecclesia Nigeriana," *Bible Bhashyam* 18/4 (1992): 221–32. [abstract: *NTA* 38/1 (1994): #356.]

Olekamma, Innocent U.

1991   "The Parable of the Unforgiving Servant (Matt 18:23–35) and

Igbo Concept of Forgiveness," (M.Th. thesis, CIWA/University of Calbar, Calabar, Nigeria).

Olorumolu, Martin D.A.
1988 "Walking in the New Life in Christ: A Study of Romans 6–8 and Its Pastoral Implications for Nigerians Today," (S.T.L. thesis, CIWA/Pontifical Urban University, Rome).

Olowola, Cornelius
1988 *The Last Week: A Study of the Last Week of Jesus Christ on Earth* (Jos: Challenge Publications).
1991 "Sacrifice in African Tradition and in Biblical Perspective," *AJET* 10/1: 3–9. [abstract: Holter: #168.]
1995 "The Christology of the Prophet Zechariah," *ETSI* 1/1: 1–15.

Olson, Howard S.
1981 "The Place of Traditional Proverbs in Pedagogy," *ATJ* 10/2: 26–35. [abstract: Holter: #169.]
1991 "The Word in Quest of Words," *Currents in Theology and Mission* 18/5: 338–44. [abstract: *NTA* 36/2 (1992): #633.]

Olubunmo, D.A.
1991 "Israelite Concept of Ideal King: A Model of Interdependence of Politics and Religion in Nigeria," *AJBS* 6/2: 59–67. [abstract: Holter: #170.]

Omodunbi, Amos Abiodun
1975 "The Idea of a Dying Saviour in Biblical Theology and in Yoruba Religion," (Master's thesis, University of Ife).

Omoge, Patrick F.
1985 "Christian Understanding of Salvation in the Light of Romans 5:1–11 and the Ikale People of Ondo State of Nigeria," (S.T.L. thesis, CIWA/Pontifical Urban University, Rome).

Onah, A.O.
1991 "Prophet Ezekiel's Concept of Individuality: Guidelines for Nigeria" *AJBS* 6/2: 68–78. [abstract: Holter: #171.]
1992 "Christianization of Yala Traditional Marriage," *AJBS* 7/1: 115–27.

Onaiyekan, John
1981 "Marriage Customs in the Old Testament," *B-PB* 4: 15–26.
"Biblical Attitudes towards Children and Youth," *B-PB* 4: 44–54.
1989 "Ministries in the Acts of the Apostles," *RAT* 13/25: 41–57; reprinted in Amewowo, et al., 1990: 139–64.
1990 "The Bible and Other Religions," Amewowo, ed.: 25–32.
"Priestly Formation for Evangelization. A Biblical Perspective," *WAJES* 2/1: 95–110.

Onibere, S.G.A.
1988 "Old Testament Sacrifice in African tradition: A case of Scapegoatism," M. Augustin & K.-D. Schunk, eds *'Wünschet Jerusalem Frieden.' Collected Communications to the XIIth Congress of the International Organization for the Study of the Old Testament, Jerusalem 1986* Beitrage zur Erforschung des Alten Testaments und des Antiken Judentums,

13 (Frankfurt am Main.: Peter Lang) 193–203. [abstract: Holter: #172.]

Onoh, Torty O.
  1989 "A Critical Analysis of the Old Testament Doctrine of Man and African Tradition Religion" *TCNN Research Bulletin* 20: 22–33.

Onunwa, Udobata R.
  1986 "Biblical Basis for Some Healing Methods in African Traditional Society," *ATJ* 15: 188–95; reprinted in *EAJET* 7/1 (1988): 56–63. [abstracts: *NTA* 31/3 (1987): #1288; *NTA* 33/1 (1989): #372; Holter: #173.]
  1987 "The Nature and Development of Early Israelite Prophecy: A Historical Prolegomenon," *Bible Bhashyam* 13: 79–88. [abstract: *OTA* 11/2 (1988): #756.]
  1988 "Individual Laments in Hebrew Poetry: A Positive Response to the Problem of Suffering," *Jeevadhara* 17: 101–11. [abstract: *OTA* 15/3 (1992): #1423.]
  1991 "Paul, Social Issues and Future Salvation: Challenge to the Modern Church," *Bible Bhashyam* 17/1; 5–13. [abstract: *NTA* 36/1 (1992): #292.]

Onuoha, Stephen E.
  1987 "Preaching the Gospel Free of Charge: An Exegetical Study of 1 Cor 9, and Its Implications for the Life of the Priest in Abakaliki Diocese of Nigeria," (S.T.L. thesis, CIWA/Pontifical Urban University, Rome).

Onwu, Nlenanya
  1980 "The Distorted Vision: Reinterpretation of Mark 8: 22–26 in the Context of Social Justice," *WAR* 19/1–2: 46–52.
  1983 "The Social Implications of 'Dikaiosune' in Saint Matthew's Gospel," (Doctoral dissertation, University of Nigeria, 1983). [abstract: *AJBS* 1/2 (1986): 184–85.]
  1985 "Jesus and the Canaanite Woman (Matt. 15:21–28). Toward a Relevant Hermeneutics in African Context," *Bible Bhashyam* 11/3: 130–43. [abstract: *NTA* 30/3 (1986): #1054.]
         "The Widow's Mites: A Reconsideration of its Meaning" *JARS* 2: 55–63.
  1986 "The Divine Commonwealth in Paul's Thought: A Critical Reflection in an African Context," *NJOT* 1/3: 61–71.
         "'Don't Mention It': Jesus' Instructions to Healed Persons," *AJBS* 1/1: 35–47. [abstract: *NTA* 33/1 (1989): #138.]
         "Mimetes Hypothesis: A Key to the Understanding of Pauline Paraenesis," *AJBS* 1/2: 95–112. [abstract: *NTA* 33/1 (1989): #241.]
  1987 "The Eucharist as Covenant in the African Context," *ATJ* 160/2: 145–158.
         "Righteousness in Matthew's Gospel: It's Social Implications," *Bible Bhashyam* 13/3: 151–78. [abstract: *NTA* 32/2 (1988): #577.]

1988 "Ministry to the Educated: Reinterpreting Acts 17: 16–34 in Africa," *ACS* 4/4: 61–71. [abstract: *NTA* 34/1 (1990): #235.]

"The Parable of the Unmerciful Servant (Matt. 18: 21–35)," Ukpong: 43–51.

"The 'Neighbour' as a Theological Paradigm for Resolving Conflicts in Africa," *B-PB* 2/7: 2–15.

"Righteousness and Eschatology in Matthew's Gospel: A Critical Reflection," *Indian Theological Studies* 25/3: 213–35. [abstract: *NTA* 33/2 (1989): #589.]

1991 *A Critical Introduction to the Traditions of Jesus* (Enugu, Nigeria: CECTA Publishers).

Onwurah, Emeka

 1987 "Isaiah 14: It's Bearing on African Life and Thought," *Bible Bhashyam* 13: 29–41. [abstract: Holter: #175.]

 1992 "Coarchy: Partnership and Equality in Male Female Relations," *Bible Bhashyam* 18/2: 96–104. [abstract: *NTA* 37 (1993): #1486.]

"The Ethico-Moral Perspective in Nation Building," *AJBS* 7/2: 43–53.

"The Original Sin: A Historico-Theological Reflection on the Fall of Man," *AJBS* 7/1: 9–19.

 1993 "The Sermon on the Mount: The Way of the Cross," *AJBS* 8/1: 36–46.

Onyedika, Chima Raymond O.

 1985 "Sin and Sickness in the New Testament and Among the Igbo: A Comparative Study of Sin-Sickness Relationship in the New Testament and in Igbo Traditional Thought," (S.T.L. thesis, CIWA/Pontifical Urban University, Rome).

Onyeocha, Anthony E.

 1992 *The Most Blessed Eucharist (Celebrating the 2nd Nigeria National Eucharistic Congress—Owerri 1992)* (Aba, Nigeria: Okpala Seminary Publications). [chapter ten: "The Eucharist in the Light of the Bible": 71–89.]

 1994 *The 4th Word of the Cross* (Owerri, Nigeria: Okpala Seminary Publications).

Opeloye, M.O.

 1988 "Predestination and Freewill in the Bible and the Qur'an. A Comparative Appraisal," *Orita* 20/1: 15–34.

O'Reilly, K.

 1988 "The Parable of the Labourers in the Vineyard Matthew 20: 1–16," Ukpong: 19–24.

Osei-Bonsu, Joseph

 1986 "Does 2 Cor. 5:1–10 Teach the Reception of the Resurrection Body at the Moment of Death?" *JSNT* 28: 81–101. [abstract: *NTA* 31/2 (1987): #743.]

 1987 "Anthropological Dualism in the New Testament," *SJT* 40/4: 571–90. [abstract: *NTA* 32/2 (1988): #847.]

"The Intermediate State in the Luke-Acts," *Irish Biblical Studies* 9/3: 115–30. [abstract: *NTA* 32/1 (1988): #159.]

1989 "The Spirit as Agent of Renewal: The New Testament Testimony," *Ecumenical Review* 41/3: 454–60. [abstract: *NTA* 34/1 (1990): #369.]

1990 "The Contextualization of Christianity: Some New Testament Antecedents," *Irish Biblical Studies* 12/3: 129–48. [abstract: *NTA* 35/1 (1991): #347.]

1991 "The Intermediate State in the New Testament," *SJT* 44/2: 169–94.

1994 "A Reflection on Paul's Speech at the Areopagus (Acts 17: 22–32)," (unpublished paper presented to the Bible in Africa Project Glasgow Consultation held on 13th–17th August 1994 at Scotus College, Bearsden, Glasgow, Scotland), typescript 7pp.

Osei-Mensah, Gottfried

1984 "An Interpretation of the Book of Revelation," *Church in Africa Today and Tomorrow: Proceedings of The Association of Evangelicals of Africa and Madagascar 4th General Assembly, Malawi 1981* (Nairobi: AEAM/Evangel Publishing House): 21–51.

1985 *God's Message to the Churches: An exposition of Revelation 1–3* (Achimota, Ghana: African Christian Press).

Osuji, Boniface Anthony

1967 "The Hebrew and Igbo Concept of Religion and Sin Compared in the Light of Biblical and Rabbinic Material," (Doctoral dissertation, Pontifical Urban University, Rome).

Osume, Charles Ereraina

1984 "A Study of Okpe Theophanies and Their Correspondence in the Old Testament," (Ph.D. dissertation, University of Aberdeen).

Osun, C.O.

1992 "Christian Ethics and Morality in Nation-Building: An Update on Nigeria," *AJBS* 7/2: 10–29.

Osunwokeh, Clement I.

1997 *A Study of the Catholic Charismatic Renewal in Nigeria in the Light of 1 Cor. 12, 13 and 14* (Lagos: Mbeyi & Associates (Nig.) Ltd.).

Owan, Kris J.N.

1991 "Biblico-Theological Basis for Church Teaching on Demonology: Substratum for Deliverance Ministry in Nigeria," *AJBS* 6/2: 36–58.

1992 "African Proverbial Wisdom and the Good News of Christ the Wisdom of God," in Brookman-Amissah, et al.: 111–32.

1993 "Contribution of the Catholic Priest to the Material Development of Society: A Biblical and Pastoral Perspective," *ACS* 9/3: 64–78. "Human Promotion in the Light of the Prophet Amos," *AJBS* 8/1: 121–37.

1994 "Manifestations of Wisdom in the Old Testament and in African Religious Traditions," *JIT* 1/1: 54–72.

1995 "The Catholic Priest and the Material Development of Society: Biblical and Pastoral Perspectives," *WAJES* 3/1: 20–33.

"The Magnificat and the Empowerment of the Poor: A Theological Reflection on Lk 1:46–55 in the Context of Contemporary Church Social Teaching on Justice and Peace," *Vidyajyoti Journal of Theological Reflection* 59: 647–62.

1996 "Jesus, Justice and Jn 10:10. Liberation Hermeneutics in the Nigerian Context," *NJOT* 10/1: 18–42.
"Jewish Patterns of Biblical Interpretation: Implications for African Contextual Interpretation of the Bible," *RAT* 20/40: 171–86.
"The Sage, the Theologian and the Liberation of a People. Biblical Thematic Reflections in the Light of Jesus ben Sira," *JIT* 3/2: 109–26; [reprinted in *Vidyajyoti* 61/2 (1997): 95–109. [abstract: *NTA* 42/1 (1998): 649.]

1997 "African Proverbial Wisdom & Biblical Proverbial Wisdom: Wholesome Bedfellows and More," *Bible Bhashyam* 23/3: 151–73. [abstract: *OTA* 22/1 (1999): #310.] Also published as "African Proverbial Wisdom and Biblical Proverbial Wisdom," in *NJOT* 11/1 (1997): 25–48. [abstract: *NTA* 43/1 (1999): #481.]

Owanikin, R.M.
1987 "Colossians 2:18: A Challenge to Some Doctrines in Certain Aladura Churches in Nigeria," *AJBS* 2/1–2: 89–95. [abstract: *NTA* 34/3 (1990): #772.]

Owoh, Gabriel John Obazi
1992 "The Ritual of Circumcision Among the Abakaliki People of Nigeria and the Challenges to Evangelization: A Perspective from Acts 15: 1–21," (M.Th. thesis, CIWA/University of Calabar, Calabar, Nigeria).

Paradza, Bernadette Vonai
1993 *The Four Gospels and Acts* (Gweru, Zimbabwe: Mambo Press).

Parrinder, E. Geoffrey
1958 *The Bible and Polygamy: A Study of Hebrew and Christian Teaching* (London: S.P.C.K.).

Patai, R.
1947 "Hebrew Installation Rites: A Contribution to the Study of Ancient Near Eastern—African Culture Contact," *Hebrew Union College Annual* 20: 143–225. [abstract: Holter: #182.]
1962 "The Ritual Approach to Hebrew—African Culture Contact," *Jewish Social Studies* 24: 86–96. [abstract: Holter: #183.]

Personn, Mch. H.
1956 *Msaidizi Mfupi wa Kuifahamu Biblia Yako: Maneno machache ya Biblia kama tulivyoonyeshwa nayo maana na msingi wa Imani yetu* (Soni, Tanganyika: Vuga Mission Press, 1956).

Peters, Adrian
1961 "Cham and Chanaan," *AFER* 3/3: 199–202.
1964 "St. Paul and Marriage," *AFER* 6/3: 214–24.

Phillips, G.E.
1942 *The Old Testament in the World Church. With Special Reference to the Younger Churches* (London). [abstract: Holter: #185.]

Pinto, Henrique
  1989   "Isaiah 61:1–2a in Liberation Theology," *ACS* 5/2: 11–42.
Phiri, Isabel Apawo
  1997   "Women in the Gospel of Luke: A Woman's Perspective,"
             JCT 3/1: 35–48.
Pluddemann, G.
  1978   "Aspects of the Theology of Exodus in the Old Testament,"
             Lutheran World Federation [Gaborone]: 167–79.
Pobee, John Samuel
  n.d.   "African Theology and the Proclamation of the Gospel in
             Africa Today" *Preparatory Documents for the All Africa Lutheran
             Consultation on Christian Theology and Strategy for Mission 10–18
             April 1980 Monrovia, Liberia* (n.p.: Lutheran World Federation
             Department of Church Cooperation).
  1969   "Mark 15:39. The Cry of the Centurion—A Cry of Defeat"
             pp. 91–102 in E. Bammel, ed. *The Trial of Jesus: Cambridge
             Studies in Honour of Professor C.F.D. Moule* (London: S.C.M.).
  1972   "Morality in the New Testament," *GBT* 4/3: 14–25. [abstract:
             NTA 18/2 (1974): #668.]
  1980–81   "The Skenosis of Christian Worship in Africa," *Studia Liturgica*
             14/1: 37–52.
  1984   "Bible and Human Transformation," *Mission Studies* 1/2: 4–12.
  1985   "The Bible and Human Transformation," *Mission Studies* 2/1:
             67–70.
             "Human Transformation: A Biblical View," *Mission Studies* 2/1:
             5–9.
             "Biblical Studies and Mission (BISAM)," *Mission Studies* 2/1:
             121–23.
             Persecution and Martyrdom in the Theology of Paul JSNT supple-
             ment series, #6 (Sheffield: JSOT). [reviews: M.E. Thrall *Expository
             Times* 97/3 (1985): 88; D. Tiede *CBQ* 48 (1986): 565–66;
             J. Green *Asbury Theological Journal* 42 (1987): 127–29; C.J.A.
             Hickling *Journal of Theological Studies* ns 38/1 (1987): 173–75;
             J.D. Kingsbury *Interpretation* 41/1 (1987): 102–103; M. Greene
             Perspetives in Religious Studies 16 (1989): 169–72; *BookNotes* 4
             (October 1997): #4.35; abstracts: *NTA* 30/1 (1986): 108; *RSR*
             12/2 (1986): 164.]
  1987   *Who are the Poor? The Beatitudes as a Call to Community* Risk Book
             Series, 32 (Geneva: WCC). [reviews: J. Ansaldi *Etudes Théologiques
             et Réligieuses* 63/2 (1988): 321; David Bosch *Missionalia* 16 (1988):
             51; J. Murishwar *Social Action* 38 (1988): 105–106; T. Presler
             Anglican Theological Review 70 (1988): 285–86; N.C. Capulong
             Asia Journal of Theology 3 (1989): 358–61; C. Nessan *Currents in
             Theology and Mission* 16 (1989): 128–29; abstract: *NTA* 32/1
             (1988): 108–109.]
  1988   "Hoping against Hope? A Biblical Perspective," *Mission Studies*
             5/2: 40–54. [reply by J.K. Riches: 55–65.]

"Reports on IAMS Projects and Activities," *Mission Studies* 5/2: 132–48.

1989 "Turning the Cheek: Why Not Retaliate?" *One World* 145: 19–21.

1992 "In Search of Christology in Africa: Some Considerations for Today," Pobee: 9–20.

"No Longer Strangers: An Alternative Community" *One World* 179: 8–9.

Pobee, John Samuel, ed.

1992 *Exploring Afro-Christology* Studies in the Intercultural History of Christianity, 79 (Frankfurt am Main/N.Y.: Peter Lang). [reviews: H.W. Huppenbauer *Zeitschrift fhr Mission* 19/4 (1993): 253–54; John Parratt *IRM* 82/326 (1993): 243–44; C.H. Rever *Missiology* 22 (1994): 119–20.]

Pobee, John Samuel, & Barbel von Wartenberg-Potter, eds

1986 *New Eyes for Reading: Biblical and Theological Reflections by Women from the Third World* (Geneva: WCC). [reviews: D. D'Souza *Bulletin of the Henry Martyn Institute of Islamic Studies* 9 (1986): 91–92; D. Ackermann *Missionalia* 15/2 (1987): 98; J. Bost *Etudes Theologiques et Religieuses* 62/2 (1987): 313–14; Dew Esther Byu *Asia Journal of Theology* 1 (1987): 572–73; D. D'Souza *Sojourners* 16/7 (1987): 41–42; Lucy Loh *Ching Feng* 30/3 (1987): 175–77; A.L.A. Olson *ATJ* 16/1 (1987): 96–97; M. Riley *IBMR* 11/3 (1987): 134–35; E.E. Thackray *Expository Times* 98/12 (1987): 380; Letty Russell *Horizons* 15 (1988): 418; B.B. Zigmund *Critical Review of Books in Religion* 1 (1988): 434–35; D.C. Benjamin *BTB* 20 (1990): 43; Mary Geok Tee Goh *Asia Journal of Theology* 4 (1990): 10–11; T.M. Eugene *Chicago Theological Seminary Register* 81 (1991): 39; abstract: *NTA* 31/3 (1987): 379.]

Polet, J.-Cl.

1983 "Questions sur le Mythe. A propos d'Adam et Eve et d'une Genese Pygmee," *Au Coeur de l'Afrique* 23/3: 177–202.

Poucouta, Paulin

1991 *La Perspective Missionaire de l'Apocalypse Johannique* (Paris: Cerf.).

"Les Communautés Johanniques et le Pouvoir Imperial dans Apocalypse," Amewowo, et al., 1991: 242–264.

1993 "Une Parole Douce et Amere (Ap 10, 8–11)," Association Panafricaine: 245–62.

Preus, Jonathan

1997 "Eating and Drinking Judgement: 1 Corinthians 11:17–34," *TCNN Research Bulletin* 30: 21–27.

Priest, Douglas Dunbar

1989 "The Problem of Animal Sacrifice among Maasai Christians," (Ph.D. dissertation, Fuller Theological Seminary).

Quarshie, B.Y.

1993 "St. Paul and the Contextualization Imperative: the Christian Faith, Religion and Culture," *TJCT* 3/2: 1–16.

Rabemanantsoa, N.
    "Etude Biblique I: Le Livre de Jonas" in Federation Lutherienne
    Mondiale [Antsirabe]: 178–86.
Rabenorolahy, Benjamin
    "Etude Biblique II: Les sept Eglises de l'Apocalypse (Apocalypse
    1:20–3–22)" in Federation Lutherienne Mondiale [Antsirabe]:
    187–91.
Rajuli, Moshe
    1989   "The Jubilee Motif As A Paradigm for Mission. An Exegetical
            and Hermeneutical Study of Luke 4: 16–30" (M.A. thesis, London
            Bible College, London, England).
Ramahatradraibe, Barnabe
    1996   "The Church as Family in the Gospel of Matthew," *Hekima Review*
            14: 33–47.
Ramashapa, J.M.
    1990   "Entering the Church in Africa Through Israel and Paul: A Com-
            parative Look At the Corporate Salvation in the African King
            (Chief) and its Related Meaning to the Church in Africa," *Nederduitse
            Gereformeerde Teologiese Tydskrief* 31: 582–88. [abstract: Holter: #188.]
Randrianarimalala, R.
    1996   "'The Lord is the Spirit,' 2 Cor 3:17a," *Hekima Review* 15: 29–36.
            [abstract: *NTA* 41/2 (1997): #1051.]
Rath, Jos. Th.
    1961   "Die Bemühungen der Patres vom Heiligen Geist um die Bibel,"
            NZM 17: 51–55; reprinted in Beckmann, ed.: 266–70.
Razafijaonimanana, [ ]
    "The Twelve," Lutheran World Federation [Gaborone, 1978]:
    180–85.
Reaume, W.D.
    1997   "Bush Justice in Biblical Perspective," *UMTC—JTS* 2: 43–58.
Reyburn, William
    1960   "The Message of the Old Testament and the African Church-1,"
            PA 7/4: 152–56. [abstract: Holton: #191.]
            "Sickness, Sin, and the Curse: The Old Testament and the African
            Church," *PA* 7: 217–22. [abstract: Holton: #190.]
Riches, John K.
    1988   "Hoping against Hope: Mission towards the End of the Twentieth
            Century. A Response to John Pobee," *Mission Studies* 10, 5/2: 55–65.
Ritchie, Ian D.
    2000   "The Nose Knows: Bodily Knowing in Isaiah 11:3," *JSOT* 87:
            59–73.
Roberts, D.
    1964   "An Exposition of Hebrews 1–4 Part I," *GBT* 2/7: 9–15.
    1965   "An Exposition of Hebrews 1–4 Part II," *GBT* 2/8: 11–16.
Robinson, Philip
    1977   "In Christ—A New Community," Lutheran World Federation
            [Gaborone]: 18–20.

Roeder, Gabriel
  1988 "The Parable of the Great Supper Luke 14:15–24; Matthew 22:
         1–14," Ukpong: 25–34.
Rogers, Robert G.
  1990 "Biblical Images of Peoplehood in African Christianity," *Abstracts:
         American Academy of Religion/Society of Biblical Literature 1990* J.B.
         Wiggins & D.J. Lull, eds (Scholars Press): 162–63.
Rosenkranz, Gerhard, ed.
  1967 *Beitrage zur Biblischen Theologie* Hans-Werner Gensichen, Gerhard
         Rosenkranz, Georg F. Vicedom, eds "Theologische Stimmen
         aus Asien, Afrika und Lateinamerika," Band II (Mhnchen: Chr.
         Kaiser Verlag).
Rowling, F.
  1930 *The Parables for Africans (Part I): Lessons on the Parables of Our Lord
         adapted for African Readers* (London: S.P.C.K.).
  1932 *The Parables for Africans (Part II): Lessons on the Parables of Our Lord
         adapted for African Readers* (London: S.P.C.K.).
Rubinga, Paluku
  1986 "The Concept of God as Father in the Bible and in African
         Religion," Gitari & Benson: 98–118.
Rubombora, Dora
  1998 "Bible Studies to Help Christians for Dealing with Spiritual Prob-
         lems that Result from Occultic Practices" (M.Div. thesis, NEGST).
Ruhamanyi Bisimwa, Deogratias
  1993 "L'universalisme dans le Psaume du Regne 97," Adeso, et al.,
         1993: 40–67.
Ruhindi, Y.K.
  1963 "Philippians 3:10–11: Knowing the Risen Christ," *Ministry* 3/3:
         123–24.
Rupper, Gerold
  1990 "The Missionary Printing Press and the Bible in Tanzania,"
         Amewowo ed.: 108–10.
Rwehumbiza, Rulange K. Philibert
  1988 *Patriarchal and Bantu Cults Compared* Spearhead #103 (Eldoret, Kenya:
         AMECEA Gaba Publications). [abstract: Holter: #197.]
  1991 "Presence and Activity of the Holy Spirit in Johannine Community,"
         Amewowo, et al., 1991: 202–241.
  1994 *Jesus' Baptism: Its Meaning and Significance For Christians Today* Spear-
         head #134 (Eldoret, Kenya: AMECEA Gaba Publications).
Rwito, Joyce Nki
  1984 "Levirate Marriage in the Old Testament and in the African
         Context with Special Reference to North Imenti Division of Meru
         District," (B.D. thesis, St. Paul's United Theological College,
         Limuru, Kenya).
Ryan, C.P.
  1992 "Problems in Christian Moral Leadership in Nigerian Secular
         Society—Biblicism and Fundamentalism," *AJBS* 7/2: 1–9.

Ryan, P.J.
1980   "'Arise, O God!' the Problem of 'Gods' in West Africa," *JRA* 11:
       161–71. [abstract: Holter: #198.]
Saakana, Amon Saba, ed.
1988   *Afrikan Origins of the Major World Religions* (London, United Kingdom:
       Karnak House).
Safo-Kantanka, Osei
1993   *Can a Christian become a Chief? An Examination of Ghanaian Ancestral
       Practices in the Light of the Bible* (Accra: Pentecost Press).
Samwel, Christopher Alfred
1991   "The Old Testament Attitudes to Sickness and Healing in Relation
       to the New Testament," (B.D. thesis, Lutheran Theological Semi-
       nary, Makumira, Tanzania).
Sandblom, Alice
1993   *La Tradition et la Bible Chez la Femme de la CEZ: Influence de l'Anci-
       enne Culture et de la Pensée Biblique dans le Maintien d'une Certaine Con-
       ception de la Femme au sein de la Communauté Evangelique du Zaire*
       Uppsala Studies in Faiths and Ideologies, 2 (Uppsala: Almqvist &
       Wiksell International, 1993). [review: *BookNotes* 1 (March 1996):
       #1.35.]
Sarah, Robert
1988   "Les Aspects Theolgico-Bibliques de la Famille," *Cahiers Bibliques
       Africains* 3/Jan: 4–16.
1989   "Les Actes des Apotres et les Jeunes Églises," *RAT* 13/25: 7–16;
       reprinted as "Les Actes des Apotres—L'Eangile du Saint-Esprit,"
       Amewowo, et al., 1990: 3–19.]
Sarpong, Peter Kwesi
1980   "African Values That Enrich Family Life," *B-PB* 3: 7–11.
Sawyerr, Harry
1959   "Was St Paul a Jewish Missionary?" *Church Quarterly Review* 160/337:
       457–63.
1961   "The Marcan Framework: Some Suggestions for a New Assessment,"
       SJT 14/3: 279–94.
1963   "The Basis of a Theology for Africa," *IRM* 52/207: 266–78.
1964   "Sin and Forgiveness in Africa," *Frontier* 7: 60–63.
1968   *Creative Evangelism: Towards a New Encounter with Africa* (London:
       Lutterworth).
1969   "Sacrifice," Dickson & Ellingworth: 57–82.
1971   "What is African Christian Theology? A Case for Theologica
       Africana," *ATJ* 4: [?] [Republished in J. Parratt, ed. *The Practice
       of Presence: Shorter Writings of Harry Sawyerr* (Grand Rapids: Eerdmans
       1996).]
Schapera, I.
1955   "The Sin of Cain," *Journal of the Anthropological Institute* 85: 33–43;
       reprinted in B. Lang, ed. *Anthropological Approaches to the Old Testament*
       Issues in Religion and Theology, 8 (Philadelphia: Fortress, 1985):
       26–42. [abstract: Holter: #199.]

Schellevis, L.
1993 "Les 'Miracles' dans le Ministere de Jésus," *Flambeau* n.s. 1: 27–37.
Schineller, Peter & Justin S. Ukpong, eds
1982 *Eucharist—Source and Summit of Christian Life: Reflections on the Eucharist in Relation to Christian Life* (Port Harcourt: CIWA publications).
Sebiomo, Francis Adeleke
1992 "Walking by the Spirit: Galatians 5: 16–26 and Its Implications for Yoruba Christians," (M.Th. thesis, CIWA/University of Calabar, Calabar, Nigeria).
Segovia, Fernando F. & Mary Ann Tolbert, eds
1995 *Reading from this Place. Volume 2: Social Location and Biblical Interpretation in Global Perspective* (Minneapolis: Fortress). [abstract: *OTA* 19/3 (1996): #1881.]
Sempore, Sidbe
1993 "Le Noir et le Salut dans le Bible," Adeso, et al., 1993: 17–29.
Senya, Patrick K.
1987 "The Pauline Concept of Justification and Its Relevance in the Context of Ashanti Traditional Religion," (S.T.L. thesis, CIWA/ Pontifical Urban University, Rome).
Senavoe, J.
1998 "Ministry of Women in the Church: An Understanding of Some Prohibitions," *AJET* 17/2: 127–40. [abstract: *NTA* 43/2 (1999): #1224.]
Seynaeve, J.
1977 "Les Citations Scripturaires en Jn. 19, 36–37: Une Preuve en Faveur de la Typologie de l'Agneau Pascal?" *RAT* 1/1: 67–76.
1983 "Le Thème de 'l'heure' dans le Quatrième Évangile," *RAT* 7/13: 29–50.
1985 "La Thème de 'l'heure' dans le Quatrième Évangile (suite)," *RAT* 9/17: 43–58.
Shorter, A.
1978 "Africa's Old Testament," Smith, ed.: 66–68. [abstract: Holter: #203.]
Shorter, A. & J.M. Waliggo, et al., eds
1987 *Towards African Christian Maturity* (Nairobi, Kenya: St. Paul Publi- cations-Africa/Daughters of St. Paul).
Sicard, H. von
1952 *Ngoma Lungundu. Eine afrikanische Bundeslade* Studia Ethnographica Upsaliensia, 5 (Uppsala). [abstract: Holter: #204.]
Sidhom, Swailem
1969 "The Theological Estimate of Man," Dickson & Ellingworth: 83–115.
Sidwaka, Francis Juma Ogeke
1988 "Towards an African Biblical Theology of Death and the Dead with Application for the Abamaraki of Western Kenya" (M.Div. thesis, NIST).
Simbandumwe, Samuel S.
1992 *A Socio-Religious and Political Analysis of the Judeo-Christian Concept of*

Prophetism and Modern Bakongo and Zulu African Prophet Movements (Lewiston, N.Y.: Edwin Mellen). [revision of 1989 University of Edinburgh Doctoral dissertation: "Israel in Two African Prophet Movements."]

Sindima, H.J.
1990 "Moyo: Fullness of Life: A Hermeneutic of the Logos in John's Prologue," *ACS* 6/4: 50–62.

Sisay Desalegn Berhe
1995 "Interpretation of Wealth and Poverty in Luke's Gospel with Special Reference to the Christian Elements in Ethiopian Poverty" (M.Th. thesis, London Bible College, London, England).

Skweres, D.E.
1979 "The Child in the Bible," *B-PB* 1: 19–24.

Solanke, S. Kolawole
1992 *The Suffering of the Innocent: A Study in the Beliefs of the Yoruba and the Hebrews* (Ibadan: Daystar Press). [review: Clare Fuller in *UMTC—JTS* 2: 79–81.]

Souza, I. de and J. Camus
1984 "Notion et Réalité de la Famille en Afrique et dans la Bible," *Savanes-Forets* 3: 131–64.

Spindler, M.R.
1981 "Politieke lezing van de Bijbel im Madagascar," *Schrift* 78: 203–13. [abstract: Holter: #208.]

Steemers, J.C.
1964 "The Ministry in the New Testament," *GBT* 2/6: 17–24.

Sugirtharajah, R.S., ed.
1995 *Voices from the Margin: Interpreting the Bible in the Third World* 2nd ed. (London and Maryknoll: S.P.C.K. and Orbis [1991]). [reviews: A. Laffey *CBQ* 54 (1992): 828–29; A.C. Leder *Calvin Theological Journal* 27 (1992): 177–78; C. Rowland *Theology* 95 (1992): 45–46; J. Penney *Epworth Review* 19 (1992): 117–18; K.M. Ruppar *Military Chaplain's Review* (1992): 114–15; G. West *Modern Theology* 8 (1992): 315–17; Anon. *Irenikon* 66/4 (1993): 584; M.D. Carroll R. *Themilios* 19 (1993): 31; J. Dupuis *Gregorianum* 74/3 (1993): 566–67; C.A.J. Pillai *Missiology* 21 (1993): 365–66; D. Soesilo *Interpretation* 48 (1994): 220; Jeffrey Kah-Jin Kuan *Voices* 19/1 (1996): 242–46; T. Mackenzie *Pacific Journal of Theology* 15 (1996): 115–16; J.C. Okoye *CBQ* 59/4 (1997): 815–16; abstracts: *NTA* 36/1 (1992): 106; *RSR* 19/4 (1993): 330; *RSR* 20/3 (1996): 239.]

Sundermeier, Theo
1987 "The Cross in African Interpretation," *ATJ* 16/2: 136–44.

Swidler, L.
1971 "Jesus and His Encounter with Women," *AFER* 13: 290–300.

Tabi, Emmanuel Gansa
1987 "The Healing Ministry of Jesus in the Synoptic Gospels: Its Pastoral Implications for Contemporary Church with Specific Reference

to the Akan of Ghana," (S.T.L. thesis, CIWA/Pontifical Urban University, Rome).

Taiwo, M.O.
1991 "Servant Role in Leadership: A Solution to the Leadership Problem in Nigeria," *AJBS* 6/1: 94–104.

Tanko, Peter B.
1985 "The Kaje Marriage Cutom and Christian Marriage in the Light of Eph 5: 21–33," (S.T.L. thesis, CIWA/Pontifical Urban University, Rome).

Tappa, Louise K.
1986 "God in Man's Image," Pobee & Wartenberg-Potter: 101–106.
1990 "An African Woman's Reflection on the Christ Event," *Voices from the Third World* 11/2 (1988): 76–83; reprinted as "The Christ-Event from the Viewpoint of African Women II: A Protestant Perspective," Fabella & and Oduyoye: 30–35.]

Tarr, Del
1994 *Double Image: Biblical Insights from African Parables* (Mahwah, N.Y.: Paulist Press).

Taylor, John B., ed.
1976 *Primal World Views: Christian Dialogue with Traditional Thought Forms* (Ibadan: Daystar Press).

The Theological Advisory Group (TAG)
1994 *A Biblical Approach to Marriage and Family in Africa* TAG Theological Reflections #5 (Machakos, Kenya: Theological Advisory Group (TAG), Scott Theological College).

Thibanda Mukenji, M.
1980 "Le Christianisme comme Religion Historique: Rapport de Carrefour," Atal sa Angang, et al., eds: 245–46.

Thomas, J.C.
1978 "Presuppositions without Exegesis," *Orita* 12/2: 96–107.

Thompson, Prince E.S.
1967 "Die Damonen in der biblischen Theologie," Rosenkranz: 148–63.
1971 "Yahwist Creation Story," *Vetus Testamentum* 21: 197–208.
1974 "The Anatomy of Sacrifice: A Preliminary Investigation," Glasswell & Fashole-Luke: 19–35. [abstract: Holter: #212.]

Thomsen, Mark W.
1965 *Introducing New Testament Theology* 2nd edition (Ibadan: Daystar).

Torrend, J.
1910 "Likenesses of Moses' Story in the Central Africa Folk-lore," *Anthropos* 5: 54–70. [abstract: Holter: #214.]

Tossou, Raphael Kossi Ametonu
1977 "La Martyria dans l'Apocalypse de Saint-Jean. Temoignage Divin—Temoinage Humain," (Doctoral dissertation, Pontifical Urban University, Rome).
1981 "Parole de Dieu et Théologie Africaine," *Saanes-Forets* 3: 85–98.

Tshibinkufua Kabundi
1984 "Une Comparison Biblique dans 'sans tam-tam' de Henri Lopes," *CRA* 18/36: 229–43.
Tshipungu, J.
1969 "Le Coeur chez l'homme Biblique et l'homme Tshokwe," *OP* 124: 181–87.
Tshisungu Balekelayi, Daniel
1993 "Message de l'Epitre à Philemon et ses Implications pour les Eglises en Afrique Aujourd'hui," *Flambeau* n.s 1: 47–53.
Tundu-Kialu, Gertrude
1990 "Human Sexuality (Genesis 1:26–31; John 2:1–12; Matthew 19:10–12)," Oduyoye & Kanyoro: 80–83.
Tzabedze, Joyce
1990 "Women in the Church (1 Tim. 2:8–15, Eph. 5:22)," Oduyoye & Kanyoro: 76–79.
Udechukwu, Basil I.
1988 "Hospitality in 3 John 5–8 and in Igbo Culture," (S.T.L. thesis, CIWA/Pontifical Urban University, Rome).
Udo, M.E.
1992 "The Challenges of Leadership in Nation Building: A Christian View," *AJBS* 7/2: 139–49.
Udoette, Donatus
1991 "The Flesh and the Spirit in Galatians 5: 16–26" (Master's thesis; Pontifical Urban University, Rome).
1993 *Prophecy and Tongues: A Pauline Theology of Charismata for Service in the Church [1 Cor 14]* (Rome: Pontifical Urban University). [Theological and pastoral implications of this thesis for the life of the Catholic community in Nigeria are developed by Udoette in a separate article: "Towards a Theology of Charismata for the Nigerian Church" *Encounter: A Journal of African Life and Religion* 2 (1993): 16–28.]
Ugobeze, John
1995 "To Heal as Jesus Healed: A Case for the Catholic Priest," Obinwa & Obilor, eds: 74–83.
Ugwueze, Oko Francis
1976 "Igbo Proverbs and Biblical Proverbs," (Doctoral dissertation, Pontifical Urban University, Rome).
Uhlin, Herbert
1946 *Masomo ya Injili kama Ilivyoandikwa na Mwinjilisti Marko* Lushoto, Tanganyika: Vuga Lutheran Mission Press).
1953 *Biblia Ilivyoandikwa* (Makanisa ya Kilutheri ya Tanganyika).
1954 *Maelezo ya Agano Jipya: Ufunuo* (Makanisa ya Kilutheri ya Tanganyika).
Uko, Ignatius
1995 "Pastoral Perspective on the Use of the Bible," Obinwa & Obilor, eds: 84–95.
Ukpong, Justin S.
1981 "Background to the New Testament Concept and Language of

Resurrection," Michael Samuel, ed. *The Life and Ministry of Jesus in the Gospels* (London: Campbell Publishers): 120–28.

"Christian Worship: A Perspective from Matthew's Gospel," Samuel, op. cit.: 29–40.

"A Critical Examination of Willi Marxen's Resurrection Hypothesis," Samuel, op. cit.: 158–66.

"The Significance of Jesus' Passion for Suffering Humanity," Samuel, op. cit.: 107–14.

1982   "The Eucharist: The Christian Passover," in Schineller & Ukpong: 3–11. [reprinted in *Proclaiming the Kingdom*, 1993: 75–85.]

1983   "Redemption. A Biblical Hermeneutical Reflection," *Catholic Witness* 4: 14–26. [reprinted in *Proclaiming the Kingdom*, 1993: 64–74.)

1985   "Contemporary Theological Models of Mission: Analysis and Critique," *AFER* 27/3: 162–71.

1987   *Sacrifice: African and Biblical. A Comparative Study of Ibibio and Levitical Sacrifices* (Rome: Urbaniana University Press).

1988   "The Christian Laity in Nigerian Politics," *NJOT* 1/2: 39–46

"The Letter to the Galatians and the Problem of Cultural Pluralism in Christianity," *RAT* 12: 67–77; reprinted in *Proclaiming the Kingdom*, 1993: 16–27.

"Mission in the Acts of the Apostles: From the Perspective of the Evangelized," *ATJ* 17/1: 72–88; a longer version appears as "Mission in Acts of the Apostles: A Study from the perspective of the Evangelized," in *RAT* 13/26 (1989): 171–207; also published in Amewowo, et al., 1990: 165–96; and in *Proclaiming the Kingdom*, 1993: 125–48. [abstract: *NTA* 32/3 (1988): #1200.]

"The Nature and Function of Parable," Ukpong: 3–11; reprinted in *Proclaiming the Kingdom*, 1993: 86–94.

"The Parable of the Talents/Pounds (Matt. 25:14–30; Lk 19:12–27)," Ukpong: 59–68; reprinted in *Proclaiming the Kingdom*, 1993: 95–104.

1989   "Jesus' Prayer for his Followers (Jn. 17) in Mission Perspective," *ATJ* 18/1: 49–60; reprinted in *Proclaiming the Kingdom*, 1993: 114–24. [abstract: *NTA* 34/1 (1990): #218.]

"Pluralism and the Problem of the Discernment of Spirits," *Ecumenical Review* 41/3: 416–25; reprinted in *Proclaiming the Kingdom*, 1993: 3–15.

1990   "Charismatic Gifts and Pastoral Ministry in New Testament Perspective," Peter Thompson, ed. *Christian Witness in Contemporary Society* (London: Campbell Publishers): 129–40.

"Jesus and the Exercise of Authority," Thompson, op. cit.: 104–15.

"The Political Dimension of Jesus' Ministry—Implications for Evangelization," Thompson, op. cit.: 40–54.

"The Poor and the Mission of the Church in Africa," Thompson, op. cit.: 11–28.

1992   "Christian Mission and the Recreation of the Earth in Power and Faith: A Biblical-Christological Perspective," *Mission Studies* 9/2: 134–47.

"The Immanuel Christology of Matthew 25:31–46 in African Context," Pobee: 55–64; reprinted in *Proclaiming the Kingdom*, 1993: 55–63.

"Inter-religious Dialogue: A Biblical Perspective," Ukpong & Okure, et al.: 42–51; reprinted in *Proclaiming the Kingdom*, 1993: 28–42.

"Inculturation and Evangelization: Biblical Foundations for Inculturation," Brookman-Amissah, et al., eds: 9–19.

1993   "Biblical Perspectives on Human Work and Creation," *Proclaiming the Kingdom*, 1993: 105–13.

"Charisms and Church Authority: A New Testament Perspective," CATHAN, 1993: 26–38.

"Creation Nouvelle. Perspectives Bibliques et Christologiques," *Spiritus* 34/131 (1993): 149–60. [abstract: *NTA* 38/1 (1994): #452.]

"Jesus' Prophetic Ministry and Its Challenge to Christian Ministry," *Proclaiming the Kingdom*, 1993: 43–55.

Proclaiming the Kingdom: Essays in Contextual New Testament Studies (Port Harcourt: CIWA Publications).

"Proclaiming the Kingdom of God in Africa Today," *Proclaiming the Kingdom*, 1993: 149–58.

"Review of [African Synod] 'Lineamenta' on Proclamation of the Good News," Ukpong, et al., 1993: 160–66.

1994   "Option for the Poor: A Modern Challenge for Church in Africa: Poverty and its Effects on People," *AFER* 36/6: 350–65.

1995   "The Problem of the Gentile Mission in Matthew's Gospel," *Vidyajyoti* 59/7: 437–48. [abstract: *NTA* 40/2 (1996): #809.]

"Tribute to Caesar, Mark 12: 13–17 (Matthew 22:15–22; Luke 20:20–26)," *Bible Bhashyam* 21/3: 147–166. [abstract: *NTA* 40/3 (1996): #1485.]

"The Political Dimension of Jesus' Ministry: Implications for Evangelization in Africa," *WAJES* 3/1: 1–10.

1996   "Jesus and the Exercise of Authority," *ACS* 12/3: 1–16. [abstract: *NTA* 41/2 (1997): #852.]

"The Parable of the Shrewd Manager (Luke 16:1–13): An Essay in Inculturation Biblical Hermeneutic," *Semeia* 73: 189 210. [abstract: *NTA* 42/1 (1998): #272.]

Ukpong, Justin S., ed.

1988   *Gospel Parables in African Context* (Port Harcourt: CIWA Press).

Ukpong, Justin S. & Asahu-Ejere

1988   "The Letter to the Galatians and the Problem of Cultural Pluralism in Christianity," *RAT* 12/23–24: 67–77. [abstract: *NTA* 33/3 (1989): 1276.]

Ukpong, Justin S., Teresa Okure, John E. Anyanwu, Godwin C. Okeke, Anacletus N. Odoemene, eds

1992   *Evangelization in Africa in the Third Millenium: Challenges and Prospects. Proceedings of the First Theology Week of the Catholic Institute of West Africa Port Harcourt, Nigeria, May 6–11, 1990* (Port Harcourt, Nigeria: CIWA Press, 1992).

1993   *The Church in Africa and the Special African Synod: Proceedings of the Second Theology Week of the Catholic Institute of West Africa, Port Harcourt, March 4–8, 1991* (Port Harcourt, Nigeria: CIWA Press).

Uloko Okulungu
1982   "La Formation Religieuse Traditionnelle de l'Enfant Tetela du Sankaru Comparee aux Textes Veterotestamentaires," Memoire de Licence en Theologie, Kinshasa, Facultes de Theologie Protestante au Zaire).

Umeagudosa, Margaret Azuka
1990   "Pauline Teaching on Women: its Relevance to the Role of Christian Women in the Nigerian in the Nigerian Ecclesiastical Context,' (Ph.D. dissertation, University of Nigeria, Nsukka).
1992   "An Exegetical Analysis of Women Evangelists in the Bible," Umeagudoso & Edet (1992): [?]
        "Power, Empowerment and Cultural Acquiescence: Biblical Expositions," Umeagudosa & Edet (1992): [?]
        "St. Paul's Injunctions to Widows in 1 Cor. 7," Edet & Dipe (1992): [?].
        "Women as Prophets: Acts 21:9, Biblical Exegesis," Edet & Dipe (1992): [?]; also published as "Women as Prophets (Acts 21:9): An Exegetical Analysis," Adeso, et al., 1993: 228–44.
1996   "The Healing of the Gerasene Demoniac From a Specifically African Perspective," *ACS* 12/4: 30–37; originally presented at the Bible in Africa Project Glasgow Consultation held on 13th–17th August 1994 at Scotus College, Bearsden, Glasgow, Scotland), 15pp.

Umeagudosa, Margaret Azuka & Rosemary N. Edet, eds
1992   *Women Development is Human Development: Biblical Expositions* (Ibadan: Daystar).

Umoh, Camillus R.
1991   "Paul's Response to Idolatry in 1 Cor 10:14–22 and Its Implications for Annang Christians of Nigeria," (M.Th. thesis, CIWA/ University of Calabar, Calabar, Nigeria).

Umorem, Anthony
1993   "Being Born Again: An Interpretation of Jn. 3:3, in relation to Christian Religious Experiences," CATHAN, 1993: 125–32.

Uzueze, Francis O.
1976   "Igbo Proverbs and Biblical Proverbs: Comparative and Thematic Research," (unpublished doctoral dissertation, Rome).

van der Beken, Alain
1982   *Les Proverbes Yaka au Service de l'Annonce de l'Evangile* Studia Instituti Missiologici Societas Verbi Divini, n. 31 (S. Augustin: Steyler).

van Rheenen, Gailyn
1993   "Cultural Conceptions of Power in Biblical Perspective," *Missiology: An International Review* 21/1: 41–53.

Vonck, Pol
1981   *The Parables: Stories for Re-Telling* Spearhead #66 (Eldoret, Kenya: AMECEA Gaba publications).

1983   "An Adult Christ at Christmas: The Christmas Gospels," Hearne: 4–21.

1984   "All Authority Comes from God: Rom 13:1–7—A Tricky Text about Obedience to Political Power," *AFER* 26/6: 338–47.

1985   "Imagining the Unimaginable: Biblical Rootage of Art," *AFER* 27/5: 260–67.

1990   *Understanding 42 Gospel Parables* Spearhead #110–11 (Eldoret, Kenya: AMECEA Gaba publications).

Wabukala, Eliud
1988   "The Idea of Hanging on a Tree among the Babukusu People of Kenya & Implications for the Teaching of the Message of the Crucifixion of Jesus Christ," (B.D. thesis, St. Paul's United Theological College, Limuru, Kenya).

1994   "Crisis in the African Understanding of Sin: An Interaction of Biblical Faith and the Traditional Religion of the Babukusu," (Master's thesis, Wycliffe College, University of Toronto); especially chapter 4, "Sin in the Bible," 82–95.

Wachege, P.N.
1992   *Jesus Christ Our 'Muthamaki' (Ideal Elder): An African Christological Study Based on the 'Agikuyu' Understanding of Elder* (Nairobi, Kenya: Phoenix Publishers, 1992); especially chapter 4, "Jesus' 'Uthamaki' (Ideal Elderhood) in the Bible." [review: E. Wendland *AJET* 14/2 (1995): 113–23.]

Wagner, Gunter
1984   "Paul and the Apostolic Faith," *ATJ* 13/2: 115–35.

Waigwa, Solomon W.
1993   "Pauline Pneumatology and its Relevance to the Akorino Church," (B.D. thesis, St. Paul's United Theological College, Limuru, Kenya).

Waliggo, J.M.
1990   "Acts of the Apostles and a Hundred Years of Evangelization in Africa," Amewowo, et al., 1990: 25–45.

1997   "Bible and Chatechism [sic] in Uganda," Kinoti & Waliggo: 179–95.

Walls, Andrew F.
1996   "Romans One and the Modern Missionary Movement," *The Missionary Movement in Christian History: Studies in the Transmission of Faith* (Edinburgh: T & T Clark/Maryknoll: Orbis): 55–67. [originally published as "The First Chapter of Romans and the Modern Missionary Movement," in W.W. Gasque and R.P. Martin, eds *Apostolic History and the Gospel* (Grand Rapids: Eerdmans/Exeter: Paternoster, 1971).]

Wanamaker, Charles A.
1994   "Towards the Development of an Ancestor Christology in Africa," *Abstracts: American Academy of Religion/Society of Biblical Literature 1994* (Scholars Press, 1994): 348.

1997   "Jesus the Ancestor: Reading the Story of Jesus From An African

Christian Perspective," *Scriptura* 62; 281–98. [abstract: *NTA* 42/2 (1998): 805.]

Wangoya, Sange
  1990   "Wisdom and Law: Similarities between Luo Traditions and the Hebrew Scriptures," (M.Rel. thesis, Wycliffe College, Toronto School of Theology).

Wambutda, Daniel
  1976   "Bible Studies: 'Man,' 'Community,' 'Healing,'" Taylor, ed.: 29–41.
  1979   "Bible Knowledge Teachers and Politics in Nigeria," *Source* [?]: 25–36.
          "Monogamy and Polygamy: Biblical Investigation with Particular Reference to Africa," *WAR* 18: 70–91.
  1984   "Critical Apparatus and Bible Versions," *Religions* 9: 20–31.
  1985   "The Work of the Holy Spirit and Mission as Reflected Specially in the Old Testament," *Life in the Spirit* (Grand Rapids: Zondervan).
  1986   "Rationalisation and the Ascendancy of Yahweh in the Old Testament," Gitari & Benson: 1–17.
  1987   "'Hebrewisms of West Africa': An Ongoing Search in the Correlations Between the Old Testament and African Weltanschauung," *OJOT* 2: 33–41. [abstract: Holter: #223.]
  1991   "Leadership and Biblical Studies," *AJBS* 6/1: 16–26.
  1992   "Biblical Perspectives of Ethics and Morality in Nation Building: A Keynot Address," *AJBS* 7/2: x–xii.
  1993   "The Holy Spirit and Missions as reflected in the Old Testament," *AJBS* 8/1: 1–11.

Warmoes, P.
  1978   "Israel 'crut' en Yahve," Facultes Catholiques de Kinshasa, 1978: 84–85.

Waruta, Douglas W.
  1989   "Who is Jesus Christ for Africans Today? Prophet, Priest, Potentate," *Jesus in African Christianity: Experimentation and Diversity in African Christology* J.N.K. Mugambi & Laurenti Magesa, eds (Nairobi, Kenya: Initiatives): 40–53.

Weber, Hans-Ruedi
  1966   "Trustees of the Universe: Bible Studies on the Ministry of the Laity," *Ministry* 7/1: 3–8.
  1993   "The Bible and Oral Tradition," Olupona & Nyang: 165–75.

Welch, Eileen
  1980   *Jeremiah* (Nairobi: Uzima Press).

Welshman, F.H.
  1974   "Psalm 91 in Relation to A Malawian Cultural Background," *JTSA* 8: 24–30. [abstract: Holter: #224.]
  1976   "A Study of Psalm 72 in Relation to A Malawian Cultural Background," *Biblical Theology* 26/2: 25–36. [abstract: Holter: #225.]

Werblowsky, R.J.Z.
  1993   "Africa and Judaism: Retrospect, Problems, and Prospects," J.K.

Olupona & S.S. Nyang, eds *Religious Plurality in Africa: Essays in Honour of John S. Mbiti* (Berlin: Walter de Gruyter): 311–16. [abstract: Holter: #227.]

Willenge, Bas
  1989   "Bible et Liberation: Une Perspective Biblique sur la Question de la Violence," *Select* 22: 62–79.

Williams, David and Bridget
  1982   *The Gospel of Matthew* Bible Knowledge for the West African School Certificate (London: Collins).

Williams, Joseph John
  1930   *Hebrewisms of West Africa: From Nile to Niger with the Jews* (New York: Lincoln MacVeach, 1931/The Dial Press, 1967). [abstract: Holter: #230.]

Windibiziri, David
  1989   "Matthew 9: 35–38," Lutheran World Federation [Yaounde]: 228–231.

Wirisy, Wilfred Tatah
  1995   "The Influence of African Traditional Religions on Biblical Christology: An Evaluation of Emerging Christologies in Sub-Sahara Africa," (Ph.D. dissertation, Westminster Theological Seminary).

Workshop Report
  1993   "The Holy Spirit in the New Testament," in Nebechukwu: 44–46.

Wright, G.D.
  1986   "On Saints and Suffering: A Reconsideration of the Message and Meaning of Philippians," *OJOT* 1: 41–45.

Yamsat, Pandang
  1992   "Ekklesia as Partnership: Paul and Threats to Koinonia in 1 Corinthians," (Doctoral dissertation, University of Sheffield).
  1997   "The Authenticity of the Pauline Thanksgiving in 1 Corinthians 1:4–9," *TCNN Research Bulletin* 30: 4–20.
           Church Discipline in the New Testament (Bukuru, Nigeria: Biblical Studies Foundation/TCNN Publications).
           Ikklisiya da Siyasa Bisa ga Koyarwa Littafi Mai Tsarki (Bukuru: Biblical Studies Foundation/TCNN Publications).
           Partners Not Rivals, Vol. 1: A Study of 1 Corinthians 1–6 (Bukuru, Nigeria: TCNN Publications).
           Yan'uwa da Abokan Aiki ba Abokan Gaba ba: Fassarar 1 Korintiyawa (Bukuru: Biblical Studies Foundation/TCNN Publications).

Yeboah, Abena Fosuah
  1992   "Circumcision in the Old Testament: A Study of Theory and Practice" (M.Th. thesis, University of Aberdeen, Scotland).

Yide, S.O. & T.G. Groenewegen
  1984   *Luke's Gospel and its Relevance for Africa Today* (Nairobi: Longman Kenya).

Yohanna, Nathan
  1995   *Is the Bible a Legal Instrument?* (Lagos, Nigeria: n.p.).

Yorke, Gosnell
  1993 "1 Corinthians 13:1 Revisited: Some Afro-liturgical and Missio-logical Implications," *Missionalia* 26/3: 378–91. [*NTA* 43/3 (1999): #1828.]
Yri, Norvald
  1987 "I Believe in the Biblical-Historical Jesus," *EAJET* 6/1: 23–32. [published the same year in Kalugila & Stevenson: 18–29.]

5. *Bible Translation in Africa*

Abegunde, Solomon Oladeji
  1987 "The Forms and Functions of Some Channel-Checking Devices in Two West African Languages," *UBS Bulletin* 148/149: 96–104.
  1991 "Curses and Blessings in Genesis in the Light of the Extension of Personality," *BT* 42/2: 242–47. [abstract: Holter: #008.]
Adamo, David T.
  1984 "Translating Hebrew Old Testament Book Titles into the Yoruba Language," *BT* 35/4: 418–24. [abstract: Holter: #012.]
Adjekum, Grace
  1989 "Beyond Literacy: Functional Equivalence for Scripture Use in Ghana" (M.A. thesis, Fuller Theological Seminary).
Akou, Mateso
  1991 "An Examination of Progress of the New Testament Transla-tions into Vernacular Languages of Zaire from 1891–1990" (M.Th. thesis, NEGST).
Alexander, J.M.
  1962 "The Effects of the Translation of the Bible in Efik on the Minds, Culture and Life of the Efik People and their Neighbours," *UBS Bulletin* 51: 118–20.
All Africa Conference on Christian Literature and Audio-Visual Communi-cation
  1962 "Literature in Africa," *BT* 13/4: 225–26.
Amegadzi, E.
  1990 "The Ewe Bible Translation Project: An Interconfessional Ex-perience," Amewowo, ed.: 50–52.
Amukobole, Micah
  1990 "The Bible Translation: A Challenge in the New Evangelization of Africa," Amewowo, ed.: 39–44.
Angogo, Rachael M. (cf. 'Kanyoro')
  1982 "Dialect Problems and Bible Translation: A Case Study of a Union Version," *BT* 33/1: 127–34.
Anon.
  1966 "Bible Society Work in Africa," *UBS Bulletin* 66: 51–58.
  1968 "Africa—a Bible Society Survey," *UBS Bulletin* 74: 52–67.
         "Scripture Distribution in Africa," *UBS Bulletin* 74: 75–78.

1985   "La Bible Malgache fete ses 150 ans," *Journal des Missions Evangeliques* 160/4: 159–63.

1994   *150 Years of Kiswahili Bible Translation* (Dodoma: Bible Society of Tanzania/Nairobi: Bible Society of Kenya). [I was informed orally by the translators in the Nairobi United Bible Society office that "Bible Translation and Some of its Principle," (pp. 1–8) was written by A.O. Mojola, "The History of Swahili Translations," (pp. 9–14) by L. Kalugila, and "Assessment and Comparison of Bible Translations," (pp. 15–21) by P. Renju.]

Ansre, Gilbert
    1988   "To Unify of Dialectize? Some Sociolinguistic Psycholinguistic Factors in Language Development for Bible Translation," Stine: 187–206.

    1995   "The Crucial Role of Oral-Scripture: Focus Africa," *International Journal of Frontier Missions* 12: 65–68.

Appleby, Lee
    1955   "Luyia Old Testament Translation, Part I," *BT* 6/4: 180–84.
    1956   "Luyia Old Testament Translation, Part II," *BT* 7/1: 25–30; "Luyia Old Testament Translation, Part III," *BT* 7/2: 85–90; "Luyia Old Testament Translation, Part IV," *BT* 7/3: 101–103. [abstract of all four articles above: Holter: #035.]

Ashley, Lynn V.D.
    1952   "The Bible in Ethiopia," *UBS Bulletin* 10: 9–13.
    1953   "A Neglected Corner of Africa," *UBS Bulletin* 16: 29–30. [Somalia]

Awoniyi, Joel
    1989   *The Story of the Yoruba Bible* (Ibadan, Nigeria: Daystar Press).

Badnock, W.J.
    1957   "Bible Translation Work in Africa Today," *UBS Bulletin* 32: 160–64.

Barlow, A.R.
    1952   "Some Problems of Translation in Kikuyu," *BT* 3/1: 29–33.

Barnwell, Katharine
    1989   "Report on the Africa Area Old Testament Seminar," *Notes on Translation* 3/2: 1–4.

Barrett, David B.
    1967   "The African Independent Churches and the Bible," *UBS Bulletin* 72: 184–92.

    1968   *Schism and Renewal in Africa: An Analysis of Six Thousand Contemporary Religious Movements* (Nairobi, Kenya: Oxford University Press); especially the section entitled "Vernacular Scriptures": 127–34.

    1982   "The Spread of the Bible and the Growth of the Church in Africa," *UBS Bulletin* 128/129: 5–15.

Beardslee, H.M.
    1970   "Distribution and Selections in Africa," *UBS Bulletin* 84: 197–202.

Beck, H.
    1960   "Problems of Orthography and Word Division in East African Vernacular Bantu Languages," *BT* 11/4: 153–61.

Bedford, Frank J.
1954   *The Bible in East Africa* (London: The British and Foreign Bible Society).
1955   "The Bible in East Africa," *UBS Bulletin* 23: 7–10.
1959   "Translation Work in Equitorial and Central Africa," *UBS Bulletin* 39: 112–16.
1963   "Opportunities for Distribution in Africa," *UBS Bulletin* 53: 7–9.
1968   "Looking Ahead in Africa," *UBS Bulletin* 74: 68–72.
Bediako, Kwame
1996   "Epilogue," Schaaf: 243–54.
Beecher, Leonard
1964   "Christian Terminology in the Vocabulary of an Animist Society," *BT* 15/3: 117–27.
Bessem, J.
1962   "Scripture Translations in East Africa," *AFER* 4/3: 201–11.
Blois, K. de
1985   "Metaphor in Common Language Translation of Joel," *BT* 36/2: 208–16. [abstract: Holter: #041.]
Bontinck, Fr.
1978   "Donzwau M.D. Nlemvo (1871–1938) et la Bible Kikongo," *RAT* 2/3: 5–32.
Booth, M.W.
1963   "African Problems," *UBS Bulletin* 53: 10–11.
Brown, Mildred
1960   "The Lwo Bible," *BT* 11/1: 31–42.
Browne, George
1859   *The History of the British and Foreign Bible Society from its institution in 1804, to the close of its Jubilee in 1854* 2 vols. (London: Bagster and Sons).
Bruns, P.C.
1985   "Some Problems Encountered in Translating the Book of Joel Into the Bokyi Language," *BT* 36/2: 241–43. [abstract: Holter: #044.]
Buhlmann, Walbert
1962   "Die heilige Schrift im Swahili-Sprach-gebiet," *NZM* 18: 117–26; reprinted in Beckmann, ed.: 279–88.
Bukas-Yakabuul, B.
1989   "Comment Traduire les Noms Divins en Kanyok," *CTB* 12: 3–11.
1996   "Etude de Matthieu 2.16," *CTB* 25: 3–7.
Burmeister, J.L.
1978   "Traduction de la Bible en Afrique Aujourd'hui," *Afrique et Parole* 53: 23–26.
Busia, K.A.
1968   "The Church and Social Change," *UBS Bulletin* 74: 81–83.
Canton, W.
1904–10   *History of the British and Foriegn Bible Society* 5 vols. (London: John Murray).

Carle, H.
  1983   "La Traduction Lomongo de la Bible," *RAT* 7/13: 83–84.
Casler, Herbert W.
  1968   "The Future in Africa: The Answer is Training," *UBS Bulletin* 76:
         188–89.
Cook, C.L.
  1955   "Languages in the Southern Provinces of the Sudan," *BT* 6/3:
         122–27.
Coldham, Geraldine E.
  1966   *African Scriptures: A Bibliography of Scriptures in African Languages. Volume
         1: Acholi—Mousgoum* (London: The British and Foreign Bible
         Society).
         *African Scriptures: A Bibliography of Scriptures in African Languages. Volume
         2: Mpama—Zulu. Indexes.* (London: The British and Foreign Bible
         Society).
Combrink, H.J.B.
  1996   "Translating or Transforming—Receiving Matthew in Africa,"
         Scriptura 58: 273–84. [abstract: *NTA* 41/1 (1997): #187.]
Cosmao, V., et al.
  1969   *Afrique et Parole. Etudes et Enquetes sur la Traduction de la Parole de
         Dieu dans les Langues Negro-Africaines* (Paris: Presence Africaine).
Dahunsi, Emanuel A.
  1972   "The Problem of Translating the Bible Into African Languages,"
         Mveng & Werblowsky: 117–120. [abstract: Holter: #059.]
Dammann, Ernst
  1954   "The Translation of Biblical and Christian Personal Names into
         Swahili," *BT* 5/2: 80–84.
  1960   "Some Problems of Translating the Bible into African Languages,"
         GBT 1/8: 29–38.
  1961   "Some Problems of Translating the Bible into African Languages—
         Part II," *GBT* 1/9 (1961): 1–6.
Dapila, N. Fabian
  1998   "The Need for Indigenization of Bible Translations for African
         Christians," *AFER* 40/1: 21–43.
Diagouraga, Elsbeth
  1995   "Parole de Vie: Parole de Dieu pour tous?" *CTB* 23: 3–9.
Dion, G.-M.
  1968   "Documents pour une Nouvelle Traduction en Kinyarwanda du
         'Notre Pere,'" *TPRB* 8: 136.
         "La Bible en Kirundi," *TPRB* 8: 136.
  1991   "La Bible en Kinyarwanda," *Dialogue* 148 (1991): 65–83.
Doke, C.M.
  1954   "The Concept of Hope among the Bantu," *BT* 5/1: 9–19.
  1956   "The Points of the Compass in Bantu Languages," *BT* 7/3: 104–13.
  1957   "De Certaines Difficultés dans la Traduction de la Bible en une
         Langue Bantou," *Scientia* 92: 111–17.
  1958   "Scripture Translation into Bantu Languages," *AfSt* 17: 82–99.

"Some Difficulties in Bible Translation into a Bantu Language,"
BT 9/2: 57–62.

1966 "The Translation of 'The Holy Spirit' in Bantu Languages," *BT*
17/1: 32–38.

Duitsman, J.
1982 "A Plus for Plurals in Writing Liberian Krahn," *BT* 33/2: 235–38.

Dwight, Henry Otis
1916 *The Centennial History of the American Bible Society* (New York:
Macmillan).

Edmonds, P.
1980 "The New Shona Bible," *B-PB* 3: 22–24.

Ellington, John
1977 "Translator's Nuisance: Chapter and Verse Division in the Bible"
Practical Papers for the Bible Translator 28/2: 207–13.
1978 "Translating the Old Testament Months into Zairian Languages,"
BT 29/4: 409–13. [abstracts: *OTA* 2/1 (1979): #12; Holter: #073.]
1990 "Kissing in the Bible," *BT* 41/4: 409–16.

Fabian, Dapila N.
1998 "The Need for Indigenization of Bible Translations for African
Christians," *AFER* 40/1: 21–43.

Fehderau, Harold W.
1964 "Defining the Kituba Language for a Translation Project," *BT*
15/1: 27–30.

Ford, William H.
1957 "Some Reflections on the Revision of the New Testament in
Lokele," *BT* 8/4: 203–206.

Gaiya, Musa
1993 "The History of the Hausa Bible: 1980 Edition," *AJET* 12/1:
54–65. [abstract: *NTA* 38/3 (1994): #1268.]

Giesekke, D.W.
1970 "Venda Names for God," *BT* 21/1: 180–85.

Goerling, Fritz
1990 "La Traduction de 'Christ' et 'Messie' en Dioula," *CTB* 13: 8–17.
1991 "Traduction de l'Expression 'Fils de Dieu' en Dioula," *CTB* 16:
20–26.

Greaves, L.B.
1957 "The Challenge of Opportunities in Africa," *UBS Bulletin* 31:
106–109.

Grimes, Barbara, ed.
1988 *Ethnologue: Languages of the World*, 11th ed., (Dallas).

Guillebaud, Philippa
1965 "Some Points of Interest and Difficulty Experienced in Translating Genesis into Bari," *BT* 16/4: 189–192. [abstract: Holter:
#086.]

Guillebaud, Rosemary
1965 "The Work of Women Translators: In Rwanda—'Behind Every
Sentence a Prayer,'" *UBS Bulletin* 61: 24–25.

Hargreaves, John
	1965	"The Story of the Yoruba Bible," *BT* 16/1: 39–43.
Harries, Lyndon
	1954	"Two Important Swahili Translations," *BT* 5/2: 78–80.
Hein, Charles
	1975	"Food for Hungry Minds," *UBS Bulletin* 99/100: 14–15.
Hermanson, Eric A.
	1991	"The Transliteration of New Testament Proper Nouns Into Zulu,"
		(M.A. thesis, University of South Africa, Pretoria).
	1997	"The Transliteration of New Testament Proper Names into Zulu,"
		BT 48/1: 138–43.
Hope, Edward
	1990	"The United Bible Societies (U.B.S.) and the New Evangelization
		in Africa," Amewowo, ed.: 45–49.
Hope, Edward & Ignatius Chidavaenzi
	1984	"Translating the Divine Name YHWH in Shona," *BT* 35/2: 211–15.
Hopgood, Cecil R.
	1954	"Hope: A Brief Study from the Standpoint of a Translator into
		Tonga," *BT* 5/1: 19–22.
Hulstaert, G.
	1961	"Traduction de l'Ecriture Sainte dans une Langue Africaine
		(Congo)," *NZM* 17: 48–50; reprinted in Beckmann, ed.: 296–98.
Hunter, N.H.
	1959	"Scripture Distribution in British West Africa," *UBS Bulletin* 39:
		120–23.
Ibiam, Akanu
	1971	"The Bible Society of Nigeria the Way I Saw it," *UBS Bulletin*
		86: 79–82.
Iyoki, Samuel
	1977	"Check the Word," *BT* 28/4: 404–407.
Kalugila, Leonidas
	1997	*Historia ya Tafsiri za Kiswahili za Biblia* (Nairobi: n.p.).
Kanyoro, Rachael M. Angogo (cf. 'Angogo')
	1983	"A Proposal for Translation Research Strategy for Africa," *BT*
		34/1: 101–06; reprinted as "Proposition de Lignes Directrices
		pour la Recherche en Matiere de Traduction en Afrique," *CTB*
		3 (1984): 13–19. [abstract: Holter: #098.]
	1985	"Translation Problems in Joel with Special Reference to Some
		East African Languages. Part 1," *BT* 36/2: 221–26. [abstract:
		OTA 8/3 1985): #855; Holter: #099.]
	1991	"Indigenizing Translation," *BT* 42/2a: 47–56. [abstract: *NTA* 36/1
		(1992): #69.]
Karanja, John K.
	1990	"The Bible and Kikuyu Christianity," *Founding an African Faith:
		Kikuyu Anglican Christianity 1900–1945* (Nairobi: Uzima Press):
		129–69. [The book is the published version of the author's
		Cambridge Ph.D. dissertation.]

Kaumba Lafunda
  1995 "Inculturation et Traduction de la Bible en une Langue Africaine.
        A propos de la These du Pr. Muraruka," *RAT* 19/37: 109–21.
Kawale, W.R.
  1987 "Some Theological and Hermeneutical Problems in Chichewa
        Bible Translation with Special Reference to Spirit World," (B.D.
        thesis, St. Paul's United Theological College, Limuru, Kenya).
  1996 "Challenges of the Translation of Genesis 1–3 into Chichewa,"
        paper presented to the International Colloquium on Bible Trans-
        lation in Africa, University of Stellenbosch, September 5–6, 1996:
        forthcoming.
Kealy, Sean P.
  1979 "The Canon: An African Contribution," *Biblical Theology Bulletin*
        9/1: 13–26. [abstract: Holter: #102.]
Kilgour, R.
  1939 *The Bible throughout the World* (London: British and Foreign Bible
        Society).
Kimuhu, Johnson Maigua
  1990 "Some Theological and Hermeneutical Problems in the Kikuyu
        Bible Translation with Special Reference to Sin in the Old Testa-
        ment," (B.D. thesis, St. Paul's United Theological College, Limuru,
        Kenya).
  1996 "The Kikuyu Bible Rendering of Hebrew Words That Function
        to Mark Off an Untouchable Zone Or Objects Or Impose Restric-
        tions in Relation to Sancta," (Master's thesis, University of Glasgow,
        Scotland).
Koffi, Ettien
  1998 "There is More to 'And' than Just Conjoining Words," *BT* 49/3:
        332–43.
Koops, R.
  1995 "Of Gopher and Galbanum: Translating Biblical Flora into Nigerian
        Languages," *BT* 46/4: 423–27. [abstract: Holter: #105.]
  1998 "'The Oil Tree' and 'Dove's Dung': Translating Flora in 1–2
        Kings," *BT* 49/2: 207–15.
Law, J.R.S.
  1960 "The Translation of the Bible into Mende," *Sierra Leone Bulletin of
        Religion* 2: 40–44. [abstract: Holter: #107.]
Lerbak, A.E.
  1954 "Translating the Psalms into Uruund," *BT* 5/2: 84–87. [abstract:
        Holter: #108.]
Likeng, P. Bitjick
  1998 "The Use of Animal Imagery in Proverbs," *BT* 49/2: 225–32.
Loewen, Jacob A.
  1983 "An Annotated West African Psalm," *BT* 34/4: 420–24. [abstract:
        Holter: #109.]
         "Clean Air Or Bad Breath? Translating the Concept of Spirit in
        African Languages," *BT* 34/2: 213–19.

"The 'World' in John's Gospel through West African Eyes," *BT*
34/4: 407–13.
1985   "Translating the Names of God: How to Choose the Right Names
in the Target Language," *BT* 36/2: 201–07. [abstract: Holter:
#110.]
"A New Look at Section Headings in West African Translations,"
BT 36/2: 237–41.
Long, D.B.
1954   "Further Comments on the Chokwe Translation," *BT* 5/2: 87–96.
Louw, Johannes P.
1991   "A Receptor's Understanding of a Reasoned Discourse," Louw:
87–107.
"Bible Translation and Receptor Response," Louw: 1–7.
"Translating a New Testament Narrative Text," Louw: 68–86.
Louw, Johannes P., ed.
1991   *Meaningful Translation: Its Implications for the Reader* (Reading, U.K./
N.Y.: United Bible Societies).
Louwen, Jacob A.
1974   "Why Bantu Translators use RSV and TEV as their Textual
Base," *BT* 25/4: 412–16.
"The 'World' in John's Gospel through West African Eyes," *BT*
34/4: 407–13.
1986   "The Translation of Holy in Monkole: Solving a Problem," *BT*
37:2: 222–27.
Louwen, Jacob A. & Ansre, G.
1982   "Adjusting Biblical Names: The Nzema Case," *BT* 33/2: 229–34.
[abstract: Holter: #111.]
Lufunda, Kaumba
1995   "Inculturation et Traduction de la Bible en une Langue Africaine.
A propos de la These du Pr Mugaruka," *RAT* 19/37: 109–21.
Luke, K.
1985   "The Ethiopic Version of the Bible," *Bible Bahashyam* 11: 170–88.
Lupas, Liana & Erroll F. Rhodes, eds
1995   *Scriptures of the World 1994: A Compilation of the 2,092 Languages in
Which at Least One Book of the Bible Has Been Published Since the Bible
Was First Printed by Johann Gutenberg* (Reading/New York: United
Bible Societies, 1995). [Fifteenth biennial publication; includes
publications up to Dec. 31, 1994.]
MacGaffey, Wyatt
1997   "Prophecy in a Spiral Universe: Central African Translations of
the Bible," lecture presented in the "Frontiers of Biblical Scholarship: The Endowment for Biblical Research Lecture Series," at
the Annual Meeting of the American Academy of Religion/Society
of Biblical Literature, San Francisco, Nov. 23, 1997. Responses
by Robert R. Wilson and James Ross.
Maclure, A. Seton
1959   "Translating the Lugbara Bible," *BT* 10/3: 124–27.

Makonnen, Lij Endalkachew
  1968 "The Message of the Church in Emergent Africa," *UBS Bulletin*
         74: 79–80.
Maleme, T.-A.
  1985 "Translating the Locust Invasion in the Book of Joel Into Kituba,"
         BT 36/2: 216–20. [abstract: Holter: #116.]
Mallo, E.
  1972 "La Traduction de la Bible en Langues Africaines," Mveng &
         Werblowsky: 134–44. [abstract: Holter: #117.]
Manning, Ross
  1967 "The Bible Society of Nigeria," *UBS Bulletin* 69: 9–11.
Marthinson, A.W.
  1957 "Bible Translations in Belgian Congo, Ruanda-Urundi, and Angola,"
         BT 8/4: 191–202.
  1963 "Widespread Needs for the Scriptures in Congo," *UBS Bulletin* 53:
         12–13.
  1965 "In Congo—Can't Keep A Bible in Stock," *UBS Bulletin* 64:
         172.
  1968 "Les Societes Bibliques au Congo," *RCA* [?]: 34–41.
Matthew, A.F.
  1956 "The Revision of the Amharic New Testament," *BT* 7/2: 72–76.
Mbogori, J.
  1971 "Church Involvement in Scripture Distribution in Africa," *UBS
         Bulletin* 88: 211–13.
Mettler, Lukas
  1962 "Katholische Bibelhbersetzungsarbeit in der Zulu Mission," *NZM*
         18: 22–31; reprinted in Beckmann, ed.: 300–309.
Metzler, J.
  1961 "Madagassische Bibelhbersetzungen," *NZM* 17: 135–39; reprinted
         in Beckmann, ed.: 318–22.
Michaeli, F.
  1954 "Bible Problems in Central Africa," *UBS Bulletin* 18: 9–11.
Mikre-Selassie, G.A.
  1985 "Repetition and Synonyms in the Translation of Joel—with Special
         Reference to the Amharic Language," *BT* 36/2: 230–37. [abstract:
         Holter: #129.]
Mojola, Aloo Osotsi
  1985 "Translation Problems in Joel with Special Reference to Some
         East African Languages: Part 2," *BT* 36/2: 226–29. [abstract:
         OTA 8/3 (1985): #856; Holter: #131.]
         "Translation and Belief," *UBS Bulletin* 140/141: 25–34.
  1988 "Peasant Studies and Biblical Exegesis: A Review with Some
         Implications for Bible Translation," *ATJ* 17/2: 162–73. [abstracts:
         NTA 33/3 (1989): #1026.] Holter: #132.]
  1989 "Translating the Term 'Tribe' in the Bible—with Special Reference
         to African Languages," *BT* 40/2: 208–11. [abstracts: *OTA* 13/2
         (1990): #470; Holter: #133.]

1990   "The Traditional Religious Universe of the Luo of Kenya: A Preliminary Study," Stine & Wendland: 154–74.

1993   "Theories of Metaphor in Translation with Some Reference to John 1:1 and 1 John 1:1," *BT* 44/3: 341–47. [abstract: *NTA* 38/2 (1994): #678.]

1994   "A 'Female' God in East Africa—Or the Problem of Translating God's Name Among the Iraqw of Mbulu, Tanzania," *UBS Bulletin* 170/171: 87–93; also published as "A 'Female' God in East Africa: The Problem of Translating God's Name Among the Iraqw of Mbulu, Tanzania," *BT* 46/2: 229–36. [abstract: Holter: #134.]

1996   *150 Years of Bible Translation in Kenya, 1844 to 1994: An Overview and Reappraisal* (Nairobi: Bible Society). [review: *BookNotes* 5 (March 1998): 5.20; abstract: *NAOTS* 1 (1996): 7.]
       150 Years of Bible Translation in Tanzania, 1866–1996: An Overview and Reappraisal (Dodoma: Bible Society of Tanzania).
       150 Years of Bible Translation in Uganda, 1986–1996: An Overview and Reappraisal (Kampala: Bible Society of Uganda).

1998   "Interaction Between Exegete and Translator: A Translator's View," *NAOTS* 4: 2–4. [abstract: *OTA* 21/3 (1998): #1248.]
       "The 'Tribes' of Israel: A Bible Translator's Dilemma," *JSOT* 81/4 (1998): 15–29. [*OTA* 22/2 (1999): #748.]

Momo Tambulamanga
1982   "Etude et Traduction des Actes des Apotres en Swahili du Shaba (concerne les chapitres 1,2,7,9,15,22,26)," (Memoire de Licence en Théologie et Sciences Humaines, Facultés de Theologie Catholique de Kinshasa).

Monticchio, Fr.
1983   "La Parola di Dio in Lingua Ekarungu e Chisena," *Continenti* 69: 398–402.

Moomo, David O.
1993   "Hebrew and Ebira Poetry," *Notes on Translation* 7/4: 9–25. [abstract: *OTA* 17/2 (1994): #1200.]

Moore, Carrie J.
1965   "The Work of Women Translators: West Africa—The Word of Life for the Kissis," *UBS Bulletin* 61: 26–27.

Moore, Hyatt, ed.
1984   *Pass the Word. 50 Years of Wycliffe Bible Translators* (Huntington Beach).

Mugaruka Mugarukira-Ngabo, Richard
1992   A La Traduction de la Bible comme Moment d'Inculturation du Message Revelé: Application à la Version Shi de Mt 5,1–2," *RAT* 16/31: 5–31.

Mulago, Vincent
1966   "Le Nouveau Testament en Mashi," in Beckmann, ed.: 299.

Muller, P.G.
1980   "Die Bible fur Agypten," *Bibel und Kirche* 35:90–91.

Munthali, Priest
  1981 "Is Your Bible Disfigured? Transliterating Biblical Names," *BT* 32/2: 225–27.
Munthe, Ludwig
  1969 *Le Bible à Madagascar. Les Deux Premières Traductions du Nouveau Testament Malgache* (Oslo, Norway: Egede Instituttet). [review: Olivier Beguin, *UBS Bulletin* 85: 46.]
Muzungu, B.
  1965 "La Traduction en Kinyarwanda du Nom 'Pere,'" *TPRB* 20: 229–36.
Mwanga, G.
  1984 "A Bible Translation Survey of Kikongo Ya Leta—Methodological and Cultural Difficulties," (M.A. thesis, Universite de Paris, Paris, France).
Nabofa, M.Y.
  1995 "The Urhobo Bible," *Orita* 27/1–2: 13–21. [abstract: Holter: #138.]
Nelson, Quentin D.
  1957 "Ngbandi Terminology in Translating Christian Ideas," *BT* 8/4: 145–49.
Nida, Eugene A.
  1955 "A Changing Africa," *UBS Bulletin* 23:3–7.
       "Problems of Translating the Scriptures into Shilluk, Anvak and Nuer," *BT* 6/2: 55–63.
Noss, Philip A.
  1976 "The Psalms and the Gbaya Literary Style," *BT* 27/1: 110–21. [abstract: Holter: #146.]
  1981 "The Oral Story and Bible Translation," *BT* 32/3: 301–18.
  1988 "Quotation, Direct, Indirect and Otherwise in Translation," Stine: 129–45.
  1990 "Wooden Spears and Broken Pottery: Symbols of Gbaya Faith," Stine & Wendland: 202–25.
  1996 "The Stain of Blood," *BT* 47/1: 139–41.
  1998 "Scripture Translation in Africa: The State of the Art," *JNSL* 24: 63–76. [originally: "The State of the Art: Scripture Translation in Africa," unpublished paper presented at the Colloquium on Bible Translation in Africa, Stellenbosch University, Stellenbosch, South Africa, 5–6 September, 1996.] [abstract: *OTA* 22/3 (1999): #1375; *NTA* 43/3 (1999): #1591.]
Nothomb, D.
  1970 "Le Sens du Mot 'Uwemera' dans la Biblia Yera," *Foi et Culture* 6/2: 63–72.
Oddy, Berenice
  1965 "Helping Fingers to Read in Central Africa," *UBS Bulletin* 61: 30–31.
Ofulue, Y.
  1998 "Translating Exclamations," *BT* 49/2: 201–207.

Olson, Howard S.
  1980   "The Kiswahili Common Language Version of the New Testament,"
         ATJ 9/2: 77–88.
Omollo, Maurice O.
  1994   "Acceptability of Swahili Union Version *Habari Njema* and Neno
         New Testament" (M.Th. thesis, NEGST).
Payle, Kenneth D.
  1997   "Ideology, Politics, and the Afrikaans Bible Translation," *Abstracts:*
         American Academy of Religion/Society of Biblical Literature 1997 (Scholars
         Press): 45.
Persson, Janet
  1997   *In Our Own Languages: The Story of Bible Translation in the Sudan* Faith
         in Sudan No. 3 (Nairobi: Paulines Publications Africa). [review:
         BookNotes 5 (March 198): 5.31.]
Plangger, Albert
  1961   "Die Heilige Scrift in Shona: Uebersicht und Wertung kath.
         Bemhhungen," *NZM* 17: 140–46; reprinted in Beckmann, ed.:
         289–95.
Psiloinis, Christo
  1958   "The Relationship of the Bible Society to Churches and Missions:
         II. in Egypt," *UBS Bulletin* 36: 172–73.
Rabin, Chaim
  1972   "The Uniqueness of Bible Translation," Mveng & Werblowsky:
         108–116. [abstract: Holter: #187.]
Pakendorf, Gunther
  1993   "From Berlin to Bethel: Albert Kropf and the Berlin Mission in
         the Eastern Cape," *Missionalia* 21/3: 229–35.
Reguin, O.
  1968   "Les Societes Bibliques et la Cooperation avec l'Eglise Catholique,"
         TPRB 8: 55–60.
Reisenberger, Azila T.
  1996   "Observations on Xhosa Translations of the Bible," *Abstracts:*
         American Academy of Religion/Society of Biblical Literature Abstracts 1996
         (Scholars Press): 211.
Renju, Peter Masumbukom
  1986   *A Semantic Analysis of 2 Corinthians 2:14–3:18* (Utrecht: Nederlands
         Bijbelgenootschap, 1986). [review: J. Callow *BT* 38/3: 335–37;
         W. Weren *Nederlands Theologisch Tijdschrift* 43 (1989): 147–48.]
  1988   "Communication Triggers As Bases for Some of the Notes for
         Study Bibles," *BT* 39/2: 242–46.
  1993   "Context Sensitive Study Bible Notes," *BT* 44/4: 411–17. [abstract:
         NTA 38/2 (1994): #680.]
  1995   "The Exodus of Jesus (Luke 9:31)," *BT* 46/2: 213–18.
  1998   "The Lamb of God (John 1.29, 36)," *BT* 49/2: 232–39.
Reyburn, William D.
  1958   "Certain Cameroun Translations: Analysis and Plan," *BT* 9/4:
         171–82.

1959   "The Role of the Heart in the Translation of Acts in Some Northern Bantu Languages," *BT* 10/1: 1–4.
        "The Significance of the African Bibleless Tribes for the Bible Societies Today," *UBS Bulletin* 39: 117–120.
1965   "A Translations Consultant in West Africa," *UBS Bulletin* 62: 56–57.
1967   "Translation in West Africa," *UBS Bulletin* 72: 178–81.

Roe, James Moulton
1965   *A History of the British and Foreign Bible Society 1905–1954* (London: The British and Foreign Bible Society).

Roulet, E.
1956   "Translating Work in Fulfulde (Fulani)," *BT* 7/1: 30–33.
1959   "Problems in Islamic Countries South of the Sahara," *UBS Bulletin* 39: 129–32.

Rwamping, J.
1968   "Cursing Psalms Are Inspired, So What?" *AFER* 10: 68–70.

Sanderson, C.
1959   "The Hausa New Testament," *UBS Bulletin* 39: 116–17.

Sanneh, Lamin
1987   "Christian Missions and the Western Guilt Complex," *The Christian Century* April 8, reprinted in *ERT* 19/4 (1995): 393–400.
1989   *Translating the Message: The Missionary Impact on Culture* (Maryknoll: Orbis). [reviews: A.B. Anderson *Critical Review of Books in Religion* 1 (1988): 273–76; J.B. Carman *Christian Century* 106 (1989): 768, 788–91; J. Kirkwood *Touchstone* 8 (1990): 49–51; J.A. Loewen *Missiology* 18 (1990): 229–30; R.R. Recker *Calvin Theological Journal* 25 (1990): 139–42; A.C. Ross *Theology Today* 46 (1990): 444–45; J.D. Ellenberger *IBMR* 15 (1991): 86–87; M.R. Waldman *JRA* 22 (1992): 159–64; O.B. Yai *JRA* 22 (1992): 164–68; Sanneh *JRA* 22 (1992): 168–72 [reply to Waldman]; K. Thomas *BT* 43 (1992): 151–53; T.S. Maluleke *Missionalia* 21 (1993): 192–93; *BookNotes* 1 (March 1996): #1.36.]
1990   "Gospel and Culture: Ramifying Effects of Scriptural Translation," Stine, 1990: 1–23.
1994   "Translatability in Islam & in Christianity in Africa: A Thematic Approach," Thomas D. Blakely, Walter E.A. van Beek & Dennis L. Thomson, eds *Religion in Africa: Experience and Expression* (London: James Currey/Portsmouth, N.H.: Heinemann): 23–45.

Sarndal, O.
1955   "Translation of Certain Biblical Key-words into Zulu," *BT* 6/4: 173–78.

Schaaf, Ype
1968   "Make the Bible African," *UBS Bulletin* 74: 72–74.
1996   *On Their Way Rejoicing: The History and Role of the Bible in Africa* (Carlisle, U.K.: Paternoster)' *L'Histoire et le Role de la Bible en Afrique* (Lavigny, Switzerland/Nairobi, Kenya: Les Editions des Groupes Missionaires/la Collection Defi Africain). [reviews: Leny Lagerwerf *Exchange* 24 (1995): 85–86; *BookNotes* 2 (October 1996): #2.34;

Jacques Blandenier *CTB* 25 (1996): 23; abstracts: *Theology in Context* 13/2 (1996): #960; *NAOTS* 1 (1996): 7.]

Schlosser Katesa

1977 *Die Bantubibel des Blitzzauberers Laduma Madela, Schöpfungsgeschichte der Zulu* (Kommissionsverlag Schmidt und Klauning, Kiel).

Schneider, Theo R.

1970 "The Divine Names in the Tsonga Bible," *BT* 21/2: 89–99.

1982 "Translating Ruth 4.1–10 among the Tsonga People," *BT* 33/3: 301–308. [abstract: Holter: #200.]

1986 "From Wisdom Sayings to Wisdom Texts-I," *BT* 37/1: 128–35.

1987 "From Wisdom Sayings to Wisdom Texts-II," *BT* 38/1: 101–17. [abstract (of the above two articles): Holter: #201.]

1991 "Tackling an Old Testament Text," Louw: 41–67.

1992 *The Sharpening of Wisdom: Old Testament Proverbs in Translation* (Pretoria: Old Testament Society of Southern Africa). [review: *BookNotes* 5 (March 1998): 5.36.]

1998 "Containers and Contents: A Case of Functional Equivalence," *BT* 49/2: 215–25.

Slager, Donald

1989 "Discourse Analysis of Ruth 2:4–17," *Notes on Translation* 3/2:29–33.

Smalley, William A.

1958 "Dialect and Orthography in Kipende," *BT* 9/2: 63–69.

1959 "Orthography Conference for French West Africa," *BT* 10/4: 181–87.

1991 *Translation as Mission: Bible Translation in the Modern Missionary Movement* (Macon, Georgia: Mercer University Press). [reviews: A.A. DiLella *Catholic Historical Review* 77 (1991): 663–65; R.G. Bratcher *Faith and Mission* 9 (1992): 108–109; W.H. Fuller *Evangelical Missions Quarterly* 28 (1992): 429–430; J.A. Loewen *Missiology* 20 (1992): 401–402; E.A. Nida *IBMR* 16 (1992): 133; V. Kruger *Missionalia* 21 (1991): 95–96; R.J. Sims *AJET* 13/1 (1994): 55–56; J.C. Anderson *Church History* 64 (1995): 149–50.]

Smit, A.P.

1970 *God Made it Grow: The History of the Bible Society Movement in Southern Africa from 1820 to 1970* W.P. Vos, trans. (Cape Town: Bible Society of South Africa, 1970)' *God Laat Het Groei: Geschiedenis van die Bijbelgenootskapsbeweging in Suider Afrika 1920–1970* (Cape Town: Bible Society of South Africa). [review: *UBS Bulletin* 85: 47.]

Smith, A.

1974 "The Biblical Apostolate," *AFER* 16: 325–28.

Souriany, Makary el

1958 "The Place of the Bible in the Coptic Orthodox Church of Egypt," *UBS Bulletin* 36: 160–64.

Stamm, W.A.

1956 "Revision of the Twi Bible in the Gold Coast," *BT* 7/1: 34–38.

Stennes, Leslie H.

1987 "Foregrounding and Backgrounding of Participants in Fulfulde," *UBS Bulletin* 148/149: 81–95.

Stine, Philip C.
1974 "On the Restructuring of Discourse," *BT* 25/1: 101–106.
1988 "Sociolinguistics and Bible Translation," Stine: 146–71.

Stine, Philip C., ed.
1988 *Issues in Bible Translation* United Bible Societies monograph series, 3 (London/N.Y./Stuttgart: United Bible Societies). [reviews: P. Ellingworth *Journal of Theological Studies* ns 41 (1990): 215–17; S.E. Porter *JSNT* 42 (1991): 118; Ronald Sim in *AJET* 12/1 (1993): 70–74; abstract: *RSR* 16/2 (1990): 151; *OTA* 14 (1991): #1180.]
1990 *Bible Translation and the Spread of the Church. The Last 200 Years* Studies in Christian Mission 2 (Leiden: Brill). [reviews: H.K. Goodpasture *Interpretation* 46 (1992): 434–35; D. O'Conner *IRM* 81/1 (1992): 131–32; G. Schwartz *Evangelical Missions Quarterly* 28 (1992): 92–93; W. Smalley *IBMR* 16 (1992): 173–74; abstract: *NTA* 36/1 (1992): 106.]

Stine, Philip C. and Ernst R. Wendland, eds
1990 *Bridging the Gap: African Traditional Religion and Bible Translation* United Bible Societies monograph series, 4 (Reading/N.Y.: United Bible Societies). [reviews: J. Sharp *Missiology* 21 (1993): 88; R. Sim *AJET* 12/1 (1993): 70–74; *BookNotes* 2 (1996): #2.36.]

Studerus, Rafael
1963 "Das Werden einer Bibelhbersetzung: Erfahrungen mit der Zulu Sprache," *NZM* 19: 122–29; reprinted in Beckmann, ed., 310–17.

Tanner, Ralph E.S.
1991 "The Reception of the New Testament in Swahili: Some Criticisms and Comments on its Use Among the Sukuma of Tanzania," *Missionalia* 26/2 (1998): 245–259.

Tattersall, Bernard N.
1954 "West Africa—A First Impression," *UBS Bulletin* 20: 24–26.

Tshipungu, J.
1969 "Pour une Bible Oecumenique au Congo," *OP* 125: 230–35.

van der Jagt, Krijn
1990 "Equivalence of Religious Terms Across Cultures: Some Problems in Translating the Bible in the Turkana Language," Stine & Wendland: 131–53. [abstract: Holter: #095.]

Van der Merwe, Du Toit
1978 "The Problem of Interference between Languages in Translation. Examples of Unnatural Translation from the Shona Bible," *BT* 29/4: 443–46.
1998 "The Centre for Bible Translation in Africa," *NAOTS* 4: 4–6. [abstract: *OTA* 21/3 (1998): #1247.]

Van Rooy, J.A.
1972 "Venda Semantics I. Terms Reflecting Primarily One Feature From the Traditional World View," *BT* 23/4: 418–30.
"Venda Semantics II. Terms Reflecting Primarily One Feature of the Traditional World View," *BT* 23/4: 431–48.

van Steenbergen, G.
1991 "Translating 'Sin' in Pokoot," *BT* 42/4: 431–37.

van't Velt, H.
  1966 "Towards a Revised Translation of the Bible in Swahili," *BT* 17/2: 74–80.
Venberg, Rodney
  1971 "The Problem of a Female Diety in Translation," *BT* 22/2: 68–70; reprinted 35/4 (1984): 415–17.
Vermeulen, J.
  1964 "Scripture Translations in Northern Nigeria," *AFER* 6/1: 66–73.
Verryn, T.D.
  1977 "'Soul' and 'Spirit' in Sotho Bible," *Theologica Evangelica* 10/1: 65–73.
Waard, Jan de
  1969 "The Translation of Some Figures of Speech from Psalms in Bamileke and Bamoun," *BT* 20/4: 143–49. [abstract: Holter: #218.]
  1971 "Do You Use 'Clean Language'? Old Testament Euphemisms and their Translation," *BT* 22/3: 107–15. [abstract: Holter: #219.]
       "Selected Translation Problems from the Prophets with Particular Reference to Bamileke," *BT* 22/4: 146–54. [abstract: Holter: #220.]
Walls, A.F.
  1992 "The Translation Priniciple in Christian History," in Stine, ed.: 23–39.
Wambutda, Daniel N.
  1981 "The Hausa Bible," *IRM* 70: 140–42. [abstract: Holter: #221.]
Warmoes, P.
  1983 "La Parution de la Premiere Bible Complete en Lingala," *RAT* 7/13: 67–82.
Waruta, Douglas W.
  1975 "Scripture Translation in Kenya," (M.A. thesis, University of Nairobi, Kenya).
Watson, John T.
  1952 "Africa Revisited," *UBS Bulletin* 11:32–34.
  1959 "The Task in Africa Today," *UBS Bulletin* 39: 107–111.
  1960 "Reflections on Secretaries' Conference in Africa," *UBS Bulletin* 42: 48–49.
Weiss, Lowell
  1995 "Speaking in Tongues," *Atlantic Monthly* (June): 36–42. [Survey of missionary linguistic work.]
Wendland, Ernst R.
  1985 *Language, Society, and Bible Translation* (Capetown: Bible Society of South Africa). [review: R. Sim *AJET* 12/1 (1993): 70–74.]
  1987 *The Cultural Factor in Bible Translation: A Study of Communicating the Word of God in a Central African Cultural Context* United Bible Societies Monograph Series, 2 (London/N.Y./Stuttgart: United Bible Societies). [reviews: P. Bennett *Hebrew Studies* 29 (1988): 213–15; J.A. Emerton *VT* 38 (1988): 252; C.H. Kraft *Critical Review of Books in Religion* 1 (1989): 146–47; P. Meyerink *Reformed Review* 42 (1989):

155; K. Schoville *JBL* 108 (1989): 319–20; L. Alexander *JSNT* 42 (1991): 118–19; R. Sim *AJET* 12/1 (1993): 70–74; *BookNotes* 2 (October 1996): #2.42; abstract: *NTA* 32/2 (1988): 239.]

1988   "Structural Symmetry and its Significance for the Book of Ruth," Stine: 30–63.

1991   "Culture and the Form/Function Dichotomy in the Evaluation of Translation Acceptability," Louw: 8–40.

1992   "Elijah and Elisha: Sorcerers or Witchdoctors?" *BT* 43/2: 213–23. [abstracts: *OTA* 16 (1993): #313; Holter: #226.]
"*Yahweh*—the Case for *Chauta* 'Great-[God]-of-the-Bow,'" *BT* 43: 430–38. [abstract: *OTA* 16 (1993): #773.]

1993   *Comparative Discourse Analysis and the Translation of Psalm 22 in Chichewa, a Bantu Language of South-Central Africa* Studies in Bible and Early Christianity, 32 (Lewiston/Queenston/Lampeter: Edwin Mellen Press). [abstracts: *OTA* 17 (1994): #835; *BookNotes* 3 (March 1997): 3.40.]

1994   "Oral-Aural Dynamics of the Word with Special Reference to John 17," *Notes on Translation* 8/1: 19–43. [abstract: *NTA* 39/3 (1995): #1541.]

1996   "Obadiah's Vision of 'The Day of the Lord': On the Importance of Rhetoric in the Biblical Text and in Bible Translation," *JOTT* 7: 54–86. [abstract: *OTA* 20/1 (1997): #431.]
"A Review of 'Relevance Theory' in Relation to Bible Translation in South-Central Africa, Part I," *JNSL* 22/1: 91–106.

1997   "Five Key Aspects of Style in Jonah and (Possibly) How to Translate Them," *BT* 48/3: 308–28.
"A Review of 'Relevance Theory' in Relation to Bible Translation in South-Central Africa, Part II," *JNSL* 23/1: 83–108. [abstract: *OTA* 21/1 (1998): #39.]

1998   *Analyzing the Psalms: With Exercises for Bible Students and Translators* (Winona Lake: Eisenbrauns). [review: K. Holter *NAOTS* 4 (1998): 21–22.]

Westberg, Sigurd F.
1956   "Some Experiences in the Translation of Genesis and Exodus into Lingala," *BT* 7/3: 117–22. [abstract: Holter: #229.]

Wilson, W.A.A.
1964   "Some Frequently Neglected Syntactical Features of West African Languages," *BT* 15/1: 11–18.

Wilt, Timothy
1989   "Two Zairean Swahili Bibles: Dealing with Diglossic Distances," *BT* 40/3: 321–31.

1995   "Quelques Observations sur la Repetition Thematique," *CTB* 24: 3–8.

Yakabuul, B.
1984   "Translating God's Names into Kanyok," *BT* 35/4: 401–409. [abstract: Holter: #231.]

Yorke, Gosnell L.O.R.
  1998   "Translating the Old Testament in Africa: An Afrocentric Ap-
         proach," *NAOTS* 4: 10–13. [abstract: *OTA* 21/3 (1998): #1260.]
Zinkuratire, Victor
  1998   "The African Bible Project," *NAOTS* 4: 7–9. [abstract: *OTA* 21/3
         (1998): #1261.]
         "Morphological and Syntactical Similarities between Hebrew and
         Bantu Languages," *NAOTS* 4: 14–19.
Zogbo, Lynell Marchese
  1988   "Advances in Discourse Study and their Application to the Field
         of Translation," Stine: 1–29.
  1989   "Pronouns for God: He, She, Or It?" *BT* 40/4: 401–405.
  1990   "The Religious World of the Godie with a View to Bible Trans-
         lation," Stine & Wendland: 175–201. [abstract: Holter: #232.]

6. *Homiletic, Devotional and "Popular" Material*

Abasika, Etiese T. Mkpa
  1993   *"This Black Jesus": The Conspiracy and the World's Best Kept Secret.
         Analysis and Evaluation of His Life From the Pyramid of Power to Human
         Freedom* (Lagos, Nigeria: Newswatch Books).
Abdu, Grace
  n.d.   *Proverbs 31: The Virtuous Woman* (Jos, Nigeria: Savanna Press).
Abuyi, Sapana Aguli
  1993   *Toma Mi Akugu'ba Yowani* [In Jur Modo (Sudan): "Book of Gospel
         according to John"] Sudan Bible Guides (Nairobi: Privately
         Published).
  1994   *Toma Mi Tisaki* [In Jur Modo (Sudan): "Book of Genesis"] Sudan
         Bible Guides (Nairobi: Privately Published).
Ackermann, Denise
  1992   "A Time to Hope [Lam 3: 22–25; Romans 5: 1–5; a sermon],"
         JTSA 81: 66–70.
Adeboye, E.A.
  1994   *The Last Days: A Study of the Book of Revelation* (Lagos, Nigeria: The
         Book Ministry).
Adejobi, E.O. Adeleke
  1950   *The Bible Speaks on the Church of the Lord* (Lagos, 1945; 2nd ed., 1950).
  1955   *The Daily Bible Guide for 1956* (Freetown).
  1965   *The Observances and Practices of the Church of the Lord (Aladura) in the
         Light of Old and New Testament* (an extensive revision of *The Bible
         Speaks . . .*, 1950; Lagos).
Adekola, Adeoye
  1990   *Amazing Grace: Twelve Messages of Divine Love and Compassion* (Ibadan,
         Nigeria: Daystar).
  1993   *Lo . . . He Comes! A Biblical Perspective on the Second Coming of Jesus
         Christ* (Ibadan: Daystar Press).

Adewole, Samuel Akin
  1995   *The Lost Facts and the Forgotten Powers of Jesus Christ for Instant Results without Candles. (Plus The Secrets of Some Religious Leaders)* (Lagos, Nigeria: privately published).
         The Man in the Synagogue vs Some Religious Leaders. (Plus A Short Dictionary of Dreams and some Selected Psalms for Prayers) (Lagos, Nigeria: privately published).
Ajijola, Alhaji A.D.
  1992   *Who Instituted the Eucharist (Holy Communion) Jesus or St. Paul?* (Kaduna, Nigeria: Straight Path Publishers).
  n.d.   *Did Jesus Perform any Miracles?* (Kaduna, Nigeria: Straight Path Publishers).
Akanni, Gbile
  1994   *God's Pattern for Christian Service: With Illustrations from the Life and Ministry of Deborah* (Jos, Nigeria: Peace House Publications).
Alan, K.
  1988   *Contradictions and Fallacies in the Bible* (Ibandan, Nigeria: Al-furqa'an Publishers).
All Africa Conference of Churches
  1996   *Troubled but not Destroyed. Devotional Guide: AACC 7th General Assembly* (Nairobi: AACC).
Allen, Ronald J.
  1991   "African Homiletics: A Soft Report," *Homiletic* 16/1: 5–9.
Aluko, J. Sunday
  1996   *The True Nature of God (In John's Gospel)* (Lagos: CSS Bookshops Limited).
Asahu-Ejere, Kinsley
  1988   "Reading Guide for February, 1988: Mark 14–16," *Bible and Life* (January–March, 1988): 14–26.
Awoyemi, Valentine
  1985   "Reading Guide for July, 1985: John 9–11, Mark 6," *Bible and Life* (May–August, 1985): 35–47.
  1986   "Reading Guide for July, 1986: Gen 21–25," *Bible and Life* (May–August, 1986): 27–42.
Baitu, Juvenalis
  1998   "An African Perspective," Joseph Anfossi & John Villata *I Am the Lord Your God. You Shall Not Have Strange Gods before Me: Reflections on the First Commandment* (Nairobi: Paulines Publications Africa): 76–77.
         "An African Perspective," Paul Tammi *You Shall Not Take the Lord's Name in Vain: Reflections on the Second Commandment* (Nairobi: Paulines Publications Africa): 38–39.
         "An African Perspective," John Villata *Remember to Keep Holy the Sabbath Day: Reflections on the Third Commandment* (Nairobi: Paulines Publications Africa): 51–52.
         "An African Perspective," Paul Tammi *Honour Your Father and Your Mother: Reflections on the Fourth Commandment* (Nairobi: Paulines Publications Africa): 53–54.

"An African Perspective," Edward Menichelli & Lionel Crocetta *You Shall Not Kill: Reflections on the Fifth Commandment* (Nairobi: Paulines Publications Africa): 54–55.

"An African Perspective," David D'Aria *You Shall Not Steal, Nor Covet Your Neighbour's Goods: Reflections on the Seventh and Tenth Commandments* (Nairobi: Paulines Publications Africa): 52–53.

"An African Perspective," David D'Aria *You Shall Not Bear False Witness: Reflections on the Eighth Commandment* (Nairobi: Paulines Publications Africa): 53–54.

Boesak, Allan A.

1979 *Finger of God: Sermons of Faith and Political Responsibility* (Johannesburg: Raven; Maryknoll: Orbis, 1982).

"The Relationship Between Text and Situation, Reconciliation and Liberation, in Black Theology," *Voices* 2/1: 30–40.

1981 "A Question for Peasants [the prophet Habakkuk and a Peasants' revolt in England]," *One World* 69: 19–20.

1983 "The Eye of the Needle [Mark 10:13–15]," *IRM* 72: 7–10.

"Falling out of Step with a World of Wanderers [Eph 2:14–22]," *One World* 87: 21–22.

1985 "If you Believe [sermon, 1st Sunday after release on bail from Pretoria Central Prison; Mark 9: 14–27]," *Reformed Journal* 35/11: 10–14.

"In the Name of Jesus: Acts 4:12," *JTSA* 52: 49–55; reprinted as "In the Name of Jesus: A Sermon for 16 June," Boesak & Villa-Vicencio, 1986: 30–40.

"Proclamation and Protest: The Lost Sons, and Outside the Gate [Luke 15:11–32; Hebrews 13:13]," *Resistance and Hope: South African Essays in Honour of Beyers Naude* C. Villa-Vicencio & J. de Gruchy, eds (Cape Town: D. Philip/Grand Rapids: Eerdmans): 74–82.

"With Fear and Trembling [Luke 14:26]," *Other Side* 21/9: 15–17.

1986 "What Belongs to Caesar? Once Again Romans 13," Boesak & Villa-Vincencio: 138–56.

1988 "Your Days are Over: The Promises of God Confront the State [1 Kings 19:4]," *Sojourners* 17: 19–20.

1987 *Comfort and Protest: The Apocalypse from a South African Perspective* (Philadelphia: Westminster) = *Comfort and Protest: Reflections on the Apocalypse of John of Patmos* (Edinburgh: Saint Andrew Press). [reviews: P. Nelson *Christian Century* 104/33 (1987): 1006–1007; W. Pilgrim *Book Newsletter of the Augsburg Publishing House* 529 (1987): 4; A. Boers *Other Side* 24 (1988): 53–54; R. Miller *Saint Luke's Journal of Theology* 31 (1988): 237–39; J. Walvoord *Biblitheca Sacra* 145 (1988): 117; J.A.L. Saunders *Perspectives in Religious Studies* 16 (1989): 272–75; abstracts: *NTA* 32/1 (1988): 114; *BCT* 3/1 (1996): 24.]

"The Woman and the Dragon: Struggle and Victory in Revelation 12," *Sojourners* 16: 27–31.

1989 "Opening sermon (Mark 8:27–30)," *Reformed World* 40/8: 167–72.

Boesak, Allan A. & Charles Villa-Vicencio, eds
1986 *When Prayer Makes News* (Philadelphia: Westminster).

Bolarinwa, J.A.
n.d. "Potency and Efficacy of Psalms," (Ibadan: Oluseyi Press).

Brown, David Maughan
1997 "'Except A Corn of Wheat Fall Into the Ground and Die ...':
The Bible and Christianity in Ngugi's novels," *BCT* 4/3: 30–35.

Bujo, Benezet
1998 "An African Perspective," Joseph Anfossi *You Shall Not Commit
Adultery, Nor Covet Your Neighbour's Wife: Reflections on the Sixth and
Ninth [sic] Commandments* (Nairobi: Paulines Publications Africa):
60–63.

Burkle, Horst
1971 "Patterns of Sermons from Various Parts of Africa," David B.
Barrett, ed. *African Initiatives in Religion: 21 Studies from Eastern and
Central Africa* (Nairobi, Kenya: East Africa Publishing House):
222–31; originally presented as "A Theological Analysis of Sermons from Various Parts of Africa: A Contribution to the Problem
of 'Indigenous Theological' Thinking," in "An Interdisciplinary
Workshop . . .": 213–22. [abstract: Holter: #049.]

Bussey, Martin K.
1992 *The Message of Romans: A Commentary for Today's Church* (Abak, Nigeria:
Samuel Bill Theological College).

Cherubim and Seraphim, Eternal and Sacred Order of
1965 *Daily Bible Reading Pamphlet 1965* (14th ed.; Lagos, Nigeria: Mount
Zion House of Prayer).

Connolly, D.
1985 "Reading Guide for December 1985: Romans 1–4, Luke 1–3,"
Bible and Life (September–December, 1985): 48–60.
1987 "Reading Guide for June, 1987: Rev 17–22," *Bible and Life* (April–
June, 1987): 31–43.
1988 "Reading Guide for July, 1988: Matt 1–4," *Bible and Life* (July–
September, 1988): 1–25.

Dayok, Denis
1985 "Reading Guide for October, 1985: Gen 6–12," *Bible and Life*
(September–December, 1985): 19–34.

Deedat, Shayk Ahmed
n.d. *Combat Kit Against Bible Thumpers* (n.p.: Hasbunallah Islamic
Publishers).
1976 *What the Bible Says About Mohummed (Peace Be Upon Him)* (Durban,
South Africa: Islamic Propagation Centre).

Drouin, Alphonse
1991 *Fifty Bible Playlets for Schools and Church Services* (Ondo, Nigeria: De
La Salle Centre). [mineographed duplication]

Echeru, Michael J.C.
1997 "Chinua Achebe's *Anthills of the Savannah*, Post-History and Biblical
Example," *BCT* 4/3: 36–44.

Edet, Rosemary
  1988 "Reading Guide for August 1988: Matt 5–7, Mark 7," *Bible and Life* (July–September, 1988): 26–46.
Eluchie, A.
  1988 "Reading Guide for September, 1988: Pss 72–78," *Bible and Life* (July–September, 1988): 47–61.
Esomonu, Lazarus Ewenike
  1987 *Preaching the Sunday Homily* (Enugu, Nigeria: Snaap Press); especially chapter 3, "The Sacred Scriptures and Preaching."
Etim, Leo E.
  1985 "Reading Guide for February, 1985: Joel, Mark 1 & 9," *Bible and Life* (January–April, 1985): 24–35.
Gacege, Peter D. Njoroge
  1997 "Initiating Biblical Apostolate in a Parish," *AMECEA Documentation Service* #467: 12–14.
Gitari, David M.
  1988 *Let the Bishop Speak* (Nairobi, Kenya: Uzima). [expositional sermons printed with the newspaper reports of the political reaction.] [reviews: John Ball *Transformation* 5/3 (1988): 32; Grant LeMarquand *BookNotes* 7 (March 1999: 7.13.]
  1996 *In Season and Out of Season: Sermons to a Nation* (Carlisle: Regnum). [abstract: *BookNotes* 3 (March 1997): #3.18.]
      "Blessed are the Peacemakers (Live Broadcast from All Saints Cathedral Nairobi on 3rd October 1982," Gitari, 1996: 43–47.
      "Blessed are the Peacemakers: Matthew 5:9," Gitari, 1996: 86–90.
      "Cain Strikes Again," Gitari, 1996: 59–64.
      "Called to be Peacemakers (Sermon Preached on 5th December, 1993 at St. James & All Martyrs Cathedral, Muranga, during the Consecration of Bishop Gatambo," Gitari, 1996: 141–144.
      "Crisis Countdown," Gitari, 1996: 29–35.
      "Do not be Conformed to this World," Gitari, 1996: 54–58.
      "Duties of the State and Obligations of Citizens: 1 Peter 2:13–17," Gitari, 1996: 91–96.
      "Get Yourself Ready: The Call of the Prophet Jeremiah," Gitari, 1996: 131–35.
      "God of Order, not of Confusion: 1 Corinthians 14:33," Gitari, 1996: 81–85.
      "The Good Shepherd: Ezekiel 34; John 10," Gitari, 1996: 128–30.
      "Let the Farmer Have the First Share of His Labour," Gitari, 1996: 145–53.
      "May We Dwell in Unity," Gitari, 1996: 13–21.
      "Overcoming Satan's Strategies of Ruining the Church: Acts 4–6," Gitari, 1996: 136–40.
      "Render to Caesar . . .," Gitari, 1996: 71–76.
      "St. Stephen," Gitari, 1996: 77–80.
      "Season for Seeking Advice: 1 Kings 12," Gitari, 1996: 97–101.
      "Shattered Dreams: Romans 15:20," Gitari, 1996: 22–28.

"Shattered Dreams Realized Hopes," Gitari, 1996: 65–70.

"Stewardship of Creation," Gitari, 1996: 120–127.

"The Tower of Babel: Genesis 11:1–9," Gitari, 1996: 116–19.

"Was There No Naboth to Say No?" Gitari, 1996: 102–10.

"The Way of Peace," Gitari, 1996: 48–53.

"You are Doomed, You Shepherds of Israel: Ezekiel 34," Gitari, 1996: 111–16.

Idoko, Alhassan

1989   *The Gospels Amplified: Volume 1 Matthew and Mark* (Jos, Nigeria: Challenge Press).

1993[?]   *The Epistle of James Amplified* (Makurdi, Nigeria: Sato's Offset Press).

Ifenatuora, Christopher

1986   "Reading Guide for February, 1986: Dan 1–4, Luke 4–5," *Bible and Life* (January–April, 1986): 18–30.

Kariuki, Charles Karuga

1991   "A Critical Analysis of the Sermons of the Rev. Dr. Timothy Murere Njoya," (B.D. thesis, St. Paul's United Theological College, Limuru, Kenya).

Kattey, Ignatius C.O.

1992   *Handbook of Biblical Preaching (Homiletics)* (privately printed in Nigeria).

Keyi, Kojo Gyinayi and Hannah Screckenbach

1975   *No Time to Die* (Accra: Catholic Press). [A book of poems depicting slogans, many biblical, on lorries.]

Kistner, W.

1973   "A Sermon on Lk 10:25–37," Becken, 1974: 65–68.

Kurewa, John Wesley Zwomunondiita

1995   *Biblical Proclamation for Africa Today* (Nashville: Abingdon).

Kwashi, Benjamin

1996   "Identifying and Dealing with Distractions," *ANITEPAM Bulletin* 12 (October 1996): 3. [part 1, a bible study on Matthew 28: 19–20.]

1997   "Identifying and Dealing with Distractions," *ANITEPAM Bulletin* 13 (January 1997): 4–5 [part 2, a bible study on Acts 6:1–7.]

M. Kouam Maurice

1993   "Ne Craignez pas (Mat 10,26–33): Mot d'Exortation aux Nouveaux Maitres en Theologie a Yaounde (Promotion de 1992–1993)," *Flambeau* n.s. 1: 71–72.

Manus, Chris Ukachukwu

1986   "Reading Guide for January 1986: Romans 5–15, Luke 3–4," *Bible and Life* (January–April, 1986): 2–17.

McGhee, Quentin R.

1990   *Preparing Illustrated Sermons with the Five Step Method* (Nairobi, Kenya: East Africa School of Theology, 1990).

Morgan, Richard

1994   *Pray with Paul: Prayers from Galatians and Ephesians* (Nairobi: Uzima).

Muhsin, Ali
    n.d.   *Let the Bible Speak* (Privately published, purchased in Nigeria).
Musa, Thomas
    1962   *The Words from the Cross* (Rock Island, Ill.: Augustana Press).
Mhagama, Christian
    1996   *God Bless Africa: Praying the Gospels for Africa's Well-being* (Nairobi:
            Paulines Publications Africa).
Ncube, Zebron M.
    1995   "The Text, the Pulpit and the Pew: Let No One Put Asunder,"
            JATA 1/1: 30–40.
Ngene, G.O.
    1993   *How to Interpret the Bible* (Okposi, Nigeria: Gonc Books International).
Njoya, Timothy Murere
    1987   *Out of Silence* (Nairobi: Beyond Magazine Press).
Nurayn Ashafa El-Nigeriy, Ustaz Muhammad
    1994   *Is Jesus God's Servant According to the Bible?* C.I.P. Enlightenment
            Series No. 01 (Kaduna, Nigeria: Centre for Islamic Propogation).
Nwankiti, Benjamin C.
    1989   *African Paul, European Barnabas: The 1989 CMS Annual Sermon Preached
            on 8 May 1989 at Partnership House* (London: Church Missionary
            Society).
Nwokoro, E.O.
    n.d.   *The Mystic Power of the Psalms on Selected Chapters for Daily Use* (Calabar,
            Nigeria: MAP Publishers).
Nyomi, Setri, Phyllis Byrd, Harold Miller, eds
    1996   *Troubled but Not Destroyed: Devotional Guide, AACC 7th General Assembly*
            (Nairobi: All Africa Conference of Churches).
Nyoyoko, Vincent
    1985   "Reading Guide for March 1985: John 1–4," *Bible and Life* (January–
            March, 1985): 36–49.
Obinwa, Ignatius M.C.
    1995   "The Means of Preaching the Word," Obinwa & Obilor, eds:
            189–204.
Odanike, Paul O.
    1991   *Spiritual Lessons from The Book of James* (Ibadan: Grace and Glory
            Publications, 1991).
Ogunfuye, Chief J.O.
    n.d.   *The Secrets of the Uses of the Psalms* (Ibadan: Ogunfuye Publications).
Ogunyomi, Peter Adeboye
    1991   *Women of the Bible* (Ibadan, Nigeria: Afolabi Press).
    1995   *Biblical Encouragement, Upliftment, and Promises for Times Like This*
            (Ibadan, Nigeria: Afolabi Press).
O'Hagan, A.
    1988   "Reading Guide for June, 1988: 1 & 2 Peter," *Bible and Life* (April–
            June, 1988): 27–42.
Okafor, Jude
    1985   "Reading Guide for September 1985: Gen 1–5, Mark 7–9," *Bible
            and Life* (September–December, 1985): 6–18.

Okedeji, Oladejo O.
 1991   *On Spiritual Madness: A Biblical Perspective* (Ikeja, Nigeria: Triumphal Press).
Oko, Azu K.
 1992   *Ancestor Worship: Roots/Biblicity* (Aba, Nigeria: n.p.).
Okon, Pius A.
 1986   "Reading Guide for June 1986: Gen 17–20," *Bible and Life* (May–August, 1986): 14–26.
Okure, Teresa
 1986   "Reading Guide for April 1986: Dan 8–14, John 10–13," *Bible and Life* (January–April, 1986): 45–61.
Olawore, Ola
 1988   *Children of the Covenant: We are Not Ordinary People* (Ibadan: Adura House Publishers).
Olson, Howard S.
 1989   "Amazing Grace: A Homily on John 8:1–11," *ATJ* 18/3: 224–29.
Omonge, Patrick
 1985   "Reading Guide for October 1985: Gen 13–16," *Bible and Life* (September–December, 1985): 35–47.
 1986   "Reading Guide for August, 1986: Gen 26–28," *Bible and Life* (May–August, 1986): 43–55.
Onyedika, Raymond
 1986   "Reading Guide for May, 1986: Ephesians," *Bible and Life* (May–August, 1986): 1–13.
Onyeocha, Anthony E.
 1992   *I Thirst: The Fifth Word on the Cross & The Eucharist* (Aba: Okpala Seminary Publications, 1992).
O'Reilly, K.
 1987   "Reading Guide for February 1987: Rev 6–11," *Bible and Life* (January–March, 1987): 17–29.
 1988   "Reading Guide for April, 1988: Pss 51–57," *Bible and Life* (April–June, 1988): 1–13.
Oyenuga, V.A.
 1995   *Choose You This Day Whom You Will Serve* (Ibadan, Nigeria: Y-Books). [Much of this book is taken up with a Biblical justification of the practices of the Celestial Church of Christ.]
Otabil, Mensa
 1992   *Beyond the Rivers of Ethiopia: A Biblical Revelation on God's Purpose for the Black Race* (Accra, Ghana: Altar International).
Otijele, P. Yakubu
 1989   "The Power of the Spoken Word in the Gospel Ministry," *OJOT* 4: 10–17.
Owan, Kris J.N.
 1986   "Reading Guide for March, 1986: Dan 5–7, Is 52," *Bible and Life* (January–March, 1986): 31–44.
Power, J.
 1987   "Reading Guide for March 1987: Gen 29–32," *Bible and Life* (January–March, 1987): 30–43.

1988   "Reading Guide for March 1988: Pss 41–50," *Bible and Life* (January–March, 1988): 27–42.

Ratz, Calvin C.

1972   *Sermons for Africa* (Kisumu, Kenya: Evangel, 1972).

Roeder, G.

1987   "Reading Guide for October, 1987: Pss 17–23, Matt 22–23," *Bible and Life* (October–December, 1987): 1–13.

Ryan, Patrick J.

1994   *Jesus in the Bible and the Qur'an* (Ibadan: Ambassador Publications).

Schilling, Harald

1995   *An Exposition of Paul's Letter to the Philippians* (Port Harcourt: Samuel Bill Theological College).

Segun, F.O.

1967   *Cry Justice! Interviews with Old Testament Prophets about a Nation in Crisis* (Ibadan: Daystar).

Seruyange, Lazarus

1985   "A Study Guide towards Effective Biblical Preaching in Africa," (D.Min. dissertation, Western Conservative Baptist Seminary, Portland, Oregon).

Shorter, Aylward

1969   "Form and Content in the African Sermon: An Experiment," *AFER* 2: 265–79.

1995   "Homiletics and Preaching in Africa," William H. Willimon & Richard Lischer, eds *Concise Encyclopedia of Preaching* (Louisville: Westminster John Knox Press): 229–31.

Simopoulos, Nicole

1997   "David's Kingdom: The Congo's Inferno. An Examination of Power from the Underside of History," *BCT* 4/3: 9–25.

Smit, Dirk J.

1989   "Those Were the Critics, What About the Real Readers? An Analysis of 65 Published Sermons and Sermon Outlines on Luke 12: 35–48," *Neotestamentica* 23: 61–82. [abstract: *NTA* 34/3 (1990): 1181.]

Tanko, Peter

1985   "Reading Guide for August 1985: John 6–12," *Bible and Life* (May–August, 1985): 48–63.

Tunmiti, Bayo

1996   *Tearing the Veil Apart: with Holy Bible and Al-Quran* (Ibandan: Effective Publishers).

Turner, H.W.

1965   *Profile Through Preaching* (London: Edinburgh House Press).

Tutu, Desmond

1995   "The Good Samaritan: Luke 10:25–37. (A sermon preached by Archbishop Desmond Tutu at the Primates Eucharist, at St. Martin in the Fields, London, on March 13, 1995)," *Anglican World* 78: 6–7.

Ukpong, Justin S.

1985   "Reading Guide for January and April 1985: Galatians," *Bible and Life* (January–April, 1985): 8–23; 50–63.

"Reading Guide for May 1985: John 5–6," *Bible and Life* (May–August, 1985): 6–21.

1987   "Reading Guide for January 1987: Revelation 1–5," *Bible and Life* (January–March, 1987): 1–16.

"Reading Guide for April and May 1987: Gen 33–40; Rev 12–16," *Bible and Life* (April–June, 1987): 1–12; 18–30.

"Reading Guide for November and December 1987: Pss 24–31; 32–40," *Bible and Life* (October–December, 1987): 13–42.

1988   "Reading Guide for January 1988: Mark 1, John 1," *Bible and Life* (January–March, 1988): 1–13.

"Reading Guide for May 1988: Pss 58–65," *Bible and Life* (April–June, 1988): 14–26.

Yamsat, Pandang

1993   "Preaching to the Whole Person," *TCNN Research Bulletin* 26: 21–41.

7. *Educational Material [including secondary school texts, T.E.E. materials, Bible study notes]*

Adewale, 'Biyi

n.d.   *The Praxis of Biblical Interpretation* (Ibadan: Baptist Press).

1996   *The Message of the Prodigal Son: A Quest into the Dynamics of Forgiveness, Repentance and Restoration* (Ibadan: n.p.).

Adjei, Grace, Mwene-Batende, John Ng'andu, Owanga-Welo, Rosalia Achieng Oyweka, Ester Agbola, Joan Rose

1979   "Introducing the Bible to Children in the family," *B-PB* 2: 13–18.

Aghaegbuna, E.O.N. & R.H. Horton

1982   *Acts of the Apostles* (Bible Knowledge: a series for the West Africa School Certificate; London: Edward Arnold in association with African Universities Press).

St. Matthew's Gospel (Bible Knowledge: A series for the West Africa School Certificate; London: Edward Arnold in association with National Association of Bible Knowledge Teachers of Nigeria & African Universities Press).

Amewowo, Wynnand

1980   "Biblical Exercises Besides Devotional Bible Sharing," *B-PB* 3: 31–34.

Andersen, Oeyvind

1990   *Msingi wa Wokovu: Ufafanuzi juu ya Waraka wa Paulo Mtume kwa Warumi Milango 1–8* (Nairobi, Kenya: Scripture Press).

Anderson, Keith

1983   *The Theology of the Bible* (Theological Education by Extension, Book 2; Nairobi: The Provincial Board of Theological Education, Church of the Province of Kenya/Evangel Publishing House).

1984   *Old Testament and New Testament* (Theological Education by Extension, Book 3; Nairobi, Kenya: Church of the Province of Kenya).

Anon.

1987   "The Bible in the Family. Biblical Workshop for the Catholic Women's Association (CWA) of the Ecclesiastical Province of Bamenda, at Our Lady of Lourdes Secondary Schools, Mankon, Cameroon, July 20–25, 1987" *Biblical Apostolate* 4: 4, 6–8.

Anum, Eric

1988   *The Book of Job* (Nairobi, Kenya: OAIC).

        The Letter to the Philippians (Nairobi, Kenya: OAIC).

1989   *Introduction to the Gospels* (Nairobi, Kenya: OAIC).

1990   *The Book of Judges* (Nairobi, Kenya: OAIC).

1995   *Amos* (Nairobi, Kenya: OAIC [1988]).

        The Book of Joshua (Nairobi, Kenya: OAIC [1988]).

        The First Five Books of the Bible (Part One) (Nairobi, Kenya: OAIC).

        The First Five Books of the Bible (Part Two) (Nairobi, Kenya: OAIC).

        The Prophet Hosea (Nairobi, Kenya: OAIC [1988]).

Assani, Samson A.B., Florence Claudia Ferguson, Germain Coffi Gbankpan, Manoah L. Keverenge, Bernice Ntombemhlophe Ntuli, Obed Ochwanyi

1990   *Hebrews: An Inter-Church Guide for African Preachers and Teachers* (African Bible Guides; Birmingham: INTERACT/Selley Oak Colleges).

1990   *James: An Inter-Church Guide for African Preachers and Teachers* (African Bible Guides; Birmingham: INTERACT/Selley Oak Colleges).

Ayongo Tawiah

1990   *Luke: An Inter-Church Guide for African Preachers and Teachers* (African Bible Guides; Birmingham: INTERACT/Selley Oak Colleges).

Batlle, Aguste

1981   *Discovering the Bible* TEE course (Nairobi, Kenya: OAIC).

        More About the Bible TEE course (Nairobi, Kenya: OAIC).

1983   *A Guide to a Personal Bible Study* TEE course (Nairobi, Kenya: OAIC).

Batlle, Rosario

1987   *How Jesus Sees Women (Part One)* TEE course (Nairobi, Kenya: OAIC).

        How Jesus Sees Women (Part Two) TEE course (Nairobi, Kenya: OAIC).

Bisong, Kekong

1984   *Come and See in the Bible Why I am a Catholic* (Ogoja, Nigeria: n.p.).

Boston, Frances

1979   "Introducing Children to the Bible At School" *B-PB* 2: 19–22.

Chabane, Jacob S.

1997   "Teaching Biblical Hebrew to Non-theological Students," *NAOTS* 2: 8–9.

Dain F. Ronald & Jac van Diepen

1972   *Luke's Gospel for Africa Today. A School Certificate Course Based on the East African Syllabus for Christian Religious Education* (Nairobi: Oxford).

Dickson, Kwesi A.

1969   *An Introduction to the History and Religion of Israel From Hezekiah to the Return from Exile* (London: Darton, Longman and Todd).

1976   *The Story of the Early Church as Found in the Acts of the Apostles* (London: Darton, Longman and Todd).

Enyioha, B. Uche
1997   *Living by the Word: A Study of the Book of 2 Timothy* (Ibadan: Publications Department, Nigerian Baptist Convention).
       Victorious Christian Life: Challenges from Revelation (Ibadan: Publications Department, Nigerian Baptist Convention).

Fawole, S.L.
1972   *Essentials of Bible Knowledge* (Ibadan: Daystar).

Forslund, Eskil
1993   *The Word of God in Ethiopian Tongues: Rhetorical Features in the Preaching of the Ethiopian Evangelical Church Mekane Yesus* (Uppsala: Swedish Institute for Missionary Research). [review: *BookNotes* 4 (October 1997): #4.14; R.J. Sim *AJET* 17.2 (1998): 154–57.]

Gallo, Luis A.
n.d.   "Jesus de Nazareth: Son Histoire et sa Passion pour la Vie de l'Homme," (Mbegu dossiers jeunes) *Revue de Pastorale des Jeunes* no. 40 (Lubumbashi). [A French translation of an Italian work published as a study booklet for African youth.]

Ganey, J.C.
1980   "Bible Discussion Sharing at Outstations," *B-PB* 3: 20–21.

Gitau, Samson, Tewoldemedhin Habtu, Victor Zinkuratire, and Knut Holter
1997   "Contextualized Old Testament Programmes?" *NAOTS* 2:3–7.

Groenewegen, T. & R. Githige
1988   *Christian Religious Education Book Three* (Nairobi, Kenya: Longman Kenya). [selected themes from the OT, the African religious heritage and the NT.]

Healey, Joseph G.
1989   "Towards an Effective Bible Reflection Method in African SCCs," *B-PB* 8: 25–28.
1995   "The Need for an Efective Bible Relection Method in SCCs in Africa," *AFER* 37/3: 156–59.

Hirmer, Oswald
1980   "From Gospel Groups to Small Christian Communities," *B-PB* 3: 16–21.

Hooper, Helena M.
1992   *The Letter of James* TEE course (Nairobi, Kenya: OAIC).

Hooper, Helena M. & Elaine Dow
1992   *The Gospel of John* TEE course (Nairobi, Kenya: OAIC).

Howat, L.
1974   "The Talking Bible. Communicating the Bible to Illiterates in Ethiopia," *Missiology* 2: 437–53.

Ijaduola, Olajide
n.d.   *St. Mark's Gospel* (privately printed; Abeokuta, Nigeria).

Klem, Herbert
1977   "Toward the More Effective Use of Oral Communication of the

Scriptures in West Africa," (D.Miss. dissertation, Fuller Theological Seminary School of World Mission).

1982   *Oral Communication of the Scriptures: Insights from African Oral Art* (Pasadena: William Carey Library).

Levi, L.
1988   *God Meets Us: Christian Religious Education Form 1* (Nairobi: Heinemann Kenya).

Lombaard, Christo J.S.
1997   "Developing Old Testament Diploma Courses at TEEC(SA)," *NAOTS* 2: 9–12.

Mallia, Paul
1990   *Welcome to the Bible: An Introduction* (Nairobi, Kenya: St. Paul Publications—Africa).

Markos, Antonious
1983   *The Bible and Healing* TEE course (Nairobi, Kenya: OAIC).

Mbukanama, Jude O.
1978   *Is It In The Bible? Doing Dialogue with Friends* (Lagos, Nigeria: St. Dominic's Book Centre).

McCain, Danny
1996   *Notes on Old Testament Introduction* (Jos, Nigeria: African Text Books [ACTS]).

McGrath, Michael & Nicole Gregoire
1976   *Africa: Our Way through the Bible (Book 1: Old Testament)* (n.p.: McGrath & Gregoire, 1976).
        Africa: Our Way through the Bible (Book 2: New Testament) (n.p.: McGrath & Gregoire, 1976).

Mutema, E.
1987   *The Good News of Liberation: Studies in the Gospel of Luke* (Harare: Longman Zimbabwe).

Neill, Stephen
n.d.   "Teaching the Bible to Fundamentalists" (unpublished paper on file in St Paul's United Theological College, Limuru, Kenya; 8pp.).

Newing, Edward G.
1970   "A Study of Old Testament Curricula in Eastern and Central Africa," *ATJ* 3: 80–98; originally given as "A Comparison of Old Testament Curricula in Seminaries and Universities in Eastern Africa," in "An Interdisciplinary Workshop . . ." (n.d.): 236–48. [abstract: Holter: #142.]

Oduyoye, Modupe
1977   *When Kings Ruled and Prophets Spoke in Israel* Daystar School Certificate Texts 2 (Ibadan, Nigeria: Daystar).
1979   *Judah Alone: the People of the Book Before the Exile and After* Daystar School Certificate Texts 3 (Ibadan, Nigeria: Daystar).
1979   *The Promised Land: from the Call of Abraham to the Fall of Samson* Daystar School Certificate Texts (Ibadan, Nigeria: Daystar).

Para-Millam, Gideon
1996   *Getting into Scripture: A Fresh Approach to Re-Discovering Biblical Truth* (Jos, Nigeria: Nigeria Fellowship of Evangelical Students).

Partain, Jack
  n.d.   "An Approach to Teaching Swahili Certificate Students to do
         'Exegesis,'" (unpublished paper, on file in St. Paul's United Theo-
         logical College, Limuru, Kenya, 7pp.).
Pauw, C.M.
  1994   "Theological Education in Africa," *OTEssays* 7: 13–24. [abstract:
         Holter: #184.]
Plueddemann, James
  1994   "Do We Teach the Bible Or Do We Teach Students?" *AJET*
         13/1: 44–53.
Quarcoopome, T.N.O.
  1985   *The Synoptic Gospels: Life and Teaching of Jesus* ('A' Level Christian
         Religious Studies; Ibadan: African Universities Press).
Roldanus, H.
  1987   "Het theologisch onderwijs zet voor Afrika zijn bestek uit," *Wereld
         en Zending* 16: 164–68. [abstract: Holter: #196.]
Schrurs, M.
  1969   "Projet d'une Catechese Biblique Existentielle pour la Première
         Année Scolaire (Region Bangala)," *OP* [?]: 24–30.
Simalenga, John
  1982   *What is the Bible? New Testament* TEE course (Nairobi, Kenya: OAIC).
  1995   *What is the Bible? Old Testament* TEE course (Nairobi, Kenya: OAIC
         [1982]).
Simson, Pierre
  1974   *Bible Catechesis 1: Gospel Miracles* Spearhead 34 (Kampala, Uganda:
         Gaba).
         Bible Catechesis 2: Authority, Reconciliation Spearhead 35 (Eldoret,
         Kenya: Gaba).
  1975   "The Gospels in the Making: From Jesus of Nazareth to Our
         Gospels," *AFER* 17/5: 258–69.
         "The Church in the New Testament," *AFER* 19/5: 280–88.
  1983   *Bible Reflections 3: Poverty, Celibacy, Obedience* Spearhead 43 (Eldoret,
         Kenya: Gaba); the second printing of the same booklet is enti-
         tled *Biblical Reflections 3: Religious Vows*.
Smith, E.W.
  1936   *African Beliefs and Christian Faith. An Introduction to Theology for African
         Students, Evangelists and Pastors* (London: United Society for Christian
         Literature). [abstract: Holter: #206.]
Steenberghen, R.
  1956   "Bible, Liturgie et Catéchese en Afrique (Chronique Catéchetique),"
         RCA 11: 381–86.
Thorpe, Shirley
  1996   *Through the Eyes of Women* (Cape Town: The Ecumenical Action
         Movement [TEAM]). [abstract: *BCT* 4/2 (1997): 49.]
Umtata Women's Theology Bible Study Booklets
  1994   *God our Loving Parent: Bible Studies on AIDS* (Umtata, South Africa).
         [Xhosa: "Uthixo, Ongubawo Wethu Onothando: Izifundo zeBhayi-
         bhile nge-AIDS"; Zulu: "Nkulunkulu Mzali Wethu Onothando;

Izifundo zeBhayibheli Malungana Nengculazi."] [abstract: *BCT* 4/2 (1997): 49.]

1994   *Towards a Theology of Sexuality: Sexuality & Pregancy, Abortion & Contraception, Rape & Battering* (Umtata, South Africa). [Xhosa: "Ubuni Bethu Phambi Kouso Bukathixo: Izifundo zeBhayibhile ngobuni nokukhulelwa, ukuqhomfa nokuthintela ukumitha, ukudlwengula nokulimaza."] [abstract: *BCT* 4/2 (1997): 49.]

1994   *Women, the Bible and the Contemporary Church: An Introduction to Women's Theology* (Umtata, South Africa). [Xhosa: "Amabhinqa, Ibhayibhile Nenkonzo Yale Mihla: Ukwaziswa kwizifundo zeBhayibhile ngamabhinqa"; Afrikaans: "Vroue, die Bybel en die Kerk Vandag."] [abstract: *BCT* 4/2 (1997): 49.]

1995   *When Two Become One: Bible Studies on Marriage* (Umtata, South Africa). [Xhosa: "Xa Ababini Besiba Mntu-Mnye: Izifundo ze Bhayibhile ngomtshato."] [abstract: *BCT* 4/2 (1997): 49.]

1996   *Matriarch, Judge, Stranger and Liberator: Four Women of the Old Testament* (Umtata, South Africa). [Afrikaans: "Matriarg, Rigter, Vreemdeling en Bevryder."] [abstract: *BCT* 4/2 (1997): 49.]

1996   *The Other Disciples of Jesus* (Umtata, South Africa). [abstract: *BCT* 4/2 (1997): 49.]

1996   *When Two Become More: Bible Studies on Parenting* (Umtata, South Africa). [Xhosa: "Xa Ababini Bandile: Izifundo zeBhayibhile ngobyzali."] [abstract: *BCT* 4/2 (1997): 49.]

Uwalaka, Mary Angela
1993   *My Bible and Me* (Ibandan, Nigeria: St Pauls).

Van Zyl, Danie C.
1994   "The Old Testament in the Training Programmes for African Independent Churches," *OTEssays* 7/4: 52–61.

Vonck, Pol
n.d.   "Reflections on the Teaching and Preaching of Jesus' Miracles," (unpublished paper, Kipapapala Senior Seminary, Tabora, Tanzania, 7pp.)

Wambutda, Daniel
1978   *Old Testament History and Religion: From the Institution of the Monarchy to the Fall of the Northern Kingdom* (Ibadan: Daystar).

Welch, Eileen & S.N. Clements
1972   *God Speaks to Men: A Textbook on the Old Testament Syllabus for the Kenya Certificate of Education* (Nairobi: Oxford University Press).

8. *South African Exegesis*

Abrahams, S.A., J. Punt, & D.T. Williams, eds
1997   *Theology on the Tyume* (Alice: Lovedale Press). [reviews: K. Holter *NAOTS* 5 (1998): 27; *BookNotes* 7 (1999): 37.01.]

Abrahams, Samuel P.
1994   "A Black Theological Perspective on the Old Testament," *OTEssays* 7/4: 244–53.

1997 "Reconciliation: Paths to Peace and Healing: An Old Testament Paradigm," in Abrahams, et al.: 36–46.

Ackermann, Denise
1989 "Hagar and Sarah—Symbols of Our Times," pp. 132–38 in *God se genade is genoeg* H.J. Pieterse Heyns L.M. & J.T. de Johgh van Arkel, eds (Pretoria: Nederduits Gereformeede Kerkboekhandel). [abstract: *BCT* 4/2 (1997): 32.]
1993 "Liberating the Word: Some Thoughts on Feminist Hermeneutics," *Scriptura* 44: 1–18. [abstracts: *NTA* 38/3 (1994): #1204; *BCT* 4/2 (1997): 33.]

Ackermann, Denise, Jonathan Draper & Emma Mashinini, eds
1991 *Women Hold Up Half the Sky: Women in the Church in Southern Africa* (Pietermaritzburg, South Africa: Cluster Publications, 1991). [abstracts: *BookNotes* 3 (March 1997): 3.02; *BCT* 4/2 (1997): 34–35.]

Amaoti Group
1993 "Temptations in the Townships," *Challenge* 13: 12 [abstract: *BCT* 3/1 (1996): 24.]

Ashby, Godfrey
1988 "The Chosen People: Isaiah 40–55," *JTSA* 64: 34–38.

Assad, M.
1994 "Culture, Oppression and Liberation Reflections Based on Old Testament Texts and Events," Simon S. Maimela, ed. *Culture, Religion and Liberation: Proceedings of the EATWOT Pan African Theological Conference, Harare, Zimbabwe, January 6–11, 1991* (Pretoria: AACC): 48–64.

Baker, David Weston
1984 "The Old Testament and Criticism," *JTSA* 48: 13–20.

Bax, Douglas
1983 "The Tower of Babel in South Africa Today," *JTSA* 42: 50–58. "The Bible and Apartheid 2," John W. de Gruchy & Charles Villa-Vicencio, eds *Apartheid is a Heresy* (Cape Town/London/Grand Rapids: David Philip/Lutterworth/Eerdmans): 112–43.
1990 "'Let Us, Then, Go to Him Outside the Camp . . .' (Heb. 13:13)," *JTSA* 71: 69–74.

Becken, Hans-Jurgen, ed.
1974 *Salvation Today for South Africa: Report on a Consultation of the Missiological Institute at Lutheran Theological College, Mapumulo, Natal, September 11–20, 1973* Paperbacks of the Missiological Institute at LTC, Mapumulo, No. 2 (Durban, South Africa: Lutheran Publishing House).

Boesak, Willa
1988 "Psalm 82: God Amidst the Gods," *JTSA* 64: 64–68.

Bosch, David J.
1987 "The Problem of Evil in Africa: A Survey of African Views on Witchcraft and of the Response of the Christian Church," de Villiers, ed. *Like a Roaring Lion*: 38–62.
1989 "Mission in Jesus' Way: A Perspective From Luke's Gospel," *Missionalia* 17/1 (1989): 3–21. [abstract: *NTA* 34/1 (1990): #158.] "The Scope of the BISAM Project," *Mission Studies* 11, 6/2: 61–69.

1991 *Transforming Mission: Paradigm Shifts in Theology of Mission* (Maryknoll: Orbis), especially Part 1: "New Testament Models of Mission." [review: *BookNotes* 1 (March 1996): #1.04; abstract: *RSR* 18/2 (1991): 130.]

1993 "Hermeneutical Principles in the Biblical Foundation for Mission," *ERT* 17/4: 437–51. [abstract: *NTA* 38/2 (1994): #1001.]

Botha, Jan

1991 "Contextualization: Locating Threads in the Labyrinth," *Scriptura* Special Issue 9: 29–46. [abstract: *NTA* 38/2 (1994): #610.]

1992 "Creation of New Meaning: Rhetorical Situation and the Reception of Romans 13:1–7," *JTSA* 79: 24–37. [*NTA* 37 (1993): #560.] "The Ethics of New Testament Interpretation," *Neotestamentica* 26/1: 169–94. [abstract: *NTA* 37/2 (1993): #560.]

1993 "Aspects of the Rhetoric of South African New Testament Scholarship anno 1992," *Scriptura* 46: 80–99. [abstract: *BCT* 3/1 (1996): 24.]

1994 "How Do We 'Read the Context'?" *Neotestimentica* 28/2: 291–307. [abstract: *BCT* 3/1 (1996): 24.] "Social Values in the Rhetoric of Pauline Paraenetic Literature," *Neotestimentica* 28/1: 109–26. [abstracts: *NTA* 39/2 (1995): #945; *BCT* 3/1 (1996): 24.] *Subject to Whose Authority? Multiple Readings of Romans 13* Emory Studies in Early Christianity, 4 (Atlanta: Scholars Press); revision of "Reading Romans 13. Aspects of the Ethics of Interpretation in a Controversial Text," (D.Th. dissertation; University of Stellenbosch, 1992). [review: H. Moxnes, *Biblical Interpretation* 5/2 (1997): 214–16.]

1996 "The Bible in South African Public Discourse—With Special Reference to the Right to Protest," *Scriptura* 58: 329–43. [abstract: *NTA* 41/1 (1997): #243.]

Botha, P.J., H.L. Bosman, J.J. Burden, J.P.J. Olivier, eds

1994 *Understanding the Old Testament in South Africa* special edition of *OT Essays* 7/4. (Pretoria: OTSSA).

Botman, H.R. & D.J. Smit

1988 "1 Corinthians 7:29 30 'To Live . . . As If it Were Not!'" *JTSA* 65: 73–79.

Breytenbach, Cilliers

1990 "On Reconciliation: An Exegetical Response," *JTSA* 70: 65–68.

Breytenbach, Cilliers, ed.

1988 *Church in Context: Kerk in Konteks: Early Christianity in Social Context* (Pretoria, Republic of South Africa: NG Kerk Boehandel). [abstract: *BCT* 3/1 (1996): 24.]

Burden, J.J.

1993 "Social Science and Recent Trends in Old Testament Research: It's Relevance for South African Old Testament Scholarship," *OT Essays* 6/2: 205–32. [abstracts: *OTA* 17/3 (1994): #1624; *BCT* 3/1 (1996): 24.]

Burden, J.J. ed.
> 1987 *Exodus 1–15: Text and Context. Proceedings of the 29th annual congress of the Old Testament Society of South Africa* OTSSA 29 (Pretoria: University of South Africa). [abstract: *OTA* 11//1 (1988): #328; *BCT* 3/1 (1996): 24–25.]

Buthelezi, Manas
> 1969 "Polygyny in the Light of the New Testament," *ATJ* 2: 58–70.
> 1977 "Towards a Biblical Faith in South African Society," *JTSA* 19: 55–58.

Chikafu, P.T.
> 1993 "The Audience Presupposed in the Conquest, Infiltration and Revolt Models: A Sociological Analysis," *JTSA* 84: 11–24.

Cloete, A.A.
> 1973 "Bible Study: John 14:1–11," Becken, 1974: 57–60.

Cloete, Daan
> 1985 "In the Meantime, Trouble for the Peacemakers: Matthew 5:10–12," *JTSA* 52: 42–48. [abstract: *NTA* 30/2 (1986): #567.]
> 1993 "Exegesis and Proclamation. Christmas: Heirs of God, the Father, through Jesus Christ, Incarnated (Galatians 4:4–7)," *JTSA* 85: 53–60. [abstracts: *NTA* 38/3 (1994): #1526; *BCT* 3/1 (1996): 25.]
> 1996 "Response to Bobby Loubser's Article [Loubser, 1996]," *BCT* 3/1: 11.

Cloete, G. Daan & Dirk J. Smit
> 1989 "'Rejoicing with God . . .' (Luke 15:11–32)," *JTSA* 66: 62–73. [abstract: *NTA* 34/1 (1990): #176.]
> 1992 "'And I Saw A New Heaven and A New Earth, for the First . . . Were Passed Away . . .' (Revelation 21:1–8)," *JTSA* 81: 55–64. [abstracts: *NTA* 37/3 (1993): 1441; *BCT* 3/1 (1996): 25.]
> 1994 "'Its Name Was Called Babel . . .'—'Therefore its Name Was Called Babel Because There the Lord Confused the Language of All the Earth . . .' (Gen 11:9) . . .' 'How is it That . . . We Hear Them Telling in Our Own Tongues the Mighty Works of God . . . What Does this Mean' (Acts 2:8,11–12)," *JTSA* 86: 81–87. [abstracts: *NTA* 39/1 (1995): #258; *BCT* 3/1 (1996): 25.]

Cochrane, James R. & J.A. Draper
> 1987 "The Kairos Debate. The Parting of the ways: Reply to John Suggit," *JTSA* 59: 66–72.

Cochrane, James R. & Gerald O. West
> 1993 "War, Remembrance and Reconstruction," *JTSA* 84: 25–40. [abstract: *BCT* 3/1 (1996): 25.]

Cochrane, James R. & Gerald O. West, eds
> 1991 *The Three-Fold Cord: Theology, Work and Labour* (Pietermaritzburg: Cluster Publications). [review: G.J. Rossouw *HTS* 50 (1994): 845–48; abstract: *BCT* 3/1 (1996): 25.]

Cochrane, Renate
> 1991 "Equal Discipleship of Women and Men: Reading the New Testament from a Feminist Perspective," Ackermann, Draper & Mashinini: 21–36. [abstract: *BCT* 4/2 (1997): 36.]

"The Equality of Women—A Biblical Perspective," pp. 126–36 in A *Democratic Vision for South Africa* Klaus Nurnberger, ed. (Pietermaritzberg: Encounter Publications). [abstract: *BCT* 4/2 (1997): 36.]

Colenso, John William

1861   *St. Paul's Epistle to the Romans: Newly Translated and Explained from a Missionary Point of View* (Ekukhanyeni: Mission Press).

1862–63   *The Pentateuch and the Book of Joshua Critically Examined* (Ekukhanyeni: Mission Press). [reprinted: London: Longmans, Green, 1865]

Combrink, H.J.B.

1986   "The Changing Scene of Biblical Interpretation," Hartin & Petzer: 9–17.

1994   "The Future of Old Testament Studies Through New Testament Eyes," *OTEssays* 7/4: 269–81. [abstract: *OTA* 18/3 (1995): #1371.]
            "The Use of Matthew in the South Africa Context During the Last Few Decades," *Neotestamentica* 28: 339–58; also published as "Resente Matteusavorsing in Suid-Afrika," *HTS* 50/1–2: 169–93.

1996   "A Social-scientific Perspective on the Parable of the 'Unjust' Steward (Lk 16:1–8a)," *Neotestamentica* 30/2; 281–306. [abstract: *NTA* 42/1 (1998): #270.]

Combrink, H.J.B. & B.A. Muller

1991   "The Gospel of Matthew in an African Context," *Scriptura* 39: 43–51.

Cook, C.

1989   "Rizpah's Vigil—Stabat Mater," *JTSA* 67: 77–78. [abstract: *BCT* 3/1 (1996): 25.]

Craffert, P.F.

1993   "Nuwe-testamentiese Studies—'N Paradigm vir Saamwees in Afrika," [New Testament Studies—A Paradigm for Being Together in Africa], *Theologia Evangelica* 26/3: 10–21. [abstract: *NTA* 38/2 (1994): #613.]

Darby, I.D.

1981   "The Soteriology of Bishop John William Colenso," (Doctoral dissertation, University of Natal, Pietermaritzburg, South Africa).

Deist, F.E.

1983   "Probleme theologischer Verstandigung in Sudafrika," *OTEssays* 1: 1–25. [abstract: *OTA* 7/1 (1984): #9.]

1987   "How Does a Marxist Read the Bible?" de Villiers, ed. *Liberation Theology and the Bible*: 15–30.

1990   "Genesis 1–11, Oppression and Liberation," *JTSA* 73:3–11. [abstract: *OTA* 14/3 (1991): #963; *BCT* 3/1 (1996): 25.]

1991   "The Bible in Discussion: Three Recent South African Publications on Scripture," *HTS* 47/4: 930–49. [abstract: *NTA* 36/3 (1992): #1109.]

"'Contextualization' as Nomadic Existence," *Scriptura* Special Issue 9: 47–66. [abstract: *NTA* 38/2 (1994): #614.]

"Objektiewe Sjrifuiteg? Kanttekeninge by Skrifuitleg in die Neg Geref Kerk 1930–1990 [Objective interpretation of Scripture? Marginal Notes to the Interpretation of Scripture in the Dutch Reformed Church 1930–1990]," *HTS* 47/2: 367–85. [abstract: *NTA* 36/2 (1992): #571.]

"South-Africanising Biblical Studies. An Epistemological and Hermeneutical Inquiry," *Scriptura* 37: 32–50.

1993 "Teaching Old Testament in South Africa in a Relevant Manner: A Personal View," *Scriptura* Special Issue 11: 18–27. [abstract: *OTA* 17/2 (1994): 1629.]

1994 "The Dangers of Deuteronomy: A Page from the Reception History of the Book," F. Garcia Martinez, et al. eds, *Studies in Deuteronomy: In Honour of C.J. Labuschagne on the Occasion of His 65th Birthday* VTSup 53 (Leiden/New York: Brill): 13–29. [abstract: *OTA* 18/1 (1995): #219.]

"Post-modernism and the Use of Scripture in Theological Argument: Footnotes to the Apartheid Theology Debate," *Neotestamentica* 28/3: 253–63. [abstract: *BCT* 3/1 (1996): 25.]

"South African Old Testament Studies and the Future," *OTEssays* 7: 33–51.

1996 "Biblical Interpretation in Post-Colonial Africa," *Svensk Teologisk Kvartalskrift* 72/3: 110–18. [abstract: *NTA* 41/2 (1997): #727.]

de Villiers, Pieter G.R.

1987 "The Gospel and the Poor. Let Us Read Luke 4," de Villiers, ed. *Liberation Theology and the Bible*: 45–76.

1989 "New Testament Scholarship in South Africa," *Neotestamentica* 23: 119–25.

1990 "'God Raised Him on the Third Day and Made Him Manifest . . . And He Commanded Us to Preach to the People . . .' (Acts 10:34–40)," *JTSA* 70: 55–63.

1993 "The Bible and the Struggle (for Power)," *Scriptura* 45: 1–28. [abstract: *NTA* 38/2 (1994): #615.]

de Villiers, Pieter G.R., ed.

1987 *Liberation Theology and the Bible* (Pretoria: University of South Africa). [abstract: *NTA* 32/3 (1988): 382.]

Like A Roaring Lion . . . Essays on the Bible, the Church and Demonic Powers (Pretoria: University of South Africa). [abstract: *NTA* 32/3 (1988): 382.]

Domeris, W.R.

1986 "Biblical Perspectives on Forgiveness," *JTSA* 54: 48–50.

"Biblical Perspectives on the Role of Women," *JTSA* 55: 58–61. [abstract: *NTA* 31/2 (1987): #816.]

"Biblical Perspectives on the Poor," *JTSA* 57: 57–61. [abstract: *NTA* 31/3 (1987): #1275.]

"Jesus, Prayer, and the Kingdom of God," Boesak & Villa-Vicencio: 113–24.

1987   "Biblical Perspectives on Reconciliation," *JTSA* 60: 77–80. [abstract: *NTA* 32/2 (1988): #835.]
        Matthew Portraits of Jesus: A Contextual Approach to Bible Study (London: Collins, 1987). [abstract: *NTA* 33/3 (1989): 384.

1989   "Biblical Perspectives on the Use of Force," *JTSA* 62: 68–72.
        "Christology and Community: A Study of the Social Matrix of the Fourth Gospel," *JTSA* 64: 49–56.
        "The Paraclete as an Ideological Construct. A Study in the Farewell Discourses," *JTSA* 67: 17–23. [abstract: *NTA* 34/1 (1990): #217.]

1990   "'Blessed are you . . .' (Matthew 5:1–12)," *JTSA* 73: 67–76. [abstract: *NTA* 35/3 (1991): #1127.]

1991   "Reading the Bible Against the Grain," *Scriptura* 37: 68–81. [abstract: *BCT* 3/1 (1996): 26.]

Domeris, W. & R. Wortley
1987   *John* Portraits of Jesus: A Contextual Approach to Bible Study (London: Collins, 1987). [abstract: *NTA* 33/3 (1989): 384.

Draper, Jonathan A.
1987   "The Tip of the Ice-Berg: The Temple of the Holy Spirit," *JTSA* 59: 57–65. [abstract: *BCTA* 1 (1993): 19.]

1988   "'In Humble Submission to Almighty God' and its Biblical Foundation: Contextual Exegesis of Romans 13: 1–7," *JTSA* 63: 30–41. [abstract: *BCTA* 1 (1993): 19.]
        "The Social Milieu and Motivation of the Community of Goods in the Jerusalem Church of Acts," Breytenbach [abstract: *BCTA* 1 (1993): 19.]

1989   "Church-State Conflict in the Book of Acts: A South African Perspective," *Reading the Bible in South Africa* C. Wanamaker & W. Mazamisa, eds (Braamfontein: Skotaville).

1991   "Christ the Worker: Fact or Fiction?" Cochrane & West: 121–41.
        "'For the Kingdom is inside of you and it is outside of you': Contextual Exegesis in South Africa," P.J. Hastin & J.H. Petzer, eds *Text and Interpretation: New Approaches in the Criticism of the New Testament* (Leiden: Brill): 235–58. [abstract: *BCT* 3/1 (1996): 26.]
        "The Johannine Community and Its Implications for a Democratic Society," Nurnberger, ed.: 115–136. [abstract: *BCTA* 1 (1993): 19.]

1992   "'Go sell all that you have . . .' (Mark 10:17–30)," *JTSA* 79: 63–69. [*NTA* 37 (1993): #1291.]
        "The Sociological Function of the Spirit/paraclete in the Farewell Discourses in the Fourth Gospel," *Neotestamentica* 26/1: 13–29. [abstracts: *NTA* 37 (1993): #803; *BCT* 3/1 (1996): 26.]

1994   "Jesus and the Renewal of Local Community in Galilee: Challenge to a Communitarian Christology," *JTSA* 87: 29–42. [abstract: *BCT* 3/1 (1996): 26.]

1995   "Wandering Radicalism or Purposeful Activity? Jesus and the Sending of Messengers in Mark 6:6–56," *Neotestimentica* 29/2: 187–207. [abstract: *BCT* 3/1 (1996): 26.]

1996   "Great and Little Traditions: Challenges to the Dominant Western Paradigm of Biblical Interpretation," *BCT* 3/1: 1–2.

"Voices from the Margin in the Corridors of Power," *BCT* 1/3: 12–13.

"Confessional Western Text-Oriented Biblical Interpretation and an Oral Residual-Oral Context," *Semeia* 73: 59–77. [abstract: *NTA* 42/1 (1998): #25.]

1997   "The Bible in African Literature; A 'Contrapuntal Perspective,'" [editorial] *BCT* 4/3: 1–3.

"Church-State Conflict in the Book of Acts: A South African Perspective," *JTSA* 97: 39–52. [abstract: *NTA* 42/2 (1998): #1063.]

"Archbishop Gray and the Interpretation of the Bible," in *Change and Challenge: Essays Commemorating the 150th Anniversary of Robert Gray as First Bishop of Cape Town (20 February 1848)* J. Suggit & M. Goedhals, eds (Johannesburg: CPSA): 44–54.

"Hermeneutical Drama on the Colonial Stage: Liminal Space and Creativity in Colenso's *Commentary on Romans*," *JTSA* 103/1: [?].

Draper, J.A. & G. West

1989   "Anglicans and Scripture in South Africa," F. England & T. Paterson, eds *Bounty in Bondage: The Anglican Church in Southern Africa. Essays in Honour of Edward King, Dean of Cape Town* (Johannesburg: Ravan): 30–52.

1991   "The Bible and Social Transformation in South Africa: A Work-In-Progress Report on the Institute for the Study of the Bible," Eugene H. Lovering, Jr., ed. *Society of Biblical Literature 1991 Seminar Papers* (Atlanta: Scholars Press): 366–82. [abstract: David J. Lull & James B. Wiggins, eds *Abstracts: American Academy of Religion/ Society of Biblical Literature 1991* (Scholars Press): 58–59.]

Du Preez, Jannie

1973   "The Exodus Character of Biblical Salvation," Becken, 1974: 19–40.

1984   "People and Nations in the Kingdom of God According to the Book of Revelation," *JTSA* 49: 49–51.

1996   "All Things New: Notes on the Church's Mission in the Light of Revelation 21: 1–8," *Missionalia* 24/3: 372–82.

1997   "Interpreting Psalm 47. Some Notes on its Composition, Exegesis and Significance for the Church's Mission at the End of the Century," *Missionalia* 25/3: 308–23.

Du Rand, J.A.

1992   "An Apocalyptic Text, Different Contexts and An Applicable Ethos," *JTSA* 78: 75–83. [abstract: *NTA* 37/1 (1993): #335; *BCT* 3/1 (1996): 26.]

"A Story and A Community: Reading the First Farewell Discourse (John 13:31–14:31) From Narratological and Sociological Perspectives," *Neotestamentica* 26/1: 31–45. [abstract: *BCT* 3/1 (1996): 26.]

Durand, J.J.F.

1978   "Bible and Race: The Problem of Hermeneutics" *JTSA* 24: 3–11.

Du Toit, A.B.
1993 "The Rise and Current State of New Testament Research in South Africa: Part 1," *HTS* 49/3: 503–14. [in Afrikaans; includes extensive bibliography; abstract: *NTA* 38/3 (1994): #1283.]
"The Rise and Current State of New Testament Research in South Africa: Part 2," *HTS* 49/4: 786–809. [in Afrikaans; includes extensive bibliography.]
"Oppressive and Subversive Moral Instruction in the New Testament," Ackermann, Draper & Mashinini, eds: 37–54. [abstract: *BCT* 4/2 (1997): 37.]

Du Toit, C.
1996 "The Place of African Hermeneutics in Understanding the Dynamics of African Theology," *Scriptura* 67: 363–85. [abstract: *NTA* 43/3 (1999): #1522.]

Du Torr, C.W., ed.
1997 *Images of Jesus* (Pretoria: Unisa).

Emslie, B.L.
1985 "The Methodology of Proceeding From Exegesis to an Ethical Decision" *Neotestamentica* 19: 87–91.

Engelbrecht, Ben
1987 "The Ultimate Significance of the Torah" *JTSA* 61: 45–58.

Farisani, E.
1993 "Land in the Old Testament: The Conflict Between Ahab and Elijah (1 Kings 21:1–29), and its Significance for Our South African Context Today," (Master's thesis, University of Natal, Pietermaritzburg, South Africa.) [abstract: *BCT* 3/1 (1996): 26.]

Flint, P.
1987 "Old Testament Scholarship from an African Perspective," Burden, Botha & van Rooy: 179–214.

Gardner, Colin
1997 "Alan Paton and the Bible," *BCT* 4/3: 26–29.

Gaybba, B.
1987 "The Development in Biblical Times of Belief in Demons and Devils and the Theological Issue Raised by Such A Development," de Villiers, ed. *Like a Roaring Lion*: 90–101.

General Synod of the Dutch Reformed Church
1976 *Human Relations and the South African Scene in the Light of Scripture* (official translation of the report *Ras, Volk en Nasie en Volkereverhoudinge in die Lig van die Skrif* approved and accepted by the General Synod of the Reformed Church October 1974; Cape Town/Pretoria, Republic of South Africa: Dutch Reformed Church Publishers); especially Chapter 1, "Scriptural data": 12–38.]

Germond, Paul A.
1987 *Luke Portraits of Jesus: A Contextual Approach to Bible Study* (London: Collins, 1987). [abstract: *NTA* 33/3 (1989): 384.]
1994 "Biblical Exegesis and Social Change in Contemporary South

Africa," *Abstracts: American Academy of Religion/Society of Biblical Literature 1994* (Scholars Press): 355.

Geyser, Albert
  1980 "The Place of the Bible in Religious Education," *JTSA* 33:16–23.

Goba, Bonganjalo
  1986 "The Use of Scripture in the Kairos Document: A Biblical Ethical Perspective," *JTSA* 56: 61–65.

Gous, I.G.P.
  1993 "Old Testament theology of reconstruction: Socio-cultural anthropology, Old Testament theology and a changing South Africa," *OTEssays* 6/2: 175–89. [abstract: *BCT* 3/1 (1996): 26.]

Govender, Shun
  1986 "The Sermon on the Mount (Matt 5–7) and the Question of Ethics," Tlhagale & Mosala: 173–84.

Group from Claremont, Cape Town
  1991 "A South African Example: Jesus' Teaching at Nazareth—Luke 4.14–30," Sugirtharajah, 1st ed.: 423–30; 2nd ed.: 447–53.

Guttler, Michele Y.
  1987 *Mark* Portraits of Jesus: A Contextual Approach to Bible Study (London: Collins, 1987). [abstract: *NTA* 33/3 (1989): 384.]
  1988 "Towards a feminst hermeneutic of Mark 7: 24–30," (unpublished Masters thesis, University of Cape Town, South Africa). [abstract: *BCT* 4/2 (1997): 39.]

Guy, J.
  1983 *The Heretic* (Johannesburg: Ravan).

Hale, Frederick
  1992 "Romans 13: 1–7 in South African Baptist Social Ethics" *SAB-JOT* 1: 66–83.

Hartin, Patrick J.
  1987 "New Testament Ethics: Some Trends in More Recent Research" *JTSA* 59: 35–41.
  1988 "Apartheid and the Scriptures: The Contribution of Albert Geyser in this Polemic" *JTSA* 64: 20–33.
  1991 "Methodological Principles in Interpreting the Relevance of the New Testament for a New South Africa" *Scriptura* 37: 1–16.
  1993 "Exegesis and Proclamation. 'Come now, you rich, weep and wail . . . (James 5:1–6)" *JTSA* 84: 57–63. [abstract: *NTA* 38/2 (1994): #950.]

Hartin, Patrick J. & J.H. Petzer, eds
  1986 *A South African Perspective on the New Testament: Essays by South African New Testament Scholars presented to Bruce Manning Metzger during his Visit to South Africa in 1985* (Leiden: Brill). [reviews: W. Beardslee *Princeton Seminary Bulletin* ns 9 (1988): 73–75; P. Ellingworth *BT* 39 (1988): 139–40; J.K. Elliot *Novum Testamentum* 30 (1988): 95–96; D.A. Black *Filoloia Neotestamentaria* 1 (1988): 117; E.V. Gallagher *CBQ* 51 (1989): 776–77; I.S. Robinson *Journal of Ecclesiastical History*

42 (1991): 259–82; abstracts: *NTA* 32/1 (1988): 95–96; *RSR* 14/3 (1988): 251–52; *BCT* 3/1 (1996): 27.]

Hawkes, Gerald
1988 "Beyond Criticism: Bible Study Today," *JTSA* 65: 60–72. [abstract: *BCT* 3/1 (1996): 27.]

Heyns, Dalene
1997 "Considering Aspects of History, Knowledge and World-view: Is Old Testament History Relevant for South Africa?" *OTEssays* 10: 387–400. [abstract: *OTA* 22/1 (1999): #147.]

Hofmeyer, J.W. & W.S. Vorster, eds
1984 *New faces of Africa: Essays in honour of Ben Marais* (Pretoria: UNISA).

Human, D.J.
1998 "Interpreting the Bible in the 'new' South Africa: Remarks on Some Problems and Challenges," *HTS* 53/3: #1532.]

Hunter, D.
1991 "Time, Narrative and Liberation Discourse: A Brief Review and Assessment of Aspects of the Recent Hermeneutical Writings of Paul Ricoeur," (Master's thesis, University of Cape Town, Cape Town, South Africa). [abstract: *BCT* 3/1 (1996): 27.]

Institute for the Study of the Bible
1992 *Repentance and Conversion: Working in the Church and the Community on "The Road to Damascus"* (Bible Studies in Context #1; Pietermaritzburg, South Africa: Institute for the Study of the Bible in collaboration with Cluster Publications).
1996 "Women and the Bible in South and Southern Africa," Report of the ISB Biennial Workshop September 1996 (Pietermaritzberg, University of Natal). [abstract: *BCT* 4/2 (1997): 39.]

Isaac, Jean, Louise Kretzschmar, Margie Pigott & Nelda Thelin
1991 "A Case Study: The Umtata Women's Theology Group" in Ackermann, Draper & Mashinini: 64–75.

Jobling, David
1997 "Searching for Colonialism's Sacred Cows: An Intertextual Reading of 1 Samuel and H. Rider Haggard's *Nada the Lily*," *BCT* 4/3: 4–8.

Joubert, S.J.
1992 "Van werklikheid tot werklikhein: Die interpretasie en interkulturele kommunikasie van Nuwe-Testamentiese waarde" [From Reality to Reality: The Interpretation and Intercultural Communication of New Testament Values] *Scriptura* 41: 55–65. [*NTA* 37 (1993): #576.]

Kameeta Zephanja
1973 "Bible Study: Romans 3:21–31," Becken, 1974: 71–74.

Khabela, M.G.
1997 "Biblical Hermeneutics of Black Theology: An Unfinished Debate," in Abrahams, et al.: 95–111.

King, N.
1995 *Setting the Gospel Free* (Pietermaritzburg: Cluster Publications.) [abstract: *BCT* 3/1 (1996): 27.]

Landman, Christina
1996 "A Land Flowing with Milk and Honey: Reading the Bible with
       Women who are Breastfeeding," pp. 99–111 in *Groaning in Faith:
       African Women in the Household of God* Musimbi R. Kanyoro &
       Njoroge Nyambura, eds (Nairobi: Acton Publishers). [abstract:
       BCT 4/2 (1997): 42.]
Lapoorta, Japie
1989 "'. . . Whatever You Did for One of the Least of These . . . You
       Did for me' (Matt. 25:31–46)," *JTSA* 68: 103–109. [abstract: *NTA*
       34/2 (1990): #637.]
Larsen, T.
1997 "Bishop Colenso and His Critics: The Strange Emergence of
       Biblical Criticism in Victorian Britain," *SJT* 50/4: 433–58. [abstract:
       NTA 42/3 (1998): #1536.]
Lategan, Bernard C.
1984 "Current Issues in the Hermeneutic Debate," *Neotestamentica* 18:
       1–17. [abstract: *NTA* 29/3 (1985): #842.]
1990 "Introducing a Research Project on Contextual Hermeneutics,"
       Scriptura 33:1–5.
1991 "The Challenge of Contextuality," *Scriptura* Special Issue 9: 1–6.
       [abstract: *NTA* 38/2 (1994): #636.]
1996 "Scholar and Ordinary Reader—More Than a Simple Interface,"
       Semeia 73: 243–55.
1997 "Possible Future Trends From the Perspective of Hermeneutics,"
       JTSA 99: 116–21. [abstract: *NTA* 42/3 (1998): #1537.]
1998 "The *Studiorum Novi Testamenti Societas* comes to Africa," *Scriptura*
       67 (1998): 419–27. [abstract: *NTA* 43/3 (1999): #1607.]
Lategan, Bernard C., ed.
1992 *The Reader and Beyond: Theory and Practice in South African Reception
       Studies* (Pretoria: HSRC).
Lederle, H.I.
1987 "Better the Devil You Know? Seeking A Biblical Basis for the
       Societal Dimension of Evil And/or the Demonic in the Pauline
       Concept of the 'Powers,'" de Villiers, ed. *Like a Roaring Lion*: 102–20.
Lefeuvre, Philip
1996 "A Biblical Vision for Diocesan Life: The Diocese of St Mark the
       Evangelist (Province of Southern Africa)," in Stott and Others:
       144–51.
le Roux, J.H.
1987 "Two Possible Readings of Isaiah 61," de Villiers, ed. *Liberation
       Theology and the Bible*: 31–44.
1993 *A Story of Two Ways: Thirty Years of Old Testament Scholarship in South
       Africa* OTE, Supplement number 2 (Pretoria: Verba Vitae). [review:
       J.A. Loader *SK* 15 (1994): 391–413; abstract: *OTA* 19/1 (1996):
       #587.]
Lienbenberg, Jacobus
1999 "Images of Jesus. A Report on a Seminar," *R&T* 5/1: 101–106.

Loader, J.
1987 "Exodus, Liberation Theology and Theological Argument," *JTSA* 59: 3–18.

1994 "Die Weg van die Here in die Woestyn oftewel God se Grootpad in die Wildernis: Oor A *Story of Two Ways* [The Lord's Way in the Wilderness or God's Highway in the Wilderness. Concerning A *Story of Two Ways*]," *SK* 15: 391–413. [abstract: *OTA* 18/2 (1995): #635.]

Long, T.M.S.
1990 "Reading Paul in the South African Context of Struggle for Liberation: Some Insights From Latin-american Liberation Theology," (Master's thesis, University of Natal, Pietermaritzburg, South Africa). [abstract: *BCT* 3/1 (1996): 27.]

1992 "Deconstruction and Biblical Studies in South Africa," *Scriptura* 42: 50–64. [abstract: *NTA* 37/3 (1993): #1128.]

1993 "Reading the Book of Revelation in South Africa: Some Methodological and Literary Observations in Response to Du Rand," *JTSA* 83: 78–86. [abstract: *NTA* 38/2 (1994): #964; *BCT* 3/1 (1996): 27.]

1994 "A Real Reader Reading Revelation," *Neotestamentica* 28/2: 395–411. [abstract: *BCT* 3/1 (1996): 27–28.]

1996 "A Real Reader Reading Revelation," *Semeia* 73: 79–107. [abstract: *NTA* 42/1 (1998): #454.]

Loubser, J.A.
1987 *The Apartheid Bible: A Critical Review of Racial Theology in South Africa* (Cape Town, Republic of South Africa: Maskew Miller Longman, 1987). [abstract: *BCT* 3/1 (1996): 28.]

1991 "Winning the Struggle (Or: How to Treat Heretics) (2 Corinthians 12:1–10)," *JTSA* 75: 75–83. [abstract: *NTA* 36/1 (1992): #308.]

1993 "Orality and Pauline 'Christology': Some Hermeneutical Implications," *Scriptura* 47: 25–51.
"The Oral Christ—Believing in Jesus in Oral and Literate Societies," (paper presented to the Theological Society Congress, University of Cape Town, 18–20 August 1993).

1994 "Wealth, House Churches and Rome: Luke's Ideological Perspective," *JTSA* 89: 59–69. [abstract: *BCT* 3/1 (1996): 28.]

1996 "The Apartheid Bible Revisited," *BCT* 3/1: 8–10.

Maartens, P.J.
1995 "The Relevance of 'Context' and 'Interpretation' to the Semiotic Relations of Romans 5:1–11," *Neotestamentica* 29/1: 75–108. [abstract: *BCT* 3/1 (1996): 28.]

Maimela, Simon S.
1982 "The New Testament Forms of Ministry and the Lutheran Concept of Ministry," *ATJ* 11/2: 121–32.

1986 "The Concept 'Israel' in White Theology: A Theological Critique," *ATJ* 15/2: 79–90.

1991 "Images of Liberation in Black and Feminist Theologies of Liberation," *Theologia Evangelica* 24/2: 40–47. [abstract: *BCT* 3/1 (1996): 28.]

Maimela, Simon S. & S. Hopkins, eds
 1989 *We Are One Voice* (Braamfontein: Skotaville Publishers). [abstract: *BCTA* 1 (1993): 28.]

Malan, Jannie
 1987 "A Complement to the Exodus Motif in Theology," *JTSA* 61:3–13.

Mandlate, B.
 1994 "Poverty and Riches in the Book of James: A Contextual Exegetical Approach of Chapters 2:1–7 and 5:1–6, in Relation to South Africa," (Master's thesis, University of Natal, Pietermaritzburg, South Africa). [abstract: *BCT* 3/1 (1996): 28.]

Masenya, Madipoane J.
 1989 "In the School of Wisdom: An Interpretation of Some Old Testament Proverbs in a Northern Sotho Context," (unpublished Masters thesis, University of South Africa).
 1991 "In the School of Wisdom: An Interpretation of Some Old Testament Proverbs in a Northern Sotho Context," *OTEssays* 4: 41–56. [abstract: *OTA* 15/2 (1992): #808.]
 1994 "A Feminist Perspective on Theology with Particular Reference to Black Feminist Theology," *Scriptura* 49: 64–74. [abstract: *BCT* 4/2 (1997): 43.]
 "Freedom in Bondage: Black Feminist Hermeneutics," *JBTSA* 8/1: 35–48. [abstract: *BCT* 4/2 (1997): 43.]
 "Wisdom Meets Wisdom: Selected Old Testament Proverbs Contextualized in A Northern Sotho Setting," *NGTT* 35: 15–23. [abstract: *OTA* 18/1 (1995): #330.]
 1995 "African Womanist Hermenuetics: A Suppressed Voice from South Africa Speaks," *Journal of Feminist Studies in Religion* 11: 149–55. [abstract: *BCT* 4/2 (1997): 43–44.]
 "The Bible and Women: Black Feminist Hermeneutics," *Scriptura* 54: 189–201. [abstract: *NTA* 40/2 (1996): #694; *BCT* 4/2 (1997): 44.]
 "Proverbs 31:10–31 in a South African Context: A Black (Northern Sotho) Woman's Reading," *Abstracts: American Academy of Religion/ Society of Biblical Literature 1995* (Scholars Press): 150–51.
 "African Womanist Hermeneutics: A Suppressed Voice From South Africa Speaks," *Journal of Feminist Studies in Religion* 11: 149–55.
 1996 "Proverbs 31:10–31 in a South African context: A *Bosadi* (Womanhood) Perspective," (Doctoral dissertation, University of South Africa, Pretoria). [abstracts: *NAOTS* 2 (1997): 15–16; *BCT* 4/2 (1997): 44.]
 1997 "A *Bosadi* (Womanhood) Reading of Genesis 16," *Abstracts: American Academy of Religion/ Society of Biblical Literature 1997* (Scholars Press): 6.
 "Reading the Bible the *Bosadi* (Womanhood) Way," *BCT* 4/2: 15–16.

"Proverbs 31:10–31 in a South African Context: A Reading for the Liberation of African (Northern Sotho) Women," *Semeia* 78: 55–68. [abstract: *OTA* 22/2 (1999): #902.]

1999   "A Mosadi (Woman) Reading of Proverbs 31:10–31," *NAOTS* 6: 2–4. [abstract: *OTA* 22/3 (1999): #1640.]

Masenya, Madipoane J. & Christina Landman
1997   *Their Story and Ours: Biblical Women and Us* (Pretoria: CB Powell Bible Centre). [abstract: *BCT* 4/2 (1997): 44.]

Masipa, Lekoapa P.
1999   "The Use of the Bible in Black Theology with Reference to the Exodus Story," (M.Th. thesis, University of Natal).

Masoga, M.A.
1995   "A Critical Analysis of the Function of Hebrews 9:1–28, in the Light of Sacrificial Yoruba ritual, and with Special Reference to the Pedi Responses to the Text," (Master's thesis, University of Natal, Pietermaritzburg, South Africa). [abstract: *BCT* 3/1 (1996): 28.]

Mazamisa, Llewellyn Welile
1988   *Beatific Comradeship: An Exegetical-Hermeneutical Study on Luke 10:25–37* (Kampen, Netherlands: J.H. Kok-Kampen). [abstracts: *NTA* 33/1 (1989): 109; *BCTA* 1 (1993): 30.]

1991   "Reading from this Place: From Orality to Literacy/Textuality and Back," *Scriptura* Special Issue 9: 67–72. [abstract: *NTA* 38/2 (1994): #637.]

1995   "Re-reading the Bible in the Black Church: Towards a Hermeneutic of Orality and Literacy," *JBTSA* 9/2: 1–26. [abstract: *NTA* 41/2 (1997): #738.]

Meyer, Wilhelm H.
1995   "Taking Reader Response to its Logical Conclusion: Reading Romans with Ordinary Readers in Pietermaritzburg." (Master's thesis, University of Natal, Pietermaritzburg, South Africa).

1997   "Christianity and the Bible in South African Literature: Interviews with Mandla Langa and Mongane Wally Serote," *BCT* 4/3: 45–51.

Mitchell, Gordon
1993   "Abraham in World Religions: Perspectives From Biblical Scholarship," *JTSA* 85: 47–52. [abstract: *BCT* 3/1 (1996): 28–29.]

1994   "Towards A New Curriculum for Biblical Studies in South Africa," *OTEssays* 7/4: 321–26.

Mngadi, C.S.
1973   "Bible Study: Isaiah 52:13–53:12," Becken, 1974: 41–45.

Moela, D.O.
1973   "Bible Study: Revelation 21:22–27," Becken, 1974: 98–102.

Mofokeng, Takatso Alfred
1983   *The Crucified among the Crossbearers: Towards a Black Theology* (Kampen, Netherlands: J.H. Kok-Kampen). [review: J.S. Mbiti *IRM* 71 (1982): 521–28.]

1987 "Black Christians, the Bible and Liberation," *Voices* 10/4: 15–24; reprinted in *JBTSA* 2 (1988): 34–39.
1992 "Discovering Culture and its Influence on the Bible," *JBTSA* 6/1: 1–14;
reprinted in *Voices* 16/2 (1993): 61–76.
1994 "Culture and its Influence in the Bible: Hermeneutical Explorations," Simon S. Maimela, ed. *Culture, Religion and Liberation: Proceedings of the EATWOT Pan African Theological Conference, Harare, Zimbabwe, January 6–11, 1991* (Pretoria: AACC): 65–76.
Moore, Basil, ed.
1973 *Black Theology: The South African Voice* (London: C. Hurst & Co.).
Mosala, Bernadette I.
1984 "Biblical Hermeneutics and the Struggle of Women," pp. 22–25 in *Women's struggle in South Africa* (Johannesburg: Institute for Contextual Theology). [abstract: *BCT* 4/2 (1997): 45.]
Mosala, Itumeleng J.
1983 "African Traditional Beliefs and Christianity," *JTSA* 43: 15–24.
1985 "The Biblical God from the Perspective of the Poor," *God and Global Justice* F. Ferr and R. Mataragnon, eds (N.Y.: Paragon House): 160–68.
1986 "Black Theology Versus the Social Morality of Settler Colonialism: Hermeneutical Reflections on Luke 1 and 2," *JBTSA* 1: 26–42.
"Social Scientific Approaches to the Bible: One Step Forward, Two Steps Back," *JTSA* 55: 15–30; reprinted as chapter 2 of Mosala, 1989. [abstract: *NTA* 31/2 (1987): #511; *OTA* 10/3 (1987): #633.]
"The Use of the Bible in Black Theology," I. Mosala & B. Tlhagale, eds *The Unquestionable Right to Be Free: Essays in Black Theology* Johannesburg: Skotaville): 175–99; reprinted in *Voices* 10/2 (1987): 90–109; as chapter 1 of Mosala, 1989; in Sugirtharajah, 1st ed.: 50–60, in *Black Theology: A Documentary History* vol. 2; James Cone, & Gayraud S. Wilmore, eds (Maryknoll: Orbis, 1993): 245–54.
1987 "The Meaning of Reconciliation: A Black Perspective," *JTSA* 59: 19–25.
1988 "The Implications of the Text of Esther for African Women's Struggle for Liberation in South Africa," *JBTSA* 2/2: 3–9; reprinted in David Jobling & Tina Pippin, eds "Ideological Criticism of Biblical Texts," *Semeia* 59 (1993): 129–37; in Sugirtharajah, 2nd ed.: 168–78; published in French as "Les Implications de Texte d'Esther pour la Lutte des Femmes Africaines pour la Liberation en Afrique du Sud," *RZTP* 5 (1991): 7–15. (translated by Tim Bulkeley and Anthony Staines) [see comments by Lillian R. Klein in "Esthers's Lot," *Currents in Research: Biblical Studies* 5 (1997), pp. 114–15; abstracts: *OTA* 17 (1994): #439; *BCTA* 1 (1993): 31–32; *BCT* 4/2 (1997): 45.]
"Violence and the Prophets," *Theology & Violence: The South African Debate* C. Villa-Vicencio, ed. (Grand Rapids: Eerdmans): 103–109.

1989   *Biblical Hermeneutics and Black Theology in South Africa* (Grand Rapids: Eerdmans); revision of 1987 University of Cape Town Ph.D. dissertation. [reviews: P. Schrotenboer *Calvin Theological Review* 25 (1990): 292–95; G. Snyder *Chicago Theological Seminary Register* 80 (1990): 41–42; David Bosch *Missionalia* 19 (1991): 87–88; P. Capp *Missiology* 19 (1991): 236; Emmanuel Martey *ATJ* 21/1 (1992): 103–106; Ambrose Mavingire Moyo *CBQ* 54/3 (1992): 582–83; M.C. Parsons *Journal of Church and State* 34 (1992): 392–93; G. LeMarquand *BookNotes* 2 (October 1996): #2.26; abstracts: *NTA* 34/2 (1990): 239; *BCTA* 1 (1993): 32; *BCT* 3/1 (1996): 29.]

1991   "Bible and Liberation in South Africa in the 1980's: Toward an Antipopulist Reading of the Bible," David Jobling, ed. *The Bible and the Politics of Exegesis: Essays in Honor of Norman K. Gottwald on His Sixty-Fifth Birthday* (Cleveland: Pilgrim): 267–74.
        "Biblical Hermeneutics of Liberation: The Case of Micah," Sugirtharajah, 1st ed.: 104–16 [an abbreviation of chapter 4 of Mosala, 1989.]
        "Ethics of Economic Principles: Church and Secular Investments," Cochrane & West: 109–20.
        "Land, Class and the Bible in South Africa Today," *JBTSA* 5/2: 40–45.
        "Wealth and Poverty in the Old Testament—A Black Theological Perspective," *JBTSA* 5: 16–22. [abstract: *BCT* 3/1 (1996): 29.]
        "Why Apartheid Was Right About The Unliberated Bible," David J. Lull & James B. Wiggins, eds *Abstracts: American Academy of Religion/Society of Biblical Literature 1991* (Scholars Press): 57.

1993   "Good News for the Poor: A Black African Biblical Hermeneutics," *Epworth Review* 20/3: 85–91; republished in *The Portion of the Poor: Good News to the Poor in the Wesleyan Tradition* M. Meeks, ed. (Nashville: Abingdon): 37–48, 117. [abstract: *RTA* 39/2 (1996): #1837.]

1994   "Why Apartheid Was Right About the Unliberated Bible: Race, Class and Gender as Hermeneutical Factors in the Appropriation of Scripture," *Voices* 17/1: 151–59.

1996   "Race, Class, and Gender as Hermeneutical Factors in the African Independent Churches' Appropriation of the Bible," *Semeia* 73: 43–57. [abstracts: *BCT* 4/2 (1997): 45; *NTA* 42/1 (1998): #62.]
        "Reconstructing the Azanian *Mispahot* (Class): Land, Class and Bible in South Africa Today," Smith-Christopher: 238–46.

Mosothoane, E.K.
1979   "The Use of Scripture in Black Theology," Vorster: 28–40.

Motlhabi, Ephraim K.
1979   "The Use of Scripture in Black Theology," *Scripture and the Use of Scripture* (Pretoria: University of South Africa).

Motlhabi, Mokgethi
1987   "Liberation Theology: An Introduction," de Villiers, ed. *Liberation Theology and the Bible*: 1–14.

Moulder, James
  1977   "Romans 13 and Conscientious Disobedience," *JTSA* 21: 13–
         23.
Mtetwa, C.N.
  1973   "Suffering and Christian Hope," Becken, 1974: 46–49.
Myrick, P. Allen
  1965   "Jeremiah 4:13–26: God's Judgement on South Africa," *Ministry*
         5/3: 121–23.
Ncube, Bernard SR.
  1984   "Biblical Problems and the Struggle of Women," Pp. 26–29 in
         Women's Struggle and South Africa (Johannesburg: Institute for Con-
         textual Theology). [abstract: *BCT* 4/2 (1997): 44.]
Nel, P.J.
  1987   "The Conception of Evil and Satan in Jewish Traditions in the
         Pre-christian Period," de Villiers, ed. *Like a Roaring Lion*: 1–21.
Nelumbu, M.
  1994   "Analytical Study of the Theme of Liberation in the Psalms,"
         (Doctoral dissertation, University of Natal, Petermaritzburg, South
         Africa). [abstract: *BCT* 3/1 (1996): 29.]
Nesvaag, J.
  1973   "Bible Study: Luke 24: 44–49," Becken, 1974: 50–53.
Nolan, Albert
  1982   *Biblical Spirituality* (Springs: Order of Preachers, South Africa).
         [abstract: *BCTA* 1 (1993): 34.]
  1988   *God in South Africa: The Challenge of the Gospel* (Claremont, South
         Africa: David Philip; Gweru, Zimbabwe: Mambo Press; London,
         United Kingdom: Catholic Institute for International Relations;
         Grand Rapids: Eerdmans); especially chapter 2, "Sin in the Bible"
         and chapter 6, "Salvation in the Bible." [reviews: T.O. Balcomb
         JTSA 68 (1989): 113–18; G. Markus *New Blackfriars* 70 (1989):
         307–308; R.K. DeHainaut *Christian Century* 107 (1990): 225–27;
         J. Donders *Commonweal* 117 (1990): 90–91; R.J.R. Mathies *Conrad
         Grebel Review* 8 (1990): 93–95; C. Murray *Pacifica* 3 (1990): 353–55;
         S. Snook *Missiology* 18 (1990): 225–26; P.L. Kjeseth *Currents in
         Theology and Mission* 18 (1991): 331–37; D. Moodie *IBMR* 15 (1991):
         91; A. Tafferner *Zeitschrift für Missionswissenschaft und Religionswissenschaft*
         77/3 (1993): 254–55; abstract: *RSR* 16/1 (1990): 56.]
  1991   "A Worker's Theology," Cochrane & West: 160–168.
  1992   "Jeremiah: The Life and Struggles of An Old Testament Prophet,"
         Challenge 6: 2–4. [abstract: *BCT* 3/1 (1996): 29.]
  1992   *Jesus Before Christianity* revised ed. (Maryknoll: Orbis [Claremont,
         South Africa: David Philip, 1976; London: Darton Longman &
         Todd, 1977; Maryknoll: Orbis, 1978]). [reviews: D. Tutu *JTSA*
         19 (1977): 68–69; J.A. Kirk *Churchman* 2/1 (1978): 70–71; J.K.S.
         Reid *SJT* 31/1 (1978): 80–82; J.A. Berquist *Missiology* 7 (1979):
         250–52; D. Hamm *Currents in Theology and Mission* 6 (1979): 182–83;
         M. Bouttier *Etudes Théologiques et Réligieuses* 55/4 (1980): 607–609;

G. Snyder *Chicago Theological Seminary Register* 85 (1995): 46–47; abstracts: *RSR* 5/3 (1979): 223; *NTA* 37/2 (1993): 282.]

1996   "Work, the Bible, Workers, and Theologians: Elements of a Workers' Theology," *Semeia* 73: 213–20. [abstract: *NTA* 42/1 (1998): #531.]

Nopece, N. Bethlehem

1986   "Romans 13 and Apartheid: A Study of Rom. 13:1–7 in Relation to the Modern Political Situation in South Africa," (M.Th. thesis, University of Glasgow, Scotland).

Nurnberger, Klaus

1973   "The People of God and the State," Becken, 1974: 103–16.

1987   "Theses on Romans 13," *Scriptura* 22: 40–47. [abstract: *BCT* 3/1 (1996): 29.]

1992   "The Royal-Imperial Paradigm in the Bible and the Modern Demand for Democracy: An Exercise in Soteriological Hermeneutics," *JTSA* 81: 16–34. [abstract: *BCT* 3/1 (1996): 29.]

1997   "The Conquest of Chaos: The Biblical Paradigm of Creation and its Contemporary Relevance," *Missionalia* 98: 45–63.

Nurnberger, Klaus, ed.

1991   *A Democratic Vision for South Africa* (Pietermaritzburg, Republic of South Africa: Encounter Publications).

Nurnberger, Margaret, ed.

1992   *I Will Send You to Pharaoh* Bible Studies in Context #2 (Pietermaritzburg, South Africa: Cluster Publications/Institute for the Study of the Bible). [abstract: *BCT* 3/1 (1996): 29.]

Odendaal, B.J.

1973   "Christian Identity and Racial Identity," Becken, 1974: 75–82.

Odendaal, Maria S.

1994   "A Feminist Understanding of the Old Testament," *OTEssays* 7/4: 254–58. [abstract: *BCT* 4/2 (1997): 46.]

Oosthuizen, G.C.

1987   "The Interpretation of and Reaction to Demonic Powers in Indigenous Churches," de Villiers, ed. *Like a Roaring Lion*: 63–89.

1989   "Hebraies-judaistiese Trekke in die Onafhanklike Kerke (Ok) en Religieuse Bewegings op die Swart Bevolking in Suid-afrika," *NGTT* 30: 333–45. [abstract: Holter: #176.]

Oosthuizen, M.J.

1988   "Scripture in Context: The Use of the Exodus Theme in the Hermeneutics of Liberation Theology," *Scriptura* 25: 7–22.

1996   "The Deuteronomic Code As a Resource for Christian Ethics," *JTSA* 96: 44–58.

Oosthuizen, Rudolph de W.

1993   "African Experience of Time and its Compatibility with the Old Testament View of Time As Suggested in the Genealogy of Genesis 5," *OTEssays* 6:190–204. [abstracts: *OTA* 17/3 (1994): #1878; Holter: #177.]

1997   "'The Eleventh Commandment Is: Thou Shalt Take Care of the
       Earth,'" in Abrahams, et al.: 47–58.
       "'Umntu Akazingewabi': The Living Dead in the Old Testament
       and in Africa," in Abrahams, et al.: 47–58.
1996   "What 'African' Means for South African Old Testament Scholar-
       ship," *NAOTS* 5: 12–19. [abstract: *OTA* 22/2 (1999): #647.]

Parratt, John
1989   "The Marxist Trend in Recent South African Black Theology: Is
       Dialogue Possible?" *Mission Studies* 12, 6/2: 77–86.

Pauw, C.M.
1994   "Theological Education in Africa," *OTEssays* 7/4: 13–24.

Peace, R.V.
1990   "A Contemporary Evangelical Account of Conversion," (Master's
       thesis, University of Natal, Pietermaritzburg, South Africa). [abstract:
       BCT 3/1 (1996): 29–30.]

Philpott, Graham
1993   *Jesus is Tricky and God is Undemocratic: The Kin-dom of God in Amawoti*
       (Pietermaritzburg: Cluster Publications); especially the verbatim
       reports of 13 Bible studies: 130–98. [abstract: *BCT* 3/1 (1996): 30.]

Plaatjie, Gloria Kehilwe
1997   "Mary Magdalene in the Gospel of John in the Context of Readings
       by Southern African Township Women," (unpublished Masters
       thesis, University of Natal, Pietermaritzberg). [abstract: *BCT* 4/2
       (1997): 47.]

Punt, J.
1997   "Biblical Studies in South Africa? The Case for Hermeneutics,"
       Scriptura 60: 15–30. [abstract: *NTA* 42/1 (1998): #69.]
       "Biblical Studies in South Africa? The Case for Moral Values,"
       Scriptura 60: 1–13. [abstract: *NTA* 42/1 (1998): #70.]
       "Reading the Bible in Africa: Towards a hermeneutic of Ubuntu,"
       in Abrahams, et al.: 14–35.
       "'[Ara ge Ginoskeis ha Anaginoskeis;]' (Ac 26 [Sic;'8]:30b]: The
       Biblical Languages and Theological Education in Africa," in
       Abrahams, et al.: 126–34.
1998   "The Bible, Its Status and African Christian Theologies: Foun-
       dational Document or Stumbling Block?" R&T 5/3: 265–310.
       [abstract: *NTA* 43/2 (1999): #804.]
       "New Testament Interpretation, Interpretive Interests, and Ideology:
       Methodological Deficits Amidst South African Methodolomania?"
       Scriptura 65: 123–52. [abstract: *NTA* 43/2 (1999): #805.]

Reve, N.
1997   "The Illegitimacy of Jesus. An Afrocentric Reading of the Birth
       of Jesus," *Theologia Viatorum* 24: 15–46. [abstract: *NTA* 43/3 (1999):
       1644.]

Robertson, A.C.
1986   "'Hope' in Ephesians 1:18," *JTSA* 55: 62–63.

Robinson, P.J.
   1994   "The Future of Old Testament Studies Through the Eyes of Missiology," *Old Testament Essays* 7/4: 305–13.
Rowland, Christopher
   1993   "In Dialogue with Itumeleng Mosala: A Contribution to Liberation Exegesis," *JSNT* 50 (1993): 43–57. [abstract: *NTA* 38/2 (1994): #640r.]
Ruf, M.
   1991   "Kontextuelle bibelarbeiten zu dem thema 'Jungersein/Nachfolge nach dem Markus evangelium,'" (Master's thesis, University of Natal, Pietermaritzburg, South Africa). [abstract: *BCT* 3/1 (1996): 30.]
Schutte, J.A.
   1977   "Amos, Israel and South Africa (A Bible Study)," *Missionalia* 5/2: 5–7.
Sampson, Courtney
   1991   "The Bible in the Midst of Women," Ackermann, Draper & Mashinini: 55–63. [abstract: *BCT* 4/2 (1997): 47.]
Sebothoma, Wilfred A.
   1989   "Contextualization: A Paradigm Shift?" *Scriptura* 30: 1–14. [abstract: *NTA* 34/1 (1990): #39.]
           "Koinonia in 1 Cor. 10:16: its Significance for Liturgy and Sacrament," *Questions Liturgiques* 70/4: 243–50. "'Koinonia' in 1 Corinthians 10:16," *Neotestimentica* 24/1 (1990): 63–69. [abstracts: *NTA* 34/2 (1990): #742; *NTA* 35/2 (1991): #757.]
   1991   "From Babel to Pentecost: An Analysis of Inter-group Dynamics in South Africa," David J. Lull & James B. Wiggins, eds *Abstracts: American Academy of Religion/Society of Biblical Literature 1991* (Scholars Press): 1.
   1994   "Why did Paul Make so Little of the Birth of Jesus?" *HTS* 50/3 (1994): 655–68. [abstract: *NTA* 39/3 (1995): #1566.]
Shutte, Augustine
   1986   "How Jesus Saves Us," *JTSA* 55: 3–14.
Sibeko, Malika & Beverley Haddad
   1996   "Reading the Bible 'with' African Women in Poor and Marginalised Communities in South Africa," *BCT* 3/1: 14–18. [abstracts: *Abstracts: American Academy of Religion / Society of Biblical Literature* (Scholars Press, 1995): 152; *BCT* 4/2 (1997): 48.]
   1997   "Reading the Bible 'with' Women in Poor and Marginalized Communities in South Africa (Mark 5:21–6:1)," *Semeia* 78: 83–92. [abstract: *NTA* 43/2 (1999): #998.]
Smit, Dirk J.
   1988   "Responsible Hermeneutics: A Systematic Theologian's Response to the Readings and Readers of Luke 12:35–48," *Neotestamentica* 22: 441–84.
   1989   "Through Common Stories to a Common Language? Interpreting Biblical Narratives in an Ideological Conflict," J.B. Wiggin & D.J.

Lull, eds *Abstracts: American Academy of Religion/Society of Biblical Literature 1989* (Scholars Press): 279.

1990 "The Ethics of Interpretation—New Voices from the USA," *Scriptura* 33: 16–28. [abstract: *NTA* 35/1 (1991): #60.]
"The Ethics of Interpretation—and South Africa," *Scriptura* 33: 29–43. [abstract: *NTA* 35/1 (1991): #59.]
"'Show No Partiality . . .' (James 2:1–13)," *JTSA* 71: 59–68. [abstract" *NTA* 35/2 (1991): #797.]

1991 "The Bible and Ethos in a New South Africa," *Scriptura* 37: 51–67. [abstract: *NTA* 36/1 (1992): #46.]

1994 "The Future of Old Testament Studies in South Africa: An Ethicist's Perspective," *OTEssays* 7/4: 286–92. [abstract: *OTA* 18/3 91995): #1395.]
"A Story of Contextual Hermeneutics and the Integrity of New Testament Interpretation in South Africa," *Neotestimentica* 28/2: 265–89. [abstracts: *BCT* 3/1 (1996): 30; *NTA* 40/1 (1996): #53.]
"Reading the Bible and the (Un)official Interpretative Culture," *Neotestimentica* 28: 265–89.

1996 "Saints, Disciples, Friends? Recent South African Perspectives on Christian Ethics and the New Testament," *Neotestamentica* 30/2: 451–64. [abstract: *NTA* 42/1 (1998): #546.]

Smit, J.A.
1991 "New Avenues: The Dialogical Nature and Method of Bible Instruction," *Scriptura* 38: 39–59. [abstract: *NTA* 36/2 (1992): #600.]
"Theoretical Perspectives: Contextualization as Metaphoric Activity," *Neotestimentica* 25/1: 1–15. [abstract: *NTA* 36/2 (1992): #601.]

Snyman, S.D. (Fanie)
1994 "Old Testament Theology: Fabulous Dreams of the Other Side of Time and Place," *OTEssays* 7/3: 453–65. [abstract: *BCT* 3/1 (1996): 30.]
"Political Reading As A Means of Understanding the Old Testament," *OTEssays* 7/4: 173–80.

1997 "On Opening Windows and Doors of Old Testament Studies in South Africa," *OTEssays* 10: 474–93. [abstract: *OTA* 22/1 (1999): #62.]
"Spiritualiteit—'n Perspektief Uit die Oude Testament" [Spirituality B a perspective from the Old Testament], *IDS* 31: 375–87. [abstract: *OTA* 21/3 (1998): #1658.]

South African Council of Churches
1989 *Confessing Guilt in South Africa: The Responsibility of Churches and Individual Christians* (Johannesburg: South African Council of Churches). [abstract: *BCTA* 1 (1993): 44.]

Southern African Theological Commission
1995 "The Land and its Use in Southern Africa," (unpublished paper, University of Natal). [abstract: *BCT* 3/1 (1996): 30.]

Spannenberg, I.J.J.
1995 "Paradigm Changes in the Biblical Sciences and the Teaching of

Biblical Studies in the New South Africa," *Scriptura* 52: 1–10. [abstract: *NTA* 39/3 (1995): #1333.]

Speckman, McGlory

1993   "The Kairos Document and the Development of A Kairos Theology in Luke-acts, with Particular Reference to Luke 19:41–44," (Master's thesis, University of Natal, Pietermaritzburg, South Africa). [abstract: *BCT* 3/1 (1996): 30.]

1996   "Beyond the Debate: An Agenda for Biblical Studies in the New South Africa," *R&T* 3/2: 135–51. [abstract *NTA* 41/ (1997): #69.]

1998   "The Kairos Behind the Kairos Document. A Contextual Exegesis of Luke 19:41–44," *R&T* 5/2: 195–221. [abstract: *NTA* 5/2 (1999): #1030.]

Strijdom, P.D.F.

1997   "What Tekoa Did to Amos," in Abrahams, et al.: ???

Suggit, John N.

1984   "'The Right Hand of Fellowship' (Galatians 2:4)," *JTSA* 49: 51–54.

1985   "An Incident From Mark's Gospel," *JTSA* 50: 52–55.

1991   "Bartimaeus and Christian Discipleship (Mark 10:46–52)," *JTSA* 74: 57–63.

1993   *The Sign of Life: Studies in the Fourth Gospel and the Liturgy of the Church* (Pietermaritzburg: Cluster Publications). [abstract: *BCT* 3/1 (1996): 30.]

Sundermeier, Th.

1973   "Bible Study: Romans 6:1–11," Becken, 1974: 83–86.

Synge, F.C.

1980   "A Plea for the Outsiders: Commentary on Mark 4.10–12," *JTSA* 30: 53–58.

Szesnat, Holger

1992   "The Apostle Paul and His Community in Corinth: A Study in Selected Issues of Socio-Economic Context and Practice," (Master's thesis, University of Natal, Pietermaritzburg, South Africa). [abstract: *BCT* 3/1 (1996): 30.]

1993   "What Did the Skenopoios Paul Produce?" *Neotestamentica* 27/2: 391–402. [abstract: *BCT* 3/1 (1996): 30.]

1995   "In Fear of Androgyny: Theological Reflections on Masculinity and Sexism, Male Homosexuality and Homophobia, Romans 1:24–27 and Hermeneutics (A Response to Alexander Venter)," *JTSA* 93: 32–50. [abstract: *BCT* 3/1 (1996): 30–31; *BCT* 4/2 (1997): 48.]

Taki, Nondyebo

1991   "Elements of a Theology of Work," Cochrane & West: 169–176.

Tlhagale, Buti & Itumeleng Mosala, eds

1986   *Hammering Swords into Ploughshares: Essays in Honor of Archbishop Mpilo Desmond Tutu* (Johannesburg/Trenton, N.J./Grand Rapids: Skotaville/Africa World Press/Eerdmans). [abstract: *RSR* 13/4 (1987): 332.]

Transkei Council of Churches
n.d. *God Our Loving Father: Bible Studies on Aids* (Umtata, South Africa).
n.d. *Towards a Theology of Sexuality: Sexuality & Pregnancy, Abortion & Contraception, Rape & Battering, Aids* Women's Theology Bible Studies Series, Booklet No. 4 (Umtata, South Africa).

Tutu, Desmond Mpilo B.
1972 "Some African Insights and the Old Testament," *JTSA* 1: 16–22; reprinted in Becken, 1973: 40–46. [abstracts: *BCTA* 1 (1993): 45; Holter: #216]
1977 *Vers`hnung ist unteilbar. Interpretationen biblischer. Texte zur Schwarzen Theologie* (Wuppertal: P.Hammer Verlag).
1983 "Liberation as a Biblical Theme," idem *Hope and Suffering: Sermons and Speeches* (Johannesburg: Skotaville; Grand Rapids: Eerdmans, 1984): 48–87.

van Aarde, A.G.
1987 "Demonology in New Testament Times," de Villiers, ed. *Like a roaring lion*: 22–37.
1993 "A Silver Coin in the Mouth of A Fish (Matthew 17:24–27)—A Miracle of Nature, Ecology, Economy and the Politics of Holiness," *Neotestamentica* 27/1: 1–26. [abstract: *BCT* 3/1 (1996): 31.]
"Recent Developments in South African Jesus Research: From Andrie Du Toit to Willem Vorster," *HTS* 49/3: 397–423. [abstract: *NTA* 38/3 (1994): #1329.]
"Recent Developments in South African Jesus Research: From Willem Vorster to Andries Van Aarde," *HTS* 49/4: 942–62. [abstract: *NTA* 39/1 (1995): #110.]
1994 "The Epistemic Status of the New Testament and the Emancipation of the Historical Jesus in Engaged Hermeneutics," *Neotestamentica* 28/2: 575–96. [abstract: *BCT* 3/1 (1996): 31; *NTA* 40/1 (1996): #129.]

van Eck, E. & A.G. van Aarde
1993 "Sickness and Healing in Mark: A Social Scientific Interpretation," *Neotestamentica* 27/1: 27–54. [abstract: *BCT* 3/1 (1996): 31.]

Van Rooy, J.A.
1994 "God's Self-revelation in the Old Testament and African Concepts of God," *IDS* 28/2: 261–74. [abstract: *RTA* 38/1 (1995): #349.]
1999 "The Covenant with Abraham in the Context of Africa," *IDS* 31: 311–26. [abstract: *OTA* 21/3 (1998): #1652.]
"Scriptural Ethical Principles and Traditional African Ethics," *IDS* 31: 93–106. [abstract: *OTA* 21/3 (1998): #1651.]

van Staden, P. & A.G. van Aarde
1991 "Social Description or Social-Scientific Interpretation? A Survey of Modern Scholarship," *HTS* 47/1: 55–87.

Villa-Vicencio, Charles
1981 "Israel: An Image of Captivity for Contextual Theology," *Theologia Evangelica* 14/2: 48.
"The Use of Scripture in Theology: Towards a Contextual Hermeneutic," *JTSA* 37: 3–22.

Visser't Hooft, W.A.
  1963 "1 Peter 1:3: A Living Hope by the Resurrection of Jesus-Christ,"
        Ministry 3/4: 149–50.
Vledder, E.J. & A.G. Van Aarde
  1994 "The Social Stratification of the Matthean Community," *Neotesta-
        mentica* 28/2: 511–22. [abstract: *BCT* 3/1 (1996): 31.]
Vorster, Willem S.
  1980 "Mark: Collector, Redactor, Author, Narrator," *JTSA* 31: 47–61.
  1983 "The Bible and Apartheid 1," John W. de Gruchy & Charles
        Villa-Vicencio, eds *Apartheid is a Heresy* (Cape Town/London/
        Grand Rapids: David Philip/Lutterworth/Eerdmans): 94–111.
  1984 "The Use of Scripture and the N.g. Kerk: A Shift of Paradigm
        Or of Values?" Hofmeyer & Vorster: 204–19.
  1987 "On Early Christian Communities and Theological Perspectives,"
        JTSA 59: 26–34.
Vorster, Willem S., ed.
  1979 *"Scripture and the Use of Scripture* (Pretoria: University of South Africa,
        1979).
Walker, Megan
  1996 "Engaging Popular Religion: A Hermeneutical Investigation of
        Marian Devotion in the Township of Mpophomeni," *Semeia* 73:
        131–58.
Wanamaker, C.A.
  1983 "A Case Against Justification by Faith," *JTSA* 42: 37–49.
  1988 "Romans 13: A Hermeneutic for Church and State," Charles
        Villa-Vicencio, ed. *On Reading Karl Barth in South Africa* (Grand
        Rapids: Eerdmans): 91–104. [abstract: *BCT* 3/1 (1996): 31.]
  1989 "Right Wing Christianity and the Bible in South Africa," *JTSA*
        69: 17–27.
Wanamaker, C.A. & W. Mazamisa, eds
  1989 *Reading the Bible in South Africa* (Braamfontein: Skotaville).
Warwick, G.W.
  1966 "The Contribution of Bishop Colenso to Biblical Criticism,"
        (Master's thesis, University of Natal, Pietermaritzburg, South Africa).
Wessels, W.J.
  1992 "Skifgebruik en samelewing Die Apostoliese Geloofsending van
        Suid-Afrika," *IDS* 26/3: 369–384. [In Afrikaans; English abstract:
        RTA 38/1 (1995): #320.]
West, Gerald O.
  1990 "Can A Literary Reading Be A Liberative Reading?" *Scriptura* 35:
        10–25. [abstracts: *BCT* 3/1 (1996): 31; *BCT* 4/2 (1997): 50.]
        "Reading 'the Text' and Reading 'Behind-the-Text': The Cain
        and Abel Story in a Context of Liberation," in David J.A. Clines,
        Stephen E. Fowl, and Stanley E. Porter, eds *The Bible in Three
        Dimensions: Essays in Celebration of Forty Years of Biblical Studies in the
        University of Sheffield* JSOTSup 87 (Sheffield: JSOT Press): 299–320.
        [abstract: *OTA* 14/1 (1991): #354.]

"Two Modes of Reading the Bible in the South African Context of Liberation," *JTSA* 73: 34–47. [abstracts: *OTA* 14/3 (191): #869; *NTA* 35/3 (1991): #1061.]

1991   "Hearing Job's Wife: Towards a Feminist Reading of Job," *OTEssays* 4: 107–31. [abstracts: *OTA* 15/1 (1992): #286; *BCT* 4/2 (1997): 50.]
"The Presence of Power in the Joseph Story," David J. Lull & James B. Wiggins, eds *Abstracts: American Academy of Religion / Society of Biblical Literature 1991* (Scholars Press): 140.
"The Relationship Between Different Modes of Reading (the Bible) and the Ordinary Reader," *Scriptura* Special Issue 9 (1991): 87–110. [abstract: *NTA* 38/2 (1994): #656.]
"Silenced Women Speak: Feminist Biblical Hermeneutics," Ackermann, Draper & Mashinini: 76–90. [abstract: *BCT* 4/2 (1997): 50.]

1992   "Some Parameters of the Hermenuetical Debate in South African Context," *JTSA* 80: 3–13. [abstracts: *NTA* 37 (1993): #608; *BCT* 3/1 (1996): 31.]
"Interesting and Interested Readings: Deconstruction, the Bible, and the South African Context," *Scriptura* 42: 35–49. [abstracts: *NTA* 37/3 (1993): #1147; *BCT* 4/2 (1997): 50.]

1993   *Contextual Bible Study* (Pietermaritzburg: Cluster Publications). [Review: Hermann Hauser *ACS* 10/4 (1994): 68–69; abstracts *BCT* 3/1 (1996): 32; *BCT* 4/2 (1997): 50.]
"Engagement, Criticality, and Contextualization: Core Concepts in the Teaching/Learning of Biblical Studies in A South African Context," *Scriptura* Special Issue 11: 1–17.
"The Interface between Trained Readers and Ordinary Readers in Liberation Hermeneutics. A Case Study: Mark 10:17–22," *Neotestimentica* 27/1 (1993): 165–80. [abstract: *NTA* 38/2 (1994): #800; *BCT* 3/1 (1996): 31.]
"No Integrity Without Contextuality: The Presence of Particularity in Biblical Hermeneutics and Pedagogy," *Scriptura* Special Issue 11: 131–46. [abstract: *NTA* 39/1 (1995): #33.]

1994   "The Challenge of Ideologirkritik: The Biblical Text As A Site of Struggle," *The Relevance of Theology for the 1990's* Johann Mouton & Bernard Lategan, eds (Stellenbosch): 273–89.
"Difference and Dialogue: Reading the Jospeh Story 'With' Poor and Marginalized Communities in South Africa," *Biblical Interpretation* 2/2: 152–70. [abstract: *OTA* 18/2 (1995): #821.]

1995   *Biblical Hermeneutics of Liberation: Modes of Reading the Bible in the South African Context* Monograph Series Number 1 (Pietermaritzburg: Cluster Publications and Maryknoll: Orbis [1991]). [reviews: David Walker *SABJOT* 1 (1992): 103–104; Dianne Bergant *CBQ* 55/1 (1993): 189–90; M. Brett *Modern Theology* 9 (1991): 426–27; Ernst Conradie *JTSA* 85 (1993): 61–65 {Conradie's review article is abstracted in *RTA* 38/1 (1995): #286}; Hermann Hauser *ACS* 10/4 (1994): 68–69; W. Sebothoma *Missionalia* 22 (1994): 87–88; P.M. Venter *HTS* 50 (1994): 853–55 *BookNotes* 8 (October 1999):

8.39; abstracts: *BCTA* 1 (1993):47; *BCT* 3/1 (1996): 32; *BCT* 4/2 (1997): 51.]

"Constructing Critical and Contextual Readings with Ordinary Readers: Mark 5:21–6:1," *JTSA* 92: 60–69. [abstracts: *BCT* 3/1 (1996): 32; *BCT* 4/2 (1997): 51; *NTA* 42/2 (1998): #966.]

"Reading the Bible in Africa: Constructing Our Own Discourse," *BCT* 2/2: 1–5.

"Reading the Bible and Doing Theology in the New South Africa," *The Bible in Human Society: Essays in Honour of John Rogerson* M. Daniel Carroll, David J.A. Clines, Philip R. Davies, eds JSOT sup, 200 (Sheffield: Sheffield Academic Press): 445–58.

1996   "And The Dumb Do Speak: Articulating Incipient Readings of the Bible in Marginalized Communities," *The Bible and Ethics: The Second Sheffield Colloquium* John W. Rogerson, Margaret Davies & M. Daniel Carroll, eds JSOTSup 207 (Sheffield: Sheffield Academic Press): 174–92. [abstract: *BCT* 4/2 (1997): 51.]

"The Effect and Power of Discourse: A Case Study of Metaphor in Hosea," *Scriptura* 57: 202–12. [abstract: *BCT* 4/2 (1997): 51.]

"The Place of Post-Colonial Biblical Criticism in a Post-Apartheid, Post-Liberation, and And Post-Modern South Africa," *Abstracts: American Academy of Religion/Society of Biblical Literature 1996* (Scholars Press): 257–58.

"Power and Pedagogy in a South African Context: A Case Study in Biblical Studies," *Academic Development* 2; 47–65.

"Reading the Bible Differently: Giving Shape to the Discourses of the Dominated," *Semeia* 73: 21–41. [abstract: *NTA* 42/1 (1998): #85.]

1997   "Finding a Place among the Posts for Post-Colonial Criticism in Biblical Studies in South Africa," *OTEssays* 10: 322–42. [abstract: *OTA* 22/1 (1999): #64.]

"On the Eve of an African Biblical Studies," *JTSA* 99: 99–115. [abstracts: *Theology in Context* 15/2 (1998): #986; *NTA* 42/3 (1998): #1558.]

"Reading on the Boundaries: Reading 2 Samuel 21:1–14 with Rizpah," *Scriptura* 63: 527–37. [abstract: *OTA* 21/2 (1998): #801.]

"Re-membering the Bible in South Africa: Reading Strategies in a Postcolonial Context," *Jian Dao* 8:37–62. [abstract: *NTA* 42/2 (1998): #806.]

1998   "Re-reading the Bible with African Resources: Interpretive Strategies for Reconstruction in a Post-Colonial, Post-Apartheid Context on the Eve of Globalization," *JCT* 4/1: 3–32. [abstract: *NTA* 43/3 (1999): #1569.]

1999   *The Academy of the Poor: Towards a Dialogical Reading of the Bible* Interventions, 2 (Sheffield: Sheffield Academic Press). [reviews: K. Holter *NAOTS* 7 (1999): 12–13; Grant LeMarquand *BookNotes* 8 (October 1999): 8.40.]

West, Gerald, Bafana Khumalo, McGlory Speckman
1994   "Report on South Africa," Bible in Africa Project: 25–27.

Wielenga, B.
   1992   "The Bible in a Changing South Africa: The Quest for a
          Responsible Biblical Hermeneutic in Mission," *Missionalia* 20/1:
          28–37. [abstract: *NTA* 37/1 (1993): #43.]
Williams, Jacqueline
   1992   "And She Became 'Snow White,'" *JBTSA* 6: 46–52. [abstract:
          BCT 4/2 (1997): 51.]
Wittenberg, Gertrud
   1991   "The Song of a Poor Woman: The Magnificat (Luke 1:46–55),"
          Ackermann, Draper & Mashinini: 3–20. [abstract: *BCT* 4/2 (1997):
          51.]
   1996   "Women of Corinth Will Not Be Silenced," *Challenge* 39 (December).
          [a play] [abstract: *BCT* 4/2 (1997): 51.]
Wittenberg, Gunther H.
   1973   "Bible Study: Deuteronomy 26:1–11," Becken, 1974: 12–18.
   1987   "Amos 6:1–7: 'They Dismiss the Day of Disaster But Bring You
          Near the Rule of Violence,'" *JTSA* 58: 57–69. [abstract: *OTA*
          10/3 (1987): #871.]
          "The Situational Context of Statements Concerning Poverty and
          Wealth in the Book of Proverbs," *Scriptura* 21: 1–23. [abstract:
          BCT 3/1 (1996): 32.]
   1988   "King Solomon and the Theologians," *JTSA* 63: 16–29. [abstract:
          BCT 3/1 (1996): 32.]
   1989   "The Rule of Justice Versus the Rule of Violence," K. Nurnberger,
          J. Tooke & W. Domeris, eds *Conflict and the Quest for Justice* (Pieter-
          maritzburg: Encounter Publications): 76–93. [abstract: *BCT* 3/1
          (1996): 32.]
   1991   "Authoritarian and Participatory Decision-making in the Old
          Testament," K. Nurnberger, ed. *A Democratic Vision for South Africa*
          (Pietermaritzburg: Encounter Publications). [abstract: *BCT* 3/1
          (1996): 32.]
          I Have Heard the Cry of My People: A Study Guide to Exodus 1–15 The
          Bible in Context Series Number 1 (Pietermaritzburg, South Africa:
          Institute for the Study of the Bible/Cluster Publications). [abstract:
          BCT 3/1 (1996): 32.]
          "'. . . Let Canaan be his Slave.' (Gen 9:26) Is Ham also Cursed?"
          JTSA 74: 46–56.
          "The Significance of Land in the Old Testament," *JTSA* 77:
          58–60. [abstract: *OTA* 15/2 (1992): #930.]
          "Old Testament Perspectives on Labour," Cochrane & West:
          91–108.
          Prophecy and Protest: A Contextual Introduction to Israelite Prophecy
          The Bible in Context Series Number 2 (Pietermaritzburg, South
          Africa: Institute for the Study of the Bible/Cluster Publications).
          [review: Hermann Hauser *ACS* 10/4 (1994): 67; abstract: *BCT*
          3/1 (1996): 32.]
   1994   "The Ideological/Materialist Approach to the Old Testament,"
          OTEssays 7/4: 167–72. [abstract: *OTA* 18/3 (1995): #1399.]

1995 "Legislating for Justice—The Social Legislation of the Covenant Code and Deuteronomy," *Scriptura* 54: 215–28. [abstract: *OTA* 19/1 (1996): #234.]

1996 "Old Testament Theology, for Whom?" *Semeia* 73: 221–40.

Worsnip, Michael, ed.

1992 *Repentance and Conversion: Working in the Church and in the Community 'On the Road to Damascus'* Bible Studies in Context #1 (Pietermaritzburg: Cluster Publications/Institute for the Study of the Bible).

INDEX OF BIBLICAL REFERENCES

Old Testament

Apocrypha

New Testament

INDEX OF NAMES

INDEX OF SUBJECTS